# Management Information Systems

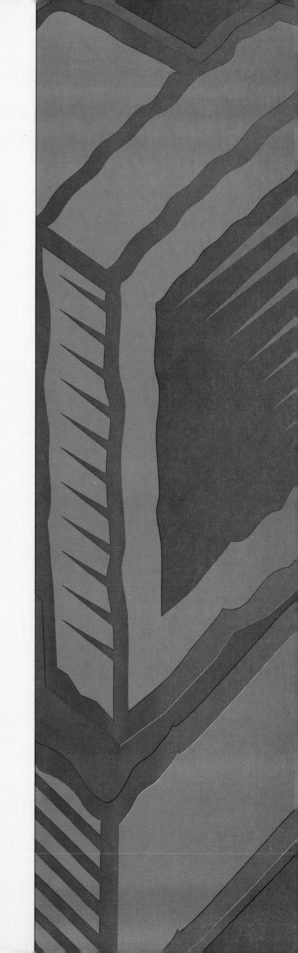

# Management Information Systems

## Solving Business Problems with Information Technology

**GERALD V. POST**
*Western Kentucky University*

**DAVID L. ANDERSON**
*DePaul University*

*IRWIN*

Chicago · Bogotá · Boston · Buenos Aires · Caracas
London · Madrid · Mexico City · Sydney · Toronto

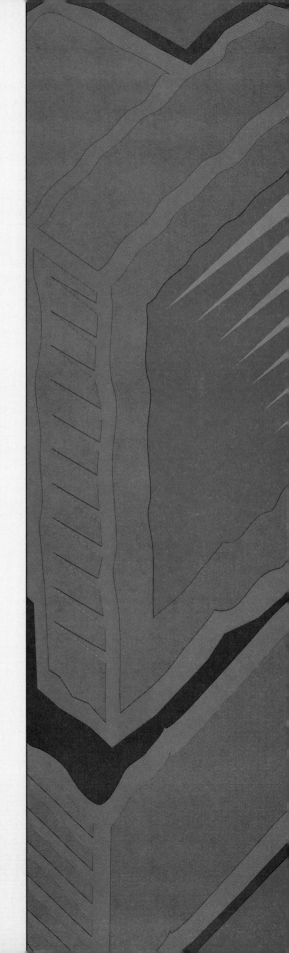

**Irwin Book Team**

Publisher: *Tom Casson*
Senior sponsoring editor: *Rick Williamson*
Developmental editor: *Christine Wright*
Associate marketing manager: *Michelle Hudson*
Project supervisor: *Karen J. Nelson*
Production supervisor: *Pat Frederickson*
Art director: *Keith McPherson*
Photo research coordinator: *Keri Johnson*
Prepress Buyer: *Charlene R. Perez*
Compositor: *PC&F, Inc.*
Typeface: *10/12 Garamond Text*
Printer: *Von Hoffmann Press, Inc.*

**Times Mirror**
**Higher Education Group**

**Library of Congress Cataloging-in-Publication Data**
Post, Gerald V.
    Management information systems : solving business problems with information technology / Gerald V. Post, David L. Anderson.
        p.    cm.
    Includes indexes.
    ISBN 0-256-17956-5
    1. Management information systems. I. Anderson, David L. (David Lee), 1953-   . II. Title.
HD30.213.P67   1997
658.4' 038—dc20                                        96–38550

*Printed in the United States of America*
1 2 3 4 5 6 7 8 9 0 VH 3 2 1 0 9 8 7 6

*To my parents,*
*for emphasizing the value of education,*
*and the joy of a good book.*

Jerry

*To my father and mother,*
*sister and brother-in-law,*
*for their support and encouragement*
*throughout the education and writing process.*

David

# Preface

## A TALE OF TWO CAREERS

Jack Lewis had it made. Or so he thought. A number of well-timed promotions at his Midwest publishing firm, W.C. Green, Inc., had landed him comfortably in the role of marketing director of the educational book division. Unlike many of his colleagues, Jack tried to keep up with the latest changes in information technology. He entered data into spreadsheets to create color graphs for budgets and expenses. His reports were created with professionally designed word processing templates. The dark mahogany desk, the 180-degree view of the duck pond, and the $30,000 of computer hardware and software in his office were testament to his success. Then it happened. A competitor developed an information system that used advanced technology to deliver custom books to students on demand over the Internet. Caught without a competitive marketing strategy, sales at W.C. Green dropped dramatically. Driving home after losing his job, Jack still could not figure out what went wrong.

Julie Nilar just wouldn't quit. She too had a marketing degree like Jack, but decided not to pursue a traditional career right out of college. A nationally ranked bicycle racer, on graduating she chose to develop her cycling skills in international competition, maybe to be chosen for the U.S. Women's Olympic Road Team in the year 2000. To pay the bills she got a part-time job as a marketing representative for Rolling Thunder bicycles, a small Colorado mail order service providing custom-made bicycles to a national customer base. As international competition kept Julie away for long periods, she always took her laptop with her to keep in touch with the office. No stranger to information technology, one project she developed during these long absences was a powerful database application which kept track of Rolling Thunder's suppliers, customers, and their orders. This application became a powerful tool for Rolling Thunder and one which led to greatly increased productivity for the company.

## INTRODUCTION

The next few years promise to bring exciting changes to managers. Increased competition forces organizations to cut costs and operate with fewer managers. The growth of small businesses encourages entrepreneurs to run their own businesses and consulting firms. Continued change in Information Technology (IT) is encouraging even more changes to business and society. IT changes such as continual performance improvements, expanded storage capacity, expanded capabilities of software, and the Internet affect all aspects of management.

The exponential growth of the Internet is exceeding all forecasts. The Internet holds the potential to revolutionize virtually all aspects of business. Consumers are presented with more choices and more data. Companies have more ways to track customer actions and preferences. Investors have instant access to data around the world. Managers have more ways to communicate and share ideas.

Changing IT presents two challenges: learning to use it, and finding new opportunities to improve management. Most students have taken a hands-on course that teaches them how to use a computer. Many expect the introductory MIS course to be more of the same—hands-on computer usage tied to specific needs. However, there are more complex and interesting problems to be solved. Managers need to apply their knowledge of IT tools to solve management problems and find new opportunities to improve their organizations. Hence, the focus of this book is to investigate the more complex question: How can we use IT to improve our jobs as managers?

**ORGANIZATION**  The text is organized into four parts to explore answers to the question of how information technology can improve management. (I) Information technology is used to improve business transactions and operations. (II) IT is fundamental in the communication and integration of data across an organization. (III) IT plays a crucial role in building models, analyzing situations and making decisions. (IV) How information systems are developed and organized.

---

### ORGANIZATION

Chapter 1:      Introduction
Part 1:       Personal Productivity and Business Operations
Chapter 2:      Personal Productivity
Chapter 3:      Solving Problems
Chapter 4:      Operations and Transactions
Chapter 5:      Database Management
Part 2:       Business Integration
Chapter 6:      Networks and Telecommunications
Chapter 7:      Integration of Information
Part 3:       Decisions and Models
Chapter 8:      Models and Decision Support
Chapter 9:      Decisions in Business Areas
Chapter 10:     Complex Decisions and Artificial Intelligence
Chapter 11:     Strategic Analysis
Part 4:       Designing and Managing Information Systems
Chapter 12:     Systems Development
Chapter 13:     Organizing Information System Resources
Chapter 14:     Information Management and Society

---

Chapter 1 (Introduction) examines the changing nature of IT, business and society. These changes highlight the need for business managers to understand how IT can be used to improve decisions, jobs, and the entire organization.

To begin, Part 1, Chapter 2 (Personal Productivity) presents a review of hardware and software that shows how managers use IT for personal tasks. Instead of simply describing technology and defining terms, the chapter focuses on advantages, disadvantages, and appropriate uses of the various hardware and software tools.

Chapter 3 (Solving Problems) discusses how to analyze and solve business problems, emphasizing the systems approach to give students experience with the subjective side of managing IT. The chapter also introduces students to business object-oriented design.

Chapter 4 (Operations and Transactions) emphasizes the importance of transaction processing systems. It presents common problems and demonstrates how IT is used to collect, process, and store quality data.

Most systems rely on databases for transaction processing, so Chapter 5 (Database Management) concludes this section. It includes hands-on applications that illustrate the use and management of databases, focusing on the importance of managers' understanding of database queries. The appendix illustrates the basic techniques of data normalization.

Part 2 covers a crucial component of MIS that is often ignored or treated lightly in other texts: communication and integration of information. Today's managers work in teams and rely on information systems to capture, transmit, and analyze information from diverse locations and in various formats.

Chapter 6 (Networks and Telecommunications) focuses on the various choices, relative merits, and costs of networks and telecommunications systems, as well as how computers can be physically connected to share data. A separate appendix explains the technical details in more depth.

Chapter 7 (Integration of Information) shows that businesses can make substantial gains through using technology to integrate the data across the company. Integration and technology can change the way business operates and improve decision-making. The chapter also discusses the challenge of combining various forms of data (text, images, sound and video) into information a manager can use.

Part 3 focuses on making decisions. It emphasizes the importance of models in management. Beginning with basic uses of models, the part examines the various IT tools available to help managers examine various aspects of making decisions.

Chapter 8 (Models and Decision Support) introduces models and highlights their importance in making tactical level decisions. The chapter discusses the common uses of models in making decisions. It concludes by examining enterprise-wide models and the use of enterprise information systems to examine problems across the entire organization.

Chapter 9 (Decisions in Business Areas) integrates MIS with courses in other disciplines by examining common problems in accounting, marketing, finance, human resource management, production, and design. The basic problems are described along with the appropriate model. A hands-on version of the problem is developed using common IT tools. The application exercises encourage students to explore the models and tools in more depth. A technical appendix reviews the basic financial ratios and computations used to analyze companies. Students are encouraged to analyze the financial aspects of the cases in each chapter.

Chapter 10 (Complex Decisions and Artificial Intelligence) emphasizes the issues and problems involved in more complex decisions, decisions that involve more complex analysis, greater accuracy, or faster responses. The text then shows how basic AI techniques, including Expert Systems, can be used by managers to reach better decisions.

Chapter 11 (Strategic Analysis) examines difficult decisions—unstructured problems involving strategy. The chapter focuses on common problems in strategy (utilizing Porter's five-forces model), and explores the ways in which IT is used to help organizations gain a competitive advantage.

Part 4 discusses how information systems are designed and created. Again, the focus is on the role of managers in the development process.

Chapter 12 (Systems Development) examines basic issues in developing and implementing systems. The text emphasizes the role played by managers in helping design new systems. It examines the various development methodologies in terms of their strengths and weaknesses so managers can help determine which method should be used to develop systems they need. The chapter also emphasizes the increasing role of end-user participation in all of the development methodologies.

Chapter 13 (Organizing Information System Resources) examines the various methods of organizing MIS resources. It focuses on the fundamental issues of centralization and decentralization. By emphasizing the strengths and weaknesses of various IT organizational schemes, managers can learn to solve organization problems and can determine how to align MIS to fit their needs.

Chapter 14 (Information Management and Society) examines the ways in which IT is changing society. It also encourages managers to think about the effects of their choices on various members of society. Basic issues include privacy, security, and ethical issues in IT related to managers, programmers, and organizations. Common methods used to provide information security are also presented.

**PEDAGOGY**     The organization of the text is based on two features. First, each chapter emphasizes the goal of the text: applying information technology to improve management and organizations. Second, the text is organized so that it begins with concepts familiar to the students and builds on them.

Each chapter is organized in a common format: (1) the introduction which ties to the goal and raises questions specific to that chapter; (2) the main discussion which emphasizes the application of technology and the strengths and weaknesses of various approaches; and (3) the application of the technology in various real-world organizations with end-of-chapter cases.

Each chapter contains several sections to assist in understanding the material and in applying it to solve problems and analyze business problems:

- **What you will learn in this chapter.** A series of questions that highlight the important issues.
- **Lead case.** Illustrates the problems explored in the chapter.
- **Overview.** A brief summary of the chapter's goal and outline.
- **Trends.** A section that presents the major changes, brief history, and trends that affect the topics in the chapter.
- **Reality Bytes.** Brief applications, cases and discussion that emphasize a specific point, highlight international issues, business trends, ethics, or illustrate problems and solutions in the real world.
- **Chapter summary.** A list of the chapter topics.
- **A Manager's View.** A short summary of how the chapter relates to managers and to the overall question of how information technology can improve management.
- **Key Words.** A list of words introduced in that chapter. A full glossary is provided at the end of the text.
- **Review Questions.** Designed as a study guide for students.
- **Exercises.** Problems that apply the knowledge learned in the chapter. Many utilize common application software to illustrate the topics.
- **Additional Reading.** References for more detailed investigation of the topics.

- **Cases.** In-depth discussion of the lead case and several other companies. Each chapter highlights a specific industry and compares different approaches to the problems faced by the firms.
- **Discussion Issue.** A brief dialog between managers to highlight a specific topic. Most emphasize ethical issues. The discussion and related questions form a starting point for class discussions.

| CHAPTER | CASE FOCUS: INDUSTRY |
|---------|----------------------|
| 1 | Fast Food |
| 2 | Small Business |
| 3 | Railroads |
| 4 | Retail Sales |
| 5 | Service Firms |
| 6 | Distributors and Inventory Management |
| 7 | Large-scale Manufacturing |
| 8 | Design and Marketing |
| 9 | Delivery Companies |
| 10 | Customer Service |
| 11 | Airlines |
| 12 | Government Agencies |
| 13 | Financial Institutions |
| 14 | Health Care |

**PRIMARY FEATURES OF THE TEXT**

- All of the chapters emphasize the goal of understanding how information technology can be used to improve management. The focus is on understanding benefits and costs of technology and its application.
- The role and importance of *objects* in understanding information technology is emphasized. The object approach is bringing major changes to the application and use of technology. A firm grasp of the concepts makes it easier to use new applications; analyze business situations; and communicate with IT developers. The use and managerial importance of object-oriented technology are highlighted throughout the text.
- An emphasis on the importance of database management systems. Increasingly, managers need to retrieve data and utilize a DBMS to investigate, analyze, and communicate.
- An emphasis on the importance of communication and integration of data. Understanding information technology requires more than knowledge of basic application packages. Students need to use and understand the applications of technologies like OLE, Notes, and the Internet.
- Students increasingly want to know how technology is used to solve problems in their chosen major/functional area. Several current applications, including hands-on exercises are highlighted in Chapter 9. The application can be expanded to even more detail depending on the background of the students.

- In-depth cases that illustrate the use of technology. By focusing each chapter on a specific industry, students can understand and evaluate a variety of approaches. Many cases illustrate companies varying over time, so students can see the changes occurring in business, and understand the evolving role and importance of information technology.
- Rolling Thunder Database. A medium-sized, detailed database application of a small business is available on disk. Specific exercises are highlighted in each chapter. The database contains data and applications suitable for operating a small (fictional) firm. The database also contains data generation routines so instructors can create their own scenarios.

## INSTRUCTIONAL SUPPORT

- A test bank with true/false, multiple choice, and short answer questions is available for use with the Irwin electronic test bank software.
- Lecture notes and overheads are available as slide shows in Microsoft PowerPoint format. The slides contain all of the figures along with additional notes. The slides are organized into lectures, and can be rearranged to suit individual preferences.
- Several databases and exercises are available on disk. The instructor can add new data, modify the exercises, or use them to expand on the discussion in the text.
- The Rolling Thunder database application is available in Microsoft Access format (version 2.0 or 7.0 [Windows '95]). It is a self-contained application that illustrates many of the concepts and enables students to examine any facet of operating a small company.
- The Irwin IS Video Library contains 14 10–12 minute videos and is available to adopters of the text.
- An Internet site for direct contact with the authors: http://cis.coba.wku.edu/faculty/post
- An Internet site for contact with the publisher: http://www.Irwin.com

## ACKNOWLEDGMENTS

Like any large project, producing a book is a team effort. In developing this book, we have had the privilege of working with dedicated professionals. The contributions of many people have resulted in an improved book, and made the process enjoyable.

First, we thank our students over the years who encouraged us to explore new technologies and to focus on how IT can benefit students, managers and organizations. We are grateful to David Witty for his contributions to the review questions. We are indebted to reviewers who offered many improvements and suggestions. Their ideas and direction substantially improved the book.

David Bateman, Saint Mary's University

Linda J. Behrens, University of Central Oklahoma

Michael K. Bourke, Houston Baptist University

Kevin Brennan, University of Rochester

Jane M. Carey, Arizona State University—West

Drew S. Cobb, Johns Hopkins University

Virginia R. Gibson, University of Maine

Mark R. Gruskin, University of Michigan—Dearborn

William L. Harrison, Oregon State University

Thomas Hilton, Utah State University

Betsy Hoppe, Wake Forest University

James E. LaBarre, University of Wisconsin—Eau Claire

Louis A. LeBlanc, University of Arkansas—Little Rock

Yvonne Lederer-Antonucci, Widener University

Douglas C. Lund, University of Minnesota

Jane Mackay, Texas Christian University

Dick Ricketts, Lane Community College

This text has been substantially improved through the dedication and professionalism of the editors and staff at Irwin. It is a pleasure to work with people like Christine Wright, Rick Williamson, and Michelle Hudson whose guidance, support, ideas, and answers to innumerable questions were invaluable to the project.

# Brief Contents

# Contents

# CHAPTER 1

# *Introduction*

McDonald's uses a considerable amount of information technology to maintain consistency, monitor employees, and track sales.

## MCDONALD'S

Since 1955, McDonald's Corporation has sold more than 100 billion hamburgers. From a single drive-in in Des Plaines, Illinois, to today's franchise system of more than 7,000 restaurants, McDonald's has become synonymous with a quality product at a reasonable price. Equally important, it has been marketed as more than a place to get a hamburger. Ronald McDonald, the clean restaurants, and each new product or promotional theme adds to the fun that keeps millions of customers of all ages coming back around the world.

McDonald's is a franchise. Each restaurant meets strict requirements to make it the same as all others. This ensures that each time you drive or walk into a McDonald's, no matter where you are, the Big Mac that you order will always be the same size, weight, and quality. In most cases, it will also be approximately the same price.

Legal contracts, quality standards, and performance specifications help to ensure that individual restaurants and food orders will be the same. What most individuals do not think about when they walk or drive into McDonald's is that McDonald's management information system (MIS) plays an important role in insuring the quality and consistency of each Big Mac. McDonald's has a strict requirement that food be fresh and not stored more than a certain number of days. Management information systems assist managers to order and track inventory. Because restaurants are not consistently busy throughout the day, management information systems also help the manager to maximize the scheduling of individuals to cook and serve the food. A large amount of cash flows through each restaurant each day. Management information systems further help track the cash flow and guard against fraud and waste. As McDonald's adds new products and addresses increasingly specific market segments, the manager must make more complex decisions about the best mix of products to serve at each meal and throughout the day. Special promotions and community events add additional factors to the equation that can be addressed more realistically through management information systems.

**OVERVIEW**     Welcome to the information age. Going shopping? As a consumer, you have instant access to millions of pieces of data. With a few clicks of the mouse button, you can find anything from current stock prices to video clips of current movies. You can get product descriptions, pictures, and prices from thousands of companies across the U.S. and around the world. Trying to sell services and products? You can purchase demographic, economic, consumer-buying-pattern, and market-analysis data. Your firm will have internal financial, marketing, production, and employee data for past years. This tremendous amount of data provides opportunities to managers and consumers who know how to obtain it and analyze it to make better decisions.

There is no question that the use of computers in business is increasing. Walk into your local bank, grocery store, or fast food restaurant and you will see that the operations depend on computers. Go into management offices and you will find computers used to analyze marketing alternatives, make financial decisions, and coordinate team members around the world.

The expanding role of technology raises some interesting questions. What exactly are computers being used for? Who decided to install them? Do computers increase productivity or are they just expensive paperweights? Are there new uses that you should be considering? Are there some tasks that should be performed by humans instead of computers? How can you deal with the flood of data that you face every day?

**THE EXPANDING ROLE OF INFORMATION TECHNOLOGY**     Technology is changing society, business, and jobs. The next few years will be exciting for managers. You will have the opportunity to use new technologies to solve problems, expand your knowledge, change society, and make money in the process.

This text illustrates how people use computers to make decisions. These decisions and the use of computers increasingly affect all our lives. As prices drop and capabilities increase, computers are used in increasingly diverse fields. Musicians use computers to create music scores, generate new sounds, and to play passages that no human could ever play. Artists use computers to create new techniques and design or modify their work. Computer artwork has become a crucial part of business presentations, especially in marketing campaigns.

Computers have many uses in business. The Wells Fargo Bank Reality Byte (1-1) illustrates some common uses. People in many other disciplines use computers for additional tasks.

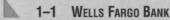

### Reality Bytes ▲ 1-1 WELLS FARGO BANK

Wells Fargo Bank, based in San Francisco, California, uses information systems to reduce operating costs, efficiently absorb acquisitions, and offer new services to customers. Because of its focus on consumers and small- and medium-sized businesses in California, the bank is one of the largest investors in automated teller machines (ATMs) and basic computer systems. Currently it has 1,246 ATMs itself. It also grants its customers access to more than 25,000 machines at other banks through the Plus and Star systems.

Branch employees can access central records and processing systems through the Wells Fargo Electronic Banking System. This enhances security and increases the speed and ease of account transfers. Corporate customers can use the computers to bill one another, make automatic payments, and monitor their accounts.

Researchers in history, philosophy, and political science use computers to track documents, search for data, or look for correlations among various events. Computer software also assists in language translations. The software makes the initial translation; human interpreters work on the complicated passages and idioms to clean up the result. Existing computer translators supply fairly rigid substitutions and do not evaluate the semantic content of the documents, so humans still must polish the result.

It is hard to imagine health care delivery without the use of computers. Computers track patients' treatments, pharmaceuticals, and appointments. Computers control machines such as x-rays, radiation therapy, and magnetic resonance imaging scanners. Computer image-enhancement techniques provide clearer pictures and 3-D images. Computers are even being used to treat medical problems. Computers are wired to muscles to provide exercise and control for injured or paralyzed patients. Other techniques such as virtual reality are used to provide surgeons three-dimensional visualizations of complex body components to help guide laser and gamma "knives."

Even though we will not dwell on the thousands of specialized uses of computers, the techniques presented in this book are valuable for anyone who wants to learn to evaluate situations and find useful applications of information systems. The ability to analyze situations and solve problems is needed by everyone, regardless of specialty.

An effect of changing technology is that it alters the way businesses operate, which changes the jobs that people perform, our leisure activities, politics, crime, and society in general. Many of the changes will be beneficial; some can have deleterious side effects. As managers, we have an obligation to examine the potential side effects of our decisions. In particular, we need to consider how our use of technology affects customers, employees, and society at large. We must consider the effects computers have on privacy and understand the ethical problems that arise. These issues are explored in-depth in Chapter 14 but also arise in cases throughout the book.

Computers are everywhere. In 1995, over one-third of U.S. households possessed at least one personal computer. In business, almost all employees who work at desks (in the industrialized nations) are using computers in their jobs. In 1990, the Gartner Group reported that 76 percent of all desk workers were using computers. In larger corporations, the number was 84 percent. In total, 26 percent of the 113 million U.S. employees were using computers in their jobs. Figure 1.1 presents the average usage

**FIGURE 1.1**

Regardless of the industry, most employees can expect to use computers to help with their jobs. These percentages reported by *Computerworld* include all employees, including line workers. For management jobs, the percentages are much closer to 100 percent.

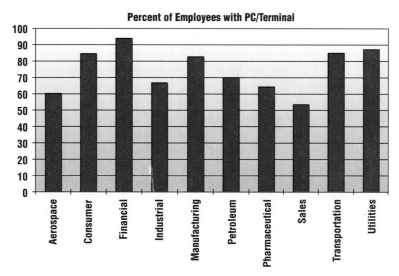

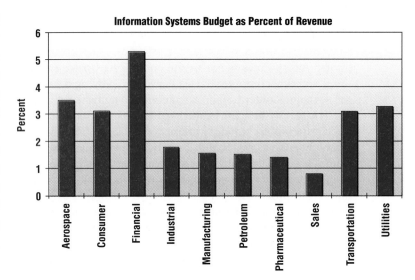

figures by industry for 1993 (the most recent figures available). Even among manufacturing and industrial firms (which have thousands of production workers), the use of computers exceeded 60 percent.

All of this technology is not cheap. Spending on information technology (computers, associated equipment, and software) constitutes a major expense for most businesses. Figure 1.2 displays the average spending on information technology by industry in 1993 (most recent year's figures available). Comparing the number to other business costs, note that spending on information resources accounted for 14 percent of the total U.S. capital investment by businesses in 1992. In some industries, the figure is as high as 50 percent.

Why do firms spend so much money on information systems? Are these investments profitable? The short answer to these questions is that spending money on computer hardware and software does not guarantee success. For this investment to pay off, managers need to learn to use the technology. Knowing how to operate various hardware and software packages is only one step. The key to building and using effective information systems is that managers need to know how to apply technology to solve problems and make decisions. Hence, we need to understand the role of managers and the decisions they make. Before examining the roles of managers, we will first clarify the definition of information systems.

**WHAT IS MIS?**  The first step in learning how to apply information technology to solve problems is to get a broader picture of what is meant by the term *management information system.* You probably have some experience with using computers and various software packages. Yet, computers are only one component of a management information system. A **management information system (MIS)** or *computer information system (CIS)* consists of five related components: hardware, software, people, procedures, and collections of data. The term **information technology (IT)** represents the various types of hardware and software used in an information system, including computers and networking equipment. The goal of MIS is to enable managers to make better decisions by providing quality information.

The physical equipment used in computing is called **hardware.** The set of instructions that controls the hardware is known as **software.** In the early days of computers, the **people** directly involved in MIS tended to be programmers, design analysts, and a few external users. Today, almost everyone in the firm is involved with the information system. **Procedures** are instructions that help people use the systems. They include items such as user manuals, documentation, and procedures to ensure that backups are made regularly. **Databases** are collections of related data that can be retrieved easily and processed by the computers. As you will see in the cases throughout the book, all of these components are vital to creating an effective information system.

So what is information? One answer to that question is to examine the use of information technology on three levels: (1) data management, (2) information systems, and (3) knowledge bases. **Data** consists of factual elements (or opinions or comments) that describe some object or event. Data can be thought of as raw numbers or text. Data management systems focus on data collection and providing basic reports. **Information** represents data that has been processed, organized, and integrated to provide more insight. Information systems are designed to help managers analyze data and make decisions. From a decision maker's standpoint, the challenge is that you might not know ahead of time which information you need, so it is hard to determine what data need to be collected. **Knowledge** represents a higher level of understanding, including rules, patterns, and decisions. Knowledge-based systems are built to automatically analyze data, identify patterns, and recommend decisions. Humans are also capable of **wisdom,** where they put knowledge, experience, and analytical skills to work to create new knowledge and adapt to changing situations. To date no computer system has attained the properties of wisdom.

To create an effective information system, you need to do more than simply purchase the various components. Quality is an important issue in business today, particularly as it relates to information systems. The quality of an information system is

## DATA, INFORMATION, KNOWLEDGE, AND WISDOM

Consider the case of a retail store that is trying to increase sales. Some of the data available includes sales levels for the last 36 months, advertising expenses, and customer comments from surveys.

By itself, this data may be interesting, but it must be organized and analyzed to be useful in making a decision. For example, a manager might use economic and marketing models to forecast patterns and determine relationships among various advertising expenses and sales. The resulting information (presented in equations, charts, and tables) would clarify relationships among the data and would be used to decide how to proceed.

Determining how to analyze data and make decisions requires knowledge. Education and experience create knowledge in humans. A manager learns which data to collect, the proper models to apply, and ways to analyze results for making better decisions. In some cases, this knowledge can be transferred to specialized computer programs (expert systems).

Wisdom is more difficult to define but represents the ability to learn from experience and adapt to changing conditions. In this example, wisdom would enable a manager to spot trends, identify potential problems, and develop new techniques to analyze the data.

measured by its ability to provide exactly the information needed by managers in a timely manner. The information must be accurate and up-to-date. Users should be able to receive the information in a variety of formats: tables of data, graphs, summary statistics, or even pictures or sound. Users have different perspectives and different requirements, and a good information system must have the flexibility to present information in diverse forms for each user.

## Collecting, Analyzing, and Sharing Data

There is an enormous amount of data available to managers—generated internally and externally. It is impossible to deal with this volume of data without information technology. But the power of information technology extends beyond these basic tasks. As a manager, you will face a quickly changing world. The people and firms that can quickly respond to these changes will profit. The best managers will understand the business, their role in it, and the ways that changes in the world affect the firm.

It is tempting to believe that once you learn how to use a word processor, spreadsheet, and a database management system, you have all the computer knowledge needed to solve business problems. In fact, these are powerful tools that will help you solve business problems that arise at a personal level. But businesses have many more levels of problems, such as data collection, departmental teamwork, information shared throughout the corporation, and uses of IT that help the business gain a competitive advantage.

To create and use information systems to their full advantage, it helps to have a basic knowledge of the technology. All hardware and software has limitations, advantages, and disadvantages. The first step toward successful use of any technology is to choose the correct tool for each job or problem. For example, after being introduced to spreadsheets, many people automatically try to generate a spreadsheet to solve every problem when there might be better tools available. By understanding the advantages and limitations of each tool you will be able to choose wisely.

## Analyzing and Building Systems

Managers are also responsible for improving their jobs and extending their company's influence. Information technology will play a key role in any organization. Successful managers will continuously evaluate current operations and explore new alternatives.

The scientific approach is a method that is useful for analyzing systems, identifying problems, and generating possible solutions. The scientific approach has been refined over thousands of years. **Systems analysis and design** is a refinement of these methods, and represents a field of study closely associated with information systems. Analysis and design techniques used by MIS professionals are useful to any business manager or student who needs to understand and solve complex problems. Even if you do not intend to become an MIS professional, these techniques will help you solve problems in any business discipline.

Similarly, you need to recognize what types of problems can be solved by users (such as yourself) and which are so complex that they require the support of a trained MIS staff. Attempting to solve problems that are too complex can lead to costly mistakes. Calling in expensive MIS professionals for simple projects that you can do yourself is equally a waste of time and money. Along the same lines, the more you know about MIS, the easier it is to communicate with MIS professionals. This communication is essential to developing systems that meet your needs.

## Traditional Management and Observations

To create useful information systems, it is helpful to examine the various roles of management. Traditional concepts of management focus on organizing, planning, and control. However, when observed at their jobs, managers appear to spend most of their time in meetings, talking on the phone, reading or preparing reports, discussing projects with their colleagues, explaining procedures, and other activities that are difficult to fit into the traditional framework.

Henry Mintzberg, a psychologist who studies management, classifies managerial tasks in three categories: (1) interpersonal, (2) informational, and (3) decisional. Interpersonal roles refer to teaching and leading employees. Informational tasks are based on the transfer of information throughout the organization, such as relaying information to subordinates or summarizing information for executives. Decisions involve evaluating alternatives and choosing directions that benefit the firm.

Other researchers have studied managers and developed alternative classifications. Fred Luthans uses three classifications of management activities. He indicates that approximately 50 percent of a manager's time is spent on traditional management activities (planning, organizing, etc.), 30 percent in formal communications, and 20 percent in informal networking. Formal communications include attending meetings and creating reports and memos. Informal networking consists of contacts with colleagues and workers that tend to be social in nature but often involve discussions regarding business and jobs.

## Making Decisions

In many ways managers expend a lot of their effort in making decisions or contributing information so others can make decisions. When you look at courses offered for future managers, you will find a focus on administration, human behavior, quantitative modeling and problem solving, decision theory, and elements of business ethics and globalization. Typically, these courses are designed to help

Managers and professionals spend considerable time in meetings. Providing support for teamwork and group decisions is an important issue in MIS.

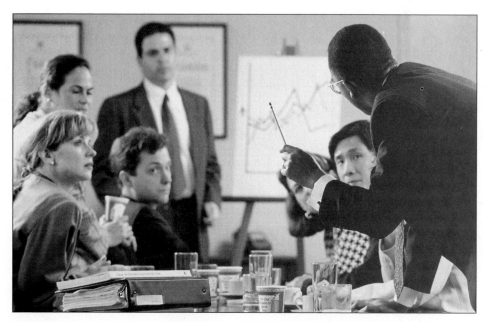

managers solve problems and make decisions. Yet, if you ask managers how much time they spend making decisions, they are likely to say that they seldom make decisions. That seems like a contradiction. If managers and executives do not make decisions, who does?

In many organizations, day-to-day decisions are embodied in the methodology, rules, or philosophy of the company. Managers are encouraged to collect data and follow the decisions that have resulted from experience. In this situation and in many others, the managers are directly involved in the decision process, even though they may not feel they are making the final choice.

The broader **decision process** involves collecting data, identifying problems, and making choices. One more step is often involved: persuading others to accept a decision and implement a solution. With this broader definition, many of the tasks performed by managers are actually steps in the decision process. Meetings, phone calls, and discussions with colleagues are used to collect data, identify problems, and persuade others to choose a course of action. Each of these steps may be so gradual that the participants do not feel they are actually making decisions.

Because of the subtlety of the process and the complexity of the decisions, it is often difficult to determine what information will be needed. As pointed out by the founder of Market Facts in Reality Bytes 1–2, decisions often require creativity. Because data generally need to be collected *before* problems arise, it is challenging to design information systems to support managers and benefit the organization. One important job of management is to examine the need for information and how it can be used to solve future problems.

## BUSINESS AND TECHNOLOGY TRENDS

Several important trends are affecting the role of managers and the organization of business. To understand the current state and future prospects of management information systems, it is helpful to examine how technology, business, and management have changed over time. Two important concepts stand out in information systems. First, there is still much that we do not know. Second, technology changes rapidly.

---

 **Reality Bytes**    1–2   MARKET FACTS

Established in 1946, Market Facts conducts survey research of consumers. The major data-collection facilities include Consumer Mail Panels, a fixed mail panel of 450,000 households; Consumer Opinion Forums, a network of six mall interviewing sites; a national telephone interviewing center; and Marketest, a controlled store auditing facility for custom test marketing and in-store experimentation. Market Facts has distinguished itself as challenging clients' assumptions about the need for research, the optimum size of a project, and the potential benefits to be derived from it. As a result, Market Facts emphasizes helping clients optimize the allocation of their research dollars.

One example of the efficiency of the company is Consumer Mail Panels. Because the company relies on mail panel questionnaires, it has been able to gather consumer information at one-third the cost of personal interviews. When asked for advice regarding the market research industry, William F. O'Dell, the founder of Market Facts, states:

Creativity is the most important ingredient in decision making, bar none. My advice to people getting into the industry today is to view market research from a management point-of-view. In other words, look at the need for the information and how it might be used. Let technology be the last thing you worry about. Understanding people is as important as the decision-making process itself.

You have probably experienced the fact that software and hardware you studied in earlier courses have already become obsolete.

Businesses and management have been changing as well. Difficult economic times provide even more incentive to change. To be better managers and to understand the role of technology in business, you must be aware of how this environment is changing. Success in business comes from identifying patterns and being the first to take advantage of them.

As described in Figure 1.3, we will focus on six basic trends: (1) specialization, (2) management by methodology, (3) decentralization and small business, (4) reliance on temporary workers, (5) internationalization, and (6) the increasing importance of service-oriented businesses. These trends will be discussed throughout the text to illustrate how they affect the use of information systems and how managers can use information systems to take advantage of these trends. The tightening job market (Reality Bytes 1–3) also means that managers must continually work on self-improvement. To survive, you must provide value to the organization.

## Specialization

The basic advantages of specialization and division of labor in manufacturing were discussed by Adam Smith more than 200 years ago. The concepts are now being applied to managers. As functional areas (such as marketing or finance) become more

**FIGURE 1.3**

Changes occurring in the business world affect the use of information technology. These trends and their implications are discussed throughout the book. Managers who understand these trends and the relationship with technology will make better decisions.

| BUSINESS TREND | IMPLICATIONS FOR TECHNOLOGY |
|---|---|
| Specialization | • Increased demand for technical skills<br>• Specialized MIS tools<br>• Increased communication |
| Methodology & Franchises | • Reduction of middle management<br>• Increased data sharing<br>• Increased analysis by top management<br>• Computer support for rules<br>• Re-engineering |
| Decentralization & Small Business | • Communication needs<br>• Lower cost of management tasks<br>• Low-maintenance technology |
| Temporary Workers | • Managing through rules<br>• Finding and evaluating workers<br>• Coordination and control<br>• Personal advancement through technology<br>• Security |
| Internationalization | • Communication<br>• Product design<br>• System development and programming<br>• Sales and marketing |
| Service Orientation | • Management jobs are information jobs<br>• Customer service requires better information<br>• Speed |

complex, they also become more specialized. Area managers are expected to understand and use increasingly sophisticated models and tools to analyze events and make decisions. As a result, the demand for managers with specific technical skills is increasing, whereas the demand for general business managers is declining. This trend is reflected in MIS by the large number of specialized tools being created, and the increased communication demands for sharing information among the specialists.

## ▼ MANAGEMENT TRENDS ▲

For thousands of years, there was little need for management in firms. Business primarily consisted of small firms in agriculture, retail, or various trades. Workers were typically hired based on their specific skills. Unskilled workers were hired on a temporary basis for simple manual labor.

The spread of mass production techniques in the early 1900s encouraged firms to expand in size to take advantage of economies of scale. Firms then needed huge numbers of low-skilled workers on a permanent basis. The production process had to be efficiently organized and supervisors were needed to control and manage the workers. Managers were also needed to coordinate the huge flow of raw materials and inventories needed to keep the production lines moving. Frederick Taylor devised his *Principles of Scientific Management* (1911) to make production as efficient as possible. Partly in response to this rigid doctrine, in the 1930s several researchers explored the psychology of work and employee motivation.

Mass production requires mass marketing and mass consumption, which means that firms needed retail outlets to carry their products and distribution channels to deliver the products. Improved communication enabled firms to create regional and national advertising campaigns. All of these tasks required more middle-level managers to make decisions and control the process. As organizations grew in size and complexity, financial and accounting controls became increasingly important—hence the need for more managers and more information. Alfred Sloan, head of General Motors, devised a centralized organizational structure to help him run his enormously complex corporation. He relied on layers of middle managers in a hierarchical chain-of-command to

solve ordinary problems and collect and summarize data for upper management.

Some of the nationwide firms in the retail sector (e.g., Sears, Kmart, and Woolworth), were organized in a similar fashion. The hierarchical system allowed central management to set overall strategies, purchase products in bulk, and store large quantities in warehouses. However, individual store managers made their own decisions about which products to stock, how to arrange merchandise, and how to market products at the local level. Adapting concepts developed in World War II, and with the advent of computers, the field of operations management was formed to create and analyze quantitative models.

In the 1950s, Ray Kroc, founder of McDonald's, chose a different approach and relied on the franchise model to build and control his company. With the franchise approach, typical operating decisions are reduced to a set of rules and procedures. Control and decisions are centralized, and local managers simply carry out standard instructions. Management theory began concentrating on systems analysis, with special attention on dynamic systems, feedback, and control.

As Leavitt and Whisler pointed out in 1958, increased use of computers enables firms to decrease the number of midlevel managers and increase centralized control. Although it took several years for technology to progress far enough to support these changes and for managers to take advantage of the technology, several companies have begun to emphasize this approach. For example, Wal-Mart, Mrs. Fields Cookies and Service-Master have relied on technology and management by methodology to provide efficient centralized control.

Reality Bytes     1–3  THE PERFECT FIT?

Ten years ago, new managers had six months to a year to prove their value to the company. Today, new hires are being terminated after only days or a couple weeks on the job. A 1994 study by the American Management Association revealed that in the prior two years, 22 percent of the employers contacted had fired a professional or manager within 90 days of hiring him or her.

Reasons for the change include increased business competition, attempts to avoid lawsuits, and the desire to find exactly the right person for the job. Edward Wild, the head of a newsletter publishing company notes: "With such a tremendous pool of talented people out there, you might as well get the one who will work out best."

Other problems arise when employees do not have the skills they claim on their resumes. Jerome Rosow, president of a nonprofit research group in New York, fired an accountant after one week, because she did not really know how to operate a spreadsheet program that she claimed to know.

## Management by Methodology and Franchises

An important result of specialization is the reduction of management tasks to smaller problems. Using specialization coupled with technology, firms have reduced many management problems to a set of rules or standard operating procedures. Day-to-day problems can be addressed with a standard methodology. For example, the manager's guidebook at Wal-Mart or the cookie directions at Mrs. Fields Cookies explain how to solve or prevent many common problems. These rules were created by analyzing the business setting, building models of the business, and then creating rules by anticipating decisions and problems. This approach gives less flexibility to the lower-level managers but encourages a standardized product, consistent quality, and adherence to the corporate philosophy.

Management by methodology also allows firms to reduce their number of middle managers. By anticipating common problems and decisions, there is no need to call on trained managers to solve the daily problems. Franchises like McDonald's or Mrs. Fields Cookies carry this technique one level further by making the franchisee responsible for the financial performance of individual units. Yet the common management tasks are defined by the central corporation.

As companies have changed, so have the jobs of managers. College graduates 20 years ago often looked forward to lifelong careers with large companies. The goal was to start at some lower level in the firm, work diligently, and progress up the ladder to higher levels of management. Although only a few people would ever make it to the level of vice-president or chief executive officer (CEO), there was always the hope of becoming a regional or district level manager. Figure 1.4 illustrates this traditional hierarchy and highlights the typical middle management roles of data collection and analysis performed for this type of organization.

Today, companies are making major changes. Figure 1.5 shows a company divided into smaller, decentralized teams. Individual teams follow predefined procedures and are responsible for the performance of their team. Technology is used to facilitate communication and share data between the teams. Individual managers succeed as their team succeeds. Although some talented managers may eventually be promoted to higher-level teams, most workers will remain within the lower-team levels. Many of these workers could become part-time or contract employees who work

**FIGURE 1.4**

In a traditional organizational structure, lower-level managers deal with customers and collect basic data. Middle-level managers analyze the data, create reports, and make suggestions to upper-level managers. The higher-level managers make decisions and set rules to guide the other managers.

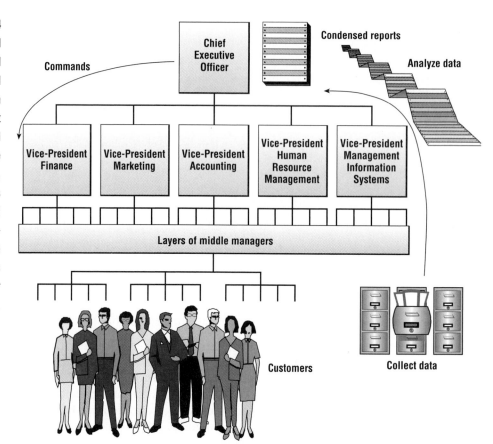

Traditional management of companies often created layers of bureaucracy—middle-level managers who spent their careers overseeing lower-level managers, creating reports, and interpreting commands from higher-level managers. A fundamental purpose of re-engineering is to use technology to eliminate these jobs.

In an interview in *The Wall Street Journal,* Michael Hammer and James Champy, leading proponents of re-engineering, commented on the future roles of managers. Hammer observes:

I think there are a lot of people who will never find a job again. The market is over for bureaucrats. If you can't design or sell products, if you can't do real work, I'd get real nervous. . . A successful career will no longer be about promotion. It'll be about mastery. What is a successful career for a lawyer?

Very few people want to be managing partner; it's about being the best tax attorney you can be.

Champy notes that future workers need to thoroughly understand the entire business:

We want workers to make decisions, and they can't do that without a knowledge about the business context. You also have to [learn] more behavioral things. Now that we've given you more control, how do you behave and make decisions—from how do you deal with a worker who isn't functioning, to what do you do when a customer asks for something that isn't in the rule book?

**FIGURE 1.5**

In the last few years, many companies have moved toward a more decentralized form of management. They have removed the middle-layers of management and replaced them with smaller teams. Franchises and smaller teams have become the primary service contact with customers. Information sharing becomes crucial in this environment. Teams communicate directly and share data across the company.

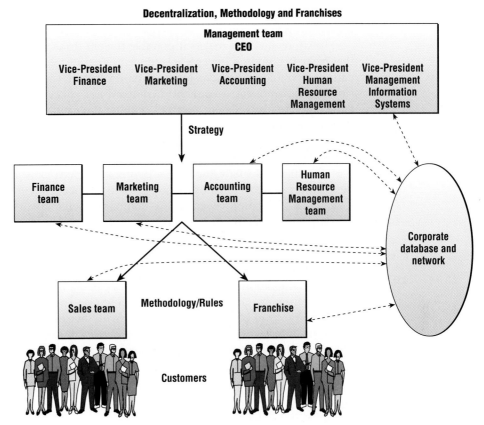

**Decentralization, Methodology and Franchises**

with a team at one company to solve a specific problem, then move on to a new assignment with another company. As emphasized by Hammer and Champy (Reality Bytes 1–4), in this environment, an individual's skills become crucial to getting and keeping job assignments.

## Decentralization and Small Business

Up to the late 1800s and early 1900s, most businesses were small, having markets limited to small geographic regions. A brief history of industrial organization reveals that there were three waves of mergers in the U.S.: (1) the horizontal mergers of the late 1800s epitomized by the oil and banking industries; (2) the vertical integration of the early half of the twentieth century, illustrated by the oil, steel, and automobile companies; and (3) conglomerate mergers of the 1950s and 1960s, in which firms like IT&T (an international telecommunications giant) acquired subsidiaries in many different industries (including a bakery!). All of these mergers arose to take advantage of economic power, but technology made them possible. Without communication (telegraph and telephones earlier, computer networks later), firms could not grow beyond a certain size because managers could not monitor and control lower-level workers.

In the mid-1990s, two additional waves of mergers appear to be expanding: (1) consolidation within the banking industry and (2) mergers among telecommunications firms and companies in the entertainment industry. The mergers in the banking industry were enabled by changing legislation and supported by improved communications, which aided managers to control branches across wider areas. The mergers among telecommunications giants and companies in the entertainment industry (such as ABC and Disney) seem to represent an attempt to profit through vertical integration. However, it is still too early to determine the true impact of these mergers.

Today, technology makes it possible to split firms into smaller managerial units that make decisions at lower levels (decentralization). In addition to faster communication, technology provides low-cost hardware and software available to each division. It is now possible to operate a company as a collection of small teams and maintain complete management statistics without the need for hundreds of bookkeepers and accountants. In the past, with limited information technology, small divisions were expensive to maintain because of the cost of collecting and processing the basic accounting and operating data.

Since the mid-1980s, the largest corporations have drastically cut the number of people they employ. Most of the job growth has occurred in small businesses (with fewer than 200 employees). A few companies have taken a similar approach by decentralizing specific operations into teams of workers. In this situation, departments operate relatively independently, "selling" services to other departments by competing with other teams. They often perform work for outside firms as well—essentially operating as an independent business unit within the corporation.

Decentralization and smaller businesses can eliminate layers of middle managers in an organization. One goal of decentralization is to push the decisions and the work down to the level of the customer, to provide better customer service, and faster decisions. Information systems enable executives to gather and manipulate information themselves or with automated systems. As a result, there is less need for middle managers to prepare and analyze data.

## Temporary Workers

So what happens to the people who are no longer needed as middle-level managers? At various times in the past, some companies provided a form of lifetime employment for their workers. As long as workers continued to do their job and remained loyal to the company, their jobs would be secure. Even in more difficult times, when employees were laid off, they were often encouraged (through extensions of unemployment benefits) to wait until the economy improved and they could be rehired. Companies in other nations, especially Japan, had stronger commitments to workers and kept them on the payroll even in difficult times.

Today, in almost every industry and in many nations (including Japan), companies increasingly rely on a temporary workforce. Individuals are hired for specific skills and tasks. When these basic tasks are completed, the employees take other jobs. Increasingly, even executives are hired because of their specific expertise. Consultants and other professionals are hired on a contract basis to solve specific problems or complete special assignments.

In many ways, it is more difficult to manage a company that relies on temporary workers. Special efforts must be made to control quality, keep employees working together, and ensure that contract provisions are met. Technology can play an important role in these situations. It can improve communications, maintain easy (but controlled) access to data and contracts, and help to institute corporate standards.

To individual workers, firms' reliance on temporary workers means that to achieve a position with more responsibility and command higher rates of pay, workers will need to possess more analytic skills than other potential employees. Even as a manager, you will need your own competitive (professional) advantage. Along with additional education, your use and knowledge of technology can give you an advantage. For example, personal productivity tools such as word processors and spreadsheets enable workers to complete jobs faster and with better quality. At the next level, programming tools such as Power Builder and Visual Basic and database management systems (see Chapter 5) enable you to create custom systems with the help of previously written modules. Knowing how to use information technology to communicate (Chapter 6) and solve problems (Chapters 8 and 9) will help you get jobs and help you perform them more efficiently and with better quality.

## Internationalization

Several events of the early 1990s demonstrated the importance of international trade: closer ties forged with the European Union, creation of the North American Free Trade Agreement (NAFTA), and the continued relaxation of trade restrictions through GATT (General Agreement on Tariffs and Trade) and the World Trade Organization (WTO). Although barriers to trade remain, there is no doubt that the international flow of trade and services plays an increasingly important role in many companies. Even small firms are buying supplies from overseas and selling products in foreign markets. Trade also brings more competition, which encourages firms to be more careful in making decisions.

As Figure 1.6 shows, the role of exports and imports has expanded rapidly in the United States since 1970. In European nations, international trade is even more important. Today, internationalization is a daily fact of life for workers and managers in almost every company. Even small businesses have links to firms in other nations. Many have set up their own production facilities in other nations. Much of this global expansion is supported by technology, from communication to transportation, from management to quality control.

Communication facilities are one of the most prominent uses of information technology to support the move to international operations. Communication technology is especially important for service industries like consulting, programming, design, marketing, and banking. Several years ago, services were often considered to be nontradable goods because they tended to have high transportation costs, making them difficult to export. Today, improved communication facilities have made certain types of services easy to export. For example, financial institutions now operate globally. Although not on the same level as banks, software development is also beginning to achieve an international presence. Some U.S. firms are turning to programmers in Ireland, India, and Taiwan. Through the use of programmers in India, a U.S.-based firm can develop specifications during the day and transmit them to India. With the

**FIGURE 1.6**

By almost any statistic, in almost every nation, the level of international trade has increased dramatically during the last 20 years. International trade brings more choices, more competition, more data, more complexity, and more management challenges.

**U.S. Merchandise Trade**

time difference, the programmers work during the U.S. night hours and the U.S. workers receive updates and fixes the next day.

Internationalization also plays a role in selling products. Groups of countries have different standards, regulations, and consumer preferences. Products and sales techniques that work well in one nation may not transfer to another culture. Information technology can track these differences, enabling more flexible manufacturing systems that can customize products for each market.

The increased competition created by internationalization and decentralization requires corporations to be more flexible. Flexibility is needed to adapt products to different markets, choose suppliers, adopt new production processes, find innovative financing, change marketing campaigns, and modify accounting systems. Firms that attain this flexibility can respond faster to market changes, catch opportunities unavailable to slower firms, and become more profitable.

## Service-Oriented Business

Another trend facing industrialized nations is the move toward a service-oriented economy. As shown in Figure 1.7, in 1920 the U.S. census showed 29 percent of the employed were in farming. By 1990, that figure had shrunk to 3 percent. In the early 1900s, people were afraid that this trend would cause food shortages throughout the U.S. and the world. Improvements in technology in the form of mechanization, transportation, growing techniques, chemicals, and crop genetics proved them wrong.

A similar trend in manufacturing has produced similar consternation. Although the number of workers employed in manufacturing has varied over time, it is clear that the largest increase in jobs has been in the management, clerical, and service sectors. In 1993, 26 percent of the jobs were in manufacturing, with 71 percent in service and management jobs. The largest increase in new jobs has been in the management, clerical, and service sectors.

These trends represent changes in the U.S. economy and in demographics such as age characteristics of the population. The importance of the service sector has to be considered when we examine how MIS can benefit the firm and its workers. Genuine Parts (NAPA) (Reality Bytes 1–5) provides just one example of how informa-

**FIGURE 1.7**

Over time, Americans have moved from agricultural to manufacturing to service and management jobs. (Year 2000 shown here is a forecast.) Management and service jobs are often dedicated to collecting and analyzing data. Just as the decline of workers in agriculture did not create a shortage of food, the relative decline in manufacturing did not create a shortage of products.

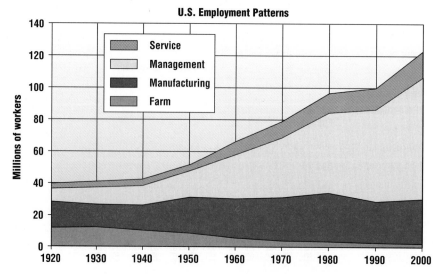

**Reality Bytes**  **1–5** GENUINE PARTS (NAPA)

If you are like most Americans today, you are keeping your car for more years and driving it for more miles. (Eight years in 1989 versus seven in 1982 and 9,200 miles per year in 1986, up 3 percent from 1986.) As your car gets older, it gets more difficult to find repair parts. Dealerships are more interested in selling you a new car than in repairing an old one. It is advantageous to the automobile companies to develop new parts and phase out the old ones.

Not so for Genuine Parts, which distributes more than 100,000 items under the NAPA Auto Parts line. The company carries complete replacements for nearly every make and model of car on the road. Their 61 nationwide distribution centers guarantee delivery overnight to more than 6,000 jobbers, gas stations, auto parts stores, and independent mechanics. President Larry Prince loves to relate stories of how even automobile dealerships come to them when they really need a part.

Since 1986 the auto replacement parts market has grown substantially to $68 billion dollars in 1992. Yet it has also grown more competitive with more and more suppliers entering an inventory-intensive marketplace.

Even with these pressures, Genuine Parts has boosted its dividend, increased sales by 33 percent, and raised earnings by 36 percent.

Genuine Parts's secret is its service. This service is made possible by the continuously updated market research it integrates into its computer inventory system. On any given day it can tell any dealer how many new and used Fords or Chryslers are in the dealer's service area and, as a result, how many replacement parts the dealer is likely to need for each model. This computerized market and inventory information even enables Genuine Parts to service its competitors. Montgomery Ward, Sears, Midas, and Pep Boys have come to rely on Genuine Parts for hard-to-find or emergency replacements.

Based on this marketing information, Genuine Parts has developed a strong brand identity for its products. This has involved an upgrade for the brand image through spruced-up stores, redesigned sales floors, and a new color scheme. One hundred company-owned retail outlets opened in 1994 and another 100 stores were scheduled to open in 1995.

tion can be used to provide better service and respond to market forces. Their information system gives them advantages over their competitors. Even manufacturing companies are beginning to focus their efforts around the concept of providing services to the customer.

**RE-ENGINEERING: ALTERING THE RULES**

We have already noted that many companies are managed by rules and procedures. It would be virtually impossible to do otherwise—the cost of intense evaluation of every single decision would be overwhelming. Hence, upper-level managers establish procedures and rules and an organizational structure that automatically solves typical problems. More complex problems are supposed to be identified by managers and forwarded up the chain-of-command for answers.

Of course, this type of management creates a fixed approach to operations and to solving problems. However, the business environment rarely remains constant. Over time, new technologies are introduced, new competitors arrive, products change, old markets shrink, and new markets arise. At some point, firms that have been guided by relatively static methodologies find their methods no longer match the marketplace. Hence, they decide to re-engineer the company: Beginning from scratch, they identify goals along with the most efficient means of attaining those goals, and create new processes that change the company to meet the new goals. The term **re-engineering** and its current usage were made popular in 1990 by management consultants James Champy and Michael Hammer. Many of the underlying concepts have been in use for years.

**Reality Bytes** ◥    1–6   RE-ENGINEERING AT COMPAQ

Compaq Computer began life in 1982 with Rod Canion at the helm as one of the fastest growing companies in the U.S. Within six years, annual sales had exceeded $2 billion. In 1991, the easy life changed as sales and profits plummeted due to competition from low-priced generic computers. In 1991, the board replaced Mr. Canion with Eckhard Pfeiffer, formerly the chief operating officer. In June 1992, Compaq launched a major price cutting offensive, dropping prices almost 30 percent per year. Although profit margins have dropped from 43 percent of sales in 1990 to 27 percent in early 1994, net profit has increased from the increase in market share. Estimated sales in 1994 could top $10 billion.

How did Mr. Pfeiffer turn Compaq around? The simple answer is that he figured out how to cut the costs of production, partly by expanding production in overseas plants (Singapore, Scotland, China, and Brazil), also by re-engineering the production at the main plant in Houston. In 1993, the Houston factory operated six production lines for 60 hours a week in 3 million square feet of space. In 1994, the factory operated 13 lines, 24 hours a day in only 2.4 million square feet of space. The sales force was one-third smaller in 1994 than it was in 1991 and worked mostly from home to reduce office costs. Inventory costs were reduced by establishing just-in-time contracts with the suppliers. By re-engineering the production, labor, and overhead, costs per computer have been reduced by 75 percent over two years.

Sometimes re-engineering is undertaken by internal management as a means to improve the company. For example, in the early 1990s, Compaq Computer (Reality Bytes 1–6) altered its strategy and re-engineered its operations and management to cut millions of dollars in costs and save the company. Sometimes, re-engineering is forced on the company when it is taken over by another corporation. In a few rare cases, managers continuously evaluate the firm to make several small changes instead of relying on a major overhaul.

Re-engineering can be a highly complex process, requiring thousands of hours of time to analyze the company and its processes. In addition to the complexity, re-engineering often faces resistance because it results in a change in the organization's structure, which affects the authority and power of various managers.

Like any management technique, re-engineering is not guaranteed to work. A report by CSC Index, a major re-engineering consulting company, which surveyed 497 large companies in the U.S. and 124 in Europe, noted that 69 percent of the American and 75 percent of the European companies have already undertaken re-engineering projects. Several of these projects have not been successful. CSC Index notes that three factors are necessary for success: (1) overcome resistance by managers who are afraid of losing jobs or power; (2) earn strong support from upper management; and (3) aim high and go for major changes instead of small rearrangements.

Re-engineering has a close relationship with management information systems. In many cases, the new processes will rely on new computer systems to transfer and manipulate information. The important tie between re-engineering and information technology is that it is not sufficient to install new computers; the company must also re-engineer its underlying processes. A common situation occurred throughout the 1980s and 1990s when companies purchased millions of dollars of personal computers but failed to re-organize business operations to capitalize on computerization. As a result, the companies showed little or no gain in productivity from the use of the computers. For automation to be useful, managers need to understand how the computers will alter the tasks and management of the firm.

**MANAGEMENT AND DECISION LEVELS**

To understand management, re-engineering, and information systems, it helps to divide the organization into three levels: strategy, tactics, and operations. Each level has unique characteristics, which use different types of support from information technology. These levels were explained by Robert Anthony in 1965. In 1971, Gorry and Scott Morton added a detailed explanation of how information systems at that time could support the various levels of management. Figure 1.8 is an updated picture of the typical pyramid shape of most organizations involving operations and tactical and strategic decisions. As is typical with most management models, the various levels are not strictly delineated. Some problems will encompass all levels of the firm. Similarly, making a change at one level may have unexpected repercussions on the other levels. Classifying a problem by its most relevant level makes it easier to concentrate on a solution. Once the primary problems are solved, the other effects are easier to handle. This text begins by discussing operations and works up to strategy. The cases in each chapter will help you identify problems at each level.

## Operations

The *operations level* consists of day-to-day operations and decisions. In your first job, you will typically concentrate on the problems that arise at this level. For example, in a manufacturing firm, machine settings, worker schedules, and maintenance requirements would represent management tasks and decisions at the operational level. Information technology at this level is used to collect data and perform well-defined computations. Most of the tasks and decisions are well **structured,** in the sense that they can be defined by a set of rules or procedures. For example, a clerk at Wal-Mart follows the procedures in the guidebook to deal with typical operations. Common problems are also anticipated, with actions spelled out in the guidebook.

As summarized in Figure 1.9, managers in other disciplines, such as accounting, marketing, or finance, also face operational decisions. Personal productivity tools, such as spreadsheets, word processors, and database management systems help managers collect and evaluate data they receive on a daily basis. The use of these tools is reviewed in Chapter 2.

An important task at the operations level is to collect data on transactions and operations, hence **transaction processing systems** are a crucial component of the organization's information system. The data collected form the foundation for all other information system capabilities. As discussed in Chapter 4, an important characteristic

**FIGURE 1.8**

There are three primary levels of decisions in business. Business operations consist of tasks to keep the business operating on a day-to-day basis. Tactical decisions involve changes to the firm without altering the overall structure. Strategic decisions can alter the entire firm or even the industry. Information system tools exist to help with each type of decision.

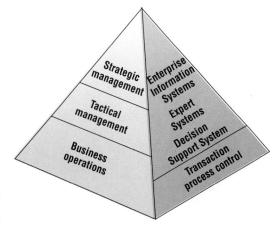

| SECTOR | OPERATIONS | TACTICS | STRATEGY |
|---|---|---|---|
| Production | • Machine settings<br>• Worker schedules<br>• Maintenance schedules | • Rearrange work area<br>• Schedule new products<br>• Change inventory method | • New factory<br>• New products<br>• New industry |
| Accounting | • Categorize assets<br>• Assign expenses<br>• Produce reports | • Inventory valuation<br>• Depreciation method<br>• Finance short/long term | • New GL system<br>• Debt vs. equity<br>• International taxes |
| Marketing | • Reward salespeople<br>• Survey customers<br>• Monitor promotions | • Determine pricing<br>• Promotional campaigns<br>• Select marketing media | • Monitor competitors<br>• New products<br>• New markets |

**FIGURE 1.9**

Each functional area of management faces the three categories of decisions and problems. Only a few examples are presented here.

of transaction processing systems is the ability to provide data for multiple users at the same time. Database management systems are increasingly used to control data and build systems to share data. Their role is explained in Chapter 5. Chapter 6 shows how communication networks are used to provide access to data throughout the organization. Along the same lines, different types of data (e.g., text, graphs, pictures) are often combined to create complex reports or compound documents, which are illustrated in Chapter 7.

Operational decisions are often the easiest to understand. They deal with structured problems over relatively short periods of time. The Weyerhaeuser situation (Reality Bytes 1–7) provides a small example of how one company improved its production process by giving managers better access to data when making day-to-day decisions about the production process.

## Tactics

As you move up in your career to project leader or department manager, you will encounter a different level of decisions, where the types of problems will depend on your specialization, but some common features will stand out. At the *tactical level*, decisions typically involve time frames of less than a year. These decisions usually

◤ **Reality Bytes** ◥   1–7   WEYERHAEUSER PAPER MILL

Weyerhaeuser Paper Mill in North Carolina upgraded its computer systems to eliminate network crashes, improve responsiveness to the customers, lower costs, and speed up troubleshooting. A plant-wide computer integrated manufacturing system was installed. Networks link minicomputers to increase information flow throughout the construction floor. Most importantly, decision making can be placed with the manager who is closest to the problem. The technology gives the manager the information and the alternatives to choose the best decision to expedite the paper production process. All of the computers and control systems are networked and controlled by the Mill Information System. Economies are so great that the payoff for the system is expected in less than 18 months.

result in making relatively major changes, but stay within the existing structure of the organization.

A manufacturing tactical-level decision might involve rearranging the work area, altering production schedules, changing inventory methods, or expanding quality control measures. These changes require time to implement, and represent changes to the basic methods of the firm. What distinguishes them is that they can be made without altering the overall characteristics of the organization. For example, in most cases, expanding quality control measures does not require the firm to expand into new industries, build new facilities, or alter the structure of the industry.

Tactical decisions are less structured and more complex than operational decisions. Researchers have created models to evaluate various management situations. Chapter 8 explains how **decision support systems** use the data collected by transaction processing systems to evaluate these models and assist managers to make tactical decisions. Chapter 9 surveys some of the models that you encounter in your other courses and presents cases that show decision support systems can make your job easier.

Other types of problems occur in business that involve more complex models. For instance, **diagnostic situations** consist of spotting problems, searching for the cause, and implementing corrections. Examples of these situations include responding to problem reports from operations to identify the cause of the problem and potential solutions. For instance, a marketing manager might be asked to determine why the latest marketing approach did not perform as well as expected. Tactical-level decisions tend to involve specialized problems, and can often be solved with the help of an expert. Chapter 10 presents **expert systems** to make this knowledge more accessible to an organization.

## Strategy

The next step on the pyramid moves up the corporate ladder to executive-level decisions. Although you may never be a CEO, you might be in a position to advise upper-level management about strategic opportunities—especially in small businesses. **Strategic decisions** involve changing the overall structure of the firm to give it an advantage over the competition. They are long-term decisions and are unstructured. In other words, they are usually difficult and risky decisions. Examples of strategic decisions in the manufacturing arena include building new factories, expanding to new products or industries, or even going out of business. Strategic decisions represent an attempt to gain a competitive advantage over your rivals. Because of the complexity and unstructured nature of executives' decisions, it is difficult to determine how information systems can help at the strategic level. However, Chapter 11 explores information system techniques that firms have used to gain a competitive advantage.

**AN INTRODUCTION TO STRATEGY**  Firms are constantly searching for ways to gain an advantage over their rivals. Finding these opportunities is hard—it requires extensive knowledge of the industry, and it requires creativity. Managers also have to be willing to take risks to implement strategic options. Strategic uses of IT often involve the use of new technology and development of new software. Being the first company to implement a new idea can be risky. However, it can also bring substantial rewards.

We will discuss strategic uses of IT in detail in Chapter 11 because you need to understand the technology before trying to solve difficult problems. On the other hand, to stimulate the imagination needed for creativity, it helps to begin thinking about the basic ideas right from the start. Many cases used throughout the book will illustrate how firms have used technology to gain substantial advantages. These examples should help you solve other problems. If you can recognize a pattern, or similarity, between your problem and actions taken by other firms, the association may help you create a solution.

Michael Porter noted that often the first step in searching for competitive advantage is to focus on *external agents,* or entities that are outside the direct control of your company. Porter's Five Forces model in Figure 1.12 illustrates that typical external agents are customers, suppliers, rivals, and governments. For instance, competitive advantages can be found by producing better quality items or services at a lower cost than your rivals. Also, many firms have strengthened their positions by building closer ties with their suppliers and customers. An excellent example of this situation is provided by Baxter Healthcare (Reality Bytes 1–8), as illustrated in Figures 1.10 and 1.11. Information technology can be used to exchange information with suppliers or customers. Over time, the customers and suppliers will come to rely on this information and the capabilities you provide. Even if a competitor eventually offers similar ties, your new partners (customers and suppliers)

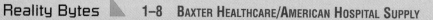

## Reality Bytes ▶ 1–8 Baxter Healthcare/American Hospital Supply

Hospitals use a large amount of routine supplies such as bandages and antiseptics. Originally, they purchased them from various suppliers, held them in inventory, and distributed them throughout the hospital as they were needed. This relationship is shown in Figure 1.10. American Hospital Supply (AHS) was one of these suppliers. To gain an advantage over their competitors, AHS created a new system and made an offer to the hospital managers. AHS placed computer terminals in hospital locations where the supplies were used (emergency, operating rooms, nursing stations, etc.). As shown in Figure 1.11, these terminals were connected to the AHS computer.

As hospital personnel removed supplies, they recorded them on the terminals. The computer kept track of the amount of supplies in each location. A list would be printed at the warehouse, and drivers delivered the necessary supplies to each location in the hospital. Monthly usage statistics were sent to the hospital.

The hospital gained because the facility did not need to maintain extra inventory, which saved money and space. Fewer hospital employees were needed, because the supplies were delivered directly to the needed locations. Additionally, the hospital received detailed usage records.

To offer this service, AHS incurred higher costs—largely the cost of creating and maintaining the information system. What did AHS gain in return? As long as it was the only company offering this service, AHS gained a competitive advantage by providing a new service. Hospitals were more likely to choose AHS over the rivals. But what would happen if a competitor created a similar system? Would the hospitals stay with AHS or switch to the rivals?

Although the answer depended on the prices, hospitals had a strong incentive to stay with AHS. They would encounter various *switching costs* if they chose another supplier. For example, daily operations would be disrupted while the system was changed. Employees would have to be retrained to use the new system. Managers who used the monthly usage reports would have to adapt to the new system. A rival would have to offer strong price advantages to overcome these costs.

Of course, over time Baxter had an incentive to cut its costs to maintain higher profits. In the process their delivery service might suffer. Some hospitals apparently experienced problems and returned to in-house stock rooms to eliminate shortages of basic supplies.

**FIGURE 1.10**

American Hospital Supply began as an intermediary that bought various medical supplies and distributed them in bulk to hospitals. The hospital distributed supplies throughout the hospital and was responsible for maintaining its own inventory.

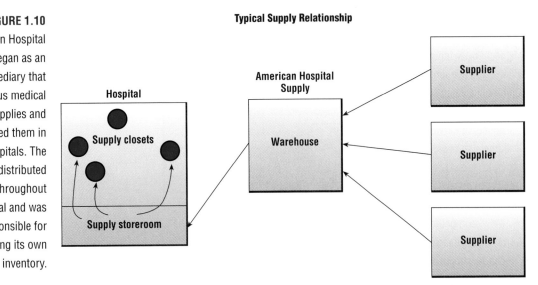

**Typical Supply Relationship**

will be reluctant to deal with a different firm because it will be difficult to change their systems and processes.

It can be difficult to identify strategic opportunities, and it requires practice to learn to analyze a complex problem. Figure 1.13 can be used to organize your thoughts as you approach strategic problems. Additional techniques and ideas are discussed in Chapter 11.

Information technology can also play a role in helping managers seek competitive solutions that might not directly employ the new technology. This support for strategic decisions typically consists of gathering, analyzing, and presenting data on rivals, customers, and suppliers.

**FIGURE 1.11**

American Hospital Supply changed the industry by providing a just-in-time inventory delivery service. Supplies then were delivered directly to where they are used within the hospital. AHS could offer this system only by maintaining a computer link between supply usage and the local warehouse. The computer data also provided summary reports to management. By purchasing AHS, Baxter Healthcare gained immediate access to that sales data.

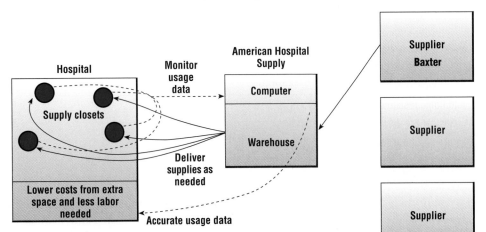

**AHS/Baxter Computer Link**

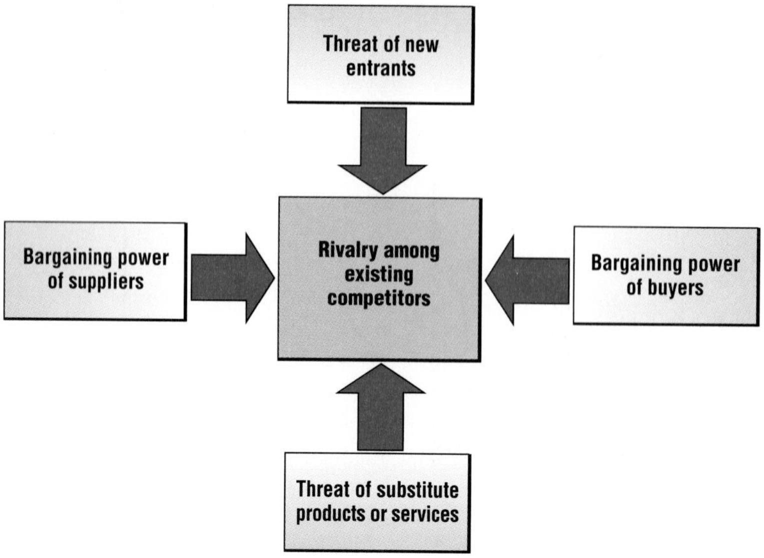

**FIGURE 1.12**

In analyzing strategies, Michael Porter focuses on the five forces: threat of new entrants, threat of substitute products or services, bargaining power of suppliers, bargaining power of buyers, and rivalry among existing competitors. Competitive advantage can be obtained by using these forces or altering the relationships between these external agents.

SOURCE: Adapted from Michael Porter, *Competitive Strategy: Techniques for Analyzing Industries and Competitors,* (New York: Free Press), 1980.

**FIGURE 1.13**

A useful method to analyze strategic problems is to begin by listing all of the strengths and weaknesses of the organization. Then analyze each category in detail. You will often have to perform additional research to answer the detailed questions.

| STRENGTH | |
|---|---|
| Source of strength | |
| Value of strength | |
| How can it be developed? | |
| What could undermine it? | |
| Development costs | |
| Additional benefits (opportunities) | |

| WEAKNESS | |
|---|---|
| Effect on company | |
| Possible solutions | |
| Cost of solution | |
| Result and cost of leaving as-is | |

**MANAGEMENT INFORMATION SYSTEM ROLES**

Information systems do not magically appear in an organization. Considerable effort, time, and resources must be devoted to building and maintaining information systems. One of the most important considerations in designing information systems is to solve the right problem. Identifying business problems and potential solutions is the main purpose of *systems analysis,* described in Chapter 3. These techniques can also help you analyze business cases and problems in other business functions. Chapter 12 introduces the main techniques used to build information systems. It focuses on the advantages and disadvantages of techniques to build information systems, such as *systems development life cycle, prototyping,* and *end-user development.*

The diverse roles of the MIS department are described in Chapter 13, along with problems that are often encountered. A common issue in many firms today is centralization versus decentralization—should major decisions be made by a core group of managers for the entire company, or should decisions be left to the managers within each subdivision of the firm? For many years business functions, including MIS roles, were centralized. As businesses have pursued decentralization in the last few years, managers have searched for new information technologies that can support both centralized and decentralized operations.

Chapter 14 outlines some of the social impacts of information technology. Users and managers need to remember that business information systems can also adversely affect workers and consumers. Firms, managers, and developers have responsibilities to insure that information systems continue to benefit everyone.

## SUMMARY

Information technology is altering jobs, businesses, and society. Managers who understand and use this technology will be able to improve companies and advance their personal careers. Information systems consist of hardware, software, people, procedures, and collections of data. These components work together to provide information and help managers run the firm, solve problems, and make decisions. Studying information systems will also teach you to analyze business operations and solve problems.

The role of a manager is changing, but at a basic level all managers spend time organizing resources, planning, motivating workers, and communicating with other employees and managers. Several business trends will affect individual jobs, business operations, and society. Important trends include specialization, management by methodology and franchising, decentralization, the increased importance of small businesses, the use of temporary workers and consultants, the growing international scope of business, and the rise in service-oriented businesses. Information technology is used to support these trends and provide new management alternatives.

Like many problems, management and information technology can be studied by breaking them down into smaller pieces. There are three basic levels to management: operations, tactics, and strategies. The operations level is concerned with day-to-day operations of the firm. Tactics involve changes and decisions that improve opera-

> ### A MANAGER'S VIEW
>
> To be a successful manager, you must understand the roles of a manager in a modern company. There are several views of managers: as organizers and planners, as decision-makers, or as facilitators and team-leaders. As a worker and a manager, you need to understand several trends in business and how they affect the ways managers do their jobs.
>
> You also need to know how information technology can be used to make you a better manager. Technology is helpful in personal tasks, collecting data, sharing information, analyzing problems, making decisions, and in giving your company a competitive advantage.

tions but do not require a major restructuring of the firm. Strategies are designed to give a firm a competitive advantage.

Strategy typically involves examining external forces: rivals (competitors within the industry), customers, suppliers, potential new competitors, and potential substitute products or services. Information technology can be used strategically to strengthen links between customers and suppliers. It can also be used to create new products and services and to improve the quality of the operations.

Information technology can be the foundation of a business, but it can also be expensive. It is important that the information system be designed and organized to match the needs of the firm. Designing and creating effective information systems is a complex task, and several techniques have been developed to analyze organizations and build information systems. Common techniques include the systems development life cycle, prototyping, and end-user development. Business managers need to understand the strengths and limitations of the various methodologies to ensure that companies get an information system that meets their needs.

## KEY WORDS

| | | |
|---|---|---|
| data, 7 | information, 7 | software, 7 |
| databases, 7 | information technology, 6 | strategic decisions, 23 |
| decision process, 10 | knowledge, 7 | structured decisions, 21 |
| decision support systems, 23 | management information system, 6 | systems analysis and design, 8 |
| diagnostic situations, 23 | people, 7 | transaction processing system, 21 |
| expert systems, 23 | procedures, 7 | wisdom, 7 |
| hardware, 7 | re-engineering, 19 | |

## REVIEW QUESTIONS

1. What is the main purpose of MIS?
2. Why do students who are not MIS majors need to study MIS?
3. Describe how six basic trends in today's business environment are related to MIS.
4. Describe the five components of a management information system.
5. What is meant by the phrase *management by methodology?* How will it affect you in the next five years?
6. Describe the three basic levels of management decisions.
7. How can an understanding of the levels of management decisions help you solve business problems?

8. What is the purpose of re-engineering? What are the costs and benefits of re-engineering?
9. Using the information given in your text and the knowledge you have gained in your previous business classes, explain why the concepts in this text are important to all students of management.
10. Outside the business environment, what are some uses of computers?
11. How are information systems used at the various levels of business management?
12. What is the main purpose of system analysis?

## EXERCISES

1. Interview a local manager (or a student who has recently graduated) to discover which business trends most affect them. Are there any other patterns that affect their industry?
2. Using the resources of your library (government data, annual reports, business publications, etc.), find statistics to document at least two business trends. Draw graphs to reveal the patterns.
3. Choose one large company. Using annual reports, news articles, trade journals, and government data (e.g., 10K reports), research this company. Identify any changes that have been made in response to business trends in the last few years.
4. Choose a specific industry. Read news articles and trade journals to identify the major companies in that industry. Extend your research to include the primary international firms in the industry. Compare the growth rates of the two types of firms during the last five years.
5. Identify three common decisions within a specific industry. Identify one decision at each level (operations, tactical, and strategic).
6. Interview a recent graduate in your major (or a relative or friend). Find out what they do on a daily basis. Ask them what their managers do. Do managers have operations tasks to perform as well as management duties? For instance, does a manager in an accounting firm work on tax returns?
7. As an entrepreneur, you decide to open a fast food restaurant. You can purchase a franchise from one of the established corporations (as discussed in the McDonald's case) or create your own restaurant.

Compare the choices by identifying the decisions you will face with each approach. What data will you need to collect?

8. Think of a part-time job you have or have had. How does your manager break down his or her time among categories of communication, traditional management, networking, and human resource management? What issues have you felt your manager has dealt with effectively? On what issues could your manager spend time to improve?

9. The data disk contains the file C01EX09.txt for this problem. You have been hired as a consultant to a fast food store. The store manager has listed the cash received and the number of orders for each half hour of the day during one week of operations. Read the file into a spreadsheet.

   a. Format the columns, then compute daily and weekly totals.

   b. Create two line charts: one for cash, one for orders. Show transactions by the half hour. (There should be seven lines on each chart.) Highlight the line for Saturday.

   c. Create a separate schedule that shows the cumulative cash and orders through the day.

   d. Draw a graph for the cumulative cash flow. Indicate on the graph when the manager should take the cash to the bank (any time the total exceeds $2,000).

   e. The manager wants an estimate of the number of workers needed at any time of the day during the week. Create a table that displays the total number of counter workers and kitchen staff needed at each half hour (two columns per day). For every 25 orders during a half hour, we need two kitchen workers. For every 15 orders during the half hour, we need one counter worker.

## ADDITIONAL READING

"1,000 Served," *PC Week*, June 5, 1995, p. E7. [Burger King]

Anthony, Robert N. *Planning and Control Systems: A Framework for Analysis*. Cambridge: Harvard University Press, 1965. [Early MIS]

"Bank Services: Many Offer Rudimentary Options, But More Are Coming," *PC Week*, October 30, 1995, p. 104. [Wells Fargo Bank]

Bartholomew, Doug. "A Better Way to Work," *Information Week*, September 11, 1995, pp. 32–37. [Compaq]

Booker, Ellis. "Baxter Gets PC Smart, Ousts Dumb Terminals," *Computerworld*, April 3, 1989, p. 33. [Baxter Healthcare]

"Bringing Methodology to Client/Server Madness," *Software Magazine*, March 1995, pp. 35–44. [Market Facts]

"Chicken Soup and Fries," *Datamation*, November 1, 1995. [Boston Market]

"Compaq's Innovate Forum 95 Kicks Off Oct 16," *Newsbytes*, October 13, 1995, p. New10130038. [Compaq]

Dodge, Marc. "IT Payoff? Sure, We Can Measure It," *PC Week*, June 5, 1995, p. E8. [Hardee's and Denny's]

"Dynamic Corporate Networks Have Managers on a Tightrope," *Software Magazine*, December 1994, p. 45. [Compaq]

Fitzgerald, Michael. "Compaq Struggles with Success," *Computerworld*, June 21, 1993, p. 123. [Compaq]

"Give Me My Mini-Satellite Dish, Survey Respondents Say," *Information Industry Bulletin*, April 6, 1995, pp. 2–5. [Market Facts]

"Global Communications Get Real," *Information Week*, November 13, 1995, pp. 34–39. [Burger King]

Goldman, Kevin. "McDonald's Joins America Online to Send Information to PC Users," *The Wall Street Journal*, September 5, 1995, p. B7. [McDonald's]

Gorry, G.A. and M. Scott Morton. "A Framework for Management Information Systems," *Sloan Management Review*, Fall 1971, pp. 55–70. [Early MIS]

"Health-Care Guys Can Make Good on Retail IT," *PC Week*, August 21, 1995, p. 11. [Baxter Healthcare]

"Integration Studies," *Computerworld*, June 4, 1990, p. 69. [NAPA]

Lancaster, Hal. "Managers Beware: You're Not Ready For Tomorrow's Jobs," *The Wall Street Journal*, January 24, 1995, p. B1. [Interview with Hammer and Champy]

Leavitt, Harold J. and Thomas L. Whisler. "Management in the 1980's," *Harvard Business Review*, November 1958, pp. 41–48. [Prediction of decline in middle management]

Luthans, Fred. *Organizational Behavior: A Modern Behavioral Approach to Management*. New York: McGraw Hill, 1973. [Management]

Main, Jeremy. "The Winning Organization," *Fortune*, September 26, 1988, p. 50. [Trends for business and management]

"Matchmaker, Matchmaker, Make Me an App: Outside Consultants Can Orchestrate Timely Delivery of a Client/Server Project," *PC Week*, January 16, 1995, p. 67. [Boston Market]

"McDonald's Creates McCyberspace," *Electronic Marketplace Report*, September 5, 1995, p. 4. [McDonald's]

Mintzberg, Henry. *The Nature of Managerial Work*. New York: Harper & Row, 1973. [Management]

Nash, Jim. "Just What the Doctor Ordered," *Computerworld*, June 1, 1992, p. 79. [Baxter Healthcare]

Porter, Michael. *Competitive Strategy: Techniques for Analyzing Industries and Competitors*. New York: Free Press, 1980. [Strategy]

"Premier 100," *Computerworld*, September 13, 1993 [IS spending and other statistics]

"Re-engineering Reviewed," *The Economist*, July 2, 1994, p. 66. [Evaluation of Re-engineering projects]

Richardson, Bruce. "Weyerhaeuser Paper Mill: From Back Issue to Front Line," *Computerworld*, January 30, 1989, p. 28. [Weyerhaeuser]

Serwer, Andrew. "McDonald's Conquers the World," *Fortune*, October 17, 1994, pp. 103-116. [McDonald's]

Sherman, Stratford. "How to Bolster the Bottom Line, (Information Technology Special Report)," *Fortune*, Autumn 1993, pp. 14-28. [IT uses]

Sloan, Alfred. *Adventures of a White-Collar Man*. New York: Doubleday, 1941. [Management]

"Systems Management Match-Up: Independent Vendors Vie for Leadership," *Open Information Systems*, December 12, 1994. [Weyerhaeuser]

"The 1001 Best Web Sites," *PC/Computing*, December 1995, pp. 121-135. [NAPA]

"The Discipline of Market Leaders: Choose Your Customers, Narrow Your Focus, Dominate Your Market," *Electronic News*, June 12, 1995, pp. 46-48. [McDonald's]

"The Testing Loop," *PC Week*, November 20, 1995, pp. 17-18. [Weyerhaeuser]

"The Texas Computer Massacre," *The Economist*, July 2, 1994, pp. 59-60. [Computer security]

"Top 50 Network Technology Drivers," *Network Computing*, September 15, 1995, pp. 65-70. [Compaq and McDonald's]

"Virtual Masterpieces," *PC Week*, July 31, 1995, p. E5. [NAPA]

Wilder, Clinton. "Security Pacific Nets Baxter Exec," *Computerworld*, April 2, 1990, p. 1. [Baxter Healthcare]

Yamada, Ken. "Net Profits: Making More Money Online; Industry Contemplates Web Uncertainty," *Computer Reseller News*, August 14, 1995, pp. 41-42. [NAPA]

# CASES  *The Fast Food Industry: An Overview*

Food service workers do not use computers as much as other workers. The most common uses are sales and inventory systems.

SOURCE: Computer Use in the United States, U.S. Bureau of the Census.

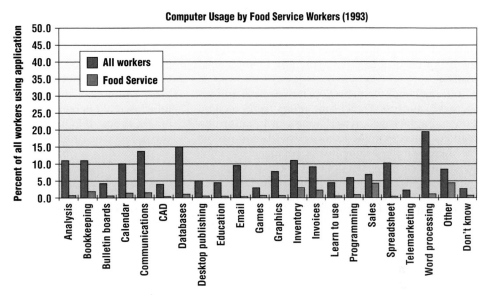

**Computer Usage by Food Service Workers (1993)**

Projections show that the fast food industry will continue to be ranked among the top industries for growth. The industry is highly dependent on commodity prices, which have remained relatively stable during the past several years. This absence of significant food cost pressure has helped fast food restaurants to gain volume increases through lower menu prices and increased marketing. With the competition for customers, many chains have kept price increases low or even reduced them. In doing so, value pricing and "value meals" have become the watchword of the industry.

The fast food industry remains very competitive. Making management even more difficult is the inability to prevent competitors from copying innovative features. The introduction of breakfast in one chain soon results in breakfast being offered in many chains.

Demographic trends have contributed to the profitability of fast food restaurants. The increasing number of people, particularly women, working outside the home has meant that less time is available for at-home food preparation. If past trends continue, the aging of the population will move individuals from fast food to midscale restaurants.

Sales growth in fast food franchises comes from three sources:

- The opening of new units.
- Higher contributions from older restaurants.
- Acquisitions.

When examining the stock prices for fast food corporations, it is important to remember that many of them are franchisers. This means that their revenue figures include royalty income from the franchisees. These operators pay a percentage of sales to the company. Franchise revenues also include one-time fees that are paid by franchisees when they join the system or open a new unit.

Franchise fees make the fast food industry particularly attractive to investors at the beginning. If the franchiser is expanding at an accelerating rate, the upfront fees magnify the franchiser's profits in the short-run. Once the growth rate flattens or declines, the upfront franchise fees become scarcer with the resulting narrowing of margins.

Franchise royalties provide much higher operating margins than company-owned restaurants, because the costs associated with royalty income are minimal. As a result, when examining restaurant chains, it is important to distinguish between sales from company-owned units and franchise royalty income. A good way to judge a business's overall health is to look at year-to-year sales among outlets open in both periods.

Another important consideration is the distinction between sales at new versus established units. Fixed costs, such as rent, utilities, and property taxes, are already covered at established units. An increase in customer traffic can be accomplished without a large amount of additional labor, a variable cost. Thus, a gain in same store sales often results in a significant impact to the bottom line.

In contrast, sales from new units can result in increased revenue figures. However, the increased costs of startup may result in narrowing margins. As a result, increased emphasis will be placed on reducing the development costs for new restaurants. This reduction will improve the corporation's return on investment as well as better enable the firm to enter small markets.

Internationally, franchise operations have enjoyed increased success. Franchising offers name recognition and a packaged, tested approach to enter new markets. Success in the former Soviet Union nations has increased the willingness of companies to enter other Eastern European countries. The passage and implementation of the North American Free Trade Agreement (NAFTA) has made further expansion into Canada and Mexico even easier.

From an information technology standpoint, restaurants thrive only when they have effective human teamwork. Although traditionally restaurants do not employ leading-edge technology, owners are increasingly discovering that adding computers to the team drives down costs and increases profits.

The computerization of the industry has been slow, however. According to Chris Wotell, vice president of Coconut Code, a restaurant-specific software developer in Deerfield Beach, Florida: "The industry is traditionally three to four years behind in terms of automation. But right now, the [restaurant] industry is light years ahead of where it was 10 years ago."

Restaurants started computerizing by adding electronic cash registers to the front of the house; these devices typically offered little more than a fancy method of input. Although such devices allowed easy information entry, that information wasn't necessarily saved or processed.

In 1990, sophisticated point-of-sale (POS) systems rapidly began replacing registers, bringing with them a full range of computer-based services. Sales of those systems have been fueled by the implementation of easy-to-use touch-screens for input.

## CASE  *McDonald's: Using Technology to Sell Hamburgers*

People who think of McDonald's associate it with hamburgers. When they walk into a McDonald's customers usually do not conclude that it takes a lot of technology to make and sell hamburgers. Until 1980 that was in fact the case. The company followed a traditional path and used computers for basic financial recordkeeping applications and personnel administration. As long as the monthly books were closed on time and the staff were paid, people did not place much importance on the role of the technology services group.

Today McDonald's is a multinational corporation with 137,000 employees in 68 offices and 14,000 restaurants in 72 countries. There are more than 7,300 restaurants in the United States with $9 billion in revenue and some 7,000 restaurants overseas with $3 billion in revenue. McDonald's opens three new stores every 24 hours. Eighty percent of the restaurants are franchised; 20 percent are corporately owned. Based in Oak Brook, Illinois, the $4 billion dollar company was founded on April 15, 1955.

McDonald's is one of the few service companies thriving in the global market. It deals with the international complexity with a straightforward strategy:

- Gather your people often for face-to-face meetings to learn from each other.
- Put your employees through arduous and repetitive management training.
- Form paradigm-busting arrangements with suppliers.
- Know a country's culture before you hit the beach.
- Hire locals whenever possible.
- Maximize autonomy.
- Tweak the standard menu only slightly from place to place.
- Keep pricing low to build market share; go for economies of scale.

### Automation of Store Procedures

In 1980, Ed Rensi, McDonald's chief operating officer, developed a vision of the strategic role that computers could play in the McDonald's organization. Rensi felt that a tremendous amount of time was spent on paperwork and administrative activity. He asserted that strategic advantage could be achieved through the reduction of the time managers spent counting inventory, figuring out payroll, or doing a manual crew schedule. Because the rest of the industry was not technology-intensive, anything that could be done to improve efficiency and control costs could be duplicated across all of McDonald's stores, which would lead to substantial increases in the profit margin. Ted Nagengast, a senior systems developer, summarized the focus of the MIS department at McDonald's:

The focus is on selling hamburgers. Our business is selling hamburgers. Everything we do is geared toward helping our store managers sell hamburgers. So we didn't want to cause any burden for MIS people in our local offices or abroad.

McDonald's implemented technology into the restaurant business in four phases. First, the International Business System (IBS) was developed in Europe and Asia. Installed in March 1984, the IBS is now used in approximately one-half of McDonald's overseas restaurants. This system uses IBM midrange computers to get financial jobs done. A key concern in the development of the program was that end users would not be able to change the key business application. According to John Osvath, director of information processing, "We try to insulate the end user from anything outside the application itself." In doing so, McDonald's has avoided on-line, real-time updates of its operations around the world, consolidating its financial reports monthly, as sales figures are reported.

Second came the Store Management Business System (SMBS). It managed inventory management, case control, and sales reporting for all of the company-owned restaurants.

The In-Store Processor (ISP) was the third step. This system performs cash management, inventory management, and order and crew labor scheduling for the restaurants. It is built on an AT&T Unix-based system that will serve as the foundation for future enhancements to the retail system. Moving the computer into the store provided additional functions that were previously too processor-intensive to do on a centralized time-sharing basis through a communications network. One example of the use of this program might be crew labor scheduling. The number of part-time workers that McDonald's employs limits the ability to transmit this information over telephone lines. Through the ISP, relevant data is directly tied to the point-of-sale cash registers. This means that sales, accounting, and inventory updates can be calculated directly from the sales data rather than being manually determined and entered. As a result, three important functions can occur at the same time:

- Online link to the point-of-sale register.
- Connection to the store manager for information processing.
- Link back to corporate headquarters.

This system also enables a variety of devices in the store to be connected to the network. Eventually, these will include the point-of-sale register, the time and attendance recorder, security, time reports, and other management items.

### Communications Technology

The fourth installation is the Integrated Services Digital Network (ISDN). ISDN is a high-speed communication system offered through existing telephone connections. In January 1988, McDonald's corporate headquarters announced that the facility had reached the full power and feature capabilities of ISDN. The company converted all 100 of the installed telephone lines to AT&T's software.

The major features that the system provides are calling-number identification, which enables users to see the number of the person who is calling; message waiting and retrieval, which notifies employees when messages have been left for them; and an electronic directory, which helps users to look up company telephone numbers and place calls with the touch of a button. This system is providing more enhanced, reliable, and flexible interfaces to messaging systems like voice mail, message-dial service, and leave-word calling service.

Today, nearly all information and communication systems at McDonald's headquarters in Oak Brook, Illinois, are linked into the ISDN network. This includes mainframes, communications controllers, personal computers, office automation equipment, telephones, and faxes. In all, there are 1,300 digital lines serving 1,110 user stations.

In terms of network integration, ISDN allows McDonald's to migrate from existing separate networks to a single, integrated, all-digital network. The primary benefit is the elimination of network confusion through the adoption of a single approach to all communications. This single-network approach will control, stabilize, and reduce overall communications expenses. Secondly, using the communication services of the telephone company rather than those of a private system avoids the operational costs and staffing associated with a premise-based switching system. As Carl Dill, vice-president of information services, has stated, "McDonald's does not want to spend money on telecommunications expertise. We want to sell hamburgers."

ISDN is important to businesses like McDonald's because it has many small restaurants rather than a few large ones. All of the restaurants are basically the same and provide identical services and food. As a result, McDonald's regional offices and restaurants do not need a high-capacity network. Thus, a network installed and maintained by the telephone company is particularly applicable to McDonald's mix of owned and franchised outlets and rapid but predictable growth. ISDN makes more than 300 voice, data, and video services available to McDonald's to link its restaurants to its corporate headquarters.

Future applications include voice/video presentation for training and new sales promotions. McTV, a private television channel, provides news and entertainment for customers while they are in the restaurant. Other uses include increased control over measurable, but variable, items such as soft-drink dispensing. ISDN is structured to make information systems easier to work with, the data more accessible, and the provision of more features.

The complexity of the systems involved and the number of vendors supplying the network equipment have increased dramatically. Unfortunately, the maintenance and management tools necessary to monitor and control faults in the performance of the network have not been developed.

The transition to ISDN has not been entirely smooth. For ISDN to function properly, there needs to be management and maintenance tools and test equipment to monitor and control faults during ISDN's performance. Managers with the technical background to implement ISDN are difficult to find and retain. The lack of test equipment is driving problem-resolution times to a critical level. Part of the problem rests in the failure of the individual suppliers to work together to address the overall issues of network management. Each supplier guarantees that its system works. No one is willing to take ownership to make sure that the entire system is successful.

In conjunction with ISDN, Designing Business Systems (DBS) is developing customized software for McDonald's restaurants. This will include a statistical reporting database with the ability to automatically track hundreds of items that McDonald's sells. A data management database, a personnel database for payroll, and a telecommunications program will also be included.

Carl Dill believes that the power of ISDN will enable inventory, sales, and employee assignments to be integrated and monitored more successfully. This will continue to give McDonald's a competitive advantage to successfully market its hamburgers and fries.

## McDonald's Creates McCyberspace

Since summer 1994, McDonald's has been involved in Internet marketing with McDonald's Interactive, an area within NBC Online on America Online (AOL). The company has also debuted "McFamily" on America Online and on the Microsoft Network.

The McFamily online site is an effort to incorporate more than advertisements in its online marketing strategy. McFamily is designed more for entertainment and education than previous efforts, which were commercially focused. McFamily offers family activity suggestions, contests, art galleries for children, and safety tips. McFamily's messages center around parenting and family information, including "seasonal ideas for fun family activities," such as block parties, travel games, and household safety information. The "Auditorium" sponsors monthly guest speakers, celebrities, and parenting experts. The "Hey Kids" area houses a gallery with McArt submitted by children, downloadable games, and contests.

McDonald's is not selling hamburgers through the Internet; however, it is using the AOL site to market brand-related products. Online services may be the best venue to build good will and an image, even though McDonald's already spends millions of dollars promoting its image through traditional media.

McFamily's "McStuff for You" section features a catalog of licensed McDonald's merchandise. Products available include gear from its NASCAR and NHRA racing teams, and 1996 Olympic Summer Games merchandise. Users place product orders through a toll-free number. The site may also eventually be used to capture customer information. Marketing surveys could be distributed online and answered in a matter of hours. Coupons could be used as rewards for answering demographic questions.

McFamily's "Helping Others" section has information on Ronald McDonald House and Ronald McDonald Children's Charities. The "McFacts about McDonald's" contains nutritional information about its food products and promotional information on what McDonald's is doing to aid the environment.

To ensure that McFamily remains a family-friendly environment, an on-screen message warns all participants that "suggestions from users will be reviewed by the McFamily editor."

In summer 1994, McDonald's completed its first attempt at online marketing with McDonald's Interactive. Located on AOL's NBC Online site, the Web page was developed by ad agency Leo Burnett. The area focused on brand-building success by including an e-mail function to dialog with customers, sweepstakes to generate names and addresses for further promotions, and a connection with Ronald McDonald House to establish McDonald's as a company with a social conscience. At the time, McDonald's was praised for taking the risk of becoming one of the first mainstream advertising giants to try electronic marketing. McDonald's Interactive did not work, however, because it did not have the staff in place to respond to the e-mail messages it received. Instead, McDonald's posted an online warning that because it was getting so much e-mail, it was unable to answer each message personally. This posted warning sent two negative messages:

- User feedback was not important to the company.
- Users wondered why McDonald's was getting such a deluge of mail. When they accessed McDonald's Web page and saw such a stern message, they could only presume that customers were sending complaints.

## QUESTIONS

1. How will telecommunications at McDonald's help managers to better plan, organize, coordinate, and control management functions?
2. How will the implementation of information technology at McDonald's enable managers to spend more time enhancing their interpersonal, informational, and decisional roles?
3. What specific information does the management information systems at McDonald's provide to give objectivity to the evaluation of each manager?
4. Why was McDonald's MIS implemented using four phases rather than one decision at the beginning of the process?
5. What has been the problem that McDonald's has been trying to solve in the development of its MIS?
6. On which of the five vital components (hardware, software, people, procedures, and databases) has McDonald's focused the most effort in the development of its MIS? On which of the five areas has the corporation stated it has concentrated? How do you know?
7. How are the typical applications listed in the chapter met by McDonald's management information system?
8. Identify the operational, tactical, and strategic decisions faced by McDonald's. Identify one information system component designed to help managers at each level.
9. What does McDonald's gain by being one of the first companies to use Internet advertising?
10. What improvements has McDonald's made to its Internet page? (Hint: Check it out on the Internet.)

## CASE    *Boston Market*

Just when many analysts felt that the fast food market was completely saturated and closed to any major newcomers, Boston Market has moved into the fast food market with a new way to roast chicken. In doing so, it created a new market segment of fresh convenient meals distinctive from casual-theme restaurants. Quality is also a distinguishing feature.

Boston Market Inc. is the largest restaurant chain specializing in rotisserie chicken. Founded in Newton, Massachusetts, in 1985, Boston Market began franchising in 1988. It first realized a profit in the second quarter of 1993. In October 1993, it topped $150 million in system-wide sales. As of January 1994, it had 241 units, 40 of which are company owned.

It reported $40 million in sales for 1993 and doubled in size to 400 outlets by December 1994.

Boston Market made headlines in November 1993 when its $42-million initial public offering was priced at $20, only to see the shares change hands for as much as $51 on their first day of trading. Shares closed that day at $49½ for a 143 percent paper profit for anyone who purchased the stock. It was the best first-day performance in the initial market in two years. Only two months after its initial public offering, Boston Market filed plans for a $100-million convertible debt deal. Capital market professionals said that they could not remember a company ever coming back to the market with a convertible so quickly after its initial offering.

Boston Market roasts its chickens whole on a rotisserie instead of frying separate pieces as traditional chains do. The preparation techniques use a unique combination of marinades, dry rubs, and glazes to make signature flavors. The chicken is then marinated overnight in a secret sauce and rotisserie roasted in a brick-fired oven for more than two hours. This results in chicken with the convenience of fast food but without the grease. In addition to chicken, Boston Market offers mashed potatoes, an assortment of hot vegetables, and a selection of deli salads. All food is prepared fresh, then roasted, steamed, or baked. Resources are maximized by using leftover chicken and vegetables for chicken pot pies, old-fashioned chicken soup, and two kinds of chicken salad. Customers can call their orders in or they can stop by the restaurant and place their orders in person. Chalk-style boards overhead serve as a supplement to printed menus. The chicken rotates in full view of customers who are making their decisions. The core concept is that of a suburban restaurant serving home-style meals at reasonable prices. The chain prides itself on the diversity of its side dishes, featuring from 16 to 22 side dishes. Management continually touts this diverse menu of sides as one of its strongest points of distinction.

Because it is a young company, Boston Market uses information technology to respond to changing consumer needs. Customers' opinions about food, service, and cleanliness are entered through a touch-screen application. Around 500 responses a week are received from each customer terminal. Upcoming promotions will revolve around new salads and sandwiches, lunch items, and a children's menu.

Boston Market Inc. is among the leaders in using information technology (IT) to improve its customer service. Correspondence and group decision making is built upon a Lotus Notes application. All of Boston Market's applications and databases are run from Unix-based servers. This provides management with online access to information and helps to streamline all business processes.

The information systems area of Boston Market has gone a long way to integrate the information from the point-of-sale terminal with scheduling, inventory, sales analysis, and recipe-tracking modules. An example of how the system works would be when the POS terminal says 100 chicken sandwiches were sold. It sends an ASCII file to the program, which knows the recipes and can deduct 100 buns and 50 pounds of chicken from the inventory. It then looks over the inventory and automatically orders enough buns and chicken to be ready for projected demand for the rest of the day. Software also enables recipes to be standardized and tied to food costs. This allows "what-if" analyses to be completed. For example, if the price of chicken goes up 10 cents a pound, the owner can decide how to cover this cost. He or she can adjust the item cost or put less on the plate.

Although specialized hardware packages exist for the restaurant market, the major software developers are turning more to the PC, a low-priced, versatile platform.

## QUESTIONS

1. Why has Boston Market become such a phenomenal success?
2. Why did the management of Boston Market place so much emphasis on computer technology in establishing the business?
3. What software applications are used at Boston Market?
4. Identify the operational, tactical, and strategic decisions faced by Boston Market. Identify one information system component designed to help managers at each level.
5. How does the computer system give Boston Market an advantage over its competitors?
6. What advantages are created by individual software applications, and what advantages arise from sharing data?

## CASE  *Burger King Corporation*

Fast food restaurants get approximately one-half of their sales from drive-through customers. Customers use the drive-through because it is quick and they do not have to get out of the car. Yet, this important area has changed little during the last 15 years. It is no wonder that most customers' memories of drive-through service involve garbled speakers.

To improve communication, most restaurants have implemented wireless headsets for order-takers to wear. These headsets reduce background noise from menu-board speakers and have helped to cut down on the number of errors in orders.

Another complaint is the impersonal nature of the drive-through. The customer only hears a voice; there is no face-to-face contact until the customer reaches the window. The number one customer complaint is arriving at the takeout window or driving away with the wrong order or less than what was paid for.

Burger King is turning to technology to resolve these problems, improve customer service, and sell more products. Burger King is testing two-way color television monitors that will enable customers and the order-takers to see each other, an enhanced sound system, and a screen display of the customer's order. When the order is entered into the computer, it shows up on the customer's terminal to be confirmed. The investment in technology is important because even small enhancements such as video screens can influence sales.

Also being tested are video boards on the menus at the drive-through windows. These video systems will make it possible for Burger King to run point-of-purchase displays on specials. The menu boards will be able to highlight different specials depending on the time of day.

In their efforts to address drive-through needs, McDonald's is testing double-lane configurations, one-way television monitors, and booths outside the menu board where an employee can take the orders.

## QUESTIONS

1. What problems do restaurants face with their drive-through areas?
2. What are the most important features of successful drive-through service?
3. How are restaurants using technology to improve the drive-through areas?
4. What are the differences between *Burger King's* and *McDonald's* approaches?
5. As a customer, are there additional improvements you would like to see?

## CASE  *Hardee's*

Nearly all the major multiunit restaurants are combining local and wide area networks to coordinate both in-house and collective information. Boddie-Noell Enterprises (Rocky Mount, NC) has linked its 336 Hardee's restaurants with XcelleNet's (Atlanta) RemoteWare Communications Management System, which provides remote polling of the individual locations as well as electronic software distribution. Two linked servers at Hardee's headquarters manage the flow of calls from stores; each store works from a 286-based PC networked to the POS system.

## CASE *Denny's*

Networks are the backbone of the Denny's chain. Denny's, for example, went through a major installation of POS equipment, no easy feat considering that each of the restaurants is a 24-hour-a-day operation. According to Bill Hamby, manager of restaurant information systems for Denny's parent company, Flagstar (Spartanburg, SC), the change affected more than 1,000 units in 46 states, and it was accomplished at the rate of one unit per day.

The PC-based network, called Restaurant Automation for Denny's Success (RADS), was designed to track sales data, improve labor costs through more efficient recording of employee hours, and reduce managerial paperwork. All of the transactions now are made through the computer. Hamby's advice is to choose the vendor wisely, especially if a nationwide changeover is involved. He recommends finding someone who can easily service the various locations, is aware of the special power and cabling needs of a retail POS system, and, especially, can interact with a constant flow of customers.

### QUESTIONS

1. Why would a franchise be concerned about communication? What data would be transferred?
2. What special problems do franchises have compared to other industries and other businesses?
3. Why did franchises wait until the 1990s to implement these networking strategies? (Hint: What were the costs and benefits of the networks, and how has technology changed over time?)

## *A Comparison of Three Small Restaurants*

The following three cases demonstrate the very different approach that small entrepreneurs can take with the integration of technology.

Jim Rua runs Cafe Capriccio, a small, white-linen restaurant in Albany, New York: "I wouldn't dream of putting a computer in here. We're small and very nontechnical here. We seat fewer than 60 people. We pride ourselves on personal service."

Because he cooks most nights, he wants his floor staff to place their orders directly—not through an electronic device. Even the argument of better inventory control doesn't appeal to him: "There isn't any inventory here. I buy food every day and write a menu every evening. I don't want to have to depend on something that might go down in the middle of dinner. Then what do you do?"

If Rua ran a larger business, he says, the idea might tempt him.

Jim Truscello opened Teller's Restaurant in Lawrence, Kansas, in the summer of 1993. It includes a custom-designed network with a pen-based interface. Unlike Rua, Truscello is completely dependent on his computer: "I couldn't operate without it. I've been in this business for 13 years, and I've worked with a lot of different systems. This one is the best."

The system was developed by another of the owners, Brad Nelson, a computer programmer who developed an interest in the restaurant business. Nelson also wrote proprietary network software for the system. As Truscello explains,

> We have bar codes on the menus and a special list of modifiers on a chart nearby. If a customer asks for something not on the chart, the server scans a "see me" code. The server uses a light pen tied into the CPU to scan the code, and it's relayed over the network into the kitchen.

Because it has no keyboard, the system requires little training—sometimes as little as 20 minutes. Each station has a 386-based CPU with a monochrome monitor, a light pen, and a printer. The network allows the users to call up information on any check from any machine. Each server carries a bar-coded card, and each ordering ticket also sports a code.

According to Mike Holguin, owner of Mitler's Homestead Restaurant in Eugene, Oregon, the computer is much better than the old way of doing things. Mike installed a network-based system when he first opened his restaurant in 1990. The network has now become the backbone of his business.

> We were one of the first restaurants in Oregon to get a touch-screen system. Everyone had used plain old tickets, and some had micros in their restaurants. This was a first. From an owner's standpoint, it's been very beneficial. To the employees, it was a real inconvenience at first, a novelty, until they got used to it. Now they couldn't think of doing it any other way.

Mike's 180-seat restaurant uses a straightforward system. Three PCs with touch-screens are stationed on the floor, with the server in the back office. The machines are all 286s running LANtastic. According to Mike,

> At the time we set this up, a 386 was out of our league. We were running it all with a 40MB hard drive. Here we're dealing with the human element. No matter how fast the computer is, people will slow it down. The reliability has been good. In three years, we haven't shut down the system more than three times.

Versatility has been the biggest payoff. We can manipulate the wording of everything, which helps because we have a lot of Spanish-speaking people in the kitchen. We can have English input in the front of the restaurant and Spanish in the back. Then, a few months after the cooks get acclimated, we switch it back to English. Computing is not just for processing the orders on a daily basis, it's also accumulating information, so you can do projections and scheduling.

The computer has become a volume builder for the restaurant. Mitler's has a regular customer named Joyce who has a special way of ordering her sourdough. Mike put her name on the order, and the cook knows how she likes it. On the bill it reads "Joyce's Meal." She loves it and brings her friends in to see it.

Mike is now 40 and has been in the restaurant business since he was 16. He started as a dishwasher and worked his way through the ranks. When the software was first installed, he was dismayed to see that it was configured more for a bar than a breakfast restaurant. His consulting firm was eager to work with him to adapt the configuration to his needs. Recently, they added the ability to obtain hourly readings from the system instead of having to do it by hand.

The software also allows innovation in the kitchen. If one of the cooks comes up with a new recipe, the program can analyze it and determine the best selling price. The computer already knows what the food costs. Mike only has to enter recipe information to get results. In Mike's view, "This system is a tool, like a spatula or a mop. As such, it is something you eventually take for granted, but it has to be good."

## CASE  *Small Restaurant*

Jim Landau owns and manages the Brown Bottle in Cedar Falls, Iowa. He sees the computer as one of his most important tools, giving him unprecedented control over his operation.

I think back to the days when I just had a cash register. I can't believe I ever did it that way. I can pull up an order I placed with a vendor a

year ago and say, "Yeah, I wrote that check." I can do my accounts payable and my payroll—I'd never go back to the old way. People learn this system quickly, which saves in the time needed for training.

Software has to be as user-friendly as possible, because the restaurant industry is not a computer-savvy business and personnel turnover is high. Because items are entered in a real-time environment, it has to be reliable.

Landau sees his network and restaurant software as crucial to his continued business success:

The big chains are squeezing us little guys out of the market. Look at the cost control they have. The district manager can take a sales report off a store every hour, even from another state. They have inventory control and personnel control we never had access to. That's changing, and it makes a big difference for us on the bottom line. With networked computers, we can now have the same power as the big chains.

### QUESTIONS

1. Why would a small restaurant choose to avoid using computers? What are the costs of computers?
2. Do you think there is some business size at which computers are unnecessary? Can they provide advantages even for small restaurants?
3. Is Cafe Capriccio different from Teller's and Mitler's? Is Rua correct in his opinion or is he just afraid of computers?
4. How is the system at the Brown Bottle different from that at Teller's? Could Brown Bottle benefit from Teller's system?
5. What special features are in Mitler's system? Would these features be useful at other restaurants?
6. Assume you are in charge of marketing for a software company that sells information systems to restaurants. Describe the features of a system that you would be able to sell to a wide variety of restaurants.

## DISCUSSION ISSUE

### *Why Don't Computers Understand English?*

Ever since the invention of computers, people have dreamed of communicating with them the same way we communicate with other humans. Business people often complain about how hard it is to learn to use

computers. Imagine how easy it would be if you could just type in a couple sentences in English (or some other natural language) and get the results you want. Advances have been made to develop natural language interfaces. However, as the following interaction between a human and a computer demonstrates, some problems may result.

Bowman: Who are our best clients?

HAL: I do not understand the word *clients*.

Bowman: I mean customers.

HAL: I cannot compute the mean of customers. To calculate averages, you must specify a numeric attribute. For example, *average income of customers*.

Bowman: No, no. I do not want the average.

HAL: Please restate the question as a positive statement. You want . . .

Bowman: Who are our best customers?

HAL: Searching . . . There are no customers named *Best*.

Bowman: No, I want the top customers.

HAL: Searching . . . The following customers match your request:

| NAME | CITY | PHONE | ACCOUNT BALANCE |
|---|---|---|---|
| Mike Top | Ames | 222-2222 | 1452.35 |
| Sidra Top | Gainesville | 444-4444 | 3352.92 |
| Susan Top | Fargo | 333-3333 | 1093.52 |

Bowman: Wait a minute.

HAL: Entering sleep mode for one minute. Further input ignored until 13:42.

Bowman: No!

HAL: 13:42. Please enter your request.

Bowman: Why are all of the customers named Top?

HAL: Searching . . . Unable to answer question. There is an incorrect premise. There are currently 7,354 customers. Only three of them are named Top.

Bowman: I get it. Okay. Which customers have the most sales?

HAL: Searching . . . There are no customers with sales.

Bowman: What?

HAL: Rephrasing result: There is no salesperson named *customers,* so *customers* has no sales.

Bowman: No. Which customers have bought the most?

HAL: Searching . . . There are no products called *most.*

Bowman: Arghh! Which customers have spent the largest amount of money?

HAL: Searching . . . Unable to access customers' computers. Please supply the proper passwords.

Bowman: What?

HAL: Retrying access . . . Incorrect passwords. Notification has been received from four customers that security violation has been logged. Network security command has shut off our access to the EDI network. Details have been forwarded to the computer security supervisor.

Bowman: No! Cancel the request.

HAL: Query canceled.

Bowman: Why did you try to access the customers' computers?

HAL: The request required calculation of total corporate spending by each of the customers. That data is stored on the customers' computers.

Bowman: Okay, try this: Which customers have bought the most products from us?

HAL: Searching . . . This company sells no products called *most.*

Bowman: Nuts. Which customers have spent the largest amount of money on all of our products?

HAL: Searching . . . The following customer matches your request:

| NAME | CITY | PHONE | PURCHASE | DATE |
|---|---|---|---|---|
| Robert Jones | Atlanta | 777-6666 | 8734.99 | 12/12/92 |

Bowman: It's about time. Thank you. I quit.

HAL: The time is 14:37. Closing the session. Logging off.

## QUESTIONS

1. Did Bowman finally get what he wanted? What did he want? There are at least three possibilities: (1) the most expensive item ever purchased by a customer; (2) the most amount of money spent at any one time by a customer; and (3) the highest total purchases by a customer over some specified time period.

2. Can you write a question that Bowman could ask that will give him the information he wanted—with no room for misinterpretation?
3. Assuming that it would be possible, what would be the drawbacks of making computers "more like humans?"

One of the first lessons you have to learn in dealing with computers is the importance of being precise.

The second lesson is that computer software is created by humans—analysts who make many decisions about the expected user interaction. Software designers generally attempt to build systems that match the jobs and needs of the users. However, the software is usually less flexible than humans, so people will typically have to adjust their own processes to adapt to the computer.

# Personal Productivity and Business Operations

**How do information systems help managers perform basic tasks?** Computers are particularly useful in helping managers with personal tasks and routine transactions. These systems have been in use for several years, and many businesses could not survive without them.

All managers perform tasks like writing, scheduling, calculating, and graphing. One of the most powerful uses of information systems lies in helping managers with these personal applications. Hundreds of tools exist to help managers with their daily tasks.

Another key role of managers is to analyze the business to solve problems and identify new opportunities. Several systems analysis techniques have been developed to help us understand complex systems. The methods and diagrams can be used by managers to understand how their actions affect the entire company.

The heart of any company is its daily operations. Whether the company manufactures products or provides services, basic operations must be performed continuously. These operations give rise to transactions with suppliers, customers, employees, other firms, and governmental agencies. Transactions must be recorded, aggregated, and analyzed. Information systems are crucial to maintaining, searching, and analyzing transactions.

A firm could have many separate transaction-processing systems. Data might be collected from thousands of sources and stored in hundreds of locations in the firm. A database management system can help managers find data. It makes it easier to share data with other workers. A database management system provides several tools to create reports and build input forms with minimal programming.

CHAPTER 2

# *Personal Productivity*

**WHAT YOU WILL LEARN IN THIS CHAPTER**

What is a computer? What types of data can a computer handle? What options are available, and do you need them? How can computers help you with common personal tasks? How can they make you more efficient? Can they help you make better decisions?

Small businesses are beginning to rely on microcomputers because of their low costs and off-the-shelf software applications.

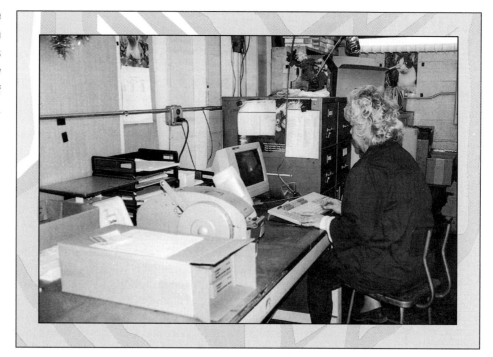

## SMALL BUSINESS

In 1988, the South Carolina Student Loan Corp (SC SLC) relied on remote access to a large computer for all of its information needs—primarily accounting reports. The not-for-profit company insures more than $300 million in student loans. Laura Rowell, the accounting manager, noted that she often put in 60- to 80-hour weeks to produce quarterly treasurer's reports.

In 1990, SC SLC decided to hire an accountant to help automate the reports with spread-sheets, and management brought in Gene Byers. By 1991, the company had 10 personal computers running spreadsheets with a template that Byers wrote to produce the treasurer's reports. The accounting officer estimates that the template saves two or three days each quarter. Byers also created a template to track money transfers needed with the state. As a result, SC SLC has reduced the number of transfers from the state treasurer's office to once a week instead of thousands per year.

Old Town Builders in Visalla, California, constructs houses for individuals. When potential customers talk to the builder, they often have difficulty determining how much the house will cost. There are hundreds of options for each house design. Customers have a limited amount of money, and they often want to trade off among options to get the features they want. For example, some people might opt for a smaller kitchen in exchange for a jacuzzi in the bathroom.

To help customers make decisions and to speed the cost-estimating process, Jeffrey Englund, a computer analyst, built a spreadsheet application that enables users to select various options. In addition to the construction options, it considers different financing methods, the subdivision, and lot size. At each step, the 1,500-line macro computes the monthly payment. The payment amount is updated automatically as customers examine each option. The spreadsheet also prevents buyers from inadvertently choosing options that do not exist or that are incompatible with other choices. When they are satisfied, the program prints out a listing of the choices and the costs.

Professionals such as dentists and doctors typically have to complete a significant amount of paperwork. In addition to typical accounting and billing records, they have to file the proper forms with the insurance companies. Additional government reports are also needed. Several companies offer packages tailored for specific tasks. For example, Excalibur Software offers the Medical Office System for the Macintosh. It can electronically transmit insurance forms for major insurance companies, Medicare, and Medicaid over modems, reducing time and error in the billing process. In 1992, the software price was listed as $4,300 for a single-physician version, and about $6,000 for a network, multi-physician version.

**OVERVIEW** The past decade has given the typical manager an incredible array of tools—both hardware and software—to improve day-to-day work. At first glance, it might seem that the value of the computer depends heavily on the specific job you have. Marketing managers, financial analysts, CPAs, and retail store managers all appear to have different uses for computers because their jobs are different. They might even need different types of computers. However, many jobs have similar features, so hardware and software tools have been created to help with specific personal tasks. Most managerial jobs involve four basic functions: research, analysis, communication, and organizing resources. Shown in Figure 2.1, managers perform several common tasks, including data searches, computations, writing reports and memos, drawing graphs, communication, and scheduling workers and appointments. Common application software packages were created to help managers with these tasks.

**FIGURE 2.1**

Every manager must perform certain basic personal tasks, including searching for data, communicating, scheduling, writing, and various computations. Several software packages have been designed to help with these basic tasks.

## TRENDS

The first computers were simple pieces of hardware. Like all computers, they had to be programmed to produce results. Programming these machines was a time-consuming task, because all of the pieces were connected by individual wires. Programming the computer consisted of rearranging the wires to change the way the pieces were connected. As computer hardware improved, it became possible to program the processor without having to change the internal wiring. These new programs were just a list of numbers and short words that were input to the machine. These lists of commands were called *software,* because they were easier to change.

Programmers soon learned that some tasks needed to be performed for most programs. For example, almost every program needs to send data to a printer or retrieve information stored on a disk drive. It would be a waste of time if every programmer or user had to write a special program to talk to the printer. By writing these common routines only once, the other programmers could concentrate on their specific problems. As a result, every computer has a basic collection of software programs called an **operating system.** The operating system handles jobs that are common to all users and programmers. It is responsible for controlling the hardware devices, such as terminals, disk drives, and printers.

As machines became faster and added new capabilities, operating systems evolved. These new capabilities have changed the way that we use the computer. The early computers could only recognize individual characters and numbers, so keyboards were used to type information for the computer. Printers that could handle only characters and numbers were the only way to get output from the computer. Eventually, television screens were used for output, but most of this output remained as characters. With the introduction of microcomputers, low-cost graphics hardware allowed the television screens to display pictures that were created by the computer. Today, many operating systems are completely graphical, which enables users to work with pictures and icons.

As the use and capabilities of computers expand, the ways we use computers change. Early programs were written by users. Later programs were written so users followed steps and answered questions in a fixed order. Eventually, users were given some control over the programs through the use of menus. More recent software focuses on an event-driven approach, where the user controls the sequence and the software responds to these events.

**INTRODUCTION**   Why do you care how computers work? After all, it is easy to use a photocopy machine without understanding how it works. Automobiles cost more than many computers, yet you can buy an automobile without knowing the difference between a manifold and a muffler. You can make phone calls without understanding fiber optic cables and digital transmissions.

On the other hand, when you buy an automobile you need to decide if you want options such as power windows, a turbo charger, or a sun roof. Similarly, many options are available for telephone services. If you do not understand the options, you might not end up with the car, telephone service, photocopier, or computer that you need. Or, you could end up paying extra money for services that you will not use. To choose among the various options, you need to know a little about how computers work.

Computers are typically discussed in terms of two important classifications: hardware and software. *Hardware* consists of physical items; *software* is the logical component such as a set of instructions. Of course, many functions can be provided in either software or hardware and a computer user often cannot tell which has been used, and most often does not care. The one main difference is that it is easier to make changes to software than to hardware—especially because software patches can be transmitted across phone lines.

**TYPES OF DATA**  Computers are used to process five basic types of data: numbers, text, images, sound, and video. Because of limited speed and storage capacity, early computers could only handle simple text and numbers. Only recently have computers become fast enough and inexpensive enough to handle more complex sound and video data on a regular basis. As computers continue to improve, these new capabilities will alter many aspects of our jobs and society.

As always, the business challenge is using technology to add value. For example, putting music and video footage in an accounting presentation might be entertaining, but in many cases it would not add value to the presentation itself. On the other hand, holding meetings with digital video links could save money by eliminating travel to a face-to-face meeting. You need to understand the concepts and characteristics of these emerging technologies so that you understand their merits and costs and learn to identify worthwhile uses.

## Object Orientation

One of the most important concepts to understand with existing computers is that all information is represented as **binary data.** Binary data, or digits, may be written as a collection of ones and zeros, and the name is shortened to *bits*. A set of 8 bits is called a *byte*. Data that are not in binary form are converted during data entry with various **input** devices. **Output** devices then change this data back to a form that humans can understand. Even complex objects can be represented by binary data. Figure 2.2 illustrates the five basic data types.

**FIGURE 2.2**

We use five basic types of data. Because processors only deal with binary data, each format must be converted or digitized. Computer peripheral devices are used to convert the binary data back to the original format.

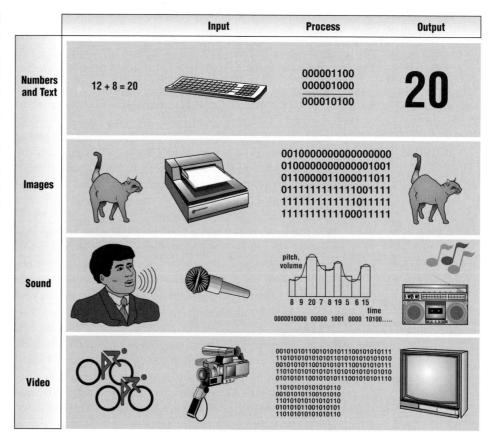

Recent software development has strongly embraced the concept of *object orientation*. The designers create objects for each software package. Each object has its own properties and methods or functions. Users can change properties and call the predefined functions. Although objects can become complex, most software begins with the five basic data types as fundamental objects. Software designers are beginning to standardize the properties and functions of these five data types. Once you learn these basic features, it will be easier to use software.

Note in Figure 2.3 that each of the basic data types has its own characteristics. Numbers have a precision and usually a scaling factor. Text has a typeface and display size, as well as appearance attributes such as bold, underline, and italic. Pictures can be described by their resolution and the number of colors. Digitized sound is based on a specified sampling and playback rate, and fits into frequency and amplitude ranges. Video combines the attributes of pictures with a frames-per-second definition. Any computer program dealing with these objects must understand their basic attributes. As a manager, once you understand the attributes it will be easier to use most new software packages.

Along with the attributes, several predefined functions can operate on each data type. Basic functions dealing with numbers include totals, calculations, and comparisons. Standard methods to manipulate text include searching, formatting, and spell-checking. Methods dealing with pictures involve artistic alterations such as color or lighting changes, rescaling, and rotation. Existing functions for sound and video are often limited to recording, playback, and compression/decompression. As shown by Phoenix Baptist Hospital (Reality Bytes 2–1), the use of graphics and video have become important in many fields.

Most application packages create their own objects as combinations of the basic data types. For example, graphs consist of numbers, text, and pictures. As a result, all of the attributes and functions that apply to the basic types also apply to derived graph objects. Hence, graphing packages can perform calculations on numbers, select fonts for displaying text, and enable you to set colors and rotation for the graph. Other applications, such as slide shows, provide additional functions, like controls for how one slide is replaced by another (e.g., fades, dissolves, and wipes).

The point is, once you understand the properties and functions of the basic data types, you can learn how to use any new application by concentrating on the

**FIGURE 2.3**

The basic data types can be thought of in terms of objects. Every object has attributes or properties that you can set. Each object has predefined functions or methods that it can perform. With compatible software, once you learn how to manipulate an object, you can use the same commands whenever you deal with that object.

| OBJECT | ATTRIBUTES | FUNCTIONS |
|---|---|---|
| All | | Cut, copy, paste, edit, save, retrieve, align |
| Numbers and Text | Precision, scale<br>Typeface, size, bold, italic, etc. | Total, calculate, compare, search, format, spell-check |
| Image | Resolution, number of colors<br>bit-map or vector | Color and light changes, rescale, rotate, blend, etc. |
| Sound | Sample rate, frequency and amplitude, MIDI or sample | Record, play back, frequency and amplitude shifts |
| Video | Inherit image and sound attributes and functions, frames per second | Record, play back, compress, decompress |

## Reality Bytes    2–1  PHOENIX BAPTIST HOSPITAL AND MEDICAL CENTER

A major task of any physician today is to communicate with patients. As medical technology advances and procedures become more complicated, it becomes increasingly difficult to obtain "informed consent" from patients. The U.S. government has also been encouraging doctors to improve explanations with "right-to-know regulations" that require physicians to explain procedures, potential side-effects, and risks.

The staff at Phoenix Baptist Hospital and Medical Center assist the physicians by building computer slide shows to instruct patients. Ray Litman is coordinator of photography and audiovisual services at the hospital which employs 900 doctors. His staff has been using Harvard Graphics software to build patient demonstrations as well as other presentations for physicians.

Prior to the slide shows, physicians often used actual photographs of surgical techniques, which tended to upset patients. The slide shows can also depict views that cannot be seen with typical photographs. For example, the physicians use cutaway views of the heart to show the objectives of angioplasty. The computer slide shows can be recorded on videotape. The doctors can then play back the tape in their offices with the patients, or they can let the patients review the tapes in their homes.

software's new objects, their attributes and functions. This approach is especially true today when many applications are designed and built using object-oriented methods.

Of course, the process of learning how to use new software would be much easier if software designers always chose the same set of commands to perform the same functions. Although the world does not quite work that way, you can come close by purchasing software *suites* (e.g., Microsoft Office Pro, Lotus Smart Suite, or WordPerfect Office) which are a combination of software packages sold by a single company. Commands to perform basic functions, such as setting text attributes, are the same for all the suite's applications. The suites also make it easier to exchange data between applications.

### Numbers and Text

Numbers and text are still the most common type of computer data used in business—for example, each cell in a spreadsheet can display a number or text (labels). Most business reports consist of tables of numbers with supporting text.

Computers handle numbers differently than do humans. Our base 10 (decimal) numbers are first converted to base two (binary). However, some decimal numbers do not convert to an exact binary value, so you will occasionally run into round-off problems. Most of the time the computer uses enough precision to avoid problems, but if you are dealing with very large or very small numbers, the errors can accumulate.

The reliance on binary numbers explains the limits experienced with some software. For instance, you might have a program that allows you to enter up to 256 lines of text. That number arises because 256 is 2 raised to the eighth power, which is the largest number that can be counted with one byte.

Alphabetic characters are represented internally by numbers. The simplest method is to number the characters alphabetically, so *A* is 65, *B* is 66, and so on. These numbers are then stored in binary form. Two basic complications exist. First, large IBM machines use a different numbering sequence (EBCDIC) than do most other computers (ASCII). Fortunately, most existing methods of transferring data to and from IBM machines automatically convert between these numbering schemes.

The second problem is that different countries use different characters. Today's hardware and software can be configured with special character sets for each country, but it can cause problems in conversion of files for people in different nations.

## Pictures

Pictures, graphics, and icons are used to display graphs and charts. Pictures are sometimes used as backgrounds or as icons in presentations that are used to help the audience remember certain points. In fact, almost all of the computer work that you do today is based on a graphical perspective. Video screens and printers are designed to display everything, including text, in a graphical format. The graphical foundation provides considerably more control over the presentation. For example, you can change the appearance of characters or combine figures and graphs in your reports.

There are two basic ways to store images: bitmap or vector format. The easiest to visualize is bitmap (or raster or pixel) format. A **bitmap image** is converted into small dots or *pixels* (picture elements). If the picture is in color, each dot is assigned a (binary) number to represent its color. This method is often used to display photographic pictures where subtle changes in color (such as blends) are important. Figure 2.4 is an example of a bitmap picture. Bitmap pictures are evaluated in terms of the number of colors and resolution of the picture. Resolution is often measured in *dots-per-inch (dpi)*. There are certain problems you will encounter with bitmap images. Consider what happens if you create a bitmap picture in a square that has 50 pixels per side. Examine Figure 2.4. How do you make the image larger? Use larger dots? Then the lines are very rough. How can you stretch the picture into a box that is 100 by 200 pixels? Although these operations are possible, they do not usually produce good results.

When you need to change the size of pictures and keep fine lines and smooth edges, it is better to store pictures in vector format. Figure 2.5 is an example of line-art or a vector drawing. **Vector images** consist of mathematical descriptions instead of dots. In most cases, they take up less storage space than bitmaps do. For example,

**FIGURE 2.4**

Bitmap pictures are typically used for photographic images. They are used for pictures that contain subtle color changes and detailed images. However, they can take up considerable amounts of disk space and can be hard to rescale.

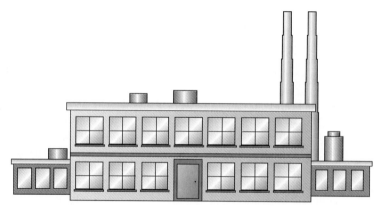

**FIGURE 2.5**
Sample vector image. The figure is defined as a collection of equations, which makes it easy to rescale, rotate, or alter its shape. It can be stored in a minimal amount of space. It is created and manipulated with typical drawing commands; users do not see the underlying mathematics.

a line is described by a statement such as: *line from (0,0) to (10,10) in yellow.* Don't worry, you don't have to be a mathematician to use vector images. Most of the current drawing packages store their work in vector format.

## FRACTALS

Fractals are a relatively new mathematical invention. Benoit Mandelbrot did much of the original work at IBM's Watson Research Center, resulting in his book, *The Fractal Geometry of Nature* in 1977. Fractals have a geometrical definition but can be thought of as highly irregular shapes that can be expressed by relatively simple mathematical functions. Fractals can be used to create realistic pictures of landscapes. They are also used to create fills in drawing packages that look realistic. They can be used to approximate geographic data, such as an outline of an island. Although they result in the loss of actual data points, fractal-based compression algorithms can produce relatively accurate pictures with only a few data points.

**FIGURE 2.6**
PHOTO-CD
RESOLUTIONS
Bitmap images are evaluated by their resolution and number of colors. Photographic quality requires 24-bit color (16.7 million colors). The Kodak Photo-CD standards define six levels of resolution, each requiring more bits of storage.

In recognition of the usefulness of digital images, Kodak created a standardized system to convert photographs to digital (bitmap) form and store them on optical disks. The system is known as **Photo-CD.** Several commercial firms convert photographs to a Photo-CD format. Depending on how you want to use the pictures, you can choose among the resolutions listed in Figure 2.6. All of the resolutions use 24-bit color. Higher resolution means that fewer pictures can be stored on one compact disk (CD).

| IMAGE PAC | NAME | RESOLUTION (V × H) | DOTS PER INCH AT 3 × 5 |
|-----------|------|--------------------|-----------------------|
| Base/16 | Thumbnail | 128 × 192 | 40 |
| Base/4 | Thumbnail | 256 × 384 | 80 |
| Base | TV | 512 × 768 | 160 |
| Base*4 | HDTV | 1024 × 1536 | 300 |
| Base*16 | Digital Print | 2048 × 3072 | 600 |
| Base*64 | Pro | 4096 × 6144 | 1200 |

## Sound

Digitized sound is a relatively new feature for personal computers. Some companies are using sound capabilities much like telephone answering machines. You can use your computer to send **voice mail** messages to coworkers. There are tools that will even read e-mail and fax messages over the phone, so managers can stay in touch while they are away from the computer. Software also enables users to attach voice notes to spreadsheets or documents. Colleagues can play back your comments while they read the report. Music and sound effects can be incorporated into presentations to make them more interesting. Professional Data Management (Reality Bytes 2–2) illustrates one of the powerful features of using computer-controlled sound in business.

 **Reality Bytes** ◣    2–2 PROFESSIONAL DATA MANAGEMENT

Professional Data Management introduced a hardware and software solution for a problem encountered in professional offices. Physicians and dentists need a way to remind patients about their scheduled appointments. Each missed appointment means lost revenue. If the office knows ahead of time that a patient needs to reschedule, other patients will be able to receive treatment earlier.

The new system is based on personal computers and uses a sound card to record and play back messages to patients. The computer automatically calls the patients and reminds them about appointments. It offers patients the ability to change the appointment by pressing keys on the phone or to leave their own message. By using the computer, the messages can be personalized for each patient. Recordings of patient names are stored in a file. The physician or staff member simply records pieces of greetings and messages. Then the computer combines the appropriate segments when making the call.

Increased storage capacity and declining costs make it easier for sound to be stored in digital format. The conversion of sound to digital form is best illustrated with CDs. Cambridge Savings Bank (Reality Bytes 2–3) highlights the use of sound cards for adding voice notes to work.

Sound consists of two basic components: volume and pitch (frequency). These two values are changed over time to produce words and music. To digitize sound, these two values are measured several thousand times per second. The resulting binary numbers are stored in sequence. The challenge is to sample the source often enough so no important information is lost. The music (or speech) is reproduced by

**Reality Bytes** ◣    2–3 CAMBRIDGE SAVINGS BANK

Cambridge Savings Bank purchased 80 Compaq PCs that included sound cards and microphones. The Cambridge, Massachusetts, bank did not have concrete plans for how to use the audio capabilities but was not concerned because they added little to the cost of the machine. Many employees of the bank now use the audio capabilities to add notes to spreadsheets and word processing documents. The audio notes are easier to create than written notes and remain attached to the documents. The systems are also used to enhance training by providing verbal feedback to users. For the future, the bank wants to merge its phone system into the computer network.

synthesizers that convert the numbers into the appropriate sounds and play them through amplifiers and speakers.

If you intend to use music in your presentations, you need to understand that there are two basic ways to store music data. One basic format is to digitize the raw sound waves by measuring the amplitude and frequency. These files can rapidly become huge, but the method can capture any sound. For music (not voice), there is a second means of storing files. Many musicians today create music using electronic keyboards. Much like typewriter keyboards, these music keyboards transmit numbers indicating which key has been pressed, how hard, and for how long. This process is supported by several standards known as *musical instrument data interchange (MIDI)*. By transmitting these numbers and messages to a synthesizer, the music can be recreated.

The difference between the two methods is like the difference between a tape recorder and sheet music. Digitized wave files are like tape recorders in that they record everything exactly as it was created. MIDI files are like sheet music—they tell a synthesizer which notes to play, and the synthesizer creates the music on demand. In addition to taking up less disk space, MIDI files are easy to modify and can be printed as sheet music. In using music files, you will have to make a choice between the two formats. The MIDI format takes substantially less space, but you need a synthesizer to reproduce it. Sampled music requires less sophisticated hardware. Also, with MIDI files, because of differences among synthesizers, you might get different sounds if you play the presentation on a different machine.

## Video

The use of computerized video signals is still in its infancy. Several recent technological changes will lower the cost of digitized video, which will ultimately increase its usage in business. One use with incredible possibilities is the ability to instantly transmit motion pictures over standard telephone lines. For instance, physicians could send images to specialists for consultation. Engineers could use video transmissions to diagnose problems over phone lines. Managers can carry on face-to-face conversations. Computer imaging tools (Reality Bytes 2–4) also make it easier for workers to create animated presentations for demonstrations or for analyzing designs and layouts.

Although it is possible to convert motion picture and television signals to binary form, the conversion results in a tremendous amount of data. The process is similar to that for single pictures, except standard movies display 24 frames (images) per second, while U.S. televisions display 30 frames per second. Perhaps you have heard of *high definition television (HDTV)*. The U.S. government, in cooperation with industry leaders, has defined standards for HDTV broadcasts in the United States—other countries use different standards. Television broadcasts are being converted to digital form for transmission. In the United States, Hughes Corporation established the first commercial digital TV broadcasts in 1994 with direct broadcast satellites to small satellite receivers with special decoders to convert the signals back to standard TV format. Much like audio CDs, HDTV provides improved quality with bigger yet sharper pictures, less interference, and more channels. Another major advantage to digital signals is that they can be compressed, allowing broadcasters to send more channels in the same space. With digital technology, cable TV companies can broadcast 500 channels over existing connections.

Digital video signals also enable you to alter the image. In fact, it is now common to create entire digital scenes that never existed in nature. These techniques are commonly used in marketing. They are also used by engineers to develop and market-test new products.

**Reality Bytes**    2–4   COMPUTER IMAGING TOOLS

Architect Jim Lennon of Del Mar, California, uses off-the-shelf software tools for the Apple Macintosh to design and illustrate new buildings. In the process of designing the new Children's Hospital of Orange County, Jim used several powerful graphics tools to illustrate his design for the hospital.

He began by photographing the proposed building site from several directions. He used a Microtek II scanner to read two of the photos into the computer. He next used Adobe's Photoshop to crop out the weeds in the photos. He used a rubber-stamp tool to touch up the parking lot and blur the seam between the two photos.

Using formZ, a 3-D drawing package, he drew in the building perimeter and the floor plan. The software then enabled him to extrude the walls and create a 3-D view of the building. He saved and transferred the image to StudioPro, where he added textures to the building. This software enabled him to show windows and skylights. Using his photographs, he used computer light sources to match the local light. The drawing was polished (with an antialiasing tool) to soften edges and minimize jagged lines.

Jim transferred the finished picture back to Photoshop. By altering photos of some cars in the foreground, Jim positioned the building to show it in the proper 3-D perspective and give the picture the correct depth. Feather tools enabled him to blend the images without harsh lines. He then experimented with various background focus tools and printed the results on a color ink-jet printer. Examining the results, he realized that the entrance needed to be redesigned. The new version gave a more dramatic effect and blended better with the existing surroundings.

Not satisfied with a fixed presentation, Lennon built a QuickTime animated fly-through of the model. First he built a short presentation where the building arose from the existing empty lot. Then he created an animation to show an approach from the parking lot, through the front entrance, and into the lobby. This second animation was only 10 seconds long but took the system 10 hours (overnight) to build. The result was output to a videotape for presentation to the client. The entire process took about a day to create—the animation was automatically generated overnight.

## Multimedia

The combination of the five basic data types—text, numbers, sound, video, and images (animation)—is known as **multimedia.** In its broadest definition, multimedia encompasses virtually any combination of data types. Today, it typically refers to the use of sound, text, and video clips in digitized form that are controlled by the computer user. Multimedia applications tend to use huge amounts of data.

Multimedia applications available include encyclopedias and similar presentations, including discussions of animals, cities, and historical figures. To date, there have not been many commercial management applications of multimedia. Some educational courses have made good use of multimedia tools. For example, anatomy classes and medical courses have access to multimedia explorations of the human body. Some software tools even enable students to perform "surgery" on a multimedia "patient" and observe the results. Some people have used multimedia tools to build presentations. As demonstrated by The Good Guys! (Reality Bytes 2–5) they are useful for initial designs in marketing because an initial video presentation can be created in a few days, instead of months. Multimedia tools are also being used in business training.

Currently, multimedia presentations are difficult to create. The techniques required are similar to those used in creating movies. In fact, if you want to learn how to create a professional multimedia presentation, it would be wise to take a course in film making. It is easier to edit presentations on a computer than with film, but the concepts of scripts, storyboards, camera angles, lighting, movement, and aesthetics still apply.

**Reality Bytes** ◤ 2–5  THE GOOD GUYS!

The Good Guys! is a chain of 37 consumer-electronics stores based in Burlingame, California. Since 1991, Gerard Chateauvieux, a sales counselor for the company, has produced four multimedia projects that promote the products and services of the retailer. Ken Weller, vice president of sales, chose Chateauvieux because of his enthusiasm for the idea, nine years of experience at the company, and good working knowledge of Macintosh software and video equipment.

Multimedia was chosen for the promotion packages because sound and motion convey ideas much more quickly than do printed brochures.

In-store training videos illustrate how "shrinkage" or missing parts and goods reduce employees' profit sharing. Chateauvieux uses many different graphics and animation because different people respond differently to multimedia. The variety increases the probability that the message will be successfully understood. The particular format that he used for the training film was a simulated newscast. To make the "newscast" more realistic, Chateauvieux used overlay and flyby graphics.

Sales-support videos use 3-D animation to explain the video and audio cables. Every video and audio cable in the store is included with a description of the best use for each cable. Another video parodies the "Unsolved Mysteries" television show format to explain the complexities of the Good Guy's payment program.

You need several hardware tools to create multimedia presentations. You will need an optical disk drive, a sound board that records and plays back digitized sound, a high-resolution color display system, and a computer with a fast processor and plenty of memory. Additionally, to create your own video images, you will need a camera and a video capture board to digitize the images.

Several software tools are specifically designed to create multimedia presentations. Most of them are in their infancy, and you can expect to see several improvements. For now, look for tools that can handle large projects, manage all of the data types you need, and are easy to use. In particular, look for tools that enable you to make extensive changes, so that you can move scenes around, copy portions of one scene to use as a foundation for another one, and so on. You can buy images, sound clips, and even video clips to make your job easier, but remember that film studios spend millions of dollars to create films.

One major business use for multimedia tools is for training. A human resources department is often responsible for creating and administering training for all the employees. Computer-based training provides the ability to offer training to individuals on their schedule. It also provides a consistent approach that can be tested and verified for accuracy.

Computer-based training makes it easier to track employee progress to determine which staff need refresher courses and to help in promotion decisions. Because of the flexibility in scheduling, it gives the employees the ability to plan their own education and choose their own direction in the company. As noted in the situation of Steelcase (Reality Bytes 2–6), all of these benefits can be achieved at lower cost with computer-based than with traditional training methods.

If computer-based training lessons are used by enough people, it can be a cost-effective teaching technique. However, it can also be expensive and time consuming to create the individual lessons. Because of the costs, computer-based lessons may not be updated as often as conventional handouts and textbooks. Additionally, because the tools are not yet standardized, companies run the risk of creating lessons using hardware and software that may rapidly become obsolete, requiring the project

**Reality Bytes**          2-6   STEELCASE IMPROVES TRAINING PROGRAM

Steelcase, Inc., is the world's largest manufacturer of office furniture. Each year the company spends more than $100,000 on outside personal computer training for its employees. Even with this expenditure, only 600 out of an employee population of 4,000 are able to take advantage of the training each year.

To address the size of this expenditure for the few number of people involved, Phil Camillo, head of Steelcase's training program, designed a learning center within Steelcase's offices. His goal was to enable end users from within the company to teach themselves in a state-of-the-art media environment. Camillo's goal was to turn the learning responsibility over to the student. This would enable the student to "schedule his own time, plan his own curriculum, and manage his own education."

Camillo sold his plan to senior management by promising a reduced training budget with far more participation and payoff. Once he had this approval, he worked closely with the information systems staff to set up "The Learning Curve." This in-house multimedia training room was filled with computer-based training,

video and audio learning modules, IBM personal computers, Macintoshes, laser discs, books, and periodicals. The center's software covers everything from personal computer software to project management and leadership skills.

In the first four years since it opened in May 1990, the Learning Curve served more than 4,000 students. To track and direct these students, Camillo set in place some unique techniques. Each visit and use of the center is tracked with student identification cards that contain bar codes.

Students begin their training with an introduction by an on-site counselor who helps them get accustomed to the workstations. Students then run a two-tier expert system program. The first module is named the Learning Style Advisor. It does a right brain/left brain analysis and gives students a chance to determine their best learning style. The second module is named the Training Plan Advisor. It questions students about the tasks they want to perform and determines their level of experience with the technologies at Steelcase.

to be discarded or rebuilt from scratch. Despite these drawbacks, computer-based training can be a useful technique to train employees. As the variety and quality of software tools and libraries improve, it will become easier and cheaper to build lessons.

## Virtual Reality

Periodically, a computer concept captures the public's imagination and receives massive press coverage and speculation. Virtual reality (VR) is one of those concepts. *Virtual reality* represents the use of computer technology to produce a simulated world that appears to be real to the participants. Technology is used to shut out the existing world and feed the human senses so that people perceive only what is generated on the computer. The human participants can also affect the computer simulation through nontraditional input devices such as computer gloves.

It is difficult to generate inputs for the five human senses (sight, sound, touch, smell and taste). Most existing VR simulators concentrate on sight and sound. The mechanical flight simulators used to train pilots might be considered to be the earliest virtual reality devices. They relied on taped video displays, multiple speakers for sound effects, and hydraulic lifters to simulate the motion of the plane. With the advent of small (5-cm) liquid crystal displays (LCDs), it became possible to shrink the hardware required to produce virtual reality sensations. Current versions are based

Workers at LISITT (Laboratorio Integrado de Sistemas Inteligentes y Technologias de la informacion en Trafico) have developed a virtual reality driving simulator (SIRCA) to evaluate driver learning and road safety.

on a headset that contains a video display for each eye and multiple speakers to fool the ears into hearing directional sounds.

The quality or realism of the simulation depends largely on the quality of the video display. Ideally, the display units need sufficient resolution to provide photo-realistic, true color pictures. Keep in mind that to be realistic, a good headset needs more than two screens in order to feed peripheral vision. In addition to the cost of these high-resolution displays, the large amount of data to be generated and transmitted puts a heavy burden on the computer. The simulation needs to show 3-D moving scenes, and it has to update them in response to actions by the participants. Plus, it has to generate scenes so that each eye sees the images from a slightly different angle.

In order for humans to interact with VR screens, we need different input devices. Two-dimensional pointers are cumbersome to use in 3-D space. One common input method is a computer glove. The glove has small automatic switches inside it that turn on and off as the wearer moves his or her hand. The computer reads the switches and determines the position of the fingers. It then displays a representation of the glove on the video screens. Theoretically, similar devices could be made for other parts of the body. However, the user has to learn to associate the video image with the position of the glove. In real life, we have muscle control and touch that tell us where our hands are. On the VR screen, you lose some of this feedback and have to rely on your eyes.

Another common input device is to mount a small laser on top of the participant's head. The computer then determines which way the wearer is looking by the position of the laser. Hence, the computer can change the display to correspond to the proper direction. An even more sophisticated laser device exists that can read eyeball movements and pick up sight lines directly.

There are many public displays of fairly crude VR devices in the form of arcade game machines. There are also some military and commercial uses of VR, such as flight simulators. One enlightening use of VR is in a device called a gamma knife (Reality Bytes 2–7). To date, few business uses of VR have appeared. Perhaps as the cost decreases and realism improves there will be more uses.

◤ **Reality Bytes** ◢ 2–7 THE GAMMA KNIFE AND VIRTUAL REALITY

The gamma knife is a medical tool used to perform operations on the human brain. It uses gamma rays to cut out small tumors. The surgeon needs to align the rays so that they intersect at the proper location for each specific patient, but it is difficult to make the proper settings with such a small scale. That's where VR becomes useful. Internal images of the patient—both CAT (computer-aided tomography) and MRI scans (magnetic resonance imaging)—are fed into a computer program that generates a large-scale 3-D image. The surgeon uses a VR headset to view the image and computer-generated lines representing the gamma rays. The surgeon uses a VR glove to grab each gamma ray and move it to the proper location. When the process is finished, the computer reads the gamma ray locations and programs the gamma-ray generator. The patient is placed in the device and the computer delivers the rays to the preassigned locations.

## Size Complications

To understand the importance of the four types of data, it helps to examine the size of each type. For many years, computers predominantly handled numbers and limited text. Over time, usage has gradually changed to include images, sound, and video. The more complex data types require much greater storage space, processing power, and transmission capacity.

Consider a typical single-spaced printed page. An average page might contain 5,000 characters. A 300-page book would hold about 1.5 million characters. Now, consider a picture. At 300 dots per inch, a full 8.5 by 11-inch page would require a little over a million bytes if it were scanned in black and white. A photograph in Kodak Base∗16 resolution with 16 million colors (24 bits per pixel) would require 18 **megabytes** (million characters) of storage space. Fortunately, most pictures have a lot of repetitive (or empty) space, so they can be compressed. Even so, high resolution pictures often fill more than one megabyte of space. Kodak's compression technology reduces Base∗16 images to 4.5 megabytes.

Sound and video require considerably more storage space. Remember that thousands of numbers are being generated every second. A typical CD holds 650 megabytes of data, which can store one hour of stereo music. The current standard for digitizing telephone conversations generates 64 kilobits per second, almost half a megabyte per minute. Video generates approximately 1.5 megabytes of data every second. However, some compression systems reduce the amount of data needed to transmit video. They start with the first frame and store just the parts that change for each succeeding frame. To address this issue, Intel has a software-based technology called Indeo that compresses and decompresses video pictures in real time. It reduces a one minute video to about 9 megabytes on average. Several other companies are producing customized processors that will convert and compress video signals faster. These techniques also provide automatic picture scaling, to let the user choose the size of the final picture—from a small window up to the full screen. Figure 2.7 illustrates the importance of the processor in software-based video performance.

Finally, many companies like Royal LePage (Reality Bytes 2–8) are experimenting with multimedia applications. The combination of these data types requires a computer having a large amount of storage capacity and fast processing speed. Multimedia applications are typically stored and distributed on CD-ROMs.

| PROCESSOR | FULL SCREEN 640 × 480 | ¼ SCREEN 320 × 240 | ¹⁄₁₆ SIZE 160 × 120 |
|---|---|---|---|
| 486SX-25 | 1 fps | 15 fps | 30 fps |
| 486DX2-66 | 10 fps | 30 fps | 30 fps |
| Pentium-60 | 20 fps | 30 fps | 30 fps |
| Pentium-120 | 30 fps | 30 fps | 30 fps |

**FIGURE 2.7**
INDEO VIDEO PERFORMANCE BY INTEL

Video quality is measured in resolution and number of frames per second (fps). The U.S. television standard is 30 fps. Movies use 24 fps. Anything less results in slow-motion or jerky effects. However, 30 fps requires a relatively fast processor—especially if you want to enlarge an image to full screen size.

 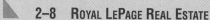

**Reality Bytes**     **2–8** ROYAL LePAGE REAL ESTATE

Many businesses deal with data that extends beyond simple words and numbers. Real estate sales is a prime example. As a result, Royal LePage, a Canadian Realtor, has purchased a multimedia system for use by its commercial property division. In addition to market data, the system enables agents to retrieve full-color pictures of the properties, detailed floor plans, and locator maps. The information can then be merged into a word processor, spreadsheet, or a desktop publishing system. Brokers can also use the system to fax the data and photographs directly to interested clients. Future enhancements include the ability to create CD-ROMs and to store video clips of the properties.

**HARDWARE COMPONENTS**

Regardless of the job you have, there are certain hardware components your computer will need. The four main components are devices that manage input, process, output, and secondary storage. Of course, for each component, there are hundreds of options, which means you can tailor a computer to your specific job. The features and costs of each component are continually changing, so it is difficult to derive simple rules that you apply when choosing a computer for your job. However, the basic roles of the four components are likely to remain relatively constant for the next few years. One trend that you have to remember is that the hardware industry changes rapidly, especially for small systems. Most computers that you buy today will have a short economic life—perhaps three years. At the end of that time, each component will have changed so much that you will typically want to replace the entire computer.

The relationship among the four components is summarized in Figure 2.8. Note that the process subsystem consists of **random access memory (RAM)** and at least one processor. In many ways, the **processor** is the most important component of the computer. It carries out instructions written by various programmers. It uses RAM to temporarily store instructions and data. Data and instructions that need to be stored for a longer time are transferred to secondary storage. The capabilities, performance, and cost of the computer are affected by each of these components.

For most components, there are three important characteristics you need to know: speed, capacity, and cost. As illustrated in Figure 2.8, each component operates at a different speed. For example, how fast can you type? If you type 60 words per minute, then the computer receives five characters in one second, or one character every two-tenths of a second. However, the processor runs much faster. Some

**FIGURE 2.8**

Computer performance and capabilities are highly dependent on the peripheral devices. Most computers will use several devices in each of the four major categories. Technological progress in one area often results in changes to all four types of components.

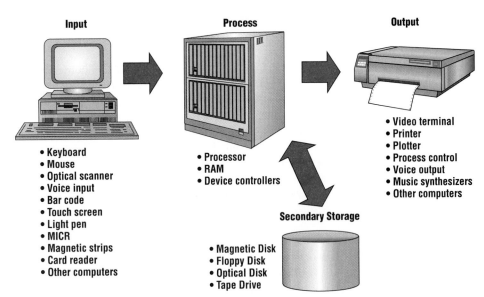

**Input**

- Keyboard
- Mouse
- Optical scanner
- Voice input
- Bar code
- Touch screen
- Light pen
- MICR
- Magnetic strips
- Card reader
- Other computers

**Process**

- Processor
- RAM
- Device controllers

**Output**

- Video terminal
- Printer
- Plotter
- Process control
- Voice output
- Music synthesizers
- Other computers

**Secondary Storage**

- Magnetic Disk
- Floppy Disk
- Optical Disk
- Tape Drive

processors can perform more than 300 **million instructions per second (MIPS).** Between each of your keystrokes, the computer processor could execute 60 million instructions! The same concept applies to most output devices because their speed is often measured in characters per second. Speed of most secondary storage devices is measured in **milliseconds** or thousandths of a second. That's still pretty slow when compared to billionths of a second (**nanoseconds**) that measure processor speed.

**FIGURE 2.9**

When one device is faster than another, overall system speed can be improved by adding a cache memory or buffer. Disk drives often use cache memory because they are much slower than the processor. When the computer retrieves data from the drive, it reads bulk data, guessing at what might be needed. The processor then retrieves data from the cache. Modern personal computers also have a cache built into the processor to speed retrievals from slower RAM chips.

One common technique to compensate for speed differentials is the use of a cache. Displayed in Figure 2.9, a *cache* is short-term storage between the processor and a slower device such as a disk drive or slower memory chips. The cache generally consists of high-speed memory. Data is transferred in bulk to the cache. It is then pulled out as it is needed, freeing up the processor to work on other jobs instead of waiting for the slower device to finish. Many current processors have their own cache built into the processor to speed up data transfers to the chip.

RAM speeds are almost as high as processor speeds. Imagine what would happen if the computer had no RAM and relied on secondary storage to hold all instructions and data. The processor would always have to wait for data from the

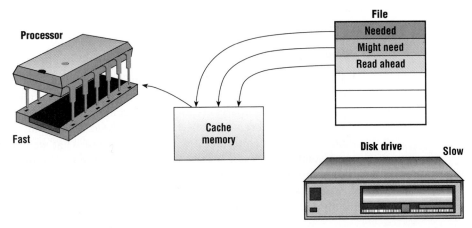

**Processor**

**Fast**

**Cache memory**

**File**

| Needed |
| Might need |
| Read ahead |

**Disk drive**          **Slow**

## A TECHNICAL NOTE ON RAM

Although RAM chips are made separately, most current PC manufacturers use a collection of chips known as *SIMMs (single in-line memory modules)*. A SIMM is a small board that contains several chips. The amount of memory contained on a SIMM depends on the type of chips used. For instance, a SIMM with nine 4 megabit-sized chips can hold 4-megabytes of data.

Notice that although there are 8 bits in a byte, it takes 9 data chips instead of 8 to get the desired number of bytes. The ninth bit is known as a *parity bit*, and it is used to identify and control for errors in memory. When data is stored in memory, the parity bit is set on or off depending on the other 8 bits. If one of the bits fails, the parity bit will not match, so the computer knows an error has occurred.

secondary storage, so the entire computer would run only as fast as the storage device (millisecond speed). The same problem arises if you buy a computer that does not have enough RAM. The computer will not be able to hold enough instructions in RAM and will have to retrieve them from secondary storage, which can take a thousand times longer.

Why are there secondary storage devices? Why not just store everything in high-speed RAM? The main reason is cost. Although prices vary, memory chips cost somewhere around $30 per megabyte. Typical storage devices cost around $1 to $5 per megabyte (or less). Also, there are two basic kinds of memory chips: static and dynamic. Dynamic chips cost less, but lose their contents when the power is turned off, so they are not useful for long-term storage.

## Processors

Processors come in a wide variety of formats. Some computers use one processor that consists of a single silicon chip (microprocessor). Others use several different chips to make up one processor. Still other computers use multiple processors. The critical point to remember is that each type of processor is unique. Each manufacturer creates its processor in a certain way and designs it to follow a specific set of instructions. For instance, a processor made by Intel works differently than one made by Motorola. As a result, instructions written for one processor cannot be used directly by the other processor. Note that some companies (especially in the personal computer world) produce "clones" of the leading chip manufacturer. For example, Advanced Micro Devices and NexGen make chips that are compatible with Intel processors and can run the same programs.

### Comparing Processors

Whenever you buy a computer, you want to have some idea of how fast it can operate. Because all of the components interact, it is hard to measure speed. It is even harder to make comparisons among different types of processors—especially when they operate differently. Nonetheless, it would be difficult to justify spending the money for a new computer if we have no idea of what we might gain. Hence, there are several measures of speed. Some measures focus on individual components, others attempt to evaluate the entire system.

Because the processor is an important factor in speed of a computer, a commonly used measure is the number (millions) of instructions they can complete in

**Reality Bytes** ▲ **2–9** BUILDING PROCESSORS AND MEMORY CHIPS

Building processors and memory chips involves growing silicon crystals and slicing them into wafers. The internal circuits are then etched onto these wafers using chemical deposition techniques. The catch is that cramming more storage on a chip requires finer and finer circuit lines. Common RAM chips in 1994 held 4 megabits of data, with leading-edge chips at 16 megabits. Because of capital costs, manufacturers will only produce new chips if they can gain four times the amount of storage.

Researchers in the mid-1990s were beginning work on a 1-gigabit chip (64 times the storage of a 16-megabit chip, or 3 generations improved). For this chip to work, it needs lines that are 0.15 microns wide (1/200,000 of an inch).

Using conventional laser lithography to etch patterns onto the chip becomes difficult as the lines get smaller. Conventional methods rely on a mask to cover parts of the chip that are then exposed to laser light, which removes a photoresistive material on the uncovered sections. The main difficulty with small sizes is that the light waves are too wide. Modern chip technology relies on ultraviolet rays because they are narrower, but they are still 0.193 microns wide. Manufacturers are experimenting with smaller wave x-rays or electron beams.

A second problem is that the etching size is coming closer to the size of a single molecule, which brings in quantum physics effects, where atoms randomly "tunnel" through barriers.

Some companies, like Cray Computer, have switched from silicon to gallium arsenide (GaAs), because it has smaller molecules that allow finer etchings. The GaAs chips also operate faster. However, GaAs crystals currently are more difficult to work with.

one second (MIPS). Other measures, called *benchmarks* have been created to compare different computers under a variety of situations. Although benchmarks give a better indication of performance than do MIPS for certain tasks, they are more complex to administer and they tend to change over time. They are useful if you can find one to match your application and you want to compare several machines at the same point in time.

Some people use the internal clock speed as a measure of processor performance. For example, the Intel Pentium processor was available at different clock speeds, such as 60 MHz, 75 MHz, and 120 MHz. Although the clock speed does directly affect the performance of the processor, you must be careful to use it only to compare processors from the same family. For instance, a Pentium at 66 MHz is faster than a 486 processor running at 66 MHz. Clock-speed comparisons between manufacturers are essentially meaningless.

Price is another important feature of processors. Consider the approximate measure of price and performance shown in Figure 2.10. Because the personal computer values are hard to see, the numbers are shown in the accompanying table. The graph shows the average cost of buying one million instructions per second (cost/MIPS). It is not completely fair to compare large IBM computers designed to handle multiple users to personal computers. Also, the costs are approximate because they include peripheral equipment. However, notice that the price differential is enormous. Also notice in Figure 2.11 that price per MIPS for all types of machines have dropped considerably over time.

The important features of the table and graph are the speed and prices of the microcomputers. Notice how the personal computer speeds compare to those of the large IBM computers. Although these machines are designed and used for different purposes, because the differences are so large, we would expect this pattern to affect the way businesses use computers. These changes will be examined in later chapters.

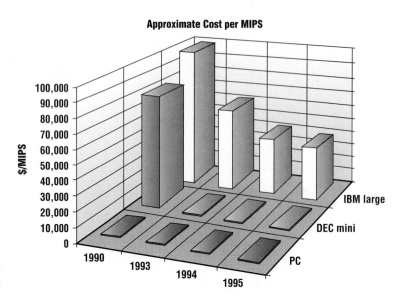

In the mid-1980s, the Intel 80286 machines performed at less than 1 MIPS. Today, the Intel Pentium machines can process over 100 MIPS. Intel has developed its own rating system to help personal computer buyers understand the potential value of new processors. Some examples are shown in Figure 2.12. The numbers do not signify any absolute level of performance but are designed to allow comparison to earlier Intel chips. There are many differences among the chips, and without the iCOMP measure, it would be hard to tell which chip might be faster.

The catch is that these numbers represent only the speed of the *processor,* but system performance also depends on the speed of peripheral devices, amount of system memory, and type of internal connectors (buses, as described next). Nonetheless, the graph does illustrate the improvements made for each generation, with the 386 popular during 1989–1993, the 486 during 1993–1995, and the Pentium from 1994 on.

### Connections

Even if two computers have the same basic components, it is still possible for one machine to be substantially faster than the other. The reason is because the components need to exchange data with each other. This communication requires an electrical connection. Most computers have special slots that form the connection between add-on boards and the processor *bus.* Various manufacturers make boards that fit into these slots. The processor can exchange data with these other devices, but it is constrained by the design of the bus. For example, even if a processor can handle 64 bits of data at a time, the bus might not have the connections to allow it

| | 1990 | | 1993 | | 1994 | | 1995 | |
|---|---|---|---|---|---|---|---|---|
| | COST/ MIPS | (MIPS) | COST/ MIPS | (MIPS) | COST/ MIPS | (MIPS) | COST/ MIPS | (MIPS) |
| PC | $1000 | 1 | $400 | 5 | $80 | 25 | $20 | 150 |
| DEC mini | $80,000 | 25 | $700 | 100 | $500 | 200 | $200 | 1000 |
| IBM large | $100,000 | 120 | $59,000 | 150 | $41,000 | 150 | $39,000 | 150 |

**FIGURE 2.12**

To assist buyers, Intel
provides a measure of
its own processors.
The rating is an index
that measures relative
performance. For
instance, a Pentium-
100 with a rating of
800 is about 8 times
faster than a 486SX-25
with a rating of 100.

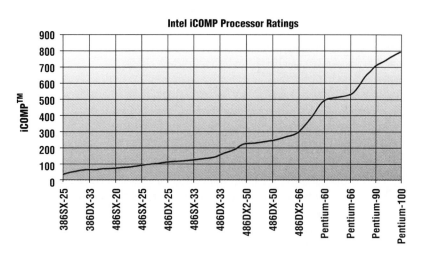

to transfer that much data at a time. Each computer manufacturer has to choose
how to design the bus. Standards enable users to transfer cards and devices from
one computer to another, especially if users buy a new computer. The problem is
that a bus designed for today's computers will eventually become obsolete as the
processor improves. At some point, the standards need to be changed. In the personal computer market, standards for the bus have been gradually evolving. The
original, IBM-designed bus, known as the *Industry Standard Architecture (ISA)*
still exists in some computers today—despite the fact that it was designed to transfer only 8-bits at a time. With the introduction of the Pentium processor, the industry has generally adopted an Intel-sponsored design known as *Personal Computer
Interconnect (PCI)* bus. PCI was also designed to make it easier for users to set up
their computers. In conjunction with the operating system, the computer determines which cards the computer contains and configures them automatically—a
process known as *plug-and-play*. In the past, users had to read obtuse documentation and set switches on every card, hoping that a new card did not conflict with
an existing one.

### Parallel Processors

In the past, when processors were more expensive, designers used only one processor in a machine. Today, many computers contain multiple processors. Although it
can be a desirable feature, you must be careful when evaluating parallel-processing
machines. If a computer has four processors and each can process 100 MIPS, then it
is tempting to say that the computer in total can process jobs at 400 MIPS. Indeed,
many computer companies advertise their computers this way. MIPS data for large
IBM computers use this method.

Can a computer with four processors really do your job four times faster? The
answer is that it depends on your job. Consider an example. A computer with two
processors has to add two sets of numbers together. Each processor works on one
pair of numbers, and finishes in half the time of a single processor. Now, the same
two computers have to work the problem in Figure 2.13.

Notice that the second calculation depends on the outcome of the first one. The
second one cannot be computed until the first one is finished. Even if we assign one
processor to each calculation, the parallel-processing machine will take just as long as
the single processor.

**FIGURE 2.13**

Some computations must be performed in sequence, so there is little to be gained with multiple parallel processors. In this example, the second computation (yyy) must wait for the first one to finish.

| 23 | *xx* |
|----|------|
| +54 | +92 |
| *xx* | *yyy* |

A parallel-processing computer is faster than a single processor only when the job can be split into several independent pieces or there are several jobs and each processor can be assigned to different jobs—several examples are presented (Parallel Processing Examples). There is one more problem: The computer has to spend some time assigning jobs and collecting the results. For a small number of processors, this may not be a major problem. However, some companies are selling computers that contain as many as 32,000 separate processors. Seymour Cray of Cray Computer Corporation in 1994 indicated that by 1999 he wants to produce a machine with 32 million processors, capable of performing 1 quadrillion (billion, million) operations per second. Two important questions should leap into your mind at this point: (1) For what types of jobs would these massively parallel computers be useful? (2) How much will the computer cost? As a partial answer for the first question, at the end of 1994, another computer manufacturer, NEC, announced that that firm could build a machine that performed 1 trillion operations per second. However, analysts estimated that it would cost $100 million and would probably never be built, because no one would buy one at that price. Although there are many interesting uses for supercomputers, companies are increasingly faced with the question of determining how much value such expensive machines contribute. An additional answer to the question comes by noting that Cray Computer filed for bankruptcy in 1995. In 1996, Cray Research (the leading supercomputer manufacturer) was sold to Silicon Graphics, Inc.

Some of the commercial uses for massively parallel machines are listed here (Parallel Processing Examples). The common feature is that the tasks can be split into thousands of smaller pieces, and there is a huge amount of data to examine. Two other large users of supercomputers are: (1) governments for code breaking, and (2) special-effects studios, such as Industrial Light & Magic.

## RISC Processors

Until a few years ago, there was one major trend in computer processors: new designs ran faster and contained more circuits than earlier versions. Each generation of processor was more complex and contained more instructions. For example, an older processor might only be able to add two small integer numbers together, while an improved version would be able to perform calculations with floating-point (real) numbers. Although this tendency to make bigger and faster processors continues, several manufacturers have added an additional approach. They are now making simpler processors, known as *reduced instruction set computers (RISC)*.

When designing a RISC processor, the manufacturer deliberately limits the number of circuits and instructions on the chip. The goal is to create a processor that performs a few simple tasks very rapidly. More complex problems are solved using software. Because RISC processors require fewer circuits they are easier to produce. Examine Figure 2.10 again and look at the figures for Digital Equipment Corporation (Digital). The drop in price per MIPS from 1990 to 1993 was largely due to the introduction of the RISC-based Alpha processor.

Except for compatibility, it typically does not matter to users whether the computer uses a complex or RISC processor. Most people simply look at cost and performance comparisons. On the other hand, the expanding production of RISC proces-

## ◥ PARALLEL PROCESSING EXAMPLES ◤

According to a study by International Data Corp, the total revenue for manufacturers of massively parallel computers was approximately $261 million in 1991. Partly because of high cost, partly due to lack of commercial objectives, massively parallel machines were largely limited to facilities performing scientific research. They are used to simulate molecules in chemistry and to study weather patterns. However, commercial use of the machines is increasing.

Chevron Oil Field Research uses a Maspar Corp. MP-1 for oil exploration. Chevron uses the parallel processors to search huge quantities of 3-D seismic data. A typical survey consists of 2,000 tapes holding 200 MBytes of data each.

NASA used a Maspar Corp. MP-1 to improve the initial images from the Hubble Space Telescope. The lens on the $1.5 billion telescope was not ground correctly and the initial images were blurry. With 8,192 processors, the MP-1 delivers 650 mega-FLOPs (million floating-point operations per second). Software analyzes each portion of the image and estimates the amount of spherical distortion from the lens to correct the image. The process takes about three hours per picture and would not be practical without the massively parallel system.

The OnLine Computer Library Center provides computer support for 11,000 member libraries. It maintains a card-catalog database of more than 24 million books. Roger Thompson is in the process of converting the database search system to run on a parallel computer to shorten the search times.

Dow Jones News/Retrieval is a division of the company that publishes *The Wall Street Journal.* They created a search system called DowQuest that uses a Thinking Machine Corp. computer with 32,000 processors. The system is a database that stores full-text articles from more than 184 publications (e.g., *The Wall Street Journal*, *Barron's*, and *Fortune*). The system asks users for a search topic, then each processor searches a portion of the database. The results are immediately presented to the user. The user can then prioritize the list, or select one or two articles. The system then uses the rankings and the words in the chosen articles to perform another search of the database. With this iterative search, the system is better at finding related articles that might use synonyms. The parallel processors make the search significantly faster, giving the user more opportunities to revise the conditions.

By using thousands of low-cost processors instead of one or two expensive, high-speed processors, massively parallel systems can be cheaper to use. A benchmark comparison of the Oracle Corp. database provides one example. The best large-computer performance in 1992 was 419 transactions per second, costing about $50,000 per transaction. The same process on a 64-node NCube parallel machine yielded 1,073 transactions per second at a cost of $2,482 per transaction—a substantial improvement in price and performance.

sors creates additional competition for chip manufacturers, which has led to faster computers at lower prices.

### Input

Because there are several types of data, many input devices are available. The purpose of an input device is to convert data into electronic binary form. Keyboards are the most common method of entering new text and data. Note that you can purchase different types of keyboards to suit individual users. For example, some keyboards enable you to change the layout of the keys. Keyboards have their own "feel"; some individuals prefer sensitive keys with using a light touch, others like stiffer keys to support their hands. Some manufacturers have gone further and have experimented with keyboard designs that accommodate nontraditional placement of the hands. Figure 2.14 provides one example.

**FIGURE 2.14**
There have been
increasing complaints
about injuries "caused"
by repetitive typing
tasks. Several
manufacturers have
experimented with new
keyboard designs that
are claimed to relieve
physical stress.

**Ergonomics** is the study of how machines can be made to fit humans better. One of the main conclusions of this research in the computer area is that individuals need to be able to adjust input (and output) devices to their own preference. Forcing people to adapt to rigid devices can lead to complaints and even physical injuries. Since the mid-1980s, many workers have encountered a disabling condition known as *repetitive stress injury*, which some people claim results from extended use of tools that do not physically match the worker.

Although there is limited scientific study of these injuries and causes, some people have found relief after ergonomic changes to their work environment. Complaints typically involve back pain, eye strain, headaches, arm and shoulder pain, and finger or wrist pain due to carpal tunnel syndrome. Common ergonomic suggestions include adjustable chairs, foot rests, arm rests, adjustable keyboards, high-resolution low-flicker monitors, and improved lighting.

Of course, all of these adjustments cost money—especially if they are added as an afterthought. The key to the problem is to evaluate individual requirements and adjust the environment *before* installing computers.

### Pointing Devices

With the increased use of graphics and pictures, it is common for computers to use pointing devices for input. A mouse is the most popular device in use today, although light pens, touch screens, and digitizer tablets are heavily used in some applications. Touch screens are commonly used for displays that involve customers or other atypical computer users. Many tourist bureaus, hotels, and shopping areas use computer displays with touch screens to give directions to visitors. Besides the fingerprints, the biggest problem with touch screens is that the tip of your finger is often too large to be a useful pointer. For more detailed use, an engineer designing a wiring diagram for an automobile would use a digitizer tablet with a special pen to draw fine lines and select individual points that are close together.

### Scanners

When you are dealing with pictures, it is often helpful to have a scanner convert a paper-based image into digital (bitmap) form. For certain types of images (line-drawings and text), there is software to convert the bitmap image into vector form.

The quality of a scanner is measured by the number of pixels per inch that it can distinguish as well as the number of colors. Most scanners can read at least 300 dots per inch. More dots mean better resolution: finer lines and sharper pictures.

Several types of scanners are available. It is possible to get a small hand-held scanner for less than a couple hundred dollars. These scanners only read a few rows of dots at one time. You have to pull the scanner across the picture by hand. They work best if you can pull it in a straight line at a constant speed. More expensive flatbed scanners scan the entire page automatically.

Scanners also can be used to input text and data into a computer. The scanner first converts the page into a picture of dots. Then **optical character recognition (OCR)** software examines the picture and looks for text. The software checks each line and deciphers one character at a time. OCR software is still slow and error-prone, but it is improving. Some systems automatically look up each word in a dictionary to spot conversion errors and improve accuracy. Even then, users report about a 90 percent accuracy rate—which is highly dependent on the quality of the original document.

### Pen-based Systems

A new category of computers is being created. Some hand-held, notebook-size computers use a pen as the primary input device. The pen is used to point to objects on the screen, make changes to documents, and even write notes. In some cases, the machines can convert your handwriting to computer text—much like OCR converts typed papers. Of course, deciphering individual handwriting is much more difficult than reading typed characters, and the accuracy of data can be limited. Despite the hype about potential applications for traveling managers (and salespeople), the first versions of pen-based computers did not sell well. As processors, storage, and display technology and telecommunications improve, we will probably see more acceptance of pen-based hand-held computers.

### Sound

Sound is initially captured with a microphone that converts sound pressure waves into electrical signals. A *sampler* then converts these signals into numeric data that can be stored on the computer. Musical **synthesizer** technology is used to convert the numbers back to electrical signals that can be heard with speakers. Sound boards can be purchased for personal computers that contain both the sampler and synthesizer technology. Digital sound conversion occurs on almost every long distance telephone call you make. Your voice is converted to ones and zeros to be sent across fiber optic phone lines.

### Voice Recognition

As long as computers have existed, individuals have dreamed of being able to talk to them and have the words translated into text. Although computers can digitize and record speech, it is still difficult to convert the spoken words into text. Some problems are the use of homonyms, variations in speech patterns or dialects, and the effects of punctuation on meaning. Many companies are working on improving voice recognition, and software exists to convert voice into text. The best systems are still expensive. The lower-cost systems understand a limited number of words and generally have to be trained to respond to only one user. In most cases, the person must pause after speaking each word. Nonetheless, the systems are useful in occupations that require notetaking along with two hands to do the job. Quality control inspectors and surgeons use them regularly.

## VOICE RECOGNITION EXAMPLES

Public familiarity with voice recognition devices increased in 1993 when Sprint Corp. began selling a voice-activated calling card that recognizes user commands to dial up to 10 numbers. In a similar vein, several car phones offer voice-dialing as a safety feature for drivers. AT&T eliminated 2,000 telephone operator positions with the use of voice recognition.

The U.S. Bureau of Labor Statistics replaced paper reports by using a voice recognition system to collect monthly data from 390,000 businesses.

Auralogy S.A., a French software company, developed a system to teach foreign languages. If the program does not recognize a student's phrase, it uses a pronunciation lesson to assist the student.

ADGA Quebec Ltd. is an engineering firm that uses voice recognition to train airport ground personnel how to use and respond to radio orders.

### Video Capture

As technology improves, companies are increasingly adding video clips to presentations. Probably the most common use of video lies in computer-based training (CBT). Users interact with scenarios described in video clips to solve problems or learn new techniques. Digital video transmissions are also being used for communication.

Because computer monitors and television sets are loosely based on the same technology, it would seem easy to merge the two. However, computer monitors deal with different types of video signals. Computers need special video boards to convert and display TV signals on the computer monitor. These cards accept standard coaxial video output from a VCR, camcorder, and television receiver. Not only can the signal be displayed on your monitor but also converted to digital form and saved or replayed. Hence, you can change the images, add text and graphics, or design special effects such as a metamorphosis that turns a person into a car *(morphing)*.

The fact that computer monitors use signals differently from televisions causes an additional challenge in an international environment. The United States, Europe, and Japan have different television signals. Videotapes recorded in the United States cannot be played on European VCRs. That means that a video capture board built for the U.S. market might not work in other countries. A few boards, however, support several different signals. So, if you are dealing with offices in different countries, be careful when purchasing video hardware and software to ensure that it supports all of the standards you need.

### Output

Most people are interested in two types of output: video and paper copy. Video output is created by a video card and displayed on a monitor. The quality is measured by the **resolution**, which is the number of pixels and colors it can display. Resolution is established by the video card, but higher resolutions require more sophisticated (and more expensive) monitors. Common personal computers today can support 1,024 horizontal and 768 vertical dots at 256 colors, which requires a video card with almost 1 megabyte of memory. There are video cards available that support 16 million different colors. This level of color is called **true color**, because it represents the typical range of colors that can be distinguished by the human eye. It requires 24 bits (3 bytes) per pixel to attain this level of color. A video card with a resolution of 1,024 by 768 pixels requires slightly more than 2 megabytes of video

RAM to display 16 million colors. By comparison, older video cards that displayed 640 by 480 pixels at 16 colors required only 150 *kilobytes* (thousands of bytes) of video RAM.

High-resolution screens with multiple colors can display beautiful pictures and excellent quality text. They do have some drawbacks. They are relatively expensive, especially because large-screen monitors (19 inches or more) are often needed to display text in a legible size. Because high-resolution true-color screens require over 15 times more data than the older video boards, the higher-resolution boards can also be slower. Manufacturers have compensated by building special hardware and software to accelerate them, but for some applications it is better to shift them into a lower-resolution mode.

The other common output device is the printer. Printers come in many different forms. Three popular formats are lasers, ink-jets, and dot matrix. In all three cases, the output is created by printing dots on the page. Resolution is measured by dots per inch. Common resolutions include 300 and 600 dots per inch, and 1,000 dot-per-inch lasers are available. In contrast, standard typesetters, such as those that are used to print books, operate at resolutions of at least 2,400 dots per inch. Again, higher-resolution devices are more expensive. Also, the increased amount of data being displayed takes longer to print (for the first copy).

Laser printers operate much like photocopiers. A multifaceted mirror reflects a laser light onto a drum. This drum rotates and picks up the toner (a dry ink). As the paper feeds through, it is given an electric charge that attracts the toner. The toner is then heated and fused to the paper. It is not crucial that you understand the process; the important point is that there are few moving parts in laser printers. As a result, they are relatively trouble free and significantly quieter than older types of printers. Because they use toner instead of ribbons, they are often cheaper to operate.

Dot matrix and ink-jet printers have a print head that moves across the page and prints each character or graphics dot. A dot matrix printer has wires that physically press a ribbon to the paper to print dots and form each character. An ink-jet print head does not touch the paper but relies on electrostatic charges to attract the ink from a nozzle to the paper. Both printers operate more slowly than laser printers, but prices tend to be lower. More importantly, it is easier to create color output with ink-jet printers because they use liquid ink instead of dry toner. Color laser printers exist, but be sure to check the cost of printing a page. Approximate comparisons of the three major types of printers are displayed in Figure 2.15.

| PRINTER | INITIAL COST (DOLLARS) | COST PER PAGE (CENTS) | QUALITY (DOTS/INCH) | SPEED (PAGES/MIN.) |
|---|---|---|---|---|
| Laser | 600–200,000 | 0.6–3 | 300–1,200 | 4–8–100+ |
| color | 2500+ | 15–75 | 300–600 | 0.5–8 |
| Ink jet | 300–2,000 | 5–50 | 300–600 | 0.25–7 |
| color | 500–2,000 | 25–150 | 300–600 | 0.1–4 |
| Dot matrix | 200–2,000 | 1.5–3 | 100–300 | 0.5–4 |

**FIGURE 2.15**

Printer evaluations. Printers are evaluated in terms of initial cost, cost per page, resolution, and speed. There are many types of printers, led by laser, ink jet, and dot matrix printers. Prices vary depending largely on speed and resolution. Technological changes are leading to new varieties of printers that can produce full color at a cost of around 5 to 10 cents per page.

## Secondary Storage

Except for prices (declining) and capacity (expanding), typical secondary storage devices have changed little during the last few years. Secondary storage is needed to hold data and programs for longer periods. Secondary storage is evaluated by three attributes: capacity, speed and price. The values for different types of storage are summarized in Figure 2.16.

The device most commonly used today is the magnetic hard drive. *Magnetic hard drives* consist of rigid platters that store data with magnetic particles. Data is accessed by spinning the platters and moving drive heads across the platters to access various tracks. Hard drives come in a variety of sizes, ranging from 80 megabytes up to 15 gigabytes (billions of bytes). One thousand gigabytes are called a terabyte (trillion bytes). Typical drive prices range from $0.35 to $10.00 per megabyte. **Access speed** is the time needed for the drive to move to a particular location and begin transferring data. Typical access speed is around 10 milliseconds.

With the increasing importance of data, companies are searching for ways to prevent loss of data by providing continuous backups. One straightforward method is to install an extra disk drive and keep duplicate copies of all files on this *mirror drive.* If something goes wrong with one of the drives, users simply switch to the other drive. A second method of protecting data is known as a **redundant array of inexpensive drives (RAID).** Instead of containing one large drive, this system consists of several smaller drives. Large files are split into pieces stored on several different physical drives. At the same time, the pieces can be duplicated and stored in more than one location. In addition to the duplication, RAID systems provide faster access to the data, because each of the drives can be searching through its part of the file at the same time.

On personal computers, another common storage device is the floppy disk drive. These use thin, removable disks to store data. They operate similarly to magnetic hard drives, but much slower. Typical capacity is around 1.5 megabytes per disk,

| Drive | Capacity (megabytes) | Speed (milliseconds) | Initial Cost (dollars) | Cost/Mbyte (dollars) |
|---|---|---|---|---|
| Magnetic Hard | 80–15,000 (200) | 9–35 (13) | | 0.25–5.00 (0.35) |
| Floppy | 1–2 (1.44) | 80–200 (120) | 50–100 | 0.15–0.50 (0.20) |
| Solid State/RAM | 20–1,000 | 0.00006–0.006 | | 45–100 |
| Tape | 250–2,000 | sequential | 300–5,000+ | 0.04–0.25 |
| Optical ROM Write Once | 650 | 200 | 250–500 1,000–2,000 | 0.05–.10 |
| Optical Erasable | 128–3,000 | 25–100 | 1,000–3,000 | 0.10–1.00 |

**FIGURE 2.16**

Disk drives are evaluated in terms of capacity, speed, initial cost and cost per megabyte—especially for removable media. A wide variety of drives is available in each category so a range is displayed for each feature. Values for a typical personal computer are in parentheses. Note there has been a strong downward trend in hard drive costs in the last few years.

which costs less than $0.25 per megabyte when bought in quantity. However, the access speed is around 100 milliseconds, or 10 times slower than hard drives.

Magnetic tapes are also used to store data. Their biggest drawback is that they can only store and retrieve data sequentially. That means you have to search the tape from the beginning to find any data. A single tape can hold a gigabyte of data at a cost of 4 to 10 cents per megabyte. Because of these two features, tapes are most commonly used to hold backup data.

With the increased use of images, sound, and video, there is a need for substantially greater storage capacity for data files. Optical disks have provided substantial capacity at relatively low costs. The optical (or magneto-optical) disk drive uses a laser light to read data stored on the disk. There are three basic forms of optical drives: CD-ROM, WORM, and erasable. **CD-ROM** stands for compact disk-read only memory, the format used to store music CDs. The ROM portion of the name means that you can only read data from the disk. A special machine is required to store data on a CD-ROM. One side of a CD can hold 650 megabytes of data and costs a couple dollars to produce in quantity. The biggest drawback is that a *fast* access speed is 200 milliseconds (one-fifth of a second). Hence, it could take a full second to find five different pieces of data. CD-ROMs are most useful for storing large quantities of data that will not change. CDs are available that contain text, pictures, sound, and video for an entire encyclopedia.

Manufacturers have tried to improve the access speeds on CDs, but they are limited by the existing standards. In the 1980s, to ensure compatibility, the major manufacturers agreed on how data would be stored on CDs. As part of this process, they decided to maintain compatibility with audio CDs, so that computer-based CD readers could also play musical selections. Although this decision helped create multimedia applications, it currently limits the speed of CDs. To meet the standards, the CD must spin at a predetermined speed. This spin rate is a major factor in determining access times, because

## ◀ UPGRADE DECISIONS ▶

Not counting printing and input devices, we can think of the computer as four major subsystems (processor, memory, secondary storage, and video). These four systems strongly affect the computer's performance. With current system designs, it is possible to upgrade a computer by replacing one or more of these components. How much you gain in speed depends on the improved speed of the new component and on how you use the computer.

For example, Mark VanName and Bill Catchings *(Computer Shopper)* note that for a typical user task that might take 100 seconds, about 60 seconds will be used by the processor and memory, 20 in the disk drive, and 20 in the graphics subsystem. Assume you buy a new video card that can display information twice as fast as the old one. The time spent in the video subsytem would be cut from 20 to 10 seconds, but that's only a 10 percent increase in system speed. On the other hand, if you doubled your processor/memory speed, you would cut 30 seconds from the overall time.

Keep in mind that not all machines and people use the subsystems in the same proportions. If you work on highly graphic-intensive applications, you might gain even more by buying a faster video subsystem.

Finally, note that after about three years, virtually all of the subsystems will be outdated. In such a case, upgrading one or two components might not be sufficient. To seriously improve system performance, you will want to upgrade the entire computer.

data can only be found and retrieved when it is spun under the read head. A common method to speed up CDs is to build in two spin rates: the standard speed to read the data, and a faster rate (two, three, or four times faster) to search the CD indexes.

The name **WORM** is an acronym for write once, read many. A WORM drive is similar to a CD-ROM drive, except that it does not require a special machine to create the original data. You can store data one time, but cannot change it. Current access speeds are slightly faster than for floppy drives. WORM drives are an intermediate step toward an erasable (or read/write) optical drive. Erasable optical drives are available, but the drive mechanism is more expensive than for CD-ROM or WORM drives. On the other hand, the removable disks can store from 128 megabytes to 1 gigabyte depending on the size of the disk, at a cost ranging from $0.10 to $1.00 per megabyte. Access speed is around 30 milliseconds, which is about the speed of a slow magnetic drive. Optical jukeboxes are available that can automatically load several disks and hold hundreds of gigabytes of storage. Optical storage devices provide enormous amounts of storage at low cost.

The biggest drawback to all forms of disk drives is that they are sensitive mechanical components. They can be damaged if dropped, they wear out with use, and there are limits to how fast they can store and retrieve data.

Due to speed constraints and the declining costs of memory chips, some applications are beginning to use memory chips as secondary storage. Although the cost can be as high as $30 per megabyte, data can be stored and retrieved a thousand times faster. One increasingly common version is the PCMCIA (Personal Computer Memory Card International Association) card that is used with laptop and notebook computers. PCMCIA cards are about the size of a thick credit card, ranging from 3-mm to 16-mm thick. The cards can hold 20 megabytes of data in a type of memory chip that does not lose its contents when the power is turned off. The larger cards can hold tiny hard disk drives.

## OPERATING SYSTEMS

Computers follow instructions called software that are written by programmers. Every computer needs one special type of software known as the operating system. The operating system is software that is responsible for communication among the hardware components. The operating system is also a primary factor in determining how the user deals with the machine.

In the past, you had no choice about the operating system; when you bought the computer, the manufacturer included its proprietary system. Today, with almost any computer, you can choose between at least two operating systems (proprietary and Unix). With personal computers there are many choices (such as DOS, OS/2, Unix, Windows-95, and Windows NT). They largely differ in three areas that will affect you directly: multitasking, user interface, and security.

### Multitasking

Picture a manager working on a major report that is due tomorrow. The computer is tied up with four hours of copying data from the central computer when the boss calls and asks for sales information on a different project. The data is stored on a personal computer, but if the copy job is interrupted, the project will not be finished on time. What should the manager do? The answer is easy if the manager's computer includes an operating system that can do **multitasking** and work on more than one job at a time. The manager presses a couple of keys and looks up the data for the boss. All other jobs continue to run in the "background."

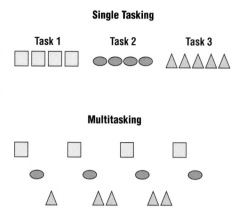

**FIGURE 2.17**

A multitasking operating system can tell the processor to work on small portions of each task and switch among them. Because the processor is so much faster than the other components, it appears to be working on several tasks at the same time.

Multitasking is a feature of operating systems that enables you to run more than one task or application at the same time. Technically, they do not run at exactly the same time, but it is close enough so you cannot tell the difference. Consider three tasks that you need to run. As Figure 2.17 shows, without multitasking the second task cannot be started until the first one finishes. With multitasking, the computer can work on part of task 1, then part of task 2, followed by task 3. By rotating among each of these tasks, the computer will appear to be working on all three at the same time.

At first glance, it might seem that nothing is gained by multitasking. If three jobs need to be completed, what difference does it make if we do one at a time or rotate among the various pieces? It sounds as if the computer will take the same amount of time to finish all three jobs. However, recall that the computer processor is faster than any of the other components. For example, with an average typist, the processor could execute 60 million other instructions while waiting for another keypress. While the processor is waiting for you to type in a request, it also could be printing a graph and looking up information in a database. Of course, if the processor has to switch among too many tasks, it will slow down. The speed of the processor, amount of memory, and quality of the operating system determine how many jobs can be performed at the same time.

Multitasking does present problems, especially since most personal computers were originally designed to do only one task at a time. For example, what happens if two programs want to change a number in a data file at the same time? The situation is similar to what would happen if you and a friend both try to sign your names on the same line at the same time. The result will be meaningless. To prevent these problems, a multitasking operating system will prevent you from accessing a file when it is being changed by another task.

*Multithreading* is similar to multitasking. It represents splitting a single application into several components or threads. Each thread can be processed independently of the others. For example, your word processor might use a separate thread to spell-check your document in the background as you continue writing.

## Graphical User Interface

There are many different varieties of operating systems. Although they perform similar tasks, the user deals with each system using different commands. A small sample of commands is presented in Figure 2.18. Many operating systems support a windows environment. For example, OS/2, Windows 95, Windows NT, X-Windows on Unix,

| TASK | PC-DOS | UNIX | IBM CMS | WINDOWS |
|---|---|---|---|---|
| Start application | Enter its name | Enter its name | Enter its name | Double-click icon |
| Copy a file | copy drive:file.suffix drive:new.suffix | cp file new | copy file suffix disk new suffix disk | Drag icon while pressing CTRL key |
| List files | dir | ls | list or filelist | On screen or start file manager |
| Change directory | cd directory | cwd directory | Not exist | Double-click directory name |
| Edit or examine a text file | edit file | ed file | edit file | Double-click file |

**FIGURE 2.18**

COMMON OPERATING SYSTEM TASKS

For many years, computers have relied on proprietary operating systems. Each system uses different commands to perform certain tasks. You need to learn several basic commands to use these systems. The problem becomes more acute if you must use several different types of computers. For example, you can encounter many different computers if you regularly use the Internet.

and the Apple Macintosh all rely on visual presentations and mouse controls instead of typed commands.

Operating systems have seen major changes over time. Think about the problems of using a computer where you have to type the following command to see what is stored in a file: *cat myfile.text | more.* There might be hundreds of commands like this one that you would have to memorize. Every major brand of computer has a different operating system, so you need to learn different commands for each machine. Instead of these command line interfaces, most modern operating systems provide a **graphical user interface (GUI).** One of the more powerful features of GUI operating systems stems from the first word, *graphical.* It means the system is based on a graphics screen instead of simple text. As a result, the screens displayed include pictures, lines, graphs, and text that is displayed in special fonts. By using graphics, it is possible to see exactly how your reports will look before they are printed. Many times it is easier to create and edit reports if they appear the same on the screen as they do when printed. This type of display is called **WYSIWYG,** which stands for *what you see is what you get.*

Instead of users memorizing command words, the graphics screen enables the operating system to display choices in menus based on icons that users click with a mouse to enter choices. **Icons** are pictures that illustrate a concept instead of using words. For instance, a pair of scissors might be used instead of the command Cut. Some people prefer dealing with icons; others find it easier to read words; some others prefer the time efficiency of entering command lines. Most GUIs list icons and words, too. Almost all actions are performed by selecting an icon or word from a menu. To start an application you look for a picture on the screen that represents what you want to do. By pointing to that item and clicking the mouse button, you tell the operating system to start the application. Many applications also support *shortcut* keys that execute a command with one or two keystrokes, such as CTRL+C for copying objects.

The GUI interface also spawned a new approach to operating systems. One of the goals of the GUI approach is to emphasize a visual approach to giving the computer instructions. For example, when a user marks an item, it is highlighted. To delete an object, it is dragged off the screen or to a trash can. To move an object, you simply drag it to a new location. These "commands" became standardized across the applications. By learning a few basic techniques, users have a head start at learning new applications.

GUIs support multiple windows. A *window* is a portion of the computer screen. You can move each window or change its size. By using windows, you can have several applications displayed on the screen at one time, which makes it is easier to copy data from one application into a second one. It is also easier to compare information from two applications if they are displayed side-by-side in windows. However, one drawback of GUI applications is that they require considerably more processing power than simple text-based applications.

## Standardization and Compatibility

Historically, each computer manufacturer created its own operating system tailored for that specific hardware. Knowing how to use one set of operating system commands might not help if a user bought a machine from a different vendor. Likewise, changing vendors typically required purchasing new application software. AT&T researchers began to solve this problem when they created a hardware-independent operating system. It is known as *Unix* and is designed to work with computers from many different manufacturers. However, Unix is not a complete standard, and application software must generally be rewritten before it can function on different computers. Standards have been an important contributor to the declining cost of personal computers, which has led to their widespread use throughout the world (Reality Bytes 2–10).

### Reality Bytes    2–10 INTERNATIONALIZATION

The increased power and decreased cost of personal computers have contributed to the use of computers in smaller and developing nations. It is enabling small companies to expand and to participate in the global economy.

Consider the case of Mexico. It has the thirteenth largest economy in the world but has become the sixth or seventh largest personal computer market. Companies there are using computers to track market research, keep track of inventory, and collect information on other firms as well as monitor global commodity and financial markets.

Jorge Melendez Ruiz, an executive at El Norte/Reforma, which collects and electronically distributes financial data, notes: "A country isn't in the First World because it has better people or better manufacturing or better systems. It's in the First World mainly because it has better information."

Consider one pilot program sponsored by the government, the village of Jalapa de Diaz in Oaxaca. The village consists of a few huts and a two-room schoolhouse. Inside is a personal computer, hooked to a microwave dish on a 60-foot tower next to the outhouse. The farmers can use the computer to track prices of the fruit they grow (apples, limes, papayas, and mangos). They are also using the machine to track the amount of coffee grown by surrounding farmers so they can sell it collectively to get a better price.

Another approach to the compatibility (portability) problem is being taken by Microsoft Corporation, which created an independent operating system called Windows NT. Windows NT was designed to operate on a variety of hardware platforms. It was also designed to be relatively easy to adapt to processors that might be invented later. A key difference with the Windows NT operating system is that application software written for one version will run without changes on other computers, regardless of the processor used. For example, a small company could begin by using personal computers. As the company grows, the amount of data increases. The company could switch to a RISC-based computer running Windows NT simply by copying the application software and data to the new machines. This *scalability* can be a useful feature for any company, because it minimizes the problems and trauma arising from changing computer systems.

## APPLICATION SOFTWARE

The main reason for buying a computer is because of its application software. It is good software that makes your job easier. Regardless of your job, there are certain tasks that you will always perform. As a manager and decision maker, you first have to gather data (research). Then you analyze the data and determine alternatives (involving calculations). Next you will make decisions and implement them (requiring writing, communication, and organizing resources). Each of these tasks can be supported by computer resources. The trick is to use the appropriate tools for each task. The objective is to use the tools to make you more productive in your job.

The catch is that productivity is a slippery problem in business—especially with respect to computer tools. One measure of productivity involves efficiency: Can you perform tasks faster? A second, more complicated measure of productivity involves effectiveness: Can you make better decisions? Early uses of computers focused on improving efficiency by automating manual tasks. The tools were often justified on the basis of decreased labor costs. Today, managerial uses often focus on effectiveness, which is harder to measure.

An important concept to remember with application software is that it was created by teams of designers and programmers. In the "old" days, when software was custom-written for specific companies and users, users could tell the designers how the software should behave. Today, we are moving rapidly to off-the-shelf software that is created to support the needs of millions of different users. In creating the software, designers had to make thousands of decisions about what the software should do and how it should appear. Sometimes their final choices might seem strange, and software does not always work the way you might prefer. Some issues can be resolved by customizing the software to your particular situation. Other times, just remember that you acquired the software for a tiny fraction of the price you would have paid for custom software.

### Research: Databases

Almost any job involves workers searching for information. This search could involve any of the five basic types of data. Computers have made it substantially easier to find, compare and retrieve data. Two important strengths of a database management system (DBMS) are the ease of sharing data and the ability to search for data by any criteria. In terms of productivity, a DBMS can make you both more efficient and improve your decisions. It improves efficiency by providing easier and faster data retrieval. By providing more complete access to data, a DBMS helps ensure that your decision incorporates all relevant data.

One complication with research is that you must first determine where the information is located. It could be located on your personal computer, the group's networked server, the company's central computers, a computer run by the government, or one purchased from another company. Unless all of these databases are connected, you must first determine which database to search. Chapter 5 focuses on the use of database management systems. Most DBMSs can handle numbers and simple text well. Only recently have they begun to tackle large text files, pictures, sound, and video.

## Analysis: Calculations

Almost everyone performs computations in their job. Although simple calculators are useful, they have some drawbacks. For example, it is difficult to go back and change a number entered previously. Also, most calculators cannot save very much data, and it is hard to print out the results. Finally, because of their small screens, they can display only a few numbers at a time. Spreadsheets were initially designed to overcome these limitations. These features are designed to make you more efficient at making calculations.

Most people find spreadsheets useful because their disciplines began with models on paper that used columns and rows of numbers. For instance, most accounting systems and financial models were designed for ledgers in this way. Whenever software mimics the way you already work, it is easier to learn.

Spreadsheets have many additional features. Graphs can be created with a couple of mouse clicks. Most packages enable users to modify the graphs by adding text, arrows, and pictures. Spreadsheets also perform various statistical and mathematical analyses. You can perform basic matrix operations like multiplication and inversion. Statistics capabilities include multiple regression to examine the relationship among different variables. Linear programming can be used to search for optimum solutions to problems. These additional features are designed to help you make better decisions by providing more powerful decision-evaluation tools.

## Communication: Writing

The primary gain from word processing is increased efficiency. Word processors improve communication by making it easier to revise text, find writing errors, and produce legible reports. Word processors today also include a spell-checker, a thesaurus, and a grammar checker. Although they are not the same as having a human editor correct your writing, they are all useful tools for writers. Grammar checkers use standard measures to estimate the reading difficulty level of your writing. For instance, if you write an employee policy manual, you want to make sure that an average employee can understand it. Most word processors also have outline tools that help you organize your thoughts and rearrange a document, improving the communication.

The proliferation of word processors creates additional advantages. At some point, a company finds that almost all of its reports, data, and graphs are being created and stored on the computer. If this transition is handled carefully, managers can use the computer to search for any prior reports or data. It also becomes easier to send reports and notes to other managers. It sounds as though companies would use less paper and rely on electronic transmissions. Most organizations have not made it to this stage yet, and some people believe we never will. In fact, the use of personal computers has dramatically increased the usage of paper by U.S. companies.

Software companies have continued to add features to their products. The biggest trend in word processors is the addition of desk-top publishing features.

**FIGURE 2.19**

Typefaces fall into two main categories; serif and sans serif. *Serifs* are little curls and dots on the edges of letters. They make text easier to read; however, sans serif typefaces are useful for overheads and signs because the added white space makes them easier to see from a distance. Ornamental typefaces can be used for headlines. Size of fonts is measured in *points.* Characters in a 72-point font are about 1 inch tall, and most books and newspapers use a font between 10 and 11 points.

**Typefaces**

**Sample Typefaces**

| serif | sans serif |
|---|---|
| Times Roman 24 | Arial 24 |
| Century Schoolbook 24 | AvantGarde 24 |
| New Aster Bold 24 | |
| Garamond 24 | Futura Oblique 24 |
| Courier 24 | |

*Ornamental*

Madrone 24          DORIC 36

Bodoni 24          RIGAMAROLE 36

**Desktop publishing (DTP)** provides more control over the final print. For example, you can choose a typeface, like the ones in Figure 2.19, to convey a certain image. You can include graphics images, tables, special characters, equations, and borders. You can automatically build an index and a table of contents. One problem that some companies have experienced with desktop publishing is that it appears to decrease the efficiency of employees. It takes employees longer to create reports, because they spend more time experimenting with layouts and presentation. The trade-off is that the reports now contain more information or communicate it better so that the effectiveness has improved and managers can make better decisions. Be careful when you communicate with documents that will be transferred to other nations. Even if the language is the same, some systems will replace characters with the local alphabet—which can be a major problem with currency signs (Reality Bytes 2–11).

One interesting impact of low-cost computers is that it is increasingly difficult to evaluate organizations by the quality of their publications. Even small groups can afford to produce high-quality reports and brochures. In the past, people tended to dismiss poorly typed and handwritten papers because they obviously came from small organizations. Now, one person can produce a report that looks like it came from a major organization.

## Communication: Presentation and Graphics

In many cases, the difference between a good report and an outstanding report is the presence and quality of the artwork. Graphs and pictures are used to communicate information and feelings. Charts and graphs are easy to create, store and modify using graphics software. Even if you are not an artist, you can buy **clip art** that was created by someone else and use it in your reports or charts. By using existing art libraries, reports and presentations can be created in a few hours. In the past, reports and presentations took days or weeks to finish by a staff of artists. By improving the appearance, a well-designed graphic can also improve communication and decision making.

To create or modify your artwork, you need a graphics package and an input device such as a mouse that enable you to draw on the computer screen. Most commercial artists use scanners so they can draw the original on paper and convert it to computer form. The digitized form enables you to make very precise changes, since you can *zoom* into a specific area. Zooming is helpful if you need to force lines to meet exactly or you want to make changes to small items, such as eyelashes on a person.

## ◤ Reality Bytes ◣    2–11  INTERNATIONAL NOTATIONS

Most applications today have the ability to use characters that are not found in the U.S. alphabet. For instance, in France or Mexico, you might need to use an acute mark (é). However, different software packages handle the characters differently, so you might have trouble converting a document from one word processor to another or to a different computer. For example, if a French subsidiary is using *WordPerfect* and the Canadian headquarters is using *Microsoft Word,* they can both print reports using the special characters. However, the document might change when the Canadian users attempt to retrieve a French document electronically.

Additionally, if you work for an international organization, remember that people in different countries write dates differently. For example, 5/10/93 means May 10, 1993, in the United States but would be interpreted as October 5, 1993, in Europe. Most word processors enable you to choose how automatic dates should be displayed.

Numbers are also handled differently in European nations. The use of commas (,) and points (.) is reversed from the U. S. version where commas separate thousands and the decimal point delineates the fractional component. (126,843.57 in the United States should be denoted as 126.843,57 in Europe.)

Two other problems often arise with spreadsheets: currencies and denoting billions. When you transfer documents to other languages or fonts, be sure to check any currency symbols. A few systems will automatically change the symbol to the local units (e.g., change $ to £,) but unless the numbers are converted by exchange rates, these changes would be incorrect. A second complication arises when a graphing package or spreadsheet automatically converts numbers to billions. In the United States and France, the number 1 billion has 9 zeros. In the UK (and nations like India), 1 billion has 12 zeros. An automatic conversion of 2,700,000,000 to 2.7 billion would result in a misinterpretation if the graph is sent to Great Britain.

Color often presents problems to computer artists. Colors on display screens are usually different from those generated by the printer. If you are serious about exact color matching, there is a color standard known as *Pantone*® that is supported by some printers (especially those used by commercial printshops), graphics software and even some monitors. By choosing colors according to these definitions, you are assured of getting the precise color on the final copy. Some software packages also support color separation. In modern four-color presses, color is created based on four different masks (cyan [blue], magenta [red], yellow, and black [key]—abbreviated CMYK). Other colors are created by blending portions of these colors, as controlled by the masks. Software that supports color separation can use a special machine to print the separate masks, which go directly to a commercial printing press.

Although you do not have to be an artist to incorporate artwork into your reports and documents, you do need an element of artistic sensibility. The goal is to use art to enhance your presentation, not clutter it. Knowing what looks good and using restraint are signs of artistic talent. Remember that faster does not always mean better. Use some of the time savings to put more thought into your presentations.

### Communication: Voice and Mail

All jobs require communication—with co-workers, managers, and customers or clients. Word processors help with reports and memos, but much of our communication is less formal. Everyone is familiar with answering machines for telephones. Businesses have taken this concept a step farther by using voice mail systems. Voice mail systems record messages much like an answering machine, but they store the messages in digital form on computers. They usually give the caller control over where the message is sent. Most people in the United States have dealt with systems that direct you to press buttons on the telephone to make choices. Some voice mail systems enable you to send the same message to several people. Some systems also allow you to skip messages or fast forward to the end.

Networked computers can be used to send messages directly to other users. These **electronic mail (e-mail)** systems are typically used to send written notices to various people. They can be used to send pictures, facsimiles (faxes), or even voice messages if the computers have sound boards and speakers. The basic problem with any communication system is that sooner or later it becomes cluttered with junk mail. One of the advantages of text e-mail is that the recipient can have the computer scan the messages to search for items that are important or interesting. With the appropriate mail filters, junk mail can be discarded automatically. Messages also can be retrieved and stored for future reference or forwarded to other people.

## Organizing Resources: Calendars and Schedules

An important task of managers is to organize company resources so that they are used most effectively. An important function is scheduling workers. Schedules involving line workers entail making sure that there are enough employees to get the job done, but no extra employees. Schedules involving managers typically involve meetings and require trade-offs between competing demands for a manager's time. Several software tools are available to improve both types of scheduling and make more efficient use of the human resources. The *Right Start Catalog* (Reality Bytes 2–12) illustrates the importance of choosing the proper tool for each job.

Most managers spend a considerable amount of time in meetings. In fact, it becomes difficult to keep track of appointments, set up new meetings, and reschedule meetings. The process is even more difficult when some participants are traveling, or are based in another city or country.

Several software packages store appointments and schedules on electronic calendars. Electronic calendar and scheduling software enables data to be shared with other people. For instance, each person in a department would use the electronic calendar to keep track of his or her personal, departmental, and corporate appointments. To schedule a meeting with departmental members, the manager selects an approximate time, specifies the priority of the meeting, and fills in the participants, location, and subject information. The calendar software then searches each personal calendar for the best time for the meeting. It overrides lower-priority meetings and places the complete notice on each person's calendar in a matter of seconds. Employees have to check their calendars periodically to see whether meetings have been added or changed.

◤ **Reality Bytes** ◣    **2–12** RIGHT START CATALOG

The *Right Start Catalog* is a direct merchandiser selling baby products. There are 170 employees, most of whom work the phone lines and process orders. Janet O'Donnell, the telemarketing director, originally used a spreadsheet to keep track of employee hours, vacations, and sick days. Even with the spreadsheet, it took half her time just to schedule the employee hours. She switched to PeopleScheduler, a software tool specifically designed for employee relations, and has reduced the time to half an hour a day. The system makes it easy to schedule hours, breaks, vacations, and absences. Managers can use the reports to track employee time and can modify the schedule instantly if someone calls in sick.

## SUMMARY

One of the original purposes of computers was to make it easier to perform basic tasks. Over time, as computers have become more powerful, they have come to support increasingly complex tasks. Today, in addition to increasing efficiency, computers can help you make better decisions. One major change lies in the type of data routinely processed. The five major types of data are numbers and text, images, sound, and video. To handle more sophisticated data and more difficult tasks, computer hardware and software have grown increasingly complex.

To choose a computer that best meets your needs, you must evaluate the four basic hardware components: input, processor, output, and secondary storage devices. Each component is measured by slightly different characteristics. Input devices are selected based on the specific task (such as a keyboard for typing, mouse for pointing, or a microphone for voice input). Processors are often selected based on speed and price. Output device quality is appraised by resolution and color capabilities as well as initial and ongoing costs. Secondary storage is evaluated based on speed, capacity, and price.

Although computer hardware and software are becoming more complex, operating systems are being improved to make them easier to use. Through graphical user interfaces and standardized menus, operating systems make it easier to use common applications. When choosing an operating

> ### A MANAGER'S VIEW
> There are many tools available for personal computers that will help you in your daily tasks. Every manager needs to write reports and memos. Most also deal with numbers on a regular basis. Calendars, schedules, and personal notes are used by most executives. Contact managers and phone lists are particularly important for sales managers.
>
> You need to know how to use all of these tools. You also need to keep up with changes in the industry. Many times in your career, you will need to purchase computer hardware and software. You can make better decisions if you understand the technology and trends.

system, you should also evaluate its ability to run several applications at once (multitasking).

Application software is the primary source of improved productivity. Packages exist to assist in research, analysis, communication, and organizing resources. Database management systems are used for research and data sharing. Spreadsheets and other analytical tools assist in calculations. Word processors, desktop publishing, drawing packages, voice mail, and e-mail are used for communication. Electronic calendars and scheduling software are used to help organize human resources. There are hundreds of other software applications for specific tasks, but most people begin with these basic tools.

## KEY WORDS

access speed, 70
binary data, 46
bitmap image, 49
CD-ROM, 71
clip art, 78
desktop publishing (DTP), 78
electronic mail (e-mail), 80
ergonomics, 66
graphical user interface (GUI), 74
icons, 74
input, 46
megabyte, 57

million instructions per second (MIPS), 59
milliseconds, 59
multimedia, 53
multitasking, 72
nanoseconds, 59
operating system, 45
optical character recognition (OCR), 67
output, 46
photo-CD, 50
processor, 58

redundant array of inexpensive drives (RAID), 70
random access memory (RAM), 58
resolution, 68
synthesizer, 67
true color, 68
vector image, 49
voice mail, 51
write once, read many (WORM), 72
WYSIWYG, 74

## REVIEW QUESTIONS

1. Describe the differences between hardware and software.
2. List and describe the four basic types of data. How much space would it take to store a typical example of each type of data?
3. Explain why speed and cost are important characteristics of computers.
4. What current processor gives the best performance for the price? Explain your answer.
5. The computer for Letterman Co. has three 100-MIPS processors. Is it safe to assume that this computer operates at a constant rate of 300 MIPS (100 MIPS * 3)? Explain your answer.
6. List and describe four common input devices. Using the knowledge you have gained thus far, what do you think is the most common type of input device? What input devices do you think will become more popular in the future?
7. List and describe two common output devices. Give an example of their use in business.
8. What is a secondary storage device? Give two examples of secondary storage devices.
9. Assume you are an employee for XYZ company. The director of MIS for XYZ company wants you to evaluate two different secondary storage devices to determine which best fits the needs

of XYZ. What criteria will you use in your evaluation of the two storage devices?
10. What is multitasking? Give some advantages of multitasking. What are some potential problems of multitasking?
11. How does a graphical user interface (GUI) help end users operate their systems more effectively?
12. Identify at least three possible uses for a massively parallel processing supercomputer. Explain how the tasks can be split into the necessary pieces.
13. You find that your company's staff now spends more time producing reports than they did before using personal computers. Should you get rid of the computers?
14. On a quick tour through a company, you notice that only 10 percent of the personal computers were being used. The rest sat on desks, either turned off or running a weird screen saver. Based on these numbers, you are thinking about selling half the machines and asking workers to share. Is this a good idea?
15. How do computers improve productivity in communication? What is the difference between increased efficiency and effectiveness (better decisions)?

## EXERCISES

1. Why don't companies build processors that follow the same instructions?
2. Estimate the current costs of operating these printers (cost per page): laser, dot matrix, ink-jet, and color laser.
3. Give three reasons why the use of personal computers could increase the usage of paper.
4. A software package enables you to define rows of data, but it uses an integer to count the rows. This value is stored in 2 bytes. If half the values can be negative, what is the largest positive value that can be held in the 2 bytes? If the counter is increased to 4 bytes, what is the largest positive value?
5. You have just been hired in a new job, and you will need a personal computer in your work. The company will pay up to $3,500 for hardware and software. Your new boss is willing to let you choose whatever components you want. Using current business and computer magazines, select the basic hardware and software elements you will need. At a minimum, your software should include an operating system, word processor, graphics package, and a spreadsheet. You might not need to purchase a printer. Describe the

basic components you chose. Be sure to justify any unusual choices.
6. Using reviews in computer magazines, identify at least two software packages in the following categories: word processor, spreadsheet, graphics, calendar, communications, and database management. Identify five major features of each package. Find the current lowest price (and source) of each product.
7. You have just been asked to explain word processors, spreadsheets, and graphics packages to a computer novice. In particular, he wants a reference sheet that will help him.

8. You are trying to decide on raises for your departmental employees. The table on the next page lists the performance evaluations they received along with an estimate of the percentage raises that you wish to give. To review your spreadsheet skills, enter the formulas necessary to complete the table, including the totals and averages. Also, create a graph that displays the percentage

C02Ex08.txt

| | A | B | C | D | E | F |
|---|---|---|---|---|---|---|
| 1 | Name | Salary | Evaluation | Raise% | Raise | New Salary |
| 2 | Mandelbrot | 97600 | 5.8 | 12 | | |
| 3 | Gardner | 82000 | 6.5 | 9 | | |
| 4 | Thom | 61300 | 4.9 | 6 | | |
| 5 | Russell | 53200 | 5.2 | 5 | | |
| 6 | Whitehead | 45000 | 5.3 | 8 | | |
| 7 | Goedel | 39400 | 6.8 | 7 | | |
| 8 | Hardy | 38400 | 7.2 | 7 | | |
| 9 | Cauchy | 27600 | 4.5 | 5 | | |
| 10 | Ramanujan | 37500 | 7.8 | 11 | | |
| 11 | Gauss | 21300 | 8.9 | 10 | | |
| 12 | Euler | 16400 | 6.7 | 8 | | |
| 13 | | total | average | average | total | total |

raise and the performance evaluation for each employee. (One extra credit point for identifying all of the employees.)

9. Estimate the storage space (number of bytes) required for each of the following items:

 a. A telephone book with 10,000 entries consisting of name, address, and phone number. Use your phone book to estimate the average length of an entry.

 b. A fax transmission of a 30-page report at high resolution (200 x 200 bits per inch). What is the raw size? What is the size if you can use a compression algorithm that reduces each page to $\frac{1}{20}$ the original size?

 c. You have a 4 x 6 inch color photograph scanned in high resolution at 2,400 dots per inch and 16 million colors (24 bits for color). How far (percentage) would you have to compress this image to fit into 4 megabytes of available RAM?

 d. Kodak has a system that transfers photographs to a CD-ROM. Using the Base∗16 resolution and the compression ratio described in the text, how many pictures can be stored on a CD-ROM that holds 650 megabytes? How many Base (TV) resolution pictures could be stored?

 e. If you wanted to store your favorite half-hour TV show in digital form, how many bytes of storage would it take? Extra credit: How much space would it take if you remove the commercials? (Hint: Time the commercials).

10. To review your word processing skills, write a short report to the CEO similar to the one shown

## RENOVATION SCHEDULE

| | | EST. RENOVATION DATE | |
|---|---|---|---|
| FACTORY | MANAGER (PHONE) | START | END |
| Spindle Prod. #7 | Sanchez (4327) | 4/9/97 | 6/7/97 |
| Planing #1 | Mirabel (1135) | 12/13/97 | 3/20/98 |
| Chair Assembly #12 | Gruntag (7893) | 6/3/97 | 9/17/98 |
| Upholstery #16 | Bachnel (8876) | 10/5/97 | 12/11/97 |
| Spring Prod. #3 | Coorda (3352) | 8/9/97 | 9/8/97 |

To:    J. Kevorkian

From: _____

Date:

After talking with the engineers and plant managers, the renovation committee has arrived at the enclosed schedule. With this schedule, we believe that we can complete the needed renovations without disrupting production. As you can see, it will take us almost a year to finish the remodeling. It is possible to speed up the process, but we would have to sacrifice production—which would cause us to be late on the **Werner contract** and we would be forced to pay a penalty fee.

below. It should include a properly formatted table. If possible, use a laser printer and a proportional typeface. Use a larger font for the title and include the underline and bold attributes.

11. A spreadsheet is an important tool that can be used to manage your personal finances. A simple plan that you can implement is a personal balance sheet. The top of the balance sheet includes your income. In it you can list all of the money that you have coming in each month. The bottom of the balance sheet is your expenses. Using it, you can list all the expenditures that you were required to make each month. Access the Internet, locate the home page for this text, and call up the sample outline to fill in with your personal data. Of course, you can enter additional lines in each category.

CO2Ex11a.xls

*a.* An important part of financial analysis is the ability to compare your financial statement to those of others. Several sample worksheets are included on the sample disk. Examine several worksheets. They are each listed by

student name. How do these worksheets compare to your income and expenses?

CO2Ex11b.xls

*b.* Graph the most significant items in your worksheet. These would include those items that seem to have the most variance or the widest range of dispersion. What difficulties occur when you graph these items against the totals in each category?

### Rolling Thunder Database

1. Using the Export Data form, copy the data to a spreadsheet and create graphs for the following situations. (Choose the type of graph you feel is best suited to present the data.)
   *a.* Sales by model type.
   *b.* Sales by month.
   *c.* Sales by model type for each month.
   *d.* Sales by state.
   *e.* Sales by employee by month.
2. Using the existing forms, enter data for a new bicycle order.

## ADDITIONAL READING

Adams, S., R. Rosemier, and P. Sleeman. "Readable Letter Size and Visibility for Overhead Projection Transparencies, *AV Communication Review*, 1965, 412–417. [An early discussion of creating good presentations]

Anthes, Gary H. "Cray Envisions New Frontier," *Computerworld*, July 18, 1994, p. 121. [Parallel processing examples]

Ashford, Janet. "Built in a Day," *MacUser,* January 1994, pp. 152–154. [Description of architect designing a new hospital]

Bass, Steve. "The Economics of Ergonomics, *PC World*, July 1993, p. 340. [Examples of ergonomic furniture, chairs, and arm rests]

Booker, Ellis. "Ads Are the Trade-Off For Lower System Prices," *Workgroup Computing*, May 4, 1992, p. 41. [Physicians Computer Network]

Bozman, Jean. "IBM Tweaks AIX, RS/6000 Servers," *Computerworld*, July 19, 1993, p. 8. [The Good Guys]

Buchok, James. "Real Estate Company Finds an OASIS Through Use of Video Over LANs," *Computing Canada*, February 16, 1994, p. S15. [Royal LePage Realty]

Bulkeley, William M. "Speech Recognition Gets Cheaper and Smarter," *The Wall Street Journal*, June 6, 1994, pp. B1, B6. [Speech recognition applications]

"Chips: TRW Wins $22 Million Contract to Make High-Performance Chips & Multi-Chip Modules Faster, Cheaper," *EDGE: Work-Group Computing Report*, September 18, 1995. [TRW]

Farace, Joe. "Photo CD and the Next Big Thing," *Computer User*, June 1994, pp. 7–9. [Kodak Photo-CD data]

Felsenthal, Edward. "An Epidemic or a Fad? The Debate Heats Up Over Repetitive Stress," *The Wall Street Journal*, July 14, 1994, pp. A1, A7. [Uncertainty over causes of RSI, including legal cases and implications]

Hamilton, David P. "Memory-Chip Man Must Tame Electrons," *The Wall Street Journal*, June 21, 1994, p. B10. [Building memory chips]

Hildebrand, Carol. "Computer Graphics Help Carry Physicians' Message," *Computerworld*, June 1, 1992, p. 35. [Slide shows for patient education]

Keyes, Jessica. "Living in Parallel," *AI Expert*, February 1992, pp. 42–47. [Parallel computing issues]

Laver, Andrea. "Mapping the Future of the Virtual Office," *Engineering Times*, July 31, 1995, pp. 120–122. [Steelcase]

Mayor, Tracy. "Spreadsheet Heroes," *Lotus Magazine*, December 1991, pp. 33–40. [Awards given for spreadsheet applications]

"NASA Work Highlights MCM Usage," *Electronic News*, February 13, 1995. [TRW]

O'Malley, Christopher. "Don't Get All Bent Out of Shape by Your Computer: Do Ergonomically Correct Products Really Help?" *PC Computing*, March 1992, pp. 268-270. [Comments and evaluation of some ergonomic alternatives]

Pope, Kyle. "Keyboard Users Say Makers Knew of Problems," *The Wall Street Journal*, May 4, 1994, pp. B1, B5. [Repetitive Stress Injuries (RSI) and keyboards]

Rohrbough, Linda. "House Calls for PC—Automated Calls for Doctors," *Newsbytes*, May 4, 1994, p. NEW2356427. [Professional Data Management]

"Satellite: FCC Responds to TRW Petition, Requires Comsat Application for Participation in Inmarsat-P Procurement," *EDGE, On & About AT&T*, January 16, 1995. [TRW]

Schroeder, Erica. "Bank's Interest Is Rising as It Taps PC Audio Capabilities," *PC Week*, September 20, 1993, p. 29. [Using audio to attach notes to documents]

"Science: The Numbers Game," *Time*, February 20, 1988, pp. 54-58. [Short history of computers]

Serwer, Andrew E. "Lessons from America's Fastest-Growing Companies," *Fortune*, August 8, 1994, pp. 42-60. [Small businesses]

Simonds, D. and L. Reynolds. *Computer Presentation of Data in Science: A Do It Yourself Guide*, Boston: Kluwer Academic, 1989. [Ideas for presentations]

"Spreadsheet Heroes," 1991, *Lotus*, December 1991, pp. 33-40. [Spreadsheet examples]

Sprout, Alison L. "Scheduling Your Forces with a PC," *Fortune*, May 30, 1994, p. 131. [PC scheduling tool at The Right Start]

"Steelcase Creates a Magic Client/Server Ordering System; This Just In—Large Office Furniture Manufacturer Goes Client/Server with Magic," *Data Based Advisor*, January 1995, p. 68. [Steelcase]

Stix, Gary. "Toward 'Point One,'" *Scientific American*, February 1995, pp. 90-95. [Designing memory chips]

Streeter, April. "Excalibur Ships App for Doctors' Offices," *MacWEEK*, March 16, 1992, p. 8. [Excalibur physician office software]

Taft, Darryl K. "Supercomputer Helps Scientists Deblur Telescope's Fuzzy Images," *Government Computer News*, March 16, 1992, p. 41. [Graphics uses of parallel computing]

Van Name, Mark and Bill Catchings. "Don't Brag—Benchmark," *Computer Shopper*, August 1994, pp. 68, 76. [PC upgrade advice]

"Wireless: TRW Issued Patent for Odyssey Satellite-Based Worldwide Cellular Telephone System," *EDGE, On & About AT&T*, July 24, 1995. [TRW]

# CASES *Small Businesses*

Small business owners and sales supervisor tend to use computers more than the average worker. In particular, they are heavy users of computers for inventory, invoices, sales, and bookkeeping.

SOURCE: Computer Use in the United States, U.S. Bureau of the Census.

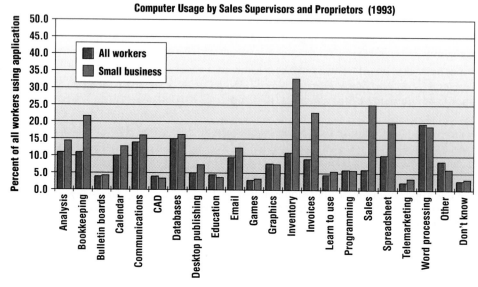

**Computer Usage by Sales Supervisors and Proprietors (1993)**

Legend: All workers / Small business

Y-axis: Percent of all workers using application (0.0 to 50.0)

X-axis categories: Analysis, Bookkeeping, Bulletin boards, Calendar, Communications, CAD, Databases, Desktop publishing, Education, Email, Games, Graphics, Inventory, Invoices, Learn to use, Programming, Sales, Spreadsheet, Telemarketing, Word processing, Other, Don't know

Although large companies are often in the news, in the past decade, it has been the small companies that have created most of the jobs. Large companies have been shedding workers, both in manufacturing and in layers of middle management.

There are several definitions of small businesses. One standard says that a firm with fewer than 200 employees is considered to be "small." The current U.S. Small Business Administration definition defines a company as "small" if it has less than $6 million in net worth and less than $2 million in profit. Applying these numbers to 1993 data, 98 percent of all U.S. firms were classified as small businesses. By comparison, the company that was number 500 on the Fortune 500 list of the largest U.S. companies in 1993 (Texas Industries with sales of $614 million and 2,700 employees) had $283 million in stockholders' equity, with $1.1 million in profits. In terms of employees, note that in 1989, the Fortune 500 companies employed about 12.5 million people in total. By 1993, that number had dropped to about 11.5 million. Sales by the Fortune 500 companies had a total increase of about $70 billion to $2.4 trillion. But that number represents a decline in real (after inflation) terms. In other words, the major component of growth in the U.S. economy in terms of sales and employment has been small businesses. In contrast, certain small businesses that David Birch (president of the economic research firm Cognetics) calls *gazelles* added more than 4 million jobs between 1989 and 1993. These companies with at least $100,000 in sales and are growing at over 20 percent a year.

In addition to the usual difficulties of operating a business, small firms have some special problems. In particular, with fewer employees, each employee is generally responsible for several tasks. It is harder to call on an expert to solve problems. With less financial capital, and an overwhelming desire to cut costs, small businesses tend to skimp on purchases of capital items such as information technology. With success or failure a mere heartbeat away, small firms tend to emphasize short-run problems, leaving little time and resources to contemplate longer solutions involving strategy. Consider the plight of Acme Thread and Supply, Inc. In 1991 the company installed an IBM PS/2 in its Honolulu office. Dennis Love, the IS manager, notes that lacking an internal support staff: "When installing a PC that will be used for order entry, invoicing, and so on, in a small business, I would plan on the installation costs being at least as much as the hardware and software—probably more."

On the other hand, with fewer layers of management and typically a looser organization structure, smaller firms can change direction rapidly to take advantage of new opportunities. Many small firms are strongly controlled by the owner/manager. The firm quickly takes on the personality of the CEO. Hence, solutions to problems must fit with the style of the CEO. Having an "answer" to a problem is often not sufficient; you must also have a solution that appeals to the CEO.

SOURCE: Adapted from "Big Surprises for Small Firms," by Lucie Juneau, *Computerworld*, June 24, 1991, p. 116. Copyright © 1991 by Computerworld, Inc., Framingham, MA 01701. Reprinted from *Computerworld*.

## CASE  *Dr. Randall Oates*

Although there are problems with current voice recognition systems, Dr. Randall Oates of Springdale, Arkansas, used off-the-shelf Macintosh tools to create a useful system for his family-practice office. He first used HyperCard (a hypertext design program) to create a system to track patient histories, generate handouts for patients, keep medical chart notes, and print prescriptions. When Articulate Systems Inc. introduced the Voice Navigator, a voice recognition system for the Macintosh, he decided to make his system respond to basic voice commands. Now he has a hands-free system with a microphone in each examining room. As he speaks key phrases, the computer records medical notes, attaches voice files to patient records, and prints prescriptions. About 80 percent of the functions can be accessed through voice commands.

Dr. Oates observes that both his patients and other doctors are interested in the technology: "During the first month I had it operating, I'd get calls from people who said 'I hear you got a talking computer. I want one of them things.'"

He has begun to distribute the medical application to other doctors. However, he is starting them out with just the keyboard/mouse version, noting: "I figure they need six months of training before they'll be ready for the voice interface. It's a pretty complicated system."

Ultimately, he would like to use a pen-based system that can be tied into medical databases. Having a small, easy-to-use system would improve quality of care, keep costs low, and help control legal liability.

Although Dr. Oates is successfully using a voice input system, other users have experienced problems. Gordon Campbell, manager of emerging technology for Connaught Laboratories, a vaccine maker, experimented with the Voice Navigator hardware. He notes that he found it time-consuming to train the system to recognize the commands. He is also concerned about environmental noise interfering with the microphone and the ability to recognize commands.

SOURCE: Adapted from "Voice Technology Beckons," by Robert Hollis, *MacWeek*, March 16, 1992, pp. 33–34. Reprinted from *MacWeek*. Copyright © 1992 Ziff-Davis Publishing Company.

### QUESTIONS

1. If you were a health-care provider or similar professional, would you create your own management system as Dr. Oates did? What are the costs and benefits?

2. What are the advantages of the voice input system used by Dr. Oates? What are the potential drawbacks? What problems could occur with a voice input system in the examination rooms?

3. Dr. Oates' statement that it will take other doctors six months to learn his system would worry many MIS professionals. Why? What problems might arise?

4. Medical and dental systems routinely provide basic accounting and billing functions. What other useful features could be added? (Hint: Consider the different types of data.) What benefits, costs, and complications might arise in trying to provide these additional features?

5. It was reported that in 1992 only 50 percent of the dentist and doctor offices had computerized management systems. Why do you think the other 50 percent have avoided them?

## CASE  *Physicians Computer Network, Inc.*

Physicians Computer Network, Inc. (PCNI) leases hardware and software to physician offices. The systems provide basic accounting and insurance filing functions to help manage the office paperwork. The company intends to add connections to other computers, such as ties to hospitals and medial associations. The basic features do not differ much from other systems.

The PCNI system is different from other systems in one major area: the price. The annual license fee for a single physician is $2,760. This fee covers the cost of all the hardware, software and support. As a result of the price, in 1992 the company had 1,800 subscribers, 82 percent of them are solo practitioners. According to PCNI chairman, Jerry Brager, there are 60,000 doctors' offices with one to five physicians. Hence, there is room to grow.

Aside from the fact that PCNI is 25 percent owned by IBM, how can the company offer the system, including two personal computers, for such a low price? The answer is that the system includes paid advertisements from drug companies, laboratories, and insurance companies. The doctors are required to view 90 minutes of the advertising (32 ads) every month. To ensure compliance, they have to answer questions on the ads. The ads are sent to the office computers each month, and the companies pay a fixed fee as well as a per-ad fee. The ads use multimedia techniques and are designed to attract attention. Physicians can also view additional information on the products (such as drug interaction effects). Summaries of the viewing histories are sent to the advertisers. So far, none of the doctors have asked to have the system removed.

## QUESTIONS

1. Why did PCNI choose to use advertising on the information system?
2. From a physician's standpoint, why would you adopt the PCNI system? What are the potential drawbacks?
3. Do you think accepting a reduced cost item that is provided by pharmaceutical companies is ethical on the part of the doctor?
4. If you were working for PCNI, what additional features would you add to the system?

## CASE *Azar Family Restaurant*

Azar Family Restaurant is located in the northwest suburbs of Chicago. Like many restaurants, it is a relatively new operation that has been open for only a few months. Azar's current target market is those individuals in the area who are 21 to 55 years of age. Because the restaurant has a sports orientation, it is also interested in those individuals who participate in or follow sports. The income level of most of the patrons is from $20,000–$70,000. Within a 10-mile radius of the restaurant are approximately 500,000 inhabitants, with a median income in the area of $33,000 dollars per household.

The menu offered by Azar is quite broad. Fish, meat, and poultry are all listed. Daily specials are posted on a board as the diners enter the restaurant. Compared to other restaurants in the area, prices are medium to high. Four other restaurants are located within a three-mile radius. Each of the four restaurants is focused differently:

- *Le Petite Le Lamb* is a French restaurant serving only the finest Continental cuisine.
- *Rocky's* is a sports grill that features big-screen televisions and sports specials for each night of the week.
- *Mama Tische's* features Italian spaghetti, pizza, and lasagna.
- *McDonald's* has a large installation at the intersection of one of the two major highways on which Azar is located.

Technologically, Azar has a single register with no cost-control functions. A computer with word processing and spreadsheet packages is kept in the back office. The inventory system is kept on paper by the owner when she checks supplies each week. All financial information regarding business inflow and outflow is handled by a local accountant since the restaurant owner "wants to cook, not work with numbers."

There is no central control function or single place where records regarding financial information,

employee wages, and inventories are kept. All interaction with suppliers is done through the telephone and paper bills.

Customer complaints regarding the rudeness of the wait staff have increased. Currently, the waitpersons from the lunch shift are women who work while their children are in school. The evening shift is primarily made up of local high school students.

Daily business pressures vary from business to business; nevertheless, they all have a few pressures in common: competition, service, and satisfaction are arguably the three most important factors faced by businesses today. In the case of Azar, it has to face competition from the other restaurants in the area that are offering the same foods or ambience as Azar. Competition pressures Azar in many ways for example; pricing, menu style, atmosphere, and sales.

Currently, the surrounding businesses have extremely competitive prices with special attention to value meals. Also due to the summer weather, catering indoor and outdoor services have been added by the two restaurants. The menu offering at Azar is very broad, and prices are relatively high. Service is another pressure that they have to face. Are the personnel trained enough whereby they understand the process and are then able to act on it? Currently Azar has high school and college students working as wait staff, and off-the-street cooks working in the kitchen.

The final pressure facing Azar is customer satisfaction. Azar needs to make this the cornerstone of its methodology. Total customer satisfaction is the key. There are complaints from customers about the food coming out undercooked and service being poor. Management is rude at times to customers and employees.

Technologically, Azar is anemic. The business has an old register with no cost-control functions, a computer in the back room for show purposes only, and no inventory system. There is also no financial accounting programs for business inflow, outflow, and so on. There is no employee recordkeeping for wages, and there is also no database by which the manager can order stock.

[Note: Although the restaurant is real, the numbers given here are fictional.]

## QUESTIONS

1. What recommendations would you make to the owners of Azar regarding the best steps to take to improve customer satisfaction and the bottom line?

 C02Azar.xls

2. Examine the balance sheets for Azar's restaurant. What problems are immediately evident?

3. Based on the financial data, what recommendations could you make to the owners of the restaurant?
4. As a worker at the restaurant, what steps could you implement to improve the efficiency of the operation?

## CASE  *Scoozi's Restaurant of Chicago*

Scoozi's Restaurant is owned by the Richard Melman chain of restaurants. Melman owns a series of restaurants throughout the Chicago area. He has sought to make each restaurant unique for particular market segments. Some focus upon Italian cuisine, whereas others focus on 1950s-style entertainment.

Scoozi's is a peasant-style restaurant in the former riverfront warehouse section of Chicago. Because it was built in this area of the city, it has plenty of room for expansion. However, it must work harder to attract customers because they must decide ahead of time to eat at Scoozi's.

Scoozi's often serves as Melman's test restaurant for his technological innovations. As such, it currently uses a computer system to record and print guest checks. Once entered into the computer, the order is immediately printed on a monitor in the kitchen. The monitor indicates the order, table number, and waitperson. Once the order is filled, a light with the waitperson's number is turned on.

At the beginning, everyone was excited about the way that the new technology would affect the staff's jobs. The waitpersons felt that they would spend less time recording orders, leaving more time to serve their customers, resulting in larger tips. The kitchen staff felt that the new technology would enable them to predict orders and get them out much faster, leading to the faster delivery of warmer food. The accountants were of course pleased because they would no longer have to decipher handwritten messages. Inventory control and replenishment would be much improved.

Unfortunately, the opposite happened. The new system required the waitpersons to type their orders into the computer. Although this kept them on the floor and avoided the necessity of going to the kitchen to check on orders, it actually took more time. The waitpersons had to write the order on a tablet, like always, then transfer the order to the computer. Rather than having touch screens or menu items premarked on the computer, each item had to be typed in. This often led to a backup while waitpersons waited to enter their orders. The backup became so severe that Scoozi's was forced to hire more waitpersons. This helped to alleviate some of the backup, but it ultimately reduced the tips for each individual because now the same number of tables and the resulting tips were being spread over a larger number of individuals.

[Note: Although the restaurant is real, the numbers given are fictional.]

### QUESTIONS

1. What went wrong with Scoozi's planning process for the new computer system?
2. In your opinion, what was wrong with Scoozi's system? Who should be responsible for this situation?
3. What changes would you recommend?

C02Scooz.xls

4. Using the Scoozi's spreadsheet, what does the financial information tell you? Based on the financial records, what changes would you recommend?

## CASE  *Data Entry: Touch-Screen Displays Produce New Capabilities*

Data entry remains the "last frontier" of labor-intensive interaction with the computer. OCR technology, voice recognition, and touch screens are rapidly changing the way in which we interact with computers.

Following are just a few examples of the way in which we interact with computers through touch screens.

- Realtors place full-color pictures of homes for sale in front of prospective buyers without having to travel to the homes themselves.
- Card manufacturers like Hallmark and Gibson let users make their own personalized cards in local card shops without previous training.
- Restaurants like McDonald's and TGI Friday's have simplified their data-entry process and reduced their training time by using touch screens on their point-of-sale terminals.
- Government agencies like the Connecticut Department of Motor Vehicles use touch screens to increase the speed and sophistication of their driver's license exams.
- Medical schools use this new technology to teach student nurses to respond to crisis situations.
- Retailers use this technology to speed customer transactions and eliminate operator errors. Not only are they more rugged than keyboards or keypads, they also reduce training time.
- Music stores like MusicLand have installed kiosks to enable customers to sample songs and video clips of recent recordings.

Touch-screen sales now approximate $150 million per year. Dataquest estimates the touch-screen market is expanding by 40 percent annually, forecasting a growth to more than $300 million dollars in sales by 1998.

Touch screens were first brought to market by Elo TouchSystems in the 1970s. Since that time, the technology has improved in terms of durability and reliability, and cost.

*Durability.* In the past five years, durability has increased from 2 to 20 million touches. Applying surface wave technology increases the durability to 50 million touches without error.

*Reliability.* Reliability is an important issue for touch-screen technology, as is durability. In this marketplace, reliability is defined as MTBF (mean time between failures). In the past five years, the average rating on a touch-screen controller has gone from 60,000 to 200,000 hours.

*Cost.* Costs of this technology have fallen with the increase in demand and production volumes. Since the early 1980s, the prices for a touch system—including a controller card, software driver, and touch screen—have fallen from $1,000 to $100.

*Pen Capability.* The next step in this technology is its combination with pen capabilities. The only thing that is preventing the complete elimination of the credit card paper trail is the customer's signature on the credit card slip. The ability to capture a customer's signature electronically on the point-of-sale display will enable the retail operation to immediately call up the signature for verification, eliminating the labor-intensive search for the actual paper receipt that the customer signed.

To address this need, Elo TouchSystems and a major point-of-sale manufacturer have jointly developed a touch-screen system that captures electronic signatures within the efficiency of a point-of-sale system activated by a finger touch.

*Flat-Screen Technology.* The value of this system stems from the requirement for accessibility. Warehouse managers want portable, flat-panel devices equipped with touch screens to enable them to better manage inventory, shipping, and receiving logistics. This will enable warehouse personnel to update inventory records in real time as new shipments arrive or finished products are sent. Service workers will be able to quickly access a technical manual from the field or check a parts database without relying on a keyboard.

The problem with liquid crystal display (LCD) flat screens has been that they emit less light than traditional CRTs. LCD flat-screen manufacturers have begun to address this issue by introducing touch screens that are significantly brighter than previous screens.

Kiosk manufacturers want larger interactive displays for maximum visual impact. Examples include airport information directories, bridal registries, and interactive museum displays. Further demands are placed on these systems because they demand clear, high-resolution displays for multimedia full-motion video and still images.

*Surface-Wave Technology.* Surface-wave technology addresses the need for high-level graphics. Constructed entirely of glass without the traditional plastic overlay, they provide superior image clarity because everything between the user and the image on the screen has been eliminated.

## QUESTIONS

1. What are the strengths and weaknesses of touch-screen systems?
2. For what uses are touch screens best suited? What are the similarities in the examples?
3. Some fast food restaurants have installed touch screens for customers to place their own orders. Why? What objections might people have to these systems? What problems are likely to arise?
4. Why does it typically require less training to use a touch-screen application?

## CASE *TRW: Voice-Based Input*

The TRW Automotive Parts Remanufacturing Plant in McAllen, Texas, reworks and rebuilds used automotive parts. Once completed, it redistributes them to aftermarket retailers where they are sold for 25 to 50 percent less than comparable new products. The used parts include brake shoes, starter motors, alternators, and rack and pinion steering gears.

Technology has helped new part suppliers by tracking incoming goods against purchase orders. This is not possible in the remanufacturing business. Used parts, or cores, arrive in unknown quantities and unknown conditions from known customers. These parts are as varied as brake shoes, starter motors, alternators, and rack-and-pinion steering gears. On receipt, these parts need to be sorted, described, and distributed to the appropriate area. They then must be entered into the production planning schedule, the warehouse management system, and the customer credit department. The parts are then physically transported to facilities where they are rebuilt and distributed to aftermarket retailers, where they are subsequently sold for 25 to 50 percent less than new parts of the same kind.

Before the automation process was installed, each part was assigned a document and customer or supplier number and quantified. Each core was individually handled by an inspector, who called the core number to a recording inspector, who manually marked the record on a "core tick sheet" that included more than 500 part numbers. The core tick sheet was used as the inventory mechanism for the process. This paper was then used by a data-entry clerk who entered the information into a materials management system.

This process created many delays. One record-keeper recorded verbal data from 12 inspectors. Often the inspectors had to wait for the recorder to note the information from another inspector. There was often a one- to three-day delay in typing the material into the system.

In response to these delays, TRW instituted a program based on two Talkman voice terminals. Manufactured by Vocollect, Inc., the Talkman understands voice data, asks the operator questions according to a logical flow, and responds with its own voice. Expert systems enable the flow of questions to branch according to recognized answers. The Talkman is trained to recognize a speaker's voice. Tables with valid part numbers, descriptions, and Zip codes are stored. As a result, invalid answers—such as incorrect parts numbers—can be rejected. Answers are digitized by the Talkman and stored in an in-board memory. The information is uploaded to a personal computer at the end of a shift. The personal computer then uses a Clipper database to export data to an MRP program. This approach has completely eliminated the old system of tick sheets and transcription. Inspectors now work at a faster, smoother pace without dependence upon synchronization with the recording operation.

An additional advantage of the Talkman is the ability to accept bar code and speech input. The use of this data-input component will provide an additional increase in speed in data-input. Further economies can be achieved through scanning part numbers and speaking condition descriptions or defects. This will lead to savings through improved data accuracy and the elimination of redundant data-handling operations.

### QUESTIONS

1. What problems was TRW experiencing?
2. Why was voice input an effective solution to TRW's problems? How does TRW overcome the limitations of voice input?
3. Draw a picture to show the flow of parts through the TRW system. Indicate the data that is collected at each step.

### DISCUSSION ISSUE

*Are Graphs Misleading?*

Graphics images convey ideas. As such, they are not always precise. Hence, there are many ways in which graphics can be misleading. In order to avoid sending the wrong impression, you need to carefully examine each image. Look at both the detail and the overall perception that is conveyed by the graph. Consider an example where the CEO (Mr. Cruddock) has called a meeting to discuss sales for the different divisions. Kwilla-June Holmes (the head of marketing) has stated that the dog food division should be sold because its sales and profits are lower than in the other divisions. The head of the dog food division (Vic) is also at the meeting.

Ms. Holmes: And this graph shows the sales for the last three years for each of our product divisions. Notice that the dog food division is lower than the others.

Cruddock: Uh, I can't quite read that graph. Are those bars made up of little dogs?

Ms. Holmes: *(smiling)* Yes they are. The new graphics package let me put different objects in for the bars.

Cruddock: Hmmm. Well, is the top supposed to be at the dog's head or the tail? The tail is quite a bit higher . . .

Ms. Holmes: Ah . . . I guess I don't know.

Vic: Our actual sales numbers are slightly below the other divisions, but only by 2 to 5 percent. Because she used those tall thin candles for the bars in the wax division, it makes it look higher compared to the wider bar for the dog food division.

Ms. Holmes: Sure, sure. I'm not criticizing your department. It just has less sales. Let's look at the next graph. Here I created four graphs—one for each division. Each graph has sales for the last five years. One bar for each year. Oh, notice that all the bars in the dog food graph use the dog symbol and are the same width, so it should be easier to compare.

Cruddock: Now, in this graph, it looks to me like the dog food division is doing better than the others. See how the sales for all five years are near the top. But in the cat food division they have two good years, but the other three are quite a bit lower. Maybe we should solve the cat food problems first.

Ms. Holmes: But . . . oh, I see the problem. Look at the numbers on the left. See, all of the numbers for cat food are higher than those for dog food. These graphs are just designed to show what happened in each division over five years. Let's just look at one graph at a time. See how the dog food division hasn't changed much. Its sales have stayed flat.

Vic: Wait a second, that's not right. Here, I've got the actual sales numbers. We've increased sales by an average of 6 percent each of the last five years. Are you sure you have the correct numbers in your graphs?

Ms. Holmes: Oh yes. I took them out of your report to Mr. Cruddock. See, check the numbers on the Y-axis.

Vic: Well, something's wrong with your graph.

Ms. Holmes: Maybe the next graph will make it clear. These four pie charts show the breakdown of expenses for the last two years for the wax products division and the dog food division. See this slice that I exploded out from the pie . . . it's personnel expense. Notice that it takes a much bigger share of the pie in the dog food division, and it's even larger in the next year. This increase in labor cost is expensive because the division is not really growing.

Vic: Now wait a minute. I thought we settled that. We have been growing, that's why we hired more people. And . . .

Cruddock: Hang on. Ms. Holmes, the slices for personnel in the dog food division appear to be smaller than the slices in the wax products division. Why do you say that the dog product's costs are higher?

Ms. Holmes: Oh that. I scaled the pie charts to match the overall sales of the division. Notice that the entire pie for the wax products division is larger than for the dog food. What I'm saying is you need to compare the percentage of the cost in each case, not the actual size of the pie. I wanted to be sure to include all of the information. It's a little confusing at first . . .

Vic: It's not confusing. It's just wrong. I don't know what you're trying to do, but I'm not putting up with these inane graphs. Just look at the actual numbers. Sure, we're not as large as the other divisions, but we're a whole lot more stable. We've had five straight years of growth.

Cruddock: Ms. Holmes, thank you for the presentation, but I'm inclined to agree with Vic. There might be some problems in the dog food division, but I don't really understand your graphs. Next time, be a little more careful when you create them.

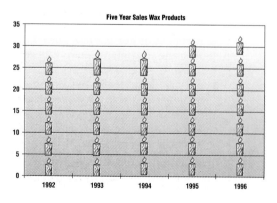

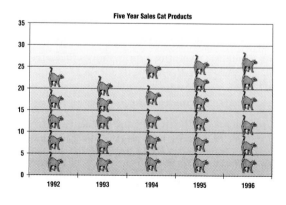

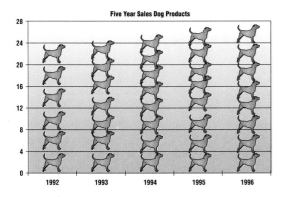

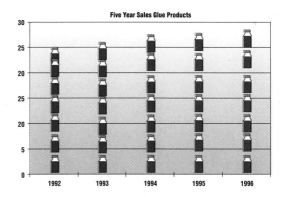

## QUESTIONS

1. Do you think the graphs created by Ms. Holmes accurately portray the status of the dog food department?
2. Do you think graphs with pictures are more interesting than simple bar graphs?
3. Do you think changing the size of the pie charts is a good way to show how the total expenses are higher for the wax products division?
4. Can you find graphs in newspapers and magazines that use pictures instead of bars to display the data? Are they more interesting? Are they misleading?
5. Do you think Ms. Holmes deliberately made the graphs so they are misleading?
6. Can you find a graphics package that enables you to draw graphs like those created by Ms. Holmes?

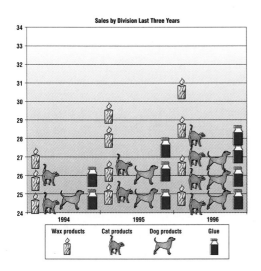

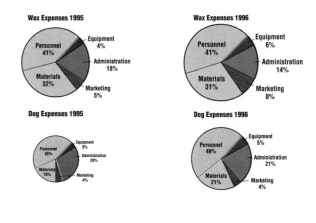

# Solving Problems

Amtrak is using their Web page (http://www.amtrak.com) to provide general information, but they are working on a schedule and reservation system for Web use.

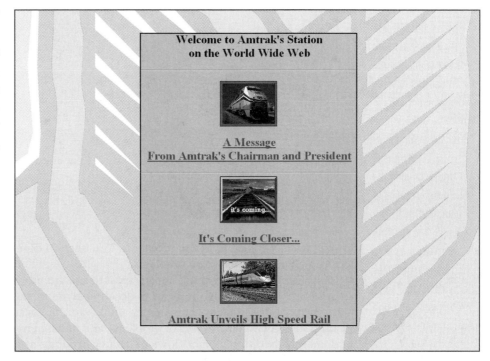

## AMTRAK

The Amtrak train system relies on filling its seats to run successfully. To do so, it must strike a precise balance between selling as many seats as possible at the highest price that the market will bear and selling reduced price seats at a price low enough to ensure that all the seats will be taken. Thus, a single seat on the same route may sell for three prices: $100, $75, or $50. Six classes of tickets exist. These range from full fare or heavy advance-purchase discounts to special promotions or excursion fares.

All of these price differentials require a great deal of sophistication on the part of the computer system that prices them. Named the Arrow system, Amtrak's reservation system handles an average of 1.2 million transactions per day. Put on line in 1981, the system was designed to provide fare, schedule, and seat-availability information. Since that time the demands on the system have increased not only in terms of numbers of reservations handled but also in relation to the decisions that must be made with the information.

Currently, $40 million are being spent to design and install a Centralized Electrification and Traffic Control System. When finished, this system will control the dispatching of trains from a central location. Large-screen monitors will enable dispatchers to watch the progress of 250 trains a day as they move through the system circuit by circuit. This will enable trains to be routed and rerouted for the most efficient use of the system. Scheduling, data, routing, and power changes will be made simultaneously. Equally important, data will be tracked and used to make future routing, scheduling, and pricing decisions.

**OVERVIEW**　Throughout your career, you will face many business problems. Some will be easy to solve; others will be more complex. As illustrated in Figure 3.1, the problems that are the hardest to solve are those that have impacts in several areas. It becomes especially

**FIGURE 3.1**

As a manager, you need to analyze the business to solve problems and make the firm more efficient and effective in pursuit of its goals. Understanding the business is crucial to using MIS to its full potential. The systems approach is used to analyze business decisions, solve problems, and design new computer systems to support the business.

difficult to find the cause of the problems. You need to develop a method that will help you understand and solve problems.

Fortunately, several methods already exist to analyze problems and evaluate alternatives. One useful technique is an in-depth analysis of business processes. This methodology is based on systems theory and is valuable for understanding complex organizations, identifying causes of problems, and finding errors in methodologies. It is commonly used to highlight flows of data or products as they travel through the system.

You will learn how to analyze a complex business system by dividing it into pieces. *Systems* can be described as collections of processes that have inputs and produce outputs. They also can be described in terms of the properties and functions of various business objects. This chapter presents a diagramming technique that will help you analyze the systems you study. You will learn to identify common systems problems.

Solving problems often entails learning to ask the right questions. Questions can help organize your thoughts and encourage you to consider new directions when looking for answers. The chapter provides hints on how to approach cases and application problems. The first step is to search for the primary problems and their cause. Systems theory helps you divide problems into interrelated subproblems. These smaller subsystems are easier to analyze and can be examined for common problems. Once the main problems have been identified, the next step is to choose the proper tools and implement a solution. Also, it is important that you learn how to test your work to avoid costly errors.

## INTRODUCTION

A common theme arises when talking with business people who hire recent college graduates. Many people believe that although college students are bright, they have trouble dealing with unstructured problems. In most courses, you learn a specific tool in each section and complete assignments at the end of the chapter using that tool. At the most, you might have a comprehensive final or a final paper that requires you to analyze the problem and select from the tools in the course to solve that problem.

In the business world all you see are symptoms. Before you can make a decision or develop a solution, you first have to use all of your knowledge to determine the causes and nature of the problem. How do you determine the cause of the problem? How do you know whether the solution involves accounting, production management, marketing, or some combination of many disciplines? Where do you start?

Hundreds of years ago, almost all businesses were small shops with few employees. The managers were also the owners. Management and problem solving were focused on day-to-day operations. As firms became larger and more complex, new management structures were created to enable a small group of managers to control the organization. Larger businesses and more complicated management structures led to more complex problems and a need for more and better information.

In the early days of computers, they were primarily used for simple mathematical computations. The programs were technical, but involved well-defined problems. The initial uses in business were to automate repetitive manual tasks such as bookkeeping and tracking customer data and orders. As computer prices dropped, the machines were used for more complex business tasks. Today, a main function of computers is to provide information to manage the firm.

Several problems quickly arose in creating these new information systems. New software projects were usually over budget and late. Worse yet, the new systems were hard to use and not very helpful. Part of the problem was that individual programs written by different people could not work together. New systems often did not solve business problems because the designers did not fully understand how the business operated.

In response to these problems, MIS researchers used general systems theory to create a new way to design software. The goal of the systems approach is to first determine how the business system works, and then use computer hardware and software to make it work better. The process of re-engineering extends this idea to the entire organization and seeks to redesign the company.

A more recent problem is the need to create new systems faster and with fewer errors. Companies are searching for ways to create a base set of systems definitions that can be used over again, instead of starting every system from scratch. Although the goal has been around for years, it has proven to be elusive. Systems designers are hoping that object-oriented design techniques might be an answer to this problem.

Solving unstructured problems is a technique required in any discipline. Physicians use symptoms to identify causes every day. An automobile mechanic needs to determine whether your car's problems are due to electrical, fuel, or transmission errors. In business, you often need to determine whether a problem should be approached through marketing, finance, human resources, accounting, or management information systems. The systems approach helps you classify problems and identify their causes and organize decisions.

**A SYSTEMS APPROACH**

To solve business problems, you first have to understand how the business operates. The difficulty occurs because large businesses can be complex and each organization is different. It would take years to learn all the details of how a business functions. As a result, it is important to approach problems with a plan. The systems method is one approach that can be used to analyze any system. The basic idea is that large systems consist of smaller, interdependent subsystems. Each of these subsystems is connected to and dependent on the others. At the same time, each system is itself a subsystem of an even larger system.

The method can be used to look at the "big picture" and see how a system works in total. It also can be used to examine the details that occur within each process. Examining organizations at both levels provides a relatively complete picture of the

**Reality Bytes** ◣    3–1   THE ZOO

Everyone recognizes the animals at a zoo, but managing a zoo involves more than just feeding the animals. For example, zoos track money, monitor breeding programs, and educate visitors.

Consider the situation of a zoo. Its primary function is to educate and entertain people. It might receive some funds (or tax breaks) from government agencies. It makes money by charging admission. It also has a membership program, where members receive admission and other benefits by paying an annual fee. There is also an "adopt an animal" program where organiza-tions donate money to cover care and feeding of vari-ous animals.

The zoo is the primary system we wish to examine. Its environment consists of the physical environment (air, land, and water) as well as the laws, customs, and other organizations competing for education/entertain-ment money.

problems and potential solutions. The use of systems analysis is illustrated by evaluating a small system for a zoo (Reality Bytes 3–1).

### Input, Process, Output

One useful approach to systems is to look at them as a collection of processes or activities. The most important step in solving problems is to find the cause of the problems. Identifying the major processes in a system will help you understand how the system works. Examining input and output objects helps you spot problems and trace them back to their source. As illustrated in Figure 3.2, systems receive **input** and **process** them to produce **output.** The process could be mechanical, such as manufacturing using raw materials, workers, and power. Alternatively, it might be a process involving symbolic processing instead of physical activity. For example, accounting systems receive sales data and process it into cash flow statements. In many cases there are two types of input and output: physical and data. In many

**FIGURE 3.2**

Each system can be decomposed into three major components: input, process, and output.

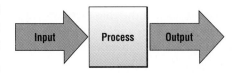

cases physical flows are accompanied by data. For instance, raw materials are shipped with an invoice that describes the products and the shipping information. Systems theory can be used to examine both types of flow. However, this is an MIS text, so most of the problems presented here will deal with flows of data.

Systems are described by collections of these processes. Each system operates in an environment that is somewhat arbitrarily defined by the boundaries of the system. For most problems, anything directly controlled by the firm is considered part of the relevant system. Everything else exists in the environment outside of the firm. The environment typically includes at least the physical space, laws, customs, industry, society, and country in which the firm operates. The firm can influence the physical environment, laws, and customs, but it does not have direct control over them.

In terms of the zoo example, input and output are less concrete because the zoo primarily produces services instead of products. Figure 3.3 shows the basic inputs of food, money, and health data for potential new animals. Output objects include education, educational materials, and baby animals for other zoos. For most purposes, the system boundary is relatively clear. Visitors, suppliers, and other zoos are outside the direct control of the zoo, so they are in the environment. If the zoo was operated by a governmental agency, it would be harder to identify the boundary. Government systems tend to reach into many different areas and it can be hard to identify their exact limits, especially since they can be extended or contracted by political decisions.

If a system is entirely self-contained and does not respond to changes in the environment, it is called a **closed system.** An **open system** learns by altering itself as the environment changes. Systems are almost never completely closed because closed systems cannot survive for long. However, some systems (or companies) are more responsive to changes in the environment than others. Consider two companies that make a similar product in the United States. What happened when Mexico, Canada, and the United States signed the North American Free Trade Agreement (NAFTA) that removed barriers to trade? One of the companies responded to this change in the environment and added a new plant in Mexico to be closer to the new customers. The other ignored the changes. If Mexican income increases as a result of the trade agreement, which company will make the most money? If Mexican

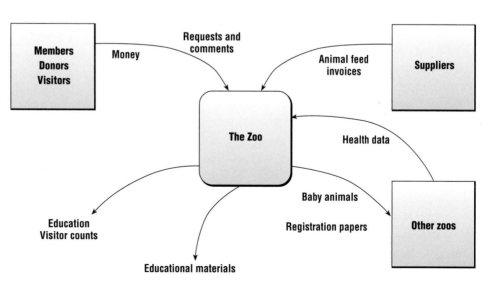

**FIGURE 3.3**

System boundary at the zoo. As we build systems, we must identify the components that make up the primary system. There will be many other entities that interact with the system. However, these entities are beyond our control, so they are outside of the system.

income decreases, can that company alter its strategy to continue making profits? Remember that a key component of strategy is to search the environment for potential advantages.

## Divide and Conquer

Most problems are too complex and too large to deal with all at once. Even if you could remember all the details, it would be hard to see how everything was supposed to fit together. A crucial step in analyzing a system is to carefully break it into smaller pieces or a collection of subsystems. Each subsystem is separate from the others, but they are connected and interdependent.

Figure 3.4 shows the five primary subsystems within the zoo. Of course, there could be many possible subsystems for the zoo. The actual division depends on how the organization operates. Each subsystem is defined by identifying the input and output flows. How do you know how to divide a system into smaller parts? Fortunately, most complex systems have already been subdivided into different departments and tasks. Many companies are organized by business functions: accounting, finance, human resources, marketing, MIS, and production. Others are split into divisions according to the type of product. Procter & Gamble's divisions might include baby products, personal hygiene, laundry detergents, and paper products.

Once you have determined the major components of the system, each subsystem can be divided into even smaller pieces. An accounting department might be split into management reporting, tax management, quarterly reporting, and internal auditing. Each of these areas might be split into even more levels of detail. At each step, the subsystems are defined by what they do (process), what inputs are used, and what outputs are produced.

There are some drawbacks to the divide-and-conquer approach. It is crucial that you understand how the components work together. If a project is split into small parts and given to independent teams, the teams might lose sight of the overall goals. Important components might not be completed, or the individual pieces might not meet the overall objectives of the system.

## Goals and Objectives

Subsystems have goals or purposes. A goal of a manufacturing firm might be to sell more products than any rival (increasing sales). Or it might be to make as much

**FIGURE 3.4**

Primary subsystems of the zoo. The first step in analyzing a system is to identify the major subsystems. In most organizations, this step is relatively easy because the organization will consist of several departments or functions.

money as possible for its owners (increasing revenues). Another goal might be find an entirely new area in which to sell products (new market segments). The goals should be defined by the owners of the system. If the system does not have a goal, it has no purpose, and there is no way to evaluate it. In fact, by definition, it would not be a system. When you are observing a system, you will need to evaluate performance, which means you have to identify the goals.

Typical spreadsheets give us the ability to ask "What-if?" questions. For example, you might want to know what happens if you increase sales commissions by 10 percent. Goals help focus the answer by providing the ability to ask questions about Why? and So what? The answer to the What-if? question involving commissions might be that revenue increases by 5 percent. But what does that result mean? If we also know that a goal of the company is to increase profits, we could look more carefully and find that increasing commissions by 10 percent leads to a 3 percent increase in profits. That result is important because it brings the system closer to one of its goals. Hence, it would make sense to increase the commissions.

It is clear that to solve business problems, you must first identify the organization's goals. The catch is that there are often conflicting ways to measure the goals. For instance, improved customer satisfaction or product quality might be useful goals. But how do we measure them? Managers who measure customer satisfaction by the number of complaints they receive will make different decisions than someone who actively surveys customers. In other words, the measurement of our performance with respect to the goals will depend on the data we collect.

## Control and Feedback

Once a system has goals, the processes can be developed or modified so the system fulfills the goals. Occasionally a manager will invent a modification out of thin air. However, most controls are made in response to information about how the system is performing. This information is known as **feedback** and is shown in Figure 3.5. As long as the system has a defined goal, a subsystem can monitor the system's performance and provide feedback to the control subsystem. The control subsystem then modifies the system to meet the goal.

The most common example of a feedback loop is a thermostat. You define the goal by setting a desired temperature. The thermostat monitors the temperature, if the temperature drops too far, a control signal is sent to turn up the heating subsystem. This example is a **closed loop** because signals stay within the loop and make changes automatically. Another example of feedback would be a marketing

**FIGURE 3.5**

Feedback and control. Processes are evaluated according to some goal. The system will have a feedback measure that compares the system to the goal, analyzes the data, and makes changes to the process.

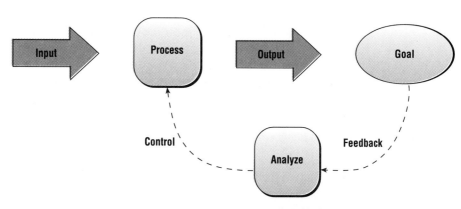

organization that provides rewards to its best salespeople. For instance, every month a manager could review the sales goals, compare the performance of the sales people and give a bonus to certain people. If the bonus is not automatically tied to the sales numbers, this example would represent an open loop because there is a break (opening) in the process—where it is controlled by the manager. A specific example is provided by Levi Strauss (Reality Bytes 3-2) which designed an information system to enable its employees to respond more quickly to information on customer demands.

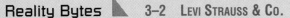

## Reality Bytes  ▲  3-2  Levi Strauss & Co.

In 1989, Levi Strauss integrated the retailer cash register, factory floor, and back-room systems and databases into its computer system. This was done to provide a mechanism for its employees to become more responsive to its customers and the fast pace of change in the clothing industry. Equally important, Levi Strauss plans to connect with trading partners, suppliers, manufacturers, and retailers to smooth the flow of information between each group. Information will be entered using universal product codes, point-of-sale scanners and terminals, and electronic data interchange. The information will be integrated backward to computer-integrated manufacturing and forward to an advanced business system.

## Diagramming Systems

We often represent systems graphically to gain insights and spot problems. We also use diagrams to communicate. Communication is of critical importance in MIS and all areas of business. Users describe their problems to systems analysts, who design improvements and describe them to programmers. Ideas and comments can be misinterpreted at any step. We can minimize problems by using a standard diagramming technique. The data flow diagramming approach presented in this section is commonly used because it focuses on the logical components of the system and there are few rules to remember, so almost anyone can understand the diagrams.

Although you could invent your own diagramming technique, a method called a **data flow diagram (DFD)** has been developed to represent information systems. It is designed to show how a system is divided into smaller portions and to highlight the flow of data between those parts. Because there are only three graphical elements (five if you count the two arrow types), it is an easy technique to learn. The DFD illustrates the systems topics in this chapter.

The basic elements of a DFD are external entities (objects), processes, data stores (files), and data flows that connect the other items. Each element is drawn differently, as shown in Figure 3.6. For example, data flows are shown as arrows. Feedback and control data are usually drawn as dashed lines to show that they have a special purpose.

Figure 3.7 presents the main level of subsystems for the zoo. Notice that it contains external entities, processes, and data flows. This level does not show data files or control flows. They can be incorporated in more detailed presentations.

### External Entity

When you identify the boundary of a system, you will find some components in the environment that communicate with your system. They are called *external entities*. Although each situation is different, common examples include customers, suppliers, and management. External entities are objects so they are labeled with nouns.

**FIGURE 3.6**
Only four or five objects are used to create a data flow diagram. External entities are objects that are independent and outside the system. Processes are functions and actions applied to data. A data store or file is a place to hold data. Data flows are shown as solid lines with arrows to indicate the data movement. Control flows are marked with dashed lines.

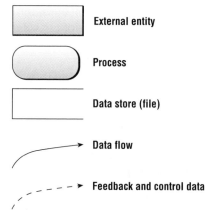

In the zoo example, the primary entities are management, certification agencies, other zoos, and members of the public (visitors, donors, and members). All relevant external entities need to be displayed on the first-level diagram.

**Process**

In a DFD, a process is an activity that involves data. Technically, DFDs are used to show systems that involve data, not products or other materials. However, in business today, virtually all physical processes have data processing counterparts. When

**FIGURE 3.7**
The zoo: Level 0. The primary processes and data flows of the zoo.

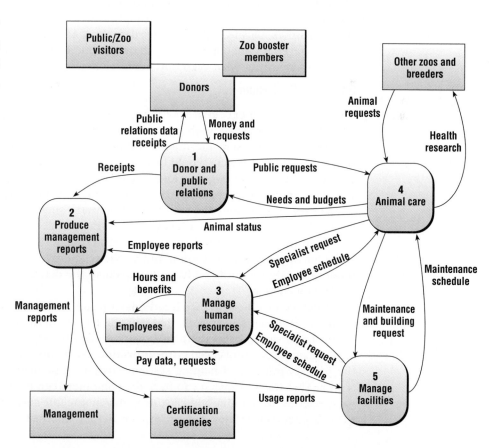

customers buy something, they get a receipt. In a manufacturing process, the amount of raw materials being put to a machine, measures of the volume of output, and quality control values are recorded. The DFD process is used to represent what happens to the data, not what occurs with the raw material.

Because processes represent actions, they are typically labeled with verbs, such as *Sell products,* or *Create tax reports for management.* There are two important rules involving processes. First, a process cannot invent data. That means every process must have at least one flow of data entering it. Second, a process cannot be a black hole; every process must transfer data somewhere else. If you look at your DFD and find one of these two problems, it usually means that you missed a connection between the processes. On the other hand, processes that do not export data might be data stores or external entities.

### Data Store

A data store or file is simply a place to hold data for a length of time. It might be a filing cabinet, a reference book, or a computer file. In a computerized system, data is likely to be stored in a database management system (DBMS). Chapter 5 provides more detail on the capabilities and uses of a DBMS. For now, it is important to note that data is a valuable resource to any company. In drawing a DFD, try to list exactly what needs to be stored, how long it should be held, and who should be able to read or change the data.

### Data Flow

The data flows represent the inputs and outputs of each process or subsystem. The data flows are easy to draw. They are simply arrows that connect processes, entities, and data stores. Be sure to label every data flow. The diagram might seem obvious *now;* however, if someone else reads it or you put it away for several months, it can be hard to figure out what each flow represents.

### Division of the System

A DFD provides an excellent way to represent a system divided into smaller components. First, each task is shown as a separate process. The data flows between the processes represent the inputs and outputs of each subsystem. Second, the DFD for a complex system would be too large to fit on one page. Hence, the DFD is displayed on different pages or levels. The top level or **context diagram** acts as a title page and displays the boundaries of the system and the external entities that interact with the system. The next level *(level zero)* shows the primary subsystems. Figure 3.7 is an example of a level-zero diagram. Each of these processes is then exploded into another level that shows more detail. Figure 3.8 is the exploded detail for the first process (donor and public relations). These explosions can continue to any depth until you have displayed all the detailed operations needed to explain the system.

A detailed DFD could take hundreds of pages to show all the levels for a large business. Although it is unlikely that you will have to draw or maintain such a large diagram, you should know there are computer tools to help keep track of these drawings. An automated tool called **computer-aided software engineering (CASE)** has the primary purpose of helping systems analysts draw diagrams on the computer screen. That way the analyst can have the computer keep track of the pages and the various levels. By pointing and clicking with a mouse, the analyst or user can see how the subsystems are related and retrieve any desired information about the system.

**FIGURE 3.8**

Each process can be expanded into more detail. This diagram shows the interactions with various members of the public. Note that data flows from the higher level must appear on this level.

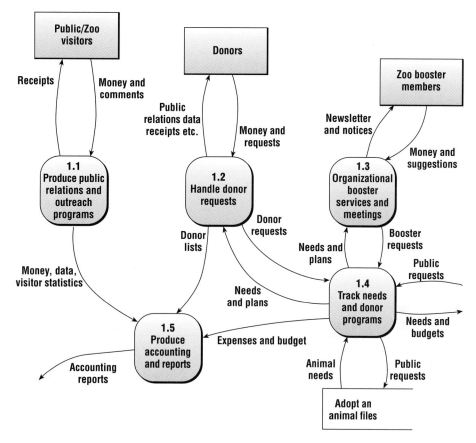

## Data Dictionary

In any project, you need to remember additional pieces of information about each object. You might want to keep a sample report for a management tax report data flow, along with any deadlines that must be met. For data stores, you need to record information such as who controls it, who needs access to the data, how often it should be backed up, and what elements it contains.

A **data dictionary** or **repository** contains all of the information that explains the terms you used to describe your system. A good CASE tool will maintain the dictionary automatically and help you enter longer descriptions for each item. Without these tools, you will have to keep a notebook that contains the full descriptions. For convenience, the entries should be sorted alphabetically. A word processor can be used to hold and print the dictionary. Figure 3.9 has sample entries for the zoo system.

## Some Simple Rules

For a DFD to be useful, you need to follow a couple of rules, as illustrated in Figure 3.10. The first one is that data flows between entities that are external to the system do not need to be shown. If a customer buys a product from a retail store, the customer and the manufacturer are external entities to the retail store. Therefore, when the customer sends a warranty registration card directly to the manufacturer, we should not include it in the retail store's data flow diagram because the data is completely outside the system. When we set the boundaries of the system, we decided that customers and manufacturers would not be

**FIGURE 3.9**
SAMPLE DATA
DICTIONARY ENTRIES
(PARTIAL)
A few sample entries
from the zoo's data
dictionary. A data
dictionary records
details on all of the
organization's objects.
It is typically organized
by type of object. It is
easiest to maintain if it
is stored in a computer
database.

| PROCESSES | DESCRIPTION . . . |
|---|---|
| Animal care | Feed, clean, and vet care |
| Donor and public relations | Handle public requests and provide educational information |
| Employee relations | Schedule employees, process benefits, handle government reports |
| Facility management | Handle maintenance, new construction, planning |
| Produce management reports | Collect data and produce summary reports for management |
| **ENTITIES** | |
| Certification agencies | Government and private agencies that create rules and regulate zoos |
| Donors | People and companies who donate money to the zoo |
| Employees | Primary (paid) workers, full-time and part-time |
| Other zoos and breeders | Zoos we trade with and share data with |
| Public/zoo visitors | Daily visits, we rarely keep data on individuals |
| Zoo booster members | Members who donate money and time for minor benefits |
| **DATA** | |
| Accounting reports | Standard (GAAS) accounting reports for management |
| Certification reports | Reports for certification agencies; produced annually |
| Facility reports | Summaries of work done and plans, mostly weekly |
| Needs and budgets | Budgets and special requests from animal care |
| Public requests | Suggestions and comments from the public |

included. Now, if you start drawing the diagram and decide that it is important to show this flow of data, it means that the boundary was incorrect, and you will have to expand the system to include at least one of the two (probably the manufacturer in this example).

**FIGURE 3.10**
Basic rules for creating data flow diagrams. Three common errors arise in drawing a data flow diagram. Check your work to avoid these errors. If these errors exist in the initial design, they will probably be carried into the "solution," and cause additional problems for users and customers.

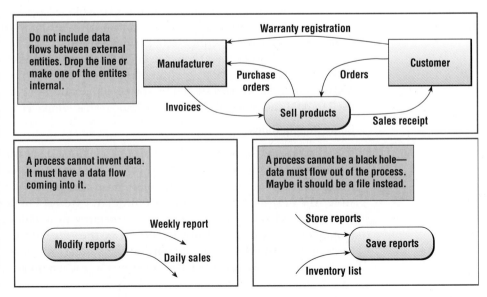

**FIGURE 3.11**

Problem boundary definition. It is hard to solve complex problems, so we often examine a portion of the overall system. Be careful to identify the root causes of problems so that your analysis includes all of the objects involved in the problem.

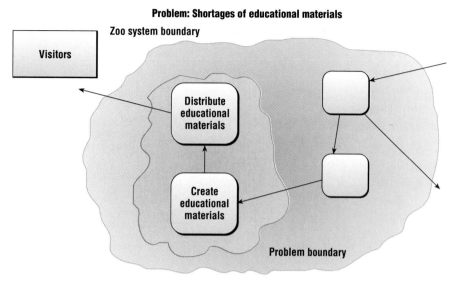

**Problem: Shortages of educational materials**

Zoo system boundary

Visitors

Distribute educational materials

Create educational materials

**Problem boundary**

## Problem Boundary

Searching for solutions raises the issue of another type of boundary: the problem boundary. The *problem boundary* marks the areas that need to be examined in order to solve a specific problem. In many cases, it will be smaller than the system boundary. If the zoo is receiving visitor complaints about shortages of educational materials, you would concentrate on one or two subsystems shown in Figure 3.11. On the other hand, if the zoo is experiencing health problems with the animals, they are most likely related to nutrition, veterinary care, and exchanges with other zoos. In this situation you might have to examine entities (other zoos and suppliers) that are outside of the primary system. As a manager, your goal is to find everything relevant to the problem and its solution, so the problem boundary can be larger than the system boundary.

## Common Systems Problems in Business

Examining problems with the systems approach provides unique advantages. Several problems occur so frequently that they are worth remembering. As summarized in Figure 3.12, there are four basic items to begin searching for problems: within specific subsystems, between subsystems, within feedback and control, and in interactions with the environment.

It would be relatively easy to run a business if nothing ever changed. Many of the problems experienced by businesses arise because of changes in the environment or changes in the operations. In the last few years, the rate of change in business has increased, so companies are more likely to experience problems. Any system that changes over time is going to experience problems. Changes can alter a subsystem so that it no longer functions properly. Problems can arise between subsystems, where the outputs provided by one system no longer match the requirements of another subsystem. Errors can arise in feedback and control loops so that the subsystems are pursuing different goals. Additionally, the system may not interact correctly with its environment.

### Defective Subsystems

Of all the problems that can arise, those that occur within a specific subsystem are usually the easiest to identify and to correct. They arise because a subsystem is not

**FIGURE 3.12**

Common sources of problems. When analyzing an organization, check for each of these problems. When you find one, mark it on the data flow diagram. The resulting diagram will show you where to concentrate your efforts.

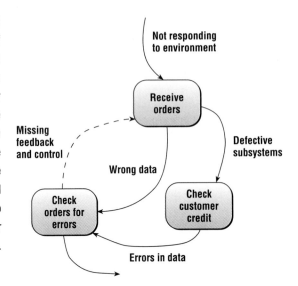

operating correctly. The main problem is to identify the proper subsystem. If each system has clearly defined goals, you can check each subsystem to make sure it is processing the inputs correctly. One system may appear to be faulty when the problems are actually due to a system that provides the input. The problems are usually resolved by fixing the specific subsystem. This system can be repaired or even replaced without affecting the other subsystems. The example of the accounting and finance departments illustrates a faulty subsystem.

### Problems among Subsystems

It is much more likely that problems will involve several subsystems. These problems are harder to identify. Whenever you spot problems in more than one subsystem, you need to ask whether the problems are related. If they are related, the solution will be more complex, and you might have to reorganize several subsystems at the same time. You are likely to encounter two types of problems. The first is when the output from one subsystem is not really what another system needs as input. The second

### ◤ FAULTY SUBSYSTEM ◢

The accounting department is producing a quarterly sales report, but the finance department really needs a weekly report to estimate cash-flow needs. In response to this problem, the finance department hires additional workers to help create its own reports. For a while, everything runs smoothly. However, at some point, the finance department is producing an estimated sales report that is radically different from the marketing estimates. As a result, the finance cash-flow projections are incorrect, and the company pays a substantial fee to borrow additional short-term funds. The personnel costs in the finance department increase because of the need to produce the extra reports. By the time management becomes aware of these two problems, it takes considerable time and effort to track down the true cause of the problem: Accounting is not producing the correct reports for finance.

occurs when the system itself is not functioning properly. In this situation, it becomes difficult to think of the system as a collection of independent pieces because they do not work.

The problem with either dependently or independently mismatched inputs and outputs is common and usually is not difficult to correct. Each subsystem is operating reasonably well; however, some subsystem may not be able to get the inputs it needs, or perhaps not in the correct format. These problems are even harder to spot when the outputs are processed by several different subsystems before the result is actually used. As illustrated in Mismatched Inputs (Reality Bytes 3–3), these problems can arise if changes are made to inputs without considering their impact on the entire system.

 **Reality Bytes**          **3–3  MISMATCHED INPUTS AT MATSUSHITA**

Matsushita is a large Japanese conglomerate. U.S. consumers are most familiar with the company's Panasonic line of electronic equipment. Like many other Japanese companies, the operations within Japan operate differently from those in the U.S. In particular, distribution of products in Japan is handled by trading companies. In fact, Matsushita distributes its products through 28 separate trading companies in Japan.

To make the process more efficient and to track sales data with each distributor, Matsushita established electronic data interchange (EDI) links to each of the 28 trading companies. This subsystem worked well and provided needed communication and monitored total sales by each of the trading companies.

However, none of the 28 links were connected. As a result, Matsushita could not get up-to-date sales data by product line. To make production and inventory decisions, managers needed a listing of sales by product item. Consequently, they were forced to hold large inventories of products. Even then, they occasionally ran out of stock on popular items.

In response to the problem, Matsushita outsourced its mainframe and order-entry system to Nippon Telephone and Telegraph (NTT). NTT built a unified order-entry system that tracked items sales and produced consolidated reports for Matsushita.

Organizations that experience major changes often encounter another problem: subsystems that are too tightly intertwined. In this situation, it is difficult to split the system into pieces because the organization is so interdependent. Similarly, a company might be organized one way, but the production or data could be split in a different direction.

These problems will be explored in more detail in later chapters. Typical symptoms include excessive duplication, missing subsystems, inability to get data, and arguments among managers over control and responsibility. As illustrated in Intertwined Subsystems (Reality Bytes 3–4), these problems can arise when two companies are merged.

### Feedback and Control

Systems can experience several problems if they do not have feedback and control loops in place, or if these controls are defective. For instance, imagine what would happen if a heating thermostat was defective in such a way that its control commands were reversed. Whenever the temperature dropped below the control value, the thermostat would turn on the air conditioner. If the temperature rose, the furnace

**Reality Bytes**   **3–4** INTERTWINED SUBSYSTEMS

Retailer Z-Stores just purchased competitor Q-Up. Unfortunately, the two accounting departments work completely differently. Z-Stores cannot afford to immediately retrain all of the sales and accounting personnel from the old Q-Up stores, so they decide to keep both systems and hire more accountants to combine the two sets of data into a consolidated report. Everything goes well until management decides to combine operations from two different warehouses.

The old Q-Up stores are operated differently from Z-Stores. They get merchandise on a regular basis from the warehouse and place it on the shelves. If it takes too long to sell, they just cut the price. The Z-Stores focus on individual items and get orders from customers. They fill these orders by relaying them to the warehouses, which deliver the items.

Managers from the old Q-Up stores are complaining that they can't get products anymore. The Z-Stores managers say it takes longer to get products and the wrong ones are often delivered. The warehouse managers say they can't keep track of which products go to which store and they are having trouble deciding what to reorder.

would be activated. The feedback loop makes the problems worse. In a system that operates as rapidly as a heating unit, it is easy to spot these errors before they get out of hand. However, in a business, the responses may be more complex, meaning that it could take much longer for the problem to become evident. As shown in Conflicting Goals example (Reality Bytes 3–5), the situation also can arise when the goals of some participants do not support the goals of the overall organization.

  **Reality Bytes**   **3–5** CONFLICTING GOALS

In 1993, managers of the British subsidiary of the vacuum cleaner manufacturer Hoover determined that current sales were below the target rates they wanted to meet. They came up with a strong promotional offer: If you buy any vacuum cleaner from us, we'll give you a free round-trip flight to the United States. Sales skyrocketed because people were buying vacuum cleaners just to get the free flights. Thousands more people filed claims for free tickets than expected.

From Hoover's perspective, the problem was that customers were buying the cheapest vacuum cleaners (retail cost of about $80), but the lowest air fares were around $400. The company was losing hundreds of dollars for every sale.

The managers who concocted the scheme lost their jobs. Hoover chartered special flights for the customers, but still lost $70 million. In 1995, Maytag sold Hoover-Europe to an Italian firm (Candy) at an additional loss of $130 million.

### Interaction with the Environment

A fundamental proposition of systems theory is that any closed system will eventually decay and die. The environment rarely stays constant, and eventually it will change enough to cause a closed, isolated system to fail. Partly for that reason, there are no truly "closed" systems. Even though most businesses are open systems and respond to changes in the environment, they may not always respond quickly enough or in the needed direction, which causes some distinct problems. For example, the Environmental Changes situation (Reality Bytes 3–6) shows how

**Reality Bytes** ◣ 3–6 ENVIRONMENTAL CHANGES

The mini- and mainframe computer industry in the 1980s represents a classic example of slow response to fundamental shifts in the environment. Throughout the 1980s, technology changed so rapidly that the capabilities of small computers were doubling every year. These computers were relatively inexpensive and were used for more and more functions. Customers started questioning why they needed to continue spending money on their large central computers.

The large computer companies were systems that were organized around selling large central computers at relatively high profit margins. Large sales staffs dealt directly with customers' MIS managers. The computer firms spent a great deal of time and money to influence these buyers and win their loyalty. The small computers had low profit margins and were often purchased by end users outside of the MIS departments. The large computer companies were not designed to operate in this new environment and lost billions of dollars, whereas new startup enterprises earned billions of dollars in profits.

a market can change and a business might be too entrenched in its current system to respond to the changes. Similarly, the economic changes in Japan have forced companies like Kao (Reality Bytes 3–7) to respond by rebuilding their entire organizations.

It is easy to say that a system should respond to changes in the environment. However, there are several complicating factors. First, an environment might be highly variable and change several times. It is difficult to change an entire system every time the environment changes. Many people have criticized the U.S. government for changing tax codes every year. Some of these codes lead to changes in the

  **Reality Bytes** ◣ 3–7 KAO: RE-ENGINEERING IN RESPONSE TO ECONOMIC CHANGES

Kao Corp. is a Tokyo-based manufacturer of floppy disks, chemicals, personal care products, and cleaners. Like other Japanese companies, they suffered setbacks in the mid-1990s recession that hit Japan.

Although most Japanese firms heavily invested in factory automation, they are far behind the United States and Europe in automating office systems. Two reasons for the delay are the complexity in dealing with the written language, and the historical abundance of labor in Japan. As a result, U.S. companies have three times the number of personal computers per employee as Japanese companies. But changes in the Japanese economy have increased the pressure on Japanese firms to change. One major change, predicted by economic theory, is the increasing wage rate in Japan. Today's wage rates are comparable to those in the United States and Europe. The second change is the increased strength of U.S. and European manufacturers, which resulted in a drop in revenue for Japanese firms.

Yet it is not easy for companies to make incremental changes in response to changes in the environment. Instead, many companies, including Kao, are looking to re-engineering techniques to make radical changes to the entire organization. In the 1980s, management at Kao concluded that without re-engineering, costs could be reduced only 15 percent. Today, Toshio Hirasaka, director of systems development at Kao, observes that the company is seeking to change the corporate culture and abolish "authoritarian management." Along the way, managers hope to simplify the business processes and make employees more productive and creative. One step in the process is to build an integrated MIS that will make it easy for managers to get data from production, sales, and logistics.

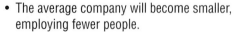

structure of the business system. These changes lead to expensive alterations in business practices, particularly if codes are changed every year.

A second problem occurs when the environment changes slowly and the changes are difficult to identify. For example, consumer tastes may change gradually over time, and companies may not recognize the changes. The problem is particularly troubling when product development is highly capital intensive and difficult to modify—as in automobile production.

The third problem caused by change in the environment is that business systems can be difficult to change. Most large corporations operate by a set of written and unwritten rules. Each job is narrowly defined and each employee knows what he or she is supposed to do. Altering the systems requires everyone to learn a new set of rules. The concept of re-engineering refers to a complete redesign of the system.

Some people believe that the business environment is going to be less stable in the coming years. They have suggested that to keep up with these changes, the typical business system will have to change. It will be smaller and more flexible, and workers will constantly have to learn new ideas and techniques.

## OBJECT-ORIENTED DESIGN

Data flow analysis concentrates on the processes within a company, identifying problems with procedures, and the exchange of data in a firm. Another approach to analyzing an organization is known as **object-oriented design.** In an object-oriented approach, the emphasis is on business objects: what they are and what they do. Objects could be anything from people to raw materials to data files or schedules. The key is that we focus on defining what an object is and what it can do. Flows of data become simple transfers of objects, which are easy to do once the object information is computerized. Because of this different perspective, an object-oriented approach breaks the problem into different pieces than the data flow method.

### Properties and Functions

Objects are defined by a set of properties (or attributes). The properties define the object. Consider the small example of a banking system. One primary object will be Accounts. A generic Account object would have basic properties like: Account Number, Account Name, Client, Manager, Date Opened, Beginning Balance, Current Balance, Ending Balance, and Interest Rate.

Each object also has functions that describe actions that can be performed by the objects and define how to alter the object. In the bank illustration, there would be functions to Open Account, Close Account, Accept Deposits, Pay Withdrawals, and Pay Interest. Note that each type of account could have a different method for computing interest payments. One might compound them daily, another weekly, and so on.

These processes are similar to the ones you encountered with the data flow approach. The main difference is that with the data flow approach the processes stand alone. With the object-oriented approach the properties and functions are combined into the definition of the object. The goal is to describe a system so that if you change a function, you only have to change one object. All of the other objects and processes remain the same.

## Object Hierarchies

Oftentimes objects are related to each other. Typically there is a base class of objects and other objects are derived from the base definitions by adding properties and altering functions. This process results in an object hierarchy, illustrated in Figure 3.13, that shows how the classes are derived from each other. The bank example has several types of accounts with each of these categories containing further subdivisions.

Figure 3.13 also shows detail in the classes by including some of the properties and member functions. The accounts have elements in common that they inherit

**FIGURE 3.13**

Objects: Encapsulation, hierarchy, inheritance, polymorphism. Object-oriented design focuses on individual objects and the data within the organization. Processes are secondary and they are usually embedded in the object. By encapsulating these definitions, the objects can be used to develop related systems with less effort. It is also easier to modify a system by making small changes to an object's behavior.

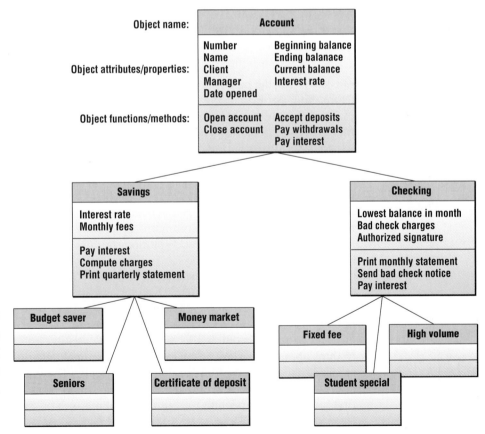

from the base class (account), such as the balance attributes. Each level adds additional detail. Each account class also contains member functions to perform operations, such as paying interest. Because the interest computations can be different for each of the accounts, the method is stored with the original definition of each account.

## Events

Another aspect of modeling objects is that they are often used in an event-driven approach. When some business event occurs, an object function is called or a property is modified. As a manager, you need to think about possible events and how they influence the objects you control. In the banking example, a customer's deposit triggers a credit to her account. This change might then force a change in a daily report object. This chain of events defines the business operations. Unfortunately, there is not yet a standardized method to diagram the event chains and their relationship with objects. As a manager, you are likely to be asked to identify the major objects and the events that affect your area of expertise in the company.

To see the usefulness of the object approach, consider what happens if the bank decides to collect additional data for the checking accounts. The only change needed is to add the new data items (and the associated functions) to the checking account class. All checking accounts will then inherit those properties and functions. None of the other operations are affected. Changes to the information system will only affect the specific accounts; the rest of the system will remain the same.

**ASKING QUESTIONS**     The key to solving business problems is to ask the right questions. In any realistic situation, you, as a manager, will never have enough information. Most of the time, several people will be involved, with their own perspectives, opinions, and biases. Although most people will not deliberately withhold information, they may not know what information is important.

You will often have to talk to the people involved at least twice. The first interview will determine the scope of the problem and identify the components of the system. When you understand the basic problem, you usually have to return and ask more specific questions to learn the details and to clarify conflicting points. You also need to try out possible solutions to determine their strengths and drawbacks. Sometimes you can have a good solution, but the people directly involved will be able to suggest improvements.

Questions serve another useful purpose. They can be used to suggest new alternatives to decision makers. This is why it is important to ask questions even when you already know the answer. Communications among people can be challenging. Each person has a mental picture of how the system works. There is no guarantee that everyone works from the same viewpoint. Questions force people to think about their view of the problem. Sometimes solving a problem is as simple as asking the right questions to define it correctly. The main point to remember is that when you approach a business problem, do not start by looking for answers; first look for the important questions. See the boxes on Symptoms and Questions for examples.

How do you know which questions to ask? The first step is to find a goal and stick to it, which generally leads to the first question: What is the primary objective? Then, if you run into conflicts or decisions: How does this action help achieve the objective? Use questions to stay focused on the goal. Another approach is to think of various alternative solutions or models. Then use questions to choose among them. Questions typically include: How do the solutions differ? Are the underlying assumptions reasonable? What happens if something goes wrong?

For illustration, consider the problem encountered at the zoo. As marketing manager, you find there is a problem in the budgets stemming from donations (Reality Bytes 3–8). Although there are some quick-and-dirty solutions, you really need to dig deeper to find the source of the problem. Figure 3.14 shows the subsystems that are affected by the problem. Reality Bytes 3–8 outlines the problems and ideas for solving them.

**Reality Bytes    3–8  PROBLEMS AT THE ZOO**

As a marketing manager at the zoo, you notice there is a problem. Some of the animal budgets contain more money than they need. Other animal budgets have no money at all. Your first response to this "problem" is to simply pull money from the large accounts and put it into the accounts with no money. Then your assistant reminds you that the accounts "promise" donors the money will be spent on the animals they specify, and it would be unethical to transfer money in the accounts. So, you need to ask: Is this the entire problem, or is it just a symptom? Why did this event occur? Does it happen often? You decide to use the DFD to trace where the money and animal requests come from. First you check to see whether total donations have changed. You examine the process that handles donor requests and verify that account balances are correct and that no major mistakes were made. You eventually work back to the donor groups

and the booster members. On questioning several prominent members, you find that some animals are more popular than others. Everyone wants to sponsor the lions and giraffes. No one wants to give money to sponsor the binturong.

On looking further, you find that the marketing department tracks only the total donations. It does not look at the breakdowns by animal. As a result, marketing promotions continue to push the "cuddly" animals, even though those animals do not need more money. You considered a proposal to change the promotions so the zoo can shift money among accounts at will. However, your legal staff advises that it might be illegal as well as unethical. You finally decide that you need to build a better feedback loop and improve the information system so that marketing knows which animals to "sell."

**FIGURE 3.14**

System problems at the zoo. Highlighting problems on the data flow diagram makes it easier to see the causes. It also makes it possible to trace the effects of changes in the system.

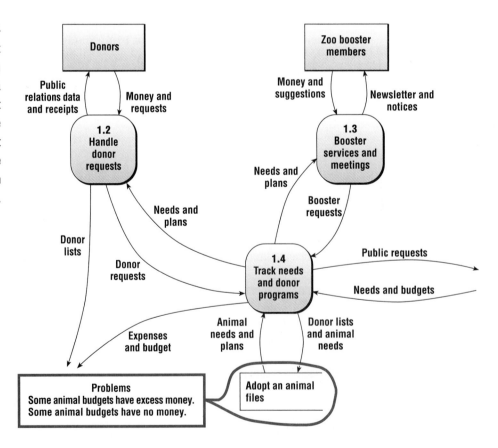

**SOLVING BUSINESS PROBLEMS AND CASES**

One of the goals of this text is to help you move a step closer to the business world and its unstructured problems. It takes time to develop your own approach to identify the important issues and search for alternative solutions with unstructured problems. Figure 3.15 illustrates one basic approach to solving problems. A useful way to learn how to solve business problems is to begin by working with smaller cases. These cases represent more compact, slightly better-defined business problems. Each chapter contains exercises and cases that reflect situations you might encounter in business. Many of these problems are loosely defined. You might be given a set of numbers and asked to create a report. In some cases, you will have to decide what problems need to be solved. Then you need to select appropriate tools to produce the report. Remember that in business, presentation is important because you will be judged both by the context and the appearance of your work.

## Solve the Right Problem

One of the first complications you encounter with unstructured problems is that there could be several problems. Especially with cases, it is not always clear which problem is the most important. You must be careful to identify causes instead of just symptoms. That is where systems theory is useful. It encourages you to look at all the components of the system. Keep in mind that almost no business runs perfectly. Some minor problems are not worth the cost to fix them. You will have to evaluate each problem and determine which ones are the most important. Remember that it is crucial to focus on the goals of the system. If there are multiple goals, you will have to assign priorities and determine how your plans relate to the goals.

## Choose the Right Tools

When the only tool you have is a hammer, everything looks like a nail. That's an old saying that has often been applied to MIS. Many students quickly see the value of spreadsheets, so they try to solve all their problems using a spreadsheet. Sometimes

**FIGURE 3.15**
You should develop a systematic plan for solving problems. The steps outlined here provide a starting point. Each step leads to increasingly detailed analysis.

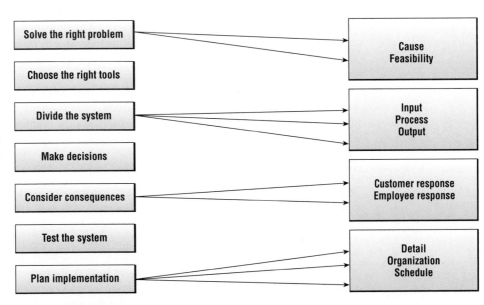

the exercise is easier to do with a database management system, or even a word processor. When you receive a new exercise, stop for a minute and decide which tool will be the easiest to use. As new tools are introduced in later chapters, there will be a section explaining the type of problems on which to use them. Chapter 5 examines the differences between spreadsheet problems and situations where a DBMS is a better choice. Chapter 7 shows how to combine the results of several tools.

## System Division: One Step at a Time

At first glance, many problems appear to be too difficult. Or you might have trouble finding a solution to a case. The trick is to split the problem into smaller pieces. For cases, use systems theory and data flow diagrams to identify the components of the system. For exercises and problems, work one step at a time. Collect the data, perform computations, create graphs, and then create the final report. If the problem is structured appropriately, try to keep the individual components separate. If you need to make a change in one section, it should not interfere with the rest of the project.

## Making a Decision

Once you have evaluated the alternatives, you must make a decision. For most problems, you can only afford to pursue one option. Your choice should be clearly defined and the relative advantages and disadvantages spelled out in detail. You also need to include a solid action plan that describes each step of your proposal. If possible, you should estimate the potential costs. At least identify the items that must be purchased, even if you do not know the costs. Also, if it is relevant, you should identify the people who will be in charge of implementing your plan.

## Consider the Consequences

Any time a system is changed, it is important to examine the participants to see who might be adversely affected and to identify how external agents might respond to the changes. For example, if you design a new system that alters the work flow within the company, some jobs and middle-level management tasks may be altered or eliminated. Although companies routinely alter jobs and occasionally reduce their workforce, a good plan will include a means to retrain workers for new jobs within the company whenever possible. Effects on external agents are more difficult to identify and harder to resolve. For example, a manufacturer might consider skipping over the retail channel and selling products directly to the final consumer. With this approach, the manufacturer could offer a lower price to consumers. However, the existing retail outlets would be upset at the additional level of competition. Many times the retailers add support through product demonstrations, comparisons with competitive products, training, and repair services. In these cases, a new system that irritates the retailers or skips them completely could be disastrous.

## Testing: Everyone Makes Mistakes

We are all familiar with the adage that "everyone makes mistakes." Hence, it generally makes sense to test our work to locate the errors. There is another side to the story, which is that we can never be 100 percent certain. Especially in developing information systems, errors will remain no matter how much we test. The problem is to do enough testing to remove the major mistakes without spending more on testing than we might save by finding all of the errors. The answer to this dilemma is to admit that you are going to make mistakes and then determine what types of mistakes will cause the most problems. Always be sure to test your work for the most important problems first.

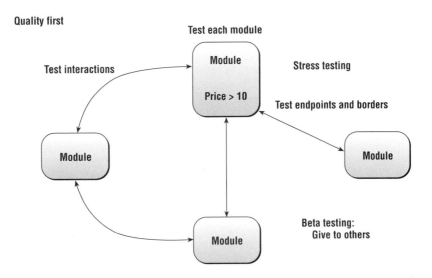

**FIGURE 3.16**
There are several tests that you should perform when creating systems. Even if a spreadsheet is the only software involved, you need to perform these basic tests. Key opportunities for errors are errors within a module, interactions between modules, endpoint values, and stresses that arise under heavy usage.

How do you test your work to find mistakes? Quality control is a large subject, but there are a few basic things to remember, as indicated in Figure 3.16. First, always keep quality in mind. Break your projects into independent pieces so you can test smaller subsets. Test endpoints and critical values. Make sure modules exchange data correctly. Stress test your work by using large amounts of data or several users. Find someone else to use your creation in a beta test. Finally, note that it is sometimes better to let errors slip through than to spend the money to find them all. Hallmark (Reality Bytes 3–9) employs a four-level approach to test large projects.

## Quality First

Most businesses today are interested in improving quality. Intensive studies during the last decade indicate that the most important aspect of quality control is that everyone in the organization has to continually work to improve quality. Quality must

All processes, whether they involve products, services, or software development, must be tested for quality at each step.

**Reality Bytes**    3–9  HALLMARK GREETING CARDS—TESTING

The computing environment at Hallmark greeting cards has traditionally been based on a large mainframe-based COBOL operation. A centralized operation builds and maintains strategic corporate systems for the finance, marketing, order processing, distribution, personnel, and manufacturing areas. More than 200 professionals generate between 40 and 60 products per year.

Since 1980, Hallmark has diversified into franchises, other lines of cards, calendars, ornaments, and other display items. The diversity of these operations has placed increased pressure on the "corporate" information system to respond to the individual needs of the diverse departments while providing information that can be consolidated easily for corporate accounting, analysis, and planning. One difficulty that Hallmark has also recognized is that the large systems do not respond quickly enough to the changing needs of the growing departments within the company.

At Hallmark, the goal of the system development area is to improve project implementation, ensure quality products, and enhance the relationship between the divisions and the information that the system provides. To accomplish this goal, the system must be able to report specific input variables such as product sales, customer traffic, and franchise order rate. In a business such as Hallmark, nonquantifiable input variables such as the strength of customer attitude and acceptance

must also be factored into the equation. To ensure that both the transformation and probabilistic relationships are included, Hallmark has defined four testing levels:

1. *Unit.* At this stage all logic paths in the programs are tested to ensure the correctness of the individual programs.
2. *Integration.* To ensure that the programs transfer information correctly between divisions, multiple programs are coordinated and tested with generated or production data.
3. *System.* The system is executed in a production-like environment to ensure that the system operates properly from both program and procedural standpoints.
4. *User Acceptance.* Users are involved in the planning and testing environment. They also assist in the implementation of test data and the review of the results. This ensures that users understand the system's operational requirements.

Following the implementation of the program, a post-implementation audit is implemented to check whether the software is able to accurately measure the goals of the individual department as they compare to the corporate directives.

be designed into the process from the beginning. Consider a manufacturing firm that only measures quality of the final product. Some of the products are tested as they come off the assembly line. Although this examination might reveal potential problems, it does nothing to improve the products' quality. The real objective is to measure quality at each step in the production process and catch mistakes before they affect the final product.

### Module Testing

Crucial to providing quality in MIS work assignments is to split your work into smaller modules. It is virtually impossible to adequately test a large, complex system. However, if the system is designed as several small components that exchange data with each other, each module can be tested separately.

Consider a spreadsheet assignment in accounting to create a balance sheet. The balance sheet needs several different types of computations. For example, it needs total sales revenue from four regions and depreciation of assets. You might include the asset values and depreciation calculations on the balance sheet. But what happens if some managers change the depreciation method? They would damage the balance sheet. It is better to create separate sections for each portion, generating a balance sheet, a depreciation schedule, and a sales report. The balance sheet would collect only the needed data from each section. As a result, if managers change the depreciation method, you only have to test the new method, making sure the data is transferred correctly to the balance sheet.

### Endpoints

Most problems you encounter will have endpoints. For example, price or quantity sold will almost always be positive numbers, so zero would be an endpoint. You might also be given a conditional statement that states that if income is greater than $32,000, the tax rate should be 28 percent. When you create a new application, keep track of these critical values. Test your application using each value, as well as numbers above and below the critical value.

If you do not have too many critical values, you can perform **exhaustive testing,** where you check every combination of the values. In the previous example, there are two critical points (prices at zero and taxes at $32,000), each with three values to test. An exhaustive test would check nine items ($3^2$). With just 20 critical points, an exhaustive test would need about 3.5 billion tests ($3^{20}$)! In this case, it is more realistic to check the 20 points separately ($3 \times 20 = 60$ tests).

### Interactions

When you are reasonably confident that each module works correctly by itself, it is important to be certain that the modules share data correctly. First, make sure that each module refers to the correct item. Then test it by changing values in one module to see whether the other modules receive the data correctly. A common error is when the receiving module expects a different type of data than you created.

Consider an example where one spreadsheet section needs to retrieve a date from another section. The person who created the first section might have stored the date as a string, but your module needs to compute the number of days between that date and today. It expects the cell to be in date format. The spreadsheet will most likely perform the calculation but treat the string as zero, giving you a meaningless answer.

### Stress Testing

Another common source of problems occurs when the application is stretched to its limits. You might create a spreadsheet that clerks use to enter data and make simple calculations. It works well for several months. As it accumulates more and more data it slows down. Similar problems can arise with spreadsheets and database management systems. You might use a word processor to create a report where every day 10 pages are added. The system works fine, but by the middle of the year it can be really slow.

### Beta Testing

Sometimes it is difficult to find errors. Most people have habits and tend to follow the same steps every time they work on a project. When your project looks like it is finished, it is important to let someone else use it for a while. Other people will almost always try some combination that never occurred to you. One example is a clerk who enters a negative value for quantity sold because someone returned an item. Although logical, such an entry could cause serious problems in an application that was not expecting it.

### Cost of Finding Errors

Although mistakes can be costly, it takes time and money to track them down. At some point, we have to stop looking and accept the fact that some errors might remain. The difficulty is deciding when to stop. The answer depends largely on the importance of the project; if someone's life depends on the outcome, we want to be much more cautious.

In some cases, it is possible to estimate the maximum amount of error. In accounting problems, double-entry provides check figures and an estimate of the maximum error in most cases. *Miscellaneous* categories are often used to correct for minor errors that are too expensive to track down. In other cases, it is not easy to place a value on the possible errors. When the Hubble Space Telescope was developed, NASA officials decided it was not worth spending a million dollars to do a final test before the 1990 launch. When it reached its 370-mile orbit, astronomers quickly realized that the main lens was incorrectly ground, and the 12.5 ton telescope could perform only a fraction of its designed capabilities. In 1993, NASA spent several million dollars on a space shuttle repair flight to refurbish the telescope and correct the lens. Was the resulting error serious enough to justify spending the amount of money it would have cost to perform the final test? Some astronomers think so. If nothing else, the bad publicity surrounding the Hubble Telescope cost NASA more than the cost of the additional tests.

### Quality versus Accuracy

The concept of quality is more complicated than just providing accurate information. In making a decision, it is important to have the correct information and timely data. Consider a situation in which your boss asked you to evaluate four different advertising media using a small spreadsheet report. You carefully collected the data and entered it into the spreadsheet. You computed total costs, returns, and profit figures for each method and wrote a short report. Throughout the process, you double-checked your work to make sure the data set was accurate and the computations were correct. However, your boss is not very happy. Apparently you left out one option and your boss wanted a graph. Even though your numbers were accurate, your report did not have the necessary quality.

## Implementation

In business, creative ideas are always useful, but without a detailed implementation plan the idea alone will not be used. Consider an idea for a new product. The idea itself is not worth much until you find a way to manufacture, market, and distribute the product. Similarly, in MIS it is easy to say that a company can achieve significant gains by installing a new computer system. However, the idea is more valuable, and the project more likely to succeed, if you include a detailed implementation plan. MIS implementation plans include hardware and software requirements, along with training, changes required in various departments, and timetables for installation. Chapter 12 explains the process in more detail.

## Hints for Solving Business Problems and Cases

Cases are often used to illustrate business problems and to show the role played by information. As you progress in your business education, you will encounter more cases. The purpose of this section is to provide an approach to solving cases. Cases

## EVALUATING TECHNOLOGY PROJECTS: INITIAL QUESTIONS

- Does the project fit with the business goals and management style?
- Does the project improve the competitive position of the firm?
- How long will any competitive advantage last?
- What value or reward is created by the system?
- What level of technology is needed to create the system (experimental, leading edge, established, or old-hat)?
- What is the probability of technical success (actually building the system)?

- What is the probability of commercial success (making money once the project is technically successful)?
- What are the costs involved in creating the system:
  - Monetary?
  - Time?
  - Additional capital, marketing, and management?

tend to be less structured than typical textbook exercises. With cases you not only have to solve the problem, you have to identify the cause of the problem, then decide what tools to use to address it. The accompanying box lists some questions to pursue when you begin your study of a new business situation.

Treat cases as if they are real business situations. First familiarize yourself with the situation and the symptoms (read the case). Next create a system view of the organization (read the case again and take notes). Divide the system into components connected by data flows. Sketch the process. You do not always have to draw a complete data flow diagram; any picture will make it easier for you to see the relationships between the components. Look for basic system problems such as defective subsystems, inputs not matching outputs, and weak interaction with the environment.

Remember that you are looking for causes of the problem. A symptom where reports contain errors could have many possible causes. Perhaps the system is not collecting accurate data. Maybe two departments are interfering with each other and altering the data. Possibly a clerk or a computer program is making the wrong computations. To find the cause in this case, you need to follow the data from the source to the final report and determine where the errors first arise. Most cases are complicated by the fact that there are many symptoms and sometimes more than one cause. A DFD can help you sort out the various relationships.

## ELEMENTS OF GOOD BUSINESS ANALYSIS

1. Identification of the root causes of problems.
2. A solid grasp of the strategic components of the problem.
3. Identification of the critical success factors.
4. An evaluation of the financial implications.
5. Thorough discussion of implementation.
6. Realistic analysis of the expected results.
7. The effect on future growth and continued development.
8. The effect on the human resources.
9. An understanding of the target markets.

There are two difficult aspects to any business problem: identifying the true problem and trying to come up with a solution. With practice, you can learn to understand systems and determine causes. Solutions, however, often require creativity. There is no easy way to learn creativity. The best way is to examine what other companies have done to solve their problems. Often, problems that you encounter will be similar to those at other firms. Each chapter in this book carries cases of how actual companies have approached various problems. You can find more case situations in common business publications such as *Computerworld, Fortune, Business Week,* and *The Wall Street Journal.*

Finally, remember there can be many different answers to any case. You might find that it is easy to suggest that a company should "Buy a new computer system." Although that statement is undoubtedly true, it is not very helpful. You really need to add more detail. The best answers describe the nature and cause of the problem, provide a detailed plan, and explain how the plan solves the problem and provides additional advantages.

A typical case will be written as a report to the managers of the company involved. Reality Bytes 3–10 lists some of the elements that are required for a good analysis of business problems and presents a useful way to organize your presentation, by beginning with a summary of the problems and a discussion of the causes. The solution should then be spelled out in detail. An implementation section should explain exactly how to arrive at the solution. This section includes a step-by-step plan of action that lists when to take each action, and specifies who is in charge. The report should also estimate the costs of the solution and describe the anticipated benefits. Some reports may need to include a contingency plan. If you make a risky suggestion that could backfire, it would be wise to give the company another option.

 **Reality Bytes** 3–10 ORGANIZATION OF CASE ANALYSIS

When you write up your case analysis, the following format will be useful. Check with your instructor to see if they want changes or additional features.

1. Statement of the facts.
2. Brief summary of the important facts of the case.
3. Description of problems.
4. Description of the problems' causes. Identify the most important problems.
5. Opportunities.
6. Listing of any additional opportunities that you might be able to pursue. In particular, look for new directions that might give your firm an advantage over the rivals.
7. Alternatives.
8. Description of the choices available. Remember to include the "do-nothing" option.
9. Decision and plan.
10. Selection of one of the alternatives and explain it in detail. Provision of an implementation plan. Include a contingency plan in case something goes wrong.

## SUMMARY

Solving business problems and cases can be a difficult task. Identifying problems and causes requires you to learn how to divide a system into smaller modules to identify the inputs, processes, and outputs. Systems have goals that are monitored, with feedback providing controls on the system. Data flow diagrams can be used to display the relationships among subsystems.

It is easier to solve problems once you have learned to analyze and diagram business systems. You can begin by examining each module to be sure that it is performing the task it was designed to do. Other sources of problems include the connections between the modules, missing or inappropriate feedback and control mechanisms, and the failure to interact with the environment. You begin to solve problems by asking questions. As you begin your study of business problems, it is important to begin collecting a list of questions that you can ask whenever you start a new case.

When approaching problems, the first step is to analyze the system by dividing it into smaller modules. The goal is to identify the most important problems and look for causes, not just symptoms.

> **A MANAGER'S VIEW**
> All managers need to solve problems. You will eventually gain experience and develop your own style. Systems theory provides a useful starting point because it encourages you to break a system into smaller pieces that are easier to understand. It also helps you focus on the causes of problems instead of the symptoms.
> The systems approach is heavily used in MIS. As a manager, if you understand this method, it will be easier to communicate with analysts from MIS when you are creating a new information system.

When you are creating a solution, be careful to choose the proper tool for each problem. That means you need to know the strengths and weaknesses of the various tools—things to focus on as you learn new tools in later chapters. Each solution should be carefully tested. Standard items to test are individual modules, endpoints, and interactions between the modules. Just remember that it is impossible to test every situation.

## KEY WORDS

closed loop, 101
closed system, 99
computer-aided software
    engineering (CASE), 104
context diagram, 104

data flow diagram (DFD), 102
data dictionary (repository), 105
exhaustive testing, 121
feedback, 101
input, 98

object-oriented design, 112
open system, 99
output, 98
process, 98

## REVIEW QUESTIONS

1. Describe all steps involved in the systems method.
2. What are the five elements of a data flow diagram (DFD) and how is it useful in MIS?
3. What two important roles do processes have in a data flow diagram?
4. As a manager at Ditka & Associates you are often called on to help solve system problems that arise. James Brooks, a team member in your department, calls you and says the system is going berserk. What four places do you tell James to check immediately?
5. Wahoo Wahoo Co. is a large manufacturer with several multimillion dollar accounts. The company's managers would like to change their computer system to help meet changes in products and pricing

to more effectively serve their customers. Do you think this complete conversion will be simple for Wahoo Wahoo? Explain your answer.
6. Explain how object-oriented design is different from the data flow approach.
7. How do object hierarchies make it easier to modify systems?
8. How does encapsulation make it easier to build and modify systems?
9. Why is it so important to ask questions when you are trying to solve a systems problem?
10. List and describe some helpful hints that can be used when you are solving business problems and cases.
11. Define the major forms of testing used in systems design.

## EXERCISES

1. Write down five questions that you might use whenever you approach a new case.

2. Interview a manager (or a friend who has a job). Identify the major processes involved in the job. Draw a diagram to show how the processes are related and to show the relevant inputs and outputs of each process.

3. Draw a small data flow diagram for the Q-Up and Z-Store case (Reality Bytes 3–4) to illustrate their problems.

4. Choose one subsystem in the zoo example and add another level to the data flow diagram. If possible, interview a manager or worker at an actual zoo.

5. Draw a data flow diagram to illustrate the course registration process at your school. Compare your diagram with those drawn by two other students.

6. Create a list of objects that would be involved in the course registration process at your school. Briefly describe some of the attributes and functions used by each object.

7. Read current business periodicals and find examples of three companies that have experienced system problems. Classify the problem in system terms (subsystem, mismatched inputs, etc.). Draw a small diagram to illustrate the problem.

8. Find an article that describes the operations or problems of a company. Write five questions that you would want to ask the CEO (or other officers) of that company if you were hired as a consultant to improve the company's operations.

9. In the bank account example, the bank wants to add a special type of checking account for people who are more than 50 years old. The interest rate will be tied to their age: a $\frac{1}{8}$ point increase for every five years over 50 ($50 = +\frac{1}{8}$, $55 = +\frac{2}{8}$, $60 = +\frac{3}{8}$ . . . ). Change the object hierarchy and add the appropriate properties and functions.

 **Rolling Thunder Database**

1. Identify the processes and activities of the Rolling Thunder Bicycle Company.

2. Diagram the overall system, showing the major subsystems, the flow of products, and the data flows.

3. Identify the primary objects involved. Specify a name, primary attributes, and possible functions for each object.

4. Identify possible constraints or bottlenecks in the system.

## ADDITIONAL READING

Alter, Allan E. "Japan, Inc. Embraces Change," *Computerworld*, March 7, 1994, p. 24. [Matsushita and Kao]

"Animated Greetings," *MacUser*, September 1995, p. 36. [Hallmark Greeting Cards]

Anthes, Gary. "Bank Sets Financial Records Straight," *Computerworld*, May 17, 1993, p. 49. [Valley Bancorp]

Battey, James. "The Web Hotlist: Web Sites Worth Checking Out," *Infoworld*, February 12, 1996, p. 33. [Levi Strauss]

Booch, Grady. *Object-Oriented Analysis and Design with Applications*, Benjamin Cummings, 1994. [Detailed methodology for object-oriented design]

Booker, Ellis. "Railroads Reroute," *Computerworld*, July 26, 1993, p. 57. [Union Pacific Railroad]

Bucker, Michael. "Test Tool Evangelists Convert IS Shops," *Software Magazine*, October 1995, pp. 42–46. [Levi Strauss]

Caldwell, Bruce. "It's No Longer Too Early to Get in," *VARbusiness*, May 1, 1995, pp. 54–60. [Amtrak]

Calvin, Robert E. "Kings of the Road," *Computer Life*, May 1995, pp. 90–96. [Santa Fe Railroad]

Coad, Peter and Edward Yourdon. *Object-Oriented Analysis*. Englewood Cliffs, NJ: Yourdon Press, 1990. [Introduction to object-oriented design and graphing techniques]

Doyle, T.C. "MCI Rolls Out Internet Electronic Commerce," *Infoworld*, April 3, 1995, p. 12. [Amtrak]

Erickson, Wayne W. "Amtrak Builds Real-Time Train Control System," *Open Information Systems*, October 1995, pp. 29–34. [Amtrak]

Garnett, Marla. "A Sneak Peek at the Future: Global On-line Links Take Off," *PC Week*, April 17, 1995, p. 58. [Santa Fe Railroad]

Gibbons, Paul L. "Beam Me Up a Straight-Leg 30/32, Scotty," *PC Week*, December 19, 1994, p. 21. [Levi Strauss]

Halper, Mark. "ISSC Tapped to Run Railroad's Systems," *Computerworld*, November 15, 1993, p. 12. [Union Pacific Railroad]

Halper, Mark. "Rivals Align to Lay Outsourcing Tracks," *Computerworld*, November 22, 1993, p. 1. [Union Pacific Railroad]

Hatelstad, Luc. "Technology, Telecommuting Demand Push PC Cards' Popularity," *Infoworld*, November 16, 1995, p. 79. [Hallmark Greeting Cards]

Haverson, Debra S. "Smarter Use of SPC," *MIDRANGE Systems*, December 16, 1994, p. 40. [Levi Strauss]

Hayes, Mary. "Focus on the Customer," *Information Week*, September 18, 1995, pp. 92-94. [Levi Strauss]

Hoffman, Thomas. "Conrail Makes Pen-based Connection," *Computerworld*, March 14, 1994, p. 55. [Union Pacific Railroad]

Hoffman, Thomas. "End Users Won't Wait," *Computerworld*, January 3, 1994, p. 28. [Union Pacific Railroad]

Hoffman, Thomas. "Union Pacific Rail Says, 'I know I can'," *Computerworld*, August 23, 1993, p. 91. [Union Pacific Railroad]

Horwitt, Elisabeth. "Amtrak Hopes PC Deal Will Stoke Profit Fires," *Computerworld*, July 9, 1990, p. 4. [Amtrak]

"How We Will Work in the Year 2000," *Fortune*, May 17, 1993, p. 38. [Job trends]

Karon, Paul. "Hallmark Welcomes Change in Handling Finances," *Infoworld*, December 19, 1994, p. 62. [Hallmark Greeting Cards]

"Kao Infosystems Increases CD-ROM Production," *Newsbytes*, April 26, 1995, p. NEW0420006. [Kao]

"Kao Infosystems Vice President of Sales and Marketing John Depuy," *Soft-Letter*, March 27, 1995, p. 5. [Kao]

Ley, Michael. "War Room: Flood Immerses the Santa Fe in Mad Race to Reroute Its Trains," *The Chicago Tribune*, July 21, 1993, pp. C1, C2. [Santa Fe Railroad]

Moad, Jeff. "Change of Course: IT Execs, Stymied by IS Schools, Are Growing Their Staffs 'Soft Skills,'" *PC Week*, April 24, 1995, p. E3. [Hallmark Greeting Cards]

Moad, Jeff. "Switching Tracks," *PC Week*, May 15, 1995, pp. E1-E3. [Santa Fe Railroad]

"Outsourcing Megadeals: More Than 60 Huge Contracts Signed Since 1989 Prove They Work," *Information Week*, November 6, 1995, pp. 34-40. [Amtrak]

Pereira, Pedro. "From Railroads to Conveyor Belts: New President Brings Experience in Mergers, High Volume and Logistics to Merisel," *Computer Reseller News*, October 9, 1995, pp. 173-174. [Santa Fe Railroad]

"Perfect Pairing," *PC Week*, October 23, 1995, p. 3. [Levi Strauss]

Parker, Rachel. "For Levi Strauss, Standard Network is a Perfect Fit," *Infoworld*, February 13, 1995, p. 78. [Levi Strauss]

Rodriguez, Karen. "Ohio Link Hooks up with DEC Network," *Computerworld*, October 14, 1991, p. 31. [Amtrak]

Schmesten, Ivy. "Financial Objects Fly, but Will the Pieces Connect," *Wall Street & Technology*, July 1995, pp. 45-47. [Santa Fe Railroad]

"Take a Web Vacation," *PC/Computing*, December 1995, p. 364. [Amtrak]

*The Economist*, June 3, 1995, p. 5. [Hoover fiasco in Britain]

Wilder, Clinton. "Amtrak Follows Airline Route," *Computerworld*, February 4, 1991, p. 8. [Amtrak]

# CASES  *Railroads*

Statistics are not collected specifically by railroad workers. In general, transportation workers use computers less than the average population. Of those who use computers, the most common uses are for inventory control and communication.

SOURCE: Computer Use in the United States, U.S. Bureau of the Census.

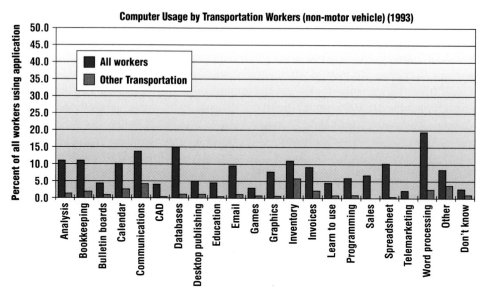

**Computer Usage by Transportation Workers (non-motor vehicle) (1993)**

Railroads hold a nostalgic and honored past in America's history. The Great Iron Horse of the 1860s played a key role in the settlement of the west and the linking of the Atlantic and Pacific coasts. Congress also realized the important role the railroads played in binding the country together and distributing raw materials and finished goods. As a result, it granted the railroads liberal land rights and right-of-ways. In the glory days of the 1930s and '40s, grand stations became the pride of New York, Chicago, St. Louis, and other major cities. Railroads were one of the leaders in the transition from small business to large corporations.

World War II brought research and investment in air travel. As a result, after the war, the airplane was positioned to become the major transporter of people across great distances. Time had become increasingly important to business travelers. As a result, they relied more heavily on the airlines as their primary means of transportation.

Another phenomenon affecting the future of the railroads was the spread of the interstate highway system. Established in 1956, this federal matching-grants program enabled Americans to travel wherever they wanted in their cars without stopping. Equally important, trucks could travel the system to carry products from the manufacturer to the warehouse and ultimately to the consumer with greater speed and convenience. The added advantage was that the trucks

could go directly to the destination's place of business. The business did not have to be located near a railroad track to be served directly.

By 1970, all of these changes left the railroads a mere specter of their glorious past. The railroads suffered many common systems problems, but a key component was their inability to respond to the significant changes occurring in the business environment. The great halls that were once the pride of the railroad moguls quickly became huge caverns of disrepair. Their great size was once a symbol of success and wealth. The increased labor costs of a new generation made the space and its decorations difficult if not impossible to clean and maintain. Even the location of the terminals became a liability. In many cities, business no longer needed to surround the train stations, and offices began to move to other sections of the city. This movement of jobs and employees also worked against train travel and left the station in a deteriorating section of the city that became increasingly undesirable and dangerous after dark.

## CASE  *Amtrak Corporation*

A series of business failures in the late 1960s sent most of the passenger railroads into bankruptcy. The failure of the Penn Central Railroad in 1970 prompted Congress to act boldly to try to maintain the railroad as a viable means of transportation. Congress was not just nostalgic in its intent. It viewed a solid railroad system as essential to the national interest during a time of war. Trips to the European Continent and Japan brought travelers back to the United States with serious questions about why America could not maintain a train system that would match the efficiency of ones found in those countries.

It was against this background of despair that Congress formed the Amtrak Corporation in 1970. This unique quasi-governmental corporation was designed to operate like the post office. Congress funded its establishment and major investments. Ultimately, Amtrak was to become a self-sufficient organization. Congress placed the assets of the now-defunct passenger trains into this organization and provided it with a charter to provide safe and efficient transportation for the American people.

The early days were far from glamorous. Little had been done to maintain the turn-of-the-century tracks since the 1930s. Trains seldom ran on time. The lack of capital investment meant that cars were old and the tracks were not well-maintained. Antiquated union contracts required workers to be on board for jobs that had long since been eliminated by modern equipment. All these factors combined to reduce the speed at which the trains could travel. Delayed schedules meant that business people could not depend on them for travel. Train stations continued to be dirty and unsafe. Several attempts to refurbish stations, particularly in Washington, D.C., for the Bicentennial in 1976, were underfunded and resulted in even more disastrous and deserted stations.

The further the trains slipped in accessibility and timeliness, the more government subsidies were needed to keep them running. As late as 1981, Amtrak revenue paid for less than one-half of the operating expenditures.

Congress realized that if the Amtrak system was to survive, efforts would have to be focused in two areas:

- Capital improvements for tracks, trains, and stations.
- A decision support system to ensure that the trains would run on time and use the most efficient scheduling and pricing techniques.

To address this need, Congress appropriated $1.6 billion to the Northeast Corridor Improvement Project in 1976. These funds were spent on basic, low-technology improvements such as relaying track, rebuilding crumbling bridges and broken down fences, and replacing drainage systems. The overhead electrification system was boosted from 12 to 25 kilovolts of power. The tracks were modified to accommodate trains running at speeds of 40 to 125 miles per hour in both directions. Funds were also directed to clean up and refurbish the 550 passenger train stations in the country. The crown jewel was to become the Washington, D.C., station, which opened as a mall/restaurant/complex in 1988. Millions of dollars were also spent to improve the tracks and make them safe to carry high-speed passenger trains once again.

Of equal importance was the programming of decision support systems to modernize the reservation, pricing, and scheduling systems. Reservations were addressed through the Computerized Reservation System (CRS). Put on line in 1981, the system cost $50 million to develop. Functionally, it acted as a scaled-down version of American Airline's SABRE system by providing agents with information about fares, schedules, and seat availability.

Scheduling was slated to be improved when a $40 million contract was awarded to the Chrysler Corporation to design and install a Centralized Electrification and Traffic Control System.

Amtrak executives soon realized the importance of optimizing inventory. This meant that variable seat pricing must be put in place to ensure that the highest price would be paid to fill a seat. In addition, the limited number of train cars had to be properly allocated to ensure that each car was being properly utilized. To do this, planners turned to yield management. This is the process of predicting where the most money is to be made, when prices should be raised, and when to offer promotions to encourage ticket sales when demand is low. A sophisticated decision support system was viewed as the only way to accomplish these goals.

To meet these new demands, Amtrak has announced Arrow II to replace its original CRS. This decision support system will facilitate variable-seat pricing and maximize inventory utilization. The new technology will enable six inventory classes of tickets to be used. These will range from full fare or heavy advance-purchase discounts to special promotions or excursion fares. Inventory control systems will distribute the cars to the routes where they can return the most revenue. Arrow will generate data that managers can use to query and forecast from. Ultimately, yield management will automatically optimize the levels of inventory for each class of ticket for each train.

## QUESTIONS

1. What parts of the Amtrak scheduling problem are structured?
2. What parts of the Amtrak scheduling problem are unstructured?
3. How does the Arrow system work to move unstructured parts of the decision-making process to a more structured framework?

4. What systems problems are demonstrated by the railroads in general and Amtrak?

5. Currently the Arrow system enables the reservation agent to query the system for the best price of a particular trip. What information might managers want to have if they were interested in setting the prices? How might the system be structured to enable them to set prices and then evaluate the response to price changes, packages, or advertising programs?

6. What components must be included in a training program for the users of the Arrow system?

7. What information would an Amtrak manager want to have included in a spreadsheet format? How would this information assist the manager in future pricing decisions?

8. How might statistical analysis be incorporated into the Arrow system? What value would statistical measures add to evaluation of the pricing and seating policy?

## CASE *Union Pacific Railroad: Advanced Train Control System*

Since 1960, the freight transportation section of American railroads has faced increasing business pressures. The interstate highway system and the growth of the trucking industry have greatly expanded the competition that railroads face in their efforts to transport heavy freight. The Staggers Rail Act, passed in 1980, deregulated the entire industry. This resulted in further consolidation and cost-cutting.

Realizing that service must be at the forefront if trains are to compete in today's marketplace, the train companies have invested in new equipment and new technologies. Mobile data links, computer-controlled heavy machinery, radio transponders, remote equipment diagnostics, and satellite communications have all been enlisted to boost productivity on the railroads.

The Advanced Train Control System (ATCS) is an industry-wide endeavor to automatically monitor and control train traffic. It is being developed as a joint effort between the U.S. and Canadian railroad trade groups. The goal of the program is to enhance safety, reduce fuel use, increase track capacity by running trains closer together, and bring the trains to a point where they can run in better compliance with the predefined schedule.

ATCS includes a set of performance specifications for suppliers of railroad equipment. The specifications are written in modules. As a result, the individual railroads can phase them in at their own pace. They can thus choose the level of investment that they can financially justify to achieve a level of compliance at a particular point in time.

The system is based on a series of transponders buried along a railroad track bed. When a locomotive passes over a transponder, an interrogator broadcasts a radio signal. The signal triggers a responding message from the transponder, which gives the train's precise location to a computer in the locomotive's cab. The train's computer then relays the information via a radio link to a central computer at the railroad's dispatching headquarters. All of this information feeds back to a "Star Wars Room" at Union Pacific's headquarters in Omaha, Nebraska. The location, speed, size, and direction of each train is presented graphically on an 8 by 80-foot-wide projection screen. This screen enables dispatchers to monitor the positions of trains on their assigned routes. Dispatchers are then able to use their desktop computers to gain even more information regarding the trains to which they are assigned.

The ATCS computers make routing decisions that will be verbally relayed to the engineers on each train. Eventually, however, the system will be upgraded to incorporate a data-radio control system.

An important asset of the new system is the ability to better control the train's braking facility. The on-board computer is programmed with an algorithm to calculate the time it takes to come to a complete stop once the command to stop is given. The calculations take into consideration variables such as speed, train weight, and track slope.

Cost justification has become a major decision issue in the development of the new system. The installation of ATCS across the entire Union Pacific Railroad Network will cost between $130 and $150 million over five years. This is a particularly difficult decision, according to Jeff Young: "Railroads usually cost-justify everything by reductions in labor costs, but there's not a lot of people savings built into ATCS."

### QUESTIONS

1. What aspects of dispatching trains for the Union Pacific Railroad are unstructured?

2. What aspects of dispatching trains for the Union Pacific Railroad are structured?

3. What procedure was used by the dispatchers to develop the algorithm to monitor the time it would take the trains to stop?

4. How might the ATCS assist Union Pacific Railroad with its budgeting process?

5. How might the dispatchers and marketing representatives use the ATCS to better respond to customers with last-minute pickup and delivery requests?

6. Define the following variables for the ATCS:

   Input variables         Output variables
   Decision variables      Feedback variables
   Transformation relationships    Time frames

7. Railroads are traditionally viewed as being conservative in their approach to change. What implementation steps would you develop to increase the likelihood of acceptance of the new program by the long-term employees of the railroad?

8. What quantitative measures would you use to evaluate the effectiveness of the ATCS package for the Union Pacific Railroad?

## CASE  *Santa Fe Railroad: Using Technology to Direct Train Routes*

The main business routes for the Atchison, Topeka, and Santa Fe Railroad run between Chicago, California, and the Gulf of Mexico. To better manage its operations, the railroad is consolidating all of its dispatching operations in its headquarters in Schaumburg, Illinois. The headquarters is a large room filled with high-tech monitors and route maps. Using the latest in decision technology and expert systems, 24 on-duty dispatchers monitor the railroad's 7,800-mile system on an array of computer screens.

The system was developed to provide one centralized location from which to direct trains and expedite service. The dispatchers keep track of every train by watching "bright red boxes" that move over white lines indicating the track. When a switch needs to be pulled or a signal changed, the operator does so by moving and clicking a computer mouse. The entire process enables trains to be directed on the most expeditious route while eliminating backlogs and delays.

The system works well when all of the trains are limited to the routes on the Santa Fe Railroad. Difficulties persist, however, when natural disasters or other events prevent the trains from following the most straightforward routes on the company's own lines. Then the dispatchers must negotiate with similar individuals on other train lines to gain access to and use of their lines.

One such natural disaster occurred during the spring 1993 floods in the Midwest. Edwin L. Harper, president of the American Association of Railroads, estimated that 25 to 30 percent of rail traffic originated in, terminated in, or passed through the flood-affected areas.

The flooding was particularly devastating for the Santa Fe Railroad. The line's bridge in Fort Madison, Iowa was partially washed away on July 10. Their bridge near Bosworth, Missouri was completely destroyed, leaving a 200-foot gap in the tracks and a hole 50 feet deep. The bridge was one of the railroad's busiest, accommodating as many as 50 trains a day. The break in the route was a major problem since, in its place, the dispatchers at Santa Fe were forced to piece together alternative routes, using tracks borrowed from other railroads.

To cover the Missouri bridge, Santa Fe dispatchers negotiated for track space using as many as 10 alternate routes. As a result, trains were rerouted through Fort Worth, Memphis, and Denver. More than 50 trains from other railroads also used its routes. The cost of this emergency exchange of tracks is covered by a standard agreement that exists for detours among railroads' tracks in emergencies.

### QUESTIONS

1. What particular problems must technology solve for the railroads?
2. How are these problems accentuated during emergencies?
3. What computer programs/tools were used to develop the routine programs for the Santa Fe Railroad?
4. What benefits were received from the computerization of the routing system compared to the previous system?
5. What systems problems are demonstrated by the Santa Fe situation?
6. Draw a DFD for the systems described by the railroad cases.
7. Using an object-oriented approach, define the basic classes (objects) that could be used to describe the railroad systems. Include basic properties and functions.
8. What is the next step for the Santa Fe Railroad in the computerization of its railroad tracking system?

## CASE  *Pepsi's Philippine Fiasco*

In late 1991, Luis "Cito" Lorenzo, Jr., was looking for a bright idea. The Wharton-educated vice chairman of Pepsi-Cola Products Philippines, Inc. (PCPPI), the independent local bottler of the multinational soft drink, needed a kind of "Operation Desert Storm" to regain Pepsi's dominance of the Philippine soft-drink market. Savvy marketing by rival Coca-Cola had ended Pepsi's reign in the early 1980s, and by 1991, Pepsi was languishing with only a 17-percent market share.

Help came from international headquarters. In December 1991, PepsiCo dispatched Pedro Vegara, then working for its promotions department in New

York, to the Philippines to help put together an effective promotion program. The scheme he came up with was called Number Fever. It had worked for Pepsi in 10 Latin American countries, and there was little reason to doubt that it would do as well in the Philippines. Number Fever combined Filipinos' penchant for gambling and the lure of instant wealth.

Buyers of Pepsi and its three other brands—7-Up, Mountain Dew, and Mirinda orange drink—would look under the bottle caps, which contained three markings: a three-digit number from 001 to 999; a cash prize ranging from 1,000 pesos (then equivalent to $40) to 1 million pesos ($40,000); and a seven-digit security code used to authenticate the caps and safeguard against tampering. PCPPI would announce the winning three-digit number daily. For the mechanics of the Number Fever promotion, Vergara referred Pepsi to D.G. Consultores, a Mexican consulting firm that had handled similar promotions in other countries.

Although all caps were imprinted with cash prizes, purchasers wouldn't know whether they had won until the three-digit number was announced. The more caps they collected, the greater their chance of winning. From February 17 to May 8, 1992, Pepsi seeded 60 winning numbers among 5,630 caps. The cash prizes amounted to a total of 25 million pesos ($1 million).

With the winning numbers preselected by computer and only ten 1-million-peso prizes available, the chance of anyone becoming a peso millionaire was one in 28.8 million. but Pepsi drinkers didn't know that. The few Number Fever winners got saturation media coverage, and entire families spent inordinate time and effort collecting tansans, or bottle caps.

Number Fever was an immediate success. It boosted sales and market share of Pepsi products to dizzying heights. Within a month, increased sales covered the $4 million in prize money and advertising costs budgeted for the promotion. By the end of March, six weeks after the start of the promotion, Pepsi products had grabbed a market share of 24.9 percent, the highest for a single month since the share had declined to 14 percent in 1989.

The sizzling success prompted the company to extend Number Fever by five more weeks. D.G. Consultores again predetermined, by computer, 25 winning numbers. The firm was convinced that a nonwinning number in the original promotion period would not come up as a winning number in the extension. It was wrong.

On May 25, Pepsi announced 349 as the winning number for May 26. Later the same night, realizing that as many as 800,000 people could be holding 349 from the first contest, the company backtracked and came out with a new winning number, but it was too late.

Angry crowds began to gather at Pepsi's offices and plants nationwide to collect their prizes. Riots, marked by bottle throwing, erupted. In a matter of hours, the world's most successful product-marketing campaign collapsed.

"I couldn't sleep the night 349 was announced as a winner," recalls Ernesto Santiago, 36, who is married with one child and jobless. He had bottle caps good for 3 million pesos. "I would buy a three-bedroom house. The balance I would use for business, maybe an auto-parts store," he told himself. The next morning, Santiago went to the Pepsi plant in Quezon City. He was surprised to see so many other 349 winners. He sensed a problem. "There has been a mistake," a Pepsi guard told them.

The promotion now threatened disaster for Pepsi. Paying the winners would have cost the company $16 billion, more than the $15-billion market capitalization of all 273 listed issues on the Philippine stock exchange as of June 1992.

Pepsi's first move was to replace 349 as a winning number with a new winning number of 134. This only added to the confusion and rage of the mobs. As a compromise, PCPPI president Rodolfo Salazar suggested that each holder of 349 caps left over from the first promotion be paid 500 pesos. The problem was finding out how many there were. The initial estimate was 600,000. It was assumed half of them would surrender their bottle caps. The estimated cost: $6 million.

The offer was good for only two weeks. As it turned out, about 500,000 winners claimed the 500 pesos, draining the company of $10 million. It was the largest corporate payoff to consumers in Philippine history. Lorenzo asked PepsiCo in New York to refund some of the $10 million. It has refused—so far. In fact, PepsiCo has threatened to pull out of the Philippines completely if made to pay the $10 million or any of the amounts being claimed by 349 cap holders.

Not every 349er has come away empty-handed. Million-peso-cap holder Jowell Roque has scored a singular victory. In 1994, after spending $1,086 in legal and other fees, the 21-year-old nursing student won a lower-court verdict ordering Pepsi to pay him $41,500. It was the first time a claimant had won against the giant multinational. In deciding in Roque's favor, Judge Valentin Cruz faulted Pepsi "for gross negligence in not ensuring that its Number Fever promotion scheme was conducted scrupulously and [was] devoid of mistakes." Pepsi is appealing the ruling.

Two years after the 349 incident, Pepsi officials still didn't know exactly what happened, or if they did know, they were not willing to discuss it fully. One thing seems clear. PCPPI did not instigate or run the promotion. Marketing and promotion were PepsiCo's responsibility. Says Lorenzo: "Our responsibility was production and distribution." The irony is that it is PCPPI that has borne much, if not all, of the public's wrath and the burden of ensuing litigation.

All together, there were more than 60 winners in the Number Fever promotion. Of these, Pepsi says, 18 were paid the top prize of 1 million pesos. However, the company says it can account for the whereabouts of only 12 of the peso millionaires. Many winners have gone into hiding, changed residence, or completely altered their lifestyles.

As for PCPPI, "The worst is over," asserts Lorenzo. "Consumer confidence is back." He says the company has recovered the market share lost as a result of the 349 fiasco. The recovery has come mostly from higher sales of 7-Up, Mountain Dew, and Mirinda orange. The cola brand itself has suffered a decline.

Pepsi has learned its lesson: "There won't be any more Number Fever," says Lorenzo. And the moral of the Pepsi 349 fiasco? "Diligence," says Jesus Celdran, president of Coca-Cola's local bottler. For Pepsi, it has been a costly lesson.

Source: Reprinted in *World Press Review* 41, no. 7 (July 1994), pp. 40–41. Copyright The Stanley Foundation, Muscatine IA 52761 written by: Antonio Lopez, from Asiaweek of Hong Kong.

## QUESTIONS

1. What systems problems are demonstrated in this case? Identify the subsystems involved.
2. What role did the computer play in creating the problems? Were they the fault of the computer or were they management problems?
3. Could a better computer system have prevented or minimized these problems?
4. Could the problem have been prevented by establishing a better methodology? What procedures would be necessary?
5. Would an object-oriented approach to the system have helped prevent the problem?

## CASE *Meridian Oil Corporation*

Meridian Oil Corporation uses a paper and mainframe-based system to track expenses. Robert Hughes, the senior regional operations accountant at the Englewood, Colorado, office is responsible for tracking costs on all Meridian activities in Colorado, Montana, North Dakota, Utah, and Wyoming. Expenses are recorded through purchase orders, sales slips, and invoices. Any time someone in the organization buys an item, the paperwork eventually flows back to Hughes and his staff.

For major projects, the proposals, expenses, and additional paperwork are collected into manila folders and sent to the appropriate departments—drilling, production, facilities, reservoir, accounting, and purchasing—before arriving at Hughes' office. Once projects are approved, clerks continue to add expenses. Corporatewide, Meridian has almost 400 projects open at one time—including some that should have been closed. Given the company's paper orientation and the large number of projects, it is difficult to determine the current status of a project's costs.

Expenses and paperwork are supposed to be tracked by a document known as the authority for expenditure (AFE) form. The AFE is supposed to list all expenses associated with a project to keep central management informed of the status of each project. Hughes is supposed to close out an AFE within 120 days of the project's completion. His staff is then supposed to do a comparison between estimated and actual costs. But he notes that "no one ever gets around to reviewing AFE costs." Additionally, because the AFE is paper-based, it is next to impossible to know where it (and the manila folder) is at any time.

Mark Hummel is a senior staff analyst who maintains 120 personal computers at the Englewood offices. He notes that there are additional problems with the current system:

People want to know if we've completed the requirements for drilling. Have we got the property staked? Have we got the drilling permit? All these things fall within the AFE tracking process, but there's no way to get a quick answer. The AFE could be sitting on a desk in operations and no one would know.

In terms of hardware, Meridian Oil Corporation has a relatively modern information system. For example, all of the personal computers in the Englewood office are connected with a local area network, which is also connected to the firm's IBM 3090 mainframe in Forth Worth, Texas. The personal computers all run Microsoft Windows applications including Word, Excel, and Powerpoint.

The problem is not really an issue of hardware and software. Any solution must revolve around the flow of the information. Consider the travels of a manila folder:

1. A drilling engineer researches a site and writes a report on the chances of successfully drilling that site. The report takes two to five days to create (not counting research).
2. The report is sent to the drilling, production, and facilities offices where it is handled by specific employees. They need the form for only

two hours, but it can sit in an in-basket for several days.

3. The engineer creates a drilling plan and makes preliminary estimates of the costs. This step takes two to five days.
4. A secretary types up the four-page base authority for expenditure (AFE) form. The process takes only 30 minutes but might sit on a desk for several days.
5. The drilling operations manager reviews and signs the AFE. It is then sent to the reservoir department. The review takes about one hour, but it can take days for the manager to get to the form.
6. The reservoir department files for drilling permits and handles other legal paperwork. It records the permits on the AFE. Depending on the drilling site, this step can take two days to two months.
7. The reservoir manager signs the AFE and returns it to drilling. Again, it only takes an hour to review but might sit for several days.
8. The drilling engineer verifies the cost estimates, signs the AFE, and forwards it to accounting. The review takes about one hour, but delays can push it to days.
9. The accountant enters the AFE into the mainframe accounting system, where it is assigned a project ID number. The data entry takes about 20 minutes, but forms often stack up for days.
10. The accountant routes copies of the completed AFE to all departments, a step that formally opens the project. At this point, money can be drawn and spent on the project. It takes two to three days for the copies to reach the departments.

SOURCE: Adapted from Alice LaPlante, "Where Have All the Profits Gone?," *PC World* 12, no. 6 (June 1994), pp. 179–184. Reprinted with the permission of PC World Communications, Inc.

### QUESTIONS

1. What are the goals and objectives of the system needed by Meridian Oil Corporation?
2. Draw a data flow diagram to illustrate the process of opening a project.
3. Expand the data flow diagram to include tracking actual expenses after the project has been opened.
4. Expand the data flow diagram to show the reports and access needed by Hughes' department.
5. Identify basic systems problems experienced by Meridian Oil Corp.
6. If the system is automated, can anything be done about the delays when the AFE is left sitting in an in-box?

7. Create an object-oriented design for the system envisioned by Mr. Hughes. (Define the base classes with initial attributes and methods.)
8. Assuming someone was hired to build an automated AFE system, how would you test the new system?

### CASE *Kickin Cookies*

As a consultant, you just received a call from this midsize company that manufactures cookies. Your initial research reveals that the company is organized in five divisions: manufacturing, purchasing, sales, distribution, and corporate management. For years, manufacturing was the heart of the company. Management goals consisted of keeping manufacturing running as efficiently as possible and creating high-quality cookies. In the early years, marketing consisted of a small group of salespeople who traveled to new stores to convince them to carry the products. As the company grew, there was never any difficulty in selling all of the output produced by manufacturing. Because of the emphasis on quality, the distribution system emphasized rapid delivery and stored products just long enough to consolidate shipments—never more than two weeks. The salespeople fill out order forms that are collected by the marketing department and forwarded to distribution. Manufacturing keeps track of daily production runs and forwards the totals to corporate accounting. Maintenance, labor, and miscellaneous costs are collected for the monthly accounting statements. Manufacturing sends requirement lists and inventory statements to the purchasing department every week. Purchasing keeps track of monthly usage and orders raw materials based on these patterns. Purchase orders are sent to the suppliers, who return confirmation notices. Production lists and estimated production targets for the following month are sent to marketing. Marketing collects shipment data from distribution and produces sales reports that are sent to corporate management.

You were called to help solve some major problems. The company has grown large enough so that it can no longer sell all that it produces. The distribution department finds that it often has cookies sitting in warehouses for more than five weeks. Some of the salespeople have talked the warehouse managers into shipping these products to special stores at discount prices. These sales are being reported directly to the accountants as *loss leaders* to avoid the quality control reviewers in the marketing department. To control some of the production problems, management has asked the marketing and distribution departments to produce monthly sales and inventory estimates and send them to manufacturing.

The manufacturing manager looks at the inventory levels and believes that the marketing reports are way too low, so production levels are still too high. Three months ago, corporate managers were concerned about the losses in the last few quarters. By comparing purchase lists to sales, they see a trend toward excessive use (or waste) of ingredients. As a result, they ordered purchasing to cut costs and reduce the amount of ingredients they buy. Now, the production manager is complaining about not having enough ingredients available. He has been using special orders, with next-day delivery to keep production up. When corporate managers saw the latest quarterly reports, sales were still down, production was up, but costs had doubled. That's when

they decided to call you. They have promised a major bonus if you can solve their problems within a month.

## QUESTIONS

1. Draw a data flow diagram to illustrate the system and the various inputs and outputs. Use a different color (or line style) for the changes that have occurred in the last year.
2. What systems problems are illustrated in this company?
3. How can the company's problems be solved? Draw another diagram to show how data should flow in this company.

## DISCUSSION ISSUE

### Resistance to Change

Changing the way an organization operates can have many repercussions. Sometimes it is difficult to decide which effects are important and which ones are major. Similarly, many people dislike change, simply because it creates short-term problems and forces alterations in their lives. Any new plan faces these problems and more. Sometimes even more than planning, overcoming these objections requires persuasion. Listen to a typical conversation at a company that distributes musical merchandise.

Jake:  We've got this great idea! We can put the team together and sell direct to the consumers. We'll computerize the entire inventory system and install an order-entry system that can be accessed with telephones or personal computers.

Elwood:  Sure, Jake, that way customers can buy directly from us, skipping the retail outlets.

Jake:  Yeah, Elwood. It'll be great. We'll be able to charge lower prices and still make more money. In addition, we'll know exactly what's hot and what's not selling. No more messing around with sales estimates. We'll have the exact numbers.

Aretha:  I don't know, you'd better think about your actions. Think!

Lou:  Aretha's right. We're not set up to handle the direct distribution. Besides, from my sales experience, most customers like to have their purchases immediately.

Jake:  We've got that worked out, Lou. We'll use overnight delivery to get them the stuff the

next morning. In the worst case, they have to wait maybe 20 hours.

Elwood:  Plus, for new music, we're planning ahead for some new tricks.

Jake:  That's right. With our computer system, the customers can listen to a few cuts over the phone before they decide. That's more than they can do in any retail store. Even better, with the new recordable disks, we could transfer the data directly over the phone to their disks. We collect the money up front, the customers get to sample the music, and they get copies immediately.

Aretha:  I'm not convinced, Jake. What about the costs? We need a huge new computer system. Plus, someone has to pay for these phone calls. What's to stop people from tying up a phone line for hours listening to different cuts?

Jake:  Those are minor details. Once we get the computer system in, we can program anything we want. We can limit the length of each call. With the new phone services, we can even place limits on the number of calls we accept from each phone number to stop repeat callers who don't buy anything.

Murph:  But what's going to happen to the distribution department? We've got salespeople, managers, and a big shipping department . . .

Elwood:  Well, if Aretha's really worried about costs, we can save a ton of money by cutting most of those departments.

Murph: But some of those people have been with us for 15 years. I'm not being sentimental, but those folks have a lot of knowledge and experience that we shouldn't just toss out.

Jake: Hey, hey. We're not just going to throw people away. In fact, after two years, we'll probably be bigger than we are now. We'll need all of those people. They'll just be doing different things.

Aretha: Sure, Jake. *If* your plan works. *If* the retailers don't get too upset. *If* the customers actually want to buy products this way. *If* we can get the workers retrained. *If* our competitors don't cut prices and knock us out of business. Then maybe we'll be better off. It sounds too risky to me.

Murph: She's got a point, Jake. If this plan fails, we're dead. Besides millions in costs, we'll lose sales. Even worse, we'll never get back into the retail stores. They'll be so upset at us that they'll never carry our products again. We have to be careful.

Aretha: Isn't there some way we can do this without betting the entire company?

Jake: Come on, folks. We have to be bold! Think about the future. We have a chance to be the first and the best. Opportunities like this don't come along every day. We need a positive outlook.

## QUESTIONS

1. Are Aretha and Murph being overly cautious, or are their comments correct?
2. Is there a way to tell whether people's comments are serious or people are merely worried about jobs and resisting change? (Hint: Does it matter?)
3. If you were running this company, would you take the risk and go with Jake and Elwood's plan?
4. What additional information might you want to collect?
5. What other problems might be encountered? Are there additional benefits?

CHAPTER 4

# Operations and Transactions

## WHAT WILL YOU LEARN IN THIS CHAPTER?

What are operations-level decisions? What are the roles of a transaction-processing system? Why are they so important? What problems are encountered when you are processing transactions? How does MIS support two primary operations: accounting and human resources? How does transaction processing provide support for the entire organization?

Transaction data. As a leading retailer, Sears recognizes the importance of collecting quality data and automating the transaction processing system.

## SEARS AND ELECTRONIC DATA INTERCHANGE

Sears, Roebuck, and Company put $5 million into a program to convert all of its suppliers to using electronic data interchange (EDI) by the end of 1992. EDI is a process of placing and paying for all orders from suppliers through an information system. Sears justified this expenditure by noting that it eliminated paper and the cost of its maintenance throughout the ordering process. Sears also asserted that EDI would reduce errors and lead to a reduction in staff.

Retail organizations like Sears went through several difficult years, beginning in the mid-1980s. On the low end, sales were squeezed by the rapid expansion of discounters—especially Wal-Mart, with its huge stores. On the higher end, sales were lost to the increased number of specialty stores, including specialty mail-order firms.

Sears and similar organizations tried many different approaches in an attempt to increase sales. In the end, they were forced to restructure their organizations. An important change was the need to reduce overhead and decrease sales costs.

**OVERVIEW**　Every business must perform certain basic tasks. Figure 4.1 illustrates that they keep track of sales and bill customers, monitor and pay employees, record expenses, and order supplies. The data collected from these transactions is also used to make all of the other decisions in the firm. If there are major mistakes in these day-to-day operations, the company will not survive. Because of the tremendous amounts of data involved, we need to carefully organize the collection and use of transaction data.

Most companies already have computerized transaction-processing systems. As a manager, you most likely will not be asked to create a new system. However, there are many times when you will have to evaluate the existing system to locate problems. You will also be asked to suggest improvements, both to decrease costs and to provide better information. It is particularly important to re-evaluate transaction systems when a company is changing—growing rapidly or undergoing structural changes through re-engineering.

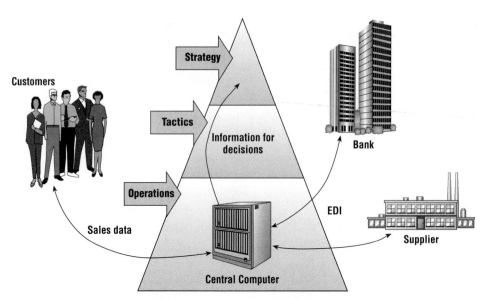

The key to collecting data is to capture it as close to the source as possible, with techniques such as point-of-sale data collection, process control, and electronic data interchange. Collecting data is a straightforward job that computers have performed for years. However, using computers does not guarantee the data will always be correct. As a manager, you have to understand the importance of maintaining the integrity of the data. Factors that complicate the task of collecting and maintaining accurate data include multiple users, huge quantities of data, summarization, and time requirements.

Because of the importance of transaction data, accounting systems were one of the earliest tasks that were computerized. In many companies, financial data collection is still the largest focus of MIS. To understand the potential opportunities and problems and how MIS helps organizations, it is important to understand some elements of accounting. Human resource management is a second area that heavily uses transaction processing. Both situations illustrate the importance of collecting, storing, and protecting key information for any company.

## INTRODUCTION

All decisions require information, but this information does not simply materialize. It must be collected, stored, and maintained. These activities take place at the operations level of the firm and are called **transaction processing.** Whenever two people make an exchange, it is called a *transaction*. Transactions are important events for a company. Examples include: making a purchase at a store, withdrawing money from a checking account, making a payment to a creditor, or paying an employee. Data from these events needs to be saved for future use. The firm needs to keep this information because transactions involve other people. Imagine what would happen if you bought an item from someone, but that person later stated that you did not pay the full amount due. Your records of the transaction would help you prove that you did indeed buy the item. The first step for computers in any firm is to capture and store this basic data. The computers also must provide a way to retrieve data and produce reports so the data is useful to decision makers. Of course the hard part is knowing which data will be needed in the future.

### ◤ TRENDS ◢

Because of legal ramifications, businesses have always collected data about transactions. Paper documents have been stored for years. Even today, copies of important transactions are kept on paper. Paper records cause problems. It takes time to make copies, they require large amounts of storage space, and they deteriorate over time. More importantly, it is difficult to use the data contained in paper records. Imagine the work involved if all sales records are on paper and you want to compute annual sales totals for each salesperson.

Accounting systems were created to generate information from the transaction data. With a paper system, transactions are recorded in a daily journal and posted to a general ledger. The accounting profession has designed reports (e.g., balance sheets and income statements) that are routinely created from this data.

Businesses quickly recognized the value of using computers to process transactions. The *back-office tasks* of computing sales totals and posting information to the accounting ledger were viewed as important uses for the computer. They were also easy to computerize. Through the 1960s, most business computers were primarily producing basic accounting reports. Raw data was punched into the computer by hand, and the computer produced totals and updated the general ledger. In effect, the computer was used as a giant calculator to automate the production of printed reports that were structured as they were before the advent of computers. The primary reason for using the computer was speed and accuracy. It was justified because it was cheaper and less error-prone than hiring thousands of people to produce the reports.

As computer capabilities increased in the 1970s, the role of the computer also increased. In transaction-processing systems, the most important change was to use the computer to collect the raw data. In retail sales, the cash register was replaced with a computer terminal and a bar code scanner. Whenever a customer purchased an item, the transaction data was immediately sent to the main computer. This automation eliminated the need to hire a person to enter the data at the end of the day. Together with fewer errors, these *online* transaction systems provided better service to the customer. Because sales were recorded immediately, the sales clerk could quickly determine whether an item was in stock. The systems also provided virtually instantaneous sales data to the managers. If some item was selling rapidly, the system could tell the employees to restock that item on the shelves.

The 1980s resulted in even more integration. Most of the changes occurred in the way data was processed into information. The largest transaction-processing change was the dramatic drop in hardware prices. This change enabled more businesses to use computers to process transactions with computers. Today, almost all businesses use computers to keep track of their transactions and produce reports and information from that data.

Several **change-drivers** have started as data-collection tools and expanded to alter the firms and industries that used them. Classic examples include: bar code scanners in retail stores, hand-held miniterminals or notebook computers by delivery firms and salespeople, and reservation systems by the travel and entertainment industries.

From the standpoint of how executives manage a company, transaction data has even more uses. Most transactions occur between the company and people outside the company (e.g., customers, suppliers, and competitors). Hence, transactions provide a way to measure the progress of the company. Companies are often measured by the amount of sales (customer transactions), costs (payments to suppliers), and market share (compared to competitors). All of this information is used to show managers the status of the company and identify where problems exist. It is used to make decisions regarding day-to-day operations as well as setting future directions for the firm.

Firms also have many internal transactions. All companies keep records on employee evaluations and promotions. Larger companies produce products in various divisions and need to track orders and shipments among the divisions. Sometimes companies use a *chargeback* system to allocate managerial costs among departments. This internal data is needed for legal purposes, and it is used to make decisions within each department.

Looking at internal processes, accounting and human resources are two subsystems in every company that make heavy use of transaction-processing systems. They also demonstrate the importance of integrating transaction data throughout the company.

## THE VALUE AND COST OF INFORMATION

Virtually any data could be collected by a company; however, it would be absurd to measure and save every piece of data. For example, it is technically possible to monitor exactly where every employee is located at every minute. But why would you want this data? It costs money to collect and store data. In addition, the more data you have, the more difficult it is to find the specific pieces that you need. The goal is to collect data that will be useful. How do you know today what data will be useful tomorrow or next year? One method that is often used to answer this question is to look at the types of decisions that companies make.

Transaction processing highlights the difference between data and information. Numbers that are collected and stored are raw data. When managers make decisions, they retrieve data and process it to provide pertinent information. If you collected all the sales transactions for a retail store, the data would simply be stored as a collection of numbers. Perhaps a manager wishes to evaluate a particular store. The manager might examine the sales level for the last five years. The computer would accumulate all the sales **data** to produce the totals for each year. The resulting **information** might show a downward trend that would lead to a decision to emphasize a different approach or to close the store. The value of information is its ability to improve decisions.

For the store-closing example, you might ask how we chose to look at five years of data. Why not more? The answer is that we always face a trade-off. Collecting more data might lead to more accurate forecasts, but it is expensive to collect, store, and analyze extensive amounts of data. Also, beyond some point, additional data merely serves to confirm the results; it does not really provide more value. Perhaps with five years' data, we can forecast sales within 10 percent. Adding more data might improve the forecast to 7 percent. In many cases, the difference will not affect our decisions, so it would not be worth the cost. Of course, all of these details are difficult to evaluate ahead of time.

One method of making decisions has been formalized with the use of statistics. When you perform tests of hypotheses, you are making a decision. As displayed in Figure 4.2, a simple hypothesis test begins by assuming the mean is at some level (e.g., zero). All tests are subject to error. A Type I error arises when you reject a null hypothesis that is actually true. You select the probability that this event will occur, which leads to the choice of a critical test value. You then gather the data and estimate basic parameters. If your test value falls above the critical level, you would reject the null hypothesis.

A second type of error can arise: You might accept (fail to reject) the null hypothesis when it is actually false. In the example, the true mean might be equal to five, but your data leads you to believe the mean is zero. The probability of this Type II

**FIGURE 4.2**
More information decreases errors. Any statistical test risks two types of errors. Changing the critical value simply trades off between the two errors. With more information, the distribution narrows and the probability of making either type of error decreases. But it costs money to acquire additional information.

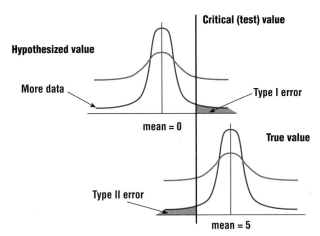

error is measured as the area under the curve to the left of the critical value in the distribution for the mean equal to five.

One fundamental theory in statistics states *for a given amount of information,* if you attempt to decrease the probability of one type of error, the probability of committing the other type of error will increase. This problem can be observed by moving the critical value line to the left or right. As the area under one of the solid curves decreases, the area under the other one will increase. However, if you collect more information by increasing the number of observations, the underlying curve will change to the (tighter) dotted line shown in the graphs. In this case, the probability of both errors decreases to the shaded areas. Statistically, you can make better decisions by increasing the amount of information. Of course, from a business standpoint, the next question you encounter is: How much does it cost to acquire the additional information and what are the potential gains?

The problem with determining the value of information is that we must collect data before we need it to make decisions. So, you have to know what decisions you might face and estimate the information needed. Because we cannot see into the future very well, most firms identify the core decisions they continually face and collect data to support those decisions. There are basic decisions and data that are used by every firm.

**DECISION LEVELS**   Managers require information to make decisions. The goal of any information system is to provide the correct information at the right time in the proper format.

Business decisions can be classified into three major categories: strategy, tactics, and operations. These levels are often displayed as the pyramid shown in Figure 4.3. MIS has created software categories that support each of these types of decisions, as shown on the enhanced pyramid.

## Business Operations

Business operations appear at the bottom of Figure 4.3's pyramid. These operations form the foundation of the business. Without this level, the business cannot survive. For example, a business needs sales to stay alive and grow. Transaction-processing systems were created to support this level of business. Without transaction processing, the rest of the MIS cannot survive. This fundamental information is used to support all of the other decisions and computer systems in the company.

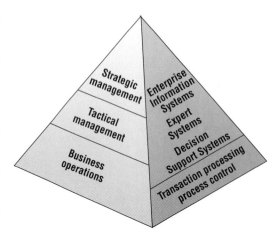

Transactions are the most common activity at the operations level. They happen on a day-to-day basis. The decisions that need to be made are short term. They affect only limited areas of the business. In a retail store, the manager needs to schedule employees and restock shelves. These decisions have to be made every day (sometimes weekly), and involve detailed data on sales.

In a factory that manufactures products such as L'eggs (Reality Bytes 4–1), there are many operational decisions such as controlling inventory and monitoring quality. A special class of software designed for factory operations is called **process control** software.

---

 **Reality Bytes**     **4–1   L'EGGS**

A part of the Sara Lee Corporation, L'eggs manufactures pantyhose and distributes them through a unique distribution system in grocery and drug stores. L'eggs installed a sophisticated computer system in an effort to encourage sales, reduce inventory, shorten product life cycles, and decentralize decision making. In its first year, the revamped distribution and manufacturing system was credited with saving the company $110 million.

In the factory, hand-held computers help speed the transfer of pantyhose from the manufacturing line to the trucks for shipping. This greatly reduces the costs normally associated with warehousing. This is in keeping with L'eggs' goal of a seamless work flow in which manufacturing was combined into one functional unit. This combination also greatly reduced the cost of overhead for the company.

---

Many production operations are performed by robots and other automated machines. Process control such as the stamping and assembly operations of Ford Escort (Reality Bytes 4–2) enables these machines to be monitored and controlled with a central computer. These activities generate large amounts of data and require special software to handle the volume and coordinate the various machines. Most of this data is useful on a day-to-day basis. Summaries (such as quality measures) may be kept for later analysis and comparison.

Many projects at the operations level are installed to reduce costs or improve speed in transaction handling. Massachusetts Mutual Insurance (Reality Bytes 4–3) is one example of how an operations-level system saved the company money.

**Reality Bytes**   4–2  Fᴏʀᴅ Eꜱᴄᴏʀᴛ Pʀᴏᴅᴜᴄᴛɪᴏɴ

The Ford Escort production plant in Wayne, Michigan, has become the first facility to combine the stamping and assembly operations. Almost all of the body welding will be done by automatic or robot welders.

To bring the identification and handling functions closer to just-in-time application, items and parts are assigned a three-digit code. When a particular part is scheduled for production, a supervisor inputs that part's three-digit number into the computer. Based on the code entered into the computer, blanking presses are automatically adjusted for the part to be pressed.

 **Reality Bytes**   4–3  Mᴀꜱꜱᴀᴄʜᴜꜱᴇᴛᴛꜱ Mᴜᴛᴜᴀʟ Iɴꜱᴜʀᴀɴᴄᴇ

Massachusetts Mutual Insurance is a $5 billion insurance company. During 1988–1990, it installed a new life and health claims adjudication system. Within several months of installation, the company was able to process 10–12 percent more claims with 35–40 percent fewer staff members. Thus, the investment in information services provided a significant cost savings with a measurable impact on the bottom line.

## Tactical Management

Tactical-level decisions affect the way the firm operates, but not to the depth of strategic changes. These decisions can change the operations of the firm without changing its overall structure. Figure 4.4 highlights the differences between the three levels. To understand the tactical level, consider a retail firm that sells bicycles. The owner/manager might be facing a decision of whether to specialize in a different line of bicycles. To make this decision, the manager of the store needs to evaluate several types of information. This information could include sales of the different bikes in the store for the last few years and the cost of the bikes. The manager would also consider comments from the customers and knowledge about the bicycle industry. Much of this information comes from the transaction records that have been stored in the computer. There are computer tools to help analyze this type of

**FIGURE 4.4**
Each decision level affects the firm in different ways. Each level uses and produces different types of information.

| Decision Level | Description | Example | Type of Information |
|---|---|---|---|
| Strategic | Competitive advantage, become a market leader. Long-term outlook. | New product that will change the industry. | External events, rivals, sales, costs quality, trends. |
| Tactical | Improving operations without restructuring the company. | New tools to cut costs or improve efficiency. | Expenses, schedules, sales, models, forecasts. |
| Operations | Day-to-day actions to keep the company functioning. | Scheduling employees, ordering supplies. | Transactions, accounting, human resource management, inventory. |

data. They are called *decision support systems (DSS)* and they are described in detail in Chapters 8 and 9.

## Strategic Management

Decisions at the strategic level alter the structure of the business and are typically designed to change the entire industry. They involve relations with external agents, such as customers, suppliers, competitors, and the government. The decisions affect the long-run future of the firm. Most of the time they are unstructured decisions. They are hard to solve and involve descriptive information, which can be hard to measure and capture.

In the example of the retail bicycle store, the owner might decide that it is time to stop selling bicycles and switch to selling motorcycles. Clearly basic sales and profit information are useful in making this decision. However, the owner also needs to estimate the long-run prospects in the bicycle and motorcycle industries. These forecasts are often hard to make because there is no accurate information available. Decision support systems play an important role by collecting, analyzing, and presenting alternatives. *Enterprise information systems* (EIS) that are used to make it easier for executives to access the data are explained in Chapter 8.

**DATA CAPTURE**    The basic components of a transaction-processing system are illustrated in Figure 4.5. The focus is twofold: accomplishing the transaction and capturing data. Data capture consists of gathering or acquiring data from the firm's operations and storing data in the computer system. Entering data into the computer can be time consuming and difficult. For instance, banks have invested heavily in automating the collection and recording of transaction data. Yet, because many transactions are based on paper, they still spend considerable time entering data. First, tellers enter the data into their terminals. Then a bank staff reads the dollar value written on checks and deposit slips. They work through the night, typing the amount into a machine that codes the number on the bottom of the check so it can be read by other computers. Automated

**FIGURE 4.5**

Data that is captured at the operations level is used throughout the firm to make decisions. If there are problems in the data or in providing access to the data, all of the decisions will suffer.

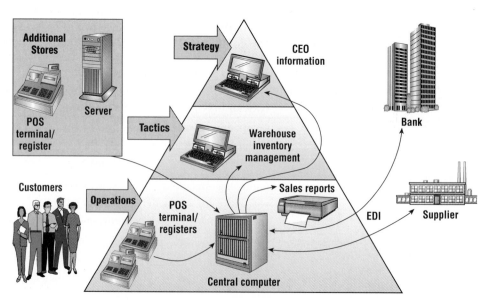

teller machines (ATMs) and debit cards save some of these steps, because the customer enters the initial numbers directly into the computer. Although the numbers must still be verified by an employee, the American Bank Association estimated that it costs banks $1 to process every check, but only $0.50 to process ATM transactions. In 1995, several banks, led by *Citicorp*, dropped all customer fees for electronic transactions but levied fees on teller-assisted transactions.

As the volume of transactions increased, businesses like Super Valu Stores (Reality Bytes 4–4) looked for faster and more accurate ways to get data into the computer. There are three basic methods to collect data, depending on its source. The data-collection method consumers are most familiar with is **point of sale (POS),** where the sales register is actually a computer terminal that sends all of the data to a central computer. On assembly lines, robots and manufacturing equipment can collect data, such as quality control measures, and return it to a computer. Typically the computer also can send control instructions to these machines. This exchange of data between manufacturing machines and computers is known as *process control.* The third way to collect data automatically involves the exchange of information with organizations outside the firm, especially suppliers and customers. Instead of dealing with paper records such as purchase orders, it is possible to send orders electronically through a process called **electronic data interchange (EDI).**

EDI represents a computer connection between various companies. Sometimes the connection is a private link between two companies; in other cases it can involve a network that connects computers between several firms.

---

### Reality Bytes ◤ 4–4 Super Valu Stores and EDI

Electronic data interchange (EDI) is a means of transferring data between suppliers and customers via direct transfers between computers instead of using paper order forms and invoices. Companies have focused on EDI for invoices, purchase orders, shipping notices, and payments. Robert Payne, an EDI consultant, estimates that it costs $10,000 to $20,000 in fixed costs to set up a basic EDI system. There are also monthly transmission costs that average $0.55 to $0.90 per transaction.

Super Valu Stores, a grocery chain headquartered in Minneapolis, reduces costs because of the chain's sheer size. The stores place about 6,000 purchase orders and receive almost 5,000 invoices every week.

Along with the cost savings from reduced paperwork, EDI speeds up the ordering process for Super Valu. The electronic system also provides better information for the company. Jeff Girard, the CFO of Super Valu, notes that without EDI, "If we order 5,000 boxes of an item that will be a special at the store, and the vendor can only deliver 4,000 boxes, we might not find out we're 1,000 short until the order is delivered and we've already put out the promotions. Once confirmations are done on EDI, we'll be able to get this information within hours of placing the order and can modify our approaches accordingly."

---

### Point of Sale

Several devices have been created to capture data at the point of the sale. Some companies rely on keyboards to enter data, but high-volume areas have switched to bar code scanners. All consumers are familiar with bar code scanners that read the universal product codes (UPCs). The scanner reads the code and sends it to the computer, which looks up the corresponding name and price. The computer prints the receipt, stores the sale information and automatically decreases the inventory count.

### Reality Bytes     4–5     STANFORD UNIVERSITY USES BAR CODES TO SECURE FACILITIES DURING THE WORLD CUP GAMES

The security force at Stanford University normally uses approximately 1,000 pieces of security equipment. During the 1994 World Cup Games, the University purchased 8,000 more items as well as borrowed 9,000 from the U.S. Department of Defense.

To track more than 18,000 pieces of equipment, the Department of Public Safety introduced a bar code-based inventory system. Bar-coded check-in/check-out cards were issued to more than 400 security personnel. This enabled the cards as well as the equipment to be laser scanned when items were checked out of the repository. Data was then fed to other personal computers to compare to the book quantities. A bar-coded wall chart provided additional information on equipment movement.

The system facilitated the return of the borrowed Department of Defense equipment at the end of the games.

As demonstrated by Stanford University (Reality Bytes 4–5) and CoreStates (Reality Bytes 4–6), bar codes can be used to track virtually any type of equipment.

Another type of scanner is used by the U.S. Postal System, which uses **optical character recognition (OCR)** to read handwritten zip codes, allowing mail to be processed and sorted faster. Even so, the Post Office hires thousands of workers to type in data that the scanners cannot read. Banks use a process called **magnetic ink character recognition (MICR)** to process checks and deposit slips. MICR readers are more accurate than straight OCR because they pick up a stronger signal from magnetic particles in the ink. A few companies are using voice recognition technology to enable workers to enter data by speaking to the computer. Voice recognition enables the users to enter data while leaving their hands free to do something else.

Several advantages arise from using automated data entry. Directly capturing data means fewer errors occur because the machines make fewer mistakes. Sometimes it

### Reality Bytes     4–6     BANKING ADDS ACCOUNTABLE MAIL

CoreStates Financial replaced its traditional mail system with a new system that will track bar-coded items, including packages shipped through Federal Express, UPS, and Priority Mail. Even more important are the statistics that the system gathers. It can measure performance; describe short- and long-term trends; support remote locations; and provide real-time, online responses to inquiries.

This new system is particularly important given the fact that the bank has 13,000 employees and is spread across six buildings. Originally, the system was designed to track "accountable specials" or time-sensitive interdepartmental mail. The system was then expanded to track registered mail, Federal Express, and UPS.

Installation was started in the mail hub in late February 1994 and rolled out to the remote locations during the ensuing year. Procedurally, a manifest is made for each piece of accountable mail that arrives at the CoreStates' mail hub. On arrival, the mail is given a bar code and scanned into the system.

Accountable mail originating inside the company is also marked with a bar coded sticker from an internally produced, five-part form. It is then sorted into six lockable tubs bound for the six different remote sites. To aid in delivery, each tub is also bar-coded. The tub is scanned again when it is locked and ready to send. An electronic packing list is then generated and transmitted over the wide area network to the destination site.

## Reality Bytes    4–7    Frito-Lay

Frito-Lay is preparing 75 local area networks in its worldwide regional offices to run customized versions of its mainframe-based Executive Information System. The system includes specialized decision support systems tailored to the local needs of management. The simplified version runs on 10,000 hand-held computers used by sales personnel. A Briefing Book module uses maps and charts to break down information by territory. The module asks for and provides informa-tion according to a number of interdependent sales variables.

The Frito-Lay sales department estimates that the hand-held computers alone save more than $20 million a year. Vice-President Charles Feld reasoned that, with the information system, Frito-Lay can track every bag of chips as it moves through any store. With similar systems in manufacturing and distribution, the system can produce data on any aspect of the company.

is not easy to collect data at the source. Consider the situation of Frito-Lay (Reality Bytes 4–7), where information at the point of sale needs to be gathered by thousands of salespeople at customer locations. Frito-Lay turned to portable scanners carried by salespeople.

POS systems also have built-in error detection methods to make certain the numbers are read correctly. By collecting the data immediately, it is easier to find and correct mistakes. If a clerk using a POS system enters an incorrect product number (or the scanner reads it incorrectly), the error can be caught immediately.

With POS data collection, the computer performs all necessary computations immediately. Hence, the job is easier for clerks and fewer errors occur. For example, a retail store might give discounts to certain customers. With a POS system, the employees do not have to keep track of the customers or discounts, because the computer can look up the discounts and apply them automatically. Similarly, prices are maintained and changed by the computer. To hold a sale, you simply change the price in the computer (one place) and put up a new sign. Of course, when there are thousands of items and prices, there are still plenty of opportunities for errors.

POS systems also can provide better service to customers. Because the sales data is captured immediately, the managers and clerks always know the inventory levels. If a customer calls to learn whether a product is in stock, the clerk can instantly determine the answer. With most systems, it is possible to tell the computer to hold that item until the customer picks it up. Some companies even connect their store computers together. If you find that one store has run out of a particular item, the clerk can quickly check the other stores in the area and tell them to hold the item for you.

A few companies even enable customers to bypass the clerks entirely. Taco Bell is experimenting with a touch-screen order system. Customers place their orders by touching items on the screen. When the order is entered, the customer pays a clerk. However, it would be straightforward to set up the kiosks to accept bank debit cards. Mail-order companies use a similar type of system but have phone order clerks to answer questions and enter the data. Similarly, a growing number of companies enable you to shop from home by using electronic networks such as Prodigy, CompuServe, and the Internet.

In addition to providing better data collection, POS systems can enable companies to collect new data and implement new strategies. For example, it is now easier for stores to offer their own credit cards. Credit cards offer three main advantages. First, the store will not have to pay the transaction cost (1 percent to 5 percent of the

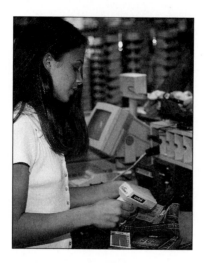

Sales data. Collecting transaction data at the point of sale ensures accurate data, speeds transactions, and provides up-to-the-minute data to managers.

sale) to a national card company. Second, in-store cards can encourage repeat business from customers. Third, the store can associate sales data with specific customers. Combining this data with geographic and demographic data enables the store to target markets for promotions and new products.

## Process Control

Manufacturing firms often deal with a different type of data. Most factories use machines that can be connected to each other and to computers. The computers can exchange data with the production machines. If you want to alter your product, you would need to change the manufacturing settings on several different machines. If the production line has 10 machines, each with five control items that need to be set, it could take several hours to reset the entire production line. Even a minor change in the product means that someone has to set each of the machines correctly. By connecting the machines to a computer, the computer can store all of the appropriate settings. When you make a change in the product, the computer sends the correct settings to all the machines. As indicated by Rocco Turkeys (Reality Bytes 4–8), computers are often used to monitor the progress of the production line. The data is used to identify problem spots and to help the firm meet production goals. Figure 4.6 illustrates the basic concept that the individual machines are controlled from one loca-

 **Reality Bytes**      4–8   Rocco Turkeys, Inc.

Rocco Turkeys, Inc. in Dayton, Virginia, uses light-emitting diode (LED) displays to regulate the progression of turkeys along the poultry processing production line. Before the computerized checking device was put in place, variances in performance at the different stations caused the production line to be either clogged or waiting for more turkeys. Because the primary production line consisted of 10 processing sta-

tions before the final packing location, the LED display indicated the production goal in bagged output for the day and the previous hour. It also calculated the percentage of the goal achieved. Using these scanners and variance controls, deviations in the processing flow were smoothed out to make the production of the processed turkeys more efficient.

**FIGURE 4.6**

Process control is the control of production machines from centralized computers. The computers monitor data from the machines and make continuous adjustments. The central control enables designers to specify all production settings from one location.

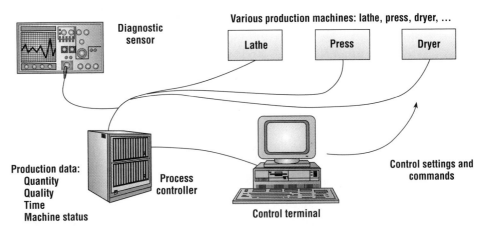

tion. Although the concept seems simple, factories have found it difficult to carry out this idea on a large scale.

Technology also can be used to collect data from manufacturing machines. With this communication, the computer can constantly monitor production levels. Managers can keep track of hourly and daily production, and even track individual products. If a customer wants to check on the progress of a special order, the manager can determine how much of the product has been produced and when it is likely to be completed.

Process control computers can also be used to monitor quality in the manufacturing process. Sensors can automatically measure almost any characteristic. They can check for items such as thickness, weight, strength, color, and size. These measurements can then be passed to a computer. If the computer notices a trend or a major problem, it can notify the operators. In some operations, the computer can send messages to the machine causing the problem and reset its controls to correct the problem automatically.

Two basic difficulties exist with process control. First, the large number of machines makes it difficult to establish standards, making it harder to connect the various machines together. Second, production machines can produce an enormous amount of data. Some machines can generate billions of bytes of data per hour. This large amount of data requires efficient communication lines, high-speed computers, and a large storage capacity. Despite these complications, process control can provide enormous advantages. It enables companies to change production processes and alter products faster and more often. It provides better information and control over quality. It enable manufacturers to create products that match the needs of individual customers: mass customization.

## Electronic Data Interchange (EDI)

EDI is a form of automated data input that supports operations by transferring documents between firms electronically. The essence of EDI is the ability to transfer data among computers from different companies. There are two basic methods to accomplish the transfer: (1) send the data directly from one computer to the other or (2) send the data to a third party that consolidates the data and sends it to the proper location. Early EDI implementations were based on direct connections as individual firms experimented with the technology. In both methods, there are two important considerations: establishing the physical links and transferring data in a format compatible to all users.

**Reality Bytes**     **4–9   GM EDI**

General Motors can electronically send a purchase order to USX Corporation to order steel for automobile production. The GM computer simply calls the USX computer on the phone and transmits the basic information. The USX computer then notifies the shipping department, which then ships out the desired items and records the shipment in the USX computer. The USX computer calls the GM computer to notify it of the shipment. The USX system also sends a bill electronically to the GM computer. After the GM computer receives the bill, it calls the bank's computer and tells the bank to transfer the necessary money to the USX account. These electronic transfers can occur without any human intervention.

SOURCE: "Automobile Industry Looks to ERP Solutions," *EDI News*, April 23, 1996, p. 3159480.

For EDI to work, each company must translate its data into a form that can be used by the other companies. If one company like Sears or GM (Reality Bytes 4-9) takes the lead and requires suppliers to send data via EDI, then they are free to define the base transaction objects. Suppliers must translate their objects into the appropriate EDI structure. Yet, a supplier might need links to several customers. If each customer used different EDI definitions, the supplier must have a conversion system for each link. Someday it might be possible to create standards for EDI connections, forcing everyone to conform to one type of data definition. Although there is some progress in this area, firms with existing EDI systems will be reluctant to spend the money to convert their data.

Data conversion might sound like an easy task, but it is complicated when the transaction systems were created over long periods of time and were poorly documented. In many cases, the programmer might have to search major portions of the corporate systems to find the appropriate data definitions. Once the appropriate data is found, it can be hard to modify. Existing programs might expect the data to maintain specific formats. Making changes to the data can require rewriting other programs.

### Proprietary EDI

As displayed in Figure 4.7, most of the early EDI systems were created independently: One large company required suppliers to provide data and accept orders electronically. The goal was to cut the costs of transactions and speed up the ordering process. EDI arrangements also enabled manufacturers to improve quality control and to implement just-in-time inventory systems. Suppliers were "encouraged" to adopt the EDI systems by threatening a loss of sales if the vendors did not comply.

With proprietary systems, the lead firm establishes the standards in terms of the hardware and the types and format of data to be exchanged. From the standpoint of the lead firm, these controls ensure that they are able to connect to each supplier with one standard technique.

To a supplier, proprietary systems created by one company can lead to problems. Imagine what happens when the supplier sells to several firms, and each firm requires the use of a different EDI system. In addition to hassles of providing data in the proper format for each customer, the supplier's employees would have to learn how to use several different systems. Purchasers face similar problems unless all of their suppliers follow a standard.

**FIGURE 4.7**

EDI can be built from individual pairwise links over proprietary connections. If the majority of transactions are between two companies, this method will work fine. If companies deal with many different suppliers or large customers, this method can cause problems when each link requires conversion to a different format.

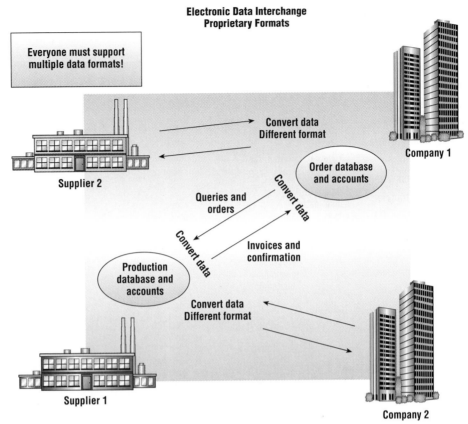

**Electronic Data Interchange
Proprietary Formats**

Everyone must support multiple data formats!

Supplier 2

Convert data
Different format

Company 1

Order database and accounts

Convert data

Queries and orders

Convert data

Invoices and confirmation

Production database and accounts

Convert data
Different format

Supplier 1

Company 2

---

## COSTS OF HANDLING TRANSACTIONS IN A HOSPITAL

Creating and handling paper-based purchase orders is expensive. Torrey Byles of the market research firm BIS Strategic Decisions notes that it costs large, 500-bed hospital $30 to $40 in overhead costs for every purchase order it issues. The supplier that receives the order incurs $24 to $28 to process each order. Switching to EDI could reduce the hospital's costs to around $12. The cost to the supplier drops to 32 cents.

"In a race to chase checks, three helicopters land in rapid succession at the airport here [Burbank, California]. Workers scramble to unload hundreds of pounds of bundled checks, hurl them into carts, and run them out to a waiting Learjet . . . On board are $600 million in checks that must get to banks in 46 cities by 8 AM or payment will be delayed a day—a costly proposition."

In addition to lower costs and more reliable transfer of data, users of EDI systems prefer the additional information available. David Smay, the treasurer of Chevron, noted problems they had with their "lockbox" bank handling paper transactions. The information provided on payments was "haphazard, incomplete or inaccurate 20 percent of the time." On the other hand, payments handled by EDI automatically identify the thousands of different invoices.

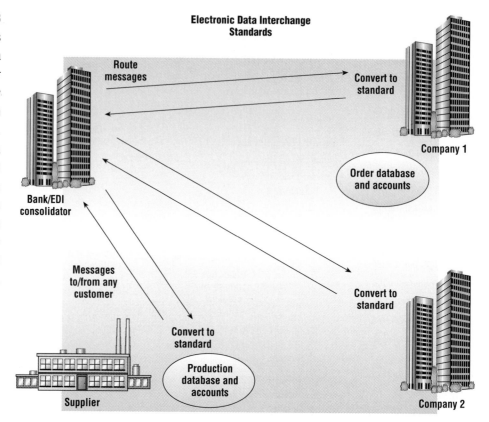

## Commercial EDI Providers and Standards

Multiple proprietary systems lead to confusion and higher costs. Consequently, companies have formed groups to define common methods to exchange data among companies. As shown in Figure 4.8, third-party providers (such as banks) have begun operating as clearinghouses for EDI transactions. In both cases, the objective is to establish common hardware and software requirements so that any company following the standards can share data with other companies.

Communication standards enable firms to share the data and automate basic transactions. However, to provide useful information, companies need to integrate this data into their management information systems. Sending purchase orders over phone lines is faster than using traditional mail, but firms can gain more advantages if the resulting data can be tied directly to their internal accounting systems.

There are two primary standards for EDI messages. The UN sponsors the Edifact standard; the United States defined the ANSI (American National Standards Institute) X12 definition. Figure 4.9 shows the overall structure of an EDI message. A significant difference between the standards is in the numbering system used to represent the types of messages, segments, and data elements. Figure 4.10 presents a partial list of the segment types available in the X12 standard. The standards also specify the exact format of the data required in each segment type.

## Additional Features and Problems

Taken to its full capabilities, EDI enables firms to electronically handle all communications among other firms. It enables managers to create and review orders without relying on paper printouts. Having data available electronically means that several

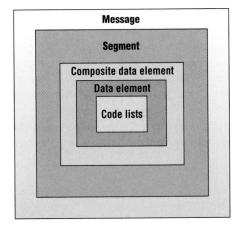

**FIGURE 4.9**

EDI standards. UN Edifact and U.S. ANSI X12 standards are similar in format; each message consists of segments and detailed data lists. Each message, segment, and data element are defined by numbers from a predefined list of possible transactions. There are substantial differences in the numbering system used for the segments and data elements.

people can work with the same form at the same time. In most companies, purchase orders and invoices are examined and altered by several people. If the form is processed on the computer, each person has access to the data at the same time. It is also much easier to store and search the electronic data. Eventually, even prices and negotiations could be handled electronically, making it much easier to sort and compare bids from various suppliers.

**FIGURE 4.10**

Sample segment codes for ANSI X12. A partial list of the codes used within X12 EDI messages. Only the number is transmitted. Each segment specifies the format of the additional data.

| | |
|---|---|
| 104 | Air Shipment Information |
| 110 | Air Freight Details and Invoice |
| 125 | Multilevel Railcar Load Details |
| 126 | Vehicle Application Advice |
| 127 | Vehicle Baying Order |
| 128 | Dealer Information |
| 129 | Vehicle Carrier Rate Update |
| 130 | Student Educational Record (Transcript) |
| 131 | Student Educational Record (Transcript) Acknowledgment |
| 135 | Student Loan Application |
| 139 | Student Loan Guarantee Result |
| 140 | Product Registration |
| 141 | Product Service Claim Response |
| 142 | Product Service Claim |
| 143 | Product Service Notification |
| 144 | Student Loan Transfer and Status Verification |
| 146 | Request for Student Educational Record (Transcript) |
| 147 | Response to Request for Student Educational Record (Transcript) |
| 148 | Report of Injury or Illness |
| 151 | Electronic Filing of Tax Return Data Acknowledgment |
| 152 | Statistical Government Information |
| 154 | Uniform Commercial Code Filing |
| 161 | Train Sheet |
| 170 | Revenue Receipts Statement |
| 180 | Return Merchandise Authorization and Notification |
| 186 | Laboratory Reporting |
| 190 | Student Enrollment Verification |

Some unresolved issues with EDI's security and ethics need further consideration. What happens when a company denies that it placed an order? How do we protect the communication links so people cannot intercept orders? Reading, changing, or deleting your competitor's orders could destroy its business. Although these actions are illegal, they can be difficult to prevent or uncover. Privacy issues also arise in conjunction with EDI. If consumer transactions are captured electronically and stored, an enormous amount of personal information will be available. What will prevent a company from acquiring or selling a list of all the items you purchase along with your salary and your home address? These questions are addressed in more detail in Chapter 14.

## DATA QUALITY

As you can see, a transaction-processing system can become quite complex. Problems are going to occur in any system—especially because all business organizations change over time. That means the computer system has to change to match the business. It is virtually impossible to change the system at exactly the same time as the business, so problems will occur. Other problems arise simply because the systems are so complex. Many processes involve humans who make mistakes. If you understand what types of problems might arise, they will be easier to solve.

The key to data quality is to focus on quality throughout the process. At input, data should be collected as close to the source as possible. For processing, data should be available to all users in a form they can use without having to reenter the data. In terms of output, reports should be linked to the databases so they always use the most recent data. Figure 4.11 lists the primary measures of data quality that you need to examine. In examining an information system, if you detect any of these problems, they are clues that you should search for ways to improve the transaction processing system.

### Data Integrity

One of the most important concepts in information processing is the issue of data integrity. **Data integrity** means keeping data accurate and correct as it is gathered and stored in the computer system. There is little value in an information system that contains out-of-date or inaccurate data. A common complaint among shoppers today is

**FIGURE 4.11**

Maintaining data quality is crucial to managing a firm. Several problems make it difficult to build good transaction-processing systems.

| Data Quality Attribute | Description and Problems |
|---|---|
| Integrity | Errors in data entry. Missing data. Failure to make updates. |
| Multitasking Concurrency | Data altered by two people at the same time, creating incorrect results. |
| Volume | Cost, difficulty of searching, transmission costs, errors harder to find, system overload. |
| Summaries | Too much detail is overkill when you only need summaries. With only summaries, you cannot recover the details. |
| Time | Many reports and decisions are subject to deadlines. Different departments getting data at different times can cause sequencing errors and additional delays. |

**Reality Bytes**          **4-10** BAR CODE SCANNERS IN MICHIGAN

Michigan state law requires that computerized scanners in stores cannot charge customers a higher price than the amount displayed on the item or shelf. In fact, if the computer charges the customer a higher price, the store is required to offer the customer a monetary reward of approximately $5. If the store refuses, the customer can take the store owners to small claims court and collect a couple hundred dollars. The law provides a strong incentive to keep accurate databases.

SOURCE: Linda Wilson, "Point of No Returns, For Most Consumer Goods Manufacturers, the Benefits of Point-of-Sale Data Hardly Seem Worth the Bother," *Computerworld*, July 17, 1995, pp. 71–72.

that stores using bar code scanners might have a different price in the computer than the amount displayed on the shelf. It is easy to change prices in the computer; it is more difficult to change the signs in the store. Shoppers will feel cheated if the computer tries to charge them a higher price than the amount listed on the shelf. Some states, like Michigan (Reality Bytes 4–10), have passed laws requiring that the scanned price cannot be higher than the amount listed on the package or display. Similar errors cause problems when the computer shows more items in stock than actually exist.

The first step to ensure data integrity lies in its capture. Each item must be correctly entered and the complete information recorded. It is sometimes possible to check the data as it is entered. Item code numbers usually include a check number that is based on the other digits. In the item code 548737, the first five digits add up to 27, so the number 7 is included as the last digit. If the person or machine makes a mistake entering one of the digits, they will probably not add up to 7, so the computer can immediately determine that there is an error. Sophisticated methods exist to catch mistakes involving more than one digit.

Even with machine entry of data, validity problems can arise. What happens when a shipment arrives, but the receiving department forgets to record it? The same problem occurs when a clerk holds an item for a customer and does not record it in the computer. Data integrity can be destroyed by indiscriminately allowing people to change the numbers in the computer. It is one of the main reasons for creating secure computers and controlling access to each piece of information.

## Multitasking, Concurrency, and Integrity

A useful feature offered by more sophisticated operating systems is the ability to perform more than one task at a time. Operating systems such as PC-DOS permit you to work on only one program at a time. In many situations it is useful to have several jobs running at the same time. What happens if you are searching a huge database and your boss calls and asks you for a sales figure? With a multitasking computer operating system, you could switch to a new program, look up the number, and allow the database to continue searching in the background.

If you use a multitasking operating system, it is important that your application software understand that other applications might be running at the same time. Each application needs to protect its data files from **concurrency** problems. Concurrency arises when applications attempt to modify the same piece of data at the same time. If two people are allowed to make changes to the same piece of data, the computer system must control the order in which it processes the two requests. Mixing the two tasks will result in the wrong data being stored in the computer. These problems can

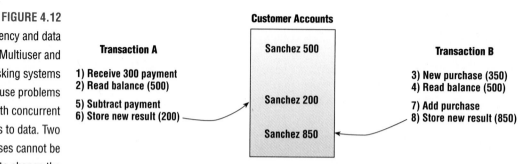

**FIGURE 4.12**

Concurrency and data integrity. Multiuser and multitasking systems can cause problems with concurrent changes to data. Two processes cannot be allowed to change the same data at the same time. Most systems will lock out transaction B until transaction A is completed. If a system becomes very busy, you can sometimes encounter delays while you wait for other users to finish their changes.

be avoided by only using software that was specifically written for multiuser (or multitasking) computers.

Consider the case of a mail-order firm shown in Figure 4.12. On the left side, customer Sanchez sent a payment on his account. At the same time the clerk begins to process the payment, Sanchez calls a second clerk and places a new order. The figure shows what happens if both transactions continue and interfere with each other. What should the final balance be? Does the computer have the correct number?

To solve this problem, the application program must know that several people might try to access the same piece of data at the same time. The software locks out all users except one. When the first process is finished, the other users can try to gain access again. To keep data accurate, applications used by many people at the same time must be written to handle these concurrency problems. Early personal computers were designed for only one user, so much of the software did not prevent concurrency problems. Software designed for computer networks generally handles this issue. When you use this software, you will occasionally receive a message that says a piece of data you desire is currently being used by another person. If you get this message, simply wait for a few minutes and try again. When the first person is finished, you should be able to proceed.

## Data Volume

A common problem experienced by a growing business is the increase in the amount of data or data volume. Consider the huge databases that have been created by Information Resources or United Parcel Service (Reality Bytes 4–11). Kenwood Stereo (Reality Bytes 4–12) faced slightly different problems with collections of paper records. It used a digital imaging system to reduce the volume of paper and make it easier to store and find documents.

 **Reality Bytes** ◣ **4–11** Huge Databases

Information Resources, Inc (IRI) in Chicago maintains a database of information collected from supermarket scanner data in more than 3,000 stores. The database tracks sales of more than 1 million products. In early 1993 storage requirements were over 1.7 terabytes and increasing.

United Parcel Service (UPS) tracks individual parcels with its Delivery Information Automated Lookup system (DIALS). It used 1.5 terabytes in 1993.

Large databases pose challenges in design, access, and maintenance. Backups require a tremendous amount of time and media (usually tapes). They require expensive disk drives to make this much data available to users. It is also difficult to devise storage strategies to provide users with fast access to the data.

**Reality Bytes** ◢ **4–12** KENWOOD STEREO AND AUDIO IMAGED WARRANTY SYSTEM

Stereo and audio distributors are required to organize and maintain warranty statements and claim forms for each of the electronic components that they sell. Warranty statements and descriptions come in all forms and sizes. A complete form can contain up to 32 individual forms and run up to 12 pages.

Stereo dealers have developed many approaches to deal with "warranty overload." Some maintain centralized filing systems; others endeavor to keep the forms with the individual products.

Customer claim forms average 100 per day. Before the system implementation, claim forms, warranties, and invoices used to be stored in microfiche, filing cabinets, and boxes in the company's warehouses.

Kenwood Stereo and Audio has addressed this problem through a local area network-based image-processing system. The IS department spent nine months presenting different imaging systems to potential users in the warehouse, accounting, administration,

service, and sales departments. It finally decided upon an Optika Imaging System that incorporated scanners, optical jukeboxes, and disks to store and retrieve the various forms. During the next four years all of the desktop computers in the company will be linked to the system. This will enable customer invoices to be downloaded from the mainframe, warranty claims scanned, and a comparison made between the two. Daily reports and shipping documents have begun to be downloaded. Proof-of-delivery documents have also been scanned into the system.

Although Kenwood expects a three-and-a-half year return on investment, managers do not believe that the only savings are financial. The new system also provides savings in file and floor space as well as in staff time and dealer and service center response rates. More importantly, the system provides the potential to improve customer service.

As the business grows, there will be an increase in the number of transactions. As the price of computers drops, more applications are placed on the computer. Additional transactions become computerized. Several problems can be created from this increase: (1) processing overload or system slowdowns; (2) greater difficulty in making sure the data is accurate; (3) insufficient storage within the computer system; and (4) data not captured fast enough.

Visa International processes more than 6 billion electronic transactions a year. By the year 2000, the company expects to handle 15 billion annual transactions. There are 18,000 banks offering Visa cards, used by 10 million customers. There is so much data generated on a daily basis that Visa cannot keep transaction data online beyond six months. All older records are moved to backup storage, making them inaccessible for additional research or decisions.

Sloppy practices and huge datasets can lead to inaccurate data. As the system slows down or the computer runs out of storage space, people avoid using it, so data is no longer up-to-date. With the increase in volume and the computerization of new types of data, it is more difficult for programmers and managers to check the data. If parts of the computer system are too slow, data may not be captured fast enough. As a result, some data might be lost. A tremendous amount of information is stored in raw data. The raw data could be analyzed to offer new services or improve quality of existing service. However, the huge volumes require too much storage space and too much processing time.

Careful planning is required to avoid these problems. At best, new computers and storage usually take a month or two to purchase. It could take a year or more to evaluate and purchase a large, expensive central computer. The MIS department would like to forecast the demands that will be placed on the computers at least a year in advance.

## Data Summaries

Another situation is commonly encountered in transaction-processing systems. In almost any company today, managers complain of having too much data. Consider the situation of a marketing manager who needs to determine the best way to increase sales for next year. Think of the amount of data that is readily available. The firm's transaction-processing system can provide detailed records on sales of every item every day, by each salesperson, broken down by city, for at least the last five years. Scanner data from marketing research firms lists itemized sales by grocery store for every product. There is also internal data from consumer surveys, production, and responses to promotions. Demographic data is available from the government.

To deal with this much data, managers are forced to rely on summaries. The marketing manager may only see a list of sales totals by each salesperson. That total might or might not include merchandise that was returned. Imagine what happens if returns are *not* included in the totals, but the manager believes that they were included. An unethical salesperson could sell extra merchandise to a friend (boosting the totals), and then return the merchandise the same day (because the returns are not subtracted from the list).

The problem multiplies as the information travels through different levels in the organization. Higher-level managers in the firm deal with data that has gone through several types of summarizing at each lower level. By the time they finally receive the information, the reports might not contain the information that is needed. The details might have been deleted or the summaries might carry the wrong set of information.

## Time

Time is another aspect of information quality in transaction-processing systems. The information system must furnish the information at the time it is needed for decision making. An information system that is overloaded or not producing properly summarized data will not be able to provide information at the right time. Consider the data needed to file tax forms. The government has a time limit for filing tax forms. Managers would be understandably upset if their computer system could not produce the annual accounting reports in time to calculate taxes. Similarly, it is difficult to place orders for new merchandise when the only available data is a three-month-old sales report.

Problems with timeliness generally arise because data is not captured early enough. The sales report might be delayed because too many people are needed to enter the data and make some of the computations. A POS system could provide a detailed sales list almost instantly. Other delays arise when the system cannot distribute data to everyone at the same time, so reports end up sitting on someone's desk.

**THE ROLE OF ACCOUNTING**    Accounting systems are important because they extend throughout the company and because they focus on money. They are used to collect data and evaluate performance. The accounting system also enables managers to combine the many divisions into an integrated picture of the entire company. Accounting systems also provide controls over the data to ensure accuracy and to prevent fraud. The primary purpose of accounting is to collect the financial data of the firm, ensure that it is accurate, and create standard reports. It is hard to capture all of the elements of an accounting

**FIGURE 4.13**
Transaction processing
is a major function of
the accounting system.
The accounting system
collects data
throughout the
company and produces
consolidated
(centralized) reports
that are used for
planning and
management.

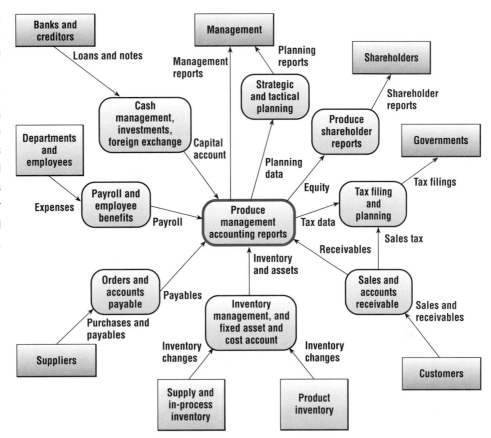

**FIGURE 4.13**
Transaction processing
is a major function of
the accounting system.
The accounting system
collects data
throughout the
company and produces
consolidated
(centralized) reports
that are used for
planning and
management.

system in one illustration, but Figure 4.13 summarizes the essential components. The accounting transaction system can be examined in terms of inputs, outputs, and processes.

## Input and Output: Financial Data and Reports

Raw financial data is collected by the accounting department and stored in an **accounting journal.** Modern accounting requires the use of a double-entry system to ensure accurate data. In a double-entry system, at least two entries must occur for every transaction. Generally, one entry records the effect of the money (e.g., cash, accounts payable, accounts receivable), and the other refers to a specific category (e.g., sales, office expenses, commissions). Each entry includes the date, amount of money, account number, the name of the person or firm involved, perhaps a comment, and the name of the person making the entry. The journal's purpose is to record all the transactions.

Journal entries represent raw data. To be useful, this data must be transformed into information. The first step is to categorize the data by *accounts* or categories. That is the purpose of the **general ledger.** The ledger is a collection of accounts that break the data down into specific categories. Common categories include *accounts receivable, accounts payable, inventory,* and *cash.* Although there are some standards, each company can define its own **chart of accounts,** which allows owners and managers to examine data on whatever categories are important to their firm.

For managers to make comparisons between divisions and other firms, accounting systems produce standardized reports. Most companies produce balance sheets, cash flow statements, and income statements every quarter. These reports are produced following standard accounting rules to enable owners, managers, and investors to compare the financial positions of various companies over time.

## Purchases, Sales, Loans, and Investments

One of the primary purposes of accounting is to record the financial transactions with external organizations. In addition to collecting the raw data, the accounting system contains controls that minimize fraud by limiting access to the data. The system also creates summary and detail reports to monitor key information.

Managers often build **exception reports** into the accounting system that are triggered when some event occurs. If sales in some region suddenly drop, if there is a major increase in the cash balance, or if inventories fall below a defined level, a message will be sent to the appropriate manager. The manager typically responds by searching the recent summary reports for a possible cause.

## Inventory

Most organizations need to carefully control inventory. Retail stores find it hard to sell items that are not in stock. Manufacturing firms need to receive and process parts as cheaply as possible. Inventory control consists of knowing exactly what items are available and where they are located. The system also needs to determine when to place new orders. It must then track the orders to make sure each item is delivered to the appropriate location at the right time. With EDI, the inventory control system can monitor current sales and automatically place orders with the supplier.

Manufacturing firms use these system to implement just-in-time inventory control. The computer system monitors the current production requirements, keeps track of deliveries, and electronically sends orders to the suppliers. The suppliers then deliver the parts just as they are needed on the production line.

Automated inventory control systems also help identify and prevent theft. By recording all movement of items from receipt to sales to shipping, management knows exactly how many items exist. Consider a retail store like a bicycle shop. The computerized inventory notes that there should be three Avocet computers in stock. Yet, when a customer asks to buy one, you notice there are only two left. If there is no mistake in your inventory report, you conclude that someone stole one of the items. Although the system did not prevent the speedometer from disappearing, it does show which items are susceptible to theft. It also helps control theft by employees, who will be less likely to steal if they know that the items are carefully monitored.

## The Accounting Cycle

An important aspect of accounting systems is that they produce information in specific cycles. Firms are required to produce reports that reflect the financial condition of the firm at the end of every quarter. Accounting systems are based on these requirements. For the most part, managers operate from quarterly reports, with intermediate monthly reports for some items. Because of the volume of data in the detail, most companies only keep current statistics and summary reports on file. Older data is shuffled off the system to make room for the current numbers. As a result, managers may not have easy access to detailed data from prior years.

## Process: Checks and Balances

### Double-Entry Systems

An important objective of accounting systems is to maintain the integrity of the financial data. The goal is to prevent mistakes and discourage fraud. Double-entry accounting provides a method to locate mistakes in data entry (Reality Bytes 4–13). If an amount is entered incorrectly, the account totals will not balance.

Because many transactions involve outside organizations, mistakes can be caught by sharing data. Every month firms receive a statement from the bank. The totals can be compared to changes in the firm's cash account. Similarly, companies typically send receipts when they receive payments from each other. Auditors periodically send verification requests to suppliers and customers to make sure the data was recorded correctly. EDI strengthens this approach, because transaction data is transmitted in computer form among the companies.

**Reality Bytes**        4–13   SMALL BUSINESS ACCOUNTING

Small businesses have to be especially careful when they attempt to computerize their information systems. The accounting records are the logical first step. Many owner/managers of small businesses use their checkbooks as the primary accounting system. To these managers, it seems logical to organize their entry into computers the same way. Some "personal financial" software packages make it easy to enter all of the checks into the computer and print out monthly reports. These methods are based on single-entry accounting systems.

Consider a small construction company that builds single-unit residential housing. The owner records his payments (checks) in the personal financial package Quicken. At the end of the month, he uses the bank statement to enter the deposits and cleared checks to balance his checkbook. He uses a code number to keep track of which house the expense is applied to but finds that he sometimes enters the wrong number. Some payments to subcontractors apply to work done on more than one project. As a result, he has difficulty tracking the true cost of each house, making it difficult to make decisions about the construction techniques.

SOURCE: Gregg Keizer, "Keeping Tabs on Your Books," *Computer Shopper*, May 1996, p. 367.

### Separation of Duties

Another type of control is the separation of duties. A manager in the purchasing department might be responsible for choosing a supplier of parts. Only the accounting department can authorize the transfer of money to the supplier. The objective is to minimize fraud by requiring a potential thief to deal with multiple employees.

Many banks take this concept a step farther. They require employees (especially tellers) to take their vacations every year. Several instances of fraud have been revealed when the employee was no longer at the job to keep the fraudulent mechanism running.

### Audit Trails

An **audit trail** is important to accounting systems. It enables investigators to track backward through the data to the source. A cash-flow statement might indicate that the company has spent twice as much money this month as last. To find out why,

**Reality Bytes**    **4–14**  FEATURES TO LOOK FOR IN ACCOUNTING SOFTWARE

**SMALL BUSINESS BASICS**

**General Ledger**
Sample chart of accounts that can be modified.
Optional automatic posting to the ledger so you don't forget.
Automatic data entry for often-used vendor account numbers.
Define fiscal years instead of forcing calendar year.
How many months can be "open" at once?
Can entries be posted for prior months or prior years?
Audit trail.
Track expenses by departments and allocate portions of bills.

**Accounts Receivable**
Granting discounts for early payments.
Charging interest for late payments.
Multiple ship-to addresses.
Sales tax (by state and locality).
Automatic payment reminder notices.

Automatic entries for monthly maintenance fees.
The ability to add notes to invoices.
Carry invoice details month-to-month, not just total balance.

**Accounts Payable**
Check reconciliation support.
Automatic recurring entries.
Monitoring and automatic notices of payment discounts.
Ability to select bills to be paid from the screen.
Ability to make payment by item, not just total bill, in case of dispute.

**General Features**
Support for printers.
Require special preprinted forms?
Custom reports.
Custom queries.
Security controls, access to various modules by password.
Technical support costs?

trace backward and find all of the raw entries that make up the number. Together with dates and amounts, the raw journal entries can contain the identity of the person responsible for the entry. By keeping this identification data, it is possible to list every article that affects an item on a report.

**HUMAN RESOURCES AND TRANSACTION PROCESSING**

Every company has employees. Companies collect hundreds of pieces of data for each employee—some for management purposes, others because they are required by law. For years, the human resources (HR) department focused on filling out and storing forms. The enormous amount of paperwork alone begs for computerization just to cut down on storage space needed. Computerized databases also enable managers to find specific data on employees. Early HR software emphasized these two benefits. Modern HR software is expanding beyond simple forms to improving data collection and providing better analyses. To illustrate the problems presented by large-scale transaction processing systems, consider the three areas of input, output, and processing.

### Input: Data Collection

Figure 4.14 illustrates the basic components of a human resource management transaction-processing system. Note that the system is even more complex because the data come from all areas of the company. To understand how the HRM systems became so complicated, begin with the obvious data that needs to be collected: num-

**FIGURE 4.14**

Most employees know that human resource management (HRM) deals with payroll and benefits. But HRM also collects data and produces reports for myriad government reports, oversees employee evaluations, and job applications. The department also handles training and education opportunities.

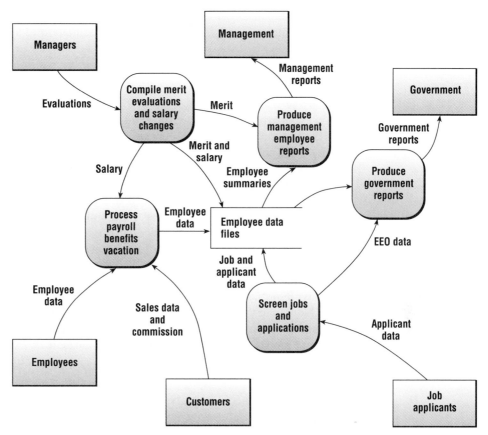

bers related to the payroll. For hourly workers, the system needs to collect and monitor hours worked. For many sales tasks, the system must compute sales by employee to determine commissions. Professional service firms often ask employees to track their time in terms of billable hours for work that is charged back to clients. In all three situations, as the number of employees increases, it becomes increasingly difficult to collect all of these statistics and verify their accuracy. It also becomes harder to find specific pieces of data.

Think about paychecks you have received. In addition to the payment amount, there could be 10 to 20 other numbers on the pay-stub. Companies monitor and report several types of payroll taxes, including federal, state, local, Social Security, and health. Also, firms monitor employee benefits, such as health care, and retirement. Most firms also handle employee deductions for employee purchases, savings plans, stock purchases, parking, meal plans, and other options. In some situations, companies must garnishee wages and forward them to a third party.

Human resource departments also track days taken for vacations, personal time, and illness. In larger companies, HRM provides training courses and offers testing of critical skills. Employee attendance and performance data is stored and incorporated into evaluations.

With expanding use of merit pay, the system must also track employee evaluations. Some performance measures are tied to productivity or output within the employee's department, so HR must relate employee work schedules to production and quality measures.

Most companies use a centralized HRM department to advertise job openings and to screen the initial applicants, verify credentials, and keep basic employment and hiring data.

## Output: Reports

There are several obvious reports related to payroll that are produced by the human resource department. Along with printing checks, HRM must provide expense reports and forecasts to the accounting system. Periodic reports are created for job vacancies and analyses of employee performance and morale.

Although the internal reports created by HRM are important, HRM departments spend a great deal of time creating reports for various government agencies. All companies must file various economic reports dealing with employment. Tax withholding data must be filed regularly with federal, state, and local agencies. The HRM department creates equal employment opportunity reports detailing characteristics of their workforce, job applicants, and hiring decisions. Then there are various reports required by the occupational safety and health administration (OSHA) regarding injuries and exposure to various hazards. If employees need to be certified, companies file aggregate reports with the various regulatory agencies. All of these reports have deadlines.

In addition to the standard reports, the human resources department is responsible for maintaining compliance with all relevant employment laws. Hence, HRM staff must continually monitor the employment data and evaluate it for exceptions and problems.

## Process: Automation

Human resources is a busy place. Keep in mind that the data and reports apply to every branch of the company. Even standard items like paychecks become complicated when the company is split into several divisions scattered across the country. Also remember that accuracy is crucial. Employees tend to get upset if their paychecks are wrong. Errors with government reports can lead to fines and lawsuits. Equally importantly, companies with good HRM departments are able to offer additional benefits to employees. With a good information system, they can offer cafeteria-style benefits where each employee selects a personal combination of benefits.

Small businesses have long complained about the burdens imposed by government reports and data collection. To alleviate some of the hassles and expense, several companies specialize in automating the data collection and report writing. Consider payroll. Because of the constantly changing laws, many companies rely on an outside agency to collect data and print the paychecks. One of the largest providers is Automated Data Processing (ADP). Even if a company chooses to maintain its own payroll records, it typically purchases the software from a third party instead of trying to keep up with the annual changes using internal programmers.

Several companies sell software that automates HRM data handling and produces government-required reports. From economics to equal-employment to OSHA reports, the basic HRM reports are being computerized. You still need to collect the data in the proper format and convert it to the purchased software. In addition to saving time in producing reports, the packages often contain the essential government rules and can analyze the data to spot potential problems.

Some newer technologies are being used to simplify data gathering. In particular, companies are searching for ways to make it easier for workers to deal with the HRM department. A system created by PRC, Inc., uses touch-tone phones and a voice-response system to enable workers to make changes directly to their base information, like changing their address or tax withholding. Another approach is to install

PC-based kiosks throughout the company, so that employees can look up information, sign up for training classes, or modify their personal data whenever they wish. Other companies are using similar software and the corporate network to allow workers to perform basic HR tasks from their desks.

The overall trend in computer support for HRM is exemplified by PeopleSoft, Inc., which is the leading vendor in moving HRM management off centralized databases and onto personal computer-based applications. The new technologies cut human resource management costs, make it easier for managers to get information, and enable companies to offer new benefits.

## SUMMARY

Every organization must perform certain basic operations: pay employees, pay bills, monitor revenue, and file government reports. Above this operations level there are tactical and strategic decisions to be made. Operations are relatively structured, short term, and easy to computerize. They form the foundation of the company. MIS supports operations by collecting data and helping to control the underlying processes.

Transaction-processing systems are responsible for capturing, storing, and providing access to the basic data of the organization. The goal is to capture the transaction data as soon as possible. Common collection methods include point-of-sale devices, process control, and electronic data interchange. Because data collection is a well-defined task, it has been computerized in most organizations for many years. Because data is the foundation for all other decisions, transaction-processing systems must maintain data integrity and minimize the threats to the data.

Financial data has always been important to any business organization. Accounting systems have been created over many years to help collect data, maintain its accuracy, and provide standardized reports to management. Financial checks and balances—such as double-entry accounting, separation of duties and audit trails—are used to maintain data

> ### A MANAGER'S VIEW
> Transaction processing is a crucial task in any company. Managers are responsible for ensuring the quality of the transaction data.
>
> Managers quickly recognized the value of using computers to collect and maintain transaction data. Two primary transaction systems in most companies are for accounting and human resource management.
>
> As a manager, you need to continually watch for problems or potential improvements that might arise in the transaction-processing systems. Because of the volume of data, mistakes are quickly multiplied. Likewise, even small improvements in efficiency or cost can provide substantial benefits.

integrity. Processing of accounting information leads to monthly, quarterly, and annual information cycles in most businesses.

Human resource systems illustrate the problems entailed in transaction processing: maintaining accurate databases and producing timely reports, and supporting employee and management needs at a low cost. They also show that good transaction-processing systems can provide additional benefits by offering new services.

## KEY WORDS

accounting journal, 161
audit trail, 163
change-drivers, 141
chart of accounts, 161
concurrency, 157
data, 142
data integrity, 156

electronic data interchange
  (EDI), 147
exception reports, 162
general ledger, 161
information, 142
magnetic ink character
  recognition (MICR), 148

optical character recognition
  (OCR), 148
point of sale (POS), 147
process control, 144
transaction processing, 140

## REVIEW QUESTIONS

1. What are the three decision levels in a firm? Give an example of a decision at each level.
2. Describe three methods of data capture.
3. What is meant by the term *data quality?* Give three examples of problems with data quality.
4. Why is data volume an important issue in transaction-processing systems? Will newer, faster machines automatically solve the problem?
5. What is meant by *concurrency,* and why is it a problem in a multiuser environment?
6. Why are so many transaction-processing systems based on accounting methods?
7. How does the accounting cycle affect decisions and operations in a typical firm?
8. What is the difference between *data* and *information?*
9. Briefly describe three ways to collect data at the point of sale.
10. How is data collection at the factory level different from data collection about consumers?
11. Why are standards so important for EDI?
12. Why is it so important to capture data close to its source?
13. How much data is represented by one terabyte? How many textbooks (the size of this one) could be stored in one terabyte of storage space? (Hint: Forget about pictures—how many words are on an average page?)
14. Why do managers and executives rely on summaries? What problems can arise with summarized data?

## EXERCISES

1. Consider a medical example related to testing. One hundred sick people are in your office. Based on their symptoms and medical statistics, you know that 90 of them have disease A and 10 of them have a rare disease B. You do not know which people have each illness, but both groups will die without treatment. Fortunately, there is a 100 percent cure for both diseases. However, if you give the wrong treatment to a person, they will die. You have a test available to indicate whether a person has disease A or B. The test is accurate 80 percent of the time. How many people will you test? Why? What is the important characteristic of this problem? How is it related to testing of information systems?
2. Find information on at least two accounting packages that could be used for a business with 100–150 employees. Identify the strengths and weaknesses of each package. Are the packages tailored to specific industries?
3. Visit at least three retail stores in your area and determine how they handle transaction processing for sales. How many checkout counters are available at each store? By counting the number of customers in a 10- to 15-minute time interval, estimate the total number of sales transactions occurring for a given day.
4. Visit a local store or factory and identify a primary set of transaction data. Describe at least three reports that a manager would want to see based on this data.
5. Go to the library and research a particular industry. Identify the major transactions that would be expe-

rienced by a typical firm in this industry. How often do the transactions occur (daily, weekly, monthly)?
6. Because of the importance of transactions, there is a large number of cases involving fraud and other legal problems with sales and other transactions. Pick an industry and find articles in business and trade journals that identify problems of this nature. How will computerization of the transactions affect fraudulent transactions? Do you think the computerization make it easier or harder to detect these problems?
7. Using articles from business, trade and computer magazines, identify three companies (in different industries) that are using imaging systems for transaction data. How large are the companies? How much storage space is used by the data?
8. Data collection can be difficult for certain industries. For example, government agencies, transportation companies, hospitals, and agricultural entities all have unique problems in collecting data. Choose one of these industries, research a firm in that industry, and explain the problems the managers encounter and how technology is being used to overcome the difficulties and collect data.

 **Rolling Thunder Database**

1. Identify the major transaction-processing components in the system.
2. Identify transaction-processing operations that need to be added to the system.
3. What features are used in the database and the forms to ensure quality of transaction data?

4. What additional data quality features should be added?

5. Explain how additional data quality features can be provided with training, procedures, and manual controls.

6. For each major transaction type, identify the sequence of steps that are performed and determine which ones are time critical.

7. For each major transaction type, estimate the frequency of the transaction and the volume of data involved.

8. Identify any transaction forms that could be improved to make them easier for clerks and other users.

9. Using the existing forms, perform the following tasks for Rolling Thunder:
   a. Take a bicycle order.
   b. Assemble a bicycle.
   c. Create a new purchase order.
   d. Record the receipt of purchases.

## ADDITIONAL READING

"A Survey of Retailing," *The Economist*, March 4, 1995. [Special section on changes in retailing. Good summary of global firms and changes]

Ahbrand, Deborah. "Client/Server: The Bedrock of New Business," *Infoworld*, September 18, 1995, pp. 53–61. [Wal-Mart]

"At Last! Retailers Nationwide Look to Cash In, as Windows 95 Finally Makes It to Market," *Computer Retail Week*, August 28, 1995, pp. 1–2. [Sears]

Bartholomew, Doug. "Think Profitability: A New Tool Assesses Sales Promotions by Comparing Critical Data," *Information Week*, May 8, 1995, p. 80. [Borden]

Baseh, Reva. "Software Measures Up," *Computer Life*, November 1995, p. 39. [Wal-Mart]

Bleakley, Fred. "Electronic Payments Now Supplant Checks at More Large Firms," *The Wall Street Journal*, April 13, 1994, pp. A1, A9. [Costs of handling checks]

Blodgett, Mindy. "Sears Hits the Road with Wireless Devices," *Computerworld*, May 29, 1995, p. 6. [Sears]

Booker, Ellis. "Imaging, Work Flow Expand at JC Penney," *Computerworld*, April 12, 1993, p. 52. [JC Penney]

Booker, Ellis. "Partners in Trade," *Computerworld*, March 19, 1990, p. 57. [Sears]

"Borden Inc. Downsizes with PowerHouse; Cognos Provides a Client/Server Solution for a Multinational Corporation that Integrates Windows with a DEC VAX, an AS/400, and UNIX," *Data Based Advisor*, January 1995, p. 66. [Borden]

Bozman, J. "Grappling with Huge Databases," *Computerworld*, May 31, 1993, p. 57. [Information Resources and UPS databases]

Braunbert, David. "Outsourcing Out There," *Network VAR*, June 1995, p. 16. [Kenwood stereo]

Bull, Katherine. "Sell Smart, Sell More," *Information Week*, September 18, 1995, pp. 176–178. [Sears, Wal-Mart]

Cafasso, Rosemary. "HR Staffs Recruit Client/Server Systems," *Computerworld*, January 16, 1995, pp. 61–62. [Brief introduction to Human Resource software and usage]

Case, Edward. "Mr. Benhamou Goes to Market," *Information Week*, September 25, 1995, pp. 96–97. [Barney's]

"Catalina Goes from the Grocery Store to the World Wide Web," *Electronic Marketplace Report*, October 3, 1995, p. 1. [Kroger]

"CompuServe Adds 4 UK Online Stores," *Newsbytes*, September 11, 1995, p. NEW09110003. [Tesco]

"CompuServe UK Prepares Online Shopping," *Newsbytes*, April 6, 1995, p. NEW04060028. [Tesco]

Demarest, Marc. "Leading-Edge Retail: Mervyn's Gains a Decision-Support Edge with Data Warehouse/Data Agent Technology," *DBMS*, December 1994. [Kmart]

Erickson, Jonathan. "Shock Treatment," *Dr. Dobb's Journal*, December 1995, p. 6. [Service Merchandise]

Ferguson, Kevin. "Where Small Publishers Can Go," *Computer Retail Week*, August 7, 1995, p. 23. [Wal-Mart]

Fitzgerald, Michael. "Retailers Try EDI Hard Sell," *Computerworld*, July 9, 1990, p. 1. [Sears]

Gambon, Jill. "Is High-Tech a Surefire Cure?", *Information Week*, September 18, 1995, pp. 164–166. [Borden]

Georgianis, Maria V. "Study Focuses on ROI of Store Renovation," *Computer Retail Week*, October 30, 1995, p. 18. [Wal-Mart]

Gill, Phillip J. "A Diet of Reengineering," *Information Week*, September 18, 1995, pp. 118–120. [Wal-Mart]

Giorishankar, Saraja. "Collaborating on the Future," *Communications Week*, July 31, 1995, pp. 4–5. [JC Penney]

Morton, Anthony and Michael Scott. "A Framework for Management Information Systems," *Sloan Management Review*, Fall 1971, pp. 55–70. [Transactions, tactical and strategic framework]

Haavind, Robert. "Taming Information Systems," *CFO*, January 1992, pp. 32–38. [Super Valu Stores]

Hanna, Mary Alice. "Getting Back to Requirements Proving to Be a Difficult Task," *Software Magazine*, October 1991, pp. 49–57. [L'eggs]

Health-Care Guys Can Make Good on Retail IT," *PC Week*, August 21, 1995, p. E11. [Kroger]

Henderson, Lisa. "Hands on Client/Server," *MIDRANGE Systems*, June 30, 1995, p. 38. [Wal-Mart]

Hoffman, Thomas. "Kenwood's New Image," *Information Week*, January 13, 1992, p. 38. [Kenwood stereo]

Horwitt, Elisabeth. "Retailer Nears End of Huge IS Overhaul," *Computerworld*, September 1992, p. 1. [JC Penney]

"Humongous Formula," *Windows Watcher*, August 1995, p. 5. [Barney's]

"I Did My Holiday Shopping Online," *Computer Life*, December 1994. [JC Penney]

"Internet Access: Catalina Marketing Announces Plans to Be the First In-store Marketer to Reach Customers Via the Internet; Major Retailers Sign on for Catalina Marketing Online Test," *EDGE, On & About AT&T*, August 28, 1995, p. 8. [Kroger]

"Japan Newsbriefs," *Newsbytes*, October 23, 1995, p. NEW10230022. [Kenwood stereo]

Kendrick, Joseph. "On the Front Lines of EDI," *MIDRANGE Systems*, September 29, 1995, pp. 27–28. [Wal-Mart]

Kukro, Rod. "Fast Track to Online Profits," *PC World*, October 1995, pp. 271–272. [Service Merchandise]

Lanetot, Roger. "Retailers Ride Windows 95 to Higher Sales," *Computer Retail Week*, July 3, 1995, pp. 61–66. [Sears]

LaPlante, Alice. "Growth Is Relative," *Computerworld*, September 14, 1992, p. 18. [Massachusetts Mutual Insurance and CoreStates Financial]

"MCI Amasses Marketers for Newly Launched Web Marketplace," *Electronic Marketplace Reports*, April 4, 1995. [L'eggs]

Medford, C. "Mom and Pop Go to War; Small Businesses Use Routers to Configure New Markets," *VARbusiness*, March 1, 1995, pp. 153–155. [Wal-Mart]

Messner, Ellen. "Banks Set Up Net for Electronic Payments; EDIBANX Poised to Compete Against GEIS and Other VANs," *Network World*, May 8, 1995, pp. 6–7. [Sears]

Mitchell, Gabrielle and Rebecca Smith. "Wal-Mart Still Alone on Ratings," *Computer Retail Week*, April 3, 1995, pp. 1–2. [Wal-Mart]

Moad, Jeff. "Blue Light Blues," *PC Week*, September 25, 1995, pp. E1–E2. [JC Penney, Wal-Mart, and Kroger]

———. "Kmart Trades in Unix POS for Win NT System; CIO Seeks to Cut Costs," *PC Week*, September 18, 1995, pp. 1–2. [JC Penney]

———. "Kmart's IT Crisis: Electronic Links Needed between Stores and Suppliers," *PC Week*, April 3, 1995, pp. E1–E2. [Kmart]

Moeller, Michael. "Sears Technicians Hit the Airwaves," *PC Week*, June 19, 1995, pp. 41–42. [Sears]

Mulgreen, John T. "Helping Retailers Build Sales: Harmonic Makes Networks Accessible to Small Retailers, Aids Marketing Strategies," *Communications Week*, October 16, 1995, pp. 63–64. [Wal-Mart]

Murdoch, John. "Use Bar Codes to Automate Data Entry in VB Apps," *Data Based Advisor*, July 1995, pp. 128–132. [Wal-Mart]

Murphy, John. "Working on the Chain Gang," *Computer Weekly*, July 20, 1995, pp. 28–29. [Tesco]

"New Gitano Chief Gets Down to Business," *Discount Store News*, August 1, 1994, p. A6. [Gitano]

Payne, Robert. "Take a Close Look before Getting on the Wire," *Computerworld*, March 26, 1990, p. 81. [Sears]

Pepper, Jon. "In the Chips," *CIO Magazine*, June 1988, pp. 38–44. [Frito-Lay hand-held computers]

Prince, Tyler and Scott Kauffman. "From Order to Loading Dock," *Information Week*, November 20, 1995, pp. 96–99. [Wal-Mart]

"Retailers Sold on NT's Potential: Microsoft Successfully Targets Industry's Reengineering Efforts," *Information Week*, January 23, 1995. [JC Penney]

Ricciuti, Mike. "Vendors to Boost OLAP Application Packages: Think Bundles Decision Support and Database," *Infoworld*, August 7, 1995, p. 28. [Borden]

Richter, Allen. "Training Top Sales Tool, Retail Execs, Reps Agree," *Computer Retail Week*, April 17, 1995, pp. 31–32. [Service Merchandise]

Richter, Allen. "Better POS Data May Help Reps Hone Pitches: Faster Systems to Cull More Shopper Info, Cut Delays," *Computer Retail Week*, March 20, 1995, pp. 49–50. [Wal-Mart]

Roberts, Bill. "Security? What Security? Policing Data Is the Exception at PowerCerv," *PC Week*, September 25, 1995, p. 26. [Wal-Mart]

Ruber, Peter. "How Computers Help K-Mart Compete," *Unix World*, May 1992, pp. S10–14. [Kmart]

"Sears Technicians to Go Wireless," *PC Week*, May 29, 1995, p. 3. [Sears]

Selz, Michael. "Big Customers' Late Bills Choke Small Suppliers," *The Wall Street Journal*, June 22, 1994, pp. B1, B2. [Accounts receivable issues]

Smith, Jan and Dylan Tweney. "Accounting Software 101 (Tutorial)," *PC-Computing*, February 1992, pp. 252–258. [Basic accounting software features]

Snell, Ned. "Top Accountants Rate Accounting Software," *Datamation*, December 1992, pp. 80–82. [Evaluating accounting packages for small businesses—find features that match your needs]

Stevens, Larry. "Front-line Systems," *Computerworld*, March 2, 1992, p. 61 [Wal-Mart]

"Tesco's New Tricks," *The Economist*, April 15, 1995, pp. 61–62. [Tesco]

"Today Wal-Mart, Tomorrow the World—AT&T Targets Decision Support," *Software Magazine*, December 1994, p. 10.

"Top Grades for Wal-Mart; Retailer Cited for Honesty in Corporate Reporting," *Computer Retail Week*, December 5, 1994. [Wal-Mart]

Wexler, Joanie M. "Get Out There and Innovate!" *Computerworld*, June 22, 1992, p. 139. [JC Penney]

Winslow, Ron. "Four Hospital Suppliers Will Launch Common Electronic Ordering System," *The Wall Street Journal*, April 12, 1994, p. B8. [EDI for hospitals, including costs]

"World Turned Upside-Down," *The Economist*, September 18, pp. 90, 93. [Visa database numbers]

# CASES  *Retail Sales*

While a few workers in the retail industry make heavy use of computers, there are still many workers who do not use them. The most common uses are for inventory control, invoices, and sales.

SOURCE: Computer Use in the United States, U.S. Bureau of the Census.

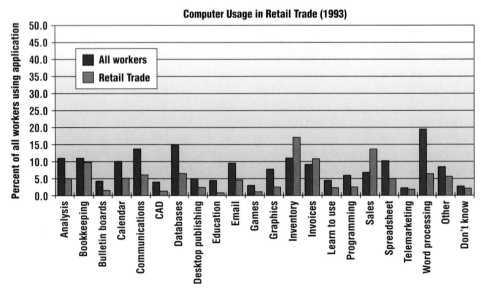

**Computer Usage in Retail Trade (1993)**

To a consumer, managing a retail store looks easy: You buy products from manufacturers, put them on the shelves, run the cash register, and count your profits. Of course, business is never that simple.

What are the most important tasks in a retail store? What are the critical success factors? The most basic concept is that the store has to stock products that the consumers will buy. That means the store needs to guess how many items to carry for every product. The hard part is that large retail stores like Sears, JC Penney, and Wal-Mart carry thousands of products purchased from hundreds of manufacturers. If a store consistently runs out of a popular product, customers will end up shopping somewhere else and might not come back. On the other hand, if the store is stuck with a large number of items it cannot sell, store managers will have to cut the price. Dumping products at clearance prices does not do much to bolster profits. Even worse, it means that the shelf space could have been better used by some other product. In most cases, the other leading factor in retail sales is competition. Whatever product the store carries, there are probably 5 to 10 other stores within a 30-mile radius that carry an identical or similar item. Each of these stores is competing for customers on the basis of convenience, location, selection, service, and price. Each store faces pressures to provide more services and additional products at ever-lower prices.

As the following cases show, information technology can play a leading role in helping retailers over-come these problems. IT can also provide a competitive advantage, by keeping costs low, locking in relationships to suppliers, and by providing better information on consumer choices.

## CASE  *Sears Roebuck and Company*

During 1991, Sears Roebuck spent $1.7 billion on information technology. This represents a larger commitment to technology that any other non-computer firm except the Boeing Company.

The cutting edge of Sears' technology is concentrated in STS, a 1600 employee spin-off. This group has directed the "store simplification" program to centralize every store's general offices, cashier, customer service, and credit functions. Another area of focus has been the centralization of the information systems operations, which was necessary because Sears now uses 2,000-plus millions of instructions per second to complete its processing requirements.

Perhaps the most far-reaching of the STS initiatives is a $60-million automation project. This program will affect each of Sears' 868 retail stores. The new system will focus on expediting the checkout and customer inquiry processes. Sophisticated computers have replaced the cash registers, and telephone inquiry kiosks will be installed throughout the stores. Sears began the project by identifying all of the manual tasks at the retail outlets. Once this was completed, Sears initiated a process of eliminating, simplifying, and automating with the goal of a paperless environment in the retail stores.

CompuAdd has received a $53 million contract for 28,000 new point-of-sale terminals as well as the enhancement of the software for 22,000 current cash registers. With the new systems, sales associates will be able to issue temporary SearsCharge cards and gift certificates, look up customer data, and process payments. The new terminals will be linked to a national database of customer information that can be accessed by name or phone number.

The original plan called for a separate vendor to receive a $7-million contract to install 6,000 new telephone information kiosks. These centers will enable customers to inquire about service, parts, and credit; check on the status of their car in the auto center; order flowers; or call the manager's office. Since the start of the project in 1991, this phase has been canceled.

Sears believes the new system will enable it to eliminate $50 million in annual back-office costs, 6,900 jobs, and the customer service desks at all stores. It will also enable Sears to gain the equivalent of seven new stores through the conversion of back office to selling space. Sears realizes, however, that the largest benefit from the system will be increased customer service, not more selling space. It is clear that Sears cannot compete based on price with deep discounters such as Wal-Mart. As a result, it is developing new systems to provide superior service for the customer.

## QUESTIONS

1. What does Sears management gain by consolidating its cash register systems into one giant system? What additional services can the stores offer customers? What information is available to managers?
2. What items does Sears have to purchase to install this new network?
3. As a customer, what services could be offered by the new system that would entice you to shop at Sears instead of one of its discount competitors?
4. Do you think Sears should install the information kiosks in each of their stores as they originally planned? Why do you think they chose not to install them?

### EDI at Sears

Sears has provided a number of incentives to encourage its suppliers to implement the EDI program.

- Based on business requirements and transaction volume guidelines, Sears has prioritized its 6,000 suppliers to determine the order in which they will be migrated to EDI.
- Sears distributes a letter to a select group of suppliers each month to ask them to set up a 90-day timetable by the end of which they will have implemented EDI.
- Within 10 days of receiving the letter, the suppliers fill out a questionnaire to determine the assistance they will need to move to EDI.
- Sears will provide the necessary software and training free of charge.
- The suppliers are moved to EDI on the predetermined schedule.

EDI does present difficulties, however. A letter from Sears requiring EDI can be quite frightening for the small supplier without even a personal computer. Sears stresses, however, that the small supplier can market EDI as an advantage when it is looking for other markets for its products.

Sears has found that many of its suppliers hold an intense opposition to change and a certain amount of ignorance about EDI. The extended conversion period has caused internal costs to mount and EDI benefits to go unrealized. By the end of 1990, fewer than half of its suppliers had adopted EDI. The longer the conversion process takes, the higher will be the internal costs and the longer it will take for the benefits of EDI to be realized.

The difficulties that Sears has encountered have occurred even though the corporation has been most constructive in its approach. It employed Andersen Consulting to develop training and documentation for EDI translation software that Sears provides free to interested partners. Sears also pays half the cost of sending partners to attend Sears' EDI seminars.

By mid-1990, Lance Dailey, Sears merchandising director of EDI implementation, realized that the enticements were not working. As a result, he decreed EDI to be an official requirement for doing business with the merchandising group. He also set a new across-the-board deadline for all suppliers to convert to EDI.

## QUESTIONS

1. Why is Sears asking suppliers to use EDI?
2. Why are suppliers reluctant to use EDI? What are the costs? What are the advantages?
3. Is Sears correct about the suppliers being able to use EDI as a tool to help sell to other companies? What problems are the suppliers likely to encounter?

4. At what point does EDI become profitable? What percentage of the suppliers need to be using EDI? What are the fixed and variable costs of EDI?
5. Do EDI connections to suppliers provide competitive advantages to Sears? Would the type of EDI network used make a difference?

## CASE *JC Penney Company*

JC Penney is a $16.4 billion retailer with 1300 stores across the country. Headquartered in Dallas, Penney's approach to management decision-aiding models is best summarized by David Evans, vice-president of information services.

"I don't care if I buy it, build it, generate it, or whatever; the end result—the important thing—is getting the software."

To meet this mandate, JC Penney uses computer-aided software engineering (CASE), fourth-generation languages (4GLs), relational databases, and programmer workstations. All of these tools are implemented to move JC Penney toward the ultimate goal of a fully integrated, fully automated retail system with electronically replenished store shelves that are never empty and back rooms that are never full. This will be accomplished through making information appropriately available at any point in the environment.

A typical transaction at JC Penney follows this procedure:

1. Bar codes on purchased items are scanned at the cash register.
2. Price look-up of merchandise.
3. Credit card validation through a magnetic stripe reader.
4. Upon validation, the system will generate a single sales slip that will eliminate the need for credit card embossing onto a separate charge receipt.
5. This information will go to the inventory management system.
6. This system ties into the purchase-order management system.
7. The purchase-order management system sends an order via electronic data interchange for non-seasonal items to one or more of 1,300 suppliers.
8. The supplier sends the order and invoices the company electronically.

JC Penney's common repository for data will enable buyers, store managers, and executives from across the country to access all of the data at the retail level to determine what is selling, what is not, and where the problems are. This common repository enables JC

Penney to integrate applications and consolidate databases to keep software maintenance costs from skyrocketing. David Evans feels this is essential to the ultimate goal of "having the right merchandise at the right time at the right price in the right place."

The task of information systems at JC Penney has been made more difficult by a corporate change in direction to better compete with local and regional stores while still retaining a national presence. This strategy has included discounting large items such as appliances, adding more and better national brand name clothing, and taking advantage of its positioning in malls to better compete with regional "anchor" department stores. To better "compete locally" local store managers have been given the authority and information to make decisions about what is and is not selling at their location.

To accomplish these changes, JC Penney must implement its integrated software on top of its current separately existing hierarchical systems that were built for single departments and business units. Currently, a number of systems operate independently. These include the POS cash-register system, which gathers information on items sold, the price-change-management and price-lookup systems, a third-party EDI system for electronic ordering, and sales-tracking and credit-authorization systems.

In an effort to expedite the development process, Penney has used Texas Instrument's Information Engineering Facility CASE tool. This high-level design language enables programmers to build applications and automatically generate code based on the chosen design elements. Whenever he can, however, Evans prefers to buy software. He always favors buying. In his opinion, "It is less expensive; it is quicker; and it takes fewer resources."

Because the company is decentralized in many cities, quality control is crucial in system development. Issues that surround rollout are much different than if everything occurs in a central office.

One concept of particular importance is the InfoStore. An extension of the repository concept, this storehouse would be based on a common relational database fed by all the transaction-processing systems of the company. Client-server architecture would enable users to access information from any location in the company. Front-end software tools would enable the user to display this information in any format. The goal of the program is to make the information available in as close to the original form as possible.

Another advantage of the InfoStore is that it would allow buyers to communicate visually with one another. An Infostore digital camera would be able to transmit clear pictures with true colors and close-ups of items to allow examination of both texture and weight. Store layouts and newspaper advertisements could also be included.

## QUESTIONS

1. How does the JC Penney approach described here differ from the Sears method described in the previous cases?
2. Diagram the flow of data at a typical JC Penney's store that results from a purchase by a consumer using a credit card.
3. How many entities are involved in a typical credit card transaction? Identify all of the information that is captured by the transaction processing system.
4. How does the decentralized management of the stores affect the flow of data at JC Penney? Are there additional problems?
5. What requirements or changes would be needed to implement the InfoStore concept that JC Penney wants to install?

## CASE *Wal-Mart*

### Cutting Costs and Prices

Wal-Mart has set industry standards for technology application in the retail field. It has a sophisticated, companywide POS and satellite communication system. Interestingly, Sam Walton was a technophobe who went along with computerization only at the urging of his top executives. The famous greeter at the door was also not Sam Walton's idea. It was recommended by an hourly worker.

Wal-Mart has become the nation's largest retail chain by breaking many rules of retailing. Founder Sam Walton popularized discount pricing, choosing to avoid the advertising and other costs associated with periodic sales. Walton introduced "low prices always" on many brand-name products. Wal-Mart also concentrated on small Southern and Midwestern towns that other retailers were not interested in. Most dramatically, he overwhelmed local merchants with low prices made possible through large economies of scale.

Some attribute Wal-Mart's success to Walton's "cheerleading management style, determined penny-pinching, and tireless devotion to getting out of the office and into stores." This style grew the company to more than 1,735 Wal-Marts. These are 80,000-square-foot discount department stores offering apparel, appliances, furniture, and prescription drugs. Also, more than 212 Sam's Clubs sell merchandise in bulk to members at near-wholesale prices.

Wal-Mart has primarily been successful in small towns and cities. Its current growth targets are the sub-urban and urban areas. Land, construction, and labor costs in these areas are higher than in the more rural areas. Competition is also stronger, reducing the potential margins. Kmart and Dayton Hudson's Target Stores have already established themselves in these markets. Customer loyalty and the best locations are currently in place. Fewer than 40 percent of Wal-Mart's stores face direct competition from Target or Kmart. In five years, with the expansion into the suburban areas, this competition will be 75 percent.

### Technology and New Services

Wal-Mart is emphasizing service as well as low prices in its new store of the future in Rogers, Arkansas. Featuring technological innovations and strategies, the store features wide aisles and classy displays. It covers 125,000 square feet and is 50 percent larger than current Wal-Marts. Seeking to blur the distinction between self- and full-service, the new technology provides information about products and helps customers locate them. The new store also includes designer names such as Estee Lauder and Calvin Klein. Instead of the traditional rows of items, related products are organized into visual "vignettes," that encourage consumers to buy "multiples," or a package of items because they fit together.

Wal-Mart was an early leader in computerizing retailing distribution. The new store will put technology in the hands of the customer. Consumerscan will give shoppers their own bar code scanners to check prices once the goods are placed in the cart.

Another innovation is the Wal-Mart Arts Report. It has a television screen to let customers preview movie and music videos. Wal-Mart Sound Associates provides information about audio products. This approach enables Wal-Mart to provide improved consumer information through technology.

Currently used in supermarkets, VideoCart provides information about products as the customer progresses through the store. VideoCart lists hundreds of product categories by department along with a department-by-department map of the store.

Based in Chicago, VideoCart, Inc, asserts that VideoCarts increase sales by $1 per visit to a supermarket. VideoCart is interested in transferring the technology to discount department stores because they are the next group of shoppers who use grocery carts.

Some analysts assert that technology is not a good substitute for knowledgeable store clerks. At its present stage, VideoCart categorizes things generically, not by specific product. Thus customers may be sent to the wrong areas for specific products. Another problem is computer downtime. If customers come to rely on a diverse group of technological guides that each come from a different manufacturer, it will be difficult to coordinate their use and maintenance.

### QUESTIONS

1. How has Wal-Mart used technology to decrease costs and gain a competitive advantage? (Hint: Do additional research.)
2. How is Wal-Mart using technology to provide new services?
3. Will consumers be attracted by these new services? Or will they see the services as a replacement for workers?
4. What are the biggest problems discount retailers like Wal-Mart are likely to face in the next 5 to 10 years? How can new technologies help solve these problems?

### CASE *Kmart Is Applying Radar to Track Customer Traffic*

To improve sales and service, Kmart is testing a radar-like system to track customer traffic. The system uses beams of infrared light to count customers as they pass under sensors mounted over the store entrance and on the ceiling. Kmart hopes to use this new system to send salespeople to crowded departments and opening more checkout lanes before long lines form. The information will also enable Kmart to determine what percentage of the visitors to the store actually make purchases. Before this test, the only data tracked was transactions from the scanner system that the chain installed at checkout counters in 1990.

The goal of the program is to convert browsers into shoppers. Departments with little traffic will be showcased through "blue-light specials" and end-of-the aisle displays. This is one of the first steps to track customer traffic with other measures than sales. In one study, 71 percent of the shoppers did not make any purchases.

For many years, Kmart was the second largest retailer in the United States (behind Sears). By 1995, sales were falling drastically—despite several changes and upgrades. Customers often complained that prices were higher than at Wal-Mart. More importantly, Kmart was having trouble providing the appropriate products. Many items were overstocked, whereas customers often complained about empty shelves for products they wanted to buy.

### QUESTIONS

1. As a customer, would you be nervous knowing that your movements are being tracked by auto-mated monitors? Do you gain benefits from the system?
2. You learn that a store has recently installed the tracking system. You know that they give discounts in slow-moving areas. You gather some friends, crowd certain areas of the store and "deter" shoppers from other areas. When the system responds by offering a discount on the item you wanted, you quickly buy it and leave the store. Are your actions ethical? Will we need laws against such behavior? Where would the line be drawn—which actions would be acceptable? Is it acceptable for one person to wander around avoiding an area until a special is offered?
3. Estimate the volume of data that would be collected by a single store in one day. How can managers keep up with this volume? How much money would be invested in a computer system to track and store this much data?
4. Given the choice of building a "radar" tracking system, and improving inventory management, what are the relative merits and drawbacks of each system?

### CASE *Applying Technology to Kroger Food Stores*

Kroger Food Stores originated the concept of universal product codes (UPC) in the early 1970s. The technology uses laser beams to scan black and white stripes of varying widths. Today, almost 100 percent of the products sold in the United States carry the UPCs. Nearly 17,000 of the nation's 30,000 supermarkets use laser scanning equipment.

A computer to store the UPC codes and their interpretation is maintained at Kroger headquarters in Cincinnati. Each file contains a 10-digit number represented by the bar code plus the current price. The first five digits stand for the manufacturer, whose number is assigned by the Uniform Code Council in Dayton, Ohio. This council maintains the database of 60,000 companies from 77 different countries. It also determines the specifications for each bar code, including the width of the stripes and the contrast between the bar and the background. The next five digits are assigned by the individual manufacturer. They signify the product, with variations for flavor, size, and weight. To ring up produce, cashiers punch in a two-digit code that prompts the computer to look up the price for that item. The data is then analyzed in the same way as the other UPC information.

To shoppers, the UPC provides an assured price check at the checkout counter. With the assumption that the computer is programmed correctly, the consumer can be assured that the correct price is entered into the register. This removes the concern that the checker will key in the wrong price. The advantages of UPC-based information systems to Kroger Food Stores are even more dynamic:

- Labor savings. UPCs reduce the labor-intensive, tedious job of pricing cans and boxes of groceries. Prices are placed on the shelves for the customer. All the stock person needs to do is unpack the groceries and put them on the shelf.
- Price identification savings. Price changes are consolidated in the computer. This eliminates the need to make the changes on individual packages before and after a sale.
- Reordering and inventory information. The computer can be programmed to reorder immediately upon the sale of a complete box of 24 cans of soup or 12 boxes of cereal. This immediate reordering program reduces the number and level of individuals involved in the reordering process.

Kroger could analyze the resulting data on a daily basis, but, according to Jerry Morton, a consultant in Lawrence, Kansas, "doesn't take the time." Each week the headquarters computer retrieves the data from the stores. The data is then sold to services that analyze it and make recommendations. Up to $1 million can be made per year for selling the data to these services.

## QUESTIONS

1. What transaction-processing advantages does Kroger gain in using bar code scanners? Do you think bar codes and scanners save time at checkout?
2. What other cost and time saving features could the use of UPCs add to Kroger Food's operations?
3. How could an individual Kroger store use UPC technology to compete successfully with supermarkets in its area who do not use this feature?
4. How might the financial analysts at Kroger Foods use the data from UPCs to make better decisions?
5. What are the base objects involved in the Kroger system? How will these objects change over time?

## CASE  *Tesco: Efficient Distribution*

Tesco is one of the largest supermarkets in Britain. Its 1994 market share of 11.4 percent was only 0.1 percent behind Sainsbury. Tesco achieved this position through efficient distribution of products to its stores. At any time, there is less than a two-week supply of products in Tesco's distribution system, which makes it the most efficient food retailer in Europe. Tesco

operates nine distribution centers. Each one uses a just-in-time or cross-docking system. Approximately 40 percent of the goods that arrive at the center are immediately dispatched to lorries and distributed to stores.

Under the prior system, suppliers delivered products directly to each store. This system raised costs because it required more transportation. Often, the lorries were half empty. Paul Bateman, Tesco's distribution director, estimates that with the old method, there could be as many as 9,000 half-empty lorries clogging the M25, the major highway circling London. With the distribution centers, Tesco has cut the traffic to 1,000 lorries a day. The drivers follow an optimized schedule that cuts the transportation time.

In late 1995, Tesco opened a new distribution center in Southampton. The new depot uses an automated conveyor system that routes incoming packages by bar code to docks for immediate distribution to each store.

Improving the distribution and handling of products does more than cut costs. It enables the stores to stock less of each item, so they can carry more product lines. Tesco is expanding into carrying clothing and flowers. Managers also claim that the chain has 7.2 percent of the British market in videotapes.

Tesco is expanding its operations internationally, buying chains in France and Hungary. As they expand, Tesco and Sainsbury are using their vehicle-scheduling models to help their suppliers improve their distribution.

Tesco is also the first British food retailer to introduce a loyalty card that gives customers a 1 percent discount. In three months, 5 million customers had signed up for the card, and sales at existing stores increased by 7 percent.

## QUESTIONS

1. What data is collected and used by Tesco's distribution system?
2. How does the improved distribution system provide benefits beyond simply cutting costs?
3. In addition to encouraging repeat sales, how can data collected via the loyalty card be used by Tesco to improve sales?

## CASE  *Barney's: Gathering Data at the Point of Sale*

Retail merchants are always looking for better ways to keep track of their customers and to link the sales of items to the inventory and ordering processes. Barney's, Inc., a New York specialty chain, has installed a sophisticated point-of-sale network system to accomplish these two goals.

To be successful, specialized retail outlets require a clear understanding of their customer base. As competition for this market segment has increased, retailers have searched for nonintrusive ways to find out more about them. This enables the retailer to offer product promotions that specifically meet the customer's buying habits.

Barney's customer profile system captures customer purchases at the point of sale and uses the data to offer customers more personalized service. Preliminary data is obtained from the credit card application. The record of purchases with the credit card enables an increasingly accurate portrayal of the customer to be developed.

Based on this record, smaller, more focused catalogs that specifically pinpoint a customer's shopping habits can be mailed. Salespersons who are particularly tuned into a customer's buying habits can begin a more suggestive selling campaign. For example, suit salespersons can call individuals who buy shirts from Barney's and ask them why they do not buy their suits there. Equally important, salespersons can do a better job of contacting customers when their favorite new merchandise comes into the store or goes on sale. Salespersons can also call with birthday and anniversary greetings and the related sales information.

On a broader scale, the consolidated information provides important data for marketing and promotion analysis. By searching the collected information by product, the buyers receive feedback much sooner about what items sell and do not sell in the store.

The second benefit of the new system includes application software for inventory control, financial software, and accounts receivable. Records are kept as each stock item is sold. Once a shipping unit of a particular item has been purchased, a new order is sent directly to the distribution center. This greatly reduces "stockouts" and decreases the amount of time involved in the order-fulfillment process.

The third benefit of the system is the improved utilization of employees. The system enables more accurate accounts of sales per employee hour. This enables employee schedules to be adjusted to reflect the number of customer sales in a selling area at a particular time. Optimal sales-staff levels can be set. Better records can be kept of which salespersons are performing most successfully. Compensation and incentive packages can be adjusted quickly to more forcefully encourage the goals of the organization.

The OS/2 operating system was chosen because of its ability to perform multitasked operations. Multitasking enables a number of operations to be run concurrently. For Barney's, this means that multiple cash register terminals can feed into a single application controller that contains terminal data and merchandise information. Standard terminals can only conduct price and credit checks. The OS/2 functions enable these checks to occur while customer data is collected and analyzed and inventories are updated. The controller supports the point-of-sale terminal data as well as pricing and other merchandise information. It logs and stores each transaction and serves as the gateway to the outside world by communicating with the host to send out data and download pricing information and e-mail. The controller also dials out to the credit network and handles online credit authorizations.

Leo Rabinovitch, vice-president of new product development at STS Systems, the Montreal-based systems-solution company that designed Barney's system, further justified the choice of OS/2 as the base platform.

> The protected environment of OS/2 helps ensure the integrity of our applications. Implementation is much simpler because you do not have the RAM constraints that you do in DOS.

> There are great salespeople out there. This system will free them. At their terminals, they do not interact with the system at all. OS/2 is under the covers in a way that the salespeople never really see it. This lets them be great salespeople and makes the not-so-great salespeople do their jobs better.

## QUESTIONS:

1. What data does Barney's new system enable the salespeople to gather on Barney's customers?
2. What obstacles did Barney's have to overcome to successfully implement its database system?
3. How does the system at Barney's enable the store clerks to use it without adjusting their normal schedules?
4. Why did Leo Rabinovitch feel it was important to stress that "OS/2 is under the covers in a way that the salespeople never really see it?"
5. What are the advantages and disadvantages for a company like Barney's to implement their new system on a new and developing operating system like OS/2?
6. How is the salesperson at Barney's different from the traditional person involved in a transaction-processing system?
7. In implementing its database management system, Barney's did not focus on hardware. According to the text, why did the designers emphasize software, data, and personnel in their implementation?
8. How will the salesperson's jobs change after the database management system is implemented?

9. What steps can Barney's management insure that the great salespeople will be freed to do a better job and the not-so-great salespeople will become better salespeople?

## CASE    *Silent Sam at Service Merchandise*

Based in Nashville, Service Merchandise operates 335 catalog showrooms in 37 states. As a catalog showroom, it is able to display more products in less retail space. The showroom only contains a sample of each item. The main inventory is stored in an adjoining warehouse, where it is accessed and delivered on customer request.

Service Merchandise was founded in 1960 by Harry and Mary Zimmerman, now the firm's honorary chairman. In 1990, it had sales of $3.4 billion. Operations are built around an annual general-merchandise catalog with more than 9,000 items. This catalog is supplemented by a 150-page spring catalog and a 100-page Christmas catalog. The catalogs are distributed to more than 14 million customers annually.

The organization employs more than 24,000 sales people nationally. Advertising itself as "the world's largest jeweler," it operates a jewelry distribution center in New York City. General merchandise is distributed from five regional centers.

Ventures into new product lines have not proved to be successful. In the early 1980s, Service Merchandise introduced lines of computer equipment, women's lingerie, and home repair. Net income plummeted; by 1986, there was a net loss of $46 million. In 1987, the organization wrote off a one-time charge of $30 million.

When catalog shopping started in the 1950s and 1960s, it was a popular alternative because it offered discounts on national brandname merchandise. In the 1970s, discount chains such as Wal-Mart and Kmart expanded nationally and offered many of the same products at the same or even cheaper prices. In the 1980s, electronic discounters such as Fretter, Inc., and Highland Superstores further cut into their markets. Fretter and Highland offered a larger array of consumer-electronic items at similarly discounted prices. The specialty chains also provided salespersons who could answer customer inquiries.

In the 1950s the lower prices reduced the inconvenience of completing an order form and waiting for the item to be brought out from the warehouse. However, the national discounters of the 1980s enabled a customer to take an item off the shelf and carry it to the checkout line without the waiting time.

These changes and pressures have led to the failure of familiar names such as McDade & Co. and W. Bell & Co. Yet Service Merchandise has remained competitive. One reason, according to Laura Walther, a company spokesperson, is "the extensive computer program that goes along with the training of their associates." The latest innovation is a fairly recent computer system that enables customers to order their own items from the warehouse and pay for them without ever talking to a salesperson.

This new system is an extension of the current Silent Sam system. This program enables customers to check the availability of items and order them directly from the warehouse. A credit-card reader lets customers charge items without having to go to a cash register. Once an item is ordered and paid for, the stock pickers are informed of the sale and the location, the inventory is adjusted, and executives are informed about what is selling best.

The advanced nature of the Silent Sam system has addressed the most listed negative aspect of shopping at Service Merchandise. Customers always listed the waiting times between selecting, purchasing, and receiving a product as compared to the discount stores where customers pick an item directly from the shelf and take it with them to a checkout. Silent Sam greatly reduces this waiting period by immediately debiting the customer's account and ordering the product to be pulled from the warehouse.

### QUESTIONS

1. What information from Silent Sam can be used to form a knowledge base for Service Merchandise? How can this knowledge base assist Service Merchandise in its efforts to strengthen its relationship with its current customers?
2. How can the Silent Sam system reduce expenditures for stocking and retrieving products?
3. How does the knowledge base assist buyers in their efforts to reduce inventory and increase the sales of the current products?
4. What enhancements would you recommend for Silent Sam to improve the training for new employees?
5. What recommendations would you give for improving the interface between the customer user and Silent Sam?
6. What enhancements would you recommend for Silent Sam in future revisions?
7. What objects are involved in the Silent Sam system? Draw an object diagram with sample attributes and methods.

## CASE    *Borden*

When Demetrius Lappas arrived at Borden as vice-president and CIO, he consolidated technology efforts across the company. The area that he identified to provide the most benefit was electronic data interchange (EDI). He asserted that customers should be dealt with from a centralized office rather than a decentralized one.

EDI consolidates standard business forms such as purchase orders, invoices, and delivery receipts into a single electronic transaction. Not only does it expedite delivery, it also greatly reduces the amount of communication needed to initiate, transact, and confirm an item for purchase.

Up until Lappas's arrival, Borden implemented EDI haphazardly. Customers had separate EDI relationships with five or six Borden divisions.

One of the reasons that Borden was slow to adopt EDI was that it dealt in the food industry. Both sales reps and Borden's own purchasers were constantly making "deals" to take advantage of shifts in the marketplace. Dealmaking artificially changed the demand for Borden products, making it difficult to forecast future sales patterns.

EDI enabled both purchasers and suppliers to share information on sales and inventory immediately. This enabled Borden to do a better job of anticipating demand and making sure that effort was not extended to simply shift product between warehouses.

On the downside, the rigor of a centralized EDI system reduced Borden's sales reps' flexibility to negotiate customer contracts. For example, when a Borden sales rep requests special pricing for customers who want to sponsor a particular product promotion, such as for Elmer's Glue, it must be incorporated into the automated EDI system. Manual adjustments to the entry must then be made. The more manual adjustments are allowed, the more checkpoints must be in place to verify that the deals are profitable and that the customers sign the original contracts.

Before EDI, the sales reps needed only to concentrate on the sale. EDI brings all of these other factors to the forefront. Some sales reps have embraced the new system; others are still listing reasons why their accounts should be excluded. Implementing EDI is really not an option, however. Key customers have already adopted policies that require their purchases and sales to be through EDI.

## QUESTIONS

1. Why did Borden switch to EDI? What were the advantages?
2. If Borden made the EDI system easier for sales reps to use, would the sales reps still have reason to complain?
3. What advantages does Borden gain by centralizing the EDI system? What advantages do customers gain?

## CASE  *Small Business Accounts Receivable*

Small businesses often run into problems when their customers delay making payments. Most small businesses do not have the resources to support themselves if receipts are late. Although the company may look solid on paper, the delayed cash flow can ruin a company. The problem is especially acute when a major portion of the sales are to a larger company, which then delays payment.

In 1994, a Dun & Bradstreet Corp. survey indicated that larger companies (those with more than 500 workers) were paying their bills more slowly than at any time in the prior four years. For example, in April 1994, Ameritech Corp. notified 70,000 suppliers that it would not pay bills for 45 days, up from 30 days. Other companies routinely pay bills 90 days after being invoiced, when the invoices are typically due in 30 days.

Al Albert, owner of a small steel-distribution company in Pennsylvania, feels the effects of these changes. He notes that two-thirds of the money due from larger companies is overdue by 45 to 60 days, forcing him to delay a planned warehouse expansion.

Thomas Re, founder of Earthly Elements Inc., encountered even more serious problems. His company sold dried floral gifts and accessories. In November 1993, the firm received a $10,000 order from a home-shopping service. The order was significant, because the firm only had a total of $50,000 in orders for 1993. However, it cost Mr. Re 25 percent more to fill the order than he anticipated. Worse yet, by the end of February he had not been paid. By March 1994 he was forced to lay off his employees and close the business. He finally received payment in April but decided it was too late to salvage the company.

Some companies, like Truck Brokers Inc, in Bethany, Oklahoma, are minimizing the problem by requiring cash at the time of the sale. Thomas Banks, the owner, notes that "We're not in the business of lending money to strangers we don't trust."

## QUESTIONS

1. What causes cash flow problems?
2. What possible solutions are there to the cash-flow problem described by these companies? Can the small businesses get the large companies to change their process?
3. Can a computer system help the small companies in this situation? Describe exactly how such a system would work.
4. Identify the benefits that would arise from using the computer system. Which of the benefits come

directly from using the computer, and which ones arise because the firm's methods were changed?

5. Would your computer solution be better or worse overall than the other alternatives? That is, what costs or problems might it cause?

## CASE *Gitano*

Morris Dabah migrated from Syria to the New York garment district in the 1970s. He worked as a middle-man buying overstocked goods and reselling them to bargain basements clothiers. Over time, he built ties with banks and manufacturers to expand his businesses. When his sons, Haim, Isaac, and Ezra graduated high school, they joined the business. In 1977, they were joined by Robert Reiss, who invested $20,000 to help them start a new line of fashion jeans. In 1979, they began marketing tight-fitting jeans under the Gitano label. The initial market for designer jeans was fueled by Calvin Klein and Gloria Vanderbilt, which sold $50 jeans in major department stores. Gitano quickly realized that there was a large market for "designer jeans" at blue-collar prices. So they began selling extensively through discount stores, notably Wal-Mart. In the 1980s, the discount stores were rapidly gaining sales against the department stores and were seeking higher-class apparel. In 1980, the company expected to have $7 million in sales. Instead, they sold $45 million.

Gitano Jeans quickly became tied to Wal-Mart. As Wal-Mart expanded, so did Gitano. At the peak in 1990, Wal-Mart was buying $300 million of Gitano goods annually, making the discounter the largest customer of Gitano. When Wal-Mart demanded price cuts, Gitano typically agreed, even going so far as selling some orders at cost—giving up an $800,000 profit on a $4 million sale.

However, Gitano was experiencing problems from its explosive growth. Almost all of the clothing was manufactured overseas on a contract basis. The factories had a habit of substituting products when filling orders. For example, they would send snap-front jeans instead of button-front jeans. Retail customers were beginning to notice the problems. Marc Balmuth, Caldor's president, noted that it took Gitano "10 or 12 months to do what other brands could do in 4 months." Gitano managers were aware of the problems, but they felt that as long as they were making money, they need not worry. The huge growth rate and ties to the rapidly expanding Wal-Mart covered up a lot of mistakes.

By the mid-1980s, competitors were stepping up sales to discount stores. The Dabahs responded by adding new apparel divisions—ending up with 11 divisions. They also started their own factories. In 1988, they opened factories in Mississippi, Jamaica, and Guatemala. Unfortunately, due to having minimal controls and lack of a business plan, the factories caused additional problems.

Each of the 11 marketing divisions would call the factories directly and place orders. The factories fell behind, constantly switching production from one apparel line to another. At headquarters, a manager notes that Isaac Dabah spent hours on the phone calling the factories. He would start and stop production from corporate headquarters. Haim later estimated that Gitano lost $11 million in sales due to the production problems. In the end, Isaac chose to run the factories at full capacity, so Gitano could respond quickly to any orders. As a result, a former manager noted that at any given time in 1989, there were at least three years' worth of inventory of jeans in storage. To get rid of the inventory, the owners opened 88 outlet stores, without paying much attention to location.

Gitano executives panicked in 1990 when Wal-Mart ordered its suppliers to attach bar-coded price tags to all merchandise. The tags would enable Wal-Mart to compare products against the original orders, and they would quickly see the problems with the factories. Haim Dabah quickly flew to Bentonville and told Wal-Mart executives that Gitano was developing its own bar-coding system, but it would take a while to be operational. Gitano never did create a bar-code system that worked, but it bought time with Wal-Mart. One Gitano manager notes that the owners had to do something to hide the problem: "We knew that it would take us years to correct the factories so that they would consistently produce what we really ordered. It was that messed up."

In addition to production problems, the company had few financial controls. Coopers & Lybrand, Gitano's accountants, found several discrepancies in auditing the 1991 data. In particular, they could not locate more than $15 million booked as profits. The audited reports were corrected, but the $15 million became known as "The Black Hole."

Additional problems with accounting, coupled with a scheme to mislabel goods to avoid U.S. Customs eventually forced the company to hire a new CEO in 1993, Robert Gregory. His observations shed some light on the "Black Hole," when he notes that salespeople often gave discounts to retailers, without notifying Gitano. The company registered the sale at an item at a 32 percent profit margin. The salespeople gave discounts on this margin, resulting in giving up 10 percent or more of the profit without Gitano even knowing it. It was an ingrained part of the culture.

After U.S. Customs agents raided Gitano headquarters, Wal-Mart stopped ordering products, claiming that they would not do business with companies that violated U.S. laws. Details of the mismanagement came out in the ensuing investigation. Shareholder lawsuits were filed claiming fraud against the Dabah family. The SEC began an investigation. Management changed from the board of directors down. Mr. Gregory, the new CEO began an extensive cost-cutting operation and is trying to negotiate new distribution deals.

In 1994, the debt-ridden company was purchased by Fruit-of-the-Loom for $100 million. The remaining 145 employees are led by president Jim Huntington. Although most of the sales are through Wal-Mart, one of his goals is to convince other retail stores to carry the Gitano brand. The Gitano name has solid brand recognition. In a survey, 90 percent of 18 to 65 year old women recognized the brand name, and 62 percent had purchased Gitano products. However, some retail stores have become reluctant to buy products from companies that are heavily tied to Wal-Mart. They fear that Wal-Mart will get better deals and undercut the retail prices.

SOURCE: Adapted from Teri Agins, "Gitano Jeans' Fall Is Saga of Corruption and Mismanagement," *The Wall Street Journal*, February 18, 1994, pp. A1, A4. Reprinted by permission of *The Wall Street Journal*, © 1994 Dow Jones & Company, Inc. All rights reserved.

## QUESTIONS

1. Create a data flow diagram to show how transaction information flowed within the Gitano company. You might want to do some additional research.
2. What systems problems are evident in the Gitano case?
3. Describe Gitano's transaction-processing system and identify the major shortcomings.
4. Design (on paper) a new transaction-processing system for Gitano.
5. Identify the primary object classes, with attributes and member functions, for Gitano.
6. Why did it take 10 years to discover the problems? Could they have been corrected earlier? Who is responsible for allowing the problems to continue?

## CASE  *Shaker Village Implements Bar Code Inventory System*

The Shakers were an important, and well-noted, component of American religious history. They received their name because they were known to "shake" in the presence of the Holy Spirit. An early offshoot of Quakerism, the sect began in England in 1747. As their numbers increased, Shakers moved to America to practice their religion more freely and take advantage of the large open areas to establish their unique, com-

munal lifestyle. The Shakers were distinguished for their industrious lifestyle. Their keen sense of practical simplicity was particularly evident in their furniture, architecture, and lifestyle.

Nineteen Shaker villages were established in the United States. Because the Shakers did not believe in having sex, their communities eventually died out. Few have survived the intervening years.

The Canterbury Shaker Village, in Canterbury, New Hampshire, is the best preserved settlement of the Shaker communal lifestyle. Dating back to the 1780s, the village is composed of a cluster of 23 buildings set atop a hill. It is surrounded by 600 acres of fields, ponds, and woods. During the commune's peak around 1860, 300 people lived, worked, and worshipped in 100 buildings on 4,000 acres. In 1992, Sister Ethel Hudson, the last Canterbury Quaker, died at the age of 96.

Even though the original settlers have all died, the village has been faithfully restored. Today it is open to the public as a nonprofit museum. Craftspeople demonstrate the Shaker skills of box making, spinning, broom-making, and basket weaving.

The museum store is located in one of the buildings. It began as a tiny outlet operated by the Shakers on an informal basis. Since then, it has expanded in size and inventory to the point that it now employs a staff of full- and part-time workers. The expansion in volume and diversity of the items for sale made inventory control, point-of-sale management, reordering, and receiving increasingly complex.

Recognizing this, John Zobel, the museum store manager, researched and implemented an automation effort. He choose WordStock, Inc., as the supplier because it provided retail inventory/POS customized software that ran on standard hardware components. The host computer is a 486 personal computer linked to a dot matrix printer for generating reports and bar codes. The POS station is a dumb terminal interfaced with a cash drawer and receipt printer. A laser scanner reads the bar codes. Credit card transactions are swiped on a magnetic stripe reader. A single controller links the POS station with the 486 personal computer.

The store carries several hundred stock-keeping units (SKUs) for a total of 50,000 inventory items. The job is made more complex by the fact that most of the merchandise is made by local artisans and small manufacturers. The first step in automating the inventory process was to enter all of the items into the database and make bar codes for everything in stock. The uniqueness of the items made this much more difficult than for stores that rely on a more traditional approach. The system was installed in March 1994. The dedication of the staff enabled completion of the entry of the inventory by May. Inventory information included item name, vendor, description, price, SKU number, and department code. Bar code labels included the item's SKU number, name, and price.

As purchases are scanned, each transaction is relayed to the controlling personal computer. Inventory counts are automatically reduced. Periodic inventory reports are issued to check stock levels on various items. Reorders are made based on these inventory reports.

The capability to generate reports enables the store manager to obtain accurate counts by SKU number, monitor sales by department, and determine outstanding purchase orders. Because a number of items are carried on consignment, the new system can evaluate the performance of consignment items and determine their profitability. The reports also enable the outside trustees to better manage the store's operation.

Other advantages include a reduction in POS errors, an increase in the speed of the transactions, and a reduction in the time it takes to complete the annual inventory. Purchase orders, formerly prepared manually on a typewriter, are now generated from the inventory system.

When problems with the system cannot be solved in house or over the telephone, the system is connected by modem to the service department where it can be diagnosed online.

SOURCE: Jeanette Brown, "Tapping Into Niche Arenas," *Computer Reseller News,* September 25, 1995, p. 89.

## QUESTIONS

1. How is the Shaker Village different from a typical retail store? What features make the Shaker Village more difficult to computerize?
2. With the new system, what types of transaction-processing problems are likely to arise? How can they be minimized?
3. If you were a manager or trustee, what types of reports would you need to manage the Shaker Village stores?
4. Why did Zobel choose a personal computer-based system instead of a system based on a minicomputer?

## DISCUSSION ISSUE

### Are Standards Helpful?

It can be difficult to combine information. One problem is the differing types of data—spreadsheets, word processor documents, databases, and graphics. A bigger problem is that there are many different brands of software in each category. There are more than a hundred different word processors available and they all store the documents in a different format. Similarly, each commercial graphics package uses its own method to store the data. The problem becomes even worse when there are different brands of hardware involved. Then the data has to be physically transferred from one computer to another. Although there are data converters, the data is often modified slightly.

One answer to these problems is to choose standard software for everyone in the company to use. By using only one brand of each type of software, it is easier to share data with other people in the company. It is also easier to combine information from the different types of software. However, there are some problems with standardization. The director of MIS (George) has just called a meeting with the head of the accounting department (Sam) and the director of marketing (Jenny).

George:  Hi, Sam and Jenny. Thanks for coming. When I talked to you earlier, I mentioned that the MIS staff has been receiving a lot of calls from your departments. It's great that your employees are using the new computers. But we're starting to see some problems with the software. Sam, how many different graphics packages are you using?

Sam:  Let's see . . . I guess about half are using Microsoft PowerPoint. The rest are using some version of Corel Draw, and a couple people are using Adobe Illustrator. But they're working on special projects.

George:  Jenny, what about the marketing department? I hear you have around eight graphics packages.

Jenny:  That's not quite true. The administrative assistants are using PowerPoint for basic presentations and Excel for graphs. We produce some early advertising drafts with our two publishing packages. But one of those is on the PCs and the other runs on the Mac. The marketing staff members use whichever graphics package they first learned, so I guess there could be five or six. What's the problem?

George:   Well, we've been getting a lot of calls from your folks as they try to share information. One of the marketing people wanted to create a report with last year's sales figures and a graph. It took us a while to find the data, and then we had to spend three days converting the graphics. And the accounting department has been screaming for a year about not being able to get access to all of the data they want. It seems everyone in the company is stashing away data in their own databases and computers. So, we've decided to choose standard software for the entire company. We just made a bulk purchase of all the software we need for the company. We'll start distributing it next week.

Jenny:    Wait a minute. That's crazy. Who picked this software? Don't we get to vote? What's wrong with a little freedom?

Sam:      I can see where it'll save money. And we really do need a corporate graphics library. I've seen 20 different versions of the corporate logo, and I know people keep creating new versions for their own software.

George:   That's right. And we'll be able to provide better training and help for everyone because there will be less software we have to handle.

Jenny:    Oh come on. How much money can you really save? Besides, I don't think my department can get by with only one graphics package. We do too many different things. We have to have a separate system for our advertising staff, and all of our copy writers use their own systems at home, and . . .

George:   We know there are going to be some problems at first. We've chosen the most flexible packages we can find. We can do everything you need using just one software package.

Jenny:    I doubt it. Besides, then it'll be impossible to use. Plus, my staff are already familiar with the software they use now.

George:   We know it will take some time. We have training sessions scheduled for the next month. I have sign-up sheets here. We want you to get everyone in your offices signed up and in a class within the next month.

*Despite the problems, the company changes to four standard software packages. A year later, there is another meeting.*

Jenny:    George, I told you it wouldn't work.

George:   Well, if your staff would just cooperate a little longer, we can still work out the small problems. Besides, we did gain the advantages I promised. The MIS department is spending less on software, training, and support than we have in the last three years.

Jenny:    Right. That's because the software and support are all coming out of my budget now. My staff know better than to call you for help. They just call the software company support lines. The phone calls are costing a fortune, but at least we get answers.

Sam:      At least everyone can share their work now. We spend a lot less time converting figures and documents, and there are fewer touch-ups. I think the standard software policy is working well.

Jenny:    Oh sure. Just because they picked the software you like. But you're stuck now. I just read where the database company you people chose is filing for bankruptcy. And George, remember that graphics package you picked? It's two years out of date. It doesn't handle Object Linking and Embedding in Windows 95 and won't run on Windows NT. So now what do we do? Pick *more* standard software?

George:   Calm down. There have been a few minor problems, but Sam's right. The system is working fairly well.

Jenny:    Sure, that's easy for you to say. Have you talked to the other departments lately?

Sam:      Look. Can't we compromise a little? I don't really care about word processors and graphics packages. I just need access to spreadsheets and databases. Let's standardize on those and you folks in marketing can use whatever graphics packages you want.

Jenny:    Oh come on. I don't see what the problem is anyway. The new versions of the software we have can share data with all of the other software. I have a package that will convert documents between 30 different word processors and 20 graphics packages. It's not perfect, but it's easy and it's fast. I still don't see why we can't just buy what we want. If you want to read my data, you can convert it to whatever format you need.

George:   But then we're back where we started. I think we'll just stick with this software for a while longer. It's going to be too hard to change now. Maybe next year we can look for a new graphics package.

Jenny:    Sure, and maybe you should look for a new job.

## QUESTIONS

1.  Do you think everyone in a company should use the same word processor? What are the advantages? What are the drawbacks?

2.  Does everyone at your university use the same software? How is student software chosen? Is there a committee? How often does it meet? When was the last time your school changed software? How often do software vendors upgrade their software?

3.  Do you think George is right in enforcing the corporate standard? Can you think of a compromise for Sam that will make everyone happier?

4.  How difficult is it to convert documents among different word processors? What software packages are available to help?

5.  Do you think this problem is common in business? Is there anything businesses can do to minimize the problem?

# CHAPTER 5

# *Database Management*

## WHAT YOU WILL LEARN IN THIS CHAPTER

Why is a DBMS a good way to store data? How do you search a database? What problems do you encounter when searching large-text databases? What tasks are better suited to a DBMS than to a spreadsheet? How does a database make it easier to share data? How can a database make you a better manager?

In addition to basic information, American Express uses its Web page (http://www.americanexpress.com) to book vacations.

## AMERICAN EXPRESS

American Express has always marketed itself as the charge card of choice for the business traveler. For tax and reimbursement purposes, business travelers must keep extensive records of amounts, places, and for whom the expense was incurred. To meet this need, American Express has always provided monthly and annual itemized statements. These statements not only list the expense but also the category in which it falls. American Express does not present itself as a credit card. Bills are to be paid each month rather than being allowed to accumulate interest charges. Income is produced from a 4 percent fee to the merchant, not through interest collected from the customer.

From the beginning, one distinguishing feature of the American Express Card was "Country Club Billing." This was the physical return of the customer's charge receipt. Users of the card relied on this service to balance their accounts by comparing their receipts with those received from American Express. When the service was begun, this labor-intensive task was accomplished by hundreds of "sorters" in Fort Lauderdale and Phoenix. However, as the use of the American Express Card grew, so did the return of the 3¾ by 5 inch blue and white slips. By 1988, the slips were flowing into Ft. Lauderdale and Phoenix at the rate of 2 million per day.

The sorting process had become tedious in the extreme. Sorting machines helped but were limited in the number of pockets that were available to receive paper. Because the charge amounts were keyed by hand, inaccuracies were high. Time was also an issue. American Express pays merchants when they receive the charge receipts but does not realize its profit until card members pay their American Express bill. Thus, any time efficiencies at this stage improve the cost of capital and the profitability of the company.

To meet this need, American Express changed to an image-processed system. Named "Enhanced Country Club Billing," card members now receive laser-printed copies of the slips they signed at the point of purchase rather than carbon copies of their receipts. This change in the system that American Express has used to return receipts to their customers has reduced the time it takes to process one card member's bill from 4 working days to one and 1.5 days.

**OVERVIEW**

Collecting and sharing data is a crucial aspect of any job. Data collection is a fundamental step in transaction processing. Data management also integrates the divisions of a company, supports teamwork, and helps to control the organization. A primary role of information systems is to collect data and make it available to managers throughout the company. As shown in Figure 5.1, when data is not integrated but controlled and protected by separate divisions, it becomes impossible to run a firm efficiently.

Companywide databases are used to set standards and make it easier for managers to access and compare the data held by various departments. With standards and well-defined databases, managers can use query languages like SQL or query-by-example to ask questions and retrieve data in any manner. As long as the data exists in the database, managers can ask any type of question and examine the data in any way they need.

For you to obtain the full advantages of databases, they need to be designed carefully—often with the help of a database professional. Once the data tables are established, it is straightforward to create data-entry screens and reports. Current database systems help users build complex reports and applications simply by placing details on the screen with a mouse.

Databases are typically supported and managed through software known as a *database management system (DBMS)*. Database management systems provide controls over the data to ensure its accuracy and control who can use or alter the data. DBMSs are designed to deal with multiple users at the same time. They have internal provisions for backup and recovery of data.

Because database management systems are so powerful, they contain many options and controls, which can be intimidating when you first encounter a DBMS. The key is to focus on the components that you need first and worry about the other details later. As a manager, the most important feature you need to learn is how to retrieve data from an existing database.

**FIGURE 5.1**

Without a DBMS, data can be scattered throughout the company, making it more difficult to share information. Inconsistent data, duplication, and errors are common. A DBMS maintains data through a common interface. Data definition, access, consistency, and security are maintained by the DBMS.

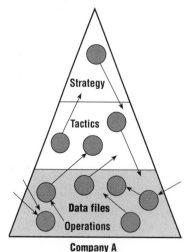

**Company A**
**Without a DBMS:**
**Hard to find and share data.**

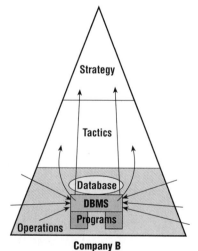

**Company B**
**With a DBMS:**
**Integrated data with shared access.**

**INTRODUCTION**  Database management systems are one of the most important tools in MIS. They have changed the way that computer applications are developed, and they are changing the way that companies are managed. The database approach begins with the premise that the most important aspect of the computer system is the data that it stores. The purpose of a database management system is to provide shared access to the data, answer questions, and create reports from the data.

A crucial factor with databases is that they can become massive. Several companies have indicated that their databases contain several terabytes (trillions of bytes) of data, as illustrated by American Express. Even small companies deal with databases with megabytes (millions) of data. The size of the database greatly affects its performance and the ability of users to find the data they need. Large databases need to be designed and maintained carefully to ensure that they run properly.

Another important characteristic of databases is that they are designed to help users to examine the data from a variety of perspectives. Instead of simply printing one type of report, they enable users to ask questions and create their own reports. Figure 5.2 illustrates how a DBMS is used in an organization. It collects data for transaction processing, creates reports, and processes ad hoc queries for managers. Figure 5.2 also indicates that databases usually require programmers to define the initial database and maintain programs to perform basic operations. The overall design is controlled by the database administrator.

Not all database systems are successful. Just as businesses fail, so do projects. There are many cases of information system projects that have failed. The reservation

---

## ◤ TRENDS ◣

In the 1960s and 1970s, companies typically built their own transaction-processing systems by writing programs in COBOL. These programs consisted of millions of lines of code. Each program created and used its own set of files. As companies expanded, more programs were created—each with its own format for files. Whenever a manager wanted a new **report** or additional information, a programmer had to modify the old code or create a completely new program.

A database management system (DBMS) presents a different approach to data, reports, and programming. The most important task is to define and store the data so authorized users can find everything they need. Report writers and input screens make it easy to enter data and create reports without relying on programmers. Data is stored in a special format so that it can be shared with multiple users.

The early forms of DBMS (hierarchical and network) limited the way in which data could be stored. The most severe limitation is that you needed to know exactly how you were going to use the data *before* you started collecting it. Database designers had to know exactly what questions people might ask regarding the data.

In the early 1970s, E. F. Codd created a flexible approach to storing data, known as the *relational model* that avoided these problems. Today, relational databases are the dominant method used to store and access data. Relational databases have a *query system* that enables managers to get answers to questions without relying on programmers.

Early databases were designed to handle business types of data, such as customer names and account data. Some modern database systems can store entire books, pictures, graphs, or even sound clips as types of data. A few companies are working on **object-oriented DBMS**s that enable users to create their own data types and continue to manipulate and search the data.

**FIGURE 5.2**

MIS employees and databases. The database administrator is responsible for defining and maintaining the overall structure and data. Programmers and analysts create applications and programs that collect data and produce reports. Business operations generate data that fills the database. Managers use the application programs and ask ad hoc questions of the data.

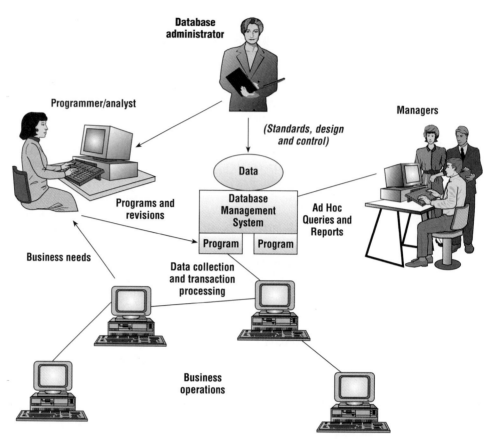

system of Continental Airlines (Reality Bytes 5–1) provides an interesting comparison to American Airlines (Reality Bytes 5–4). Although database projects are often easier to complete than projects using traditional programming techniques, it is still important to evaluate the business first and decide whether or not the project is reasonable.

 **Reality Bytes** ▶ **5–1  CONTINENTAL AIRLINE BANKRUPTCY**

A well-designed database can greatly improve the ability of a business to serve its customers' needs. This power often draws companies to develop grand plans of how the database will change the way that they do business. For the database to work, a substantial financial investment and a great deal of energy must be committed to the project. Sometimes databases are begun but not finished because the business is not stable enough to support the investment required.

In 1989, EDS entered a $4-billion contract with Continental Airlines to program a state-of-the-art

reservation system. The system promised to link Continental's reservation system with those of the automobile companies, hotels, and entertainment establishments. Unfortunately, in the days before bankruptcy, Continental became so involved in maintaining the day-to-day operation of the business that it was unable to invest the time necessary to work with EDS to ensure proper input regarding the system requirements. This, and Continental's impending bankruptcy, led to the dissolution of the contract at the early stages of the agreement.

## Relational Databases

The goal of a relational DBMS is to make it easy to store and retrieve the data you need. All data is stored in **tables,** which consist of **columns** with **rows** of data. Each table has a name and represents objects or relationships in the data. For instance, most businesses will have tables for customers, employees, orders, and inventory.

Besides storing data, a modern DBMS has several useful tools. Input screens are built to help users enter data. Reports can be created by laying out data, text, and graphics on the screen—often with no programming. You can get answers to questions with a query language or even by pointing to tables and data on the screen. You can establish security conditions by granting or denying access to portions of the data. Most systems include an application generator that can tie input screens, queries, and reports together with a menu system. A complex application can be created by typing a few titles on the screen, without writing a single line of traditional program code.

### DATABASE TERMINOLOGY

When E. F. Codd created the relational database model, he deliberately introduced new terms to describe the way that databases should store information. His terms are *attribute, tuple,* and *relation.*

Although Codd's terms are precisely defined mathematically, they can be confusing. As a result, many people use the slightly easier words: *column, row,* and *table.*

Before relational databases, several different terms were used to refer to the various parts of a database. The problem is that many of the terms had several definitions. Common terms include *field, record,* and *file.* You should avoid these terms.

## Tables, Rows, Columns, Data Types

If you understand how spreadsheets work, it is easy to comprehend relational databases. A single spreadsheet consists of rows and columns of data. Each column has a unique name, and a row contains data about one individual object. A database consists of many of these tables that are linked by the data they contain.

In a database, each table contains data for a specific entity or object. For example, most companies will have a table to hold customer data. There are certain attributes or characteristics of the customers that we want to store. In Figure 5.3 each customer has a phone number, name, address, and city. In practice, there will be more columns.

Figure 5.3 also illustrates one of the most important features of a database system: Relational databases are specifically designed to allow many tables to be created and then combined in interesting ways. If you only had one table, you could use a spreadsheet or virtually any filing system, assuming it could handle the number of rows you needed. However, most business problems involve data stored in different tables. In the example, customers can place many different orders. Each order is stored in a separate line in the Orders table.

Notice that the tables are joined or linked by the customer phone number. The phone number is the **primary key** column in the customer table. Each row in a table must be different from the rest; otherwise, it is a waste of space. Consequently, each table must have a primary key. A primary key is a set of one or more columns that

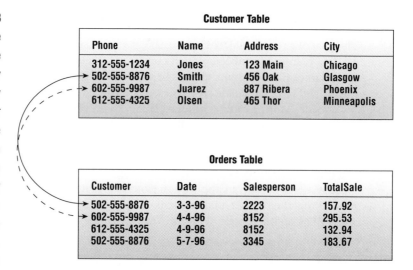

**Customer Table**

| Phone | Name | Address | City |
|---|---|---|---|
| 312-555-1234 | Jones | 123 Main | Chicago |
| 502-555-8876 | Smith | 456 Oak | Glasgow |
| 602-555-9987 | Juarez | 887 Ribera | Phoenix |
| 612-555-4325 | Olsen | 465 Thor | Minneapolis |

**Orders Table**

| Customer | Date | Salesperson | TotalSale |
|---|---|---|---|
| 502-555-8876 | 3-3-96 | 2223 | 157.92 |
| 602-555-9987 | 4-4-96 | 8152 | 295.53 |
| 612-555-4325 | 4-9-96 | 8152 | 132.94 |
| 502-555-8876 | 5-7-96 | 3345 | 183.67 |

uniquely identifies each row. If someone gives you a key value (e.g., phone number), you can immediately locate the appropriate row and find the rest of the data for that entity (name, address, city).

Each primary key value must be unique, so in this example no two customers can have the same phone number. In the Orders table, the key consists of the customer phone number plus the Date column. Keys that use more than one column are called **concatenated keys.** For this key to be unique, customers can only place one order per day. In the real world, we could avoid this problem by creating a column for Order_Number as the key.

Unlike a spreadsheet, each database column can contain only one type of data at a time. For example, in the Date column you can only store dates. You would not be allowed to put names or totals in this column. Most relational databases were designed to hold business types of data. The basic choices are: text, dates (and times), numeric, and objects (graphics, video, and sound). Some systems enable you to be more specific about how to store numeric data. For instance, you might want to store data with only two decimal places for monetary values. Whenever possible, dates should be stored in a date format instead of text. That way you can perform arithmetic on the values. For example, a formula like (today + 30) could be used to find a due date that is 30 days from today.

## ADVANTAGES OF THE DATABASE APPROACH

## Problems with the Programming Approach

To store data on a computer with a programming approach (e.g., COBOL), the programmer has to create a file. To use this file later, the programmer has to know exactly how it was created. Consider the portion of the simple data file shown in Figure 5.4. It is difficult to determine the meaning of the data stored in this file. For instance, the middle set of numbers may represent a customer ID number. However, where does it stop? Is the first address supposed to be 351 Main Street, or is it 1 Main Street? There is no way to answer this question by looking at this data file. To use this data, a programmer has to locate the file definition or program that originally created

```
Jones John 223452351 Main Street Smith Abdul 987635323 Elm Street Markan
Martha 151257362 Oak Street Stein Joshua 736346542 East Way
                              .   .   .
```

**FIGURE 5.4**
SAMPLE DATA FILE
Simple files. In a non-DBMS approach, data is often stored in files that are hard to read. To correctly retrieve the data, you need to find the file definition that is probably stored in an application program. If one program is changed, all other programs that use the file will need to be altered.

the file. Hiding somewhere in that program is a description of how this file is supposed to be read.

It gets worse. Imagine what happens when there are thousands of data files and hundreds of programs, and constant changes, as in a reservation system. If the programmers are careful, even this situation can be dealt with. However, consider what happens when the data need to be shared among several programs or multiple users. In Figure 5.5, there are only two programs and four files. Notice that the customer file is used by both programs. One dark and stormy night the program that prints customer bills encounters an error and crashes. It displays an error message on the operator's terminal. The operator promptly calls the programmer who is on duty that night. The programmer crawls out of bed, goes to work, and looks for the problem. To solve the problem, our sleepy programmer has to modify the customer file. That leaves three choices. First, if she just changes the file and this program, the invoice program will fail at some point in the future (in the middle of the night). Second, she could change all the programs that use the customer file, but it means spending several hours searching through every program to see whether it uses the customer file. Third, she can copy the customer file and modify it for the billing program. That way the billing program will be able to finish tonight and the other programs will not be affected. Of course it means creating duplicate data, but someone else can solve that problem later.

**FIGURE 5.5**
Programming difficulties. Significant problems arise in a programming environment when multiple programs try to share the same data files. The problem is multiplied when there are thousands of programs and data files.

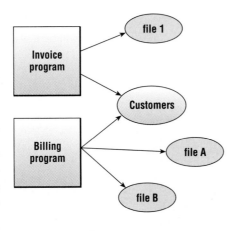

| DBMS ADVANTAGES | PROGRAM/FILE ADVANTAGES |
|---|---|
| Focus on data<br>*Data is crucial, programs change* | Existing MIS knowledge |
| Data independence<br>*Ability to change programs and data* | Support for legacy data. |
| Data integrity<br>*Accuracy, Time, Concurrency, Security* | High-speed code for some applications; can run on existing/older hardware. |
| Speed of development<br>*Report writers, Input forms, Data manipulation* | |
| Flexibility and queries<br>*User control without programs* | |

## The Database Management Approach

### Focus on Data

The database management approach is fundamentally different from the older programming methods. As noted in Figure 5.6, the most important aspect is the data, not the programs. The problems that were created with the old methods are avoided by focusing our attention on the data. Whenever someone needs a computer application, the first step is to identify the data that will be needed. Then a database management system is used to store the data. It takes care of storing the raw data, as well as information about that data. Everything you want to know is stored within the DBMS, not in an application program. This situation is illustrated in Figure 5.7.

### Data Independence

Defining the data separately from the programs is called **data independence.** The main advantage is that it is possible to change the data without having to change the programs. For instance, you might want to add a second phone number to the customer data. With a DBMS, you can make this change, and it will not affect any of the existing programs. Similarly, the reports can be modified without having to change the data. That means when the programmer is called in at 3 A.M., she only has to change one program. All the other programs will be unaffected. Besides making the programmer's life easier, the database is more likely to be accurate and there will be less duplication of data.

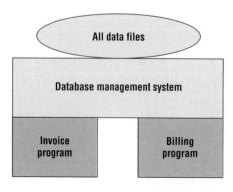

Data independence means that the data and programs are separate, which makes it possible to alter the database tables as needed, without destroying the programs. As the business grows, you might decide to collect additional data, such as keeping track of sales by salesperson or by sales route. As the company expands and changes, the underlying tables can be expanded and new tables can be added—without interfering with the existing tables or current programs. Just be careful to avoid deleting tables or removing entire columns. Of course, as the business changes, managers will undoubtedly want to modify the reports to add the new information.

### Data Integrity

As discussed in Chapter 4, data integrity is an important consideration in designing and maintaining databases. Data integrity means that the database holds accurate, up-to-date data. If there are business limits on certain values, the database should force the data entry to abide by those rules. For example, prices will always be positive numbers. Another integrity concept is the importance of identifying missing (null) data. Computations should be able to skip missing data. From a manager's viewpoint, an important integrity design element is naming columns carefully. The columns should have names and descriptions so that the users understand what is stored in the database. If a column is simply labeled *Revenue,* users might wonder if that means revenue from all products, all divisions, the current year, or perhaps just monthly totals. All of this information is stored with the database in the data dictionary.

An important component of database integrity is that the data needs to be consistent. For example, consider a table that describes products for sale. Perhaps the products are grouped into categories (cleaning supplies, paper goods, clothing, etc.). Each item belongs to only one category. What happens if the categories are not entered consistently? The *Cleaning Supplies* category might be entered as just *Cleaning,* or maybe as *Clean Supplies,* or even *Cl Sup.* These variations in the data make it difficult to search the table based on that category because the user would have to know all of the variations. A good DBMS supports rules that can be used to minimize these problems. Thus when dealing with databases, it is good practice to be careful when you enter data to ensure that your entries are consistent.

Consider the problems faced by the U.S. CIA (Reality Bytes 5-2). They collect and store data on thousands of variables for hundreds of countries. Plus, they search large blocks of textual material, which causes many problems. Different words can be

 **Reality Bytes** ▶ **5–2** THE CENTRAL INTELLIGENCE AGENCY

Data integrity and accuracy are extremely important for data bases to provide accurate information. This is particularly the case at the Central Intelligence Agency (CIA). The CIA must maintain extensive databases on a large number of foreign operatives, corporations, and activities. Up until this time they have been hindered in their searches by the diverse number of computer systems and programs that they have had to search.

One product that the CIA has adopted to search its databases is Topic, a comprehensive text and image search and retrieval program. Topic is unique because it is document-format independent. It can search most major word processing and desktop publishing packages and image formats without regard to the program in which they were written. Topic retrieves by concepts formed through a combination of words rather than a single word. Thus, it can search for information across large collections of documents stored in multiple formats on many different computing platforms. Topic uses all of the computing resources on a distributed network to result in fast retrievals.

used to describe the same concepts; the same word can have different meanings; and words can be misspelled. These inconsistencies make it difficult to search the database. Therefore, the CIA database tools have to be powerful and capable of finding matches based on inconsistent and incomplete data. Chapter 10 illustrates other tools available that the CIA uses to overcome these problems.

### Speed of Development

It is possible to create an entire database application without having to write a single line of traditional programming code. As a result, an application can be built in a fraction of the time it would take to create it by writing COBOL programs. Studies indicate that most systems can be created 10 times faster using a DBMS—if the data already exists in the database. As the commercial database products (such as Oracle, Ingres, Informix, and DB2) continue to add features, they can be used to solve even more complex problems.

Keep in mind that it is possible to use traditional programming tools (such as COBOL) in conjunction with the DBMS. If complex reports or complicated calculations are involved, it is sometimes easier to use a traditional programming language. These programs retrieve the base data from the DBMS and print their own reports or store computed values in the database for later use.

Recall that one of the most important steps of developing a solution is to break the problem into smaller pieces. One major piece of any problem is the data. A DBMS makes this portion of the problem easier to solve. By putting the DBMS in charge of maintaining the data, keeping track of security, automatically supporting multiple users and printing reports, the developer can concentrate on solving the specific business problems. By starting from scratch with COBOL, each of these features would have to be rewritten for every application that was designed, which would be expensive.

### Control over Output

Another strong advantage of database management systems is their ability to provide many different views of the output. In fact, a primary objective of the relational database approach is to store the data so that users can retrieve it any way they need. The other feature of databases is that they are designed to make it easy to combine related data. An older programming/file approach generally limits the user to using data in only one way.

With a DBMS, output can be created from report writers, which make it easy to format the data; some systems even draw graphs. The other common method of retrieving data is to use a query language such as **query by example (QBE)** or **SQL.** Queries enable managers to search for answers to questions without using a programmer to write special programs.

**QUERIES**    Most of the time, managers will be dealing with databases that have been created by someone else. You will need to learn how to retrieve data to answer questions. It might be nice to be able to ask questions in a natural language (such as English), but it turns out to be hard to make computers understand these questions and you might not always be certain that the answer is what you asked for. A DBMS provides at least one method of asking questions and retrieving data. Two common methods are QBE and SQL. SQL is an international standard method for retrieving data from database management systems. It is supported by most of the major commercial relational database management systems. By the way, according to the most recent definition, the name SQL is just three letters, not an acronym. QBE stands for query by example and is a visual method of examining data stored in a relational database. You ask ques-

**FIGURE 5.8**
FOUR QUESTIONS TO
CREATE A QUERY
To create a database
query, you will always
have to answer these
four questions. In many
cases, there will be only
one table (or view), so
the second and last
questions are easy.

- What output do you want to see?
- What tables are involved?
- What do you already know (or what constraints are given)?
- How are the tables joined together?

tions and examine the data by pointing to tables on the screen and filling in templates. As shown by the International Disaster Relief agencies (Reality Bytes 5-3), the data can be collected over many years. Queries can only answer questions for which you have collected the appropriate data.

Regardless of the method used to look up information in a database, there are four basic questions you will answer, as listed in Figure 5.8. It does not matter in which order you think of the questions. With some methods (such as QBE) it is easier to choose the tables first. With other methods (such as SQL), it is sometimes easier to choose the output first. In many cases, you will switch back and forth among the four questions until you have all of the components you need. As you learn more about databases, keep these four questions handy and write down your answers before you attempt to create the query on the DBMS.

## Reality Bytes    5–3  INTERNATIONAL DISASTER RELIEF

The Centre for Research on the Epidemiology of Disasters at the University of Louvain in Belgium has built a database of all international disasters since 1900. Researchers have also developed early warning systems to predict drought, famine, and some earthquakes. The International Red Cross notes that the early warning system helped that organization avoid famine in Ethiopia in 1994.

In Burundi in 1995, the Red Cross used its database to speed its response and provide better service.

The system enabled workers to find 40 additional workers within 24 hours. It identifies which commercial suppliers can deliver food immediately and locate trucks to deliver it. The database can even identify the quickest delivery routes.

Additional data is collected on-site and shared with other workers and the international community. Relief workers in the field use radio links to the Internet to relay data and needs to other agencies.

## Single-Table Queries

Consider a simple customer table that contains columns for CustomerID, Name, Phone, Address, City, State, and AccountBalance. Each customer is assigned a unique number that will be used as a primary key. The AccountBalance is the amount of money the customer currently owes to our company. The table with some sample data is shown in Figure 5.9.

**FIGURE 5.9**
A sample table for
customer data.
CustomerID
(abbreviated to CustID)
is the primary key and
is used to uniquely
identify each customer.

| CUSTID | NAME | PHONE | ADDRESS | CITY | STATE | ACCOUNTBALANCE |
|--------|------|-------|---------|------|-------|----------------|
| 12345 | Jones | 312-555-1234 | 123 Main | Chicago | IL | 197.54 |
| 23587 | Smitz | 206-656-7763 | 876 Oak | Seattle | WA | 353.76 |
| 87535 | James | 305-777-2235 | 753 Elm | Miami | FL | 255.90 |

**FIGURE 5.10**

Query by example for the Customer table. Checking the Show box ensures that the column will be displayed when the query is run. Conditions are entered in the Criteria row. Conditions entered on the same row are connected by an "And" clause. Conditions on separate rows are combined with an "Or" clause.

| Field: | CustomerID | Name | Phone | Address | City | State | AccountBalance |
|---|---|---|---|---|---|---|---|
| Total: | | | | | | | |
| Sort: | | | | | | | |
| Show: | X | X | X | X | X | X | X |
| Criteria: | | | | | | | > 200 |
| Or: | | | | | | | |

## Query by Example

Query-by-example systems that were designed for graphical user interfaces (GUIs) are especially easy to use. Microsoft's Access illustrates a common approach. The basic mechanism is to make selections on the screen—typically by pointing to them with a mouse. You then fill out a template like the one shown in Figure 5.10.

With a QBE approach, you will first be asked to choose the table that contains the data you want to see. You will be given a list of tables in the database and you select the one you need. Once you have selected the table, you choose the columns that you want to display in the result. You use the QBE screen to specify totals, sort the results, and place restraints (criteria) on the data.

Most of the time, you will want to see only some of the rows of data. For instance, you want a list of customers who owe you the most money. You decide to restrict the listing to customers who have account balances greater than $200. With QBE, you enter the appropriate restriction in the column as shown in Figure 5.11. You can specify other conditions for the other columns. Placing them on the same row means they will be interpreted as AND conditions. If conditions are placed on separate rows, results will be computed for rows that match at least one of the criteria (OR condition). Figure 5.11 shows the QBE screen which tells the DBMS to display the ID, City, and AccountBalance for customers who live in Denver and have account balances of more than $200.

If you are searching a text column, you might want to look for a single word, or part of a word in a sentence. There is a pattern-matching command called LIKE that enables you to search for parts of text. For example, to assign customer accounts alphabetically to your salespeople, you might need a list of customers whose names start with the letter S. In the name column, you would enter the constraint: LIKE "S*". The asterisk (*)

**FIGURE 5.11**

Query by example query. List the customers from Denver with an AccountBalance of more than $200. Results of the query can be sorted in Ascending or Descending order. Multiple levels of sorts are created by selecting additional columns. You will use multiple column sorts when the first column contains several identical values. For example, sort by City, Name.

| Field: | CustomerID | Name | Phone | Address | City | State | AccountBalance |
|---|---|---|---|---|---|---|---|
| Total: | | | | | | | |
| Sort: | Ascending | | | | | | |
| Show: | X | ☐ | ☐ | ☐ | X | ☐ | X |
| Criteria: | | | | | Denver | | > 200 |
| Or: | | | | | | | |

will match any characters that follow the letter S. You also can use a question mark (?) wildcard character to match exactly one character. Note that some database systems use the SQL standard percent sign (%) and underscore (_) instead of * and ?.

Another useful condition is the BETWEEN statement. If you have a table of orders and want to get a list orders placed in June and July, you can enter the condition for sales_date: BETWEEN #6/1/96# and #7/31/96#.

There is one additional feature of relational databases that you will find useful. In many cases, there will be data missing from your database. Perhaps you do not have the phone numbers of all of your customers. Or, maybe the marketing department has not yet set a price for a new product. Missing data is represented by the NULL value in relational databases. So if you want a list of all the customers where you do not know their phone numbers, you can enter the condition for the phone column: IS NULL.

## SQL

Another method of retrieving data from a DBMS is with the query language SQL. Although some people find SQL more difficult to learn, it has two advantages. First, it is a standard language that is supported by many different database systems, so the commands will work the same in many situations. Second, it is easier to read than QBE, so it is easier for your colleagues to understand your queries.

SQL is a moderately complex language. There are only a few major commands in SQL, but each command can have several components. We will use only a few simple SQL statements. You can take a database class to learn more SQL details. We will start by looking at a data in a single table, to introduce the SELECT statement. Then you will learn how to combine data from several tables.

The standard command for retrieving data in SQL is SELECT. To be clear, we will write SQL command words in uppercase, but you can type them into the computer as lowercase. The simple form of the command is shown in Figure 5.12. The four parts are written on separate lines here to make the command easier to read.

The first step is to decide which columns you want to see. These columns can be listed in whatever order you want. The column names should be separated by commas. If you want to see all the columns, you can use the keyword ALL or an asterisk (*). Next, you need to know the name of the table. The SQL command to retrieve all of the customer data is: SELECT * FROM Customers. The result can be sorted by adding the ORDER BY clause. For example, SELECT * FROM Customers ORDER BY City.

**FIGURE 5.12**
The SQL SELECT command is used to retrieve and display data. It is the foundation of many of the other SQL commands.

| SELECT | columns |
| FROM | tables |
| WHERE | conditions |
| JOIN | matching columns |
| ORDER BY | column {ASC|DESC} |

**FIGURE 5.13**
DATABASE
CALCULATIONS
QBE and SQL can both
perform calculations
on the data. In addition
to these aggregation
functions, new
columns can be
created with standard
algebraic operators
$(+ - * /)$.

| | |
|---|---|
| SUM | total value of items |
| AVG | average of values |
| MIN | minimum value |
| MAX | maximum value |
| COUNT | number of rows |
| STDEV | standard deviation |
| VAR | variance of items |

To get a list of customers who live in Atlanta with account balances greater than $200, you need to add a WHERE clause. The command becomes: SELECT * FROM Customers WHERE (AccountBalance > 200) and (City = "Atlanta"). Notice the similarity to the QBE command. Of course, with SQL, you need to remember (and type in) the names of the tables and columns. NULL values and BETWEEN commands are also available in SQL.

## Computations

Many business questions involve totals or other calculations. All database systems have some mechanism to perform simple calculations. However, these facilities are not as complex as those available in spreadsheets. On the other hand, the database versions are generally easier to use and can operate on millions of rows of data. Typical functions are listed in Figure 5.13.

### Query by Example

Although most database management systems provide a means to compute totals and averages, there is no standard method for entering the commands. Typically, the commands are displayed on a menu. Access uses an extended grid shown in Figure 5.14. You point to the row you want to calculate and type in the desired function. The example shows how to get the number of customers and the average account balance.

Calculations are generally combined with the selection criteria. For instance, you might want the average account balance for all customers who live in Atlanta. The QBE screen for this question is displayed in Figure 5.15. The only change you have to make is to type *Atlanta* into the city column. Combining selection clauses with calculations enables you to answer many different questions.

**FIGURE 5.14**
Query by example
overall AccountBalance
average for the
Customer table. This
query counts the
number of rows
(CustomerID) and
computes the overall
average of the
account balance.

| Field: | CustomerID | Name | Phone | Address | City | State | AccountBalance |
|---|---|---|---|---|---|---|---|
| Total: | Count | | | | | | Avg |
| Sort: | | | | | | | |
| Show: | X | ☐ | ☐ | ☐ | ☐ | ☐ | X |
| Criteria: | | | | | | | |
| Or: | | | | | | | |

**FIGURE 5.15**

QBE AccountBalance average for Atlanta customers for the Customer table. This query computes the average account balance for those customers living in Atlanta.

| Field: | CustomerID | Name | Phone | Address | City | State | AccountBalance |
|---|---|---|---|---|---|---|---|
| Total: | count | | | | where | | Avg |
| Sort: | | | | | | | |
| Show: | X | ☐ | ☐ | ☐ | X | ☐ | X |
| Criteria: | | | | | Atlanta | | |
| Or: | | | | | | | |

Another useful feature is the ability to divide the rows into groups and get subtotals or other calculations for each group. If you know there are 10 cities in the database, you could run the average account balance query 10 different times to get the values for each city. An easier method is to use the GROUP BY option and run the query once. This time, instead of specifying the city, you indicate that cities are to be treated as groups. Then the DBMS will find the average account balance for each city. You do not even have to know which cities are in the database. The group by method used by Access is shown in Figure 5.16.

## SQL

SQL can also perform simple calculations. If you have columns for Price and QuantitySold, the value of items sold can be found by computing: SELECT Price * QuantitySold. The standard functions in Figure 5.13 are available. To compute the total of the accounts, you would enter: SELECT AVG(AccountBalance) FROM Customers.

The GROUP BY clause is also available. The command becomes: SELECT AVG(AccountBalance) FROM Customers GROUP BY City. Although it might be more difficult to remember the command and the column names, using SQL has two advantages over QBE. First, SQL is a defined standard. The commands you learn for one DBMS will generally work the same on another DBMS. Second, SQL statements are sometimes easier to read. Some QBE commands are not easy to understand—especially if selection criteria are connected by AND or OR commands displayed on separate lines. Many QBE systems automatically build the corresponding SQL statement for you. It is a good idea to check this statement to make sure you placed the conditions correctly on the form.

**FIGURE 5.16**

Subtotal calculations. One powerful capability of query systems is the ability to compute summary statistics for subsets (groups) of data. This query computes the average account balance for customers and lists the results for each city in the database.

| Field: | CustomerID | Name | Phone | Address | City | State | AccountBalance |
|---|---|---|---|---|---|---|---|
| Total: | | | | | Group By | | Avg |
| Sort: | | | | | | | |
| Show: | ☐ | ☐ | ☐ | ☐ | X | ☐ | X |
| Criteria: | | | | | | | |
| Or: | | | | | | | |

**FIGURE 5.17**

Multiple tables. The true power of a database lies in the ability to combine data from multiple tables. Actual databases can have hundreds or thousands of related tables. Notice that each table is related to another table through matching columns. You should be able to draw lines between column labels that will connect each of the tables.

**Customer**

| C# | Name | Phone | City | Acct |
|----|------|-------|------|------|
| 12345 | Jones | 312-555-1234 | Chicago | 197.54 |
| 29587 | Smitz | 206-676-7763 | Seattle | 353.76 |
| 87535 | James | 305-777-2235 | Miami | 255.93 |
| 44453 | Kolke | 303-888-8876 | Denver | 863.39 |
| 28764 | Adamz | 602-999-2539 | Phoenix | 526.76 |

**Orders**

| O# | C# | S# | ODate | Amount |
|----|----|----|-------|--------|
| 117 | 12345 | 887 | 03-03-96 | 57.92 |
| 125 | 87535 | 663 | 04-04-96 | 123.54 |
| 157 | 12345 | 554 | 04-09-96 | 297.89 |
| 169 | 29587 | 255 | 05-06-96 | 89.93 |
| 178 | 44453 | 663 | 05-01-96 | 154.39 |
| 188 | 29587 | 554 | 05-08-96 | 325.46 |
| 201 | 12345 | 887 | 05-23-96 | 193.58 |
| 211 | 44453 | 255 | 06-09-96 | 201.39 |
| 213 | 44453 | 255 | 06-09-96 | 154.15 |
| 215 | 87535 | 887 | 06-09-96 | 563.27 |
| 280 | 28764 | 663 | 06-27-96 | 255.32 |

**Salespeople**

| S# | Name | YearHired | Phone | Commission |
|----|------|-----------|-------|------------|
| 255 | West | 1975 | 213-333-2345 | 5% |
| 452 | Zeke | 1994 | 213-343-5553 | 3% |
| 554 | Jabbar | 1991 | 213-534-8876 | 4% |
| 663 | Bird | 1993 | 213-225-3335 | 4% |
| 887 | Johnson | 1992 | 213-887-6635 | 4% |

**ItemsSold**

| O# | Item# | Quantity |
|----|-------|----------|
| 117 | 1154 | 2 |
| 117 | 7653 | 4 |
| 117 | 3342 | 1 |
| 125 | 8763 | 3 |
| 125 | 1154 | 4 |
| 157 | 7653 | 2 |
| 169 | 3342 | 1 |
| 169 | 9987 | 5 |
| 178 | 2254 | 1 |

**Items**

| Item# | Description | Price |
|-------|-------------|-------|
| 1154 | Corn Broom | 1.00 |
| 2254 | Blue Jeans | 12.00 |
| 3342 | Paper towels 3 rolls | 1.00 |
| 7653 | Laundry Detergent | 2.00 |
| 8763 | Men's Boots | 15.00 |
| 9987 | Candy Popcorn | 0.50 |

## Joining Multiple Tables

The true strength of a database management system lies in its ability to combine data from several tables. Part of the Customer table is shown in Figure 5.17, with additional tables that show a list of orders placed by those customers and the salespeople involved.

Notice that the tables were designed so they can be connected. For example, the Orders table can be connected to the Customer table by matching the customer number (C#). The Orders table can be matched to the salespeople table through the salespeople table number (S#). Once you have joined the tables together, the database system retrieves and displays the data as if it were stored in one table.

The chief advantage to using multiple tables is that you can connect tables that have a one-to-many relationship. For example, each salesperson may be associated with many different orders. Instead of repeating the salesperson information on every order, we only needed to include the salesperson's ID (S#) number. Joining the tables together tells the DBMS to automatically look up the corresponding data from the salespeople table.

### Query by Example

Most people find that database systems that use graphical QBE commands to join tables together are much easier to use than straight SQL commands. With a DBMS like

*Access* you join the tables together by pointing to the column name in one table and dragging it to the matching column in the other table. The DBMS displays the connection between the two columns. Whenever you want to retrieve data from more than one table, you must first join them together.

### SQL

In SQL, connections between tables are typically made with the INNER JOIN clause in the FROM statement. For example, to join the customers and orders tables by equal customer numbers and get the combined data, use the command:

```
SELECT * FROM Customers INNER JOIN Orders ON
Customers.C# = Orders.C#
```

Notice that both tables must be listed in the FROM statement. Always remember that if you list more than one table, the tables must be joined. The dot before the column (C#) separates the table name from the column name (table.column). You can use this form any time you type in a column name, but it is only required when there might be confusion about which table the column is in. In the example, both tables have a column called C#. To keep them straight, we have to specify which table we want to use.

### Examples

We now have the basics to begin asking questions of the data. Start with an easy one. Which customers (C#) have placed orders since June 1, 1996? The query and result are shown in Figure 5.18. Notice that customer number 44453 has placed two orders. Some systems will show you the order number twice; others will automatically delete the duplicates.

It can be difficult to remember each customer's number, so it is better to use the customer name and have the DBMS automatically look up the customer number. This second query is shown in Figure 5.19. Note that the Customer table is joined to the Orders table by the matching values of C#.

**FIGURE 5.18**
QBE and SQL. QBE and SQL are based on the same fundamental concepts. You build each query by asking the same four basic questions.

**Question:** Which customers (C#) have placed orders since June 1, 1996?

**QBE:**

| Field: | C# | ODate | | | | | |
|---|---|---|---|---|---|---|---|
| Total: | | | | | | | |
| Sort: | | | | | | | |
| Show: | [X] | [X] | ☐ | ☐ | ☐ | ☐ | ☐ |
| Criteria: | | > = 6/1/96 | | | | | |
| Or: | | | | | | | |

**SQL:** SELECT C#, ODate
FROM Orders
WHERE ODate > = 6/1/96

**Result:**
44453 6/9/96
44453 6/9/96
87535 6/9/96
28764 6/27/96

**FIGURE 5.19**

Multitable queries showing shared columns. Queries-that use more than one table are slightly more complex. Because columns can have any name, you must tell the database system how the tables are connected.

**Question:** What are the names of the customers who placed orders since June 1, 1996?

**QBE:**

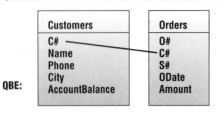

| Field: | Name | ODate | | | | | |
|--------|------|-------|--|--|--|--|--|
| Total: | | | | | | | |
| Sort: | | | | | | | |
| Show: | X | ☐ | ☐ | ☐ | ☐ | ☐ | ☐ |
| Criteria: | | > = 6/1/96 | | | | | |
| Or: | | | | | | | |

**SQL:**   SELECT   Name
         FROM   Customers INNER JOIN Orders ON Customers.C# = Orders.C#
         WHERE   ODate > = 6/1/96

**Result:**   Kolke
             James
             Adamz

Now, try a more complicated query: List the salespeople (sorted alphabetically) with the names of the customers who placed orders with that salesperson. This question sounds difficult, but the command is easy when you join all three tables together. The query and the result are shown in Figure 5.20. Notice there is no entry for the salesperson (Zeke) who has no orders at this point.

One more example and you should be ready to work on problems by yourself. Say your firm is thinking about opening a new office in Miami and your manager wants to know the total amount of orders placed from customers who live in Miami. This command uses the SUM function and is shown in Figure 5.21.

## Views

There is one important feature of queries that you will find useful. Any query can be saved as a **view.** For example, if you have a complex query that you have to run every week, you (or a database specialist) could create the query and save it as a view with its own name. The important point is that the view can now be treated like any other table. In the example, you might define a view that combines the tables for customers, orders, and salespeople, and call it SalesOrders. Then, to get the total sales from customers in Miami, you run the query on the SalesOrders view and you no longer have to worry about joining tables because the query has already performed the step.

The advantage of views is that you can look at the data in different ways without having to duplicate the data. As a manager, you can create complex views so your employees can look up information using much simpler commands. Think of a view as a mirror. If you stand in front of a three-way mirror in a clothing store, you get different views of yourself, but there is still only one person.

**FIGURE 5.20**
Multitable queries with several joins. More complicated queries follow the same basic rules. Note that some database management systems can automatically switch displays between QBE and SQL. This feature is useful so that you can check the joins and the criteria to be sure they are being interpreted correctly.

**Question:** List the salespeople (sorted alphabetically) along with the names of the customers who placed orders with that salesperson.

**QBE:**

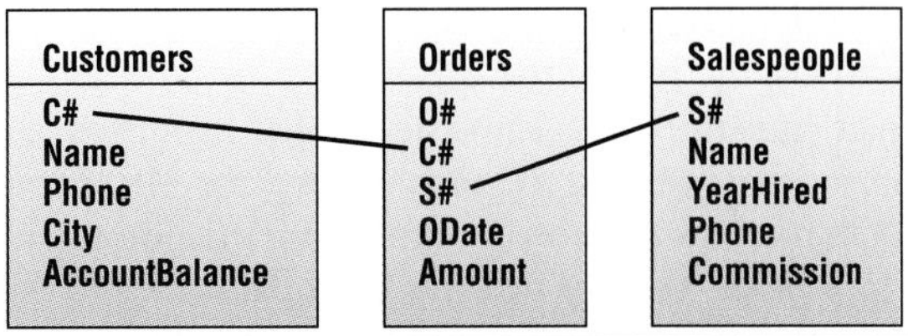

Customers: C#, Name, Phone, City, AccountBalance
Orders: O#, C#, S#, ODate, Amount
Salespeople: S#, Name, YearHired, Phone, Commission

| Field: | SalesPeople.Name | Customers.Name | | |
|---|---|---|---|---|
| Total: | | | | |
| Sort: | | | | |
| Show: | X | ☐ | ☐ | ☐ |
| Criteria: | | | | |
| Or: | | | | |

**Result:**

| | |
|---|---|
| Bird | Adamz |
| Bird | Kolke |
| Bird | James |
| Jabbar | Smitz |
| Jabbar | Jones |
| Johnson | James |
| Johnson | Jones |
| West | Kolke |
| West | Smitz |

**SQL:**  SELECT  SalesPeople.Name, Customers.Name
FROM  SalesPeople INNER JOIN
 (Orders INNER JOIN Customers ON Customers.C# = Orders.C#)
 ON SalesPeople.S# = Orders.S#
ORDER BY  SalesPeople.Name

**FIGURE 5.21**
Computations and subsets. Totals and other computations can be entered on the QBE form. Be careful about the WHERE criteria. In this example, we want the condition to be applied to each data line, so we specify the WHERE label. Some systems might try to apply the condition to the overall total, which would use the SQL HAVING label.

**Question:** What is the total amount of orders placed from customers who live in Miami?

**QBE:**

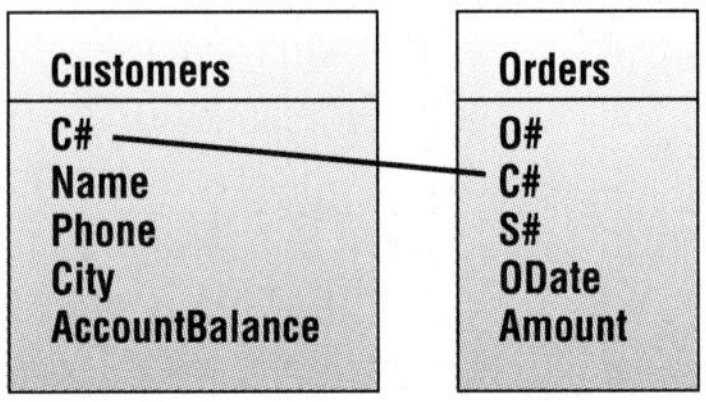

Customers: C#, Name, Phone, City, AccountBalance
Orders: O#, C#, S#, ODate, Amount

| Field: | Amount | City | | |
|---|---|---|---|---|
| Total: | Sum | Where | | |
| Sort: | | | | |
| Show: | X | ☐ | ☐ | ☐ |
| Criteria: | | Miami | | |
| Or: | | | | |

**Result**

686.81

**SQL:**  SELECT  Sum(Amount)
FROM  Customers INNER JOIN Orders ON Customers.C# = Orders.C#
WHERE  City = "Miami"

**DESIGNING A DATABASE**    In any large project, the most important first step is to determine whether the project is going to be economically and technically feasible. At this point, it is also crucial that the top levels of management fully support the project. If there is hesitation on the part of the executives, the rest of the organization will be less likely to cooperate. Also, when the project runs into delays and additional expenses, it will be difficult to obtain the additional support needed to finish the project. The developers of the Sabre reservation system obtained this support by explaining the potential advantages of the system.

An important step in dealing with databases is the initial definition when you decide exactly what columns to put in each table. If it is done correctly, the tables fit together and you can retrieve any combination of data you need. It is also easy to

 **Reality Bytes**     **5–4**    Sabre—Specifying Requirements

Computerized reservation systems are built upon the concept of linked databases. The time and expense of searching information is related to the amount of material that needs to be examined. As a result, the most efficient searching process is to break the databases into smaller parts. Each section can be individually searched and then linked for more composite travel arrangements. Storing information in individually retrievable units also enables information to be accessed from many different perspectives. For example, the agent can look for flights by airline, times, cities, or passenger.

The quickest way to evaluate the financial effectiveness of an airline is to examine its utilization ratio. This is the percentage of seats that are full on any given flight. Because seats are sold on a variable price basis, the airline's goal is to sell as many seats as possible at the highest possible rate. To list all of the seats at the highest price may cause too many seats to remain unfilled. To list all of the seats at the lowest price may cause them to sell out but at a rate that is far below what the market will bear.

Computerized reservation systems greatly improve airline utilization. They enable each "seat" to be sold at a unique price. They also automatically document the number of seats that are sold on each plane. An astute airline planner can link the marketing information from specific segments of the database with the utilization ratio on specific flights. He or she can then develop a marketing program to intercede in any routes that are not filling according to schedule. For example, if flights to the South are not full, he or she can initiate flight "bargains" to those areas. This might include prices to entice retired individuals with

flexible schedules and the desire to travel to the South but with limited resources with which to purchase tickets.

When American Airlines managers first began the design process for the Sabre system, they analyzed the business requirements for what they wanted the system to do. Then they set parameters for the system. They wanted an online database that could be accessed by travel agents across the country. The database would have to be able to be updated instantly. In setting these goals, they realized that this project would expand the current technological boundaries in database work.

The project had the potential to change the way reservations and scheduling were accomplished in the entire airlines industry. It was also the first time a database program of this magnitude had been attempted. Coupled with the expense of a project of this nature, the project team realized top management support was essential for the project to succeed.

After analysis, top management realized that the income potential from the proposed system could become so significant that the investment was worth the risk. As a result, company executives established a study team composed of users and individuals from the information technology group to examine the proposed system and make further recommendations. Management also developed a program to communicate its commitment to the individuals at the airline who were currently charged with maintaining the reservation system. Finally, the work flow documentation in the current manual system was thoroughly reviewed to determine the best way to automate the system and enhance efficiencies.

make additions and changes to the tables. On the other hand, if the tables are not defined correctly, you will end up with a mess. You will not be able to collect and store some of the data you need. You will have trouble getting answers to some types of questions. It can be time consuming to redefine tables and reports to fix the problems. Because defining tables is so important, everyone who uses a database should have some idea of what is involved. However, to become an expert you really need to take a database management course.

## Data Definition

The first step in defining tables is to identify the information that you will need to make your decisions. You can begin by collecting or designing the input forms and reports that will be used. Then the data items displayed on these forms and reports will be organized into tables.

There are some rules that each table must obey. First, every table must have a primary key, which is one or more columns that uniquely identify each row. Often we create an ID number (such as order number) to use as a short primary key. Improperly chosen database keys (Reality Bytes 5-5) can result in costly errors.

 **Reality Bytes**  **5-5** **DATABASE KEYS**

A company learned a costly database lesson in 1993. The MIS department created a database that automatically printed employee bonus checks. Managers rushed the system into place without formal testing by the accounting department. The MIS team decided to use the employee name as the primary key. However, several employees had the same name. As a result, bonus checks were sent to the wrong employees. A few of these employees refused to return them. It cost the company several thousand dollars to issue new checks to the correct employees. It pays to make sure that keys are unique and take the time to test new systems.

The second rule is there can be only one value stored in each cell. For example, if there is a column for phone number, it cannot hold a home phone number and a business phone number at the same time. In this case, the solution is to create two columns: HomePhone and WorkPhone. But what if there are more phone numbers, such as a fax number or an answering service number? How many phone number columns should we create? If most people have only one phone number, it would be a waste of space to create columns for five phone numbers. This problem is an example of repeating columns. If you do not know how many columns to use, you should create a new table to hold those columns. In this example, you could have a phone table, like the one shown in Figure 5.22. Notice that the columns for the primary key are underlined and must include the original customer number (C#). There is no wasted space if a customer does not have a certain type of phone number. For example, there is no entry for a business phone for customer number 44.

The process of defining tables correctly is called data **normalization.** You can learn more about normalization in a database course. The first steps of normalization are described in the appendix. If you want a hint, an important rule is that every non-key column must depend on the whole key and nothing but the key. Roughly, it means that each table should refer to only one object or concept. You should be able to give each table a name that reflects what is stored in the table. If you have trouble coming up with a simple name, the table might not be defined correctly, and you

**FIGURE 5.22**

Table definition. For the database approach to work correctly, all of the tables must be carefully defined. A technique known as normalization is used to properly define the tables. In this example, customers might have many different types of phone numbers. We say that phone number is a repeating attribute. Repeating attributes must be converted into rows in a new table. Hence we split the initial table into two tables: Customers and Phones.

**Customers**

| C# | Name | City | Home | Business | Fax | Service |
|----|------|------|------|----------|-----|---------|
| 11 | Johns | Chicago | 312-111-1111 | 312-222-2222 | 312-222-3834 | 312-876-3456 |
| 22 | Smith | Chicago | 312-111-4567 | | | 312-414-5353 |
| 33 | James | Chicago | 312-111-2967 | 312-222-9976 | | |
| 44 | Riosi | Chicago | | | 312-333-8765 | |

**Customers(C#, Name, City)**

| C# | Name | City |
|----|------|------|
| 11 | Johns | Chicago |
| 22 | Smith | Chicago |
| 33 | James | Chicago |
| 44 | Riosi | Chicago |

**Phones(C#, PhoneType, Number)**

| C# | PhoneType | Number |
|----|-----------|--------|
| 11 | Home | 312-111-1111 |
| 11 | Business | 312-222-2222 |
| 11 | Fax | 312-222-3834 |
| 11 | Service | 312-876-3456 |
| 22 | Home | 312-111-4567 |
| 22 | Service | 312-414-5353 |
| 33 | Business | 312-222-9976 |
| 33 | Home | 312-111-2967 |
| 44 | Fax | 312-333-8765 |

might have to split it into multiple, simpler tables. An introduction to the process of normalization is presented in the appendix to this chapter.

## Data Input Screens

Rarely is data entered directly into the database's tables. Instead, input forms are used to enter some data automatically and to present a screen that is easier for users to understand. It is common to use colors and boxes to make the screen easier to read. Input screens can be used to perform calculations (such as taxes). Longer descriptions and help screens can be included to make it easier for the user to remember what goes in each column. A sample form is shown in Figure 5.23.

### ◤ INTERNATIONALIZATION: ZIP CODES ◢

Databases often contain addresses (of customers, suppliers, employees, etc.) that typically use zip codes. In the United States, zip codes typically consist of five digits, so it is tempting to set up a Zipcode column that restricts input to five integers. However, bulk mail is often cheaper if it utilizes nine-digit zip codes (Zip + 4).

Even more importantly, if your addresses might someday include international data, you have to be more careful in column restrictions. For instance,

Canadian and British postal codes include alphabetic characters in the middle of the code. Some areas (such as Hong Kong) do not use any postal codes.

Similarly, when you set up databases that include phone numbers, be sure to allocate enough space for area codes. If international phone numbers will be listed, you need to add three extra digits on the front for the international country code.

FIGURE 5.23

DBMS input forms. Input forms are used to collect data from the user and perform basic computations. Subforms or scrolling regions are used when there is a one-to-many relationship.

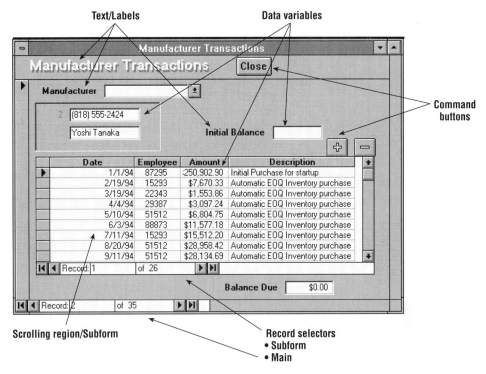

**FIGURE 5.23**

DBMS input forms. Input forms are used to collect data from the user and perform basic computations. Subforms or scrolling regions are used when there is a one-to-many relationship.

Many times, input screens look like existing paper forms. Consider a typical order form, which first collects customer information such as name and address. It also contains lines for items ordered, descriptions, and prices. These are usually followed by subtotals and totals. If these forms exist on paper, it is easy to create them as a DBMS input screen. If you are creating a completely new form, it helps to draw it on paper first to get a feel for what you want it to look like.

Most input forms begin as a screen that is empty except for a menu line or some other help message. Three types of information can be placed on an input screen: (1) simple text, (2) input blanks or (3) data retrieved from the database. A Windows-based DBMS can also include pictures, graphs, sound and video.

Paper forms have labels to tell the user what is supposed to be entered into each blank. For instance, many paper forms ask for a name: NAME _____ . The label (NAME) tells you what you are supposed to enter on the blank line. A DBMS input form works much the same way. The first step is to type in the various labels. Move the cursor to a spot on the screen and type in a label or sentence that will tell the user what needs to be entered.

Most database systems automatically enter some types of data, such as the current date. If necessary, users can change the date, but it saves time by enabling them to press ENTER to accept the displayed value. The same situation holds for sequential items like order numbers, where the DBMS can automatically generate each unique order number.

After you have typed in the basic labels, the next step is to add the data-entry boxes. Just as you would type a blank line on a paper form, you need to tell the DBMS exactly what data will be entered by the user. For instance, move the screen cursor to a position next to the Date label, then tell the DBMS to enter data at that point. You will specify the name of the column where the data will be stored. You can also specify default values. A **default value** is a value that is automatically displayed by the computer. For the case of the date, the DBMS will let you enter a name like Date() that will display the current date.

When a DBMS prints out data, it can be formatted in different ways. You can control the way the data is displayed by using a format command. A date might be displayed as 10/24/92 by entering the format MM/DD/YY. There are several common date formats; most firms tend to use one standard format. Note that many European firms use a format that is different from the common ones used in the U.S.

The next section of the order form contains basic customer information. This data is stored in the Customer table, not the Orders table. When you select the Orders table, you might have to indicate that the Orders and Customer tables are connected to each other by the phone number. Now, place the text labels on the screen (customer name, address, etc.). Then place a data entry box after each label.

Next, you can add the Sales table; it is connected to the Orders table by the order number. Type in the column names for Item#, Description, Price, and Quantity. The DBMS input form will define this part of the table as a **scrolling region** or subform. To users, this subform will behave somewhat like a spreadsheet. They can see several rows at a time, and keys (or the mouse) will move the screen cursor up and down as users enter data into any row.

The only items entered in the Sales table are the Item# and the Quantity ordered. The Description and Price can be found by creating a *look-up* in the items table. If the clerk using this screen types in the item number, the description and price will appear. With a good DBMS, it is possible to define a pop-up form or combo box in case the clerk does not know the number. This way, by pressing a certain key, a table listing each Item# and Description will be displayed in a window on the screen. The clerk can then scroll through the list to find the item.

## Reports

Most of the time, the data listed in one table is not complete enough to help managers make decisions. For example, a listing of a Sales table might provide only phone numbers, item numbers, and the quantity ordered. A more useful report would print sales grouped by customer. It would also compute total sales for each customer. Because this report relies on data from several tables, it is best to base the report on a view.

The view for the sales report example needs four tables. An OrderReport view is created that joins the Customer table to Orders by C#, Orders to ItemSold by O#, and ItemsSold to Items by Item#. The DBMS will have a "create report" option to create the sales report. The report will be based on the OrderReport view. The report writer consists of a blank screen. You can put simple text statements anywhere on the page. You also can place data values on the page, and you can compute totals and make other calculations.

Most reports can be broken into categories. For example, there might be report titles that appear only at the front of the report (such as cover pages). Other information, such as the report title, date, and column labels, will be repeated at the top of each page. All of these items are called **page headers.** Similarly, there can be **page footers** at the bottom of each page. Reports may also contain group **breaks.** For instance, the sales report needs subtotals for each customer, so you need to break the report into subsections for each customer. Generally, you can specify several levels of breaks. For instance, you might break each customer order into totals by date. Each break can have a *break header,* a **detail section,** and a *break footer.* In the example shown in Figure 5.23, the customer name is printed on the break header. There is a detail line that lists the item information. The subtotals are displayed on the break footers. The report design or layout is illustrated in Figure 5.24. The report with sample data is printed in Figure 5.25.

**FIGURE 5.24**

DBMS report writers. Reports are created in sections. The report header is printed one time at the top of the report. Data in the page header section is printed at the top of every page. There are corresponding page footers and a report footer. Primary data is printed in the detail section. Data can be organized as groups by creating breaks. Titles are often printed in the break header with subtotals in the break footer.

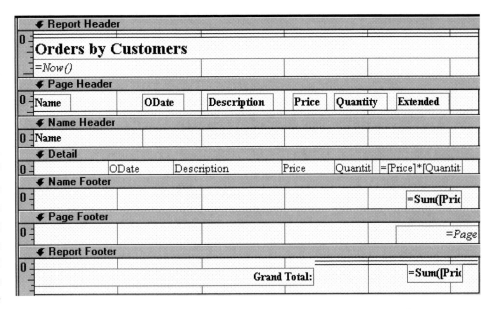

To create this report, you first tell the DBMS that the report will contain one break based on customer phone number. You also define the variable *subtot* which is price multiplied by quantity. Now you move the cursor to the top of the screen and type in the titles for the top of the page. Then place each column and variable on the report. You can format each item to make it look better. For example, you might want to format dates as MM/DD/YYYY so that all four digits of the year are displayed. Similarly, you can add dollar signs to the subtotals and totals.

When you have finished creating the report, you can print it. When you print this report, it should be sorted by customer name. The DBMS will also enable you to print the report so that it contains data just for one month. Notice that only five or six lines are needed to create a complex report. Without the DBMS report writer, it would take a programmer several hours to create this report, and it would be much harder to make changes to it in the future.

## Putting It Together with Menus

If you are creating a database for yourself with just a couple of input screens and reports, you can probably quit at this point. On the other hand, for more complex databases or for projects that other people will use, it would be wise to make the system easier to use. *Application generators* are tools that enable you to combine the various features into a single application. The resulting application can be used by selecting choices from a menu, much like users do with commercial software. The important design feature is that you can create the entire application without writing any programming commands.

Consider a simple example. As a manager, you need a sales report printed every day that shows the best-selling items. Every week you want a list of total sales for each employee to bring to your sales meetings. You also send letters to your best customers every month offering them additional discounts. You want to put your secretary in charge of printing these reports, but you do not have time to explain all the details about how to use the database program. Instead, you create a simple menu that lists each report. The secretary chooses the desired report from the list. Some

## Orders by Customers

*07-Mar-96*

| Name | ODate | Description | Price | Quantity | Extended |
|------|-------|-------------|-------|----------|----------|
| **Adamz** | | | | | |
| | 6/27/96 | Blue Jeans | $12.00 | 1 | $12.00 |
| | 6/27/96 | Paper Towels, 3 rolls | $1.00 | 3 | $3.00 |
| | | | | | **$15.00** |
| **James** | | | | | |
| | 4/4/96 | Corn Broom | $1.00 | 4 | $4.00 |
| | 4/4/96 | Men's Boots | $15.00 | 3 | $45.00 |
| | 6/9/96 | Blue Jeans | $12.00 | 1 | $12.00 |
| | 6/9/96 | Laundry Detergent | $2.00 | 1 | $2.00 |
| | | | | | **$63.00** |
| **Jones** | | | | | |
| | 3/3/96 | Corn Broom | $1.00 | 2 | $2.00 |
| | 3/3/96 | Laundry Detergent | $2.00 | 4 | $8.00 |
| | 3/3/96 | Paper Towels, 3 rolls | $1.00 | 1 | $1.00 |
| | 4/9/96 | Laundry Detergent | $2.00 | 2 | $4.00 |
| | 5/23/96 | Corn Broom | $1.00 | 1 | $1.00 |
| | | | | | **$16.00** |
| **Kolke** | | | | | |
| | 5/1/96 | Blue Jeans | $12.00 | 1 | $12.00 |
| | 6/9/96 | Blue Jeans | $12.00 | 1 | $12.00 |
| | 6/9/96 | Candy Popcorn | $0.50 | 5 | $2.50 |
| | 6/9/96 | Paper Towels, 3 rolls | $1.00 | 2 | $2.00 |
| | | | | | **$28.50** |
| **Smitz** | | | | | |
| | 5/6/96 | Candy Popcorn | $0.50 | 5 | $2.50 |
| | 5/6/96 | Paper Towels, 3 rolls | $1.00 | 1 | $1.00 |
| | 5/8/96 | Men's Boots | $15.00 | 1 | $15.00 |
| | 5/8/96 | Paper Towels, 3 rolls | $1.00 | 4 | $4.00 |
| | | | | | **$22.50** |

reports might ask questions, such as which week to use. The secretary enters the answers and the report is printed.

The first step in creating an application is to think about the people who will use it. How do they do their jobs? How do the database inputs and reports fit into their job? The goal is to devise a menu system that reflects the way they work. Two examples of a first menu are shown in Figure 5.26. Which menu is easier for a clerk to understand? The one that best relates to the job. Once you understand the basic tasks, write down a set of related menus. Some menu options will call up other menus. Some will print reports; others will activate the input screens you created.

Once you know how you want the menu structure to appear, you fill in the menu templates in the application generator. To create a menu, you type in a title and fill in the choices. Then you assign an action to each choice. Usually you just pick from a list

**FIGURE 5.26**

Designing menus for users. Which menu is easier for secretary to understand? When designing applications, you should organize the application to match the processes users perform.

| MAIN MENU |
|---|
| 1. Setup Choices |
| 2. Data Input |
| 3. Print Reports |
| 4. DOS Utilities |
| 5. Backups |

| CUSTOMER INFORMATION |
|---|
| Daily Sales Reports |
| Friday Sales Meeting |
| Monthly Customer Letters |
| Quit |

of actions and type in specific data such as the name of the report and how you want it sorted. When you are finished, the application generator creates the application.

## DATABASE ADMINISTRATION

Managing a database can be a complex job. Often there are hundreds of choices that need to be made when the database is designed. Someone needs to be in charge of defining the data, making sure that all useful facts are captured, and managing security for this valuable asset. As illustrated by the SABRE system (Reality Bytes 5–6), databases have to be evaluated and fine-tuned on a regular basis. Someone has to keep track of these maintenance changes and decide when major updates should be installed. A **database administrator (DBA)** is usually appointed to manage the databases for the firm. The DBA needs to know the technical details of the DBMS and the computer system. The DBA also needs to understand the business operations of the firm.

The database administrator is responsible for all operations involving the database. These duties include coordinating users and designers, establishing standards, and defining the data characteristics. When new programs are created, the DBA makes sure they are tested and documented. The DBA also schedules backups and recovery, and establishes security controls.

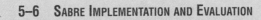

## Reality Bytes          5–6  SABRE IMPLEMENTATION AND EVALUATION

The Sabre system debuted in 1963. In that year it processed data related to 45,000 telephone calls, 40,000 confirmed reservations, and the sale of 20,000 tickets. At the beginning, it was used only for reservations made directly with American Airlines. Travel agents would call the American Airlines reservationists who would then access Sabre to book the flight. Keeping the system in-house meant American had complete control over access to the system.

Duplicate card systems were kept for six months after the Sabre system went "on-line." This ensured that few mistakes were made in the reservation system. It also provided a cross check on the accuracy of the new system. In the early days this duplicate system acted as a backup to calm management's concern

that something disastrous might happen to the new implementation.

The subsequent evaluation and fine-tuning of the system resulted in improvements in access speed, searching logistics, and ease in inquiry. Larger and improved mainframe processing power and more efficient programming techniques have enhanced the speed and accuracy with which records are accessed. The programmers at American and other companies have learned much in the intervening years about the mechanisms of database searching. They have incorporated these improvements into the Sabre system on an ongoing basis. Observation and feedback from actual users of the system have led to interface enhancements between the user and the system itself.

In a few large companies, an additional person known as the *data administrator (DA)* is charged with overseeing all of the data definitions and data standards for the company. In this case, typically several DBAs are used to monitor and control various databases. The DA is responsible for making sure data can be shared throughout the company.

## Standards and Documentation

In any company of moderate size, many different databases will be used by hundreds of workers. These databases were created at different points in time by teams of employees. If there are no standards, each piece will be unique, making it difficult to combine information from multiple databases or tables. The marketing department may refer to *customers,* whereas management calls them *clients.* The DBMS needs to know that both terms refer to the same set of data. Also, someone has to determine the key values for each table. Consider the Customer table. One department might assign identification numbers to each customer. Another department might use customers' phone numbers, and a third department might use the customer names. To prevent confusion and to be able to combine information, it is best for all users to use only one of these methods to identify the customers.

There are other standards involved in the database process. It is easier to use a database if all input screens have similar characteristics. For instance, the base screen might use a blue background with white characters. Data that is entered by the user will be displayed in yellow. Similarly, certain function keys may be predefined. ESC might be used to cancel or escape from choices. F1 might be used for help, and F3 to display a list of choices. If each application uses keys differently, the user will have a hard time remembering which keys do what with which database.

Likewise, it is helpful to standardize certain aspects of reports. It might be necessary to choose specific typefaces and fonts. Titles could be in an 18 point Helvetica font, whereas the body of reports could be printed in 11 point Palatino. To provide emphasis, subtotals and totals could be printed in boldface, with single and double underlining, respectively.

One of the crucial steps in creating a database is the definition of the data. Many important decisions have to be made at this point. Besides the issues of what to call each item, the DBMS has to be told how to store every item. For instance, are phone numbers stored as 7 digits, or should they be stored as 10 digits, or perhaps stored with the 3-digit international calling code? Postal zip codes pose similar problems. The United States uses either a five digit or nine digit zip code, but is considering adding two more digits. Other countries include alphabetic characters in their codes. Someone has to determine how to store this information in the manner that is best for the company.

There are many other aspects of database design that need standards to make life easier for the users. However, whenever there are standards, there should be a mechanism to change these standards. Technology always changes, so standards that were established five years ago are probably not relevant today. The DBA constantly reviews and updates the standards, and makes sure that employees follow them.

Even though databases are easy to use, they would be confusing if the designers did not document their work. Picture a situation where you want to find information about customers but the designers named the table Patrons. You might never find the information without documentation.

Documentation can assume many forms. Most DBMSs allow the designers to add comments to each table and column. This internal documentation can often be searched by the users. Many times it can be printed in different formats so that it can be distributed to users in manuals. Because it is maintained in the database along with the data, it is easy to find. It is also easy for the designers to add these comments as they create or change the database, so the documentation is more likely to be current. It is up to the DBA to ensure that all designers document their work.

## Testing, Backup, and Recovery

One advantage of the DBMS approach is that it provides tools such as report writers and application generators that end users can employ to create their own systems. Although it is easier for users to create these programs than to start from scratch, the programs still need to be tested. Corporate databases are extremely valuable, but only if the information they contain is accurate. It is the responsibility of the DBA to keep the information accurate, which means that all software that changes data must be tested.

Most companies would not survive long if a disaster destroyed their databases. For this reason, all databases need to be backed up on a regular basis. How often this backup occurs depends on the importance and value of the data. It is possible to back up data continuously. With two identical computer systems, a change made to one can be automatically written to the other. If a fire destroys one system, the other one can be used to continue with no loss of information. Obviously, it is expensive to maintain duplicate facilities. Many organizations choose to back up their data less frequently.

The main point of backup and recovery is that someone has to be placed in charge. Especially in small businesses, there is a tendency to assume that someone else is responsible for making backups. Also, remember that at least one current copy of the database must be stored in a different location. A major disaster could easily wipe out everything stored in the same building. There are some private companies that for a fee will hold your backup data in a secure, fireproof building where you can access your data any time of the day.

## Access Controls

Another important task in database administration is the establishment of security safeguards. The DBA has to determine which data needs to be protected. Once basic security conditions are established, the DBA is responsible for monitoring database activity. The DBA tracks security violation attempts and monitors who is using the database. Because there are always changes in employees, removing access for departed employees and entering new access levels and passwords can be a full time job.

**DATABASE AND SPREADSHEETS**
A common problem faced by computer users is understanding the difference between spreadsheets and databases. As spreadsheets get easier to use and continue to offer new features, it gets more tempting to use the spreadsheet for every job. Although spreadsheets and databases both store data in rows and columns, they are designed to solve different problems. As highlighted by Air Canada Vacations (Reality Bytes 5-7), you need to understand the comparative advantages of each tool to use either of them wisely. As explained in Chapter 7, you might want to combine both tools to solve problems.

## Data Storage versus Calculations

The main purpose of a database is to store different tables containing large amounts of data. The DBMS provides tools to combine the data from these tables. It is possible

**Reality Bytes**    **5-7** AIR CANADA VACATIONS

Air Canada Vacations is a subsidiary of Air Canada, the largest airline in Canada. Air Canada Vacations operates several offices throughout Canada to book tours and flights for individual customers. Many of the tours are conducted by independent suppliers. Air Canada Vacations books the passengers, collects their money, and pays the vendors before the flight. In more complex cases, such as a ski trip, a passenger needs airfare, lodging, lift tickets, and a rental car. Each of these items is supplied by a different vendor and Air Canada pays them separately. The entire industry is highly competitive and profit margins are slim.

Air Canada Vacations initially built a personal computer spreadsheet application for use by the booking agents. An analyst would enter the cost of each item, then add in commissions and a profit margin. The spreadsheet printed the final totals. The process was cumbersome for the agents because they had to look up component prices and manually enter the data.

In addition to being error-prone, the system was inefficient at calculating the amounts owed to suppliers and made it difficult to determine profits on each package. Air Canada's MIS director, Roger Rouse, notes that

We had hundreds and hundreds of agencies with suppliers, and each supplier had to pay $X$ number of days either before or after departure. Using a

list of bookings, somebody had to retrieve the contract for each supplier and literally use a pencil to calculate the amount due each supplier in order to generate cheques for each one. It was a terribly tedious process.

To alleviate these problems, Air Canada Vacations changed the application to the Informix database management system running on an IBM RS/6000 RISC-based minicomputer. The entire system was built with the Informix fourth-generation language. The software engineers developed applications for accounts payable and accounts receivable, as well as a pricing system. Now the agents simply select various components of a vacation, the prices are retrieved from the appropriate tables, and a total price is computed. Analysts can create package deals and modify the total price to meet the competition. Additionally, once a vacation has been booked, the payments due to suppliers are updated automatically. Rouse notes that "Within seconds of a booking, we know what our cost is, if we are making money, and, if so, how much. This information also allows us to go ahead and pay our suppliers and generate our financial statements—and it's all handled automatically."

The contents of the database are also immediately available to mangers. With the query system, they can look up any type of data they choose.

to perform calculations on the data; however, most calculations apply to sets of data, not just to one item. For example, databases are commonly used to calculate totals. On the other hand, spreadsheets were primarily designed to perform calculations. They are not good at storing large amounts of data, and it is difficult to combine information that is stored in different spreadsheets.

## Illustration

To illustrate the difference between the tools, consider three tables: Customers, Products, and Sales. The Customer table contains typical data such as phone, name, and address. Likewise, the Products table lists product numbers, descriptions, and prices. The Sales table identifies products that were bought by each customer. It holds the customer phone number, a product number, date, and the quantity purchased.

You want to produce a report that lists the customers who spent the most money last month. Producing this list means that you have to look at the Sales table first. Get the product number for each item sold this month. Look up the price in the Products table and multiply that price by the quantity sold. This value is then added to the total for the customer. When all the sales have been searched, sort the list by

**FIGURE 5.27**

Sample comparison of spreadsheet and DBMS. You are given three lists (tables) of data. You are asked to find the best customers (highest sales total). This problem is difficult to solve if you only have a spreadsheet. A DBMS can provide an answer with a single query. Problems that involve combining data from multiple tables are best solved with a database management system.

```
Tables

Customers(C#, Name,Address)
Products(P#, Description, Price)
Sales(O#, P#, Sdate, Quantity, C#)
```

Retreive the three tables (if they fit).

```
DBMS

SELECT    Sum(Price*Quantity), C#,Name
FROM      Customers INNER JOIN
          (Sales INNER JOIN Products
          ON Sales.P# = Products.P#
          ON Customers.C# = Sales.C#
WHERE     Sdate > Now() - 30
GROUP BY  C#
ORDER BY  Sum(Price*Quantity) DESC;
```

**Part 1  Sales**

| C# | P# | Q | Price | Price*Q | SubTotal |
|----|----|----|-------|---------|----------|
| 11 | 22 | 1 | 15.95 | 15.95 | 15.95 |
| 11 | 35 | 2 | 5.75 | 11.50 | 27.45 |
| 31 | 18 | 1 | 25.95 | 25.95 | 53.40 |

1) Select by date
2) Sort By O#, P#

**Part 2  Products**

| P# | Description | Prices |
|----|-------------|--------|
| 18 | shorts | 29.95 |
| 22 | shirt | 15.95 |
| 35 | laces | 4.75 |

3) Look up prices
4) Put into **Part 1**
5) Calculate total
6) Sort for highest total

**Part 3  Customers**

| C# | Name |
|----|------|
| 11 | Smith |
| 31 | Torrez |

7) Look up names

the customer totals. Finally, use the Customer table to look up the names that go with these customer numbers.

For small amounts of data, this problem can be solved using either a database or a spreadsheet; however, the spreadsheet approach is much more difficult. It involves several complicated instructions to combine the information from the three tables. With a good database, this list can be created with one or two statements. Additionally, consider what happens if there is a large amount of data. Perhaps there are thousands of customers, hundreds of products, and thousands of sales per day. It is probably not possible to store each table in a single spreadsheet. Now you have to search even more spreadsheets to combine the information. What happens if you start with a small store, but it expands? With the spreadsheet approach, you have to rewrite the entire system. With the database, you simply add more data. The commands and reports do not change.

On the other hand, if you need to perform complex analyses on the sales data, you might be better off using a spreadsheet. Perhaps you want to examine a statistical moving average and some regression statistics. Then you want to display these projections in a graph. Although it is possible to produce this type of report with a database, the statistics computations might not be available. However, the calculations are relatively easy with a spreadsheet. Because the spreadsheet also can produce the graphs, the entire report can be produced without having to leave the spreadsheet.

## Security and Data Integrity

Another important difference between databases and spreadsheets is that databases have stronger controls for data security and integrity. With most database management systems, users are asked to identify themselves (with usernames and passwords) before they can use the database. The designer can then give each user (or group) access to specific data items. For instance, consider a typical purchasing department. A security problem that has arisen in some companies is that a clerk in the purchasing department might create a fictitious supplier. The clerk then places orders with this company, fakes the receipt of products, and collects the "payment." A DBMS could be used to prevent this problem. Clerks would have the ability to create new purchase orders and correct mistakes in existing orders. However, they would not be given the ability to create new "suppliers." The DBMS would not allow purchases from companies not listed in the supplier table, so this scheme would fail.

Although spreadsheets can be encrypted, you generally are forced to give a user complete access to the spreadsheet. With some simple commands, a user can—accidentally or purposefully—delete entire rows and columns in the database. Similarly, it is hard to set integrity constraints in a spreadsheet. What happens if a user accidentally enters a negative number for a sale price? Both of these situations are easy to control with a good DBMS. The designer sets the appropriate conditions, and the DBMS handles the rest.

## COMPLEX DATA TYPES AND OBJECT-ORIENTED DATABASES

Modern database management systems can deal with data types that are more complex than simple text, dates, and numbers. Today, there are many applications where you might want to store large quantities of text, such as a book or last year's tax report. Similarly, many reports include graphs and pictures.

### Text

One problem that is being faced by many companies today is that the majority of reports are now created on computers. However, they are created on individual personal computers and stored independently in each department. There is a tremendous amount of information and analysis contained in each report. It would be useful if managers could search the old reports by computer and combine information from them to create new reports (Reality Bytes 5-9). Similarly, there is an enormous

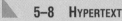

### Reality Bytes    5–8  HYPERTEXT

Hypertext promised to revolutionize access to textual data. Unlike books that are organized linearly, hypertext is formatted by the computer into a series of interrelated associative links. Users can move directly to the next topic by identifying it rather than following the predetermined path that an author presents in a book.

Macintosh computers come equipped with Hypercard software. Stacks of information are available for access or programming with sound, graphics, and animation. Help systems in Windows environments also use a hypertext approach. If you see a word you do not understand, or want more information, you point to the item, press a mouse button and the appropriate screen appears.

The downside of hypertext is its randomness. Advantages exist in allowing the mind to wander a path of interest. However, pedagogical reasons exist to follow the learning pattern and direction of a wiser, more experienced individual. Another difficulty is that it is difficult to predict all of the paths an individual may pursue in the search through new material.

Even with these two educational difficulties, hypertext media present a unique opportunity to organize the learning process in a more dynamic, experimental method.

## Reality Bytes    5–9   NATURAL LANGUAGE PROCESSING PROVIDES HELP TO DECIPHER VAGUENESS IN WORDS

Today's corporation faces an avalanche of textual information. Letters, field reports, wire-service stories, memoranda, e-mail messages, faxes, and legal documents flood corporate offices each day from any number of sources. Word processing has helped to save and organize internally generated information on disks. However, finding the information that is needed even when it is stored in a compatible source can present serious problems.

Today major computer companies such as IBM and Digital Equipment Corporation are investing vast resources in trying to discover a process that will enable them to find specific pieces of data among the vast collections of unorganized text.

Database systems enable the computer to process data that fits naturally into lists of structured records. The format enables each item to be stored with an index. Based on location, the database system can quickly find and relate data to other items.

Unfortunately, straight lines of text do not provide such a neat indexing scheme. Sentences and paragraphs convey ideas that make sense to the trained mind but are extremely difficult for the computer to grasp. As a result, textual analysis has been called the next frontier of information processing.

Much of the research in textual analysis has been funded by the U.S. military and intelligence communities. Verity, Inc.'s, workstation-based Topic enables scientists to scan National Science Foundation files on research projects and grants. General Electric uses a GESCAN machine to examine notes on phone calls to a customer hotline and identify patterns in reported problems.

Information Dimensions, Inc., in Columbus, Ohio, has established leadership in large-scale text retrieval. Its Basis software can identify text in which word combinations occur. Verity adds the advantage of weighting keywords by relative importance. Text management systems bring the benefit of collecting large amounts of information without deciding ahead of time how to organize or search it. With the reduction in the cost of storage and the high cost of organizing the data, this presents a more cost-effective way to store data. Money is only spent to access data when the information is needed rather than indexing all the data whether it is needed or not.

amount of information published each year that might be useful to have accessible via the computer. Another method to handle searches of large amounts of text is to use a hypertext approach (Reality Bytes 5–8), in which individual screens are connected to each other by keywords.

Some databases can now hold entire documents as a single piece of data. Typical search commands enable users to find documents based on keywords or phrases. By storing the text in the database, several people can have access to the data at the same time. By keeping the data in the same place, it is easier to see what reports are available, and making backups is easier because they are maintained by the DBMS.

### Pictures and Graphs

In many cases it is useful to store pictures and graphs in a DBMS. For instance, some companies store employee photographs in a database. Whenever a security guard brings up an employee record, the person's picture is displayed on the screen for additional verification. Pictures of products can be incorporated into reports to produce custom catalogs or more appealing letters. Engineers store diagrams directly in the database. Whenever they need to make a change to a component, the DBMS can bring up the correct diagram and save the changes so other engineers can see the new version immediately. Along the same lines, databases are beginning to store video clips.

## Objects

There has been a movement to define databases in terms of objects. Objects can be defined by the users to match real-world entities. In some respects, there is little difference between objects and relational tables. However, remember that with objects, not only is the class defined, but so are the commands that work on those objects. For example, an engineer might define a *blueprint* object to hold diagrams. The engineer might define commands to search, add, and subtract blueprint objects. The search command would enable engineers to compare portions of diagrams based on their graphics content. An automobile engineer might ask the computer to find all blueprints that use a particular suspension system—based on how the blueprint is drawn. Similarly, perhaps an ADD command would take smaller diagrams from different engineers and piece them together to create a complete blueprint. Similarly as Figure 5.28 shows, a doctor might use an object-oriented database to store information related to patients. Of course, creating these commands is still difficult. In any case, a true object-oriented DBMS allows the user to create databases that closely reflect the way they work, which makes them easier to understand and to use.

The term *object-oriented* means designers create their own objects, along with commands (methods or actions) that affect the objects. Many existing object-oriented databases do not allow relational queries. Instead, they rely on predefined relationships.

**FIGURE 5.28**

Sample object database. Each table represents a separate object, and each object can contain different types of data. The patient data might contain a photograph, and the x-rays can be stored in the online database so they are accessible to several physicians in different locations. The physician comments might be voice recordings.

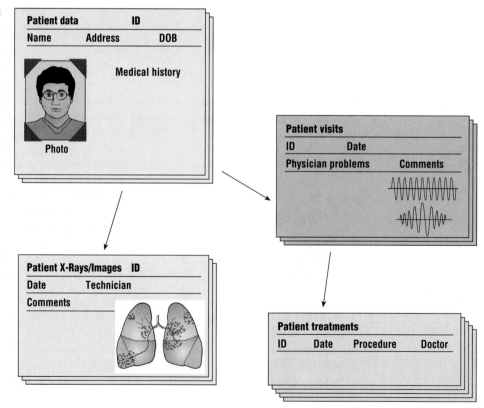

**COMMERCIAL
DATABASES**

Many types of information are impossible or expensive for individual firms to collect. Governments collect an enormous amount of data from individuals and from companies. There are private research companies that offer detailed data on almost any subject, such as customers, competitors, and international markets. Much of this data is available in commercial databases. You might want to trace the stock prices of six companies during the last five years. You can use your computer to call a computer owned by a commercial data service. Then you search for exactly the data you need and copy (download) it to your computer. Your spreadsheet and graphics software can be used to analyze the data. Several companies specialize in providing business data for computer users. Some examples are CompuServe, Dow-Jones News Retrieval, GEnie, America Online, The Microsoft Network, and Prodigy.

An enormous amount of information is available in commercial databases. Most of the data collected by different government agencies is available on tape, optical disk, and through private companies that maintain commercial databases. For example, demographic data on customers from the census bureau is available in many forms. Stock prices can be purchased from many different companies. Individual corporate data such as profit statements and other reports can be obtained electronically. The results of all legal cases in the United States are stored in computer databases as well. Westlaw and Lexis-Nexis provide online searches of cases and results. With a modem, a subscriber can copy these cases to a computer and they can be included in reports to clients. The variety and amount of information available continues to increase at a rapid rate. A considerable amount of data is also available on CD-ROMs (Reality Bytes 5–10 and 5–11).

**Reality Bytes     5–10   COMPUTER PERIODICALS DATABASE**

One of the most evident signs that knowledge is rapidly expanding is the proliferation of newspapers, journals, and magazines. The sheer volume of these materials has made storing and accessing them a major and increasingly expensive task for libraries throughout the world. Space limitations are one constraint; accessing the information is another. Each journal must be subscribed to and individually checked into the library. Then the journal issue has to be in the right place for it to be used.

The first attempt to address these high costs was an online database. A large computer stored the entire text of a number of journals in a particular area. To search and retrieve this information, the user had to dial into the system. As the power and number of journals kept increased, so did the cost of accessing the data.

Computer Library's Computer Periodicals Database is seeking to address the issue of database searches in a cost-effective manner. Computer Library's evaluation indicates that most individuals who conduct journal research do not need up-to-the-minute information. For most, monthly updates are worth the savings in online fees.

Computer Library has placed three years of major computer journals on a computer periodicals database. Using a CD-ROM drive, this information can be accessed through a cost-effective personal computer with a hard drive. Now subjects and titles can be searched as exhaustively as an individual wants. They can be defined in as many different combinations as possible with no regard for the cost of online search time.

The Computer Library presents options in storing the data. When the results are narrowed to the desired outcome, the research can be printed or downloaded to a disk. This enables the information to be accessed on the researcher's personal computer at a later date.

**Reality Bytes**    5–11    LEGAL RESEARCH DATABASES

Fees for using online databases by legal researchers can run as high as $240 per hour. Printing results can sometimes cost $1 a page. LEXIS and Westlaw, the market leaders, each offer access to more than 5,000 legal databases. The databases are updated almost constantly as new laws are introduced and court cases are resolved. Despite the wealth of information, many firms are reluctant to pay the high prices—especially small law firms or tax and legal departments in smaller companies. Large firms that use LEXIS and Westlaw typically pass the search costs on to the clients. Smaller clients tend to balk at these costs.

To increase the market and provide information to smaller firms, more than 150 companies—including LEXIS and Westlaw—now sell CD-ROM databases. Professionals can purchase the CDs for a fixed fee or pay a monthly charge to receive updates. Costs can be as low as $60 a month. The advantage of the CDs is that there is no per-search charge. Even a small firm can spread the cost out over several clients. Firms can also buy specialty databases (for a given state or technical field), paying only for the data they need.

## Advantages

Lawyers and accountants can use these sources instead of traditional libraries of books. Besides saving trees, there are several advantages to using computerized databases instead of traditional books. It is possible to squeeze several hundred books on one optical disk. These disks can be carried with portable computers to a client's office. In seconds, the computer can search the text for any phrase. Not only is the computer faster, but it is complete—you do not have to worry about accidentally missing some information. The commercial database companies can provide up-to-date information. Many of the databases are updated daily or weekly. It is impossible to change information in books that rapidly. Lastly, with dial-up services, you only pay for exactly the data that you use.

## External versus Internal Data

There are a couple of things to keep in mind when using databases that are created by someone outside your company (external). First, you have to pay for *usage* of the database. That means you have to be efficient and not waste time while you are connected to the database. Some ideas for efficient search strategies are outlined in the next section.

Another consideration with external data is that you are dependent on someone else for the accuracy of the data. Although some items can be verified through other sources, much of the data cannot be tested. Fortunately, most commercial database firms are extremely careful about providing accurate data. Additionally, remember that the data available from commercial databases is available to anyone willing to pay the price, including your competitors. You typically need to supplement the commercial data with additional research.

Commercial databases are useful for data that changes quite often. For example, it would be extremely expensive for you to personally keep track of current stock market prices. You can buy data for individual stocks from a variety of sources. Similarly, various governmental agencies collect economic and demographic data that you can purchase. In both cases, it would be difficult to collect similar data on your own, and if you could, it would be extremely expensive.

**Reality Bytes** ▶ 5–12 PRIVACY

Despite federal laws prohibiting access to and use of government data, many federal employees routinely scan government databases for their personal use. In 1994, Senator John Glenn revealed that 1300 IRS employees were investigated for violations of privacy and security regulations between 1989 and 1994. Many were charged with retrieving tax records on friends, neighbors, celebrities, and relatives. More than 500 of the cases occurred since August 1993, when 370 employees at IRS offices in the southeast were caught improperly examining tax data. Tax returns are increasingly filed electronically, which makes them available to a wider group of IRS employees.

The IRS is modernizing its tax system, and plans to improve security controls—both to ensure **privacy** and to minimize fraudulent filing. In particular, they plan to install electronic security alarms and establish access rights that restrict the use of data by IRS personnel.

Privacy presents an additional problem with large, centralized databases. Government agencies are particularly troublesome since their databases contain detailed personal data. Even the IRS, which has strict employee standards, has encountered problems (Reality Bytes 5–12).

**DATABASE SEARCH STRATEGIES**

Many modern databases, especially the commercial ones, are huge. If you are not careful, you might ask a question that takes several hours and thousands of dollars to answer. It would be silly to go to a large university library and ask for a list of all books in the subject area of *Business*. This list would contain several thousand entries. Similarly, any time you search a large database, you need to have some idea of the size of the response.

Many databases are text based. They hold written information that you can search by words or phrases. To find the information you want, you need to write down a list of keywords that describe your topic. With some systems, such as Verity's Topic (Reality Bytes 5–13), you provide weights for each word to indicate its

 **Reality Bytes** ▶ 5–13 TOPIC—AUTOMATIC USER-INTEREST RETRIEVAL

Dow-Jones, in cooperation with *Verity, Inc.*, has released a text retrieval system that analyzes and selectively routes online information to users according to pre-defined user interest profiles. This is the first step in publishing a daily, personally focused newspaper. Topic Real-Time scans documents based on content as they arrive from online information sources. If a document appears that is relevant to a particular user, Topic lets that user know that the document should be reviewed. This enables each user to receive a customized briefing each morning.

Technologically, the search is built on concept-retrieval technology rather than key words. A knowledge base of "topics" is built to define subject areas that are important to the organization. This expertise is then tapped to profile incoming information sources. Within seconds after receiving it, Topic can analyze a document for relevance to a user's profile. Potentially interested users can then be notified through e-mail that a document has been received.

importance. The system then ranks each document it finds based on those weights. Consider a small example without the use of the weights. Say you are going to be transferred to an office in Medellin, Colombia, for two years. You decide to search the newspapers and magazines in the last four years to help you learn more about Medellin.

You start by logging on to a computer database that contains computerized copies of several hundred newspapers and magazines. What happens if you ask the computer to find all references to Colombia? You would be flooded with several thousand articles containing that word. Your next step is to narrow the search by providing a more specific topic. Say you add the word *terrorism*. You have to be careful when you add this new word. If you entered both words at the same time, it would become a phrase (*Medellin terrorism*) and the computer would search until it found articles that contained those two words written exactly the same way. What you really want is a list of articles that contain the word *Medellin* and the word *terrorism* in the same article.

There is another problem. If you are looking for the word *terrorism*, you should include other words that refer to the same topic, such as *terrorist, bombing,* and *kidnap*. In other words, you want to search for all articles that refer to *Medellin* AND (*terrorist* OR *terrorism* OR *bombing* OR *kidnap*). This type of search is called a **Boolean search.**

The hardest part of searching textual databases is coming up with a list of possible keywords. You need to think about the words that are related to your topic. You might want to use a thesaurus if you have trouble thinking of related words.

Most of the large database systems provide you with a count of the number of items that match your keywords. You can use this number to tell you when to narrow or widen your search. If the computer says there are several thousand items that match your selection, you should narrow the search to a more specific topic. So you will add additional words (using AND). On the other hand, if the computer finds no items that match your conditions, you will have to try different keywords. Split phrases up into separate words, get rid of some AND conditions, and add synonyms using an OR phrase.

It takes practice to learn what combinations of keywords work best. Some companies hire specially trained librarians to help with these searches. It is a good idea to learn how to search for information in these large databases. Because of their significant advantages, eventually all important data will be stored and searched by computers.

Several companies are taking another approach to dealing with the problem of costly online searches. In many cases, it is possible to buy CD-ROMs that contain the popular databases. Because you can search a CD-ROM as often as you want for a one-time cost, you begin your search there. After you have narrowed down the topic and obtained the base data, you run a quick check with the online services to collect recent additions or changes.

## SUMMARY

Everyone needs to search for information. Computers make this job easier, but someone must set up and maintain the databases to ensure their integrity. There are many ways to search databases, and relational database management systems are a popular method. They are increasingly used as the foundation of the information system. They make it easy to share data among users while maintaining access controls. Equally importantly, the databases are easy to alter as the organization changes. Sophisticated databases can handle all the data types in use today, not just simple numbers and text.

It is relatively easy for users to obtain data using SQL or query-by-example tools. Because SQL is a recognized standard query language, it is worth remembering the basic elements of the SELECT command. The syntax is easy (SELECT columns, FROM tables, WHERE conditions, ORDER BY columns). Just remember that whenever you use more than one table, they must be joined by related columns.

An important step in databases is to design them correctly. The trick is to split the data into tables that refer to exactly one concept. Most organizations have a database administrator to help users create the initial database tables, define standards, establish access rights, and perform backups and testing. Once the tables have been defined, users can create input screens, reports, and views by using graphical tools to draw the desired items on the screen.

> ### A MANAGER'S VIEW
>
> Every manager needs to do research. Sometimes you will have to summarize and evaluate transaction data. Sometimes you will use external databases to evaluate the industry and your competitor's.
>
> Database management systems provide important capabilities to managers. One of the most useful is a query language, such as QBE or SQL, that enables you to answer questions without the need for hiring an MIS expert. A DBMS also speeds development of new systems and provides basic features such as report writers and input forms.

It is important to choose the right tool for each job. Databases excel at handling huge amounts of data and sharing it with other users. On the other hand, spreadsheets are designed to perform calculations and create graphs. One indication that a problem should be solved using a DBMS instead of a spreadsheet is when several tables of data are involved.

Every day, more information is stored in commercial databases. In many ways, they are becoming the libraries of the future. Almost any type of reference data you can imagine can be searched electronically. Just remember that you have to pay to access this data, so you have to design your search strategies carefully to save money.

## KEY WORDS

| | | |
|---|---|---|
| Boolean search, 224 | detail section, 210 | query by example (QBE), 196 |
| breaks, 210 | normalization, 207 | report, 189 |
| column, 191 | object-oriented DBMS, 189 | row, 191 |
| concatenated keys, 192 | page footers, 210 | scrolling region, 210 |
| data independence, 194 | page headers, 210 | SQL, 196 |
| database administrator (DBA), 213 | primary key, 191 | table, 191 |
| default value, 209 | privacy, 223 | view, 204 |

## REVIEW QUESTIONS

1. What does the term *Boolean search* refer to in a database? Give an example.
2. How does data independence make it easier to design and maintain computer applications?
3. What is the purpose of normalization, and why is it important?
4. What is the purpose of a primary key? What is a concatenated key? Why do we use concatenated keys?
5. What tasks are performed by a database administrator?

6. Would you prefer to use QBE or SQL to access a database? Why?
7. What is a *view* in a database?
8. What four questions do you need to answer in order to create a database query?
9. What problems are you likely to encounter when searching large text databases? What strategies will help reduce search time and costs?
10. How do you join tables with QBE? With SQL?
11. How do you enter restrictions or constraints with QBE? With SQL?
12. How do you perform computations with QBE? With SQL?

13. What is the purpose of an application generator in a DBMS?
14. Do you think users can create their own reports with a DBMS report writer? What limitations are there?
15. Why are standards important in a database environment?
16. What types of problems are better suited to using a DBMS instead of a spreadsheet?
17. What are the advantages of using an external commercial database, compared to developing and maintaining the database yourself? What are the drawbacks to both methods? What types of data are best purchased from external databases?

## EXERCISES

 **Access Database for Exercises 1–15.**

C05Ex15.mdb

It is best to answer the first 15 exercise questions using a DBMS, but if one is not available, you can use the tables in the text and write your queries by hand. If you have a DBMS that handles both QBE and SQL, you should do the exercise with both methods.

1. List the customers who live in Seattle and have an account balance less than $500.
2. List the customers who live on Main street or whose last name begins with the letter J, in descending order of account balance.
3. What is the total amount of money owed us by customers who live in Miami?
4. How many orders have been placed by customers from Denver? How many of those were placed in March 1996?
5. What is the largest order ever placed?
6. Which set of salespeople has placed the most orders: those who were hired before 1990 or those hired in 1990 or later? Hint: Use two separate queries.
7. List the names of the salespeople who sold orders worth more than $200 in descending order of the amount.
8. Calculate the total commissions owed to salesperson Johnson. Hint: You need to compute the total of commission times order.amount.
9. Get the name and phone number of customers who bought laundry detergent in June 1996.
10. Create a list of items that have been sold, along with the total quantity sold of each item, sorted by that quantity. Hint: Use GROUP BY.

11. Which (if any) salesperson sold jeans to Adams in Phoenix?
12. Create an input screen that enables a clerk to update information and add new customers to the database.
13. Using the tables in the chapter, create an order-entry input screen that can be used by a clerk who knows nothing about databases. Note: Depending on the DBMS, it might be difficult to compute the order.amount total.
14. Create an inventory report that lists all of the products, group them by category, and within each category, sort them by ID number.
15. Create the customer order report that is described in the chapter. Hint: First create a view that joins the appropriate tables together.
16. For any business, choose five entities (objects) that might be used as database tables. Identify primary keys for each table.
17. Using the CD-ROM resources at your library or perhaps access to an online database service, identify which company was the first one to issue corporate bonds with a maturity of 100 years. Include the source of your answer. Hint: It was after 1990.
18. Using the CD-ROM resources at your library or perhaps access to an online database service, how were the U.S. airlines doing in 1992? Which airline(s) had positive earnings? What major problems did the airlines face?
19. With the cooperation of a local small business, create a database for that company. Note that you should verify the initial layout of the tables with your instructor or someone who has studied database design.

**Rolling Thunder Database**

Create queries to answer the following questions. (*Difficulty level: 1 = easiest*)

1. How many bicycles have been built of each type (*2*)?
2. What is the most popular type of tubing used in the bicycles that were ordered (*3*)?
3. What is the most expensive bicycle that was sold (*2*)?
4. Who spent the most money on bicycles (*3*)?
5. Which customers still owe us money (*2*)?
6. Which employee (name) installed the most bike parts (*3*)?
7. What is the total salary cost (*2*)?
8. What is the average price we paid for Shimano XT derailleurs (rear) (*4*)?
9. List all of the managers (check their title) and the employees (names) who work for them (*5*).
10. List the purchase orders where TotalList does *not* equal the computed total of the individual items (*4*).
11. List the component items that had *no* sales in March (*5*).
12. Compute the list price of the component items for bicycle with serial number = 841 (*2*).
13. Compute the sales by model type by month (*5 Hint: Crosstab*).
14. Compute sales by month (*2*).
15. Compute the total sales taxes we owe to each state (for 1994) (*2*).
16. List all of the employees hired before 1993 (*1*).
17. List all of the bicycles ordered in March 1994 that used the LetterStyle "Flash" (*1*).
18. What is the value of our current inventory of Shimano components (*2*)?
19. List all of our employees (ID) who were involved in a transaction with a manufacturer worth more than 100,000 (*1*).
20. List all of the retail bicycle stores in your state (*2*).

## ADDITIONAL READING

"12 Years of High-Tech History on CD-ROM," *Newsbytes*, August 18, 1995, p. NEW08180015. [American Express]

"American Express Launches AOL Flight Booking," *Newsbytes*, July 27, 1995, p. NEW07180019. [American Express]

"American Express to Let Members Buy Over Internet," *Newsbytes*, July 18, 1995, p. NEW07270005. [American Express]

Anthes, Gary. "Making US Intelligence More Intelligent," *Computerworld*, April 1, 1991, p. 29. [The CIA]

Anthes, Gary H. "IRS Cracks Down on Fraud," *Computerworld*, July 25, 1994, p. 28. [Privacy and databases]

Asbrand, Deborah. "Realty Firm Takes Do-it-Yourself Approach to Database," *Infoworld,* May 2, 1994, p. 85. [John L. Scott Realtors]

Barr, Stephen. "1994, Snoops. . . 1300 IRS Workers Browsed Through Tax Returns," *The Washington Post*, reprinted in the *Louisville Courier-Journal*, July 19, 1994, p. A1. [Privacy and public databases]

Bozman, Jean S. "Verity Plots Revolution in Desktop Text Retrieval," *Computerworld*, February 26, 1990, p. 84. [The CIA]

Burelo, John A. "The CIA Home Page," *Computer Shopper*, September 1995, p. 667. [The CIA]

Caldwell, Bruce and Mary Hayes, "Banks Cash in Online: Intuit, Microsoft in Tie to Sign Up Institutions," *Information Week*, July 31, 1995, p. 30. [American Express]

Carrol, Jim. "Telecommunications Can Be Strategic Business Tool," *Computing Canada*, February 15, 1995, p. 33. [SABRE]

"Catastrophe Theory," *The Economist*, May 13, 1995, p. 80. [International disaster relief]

"Continental Airlines Adds FlightLink Phones," *Newsbytes*, March 15, 1995, p. NEW03150026. [Continental Airlines]

"Continental to Fly with Banyan ENS," *PC Week*, December 26, 1994, p. 3. [Continental Airlines]

Felsenthal, Edward. "New Places to Look for Legal Precedent," *The Wall Street Journal*, June 1, 1994, pp. B1, B3. [Legal research sources]

Horrman, Thomas. "Law Firm Makes Strong Imaging Case," *Computerworld*, November 23, 1992, p. 45. [Natural language]

"Intelligence Agencies Build Their Own Internet, with Security a Major Goal," *Government Computer News*, January 9, 1995, p. 8. [The CIA]

Maglitta, Joseph. "Information Services Update," *Computerworld*, May 28, 1990, p. 89. [Natural language]

Mapid, Lawrence. "Bank on this Personal Finance Program," *Los Angeles Times*, November 22, 1995, p. D4. [American Express]

McCarthy, Shawn P. "Cracking the Security Market," *Marketing Computers*, January 1995, p. 20. [The CIA]

Nadile, Lisa. "Ticketless Plane Reservations Fly on Client/Server System," *PC Week*, January 30, 1995, p. 1. [SABRE]

Pallatto, John. "Verity System Offers Real-time Data Retrieval," *PC Week*, May 7, 1990, p. 63. [Introduction of Verity Topic]

Pepper, Jon. "Quick Search Library," *Software Magazine*, March 1990, p. 97. [Introduction of computer periodicals database]

Perensa, Melissa. "Quicken's New Frontiers," *PC Magazine*, November 21, 1995, p. 61. [American Express]

Rostron, Jim. "System Streamlines Vacation Planning," *Computing Canada*, September 27, 1993, p. 24. [SABRE]

"Secure Credit Transactions New on Net," *PC Week*, July 24, 1995, p. 3. [American Express]

Zellners, Wendy. "Putting a Keener Edge on SABRE; The Reservation Giant Moves to Face Down New Online Rivals," *Business Week*, October 23, 1995, p. 118. [SABRE]

# CASES  *Service Firms*

There are many types of service jobs, but most of the workers make only limited use of computers.

Source: Computer Use in the United States, U.S. Bureau of the Census.

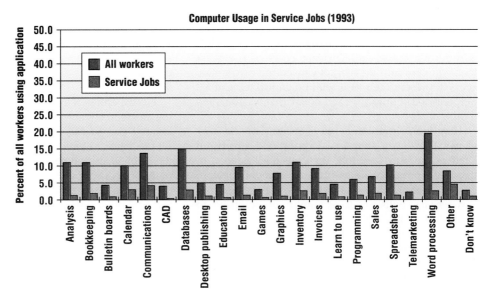

**Computer Usage in Service Jobs (1993)**

As noted by the U.S. Census figures, the importance of the service sector has been steadily increasing since the early 1900s. Information technology has played an important role in the service sector for several years.

Firms that survive by selling services instead of products often have a different set of problems and a different approach to business. For starters, many service firms are relatively small and have limited resources. More importantly, they are selling something that tends to be tailored to each specific customer. As a result, customer service and satisfaction is a critical success factor. Because of the need for close customer contact and the importance of tailoring items to each customer, service firms tend to have a high ratio of employees per sale.

The importance of tailoring services to individual customer needs has led service firms to use information technology to seek a competitive advantage. In particular, in many cases, information is a primary "product" of the service industries. Consider the credit card agencies that track bills and provide monthly and annual summaries of purchases. Or examine the information databases managed by a real estate company, or a travel planning firm. In these situations and more, a major portion of the service provided by the company is information.

Early information systems based on proprietary applications and files helped service industries provide basic data for consumers and management. However, the proprietary nature of the systems made it difficult to share information among applications and among different companies. The lack of a query system made it difficult for managers to get the information they wanted. Many mangers have complained that "the data exists in the system, but I can't get it."

The problems are more complicated for small firms because they typically do not have the information system staff to help them get at the information. In most cases, they rely on off-the-shelf applications and simply live with the limitations, or the firms adapt their business processes to match the software.

## CASE  *American Express: Imaged Copies Increase Profitability*

From its earliest days, consumer credit has been presented as a prestige item reserved for a business's best customers. The consumer had to "earn" the privilege of charging simply on the basis of his or her signature. Hotels and country clubs first introduced this concept. Fine department stores offered credit cards that were carried as an indication of the status that accompanies the opportunity to shop there. The American Express and Diners Club cards were the first to offer a credit card that was available across the country. This type of card was directed toward the business traveler who needed to keep the receipts so they could be turned in for reimbursement and tax purposes. Its annual fee and use mainly at more expensive restaurants, hotels, and department stores limited its attractiveness to a fairly wealthy traveling public.

The 1980s brought consumer credit to broader segments of the population. Visa and Mastercard offered easy, understandable credit to people with income levels beginning at $18,000, sometimes even without an annual fee. The late entry of the Sears Discover card into the market caused the card's managers to present their card with no annual fee and a 2 percent (.02) bonus for each dollar that was charged on the card.

Easy credit presented more options to the consumer. Previously American Express had advertised itself as the only card that the consumer needed to carry. In a period of a few years, consumers began to carry 4–5 credit cards at once. Visa, Mastercard, and Discover had enlisted a large number of merchants to accept their card. In many cases, these were the same merchants who also accepted American Express cards. For the first time American Express found itself competing in a marketing campaign to convince consumers to pull its card rather than another out of their wallets or purses to charge purchases.

One of the advantages that American Express presented for using its card was the physical return of the customer's receipts. Customers had grown used to the convenience of balancing their receipts with those of American Express. With 2 million receipts arriving daily at its Fort Lauderdale and Phoenix locations, American Express realized that it needed a new system if it was going to be able to continue this service in an increasingly cost-competitive environment.

The new system would have to meet several important goals. First, keyed data entry would have to be minimized due to the increasingly high cost of this process. Second, the entire receipt would have to be able to be stored and retrieved as a complete image to continue American Express's tradition of returning a copy of the entire receipt. Third, the processing time between purchase and billing would have to be greatly reduced to minimize the high cost of capital. Fourth, accuracy had to be paramount because the consumer's credit and trust in the company would be at stake. Finally, the process would have to be alterable in the future as new products and technologies were developed to be integrated into the system.

The process of using the American Express card and receiving a bill involves a number of steps. When a card member makes a purchase, the card is "swiped" through a scanner and the amount of the purchase is entered on the keyboard. Information regarding the purchase, the purchaser, and the retailer is immediately transmitted to the main computer. Customers then sign slips for the purchases. These original slips are then submitted to American Express.

When credit card slips are received from the merchant, they are scanned and the billing amounts are entered into the database. Images are sent to the system's optical disks for storage. The imaged receipts are then balanced against the billing totals to make certain that there are no mistakes. Once everything is balanced, console operators prepare the bill by calling up the images on the screen and combining them with the actual bill.

Future enhancements include the customer signing an electronic notepad. This will enable the entire imaged slip to be transmitted electronically, complete with signatures, to the billing centers. Research is also being done on character recognition technology. This will enable the dollar amounts on the slips to be read by the imager. This will eliminate the next most time-consuming step, that of keying in the dollar amounts by hand.

The change to an imaged system presented some important challenges to the way American Express traditionally interacted with its customers. These were described by Cliff Dodd, senior vice-president of billing and payment services.

> Getting a bill means you have to pay money, and that's not a very pleasant experience to begin with. But if all of a sudden you change something that is very familiar and very important to a lot of people (because they use the card as a business tool), you really run the risk of alienating people. But we found that after six months of getting the Enhanced Country Club bill, 92 percent of our card members said they liked the new system better. That's because it's a neater package now, easier to read, understand, file, and store.

The new system provides one obvious advantage. Without the receipts, the new bill provides more room in the envelope for marketing additional features of the card and other services. Another advantage occurs at the point of sale. The more information that the merchant keys into the computer system, the less will ultimately have to be entered by American Express personnel. This will improve the accuracy of the billing process and reduce American Express's cost to maintain it.

## QUESTIONS

1. What are the American Express system inputs and outputs?
2. What processing steps take place between the purchase of an item and the receipt of the bill?
3. What information must be stored in American Express's database?

4. What manual procedures have been eliminated by the new system?

5. What manual procedures do future processing improvements promise to eliminate?

6. At what points are the financial information from the database checked against the scanned image of the customer receipt?

7. Why is the financial information compared at several steps to the information on the scanned receipts?

8. What other competitive advantages might the new system provide for American Express?

## CASE *John L. Scott Realtors*

John Scott Realtors is a small real estate firm headquartered in Bellevue, Washington, with a total of 25 offices in Western Washington. The firm purchased a Hewlett-Packard minicomputer in 1989 to keep track of properties and commissions. Over time, the company acquired 250 personal computers. Given the declining prices of personal computers, staff began the process of converting to a client-server local area network, with personal computer-based servers installed in major offices.

With the old system, data was stored in proprietary formats for each application package. As a result, managers and agents could only retrieve information that is printed on the standard reports. Although most of the users have personal computers, they could transfer the data they want from the minicomputer to their spreadsheets and other applications.

The real estate offices are also connected to several local Multiple Listing Services (MLS) databases. Each MLS database has a different system to identify property features and agents. Combining information from the various databases typically requires manually re-entering the data.

Nathan McCoy, the computer services director, wanted to replace the minicomputer with several smaller personal computer-based servers running Microsoft's Windows NT. The objective was to tie the servers together with the users' personal computers on a local area network. Servers would be located in major offices. The network would provide the physical link between the machines.

To make it easier for users to find the data they need, McCoy planned to implement a relational DBMS. His goal was to provide easy access to the internal and external data. First, he needed to redesign all of the existing applications. Yet he knew that as a small company, the firm could not afford to pay tens of thousands of dollars in consulting fees to design the new system.

Mr. McCoy decided to involve the users directly and design the new database himself. After reviewing database design textbooks, he created a 25-person database design team that met regularly with end users. Initially, he tried to design the system with the traditional "normalization" approach to database design. He noted that he would start thinking right away in terms of primary keys. He wondered where he would put a particular field.

To simplify the design process, the team purchased a visual modeling tool that enabled them to specify the data and relationships as diagrams. The software then converted the diagrams into a complete database specification. In six months, the team designed four major applications: an agent master file, commissions processing, trust accounting, and transactions/sales management. McCoy estimates that the team saved $20,000 by not having to pay for approximately 200 hours of time from outside consultants.

The next step was to hire an outside team to actually build the applications. Because the basic design work is completed and users seemed to agree on the system design, the next step should be straightforward.

### QUESTIONS

1. What problems were experienced by Scott Realtors? What was the cause of these problems?

2. What advantages are provided by using a relational DBMS? How does the database approach solve the problems?

3. What are the next steps involved in creating the new system?

4. What problems might arise in the next few steps of building the applications?

5. How much time do you think McCoy and his team invested in the project up to the point of hiring the programmers? Would they have been better off hiring an outside consultant? What are the costs and benefits of hiring consultants?

6. Do you think Scott Realtors could have built an adequate system using off-the-shelf software? What are the costs and benefits of trying this approach?

7. Using an object-oriented approach to designing the new system for Scott Realtors, what would be the major object classes, in terms of attributes and functions?

## CASE *Precision Twist Drill Company*

The Precision Twist Drill Company in Crystal Lake, Illinois, began making drill bits in the 1920s for the increasingly varied demands of the automobile and truck manufacturing companies. High-quality products and the ability to respond to their buyers' needs established Precision Twist as the nation's leading manufacturer of drill bits.

The requirements of the 1980s brought an increasing demand for technology-driven manufacturing techniques to the firm. Coupled with this was the high investment cost to reach these objectives. Across the country, smaller, more limited producers of drill bits realized that they could not make the financial investment necessary to remain competitive in this environment and thus put their plants on the market.

During this same time period, Precision Twist analyzed the market in terms of the reduced competition and made a commitment to expansion. The company purchased plants in Rhinelander, Wisconsin; Montpelier, Ohio; and Tucson, Arizona. With each purchase the company gained new drill bit processes, brandnames, and customer lists.

The increased number of plants and demand for the product strained the company's current computer system. In 1972–73 the MIS group had installed a Xerox time-share system. Increasing numbers of transactions caused Precision Twist to purchase and install an IBM System 36 in 1983. This enabled them to bring transaction processing in-house. In conjunction, the company bought some accounting software from Insight Software in Dublin, Ireland. They also wrote an order-entry and inventory-evaluation system.

The system was acceptable in 1983 when the company produced less than 100,000 drills daily and had revenues less than $25 million dollars. Business was growing, however, to 315,000 drills from the Rhinelander plant alone. Equally significant was the complexity of orders that Precision Twist was receiving. The Rhinelander plant filled standard orders. These were bits that were purchased from the company's 150,000 predefined variations on 10,000 separate bits. The Crystal Lake plant concentrated on the special orders—bits that Precision Twist manufactured to meet customers' specifications. These customers included Ford, General Motors, Chrysler, Caterpillar, and Cummins Engine. In this case, the purchaser provided the specifications to the drill manufacturers and Precision had to provide the best overall bid.

Company officials categorized their efforts to computerize the accounting, customer service, distribution, and shop-floor functions as a series of "fits and starts." The inventory system worked, but had it had no link to the company's general ledger or shop-floor reporting systems. According to Joy Young, Precision Twist's auditor, "every piece of information had to be beat in by hand."

The first step that Precision Twist took was to hire a strategic planning and a shop-floor consulting firm to connect these four reporting areas of the company. Norman Margolin, executive vice-president and CFO, noted, "The firms did a good job of taking the company apart and telling us what we were doing and why we were doing it. But our manufacturing people were looking for more shop-floor rather than textbook experience."

Richard Gulbrandsen, the vice-president for engineering, added three more problems:

- A language barrier regarding specific needs on the manufacturing floor.
- The consulting firms were extremely expensive.
- Precision Twist could not see what was going to happen in the next phase.

Losing faith with outside consultants, Precision Twist employed a director of management information systems in 1987. It was not long until he was replaced with a committee that included everyone in the company who had operational responsibility and authority. The committee was composed of the organizational heads of manufacturing, accounting, scheduling, product control, traffic and distribution, and the data processing manager.

The committee spent the next year evaluating vendors and manufacturing packages. They began by examining off-the-shelf packaged software. They soon concluded, however, that their requirements were not generic to tool manufacturing. In their analysis stage, they listed four specific needs:

- *Multiplan capabilities.* Precision Twist needed to be able to take a partially fabricated set of drill bits from the Crystal Lake plant and finish them in the Rhinelander, Montpelier, or Tucson plants. This movement was necessary because of changing resource requirements. While other companies centered entire product groups in one plant, the size of Precision Twist's products enabled them to concentrate their plants on particular parts of the bit development process.
- *Customer service.* The sales force wanted the information system to provide the capacity to know where an order was in the manufacturing process and when the customer could expect to receive it.
- *Manufacturing forecast.* The manufacturing group needed to forecast what was happening on the shop floor. An accurate portrayal of where slack might be in the manufacturing process would enable the schedulers to better utilize the available equipment.
- *Work-in-progress and finished goods inventories.* Procedures needed to be in place to better plan raw material handling and work requirements. This would reduce the capital that was

involved in both work-in-progress and finished goods inventories.

After examining many products, the committee decided to implement an automation plan using Andersen Consulting's MacPac II software and a hardware configuration of the IBM AS/400, personal computers, and terminals. The pilot was based in the Crystal Lake location. It used 14 MacPac modules including design engineering, manufacturing engineering, product costing, requirements and capacity planning, inventory control and accounting, shop-floor control, master scheduling, and accounts payable.

Midway through the pilot project, the MacPac system still needed to be customized on the company's IBM AS/400 computer. With 40–60 terminals on the AS/400 and several personal computers on the accounting side, Precision Twist was most interested in using MacPac II to integrate both the inventory and accounting sides of the operation. To expedite this process, Stephen Meyer wrote an interface link between MacPac and Precision Twist's Insight accounting and internally written order-entry software.

Realizing the impact that the system will have on the total operation of the company, Richard Gulbrandsen, the vice president for engineering, summed up the integration process: "We're changing our business habits. We're learning how to collect data better, and we're taking a different approach to direct and indirect reporting of labor hours. We're learning a lot of things we can and cannot do."

SOURCE: Robert Knight, "Twists, Turns, Fits, Starts in Pursuit of Automation," *Software Magazine*, September 1990, p. 100.

## QUESTIONS

1. How does the specialized nature of Precision Twist Drill Company make it particularly in need of a database management system?
2. How did the nature of Precision Twist's products make it advantageous to focus their plants on particular parts of the process rather than manufacture different parts at different plants?
3. How will a well-constructed database management system assist Precision Twist in keeping track of the numerous parts and variations in four different plants?
4. Why is the link between the general ledger and the shop-floor reporting system particularly difficult to make?
5. How did the four specific needs listed by Precision Twist match the alternatives that were available to them?

6. Why did Precision Twist have so much difficulty making the transition from Phase 1 (the strategic plan) to Phase 3 (the implementation of the combined system)?
7. Which type of reports would management at Precision Twist be most interested in: periodic or standard reports?
8. List the individuals who need to share data at Precision Twist. What particular qualities of the financial and manufacturing data make it difficult to share?
9. During which of the four stages of database development did Precision Twist have the most difficulty formulating its goals?
10. Why was communication a problem between the financial and manufacturing individuals in the company? How was this communication issue underscored by inability of consultants that represented both sides of the issue to come to agreement?

## CASE *Ford New Holland Agricultural Machinery Division*

Ford New Holland is Ford Motor Company's agricultural machinery division in New Holland, Pennsylvania. It manufactures tractors, farm implements, and machinery under the *Ford* and *New Holland* names. Because of the different needs of farmers across the country, tractors and farm implements are diverse in their manufacturing structure. They can be customized to meet a particular area or farmer's need. For example, wheat farmers in Kansas and Nebraska need large, powerful tractors to cover the expansive area of their crops. Orange growers in Florida need smaller, less-powerful tractors and trailers to carry pruning equipment and fertilizer to the trees and to take the fruit from the fields.

Each different need requires a specific engine size and implement mix. Each variation also needs its own set of documentation, owners' manuals, and sales brochures. This presents an enormous problem, not just for the salespeople and maintenance technicians but also the individuals who must develop and write the training material and manuals. As the stacks of documentation grew, Ford was finding that printing and dissemination of the manuals became an increasingly heavy financial burden. Training the salesperson to access the data seemed to be beyond the company's reach.

To address this need, Ford examined the capability of a CD-ROM system. A CD-ROM database can store up to 660 megabytes of information per disk. CD-ROM also offers the advantages of being interactive. Rather than having to read a document in linear order, the computer can quickly search for the specific term or diagram. Although the first disk is quite expensive to produce, subsequent duplication is comparatively inexpensive. A CD-ROM makes the stores of data portable in a way that is far superior over the bulky retrieval methods of archival storage media such as mainframe tape systems or microfiche.

Based on these advantages, this division decided to build a CD-ROM application to improve its costly online catalog system. It chose Carmen J. Martin to direct this project.

The first decision that Carmen had to make was where to produce the CD-ROM application. The entire production process could be completed internally at a high startup cost but with more control for the company. Second, the responsibility could be split between an in-house program and an outside service with a gradual increase in internal investment and involvement. Third, an outside service bureau could be hired to produce the application from start to finish. This would ensure that the project would be completed at a fixed price but would not help to transfer how to accomplish the task back to Ford.

Martin chose to tackle the project herself. After a one-day training session on CD-ROM development, she went to work to develop a new manual/training application for Ford. She started by learning a development package that enabled her to build an easy-to-use, menu-driven application. The application included instant cross-referenced and indexed access to prices, descriptions, and nearly everything else people wanted to know about the 300,000 parts and components from the division's product line. The information came from tapes of raw computer data from the data processing department.

According to Martin, now when a dealer wants information,

> All he/she has to do is type in the word *hose* and the tractor's model number, and the system prints a list of all the hoses used in that tractor. The dealers wanted this information without incurring the communication charges of going online to our mainframe. CD-ROM was the only way to give them what they wanted in a cost-effective manner.

### QUESTIONS

1. What advantages does the CD-ROM technology provide compared to the more traditional printed catalogs and reference manuals?
2. Why is the power to search for particular words or concepts important for the user in the field?
3. Why were the dealers adverse to "dialing in" to the mainframe to retrieve their product information?
4. When might a "dial-in" system be necessary rather than using a CD-ROM system?
5. What are the advantages and disadvantages of building a CD-ROM application in-house versus using a service bureau?
6. What guidelines would you give a manager who was deciding whether to continue with the current paper-based catalog program or go to a CD-ROM-based system? What factors should the manager consider as he or she makes this decision?
7. What guidelines would you give a manager who was deciding whether to build a CD-ROM-based system in house versus with an outside service agency? What factors should the manager consider as he or she makes this decision?

## DISCUSSION ISSUE

### Who Should Control Corporate Data?

An interesting problem arises with the emphasis on the data provided by the database approach. Who should control the corporate data? Remember that standards are needed in order to keep the data consistent and make it useful to everyone. On the other hand, the data often come from individual users and departments. If the production department has its own collection of information, perhaps the staff should have more control over that information. Listen to Ilsa, the production manager, as she discusses her new database with Rick, the database administrator.

Ilsa:    Rick, I have to talk to you.

Rick:    Uh-huh. I saved the first report for you.

Ilsa:    We have the new robots installed. They'll be connected to the computers by the end of next week. We need to store the measurement information to use it for quality control. Also, we need access to the inventory and production schedule databases so we can configure the robots for each production run. Only we're having some problems with the database team. They said management won't let us use the customer data. We need you to talk to them.

Rick:    Yeah. Well, I try not to stick my neck out. These rules were created by a committee three years ago. We all agreed to them. You knew the rules going into this project.

Ilsa: I can understand how you feel. Before all this started, I thought I had everything I needed. But we've changed. We didn't know about the robots three years ago. We can't live in the past. I tried to go straight to marketing, but the staff said you're the only one who can help us. They seem upset that they don't own the data anymore.

Rick: Listen. Nobody owns anything here. And we all have problems. You know what it was like before. If it weren't for these standards, you wouldn't even be able to ask for the customer data. It was so poorly managed that even marketing couldn't use it. It took us almost a year to clean it up and test all the data. We can't just give you open access to it now. I'm not going through that mess again.

Ilsa: There must be something you can do. Look, if we can't get access through you, we'll just have to go around you. We can build our own customer and orders database. It'll just take longer and cost us more money.

Rick: Sure, but how are you going to keep it up to date? And how are you going to fit it in with the existing data? You'll end up duplicating everything we've already done. Pretty soon we'll be right back to the mess we had three years ago. I can't allow you to do that.

Ilsa: We don't have any choice. Our work is too important to the company. OK, we can't do it

without your help. So why can't you help us? There must be some way to set up our databases to match with yours. We'll promise not to hurt your data. We'll do whatever tests you need.

Rick: It's not that easy. Maybe we can work it out, but we can't possibly finish it by next week. See, I have to play by the rules too. If I start changing the customer database, then marketing will be in here screaming. If I touch inventory, management will be on the phone. Plus, accounting has a bunch of changes they want me to make. I don't think your modifications will match theirs. They've been complaining about security and insufficient audit trails. I have to coordinate these changes. We'll at least need a committee and several meetings.

Ilsa: All I'm asking for is a chance. Remember, Rick, this problem's bigger than both of us. Sometimes we can't play by the rules; they need to be changed.

## QUESTIONS

1. Do you think Rick is being too restrictive? Should he just give Ilsa what she wants?
2. What do you suppose will eventually happen if Ilsa "goes around" Rick and builds her own database? What if everyone else in the company does the same thing?
3. Is there a compromise position where both Rick and Ilsa can get what they want?
4. How could a good database management system help?

# *Data Normalization*

## INTRODUCTION

Database management systems are powerful tools, with the ability to present data in many ways. They are used by managers to answer many different types of questions. However, this flexibility is not automatic. Databases need to be carefully designed; otherwise, managers will not be able to get the information they need. Poor design also leads to unnecessary duplication of data. Duplication wastes space and requires workers to enter the same data several times. *Normalization* is an important technique to design databases.

To understand the process of normalization, consider a small example. We want to build a database for a small video rental store. We begin by thinking about who will be using the database and identifying what data they will need. Consider the situation of the checkout clerks. They first identify the customer, then record each movie to be rented. The computer should then calculate the amount of money due along with any taxes. Figure 5.1A shows a sample input screen that might be used.

The important point to note is that the data will have to be stored in more than one table. Each

**FIGURE 5.1A**
The order form is used in almost any firm. We need to determine the best way to store the data that is collected by this form.

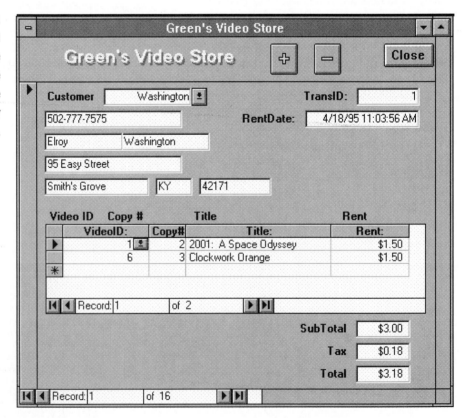

entity or object on the form will be represented by a separate table. For this example, there are four objects on the form: Customers, Videos, Rental, and VideosRented.

Before explaining how to derive the four tables from the form, there are some basic concepts you need to understand. First, remember that every table must have a primary key. A primary key is one or more columns that uniquely identify each row. For example, we anticipated problems with identifying customers, so each customer is assigned a unique ID number. Similarly, each video is given a unique ID number. Note that we might have more than one copy of each title, so we have also assigned a copy number to each video. There is one drawback to assigning numbers to customers: We cannot expect customers to remember their number, so we will need a method to look it up. One possibility is to give everyone an ID card imprinted with the number—perhaps printed with a bar code that can be scanned. However, we still need a method to deal with customers who forget their cards.

The second aspect to understand when designing databases is the relationships between various entities. First, observe that there are two sections to the form: (1) the main Rental which identifies the transaction, the customer and the date, and (2) a *repeating section* that lists the videos being rented. Each customer can rent several different videos at one time. We say there is a *one-to-many* relationship between the Rental and the VideosRented sections.

As you will see, identifying one-to-many relationships is crucial to proper database design.

In some respects, designing databases is straightforward: There are only three basic rules. However, database design is often interrelated with systems analysis. In most cases, we are attempting to understand the business at the same time the database is being designed. One common problem that arises is that it is not always easy to see which relationships are one-to-many and which are one-to-one or many-to-many.

## NOTATION

It would be cumbersome to draw pictures of every table that we use, so we usually write table definitions in a standard notation. The base customer table is shown in Figure 5.2A, both in notational form and with sample data.

Figure 5.3A illustrates another feature of the notation. We denote one-to-many or repeating relationships by placing parentheses around them. Figure 5.3A represents all the data shown in the input screen from Figure 5.1A. The description is created by starting at the top of the form and writing down each element that you encounter. If a section contains repeating data, place parentheses around it. Preliminary keys are identified at this step by underlining them. However, we might have to add or change them at later steps. Notice that CustomerID is marked with a dashed line to indicate that in the RentalForm, it is not the primary key, but it might be

**FIGURE 5.2A**

Notation for tables. Table definitions can often be written in one or two lines. Each table has a name and a list of columns. The column (or columns) that makes up the primary key is underlined.

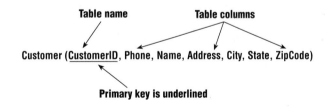

| CustomerID | Phone | LastName | FirstName | Address | City | State | ZipCode |
|---|---|---|---|---|---|---|---|
| 1 | 502-666-7777 | Johnson | Martha | 125 Main Street | Alvaton | KY | 42122 |
| 2 | 502-888-6464 | Smith | Jack | 873 Elm Street | Bowling Green | KY | 42101 |
| 3 | 502-777-7575 | Washington | Elroy | 95 Easy Street | Smith's Grove | KY | 42171 |
| 4 | 502-333-9494 | Adams | Samuel | 746 Brown Drive | Alvaton | KY | 42122 |
| 5 | 502-474-4746 | Rabitz | Victor | 645 White Avenue | Bowling Green | KY | 42102 |
| 6 | 615-373-4746 | Steinmetz | Susan | 15 Speedway Drive | Portland | TN | 37148 |
| 7 | 615-8884474 | Lasater | Les | 67 S. Ray Drive | Portland | TN | 37148 |
| 8 | 615-452-1162 | Jones | Charlie | 867 Lakeside Drive | Castalian Springs | TN | 37031 |
| 9 | 502-222-4351 | Chavez | Juan | 673 Industry Blvd. | Caneyville | KY | 42721 |
| 10 | 502-444-2512 | Rojo | Maria | 88 Main Street | Cave City | KY | 42127 |

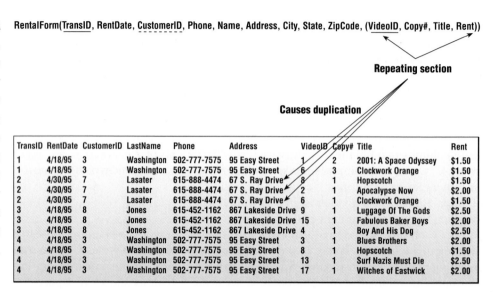

**FIGURE 5.3A**

Converting to notation. Repeating sections are indicated by the inner parentheses. If we try to store the data this way, notice the problem created by the repeating section: Each time a customer checks out a video we have to re-enter the phone and address.

used as a key in another table. Because TransID is unique for every transaction, there is no need to make CustomerID a key. We can already see some problems with trying to store data in this format. Notice that the same customer name, phone, and address would have to be entered several times.

Remember that some repeating sections are difficult to spot and might consist of only one column. For example, how many phone numbers can a customer have? Should the Phone column be repeating? In the case of the video store, probably not, because we most likely want to keep only one number per customer. In other businesses, we might want to keep several phone numbers for each client. Data normalization is directly related to the business processes. The tables you design depend on the way the business is organized.

## First Normal Form

Now that we have a way of writing down our assumptions, it is relatively straightforward to separate the data into tables. The first step is to split out all repeating sections. Think about the problems that might arise if we try to keep the repeating VideosRented section with the customer data. If we design the database this way, we would have to know how many videos could be rented by each customer, because we would have to set aside space before hand. If we do not choose enough space, we will have to throw out transaction data. If we set aside too much, there will be wasted space. Figure 5.4A illustrates the problem.

The answer to this problem is to pull out the repeating section and form a new table. Then, each

**FIGURE 5.4A**

A table that contains repeating sections is not in first normal form. If we try to store data in this form, we are faced with the question of deciding how many videos might be rented at one time. We will waste a lot of space with missing data.

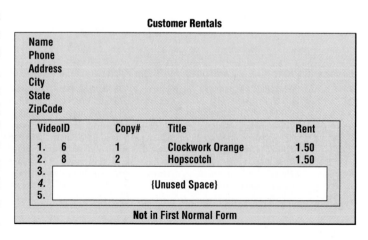

movie rented by a customer will fill a new row. Rows do not have to be preallocated, so there is no wasted space. Figure 5.5A uses the notation to show how the table will split. Notice that whenever we split a table this way, we have to bring along the key from the prior section. Hence, the new table will include the TransID key as well as the VideoID key.

When a table contains no repeating sections, we say that it is in *first normal form.*

## Second Normal Form

Even if a table is in first normal form, there can be additional problems. Consider the RentalLine table in Figure 5.5A. Notice there are two components to the key: TransID and VideoID. The nonkey items consist of the Copy#, Title, and the Rental rate for the movie. If we leave the table in this form, consider the situation of renting a movie. Every time a movie is rented (new TransID), it will be necessary to enter the VideoID, Copy# *and* the title and rental rate. It means that we will be storing the video title every time a video is rented. Popular movies might be rented thousands of times. Do we really want to store the title each time?

The reason we have this problem is that when the TransID changes, the movie title stays the same. The movie title depends only on the VideoID. It is tempting to say that the same problem arises with respect to the rental rate. Indeed, in some video stores, the rental rate might depend only on the VideoID. However, what if the store offers discounts on certain dates, or to specific customers? If the rental rate can vary with each

**FIGURE 5.5A**

Splitting a table to solve problems. Problems with repeating sections are resolved by moving the repeating section into a new table. Be sure to include the old key in the new table so that you can connect the tables back together.

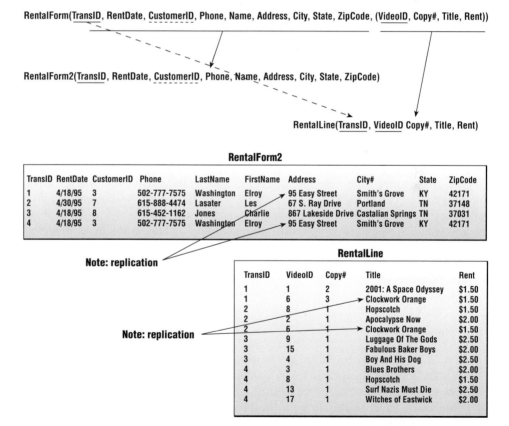

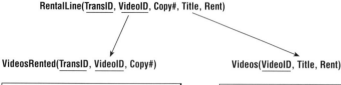

RentalLine(<u>TransID</u>, <u>VideoID</u>, Copy#, Title, Rent)

VideosRented(<u>TransID</u>, <u>VideoID</u>, Copy#)          Videos(<u>VideoID</u>, Title, Rent)

| TransID | VideoID | Copy# |
|---------|---------|-------|
| 1 | 1 | 2 |
| 1 | 6 | 3 |
| 2 | 2 | 1 |
| 2 | 6 | 1 |
| 2 | 8 | 1 |
| 3 | 4 | 1 |
| 3 | 9 | 1 |
| 3 | 15 | 1 |
| 4 | 3 | 1 |
| 4 | 8 | 1 |
| 4 | 13 | 1 |
| 4 | 17 | 1 |

| VideoID | Title | Rent |
|---------|-------|------|
| 1 | 2001: A Space Odyssey | $1.50 |
| 2 | Apocalypse Now | $2.00 |
| 3 | Blues Brothers | $2.00 |
| 4 | Boy And His Dog | $2.50 |
| 5 | Brother From Another Planet | $2.00 |
| 6 | Clockwork Orange | $1.50 |
| 7 | Gods Must Be Crazy | $2.00 |
| 8 | Hopscotch | $1.50 |

**FIGURE 5.6A**

Second normal form. Even though the repeating sections are gone, we have another problem. Every time we enter the VideoID, we have to re-enter the title. That would waste a lot of space. There is a more serious problem: If no one has rented a video yet, we have no way to find its title since it is not yet stored in the database. Again, the solution is to split the table. In second normal form, all non-key columns depend on the whole key (not just part of it).

transaction, the rate would have to be stored with the TransID. The final choice depends on the business rules and assumptions. For now, we will assume that rental rates are like the title and depend only on the VideoID.

When the nonkey items depend on only part of the key, we need to split them into their own table. Figure 5.6A shows the new tables.

When each nonkey column in a table depends on the entire key, we say that the table is in *second normal form.*

## Third Normal Form

Examine the RentalForm2 table in Figure 5.5A. Notice that because the primary key consists of only one column (TransID), the table must already be in second normal form. However, a different problem arises here. Again, consider what happens when we begin to collect data. Each time a customer comes to the store and rents videos there will be a new transaction. In each case, we would have to record the customer name, address, phone,

city, state, and zip code. Each entry in the transaction table for a customer would duplicate this data. In addition to the wasted space, imagine the problems that arise when a customer changes a phone number. You might have to update it in hundreds of rows.

The problem in this case is that the customer data does not depend on the primary key (TransID) at all. Instead, it depends only on the CustomerID column. Again, the solution is to place this data into its own table. Figure 5.7A shows the split.

Splitting the table solves the problem. Customer data is now stored only one time for each customer. It is referenced back to the Rentals table through the CustomerID.

The four tables we created are listed in Figure 5.8A. Each table is now in *third normal form.* It is easy to remember the conditions required for third normal form. First: There are no repeating groups in the tables. Second and third: Each nonkey column depends on the whole key and nothing but the key.

Note in Figure 5.8A that we could technically split the Customers table one more time. Because

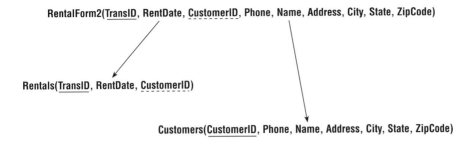

RentalForm2(<u>TransID</u>, RentDate, <u>CustomerID</u>, Phone, Name, Address, City, State, ZipCode)

Rentals(<u>TransID</u>, RentDate, <u>CustomerID</u>)

Customers(<u>CustomerID</u>, Phone, Name, Address, City, State, ZipCode)

**Rentals**

| TransID | RentDate | CustomerID |
|---------|----------|------------|
| 1 | 4/18/95 | 3 |
| 2 | 4/30/95 | 7 |
| 3 | 4/18/95 | 8 |
| 4 | 4/18/95 | 3 |

**Customers**

| CustomerID | Phone | LastName | FirstName | Address | City | State | ZipCode |
|------------|-------|----------|-----------|---------|------|-------|---------|
| 1 | 502-666-7777 | Johnson | Martha | 125 Main Street | Alvaton | KY | 42122 |
| 2 | 502-888-6464 | Smith | Jack | 873 Elm Street | Bowling Green | KY | 42101 |
| 3 | 502-777-7575 | Washington | Elroy | 95 Easy Street | Smith's Grove | KY | 42171 |
| 4 | 502-333-9494 | Adams | Samuel | 746 Brown Drive | Alvaton | KY | 42122 |
| 5 | 502-474-4746 | Rabitz | Victor | 645 White Avenue | Bowling Green | KY | 42102 |
| 6 | 615-373-4746 | Steinmetz | Susan | 15 Speedway Drive | Portland | TN | 37148 |
| 7 | 615-888-4474 | Lasater | Les | 67 S. Ray Drive | Portland | TN | 37148 |
| 8 | 615-452-1162 | Jones | Charlie | 867 Lakeside Drive | Castalian Springs | TN | 37031 |
| 9 | 502-222-4351 | Chavez | Juan | 673 Industry Blvd. | Caneyville | KY | 42721 |
| 10 | 502-444-2512 | Rojo | Maria | 88 Main Street | Cave City | KY | 42127 |

**FIGURE 5.7A**

Third normal form. There is another problem with this definition. The customer name does not depend on the key (TransID) at all. Instead, it depends on the CustomerID. Because the name and address do not change for each different TransID, we need to put the customer data in a separate table. The Rentals table now contains only the CustomerID which is used to link to the Customers table and collect the rest of the data.

Zipcodes are uniquely assigned by the Post Office, the City and State could be determined directly from the ZipCode (they do not depend on the CustomerID). In fact, most mailorder companies today keep a separate Zip Code table for that very reason. For our small video firm, it might be more of a nuisance to split the table. Although we can purchase a complete Zip Code directory in computer form, it is a very large database table. For small cases, it is often easier to leave the three items in the customer table and use the database to assign default values so clerks can simply press ENTER and accept the common values.

**CHECKING YOUR WORK**

To double-check the tables, first look for items that might be one-to-many relationships. They should be signified by keys (underlined). For instance, in the VideosRented table, each transaction can show rentals for many videos. If you find you have to add a new key, you will have normalize the table again.

When you are satisfied the keys adequately represent the one-to-many rules of the business, go through each column and ask: Does it depend on the whole key and nothing but the key? If not, split the table into smaller pieces.

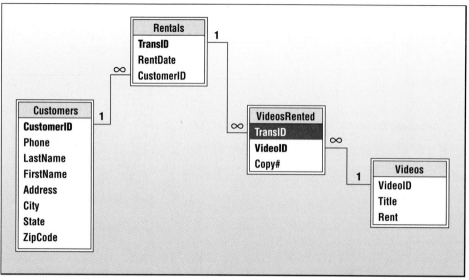

**FIGURE 5.8A**

Third normal form tables. There are no repeating sections and each non-key column depends on the whole key and nothing but the key. This figure also shows the relationships between the tables that will be enforced by the DBMS. When referential integrity is properly defined, the DBMS will ensure that rentals can be made only to customers who are defined in the Customers table.

Finally, be sure that the tables can be rejoined to create the original form or report. Notice in Figure 5.8A that you can draw lines that reconnect all of the tables. If you find a table standing alone, it generally means that you forgot to bring along a key value when you split the table. Be especially careful when you are pulling out repeating sections to carry along the key from the main table.

Another way to test your tables is to look at the table names. Each table should represent one entity or object. If you have trouble deciding what to name a table, it might be because the table is trying to describe more than one entity—like the RentalForm2 table in Figure 5.5A. You will also see similar problems as you try to enter data into the tables. If you find yourself entering the same data more than once, you probably made a mistake.

# *Business Integration*

**How do information systems help managers integrate business tasks?** A hundred years ago, there were very few large businesses. As firms became larger, owners needed a way to manage and control the huge number of employees. Managers needed assistance with hundreds of daily operational decisions. The primary approach was to build a hierarchical structure where each division was divided into ever-smaller departments. With guidelines and standard procedures, each department was independent and was responsible for its own operations.

Technology provides managers with virtually instantaneous communication. This communication enables managers to integrate the business operations. Managers can reorganize the business to solve problems from a broader perspective. Technology also enables managers to integrate information in different formats from multiple locations around the company.

CHAPTER 6

# *Networks and Telecommunications*

**WHAT YOU WILL LEARN IN THIS CHAPTER**

What are the primary components of a network? What are the differences between a client-server and a peer-to-peer network? What problems and complications are encountered with networks—especially enterprise networks? Why are standards necessary? What is the Internet and how can it help you? What telecommunications problems might you encounter in a global setting? How are networks used to solve business problems?

244

Magna International directs its Web page (http://www.magnaint.com) primarily at prospective investors, along with basic information on the products and services they provide.

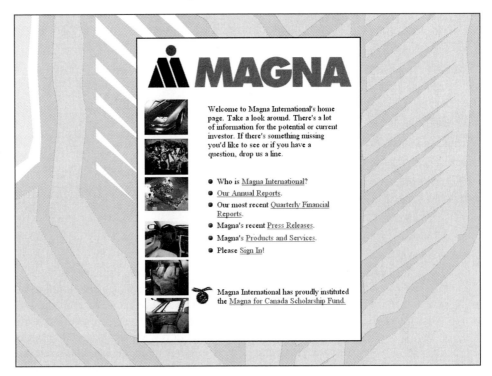

## MAGNA INTERNATIONAL

Magna International is a large manufacturer that sells automobile parts to a Chrysler Corporation assembly plant. Chrysler has adopted a just-in-time (JIT) inventory system and generally requires that parts be delivered to the plant within four hours of placing the order. It typically takes Magna one hour to find the part in inventory and pack it, and another hour to ship the item to the Chrysler plant. That does not leave any room for error. Mistakes or late shipments resulting in a shutdown of the Chrysler line result in huge penalties paid by Magna.

Obviously Magna has to be extremely careful with its inventory management. To make a profit, the supplier needs to maintain low inventory levels, but the company must always have the product ready to ship. Magna also has to forecast product demand. So far, Magna has been successful and inventory turnover is every two or three days.

To meet this demanding production schedule, Magna uses several networks. Electronic data interchange is used to receive orders from the Chrysler plant. An internal radio network is used to maintain up-to-date data on shipments.

**OVERVIEW** "The network *is* the computer." Scott McNealy, CEO of Sun Microsystems, built his company on this philosophy. In any business, buying computers and collecting data is not enough. To produce information, we must be able to share. As illustrated by Figure 6.1, networks are used to share data, software, and hardware and to communicate throughout the company. The ultimate goal is to eliminate distance as a factor in managing a business.

The importance of teamwork is easy to understand. Why would anyone disagree? Why would a company (or a nation) not have a state-of-the-art network? Like many questions in MIS, there are two basic problems: cost and changes in technology. Most networks

**FIGURE 6.1**
Managing an organization requires communication. Increasingly, communication uses computer networks to collect data, transmit messages, store collective knowledge, search for answers, coordinate work, and connect to external agents.

rely on cables to transmit data. Installing cables in a building is time-consuming, expensive, and disruptive. Additionally, there are several possible ways to link computers together. As we gain knowledge and technology improves, companies eventually have to replace components in their networks. Managers need to plan and predict how the company will grow and how technology might change. Between the costs and uncertainties, there is plenty of room for disagreement and several decisions to be made.

Consider the brief history of networks in most companies. Years ago, companies installed lines for telephones. Then they installed lines for dumb terminals connected to central computers. Then they installed lines for video. Then they installed **local area networks (LANs)** to connect personal computers. Every time the company grows, it has to expand these networks.

Consider the dream of a full-service, integrated network that would combine voice, fax, computer data, images, and video on one integrated system. We would like instant access to the system from anywhere in the world. We could send or receive any type of data anywhere, then copy it, edit it, search it, and route it to additional people. Oh yes, we would have access to the network 24 hours a day with no failures, no transmission errors, and no loss of data, and it would cost very little.

We actually come close to having all of these capabilities today, except that the cost of using such networks is not as low as in our dream. In the early 1960s, it was technically possible to build a network of videophones. But it was too expensive—not enough people were willing to pay the price. Over time, technology improved and costs declined so that phone companies are now building networks to carry video data. Thus, as a manager, you need to be aware of the changing capabilities of networks, but you must also evaluate the benefits and compare them to the costs.

**INTRODUCTION**

Communication is important to companies. There are two major categories of communication: internal and external. Internally, communication is used to keep the business running as one cohesive organization. Messages and data constantly travel among workers and managers. Workers collect data and share it with colleagues and summarize it for managers. Managers use the data to make decisions and change the organization. Changes are implemented as new policies and procedures, resulting in messages that are distributed throughout the company. There are many reasons for external communication, including collecting data about customers and suppliers and providing information to shareholders and governmental agencies.

## ▼ TRENDS ▲

The telephone system was originally designed to transmit sound by converting sound waves into electrical signals. Certain limitations were built into the system to keep costs down. An important feature of the phone system is its ability to handle multiple phone calls on one line. In the very early days of telephone, phone calls were connected by giant switchboards that required separate physical connections for each call. Over time, these switchboards were replaced with electronic switches. Today, the switches are the heart of the phone system network. Most of the switches in the United States are actually dedicated computers. To carry voice calls, the switches first convert the electrical signal into packets of digital data. These packets are then sent to the appropriate destination. An interesting feature of the digital-packet switches is that the packets can be separated and sent via different routes. The receiving switch puts them back together in the proper order. For example, a message from New Orleans being sent to New York could be routed through Atlanta and some parts might be sent through St. Louis. All of these conversions happen so fast that the caller and recipient do not know they are happening.

Another major change is the use of cellular telephones. In the 1980s, cellular telephone networks were installed in U.S. cities. They enable people to carry portable telephones. These phones transmit and receive signals with radio waves instead of wires. Computers are used to identify phones and maintain the connections.

A more recent trend that will affect personal communications is the rapid growth of cable television. Over 60 percent of U.S. households can receive cable television. In 1996, the government removed almost all barriers in the telecommunications industry. Consequently, the major cable television providers are considering using their systems to transmit phone calls, and the phone companies are also attempting to transmit television programs over the phone lines. The competition could be interesting. Cable television uses wiring that can carry more data (or channels). However, the cable systems do not have the routing capability of the phone companies.

Originally, computers were expensive. As a result, most companies owned only one computer. Because input and output were located at one point, there was little reason to transmit data. Eventually, video terminals and personal computers were placed on manager's desks, and these computers needed to share information.

The late 1980s saw a significant increase in the number of companies connecting computers with local area networks (LANs). Many computers are also connected across longer distances. These connections often use the services of the telephone companies. The digital phone switches make it easier to transmit computer data.

Some companies are experimenting with radio networks that connect portable personal computers without wires. At the other end of the scale, several countries are investing money in high-speed computer networks. These communication lines will make it easier for researchers and businesses to exchange information.

To understand the importance of telecommunications, note that AGS Information Services (a consulting firm) estimates that 48 percent to 68 percent of corporate technology budgets are spent on telecommunications. Some firms, like travel agents and brokerage firms, rely heavily on telecommunications and spend even more for them. Telecommunications expenses represent 2 percent to 7 percent of these businesses' total operating budget—which amounts to more than $10 million a year for a $500 million firm.

Sharing data and resources can cause problems. For example, there are security issues concerning who should be able to use and change the data. Additionally, there are political problems regarding ownership and control over the data. These con-

**Reality Bytes** ◣  6–1  DILLARD'S OF ARKANSAS

In 1989, Dillard's Department Stores achieved a 25 percent growth rate in profits to $114 million. Since 1980, they have accumulated a 25 percent compound annual growth rate in earnings per share and a 37 percent annual return to investors.

Bill Dillard insists on tight cost controls and centralized administration of everything from payroll to buying. The other thing he is focused on is computer technology. He prides himself in knowing how much business any of his stores has done at any time of the day by simply entering the request into a computer at the headquarters. Equally important is the ability of the information system to get products onto the selling floor faster than any other retailer. Using a program called Quick Response, any basic item can be electronically reordered from the vendor every week—based on the previous week's sales—without human intervention. What takes a month to restock in other stores can be completed in 12 days with Quick Response.

Dillard's is extremely loyal to its current suppliers. Quick Response cements that loyalty. Some have criticized the computer program for causing Dillard's to be too committed to its current line of products. One national sales manager from a women's sportswear firm put it like this: "We know who's selling to them and some of them aren't that great. But Dillard's just keeps reordering from them. They are one of the toughest stores in the industry to crack."

Technology also allows Dillard's to quickly integrate its new acquisitions into its current chain of stores. When they acquired the D. H. Holmes chain of 18 department stores in New Orleans, employees descended on the store on a Friday afternoon. By the next Monday, all new point-of-sales registers had been installed with a linkage to the Little Rock headquarters. Existing merchandise was retagged with bar-coded labels that enabled Dillard's to immediately capture sales information at the checkout registers.

SOURCE: Lucie Juneau, "Luring Consumers with Conspicuous Efficiency," *Computerworld*, September 14, 1992, p. 37. Copyright 1992 by Computerworld, Inc., Framingham, MA 01701—Reprinted from *Computerworld*.

cerns are multiplied in an international environment, because national governments may impose constraints on how companies can use the data they collect.

The objective of a network is to connect computers transparently, so that the users do not know the network exists. The network provides access to data on central computers, departmental computers, and sometimes on other workers' personal computers. Networks can create shared access to fax machines, modems, printers, scanners, and other specialized hardware. To the user, it does not matter where these devices are located. The network makes them work the same as if they were on any desktop. Department stores such as Dillard's (Reality Bytes 6–1) were early users of networked systems to enable tracking sales by each store.

### Sharing Data

Sharing data is one of the most obvious uses of networks. It also has the ability to make profound changes in the way an organization works. For hundreds of years, companies have been organized as hierarchies, divided into smaller organizations that are easier to manage. Dupont and General Motors quickly learned that as the size of an organization increases, it becomes increasingly difficult to manage, so their executives invented the structure of the modern corporation. Much like a military organization, dividing the company into subsections with well-defined tasks enables top executives to focus on direction while lower-level managers implement solutions. In this type of organization, data flows up and down the hierarchies, whereas only limited data flows across the various departments. Enterprising managers often build informal connections with managers in other departments to improve their personal access to data.

Implementing networks in a corporation changes the way employees and managers communicate. A well-designed information system can radically increase the flow of data throughout a company. Managers can see customer and marketing data immediately as it is collected. Employees in one department can easily share data with other departments. Globally located firms can use networks to operate on problems around the clock, sharing data and bringing in teams as each day begins around the world. Changing the way people communicate can alter the entire structure of the company. In particular, the increased flow of data across organizational lines reduces the importance and power of the hierarchical structure. It also means that managers have to trust employees. By giving employees access to the data they need, jobs can be accomplished faster and with higher quality. A network also facilitates the use of teams. In particular, it allows informal teams to spring up throughout the company to solve problems as they arise. Instead of waiting for a higher-level manager to appoint a team, employees can use the network to ask questions, notify others involved, and find in-house experts.

### Transactions

One of the most important reasons for connecting computers is the ability to share data. Consider a retail store with five checkout registers. Each register is actually a computer. If these computers are not connected, it is difficult to compute the daily sales for the store. At the end of the day, someone would have to manually collect the data from each computer and enter it into another computer. Also, imagine what would happen if a customer asked a clerk to determine whether a product was sold out. The clerk would have to check with each of the other clerks or perhaps call the storeroom. Collecting data from point-of-sale devices was a primary motivation for installing computers in the retail environment. A simple network is shown in Figure 6.2. The American Express network (Reality Bytes 6–2) illustrates some of the advantages of using a network for transaction processing.

Connecting the firm's computers enables a central database to maintain the current inventory and sales data. Current sales totals will be instantly available from any terminal. When a customer asks whether an item is in stock, the clerk simply looks up one number. If several stores are connected with a network, the clerk's computer can instantly check inventory at the other stores as well. Similarly, the manager could

**FIGURE 6.2**
Network for transaction processing. Networks are often used to collect data in a central database. From there, the data can be queried and analyzed by managers.

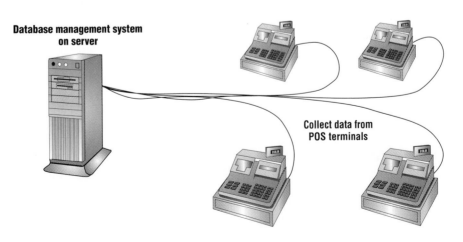

Database management system on server

Collect data from POS terminals

## Reality Bytes    6-2    AMERICAN EXPRESS HUMAN RESOURCES NETWORK

American Express has implemented HR Express to better address its human resources needs. This LAN-based, multivendor system independently maintains payroll and benefit data while sending common employee demographics to the corporate office. Using an integrated system enables packages from a number of different vendors to be included in the system. Equally important to senior management, the software does not stand in the way of an acquisition or divestiture.

Running on Novell NetWare on LANs, the system is installed in 22 locations. It depends on an interface that automatically takes data from the unit systems and updates the centralized human resources database.

A catalyst for the new system was the increasing inability of the old system to correctly process checks. Set up for a business unit of 5,000 people, it was processing data for 12,000. Another problem was its inability to maintain corporatewide data. HR Express addressed this concern by defining 102 data elements that are fed via e-mail to the corporate system.

get daily sales from each location without leaving the office. Increasingly, consumers are gaining direct access to merchants and banks. Consequently, automated bill payments will become increasingly popular (Reality Bytes 6–3).

### Decisions and Searches

Many types of data need to be shared in a company. Look at the problem from a manager's viewpoint. Each level of management has its own decisions to make, and each requires information from the rest of the company. Consider a situation in which a manager is told to close down 3 stores out of 200. Selecting those stores can be a tough decision. It requires knowing sales volume for every store and projected future sales as well as operating costs. The manager will bring this basic information to a personal computer to create graphs and evaluate models. It is possible to collect all of the data from each store by hand and enter it into the computer. However, it would be much more efficient if the manager could simply transfer the data directly from the central database to the personal computer. Not only is this method faster, it prevents errors. The database should have the most recent information. Additionally, all managers will use the same data. A portion of a network for making decisions and sharing work with team members is illustrated in Figure 6.3. Without networks and central-

## Reality Bytes    6-3    E-MAIL AND POST OFFICES

Every day, more transactions are carried by computer communications. Many people are asking at what point does e-mail start hurting the national post offices or "snail mail" as it is sometimes called. As any homeowner can testify, the bulk of current mail consists of advertising or "junk mail." In the United States, the post office estimates that only 5 percent of the mail consists of personal messages. To date, most U.S. consumers still use postal mail for bills. However, as interstate banking increases, even this usage will change.

In England, British Gas estimated that in 1991 almost one-third of customer payments were in the form of automatic bank transfers. Only 10 percent were carried by the post office workers. In response to these competitive threats, many European postal companies are considering privatization to decrease costs.

**FIGURE 6.3**
Network for decisions and collaboration. The file server holds basic data and software tools. Managers retrieve data and create reports. The reports can be shared with other managers. With collaborative software, revisions are automatically tracked and combined to form the final document.

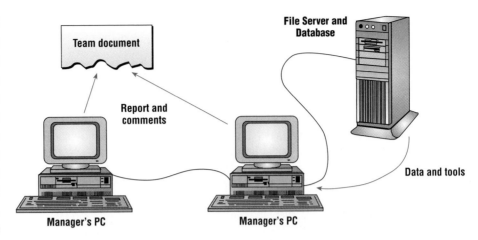

ized data sharing, many companies experience problems when managers have different versions of the data. American Express implemented a LAN in its human resources department to help the staff consolidate information and process data more efficiently.

## Messages

Computer networks can be used to send messages to other people, much like telephone or mail systems. This technique is called **electronic mail** or **e-mail** for short. By connecting computers, one person can send a message to any other user connected to the mail system. Current mail systems enable you to send files, pictures, or even sound to other computer users. As shown in Figure 6.4, e-mail systems often rely on one machine to hold messages, which are then distributed to other computers when the users sign on.

**FIGURE 6.4**
Networks for communication. E-mail messages and scheduling are two common forms of communication in business. With e-mail, one machine holds the mail for the group. Mail is held until the recipient logs on and can receive the message. For scheduling, each user maintains a personal calendar. To schedule a meeting with a group of people, the computer examines the calendars for the desired participants to locate an open time slot.

Many companies have their own internal e-mail systems. Common interoffice communications (such as meeting notices) are sent over the computer. E-mail is much faster than traditional mail. Many times it is more convenient than using telephones—there are never any busy lines with e-mail. E-mail users can send or receive messages at

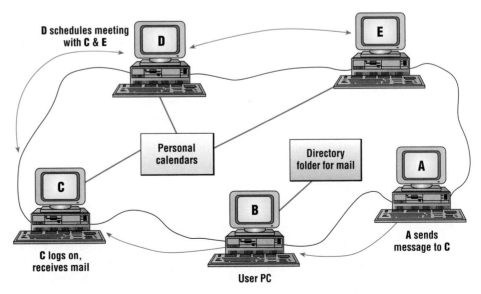

**Reality Bytes**    6–4    E-MAIL: MILLIONS OF MESSAGES

With more than 20 million people able to send messages on the Internet, it can be risky to make your e-mail address public, especially because many of those people can send messages free or for a few cents. When the *New Yorker* published the e-mail address for Microsoft's CEO Bill Gates, he received more than 5,000 messages. Problems also exist within companies. There are employees who choose to send copies of their messages to everyone in the company. Of course, the CEO is at the top of everyone's list.

Mitch Kertzman, chairman of Powersoft Corp., notes that he receives hundreds of messages in one week, including one by an employee trying to sell a dog. Charles Wang, CEO of the giant software company Computer Associates, cuts off access to the internal e-mail system for five hours a day—so employees can work. As e-mail proliferates, more people are using filters that scan incoming mail to weed out unwanted messages.

any time. Electronic messages can be sent to many people at the same time by creating a mailing list. Messages can be stored, retrieved, and searched for later usage. In most systems, the computer can automatically notify you when the recipient reads the message. You never have to worry about whether your message was received.

Voice mail systems, which resemble answering machines, have some of these same advantages. However, e-mail takes less space to store. More importantly, e-mail can be scanned electronically to search for key topics. Similarly, there are e-mail filters that automatically read your mail and focus on the topics you have chosen. They cut down on the amount of junk e-mail messages.

There are also public networks that enable organizations to communicate electronically. In particular, there is a large international network called the **Internet.** The Internet is a worldwide data communications network that links together millions of computers. With this system, managers can easily communicate with researchers at universities and with other managers around the world. Sometimes, people are too easy to reach by e-mail—executives and researchers are increasingly swamped by e-mail messages (Reality Bytes 6–4).

There are some drawbacks to e-mail. Some people are still reluctant to use computers, so they do not check the computer often enough to keep up with their mail. Another problem is that in 1991, the U.S. courts ruled that public transmission systems such as e-mail are not subject to same legal protections for privacy as paper mail and phone calls. Unless the laws are rewritten, it is legal for employers (and almost anyone else) to read everyone's e-mail messages. Of course, being legal does not make it ethical. The best solution to open communication systems is to encrypt the messages. Most word processors and spreadsheets make it easy to encrypt the files when they are saved. An interesting twist on this situation is that some courts have ruled that public officials *cannot* encrypt their messages—in fact, in some situations, it is illegal for public officials to communicate via e-mail (Reality Bytes 6–5).

### Bulletin Boards

An electronic **bulletin board system (BBS)** is similar to a physical bulletin board, except that people access it from computers. The BBS allows users to post comments, pictures and files for other people to view or copy. Bulletin boards are usually organized by topics, and you can search them for specific phrases or com-

◤ **Reality Bytes** ◤    6–5   Government E-mail

Government agencies (and universities) have been quick to adopt e-mail. Many agencies have offices scattered across a state or around the nation. Most have easy computer access and networks, so adding e-mail is relatively straightforward. But there are some interesting problems.

In Palo Alto, California, city lawmakers received a stern warning from the city attorney. Council members used e-mail to discuss a land-use proposal. The attorney indicated that such communication constituted a "meeting" and was thus subject to the state's open meeting laws. Most states have laws stating that all public meetings must be publicly scheduled and open

to public access. Lawmakers are not allowed to debate issues in private. The laws vary by state. Sometimes a "meeting" requires several lawmakers. Other times, as in Florida, the laws apply even to two officials.

Another problem facing governments are the issues of when to delete e-mail and what e-mail can be deleted. The courts have regularly ruled that e-mail is subject to the Freedom of Information Act and must be provided to citizens on request. They have also ruled that officials must keep copies of e-mail messages as part of the public record. However, most computer systems are not good at organizing and archiving the thousands of e-mail messages created every day.

ments. They are a useful way to disseminate information that is of interest to many different people. As indicated in Figure 6.5, bulletin board systems are often accessed over phone lines using modems. The bulletin board operator (or *sysop*) buys the BBS software and several modems. Users can call the BBS with communication software and leave messages or copy files to the BBS (*upload*) or copy files from the BBS to their own PC (*download*). Some sysops charge users a fixed fee for access; others charge by the number of files transferred or by each minute of access time. Some service boards have no charges but limit the amount of time one user can be connected to the board.

Several commercial networks support a variety of bulletin boards. Individuals can subscribe to networks like Prodigy, GEnie, CompuServe, America Online, and the

**FIGURE 6.5**

A bulletin board system (BBS) uses a network for sharing information. It is designed as a repository of messages, files, images, and user comments. Individual boards often specialize in specific topics. Companies are beginning to create internal systems to share data within the company.

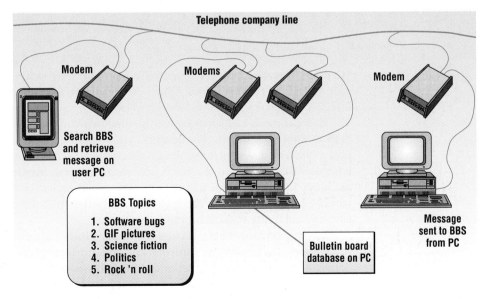

Reality Bytes      6–6   AMERICA ONLINE, COMPUSERVE, DELPHI, eWORLD, GEnie, AND PRODIGY

All of the popular online services provide stock quotes, technical support, or travel information. They can download software; use an encyclopedia; send mail and faxes; browse magazines; make airline reservations; and participate in written discussions on many topics.

### CompuServe (CIS) (800/848–8199)

CompuServe is known for its vast wealth of databases and research-oriented services for financial, legal, and medical interests. CompuServe offers a core set of services, as well as an online *Books in Print,* computer vendor forums, brokerage services, *Consumer Reports,* Associated Press news, and the electronic edition of the *Official Airline Guide.*

### Delphi (800/695–4005)

An Internet-oriented service, Delphi offers most core services, with its main omissions being vendor forums and graphical software. Delphi offers news from Reuters and United Press International; stock quotes; airline and car-rental reservations; the Computerized AIDS Information Network (CAIN); the Nynex Electronic Yellow Pages (covering businesses in the Northeast); Grolier's Encyclopedia; movie reviews; and computer vendor forums for a variety of platforms, including Macintosh.

### eWorld (800/775–4556)

eWorld contains items similar to those of other online services. The core services that eWorld will pro-

vide include news from Reuters and *USA Today,* stock quotes, movie reviews, *Grolier's Encyclopedia,* a Living Well section, and a computer center.

### GEnie Within GEnie's (800/638–9636)

In GEnie's core areas, you can access stock quotes; Dow Jones News Retrieval; the Eaasy Sabre airline-reservation system; a GEnie mall; TRW business credit profiles; *Grolier's Encyclopedia;* forums for Macintosh developers and users; discussion areas; and a searchable database of articles from newspapers published in the United States, including the *Los Angeles Times, Washington Post,* and *Chicago Tribune.*

### Prodigy (800/776–3449)

The core areas of the Prodigy service let you use an encyclopedia, read news, go shopping, discuss computer problems, and get stock quotes. More children use Prodigy than any other online service, and Prodigy's educational offerings include games, National Geographic adventures, and a Sesame Street area.

In recent years, Prodigy has come under fire for its policy of screening messages sent to message boards before posting them. Prodigy communications manager Deborah Borchert said if a message contains an obscenity or blatant bigotry or hate, the message will be returned to the sender. Borchert stressed that the screening is done only for message boards, not private E-mail.

Microsoft Network (Reality Bytes 6–6). Many of these systems maintain public bulletin boards or forums. *News groups* are available to companies connected to the Internet and cover a wide variety of topics.

Many commercial software companies provide forums that contain hints and help about their products. For instance, you might be having trouble using your word processor with a new printer. You could connect your computer to a BBS run by the company that produced the word processor. You can instantly search the board to see whether the company has already announced a solution to your problem. If not, you can send a message to the technical support staff at the company, who will usually respond to the request on the following day.

Larger companies have started using BBSs internally. For instance, there might be a board that contains information and notices from the human resources department. The board can list questions and answers about health insurance benefits. It could carry postings for internal jobs and schedules for training classes. Work schedules and holidays are often listed on bulletin boards. They also can provide contacts between employee groups, company sports teams, and other internal clubs.

Because BBSs are easy to use, they can provide information to many people. The biggest drawback is that everyone in the target audience needs to have access to a computer in order to read the bulletin board. A company planning to use a BBS has to ensure that everyone has equal access. In manufacturing firms, most managers have personal computers and access to the network. On the other hand, the factory workers might not have access and training to use the computer systems.

### Calendars and Scheduling

Managers spend a great deal of time in meetings. Yet, sometimes the greatest challenge with meetings is finding a time when everyone can get together. Several software packages use computer networks to solve this problem. Managers enter meetings and scheduled events into their personal electronic calendar file. Each event is assigned a priority number. For example, a time allotted for a haircut would be given a low priority; a meeting with a supervisor would receive a higher rating. If the CEO wants to set up a meeting, the CEO tells the computer which people are involved, sets a priority level, and gives an approximate time. The computer then uses the network to check everyone else's schedule. When it finds an open time (overriding lower priority events if needed), it enters the meeting into each person's calendar. The entire process takes a few seconds.

### Teamwork and Joint Authorship

In any job, it is rare for one person to work alone. Most businesses are arranged as teams. Individual people are given specific assignments, with each team member contributing to the final product. For instance, the marketing department might have to prepare a sales forecast for the next six months. Each person could work on a specific sales region or product category. These individual pieces would then be merged into a single document. If the computers are networked, the manager's computer can pull the individual pieces from each of the individual computers. Also, each team member can be given access to the others' work to ensure that the reports use the same data and assumptions. Iberomoldes (Reality Bytes 6–7) used a network of Portuguese, British, and Belgian units to speed the design of a new suitcase.

 Reality Bytes    6–7   IBEROMOLDES OF PORTUGAL

A Portuguese luggage manufacturer had an idea for a new suitcase—a hard-sided case designed to be stored in two pieces. One piece fits inside the other, reducing storage requirements for the retailer and the customer. The Magnum case is being marketed in Europe.

The case was designed by Iberomoldes of Portugal, a design and manufacturing company with sales of $25 million in 1993. Running 3-D CAD software, the engineers at Iberomoldes worked with British designers and a Belgian manufacturing team. Using a network that connected the three groups in real time, the teams were able to exchange up-to-date designs and comments by computer, voice, and fax.

To compete with the Japanese, Henrique Neto, Iberomoldes' managing director, turned to integrated computer technology. He notes that

an in-house subsidiary called Simultaneous Engineering Technology (SET) unified design, engineering, prototyping, and tooling on the computer. This eliminated costly errors and production modifications. As a result Iberomoldes was able to work with high quality.

## Reality Bytes    6-8    MANUFACTURER'S HANOVER TRUST COMPANY

In spring 1987, Manufacturer's Hanover Trust Company in New York automated its Corporate Banking Section. To accomplish this, the bank bought and installed local area networks, personal computers to run them, and personal computers for the individual bankers to work on.

The difficulty the bank faced was to find network software. Generic spreadsheet and word processing software provided some support. However, it was not adequate to add value to its networking needs and to address some of the sophisticated banking problems that the Bank faced.

Lotus Development provided a networking solution in its product Lotus Notes. It is *groupware,* which is software that enables workers on networks to share information and communicate electronically. The program enabled the bank to combine prepackaged pieces of Lotus Notes code to develop customized applications. Electronic address books and calendars were also integrated to streamline meetings and other scheduling problems.

Lotus Notes became a sales tool for the bank. Account representatives organized customer data, tracked client contacts, and gave salespeople and account managers information to analyze markets and prepare sales proposals. Sales forms were developed that enabled users to structure details on the services that a client was using, related financial data, evaluated marketing strategy, and informed management about key contacts.

Although Lotus Notes helps people to organize the data for the account representatives, it only works if the salespeople use the program. The biggest problem has been getting them to change the way they keep their files. In the past, each individual has kept their files in their own way. Entering data into the system and accessing it requires the managers to change their work habits and store files in a consistent fashion. This change has been difficult to implement.

**Groupware** is software that enables several people to work on the same document. Each individual computer has access to the master document. When one person makes a change to the document, the change is highlighted for everyone to read and approve. With existing international networks, each person might be located in a different country. As illustrated by Manufacturer's Hanover Trust (Reality Bytes 6-8), Lotus Notes is a groupware product that makes it easy for employees to combine data and communicate interactively with each other.

### Backup

There is another important reason for sharing data over computer networks. Most people are not very good at maintaining backup copies of their work—especially on personal computers. If each computer is attached to a network, it is possible to set up an automatic backup system for individual personal computers. There are two ways to use networks for backup. The older method relies on individual workers copying their data files to a central file server. The network manager makes daily (or hourly) backups of the data on the central server.

A newer method is significantly safer, because it is virtually automatic and does not require users to remember to transfer their files. It does require users to leave their machines running. At a predetermined time, a central computer with a large backup capacity connects to the individual machines and copies the files that have changed. This data is then stored somewhere safe (such as a tape or optical disk). If a computer or a person accidentally deletes a file, the backup computer can restore the file and send it back to the personal computer. With the communication network, the backup process is almost completely automatic.

## Sharing Hardware

Hardware items are also often shared through communication networks. For example, networks are used to provide users access to special output devices, such as high-speed printers, plotters, or color printers. Networks can be used to give people access to special computers, such as when an engineer needs to use a supercomputer.

### Printers

A common use of networks is to give users access to high-speed, high-quality printers. Even if each computer has a small personal printer attached, some jobs need to be handled by a high-speed laser printer. Some printers even provide collating and stapling of documents.

Another advantage is that if one printer breaks down, users can send their jobs to another printer on the network. Think about what happens if there is no network and your printer breaks down. You have to copy the file to a floppy disk, and interrupt someone else's work to borrow their computer to send the file to another printer. What happens if you are using a special software package that no one else has on his or her computer? You will probably have to physically move a printer from another computer desk to yours, connect the hardware, print your document, and bring the printer back to where it came from. With a network, you simply select a different printer from a list displayed on your computer and go pick up the output.

Printer sharing is often used to provide everyone access to special, expensive printers. For instance, at $5,000 each it would be expensive to buy color laser printers for everyone who might need one, yet it might be reasonable to buy one for a department to share. With a network, users can choose from among two or three different printers by selecting them on the screen. Figure 6.6 shows some of the hardware devices that are often shared.

### Storage Devices

The arguments used for network printer sharing can be applied to sharing storage devices. For instance, the firm's finance department may require access to large financial databases. Financial data and stock prices for most U.S. companies can be purchased on CD-ROM disks. It would be expensive to buy CD-ROM drives and data

**FIGURE 6.6**

Networks for sharing hardware. The workstations use the server to perform backups. Files are picked up by the server and transferred to tape. The LAN administrator can reload a tape and restore files as needed. Networks are often used to share printers and storage devices. Networks can be used to share access to supercomputers—even if they are in a different city or different country.

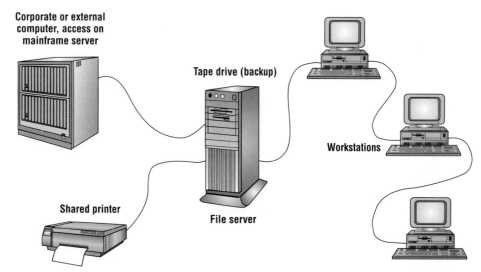

Corporate or external computer, access on mainframe server

Tape drive (backup)

Workstations

Shared printer

File server

disks for every person in the finance department. It makes more sense to connect the finance computers and the CD-ROM drive together on a network. Then, whenever someone wants to look up information in the database, the computer uses the network to transfer the information from the optical disk.

### Special Processors

Special computers that are relatively expensive can be attached to a network to save costs and make it easier for users to access these machines. Parallel-processing computers and other supercomputers can perform calculations thousands of times faster than ordinary computers, but they are expensive. Consider a small engineering company. For the most part, the engineers use their workstations to develop their designs. They occasionally need to run simulations or produce detailed graphics images. Both of these tasks could take many hours to perform on individual client computers. The company can cable each engineer's workstation to a network that can access a supercomputer. When an engineer needs to perform high-speed calculations, the job is sent directly to the supercomputer. The results are returned via the network to the workstation so they can be added to the final report. More likely, the supercomputer could be owned by a university, and the firm would lease time to run each job. If the network is designed properly, it makes no difference where the machine is located.

### Sharing Software

Another important reason for using computer networks is to enable users to share software packages. Consider a department with 25 employees who want to use Microsoft Office Pro. Each person has a computer with a 500-megabyte disk drive. Without a network, each computer would need a copy of the software. That means buying 25 copies and installing them on each computer. Each copy would require almost 200 megabytes of disk space. No one would have much space left on the hard disk to store data. Also, imagine what would happen when a new version of the software was released. Someone would have to install the new package on each of the 25 computers. If it took an hour to install the new release, someone would waste half a work week in the process. Imagine how long it would take to update a company with 10,000 copies.

Consider the same example if all of the computers were connected to each other with a network. One of the computers could be chosen to store all of the software. This machine would be a **file server.** Each application package would only be stored on the file server, which would conserve space on the other 24 machines. Figure 6.7

**FIGURE 6.7**

Networks are often used to share commercial software. Licensed software is stored one time on the file server. When (1) a workstation sends a message to use the software, (2) the server verifies access and checks the license, then (3) the software is sent over the network, and (4) loaded in the workstation's RAM where it is executed.

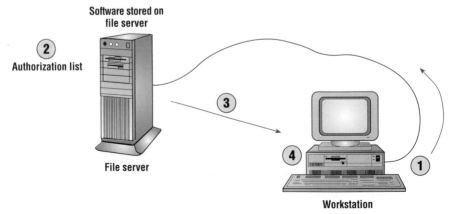

Software stored on file server

(2) Authorization list

File server

(3)

(4)

(1)

Workstation

shows the actions that are taken when a user loads software stored on a file server. To use the software, your computer takes the application package from the file server and loads it into the RAM on your computer. Only one new copy has to be installed to update the software for all users.

The issue of buying 25 copies of an application package is a little trickier. It depends on the software company and how often the software is used. Each company has its own license requirements. In some cases, if all 25 people want to use the software at the same time, you will still have to buy 25 copies. In other cases, if only 10 people will be using the software at the same time, you would only have to buy a license for 10 users. Then any group of 10 people can use the software. The software automatically counts the number of current users. When it reaches 10, no one else is allowed to use that package. The amount of money that can be saved depends on how many people will be using each package at the same time. These network license agreements are especially useful for experimenting with software that only a few people will use at one time.

## Voice and Video Communication

A major cost of telecommunications in business is for telephone calls. Despite the total expenditures, there is little doubt about the value of communication and phones. Phone calls are almost always cheaper than in-person visits. Cellular phones present a different picture because the charges are considerably higher. There are many situations where cellular phones are invaluable, as when the salesperson is more effective by being always available with a portable phone. However, in most cases you do not want to give a cellular phone to every employee in your company. Until usage costs drop considerably, managers will have to evaluate each situation to see whether the benefits of portability outweigh the costs.

Since the mid-1980s, companies have experimented with video communication or teleconferencing. The ultimate objective is to decrease travel costs by connecting people with video links. Several large companies built teleconferencing rooms that provide video links to similar centers. With several video links, participants at each center can see and hear the others, as well as view documents at each location. The centers have been useful for companies that routinely conduct business in fixed locations, such as a U.S. company with a manufacturing plant in Southeast Asia.

With improvements in technology and faster transmission of data at lower costs, it is becoming feasible to run full-service networks to each desk. These links would enable workers to communicate with others using voice, pictures, computer data, or video across the same line. Although these links are technically feasible today, they are somewhat expensive. As costs decline, you will have to decide which applications can benefit most from the technology. Look first to those requiring face-to-face communication and conferences that rely heavily on presentations and graphics.

**COMPONENTS OF A NETWORK**

At some point in your career, you might be responsible for purchasing a local area network. Similarly, you might experience problems when some component of an existing network fails. In both cases, you need to be familiar with the major components of a LAN. Illustrated by Figure 6.8, computer networks contain four basic components: computers, transmission media, connection devices, and software. In practice, there are many varieties of each component. Also, several companies manufacture each of these products, hence, sometimes products do not work well together. As a result, it can be confusing and difficult to create a computer network. It can also be difficult to track down the source of problems.

**FIGURE 6.8**

LAN components. A local area network consists of four major components: computers, transmission media, connection devices, and software. Each computer and shared peripheral must be connected to the transmission media. Network operating system software controls access to files and controls the flow of data on the network. The personal computer operating system must be modified to recognize the LAN services and process communication between the personal computer and the LAN.

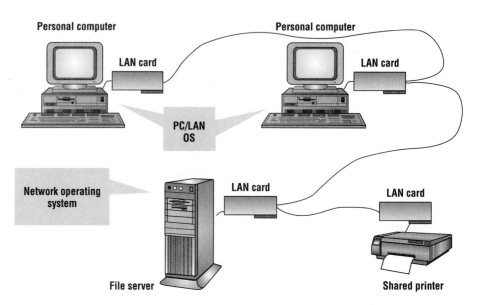

## Computers

Virtually any type of computer device can be connected to a network. Sometimes only simple terminals and printers will be used for input and output. Other times, personal computers are linked. Sometimes there will be several large central computers connected together. In some cases, all of the computers will be similar. In other cases, one computer will be faster and larger than the others.

The earliest computer networks consisted of one computer with several terminals and printers attached to it. These networks were fairly simple, because all of the work was performed by the one computer. There are substantially more problems involved in connecting several computers together. For starters, each computer needs to know that the others exist and that they have a specific location (address) on the network. The computers need to know how to send and receive information from each other. This condition presents a problem with most personal computers, because they were originally designed to operate alone. To work together, they need connection devices (LAN cards) and special software.

Computers attached to networks tend to perform one of two functions: servers or clients. **Servers** are computers that store data to be used by other computers attached to the network. **Clients** are computers used by individual people. Sometimes a computer is used as both a client and a file server. Networks where many of the machines operate as both clients and servers are called **peer-to-peer networks.**

### Servers

Consider a human resources management (HRM) department that wants to create a network of computers. This department wants to use one computer to store the data files for the employees, as well as data about training classes, new jobs, benefits, and work schedules. Managers want employees to use the computers to look for information about their jobs. On the other hand, there is some information (such as salaries) that only managers should be able to see. Before the network, each type of information was stored on a separate computer. An employee would have to check four different computers in order to find all of the basic information. However, the salary information was stored on only the manager's computer, so no

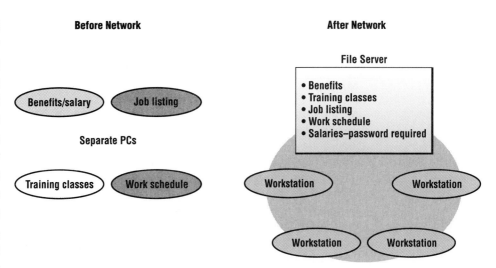

one else could use it. Figure 6.9 shows the situations before and after the installation of a network.

The department wants to buy one larger computer and use it as a file server. It will have a much bigger and faster hard disk to store all of the data files. The other computers will be used to look up any information on the file server. In this manner, employees can find all of the information they need by using one computer. Yet, there is a slight problem: The manager still wants to prevent the employees from seeing the salary data.

Actually, there are two complications for the file server. First, any computer that stores files for the others must be able to talk to them all at the same time. Second, the file server needs to have security provisions so that some information can be accessed only by authorized users. In other words, the file server has to be able to function as a multiuser computer. Remember that personal computers were originally designed to work with only one person at a time. For personal computers to function as file servers, they need a multiuser operating system. This operating system has to understand the network, provide file and printer access to the attached computers, and provide security for each of the files.

### Client Computers

The networked computers could be any type of machine. Because these computers are typically used by individual people at their own desks, they are often called *client computers.* These computers need to access the network, and be able to send information to at least one other computer. A **network interface card (NIC)** (or LAN card) is installed in each computer. These cards are connected together by some transmission medium. Additionally, most personal computers need special software to change the operating system so that it knows how to deal with the network card and can recognize the other computers.

In many client-server networks, the file server looks like a supercapacity hard disk drive to the individual client computers. Consider the HRM example. When you use the workstation, the files on the server appear to be on a new disk drive. You use the files as if they were stored on your computer, and the server delivers the data.

When you tell the application software to read a file from the server, several things happen. First, your workstation sends a message to the file server. The server decides whether you have the proper authority to use that file. If so, it sends the file over the network to your computer. All of these messages are hidden from you, and you can treat the file server just as if it were a high-capacity hard disk drive.

## Media

All communication requires a transmission medium. The people or computers involved have to be physically connected in some manner. With spoken words, individuals are connected by the surrounding air that transmits sound waves. Telephones are connected by wires. There are many different ways of connecting computers. As illustrated in Figure 6.10, common methods include electric wires, light waves, and radio waves. From a communication standpoint, all of these methods are related because they are all part of the electromagnetic spectrum. From a computer management perspective, there are some distinct advantages and disadvantages of using each of these methods. In many ways, the choice of communication medium is the most important aspect of selecting and installing a network. All of the other components can be changed fairly easily. Cables are often buried underground or run through the walls and ceilings of buildings. Once a media choice is made, it can be expensive to change your mind and install new cabling.

### Electric Cables

There are two basic types of electric cables: twisted-pair and coaxial. *Twisted-pair* is the oldest form of electrical wiring. Because electricity must travel in a closed loop, electrical connections require at least two wires. Twisted-pair wires are simply pairs of plain copper wires. There are many examples of twisted-pair wires in households, such as telephone cables. Twisted-pair is the cheapest type of cabling available. Another advantage is that some businesses have extra, unused telephone wires in buildings. In a few cases, these extra wires can be used to connect computers, which reduces the cost of installing new wires.

Twisted-pair wires have certain disadvantages. This type of cable cannot carry much information at one time. Plus, data transmitted on twisted-pair wires is subject

**FIGURE 6.10**

Signals can be sent via several types of media. They can be carried by electricity, light waves, or radio waves. All of these methods have advantages and disadvantages. Fiber optic cabling offers the fastest transmission rates with the least interference, but because it is relatively new, the initial cost tends to be higher.

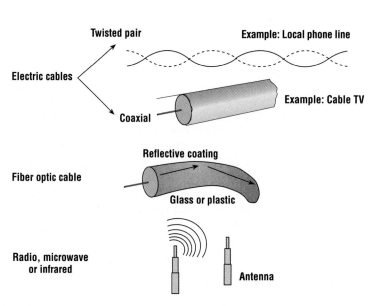

to interference from other electrical devices. Interference can distort or damage a telecommunications signal. For instance, it is best to avoid running twisted-pair wires next to electric power lines and electric motors, because these devices produce electromagnetic radiation that can interfere with the signal. On the other hand, it is possible to put several twisted-pairs into the same diameter as one coaxial cable. The overall transmission speed can be increased by sending portions of the message along each wire.

Coaxial cables were designed to carry more information than twisted-pairs, with lower chances of interference. *Coaxial cable* (often shortened to *coax*) consists of a central wire, surrounded by a nonconductive plastic, which is surrounded by a second wire. The second wire is actually a metallic foil or mesh that is wrapped around the entire cable. This shielding minimizes interference from outside sources. Cable television signals are transmitted on coaxial cables. Coax is capable of carrying more information for longer distances than twisted-pair, and it is not much more expensive. The technologies for using it are well-established, so the supporting equipment is reasonably priced and readily available.

### Fiber Optics

A relatively recent invention (early 1970s) in communication uses light instead of electricity. Because light generally travels in a straight line, it could be difficult to use for communication. Fiber optic cable allows light to travel in straight lines but still be bent around corners. A fiber optic cable consists of a glass or plastic core that is surrounded by a reflective material. A laser light (typically infrared) is sent down the cable. When the cable turns, the light is reflected around the corner and continues down the cable. Fiber optic cable provides the advantages of high capacity with almost no interference. The limitation in using fiber is the higher cost of the cable and the cost of the connectors and interface cards that convert computer electrical signals into light. For example, NICs for coaxial or twisted-pair cable can be purchased for around $80, whereas NICs for fiber optic lines run directly to personal computers cost around $1,000 (in 1995).

A thin fiber optic cable can carry as much data as 900 single copper wires, with minimal interference and superior tensile strength.

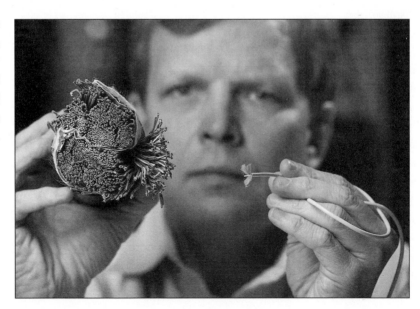

## Radio, Micro, and Infrared Waves

Radio, microwave, and infrared transmissions do not require cables. These communication methods are called **broadcasts.** The signal can be picked up by any receiver or antenna that lies in its path. However, microwave and infrared transmissions require clear line-of-sight transmission. The major advantage of broadcast methods is portability. For example, computers can be installed in delivery vehicles to receive information from corporate headquarters. On a smaller scale, individuals can carry around small computers (e.g., pen-based notebook computers). These computers can communicate with each other and with a central database via a broadcast network. For example, physicians in hospitals could carry small computers that would automatically receive information for each patient when the physician enters the room. Any instructions could be sent directly from the physician's computer to the nursing station. Commodity traders have also found portable computers and radio networks to be useful (Reality Bytes 6–9).

There are two potential drawbacks to broadcast media. First, it is more important to provide security for the transmissions. Second, broadcast transmissions carry a limited amount of data. The two problems are related. Because it is a broadcast method, the signals sent by one computer can be received by any other computer within range. There is no way to prevent other computers from physically receiving the signal. In the 1970s and 1980s (before the breakup of the Soviet Union), government spies on both sides routinely monitored telephone conversations emanating from embassies. To protect the data, broadcast transmissions need to be encrypted.

The problem of limited capacity arises because only a small number of radio frequencies can be used to carry data. Most of the radio and television frequencies are already being used for other purposes. Figure 6.11 shows some of the major frequency allocations in the United States. The Federal Communications Commission (FCC) allocated the PCS bands in late 1993 for use by personal communication devices such as laptop computers and personal digital assistants (PDAs). To provide these frequencies, the FCC had to take them away from existing users. Imagine what would happen if computers suddenly started sending information over the same

**FIGURE 6.11**

Electromagnetic frequency spectrum. Communication techniques are essentially the same on all media, because all waves physically have similar properties. However, the different frequencies affect the communication performance. Shorter wave lengths (higher frequencies) can carry more data. Some waves can travel longer distances. Others are more susceptible to interference. In any case, there are a finite number of frequencies available for communication. Hence, the frequency spectrum is allocated by governmental agencies.

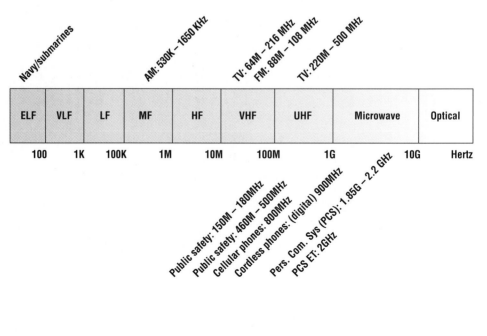

Microwave transmissions are used to provide communications for cellular phones and laptop computers. As prices of phones, portable computers, and communication costs decrease, increasing numbers of workers are choosing wireless technologies.

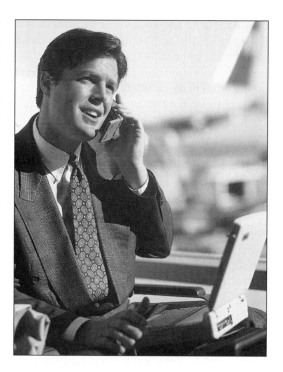

radio frequency as that used by your favorite radio station. You would not be able to hear the voices on the radio, and the computers would miss most of their data because of the interference.

All governments allocate the frequency spectrum for various uses, such as radio, television, cellular phones, and garage door openers. The PCS frequencies were auctioned off to the highest bidders in 1994, raising more than $65 billion dollars for the FCC. The frequency problem is even more complicated when the signals might cross political boundaries. As a result, most broadcast telecommunications issues are established with international cooperation. Some of the overcrowding problems are being mitigated through the use of digital transmissions that cram more calls and more data into the same amount of frequency space.

Despite these problems, an increasing amount of business communication is being carried over radio networks. For example, from 1982 to 1993, the use of cellular

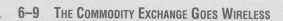

◥ **Reality Bytes** ◢ 6–9 THE COMMODITY EXCHANGE GOES WIRELESS

Prior to 1993, traders at the Commodity Exchange (ComEx) kept track of price changes by people who served as price reporters. The price reporters would listen for price changes, then signal the trading floor supervisor, who used a headset to notify a data entry operator. In 1993, trading floor staff were given hand-held computers that connected to a PC-based server via radio waves. The radio waves are collected by a ceiling-mounted antenna which communicates with the server at 56,000 bps. The initial hardware cost was $15,000, and the exchange spent about $35,000 to develop the software to process the transactions. The system enabled the exchange to increase the number of commodities listed without adding additional workers, saving about $200,000 a year in salaries of data-entry clerks.

(radio) phones expanded from almost zero to 13 million subscribers in the United States and 30 million worldwide in 70 countries. These numbers do not seem large compared to the worldwide estimate of 550 million telephone users, but the number of cellular phone users will undoubtedly increase. For starters, Motorola (a leader in radio communication) estimates that 40 million U.S. employees work away from the office for extended periods, as does 40 percent of the global workforce. Additionally, in many cases, it is much easier to connect people over radio networks instead of installing cables. As noted in *The Economist* (October 23, 1993), the $1,000 average cost of providing a radio network to a home or business is falling rapidly. In comparison, in places such as Italy or China, it costs $2,000 or more to install a basic copper wire (twisted-pair) to a home.

### Transmission Capacity

To understand the difference in the amount of information that can be carried by the three types of cables, consider a simple example. It's a hot day outside and you spray water on yourself with a garden hose (about 1-inch diameter). On the other hand, if you want to put out a house fire, you will need more water, so you use a fire hose (diameter of 3 inches). If you need enough water to supply a factory, you will want to use an even larger pipe (10 inches in diameter). The amount of water supplied by each method is loosely equivalent to the raw amount of data that can be carried by twisted-pair, coaxial, and fiber optic cables. However, the amount of data is not related to the diameter of the cables; in fact, optical cables are thinner than the electrical cables and carry substantially more data.

Capacity of transmission media is measured by the number of bits of data that can be sent in one second. In raw form, twisted-pair wires can carry about 1 million bits per second (denoted 1 Mbps). Networks based on coaxial cables typically carry 10 Mbps, while fiber optic cables can carry more than 100 Mbps. Because technology changes, these numbers increase over time. For instance, some techniques allow twisted-pair cables to transmit as high as 10 Mbps (if the cable meets certain conditions). A standard transmission protocol that uses multiple wires and data compression is known as *10 Base-T.* This system can carry up to 10 megabits per second.

In the long run, fiber optic cables offer the greatest potential bandwidth. Yet the commercial networks face limitations because of the switches and software. In 1995, AT&T noted that several of their long distance lines were running out of capacity. With the expanded use of fax machines, computers, and video conferencing, the long-distance carriers are concerned about running out of line capacity. In 1994, there were about 1.3 million long-distance calls in progress at any point in time. Bell Labs researchers are working hard to design new fiber optic cables and switches that can carry more signals. State-of-the-art research has enabled the switches to send more than 300 billion bits per second down a single fiber in the lab.

Consider an example involving two computers. You have three items that you wish to send from one computer to the other one: a small text file, a picture, and 10 seconds of a video. The text file consists of 10,000 bytes (or 80,000 bits). The picture is a bit image of about 500,000 bytes, or 4 megabits. The video generates about 1.5 megabytes per second for a total of 15 megabytes (or 120 megabits). How long does it take to send the raw data using each of the three cables? The times are displayed in Figure 6.12, assuming that the transmission can use the entire bandwidth. In practice, networks are considerably less efficient (sometimes as low as 20 percent to 50 percent of capacity). Notice that it does not really matter how the text file is transmitted.

| | | | TWISTED-PAIR 1 MBPS | COAXIAL 10 MBPS | FIBER OPTIC 100 MBPS |
|---|---|---|---|---|---|
| ITEM | BYTES | BITS | SECONDS | | |
| Text | 10,000 | 80,000 | 0.08 | 0.008 | 0.0008 |
| Image | 500,000 | 4,000,000 | 4 | 0.4 | 0.04 |
| Video-10 sec. | 15,000,000 | 120,000,000 | 120 | 12 | 1.2 |

On the other hand, only the fiber optic cable carries the video data in less than 10 seconds, so it is the only method that can show the raw, uncompressed video in real time. Other methods will force the digitized video to be shown in slow motion. One of the main reasons we do not have good video telephones yet is that twisted-pair wires cannot carry enough data to transmit real-time *raw* video data. So how are the phone companies going to deliver television signals? By compressing each picture into less data.

Transmission times become more important when more than two computers are involved, and when you want to send more than one item. For example, think about what will happen if you install a slow twisted-pair network for 60 users in a department. What happens when they all arrive at work in the morning and turn on their computers at the same time? Say the computers all go to the file server and ask for a copy of a word processor program (about 2 million bits). In the best case, it takes 2 minutes (2 seconds times 60 people) for everyone to get started. In reality, it is more likely to require at least 10 minutes. Now imagine what happens if there are 600 users on the network!

You want to use the fastest communication line that you can afford. The next important question is: how much difference is there in price? Cable costs are measured per foot. For the most part, there is little difference in prices between twisted-pair wires and coaxial cable. The actual prices depend on the specific cable—especially the type of outer coating. As a rough estimate, coaxial cable might cost two or three times more than twisted-pair. Fiber optic cable is probably two or three times more expensive than coaxial cable. However, in most cases the cost per foot does not matter. Even fiber optic cables run less than $2 per foot. In most cases, there will be only a couple thousand dollars difference between a "cheap" alternative and a faster one. Unless all of the computers are in the same room, it is considerably more expensive for the labor to install the cable.

Transmission rates for radio-based methods depend on the amount of frequency available. A typical speed for transmission over microwave transmissions from small satellite dishes is 57,600 bits per second. Cellular phone speeds are comparable to standard phone transmissions (around 28,800 bits per second). Data-compression techniques are available that can double or perhaps quadruple raw transmission speeds.

## Combinations of Media

To gain the advantages of each type of media and to deal with networks created a section at a time, most large networks use several types of media at the same time. For example, fiber optic cables are typically used as a *backbone* to connect networks over longer distances between buildings or between floors in large buildings. Use of the nonelectrical cables between buildings also helps isolate the network from lightening strikes.

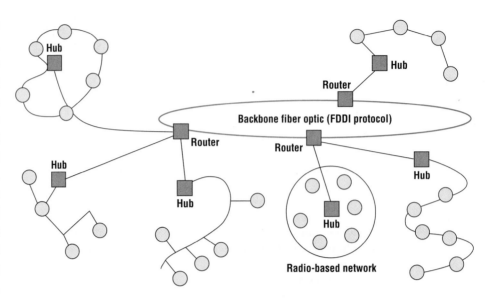

Many companies initially built smaller LANs in various departments throughout the company. As shown in Figure 6.13, a fiber optic backbone can be used to connect these individual networks into one large network to make information available to everyone in the company. Typically, each smaller LAN is connected to a *router* and the routers are connected together with fiber optic cable. The individual LANs could use twisted-pair, coaxial, or even radio connections. The router is used to convert the appropriate signals into a standard signal that can be handled by the other routers. Messages can then be sent from one workstation on a LAN to any other workstation in the company regardless of the LAN or media being used. In many ways, routers are just small computers that accept different types of signals and send (route) them to the appropriate subnetwork. This design has four major advantages. First, most of the traffic is maintained locally within each department. Second, given the appropriate security access, managers can get access to the same data and resources regardless of the computer they use. Third, if one part of the network (or a computer) fails, the other segments are unaffected and continue to operate. Fourth, one segment can be changed and updated at a time. It is not necessary to change the entire company's hardware or software at once. Each department can have exactly the resources they need.

## Connection Devices

Keep in mind that transmission speed in networks depends on the speed of all the components. As a result, it takes substantially longer to transfer files and messages than would be indicated by the published transmission speeds. In particular, as the number of computers increases, the network has to work harder at coordinating the computers. This coordination can generate an enormous amount of messages being transmitted.

In order to connect the cables (or receive radio waves), the computer needs a special communication card. This NIC or LAN card translates computer signals into messages that can be sent on the network. Each network has certain *protocols* or rules that must be followed when sending messages. The LAN card also functions as a buffer between the computer and the network to allow the two to operate at different speeds. For instance, if the network transmits messages faster than the computer can handle them, the LAN card holds incoming messages until the computer is ready.

Other connection devices are often required to connect different networks. In a business, each department might have its own network based on coaxial cable. Each department would have its own file server and printer. In order to share information with other departments, the departmental networks would have to be connected to each other. This connection could use fiber optic cable and would require a special device (router or *gateway*) that converts the electrical coaxial signals into light. Routers are used to connect different types of networks together regardless of the type of cable. They can also convert the common protocols to connect different types of networks.

## Software

### Operating Systems

Because most personal computers were designed as stand-alone machines, the older (DOS) operating systems cannot provide data to several users at the same time, and they cannot send information to or receive it from other computers.

Any computer used as a file server needs to employ a multiuser operating system. For example, Novell is a company that specializes in selling hardware and software for networks. Novell sells a multiuser network operating system (NOS) called *NetWare* that runs on the file server. It is also possible to use minicomputers as file servers. All of the minicomputer manufacturers provide software to use their machines as file servers for personal computers. Operating systems such as Windows NT, Unix, and OS/2 can handle multiple users and function as file servers.

Most personal computers also need special LAN software. Generally, this software is purchased from the same company that provides the operating system for the file server. It runs in the background of the workstation so that it can send and receive information on the network. Its job is to identify messages sent to each computer and put the incoming messages into the proper format for the workstation computer. It also converts the data so that it can be sent in the proper format for the file server to understand. If there is a printer on the network, the workstation software intercepts the workstation printer output and passes it to the network printer.

### Application Software

Almost all software companies are now selling software that functions correctly on networks. This software automatically prevents two people from trying to alter the same data at the same time. It also enables each user to configure or customize the software. For instance, you might want your word processor to edit yellow text on a black background. Someone else might want to use white on blue. The software enables each person to save these colors and other preferences on his or her own machine.

**CLIENT-SERVER AND PEER-TO-PEER LANS**

Local area networks can take a variety of forms. Two common methods of organizing LANs are client-server and peer-to-peer. There are advantages and disadvantages to each method. In some cases, it is possible to set up networks that use features from each method to gain the advantages of both methods.

## Client-Server

The client-server model illustrated in Figure 6.14 is probably the most common in use today. With this system, there are a few servers that contain the majority of the data for the company. The users work on personal computers that are clients. The two types of machines are treated differently on the network. The servers are fast, multiuser

**FIGURE 6.14**

The client-server model is a common method of organizing computers on a network. Servers are fast computers with large disk capacity and multiuser operating systems. The clients rely on the servers for most network functions. In a peer-to-peer organization, the individual client computers are powerful enough to share files and messages directly with other client machines.

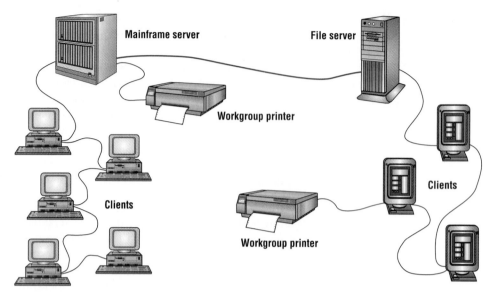

machines that share data with many users at a time. On the other hand, smaller personal computers are often used as clients. They have limited operating systems that know how to communicate only with the server. If you want to send a message to a colleague, the message first goes to the server. It is stored there until your co-worker logs into the network and the message is sent to the client computer.

If there are many servers on the network, they are often arranged with clusters of clients. The servers are connected to each other. Typically, the users deal with one main server, but the network enables them to use any of the servers once they have been given authorization. A common usage of this layout is to provide servers to each department. Each member of the department typically uses the department server but sometimes needs to share data with the servers in the rest of the company.

A drawback to this method is the amount of message traffic between the clients and the server. Similarly, because the server is almost constantly in use, it needs to be a very fast machine with large storage capacity. With several servers, some LANs require that you know the name of the server assigned to each person you want to send a message to.

## Peer-to-Peer

A second method of organizing a LAN is to treat each computer as a peer (i.e., as an equal). In a peer-to-peer network, each computer can communicate directly with the others (assuming proper security authorizations). Each computer needs to be able to communicate with other machines at the same time that it handles tasks for the primary user. Ideally, each computer should be capable of preemptive multitasking. Older machines can cause problems because they slow down too much while trying to do so many things at one time.

Peer-to-peer networks are useful for situations in which the users often exchange data with each other. The design enables them to transfer data directly to the person who needs it, without passing through an intermediate server. The main drawback is that the individual computers need to be relatively fast and have enough storage capacity to hold transfer files.

With these networks, each person essentially owns the data on his or her machine. They are responsible for controlling who can share it. For this reason, peer-to-peer networks give a considerable amount of control to the users. That control is both good and bad. If the users are well-trained, understand the complexities, and are willing to devote the time to maintaining their data, everything will work well. For example, engineers working on related projects might prefer a peer-to-peer network. On the other hand, you would not want to install a peer-to-peer network for use by temporary clerical workers.

With peer-to-peer network software, it is possible to install machines to operate as traditional servers. The servers could handle the application software and printers. Users could transfer data to the server to take advantage of automatic backup capabilities. Similarly, files that need to be distributed to many users or bulletin boards could be stored on the servers. On the other hand, data that is shared among two or three people could be sent directly to the individual machines.

## ENTERPRISE NETWORKS

Many large companies have hundreds of local area networks. Connecting personal computers is only the first step in building a telecommunications system. The next step is to facilitate communication across the company and interconnect the LANs. A network that connects various subnetworks across a firm is called an *enterprise network.*

Several types of data need to be collected and shared throughout a company. Basic transaction-processing data such as accounting and HRM data need to be collected and aggregated for the firm. Management decisions and questions need to be communicated with all employees. Planning documents and forecasts are often prepared by interdisciplinary teams.

Although it is easy to agree that all computers in a company should be able to share data, several problems arise in practice. Various departments often use different hardware, software, and network protocols. It becomes more difficult to identify the cause of problems in a network as it becomes larger. Likewise, adding more components tends to slow down all transmissions. Network management issues multiply. Small tasks such as assigning usernames and maintaining passwords become major chores when there are thousands of users and hundreds of file servers. Security becomes increasingly complex, especially when corporate data is carried across public networks. Upgrading network components can become a nightmare, resulting in either complete replacement across the firm or incompatibilities between some divisions. Even simple network functions like e-mail can quickly bog down a system when there are 50,000 users.

Enterprise networking requires a combination of standards and special hardware and software to translate data from one system to another. It also requires investing in more network personnel to install, upgrade, and manage all of the components.

As enterprise networks spread across large distances, they tend to involve wide area networks. A *wide area network (WAN)* differs from a LAN because of the geographical distance that it covers. More specifically, a WAN involves links that are controlled by public carriers (e.g., phone companies). Few individual firms can afford to build their own long-distance networks. Although some companies do have their own satellite connections, it is almost impossible for a company to install its own cables for any distance.

To establish WAN lines, you simply call a phone company or other commercial contractor. Each has several offerings in a wide range of prices, all of which change over time. Typically, you lease a line with a fixed amount of bandwidth or transmission capacity. For instance, a T1 line can transmit up to 1.544 megabits per second. A T3 line can carry about 45 megabits per second. If your carrier offers ISDN (Integrated Services Digital Network), you can lease digital lines that start at transmissions of 128 kilobits per second. Most of these choices involve communication from one fixed point to another, such as a connection from headquarters to a factory or warehouse. You can use the line to carry any type of data that you wish. However, all of your hardware and software must meet the standards supported by the public carrier.

## The Need for Standards

STANDARDS    **Standards** are important with networks. There are many different types of computers and various network types. Each computer and network company has its own idea of which methods are best. Without standards, there is no way to connect computers or networks produced by different vendors. Standards are also supposed to protect the buyers from obsolescence. If you install network equipment that meets existing standards, you should be able to buy products in the future that will work with it.

Unfortunately, there are many standard-setting organizations. Each major country has its own standards organization (such as ANSI, the American National Standards Institute). There are several international organizations, such as ISO and the ITU (International Telecommunications Organization, renamed from CCITT) charged with defining computer and communication standards. Additionally, manufacturers of computers and telecommunications equipment try to define their own standards. If one company's products are chosen as a standard, they gain a slight advantage in design and production.

It is not likely that typical managers will be involved in the issues of setting and choosing communication standards. Yet, as a consumer you need to be aware that there are many standards and sometimes variations on the standards. (In this industry, the word **standards** does not mean there is only one way to do something.) When you are buying telecommunications equipment, the goal is to purchase equipment that meets popular standards. It is not always easy to decide which standard will become popular and which ones will be abandoned.

## A Changing Environment

Why are there so many standards? It would be far simpler if everyone could agree to use one standard and build products that are compatible. The problem with this concept is that technology is continually changing. Thirty years ago, phone companies never considered using digital transmission over fiber optic cables, which is the dominant form of long-distance transmissions used today.

As each technology is introduced, new standards are created. Yet, we cannot discard existing standards because it takes time for firms to convert to the new technology. Additionally, as manufacturers gain experience with a technology, they add features and find better ways to use the products. These alterations usually result in changes to the standards. An additional complication is that many companies are modifying their products at the same time. It is hard to determine in advance which changes are worthwhile and should be made standards.

The net result is that standards can be useful, but managers have to be careful not to rely too much on a standard. First, remember that even if two products support a standard, they still might not work together well. Second, if you choose a standard for your department or company, remember that technology changes.

Corporate standards should be reevaluated every year or so to make sure they are still the best solution.

**OBJECT ORIENTATION**

At the foundation of any telecommunications system, there is a means to transfer raw bits of data. In fact, the ISO communication model is built around this fact. A primary purpose of standards is to ensure that machines can be physically connected to provide this transfer of binary data. Yet, workers are increasingly interested in transferring entire objects. Hence, each computer needs to be able not just to transfer the object but also to read and display the attributes, and to use its base functions.

Today, it is generally possible to transfer objects between computers, but there is no guarantee that each computer will be able to evaluate or use the object. In many cases, the objects are simply stored as binary files, awaiting transfer to a computer or user with the appropriate software and hardware to use the object. The rock group Aerosmith (Reality Bytes 6–10) was one of the first to offer music over a network, but at the time only a few people could use the data.

---

**Reality Bytes**     **6–10  TRANSFERRING OBJECTS OVER NETWORKS**

One problem with objects beyond simple documents is that they tend to be large. Large objects need high-speed communication lines. For example, in 1994, the rock band Aerosmith distributed a copy of one of its songs, "Head First," over CompuServe (a commercial network). The 3-minute, 14-second song was stored in a digital form that can be played on personal computer sound cards (synthesizers). Recorded in stereo, the song takes up 4.3 megabytes of storage. With a fast modem (14,400 bps) it would take about an hour to copy the file from CompuServe to a personal computer.

---

The World Wide Web (WWW) represents a step toward an object-oriented approach to telecommunications and data transfer. With the Web, every computer and its files are treated as objects. To run the Web, each computer needs client software that is capable of understanding a base "markup language" as well as a "universal" address system. The addressing system provides a means of identifying objects (what they are and where they are located.) The markup language contains commands that are used to define functions and attributes of the various objects. Currently, objects are limited to predefined text, graphics, sound, and video formats. Functions are limited to basic viewing and hypertext links. Nonetheless, the Web demonstrates how objects can be shared over a network by many people working on different computers.

Lotus Notes is another method that enables users to share and integrate objects over a network. Lotus Notes is loaded on the network, with copies running on each user's workstation. It primarily works as an enhanced mail system that makes it easy for users to mail data from a variety of objects—including spreadsheets, word processors, and voice annotation. The resulting "message" can be modified by the recipient; notes can be added, spreadsheets changed, or graphs inserted. The resulting message object can be modified by other users in the workgroup who have the proper authorizations. Lotus Notes maintains all of the objects in a database, which enables users to search for phrases, comments or other objects. Lotus Notes is discussed in more detail in Chapter 7.

## NEW TELEPHONE SERVICES

Recent and ongoing changes in the phone systems will eventually produce major changes in the way we deal with telephones, computers, and televisions. The older phone system was designed to carry voice or sound. These systems are limited in their ability to transfer computer data. With voice-based systems, the computer's electrical signals have to be converted to sound with a **modem.** The phone system converts the sound to new electrical signals that are then transmitted over the phone lines. A key issue with modems is the speed at which they can transmit basic data. Because of the way the telephone system was designed, there is a limit to how fast data can be transmitted over ordinary phone lines. Existing modems are close to this limit. Current high-speed modems can transmit raw data at 28,800 bits per second (bps). However, data-compression techniques (squeezing files into fewer bits) can increase the effective transmission speed. Some modems are available today that use compression to transmit in excess of 200 kilobits per second. Of course, to get these high speeds both the sender and receiver have to have similar modems, and they need a high-quality phone connection.

In the last few years, phone companies have converted their system to a digital (computerized) system known as **Integrated Services Digital Network (ISDN).** With this system, all transmissions are sent as digital (binary) signals. As a result, computer transmissions are faster and less subject to errors and interference. The binary computer signals are converted directly to signals for the phone system. Low-speed computer communication over ISDN lines is around 128,000 bps. Devices similar to modems are used to convert the computer signals into appropriate digital telephone signals. Again, compression methods can increase the effective speed of these devices. Additionally, it is possible to rent high-speed ISDN connections that can transfer millions of bits per second and are limited more by how much you are willing to pay than by the technology. One advantage of ISDN services is that they use existing phone lines; customers simply purchase new connection devices. ISDN links are fast enough to connect LANs across common phone lines, so that a user in Chicago would have the same access as a user in Los Angeles. As shown in Figure 6.15, one feature of modern phone systems is that they break information into small pieces called *packets.* These packets contain a destination address along with the message and are carried to the appropriate location and reassembled. Even voice conversations can be broken into pieces. This method grants the phone company greater control over the usage of its lines and better utilization of available transmission capacity.

**FIGURE 6.15**

Packet switched networks operate by partitioning all messages into small packets. Each packet contains a destination and source address, along with sequencing instructions. The packets can be separated and sent over different routes. At their destination, the original message is automatically restored by the network. Packets provide efficient use of transmission networks because they can mix packets and route transmissions over empty routes.

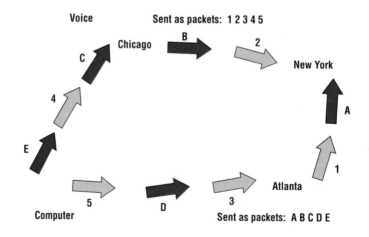

Computer networks are beginning to employ a packet-switching system in which packets can be sent over different routes at different times. It is known as **asynchronous transfer mode (ATM).** With high-speed routers it can offer transmission speeds in excess of 150 Mbps. With the appropriate devices, it can also carry sound, fax, and video on the same lines intermixed with computer data. Development of ATM networks is fairly new, and considerable work on perfecting them remains to be done. However, ATM networks offer significant gains in transmission speed and capacity for all transmission forms.

ISDN provides additional useful features. For instance, a device can be attached to your phone that automatically displays the phone number of the person who is calling—even before you pick up the phone. For businesses that rely on telephone sales, it can save a considerable amount of time. When a customer calls a mailorder company, the caller's phone number is sent directly to the computer. When the clerk picks up the telephone, the computer automatically displays all information available about the customer. As long as the customer calls from the same telephone, this process can save several seconds for each phone call. With thousands of phone calls a day, these seconds add up to substantial savings. With publicly available databases, the caller's location can be pinpointed and the salesperson can provide more personal assistance.

Several companies have been experimenting with data compression to allow video transmissions across telephone lines. With these systems, physicians could instantly send medical images to experts in distant cities for consultations. Engineers in different locations could discuss changes to diagrams. You might even be able to stay at home and attend class by using your telephone.

## THE INTERNET

The Internet is a loose collection of computer networks throughout the world. It began as a means to exchange data among major U.S. universities (NSFnet of the National Science Foundation), and connections to various military organizations and U.S. defense suppliers (Arpanet of the Advanced Research Projects Agency). No one knows how many computers or networks are currently connected by the Internet. The numbers have been increasing exponentially since the early 1990s, so any number is likely to be wrong within a few days. To give you some idea of the Internet's astounding growth, in January 1993, there were 1,313,000 host computers. In January 1994, there were 2,217,000 hosts located in more than 70 countries. Another 80 nations have e-mail access to the Internet. As of May 1994, there were more than 31,000 separate networks connected by the Internet, expanding at the rate of a new network every 10 minutes. Each network can contain hundreds or thousands of individual computers. In 1994, at least 20 million people had access to at least e-mail services. As of mid-1994, commercial use (as opposed to university and government) accounted for 50 percent of the Internet usage. International usage expanded so that since mid-1994, more than 50 percent of the networks on the Internet are located outside the United States.

More and more people are gaining access to the Internet. But what does that mean? What exactly is the Internet? At heart, the Internet is really just a communication system for computers. It is defined by a set of standards that allow computers to exchange messages. The most amazing aspect of the Internet is that there really is no single person or group in charge. Anyone who wishes to connect a computer to the Internet simply agrees to pay for a communication link (usually via a phone company), and to install communications hardware and software that supports the current

Internet standard protocols. The company is then given a base address that allows other computers to identify users on the new computer. Standards are defined by a loose committee, and addresses are controlled by another small committee. The committees are purely for the purpose of speeding the process; all decisions are up to the organizations connected to the network. Although various governments provide subsidies that operate some of the computers and cover some of the communication costs, participation in the Internet is voluntary and there are few rules, just standard practices and agreements.

As a giant communication system, the Internet offers some advantages. But all features are available only because they are offered by the owners of the computers that are attached to the Internet. Some organizations offer free services; others charge for them. There are two basic types of services: (1) mail and (2) access to data and to computer time.

### Internet Mail

One of the most popular features on the Internet is electronic mail. Virtually every machine on the Internet is capable of sending and receiving mail for registered users. As long as all participants have the appropriate software, they can send files, pictures, even sound as their message. One company even sells an Internet "phone" system that enables two people to talk to each other using the Internet links.

To send a message to any Internet user, you need to know his or her address. There are two parts to an e-mail address: the username and the computer name. Technically, Internet machine addresses consist of a set of four numbers (or one 32-bit number). However, there are *domain servers* on the network that automatically translate written names into the appropriate numbers. As a result, most people use the machine name. The complete address is written as: *username@machine*. The username is assigned by the system administrator of the computer. The machine name is assigned by the Internet committee when you apply for network access. It usually contains at least two parts, and often more. The parts are hierarchical and separated by dots. For example, a complete user address might look something like: *post@wkuvx1.wku.edu* or *president@whitehouse.gov.*

In the first example, the machine address has three parts. The *edu* tells us that it is an educational institution. The *wku* is typically the organization name. The *wkuvx1* part is the assigned name of the computer being used at that organization.

Internet offers two other services similar to e-mail: discussion groups (listserv) and newsgroups (news). Discussion groups send electronic journals to anyone who "subscribes" to the list. Typically, there is no fee for subscribing. Editors control the "publication" of a group. Comments are sent first to the editor, who decides whether to include them. Newsgroups are similar but more open. Anyone can submit a com-

---

### ▼ INTERNET ADDRESSES ▼

The last part of an Internet address indicates the type of organization:

| | |
|---|---|
| .edu | Educational/university |
| .com | Commercial/business |

| | |
|---|---|
| .gov | Government |
| .mil | Military |
| .net | Network administrative |
| .org | Miscellaneous |
| .hk | Hong Kong/or other country codes |

ment at any time to a newsgroup, which represents a giant global bulletin board. There are thousands of established topics, ranging from science to alternative lifestyles to anything you can imagine. The comments are usually uncensored and might or might not be accurate. Some people have found newsgroups useful for addressing complex computer problems. With millions of people on the Internet, there is a good chance that someone else has already encountered your problem and might have a solution. Newsgroups and bulletin boards provide useful tools to managers—especially to small business managers who have limited resources (Reality Bytes 6–11).

---

## ◥ Reality Bytes ◤ 6–11 BUSINESS ONLINE

### TO CATCH A THIEF

Although the technique is not widespread, bulletin board systems have been successful at catching criminals. Don Knutsen owns Northwest Sports Cards in Tacoma, Washington. Burglars stole some classic baseball cards, including a 1954 Willie Mays card. Along with calling the police, Mr. Knutsen reported the theft on SportsNet, a national computer network for buying and selling cards. That same morning, a man was caught trying to sell the cards to another dealer who read the report on SportsNet. The Jewelers' Security Alliance is using the same ideas to transmit pictures of thieves and stolen jewelry to its members. However, only about 9,000 of the 30,000 U.S. jewelers belong to the alliance.

### SEARCHING FOR FUNDS

Small businesses often have trouble getting startup money. Banks do not like to loan to risky ventures. There are venture capitalist firms that specialize in providing money to risky but potentially lucrative businesses. However, small businesses just starting often do not know how to contact them, and the venture capitalists have difficulty finding out about the thousands of startups every year. Specialized online systems, such as American Venture Capital Exchange, exist to help small businesses and venture capitalists exchange information and analyze potential investments. The systems allow companies to provide information to potential investors across the United States. Investors get a wider selection of companies to choose from.

---

Although messages on the Internet tend to be uncensored, be careful. If you somehow manage to insult a few thousand people, you could find yourself immersed in hundreds of thousands of mail messages that overwhelm your computer account. Also, avoid using the Internet for personal use while working for a company. In the United States, companies have the legal right to monitor your messages. In extreme situations, the computer manager can revoke accounts from people who abuse the system.

More recently, there is an Internet proposal to encapsulate EDI messages from the International (Edifact) and U.S. (ANSI X12) standards inside regular mail messages on the Internet. When this standard is approved, firms will be able to transmit their EDI messages along existing Internet links. This system should make it much simpler for firms to communicate. The Internet provides a standard, worldwide data link. By connecting to one point, a firm can reach any other company on the net. By using one of the two standards (specified in the mail header), the firms can easily exchange data.

## Access to Data on the Internet

Anyone with a computer connected to the Internet has the ability to give other users access to data stored on that computer. Read that sentence again. The owner has control over the data. Unless someone specifically grants you access to data, it is basically illegal to try and get the data, or even to use the person's computer.

There are three basic ways to give someone access to data on a computer attached to the Internet: (1) direct login or telnet, (2) file transfer or FTP, (3) database access to lists through the World Wide Web (WWW).

### Telnet

**Telnet** is a method supported on the Internet that enables users of one computer to log on to a different computer. Once logged on to the new system, the user is treated as any other user on the system. That is, the new computer does not care that the commands are coming over the Internet and treats it the same as any other terminal.

To use Telnet, you must first have an account established on the desired computer. Telnet is useful if you work for a company that has several computers in different locations. You will rarely use Telnet to connect to computers owned by other companies, because it provides users with substantial access and control over the machine. However, some companies (and universities) provide accounts for research purposes, which gives you access to a faster computer or specialized software that you might not personally be able to afford.

### FTP: File Transfer Protocol

**FTP** stands for **File Transfer Protocol.** It is a standard method of transferring files on the Internet. If you control a computer, you can give other users access to specific files on your computer without having to provide an account and password for every possible user. To obtain a data file with FTP, you first log in to the desired machine. Most of the time, you log in as an anonymous user, entering your e-mail address as a password. As an anonymous ftp user, you can download specific files to your computer.

There are two types of files you might want to transfer: text and binary (sometimes called *image*). *Text files* are character-based and typically contain messages or simple information. They can be read by almost any type of computer. *Binary files* are stored in a format for a specific purpose. They might be pictures or data files for a specific software package such as a word processor or spreadsheet. Many times files are compressed into a binary file to save space and decrease the transmission time. To transfer a binary file, be sure you set binary mode within FTP. You also need the compression/decompression program to retrieve the underlying files.

The two basic FTP commands are GET and PUT. GET transfers a file from the distant (host) computer to yours (local). PUT sends a file from your local machine to the host computer. You can often get a list of files on the host computer with the DIR or LIST command.

### WWW: World Wide Web

The **World Wide Web** is a first attempt to set up an international database of information. When you start the software on your local computer, you will see a menu that lists information you can find. Making a choice in one menu will usually connect you to another computer on the Internet and bring up its WWW menu. From there you can look at library catalogs, pictures, or whatever information is provided by that Web server. The initial versions of the Web were developed at CERN, the European particle-physics laboratory, where the staff wanted to make it easier for researchers to share their work.

## ESTABLISHING AN INTERNET SITE

Although it is still challenging to make sales over the Internet, many companies are using the Internet to market their products and to build closer links to their customers. Some Web sites get as many as 100,000 hits (visits) a day. Although only about 7 percent of American households are connected to a network, the profile user is a valuable customer. The average U.S. user is a 31-year-old male making $65,000 a year. Seventy percent of users have a college degree. These demographics are not surprising, because network connections require about $2,000 in computer equipment and a network connection. America Online (AOL), one of the leading private networks charges a base fee of $9.95 a month, but the average user spends an additional $7 for extra time—leading to an average $200 a year connection charge.

Building a site on the Internet requires that you have a fairly powerful computer. It also entails buying a router that can connect to the network at high speeds and paying communication costs. Forrester Research estimates that building a Web site costs $60,000 to $120,000 the first year. However, you can often lease space on someone else's machine for around $5,000.

The difficult part of building a Web site is attracting visitors. Internet users are notoriously fickle. Many are searching for entertaining sites. Others look for customer support or in-depth product information. Mahesh Murthy, who designed marketplaceMCI, notes that "If you bore users the first time, they'll never come back and you've lost them. Then you've wasted your resources." He points out that "entertaining" Web sites have to constantly change and offer new connections, games, and features.

Actually building a Web page is becoming easier as companies introduce new software. Web pages are based on a standardized format known as HTML: Hypertext Mark-up Language. Several word processors now support this format, and other tools make it easy to add video and graphics. HTML is a set of commands that tell the browser how to display the text. Complete documentation is available on the Web. Interactive sites are built using a special programming language called Java. Generally you need to hire trained programmers (Webmasters) to build complex interactive Web sites.

It can be hard to measure the value of building a Web site. Because it is difficult (and against custom) to charge for access to individual sites, you can receive thousands of visitors a day and see no direct profit. Reaching new customers, encouraging repeat buying, and providing better customer service are all possible goals of an Internet site. They are all difficult to quantify in terms of profits.

The easiest access to the Web is with a *browser* like Mosaic or Netscape. Browsers present a page of information that contains links to other pages on the Web. The page can contain text, graphics, video, and sound clips. By selecting highlighted words, you can move to other systems, trace topics, and transfer data. Pictures are displayed automatically, and most operations can be completed by selecting items with a mouse.

Organizations that support the Web, build a *home page.* This screen is written in a markup language that is interpreted by Internet browsers. Building a Web page is getting easier, but complex forms might require the help of experienced programmers. When you connect to someone's home page, your screen displays what it is told. From this display, you select where you want to go next: either deeper into the data on that system or to a different computer.

If you ever work with the obscure command-line statements of the older Internet utilities like FTP, you will quickly appreciate the ease-of-use of the Web. However, you are still faced with the same difficulties in terms of locating useful data. The Web

## THE INTERNET AND THE CONGRESS

The Library of Congress has introduced "Thomas," a public online access service. Named in honor of President Thomas Jefferson, the new system provides a wide range of information regarding U.S. laws and lawmakers.

When he introduced the new system, Speaker of the House Newt Gingrich said that the new system will shift the "balance of power toward the citizens and out of the Washington Beltway."

Librarian of Congress James H. Billington declared that the new service will "enable Americans to search more easily for legislation and to understand more fully the lawmaking process." In his opinion, "The system is easy to use with a unique search process."

Available free of charge to Internet users, the service is available through the World Wide Web.

The address is www.thomas.loc.gov.
Thomas includes the following:

- Full texts of bills from the previous Congress.
- The House of Representatives' gopher system, which includes directory information for lawmakers and committees, committee hearing schedules, House floor schedules, and visitor information.
- The text of House procedures.
- Full texts of bills.
- Full texts of the *Congressional Record.*
- Full texts of the *Congressional Research Service's Bill Digest,* containing summaries and chronologies of legislation.

makes it easier to move around the Internet, but you still need to find a useful starting point. Some companies publish their Web addresses; others you can find from friends or from contacts on the net. Sometimes you can stumble across an interesting server by accident. Keep a list of the useful servers that you find. With the constantly changing Internet, sometimes links disappear. If you know the full address, you can usually get back to specific servers even if connecting links are changed. Web addresses generally begin with an *http:* prefix.

### Locating Data on the Internet

Because the Internet is so large and growing rapidly, it can be difficult to find useful data. Additionally, organizations are constantly changing the type of information they provide. The data available is constantly changing, making it impossible to provide an up-to-date listing. So how do you find anything on the Internet?

Several tools can help you find data on the Internet. You might purchase a book that lists some of the major databases. It can be a useful starting point, because there are some databases that have been provided for several years. However, an easier method is to use one of the electronic search tools provided by Internet organizations.

Another method of locating files on the Internet is a utility program called **gopher.** Gopher is supported by *archie* and *veronica,* which are two search tools for finding information provided by gophers. To the user, gopher is a set of menus that you trace to find information on various machines. Although it is loosely organized by category, it is mostly used to make it easier for you to change to different machines on the Internet. As a result, you generally need to know approximately where to find the data you want. For instance, if you know that you want U.S. population data, you can use gopher menus to connect to the U.S. Census Bureau computer. Their gopher will then give you a menu showing the data available over the Internet.

The World Wide Web is a graphic-based Internet search tool. Many Web sites contain links to other sites so you can find related data. Some companies provide search

Microsoft created a new network (MSN) to provide information and resources to subscribers. Initially designed to operate as a private network, within months of its introduction, Microsoft moved the service to the Internet (http://www.msn.com) because of the rapid growth in the public network.

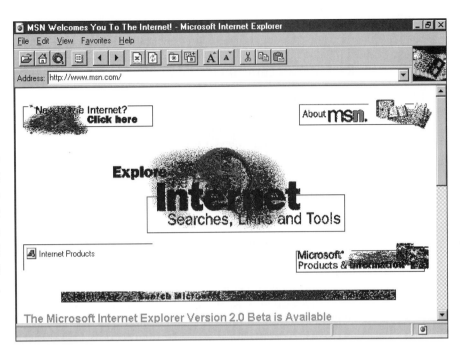

engines that help you search for specific topics. Common search sites include Yahoo, Altavista, Lycos, and Netscape. Lycos (The Wolfspider) was created in 1996 by Michael Mauldin at Carnegie Mellon University. It searches Web sites, catalogs each page it finds, and records the links for future searching. Altavista was created by Digital Equipment Corporation to search thousands of sites based on complex criteria you enter. Yahoo and Netscape organize sites by topics, making it easier to find related information.

A few specialized Web sites operate as pointers to other sites (Reality Bytes 6–12). For example, there is a site that contains a list of Web pages by major U.S. companies. There is a site with links to pages related to movies. There are several

 **Reality Bytes** ◣ 6–12 AFRICAN-AMERICAN GROUPS ON THE INTERNET

Many groups have turned to the Internet for camaraderie, to build an identity, and share information. The Internet offers many features to groups: worldwide access, low-cost connections, large databases with search capabilities, and interactive communications that enable people to exchange messages directly.

Several organizations have created Web sites geared toward African Americans. William Murrell III who oversees the African-American Culture and Arts Forum on CompuServe notes that:

*It can be very important for black people who work for largely white companies and who attend largely white schools. They feel isolated. In a way, going on line is a new way of getting the same old*

*thing: connecting with your peers. It's just that in this case your peers are other black people.*

Some of the African-American online sites are:

- African-American Culture and Arts Forum on CompuServe
- African-American Information Network on eWorld
- NetNoir Online on American Online
- African-American Home Page at http://www.lainet.com/joejones/
- AfriNET at http://www.afrinet.net
- Universal Black Pages at http://www.gatech.edu/bgsa/balckpages.html

sites that specialize in links to museums. The one complication with Web sites is that they are created and maintained by individuals, so they often change.

## Security Concerns on the Internet

Although security is an issue with all computer networks, the Internet presents a special challenge. In particular, the Internet is not owned by anyone and is really just a loose connection of computers. Virtually anyone can connect a computer to the Internet—even serving as a host computer.

Because of the design of the network and its size, messages are rarely sent directly from one computer to another. In almost all cases, messages are passed through several other computers on the way to their destination. As indicated in Figure 6.16, it is possible for someone to join the Internet and spy on all conversations that pass through that section of the network. Users on the starting computer who log in to the destination computer via Telnet will have to enter their username and password on the destination computer. Yet that information will pass, unprotected, through the interloper's computer. With a simple monitoring program, the eavesdropper could collect hundreds or thousands of accounts and passwords a day. The other difficulty is that security is the responsibility of each machine operator. With easy access to thousands of machines, hackers like Kevin Mitnick (Reality Bytes 6-13) can take advantage of any lapse in security.

One final reminder about data on the Internet. There is a tremendous amount of "fluff" on the Internet—information that is of dubious value. Additionally, many of the comments are purely personal opinions, which might or might not be accurate. As a user of the Internet, it is your responsibility to verify all "facts" and comments that are important to you.

## Business on the Internet

Hundreds of articles have been written about business use of the Internet. There are plenty of opportunities. The popularity of mailorder and television shopping points out the demand for shopping from home. Yet, these same mechanisms lead to the big question: Given the success of mailorder and television shopping, what do we gain by shopping through computer networks?

Figure 6.17 summarizes the three primary gains. First, the network could make it easier to search for data and to compare offerings from various suppliers. If data and

**FIGURE 6.16**

Internet security concerns. Data passes through many unknown servers. Any machine connected could read the data, destroy it, or fabricate a different message. Encryption techniques are available but not yet employed by the mainstream of Internet users. Rapidly changing automatic password generators are available for secure logins across insecure networks.

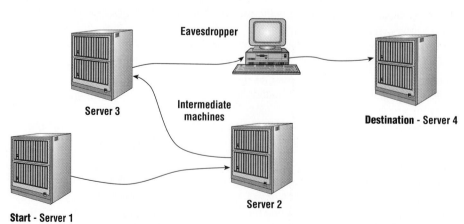

## Reality Bytes    6–13  INTERNET SECURITY

In 1995, Kevin D. Mitnick, was able to steal 20,000 credit-card records from Netcom Communications Inc., an Internet service provider. Although none of the cards were used fraudulently, Netcom Executive Vice-President Warren Kaplan noted, "We absolutely didn't know that the files had been taken." Mitnick was arrested on other charges about the same time that The Well, another Internet provider, found the copies of the files.

One common security method is to install a computer that acts as a "firewall." All Internet communications are routed through one computer. This machine examines addresses of incoming message packets. It only accepts messages from predefined sources to come through the system. However, even this protection can be circumvented, when hackers change their packet addresses and pretend to be an internal, trusted computer.

Because of these problems, John Wankmueller, director of technology assessment for MasterCard International, notes that "It's very unsettling. We wouldn't use the Internet as it is today to conduct electronic commerce."

networks could be standardized, we could build an automated search system that would track down anything consumers want. Second, the network could cut data-handling costs. With an automated order-entry and tracking system, consumers could select items themselves, without the need for phone operators. If the system were easy to use, it could save money and reduce errors. Third, computer access to catalogs and product descriptions could provide more detailed information to consumers, allowing them to get exactly the data they wanted.

There are several drawbacks to shopping over computer networks. First, households need computers—although about one-third of U.S. households now have computers, traditional sales tools such as televisions, phones, and catalogs reach millions of more people. Second, there are virtually no security provisions on the Internet, making it difficult to verify the source of transactions and easy for dishonest people to steal money and merchandise. Private networks like CompuServe and Prodigy are slightly more secure, but abuses can still occur. Third, data transmission is slow. You can pack a lot of data into one catalog, and consumers can flip pages rapidly. Public transmission networks are still slow. Even at ISDN rates of 128 kbps, it would take more than a minute to transfer a 1 megabyte picture to a consumer. Imagine how long it would take to send a 200-page catalog! Fourth, computers are not as portable as catalogs (or even televisions). It is still difficult to browse the Internet while sitting on the beach. Fifth is an interesting question: Who will pay for the network? Possibilities include consumers (directly and indirectly through higher prices), governments, and businesses (through charges or taxes). Until these drawbacks are resolved, we will see only limited business use of the Internet.

**FIGURE 6.17**

In many ways, shopping on the Internet is not much different than traditional mailorder catalogue shopping. As the Internet capabilities expand, it will offer additional advantages, such as automated searches, secure handling of money, and immediate transfers of nonphysical merchandise (data). Several issues must be resolved and improved before the Net reaches its full potential.

| ADVANTAGES | DRAWBACKS |
| --- | --- |
| Search and compare. | Availability: requires a computer. |
| Automated data handling. | Lack of security. |
| More tailored information. | Slow speed limits graphics and video. |
| | Lack of portability. |
| | Who will pay? |

Current use of the networks revolves around data and e-mail. Investors get current and historical data on stock prices and corporate performance. Researchers search professional publications, magazines, newspapers, legal decisions, and government databases. Companies provide product information. Notably, software companies use networks to answer questions and distribute bug fixes. But the most common use of networks is e-mail and chatting on bulletin boards.

**GLOBAL TELE-COMMUNICATIONS**

Business firms in the 1990s are becoming more dependent on international markets. This internationalization increases the demands on the telecommunications system. The international transmission of data is becoming part of the daily business routine. A manufacturing company may have factories in several different countries, with the headquarters located in yet another country. Supplies have to be sent to factories. Finished and intermediate products have to be tracked. Customer demands have to be followed in each country. Quality control and warranty repair information have to be followed from the supplier through the factory and out to the customers. Financial investments have to be tracked on stock markets in many countries. Different accounting and payroll rules have to be provided for each country. Basic accounting and financial data have to be available to management at any time of day, in any part of the organization.

Creating networks across international boundaries creates many problems. Some of the complications are technical, some are political or legal, and others are cultural.

## Technical Problems

The biggest technical complication is that each country may have its own telecommunications standards. For example, in the western European nations, the telephone systems are managed by governmental agencies called Postal Telephone (PTT) companies (Reality Bytes 6–14). Because PTTs are publicly run, national governments have a habit of insisting that communication equipment be purchased from manufac-

---

◤ **Reality Bytes** ◣    6–14  CHANGING EUROPE'S PTTs

The European Union (EU) established several laws that would bring European nations closer together beginning in 1992. The goal was to make it easier for companies to operate in Europe and provide more alternatives to consumers. A major thrust of the legislation was to reduce the trade barriers that exist between European nations. They removed outright barriers such as tariffs and restrictions on workers. The laws also attacked governmental subsidies and other indirect barriers. As part of these changes, in 1993 the EU Council decreed that by January 1, 1998, all state monopolies on voice telephone services must end. Data telecommunications were mostly privatized in 1993.

In the meantime, the European telecommunication giants who have already been privatized are going after markets in the other nations. AT&T formed a joint venture with Dutch, Swedish, and Swiss phone companies. One of their networks, designed for use by multinational firms, has estimated revenues of $100 million a year in 1995. Multinational companies, including Xerox, Philips Electronics and American Express expect to cut their phone bills in half. In Germany, the electric utility is building a fiber optic network to compete with the phone company.

turers within their own nation. Despite the standards, there are still technical incompatibilities among the various nations.

In developing nations, the communications equipment may be antiquated. The older equipment will not be able to handle large amounts of data transfers, and there may be an unacceptable number of errors. Also, the government-controlled power supplies may not be reliable enough to run computers and network equipment.

One possible way to avoid the public telecommunications hassles is to use microwave transmissions through satellites. This approach can be more reliable but can be expensive unless you have huge amounts of data to transfer. For developing nations located in the southern hemisphere, there may not be adequate satellite coverage. Many of the satellite channels available to developing nations are used and controlled by the individual governments. It is generally not economically feasible to put up a new satellite, and most governments would object if you attempted to bypass their control.

To transmit more than simple text and numbers, there are more potential problems to consider. The U.S., European, and Asian nations all have different video standards. Televisions made for the U.S. market will not function in Europe. If a company creates a multimedia marketing presentation in the United States, it will probably be difficult to show to clients in France. These incompatibilities are about to get worse with the introduction of high-definition television (HDTV) or digital television. Each of the national groups is working with a different technique.

## Legal and Political Complications

Some important problems can be created when a firm wants to transmit information across national boundaries. These transfers are called **transborder data flows (TBDF).** The problem arises because the information has value to the sender. Because it has value, some governments have suggested that they would like to impose a tariff or tax on that value. Besides the cost of tariff, the issue raises the possibility that the national governments may want to monitor the amount and type of data being transferred. Most businesses are reluctant to allow anyone that much access to their information.

Another important issue revolves around typical marketing data about customers. It is common for marketing departments to maintain huge databases. These databases contain customer names, addresses, phone numbers, estimated income levels, purchases, and other marketing data. Problems have arisen because the Western European nations have much stricter laws concerning privacy than does the United States. In most European nations, it is illegal to sell or trade customer data to other companies. It must also be stored in protected files that cannot be seen by unauthorized employees or outsiders. In most cases, it is the responsibility of the company to prove it is meeting the requirements of the law. In many cases, this requirement means that customer data must be maintained on computers within the original nation. Also, this data cannot then be transmitted to computers in other countries. As a result, the multinational company may be forced to maintain computer facilities in each of the nations in which it does business. It also needs to impose security conditions that prevent the raw data from being transmitted from these computers.

There is one more important political issue involving international computer centers. Many nations, especially the developing nations, change governments quite often, as well as abruptly. There are many nations where terrorist activities are prevalent. Often times, large multinational companies present tempting targets. Because computer centers tend to be expensive, special security precautions need to be established in these countries. Probably the most important step is to keep the computer center away from public access. Several U.S. security specialists publish risk factors for each country and suggested precautions. They also provide security analysis and protection—for a fee.

A host of other political complications affect any multinational operation. For example, each nation has different employment laws, accounting rules, investment constraints, and local partnership requirements. Most of these can be surmounted, but they usually require the services of a local attorney.

## Cultural Issues

All of the typical cultural issues can play a role in running multinational computer networks. The work habits of employees can vary in different nations. It may be difficult to obtain qualified service personnel at some times of the day or night. These issues can be critical for computer networks that need to remain in operation 24 hours a day. In many nations, it is still considered inappropriate to have female managers when there are male subordinates. Collecting information may be exceedingly difficult or even culturally forbidden. In some countries, you will lose a customer if you try to obtain marketing data such as age and income.

In some nations, the connections between suppliers and customers are established by culture. For instance, in Japan, distribution of products is handled by a few large firms. These companies have established relationships with the suppliers and retail outlets. In any country, it can be difficult for an outside firm to create a relationship between suppliers and customers. Trying to build computer networks with the various companies could cause severe repercussions. The established firms may think you are trying to steal their knowledge or information.

## Comment

Creating international data networks can lead to many problems. There is no easy solution to many of these problems. However, international networks do exist and they will increase in the next few years. In many cases, firms have to operate in the international environment in order to succeed. There is no choice. The company must build international telecommunications networks.

As the European Union increases the amount of interdependence between western and eastern European nations, there will be even more reasons for companies to operate in many nations. The same holds true for the conversion of the East European nations to market economies. The companies that take the lead in international computer networks will face many problems, but if they succeed, they will create the foundation necessary to be the leaders in their industry.

---

###  CULTURAL DIFFERENCES IN THE WORLD

If you invite people to a party at seven o'clock, your guests will consider it polite to turn up on the dot in Germany, 5 minutes early in the American Midwest, an hour early in Japan, 15 minutes afterward in the UK, up to an hour afterward in Italy, and some time in the evening in Greece. I deliberately avoided the more emotive word "late," because there is nothing wrong in it. It is the accepted convention.

SOURCE: John Mole, *When in Rome . . . A Business Guide to Cultures & Customs in 12 European Nations,* AMACOM: New York, 1991, p. 155.

## SUMMARY

One of the most important concepts in MIS is the importance of sharing data. Computer systems that are designed to be used by many people at the same time are more complex than single-user systems. Because of this complexity, more problems arise. Hardware and software have to be designed to be shared. Someone has to be in charge of controlling access to the machines and data. Standards have to be established to ensure compatibility among pieces of equipment.

LANs are an easy means to share data between users. They provide access to transaction data collected by central computers. They are used to send messages between users, through e-mail and bulletin boards, and scheduling meetings on electronic calendars. They make it easier for teams to share data, results, and reports for projects. LANs also make it easier to create backups of personal computer data.

As the use of personal computers increases, local area networks are frequently used to connect them together and to give individual users access to data stored on central computers. Many organizations have chosen to organize their networks as a collection of client computers that access data from a few servers. Most communication is between the client personal computers and the server. Computers can also be connected as peer-to-peer machines to transfer data directly to each other, without the use of an intermediary.

### A MANAGER'S VIEW

All workers need to communicate, both through formal channels with reports and informal conversations with other workers throughout the company. Communication is used to compensate for the barrier of distance.

Computer networks facilitate several types of communication: written, voice, image, and even video. At heart, networks are simple connections among machines. As a manager, you need to know how to use networks to share data. You also need to watch for network problems and incompatibilities.

Changes in the telephone industry are having profound effects on the connection of computers across long distances. As the availability of ISDN increases, it will become easier (and possibly cheaper) to connect computers across phone lines at much higher speeds. Even the television cable companies are considering new facilities for connecting computers.

The telecommunications facilities and prices we rely on in industrialized nations are not always available in other nations. Additionally, there are incompatibilities between equipment produced for various nations. Political restrictions are another source of complications when transferring data across international boundaries.

## KEY WORDS

asynchronous transfer mode (ATM), 275
broadcasts, 264
bulletin board system (BBS), 252
client, 260
e-mail, 251
file server, 258

File Transfer Protocol (FTP), 278
gopher, 280
groupware, 256
Integrated Services Digital Network (ISDN), 274
Internet, 252
local area network (LAN), 246
modem, 274

network interface card (NIC), 261
peer-to-peer network, 260
server, 260
standards, 272
Telnet, 278
transborder data flows, 285
World Wide Web, 278

## REVIEW QUESTIONS

1. What are three main items that can be shared with networks?
2. What business reasons do users have for sharing data?
3. What are the main components of a network?
4. What are the differences between client-server and peer-to-peer networks?

5. Why are standards so important in networks?
6. What new telephone services are available and how do they affect businesses?
7. What problems arise with global telecommunications?

8. What are the advantages and drawbacks of e-mail compared to traditional mail? Compared to telephones?

9. What is a bulletin board system? Give an example of how it can be used in business.

10. How are electronic calendars used to schedule meetings? How does their use affect workers?

11. What advantages are gained by sharing printers with a LAN?

12. What do you gain by storing software on a file server?

13. What types of transmission media are available? How do they compare in transmission rates and cost?

14. What software is needed on personal computers to connect them to a LAN?

## EXERCISES

1. First, *get permission from your LAN administrator,* then conduct a performance test of your LAN. Have five students start an application program at the same time. Measure the time it takes for the package to be loaded by all five users. Now, try the same experiment with 10, 20, 30, and as many users as you can find. Create a graph of the results.

2. Using magazine reviews and advertisements, how many major network operating system choices can you find for a 10-user LAN?

3. Using catalogs and advertisements, estimate the hardware and software costs of installing a LAN for 10 users and 1 file server. Provide a detailed list of the items you need to purchase. What would be the cost of some application packages (word processor, spreadsheet, database, etc.). Will you need to license all of the software for 10 users?

4. Use your LAN to send a message to at least five students in your class. If you have access to a BBS or USENET, post a message on the system and reply to anyone who responds to the message.

5. If you have access to the Internet or telnet, connect to a computer in a different state that you are authorized to access. For example, library computers are often open to the public, so you can search for books. See how many books you can find on a specific subject (perhaps telecommunications in Africa).

6. As a group assignment, set up a small database on a LAN. For example, create an input screen to record product orders, and create reports that display customer and inventory data. Using the LAN, have three people enter data at the same time. Make sure the database handles multiple users correctly—see whether the values are correct. Also, note whether there are any performance changes when one, two, and three people enter data simultaneously. Can two people enter orders for the same customer at the same time? What about entering the same product for different customers at the same time? Can a fourth user retrieve accurate reports at the same time orders are being taken? Are the reports automatically updated after the orders are entered? Have one user view the base table data while the orders are created. Does the user screen update automatically when the data is entered?

7. As a group assignment, write a short paper (one or two pages) on uses of LANs. Using current periodicals, each group member should find an article on local area networks. Summarize that article in one paragraph. Each person types in his or her summary with a word processor. Using a LAN, send the individual pieces to one member, who assembles them into a final document for printing.

8. Assuming that you have money, choose an automobile that you would want to buy. Use the Internet to find the list price and estimated dealer invoice of the automobile. Is it possible to purchase the automobile over the Internet? Can you apply for a loan using the Internet? Be sure to specify the address of any data you find.

 **Rolling Thunder Database**

1. Design a network for the Rolling Thunder Bicycle Company. Identify who will need access to the network, how many workstations you need (and where to place them), the data, input forms, and reports users will need. Using the existing data, estimate the storage requirements and transmission needs. Specify how changes and growth will affect the type of network needed.

2. Match purchase orders with receipts. Verify that total expenditures match. Determine whether any employees were in charge of both purchases and receipts.

3. Choose a bicycle and list all of the people who were involved with its production and shipping (e.g., we assume we received a problem/complaint on a bicycle). How would a network facilitate handling this type of query?

## ADDITIONAL READING

"Art From Russian Museum on CompuServe," *Digital News & Review*, February 6, 1995, [Museums and the Internet]

"Art Museum Goes Multimedia," *The Seybold Report on Publishing Systems*, February 13, 1995, p. 20. [Museums and the Internet]

Ball, John. "Manufacturer Provides Parts Just in Time," *Data Based Advisor*, March 1994, pp. 71-74. [Magna International]

Balteisan, Kristin U. "A Passion for Art: Magnificent Museum," *MacUser*, December 1995, p. 87. [Museums and the Internet]

Berners-Lee, T., R. Cailliau, A. Luotonen, H.F. Nielsen and A. Secret, "The World-Wide Web," *Communications of the ACM*, August 1994, pp. 76-82.

Booker, Ellis. "American Express Integrates Network," *Computerworld*, June 24, 1991 p. 66. [American Express HRM]

Bradbury, Janel. "Louvre Story," *MacUser*, January 1996, p. 34. [Museums and the Internet]

Brenesal, Barry. "Turn Your Home into an Art Museum with the Tate Gallery," *Computer Shopper*, April 1995, p. 214. [Museums and the Internet]

Brown, Bruce. "Use Your PC to Tone Up with Mayo Clinic Sports Health CD," *Computer Shopper*, October 1995, p. 216. [Medicine and IT]

Cauley, Leslie. "Scientists Search for More Room on Phone Lines," *The Wall Street Journal*, September 28, 1994, pp. B1, B8. [Fiber optic research, statistics on phone line usage, and capacity]

Claffy, K.C., H.W. Braun and G.C. Polyzos. "Tracking Long-Term Growth of the NSFnet," *Communications of the ACM*, August 1994, pp. 34-45.

Claue, Alisan, "Control Freaks," *Computer Weekly*, August 31, 1995, pp. 30-31. [Bell Atlantic and TCI]

Clavan, Barbara. "Tracking Beer No Small Job," *Computing Canada*, March 30, 1994, p. 24. [Brewers Retail]

Cobb, Nathan. "Suddenly, a Boom in Sites Geared Toward African Americans," *Boston Globe*, January 2, 1996, pp. 25, 28. [Minority use of the Internet]

Davis, Liselotte H. "Business as (Un) Usual," *Computerworld*, December 21, 1992, pp. 55-57. [Discussion of telecommunications problems in eastern Germany]

Desmond, Michael and Anne Desmond. "Second Opinion, Health Care Professionals Examine Medical CDs," *Multimedia World*," October 1995, pp. 70-73. [Medicine and IT]

*Fortune*, April 18, 1994, Special advertising section on Portugal, p. 3. [Iberomoldes]

Fox, Robert. "News Track," *Communications of the ACM*, August 1994, pp. 9-10. [Aerosmith and the Internet]

Goodman, S.E., L.I. Press, S.R.Rugh, and A.M. Rutkowski, "The Global Diffusion of the Internet: Patterns and Problems," *Communications of the ACM*, August 1994, pp. 27-31.

"Hitting the Mail on the Head," *The Economist*, April 30, 1994, pp. 69-70. [Postal statistics]

Hudson, Richard L. "European Companies Speed Shift to Phone Competition," *The Wall Street Journal*, June 24, 1994, p. B3. [Opening European phone market]

Huey, J. and A. Kupfer. "What That Merger Means for You," *Fortune*, November 15, 1993, pp. 82-90. [Mergers of telcommunications companies]

"Internet Update—Art Sites On The Web," *Newsbytes*, November 1, 1995, p. NEW11010032. [Museums and the Internet]

"Internet Update—Art Sites On The Web: St. Petersburg Salvador Dali Museum," *Newsbytes*, November 1, 1995, p. NEW11010034. [Museums and the Internet]

Kahn, Robert E. "The Role of Government in the Evolution of the Internet, *Communications of the ACM*, August 1994, pp. 15-19.

Keefe, Patricia. "Lotus Releases Note-Able Net Package," *Computerworld*, December 11, 1989, p. 7. [Manufacturer's Hanover Trust]

Kirkpatrick, David. "As the Internet Sizzles, Online Services Battle for Stakes," *Fortune*, May 1, 1995, pp. 86-96. [Establishing an Internet site]

LaPlante, Alice. "Rugby Darby," *Infoworld*, November 15, 1993, pp. S100-103. [Rugby Darby]

Lee, Louise. "E-Mail Among Officials May Be Against the Law, *The Wall Street Journal*, February 16, 1995, p. B1. [Complications and legal interpretation that e-mail might violate open meeting laws]

Leiner, Barry M. "Internet Technology," *Communications of the ACM*, August 1994, p. 32.

Meet the Finalists, *Computerworld*, May 24, 1993, p. 113. [Windows world finalists, Chicago 911 system]

Mehta, Stephanie N. "Business Owners Fight Crime as They Sit at Their Computers," *The Wall Street Journal*, June 2, 1994, pp. B1, B2. [Baseball card collector's network]

Nash, Jim. "EDI Sprinters Find Partners on Slow Track," *Computerworld*, March 5, 1990, p. 1. [Dillard's]

O'Brien, Timothy L. "Entrepreneurs Raise Funds Through Online Computer Services," *The Wall Street Journal*, June 2, 1994, pp. B1, B2. [Small business on the Internet]

Pearlstein, Joanna. "Macworld's Guide to Online Services. (America Online, CompuServe, Delphi, eWorld, GEnie and Prodigy)," *Macworld*, 11(8), pp. 90–96. [Online services]

"Prowling the Web," *The Economist*, May 13, 1995, p. 81. [Brief description of Lycos, the Web searcher (spider)]

Sandberg, Jared. "Undetected Theft of Credit-Card Data Raises Concern about On-line Security," *The Wall Street Journal*, February 17, 1995, p. B2. [Internet security]

————. "Computer Experts See Hackers Gaining an Upper Hand in Fight Over Security," *The Wall Street Journal*, January 24, 1995, p. B6. [Internet security]

Smith, Laura B. "Virtual Masterpieces," *PC Week*, July 31, 1995, p. E5. [Museums and the Internet]

Spinner, Karen. "Chemical Banks on Object Middleware for Global Trading," *Wall Street & Technology*, August 1995. [Manufacturer's Hanover Trust]

Stewart, Thomas A. "Managing in a Wired Company," *Fortune*, July 11, 1994, pp. 44–56. [Examples of companies using networks and the effects on the organization]

Teeter, Christopher. "Safeguarding Long Distance Networking," *Computerworld*, March 12, 1990, p. 47. [Telecommunications cost estimates: 2% to 7% of operating costs for "lifeblood" users]

"Telecommunications Survey," *The Economist*, October 23, 1993, pp. 1–20. [Special section on worldwide telecommunication trends, especially wireless]

Telecousur, George Gilder. "The Bandwidth Tidal Wave," *Forbes*, December 5, 1994, p. 162. [Bell Atlantic and TCI]

Tetzeli, Rick. "Surviving Information Overload," *Fortune*, July 11, 1994, pp. 60–65. [Statistics on number of information/communication devices in U.S.]

"To Your Health," *Computer Letter*, September 25, 1995, pp. 1–7. [Medicine and IT]

Wall, Thomas J. "NII Milepost: The 1995 Infobahn Progress Report," *Technology & Learning*, May 1995, pp. 52–58. [Bell Atlantic and TCI]

Wexler, Joanie M. "Exchange to Save $200,000 Annually," *Computerworld*, January 18, 1993, p. 45. [The Commodity Exchange]

Wexler, Joanie M. "Words to the Wise," *Computerworld*, January 13, 1992, p. 64. [Telecommunication cost estimates: 48 percent to 68 percent of technology budgets]

Wood, Christina. "The Virtual Doctor," *PC World*, November 1995, pp. 380–381. [Medicine and IT]

Zachary, G. Pascal. "It's a Mail Thing: Electronic Messaging Gets a Rating—Ex," *The Wall Street Journal*, June 22, 1994, pp. A1, A10. [E-mail excess]

# CASES  *Distributors and Inventory Management*

The wholesale industry and distributors in general rely on computers—especially in inventory control, processing invoices, sales, bookkeeping and general databases.

SOURCE: Computer Use in the United States, U.S. Bureau of the Census.

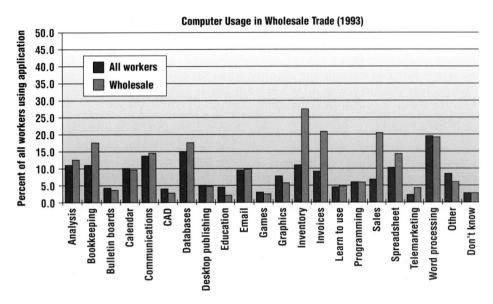

**Computer Usage in Wholesale Trade (1993)**

Many companies (distributors) avoid direct sales to consumers. Instead, their products are sold to intermediaries who either sell them to consumers or embed them in other products. These distributors face several problems. First, without direct contact with the final consumer, it is more difficult to predict demand for their products. Their sales to the intermediaries can be distorted by the decisions and guesses of the other firms. Second, it is more difficult for consumers to provide information and feedback to the original manufacturer.

A fundamental problem for the distributors is the decision of how much inventory to hold. Often there are several product variations, with combinations of features leading to a large number of products in several categories. The distributor has to forecast both total demand for the product and demand for each specific item. Guessing wrong leads to either excessively large inventories or shortage of some products. Excessive inventories cost money because of interest rate costs. They also waste expensive storage space and require additional handling. The expense of shortages is the loss of sales, including the costs associated with irritating your customers.

The role of distributor is important in many economies. Distributors often control significant sectors of the economy. The power to control distribution channels means they have a strong influence on products. Yet, distributors also face competition.

Success often depends on close relationships in both directions: to suppliers and to the customers.

## CASE  *Magna International*

Magna International faces problems similar to other companies that supply parts to the automobile industry. To compete with the Japanese firms during the 1980s, American automobile manufacturers found they could cut costs by using just-in-time inventory control. With this system, parts are supposed to show up from the suppliers just when they are needed on the assembly line. The automobile company runs the risk that if parts do not arrive in time, the line must be stopped. However, the company substantially reduces its overhead costs, because the company does not need to hold a large inventory of parts. In addition to the interest cost of holding the parts, the company saves storage space and needs fewer personnel to handle the parts.

On the other hand, just-in-time inventory management merely shifts the inventory burdens onto the parts manufacturer. Because the parts are made in batches, the manufacturer estimates the demand for each component, produces it in bulk, stocks it in inventory, and then ships the parts as they are needed. Because each supplier provides only a small number of parts (compared to the entire production), it is slightly easier to control and monitor these smaller inventories. Yet, the supplier must be very careful to never miss a delivery schedule.

To keep up with the short time schedule, Magna International built an inventory and order-tracking system on its Novell NetWare local area network. The data is stored on a RAID (redundant array of inexpensive drives) disk system that automatically creates backups and provides fast access to the data. Several different types of computers, running different operating systems are connected to the network. The EDI transmissions are handled by a Unix-based workstation. The forklift operators and inventory personnel have radio frequency-based (RF), hand-held bar code readers. These scanners transmit and receive data to base stations hooked to personal computers on the network. Each RF terminal has a unique ID. Messages are broadcast throughout the plant, but only the terminal with the proper ID responds to the message. As parts are added to or removed from inventory, the workers transmit the data to the central inventory database.

### EDI Notices

Chrysler provides four types of information during the process via the EDI connection:

1. A two-week forecast of what Chrysler planners think will be produced in the coming weeks. At Magna, this information is sent to the plant scheduler and to purchasing.
2. A 48-hour notice, which lists every vehicle to be produced in the next 48 hours, by VIN (vehicle identification number). The vehicles might not be produced in the order listed. Magna's production planner checks current inventory and adjusts production to meet the demand.
3. A ship trigger, which is the actual order for the part. Based on this notice, the desired parts are picked from inventory. A truck is loaded with 96 parts and sent to the Chrysler assembly plant. The system also prints a bill of lading identifying the parts.
4. Payment data is sent to Magna. As Chrysler installs the parts, the vehicle data is transmitted back to the appropriate suppliers, with signals sent to the banks to make payment. At Magna, the accounts receivable department matches the payment notices against the orders and shipping data. Because of the volume of data, the actual matching is handled by the computer system.

### Pick System

The inventory pick system is more complex that it seems at first glance. As items are picked from inventory, the Sequenced Delivery System monitors future shipments and production. As parts are picked from the lower levels by the workers, the RF network instructs forklift operators to move boxes from higher locations down to the lower levels. Incoming parts from the production line are slotted into the system as close to the estimated demand sequence as possible.

### Management Use of the Data

Inventory managers need to monitor the system, so they have access to an online display. The display shows the quantities and rack lanes used for each product. The system allows managers to download the shipment and EDI order data to individual personal computers. Because the main data files are stored in a standard database format, the data can be loaded into spreadsheets for estimation and graphing.

### QUESTIONS

1. How many networks are in use at Magna International? Describe them. Are they client/server, peer-to-peer, or somewhere in between?
2. What network features are provided by Magna's system?
3. Describe the flow of data at Magna International. Draw a data flow diagram.
4. What objects are transferred on the networks? From an object-oriented design perspective, describe the object attributes, functions, and the relationships among the objects.
5. What decision levels are involved in this case at Magna International?
6. What compatibility problems have to be overcome for this system to work?
7. How does the time factor complicate the network issues in this case?
8. How does Magna's system provide a strategic advantage? How does it affect competitors or firms that might want to enter the industry?

### CASE   *Brewers Retail Inc.*

In Ontario, Canada, a six-pack or case of beer can only be purchased at the local beer store operated by Brewers Retail Inc. (BRI). BRI is regulated by the Liquor Control Board of Ontario and the Liquor Licensing Board of Ontario. Until 1994, it was not difficult to operate the local stores, in large part because BRI was only allowed to sell beers that were produced in Ontario. Even beer manufacturers (such as LaBatt's and Molson) were required to have at least one factory in Ontario. This restriction limited the number of brands of beer carried by BRI, which made it easier to determine inventory levels and distribution schedules.

BRI had a batch-oriented computer system to record orders and shipments. Basic statements were produced monthly, with some weekly data available on paper reports.

Everything changed in 1994, when the North American Free Tree Agreement took effect. The Ontario government was forced to change its distribution policy and allow BRI to stock any product from North America. Suddenly BRI was faced with a much more challenging problem. Pompi Malik, the systems development manager, notes that

> The influx of new beers and related merchandise hasn't changed inventory size, but the number of different brands has risen considerably. This requires managing a much more complex inventory distribution—we now have to replenish dozens of different products in places where we previously had to restock only a few.

Unfortunately, the batch system with monthly reports did not produce timely information, and managers could not track changes fast enough to react to them. They ran the risk of having too much of one brand and watching it go stale, whereas customers complained about being out-of-stock of their favorite brand. BRI has additional complications because of the involvement of the government regulatory boards. BRI needs to communicate with these boards on a daily basis.

BRI replaced the mainframe computer system with a network of personal and minicomputers. The new inventory and ordering system was based on the Sybase relational database management system. The goal is to provide a system running on a network that connects the retail stores to the warehouses by a TCP/IP-based network. TCP/IP is one of the fundamental standards of the Internet. One of the major applications is the Store Balance System, which retrieves data each night from the outlet stores. It uses the data to record the financial books for the stores and to track systemwide beer sales. Gene Kotak, the IS director, observes

> In place of weekly balance reports, we now have daily, online transactional information that gives us an accurate, up-to-date picture of our ongoing operations. We've completely eliminated our old-style batch processing and the frustrating delays associated with it. Now we can continually stay on top of sales performance and make adjustments quickly whenever necessary.

The eventual system will run on personal computers, with the SQL-based relational database running on Sun Sparc Station servers.

## QUESTIONS

1. What advantages does BRI gain by using an SQL database system to build the new information system?
2. What role does the network play in BRI's new system? What data will be transferred?
3. Would BRI have gained the same advantages if the company had simply installed the SQL DBMS and not created the network?
4. What type of computer connections are made to the retail outlets? What advantages could be gained with a continuous online link? How much more would it cost?
5. What systems problems caused BRI to create the new network?
6. If you were a manager at BRI, what information would you want to have available on the network? What additional tools would you want?
7. What other network connections might be worthwhile? What complications might you run into when trying to expand the network?
8. Are there any unique features to this problem due to the fact that BRI is located in Canada? If you were director of IS at BRI, could you have purchased a system from the United States (or Britain or . . .) to handle the inventory problems?

## CASE *Rugby Darby Group Companies Inc.*

Rugby Darby is one of the largest suppliers of generic drugs, medical, dental, and veterinary products in the United States. Faced with increased competition and declining profits, the supplier chose to re-engineer its operations. Formed as a pharmaceuticals distributor in the mid-1940s, Rugby Darby had expanded distribution and manufacturing over the years. The privately held firm based in Rockville Centre, New York, has sales of $600 million. On the strength of its generic drug manufacturing and distribution, one of every four prescriptions in the United States is either manufactured or distributed by Rugby Darby.

In 1991, Rugby Darby was facing a difficult future as competition drove down prices and decreased profits. CEO Michael Ashkin ordered managers to find ways to cut costs. Neil Perlman, senior vice-president of information, was in charge of finding ways to use technology to decrease costs: "Our CEO knew that it was through technology that we could achieve real cost savings. In effect, he told us, he was betting the company on us."

In response, the IS department formed a virtual SWAT team that toured Darby's operations around the country, looking for problems, inefficiencies, and areas where service could be improved. Pete Bavoso, director of network services sent the SWAT team to look at everything from warehouse functions, to back-office automation, to field sales work, to pure administrative tasks. He flew people all over the country to examine Darby's computer operations.

## Returns

Some of the biggest problems the team found were in the "returns" division. Returns in pharmaceuticals are much more complex than in other industries, such as clothing. For example, because they are controlled substances, drugs can only be shipped to certain people, and opened packages cannot be resold. Yet, because of common practice, Darby is essentially required to accept returns from any customer for any reason.

Returns are further complicated by the fact that the drugs are often sold at different prices. Seasonal promotions, bulk discounts and closeout sales all affect the price paid for the products. The problem with returns was that Darby did not know what price was paid for the product—especially because invoices and pricing records were mostly paper-based and hard to search. Perlman notes that

> It wasn't uncommon for a product to sit on the shelf for three years until out of date, and then be returned to us. We wouldn't know what we sold it for. In many cases, we were giving more money back than we'd been paid in the first place. This was a nightmare.

The process was further complicated by the involvement of the government. Even if the product is unopened and not outdated, additional criteria have to be met before it can be resold. Darby needed to identify the factory that produced it, when it was produced, and the batch number. Unfortunately, many products came back without the code number, and sometimes even without the full product name. To cope with these issues, Darby maintained a department of 20 employees to handle returns.

## Computer System

In 1991, when Darby began the analysis, the company data was handled by AT&T minicomputers in the 14 remote facilities and an IBM 3090 mainframe at headquarters. The two systems were basically incompatible, and AT&T was no longer supporting the out-of-date minicomputers. There were few personal computers and no local area networks. Standard applications consisted of order entry, sales automation, and accounting.

In solving the problem with the returns, Perlman decided to shift all of the sales and order-entry operations to a relational database running on a network of high-end personal computers. A Novell network was installed with 40 servers running the then-new Microsoft Windows NT operating system. By 1993, Darby had installed almost 1,000 486-based personal computers on the network. The individual LANs were interconnected over leased digital phone lines. The IS department knew it took a risk by using the earliest version of the Windows NT operating system. Yet programmers had experimented with other products for PC-based servers and found the database management systems could not handle their data load.

The new system tracks pricing and product numbers for every order. It enables workers to look up production numbers for every item returned. By eliminating 15 workers from the returns department, the system saved more than $250,000 in salary and benefits. The company also saved $300,000 in annual maintenance costs for the AT&T machines. More importantly, mistakes from re-entering data have disappeared. The backlog in the returns department was reduced from three weeks to one day. Customers receive credit for returns immediately, instead of weeks later.

Rugby Darby is now planning to replace the IBM mainframe. Currently the personal computers are also used as terminals to the accounting system. Darby also runs a mailorder business, offering pharmaceuticals direct to customers. The objective is to move the ordering and accounting system to the LAN.

## QUESTIONS

1. What are the major benefits of the new system?
2. Why is the network important to this system? What data is transferred across the network?
3. What risks did Darby face by choosing Windows NT at that time—before it was officially released by Microsoft?
4. What complications is Rugby Darby likely to encounter if the company removes the IBM mainframe and moves all the applications to the new network?
5. Why was a relational database system important to solving Darby's problems?
6. Does it matter what transmission medium Darby uses for the network? Hint: How much data is transferred?

## CASE *The Republic of Tea*

The three founders of this Marin County, California, tea company had a yen for Zen—so much so that they wrote a book *(The Republic of Tea)* extolling the virtues of Tea Mind, a state of consciousness that cofounder and CEO Bill Rosenzweig describes as "attentive tranquillity." Computers, thought Rosenzweig, would help make Tea Mind possible, since they would handle the mundane and repetitive aspects of shipping, billing, inventory, and accounting, leaving employees free to think deep, leafy thoughts. Ray Charles said it eloquently: Uh huh.

Rosenzweig began with Macs, which he saw as the path of least resistance. What Apple says about the Mac is true: It's the only computer you can take straight out of its box and connect to another computer (as long as it's another Mac) using nothing more than phone cord. Theoretically, this saves your having to deal with different vendors and consultants. The network you get is fine for an office with a small number of users. Republic of Tea, originally, had three.

The number grew. After business opened in January 1992, orders took off, and the company quickly added people. As users joined the network, processing times slowed. Workers' frustration boiled over. Time that might better have been spent dreaming up new tea flavors (hmmm . . . wool? mackerel?) was wasted waiting, waiting, *waiting* for the network to do its stuff. Just posting a cash receipt could entail a three-minute wait.

Consultants came, stroked their chins, and announced that if speed were to be increased, Rosenzweig should buy a new, non-Apple wiring system, special modular software, and a souped-up processor to drive the network. After the software had been purchased, Rosenzweig and his consultants discovered that the module for tracking shipping wouldn't run on the Macs. Why? Apple blamed the software; the software writers blamed the consultants, who had modified it; the consultants said the software's whole selling point was that it *could* be modified.

With 700 accounts to ship to, the Republic couldn't take time to sort this out. "The last thing I wanted to do," says Rosenzweig, "was screw up deliveries." So to run the shipping software, he bought a separate computer, which runs outside the network.

Today Rosenzweig is stuck with a hodgepodge of products from a variety of vendors that requires round-the-clock tweaking. A company with 15 full-time employees has three different consultants for its accounting software alone. When a power failure sent the network crashing in April, the Republic discovered it had become so dependent on outsiders that nobody on staff knew how to get the system up again.

Rosenzweig is tranquil, but not happy. He isn't happy with his software. He isn't happy with his hardware. He isn't happy with consultants' fees. Is there anything he *is* happy with? Yes. A Southall & Smith Ltd. tea-packing machine: a glass-and-metal throwback to 19th-century technology that uses levers, gears, and brass weights to put tea in canisters. It's an old machine, but reliable. Rosenzweig prizes one attribute the most: "It's not connected to anything else."

SOURCE: Farnham, Alan, "Want a Network? Read This," *Fortune,* June 14, 1993, pp. 76, 80.

## QUESTIONS

1. What problems did Rosenzweig have with the network? What is the cause of the problems? Could they have been avoided? Is the network the main source of the problems?
2. Now that the system is in place, if Republic of Tea continues to grow, what do you think will happen to the computer systems? Will Rosenzweig be able to get the information he needs to run the company?
3. Using current network, hardware and software technology, design a new system for Republic of Tea. How much money would it cost to build it from scratch? Will it be able to handle future expansions?
4. What additional problems would be encountered if Republic of Tea wished to build a completely new system?
5. Why do you think the original network was so slow? Why do you think the staff had so many problems with the accounting software?

## CASE  *Bell Atlantic and TCI*

In the fall of 1993, *Bell Atlantic,* one of the regional telephone companies, tentatively agreed to buy TCI (Tele-Communications Inc.) for approximately $32 billion in a deal based on a stock swap and debt assumption. Also in 1993, the number-two cable operator in the United States (Time Warner) formed a $2.5 billion strategic alliance with U.S. West, another regional phone company.

Bell Atlantic gains access to the installed cable system of the largest cable company in the United States with 10.2 million subscribers. It also gains some control over the programming or items that are carried over cable. TCI had a financial interest in CNN and TBS. It also had a subsidiary known as Liberty Media Corp. that created its own programming—mostly broadcasts of regional sporting events.

Why would TCI agree to the deal? Although they had revenue of $3.9 billion in 1992–1993, TCI had minimal profits ($63 million) and a $10 billion debt. Additionally, future earnings were potentially limited by the 1992 Cable Television Consumer Protection and Competition Act, which reestablished regulation of cable rates. Also, as indicated by the fact that five other major cable companies have signed agreements with telephone companies, the cable companies were not sure they could compete head-to-head against the phone companies. Cable companies have the ability to deliver a great deal of information to households over coaxial cable instead of twisted-pair wiring. However, their networks were built to handle information flowing in only one direction. They had limited capabilities to control who received the various signals and no means for subscribers to send information back to the cable company. More importantly, there was no way for cable subscribers to treat the cable systems as a phone—to send information directly to other subscribers. The phone company networks are based on switches that are designed to provide individual services to and from each customer.

Why would Bell Atlantic want to buy TCI? With $1.5 billion earnings on revenues of $12.9 billion, it does not appear that the phone company needs to burden itself with a cable television company costing $32 billion. On the other hand, experts estimate that it would have cost Bell Atlantic around $23 billion and several years to duplicate the cable infrastructure they acquired from TCI.

Beneath all of these mergers and alliances lies a fundamental change in technology: the ability to transmit television signals in digital form. Partly from sponsorship of the U.S. government, companies have been working on high-definition television (HDTV) signals that are higher quality and transmit in digital form. Digital transmission provides clearer pictures *and* allows the signals to be compressed so they require less bandwidth. In other words, instead of the 35–50 channels available on older analog cable television lines, it would be possible to transmit several hundred different channels at the same time. Similarly, it would be possible to transmit a limited number of channels over the phone company's twisted-pair networks.

Because almost no one really needs to have 500 channels delivered to their house at one time, most companies have been working on methods to enable customers to choose which programs they want to receive. In other words, the companies are working on creating an interactive network that is based on bi-directional communication. That's where the capabilities of the phone company switches becomes useful.

There is also competition from another source. In 1993–1994 Hughes Aircraft launched a set of new satellites. These satellites can beam a strong television signal to most households in North America. The signals are so strong that consumers can receive them with a small 18-inch diameter antenna. The signals are also digital and the satellites can broadcast up to 150 channels at the same time. By including a phone line to the television decoder, Hughes can sell individual movies and sports events on a pay-per-view basis. With 150 channels, consumers have a reasonably large number of choices. Although the satellite broadcasts do not require the installation of millions of miles of cable, the ability to interact with customers is limited. A complete alliance between the phone and cable systems could theoretically provide more capabilities. Yet, by themselves, neither the phone company nor the cable companies could provide the same level of service.

The merger of phone and cable companies also offers the ability to provide entirely new services to businesses and households. For example, interactive television could become a reality, enabling consumers to alter movies and participate in nationwide discussions through their "television communication devices." The provision of faster data transfer services would make it easier for companies to connect LANs and transfer data using the public networks. Potentially, everything from banking services to health care to education could be provided and altered through the use of interactive television communication. Of course, the success and acceptance of these services will depend to a large extent on their cost to the consumer. Along the way, there are many questions that remain to be answered.

The merger was called off within two months of the original announcement. One of the reasons given was because the drop in stock value made the original deal too expensive for Bell Atlantic. However, stock prices typically respond to investor sentiments, implying that many investors decided the merger was of limited value. Other mergers between cable companies have also fallen through for similar reasons.

## QUESTIONS

1. As a consumer, what services would you like to see provided by a cable/phone company? How much are you willing to pay for these services?
2. In business, how could your company use these new services? Hint: Consider internal use, connections to customers, and ties to suppliers.
3. What about customers who cannot afford access to these services? Should everyone be guaranteed access to the new cable/phone system? Who will pay for it?
4. What changes do you think these new services will have on society? Will it change the way we work? Our entertainment or recreation? How will it affect education? Will it change or influence government of cities, states and the nation?
5. In terms of international access, what will happen if one country (the United States) is altered by this new communication network? What happens to people in other nations who do not have access to this technology? Is such a situation likely? Should the United States provide money

and patent information to other nations to give them access to the technology and to the resulting systems?

6.  If cable companies and phone companies do *not* merge, how will customers get access to the "information highway?"

## CASE    *The Internet and National Political Parties*

The Clinton Administration became the first to set up databases and bulletin boards on the Internet. This makes the daily news briefings and press releases available across the country to the academic community and to all others who access the Internet through any number of publicly available online services. This also expedites the distribution of unedited presidential speeches, statements, and interviews to home computers. You can even send a message to the U.S. president at his own Internet address.

| | |
|---|---|
| CompuServe: | Address for the White House: 75300,3115 |
| | *Go Whitehouse* connects to a large library of official White House documents. |
| | *Go Whitehouse* connects to bulletin board discussions and online debates about presidential policies. |
| America Online: | Address for the White House: Clintonpz |
| | *Whitehouse* connects to the library and bulletin boards. |
| MCI Mail: | Address for the White House: White House |
| | *View White House* for the library of documents |
| Internet: | 75300.3115@CompuServe.com |
| | Clintonpz@AOL.com |
| | President@WhiteHouse.gov |

To subscribe to electronic deliveries of White House documents, send a message to the Internet Address:

Clinton-Info@Campaign96.Org

Help is the subject of the message.

To access an online database of recent presidential documents, at the University of North Carolina,

telnet sunsite.unc.edu, log in under politics.

Many other bulletin boards are also available:

| | |
|---|---|
| CompuServe: | Go Politics |
| | Republican Party |
| | Ross Perot United We Stand Party |
| | Rush Limbaugh Talkshow |
| America Online: | Go Issues Republican Party |
| | Ross Perot United We Stand Party |

White House sources indicate that President Clinton is not a routine computer user and does not personally receive the online messages and comments. The White House does not receive the messages directly into its computer system. They are delivered to the White House on disk, are printed out, and then are answered by workers through regular paper U.S. Mail ("snail mail"). It should also be noted that the presidential staff does not regularly read the bulletin boards or participate in them.

### QUESTIONS

1.  If someone using an online bulletin board makes insulting remarks about your favorite politician, should that BBS user be censored? What if the BBS user uses "foul" language? What if the BBS user makes a false accusation about someone else? What if he or she threatens someone?

2.  Someone insults a political figure using an online system. Several hundred people retaliate by "e-mail bombing" the writer—flooding the user's mailbox with thousands of messages. What actions or rules, if any, should be taken by the online providers or governmental agencies?

3.  Some services offer users anonymity when posting messages. With the Internet, some "remailers" generate anonymous (fake) return addresses that cannot be traced. Sometimes anonymous writers make derogatory comments (e.g., racist, sexist, and accusatory: for example, one student was anonymously and publicly accused of rape). Should services permit anonymous comments? Should the services be held responsible for monitoring their bulletin boards?

4.  *America Online (AOL)* is a service provider that gives users the ability to make anonymous comments. In early 1995, it was announced that sometimes the anonymity feature did not work properly and writers true names and addresses were available to other users. Should there be rules, laws, penalties, or ethical responsibilities to prevent or punish these problems?

## CASE *Using the Information Highway to Access the Mayo Clinic*

### Consumer Medical Information

The *Mayo Clinic Family Health Book* is available in both a CD-ROM and hard-copy version. The CD-ROM version has sold more than 650,000 copies; the hard-copy version 550,000 copies.

Following up on this success, the Mayo Clinic has announced a new licensing agreement with IVI Publishing, Inc. Future plans include products and services for online networks and cable television. One plan is for a program where consumers can correspond online with Mayo clinic doctors.

Mayo and IVI plan to develop a digital library of Mayo-produced medical information. The first target is the consumer market. This library would include text of the clinic's consumer publications, medical images, and videos. A secondary market is the textbook market. A new CD-ROM named AnnaTommy, developed by anatomists and physiologists, teaches children about the body. The third market is continuing education for physicians. A new series of CD-ROMs helps primary care physicians keep up with specialty areas and meet continuing education requirements. This is particularly important because managed care is causing the primary physician to deal with more complex problems that previously might have been referred to specialists.

On the East Coast, Johns Hopkins University School of Medicine is pursuing business partnerships to develop and distribute health information through several multimedia channels. The Cleveland Clinic and Stanford University are also exploring such arrangements.

These high-profile medical centers are particularly interested in these new methods of disseminating information and identifying new sources of revenue. Efforts to contain health care costs and move to managed care have made purchasers less willing to pay the premium for medical research and education charged by research institutions.

Rodney Friedman, of Rebus, Inc., views the information highway as an important addition to the distribution of health information. The system provides a way to enable people to tailor the information that they want so they can access it at any level. Rebus publishes health newsletters for Johns Hopkins and the University of California at Berkeley.

### Online Medical Diagnoses

Primary care physicians are increasingly using online services to get ideas on tough medical cases, select tests and treatments, and stay up-to-date with medical advancements.

Medline is the most popular online service for physicians. It is a database of more than 3,700 medical journals maintained and updated by the National Library of Medicine.

The benefits of online searching have been reported in the *Journal of the American Medical Association.* In a study based on more than 450 Medline searches, physicians reported that the service proved effective in helping save lives and cure illness. In a study published in *Academic Medicine,* timely Medline searches were associated with lower costs and shorter hospital stays.

Most physicians are not using online services, however. Even the most liberal estimates show that only 20 percent of physicians are online. This number is increasing because of the increased availability of the Internet, improvements in software, and computer-savvy patients. Because patients can access the same medical databases themselves, they can influence their own care. Other factors are demand for accountability in the delivery of care and the difficulty of keeping up with the volume of research. Previously, searches would have to be done by specially trained librarians. It would take several days to get the results of the search printed and returned to the doctor.

Online services are especially important for physicians located in rural areas. Although medical textbooks are usually two years behind the latest research, online searches can provide up-to-date information on drugs and illnesses.

### QUESTIONS

1. What are the advantages and drawbacks of CD-ROM compared to paper for the distribution of medical information to consumers?
2. What are the advantages and disadvantages of online distribution of consumer medical information compared to use of a CD-ROM?
3. What advantages are offered by Medline and other services that provide online medical information to physicians?
4. Why might physicians *not* use online medical services? As a consumer, would you pay a higher fee to deal with a physician who routinely uses online services? Should medical personnel be "forced" to use online services? For example, if a physician did not use an online service, should it be easier to sue him or her for malpractice?

## CASE *The Internet Becomes Important Tool in Customer Service*

Dell Computer Corporation has committed seven individuals to regularly surf the Internet and user groups on CompuServe, America Online, and Prodigy to get a feel for consumer reaction to Dell's products. The company has found that monitoring the Internet is a way to reduce the long-distance costs of customer support lines. It also uses the online service to test reaction to corporate changes, finding the information-gathering process on the Net to be cheaper than hiring a market research firm. Dell has found that computer users are more direct on the online services than they are on the telephone. The presumed anonymity of the computer provides the computer manufacturer with more honest feedback and reactions to products and changes.

Dell and Compaq have also confessed that they use the Internet to catch up on issues facing other manufacturers. These include discussions of bugs, product delays, and new products and marketing ideas.

Microsoft, IBM, and Apple have also added home pages on the Internet's World Wide Web. The World Wide Web enables customers to browse, select, and download large amounts of product information. These companies have found this to be a cheaper and more cost-effective way to disseminate product information.

Coors is using a Web home page to provide information to browsers on the Internet. They found that by providing entertaining offerings like games, puzzles and graphics, they can attract thousands of users. By featuring their products in the games and displays, they can promote their products without being subject to traditional restraints imposed on television and print advertising.

An interesting case arose in Memphis, Tennessee, in 1994, when a California company was found guilty of violating local (Memphis) obscenity standards. A person in Memphis, using his own computer, called a computer in California. Paying by credit card, he purchased and downloaded "pornographic" figures from the computer. He then filed a complaint against the California company. A jury determined that the images were "obscene" by local standards and imposed fines and jail terms for the managers of the California database.

## QUESTIONS

1. What are the advantages and disadvantages of using the Internet for customer feedback? Hint: What do you know from statistics and marketing about "representative samples"?
2. As a consumer, what are the advantages and disadvantages of using an online service to contact vendors?
3. You are using the Internet to answer customer questions. You find that a competitor is paying employees to flood your BBS with complaints and problem claims. Is this action ethical? Knowing that many of the postings are anonymous, what

action can you take against the competitor? What could you do to prevent future problems?

4. Should Internet sites be subject to the same constraints as print, television, and video advertising? (For example, television ads for alcohol cannot show a person consuming the product.) Could such restrictions be monitored?
5. What complications are created by international companies? A global company could establish a Web site overseas and claim that it is not subject to U.S. laws. Should the U.S. laws apply to anyone in the United States who receives data, or to the providers of the data? Would U.S. companies be at a disadvantage if the United States passed restrictive laws?
6. U.S. Supreme Court rulings specify that localities must define their own standards in terms of obscenity. As the Memphis/California case illustrates, which local standards should be applied? Similarly, assume your company operates a computer Web site that you use to collect comments from customers. An anonymous "customer" places a graphic image on your machine. Someone from Memphis downloads that image and arrests you and your CEO on obscenity charges. Are you "guilty"? What responsibilities should be placed on information providers?

## CASE *Museums: Integrated Systems for Art Collection*

### An Art Network

The New York Metropolitan Museum of Art is building a new network infrastructure named the MetNet. The new system is being constructed to better track the museum's art objects. It is designed to consolidate the museum's financial operations and closely integrate its curatorial, merchandising, and registration activities.

The end goal of MetNet is to make art images and graphics available to nearly 2,000 desktops. Employees will be able to gather up-to-date relational data from a number of sources. This improvement will help employees make educated decisions regarding merchandising, exhibits, membership drives, and endowments.

Under the direction of Arthur Tisi, chief systems officer at the museum, the network development team faces the challenge of integrating 20 contiguous buildings in Manhattan, several sites in other parts of the city, and 20 retail locations across the country. The project is made more difficult by the fact that connections between the sites are not the same. Some are connected by dial-up lines; others through individual LANs; and still others are part of a separate mainframe-based system. Information systems officials describe the current network as a mishmash of disparate, incompatible systems that cannot be managed.

When completed, MetNet will be based upon a System 5000 network hub from Bay Networks, Inc. This hub will connect over 40 Microsoft Windows NT and Novell NetWare servers in 20 buildings. Internally, the museum is being rewired with fiber optic cable. T1 links will connect the remote sites with the central hub.

The hubs and routers will be managed by Bay Network's Optivity, a network management protocol based application. The software distribution and inventory management of the desktops will be managed by the Systems Management Server. Central management will further reduce maintenance chores and costs.

From a financial standpoint, the museum is testing server-based software in an effort to consolidate the financial applications and replace the mainframe-based system. Ultimately, the museum hopes to establish a relational database that will consolidate the four primary operations of the museum: financial, curatorial, registration, and merchandising.

The new model will increase the ability of separate departments within the museum to work together. This will enable the 19 curatorial departments to exchange information with merchandising, retail operations, and endowments areas. Other potential applications include a desktop imaging and a collection management program to track art objects. Internet is also being explored as a way to expand the audience for these art objects once they have been collected.

### Information Systems at the Guggenheim Museum

To facilitate the exchange of information among individuals and departments, the Guggenheim Museum has installed WordPerfect's GroupWise e-mail system. For outside connections, they have used CompuServe rather than the Internet. Internally, they chose Novell's NetWare Global Messaging server and WordPerfect's Message Handling Service Gateway to provide the connection to CompuServe. The project was initiated to improve communications between its uptown and downtown sites.

Before the installation of GroupWise, staff persons at the Guggenheim used Cubix Corporation modems and Symantec Corporation's PC Anywhere to transfer files. Staff members deposited files on the LAN using file transfer and copying functions. Then they telephoned colleagues to alert them to a file on the LAN.

The installation of GroupWise was less than smooth. Some of the problems encountered were:

- A large number of pieces of technology need to be put in place for a sophisticated enterprise e-mail system like GroupWise to become operational.
- Inherently, GroupWise has installation difficulties.

Another aspect of the Guggenheim Museum's movement toward technology is its multimedia virtual reality exhibit, using personal computers loaded with add-ons and peripherals. Because the museum did not use a DMI-like standard, the result was, in the employees' words, a management nightmare. Often, the Guggenheim was forced to use the reboot-and-pray method of PC troubleshooting.

### QUESTIONS

1. What unique problems do museums face when they build information systems and networks?
2. What problems were likely to have been experienced by the Guggenheim staff prior to the installation of the network?
3. What complications does the Met face by having such diverse networks? What are the curators' options for improving the network?
4. What advantages does the Met gain by consolidating its four main activities?
5. With a network of 2,000 desktops, what network management problems are likely to arise? How can they be handled cost effectively when people are scattered across 20 buildings?

### CASE *Chicago's New 911 System*

Chicago has implemented a new, state-of-the-art police Emergency Communications Center Network. Costing more than $215 million dollars, the system enables dispatchers to quickly transmit detailed historical and event data to police officers responding to emergencies and crimes in progress. This provides police officers with much more information about a situation before they must confront it. The new network also links firefighters and emergency medical service technicians to help them respond to emergencies.

The system promises that 99 percent of all calls to Chicago's 911 emergency number will be answered within one or two rings—most in 1.2 seconds. Under the previous manual system, only 60 percent of the 911 calls were answered within two rings. Calls took an average of three times as long to be processed.

From a technological standpoint, the secure communications network will use 155 Mbps and 655 Mbps Synchronous Optical Network (Sonet) backbones. This is the standard for high-speed data transmission over fiber optic cable. The link between the emergency dispatchers and the administrative personnel are 185

Ascom-Timeplex routers from Digital Equipment Corporation. Unix-based workstations and a Microsoft Windows NT server version 3.51 connects 215 firehouses, police stations, and public safety facilities. The Microsoft server was chosen for its ability to handle large Oracle databases.

The hub for the network's 176 miles of fiber optic cable is the Madison Avenue 911 emergency headquarters. The Ascon-Timeplex routers link more than a hundred 911 emergency dispatchers, 13,000 police officers, and 4,500 firefighters throughout the city on T1 lines. The Ascon-Timeplex routers provide speed and redundancy. They also are able to integrate a wide variety of disparate network protocols. The devices also use Express Routing software. This enables the emergency network to prioritize the various data traversing the network to deliver maximum bandwidth with the least amount of overhead.

The 108 dispatchers use Digital Unix computer-aided dispatch workstations to access electronic databases containing detailed maps of city streets and buildings.

The procedure is as follows:

1. Telephone calls to the 911 Emergency Communications Center are routed through the 176-mile, city-owned fiber optic Integrated Services Digital Network. Callers are connected in less than 1.2 seconds to one of 108 emergency 911 dispatchers.

2. Telephone calls are logged and answered. The caller's name and address are displayed on a Digital Unix-based workstation. The 911 operator verifies the information and transfers the call to the police or fire dispatcher.

3. The 911 dispatcher accesses the Oracle database to call up detailed graphic maps of any street and building in Chicago. The maps give dispatchers instant access to exact street locations, the best routes to get there, and detailed building descriptions. These include entrances, closest cross streets, nearest fire hydrant, owner's name, and whether hazardous materials are stored on the property.

4. Domestic disturbance records indicate previous criminal records. Separate computer screens display telephone numbers and addresses of municipal and governmental agencies. Touching the screen will dial the selected agency.

5. Information is transmitted through the routers and backbone to computer terminals in squad cars and fire engines and hand-held devices carried by officers, firefighters, and other personnel.

## QUESTIONS

1. What information is provided by the new 911 system?
2. How does the information help police and emergency officers? How does it help citizens?
3. Diagram the network. Identify the communication links and how data is transferred among the different workers.
4. Beyond transaction processing, how can the data be used to make better decisions by the police and emergency teams?
5. What potential security problems exist with the network? What data will need to be protected? What weaknesses or threats face the system?

## CASE *Technology and the Presidential Elections*

Bill Clinton and Al Gore will unmistakably be noted in history as the first president and vice-president to use the Internet for campaign purposes. From the early days of the 1992 campaign, they enlisted Internet experts from MIT to establish home pages and automatic mailing functions from the computers there. Press releases, news items, legislation, and regulation were regularly distributed through e-mail on the Internet.

Linkage between the use of the Internet and the Clinton/Gore win in the election is difficult. What this use did do, however, was to clearly align Clinton and Gore with the image of a younger generation that was ready to capture and use information technology. This approach was compared in the media to that of George Bush, who was just learning to use a computer that had been installed in a White House closet.

The enthusiasm for the Internet and e-mail in political campaigns has expanded exponentially in the 1996 presidential race. Five presidential campaigns and the Clinton White House had Internet home pages. These pages carried carefully scripted information about their candidate's positions and backgrounds.

Texas Senator Phil Gramm boasted of the most successful Internet page. It was opened 150,000 times. This follows Gramm's substantial investment in computer equipment from his campaign funds. After opening Gramm's home page on the Internet, a user was asked whether he or she would like to sign up to help in the campaign. A positive response was immediately transmitted to local coordinators.

Presidential hopefuls Patrick Buchanan, Richard Lugar, and Arlen Spector also had home pages.

Senator Robert Dole's campaign adopted the fax as its communications mechanism. It regularly and automatically transmitted "blast-faxes" to more than 800 radio talk-show hosts. The campaign staff could target specific faxes to anyone on a segmented list of names and numbers for more than 150,000 reporters, commentators, and supporters. These groups were further classified by geographic area and issue interest.

California Governor Pete Wilson focused on television advertisements. His ads were tailored for precise market niches.

Candidates were not the only ones opening Internet sites and Web pages. "Unofficial" Internet sites were often run by candidate's supporters who may or may not be sanctioned by the candidate him/herself.

According to Mandy Grunwald, a consultant to President Clinton during his 1992 campaign, the explosion of information outlets has made getting a message through the clutter even more difficult. To get their messages across, campaigns will have to be "repetitive" without being "boring" in their efforts to use a broad spectrum of potential communication techniques.

The 1996 campaign has been likened to both an air and ground war. The air war, or blanket approach, consisted of print and broadcast news and advertising outlets, with large amounts of television advertising. The ground war included high-tech approaches that identify narrow slices of the public. This is where the Internet and focused television cable channels came into play. The proliferation of outlets meant that most Americans received their election information unfiltered. They were be able to choose among the newsclips of the evening network news, the commentary of public television, or the gavel-to-gavel coverage of C-span.

Following the theme of air wars, Mark Merritt, director of communication for the Alexander campaign, called the elections "narrowcasting rather than broadcasting." This meant that the distribution of the messages were focused on specific target market segments, including specific states and areas within a state. Any campaign, using a desktop computer and a toll-free telephone number, could make audio and picture versions of campaign reports available to television and radio stations across the country.

According to David Bienstock, director of broadcast time for the Wilson campaign, it has become even more important to research the size and shape of the viewing audience. Bienstock feels that the election for president was essentially a local one with 300 local elections rather than one large one.

## QUESTIONS

1. How does the Internet combine the capabilities of networks and databases?
2. Describe the basic communication methods available to political candidates and the target audiences that can be reached with each method.
3. How do networks and communication affect "democracy"? Hint: Research the role of fax machines in the political transformation of the former Soviet Union.

## DISCUSSION ISSUE

### *International Data Flows*

Operating in an international environment adds several complications to MIS. Technical difficulties include problems created by differing standards and complications that arise because of transferring data over long distances. However, cultural differences and different legal environments can cause even more problems. Techniques such as marketing systems and inventory methods that work well in the United States will usually have to be changed to support the variations in other nations. Listen to the head of marketing (Toni) discuss strategy with one of her department managers (Millie) and Dobbs, the MIS manager assigned to the project.

Millie:  The way I see it, we should set one marketing plan and use it across all the markets. Besides cutting costs, I don't think there's much difference between the markets anyway.

Dobbs:  Oh come on, Millie. We'll have to translate all of the promos and the packaging anyway. I don't see where it'll cut costs.

Millie:  Well, Dobbs, for starters, it'll cut down on the number of meetings we need. More importantly, a single focus cuts down on the production diversity. For example, if we choose to focus on quality in all markets, we can limit the number of options and colors and concentrate on the base set. Plus, it'll simplify the data we need. By collecting the same data from each market, it will be easier to collect data and to perform the marketing analyses.

Toni:  Speaking of marketing data, could we get back on track? We need to identify the data you want to collect. For starters, we'll need to set up focus groups in each major city. Then track initial sales by store, along with our competition. To select initial markets, we'll also need to get geographic-based consumer data such as incomes, spending, and population by region.

Dobbs:   Whoa. Slow down. Sure, that's the way we've worked in the United States, but I think we're going to have trouble in Europe.

Millie:  How so? I don't see where it'll be much different. Overall income distributions and basic economic indicators are about the same.

Dobbs:   I'm not worried about the marketing differences right now—just the data collection. For example, France has limits on what data we're allowed to transfer out. Legally, we should set up a separate database facility in France, and we might need another one in Germany.

Millie:  So where's the problem, Dobbs? We'll have offices in each country anyway. Because we use PCs in every office, we'll just set up the local data in each office. You can build a communication network, right? Then we just transfer everything back here and do what we want.

Dobbs:   Sure, from a technology standpoint, we can do that. But what I'm trying to say is that we're not supposed to do it that way. France says we're not supposed to export this data.

Toni:    Well, I don't see how we can work that way. At some point, the managers in the United States are going to need to look at that data. What are we supposed to do? Fly to Paris every time we have a marketing decision?

Millie:  Those rules sound crazy. Does anyone actually obey them? Maybe we should just set it up the way we want. What can they do to us anyway?

Toni:    Dobbs, isn't there some way we can transfer the data without the government knowing about it? I mean, we're going to be sending tons of data back and forth. I can't believe they can monitor all of it.

Dobbs:   I don't know much about their laws yet. I just know the French government doesn't want us to transfer the data. I suppose we could think about using a coding scheme so no one can tell what we're sending. We do

have to be careful though. France also has pretty strict rules about private companies not being allowed to encrypt data. Still, you're right about the amount of data. I imagine my staff could cook up something that'll work. But I'm not sure we should work this way, Toni.

Millie:  Look, Dobbs, what's the worst that can happen? If they complain, we'll just apologize and tell them that we'll do it their way. It's not like we're stealing anything. We still pay lots of money to collect the data and organize it. How can anyone care about where we store it? Toni, it'll make it a lot easier to handle the marketing end. We can't afford to run each nation separately. The combined data will let us make decisions faster and cut our costs. Plus, it'll give you more control over the day-to-day decisions.

Toni:    Well, that's true. No matter who I send to head these departments, I'll still need to check the data and verify their decisions. If I had to travel to each agency, I'd spend all my time in airports. I don't see where we have much choice. Dobbs, check into it a little more, then come back with some options for us. We want to be careful, but we've got a right to use that data.

Dobbs:   All right, it's a little risky, but I think we can do it. Just don't tell everyone about how we're going to be transferring the data. We'll set it up to look like the data is staying in France. We can use the backup data. We'll keep the transmission time as short as possible. Once we get the data in the United States, if anyone asks, we'll just say we got it from somewhere else.

## QUESTIONS

1. Do you agree with the group's decision?
2. Is there any other way for the marketing department to operate the way they want, but still leave the data in France? What are the trade-offs?
3. If you work for the marketing department or the MIS department and you are asked to help set up this new system, what would (or could) you do?
4. What is the probability the company will be caught?
5. Do you think nations should be allowed to set up laws that restrict the transfer of data? What are the advantages and disadvantages to the country?

# APPENDIX

# *Technical Definitions*

## INTRODUCTION

In many ways, computer networks and telecommunications are highly technical fields. They are also rapidly changing fields, with new products being introduced daily. As a result, the industry has created its own terminology. Of course, the terminology changes as fast as the industry, so no description can ever be up-to-date. Nonetheless, managers might find it useful to be familiar with some of the basic technology.

There are also a few standard products available for computer networks. Although the capabilities and purposes are similar, some technical differences among the choices can affect purchase decisions.

## DIRECT CONNECTIONS

One of the earliest methods of connecting terminals to computers was with direct physical connections. For example, each terminal would be wired directly to the computer—typically with twisted-pair cable. Eventually, to provide some flexibility, these terminals were wired directly to a *front-end processor,*

shown in Figure 6.1A. This processor was a simple communications device that accepted all of the terminal wires and then assigned each user to an open communications *port* on the computer. This device decreased the number of physical access ports required on the computer. Although the front-end processor had to physically connect to every terminal, by reassigning terminals to different computer ports, the computer only needed to enough ports to handle the expected number of simultaneous users. Because not all users were expected to be on the computer at the same time, the cost of the computer was reduced.

One of the biggest drawbacks to direct connections is that separate lines had to be run from each terminal to the front-end processor. In addition to the high installation costs, many of these lines sat unused for extended periods of time.

## SWITCHED NETWORKS

There are various switched networks. At heart, they are all based on providing individual connections between any two computers (or telephones). With

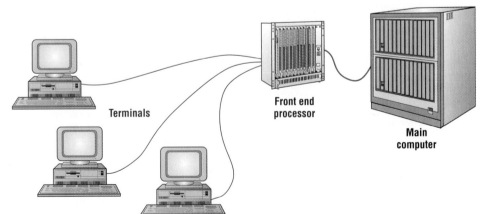

**FIGURE 6.1A**
Direct-connect (star) networks. Early networks connected terminals through individual lines to a front-end processor that controlled and organized the signals for the main computer.

Terminals

Front end processor

Main computer

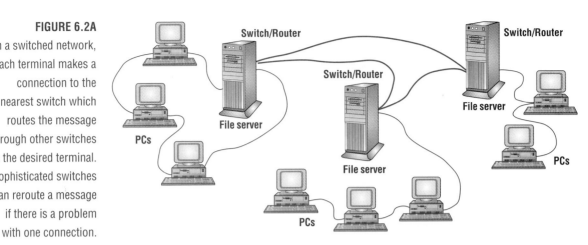

**FIGURE 6.2A**

In a switched network, each terminal makes a connection to the nearest switch which routes the message through other switches to the desired terminal. Sophisticated switches can reroute a message if there is a problem with one connection.

these systems, each device must be connected directly to a switch. The switch maintains addresses (phone numbers) for each device. The early switches actually made physical connections between devices. For example, if your terminal requested a connection to a specific computer, a physical link between the two was established and dedicated to your use. A small example of a switched network is displayed in Figure 6.2A.

Modern switches provide logical connections that do not rely on a single physical line. In particular, many of the systems are *packet switches.* Packet switches chop every transmission into small pieces. Each piece contains a source and destination address as well as a sequence number. When the switch receives a packet, the switch determines the best route and sends the packet on to the next switch. The final switch reassembles each packet in the proper order and delivers the total message to the destination machine. The packets for a single session might follow hundreds of different paths before reaching the same destination. The process happens so fast that none of the users can tell that the packets were ever separated. Modern phone systems are based on packet-switched networks. A relatively new transmission protocol known as Asynchronous Transmission Method (ATM) is essentially a packet switching network that runs at very high speeds. Using high transmission speeds and preventing collisions, it offers high speed transfers for many simultaneous users. However, because it is still new, it is relatively expensive.

## SHARED-MEDIA NETWORKS

Shared-media networks evolved from early radio networks—such as the ALOHANET created by the University of Hawaii to connect users on different islands to the university computer. Although this system was based on radio waves and avoided the high cost of installing cables, today the most popular shared-media network is *Ethernet,* which is based on coaxial or twisted-pair cables.

In many ways, a shared-media network is like a room full of people trying to talk to each other. The limitation of sharing the media (the air in the room) is that only one person or computer can talk at a time. As a result, there need to be *protocols* that establish rules of behavior to avoid common problems. The protocols need to cover four situations: (1) providing a means to address each recipient and sender, (2) who is allowed to talk (initiate a conversation), (3) how long can a single sender talk at one time, (4) what to do if there is a *collision,* when two machines (or people) try to talk at the same time. Figure 6.3A illustrates how the various computers are connected to a single cable in a shared-media or *bus* network. Radio networks are often built the same way, except the transmissions occur with radio frequencies through the air instead of through cables.

Ethernet is one of the earliest protocols to resolve these problems. It has been standardized by several national and international standard setting bodies so that a network can be built from equipment provided by different vendors. The Ethernet protocol is

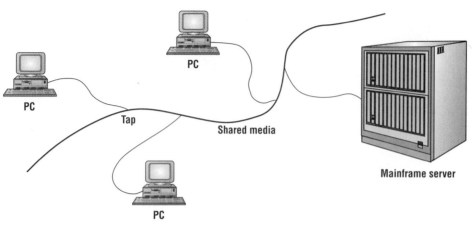

**FIGURE 6.3A**

With a bus (Ethernet) network each device is connected to a common transmission medium. Only one device can transmit at a time. Standards define when a device can transmit, how to specify a device, and how to tell whether the line is busy.

also known as CSMA/CD, which stands for *Carrier-Sense, Multiple-Access/Collision Detection.* In this system, any LAN card is allowed to transmit on the network, but first it must examine the media to see whether another card is currently transmitting (carrier-sense). If so, the second card must wait until the line is clear. Users are prevented from tying up the line for extended periods by restricting the length of time each card can transmit at any one time. This time interval is a *tunable parameter* that can be set by the LAN administrator to provide better service under different conditions. Once the line is clear, the card can begin transmission. Because of multiple access, sometimes two computers will attempt to initiate a conversation at the same time and a collision occurs. When any card detects a collision, it immediately stops transmitting and waits a random length of time before trying again. Addressing on Ethernet is handled by each interface card. Every interface card must have a unique identification number. The numbers are assigned at the time the card is manufactured.

One of the biggest drawbacks to CSMA/CD is that as the number of users increases, there will be more collisions. With many collisions, the computers end up spending more time detecting collisions and waiting than they do transmitting. It is also the reason why a high-speed medium is important to this method. The faster that every transmission can

be sent, the sooner the line is clear and ready for the next user.

A second method of dealing with shared media known as a **Token-Ring** network is shown in Figure 6.4A. The protocols here are slightly different. In this case, there is a special data packet known as *a token.* There is only one token available and it is passed around a *ring* to each machine. A machine is allowed to send a message only if it holds the token. The message contains a source and destination address, and each machine examines the address to see which packets it should keep.

The drawback to Token-Ring networks is that the computers have to continually pass the token, and they have to wait until they receive the token before transmitting. This overhead results in slower transmissions than Ethernet networks when there are only a limited number of users. However, as the number of users increases, there are no collisions with the Token Ring, so performance does not deteriorate as rapidly as under Ethernet.

In practice, the differences among network types is not as great as the theory might indicate. Of course, most networks are designed in segments to avoid putting thousands of users on the same shared media. By building a LAN in segments, most traffic remains within a smaller network and only a few messages are shared on the network backbone.

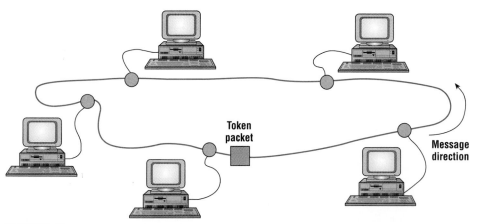

**FIGURE 6.4A**

A token ring network operates with a unique protocol. A machine is allowed to transmit data only if it holds the token packet. Messages are passed between machines until they reach they destination. Based on defined intervals, the token is passed around the ring to each machine. If a machine has nothing to send, it passes the token on. This sequential method is relatively efficient for large networks.

## CHOOSING NETWORK DESIGNS

For the most part, it is rare that you will make a direct decision between the various network types. Because there are only a limited number of network vendors, the most common practice is to identify the business needs of the users and then see how existing vendors can meet those needs. The focus of the decision is on features and prices, not on the type of network offered. For comparison purposes, a few of the popular networks are listed in Figure 6.5A.

## ISO REFERENCE MODEL

Although there are differences in network communication systems, they all have a common form that can be studied using the ISO Reference Model. In this model, there are seven basic layers to network communications: Physical, Data link, Network, Transport, Session, Presentation, and Application. Any communication between two computers must deal with these seven layers in some fashion. The basic structure is illustrated in Figure 6.6A. Each layer serves a specific purpose. Also, each layer tends to add data to the layer above.

| BRAND/VENDOR | TYPE | MEDIA |
|---|---|---|
| ATM | Switched/Token | Fiber optic (others later) |
| Digital | Ethernet | Coaxial/Twisted-pair |
| FDDI | Token Ring/Dual | Fiber optic |
| IBM | Token Ring | Twisted-pair |
| Novell | Ethernet | Coaxial/Twisted-pair |

**FIGURE 6.5A**

A brief comparison of networks that are commonly available. Offerings change constantly, so contact the vendors for specific data.

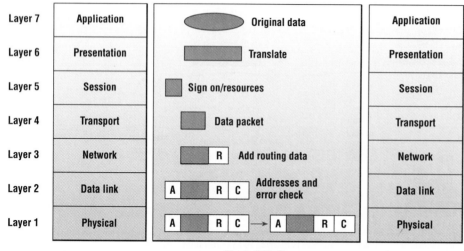

**Physical Media**

**FIGURE 6.6A**

The ISO Reference Model illustrates how data from an application on one machine is translated through seven layers, transmitted to another machine and converted to the new application. Networks involve more than just transmitting data.

The primary advantage of the OSI model is that it breaks the communication problem into smaller pieces. As long as each piece follows the appropriate standards, you can choose components from different vendors. As new components are introduced, you should be able to upgrade the appropriate section without replacing the entire network.

## Physical Layer

The purpose of the Physical layer is to make the connection between two machines. It is directly related to hardware. There are standards to specify constraints on voltage, type of wire, frequency of signals, and sizes of physical connectors. Raw data bits are transferred at this stage.

## Data Link Layer

The Data link layer is concerned with transmitting error free data to the correct destination. This level is primarily directed to hardware specifications. Standards refer to error-checking methods and means of identifying addresses. Most networking protocol standards (Ethernet, Token Ring, FDDI—fiber distributed data interface) define standards through the Data link layer.

## Network Layer

The Network layer is concerned with routing messages to the appropriate location. In particular, it selects the appropriate path for a message in networks where there is a choice. Its main advantage is that it separates the higher layers from the physical transmission of data. The Network layer handles connections across different machines and multiple networks. The Internet Protocol (IP) is an example of a Network layer standard.

## Transport Layer

The Transport layer is responsible for providing transparent services to the session layer. It hides the details of establishing connections and transmitting data. It breaks the message into packets and reassembles them on the receiving side. The Transport layer ensures that message packets are delivered correctly, in the proper order and with no duplication or lost data. Sample protocols at this layer are TCP and Novell IPX.

## Session Layer

The Session layer is the user interface to the network. It handles user identification at logon time and enables the user to select remote hardware and software. It is handled in software, by the operating system and network specific packages. For instance, you might be asked to specify which file server you want to use.

## Presentation Layer

The Presentation layer handles encryption and compression. Data is translated into formats that can be used by the two machines.

## Application Layer

The Application layer translates the underlying data into a meaningful context. It ensures that applications can talk to each other and retain the meaning of the data. For example, a sales database on one computer might provide sales data to your computer. Even though it might be reformatted and translated into a spreadsheet application, it still represents sales data.

Above the Transport layer, many existing networks use proprietary techniques to establish connections. For example, logon commands and procedures depend on the manufacturer of the network and the computer equipment. At the presentation and application layers, there are few standards. Perhaps the closest we come today is with the use of dynamic data sharing in Windows described in Chapter 7. Software that is written to Windows definitions can share data with similar software. Hence, applications can share data directly, even over networks.

# Integration of Information

Armatron uses its computer-integrated manufacturing system to integrate workers throughout the company. The improved communication changed the culture of the company and fosters teamwork and cooperation.

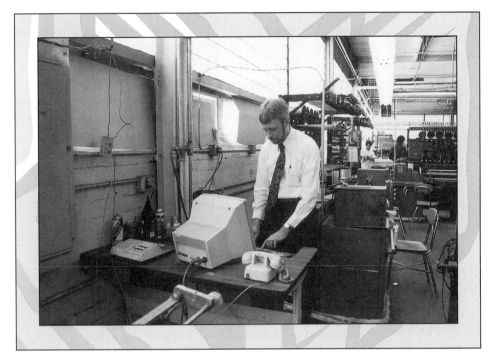

## ARMATRON INTERNATIONAL

Armatron International, Inc., began life as a manufacturer of automobile radios. In 1991, its contract for supplying (imported) radios to Chrysler Corp. was terminated. Today, most of the company's sales consist of a variety of garden products, although the research and development team has designed an obstacle avoidance system for trucks known as Echovision. The Melrose, Massachusetts, manufacturer is a leader in the production of electronic bug killers. Armatron also manufactures Flowtron electric leaf mulchers and chipper/shredders, as well as compost bins. The company supplies these garden products to major retailers such as Sears as well as direct sales to more than 3,000 customers. Virtually all of the sales are to retail outlets, with some products produced under private label for other companies.

Prior to 1990, Armatron relied on software modules its programmers had developed in-house for use on an IBM mainframe. Reports were created at various levels of assembly and at the individual stages of production. The computer system could produce standard financial, accounting, and inventory reports, along with marketing and production forecasts. However, there was limited data sharing among departments. In fact, CFO Ed Rogers notes that "We used to operate as little kingdoms without a great deal of interaction between departments."

The order-entry department exclusively handled orders from large customers, with products shipped from the finished goods area. Parts were distributed by the customer service department. If a large customer placed an order for new products and for parts, the orders had to be split and reprinted on two pieces of paper that were transferred to the two departments. Shipping employees had to put the pieces back together—if they were told the order had been split. In addition to causing problems with shipments, the process was slowing down shipping and customers were getting upset.

Many components are purchased preassembled from outside suppliers. There was some attempt to use just-in-time (JIT) inventory control for these subassemblies and for raw materials. However, managers were experiencing problems with some suppliers (both in terms of quality and timeliness). With a small number of workers and increasing production, they did not have time to examine and track products and materials from suppliers. Ed Rogers notes that the purchasing department often had trouble "processing purchase orders correctly and on time as well as scheduling delivery dates."

According to Carol Mooney, the cost accounting manager, cost accounting was another area that created problems. He explains that "I used to have to write down all the cost changes, pass them into the DP department, and they would have to manually key them in. I then would review the returned report to ensure that everything went through properly, which took a lot of time."

## OVERVIEW

Sometimes it seems that companies work together with a great deal of synergy. In other companies, departments operate independently and managers battle each other constantly. As illustrated by Figure 7.1, teamwork, cooperation and sharing are crucial to ensure profitability for most companies. Manufacturing can improve quality and cut costs by constantly examining every step of the production process. Marketing is more effective with close ties between sales, production and distribution. Finance needs to know details on current sales, marketing plans, and cost projections throughout the company.

Cooperation and teamwork seem like obvious concepts, why would companies have problems with them? One problem has always been the difficulty in sharing information throughout a firm. As a manager, how do you find the data you need, without being deluged by tons of data? It is especially difficult when most data takes the form of printed corporate reports. How are teams supposed to work together when they rely on phone calls, meetings, and office mail to communicate?

A primary task of management is to keep the company focused on a common goal with everyone working together. Information systems play a major role in this

**FIGURE 7.1**

To simplify management, firms are often split into departments. Yet, they must be able to work as a single, integrated company. Information systems can help managers improve the integration and control of their firm.

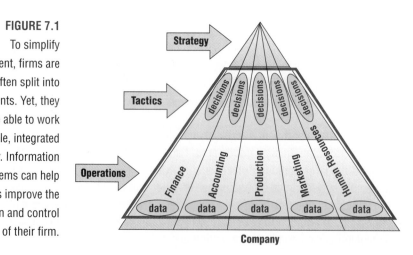

task. Creating communication networks is one step in the process of integrating the corporate components by providing the same data to all users via phone and data communication. Another helpful technique is the ability to capture data from different sources within the firm and combine them into one document—called a **compound document.**

Various software packages have been designed to handle the different types of information: word processors for text, spreadsheets for computations, databases for storing numbers, and graphics packages for pictures and graphs. Most business reports and analyses need elements from each of these packages. The goal is to collect this data from different locations and combine it into one report. An important concept involved in combining this data is the difference between static and dynamic integration. With **static integration,** you simply copy results from one system into another. If the original data changes, it does not affect the copy. Conversely, dynamic links can be created so that if the original data changes, the "copy" is automatically updated as well.

**INTRODUCTION**     Coordinating the many aspects of business requires a wide variety of information from many sources. Perhaps you need to make a decision about how to market a new product. You would retrieve a variety of customer information from the sales database. You would use reports from the production team and a collection of graphs created from the initial marketing surveys. You could use a spreadsheet to analyze this information along with various marketing strategies. Along the way, you would probably use accounting data to create graphs to display costs and projected profits for the various cases. Finally, you would use a word processor to create a formal report to your supervisors that describes the choices and your analysis. The report would contain your writing along with the graphs, spreadsheet tables, and some of the data.

**Integrated data** could be something as simple as a graph and table from the human resources department that you have included in your financial reports. That way you can see the overall patterns in the data and still have the raw numbers handy. Similarly, there are many times where you will want to include pictures in a word-processing document. In terms of databases, there are many situations in which you want to store images. An automobile insurance company could store photographs of the cars they insure. If a client's car were damaged, those pictures could also be saved.

One of the biggest difficulties that arises when you are trying to integrate information is the diversity in hardware and software. For example, each software package uses its own format to store data files. As a result, there are more than 50 different formats for word-processing documents. The problem multiplies rapidly when you consider the large number of graphics packages, spreadsheets, and database management systems that each have their own file formats. In order to integrate these different types of information, you need software that can read many different file types, or the software needs to use a common format.

The trend in software is toward packages that work together by sharing data through links. Much of this software works in conjunction with a windowing operating system such as OS/2 Presentation Manager, Windows, or X-Windows. The key is that when you change one item, the other software will automatically pick up the changes. The concept is similar to a spreadsheet formula that refers to other cells.

The key difference is that you can refer to data in different programs, such as transferring data from a spreadsheet into a word processor. With a network, the data can be located in different departments throughout the business.

---

### ◥ TRENDS ◢

Consider a sample business decision involving different types of data. You are working as a manager at a large department store. Three reports are produced daily by the central computer: the daily sales report (Figure 7.2), returned merchandise log (Figure 7.3), and a commission report (Figure 7.4). At the end of each week, you create a report that evaluates the profitability of each department in the store (e.g., housewares, women's clothing, and shoes). You also maintain a line graph that shows this net sales number for each week. At the end of the month, you write several pages of comments about the trends and the monthly activities. The report includes copies of the data and your graphs. It is sent to upper management. A small example is shown in Figure 7.5.

To see how the use of computers is changing, consider how this report might have been produced by managers at different points in time. Figure 7.6 highlights the differences in processing information in three time periods. In the 1970s, the central computer kept track of all sales. Each night, the computer printed three basic reports. At the end of the week, a manager computed the net sales by hand and drew the graph on graph paper. A secretary would then type the report on a typewriter and staple the graph at the end of the document.

In the 1980s, personal computers with spreadsheets and word processors were introduced to the business world. At this point, the manager entered the numbers from the reports into a spreadsheet. These numbers were usually entered by hand. The spreadsheet could perform the necessary calculations and create the graphs with only a few commands. A word processor was used to type the report. The spreadsheet printouts and the graphs were stapled into the final report.

Today, the process can be even simpler. First, a database management system holds the sales data.

Spreadsheet commands can be used to retrieve exactly the data that is needed. The spreadsheet performs the desired calculations and produces the graphs. The report is still typed on a word processor; however, the spreadsheets and graphs are automatically copied into the word processor document. This process is facilitated by software suites that consist of software packages designed to exchange data.

Think about what happens if some of the original data is changed. For instance, just before you send the report to management, someone calls and says that the sales figures for half the items in the housewares department are wrong. In the 1970s example, the manager had to recompute all of the totals, redraw the graphs, and rewrite the report. The 1980s manager had to change the numbers in the spreadsheet, rewrite sections of the report, and print the new graphs. With a truly integrated system, you would simply tell the word processor to reprint the report. The word processor would automatically tell the spreadsheet to get the new data, update the graphs, and transfer the results to the final copy.

The most recent trend in integrating information comes through the use of windows-oriented software and graphical user interfaces. One of the primary objectives of these operating systems is to enable you to run several different types of software at the same time (multitasking) and to share data between each package. When software vendors create software for these operating systems, they follow some standard rules. These rules allow each piece of software to "talk" to the other software you own and exchange data. As a result, you can combine information from any word processor, graphics package, or database system that follows the rules.

FIGURE 7.2
Businesses create
many different reports.
Begin with this small
excerpt of the daily
sales report. It itemizes
sales for each
department.

| DAILY SALES REPORT | | | FEBRUARY 11, 1996 | |
| --- | --- | --- | --- | --- |
| DEPARTMENT | ITEM # | Q-SOLD | PRICE | VALUE |
| House | 1153 | 52 | 2.95 | 153.40 |
| | 5543 | 13 | 0.59 | 7.67 |
| W. Clothing | 5563 | 1 | 87.32 | 87.32 |
| | 7765 | 4 | 54.89 | 219.56 |
| | 9986 | 2 | 15.69 | 31.38 |
| Shoes | 1553 | 2 | 65.79 | 131.58 |
| | 6673 | 1 | 29.39 | 29.39 |
| **Total Sales** | | | | **660.30** |

FIGURE 7.3
To evaluate customer
service and quality, the
store tracks returned
merchandise and
produces a daily report
by item number.

| RETURNED MERCHANDISE LOG | | FEBRUARY 11, 1996 | |
| --- | --- | --- | --- |
| ITEM # | Q | PRICE | VALUE |
| 1153 | 3 | 2.95 | 8.85 |
| 3353 | 6 | 27.59 | 165.54 |
| 4453 | 2 | 15.95 | 31.90 |
| 8878 | 1 | 24.95 | 24.95 |
| **Total** | **12** | | **231.24** |

FIGURE 7.4
Managers compute
daily sales by employee
and determine the
commission based on
each employee's
commission rate.

| COMMISSIONS | | | FEBRUARY 11, 1996 | | |
| --- | --- | --- | --- | --- | --- |
| EMP # | NAME | DEPT | SALES | RATE | AMOUNT |
| 1143 | Jones | House | 543.95 | 5% | 27.20 |
| 2895 | Brown | M. Clothing | 775.35 | 4% | 31.01 |
| 4462 | Smith | W. Clothing | 1,544.52 | 5% | 77.23 |
| 7893 | Torrez | Shoes | 876.93 | 6% | 52.62 |
| 9963 | Cousco | M. Clothing | 589.47 | 5% | 29.47 |

FIGURE 7.5
The weekly sales
analysis report requires
selecting and
aggregating data from
each of the other
reports. The text, data,
and graph are
combined into a final
document.

**Weekly Sales Analysis**     2/8/96 – 2/13/96
Manager comments are written in the first 10
pages, along with comments on special events.

**Department Analysis**

| Dept | Sales | Returns | Commissions | Net |
| --- | --- | --- | --- | --- |
| House | 4,113.58 | 25.35 | 205.68 | 3,882.55 |
| Women's clothing | 54,221.92 | 998.52 | 3,024.64 | 50,198.76 |
| Men's clothing | 28,664.48 | 356.24 | 1,421.58 | 26,886.66 |
| Shoes | 10,225.31 | 853.47 | 592.36 | 8,779.48 |
| **Total** | **97,225.29** | **2,233.58** | **5,244.26** | **89,747.45** |

FIGURE 7.6

Methods used to create integrated reports have changed over three decades. With simple transaction systems, managers computed the totals, drew graphs, and had secretaries type the report. With personal computers, middle managers re-entered data into spreadsheets and used a word processor to print the final report. With an integrated system, top managers use a personal computer to query the database, draw the graphs, and produce the final report.

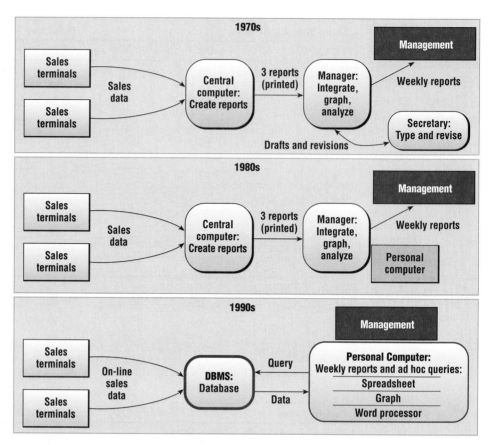

**INTEGRATION IN BUSINESS**

For a business to be successful, it needs to integrate information from all aspects of the organization. Figure 7.7 shows how data are pulled from all areas within the organization to assist each level of decision making. Figure 7.8 shows that modern management techniques of just-in-time production and mass customization require a high degree of internal integration, as well as strong links to suppliers and customers.

Most companies are split into functional departments, with varying degrees of independence. However, there are always pressures and decisions that affect the entire organization. For instance, changes in products or manufacturing schedules clearly affect the marketing department. Because these changes will probably alter the cash flows of the company, the accounting and finance departments also need to be aware of the changes. Furon Aerospace (Reality Bytes 7-1) illustrates how an integrated approach can save time and cut costs—especially in a manufacturing environment.

In the 1960s and 1970s, computer systems were built for individual departments and areas within the company. In many companies, these systems became islands. They were focused on one task and did not share data with each other. For instance, the accounting department collected the basic transaction data and produced the necessary accounting reports. Anyone in the company who wanted to use this data relied on paper printouts of the standard reports. When spreadsheets arrived in the 1980s, the basic accounting numbers were often rekeyed into spreadsheets in other departments. Besides wasting employee time to retype numbers that were already stored on a computer, this practice caused more errors from mistyping the data.

**FIGURE 7.7**

Data from all
operations must be
integrated throughout
the organization.
Transaction processing
data is available for
modeling and decision
making at the tactical
and strategic levels.
Queries are used to
retrieve data
throughout the firm.

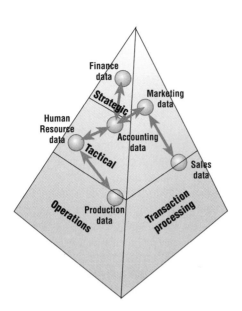

Additionally, consider what happened when the accounting department changes some of the numbers: Some users of the data might not get the updated versions, and people would attempt to make decisions on out-of-date data.

Computer use in most companies began with transaction-processing systems. Because transaction systems are structured and there is considerable experience at this level, it is a logical place to begin. However, it is also tempting to treat each transaction separately: (1) Payroll services can be purchased from a specialized data-processing company, so the data will be handled separately from the other corporate data. (2) A sales order-processing system might be constructed independently of the inventory control system. (3) Process control systems to handle manufacturing tend

**FIGURE 7.8**

Total data integration
begins with the
vendors, tracks data
through all operations
of the firm, and
incorporates
information from
customers. Each area
in the firm has easy
access to data from
any other location. This
integrated data is used
to make better
decisions by enabling
managers to focus on
the "big picture"
instead of local
solutions.

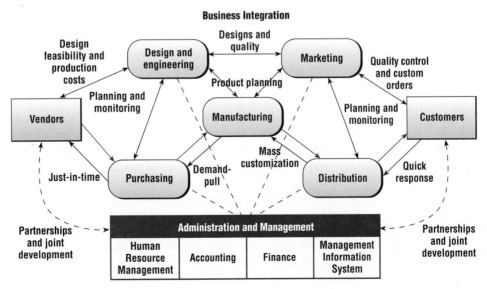

## Reality Bytes ◣ 7–1 FURON AEROSPACE COMPONENTS

Based in Seattle, Furon Aerospace Components manufactures nonmetallic components for aircraft, space, and electronics applications. They also sell services such as program management, precision mechanical assembly, fabrication, testing, and machining. Prior to installing a new computer-integrated manufacturing (CIM) system, most production and accounting reports were created on a batch system that dealt with each category independently of the others. Some reports took 10 to 12 hours to run.

To eliminate existing problems and to help integrate the business reporting and control system, Furon installed a comprehensive CIM package purchased from Jobscope. The software integrates order entry,

backlog analysis, customer service, engineering, bills of materials, routings, MRP, purchasing, receiving, quality control, stores, labor, shipping, invoicing, and the accounting functions.

Routing operations that used to take two and a half weeks are now performed in two and a half days. Accuracy in the bills of materials is above 98 percent. With the new data and nightly reports, raw material inventories have been reduced by 20 percent with a 96 percent accuracy of inventory needs. On-time deliveries have increased from 73 percent to 95 percent, and Furon managers can track every feature of the job status from order entry to customer delivery.

to be isolated because the data (e.g., robotic control signals) are different from that used in the rest of the company. (4) Similarly, the corporate accounting system is often developed as a stand-alone product. Journal entries are created by copying data in reports produced by other systems. Although each of these transaction systems offers management advantages to their respective departments, it is difficult for managers to use data from other departments. Also, independent systems make it difficult for executives to share data and evaluate interrelationships between the departments.

The amount of data integration needed in a company often depends on the management structure of the firm. Some firms are highly decentralized, so that each business unit makes its own decisions and functions independently of the others. Typically in these situations, only accounting data (profit/loss) are integrated and reported to upper management. For example, PepsiCo is a large corporation that focuses on food and beverage items. They own brands such as Pepsi, Pizza Hut, Kentucky Fried Chicken, and Frito-Lay. For the most part, each unit functions independently of the others (although the restaurants all sell Pepsi beverages). As a result, there is little need for sharing of data between two subsidiaries. For instance, why would Frito-Lay managers need to know daily sales at Pizza Hut?

On the other hand, some organizations are much more integrated. In your economics courses you were shown the difference between vertically and horizontally integrated firms. Consider a vertically integrated firm such as an oil company that functions at different levels of production (including oil exploration, drilling, transportation, storage, and retail sales). Although an oil exploration team may not need access to daily fuel sales in New York state, they do need to forecast future demand for oil. Likewise, the retail sales division does not need to know the daily costs associated with drilling for oil, yet they might need to track deliveries and communicate with the corporate office.

Consider a horizontally integrated firm such as Wal-Mart with retail stores in many different cities. They achieve lower costs by combining the buying power of all the stores. By coordinating sales, warehouses and distribution, Wal-Mart can negotiate better prices with manufacturers. Additionally, Wal-Mart reduces operating costs by standardizing management practices (and information systems) across all the stores.

---

**Reality Bytes**     **7–2** NATIONAL BICYCLE INDUSTRIAL CO., LTD. (JAPAN)

Japan's National Bicycle Industrial Company uses a highly integrated computer-driven manufacturing system to build custom bicycles. The computer handles just-in-time inventory, computer-aided design, and robot processing. When customers purchase Panasonic bicycles, their measurements are entered into the computerized ordering system. They also enter their choice of gearing, handlebar size, pedals, brakes, and color preferences. In all, there are 11,232,860 possible combinations. The specifications are sent by network to the factory, where bar-coded parts are delivered to the robot (and a few human) builders. The inventory levels are monitored by the computer, which automatically places orders with the suppliers. With this system, an entire bicycle is built in 8 to 10 days, with about 60 semicustom bicycles produced every day.

---

By integrating information from all stores, it is easier for Wal-Mart to forecast customer demands. Also, by networking the store information systems, managers who experience higher sales of certain products can request shipments from stores that are not selling the item as rapidly.

Manufacturing firms can gain additional benefits from integrating data. Benefits like just-in-time inventory, total quality management, and mass customization can only exist with tight integration of data. The National Bicycle Industrial Company of Japan (Reality Bytes 7–2) illustrates how integrated data is used to provide customized products to mass markets.

In one sense, all data in a company can be integrated—but some specific software and network capabilities make it much easier to create integrated documents. One key concept is the issue of static and dynamic integration.

**STATIC AND DYNAMIC INTEGRATION**

Two basic methods are used to combine information. It is important to understand the difference between these two methods. Say you want to produce a report that includes a graph, as illustrated in Figure 7.9. Using separate tools, you print the report first, then use a graphics package to print the graph. You combine the two by putting the printed graph at the end of the report. Now, what happens if you change the graph? The original graph page in the report cannot change, it is *static*. You have to reprint the graph, remove the old page, and replace it with the new one.

**FIGURE 7.9**

Static integration. One way to integrate data is to use a base document that contains static copies of other objects. If the original objects are changed, the user must recopy the items to the document. One advantage to separating the copy and original is the original can be changed or moved.

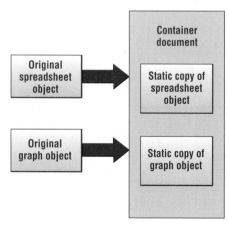

Many word processors enable you to **import** graphs or figures into your documents. You can change the size of the graph, print the correct page numbers, and adjust the margins and headers. You can even print titles for the graph in the same font as the rest of the document. There is only one catch: Usually the transfer of the graph is static. When you tell the word processor to include the graph, it literally copies the graph into your document. If you go back to the graphics package and change the graph, these changes will not be copied to the word processor's document. If you change the graph, you have to return to the word processor and recopy the image into the document.

Some software today can provide **dynamic integration** of information. The method has many names, such as **hot links, Dynamic Data Exchange (DDE),** or **Object Linking and Embedding (OLE).** Consider an example of a word-processed report displayed in Figure 7.10, where you wish to include part of a spreadsheet. You can tell the word processor to link to the spreadsheet. When the report is printed or displayed, it goes to the spreadsheet and grabs the current information. The spreadsheet information is printed as a table. If you go back to the spreadsheet and change the data, these changes will automatically be included when the report is printed or displayed again.

A more advanced version of DDE is known as Object Linking and Embedding (OLE), which is used by Microsoft Windows programs. With OLE, images, sound, data, and other objects from software can be combined using a different software package. The difference is that when the user or designer selects the object, the original software package is automatically started. The object can be edited where it sits within the new document. You do not need to know which package created the object, but you do need access to the software. A competing version is known as the *Common Object Request Broker Architecture (CORBA)* model. The CORBA model is a proposed standard that enables software to share files and data across networks of different machines. The proposed standard suffered a setback in 1995 when Microsoft announced that it would not support it in Microsoft software.

The difference between static and dynamic integration is that with dynamic integration the most recent data is automatically used when the report is produced. Another advantage arises because you do not have to remember which reports use your spreadsheets or graphs. Figure 7.11 illustrates how many different types of data can be incorporated into a compound document. Notice that there might be several levels of links. For example, a spreadsheet might pull data from a database, perform

**FIGURE 7.10**
Dynamic integration. With dynamic integration, data objects are placed in the container document. However, the document maintains a link with the original objects. If an object is changed by another user, the container document automatically picks up the new version.

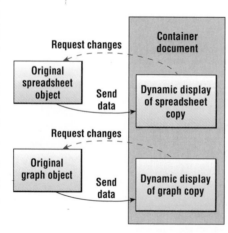

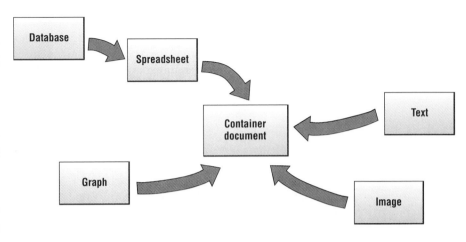

**FIGURE 7.11**

Multiple links. A container document can contain links to many other objects. There can even be multiple levels. In the example, a spreadsheet could receive data from a database, perform computations, and then pass the results to the final document.

computations, and then send the results to a word processor for formatting. All changes you make are automatically included when the report is printed. One drawback is that every time you edit your documents, the computer has to check the linked files for changes. This process can be slow if there are several spreadsheets and graphs linked to the compound document.

You need to be careful when using dynamic links to **export** data. First, a document might contain several links, some of them dynamic, others static. Just looking at the document, it is not easy to tell which links are dynamic and which are static. Even if a document contains dynamic links, you need to review the document to be sure that every item was updated properly. Second, when the data tables and graphs are updated, the textual descriptions and interpretation have to be changed manually.

When you create new documents, one of the most important decisions you will make is to determine which elements should be linked statically and which ones dynamically. You need to weigh the advantages and disadvantages summarized in Figure 7.12. Basically, once a dynamic link is created, it is maintained automatically by the document and the computer. Hence, you know the data and figures will be up-to-date. The biggest problems arise when you want to share or move the document. You might have to rebuild or cancel the links. Similarly, if you make radical changes to the underlying linked elements (database or graphs), you will probably have to rebuild any documents that use those files. Consider what would happen if you decide to

**FIGURE 7.12**

Dynamic links. Dynamic links can be convenient because the final document automatically tracks changes. Users simply print the final document, which collects the necessary updates and formats the output. However, there are some situations when it is better to use static linking. The problems become more serious as the number of people involved increases.

| ADVANTAGES | DISADVANTAGES |
|---|---|
| Data references are always up-to-date. | If you move the document, the links might have to be rebuilt or dropped. |
| Computer and document know the source of all components. You do not have to rely on users to remember. | You cannot make radical changes to the underlying components.<br>• Software upgrades cause problems.<br>• File deletions, moves, or major alterations affect other users. |
| Updates and changes are automatic, requiring minimal user training once the document is created. | Data changes can cause reformats that require fine-tuning the layouts. |

split one graph into two new graphs and delete the original. Any documents that are based on the original graph will lose their links. The problem is that you do not know which documents are linked to that graph.

The first step in creating an integrated system is to provide a system that encourages users to share data. There are two important components: (1) a network and (2) groupware software.

## INTEGRATION OVER NETWORKS

Rarely is all of the information needed for a report stored in one place. A typical report may involve data stored on the central corporate computer, text and spreadsheet results created by co-workers, and pictures or graphs created by the art department. Many times it will be necessary to download data from the commercial databases discussed in Chapter 5. It is easier to combine data from these various sources if they are connected by the networks discussed in Chapter 6.

To be effective, every piece of the data must be connected by a network. You also need the security clearances to use the data. For example, to pull data from a commercial database, you need to have an account with that company. To access information created by co-workers, they need to tell you the name of the files and make sure that the security system allows you to read the files.

Without networks, it is impossible to perform dynamic integration of data from different sources. If a co-worker changes some of the text or data, it will be necessary to copy the new file to a floppy, bring it to your computer, and modify the final document. The process is simpler with advanced software that supports networks and dynamic retrieval of data. When creating the report, you specify the names and locations of the data that you will need. Figure 7.13 shows that when the report is printed, it sends messages over the network to collect the needed information. The resulting data is formatted and printed. If someone changes the original data, you just reprint the report. At that time, the report writer picks up all of the current information. Dynamic integration is a tremendous benefit in this situation, because the document *remembers* where all of the data came from. Creating a report that uses data from 10 different locations can be difficult to keep up-to-date if you need to remember to modify it each time someone makes a change.

**FIGURE 7.13**

Dynamic links across a network. One of the powerful features of linking is that the application software can retrieve the data from any accessible computer on the network. For example, a manager might retrieve graphs, data, or spreadsheets from other departments to create a consolidated report. Individual workers in each department create the initial parts and set security rights so they can be retrieved by the team leader. With dynamic links, the team leader always has the most recent copy of the team's work.

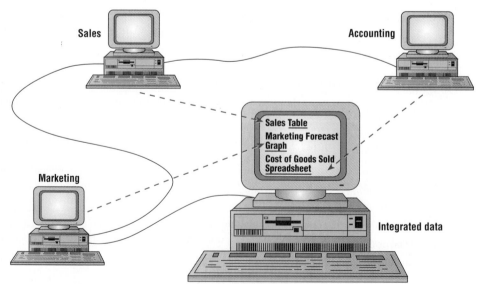

Notice that integrating data over networks requires coordination of the workers. The computers need to be networked. The software packages have to be compatible so that data can be used by many different people. Security controls are needed to specify which workers have access to each type of data.

Once the basic network is in place, additional software can be purchased that improves communication and data integration among workers. A relatively new category of software is useful at integrating workgroups, departments, and the entire firm.

**WORKGROUP INTEGRATION**

Cooperation and teamwork have always been important in managing a company. Today, as firms remove layers of middle management and as they focus on teamwork, integration and sharing become crucial. Making decisions requires input from different people. Problems that arise are solved by creating a team of workers—often from different disciplines.

Picture yourself as a manager in a modern corporation. In addition to your day-to-day tasks, you will be asked to serve on various teams to solve problems. You could be working with three or four different groups at the same time. How do you organize your work? How do you remember the status of each project? How do you keep in touch with the team members? How do you keep track of documents, comments, and revisions for each team? How do you know which team members are falling behind and need more help? Now assume that the team members are scattered across different locations. You cannot afford to schedule meetings every week. How do you keep the project moving and make sure that all important ideas are incorporated in the final decision?

Software tools known as **groupware** have been created to help answer these questions and make it easier for teams to work together. Groupware tools like Lotus Notes (Reality Bytes 7–3) are designed to make it easy for several people to work on a document at the same time, regardless of where everyone is located. There are three key components to groupware: (1) communication, (2) compound documents, and (3) databases. Groupware uses these three components to integrate and share different types of data across an organization.

**Reality Bytes**    **7–3** Four Main Groupware Categories

*Basic groupware* (Lotus Notes)—Basic groupware combines a sophisticated messaging system with a giant database containing work records and memos. It changes the way information flows in an organization. Traditional e-mail requires you to know to whom you are forwarding your idea. With Lotus Notes, the memo is forwarded instead to the appropriate bulletin board. Anyone interested in that subject can then check the bulletin board within their time frame.

*Workflow software* (ActionWorkflow, PRocessIT from NCR)—Work flow software is designed to remake and streamline business processes, eliminating much of the form-filled, paper-clogged bureaucracy. It focuses on the steps that make up processes

and redesigns those steps. Work is routed automatically from employee to employee.

*Meeting software* (GroupSystems from Ventana Corporation)—Meeting software enables meeting participants to interact simultaneously through the computer. Studies have shown that people read faster than they speak. Thus, the software dramatically speeds the process toward consensus by not waiting for individuals to speak individually. This also ensures that everyone gets a chance to take part.

*Scheduling software* (Network Scheduler 3 from Powercore)—Scheduling Software coordinates a workgroup's electronic datebooks and identifies when they can meet.

## Communication

To share data effectively, everyone involved on a team project should be connected to the others via a network. The network could be a small LAN connecting members of a department, or it could be an enterprise network that connects everyone in the company across the nation or world. Depending on the problem, the network might include radio links to traveling salespeople, or it could contain ties across the Internet to divisions in other countries.

An important aspect of the network is that it must be able to efficiently handle large transfers of data. Most groupware products operate by sending constant updates across the network. These updates can include text, images, sound, and even video clips. Remember that the more complex data types can be huge, and they require high-speed network links.

One simple use of groupware products is basic e-mail and scheduling. However, groupware products extend e-mail in several ways. Users can mail documents created with other software packages. The mail system enables recipients to sort and organize each piece of mail so that it is easy to find later. Each piece of mail can be related to other documents, so project data can be stored in one location. Users can comment on mail messages, store the comments with the original, and forward them to other workers. Some systems have a mailbox for each user that can automatically handle text, fax, and voice messages. All of these messages are sent to one address, making it easier for senders and for the recipient.

## Compound Documents

Compound documents are a key focus of groupware tools. Almost everything the user does is stored in a document. These documents can contain text, images, graphs, sound, and even video clips. Each document can be revised and shared with other members of the team. Just remember that everyone who wants to view a complex document must have access to the hardware and software needed to re-create the various elements. For team projects, each team member might be responsible for various elements of a document. For instance, one worker could find the basic data and enter it in a database. Another worker could use a spreadsheet to analyze the numbers. A third team member might create the

Computers are increasingly used to support teamwork and workgroups. Data, comments, and analysis are created and shared through networks of computers.

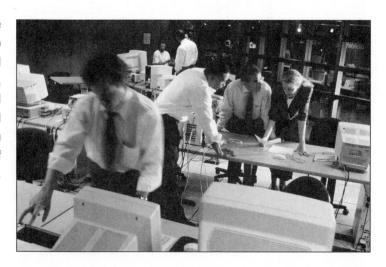

various graphs and artwork, whereas a fourth documents the analysis and writes the conclusions.

The contributions of each worker are stored in a central document. As one worker updates and revises the document, the changes are automatically noted for the other team members. Colors are often used to highlight changes recommended by each worker.

## Databases

Databases are a crucial element to the groupware approach. Their key contribution is to enable workers to share access to the same documents at the same time. Each member of the team can work on the same document. As it is updated by one person, the changes are immediately available to everyone else on the team. The database system automatically records who was responsible for each change. It provides security features by controlling who is allowed to make changes and who is allowed to see the document.

The database approach enables users to search the various documents and to link them together. From a base document, users can easily find related documents and share them with colleagues. Users can search for documents based on titles or do full-text searches. The documents can be searched alphabetically or based on topics or subjects. Banker's Trust (Reality Bytes 7–4) used this approach to speed up its operations and improve customer service.

The database approach also makes it possible to build new applications with minimal programming. By maintaining complex objects, groupware tools enable designers to create systems that collect and share data across the organization. Groupware tools have been especially useful in automating the workflow in service-

### Reality Bytes ▶ 7–4 BANKER'S TRUST

Banker's Trust manages assets for large financial institutions, with large amounts of money in various types of investments. Error detection and resolution are an important part of the process.

In the past, case histories were kept in manila folders. Error resolution meant clerks in New York had to search through big boxes of papers, consult other departments, and then mail documents to a servicing and records center in Nashville for double-checking and additional research. Someone in Nashville would then send a reply, often an annotated copy of the original request, back to New York. Finally the client would be notified of the resolution. Typically an inquiry took three to five days to complete.

Workflow software from Action Technologies helped Banker's Trust to automate this process. Electronic file folders were stored in Lotus Notes, making them accessible to everyone on the bank's com-

puter network. At the beginning of the process, the team spent two weeks analyzing the steps involved in customer queries. It then developed a workflow analysis diagram that broke out roles of the people involved. These included account administrators who received the inquiry and managed the process, the people who wanted the money, the Nashville staff, and supervisors who approved the final response.

Since the system was installed, the bank guarantees clients a maximum three-day turnaround on queries. Many are completed within one day. The process is expedited because Lotus Notes can organize cases by the status of the client's query, its position in the workflow, or the person responsible. The number of account administrators was reduced from 13 to 9 because they were no longer needed to move boxes and file manila folders.

based organizations. Think about the steps and people involved in creating a legal document, an accounting report, or a management-consulting analysis. It is difficult to automate this process with conventional MIS tools. However, groupware tools work well because they focus on the final document. Contributions from individuals are immediately available to the rest of the team, and comments can be added or changed at any time by any member of the team.

## Applications

Groupware tools have been successful in several areas. Applications can be classified into four primary types: (1) automation of teamwork, (2) discrete business solutions, (3) enterprise-wide systems, and (4) extending the enterprise.

### Automation of Teamwork

Communication is essential to teamwork. Teams are often formed to solve specific problems or for special projects. For example, to solve a problem with cost overruns in a warehouse, you would create a team that consisted of at the minimum an accountant, the warehouse manager, warehouse employees, a purchasing manager, and a production manager. The team would collect data, evaluate alternatives, and recommend solutions.

E-mail enables teams to share ideas, review work, and share comments with other members of the team. Providing 24-hour access to communication ensures that people can work whenever it is convenient for them. It also supports workers in different time zones. Providing support for complex documents, recording comments, and tracking votes enables groupware to function as a substitute for face-to-face meetings. The expanded use of video will further decrease the need for meetings.

Groupware tools enable managers to allocate tasks to the team members and then monitor the progress of each worker. By tracking changes and comments of each member, the system shows managers the contributions of each person.

Groupware products are oriented toward knowledge management. Knowledge consists of more than simple data elements. It is the product of data, rules, observations, insights, and comments by various members of the team. By storing all of these comments, the system makes them available to future teams. If a similar problem arises, workers can review the solutions and comments of earlier teams. Think about what happens in a typical company when a problem arises. Managers appoint one or two experts who solved similar problems in the past. What happens when these experts leave? Although we might keep their earlier reports, we would only know the answers to the problem. On the other hand, if all problems were analyzed and discussed with groupware tools, think of the knowledge that remains available to future managers. All of the comments, suggestions, criticisms, assumptions, and notes are stored and arranged by topic.

### Discrete Business Solutions

Applications can also be designed for individual projects or discrete solutions. Individual departments can create their own applications, providing greater communication and support within each department. By focusing on complex documents, the tools improve productivity in service jobs—an area that has always been difficult to automate.

For instance, a groupware application would be useful in a legal department. The application would track individual cases and enable managers to oversee schedules and comment on specific cases.

Given the initial network and software, workers in each department could build their own applications with support from specialized MIS personnel. Although groupware tools require the purchase of additional software for each user, they generally run on existing hardware and common networks. By using existing software applications and hardware, the costs of using workgroup software are relatively low.

A key feature of workgroup tools is that users control the entire development process. Once the groupware has been set up, users create the documents, choose topics, and create links among documents. Each team or department controls the outcome. Better yet, documents and linkages change over time to meet changing needs of the organization—without requiring programming or changes by MIS personnel.

### Enterprise Solutions

By standardizing on hardware, software, and communication protocols, groupware tools serve to connect the entire organization. The system can connect workers from different locations. It provides equal access to mobile workers regardless of their current location. It enables employees to work from home. By being accessible to all workers, it is easy to create ad hoc problem-solving teams consisting of workers from different departments.

By capturing all important communications and analyses, groupware tools can serve as a form of corporate memory. To learn how a particular decision was made three years ago, someone need only pull up the associated documents. In addition to the raw data and the ultimate decision, the system contains comments, criticisms, and viewpoints from workers throughout the company. Along the same lines, managers can review all comments to get a better understanding of the corporate culture. They can also monitor statements for potential legal problems, such as discriminatory or inflammatory comments.

### Extending the Enterprise

Because of their ease-of-use and ability to handle complex documents, groupware tools can be used to build links to other companies, suppliers, and customers. Improving ties to suppliers and customers can cut costs, speed product development, improve quality, and provide better customer service. Beyond these simple changes, closer relationships can also alter the way the business operates. Groupware systems can change business processes such as purchasing and production. As discussed in Chapter 11, information systems can provide a competitive advantage by changing the basis of competition. Closer ties to customers can keep out competitors. Closer ties to suppliers can lock out potential competitors by minimizing their access to materials.

Of course, building ties through groupware products requires that all companies involved have similar technology. Hardware and networks need to be compatible. Each company must use the same groupware tools, especially because there are few standards. The various companies might also have to use the same basic software tools (word processors, spreadsheets, and graphics packages). At a minimum, they will need to be able to store documents in some common format.

## Workgroup Example

To understand how groupware works, consider an example of an engineering consulting firm. As illustrated in Figure 7.14, the firm has headquarters in San Francisco, but a team is working with a client with headquarters in Stamford, Connecticut. The

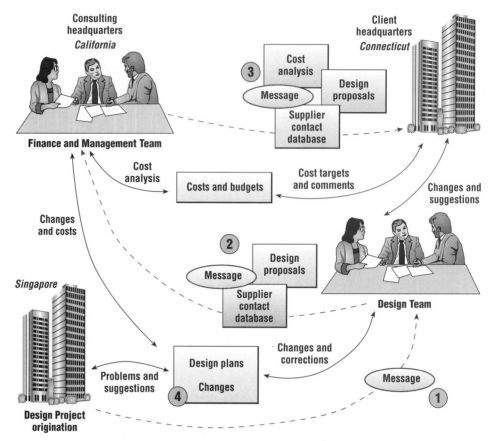

**FIGURE 7.14**

Workgroup example. A design firm uses teams to design a project for the client. The teams working in different areas can share their changes and comments with groupware tools. (1) Message and problem are sent to the design team. (2) The design team forwards two proposals to the finance team. (3) The finance team analyzes the costs and budget effects. (4) The client makes a choice and design team makes changes and notifies the project leader.

engineering firm is designing a plant for the client in Singapore. Much of the work is being performed by three engineering teams: the design team working at the client's headquarters in Connecticut, the finance team in California, and an on-site project team in Singapore.

Consider what might be a typical day. At noon, the project team encounters a problem with the design when they cannot obtain some special components described in the original design. The project team tracks down two alternatives, and at 6:00 P.M. the leader sends an e-mail message to the design team noting the problems and asking for guidance. Three hours later, at 8:00 A.M. in Connecticut, the design team consults with the client and draws up two sets of modifications to the plans. At 1:00 P.M., they add initial designs and comments to the message and send a message to the finance team in California.

The finance team takes the proposed changes and begins an analysis of the costs. Using the supplier contact database supplied by the project team, the finance team revises the budget estimates and schedule and attaches a copy of two spreadsheets to the new design. The client goes over the changes and new costs with the design team and chooses one of the options.

At 4:00 P.M. the next day, the design team revises the main design, orders the components, and notifies the project leader. Three hours later, the project team arrives at work and begins implementing the changes. An acknowledgment message is sent to the design team with the daily progress reports.

All of the messages, designs, spreadsheet analyses, and databases are transferred through the corporate network of the design firm. The related documents are tied together. For instance, the design team can retrieve the cost spreadsheets or the supplier contact database by clicking on icons in the report. There are separate LAN servers for each of the three locations. The files are replicated on each server—as changes are made in one location, they are automatically forwarded to the other servers. At any time, a person in each location can call up the related documents and check the progress or comments of the other teams.

## Problems with Sharing Documents

Although groupware tools make it relatively easy to share documents and coordinate workers, there are some problems that managers need to avoid. Even companies that are highly advanced in their use of technology have reported problems. Figure 7.15 summarizes the basic issues.

Compatibility of data and software tools is the most important issue. In most cases, all users need to use the same software tools. Many times, they will need the exact same versions of that software. There are tools that convert data files to different formats; however, if you want to keep the exact page layout or take advantage of special features on one product, you will need to use the same software.

Similarly, everyone using a document will need the same fonts. Because fonts are generally software-based, that is not a serious problem because they can be distributed to other users. However, in any organization some users will insist on collecting and using obscure fonts that might not be available to everyone else. One solution to this problem is offered by Adobe in the form of a software product called Acrobat. It is a document viewer that always displays documents the same way, even when a recipient does not have the same hardware, software, and fonts as the document's creator. All information about the document (such as fonts and graphics) is stored within the document. Acrobat also contains a full-text search engine that enables users to search all of their documents.

The problem of compatibility worsens for more complex data such as sound and video. To reproduce these objects on different machines requires each machine to have the appropriate (matching) hardware and software. In some cases, if a user does not have the appropriate hardware, the document will not open.

**FIGURE 7.15**

Problems with sharing documents. There are several technical hurdles to overcome to make it easy to share documents. One solution is to require everyone to use the exact same hardware and software. But the continual introduction of new hardware and software updates makes it difficult to achieve this harmony.

- Everyone needs current/same version of the software.
  - Data conversion tools exist.
  - To get the exact layout you need the same versions.
- Everyone needs the same fonts, displays, sound cards, and video drivers.
  - Different hardware adjusts and converts but does not always produce the same results.
  - If a driver (e.g., sound) is missing on one machine, the document might crash.
- Everyone needs access and network paths to the linked documents.
- Transmission time can be a problem with video and sound.
- Concurrency: Multiple changes at the same time.
  - Who made what changes? Good software keeps track by user and time.
  - One user might be locked out of a document while others make changes.
  - Replication minimizes lockouts but causes conflicts when two people change the same data on different servers. Which version should survive?

With dynamically linked documents, users need access and network paths to all of the relevant documents. This problem is especially important when documents are moved to other machines. With some systems, if a piece of software is unavailable, portions of the document will be blank. There is a related problem with sound and video. Even if the network connections are available, they might be too slow to support the amount of data. This problem is most common with mobile links and ties to outside companies and across international links.

Another problem exists because of concurrency—allowing several people to modify the same document at the same time. There are several solutions to this problem. The most common method used by groupware tools is to replicate the data across the organization. Each file server contains a copy of the documents. When a document is updated on one machine, the changes are sent to the other machines. The problem is that users might make changes to the same document on different machines. Then someone has to decide which version should be saved. The process is relatively automatic, but occasionally the computer cannot determine which change should be kept and you will be asked to decide which version to retain.

## INTEGRATING WITH LEGACY SYSTEMS: A DATA WAREHOUSE

In many ways, the design and implementation of an information system is easier if you are starting a new company or rebuilding one completely. With older (legacy) systems, existing data and software might be incomplete and inconsistent. Valuable information and processes are embedded in these systems; we cannot just throw them away and start over. Yet, it can be more difficult to retrieve data from these systems and integrate it into new management systems.

As business operations and management change, information systems need to be updated. Management emphasis on teamwork is a significant change in the last few years. The improved integration features of current software fit nicely with the changes in management toward teamwork and integration across the enterprise. The problem is that few companies have the opportunity or the money to completely redesign their information system to take advantage of these new features. As a result, they need to utilize the data stored in their legacy systems. This data must be made accessible to decision makers so it can be analyzed. To meet this need, some companies are creating a data warehouse. A *data warehouse* is a single consolidation point for enterprise data from diverse production systems. The data is typically stored in one large file server or a central computer.

Many older transaction processing systems store data in their own files, without using a database management system. Although transaction systems produce standard reports, managers often need to use the base data to perform additional analyses or in-depth searches. Before the widespread use of networks, managers often entered data from each report into their own spreadsheets. Installing a network offers the ability to share data across the company. However, the data must be stored in a format that is accessible to the managers. Figure 7.16 illustrates how a data warehouse copies the transaction data into a central, shared location.

### Building a Data Warehouse

The goal of a data warehouse is to hold all of the data needed by managers to make decisions. Hence, the first step is to determine the data needs and models that managers use. The next step is to identify the data sources that are available in the company. This step can be difficult when the data is stored in hundreds of different files, scattered across many different machines. It requires analyzing company data sources in depth and documenting the business processes.

**FIGURE 7.16**

Data warehouse. A data warehouse is commonly used as a method to provide data to decision makers without interfering with the transaction-processing operations. Selected data items are regularly pulled from the transaction data files and stored in a central location. DSS tools query the data warehouse for analysis and reporting.

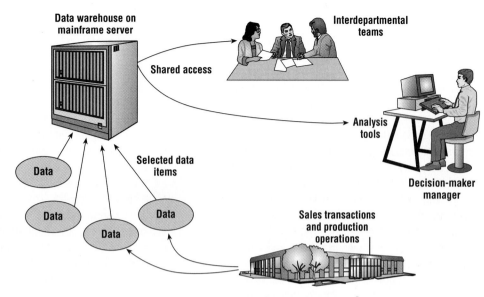

Once the data needs and data sources have been identified, the data must be transformed and integrated so that it can be searched and analyzed efficiently by the decision makers. In many cases, the data warehouse is created as a static copy of the original data. Instead of building a link to the original data files, it is easier to copy the data into new files. Special programs are run periodically to update the data warehouse from the original data.

The next step is to document the data warehouse. *Metadata* is used to describe the source data, identify the transformation and integration steps, and define the way the data warehouse is organized. This step is crucial to help decision makers understand what data elements are available. It also enables managers to find new data.

Once the data warehouse has been defined, programs are written to transfer the data from the legacy systems into the data warehouse. In some cases, managerial applications are created and distributed. Applications can be written for decisions that occur on a regular basis. For instance, finance decisions involving cash flow must be made every month or every week, and rely on standard data. On the other hand, applications for ad hoc decisions will have to be created as they are needed. U.S. West and Chase Manhattan Bank (Reality Bytes 7–5) illustrate how a data warehouse can overcome problems with large, unconnected databases.

## Limitations of a Data Warehouse

A data warehouse represents a subset of the total data in the company. In most cases, it is a static copy, not a dynamic link. Consequently, managers might not always have the most current data. Similarly, data not transferred to the data warehouse will still be difficult to find and use. Data warehouses are not always stored in relational database management systems. Instead, they are collections of files and the data items are extracted and transmitted to managers' personal computers. This type of system is relatively easy to use—managers do not have to learn data access commands (SQL or QBE). However, it is less flexible than using a database management system. Decision makers will be unable to get additional data or to compare the data in some previously unexpected way. The success of a data warehouse depends on how well the manager's needs have been anticipated.

**Reality Bytes**     7–5   DATA CONSISTENCY—BUILDING A DATA WAREHOUSE

U.S. West is one of the "baby bells" formed from the initial breakup of AT&T. It provides telephone services to people in 14 states. In 1991, U.S. West decided to consolidate the multiple terabytes of data held in the separate corporate databases. Part of the decision was driven by desperation. Because the data was not connected, orders for new service and resolution of complaints often required manual searches. Worse, phone lines and switches were not being freed up quickly enough when a customer moved or dropped services. Consequently, in fast-growing regions, U.S. West was having trouble allocating new lines. Even though the capacity was available, service personnel had no easy way to find the open switches and lines. Every database had different formats, so street addresses from one file could not be matched to addresses in the customer database. U.S. West put together a team of four full-time project managers and part-time support from 18 managers. With the help of Apertus Technologies, Inc. in Minneapolis, the team created rules, data structures,

and relationships among the data items. Apertus developed an object-oriented program to analyze the data and automate part of the process. To reduce the complexity and obtain results faster, U.S. West narrowed the problem to six databases in the fastest growing cities. Nonetheless, after four years, managers estimate they are only halfway through the project.

Chase Manhattan Bank in New York faced similar problems in reconciling myriad customer accounts. The bank's new database would pull data from 70 databases operated by 18 different business units. The goal was to consolidate all customer data so managers could retrieve and analyze data by households. The initial process required the efforts of 22 people over four years just to clean names and addresses of 20 million records. Chase used software from Innovative Systems that contains a list of 2.4 million names and more than 60,000 rules to identify duplicate names and addresses.

**OPEN SYSTEMS: INTEGRATION WITH DIFFERENT SYSTEMS**

Integrating data is difficult enough if everyone uses the same hardware and software. Integration is considerably more complex when it involves hardware from different manufacturers. Figure 7.17 illustrates some of the problems with integrating data across different systems. The problems are even more severe when the systems are owned by different people, such as suppliers or customers.

The entire technology industry is aware of these problems. Consequently, a variety of standards are designed to make it possible for different hardware and software to share data.

### Hardware

In the early days of computing, there were almost no standards. Hundreds of different companies built their own hardware that was completely independent of all the other computers. In the 1960s and 1970s, this process changed due to the dominance of IBM. As long as a company stayed with basic IBM hardware, data could be transferred among departments and different companies. Other companies built hardware that was compatible with these IBM machines. However, there were still many different computer companies that used incompatible hardware and software. Even IBM created new machines that were not directly compatible with the other primary IBM computers.

AT&T was one company that encountered problems in dealing with hardware and software from different vendors. Consequently, AT&T developed a new operating system known as *Unix*. The goal was to make this system run on hardware from different vendors. That way, it would always be possible to share data between various

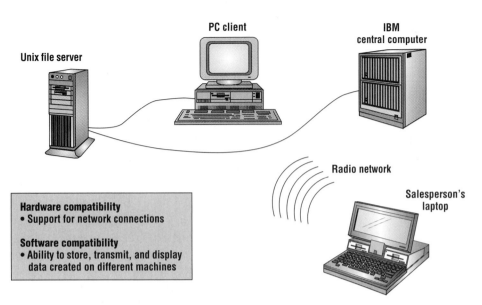

**FIGURE 7.17**
Data integration with diverse technology. It is possible to share data even though users have different hardware and software applications. At a minimum, each person must be able to connect to the network, and the software must be able to store data in a common format. Typically, the data will be transferred in ASCII format, which results in the loss of formatting and layout information.

machines. Today, you can buy a version of Unix for almost any type of computer. The catch is that there are several variants of Unix, and they are not completely compatible with each other.

An ultimate goal of creating an *open system* is to separate software and data from the hardware. If a company needs a new computer, it would be ideal to simply buy a new machine, copy all of the software and data to it, and have everything work correctly. From the beginning, Unix only solved part of this problem—just the data (and commands) were transferable among systems. Software generally needed modifications to run on new hardware.

With the advent of personal computers, the situation worsened. For a while, there were many different computer companies, all with incompatible hardware and software. By the mid-1980s, most companies (excluding manufacturers in Japan) focused on two types of computers: IBM-compatible and Apple Macintosh. Most companies focused on IBM-compatible machines. Just as in the 1960s and 1970s, this dominance of one machine made it easier for people to share data and software—but only because the machines were built exactly alike.

To expand their capabilities, computer companies are continually experimenting with new designs and new methods of building computers. One important example is the introduction of RISC processors that perform more limited computations at much higher speeds than traditional processors. The problem is that to gain speed, these processors are not completely compatible with existing designs; hence, they cannot run the huge amount of software available for typical personal computers.

## Software

To take advantage of breakthroughs in hardware design, we need a way to use common software and data on different types of hardware. Several companies are working to solve this problem. Microsoft was one of the first to provide a commercial solution with an operating system called Windows NT. This new operating system was designed from the bottom up to run exactly the same on different types of hardware. The hardware manufacturer makes a few changes to a hardware-interface layer that makes it compatible with a new processor. Application software runs the same on any hardware, so data can be shared with any user.

The problem is even more complex when you are dealing with divisions in different nations. Several business people have remarked that people outside the United States are slower to adopt new technology. For instance, if a software package is upgraded, it is most likely to be adopted by the U.S. departments, whereas the overseas workers will continue to use the old version. Data integration becomes difficult when departments are using different versions of the operating system and the application software.

## Open Standards

The common-hardware and Windows NT approaches have one major problem. They are based on proprietary definitions. In the case of the hardware, the entire computer was defined by IBM. In the case of Windows NT, the interface is defined by Microsoft. Other computer vendors are reluctant to use these definitions because they must pay royalties to the owner of these definitions.

To combat this situation, several organizations have attempted to define standards and protocols that will enable hardware and software to work together. By making the standards definitions public, all companies can use them without royalty payments and lawsuits. Over the years, several important standards have been created that have made it easier to share data.

The drawback to the open-standards approach is that it takes considerable time to develop all of the standards needed. Additionally, each vendor has an incentive to push its own definitions. It can take years for competitors to agree on a standard. By that time, the definition might be obsolete. The competition between vendors often leads to the creation of two or more competing standards-setting organizations. Half the companies agree to support one "standard"; the other half support a different "standard."

Despite these problems, standards are essential to creating integrated systems. They are especially important when you are linking machines that are owned by different organizations, such as ties between suppliers and customers.

## Management Issues

To a manager, the entire issue of computer "standards" can be confusing. The most basic issue is that it would be wonderful if everyone could immediately agree on a single standard for every definition. That way we could buy hardware and software from anyone and know that it would work together on any of our computers. As shown by Trane (Reality Bytes 7–6), this utopia will probably never exist, because of changes in technology and the constant competition among manufacturers to gain an advantage. In reality, we are forced to guess which technology will succeed and which standard will eventually dominate the others. Choosing incorrectly can result in ownership of *orphaned* products that are no longer supported. You also end up changing hardware, software, and data more often, which results in expensive and disruptive conversions.

Unfortunately, there is no simple rule that will tell you how to choose a direction or standard. Some companies avoid the issue by avoiding new technology and waiting until it is clear which technology will win. Some managers simplify their choices by always buying from the market leader. Both strategies can cause problems: In par-

**Reality Bytes** ▲ 7–6 TRANE

As a subsidiary of American Standard, Trane manufactures residential and commercial heating and cooling systems. Their manufacturing plant in Clarksville, Tennessee, typically produces mid-range commercial units up to 130-ton capacity. These units are typically used for heating and cooling at small stores, such as fast-food restaurants.

Like many other manufacturing companies, Trane has moved to just-in-time deliveries with many of its suppliers. The assembly line is automated, and demand-driven. Turning to the computer terminal at the start of the line, an operator can call up a specific order. The computer system generates instructions throughout the line and parts are tagged for that assembly. Four and a half hours later, the designated heating/cooling unit rolls off the line and into a truck for delivery.

In an effort to improve efficiency, the plant operates with only two levels of managers. The central computers of the 1980s were outsourced and replaced with an IBM AS/400 mid-range computer. By 1997, the AS/400 was replaced with a series of LAN file servers. Managers rely on the PC-based information systems to communicate and share data with workers in the plant and throughout the company.

Don Combs, manager of the MIS department, observes that this level of operation can be achieved only through the use of corporate standards for all information systems. As new technologies are added, new standards have to be implemented. For example, the plant vice-president decided that all operations would go to a paperless environment. Meetings are held in rooms with PC-based projection equipment and PCs connected to the LAN. No one is allowed to bring paper to the meetings. New standards were created for the selection of scanners, graphics file formats, and supporting software to convert and store paper documents that came from outside sources.

Combs is searching for groupware and e-mail tools that will further reduce the use of paper and improve the flow of information throughout the company. He is particularly concerned about the need to attach binary documents (e.g., images and spreadsheet files) to mail messages that can be sent throughout the company. In early 1996, few software packages provided the standards needed to enable seamless exchange of binary documents over the mail system.

ticular it means that you will always be a follower instead of a leader. Although there are advantages to being a follower, it makes it difficult to use technology to gain an advantage over the competition.

**GROUP DECISIONS** A different type of groupware tool is designed specifically to help groups (or teams) make decisions. Many business decisions involve a group of people. Often, one person might be responsible for the final decision, but meetings are used to enable everyone to have a say, analyze the potential effects on each area, and persuade others to accept a decision. Decisions that involve groups of people have additional complications. Someone has to organize and control the meeting. During the meeting, people compete to make comments and get their opinions heard. Someone has to take notes of the meetings and votes have to be counted.

Information systems can help with group decisions. Groupware tools can be used to share data and documents. Message systems can be used to share comments and early drafts of work. Bulletin boards can be used to let everyone express opinions and evaluations. In the late 1980s, an additional tool known as a *group decision support system (GDSS)* was defined. A GDSS is designed to help managers reach a consensus during meetings.

Group decision support systems can be used to coordinate meetings, record notes, take votes, and encourage participation. As shown in this system by Ventana corporation, each participant enters data in a PC, with summary results displayed on the central screen.

## Features of a GDSS

Most versions of a GDSS use a special meeting room, where each participant is seated at a networked computer. There is a facilitator who operates the network and keeps the discussion moving in the right direction. Before the meeting, the primary decision maker meets with the facilitator to establish the objective of the meeting. They set up sample questions and design the overall strategy. The facilitator enters some basic data into the GDSS.

Typical meetings begin with a brainstorming session, where participants are asked to think of ideas, problems, and potential solutions. They type each of these into categories on their computers. The basic ideas and suggestions are stored in a database and shared with the group through the networked computers.

In terms of discussion and comments, the facilitator can choose individual items and project them on a screen for the entire group to analyze. Participants can write comments or criticisms of any idea at any time. This system is particularly helpful if many participants come up with ideas and comments at the same time. The computer enables everyone to enter comments at the same time, which is faster than waiting for each person to finish speaking.

Another feature of using the computer for entry of ideas and comments is that they can be anonymous. Although each comment is numbered, they are not traced back to the original author, so people are free to criticize their supervisor's ideas. Anonymity reduces embarrassment and encourages people to submit riskier ideas.

At various points, the facilitator can call for participants to vote on some of the ideas and concepts. Depending on the software package, there can be several ways to vote. In addition to traditional one-vote methods, there are several schemes where you place weights on your choices. The votes are done on the computer and results appear instantly. Because it is so easy to vote, the GDSS encourages the group to take several votes. This approach makes it easier to drop undesirable alternatives early in the discussion.

One useful feature of conducting the meeting over a computer network is that all of the comments, criticisms, and votes are recorded. They can all be printed at the end of the session. Managers can review all of the comments and add them to their reports.

In theory, a meeting could be conducted entirely on a computer network, saving costs and travel time if the participants are located in different cities. Also, if it is designed properly, a GDSS can give each participant access to the corporate data while he or she is in the meeting. If a question arises about various facts, the computer can find the answer without waiting for a second meeting.

## Limitations of a GDSS

Perhaps the greatest drawback to a GDSS is that it requires participants to type in their ideas, comments, and criticisms. Most people are used to meetings based on oral discussions. Even if they have adequate typing skills, a GDSS can inhibit some managers.

Along the same lines, in a traditional meeting, only one person speaks at a time, and everyone concentrates on the same issues at the same time. With a GDSS, your focus is continually drawn to the many different comments and discussions taking place at the same time. People who type rapidly and flit from topic to topic will find that they can dominate the discussions.

In terms of costs, maintaining a separate meeting room with its own network and several computers can be expensive. Unless the facility is used on a regular basis, the computers will be idle a great deal of the time. When you factor in the costs for network software, the GDSS software, and other utilities, the costs multiply. One way to minimize this problem is to lease the facilities that have been established by a couple of universities and some companies (e.g., IBM).

The use of a GDSS also requires a trained facilitator—someone who can lead discussions, help users, and control the GDSS software on the network. Hiring an in-house specialist can be very expensive if there are only a few meetings a year. Using facilities from an outside agency can reduce this cost, but it means that someone outside your company is watching and controlling your meeting. Although most facilitators are scrupulously honest, there might be some topics that you do not want to discuss with nonemployees.

**SOFTWARE TO SUPPORT INTEGRATION**

The traditional tools consisting of a database, spreadsheet, graphics package, and word processor are useful tools within groupware products. The network and groupware transfer data among workers, but workers still need the traditional tools to create and modify the data. Software companies have been adding features to these packages to make them more useful for workgroups.

The most common approach to integrating data is to create a base document that displays all of the contributing information. When the document contains several types of data, it is known as a compound document. This base document could be a spreadsheet, word processing (or desktop publishing) document, a database management system report, or a slide show. This discussion explains how these different methods can be used to combine information. As illustrated by the spreadsheet link in Figure 7.19, there might be several levels of links.

**Sales Report for November**
**Data retrieved from Database**

| Region | Sales | Returns | Net |
|--------|-------|---------|-----|
| North | 1,555 | 321 | 1,234 |
| South | 5,663 | 664 | 4,999 |
| East | 8,883 | 783 | 8,100 |
| West | 3,441 | 241 | 3,200 |
| **Total** | **19,542** | **2,009** | **17,533** |

## Spreadsheets

Historically, the earliest type of integration in the personal computer world occurred within spreadsheets. Almost all spreadsheets are capable of creating graphs. Early in their development, the software designers realized that it was necessary to dynamically link the data and the graphs. Because the graphs are included in the spreadsheet, they are automatically updated when you change the spreadsheet data. Today, most spreadsheets allow the graphs to be printed alongside the data.

In many firms, users spend too much time re-entering data into spreadsheets that came from other computers. For example, a finance manager might copy summary data from the monthly accounting reports into a spreadsheet that performs cash flow projections. Obviously the report would be easier to produce if the data could be retrieved directly from the accounting database into the spreadsheet.

There are many ways for spreadsheets to obtain data. The import function is useful. It enables the spreadsheet to read data that was created by other software packages. This type of link is static. The data is immediately copied from the other files. If the original files change, the spreadsheet data is not automatically updated.

Some spreadsheets are capable of creating dynamic links to other software packages—especially to databases. With these tools, the original data is stored in a database management system. The spreadsheet is used as a report writer to produce computations and graphs. Whenever the original data is changed, the spreadsheet and its graphs are automatically updated.

As illustrated in Figure 7.20, a company may keep a central database that records all of the sales data. The database tracks customers, salespeople, inventory, and actual sales. This data is used to produce standard monthly sales and accounting reports. On the other hand, the marketing department has a spreadsheet to predict sales for the next three months. It uses the sales data for the last three months along with some economic variables. Likewise, the purchasing department combines the inventory and sales data in a spreadsheet that helps purchasers decide when to reorder each product. At the start of each day, the marketing and purchasing departments print out their spreadsheets. Because the spreadsheets are dynamically linked to the central database, they automatically have the current data. Therefore, end users simply start their spreadsheets and print the reports that are needed.

**FIGURE 7.20**
Spreadsheet link to DBMS. One of the biggest problems users encountered with early spreadsheets was the need to type data from existing reports into the spreadsheet. With dynamic linking (and networks), (1) the spreadsheet can issue a query to the DBMS, (2) receive the data and (3) perform the computations automatically. (4) The spreadsheet can query the DBMS at regular intervals to (5) collect changes in the data.

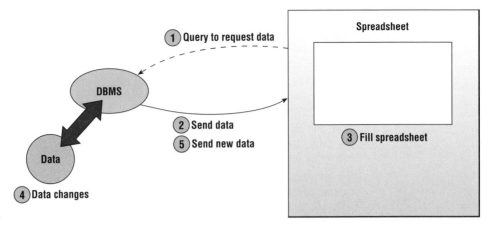

## Word Processors and Desktop Publishing Software

Word processors are used to write most reports. It makes sense to use them as the foundation to integrate additional information. If the report is primarily text but needs to incorporate diagrams, charts, or spreadsheet information, then the word processor can format and paginate the final report. Figure 7.21 shows one example.

Most word processors can read information from graphics packages and spreadsheets. The graphs can be placed anywhere on a page. Wide graphs can be rotated to print sideways (landscape mode) if necessary. Most graphs created by spreadsheets or other data packages can usually be copied to word processors with few problems. Some manipulation of the background shading may be required, such as inverting colors to print black on white instead of white on black.

As discussed in Chapter 2, bitmapped graphics cause problems when you try to integrate them into a document. The problem is that when these illustrations are copied into the word processor, the word processor often needs to resize the picture. It is difficult to change the size of bitmapped images without distorting the picture. If you want to copy graphics pictures into another document, it is best not to use bitmapped images. Instead, you should try to find line-art or vector images. If you

**FIGURE 7.21**
Word processors are commonly used to create the container document. Many reports contain written comments, and word processors (or desktop publishing packages) provide page layout, templates for consistency, and automatic numbering.

**Word Processor Integration**

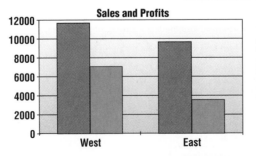

Many reports will contain large amounts of text. A word processor will be used to enter and format the pages. If you want to include a graph, it can be placed in its own box anywhere on the page. The figures can have titles, and they can be numbered automatically. Text can automatically flow around the box. You can build automatic references to the figure numbers. If you add or move a figure, the numbers and references update automatically.

Similarly, you might want to include data from spreadsheets. In this case, the best method is to create a table in the document.

| Region | Sales | Profit |
|--------|-------|--------|
| West | 11,500 | 6,814 |
| East | 9,400 | 3,415 |
| Total | 20,900 | 10,229 |

need bitmapped images for their color, experiment with the size and placement so you get the best results for your printer.

Spreadsheets are typically handled as tables. As long as there is enough space in the table cell, the word processor will format the columns correctly. If the spreadsheet data cell is too wide for the table, first change the size of the columns. If there is not enough space, you can either delete some of the data or use a smaller type size. These problems are particularly cumbersome when you are using dynamic integration. Significant changes in the original data might require you to change the layout of the table or columns.

One primary advantage of using a word processor or a desktop publishing package to integrate data is that you have access to all of the text layout features. In particular, the word processor can use one typeface throughout the document. By incorporating the spreadsheet data into the document, all of the text and numbers can be printed with the same fonts to provide a more consistent-looking document. Most word processors can automatically number the various figures and tables, generate a table of contents, and produce a list of figures and tables.

## Database Reports

Database report writers are similar to word processors; however, there is one major difference. The data printed in the report is repetitive. For example, you might want to produce a list of customers. With a word processor, the manager would copy all of the data into the document. The word processor would then format the entire document at one time. With a DBMS report writer, the manager creates a template for a single row of data (e.g., one customer). The report writer then fills in this template for every row of data. The report writer automatically takes care of formatting each item, determining page breaks and computing subtotals.

Some database report writers can print data, graphics, and text files from word processors. You would use this approach when the bulk of your report is based on data that is stored in a database. For example, an advertiser might wish to produce a catalog that describes all of the products offered for sale, such as the example in Figure 7.22. A good report writer can retrieve the product numbers and prices and descriptions from the database as shown in Figure 7.23. The report writer can set

**FIGURE 7.22**

Database report writer. A DBMS report writer is designed to handle repeating rows of data. You merely indicate where each item should be displayed on the page and insert computations and totals. The DBMS formats the data and displays the report for the rows you select in the order you specify.

**Catalog of Bicycle Parts**

**Part# 1165    Specialized Tri-Spoke Wheel**

This wheel is great for time trials. It can save over 2 minutes on a 50-mile course. No problems with crosswinds.

$750

**Part# 9978    Solid Disc Wheel**

The original high-speed wheel. Cuts wind resistance by 20% at high speeds. Best used only as rear wheel. It may cause trouble in high cross-winds. It performs slightly better than the tri-spoke in low wind conditions.

$800

**FIGURE 7.23**
Sample page from
DBMS report writer.
The overall layout was
specified by the design
page. The text and
figures were inserted
and formatted
individually.

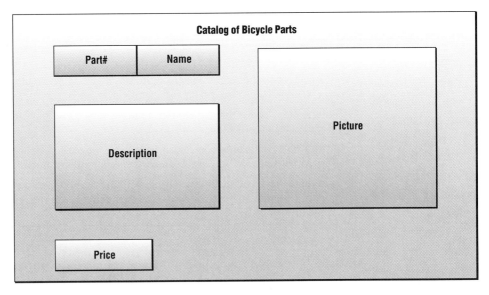

professional typefaces for the descriptions and take care of formatting the text.
Pictures of products can be printed on the report next to the descriptions. Lastly,
comments or testimonials for the products can be included in the catalog. This information could be stored in a word processor's file and printed in the final report next
to the product descriptions. Each of these components might be created by a different department and could be stored in a central database, so that everyone would
have access to the current data.

Database report writers are useful for any problems that involve repetitive types
of information. They are also useful when you need to relate or compare information
stored in different tables. For instance, pictures are usually created with the graphics
software discussed in Chapter 2. The database can combine these two sets of information by matching the items according to product number.

Sometimes it is hard to tell when you should use a word processor and when you
should use a report writer. Figures 7.24 and 7.25 outline the basic steps involved in
creating the catalog using a word processor or a report writer. As another example,
consider a human resources management (HRM) department that needs to produce a

**FIGURE 7.24**
CREATING A
CATALOG USING A
WORDPROCESSOR
Catalogs that are
created one-time in a
single layout can be
designed with desktop
publishing systems.
This method enables
the user to make
detailed design
changes, such as slight
changes in font for
certain items or color
corrections for
individual pages.
However, detail changes
are time-consuming,
and it can be difficult to
make major
reorganization changes
using a desktop
publishing program.

- Start at the top of the page. Enter the titles, then set up the page number method and
  the margins.
- Type in the first item number: its name, description, and price.
- Create a figure and tell the word processor to read in the corresponding picture.
- When you finish with the first item, do the same thing for all the others.
- Each time you want to include a picture, you have to create a new space for it and read
  it in.

Imagine the work involved when you delete the solid disk wheel. After you delete the
information for that item, you have to make sure that the pictures are still in the proper
place. The word processor may have found it necessary to shift a price or a picture to
another page. Lastly, because all of this information is stored in a document instead of a
database, it will be hard to search, and to make changes to prices and descriptions.

**FIGURE 7.25**
CREATING A CATALOG
WITH A DBMS
REPORT WRITER
With a DBMS report
writer, you specify
layouts and formats for
each generic item you
place on the report.
The report writer then
handles the details and
formats each row of
data. The DBMS
approach is particularly
good at rapidly creating
specialized catalogs
with a restricted
selection or different
ordering of the
products. However, you
must rely on the report
writer to handle the
final format. It is
usually difficult to
make detail changes to
a single page.

- Define the page by specifying margins, page numbers, headers, and footers.

- Tell the report writer where to display the information: product number, name, description, and price.

- Place a box on the screen page to show where the figure should be printed.

- These tasks are only done once. When you run the report, the DBMS will fill in the information, format the text, and load the pictures. The DBMS automatically handles pagination and formatting.

- With DBMS commands, you can sort and print the catalog in any order. For instance, one catalog could be sorted by category, another one by product number or price.

- Also note that all of the links are dynamic. The data and pictures are read at the time the report is printed. Any changes you make before you print the report will automatically be incorporated.

list of job descriptions and performance appraisal categories for all company jobs. Because these descriptions are text instead of numbers, it looks as if the best approach is to use a word processor to store all of the documents. On the other hand, many jobs will use the same descriptions, so it would be easier to store them in a database. For instance, you might have the same description of safety requirements for several jobs. Instead of retyping and storing the same paragraph many times, it can be stored once in the database. The database report writer can then select the categories that apply to each job and print them on the final form.

## Guidelines for Integrating Data

There are three primary software means to integrate data from different sources: spreadsheets, word processors, and DBMS report writers. You should choose the method that best matches your needs. If the report is primarily based on calculations and data and it simply needs a few graphs, use a spreadsheet. If the report is largely based on text that does not change, then use a word processor and include graphs and tables. If the report is based on repetitive data, use a database report writer.

Keep in mind that integrating information is still a recent advance in computer software. Different software packages have varying capabilities. For example, some word processors cannot read spreadsheets into tables. Finally, remember that there is a big difference between static copies of files and dynamic linking, in which the report always contains the most recent data.

**INTEGRATING DATA
WITH WINDOWS**

So far, the discussion has centered on using individual software packages to combine information from various sources. There is one more method of integrating data. This method relies on the operating system to share information among the software packages. As discussed in Chapter 2, most of the recent operating systems enable users to run several programs at the same time. These different programs can be displayed on the screen at the same time. For example, Microsoft Windows software exists for personal computers running DOS. OS/2 has a Presentation Manager that works much the same as the Windows interface. Unix computers can run a similar product called X-Windows. Macintosh computers and the Next operating system also allow many programs to be running and displaying information on the screen at the same time.

## Clipboard and Linking Data

Besides displaying several different software tools on the same screen, these systems allow the packages to exchange data. It is possible to make both static copies and dynamic links. Windowing operating systems have a **clipboard** to import or export data between different software packages. As an example, say that you are writing a report using a word processor in one window. You have a graph displayed using a graphics package in a second window that you would like to put in the report. Using a mouse, you click the pointer on the graph window to make it active. You then choose the **cut** option to move the image or **copy** icon to copy the graph. This copy is temporarily stored on a clipboard. Now, switch to the report and **paste** the copy of the graph from the clipboard. The graph will be included when the report is printed. However, remember that unless you make a dynamic link, if you change the graph using the graphics package, you will have to go back and recopy the graph into the report.

Many recent software packages that run in windows operating systems can also share information dynamically. Basically, the software packages talk to each other. There might be a word processor document in the left window and a spreadsheet in the right window. You can tell the word processor to retrieve part of the spreadsheet and store it in a table. The word processor sends a message to the spreadsheet and automatically collects the data. If you make a change to some of the data, the spreadsheet will instantly send that information to the word processor. So the table in the word processor will always have the correct data and will update the display on the screen as you make changes.

Similarly, some database management systems can collect and display graphs and images. For instance, in the human resources department you might create a database of employees. By including a photograph of the employee, this database can have additional uses. For instance, consider a company that needs to maintain high levels of security. The guard stations at the company gate could use the employee database. When a person wanted to enter the company grounds, the computer could read his or her magnetic stripe ID card. The database would look up the corresponding personnel data and display it on the screen for the guard. The screen could contain the name and description of the person. It could also display a picture of the employee that was stored in the corporate files. The guard could then compare the picture to the person trying to gain entry to the company. Entrance and exit data could then be stored by the security division. If problems or questions arose later, a security team could integrate data from the gate files, HRM database, and employee work records.

## Sequential Binding of Documents

When Microsoft created Windows 95 and Office 95, the designers added a new method to create reports that use data from different software packages. The *binder* is a place to combine various parts of a report. Like a large folder, each section can contain output from a different software package. Each section is edited and maintained with the original application. The binder is responsible for setting consistent page layouts such as headers, footers, and page numbers. It is useful when you need to combine large sections from various types of software packages.

Binders can be shared with other users. Keeping all of the related files within one binder minimizes mistakes such as lost files. Many applications also track changes made by each user, so you can find updates and verify changes.

## SUMMARY

Working together and sharing data are crucial in today's companies. MIS can help teams work better with tools designed to integrate data across an organization. Managers need to know how to use a variety of tools, from data sharing over networks, to dynamic linking, to groupware products.

One important concept is the difference between static and dynamic integration. Static transfers simply make copies of the data as it is now. For instance, you can paste a graph into a word processor's document. If you change the original graph, it does not change the copy stored with the word processor. Therefore, any time you change data, graphs, pictures, or documents, you have to check all of your reports to see whether they need to be corrected. Dynamic integration solves this problem. You might use dynamic integration to include a graph in a spreadsheet. If one of the numbers is changed, the graph is automatically updated, and the version printed by the spreadsheet is always up-to-date.

There are many ways to integrate various types of data. One of the earliest methods uses a spreadsheet as the foundation. For instance, many spreadsheets can import and format data stored in databases. Spreadsheets can also be used to create and print graphs. A second method to combine information is to use a word processor as the foundation. Your document can then import spreadsheet tables and graphs or pictures. A third method begins with a database report. The database report can import data, make calculations, and include spreadsheet information, word processor documents, graphs, and pictures.

Windows-based software enables you to combine information from software that is displayed in different windows on the screen. Some of these transfers use static copies; others use dynamic integration (or hot links). These systems enable you to see how all of the information is related. If you change a piece of data, the other documents and graphs will be updated automatically.

To integrate data, you need to select a base document. The way to make your other choice (spreadsheet, word processor, or database), is to identify the primary format of the finished report. If the

### A MANAGER'S VIEW

Teamwork is an increasingly important aspect of management. Integration of business units so they work together is another important issue. Effectively managed, the techniques can cut costs, improve quality, and improve response time.

Several tools will help you integrate data and share information. Software suites and operating systems like Windows enable users to integrate data from different packages across a network. Workgroup products like Lotus Notes enable workers to build complex documents and share comments with other employees.

report consists of tables of numbers with a few graphs, a spreadsheet should be used to perform the integration. If the majority of the report is written analysis that uses tables and graphs to illustrate certain points, a word processor will work best. If the report consists of information that repeats (like the catalog example), a database is the best choice. Likewise, if the report relies on combining related data from different places, a database will work best.

Integration often requires combining data from many different locations. Networks enable you to dynamically link the work done by different people. However, if everyone in a company uses different software, it becomes difficult to combine the information because each software package stores data in a unique format. As a result, companies generally create standards for how the data will be stored and accessed. Although these standards are often necessary, several problems can arise when some users have special needs or the standards need to be changed.

Workgroup software like Lotus Notes combines many features to facilitate work on group projects. It supports communication, document sharing, integration of data types, and tracking individual changes.

Group decisions can also be supported with GDSS software that is used to facilitate meetings. Its primary feature is that all managers can contribute at the same time. It also tracks comments for each idea and supports several types of votes and rankings.

## KEY WORDS

clipboard, 343

compound document, 313

copy, 343

cut, 343

dynamic integration, 320

Dynamic Data Exchange (DDE), 320

export, 320

groupware, 323

hot links, 320

import, 320

integrated data, 313

Object Linking and Embedding (OLE), 320

paste, 343

static integration, 313

## REVIEW QUESTIONS

1. What is meant by the concept of integrating information in business? Give an example of problems that can arise if business information is not integrated.
2. What is the difference between static and dynamic integration?
3. What are the differences between using a file created with a spreadsheet, word processor, or database management system as the base document when you integrate information?
4. How do windowing operating systems make it easier to integrate information?
5. What role is played by networks in integrating information in a business?
6. How do groupware tools help managers integrate data? What features do they have that support teams?
7. What problems are you likely to encounter when attempting to integrate data across the entire company? How might you solve these problems?
8. What is the goal of open systems? How does it affect sharing data and integrating the business operations? Will we ever see completely interchangeable hardware and software?
9. Why is it better to use vector images instead of bitmap graphics when you copy figures into a word processing system's document?
10. What basic steps are involved in creating a catalog using a database report writer?
11. How do the features of Object Linking and Embedding (OLE) make it easier for users to deal with compound documents?
12. Describe three features of group decision support systems.

## EXERCISES

1. Describe a report for which you would use a spreadsheet as the base for integrating other information.
2. Sometimes dynamic integration can cause problems. Identify three situations in which you would be better off using static instead of dynamic integration of data.
3. Create a spreadsheet and draw a graph. Now, copy them into a word processing system's document and dynamically link (embed) them. Make changes to the original spreadsheet to make sure the graph and the word processor's document are updated. Does your software require extra steps to make sure the changes are recorded in each location?

C07Ex04.mdb

4. Using a DBMS (CO7Ex04.mdb) and a spreadsheet, create the sample report displayed in the spreadsheet discussion. The sales and returns are stored in the DBMS and the DBMS should be used to compute the totals by region.
5. As a group project, assume that each person in the group is a manager of a different department. Each person creates a spreadsheet to list the salespeople in his or her department (4–10), their hours worked, total sales, and commissions. Compute the totals for each column. Once the individual spreadsheets have been created and stored on separate computers, the group will create a composite spreadsheet that brings in the data from each individual spreadsheet. Compute the corporate total and draw pie charts for each column. If possible, use dynamic linking across the network to capture the data from the individual spreadsheets.

## DeptStor Database

6. Using a DBMS, spreadsheet, and word processor, create the four reports shown in the introduction: daily sales report, returned merchandise log, commissions report, and the weekly sales analysis. If possible, use tools that support dynamic integration.

7. Using current business publications, find an example of a company that is experiencing problems with integrating data. Alternatively, find an example of a company that has an excellent system for integrating information. Identify data that is shared dynamically and data that is shared through static copies. (Hint: Companies are more likely to report successes than problems.)

8. Using a graphics-oriented DBMS, create a small catalog report that includes pictures and text descriptions.

9. Find descriptions of the top-selling software packages (spreadsheet, database management system, word processor, graphics). Be sure to include version (edition) numbers. What types of integration do they support? Will they share data with software written by other companies? Can each package dynamically link to any of the other packages? Will it link as both a client (accepting data) and server (sending data)?

10. Find a business situation that could benefit from the use of a groupware product. Describe the problems that exist and how they can be overcome with the groupware tools.

## Rolling Thunder Database

1. Extract sales and cost data by model type and create a spreadsheet to analyze it. (Hint: Use the Extract Data form.) Write a short report discussing profitability and any trends. Include graphs to illustrate your comments. Your spreadsheet should look at monthly sales by model and monthly material costs by model. Be sure to compute profit margins and examine percentages.

2. Assume that we are experiencing problems with quality control. Suddenly there are several complaints about the components. Write a report describing all of the data and reports we would need to help us resolve these problems.

3. Top management needs an analysis of purchases and deliveries from vendors. Begin by using queries to extract the appropriate data to create a basic spreadsheet. Write a report analyzing the data; include graphs to illustrate your points.

| VENDOR | PURCHASES ORDER TOTAL $ | PERCENT OF VENDOR TOTAL | RECEIVED $ | RECEIPTS % OF PURCHASE | AVE. DAYS TO DELIVER |
|---|---|---|---|---|---|
|  |  |  |  |  |  |
|  |  |  |  |  |  |
|  |  |  |  |  |  |

## ADDITIONAL READING

Baer, Tony. "Mister Data Clean," *Computerworld Client/Server Journal*, November 1995, pp. 48–50. [Data warehouse problems]

Bartholomew, Doug. "SAP America's Trojan Horse," *Information Week*, April 24, 1995, pp. 36–42. [Price Waterhouse]

Bell, Trudy E. "Bicycles on a Personalized Basis," *IEEE Spectrum*, September 1993, pp. 32–35. [National Industrial Bicycle Company]

"Catalina Goes from the Grocery Store to the World Wide Web," *Electronic Marketplace Report*, October 3, 1995, p. 1. [Kraft General Foods]

"Data Points: Schedule Slippage," *Soft-Letter*, October 16, 1995, p. 2. [Price Waterhouse]

Fine, Doug. "Help Desk's New Hat," *InfoWorld*, October 23, 1995, pp. 1–4. [Kraft General Foods]

Francett, Barbara. "Shrinking Space on the Retail Horizon," *Computerworld*, May 13, 1991, p. 97. [PDS and retail drug sales]

Gill, Phillip J. "A Diet of Reengineering," *Information Week*, September 18, 1995, pp. 118–120. [Kraft General Foods]

Hamilton, Rosemary. "Note Productivity Claims Eyed," *Computerworld*, June 15, 1992, p. 4. [Lotus Notes examples]

"Institutions Get New Tools to Manage Risk," *Wall Street & Technology*, December 1994. [Price Waterhouse]

LaPlante, Alice. "Growth Is Relative," *Computerworld*, September 14, 1992, p. 18. [Banker's Trust]

Liebmann, Lenny. "Writing the Book on Change," *LAN Magazine*, October 1995, pp. 163-166. [Price Waterhouse]

Major, Michael J. "Pinpoint a Profit Center and Size of Investment," *Computer Reseller News*, November 13, 1995, pp. J33-34. [Kraft General Foods]

Mehler, Mark. "Notes Fanatic," *Corporate Computing*, August 1992, pp. 160-164. [Price Waterhouse]

Nash, Kim S. "Oracle Office to Throw Down Gauntlet to Notes," *Computerworld*, September 6, 1993, p. 1. [Oracle and Lotus Notes]

"On the Job: Order-Driven Manufacturer Streamlines Production Cycle with CIM," *Midrange Systems*, July 7, 1992, p. 13. [Furon Aerospace]

Radding, Alan. "Going Down? Midrange Platforms Hold the Door Open for a More Moderate Form of Downsizing," *Midrange Systems*, October 13, 1992, pp. 23-27. [Armatron]

Radding, Alan. "The Feature Parade," *Midrange Systems*, October 10, 1993, pp. 27-28. [Fairbanks Morse]

Radosevich, Lynda. "Vendors Unite to Promote Work Flow," *Computerworld*, August 2, 1993, p. 16. [Lotus Notes examples]

Rodriguez, Moises-Enrique. "Switzerland Establishes CIM Centers to Study Technology," *Industrial Engineering*, November 23, 1991, pp. 23-24. [Switzerland's economy is based on small and medium-sized manufacturing, so the nation is paying for training in CIM to help them compete better.]

Rymer, J.R. "Dazel Goes Beyond Printing to 'Output Management'," *Distributed Computing Monitor*, April 1995, pp. 37-42. [Cummins Engine]

Smith, Laura. "Boeing to Shave IT," *PC Week*, June 12, 1995, p. E. [Lotus Notes examples]

Smith, Larry and Charles Walker. "Boeing Slated Over 777 Software Set-Up," *Computer Weekly*, May 25, 1995, p. 1. [Lotus Notes examples]

"Specialized Financial Applications," *Wall Street & Technology*, December 15, 1994, pp. 95-105. [Price Waterhouse]

Vacca, John R. "A Guide to the Future Factory," *Midrange Systems*, March 3, 1992, pp. 367-38. [Armatron]

Walker, Charles. "Are Aircraft Software Tests Up to Scratch?" *Computer Weekly*, June 22, 1995, p. 16. [Lotus Notes examples]

# CASES  *Large-Scale Manufacturing*

Large-scale manufacturers typically involve durable goods. Manufacturers use computers for the same tasks as the entire economy. There is a slight emphasis on inventory, graphics, databases, and analysis.

SOURCE: Computer Use in the United States, U.S. Bureau of the Census.

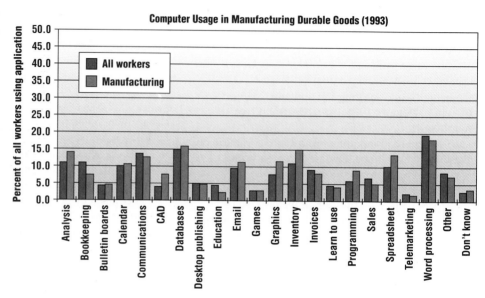

**Computer Usage in Manufacturing Durable Goods (1993)**

Large-scale manufacturing involves complex products that use thousands of parts. In this situation, even minor problems get multiplied thousands of times to become serious concerns. Simply keeping track of suppliers can become a nightmare. Monitoring engineering changes and modifications becomes crucial to the success of the firm. On the other end, there are typically a limited number of customers, particularly since the products tend to be expensive. Consequently, the customers often want customized products, which further complicates the manufacturing process.

Salespeople end up in the middle of many disputes between customers and engineers. The salespeople try to make their product fit the exact needs of the customer, but each unique option increases costs. Costs rise from engineering modifications, to custom assembly, to ordering special components.

Throw in the importance of quality control, and it becomes clear that information is crucial to every step in the production process. Every item and customized option ordered has to be tracked by customer and product. Components need to be ordered so they arrive just-in-time to minimize inventory costs. Individual parts need to be tracked at every step of the assembly process to monitor quality and suppliers. Production runs and assembly operations need to be scheduled to maximize standardization and keep costs down.

There is a tremendous amount of data to track. But equally importantly, managers need instant access to the data. They also need the ability to pull data from any section of the company and combine it into new reports.

## CASE  *Armatron International*

In 1991, Armatron had total sales of $23.6 million. The loss of sales to Chrysler Corporation hurt the company in 1990 and 1991. In 1989, the company had 195 employees and sales of more than $41 million. In 1991, the company had sales of $23.6 million and 120 employees. Charles J. Housman, the president, began emphasizing the shift to the garden products market, because he believed the increasing environmental pressures for composting and avoidance of pesticides will generate increased sales for several years.

Because of the seasonal markets for its products, Armatron operates a different production schedule than other manufacturing firms do. From January to June, it produces its bug killer products. Then from August to October, it converts production to the Flowtron leaf-eaters and chippers. Also because of the seasonal nature of the products, Armatron offers extended payment terms to its customers. According to the 1991 annual report:

> Net sales to two customers accounted for approximately $6,065,000, or 26%, of consolidated net sales in fiscal 1991, as compared to $15,532,000, or 48%, in fiscal 1990, and $25,813,000, or 63%, in fiscal 1989 . . . Net

ARMATRON BALANCE SHEET
ANNUAL ASSETS (000$)

| FISCAL YEAR ENDING | 09/30/91 | 09/30/90 | 09/30/89 | 09/30/88 |
|---|---|---|---|---|
| Cash | 5,235 | 3,141 | 22 | 79 |
| Receivables | 4,314 | 4,916 | 8,556 | 6,442 |
| Inventories | 3,766 | 5,389 | 7,107 | 6,634 |
| Other Current Assets | 536 | 398 | 259 | 891 |
| Total Current Assets | 13,851 | 13,844 | 15,944 | 14,046 |
| Prop, Plant & Equip | 7,795 | 7,135 | 6,812 | 6,530 |
| Accumulated Dep | 6,387 | 5,882 | 5,461 | 4,983 |
| Net Prop & Equip | 1,408 | 1,253 | 1,351 | 1,547 |
| Deposits & Oth Asset | 100 | 100 | 128 | 100 |
| Total Assets | 15,359 | 15,197 | 17,423 | 15,693 |

ANNUAL LIABILITIES (000$)

| FISCAL YEAR ENDING | 09/30/91 | 09/30/90 | 09/30/89 | 09/30/88 |
|---|---|---|---|---|
| Notes Payable | NA | NA | 7,400 | 7,496 |
| Accounts Payable | 1,792 | 2,318 | 1,653 | 1,010 |
| Cur Long Term Debt | 13 | 11 | 19 | 533 |
| Accrued Expenses | 585 | 680 | 757 | 631 |
| Income Taxes | NA | NA | NA | NA |
| Other Current Liab | 466 | 740 | 854 | 668 |
| Total Current Liab | 2,856 | 3,749 | 10,683 | 10,338 |
| Long Term Debt | 6,030 | 5,041 | 1,009 | 1,034 |
| Total Liabilities | 8,886 | 8,790 | 11,692 | 11,372 |
| Common Stock Net | 2,606 | 2,606 | 2,606 | 2,606 |
| Capital Surplus | 6,770 | 6,770 | 6,770 | 6,770 |
| Retained Earnings | −2,517 | -2,723 | -3,399 | −4,809 |
| Treasury Stock | 386 | 246 | 246 | 246 |
| Shareholder Equity | 6,473 | 6,407 | 5,731 | 4,321 |
| Tot Liab & Net Worth | 15,359 | 15,197 | 17,423 | 15,693 |

sales to one customer accounted for $5,978,000, or 26% of this segment's sales in fiscal 1991, primarily due to increased volume, as compared to $3,931,000, or 19%, in fiscal 1990, and $4,177,000, or 22%, in fiscal 1989.

Armatron International faced problems similar to many other manufacturing companies. The company had solid production techniques and basic information systems, as well as a growing market. What the company needed was more integration, both from a business perspective and within their information systems. They found many of their answers at the end of 1989 in a computer-integrated manufacturing (CIM) system.

In November of 1989, Armatron installed the CIM system and began training everyone in the company. In April 1990, sales, order entry, and accounts receivable were converted to the new system. By August 1990, all company operations were online on the new system. In addition to the accounting functions, the system assists inventory management, purchasing, manufacturing, shop floor control, cost accounting, master production scheduling, Materials Requirements Planning (MRP), just-in-time inventory (JIT), order processing, billing and sales analysis, accounts payable, and the accounting general ledger. The new system runs completely on an IBM AS/400 processor.

The new system provides online access to all employees from workers on the factory floor to the CFO. By keeping all data in common databases, every properly authorized employee has access to the same data at the same time. Armatron faced several challenges in installing the new system. It required convincing employees who had worked for Armatron for more than 30 years that the company needed to make the switch. As each module was implemented, project leaders were chosen within the affected areas of the company. These leaders received intensive training and were responsible for educating end users within their departments. Consultants and a helpline were used to provide quick answers to questions. To make the conversion in a four-month time period, Armatron avoided modifying the purchased software unless there was no other choice.

The JIT module is based on the finished products. It determines inventory and purchasing requirements based on final production levels. By using a common database, there is less need for subassembly reports and extraneous memos between production and purchasing. By standardizing the data and reports within the company, the system reduces wasted time, eliminates data entry errors and cuts the time needed to process orders. As a result, staff productivity has increased—for example, time from receipt of orders to shipping has been cut in half for most orders.

The system is based on a central AS/400 using dumb terminals for user input. The company has avoided personal computers, largely because managers wish to avoid the complexity of dealing with microcomputers. Herb Parsons, the IS manager, notes

that "We keep things as simple as possible. The software we use only needs a dumb terminal." He also mentioned rejecting a PC LAN solution because "I'm not a fan of PCs. It's too easy to lose control, and networking PCs is a lot of work."

By freeing up staff time from time-consuming manual tasks, the workers have more time to concentrate on improving quality. Carol Mooney, the cost accounting manager, notes that "We now have more time to pay attention to detail as material is received." Similarly, with the data online and accessible to everyone, less time is needed for review of reports, freeing managers to make better decisions and focus on improvements.

Ed Rogers, the CFO, also notes that "Implementing the new system has had a positive cultural impact on Armatron as a business and on individual areas of the company." He notes that "We had to work together to make CIM work, but it was a companywide project that fostered increased cooperation, appreciation, and consideration for each other's functions because everything we do affects somebody else in a pull-through situation."

## QUESTIONS

1. What benefits did Armatron gain from implementing the new computer system?
2. What benefits arose from changing the way Armatron operates?
3. Is it possible to separate the two previous questions? That is, could Armatron have gained the same benefits without the new information system? Or what would have happened if the com-

## ARMATRON ANNUAL INCOME (000$)

| FISCAL YEAR ENDING | 09/30/91 | 09/30/90 | 09/30/89 | 09/30/88 |
|---|---|---|---|---|
| Net Sales | 23,624 | 32,469 | 41,064 | 33,181 |
| Cost of Goods | 18,095 | 25,746 | 33,172 | 26,577 |
| Gross Profit | 5,529 | 6,723 | 7,892 | 6,604 |
| R & D Expenditures | NA | NA | NA | NA |
| Sell Gen & Admin Exp | 4,865 | 5,151 | 5,851 | 5,712 |
| Inc Bef Dep & Amort | 664 | 1,572 | 2,041 | 892 |
| Depreciation & Amort | NA | NA | NA | NA |
| Non-operating Inc | 237 | 74 | 754 | 279 |
| Interest Expense | 665 | 875 | 1,170 | 1,041 |
| Income Before Tax | 236 | 771 | 1,625 | 130 |
| Prov For Inc Taxes | 70 | 225 | 475 | 33 |
| Net Inc Bef Ex Items | 166 | 546 | 1,150 | 97 |
| Ex Items & Disc Ops | 40 | 130 | 260 | 33 |
| Net Income | 206 | 676 | 1,410 | 130 |

pany installed the new system and did not alter the business processes?

4. Are there other uses or advantages that Armatron could gain by using or expanding this system?

5. What problems would you expect to encounter during the conversion process? How can they be overcome?

6. What additional implementation procedures could you install?

## CASE *Fairbanks Morse Engine Division*

As a division of Coltec Industries, Fairbanks Morse builds large diesel engines that it sells to the U.S. Navy and to commercial engine customers throughout the world. The company was founded in 1885 and through its life has produced a wide variety of equipment ranging from windmills to washing machines and air conditioners. Today, it concentrates on high-quality, large diesel engines.

Located in Beloit, Wisconsin, Fairbanks Morse can machine individual parts up to 43 by 12 by 14 feet high to very small tolerances. The company uses a variety of conventional and numerically controlled production machines.

The Fairbanks Morse Engine Division is highly dependent on sales to the U.S. Navy and to other governmental organizations and utility companies. In 1991, sales were solid, including increased shipments of engines to the U.S. Navy Landing Ship Dock and Charleston Naval Shipyard programs. The company also experienced increased shipments to the electric utility industry, in particular the nuclear energy market.

The MIS functions in Fairbanks Morse have followed a pattern similar to many other companies. In the 1960s, the MIS group computerized financial and accounting functions such as payroll, accounts payable, general ledger, and product costing. In the 1970s MIS began to computerize production operations, beginning with inventory control and computerized bills of materials. Like other companies, the managers experienced problems with inaccurate inventories, since early inventory systems relied on workers to manually enter code numbers and quantities whenever products were added to or taken from inventory. By the early 1980s, every department in the company had its own computerized systems.

Most existing applications were in good shape. For example, the company had few problems with the accounting and financial systems. Similarly, the manufacturing people were already using basic CIM systems to control many of the production machines and for planning and materials requirements. However, each of these systems was independent. It would be highly disruptive to change these fundamental systems. The shop-floor personnel did not want to change systems and they did not want to add another terminal to every machine on the floor.

Most of the systems operated independently of the others, so information transfers from one department to another often relied on paper records. For instance, the primary control mechanism for production was the labor ticket. Each step in the manufacturing process was based on a listing of the work to be performed along with the materials needed for that step. Typically, there were more than 1,000 labor operations a day, generating more than 6,000 labor cards every week. Because of the volume and because in many cases the paper records were the only controls, a tremendous amount of incorrect data resulted. Workers also noted that parts were often not in the proper locations.

What Fairbanks Morse wanted was a better way of tracking inventory. Manufacturing also needed to track tools so workers could always find what they needed. More importantly, the managers needed to eliminate the paper labor tickets and find a better way to record manufacturing status, worker time, and materials used. Additionally, the new system had to work with the existing systems and effectively tie them together.

In 1989 they began implementing a three-year plan. By the end of 1992, the majority of the system was operational across the entire plant. There are two major features to the plan. First, a Token Ring network was installed connecting the existing CIM equipment, new personal computers, IBM AS/400, and their existing IBM mainframe. Second, *everything* in the plant was given bar codes.

Labor tickets and even worker time cards were eliminated. Every employee now wears a badge that contains a bar code. Each job is given a bar code that travels with the work in progress. Every workstation has a bar code. As employees report to work, they run a scanner across their badges. At each station, they scan the work in progress and the master code for the task they perform. All of this data is collected and routed through the network to a personal computer data collection controller that adds a time stamp and passes it to the AS/400. From there, summary data is passed to the centralized IBM mainframe. Employee time data is forwarded to the centralized accounting system to generate payroll and performance reports.

Production control is handled by creating the special bar code list that is attached to the work in progress. Job progress is tracked and can be rerouted or rescheduled. Detailed material usage data is immediately available to inventory management, purchasing, and the subassembly manufacturing teams. Tool tracking is integrated with the material tracking within the CIM. By bar coding and tracking tool usage, employees can quickly find specialized tools.

Production line managers can use their terminals to retrieve data directly from the AS/400. A special hotkey combination enables managers to switch between the CIM system and the AS/400 database. They can track employee time, production status, and material usage. Higher-level managers can print reports, examine data, and query line managers without leaving their offices.

## QUESTIONS

1. What advantages does Fairbanks Morse gain from the new system?
2. Are there other uses or future benefits that can be gained from the system?
3. Are there technological improvements or changes that might be made to improve the system?
4. What problems do you think the managers encountered while implementing the system? Why do you think it took three years to implement the project?
5. How does the system improve inventory control? How might it support JIT inventory techniques?
6. How does the Fairbanks Morse solution differ from that used by Armatron? What problems would Fairbanks Morse have encountered if the company had used a solution similar to Armatron's? Would Armatron have been better off if the company used a technique similar to that chosen by Fairbanks Morse?

## CASE  *Cummins Engine*

The automobile companies have streamlined their production processes. Beginning with Henry Ford's leadership, the automakers have used the production line to decrease the number of manufacturing variables. This technique has greatly reduced the inventory and training necessary to manufacture automobile engines.

Economies of scale are not as applicable to truck and large-equipment engine manufacturing. The sale of a large truck or an earth-moving machine is a coordinated effort of the salespeople and manufacturers of the engine, body, flatbed, and tires. The sales process is one of negotiation. The goal of the purchaser is to acquire a truck that is customized to his or her specific needs. The manufacturer strives to reduce costs by making the manufacturing process as standardized as possible.

The salesperson is caught in the middle. He or she knows that the sale is made based on the specificity with which the truck meets the needs of the pur-

chaser within a cost range. Yet the commission is based on making the truck as standard as possible to manufacture. The plant engineers become the moderators. They must take the promises of the salesperson and manufacture a truck that will satisfy the wants of the purchaser within the constraints of the manufacturer. All of these decisions must be made in a way that will meet the cost objectives for the purchaser and provide a reasonable profit for the manufacturer.

Cummins Engine Company in Columbus, Indiana, is a $3.5-billion manufacturer of diesel engine components and power systems. The highly specialized engines that it produces are noted for their reliability and power. For many years, through the mid-1980s, Cummins had been a leader in this oligopolistic field. Because the market segment seemed secure, Cummins became lax in its marketing efforts. Cummins engines decreased in quality, the time between taking an order and filling it grew exponentially, and the quality of the components decreased.

The early 1980s brought a mild recession and, for the first time, viable competition from overseas. Cummins faced a serious sales slump and layoffs for the first time in its history. Cummins' management realized the firm could no longer continue business as usual. The purchasers of large trucks and equipment had become too sophisticated to make purchase decisions based on habit. Managers decided they had to become more service-oriented. They accepted the vision that technology could be used to focus the company in this direction.

To achieve its goals, Cummins began a major computerization project to track more than 70,000 parts stocked throughout its worldwide distribution network. Its techniques have included the computerization of the processes of integrated ordering, manufacturing, warehousing, inventory polling, transportation, purchasing, and invoicing. Using this integrated computer system, Cummins has greatly improved the distribution channel by reducing inventory by 40 percent and increasing product availability by 50 percent.

For Cummins, this process has been called logistics integration. In order to deliver what the customer wants, management put the following specific techniques in place.

- Use a networked information system to move products faster and stay better informed.
- Manage by exception by calling managerial attention to things that go wrong.
- Organize from supplier to customer so that everyone in the distribution chain cooperates to improve forecast accuracy by reducing handling and cutting costs.

- Look at all jobs as customer service by providing immediate access to individuals who meet the customer and can deliver what the customer wants.
- Use technology to empower employees, flatten hierarchies, and encourage peers to confer directly to get the job done most efficiently.
- Change the management structure to emphasize a smooth product flow rather than functional distinctions between jobs.
- Adopt a long-term planning perspective to enable the manufacturing process to adapt quickly to change.

Jack Kent, director of logistics, views an integrated information system as essential to meeting the customer's needs. In his opinion, the integrated order system enables Cummins to manage the flow of materials without duplicating efforts on incompatible systems. At Cummins, order entry, inventory management, and shipping are all coordinated through computers at the Belgian, Miami, and Singapore parts distribution centers. Networking enables each sales representative to view global inventory and sales status. At all times salespeople can know the parts inventory in the channel. The ability to beat competitors in this area alone has led to a substantial increase in sales.

According to Kent, moving information ahead of product enables Cummins to keep costs low while improving delivery schedules. Workers constantly check the system for current information about what parts are coming in and what needs to happen next. According to Kent, "The better we service our distributors on a truly integrated system, the lower their and our costs will be."

Most companies view suppliers as adversaries and refuse to factor them into order processing. Cummins' integrated system has enabled the company to treat suppliers as partners who cooperate in the sales process. The system provides early information to suppliers so that they can provide orders on schedule. This process is enhanced through electronic data interchange (EDI). EDI enables every part of the ordering process to be computerized. This includes advance shipment notification, purchase orders, and electronic funds transfer. Knowing the status of parts while they are still in the production process enables Cummins to project budgets and make promises far earlier than its competitors.

Another step that Cummins has taken to improve customer service is to provide information to its warehouse workers so that they, too, can focus on the customer. Warehouse staff now pack an identification card in each box so they can be contacted if there is a problem. When distributors visit their customer ser-

vice representatives, they tour the warehouse to meet individuals who pick and pack their orders. This system provides the mechanism for the sales representatives to give and receive feedback from the individuals who make the shipment possible. To make this interchange long term, inventory for distributors is packed and shipped on the same day and hour of each week. This guarantees consistent delivery times and provides a working relationship to resolve any problems that may arise.

### QUESTIONS:

1. In what specific ways will Cummins' new computer system help the salespeople improve the service that they provide to their customers?
2. What unique problems are faced by manufacturers of large, complex products?
3. What specific information about Cummins' customers will the new computer system provide for senior management at the company?
4. How can computer technology assist companies that manufacture items with a large number of variable parts?
5. Using data flow diagrams, represent the order/build/ship cycle at Cummins Engine Company.
6. Using an object-oriented approach, identify the primary object classes, their attributes, and functions.

### CASE *Kraft General Foods*

Throughout the 1980s, tobacco companies worked to diversify their operations. They had substantial amounts of cash available but worried about the declining use of tobacco in the United States. Consequently, two of them went on buying sprees and purchased several food producers. RJ Reynolds bought Nabisco in a highly publicized takeover. Philip Morris acquired three well-known companies: Kraft Foods, General Foods, and Oscar Mayer. The resulting organization is called Kraft General Foods (KGF) and operates relatively independently. The combined organization produces hundreds of different products, sold primarily through supermarkets.

Although there are similarities in the three organizations, they all used different information systems, which caused several problems. Each company had a different ordering system. Orders arrived at General Foods by phone (45 percent), fax (20 percent) and direct computer lines (35 percent). At Kraft, 65 percent of the orders came from hand-held computers carried by the salespeople, the other 35 percent came over the phone. All of the Oscar Mayer orders came over the phone.

Even within each organization, there was little integration of information. Each brand used a separate system to track sales, and a second one to track profit and loss. Consequently, sales representatives for KGF used six different systems to track sales and inventory—none of them sharing data with the other.

In mid-1994, after several years of work, KGF had built a system that enabled local sales representatives to enter orders for Kraft and General Foods products through one source. The sales agents could check orders and warehouse inventory levels. However, Oscar Mayer products still needed to be ordered through the Madison, Wisconsin, office. Sales representatives could not get direct access to that sales data, even though Oscar Mayer has a relatively up-to-date online ordering system.

Within KGF, three groups of people were responsible for processing orders: account managers, salespeople, and service representatives. The salespeople traveled to the stores, typically restocking shelves, collecting orders, and sending information back to the headquarters. Account managers were higher-level managers in charge of advertising, promotions, and product details. The service representatives traditionally functioned as order-takers, receiving orders over the phone and entering them into the computer system.

Although the sales representatives were generally successful in using the system to deliver the appropriate orders, there were some problems. In particular, customers were given discounts based on the amount of orders and sales. The system made it hard to compute total sales, because the representatives needed to pull data from each system for each customer. A related problem is that KGF and the customers could reduce shipping costs by combining orders from the three brands.

Over several years, KGF built a computer system that uses personal computers to give sales representatives access to the six different computerized systems. The PCs were connected to an IBM AS/400 minicomputer. The system was awkward in that it required salespeople to log on to each system anytime they wanted data. It also does not allow PCs to send messages to the customers or salespeople.

Integrating the processes has resulted in personnel obstacles as well as computer problems. The three brands deal with different types of products, each with their own promotions and selling strategies. For example, products from Kraft and Oscar Mayer have short shelf lives, so promotions are common. Products carried by General Foods, like Maxwell House coffee, have longer shelf lives and are rarely discounted. Consolidating the salespeople from the different divisions requires substantial training.

KGF managers knew they needed to improve their information systems. They began work on them in 1991. James Kinney, the chief information officer, observed that simply installing new ordering systems was not sufficient. KFG also needed to reorganize the way the business operates. In his opinion, change on the part of people was the most difficult part of the entire reengineering effort." He expected the reorganization and development to continue at least until 1995. He felt that these types of projects take multiple years and are accomplished a bit at a time.

### QUESTIONS

1. Help KGF come up with a systems plan that will integrate the company's systems. Be sure to include any reorganization that might be necessary.
2. What problems need to be overcome? Which ones are the most important?
3. Using an object-oriented approach, design a system that will assist in consolidating the data at KGF.
4. In designing a new system for KGF, what resistance do you expect to encounter? Which people will experience changes in their jobs?
5. How do the variety and differences among products affect the problems at KGF? What complications are created by the size of the organization?
6. What strategic advantages could be gained by improving the information systems in the three divisions? Is it just an issue of cost savings, or are there other potential advantages? [For comparison, see Alice LaPlante, "Armour Deploys Strategic Sales Force Automation," *Infoworld* 15, no. 4 (November 29, 1993), p. 66.]

### CASE   *Technology and the Corner Drug Store*

Large drugstore chains are rapidly capturing the prescription market. Regional chains such as Walgreens and Osco promise 24-hour service and the ability to use a centralized database to fill a prescription from any of their locations. Increased inventory control made possible by linking the ordering system to the prescription process reduces the inventory carrying costs.

Another change in the marketplace is the introduction of a national, mail-based pharmacy service. Prescription Delivery Service has introduced a new, advanced mail service facility. It integrates automatic identification technology with bar codes, radio frequency data communication, and video inspection.

To a large extent, PDS is responding to the request of health maintenance organizations and other managed health care plans. In particular, PDS services self-funded corporations, unions, and non-profit organizations.

To service its customers, PDS has integrated five computer systems into its 44,000-square-foot mail service dispensing facility. The entire system is operated by 17 pharmacists and 23 staff. In all, more than 10,000 prescriptions are processed in an eight-hour workday. These prescriptions are received by telephone or modem from more than 300,000 customers nationwide.

The key to PDS's success is its concentration on using automation to fill commonly prescribed items such as hay fever or arthritis medication. The fully automated, customized system greatly increases the accuracy of the dispensing process. Using expert system technology, the computerized system is able to instantly identify drug interactions and allergic reactions between a customer's prescription and his or her medical history or other prescriptions. The PDS database contains images of pharmaceuticals to verify the filled prescriptions are correct.

Procedurally, the system uses a conveyor to move plastic totes containing prescriptions through various stations. Prescriptions are filled and checked by pharmacists. Bar code scanners along the conveyor line identify the totes. Resembling a model train, the sections of the system communicate through Ethernet connections and protocols.

Bar code technology plays an important part of the system. The first code identifies the customer and their orders. The second transfers data to the host computer that sends instructions on the exact location of the drug. Staff members follow the directions on portable hand-held terminals. The third bar code acts as a license plate to direct the tote to the mailing center. Once at the mailing center, bar code scanning verifies orders and provides quality control. A computer screen is divided into four windows for each prescription. One screen is an image of the prescription. Pharmacists monitor this screen and record incorrect orders on a bar-coded menu sheet. These could include faulty labels, incorrect amounts, or the wrong drug. Finally, Postnet bar codes are applied to mail the prescriptions.

The mail service dispensing program also offers drug utilization review information to pharmacists locally and through the mail-service program. Clinical drug utilization review programs are also available for the pharmaceutical companies themselves.

Future plans include the incorporation of EDI technology into the system. This will enable PDS to create a fully integrated clinical management/order-fulfillment process. This integrated system will enable the entire process of ordering pharmaceuticals to be streamlined. The Pharmacy Genesis Project will enable

physicians to initiate maintenance medication orders and perform other duties by accessing the system electronically.

### QUESTIONS

1. With the PDS system, how many transactions does one pharmacist handle in an average day? Per hour? Research question: How does that compare to an average pharmacist at a typical drug store?
2. Diagram the flow of data at PDS. Why is data integration important to PDS?
3. If PDS wants to expand its operations and increase sales, what options are provided by the system?

### CASE  *Price Waterhouse*

By the late 1980s, Price Waterhouse (PW), the sixth largest national accounting firm, was experiencing problems with its computer information systems. The firm was spending close to $25 million a year on microcomputers by purchasing small groups of items for $10,000 to $20,000 at a time. All offices and groups were basically independent from the others. Without corporate standards, there was a tremendous amount of incompatibility in hardware, software, and data.

Professionals in the main offices were running between floors, carrying stacks of paper to senior managers to get sign-offs. When partners from out-of-town offices visited headquarters, they could not use the local computers to modify or print their data, because the corporate machines did not have 3.5-inch disk drives. More importantly, although there was a wealth of information and knowledge in the company, it was difficult to find them. In particular, partners in smaller offices did not have the support and access to knowledge readily available to partners in the main offices.

PW hired Sheldon Laube as director of information systems to straighten out the tangled information systems. In 1989, Laube found what he had been looking for: Lotus Notes software that enabled people to share messages, data, and files easily.

Lotus Notes is classified as groupware, a product designed to make it easy for groups or teams to share information. Its three main components are e-mail, a bulletin board system, and a database of unstructured information. The system is designed to share a wide variety of information, from simple text, to numbers, to entire spreadsheets and pictures. Users can create team documents that incorporate revisions by multiple authors, enabling multiple people to insert comments and make changes at the same time. It also serves as an integration tool, creating compound documents that incorporate different types of data from various sources.

PW is using Notes to store a wide variety of information, such as

- A collection of the firm's analyses of IRS rulings and opinions.
- Information describing court rulings and the actual ruling.
- Every business proposal PW submitted to clients since 1989.

Lotus Notes is a Windows-based product, and it was designed to be easy to use. These are key features for PW, because senior partners had been reluctant to use computers. Most of the time they relied on their secretaries to collect data and create reports. As a result, virtually all information within PW was distributed in paper form. Tax decisions were usually photocopied and passed around. But information rarely made it to the right people on time. Experts in Washington had no way to notify PW partners about impending legislation. Foreign partners often learned about new developments by reading delayed issues of the *The Wall Street Journal.*

In 1990, Laube purchased 10,000 copies of the beta test version of Lotus Notes for $2 million. In January 1990, he had installed the Hot Topics bulletin board detailing trends for the financial services group. By 1992, PW had more than 700 applications on Lotus Notes. Only 100 of them were created by the MIS department.

Because of the size of the organization and the fact that staff were using beta copies of Notes, PW experienced several initial problems. With support from Lotus, Novell, and IBM, most of the problems were solved in a couple of months. By late 1992, PW was running Notes on 125 servers, supporting 11,000 personal computers connected on a wide area network. Some complications remain because of the way Notes operates. For instance, every few minutes, the Notes servers contact each other and transmit updated copies of their databases. Each server maintains a complete version of all the databases. Yet, these updates sometimes require manual intervention, especially when one item is altered by different people at the same time.

Overall, the partners are pleased with the use of Notes. They use it to generate billing reports and compile marketing data themselves, instead of relying on secretaries. A survey of 800 partners revealed that 85 percent rated the product a 7 on a scale of 10, 30 percent gave it a top rating of 10. Only 4 percent rated the product at 4 or less.

The features of Lotus Notes have proved useful at attracting and keeping clients. One client was considering going with a competitor because that firm had a larger office in the local area. Glenn Carlson, a regional director for PW, used Notes to check with everyone in the firm to demonstrate how all the resources of PW were immediately available to the client. He used a similar technique to keep a client who was concerned about PW not having enough specialists available.

## QUESTIONS

1. How does Lotus Notes help integrate information?
2. What data integration problems existed at Price Waterhouse? How were they solved through the use of Lotus Notes?
3. How is a service company like Price Waterhouse different from manufacturing companies? What are the differences in the types of information?
4. What competitive advantages has Price Waterhouse gained?
5. Could the use of Lotus Notes change the way that Price Waterhouse operates?

## CASE *Lotus Notes and Oracle Reach Database Agreement*

Lotus and Oracle have agreed to jointly develop and market a product that will allow Lotus Notes to access Oracle databases through Oracle's media-server software. Oracle is the leading builder and customizer of databases for corporate networks. Lotus Notes is the first widely available groupware tool to develop user databases and interchanges. It is used primarily to facilitate collaboration among employees, no matter where they may be physically located.

The combination with Oracle adds a multimedia dimension to workgroup computing. With this combination, Notes will be able to handle large videos and documents.

The agreement is beneficial to Oracle because it provides Oracle with a front-end access to end users. Even though it is the number-one database product, Oracle sells its products to information systems executives, not consumers. Thus, it is viewed as a database for corporations, not an end-user tool.

Oracle is also developing Oracle Documents, its own groupware tool. In addition to including many of the features found in Lotus Notes, it will also be able to access video and large documents. Another important addition will be the Context Search Engine that will enable users to search documents by theme rather than just keywords.

## QUESTIONS

1. What advantages do users gain by connecting Lotus Notes to an Oracle database?
2. As a business manager and computer user, what tasks will you perform that can take advantage of multimedia (especially video and sound)?
3. Companies have traditionally created databases to handle text and numbers. The newer database management systems, like Oracle's, can now provide full multimedia services such as video-on-demand. What business opportunities are presented by these new tools?

## CASE *Groupware: Young and Rubicon Applies Work Flow*

Advertising agency Young and Rubicon (Y&R) has used Lotus Notes to apply work flow concepts to streamline its current practices. Young and Rubicon took the approach of using Lotus Notes and work flow to change the way that people interact with each other rather than just automate the current paper flow in the organization.

Y&R began by examining how information was passed between different hands, including the actual traffic-flow patterns. In doing so, they paid particular attention to forms routing and the actual path an advertisement would travel as it moved into production.

In the process, the approval forms and estimate requests remained the same. According to Nicholas Rudd, chief information officer, what changed was the motivating force that moved the forms between people. Y&R worked to identify a core set of interactions, analyze those interactions, and then re-engineer the process.

Y&R chose Action Workflow, software that promises to break down the complex set of human interactions into four steps:

1. Client request.
2. Vendor agreement step.
3. Vendor reports completion step.
4. Customer satisfaction step.

Y&R worked with a test client, Chevron Corporation, to use the work flow software to map specific interactions between people. Parties at both companies discovered problem areas, made changes to correct them, and put these changes into the system for reference. This process eliminated the redundancy of tasks between different departments, ensuring that all steps of the new process were completed. An important component of the software was the ability to get baseline measures on productivity enhancements. The new work flow process enabled overtime to be reduced by fifty percent.

## CASE *Boeing Airlines*

Boeing Airlines conducted extensive experiments for two years regarding meeting software. The company found that meeting software could cut the time projects take by 90 percent. Yet, Boeing is not using groupware at all.

Although Boeing will not speak in detail about why groupware was dropped, managers generally attribute it to cost-cutting. Internally, Boeing states that comparison with other technology investments indicated that it offered less payback. Outside the company, analysts speculate that managers did not like finding themselves in an electronic spotlight, where decisions once made at their sole discretion became open for public inspection and comment.

## CASE *Dell Computing*

Dell Computing installed Lotus Notes in 1990 to help its designers track the progress of various assignments. Before long, there was a proliferation of Notes databases.

As the user base expanded, so did the information that was exchanged. Some was purely social. People used Lotus Notes to discuss movies or other entertainment. Rather than being a time saver, Notes became a technological way to waste time.

It was not long until Dell management imposed strict rules on how Notes was to be used. Supervisors took it away from some employees. Now it is only used where it can accomplish a specific task. Only 500 users have access to the system.

One such task is to keep track of the status of all design, marketing, and manufacturing work on different kinds of products. Employees throughout the world can follow and comment on each other's contributions to the project. Manufacturing managers now order parts, plan staffing, and learn about new products on-line.

## QUESTIONS

1. What advantages are there to using electronic databases to replace paper flows?
2. For years, people have predicted a "paperless" office, but the use of paper continues to increase. What will it take to eliminate virtually all paper from a typical office?
3. At Y&R, what gains came from reducing the use of paper, and what gains arose from changing the flow of information?

4. What potential problems exist with groupware tools? Can you find current cost figures for Lotus Notes?

5. Why did Boeing and Dell experience problems with groupware tools? Did eliminating the tools solve the underlying problems?

## DISCUSSION ISSUE

### *Telecommuting*

The last few years have given rise to a substantial increase in the capabilities of personal computers as well as improved telecommunications facilities. Many people have also observed that the type of work performed today is radically different from the manual labor required several years ago. A large portion (perhaps as much as 50 percent) of the U.S. workforce provides information services. Because this information is easy to transmit, it is theoretically possible for millions of workers to perform their current jobs from their own homes. They would not have to go to an office in order to work. However, there are many issues that need to be resolved before telecommuting becomes commonplace. Paul, a financial analyst, is asking his boss (Duncan) for permission to work at home. The CEO (Leto) also has to be convinced.

| | |
|---|---|
| Paul: | Duncan, I've been reading about some companies that are allowing the employees to work at home. They work on the PCs and trade information with the firm's computers by connecting over the phone lines. |
| Duncan: | Yes, I've heard of that. In fact, I ran into a friend at a convention who has some employees working at home. |
| Paul: | Well, I'd like to try it. You know I live out by the desert and have to drive about 50 miles to get to work. By working at home, I'd save gas and I'd be able to spend more time on my work. I already have a fast PC and a modem. Most of my job is spent analyzing numbers, and I can get those by dialing in from home. There's really no reason for me to come here every day. |
| Duncan: | I know you spend a lot of time at the computer, but I'm not sure. I'd really prefer to have you here, so I can keep an eye on your work. You've been doing a good job, but sometimes I need to check your calculations. |
| Paul: | I've already thought of that. I'll get a separate phone line in my house for the computer. That way you can call me whenever you want. With this new software on the LAN, we can even work on the same pro- |

ject at the same time. All of the information on my screen will show up on yours too. So, we can talk on the phone, and I can show you step-by-step how I did the calculations.

| | |
|---|---|
| Duncan: | Hmmm. That might work. But what about distractions? Don't you have two children? |
| Paul: | Sure; on the other hand, there'll be fewer distractions from the other workers. Plus, I can start earlier and work later at night. Look, how about if we try it for a month as an experiment? If it doesn't work out, I'll come back in. If it doesn't work, you'll have a good excuse when someone else asks. If it works, you can offer the option to other employees. Just think of the office space you'll save. |
| Duncan: | That's an interesting thought, but I'll have to clear it with the CEO. I'll set up a meeting . . . |

*At the meeting with the CEO . . .*

| | |
|---|---|
| Duncan: | Those are the basic advantages. I'm willing to try the experiment . . . |
| Leto: | Well, I'm not. I think it's foolish. Paul, you chose to live that far away and you knew how long the drive was. We'd have no way to keep track of your work if you stay at home. For instance, with all that extra time, you'll be tempted to moonlight for some other company. We need your full attention on this job. |
| Paul: | I like this job. I promise I'll spend all my time working on this job. And you or Duncan can still follow everything I do. He just has to call me. Plus, the firm's computer holds all of my work, so you can always see what I'm working on and how fast it's getting done. |
| Leto: | There are still too many problems. What about security? You work with some top-level information. How can we allow you to transfer all of this data to your home computer? What if some neighbor decides to look through your PC files? |

Duncan: But Paul takes work home now. I don't see the difference.

Leto: I still don't like the idea. Maybe we can trust Paul, but what about the next person? What happens when everyone wants to work at home? If I let Paul do it, but no one else, I'll end up with discrimination complaints.

Paul: Eventually, I think everyone will end up working at home. There are a lot of qualified workers out there willing to work part-time who can't commute to the office. We'd just be starting the new style earlier than some other companies.

Leto: Maybe so, but I think the risk is way too high. If we let our employees stay home, they might work and they might not. If they don't, we're dead. It would take too long to pinpoint the problem. Duncan, you and the other managers would just hide the delays from me. By the time all of the managers told me the problem, it would be too late. Maybe next year . . .

## QUESTIONS

1. Do you think that Leto is too strict? What advantages does telecommuting provide to the company? What advantages to the workers?

2. As a new employee, do you want to work for a company where most of the people work out of their homes? Would you accept a lower salary to work for such a company?

3. What type of jobs would be easier to perform with telecommuting? What jobs would not work well?

4. What changes will managers have to make in order for telecommuting to succeed?

5. Do you think more companies will support telecommuting in the next 5 years or 10 years? What pressures will persuade companies to use telecommuting? What social practices will lean against it?

6. What problems would be experienced by telecommuting workers? The employers?

7. If 25 percent to 50 percent of the workers eventually telecommute, how will society be changed?

# PART 3

# *Decisions and Models*

**How do information systems help managers make better decisions?** Business decisions can be complex. Complexity can arise from several areas, including: the use of huge amounts of data, difficult mathematical formulations, uncertain relationships, detailed linkages to multiple business units, and physical or procedural constraints. Middle-level managers in all functional areas face complex problems. Various models have been created to help you analyze these problems and evaluate alternative answers. Information technology provides several tools to help managers collect data, evaluate models, evaluate output, and make decisions.

Ongoing research into artificial intelligence has led to additional tools to solve specific problems. Expert systems, robotics, and neural networks are sophisticated tools to tackle complex problems.

Strategic analyses represent some of the most difficult decisions a manager can face. Strategy represents fundamental changes in the operations of the business. Information systems are used to search for useful changes. Information systems have also been useful in creating a competitive advantage.

# Models and Decision Support

Sega uses its Web page (http://www.sega.com) to highlight products and pricing—especially for new games. They also provide hints on playing games.

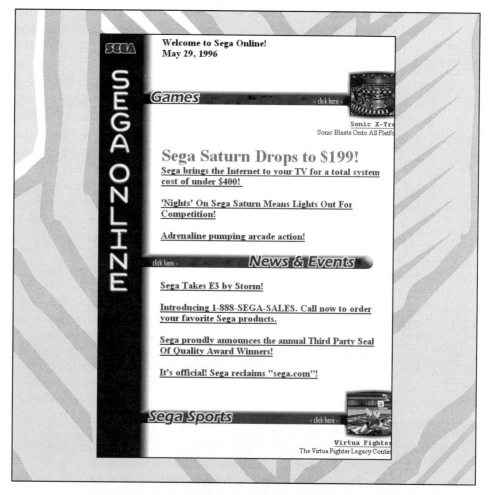

## SEGA ENTERPRISES

Most people know of the battle between giant games makers Nintendo and Sega Enterprises. In 1991, Sega was the first to introduce the Genesis game machine that used 16-bit computations for faster games and more detailed video displays. It was introduced in time for the 1991 Christmas season with several game cartridges available. Sega Genesis also maintained compatibility with older games. With the technological lead on Nintendo, it looked as if Sega was ready to take the lead in the $6 billion dollar market for home video games. By Christmas, when Nintendo introduced its own Super NES 16-bit game, Sega held the lead in sales. Sega's gain came partly from introducing the machine earlier and partly by selling it for $50 less than Nintendo's machine. It also had more games available.

By most management measures, Sega Enterprises was ready for the huge Christmas season that began in September 1991. Its inventory system was automated, using Computer Associates' software on an IBM AS/400. Executives had personal computers loaded with Microsoft's Excel spreadsheet. Each night an EDI service bureau collected sales data over phone lines from 12,500 retail stores across the United States and passed them on to the Sega AS/400. Overnight, the computer created reports detailing sales of the Genesis machines and corresponding game cartridges that were sold the day before. Additional reports could be created by the MIS department but often took days to create.

By any modern measure, Sega Enterprises had all of the information managers needed. Yet, Sega of America executives were facing a crisis in 1991. They did not have sufficient access to the data to make correct decisions. The retail stores were furious because Sega could not deliver machines to them fast enough. To salvage this crucial selling time, Sega used air freight to ship the games directly from Japanese factories to the U.S. stores. Despite helping Sega to its best year (selling 1.6 million units), this emergency airlift is estimated to have increased Sega's costs by $10 million. To that number, according to one estimate, you can add in $75 million in sales lost to Nintendo, because customers switched to Nintendo when the Genesis machines were unavailable.

Sega executives knew the cause of the problem: The corporation's internal information system did not provide sufficient access to the data. By the time managers received the daily sales reports, it was too late. Similarly, although executives could use spreadsheets to analyze the data to spot trends, the numbers all had to be rekeyed from the reports into the spreadsheets.

**OVERVIEW**

How can information systems help you make better decisions? Providing the necessary data is one step. We have already seen how personal and operations-level decisions can be improved with better access to data. Yet, some tactical business decisions are more complex. Sometimes just having the data is not enough. For example, choosing advertising alternatives, identifying investment opportunities, and determining merit pay raises are difficult decisions. Each of these decisions affects many areas of the company and involves several variables.

To deal with complexity, we build models. Models help managers visualize physical objects and business processes. As illustrated in Figure 8.1, information systems help you build models, evaluate them, and organize and display the output.

**INTRODUCTION**

What subjects are you required to study? Many of them are outside your major field; some may not seem relevant to the job you hope to have. Why do you think these subjects are required? One reason is to show you how various disciplines solve problems and make decisions. Every academic discipline has created models that describe an approach to problems and identify common solutions. Psychologists create models of how humans behave and interact. Sociologists concentrate on models of

**FIGURE 8.1**
Tactical decisions often require complicated analysis. Problems utilize forecasts, optimization and in-depth analysis. Information systems provide support through datamodeling and presentation tools. Managers use information system tools to build, evaluate, and maintain various models.

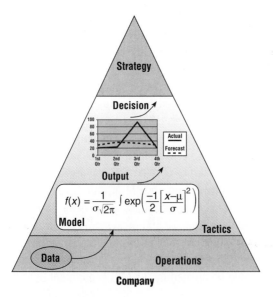

**TRENDS**

Through the 1970s, computers were largely used to assist with transaction processing. Support for making decisions was generally limited to the basic reports produced from the data. Computers were too expensive and programming too difficult to be used by every manager. As personal computers became commonplace through the 1980s, managers began transferring data from the corporate central computers to their personal computers.

Personal computers gave managers the ability to quickly examine the data from many different perspectives. They made it easy to compute totals and other statistics. Control over data on their personal machines also gave managers the ability to get reports and analyses faster. Spreadsheets also gave managers the ability to create graphs quickly and easily. Managers now have the tools to instantly evaluate data in detail. Combining basic statistics with graphs, it is easier to identify patterns and see trends. Spreadsheets also enable analysts to build models that can be used to examine the effects of changes using various assumptions and interrelationships between factors.

Another important trend that occurred during the 1980s was the increased competitiveness experienced in most industries. Every decision became more important. Winning in business now requires that answers be more precise and decisions be made as rapidly as possible. More options need to be evaluated, and potential solutions have to be measured against corporate goals.

Our knowledge of business has also increased during the last decade. Academics and businesses have created more complex models or ways of approaching problems. Computers are used to analyze the corporate data using these models.

groups and societies. Economists have models that attempt to explain how people, firms, and governments interact using money and prices. There are financial models to help you evaluate various investments. In marketing, there are models of consumer behavior that help you decide how to promote and sell products and services. General management models examine the organization of firms and interactions between workers. The point of each subject is to learn these models and recognize problems they solve. Regardless of the job you eventually perform, you will be amazed at the number of models that will prove useful.

A **model** is a simplified, abstract representation of some real-world system. Some models can be written as mathematical equations or graphs; others are subjective descriptions. Figure 8.2 shows a simple economic model that can be used in business to determine the best level of production for a firm. In actual practice, the process will be much more complex.

**FIGURE 8.2**

Sample model. Models come from several disciplines, including this one from economics. This model illustrates how a firm uses industry price and internal cost curves to determine the optimal quantity to produce.

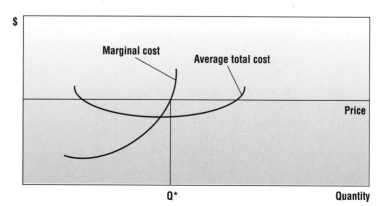

Information systems typically provide three levels of support for tactical decisions. First, they provide the data for the models. Second, technology provides support for building, evaluating, and analyzing models. Third, information systems provide the means to display the results in a variety of formats—especially graphs.

**DECISIONS**

There are many levels of decisions and problems in business. Therefore, there are many different types of models. Figure 8.3 should refresh your memory of the business decision levels. Operations problems tend to be well-defined and relatively easy to solve. They are largely supported by transaction-processing systems that collect the data. This database is used by managers at the tactical level to make less-structured decisions.

What separates operations problems from tactical level decisions? Of course, there is no hard and fast line. Yet, there are some indicators that will help you classify problems into the appropriate level. First, look at the time frame. If the decision only affects the business for a day or two, it is probably at the operations level. Decisions with a time frame of around a year or less are likely to be tactical in nature. The real key is the complexity of the model involved in making the decision. More complex, less structured models lead us to classify the decision as tactical. Detailed examples of tactical decisions in various business areas are presented in Chapter 9.

Why do you care about the level of the decision? The basic reason for the classification is to make it easier for you to solve problems. If you can identify a problem as transaction oriented, you know that the solution will focus on collection and integrity of the data. If a problem falls in the tactical decision level, the solution probably entails improving the decision support system (DSS). A major component of a DSS is the model.

**BIASES IN DECISIONS**

Making decisions can be difficult. If we ask managers to glance at a few pieces of data and make a decision, they will make mistakes. We know that people have **decision biases** and difficulties assessing data. If you understand these biases, it becomes clear that we need an organized means to evaluate data and make decisions. Additionally,

**FIGURE 8.3**
Business decisions. Tactical decisions often involve attempts to improve efficiency. Models play an important role in these decisions. Several MIS tools are used to support tactical decisions. Most are classified as decision support systems (DSS).

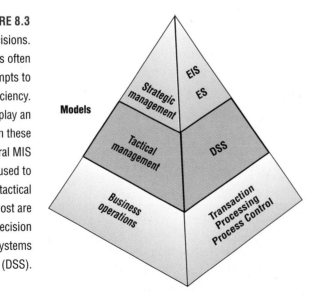

**FIGURE 8.4**

Biases in decision making. Without models, people tend to rely on simplistic "rules of thumb" and fall prey to a variety of common mistakes. These errors can be minimized with training and experience in a discipline. They can also be minimized by having computer systems perform much of the initial analysis.

| ACQUISITION/INPUT | | |
|---|---|---|
| **BIAS** | **DESCRIPTION** | **EXAMPLE** |
| Data availability | Ease with which specific instances can be recalled affects judgments of frequency. | People overestimate the risk of dying due to homicides compared to heart disease. |
| Illusory correlation | Belief that two variables are related when they are not. | Ask any conspiracy buff about the death of JFK. |
| Data presentation | Order effects. | First (or last) items in a list are given more importance. |
| **PROCESSING** | | |
| Inconsistency | Difficulty in being consistent for similar decisions. | Judgments involving selection, such as personnel. |
| Conservatism | Failure to completely use new information. | Resistance to change. |
| Stress | Stress causes people to make hasty decisions. | Panic judgments and quick fixes. |
| Social pressure | Social pressures cause people to alter their decisions and decision-making processes. | Majority opinion can unduly influence everyone else: mob rule. |
| **OUTPUT** | | |
| Scale effects | The scale on which responses are recorded can affect responses. | Ask a group of people to rate how they feel on a scale from 1 to 10. Ask a similar group to use a scale from 1 to 1,000. |
| Wishful thinking | Preference for an outcome affects the assessment. | People sometimes place a higher probability on events that they want to happen. |
| **FEEDBACK** | | |
| Learning from irrelevant outcomes | People gain unrealistic expectations when they see incomplete or inaccurate data. | In personnel selection you see how good your selection is for candidates you accepted. You do not receive data on candidates you rejected. |
| Success/failure attributions | Tendency to attribute success to one's skill and failure to chance. | Only taking credit for the successes in your job. |

as a manager, you should be aware of some of these problems, both in your own evaluations and when you make presentations to other managers.

Barabba and Zaltman analyzed decision making at General Motors and noticed that several common problems arose. In particular, they were concerned about decisions being made regarding the development of new automobiles. Figure 8.4 summarizes the biases in four primary categories: acquisition (input), processing, output, and feedback.

## Acquisition/Input

The first type of bias arises from the way we perceive data. People tend to place too much emphasis on events they just observed or on major events that receive news coverage. For example, many people are afraid of flying, whereas statistically, heart disease is a much more serious problem. People often misinterpret data statistically. They tend to discard data that does not fit their prior beliefs—thinking that it is merely an "outlier." Similarly, managers often have trouble identifying correlations between events. Even if two events happened at the same time, it does not mean they are related. If you put a new sales manager in a region and sales increase, does that mean that the sales manager was responsible? Perhaps. But the increase might also have been attributable to a change in consumer incomes. We need to carefully evaluate the data to make the correct determination.

## Processing

In processing or evaluating data, people make several common mistakes. They have difficulty being consistent from one decision to another. In evaluating new car options, managers might first prefer a streamlined, aerodynamic look. Several months later, they might decide that the aerodynamic look is too harsh, and ask designers to add rounded corners and other aspects to soften the look. Similarly, we do not always incorporate new information. If some decision has traditionally been made one way, it is hard for managers to change their methods—even though the environment has changed. Complexity causes similar problems. When faced with complex decisions under uncertainty, people tend to simplify the problem by ignoring some aspect. Hundreds of variables might affect our forecast of sales for next year. Yet, many times we simplify the problem by assuming that few things will change and we simply project a 10 percent increase. In a related manner, people often look for simple rules, as long as they can be "justified." Finally, all of our decisions are affected by stress and social pressure. Faced with the pressure of a deadline or competition, people will rush and make decisions differently than if they took the time to study the problem.

## Output

Decisions are sometimes biased by the format of the output. Scales on graphs affect our interpretation. For instance, presenting results on a small laptop screen can give a different impression and lead managers to choose a different option than they would if they saw the graph on paper. Worse yet, people often choose outcomes based on wishful thinking. Some managers examine a list of possible outcomes and gravitate to the one with the best outcome. They sometimes think that if everyone simply tries hard enough, they can reach the best outcome. Sometimes this attitude is helpful to push the company higher. Other times it causes serious problems when managers ignore more likely outcomes.

## Feedback

Managers should alter their decision-making technique based on how well they perform on each decision. Unfortunately, we sometimes incorporate the feedback incorrectly. For example, when hiring new workers, you might congratulate yourself on choosing good workers. Yet, you rarely receive data on the candidates you rejected, so you do not really know if you made the best decision. Similarly, many people only take credit for successes. Either deliberately or unintentionally, they downplay their failures.

## Models and Information Systems

There is nothing inherently good or bad about these biases, they simply exist in most people. The first step to overcoming them is to recognize their existence. The second step is to carefully collect accurate data. Finally, the biases point out the need for models. When correctly used, models can provide consistency and improve decisions by minimizing individual biases. Of course, poorly designed models might simply incorporate and institutionalize these same biases.

Information systems can help minimize problems with data acquisition. By providing access to the data and sorting it in different ways, managers get a complete picture of the situation. By making it easy to perform statistical tests, managers do not have to rely on their intuition.

If we could computerize the entire decision-making process, processing and feedback biases would be minimized. However, most situations are difficult to automate. Chapter 10 examines a few of the complex situations that we can automate. In other cases, we rely on managers to use an appropriate model. As computers become more powerful and less expensive, managers can evaluate more complex models. Simulation tools also enable managers to examine the potential outcome of their solutions *before* they are implemented. By looking at more options and evaluating the outcomes, managers identify better decisions.

The strength of information systems lies in their ability to present results in a variety of formats. By viewing results from several different perspectives and in different formats, a manager gets a clearer picture of the problems and potential solutions.

## INTRODUCTION TO MODELS

As defined earlier, a *model* is a simplified, abstract representation of some real-world system. It is simplified because we cannot handle all of the details of the real system. In fact, simplification is a major reason we build models. However, it must contain enough features of the original system so that it behaves the same way. Models represent systems, so they are built from a collection of related subsystems.

### Physical

Models are used for many different purposes, and there are several different types of models. Most people are familiar with physical models. Movie studios build physical models so they can destroy them without injuring people or expensive property. Architects construct models to help clients and builders visualize a building and its surroundings. Automobile designers build models (prototypes) so they can test consumer responses. Engineers build models to test specifications and examine aerodynamic properties. In the case of a physical model, generally the goal is to create a model that can be constructed cheaply that looks like the original system.

Physical models have limitations. They can be expensive to build, especially as you try to add more detail. A small-scale model of a building that concentrates on size and wall placement can be easy to create. But if you want to add details like interior trim, window treatments, and furniture, you need to hire talented artists to work with the small scale. Even more importantly, physical models are relatively difficult to change. For instance, automobile designers once built full-size clay models of new designs. The clay enabled them to make minor style changes, but large changes (such as length) essentially required starting over.

The declining cost and improved capabilities of technology have given designers new tools to build models. In particular, computer-aided design (CAD) tools make it easy to create visual models of physical items. These systems enable designers to create realistic, three-dimensional images of virtually any physical item. They are used to design buildings, landscapes, automobiles, airplanes, machinery, and all of the related

components. Designers and clients can view the objects from any angle, under different lighting conditions. With high-resolution displays, the designs look like photographs of a real product. Figure 8.5 shows a CAD workstation.

CAD systems overcome two of the major problems with physical models. It is easier to add details, and it is much easier to make changes to the designs. In many cases, the designer can try out various changes and immediately see the effect. This interactivity can significantly speed the design process.

CAD systems provide two additional advantages. First, they make it easy to share the designs. With networks, designers from several countries can work on the same design at the same time. Automobile manufacturers have used these techniques to cut years from their development cycles. Second, most CAD designs are more than simple drawings. The objects are stored internally as mathematical relationships. At a simple level, consider a three-dimensional drawing. The design is actually stored as a set of coordinates in three-dimensional space. The designer can use this mathematical representation to perform various tests of the model. For example, CAD systems can estimate the heating and cooling systems needed for each architectural design. They can be used to estimate the weight of an automobile. They can also be used to test the aerodynamic effects of a design.

## Process

It is relatively easy to see the uses for models of physical items, but they are only one type of model. Other models are symbolic or descriptive. Recall the data flow diagram techniques presented in Chapter 3, which are used to display business processes. These diagrams are models of the underlying system. Models of processes have been used for many years, especially in manufacturing. Figure 8.6 illustrates a small process for handling custom orders. Engineers use process models to evaluate the flow of materials and products through the production process. They examine diagrams and mathematical models to identify problems and improve efficiency and

**FIGURE 8.6**

Simple model of evaluation of custom orders. Data flow diagrams are useful models of business processes. They focus on relationships among entities and the various processes. Each process can be modeled to any desired level of detail.

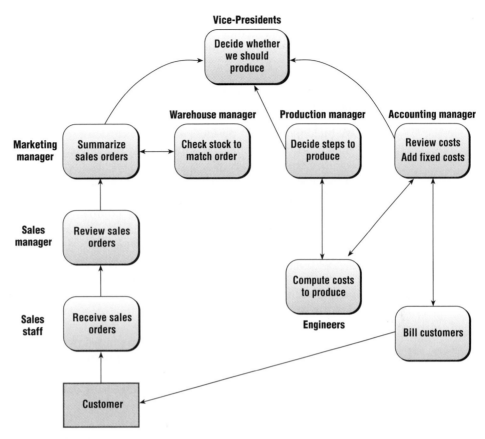

quality. For example, Bell Helicopter (Reality Bytes 8–1) redesigned a production plant and cut construction time in half.

Process models often use drawings and pictures to represent the various objects. However, at heart they typically use mathematical equations to represent the process and the various relationships. For example, an operations engineer would model a machine as a mathematical formula that converts raw materials and labor into products. Using equations for each step of the production process, the engineer could search for ways to reorganize production to make it more efficient or to improve quality.

## Business Modeling

We build models of a business or business process to help managers make decisions. Most businesses are far too complex for any single person to understand all of the details. Consequently, a variety of models may be created to present a simplified view of the business. In particular, one of the original purposes of accounting was to create a standardized model of the financial aspects of business. Another common model of business is the practice of dividing the company into functional areas. For example, a manager with experience in the finance department of one company can usually apply knowledge and problem-solving skills to finance departments in other companies and even other industries.

In the early to mid-1900s, two popular modeling techniques were derived from engineering concepts. Many companies used time-study models and work process flows to evaluate their firms and change their processes. The objective of these methods was to measure the business processes, by the amount of time spent on each task and by tracing the number of steps each item followed. By identifying the redundant steps or the components that took the most time, managers would know which items needed to be changed.

In the 1990s, one modeling technique that gained increasing attention became known as **re-engineering.** The objective of this technique is to analyze and model the critical business processes and make major changes to the operation of the business. The underlying assumption is that small changes over time can eventually cause a business to be misaligned with the ideal target. Hence, the purpose of re-engineering is to make fundamental changes to the firm, improving efficiency and quality while better meeting the needs of the customers. The key feature in re-engineering is building a model of the business processes and creating an improved model from scratch. For example, the small model in Figure 8.6 could be used to track the number of orders and amount of time products spent in each department. Backlogs and redundant reviews could be identified and eliminated, making the process more efficient.

**WHY BUILD MODELS?**

There are thousands of models in business. Some models are simple rules-of-thumb that managers use to make quick decisions. Others are highly abstract, often expressed as detailed mathematical equations. Some models are incredibly detailed and require thousands of data variables, like economic forecasting models. Other models are descriptions of situations or behavior, such as motivational recommendations based on personality types. Why do we have so many different models?

The basic goals are summarized in Figure 8.7. The main reason we need models is because reality is too complex and hard to understand. Models help us simplify the world. They help us search for similarities in different situations. Models also enable managers to predict how changes might affect the business.

Consider a small example. You have an older car with about 80,000 miles. You received a small raise in your job and are thinking about purchasing a newer car. Your initial impressions are swayed by the hundreds of automobile commercials you see and you would really like to buy a new car. You checked prices and dealer invoice costs using the Internet and are excited about buying a new car. On the other hand,

**FIGURE 8.7**
MODEL BUILDING
The four primary
reasons for building
and using models.
Descriptive, graphical,
and mathematical
models can be used for
each of these
purposes. However,
mathematical models
tend to be emphasized
for optimization and
simulation.

*Understand the Process*
Models force us to define objects and
specify relationships. Modeling is a first step in
improving the business processes.

*Optimization*
Models are used to search for the best
solutions: Minimizing costs, improving
efficiency, increasing profits, and so on.

*Prediction*
Model parameters can be estimated from prior
data. Sample data is used to forecast future
changes based on the model.

*Simulation*
Models are used to examine what might happen
if we make changes to the process or to examine relationships in more detail.

you know that new cars lose 10 to 15 percent of their value as soon as you drive
them off the lot. A friend suggested that you should keep your old car for another
year, but you are worried that it might lose too much value by next year.

You have just created a model. Part of the model is based on historical sales data
which tells you how fast new cars depreciate in value. Another part of the model
uses economic data to estimate the potential value of your used car if you keep it and
add miles for another year. To make an informed decision, you could create a simple
forecast of automobile prices to estimate what might happen to new car prices next
year. You could then create a spreadsheet to analyze the cost of buying a new car. By
using standard discount functions, you could compare the total cost of your choices.

As the decision maker, it is up to you to determine which models to use and to
make sure they actually apply to the situation. Once you have selected the appropriate
model, you apply whatever data you have, evaluate the results and make the decision.

## Understanding the Process

One of the primary reasons for building models is to help us understand how the world
behaves. Without a model or idea, how can we determine how things work? Citicorp
(Reality Bytes 8–2) uses a model to determine how well the banking firm is serving customers. By comparing the model results to actual practice and to their corporate standards, Citicorp managers get a measure of the quality of their service. By building a

 Reality Bytes  8–2 Citicorp

Citicorp applies computer models to evaluate its
effectiveness in addressing customer needs. Its distribution services division employs an enterprise
information system to address issues of customer
service and quality. Response time to customer
inquiries is tracked and updated every 30 minutes.
Written customer requests, account inquiries, cus-

tomer statements, payments, and card issuances are
also monitored. Executives can select any of these
areas to examine and view quantitatively or graphically. They can also perform "what-if" scenarios to
alter variables to simulate changes in managers or
the relationship between teller and cash machine services or charges.

model to explain how things work, we can apply the model to help solve other problems. Models are also used to determine cause-and-effect relationships.

Some models are accurate and work well in a wide variety of situations. Other models seem haphazard and generate incorrect results. One reason for the difference is that some processes are harder to understand. For example, most of the physics models that you know are concrete and work well in daily situations. On the other hand, weather forecasters have many models, but it seems that they are wrong a lot of the time. One of the reasons is because weather depends on the entire biosphere, which is exceedingly complex. Similarly, some economic models are highly accurate. We know that if the government increases taxes on gasoline, the price will rise. Some economic models will even tell you how fast and how far the price will rise—within a few tenths of a cent. Yet economic forecasts for an entire economy are often wrong, because the system being modeled is much more complex.

Along with the difficulty in understanding complex processes, some processes can never be modeled accurately. Sometimes there is too much variability in the underlying process. As a simple example, consider a roulette wheel with 38 possible numbers. Even if we build a model to explain how a roulette wheel works, it will not help us predict which number will show up next (unless the wheel is broken or rigged). The roulette wheel was designed to be a system with a large random component. We can model how it will behave on average over time, but that does not help us determine the next outcome. Many systems in the real world have large random components, particularly if they involve subjective choices by people. We might be able to predict on average how a group of 50,000 consumers will respond to a marketing approach, but randomness makes it difficult to predict how one specific consumer will react.

## Optimization

In business, an important reason for building models is to help us make the *best* choice possible. Without a model, we can experiment and we might get lucky enough to make a decision that gives us good results. But if we really want to find the optimum choice, we must first build a model that accurately describes the underlying process. Then we can find a solution for the model that gives the best result. Figure 8.8 illustrates the basic concepts with a simple model using two input variables.

There are many examples of optimization models in business operations. For instance, how many tellers should a bank have on duty at one time? What is the blend of fuels that will produce the lowest-cost gasoline? What price should we charge for a new product? The teller problem can be analyzed with a queuing theory model. Fuel blending is typically analyzed with a mathematical programming approach. The pricing problem uses models from marketing research and economic models of prices, costs, and profits.

**Optimization** is a complex subject that typically evaluates mathematical models to find a "best" solution. The average business manager will not be expected to create his or her own mathematical optimization models. On the other hand, you will be expected to know that models exist to solve certain types of problems, and you should know how to apply these basic models. Computer software can be used to solve the model and evaluate the alternatives.

## Prediction

An important use of models is for **prediction.** If a model is reasonably accurate, it can be used to predict future outcomes. For instance, in the used autmobile example it would be possible to estimate how the price of used cars changes over time.

**FIGURE 8.8**

Optimization model. Optimization models are formed by identifying the control variables and the output or goals. With a mathematical model, it is possible to locate a maximum or minimum point for the goal. Many problems are complex and highly nonlinear problems do not always have a solution.

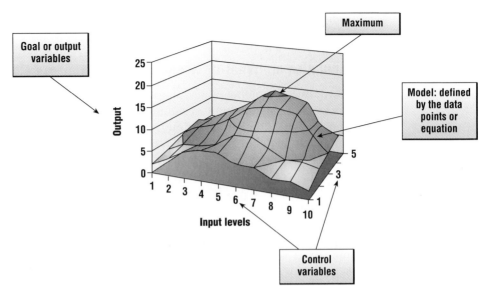

Prediction first requires that you have a model that describes the situation. Then data is collected and statistical techniques are used to estimate the **parameters** of the model for the specific problem. Next you fill in any parameters that you already know, and the model provides a prediction. Sometimes the prediction will be a specific number, other times it will be a range of possible values. Occasionally predictions are descriptive, such as "prices will increase slightly."

Statistical methods and **descriptive models** can be used to describe situations. Descriptive statistics such as means and variances are useful to help managers identify and classify problems. Prediction techniques such as regression and time series forecasting are used to examine the data, identify trends, and predict possible future changes. To use statistics effectively requires a model of the underlying system. For instance, to use regression methods you first identify the dependent variable and a set of possible independent variables. These choices come from the underlying model. Figure 8.9 illustrates how a spreadsheet or graphics package can be used to display the results of a forecast. With an integrated system, the results

**FIGURE 8.9**

Prediction model. Several statistical techniques exist for analyzing data and making forecasts. Two common methods are regression and moving averages. Both methods require substantial amounts of data. Choosing between the two requires some expertise in statistical analysis, but many times we display both methods to show a range of possible outcomes.

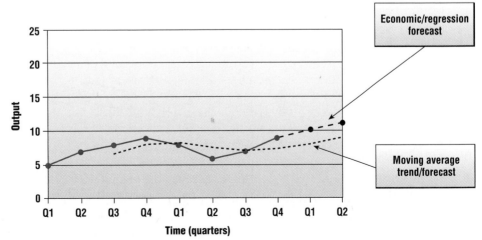

from a statistical model could be fed to the graphics package, automatically updating the graph for changes in assumptions.

## Simulation or "What-If" Scenarios

**Simulation** is a modeling technique that has many uses. Once a model is created, managers use simulation to examine how the item being studied will respond to changes. With simulation, various options can be tested on the model to examine what might happen. For example, engineers always build models of airplanes and engines before they try to build the real thing. The models are much cheaper. In fact, most engineers today start with mathematical computer models because they are cheaper to create than physical models and can contain more detail. Additionally, we can perform experiments on models that would not be safe to perform in real life. For example, an engineer could stress a model of an airplane until it broke up. It would be dangerous and expensive to try such an experiment on a real plane. Similarly, a business model could examine what would happen if prices were increased by 20 percent without worrying about losing real money.

Most simulation models are mathematical instead of descriptive models, because they are easy to evaluate. Mathematical models contain parameters, or variables that can be controlled by the managers. For instance, you might use a spreadsheet to create an accounting model of an income statement and balance sheet. When you create the spreadsheet, production quantity and price of your products are controllable parameters that affect the income and profits of the firm. You could use the model to investigate decisions, like the effect on profits if you increase production. Costs will increase, but so will revenue from sales. The net result depends on the specific details of the firm and the model. Figure 8.10 presents sample output from a simulation. Spreadsheets are often used to analyze small models and graph the results. More sophisticated simulation packages can support more complex analysis and will automatically create graphs and pictures to show interrelationships.

The more complex the model, the more alternatives that can be simulated. In the last example, a more detailed model might enable you to investigate alternatives such as increased overtime, hiring another shift, building additional plants, or subcontracting the work to another firm.

**FIGURE 8.10**

Simulation models explore many alternatives. This example shows how output might change in response to a control variable for three scenarios. The first step in simulation is to identify the input (control) and output variables. Then a (mathematical) model is built that measures the response of the output variables to changes in the inputs. The model is examined for several different levels of each input variable.

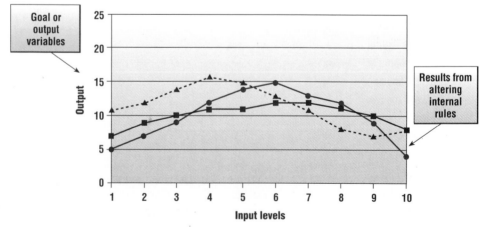

## BUSINESS TRENDS

Models are closely related to one of the business trends discussed in Chapter 1: management by methodology. To manage a large business and ensure consistency, many companies have created methods (or processes) for each task. For instance, a package-delivery company will have specific instructions for delivery people, clerks, and other line workers. Management reports are created a certain way each week or month and routed to a specified list of managers.

These rules make it easier to train new employees, provide more consistent service, and enable

managers to control the company. But how do managers create the rules? Trial and error (or experience) is one possibility. However, for more complex problems, managers begin with a model of the business. Depending on the situation, the model might be used for optimization, prediction, or simulation. By using a model, managers can examine and test alternative methodologies without harming the actual business. As the resulting methodologies are implemented, reactions can be used to alter the underlying model, improving it for future use.

**DECISION SUPPORT SYSTEMS: DATABASE, MODEL, OUTPUT**

By now you should have an inkling of how MIS can help you make decisions. **Decision support systems (DSSs)** were created to help managers make **tactical decisions.** As illustrated in Figure 8.11, a DSS provides support in three main categories: data collection, analysis of models, and presentation.

Notice that data collection is typically performed by the transaction-processing system. Thus, if the transaction system is not working properly, the DSS will not work either. Also note that a fundamental difference between a transaction system and a DSS is the support for creating and evaluating models.

You cannot make good decisions without data, so databases are a fundamental component of a DSS. The issues of data quality and availability raised in Chapters 4 and 5 apply equally well to DSS. However, decision support systems require more

**FIGURE 8.11**

Decision support systems. A DSS provides support for tactical-level decisions. It has features to query data, analyze and store models, and present results. Some systems are designed to solve specific problems. Other systems use standard components (e.g., database management system, spreadsheet, and graphics packages) with applications that are tailored to each problem.

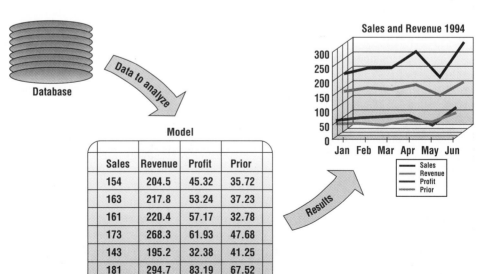

than just collecting and storing the data. It is important that the data be easily accessible to the decision maker. Frito-Lay's response (Reality Bytes 8–3) to new competition emphasizes the importance of speed. In particular, the decision maker needs to retrieve data and transfer it to the model. Similarly, the predictions, simulations, and even the model itself need to be shared with colleagues.

There are many types of models and different software packages can be used to create and analyze the various types. Specific models and modeling software are discussed in more detail in the following sections and in Chapter 9.

At first glance, it might seem strange to include output as a characteristic of a DSS. Yet, if the system cannot produce output in a format that is easy to understand, then it will not be useful. Graphs are an important feature of DSS output. Most people find it easier to spot trends and relationships on a graph than from a table of numbers.

When you are generating output to be used to make decisions, there is one feature of the corporate world you should remember: Few decisions are made by one person. A large part of the decision-making process often involves persuading other people that you are right. Reports that are concise, accurate, and visually appealing can be persuasive.

Decision support systems consist of three primary components: database, modeling tools, and presentation software. These pieces are sometimes only loosely connected. For instance, the database or **data warehouse** might have been built for transaction processing, and special software is used to extract the data and format for use in the DSS. Part of the reason for the separation is that different software is often used for each component. In these situations, the manager goes through more steps to make the decisions—including selecting the data, transferring it to a spreadsheet, evaluating the model, and designing graphs and reports. A more integrated DSS would automatically perform many of the steps. The model might automatically obtain updated data, recalculate the model, and build new graphs. Using the networks and integration techniques discussed in Chapters 6 and

 **Reality Bytes**    **8–3** Frito-Lay

The sales of Frito-Lay chips were slumping in the San Antonio and Houston supermarkets. Corporate marketers were having difficulty isolating a cause. As a result, they accessed their decision support system and quickly identified that a regional competitor had introduced El Galindo, a white-corn tortilla chip. Even though the competitor did not have the resources to advertise extensively, word of mouth was increasing demand and resulting in the allocation of expanded shelf space. Based on this competitive information, Frito-Lay rushed a white-corn version of Tostitos into the market and won back most of the lost market share within three months.

Two years ago, the marketers would have had great difficulty isolating the cause of this change in sales.

Today, Frito-Lay's decision support system gathers data daily from supermarkets, scans it for information about local and regional trends, and identifies problems and opportunities in particular markets.

The decision support system at Frito-Lay allows marketing executives to track changes in sales as current as the day before. This information is used to respond reactively and proactively much more quickly. If a competitor begins a major promotional campaign, its results can be identified almost immediately and a counter program set in place. If Frito-Lay introduces a new sales program, it can be tracked and adjusted—almost immediately—in reaction to customer purchases.

7, an integrated DSS can be much easier to use. It can also help to coordinate decisions and comments from co-workers.

**BUILDING MODELS**     Once managers have access to the data, they can build models to analyze the data and solve problems. Building models is an extension of the systems approach presented in Chapter 3. A model is built as a collection of subsystems that match the real-world system. Each subsystem consists of inputs, processes, and outputs. In mathematical models, these relationships are expressed with equations. As explained in Chapter 3, the first step is to decompose the problem into smaller pieces. The next step is to identify input and output variables. Next, define the processes and determine how they behave mathematically. The resulting model equations are usually programmed into the computer.

## Assumptions

A key feature of all models is the **assumptions** made by the builder. Models are designed to be simplifications of reality, which means that some details have been left out. Models are generally built for specific situations; they may not apply in every case. Modelers use explicit assumptions to highlight the situations where the model can be used effectively. Whenever you evaluate models, a key place to begin is to look at the assumptions. Be careful; sometimes not all assumptions are spelled out.

Students sometimes complain about studying unrealistic models. These complaints often arise because of the assumptions in the model. Keep in mind that it is far easier to understand a model if you start with a smaller, simpler version. As you modify assumptions, the models become more realistic, but they also become more complex.

## Identifying Input and Output Variables

In a model, each subsystem receives data through input variables, processes the data, and alters the output variables. Output variables are chosen with respect to our goals. Profit will be a typical output variable for a firm. There are also output variables for the various departments. For instance, quantity produced and quality ratings are common output variables for a manufacturing department. As long as the company has well-defined goals, it is relatively easy to identify the relevant output variables.

Input variables can be almost anything. In production systems, they might be quantities of raw materials, labor hours, or money invested in capital equipment. Marketing departments looking at sales relationships would examine input variables such as prices, promotions, consumer demographics, and quality ratings. Notice that output variables (e.g., quality) for one system will be input variables to other systems.

As shown in Figure 8.12, a major task in many models is to identify the important input variables. Statistical techniques (such as factor analysis and multiple regression) are often used to identify and determine weights for input variables. Statistical packages (like SAS and SPSS), and some spreadsheets have made it much easier to use statistical tools. However, statistics can only be used effectively if you understand the model. You cannot test every possible variable and hope that the statistics reveal useful relationships. You need a model to determine which variables *cause* changes in others.

Input → **Process**

Equation:
*output = f(input, time)*    **Output** →

**Define system**
    Input - Process - Output
    Simplifying assumptions
    System boundary

**Equations**
    Identify variables you can control
    Define equations

**Estimate equations from data**
**Prediction**
**Simulation**

## Processes and Equations

Functions or processes take the input data and transform it into outputs. For instance, consider metal-working machines that can take blocks of aluminum, roll it out, cut it, and produce aluminum cans. Inputs would be the aluminum blocks, electricity, the number of machines, and human labor. Output is measured by the number of cans. Based on the characteristics of the machine, there is a production function that determines how many cans will be produced from the inputs. The equation in Figure 8.13 is one possible example of the relationship.

Notice that if any of the inputs is zero, there will be no output, and output can be increased by increasing any of the inputs. The actual values of the coefficients will depend on how we measure the variables and on the machines being used. The specific values could be statistically estimated from test runs of the machine at different combinations of the inputs.

An important question arises with this example: How do we know which type of equation to use? It is not enough to know the variables; you also have to know how they fit together. Perhaps a linear equation (e.g., $Q = 9.4\,A + 1.5\,E + 4.3\,L$) would provide a better explanation of the process. A major question in modeling involves choosing the appropriate equations to explain the underlying relationships. Advanced statistical techniques offer some help in choosing functions. But the best method is to thoroughly understand the process. In this case, the engineers who designed the machine should know which mathematical model best describes the machine.

In other situations, the best method to determine the proper relationships is to refer to an expert. Recall that this chapter began by noting that one of the goals of a business education was to teach you the various models used in each discipline. Other people have already created thousands of models for you to use. You just have to understand them and know when to apply each model. To help you out, some common models and applications will be examined in the next chapter.

$$Q = (6.5)\,A^{0.7}\,E^{0.1}\,L^{0.2}$$

## Software

Once you understand models and the modeling process, it is easier to see how MIS can help build and evaluate models. Clearly the first step is to provide easy access to the data. Data is used to identify input variables, estimate model equations, and drive simulations. However, decision support systems go a step farther and help

## ▼ BUILDING QUALITY MODELS IN SPREADSHEETS ▲

Many models are built using spreadsheets. In many respects, spreadsheets are similar to more traditional computer programs. Yet, designers rarely include comments that explain their intentions. Hence, when spreadsheets are passed to other users, there is enormous potential for mistakes and problems. You need to consider these problems when you create a spreadsheet and you should check other users' spreadsheets for them.

One common problem is the use or misuse of absolute and relative addresses (using the dollar sign to keep a cell reference from changing). Say that cell B1 holds the current hourly wage rate. Other cells can use that value to compute the cost of workers: =B1*C7. To be safe, the formula should be written as: =$B$1*C7. Without the absolute address, copying the formula to a new location will cause the B1 pointer to change, yielding incorrect results. These changes can be hard for later users to spot.

Be on the lookout for hidden columns, hidden rows, or hidden worksheets. Current spreadsheet software enables users to hide portions of the spreadsheet. There might be errors in these hidden segments—look for missing rows or columns. First save a backup copy, then "unhide" all of the rows and columns.

Beware of formulas in which the cell references have been changed to "hard" numbers or literals. Walter Schmidt, a CPA, recalls the time he gave a spreadsheet to a client that computed the interest expense deduction for the client's taxes. At some point, the client discovered that the interest deduction was too low. On investigation, Schmidt learned that one of the client's employees had changed a cell reference to a constant value. When the spreadsheet was changed, the formula did not pick up the changes, leading to the wrong number.

Most current spreadsheets can present a "map view" of the spreadsheet, in which special characters indicate the purpose of each cell: value, formula, or label. These characters can help you spot formulas in which the entire cell has been accidentally replaced by a constant. You will still have to check individual formulas by hand. Other tools enable you to see how each cell depends on (or is used by) other cells. These tools are useful to spot cells that are no longer needed and to highlight circular references.

You can also protect spreadsheets by locking cells containing formulas. That way users will not accidentally overwrite your model.

Another useful trick is to make sure that any operations performed on columns have a "nice" starting and ending point. Place a line in the cell above the first row and after the last row. If the data range from B10 to B20, place a line in B9 and B21. Then any column operations should include the lines: SUM(B9:B21). The lines will not affect the computation. More importantly, if someone tries to insert a row before the first entry (B10), the new value will be included in the final total. If the original cell range only extended from B10 to B20, inserting a row before B10 would not update the total.

Cells and ranges should be given names. Then, instead of referring to a cell by its address, formulas will use the full name, making it easier to understand the purpose of the formula. Names are especially useful when you are linking spreadsheets.

Current spreadsheets make it easy to add notes to any cell. Use the notes to document the purpose of the cell and to answer questions that co-workers might have when they look at your spreadsheet. Be sure to reference the source of all equations and models.

the decision maker create and evaluate various models. There are two basic categories of DSS software: generic and preprogrammed.

### Generic Modeling Tools

The advantage to generic modeling tools is that they can be applied to any situation or business. The drawback is that you have to build the models yourself. For example, SAS is a collection of software packages that can be used to build a complete DSS. The tools include a DBMS, advanced statistical analysis, graphing support, and optimization techniques. It contains the base tools you need to create and evaluate complex models. But by themselves, the SAS programs know nothing about finance, marketing, accounting, or other business models. You apply your knowledge and equations to create the model. Other statistical software like DOE-Wisdom (Reality Bytes 8–4) help you model and statistically evaluate the processes within an organization.

Spreadsheets can also be used as generic modeling tools. Current versions provide some statistics capabilities (regression), can solve small optimization problems and can be used for simulations that involve a small number of variables. They are particularly useful for finance and accounting problems because they have several predefined functions that are commonly used in those areas.

There are several other generic modeling tools. You can purchase simulation tools such as GPSS, SIMSCRIPT, and MODSIM III. As shown in Figure 8.14, some tools enable you to build a complete graphical representation of the process and run the simulation by drawing objects on the screen and defining the interrelationships. For instance, a traffic engineer could test a traffic light system by drawing streets, cars, and the lights on the screen. After defining how each object behaves, the computer will run the simulation and display the actions on the screen. There are also tools like IMAGINE-IT that are specifically designed to help managers model the business organization. These tools are useful for re-engineering because managers can test and evaluate the effect of changes without harming the actual operations.

With a graphics-based simulation package, the objects are displayed on the screen and the simulator moves the objects so the decision maker can see the result-

**FIGURE 8.14**

Object-oriented simulation. A simple example of custom manufacturing. Each object (parts list, purchase order, etc.) and each process are defined in detail by the modeler. The simulation system generates orders, makes shipments, and orders inventory according to programmed rules. The simulator collects a wide variety of statistics that can be displayed graphically (as in Figure 8.10) or in tabular reports.

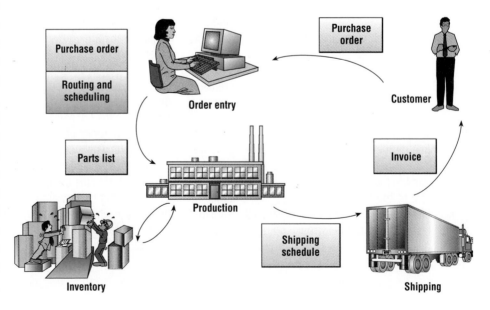

ing interactions. For example, this process could be used to display the flow of information or products through various steps in the company. As illustrated by Figure 8.14, the object can be modified at each step, or new objects can be created. By adding timing attributes, the simulator can portray the actual movement. The analyst can alter various parameters and see how they affect the overall system, looking for bottlenecks and solutions to problems.

In the example, the primary function of the customer object is to generate purchase orders. The timing and frequency of orders is a control parameter. The orders are processed by the order-entry department, which schedules the jobs and sets timetables for the production department. The order-entry department evaluates a small optimization function to set priorities for various jobs depending on the customer, type of product, and marketing objectives. In this situation, production is treated as a "black box," and we are not concerned about how production actually converts inputs into final products. In a real company, configuring optimal production lines and schedules is an important area of simulation and optimization. The inventory department uses models to determine quantities and delivery times so that the production line always has the items it needs. In the last step, the shipping department consolidates shipments by geographic area and distributes the products to the customer.

Each of these physical objects has attributes such as capacity, time required to complete a job, and cost. They have internal functions, typically created from optimization and scheduling models. The functions respond to the data objects and produce the desired outputs that are sent to the next step.

In a graphical simulation, the computer randomly generates customer orders. As the orders pass through each stage, the computer executes the processing that takes place, adding a random time element to simulate human variances. At each step, the computer monitors the number of transactions taking place, the amount of time spent waiting because of delays, and the cost of the operations. These values are displayed on graphs. The person analyzing the model can alter underlying parameters to see what happens. For instance, if the order-entry scheduling system is changed, you would want to know how it will delay production and how it will affect delivery times, as well as total costs. Likewise, you could examine the effects of decreasing the inventory levels.

Like any simulation, the greatest difficulty lies in creating the underlying models. Each component (order entry, production, inventory, and shipping) must be defined mathematically. After specifying the inputs and outputs, the internal rules and procedures need to be written as mathematical statements. Most of the time, as you make the model more realistic, the number of variables and complexity of the model increases. But once the base model is constructed, it can be used to analyze a wide variety of problems.

### Preprogrammed and Specific Models

Because there are some situations that occur in many different businesses, several companies have designed models and created software that will help you solve specific problems. Some models are *add-ins* that run with other software (such as spreadsheet macros). Other versions are *stand-alone* and handle the complete problem from data collection to evaluating models to producing output. In finance there are thousands of software packages that will capture stock market data, evaluate different finance models, and keep track of your portfolio with graphs and summary statistics.

One feature to look for with preprogrammed models is how much control you have over the underlying model. Your problem could have a slightly different twist and you might want to modify the model by altering the input variables or even the

**Reality Bytes** ◣    8–4   UNDERSTANDING PROCESSES—DESIGN OF EXPERIMENTS USING DOE-WISDOM

In any process, there are control variables (inputs) and response variables (outputs). For example, a milling machine turns metal into useful products. Each machine has settings to control factors like angles, cutting speed, and pressure. Yet it is not easy to see exactly how the input variables affect the output variables. Even in physical processes, there are so many variables and interactions that it is difficult to determine the best settings for each control level. Engineers can build mathematical models based on physics to describe the overall process, but individual machines might not perform exactly as predicted by the theory.

To maximize production, minimize costs, and improve quality we need to know more about how the control variables influence the outputs. To gain this understanding, we perform experiments—varying each control level and measuring the output variables. One problem with experiments is that they cost money and time. For instance, with a machine, we have to take it off the production line, and pay someone to try the many input combinations, measure the output variables, and analyze the results.

With any process, it is generally impossible to evaluate every combination of input levels. There are too many possible settings and it would be too expensive to test them all. Consequently, statisticians have devised several methods to evaluate processes using a smaller set of data. Each technique has certain advantages, examines slightly different combinations of input data, and uses a different statistical technique to analyze the data.

Information systems can be used to help analyze processes, design the appropriate experiment, and analyze the results. One tool specifically designed for this purpose is a PC package called DOE-Wisdom from Madcat Software. It helps the worker choose a design method. It then selects the appropriate control levels to be tested and asks the decision maker to perform the experiments and enter the resulting data. The software automatically performs several analyses of the data and presents the results in tables and a variety of graphs.

Using the data from the experiment, the software builds a model of the process. In addition to the graphical presentation, the software helps the designer evaluate predictions using the model.

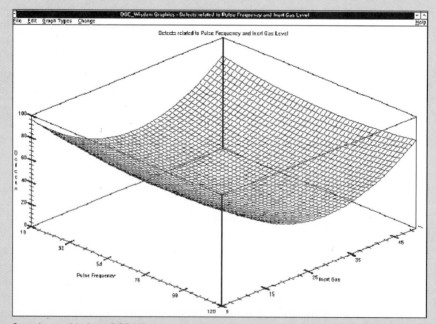

Sample graphic from DOE-Wisdom. Hypothetical data for a welding process that measures defects as a function of control levels for welder's pulse frequency and ratio of inert gas used.

equations. As with any software, try to arrange a trial period to evaluate the software and make sure it can be applied correctly to your specific problem.

How do you find software packages to help model your specific problem? Probably the easiest place to begin is with magazines or journals that are aimed at your particular specialty. For instance, accounting magazines regularly evaluate and carry advertisements for accounting software. There are magazines with reviews for almost any topic you might be interested in. Another source of advice is user groups and electronic bulletin boards that carry discussions on the topics you need. Also, some commercial firms (like Datapro) publish notices and evaluations of a wide variety of software.

## Model Complexity

There are several problems to watch for with models and simulation. The issues are summarized in Figure 8.15. First, there might be so many alternatives that it could take years to examine all of them. The catch is that more complex models tend to be more realistic, but they also take longer to evaluate. Of course, a faster computer can speed up the evaluation of the alternatives.

## Cost of Building Models

It can be expensive to build detailed models. Sometimes, it might be cheaper to make a decision (even if it is wrong) than to spend the money to build and evaluate the model. Unless you have a lot of spare time on your hands, it is probably not worthwhile to build a mathematical model to determine the optimal time for students to buy used textbooks. The cost of building models is sometimes hidden. Creating a complex new model from scratch can take considerable time. In many cases, it is not possible to create a new model in time to make a decision. The trick is to build the base models ahead of time so they are available whenever a decision must be made. But then, how do you know whether you are spending too much on the models when you do not know whether they will be useful?

## Errors in Models

The other major problem is that models are not the same as reality. G. H. Hardy (a superb theoretical mathematician) once stated (*A Mathematician's Apology*) that he felt sorry for applied mathematicians because no matter how good they were, no matter how complex the models they built, the model could always be criticized because it did not accurately reflect the real world. Remember that predictions and simulations from models do not have to be 100 percent correct. Some variables could be incorrect, relationships can be missed, or results might be misinterpreted. However, these are not sufficient reasons to discard the entire process of modeling and simulation. Even a partial understanding is better than none. In many cases, simulations enable us to investigate situations that would be impossible with any other technique. However, it is

- Model complexity
- Cost of building model
- Errors in Models
  - Data
  - Equations
  - Presentation and interpretation

**Reality Bytes**     **8–5** Modeling and Simulation Problems

The Hartford Civic Center Coliseum roof collapsed on January 18, 1978, from snow and ice. Apparently the wrong model was chosen when the beam construction was being simulated. After the collapse, the simulation was rerun with the correct model and it predicted the crash.

In development of the Handley-Page Victor aircraft, a wind-tunnel model, aerodynamic equations from a res-onance test, and a low-speed flight test all indicated that there were no tailplane flutter problems. Unfortunately, all three models contained errors, and the tailplane broke off during the first flight test, killing the crew.

On April 1, 1991, a Titan 4 rocket booster blew up on the test pad. Extensive 3-D computer simulations missed a combination of subtle factors that contributed to the engine failure.

important to understand the models being used so that you know which variables are important and which ones can be ignored. Several real-world problems (Reality Bytes 8-5) have been traced to errors in using and applying models.

There are three fundamental errors that can arise in mathematical models: (1) flaws in the data, (2) flaws in the equations, and (3) flaws in display or interpretation of the results.

Data errors can arise because of missing data, errors in collecting the data, or using the wrong data to build the model. Some models, especially those that rely on statistics, are highly sensitive to the database that was used to build the model. If someone tries to apply the model to a different problem area, it could give incorrect results. Similarly, if a model is tested with one set of data, but the actual system is exposed to completely different conditions, we cannot expect the model to provide completely accurate results.

Models based on mathematical equations can be extremely complex. For example, some economic models contain thousands of equations. It is difficult to ensure that all of the equations are correct and that they actually represent the way the original system works. Errors in even one equation could lead the decision maker to make major mistakes. Even for small models, there are horror stories of people who have lost money because of errors in their spreadsheet equations.

Presentation errors can also be difficult to spot. Chapter 2 raised the issue of interpretation of graphics. Research has shown that people are sensitive to graphics features like scale, dispersion, and color. Errors in interpretation can be the most difficult to spot, especially because different people can reach different conclusions when looking at the same output. One solution would be to have several different people examine the results. By combining their interpretations and discussing the results, you stand a better chance of avoiding misinterpretations.

## A BUSINESS MODEL: ENTERPRISE INFORMATION SYSTEMS

Many companies have moved beyond simply collecting data, and are striving to produce systems that provide useful data to the executives but are easy to use. An **enterprise information system (EIS)** is designed to use the existing transaction data and display it in a form that is easy for top-level executives to access. To achieve this objective, the EIS is based on a model of the entire company. In most cases the output from the model is presented graphically and the executives retrieve information by pointing to objects on the screen. A small portion of a sample EIS is shown in Figure 8.16. As shown by Falconbridge (Reality Bytes 8-6), an EIS can be used effectively to integrate data across the company.

**FIGURE 8.16**

Lightship specializes in
software for creating
Enterprise Information
Systems. This sample
front-end screen
enables executives to
search for data by
selecting from a few
simple controls on the
screen.

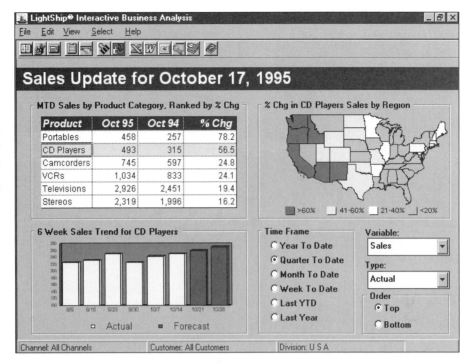

## Description of an EIS

The first screen of an EIS can be a graphical representation of the company. A CEO can then point to a portion of the company on the screen and get reports for that division. If there is a problem, or a decision to be made, the executive can **drill down** to get more detailed data by pointing to another object. For example, if the main screen shows that current sales in the west region are low, the executive can focus on the west region and bring up the last few quarters of sales data. The EIS will graph the data to highlight trends. The executive can then dig deeper and bring up sales by departments or check sales performance by each employee, highlighting unusually high or low sales figures. By pointing to customers, the CEO can get current profiles on the main customers and examine their recent purchases. With a good EIS, the executives can retrieve this information instantaneously by pointing to objects on the screen.

## How Does an EIS Work?

For starters, the EIS must be connected to the transaction processing system or data warehouse, because it is the source of the data. Many of these systems are created with special software (e.g., Pilot) that simply grabs data from the corporate databases. In one sense, the EIS is a complex model of the firm. Figure 8.17 illustrates how executives can "visit" different divisions on the computer and retrieve the data immediately. For the EIS to be useful, the computer model must be a faithful representation of the actual company.

As a model, the EIS display has inputs of raw materials and people. Outputs are typically measured by traditional accounting standards of profits, costs, and growth rates. The EIS maintains budgets and forecasts and can compare them to actual values. The functions and processes are determined from the individual departments. For instance, there could be a production model that describes the manufacturing output.

**FIGURE 8.17**

Enterprise information system. As industries become more competitive managers search for ways to evaluate and improve the overall operations. Enterprise systems collect data from across the firm and make it available to managers and top executives. Managers can start with an overview of the firm and drill down to various levels and departments to get more detailed data.

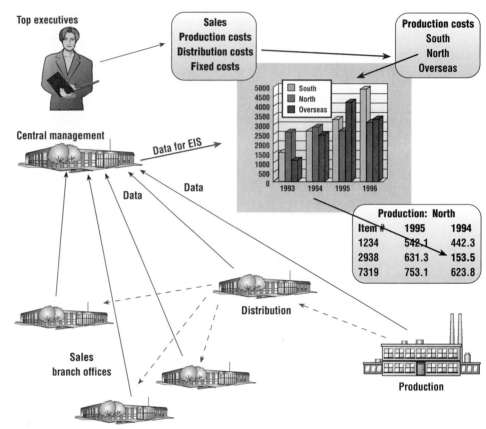

An EIS at McDonnell Douglas has a graphics screen that displays portions of airplanes as they are being built. As a wing is completed, it is drawn onto the computer model.

## Advantages of an EIS

The primary goal of an EIS is to provide easy access to corporate data for the executives. Instead of waiting for a report, the top executives can retrieve the data as soon as it is available. Also, because all the data is accessible from the same system, it is easier to examine data from different departments to produce a better view of the "big picture." Another useful feature is that the executive's use of the data is nonintrusive.

Imagine that you are CEO of a company, and you do not have an EIS. The monthly reports have just indicated that one of the warehouses is not running smoothly. You want to find out what the problems are. You suspect the warehouse manager is part of the problem, but you need to be sure. What do you do? The most direct approach is to go visit the warehouse. But what happens when you show up at the warehouse? It is likely that the manager and the workers will change the way they work. Your attempts to collect data have altered the way the system runs, so you will not get the information you wanted.

Other options include sending other people or asking for additional information via the chain-of-command. Although useful, these methods will be slower and the information you receive will be colored by the perceptions of the people collecting the data. For example, many people will try to focus on what they think you want to hear.

**Reality Bytes          8–6  FALCONBRIDGE, LTD.**

Falconbridge, Ltd is a Canadian minerals company headquartered in Toronto. It specializes in nickel, copper, and cobalt. Falconbridge's global operations include field exploration, production, refineries, laboratories, sales offices, and product warehouses. Buying and selling commodities across the globe means there are many sources of information; all of it must be tracked on a continuous basis. Yet in the late 1980s, Falconbridge did not have much of this crucial information available to managers. Dan Tuepah, director of marketing and planning, notes that

> We were relying on our accounting group to provide us with information about how we did, what we sold, where did it go. And, of course, you are dealing with a huge manual process and lot of hard-copy reports and exchange of data among groups to find out what you wanted.

Falconbridge uses a mostly decentralized approach to information systems, with more than 20 minicomputers and 2,000 personal computers. Each major facility had its own IS, with different hardware and software. Sharing data was a major challenge.

Falconbridge took the first step to solving these problems by linking all of the international sales offices with a network. Software designers built computer applications to collect the data automatically, removing much of the manual data entry and all of the rekeying efforts. Several of the sites had small Novell networks but no way of connecting to the other locations or to corporate headquarters. To overcome this limitation, Falconbridge installed an enterprise network system from Banyan known as Vines. The Vines system is designed to connect local networks to share data, e-mail, and resources from a wide variety of computers.

With the network in place, Falconbridge was faced with a problem encountered by many other companies. There were "hordes of information available to us—so what do I want to do with it all?" To provide managers with a better view of the data, Falconbridge added an EIS component to its system. The EIS collects all of the sales data and presents summaries to the managers. Through an easy-to-use personal computer interface, Tuepah can instantly "see all sales activity around the world."

The EIS component was custom-built to provide easier access to real-time data. Falconbridge avoided existing EIS software, arguing that it tended to focus too much on historical data or out-of-date information. According to Tuepah, a key feature of the EIS is the ability to share up-to-date data with everyone. Managers no longer need to rely on their personal spreadsheets to collect data.

SOURCE: Martin Slofstra, "A Tale of Two Systems," *Computing Canada* 20, no. 2 (January 19, 1994), p. 31.

The EIS minimizes these problems by providing instant access to the corporate data. The executives can produce reports and examine departments without interfering with the operations of the company. Graphs can be created automatically. The executives can set up different scenarios or simulations. Most of these activities are accomplished simply by pointing to objects on the screen.

## Limitations of an EIS

The concept of an EIS sounds good: Give the top executives immediate access to all of the corporate data. In practice, an EIS is rarely that comprehensive and is usually difficult to implement. One of the biggest limitations is that in many companies, the corporate data is handled by older COBOL-based programs. It is difficult to translate this data into a database that can be searched by the executives. Many systems simply copy portions of the data into a small database. This method typically provides only a small subset of the data.

There is also a trade-off between ease-of-use and the flexibility of the EIS. An EIS is easiest to use if the designers know ahead of time exactly what questions might be asked. Executives can then click on each item they wish to see. However, if the managers stray from the predefined report, they have to create complex queries.

In addition, although the graphical interface and drill-down capabilities are elegant and easy to use, an EIS is expensive to create and maintain. Integrating the data and formatting it for ease-of-use requires programmers and analysts behind the scenes to anticipate management needs and keep the system up-to-date.

Overall, most top executives find it easier to ask lower level managers for basic reports and information. A few executives believe that day-to-day details and computer usage should be left to lower-level managers. Standard reports are already produced by the transaction-processing system. Other questions can be investigated by midlevel executives. Many top executives believe this system leaves them free to concentrate on long-run strategy.

## SUMMARY

Managers make many different decisions. Every business discipline builds models to help people analyze problems and make decisions. Some models are straightforward; others are complex. Some are described by statements subject to interpretation; others are defined by mathematical formula. Businesses use models to improve their processes, evaluate choices, and forecast the future.

Management information systems can help managers collect data to drive the models. There are also software tools to help managers design and evaluate models. Word processors and graphics software are used to create the final reports. Decision support systems combine elements of these three tools to make it easier for managers to evaluate options, make decisions, and persuade others to accept the decision.

It is unlikely that you will have to design your own theoretical models from scratch. On the other hand, you will be responsible for understanding the basic business models. You also will have to decide which model is needed to analyze and solve various problems. Once you have determined the appropriate model, a variety of software is available to help apply the model. There are generic tools such as spreadsheets, statistics, and optimization packages.

> **A MANAGER'S VIEW**
>
> Tactical-level decisions can be complex. Managers need to make forecasts, improve operations, and search for ways to reorganize the business. Making snap decisions based on "gut instinct" rarely leads to effective solutions. Rigorous analysis can involve mathematical and statistical evaluation of operations data. Models are tools that are used to make better decisions. Although they have limitations, models can provide insight into the business. Managers use decision support systems to collect data, evaluate models, present the results, and make better decisions.

There are also thousands of packages available to solve specific problems.

In many ways, enterprise information systems are models of the entire business. They are designed to make it easy for higher level managers to monitor the performance of the firm, identify problems, and retrieve data from the corporate databases. They are graphically oriented to make them easier to use and to enable them to create graphs and images of the corporate performance.

## KEY WORDS

## REVIEW QUESTIONS

1. What are the primary reasons for creating business models?
2. What are three uses of models?
3. Describe three problems you might encounter when using models.
4. How are tactical-level decisions different from operations-level decisions?
5. List the three major components of a DSS.
6. List the major steps involved in building or using a model to solve a problem.
7. What is the major difference between generic and application-specific modeling tools?
8. What is the primary purpose of an enterprise information system?
9. List three advantages of an EIS.
10. What is the role played by assumptions in building models?
11. What is meant by the term drill down in an EIS?
12. How does re-engineering use models to improve a company?

## EXERCISES

1. Find examples of five models. List the discipline (such as economics or marketing), give an example of how modeling is used, and classify the use (optimization, prediction, simulation).
2. Find three software packages that would be useful for building decision support systems. Evaluate each in terms of the three DSS components. Are the packages generic or specific to some discipline?
3. Choose a local retail firm and identify three models that could be used by the manager to run the company. Which of these models is the most important to this firm? List the assumptions, input and output variables, and processes involved for this model.
4. You have just been hired by Eli Lilly to design a new EIS. As a first step, you need to determine the primary structure of the company. Using resources available at the library, create an outline of how the EIS will function. In particular, build a hierarchical chart that describes the primary screens and how they are related.
5. Interview a manager in your community to see what kinds of models he or she uses to make decisions. (Hint: Do *not* ask the manager to describe the models they use.) Are the models mathematical, descriptive, or heuristic (rules of thumb)? Could some of the decisions be improved by using better models? How difficult would it be to create and use these models? Who selected and created the models currently being used?
6. A marketing manager has asked you to help design a DSS for the marketing department. Every month marketers need to evaluate the effectiveness of their advertising campaigns and decide how to allocate their budget for the next month. They advertise only in the local area and have four basic choices: radio, television, local newspapers, and direct mail. Each month, they conduct random phone interviews to find out who sees their advertisements. They can also purchase local scanner data to determine sales of related products. Each month, the media salespeople give them the Arbitron ratings that show the number of people (and demographics) who they believe saw each advertisement. They also receive a schedule of costs for the upcoming month. As a first step in creating the DSS, identify any relevant assumptions and input and output variables, along with any models that might be useful.
7. A government official recently noted that the government is having difficulty processing applications for assistance programs (welfare). Although most applications are legitimate, several facts they contain have to be checked. For instance, welfare workers have to check motor vehicle and real estate records to see whether the applicants own cars or property. The agency checks birth, death, and marriage records to verify the existence of dependents. They sometimes examine public health data and check criminal records. It takes time to check all of the records, plus the agency needs to keep track of the results of the searches. Additionally, a few applicants have applied multiple times—sometimes in different localities. The office needs to randomly check some applications to search for fraud. Every week, summary reports have to be sent to the state offices. A key feature of these reports is that they are used to convince politicians to increase funding for certain programs. Describe how a DSS could help this agency. Hint: Identify the decisions that need to be made.

 **Rolling Thunder Database**

1. Identify five models that could be used to improve the management of the Rolling Thunder Bicycle company. What data would be needed to evaluate the models?

2. Identify shipments where receipts do not match the original order. Provide a count and value (and percentages) by supplier/manufacturer.
3. Using basic accounting, lists costs and revenues by month. Provide any graphs and tables to illustrate trends or patterns.
4. Analyze sales and discounts by employee and by model type. Are some employees providing higher

discounts than others? Are we discounting some models too much or not enough?
5. List a tactical-level decision in each of the main divisions of the company. How often is the decision made? Who makes it? What information is used? What types of analyses need to be performed?

## ADDITIONAL READING

Asten, Roy. "A Virtual Tug-of-War," *Computer Reseller News*, May 29, 1995, pp. 33-39. [Sega and Nintendo]

"Automakers to Build Their Own Private Internet," *Network World*, September 25, 1995, pp. 1-2. [GM design]

Barabba, Vincent and Gerald Zaltman. *Hearing the Voice of the Market*. Cambridge: Harvard Business Press, 1991. [Overcoming design biases at GM]

Bartholomew, Doug. "Scheduling Software: Manufacturing Gets a Lift—Bell Helicopter's New Scheduling System Improves Productivity, Worker Morale, and the Bottom Line," *Information Week*, January 16, 1995, p. 62. [Bell Helicopter]

Booker, Ellis. "Pushing Decision Support Beyond Executive Suite," *Computerworld*, December 20, 1993, p. 65. [Sherwin-Williams]

Carlton, Jim. "Nintendo, Gambling With Its Technology, Faces a Crucial Delay, *The Wall Street Journal*, May 5, 1995, pp. A1, A4. [Sega and Nintendo]

Carlton, Jim. "Nintendo, Video-Game Retailers Discover Treasure Trove in Donkey Kong Country," *The Wall Street Journal*, January 11, 1995, pp. B1, B8. [Sega and Nintendo]

Coctlaw, Terry and Michele Clarke. "Closing in on the Open Factory; Part II: Automakers Are Finally Beginning to Trust the PC," *Electronic Engineering Times*, April 10, 1995, pp. 1-2. [GM design]

DeJong, Jennifer and Wayne Rash Jr. "Video Madness," *Corporate Computer*, August 1992, pp. 134-144. [Sega and Nintendo]

Halper, Mark. "Nintendo Playing No Games with Holiday Product Deliveries," *Computerworld*, November 29, 1993, p. 1. [Sega and Nintendo]

Hoffman, Thomas. "Unisys Outlines Unix Strategies for 1993," *Computerworld*, February 8, 1993, p. 47. [AAA service]

Hutheesing, Nikhil. "Games Companies Play," *Forbes*, October 25, 1993, pp. 68-69. [Sega and Nintendo]

Maguiness, David. "Other People's Models," *Lotus*, February 1992, pp. 19-24. [Hints on building good spreadsheets]

Manning, Ric. "Some Sega Buyers Left Idle without New Cable," *Louisville Courier Journal*, December 30, 1994, p. D1. [Sega and Nintendo]

Moad, Jeff. "Object Lessons," *PC Week*, October 23, 1995, pp. E1-E3. [Citicorp]

Neumann, Peter G. "Modeling and Simulation," *Communications of the ACM*, June, 1993, p. 124. [Modeling problem examples]

Pastore, Richard. "Handheld PCs Aid Nintendo Sales Reps," *Computerworld*, August 7, 1989, p. 39. [Sega and Nintendo]

"PC Week Executive Guide to Teambuilding," *PC Week*, March 27, 1995, p. E9. [Frito-Lay]

"Sega Reports Record Sales, Profit (for FY Ended 3/31/92)," *Software Industry Bulletin*, May 26, 1992, pp. 1-2. [Sega and Nintendo]

"The Player: Nintendo Is a Force to Reckon With—But Not in Interactive Video," *Computer Letter*, June 21, 1993, pp. 6-9. [Sega and Nintendo]

Zaltman, Gerald and Vincent P. Barabba, "Knowledge Loom of the '90s," *Computerworld*, June 22, 1992, pp. 133, 136-137. [Overcoming design biases at GM]

# CASES *Design and Marketing*

There are no detailed statistics on design and marketing. However, engineers (like other professionals) tend to utilize computers significantly more than the general population. Word processing is a primary application, along with CAD programs, analytical tools and databases.

SOURCE: Computer Use in the United States, U.S. Bureau of the Census.

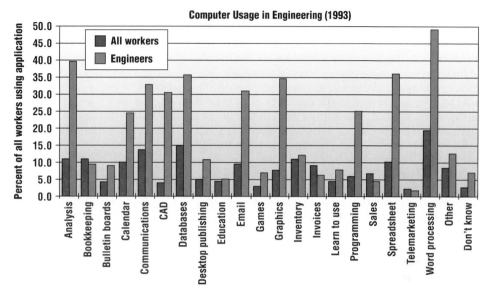

Computer Usage in Engineering (1993)

Models are employed for many different purposes in the corporate world. However, models are commonly used to evaluate alternatives and predict possible outcomes. These techniques are useful in design of products and in marketing management.

Some people think of marketing management as just collecting sales figures and motivating salespeople. Yet, in today's competitive environment, just having sales numbers is not enough. Sometimes, even yesterday's sales figures are too old; it takes time to schedule, produce, and ship products. Planning becomes a key element in marketing. Yet, planners are faced with many uncertainties and limited data. They need to evaluate various scenarios and set up contingency plans. All the options need to be examined in terms of revenues, costs, and effects on the company and competitors. Models play an important part of planning.

Design of products was once considered to be the realm of "artists," involving creativity with a nod to engineering feasibility. Today's designers still rely on creativity, but they must confront the realities of the marketplace. They must constantly be in touch with what consumers want—not an easy feat, because consumers do not always know what they want. Design teams continually evaluate survey data, conduct focus groups, and get feedback on design ideas. By the time they collect a few thousand opinions and share ideas with hundreds of team members, there is an overwhelming amount of data floating around. Being a designer essentially means making hundreds of deci-

sions. It is impossible to comb the vast databases to answer every design question. Technology can help by making it easier to search databases, showing related data, and improving communication among teams. As computer systems get better at handling more complex data (pictures, sound, and video), the use in design continues to expand.

## CASE *Sega of America: Accessing Data*

Nintendo was formed in 1889 to sell playing cards. Since 1949, it has been run by Hiroshi Yamauchi, who inherited the company from his grandfather. He made several attempts at diversification, but most of them failed. He found success by concentrating on toys and arcade games. The huge success of the 1980 Game & Watch provided money to invest in the video game market. The original game machine was sold at a low price (about $65), with the intention of making money later on the game cartridges. Introduced into the United States in 1985, it sold 440,000 the first year.

Nintendo strictly controls the production of games for its machines. In Japan, no other company can create games for the machine. The Federal Trade Commission disallowed that strict position in the United States. But even so, vendors must first get approval from Nintendo and pay a royalty fee for every cartridge sold—reportedly as much as $10 per cartridge. After eight years of selling the original machine,

Nintendo took a risk with the Super NES in 1990 by producing a machine that was incompatible with the earlier cartridges.

Sega is the dominant player in the video games market. The company was started by an expatriate American in Japan, was sold to Gulf & Western, and then sold again to a Japanese software integrator (CSK). (*Sega* is not a Japanese word; it stands for "service and games.") The company began life as a distributor and then creator of arcade machines. Sega's initial home game machine did not fare well in the market because it was introduced later than Nintendo's and cost twice as much. However, Sega's introduction of the 16-bit Genesis has given it a much higher revenue growth rate than Nintendo has.

Sega of America is the U.S. arm of the $1.6 billion Japanese Sega Enterprises, a manufacturer of video games. The American subsidiary began operations in 1989 and is headquartered in Redwood City, California. In 1991, Sega earned $106 million profit, with sales doubling from the prior year. The company expects to sell 3.6 million Genesis units in 1992 compared to 6 million units of Super NES anticipated by Nintendo. The headquarters supports about 200 people. There are distribution centers in Seattle; Hayward, California; and Newark. There are also 15 sales offices around the country. As of early 1992, when a retail customer called a Sega representative, the rep called headquarters and requested a report from a sales coordinator. The coordinator then manually prepared the report—which could take several days.

After the Christmas rush of 1991, Sega executives knew they had a problem with their information systems. They also knew they had only nine months to fix the problems before the 1992 Christmas season. Throw in the fact that Nintendo was quickly closing the gap in sales, number of 16-bit games, and an impending price war. Bill Downs, director of IS and telecommunications for Sega of America, knew he had to act quickly.

To install the system on time with minimal implementation problems, the new system had to use most of the existing hardware and software. Generally, operations had been centralized on a midsize IBM AS/400. There were also 132 personal computers scattered throughout the organization. The computers were attached to the AS/400 and functioned largely as dumb terminals, with minimal capabilities to download data. There were also 25 Apple Macintoshes connected in a small AppleTalk network. They were typically used to run Microsoft Excel and Word. Based on volume, about 60 percent of the retail outlets provided orders and received invoices through an EDI network. The EDI system had the capability of collecting more detailed data, down to cash-register sales data, but it was not being used for that purpose.

To make crucial marketing and inventory decisions, Sega executives decided they needed better access to the data. In particular, they needed to examine the data in a variety of formats, such as sales by region, store, product line, or over a period of time. The executives examined data on a case-by-case basis, so they needed a system that would enable them to manipulate the data themselves—without requiring the skills of an MIS programmer. Downs decided to evaluate proposed solutions based on these criteria:

- Understanding the business problem (product line, customers, and competitors).

- The use of proven software technology (software should be currently available). Although the company had a long history of using products from Computer Associates, its proposal called for software that was not finished and might not be available until the third quarter of 1992.

- Query capabilities (to enable managers to access data as they pleased, from several different perspectives, without requiring programming skills).

- Low ownership costs (no new staffing or specialized training).

- Use of the existing equipment, especially the AS/400 and the PS/2 machines, without having to buy more powerful workstations.

- Expanded use of EDI with retailers (expanding use of existing data and adding new data sources).

- Ease-of-use by executives (many of whom have limited computer training).

- Vendor's system knowledge and technical expertise.

- Independence from programmers. Managers and executives should be able to query the databases and create simple reports on their own.

- Decision support for executives. The system must provide the "correct" information for top executives—typically summarized, but enabling executives to drill down to any level of detail.

- A graphical user interface that is easy to use and that requires minimal training.

- Commitment to Sega and seeing the project through to completion.

- Physical portability—the ability to physically move the system because Sega has moved its corporate offices several times.

- Support for the SAA/CUA standards (largely with respect to the user interface).

At least two systems integrators have suggested installing a LAN to meet Sega's objectives. Basic costs of installing the LAN for Sega include the software, new interface cards (for about $175 a piece) and probably two file servers (at least $10,000 each). Fortunately, Sega already had the cabling needed to build the LAN. The managers considered purchasing a new computer to use as the database server that would have more flexibility and better performance than the existing AS/400. However, cost and time factors led them to keep the AS/400. Sega IS personnel were wary of the LAN approach, partly because it represented a major departure from their existing centralized system and partly because they were concerned about flexibility and lack of standardization.

The LAN proposal submitted by Lante (a systems integrator) consisted of:

- Local area network: A Novell NetWare LAN running on a token ring. The LAN would support both Sega's Macintosh computers and its PCs.
- A PC query system based on Gupta's SQL-Windows, in conjunction with Gupta's Quest. Together, the software enables executives to formulate ad hoc queries on their PCs to retrieve data from the AS/400.
- A software package called Rumba, which allows Sega to run AS/400 host applications on PCs under Windows.
- The Gupta SQLBase Server, which is a database engine based on SQL and designed to handle data efficiently, including graphics.
- Gupta SQL Windows, which is an application development system that is used to create graphics products under Windows that can query and display data in a variety of formats, including graphics and maps.
- Gupta Quest works with Gupta SQL products to access data, process queries, and create reports.
- Novell NetWare as the operating system for the LAN.
- Rochester Software Connection Showcase Vista, an optional tool to generate reports and enable users to query the AS/400 databases.

After the first round of judging, the two main candidates were Lante and SHL Systemhouse. SHL Systemhouse, a client-server consultant, had a slight edge, but Sega officials wanted to re-examine the choices. SHL's solution relied on software from many vendors. Although they recommended a switch to a LAN, their leading proposal kept the existing wiring system and used software to deliver the data from the AS/400 to the PS/2 computers. The SHL was weaker at explaining how the pieces would work together and used the following:

- The Forest and Trees SQL reporting tool that retrieves data from PCs and host databases. It presents data in a graphical format and enables users to drill down for more detail.
- AS/400 folders and PC/Support. By copying the AS/400 host data into folders every night, the PCs can access the data as if it were stored on a simple PC disk drive.
- Show-Case Vista and Show-Case EIS from Rochester Software Connection as graphical front-ends to enable the executives to query the AS/400 database.
- OS/2 as a PC operating system to allow multitasking and build custom applications. It would require upgrading several of the Sega PCs.

Overall, Bill Downs knew exactly what he needed. The problem was finding someone to create the system and get everything operational in nine months. Ultimately, he wanted a system that displayed a map on the screen for executives, showing sales in different regions. By pointing to each city, the executives could get a detailed listing of sales for that city. Digging deeper, they could eventually list sales by each store on any given day for each product. The overriding objective was to ensure that the executives had easy access to up-to-the-minute sales data.

Before Christmas sales in 1993, Sega of America controlled almost 50 percent of the video game market, compared to the 7 percent it had in 1990. Sales in the U.S. division reached $1 billion. According to *The Wall Street Journal* (June 7, 1994, p. B2), the U.S. market for video game software was growing at the rate of 30 percent a year, and would total about $4.5 billion in 1994. Sega is actively developing interactive games based on CD-ROM technology. Nintendo has announced plans to introduce a CD-ROM component, but has repeatedly delayed production.

By 1994, Sega had still not resolved all of its delivery problems. For Christmas, the company released the Sega 32X game system as an upgrade to existing systems. It provides better graphics and sound, as well as faster action. Once again, Sega beat most of its rivals to the market and demand was high. The only catch was that owners of older Sega systems needed a special cable adapter to connect the game to older televisions that do not have separate audio and video inputs. Although the 32X machines were available, the $20 cables were impossible to find. Twelve-year-old Casey Overstreet pointedly observed that "You got this great game-playing system and you're going, 'All right!' Then you find out you can't play it."

Some retailers were not aware that the cable was needed, and Sega of America simply noted that it was sold out during the holiday season.

## The Nintendo Approach

Nintendo took a slightly different approach to the distribution issue. In 1989, Nintendo had 130 merchandising representatives who traveled to retail outlets. At each store, they recorded 14 pieces of data such as sales floor inventories, prices, and allocated shelf space. The data was recorded on forms that were mailed to headquarters and entered into the central computer. It often took one to two months for the data to be compiled into a report. Mark Thorien of Nintendo noted that

> By that time, the information was so untimely that it was basically worthless . . . There are real dramatic swings between what people want one day and what they want the next. You have to stay on top of it, or you get stuck with a lot of inventory that you can't sell.

In 1989, Nintendo replaced the paper-based system with hand-held computers for all of the sales representatives. As data was entered into the machine, it was automatically transmitted back to the central computer. Messages could also be sent to from the corporate managers down to the sales representatives. Reports were now created in 24 hours. Additionally, there were fewer mistakes because of misread handwriting.

In November 1993, Nintendo of America signed a contract with Unisys to provide "Fast EDI" services between Nintendo and 15,000 retail stores. With the old methods, it took an average of five weeks for a licensee of a Nintendo cartridge to ship products to the stores. The new method was supposed to cut the time down to six days. The system gained speed by allowing licensees to store their products at the Nintendo central warehouse in North Bend, Washington. The EDI ordering system tied to the stores was capable of processing sales for 15 million cartridges a year. By centralizing the warehouse and the EDI system, Nintendo could provide faster delivery of cartridges at a lower cost than licensees could obtain on their own. At the end of 1993, 11 retail chains had signed up for the system. Almost two-thirds of Nintendo games were produced by licensees. Most were small companies. Phil Rogers, vice president of operations at Nintendo, estimates that a comparable system would cost the licensees between $20,000 and $500,000 each, which the smaller companies could not afford. With the new system, a per-cartridge fee is paid to Nintendo and a separate fee to Unisys.

## 1995 and 32-bits

By 1993, Nintendo's U.S. market share in 16-bit games had slipped to 39 percent. In February 1994 Hiroshi Yamauchi, head of the Japanese parent company, removed his son-in-law Minuro Arakawa as head of the U.S. subsidiary. He was replaced by Howard Lincoln, who was chosen to be more aggressive. By 1995, with improved marketing and new games, Nintendo's market share had risen to 57 percent.

However, 1995 and 1996 offer new challenges to Nintendo and Sega: the introduction of 64-bit game players capable of three-dimensional graphics. Sega and new rivals like 3DO were to have 64-bit systems ready for the 1995 Christmas season. Nintendo will not. A lack of 64-bit games might hold the market down for a year. The big question is whether Sega could use the six-month lead to gain a major advantage. Both Nintendo and Sega suffered in Christmas 1994 sales, with retail sales down approximately 20 percent. In October 1995, Microsoft announced a set of programming tools that would enable personal computers to function as better games machines. Microsoft's stated goal is to make the personal computer the premier video game platform.

## QUESTIONS

1. How did the original information system hurt Sega?
2. Sega's original computer system provided sales data as recent as the prior day. Why was this data not good enough? What more did Sega managers need?
3. What key features did Sega plan to add to its information system? Which capabilities do you consider most important? Place weights (from 1 to 10, with 10 the most important) on each of the 15 criteria evaluated by Sega.
4. What data will be collected by the new system? What decisions will be made based on this data? How will the system help executives make better decisions?
5. In what ways does the new system represent a model of Sega's business operations?
6. How might the new system alter the way in which Sega operates? Consider the effect on prices, customers, retailers, and the parent company in Japan.
7. What are the advantages and disadvantages of the two leading proposals (Lante and SHL)?
8. Which of the two proposals would you choose? What additional information would you like from the two companies (Lante and SHL)?

9. How will the new system alter the culture and operations in the IS department at Sega? What problems and benefits might you expect to see from these changes?
10. What additional features would you add to Sega's information system in the future?
11. How does Nintendo's approach to distribution of cartridges differ from Sega's new system? Is one method better than the other? What are the costs and benefits?

## CASE  *Sherwin-Williams*

Sherwin-Williams Co. began as a manufacturer of paint. Their Paint Stores Group is headquartered in Cleveland and had $1.5 billion in sales in 1991, which grew to $1.8 billion in 1992. This group was organized into 110 districts. Each one was headed by a district manager. Each district manager was responsible for 20 to 25 stores. These managers reported to 14 area vice-presidents, who in turn reported to 4 division heads. The overall organization is run by the CEO, John Breen. Overall, the company had a traditional management hierarchy. Individual stores were operated independently and results were reported up the command chain. Major decisions were made at the executive level. Policies were broadcast to the entire organization and messages sent through the managers to be given to individual stores. There was little horizontal communication between individual stores or districts.

Each store had an automated point-of-sale system based on NCR cash registers. The POS collected detailed sales data for each store, but each store was independent of the others. Overall, Sherwin-Williams was satisfied with the POS system. Most of the corporate computing was handled by a centralized Amdahl computer (compatible with large IBM computers). Bill Thompson, the head of MIS for the paint group, noted that almost none of the district managers used personal computers (fewer than 15 percent).

Every Monday morning, managers called each of the stores in their district to get sales figures for the previous week. The managers used these numbers to create a sales report which was forwarded up the hierarchy to the area vice-presidents. Because of the importance of staying in touch with the local stores, the weekly phone calls are important to the managers. However, the managers spend a lot of time every week producing the sales reports. Additionally, because upper management was always in a hurry to see the data, there was only enough time to collect basic sales figures. The senior executives are also interested in detailed comparisons based on sales by product category, by sales representative, and by each territory. Most of the time,

the area vice presidents and senior executives make decisions based on comparisons of aggregated sales data by territory. However, they sometimes want more detailed data from individual stores. Additionally, senior management wants to make more comparisons among regions. Similarly, district managers would like to compare their sales to those of the other districts.

### QUESTIONS

1. What basic problems are faced by Sherwin-Williams managers?
2. What level of management is most in need of better information access?
3. How can MIS help Sherwin-Williams managers get access to their data?
4. What hardware and software might be needed?
5. What additional communication facilities might be needed?
6. Will a new system alter the way the organization is managed and operated?

## CASE  *Lewin-VHI: Healthcare Analysts*

Health insurance and access to healthcare are major issues to most Americans. The cost of healthcare increased throughout the 1980s and insurance companies introduced restricted coverage and payment limits in an attempt to control expenses. By the early 1990s, the issues erupted into a national debate. Politicians like President Clinton used the issue to appeal to voters. Every side in the debate evaluated options, hired lobbyists, held press conferences, and bombarded Congress and the public with predictions on costs and quality of care for thousands of plans. After more than a year of study, the Clinton Administration released a set of proposed reforms.

No self-respecting lobbyist would approach the debate without some form of statistics to back up the opinions and complaints. For example, in 1994, every member of Congress was sent a report from a group known as Families USA that contained the headline: "Better Benefits. Millions Helped by Clinton Reform." Of course, lawmakers received many other reports, including one from the Heritage Foundation arguing that the Clinton reform "has huge hidden costs, in the form of wage reductions and job losses." The interesting feature of these two reports is that they were both based on analyses from one company: Lewin-VHI, a division of Value-Health Inc. Lewin-VHI has earned tremendous respect in Washington, with lobbyists insisting on using their analyses. Lawmakers received so many reports based on their model that Daniel Patrick Moynihan, the Senate finance committee chairman, noted "Whatever else comes out of this year, Lewin-VHI will do very well."

Industry analysts note that Lewin-VHI, located in suburban Virginia, earned around $20 million in 1993, reflecting a 30 percent increase in revenue. In addition to studies for federal and state governments, Lewin-VHI sells studies to hospitals and other health care organizations. Formed in 1970, the company built its reputation by providing fast, accurate analyses of the health care industry. For many years, it was virtually the only consulting firm providing these reports. Today, its analyses are based on a computer model (the Health Benefits Simulation Model) developed during the last 10 years. As an illustration of its capabilities, Lewin-VHI used the model to evaluate Clinton's 1300+ page reform. The company completed the analysis in one month. The Congressional Budget Office took more than three months to perform similar analyses for Congress.

One of the difficulties with such a complex model is that there are thousands of parameters to be evaluated. Hence, the results you obtain are often dependent on exactly what questions are asked and on what assumptions are made. For example, Families USA supports the Clinton plan and asked Lewin-VHI to determine the costs to an average American. The conclusion was that the plan would save an average person $695 a year in health care costs. On the other hand, the Heritage Foundation, which dislikes the Clinton proposal, had a study prepared by Lewin, and the conclusion was that families would save only $53 on average, and 53 percent of the people would see costs increase.

How can the same company, using one model, produce different results? Larry Lewin, the company's chairman, notes that "It has to do with how the question is asked." Robert Rubin, Lewin's president, also notes that "There are subtle differences in the assumptions used, or the methodology," Additionally, he observes that regardless of the results, "It's the spin the client puts on it." For these very reasons, for every study the company produces, Lewin-VHI insists on seeing all press releases issued by the client, with the ability to issue a separate press release correcting any errors in interpretation.

In the case of Families USA and the Heritage Foundation, some of the differences were due to the fact that Heritage asked them to include wages lost from the increased cost of health-care benefits to businesses. Similar, apparently contradictory findings arose with evaluations of other alternatives, such as the alternative Cooper proposal.

Mr. Lewin and Dr. Rubin insist that the firm takes pains to remain neutral. All politically sensitive reports are carefully reviewed by both of them. The company also turns down clients who want to bias the results. Dr. Rubin notes that "We're at the point now where people say our reputation for being fair is such that we're just not going to do something in a half-baked way."

Lewin-VHI charges from $25,000 to as much as $125,000 for basic reports to complex analyses. Clients typically provide assumptions, parameters, and various scenarios they want to investigate.

SOURCE: Hilary Stout, "One Company's Data Fuel Diverse Views in Health-care Debate," *The Wall Street Journal*, June 28, 1994, pp. A1, A10. Reprinted by permission of *The Wall Street Journal*, © 1994 Dow Jones & Company, Inc. All rights reserved.

### QUESTIONS

1. How can a model produce different results for different people?
2. Because most models can produce a variety of results, how do we know which conclusion is "correct?"
3. Why do we bother with models like the Lewin-VHI model when we know that the model can produce different results?
4. What types of models do you think Lewin-VHI uses? What would be some of the basic input and output variables?
5. As a member of Congress, how could you evaluate the various studies? What would you look for in each report to help you evaluate the conclusions?
6. If we did not have the Lewin's Health Benefits Simulation Model, how would lobbyists, Congress, and the public evaluate the proposed health care plans?

### CASE *General Motors Design: Inquiry Center*

In designing an automobile, it is crucial that designers provide the styles and features demanded by customers. As auto manufacturers have seen many times, guessing wrong can be a costly mistake. Ford Motor Company learned its lessons in 1957 when the auto maker introduced the Edsel. Ford's Marketers interviewed 800 consumers about automobiles, image, and some marketing ideas. Ford also spent considerable money researching the name. Virtually all of the ideas (including names) were ignored. This highly publicized episode helped persuade Ford's managers to listen to the market. By the 1970s, General Motors and most other manufacturers were designing cars mainly by committee. Managers and engineers relied on their own preferences and intuition to choose features. When gas prices tripled in the 1970s and consumers wanted smaller, more reliable cars, U.S. automakers were left with lots full of oversized, gas-guzzling cars. Even in the 1980s, the automobile companies had trouble listening to customers. Long after the Japanese manufacturers had converted to more efficient, more reliable overhead-cam engines, General Motors was relying on older push-rod engines. If asked for a reason, engineers were likely to reply that "Push-rod engines accelerate faster from a stoplight." That statement does not answer the important question: What features did consumers really want?

Sometimes auto manufacturers reap substantial benefits from understanding the market. In the late 1980s and early 1990s, Chrysler earned substantial profits by introducing the minivan. The designers listened to customers and noted that baby-boomers now had larger families and needed more space, yet wanted an easy-to-drive vehicle. Getting a jump on the other firms attracted customers. It also provided early feedback on design changes and new features, keeping Chrysler ahead of the competition in each new redesign.

In any context, it seems "obvious" that companies need to pay attention to the demands of customers. Using 20/20 hindsight, it is easy for us to find situations in which companies could have made better decisions—if only they had listened to the market. The problem is that most situations and decisions are complex, and there is rarely only one voice. The decision maker is quickly faced with thousands of "voices," conflicting opinions, and impossible demands.

It is difficult to judge consumer preferences in automobiles. It takes at least two to three years to design and build a new vehicle. Tastes and economic circumstances can change radically during that time. Plus, there are different types of customers, and many of them do not always know what they want. Or they want a supercar for no cost. The decision is further complicated by the number of workers and managers involved in the design process, each with preferences, tastes, and opinions of what the market wants. Throw in the uncertainty caused by the competition, complications from suppliers, and variances in the economy, and automakers are faced with a complex problem. Robert Stempel, a CEO of GM, expressed these problems in a speech to senior marketing managers:

> You heard the word "listening" today. A lot of people think they listen, but they don't. They're the types who seem to listen and say "I hear you, but I know better. I know how to build a great car or truck. And you've never really built one, so let me do it my way." Well, you can't really work that way. We do have to listen to what the customer is telling us. When he talks about ride/handling, we really have to under-stand what he means. He might be talking about bumps in the road, and he calls that ride/handling. When he talks about acceleration, does he mean flat-out acceleration, or does he mean getting onto expressway ramps? There are hundreds and hundreds of differences between what the customer says and what he really means.

GM, like the other automobile companies, combats these problems by collecting large amounts of data. The information is often scattered throughout the company, controlled by various groups and rarely in a format needed by the designers. Those managers trying to listen to the market, are swamped with a tidal wave of data. Trying to find the useful pieces of information and make sense of the data are difficult.

Design is not an isolated process. It involves hundreds of designers, marketers, and engineers. Designs and ideas have to be presented to focus groups of consumers for feedback. Engineers and production managers evaluate designs for production costs and feasibility. Suppliers are contacted for comments, cost projections, and availability of materials and components. Designs and features are revised and reanalyzed. Coordinating these teams and communicating elements and changes are major challenges.

To meet these challenges, companies need to develop a marketing system that is designed from the ground up to make it easier for managers to get the information they need. Creating this system entails understanding all of the design and decision stages in the company. GM instituted a specialized system known as an *inquiry center* for the design staff. The overall goal of the system is to enable GM to provide vehicles that meet the demands of the market and to encourage innovation. The inquiry center is not a physical organization, and it is set up so that it cannot be controlled by any single faction. Its purpose is to provide up-to-date, usable information for everyone involved in the design process. The market research group takes the lead in collecting and storing the market data. Marketers talk with customers, collect survey data, analyze trade-offs between attributes and work with competitive product comparisons. But the center goes beyond collecting data. It is designed to integrate data to improve the decision-making process. At its heart, the inquiry center relies on technology to share information.

Some of the data used by these decision makers is in a traditional numeric format: data from surveys, product and engineering specifications, sales data, and comments. Other data is more descriptive: news reports, reviewer critiques, and audience responses to presentations. Some data is easiest to understand visually: prototypes, colors, instrument layouts, driver and passenger body positions, and even focus group interviews and test drives.

Interpretation of the data involves many types of models. There are physical (and CAD) mockups of the designs, interior layouts, and components. Engineering models examine production, manufacturing complexity, scheduling, and quality control. Financial models are used to evaluate costs and pricing. Economic forecasts estimate demand and market conditions. Consumer marketing models detail preferences and trade-offs between features. As Robert Stempel noted, "It's not just how you collect the data. Everybody can collect the data. It's how you use the data once you have it. It takes work."

Prior to the inquiry center, research results, designs, and comments were typically held by individual groups within GM. At some companies, the political climate limits the amount of sharing that takes place: Information represents power. There are stories of executives attending meetings but hoarding current data. When other participants presented an opposing plan, the first manager would innocently ask what data supported the opposing position, then surprise them with the newer data.

Even when departments and teams cooperate, there is just so much data that it is difficult to find specific items or related information. Some departments circulate their data to virtually everyone in the company, leading to mailboxes stuffed with huge amounts of meaningless reports. No matter how carefully messages are targeted, as the amount of data increases, eventually it becomes difficult or impossible to find specific data. Even if a designer stumbles onto a useful piece of information, it is difficult to track down related information. It is also difficult to share more complex data forms, like videotapes.

Design teams in GM face problems common in other multinational corporations. Different groups refer to the same information with different terms. Even simple searches for *color* become complicated when British teams use the database (spelling it *colour*.) Similar disparities in customer names make it difficult for anyone to find all data related to one customer.

Design teams need support in three main areas: decision-making logic and evaluation, collaboration, and creativity. The systems must be easy to use to make it easy to locate and share data. The design system must also avoid encouraging (or forcing) conformity among the designers. GM still remembers the design fiasco of the 1980s when four major divisions (Pontiac, Oldsmobile, Buick, and Chevrolet) created virtually identical automobiles.

SOURCE: Gerald Zaltman and Vincent P. Barabba, *Hearing the Voice of the Market*, Boston, Mass: Harvard Business School Press, 1991.

## QUESTIONS

1. Design an information system that will support the design process at GM's inquiry center. Include details on communication and types of software and hardware. Explain how your system will solve the problems.
2. Identify the primary models involved in the GM design process. Specify the input and output components along with the primary purpose and techniques used in the models.
3. Using an object-oriented approach, describe the various objects involved in the inquiry center project. Include basic attributes and functions for each object. Also show the primary relationships between objects.
4. What complications are added because of the global aspects of GM? How can technology help overcome these problems?
5. What are the primary problems experienced by the designers and managers? Facing a limited budget, rank the problem areas to indicate the best solution process.
6. How will a new marketing and design system alter the way the organization is managed and operated?

## CASE    *Using Statistics to Improve Quality and Customer Satisfaction*

The Auto Club of New York is the eighth largest affiliate of the Automobile Association of America. Because it is a membership organization, the Auto Club was concerned about the perception of its services by its members.

Working with an outside consultant, the Auto Club chose a mail survey as its information request mechanism. A random sample of 2,500 members each received a six-page survey and, as an incentive to return it, a new $1 bill. Questions were attitudinal in scope and centered on the services used, the favored methods for service usage, competitive comparisons, and overall satisfaction indices. The goal of the survey was to rate member opinion on 16 service attributes divided into three perspectives:

- The importance of each attribute.
- The level of expectation for each attribute.
- The member's rating of the club's performance on attribute delivery.

The members were each asked to evaluate each service attribute and rate its level of importance. The expectation of service was also rated.

The returned responses from 1,241 members, or approximately 50 percent, were analyzed. SPSS was used for multivariate analysis; Lotus 1-2-3 was used for tabulation; Harvard Graphics was used for graphic presentation and perceptual mapping; WordPerfect was used for the integration of text and data. Data presentation was done through bar and pie charts and detail tables. Actual interpretation was based on the comparison between an attribute's importance mean rating and the difference between the attribute's mean performance and its mean expectation (the P-E gap).

A positive, or favorable, P-E gap for an attribute means that the performance exceeds expectations. A negative, or unfavorable, P-E gap means that the performance does not meet expectations. This scale allows the identification of attributes that have a high level of importance as defined by the mean rating but have a low performance-to-expectation deviate.

Regression analysis was used to highlight significance differences. Attributes were classified using factor analytic techniques based on how members responded to the club's performance. Significant factors were detected and described as "service access" and "service delivery." Reliability tests were performed on each factor.

The results of this statistical analysis helped the Auto Club to prioritize its quality improvement programs and allocate resources to new programs that focus on the critical issues that affect service quality. By doing so, they were better able to focus on what was important to their customers.

## QUESTIONS

1. Identify the three primary components (data, model, output) of this decision support system and the IS tools that support each component.
2. Without the IS tools, what steps would be needed to analyze this data and present the results?
3. Create four sample AAA service questions and invent 10 responses. Using a spreadsheet, estimate the means and compute the P-E gap for each question. Create graphs for each of the questions. Then multiply each gap amount by the mean of the priority values for each question. Create new graphs for this prioritized data.

## DISCUSSION ISSUE

### *Employee Privacy*

An important issue for many employees today is the extent to which companies monitor their employees' use of telephone and computer communications systems. As an example, let's listen to a hypothetical discussion between Edgar and one of his employees.

Edgar: Miles, I understand you have been using electronic mail a lot lately.

Miles: Sure. I've been working on the Robestat project, and I've been asking some of my old colleagues and a couple professors for advice. I'm building a fairly complex model and I needed some help with the math and the statistics. The e-mail system is fast and my friends aren't charging us for the advice. Besides, I thought the e-mail system was cheaper than regular mail. Is there a problem with the cost?

Edgar: Not exactly. The work you've been doing on the project is fine. That's not the problem. The problem is that you've also been using the system for personal use on company time.

Miles: I don't think I know what you're talking about.

Edgar: Do you know someone named Madeline at the University of San Francisco?

Miles: Well, sort of, but . . .

Edgar: The computer records show that in the last month, you sent her an average of five messages a day, and received about two a day from her.

Miles: Uh, sure. But she's just one of the colleagues I mentioned. We've, uh, been discussing parts of the project. She does some research for me at the library. I haven't given her any details about the project or any confidential data.

Edgar: That's not the real problem. But Miles, you're not quite telling me the whole story are you?

Miles: I, uh, don't know what you mean.

*(Edgar turns to a terminal and types a command.)*

Edgar: Well, let's see. How about this message you sent yesterday:

```
Dearest Madeline: I really miss
you. I had a great time at the
party last weekend. I can't wait
to see you again. I have a boat
reserved for the weekend. Just
the two of us. Come with me, and
we can watch the sun rise over
```

```
Alcatraz.  What  do  you  say?
Miles  ;>)
```

There's a lot more of this drivel here. I can't find anything about the project, unless you count this silly reference to some chase through the library.

Miles: But . . . where did you get those? You can't read those. They're personal property.

Edgar: Not that it matters, but we routinely monitor everyone's use of the computer. The point is that you've been using company resources for your personal use. Besides, some of these messages sound a bit immoral to me. This company doesn't need workers like you. Clean up your desk. We'll mail your final check to your home address. Here's security. They'll escort you out.

Miles: But, but, wait a minute. You can't do that. You can't read my mail messages—that's illegal. You can't tell me what I can or can't do on my time. You can't do this, I'll sue the company. I'll sue you. I'll . . .

Edgar: Go ahead. We'll win, just like all the other companies have won. It's our computer, we can do what we want. Security, I'm through with him.

*(Miles is ushered out.)*

Miles: Wait, wait! What if I pay the cost of the messages? It can't cost more than a couple cents each!

Most people know that it is illegal to intercept people's mail or to tap phone lines. Even the police need a warrant from a judge to violate privacy in this manner. However, many people are not aware that these legal protections do not extend to broadcast communication systems. Also, employees are often unaware that companies can routinely monitor their computer usage and read electronic mail messages. Similarly, companies are allowed to monitor phone calls on the systems they own.

## QUESTIONS

1. Even if it is legal, do you think companies should read employee e-mail?
2. What does the company gain by reading employee e-mail? What does it lose?
3. Do you think Miles was wrong to use the e-mail system the way he did? Would you fire him?
4. Do you think cost of the message system is an important issue?
5. Assume that you want to change the laws and restrict the ability of companies to monitor their employees' use of the information systems. How would you write a law to protect employee privacy, yet still protect the interests of the companies?

# CHAPTER 9

# Decisions in Business Areas

Federal Express uses its Web page (http://www.federalexpress.com) to provide basic information on services. It is also using it as a fundamental link to customers, who can use it to track shipments. Relying on the Web simplifies communication procedures and reduces development costs because customers pay for their own Web connections.

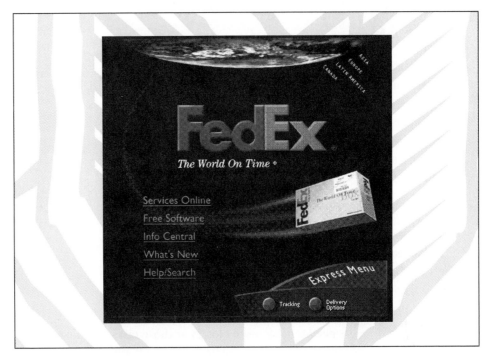

## FEDERAL EXPRESS

Federal Express promises to deliver packages overnight absolutely and positively. Its extensive fleet of trucks and planes, Memphis distribution hub, and Cosmos2 computer system enable it to accomplish these objectives. Cosmos2 keeps track of 14 million online package deliveries every day. When a customer service representative keys in a package's registration number, the system can track the package from its dropoff at any Federal Express office to its ultimate destination. The advantages that this system provides have been indispensable in Federal Express's rise to be the leading provider of overnight package delivery around the world.

A key component of the system is the menu-driven Supertracker bar code scanner. Worldwide, 60,000 Supertrackers scan packages every time a package changes hands. Data is stored in the Supertracker and relayed back to the minicomputers in the dispatch station when the Supertracker is replaced in its cradle in the van. At the end of the business day, the Supertracker is returned to a mechanical cradle in the dispatch station where its information is downloaded to the central computer. This transfer enables the master database to be automatically updated each night.

The Supertracker system provides more information than just the location of packages. Early access to the number of packages headed toward each destination enables management to allocate delivery personnel and trucks to each day's routes. Monitoring the number of pickups in a region also assists management in its efforts to evaluate advertising and other programs in an area. Quantitative measures of pickups and deliveries can also be used to evaluate offices and personnel against standards from other offices and areas.

**OVERVIEW**　It is easiest to understand the importance of models by briefly examining models from various business disciplines. You will study most of these models in greater detail in other disciplines. However, in order to see how MIS supports different tasks,

**FIGURE 9.1**

Management is often analyzed and taught as a collection of disciplines. Each functional area has its own tactical decisions and its own models. There are similarities between all of these models. Information systems support tactical decision making with access to data, evaluation of models, and presentation of results.

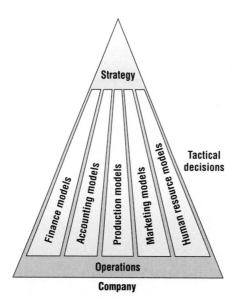

we need to look more closely at those tasks. As illustrated in Figure 9.1, each discipline uses models to evaluate tactical decisions.

As you read these examples notice that although the models are different, the support from MIS is similar in each case. Look for the DSS components: database, modeling tools, and presentation support. Once you learn the basic MIS tools and learn how to deal with models in general, you can apply these techniques to any modeling problem.

**INTRODUCTION**

Every discipline has its own set of models that characterize how it approaches problems. Models are revised and new ones are created. The study of management includes models from many areas, such as accounting, finance, marketing, human resource management, production management, economics, and statistics. Depending on your career inclinations, you will also be exposed to models from other disciplines, including psychology, art, education, philosophy, and history.

To demonstrate how MIS can help you create and evaluate models, this chapter will illustrate models from some of the important business functions. Even if you are not an expert in each subject, you should be able to understand the main concepts of the models. The problems illustrated in this chapter are small enough so that they can be solved with generic software available to you (i.e., a spreadsheet, database, and word processor). In the business world, the databases are much larger, the models more complex, and the reports can run to hundreds of pages.

Each business discipline has its own way of modeling business problems. This approach is characterized by the different objects that are used and the techniques they employ. For instance, accounting defines several standard objects, such as transactions, reports, journals, and accounts. In production management, the focus is on operations and products, with the goal of optimizing production (cutting costs, increasing efficiency, or improving quality). In each of the following examples, you should identify the primary use of the model as discussed in Chapter 8. Look for similarities between the applications. They will lead to a better understanding of how information systems can help managers use models to make better decisions.

## TRENDS

There are certain functions that every business must perform. Every company needs to account for its sales, market its products or services, reward and motivate its employees, and make investment decisions. In a small company, these functions are often performed by one or two individuals. In the development of corporations, large firms found it beneficial to create specialized departments to perform these functions. Today, with the help of information technology, many firms are working to integrate these functions across the company.

One trend stands out in the United States and in European nations: Business has become more competitive. In almost every industry, profit margins have been shrinking. For example, Sears' managers estimate that between 1980 and 1995 average gross margins in United States retailing fell by 10 percentage points (*The Economist,* March 4, 1995). In turn, the retailers have pushed manufacturers for lower prices. The emphasis on prices is strongly emphasized in retailing by the strength of discount outlets. *Discount Merchandiser* (June 1993) reported that discount stores (and wholesale clubs) in 1992 sold 22.7 percent of general merchandise such as clothing, housewares, and small appliances in the United States.

Companies are also facing more competition from international rivals. The reduction of barriers in Europe led to consolidation of retailing across

Western Europe. Between 1990 and 1993, European firms opened 610 stores in nations other than their home country. Four of the top five food retailers in Spain are now owned by French companies. (*The Economist,* March 4, 1995).

The essence of competition is that it forces companies to become more efficient. Managers have to make better decisions. Management mistakes always cause problems. With competition, they are more likely to cause the company to fail.

Researchers have been studying businesses for many years. Our knowledge of how to manage a business and solve typical problems has increased considerably during the last 30 years. Until recently, many of these solutions have been difficult to apply. Part of the problem is the lack of trained managers, and part has been due to the difficulty of evaluating and using the various models.

In the past, only large firms were able to hire specialists to build models and solve problems for that company. They were also able to afford the expensive computer time needed to collect the data and solve the models. With increased capabilities and low prices of personal computers, these same models are now available to all business managers. With the standardized computer platform, specialists have created packages that enable managers to use complex models without needing to be experts in the area.

### Transaction Processing and Tactical Management

ACCOUNTING   A large portion of the resources in accounting departments is devoted to transaction processing. Systems are designed to capture data and produce standardized reports. Tracking the financial data provides a model of the business—especially the financial aspects. Order processing, inventory, accounts receivable, and accounts payable model the acquisition and sale of products from the firm. Fixed asset reports and depreciation track the purchase, operating costs, and remaining value of major assets of the firm. Payroll, withholding amounts, and tax records monitor employee activities and payments.

Accounting departments also support tactical management throughout the company. Standard reports such as cash-flow analysis, income statements, and balance sheets provide an indication of the current financial status of the firm. By comparing current and prior reports, managers can spot trends and make changes to correct problems. Operating budgets and capital spending plans are created to

Because of the volume of data, accountants are primary users of information systems. Spreadsheets are used to evaluate the financial condition of the firm and help make decisions.

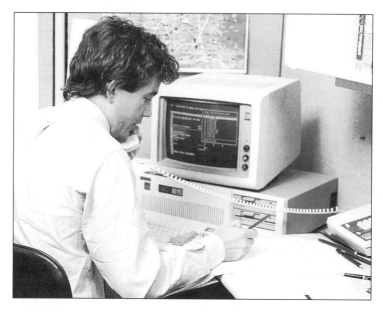

help managers compare alternatives and plan future expenditures. Similarly, the accounting departments are in charge of tax-management tactics to minimize tax bills and avoid penalties.

MIS support for transaction processing is explained in Chapter 4. The fundamental component is the use of databases to store the data, control shared access to authorized users, and produce reports for managers. In addition to providing access to the data, MIS supports tactical management with decision support systems that evaluate the various models and produce graphs and reports. Most organizations have customized accounting software packages to collect data, produce reports, and perform comparisons. Increasingly, the data can be transferred to personal computers on which models can be created and evaluated using spreadsheets and other financial modeling tools.

If there are failures in the MIS support for accounting transaction systems, some common symptoms will be observed. Reports will be delayed and inaccurate. Managers will complain about not being able to get the data they need. Meetings may degenerate into discussions of the true values of the basic financial numbers. Some managers will be forced to use their own time to adjust reports, and create graphs to make comparisons. In extreme cases, departmental managers will begin keeping their own accounting records.

## Control Systems

Because of their responsibility for the accuracy of the financial data, accounting systems also provide important control systems to minimize theft and fraud. Financial statements produced on a regular basis track the major expenses and revenues of the firm. Capital budgeting is used to monitor and allocate purchases of expensive items. Similarly, accounting systems are often responsible for analyzing costs and benefits from projects and to monitor project expenditures on a regular basis. Reports on the changes in financial position display the major sources and uses of funds in the firm. Unexpected or overly large changes in these reports could be indications of problems. Similarly, departments and projects are expected to submit and follow budgets. Variances from the budgeted amounts are closely monitored in an effort to control expenses.

---

 **BUSINESS TRENDS**

As a current or future manager, you might be asking "Why do I need to learn so many different models? I can always find an employee to take care of the details; my job is to make decisions. . ." Although this philosophy might have worked in the past, it is likely to cause serious problems in current and future jobs because of the changing business environment.

As competitive pressures increase, businesses are downsizing and decentralizing. Most growth is occurring in small business and franchise operations. In each situation, there is less need for "middle managers," and more demand for managers who collect their own data, perform analyses, and make decisions. Individuals who can efficiently perform these tasks without relying on subordinates will earn promotions and bonuses.

With increased specialization, you will probably focus on models within your discipline. However, models from other areas can sometimes lead to ideas and solutions to other problems. For instance, an investment model from finance might be used by a marketing manager as a foundation for selecting a mix of promotional strategies. Additionally, few jobs are rigidly defined in one discipline. Almost all managers need to understand the basic accounting, marketing, economic, and human relations management models.

---

MIS support for accounting controls comes from maintenance of historical data to use for comparisons and from assisting in evaluating the basic accounting models. Spreadsheets are often used to draw graphs for highlighting trends and evaluating variances between budgeted and actual expenses.

Errors in accounting control systems can be serious. If the controls are inadequate, there is increased potential for fraud or theft. For example, a county government in Tennessee lost thousands of dollars from 1990 to 1992. An employee created a fictitious company that allegedly sold several products to the government. The money was paid to the company and pocketed by the employee and no products were delivered. Better control systems and information management could have identified the discrepancy between expenses and deliveries.

Control systems can also be too strict—to the point where it is more expensive to provide the accounting paperwork than to suffer the loss. For example, most departments are allocated petty cash to spend on small items each year because it is too expensive to record small expenditures. The costs of generating purchase orders and tracking payments through a paper-based accounting system often exceed $50 per order.

## Strategic Support

Virtually every firm has its own accounting system. Although certain standards have to be met, each system is created and customized to fit the specific situation of the firm and its management and owners. These systems are defined and maintained by the accounting departments. However, because the firm changes over time, so will the accounting system. It is up to the accounting department to modify its systems as the company changes or as the *generally accepted accounting practices* are modified.

Accounting systems are used to evaluate potential mergers and acquisitions. By creating a standard financial model of the firm it is possible to compare firms, even if they are in different industries.

The accounting department is also responsible for evaluating strategic alternatives in terms of accounting and tax policies. Occasionally a firm will alter its financial structure to take advantage of changing tax laws or because of changes in the market. For example, as the interpretation of tax laws changed, not-for-profit firms were faced with a choice. To retain not-for-profit status, they were forbidden from lobbying government officials. Organizations such as Greenpeace faced a major choice: If they wished to affect legislation, donors could no longer deduct their contributions from their personal income taxes. Greenpeace changed its status and accepted the nondeductibility of donations. This change required considerable analysis of how contributors might respond.

MIS support for strategic changes is more complicated. Decision models can be used by managers to evaluate the various choices. For instance, the Greenpeace managers might have an estimate of how many contributors they would lose when the tax deductibility was dropped. They could also consider the effect of soliciting larger contributions from the remaining members. There would be some cost advantages from processing fewer checks for larger amounts of money. Similarly, any company undergoing restructuring would want to examine changes in cash flows, costs, and profitability. With a computerized model of the financial system, these changes could be simulated to identify potential problems and benefits.

## Example

The foundations of traditional cost accounting systems were designed in the 1920s. The traditional methods identify costs according to basic categories, such as salaries, fringe benefits, supplies, and fixed costs. This method works well for a manufacturing firm in which most of the costs are due to labor and the company produces a few products using the same processes. Through the 1960s, most large U.S. manufacturers fit this mold, and the standard accounting methods worked well. Today's manufacturers produce a much wider array of products and spend more on supplies, capital, and fixed costs than on labor. As explained by Terence Pare in *Fortune,* consider a company that makes two types of pens: one black, the other purple. Ten times as many black pens are produced as purple ones. It takes eight hours to reprogram the machines to switch pens, which is the major overhead cost. In traditional accounting, the overhead costs are allocated to each pen based on the levels of production, so 91 percent of the switching costs will be allocated to the black pens and 9 percent to the purple ones. This method understates the costs of producing the low-volume purple pens.

A new accounting method that is better at identifying costs for complex manufacturing processes was designed by professor Robert Kaplan called **activity-based costing (ABC).** The fundamental difference is that ABC allocates costs by examining a detailed breakdown of the production activities. In the example of the pens, each activity carries a cost. Production of purple pens would entail activities such as processing orders, buying supplies, and reprogramming the production machines. The production system is decomposed into its various subsystems, as explained in Chapter 3. Only now in ABC each activity or subsystem carries a cost. The cost of producing an item is obtained by adding the costs from each subsystem that it uses.

Figure 9.2 illustrates a traditional approach to accounting for costs. It identifies costs for each major category. The ABC method is shown in Figure 9.3. Notice the

**FIGURE 9.2**
DANA CORP. AUTO PARTS
Traditional cost accounting totals expenses in a limited number of predefined categories. It is difficult to determine how much it really costs to make a product—especially if there are multiple products.

(Terence Pare, A New Tool for Managing Costs, *Fortune,* June 14, 1993, pp. 124–129.)

| Salaries | $371,917 |
|---|---|
| Fringes | 118,069 |
| Supplies | 76,745 |
| Fixed Costs | 23,614 |
| Total | $590,345 |

**FIGURE 9.3**
ACTIVITY-BASED
COSTING
Activity-based costing
pushes accounting to
more detailed levels.
Instead of simply
recording the total
costs (bottom row), we
estimate the costs at
each processing step.
This detail provides a
better picture of where
and how costs are
incurred.

| | SALARIES | FRINGES | SUPPLIES | FIXED COSTS | TOTAL |
|---|---|---|---|---|---|
| Process sales order | $91,253 | $28,969 | $18,830 | $5,794 | $144,846 |
| Source parts | 85,882 | 27,264 | 17,722 | 5,453 | 136,320 |
| Expedite supplier orders | 45,450 | 14,429 | 9,379 | 2,886 | 72,143 |
| Expedite internal processing | 31,465 | 9,989 | 6,493 | 1,998 | 49,945 |
| Resolve supplier quality | 29,987 | 9,520 | 6,188 | 1,904 | 47,599 |
| Reissue purchase orders | 28,498 | 9,047 | 5,881 | 1,809 | 45,235 |
| Expedite customer orders | 17,481 | 5,549 | 3,607 | 1,110 | 27,747 |
| Schedule intracompany sales | 11,194 | 3,554 | 2,310 | 711 | 17,768 |
| Request engineering change | 10,524 | 3,341 | 2,172 | 668 | 16,704 |
| Resolve problems | 10,488 | 3,330 | 2,164 | 666 | 16,648 |
| Schedule parts | 9,696 | 3,078 | 2,001 | 616 | 15,390 |
| Totals | $371,917 | $118,069 | $76,745 | $23,614 | $590,345 |

increased amount of detail. In particular, the cost attributed to each process is itemized. As illustrated in Figure 9.4, these values are found by breaking the production process into smaller subsystems and then estimating the costs attributable to each step.

**FINANCE**    There are many models in finance. They are classified into two general categories: investment and corporate financial management. Most of the financial decisions in a firm occur at the tactical level. However, tracking external financial markets is typically a transaction processing problem.

## Investments

Managing portfolios of financial instruments is probably the best known finance activity. Thousands of potential investments exist for individual and corporate funds. Each investment must be evaluated on the basis of current price, price trends,

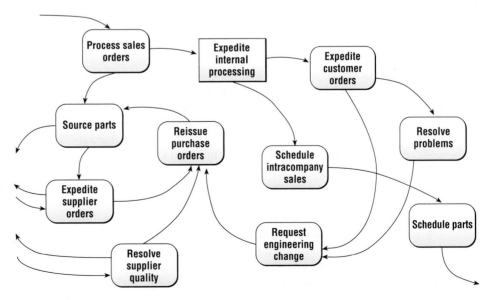

**FIGURE 9.4**
Activity-based costing.
The data flow diagram
is a useful tool to
display processes and
the flow of data (or
products) through a
system. Activity-based
costing assigns costs
to each process by
categories such as
salaries, fixed costs,
and so on.

estimated risk, and maturity date. Evaluation of these components often requires a substantial amount of additional data. To estimate the future price of a particular stock, analysts examine the current and prior financial statements of the firm, and international economic conditions. They also look at industry changes, trends in the market, and general economic data. Can you picture how much data is involved? Just consider prices of financial instruments. Even if you restrict yourself to 1,000 stocks and record hourly prices each day, you will collect 2 million prices a year. When you include the international markets, the amount of data increases substantially. One Source (Reality Bytes 9–1) has recognized the importance of this market and sells a CD-ROM product to help investors.

---

 **Reality Bytes ◥    9–1  ONE SOURCE AND THE EUROPEAN UNION**

In 1992, the European Common Market was unified and strengthened. Currency and trade restrictions among the 10 European countries were dropped. Eventually, the European nations will present a unified economic presence, similar to that of the United States. New challenges and opportunities will arise, not only for the European nations but also for the other countries of the world that must compete with them. Recognizing these opportunities, many companies have begun massive development and marketing campaigns to take advantage of the new market.

Information will play a vital role in helping companies and investors operate in this new environment. To meet the increased need for information, One Source has developed a series of CD-ROMs. This technology provides financial professionals with access to detailed financial and textual information on corporations in this European region. Based on the personal computer, One

Source was used by more than 10,000 subscribers worldwide in 1995. It is unique because it is based on CD-ROM technology rather than online access to the financial data. Because the data is segmented by country, searches are limited and can be conducted as long as the user desires without connect time or line charges. One Source is divided into three segments.

1. *CD/Private+* provides information on a list of more than 100,000 private and public companies in the United Kingdom from the past 10 years.
2. *CD/Corporate* contains textual and financial data on 5,000 publicly traded companies in the United Kingdom.
3. *CD/M&A* covers more than 10,000 mergers and acquisitions. It includes target and buyer company backgrounds, deal terms, and target company financials dating from January 1987.

---

Through the 1980s, many Wall Street banks and investment firms (Reality Bytes 9–2) hired financial analysts who became known as *rocket scientists* or *derivatives geeks.* Their job was to create models of the various markets. These models analyze the changing prices and look for certain features that indicate the best stocks to buy and sell. Some of the models operate virtually automatically. As the models monitor the prices, they evaluate thousands of rules and automatically generate buy and sell orders. These computer systems have changed the way large financial institutions deal with investments. They enable analysts to monitor more investments, identify changes, and make decisions faster. Some systems use the *Black-Scholes* equations to estimate pricing for derivatives (new financial instruments that are based on some underlying market, such as options). As an illustration of the difficulty of models, note that several firms lost millions of dollars in the derivatives market in 1994 and 1995. Some of the clients claimed they lost money because they did not have access to or understand the models created by the brokerage firms.

An excellent summary of the techniques and tools available to investment professionals is contained in a series of articles (Survey: Frontiers of Finance) in the

## Reality Bytes          9–2   BROKERAGE FIRM INVESTMENT IN TECHNOLOGY

Daniel Grant, head of Tangent International, a financial systems integrator, commented on development of information systems by brokerage firms. For example, Prudential Securities owned three massively parallel computers to analyze mortgage securities and portfolio and risk management. Prudential added a fourth machine to track arbitrage opportunities. Several other firms are running "older" Y-MP supercomputers from Cray Research.

Why do brokerage firms need so much computing power? Deborah Williams, working at a financial information consulting firm, noted that "The ability to run arbitrage schemes and develop derivatives products was almost wholly dependent on a firm's use of technology."

October 9, 1994, issue of *The Economist.* For example, Olsen and Associates, a Zurich company, has a financial model that predicts exchange rates for 53 pairs of currencies. Using the model has produced annual returns of more than 10 percent on top of the interest rate costs. The system uses second-by-second data on foreign exchange rates collected since 1986. It is updated every month with more than 50 megabytes of data from Reuters and an equal amount from Knight Ridder and Telerate. Trading recommendations are made by the system at least hourly.

Smaller versions of these systems are available to individual investors and small businesses. Primary stock market price data is available through online services such as Dow Jones News/Retrieval or from data broadcasts that can be received with a special modem. Investment analysts sell commercial versions of their modeling software that provide automatic monitoring, trend graphs, and investment advice.

At heart, finance relies heavily on information. As indicated in Figure 9.5, stock markets have to keep track of the base trading data and provide information to investors. Increasingly, they are being called on to handle computerized trading,

**FIGURE 9.5**

Financial markets. Information is the entire essence of a financial market. Its purpose is to bring buyers and sellers together. With thousands of investments and millions of buyers and sellers, brokers are surrounded by data. The problem lies in properly analyzing and evaluating this data.

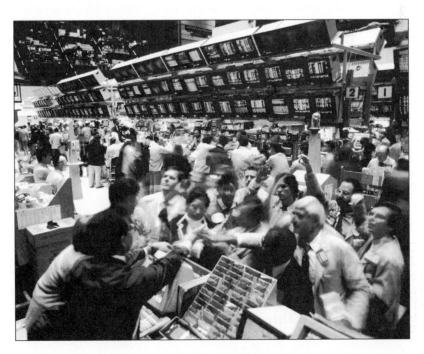

where the investors trade electronically. Creating these systems can be difficult. For example, in March 1993, the London Stock Exchange scrapped its Taurus project to computerize its operations. After six years and around £400 million ($600 million), the exchange decided the new system would not work (*The Economist,* June 12, 1993, p. 90).

## Corporate Finance

Corporate financial officers have to make many decisions beyond managing investment portfolios. They are often responsible for capital budgeting, cash management, credit control, economic forecasting, and financial performance analysis. Each of these tasks uses its own set of models. Economic models are used to forecast future conditions. Financial performance models are correlated to the economic results. Cash-flow models are based on careful monitoring of budgets and historical revenue and spending patterns. Customer credit is granted or denied based on evaluations of the current customer balance, payment history, and estimates of their ability to pay.

One obvious level of MIS support is the computerized databases that monitor the firm's financial transactions. MIS also provides access to data from external sources, such as various government agencies, stock markets, financial institutions, and credit agencies. The reports generated from these databases play an important role in financial decisions. For example, the financial officer relies on exception reports to make sure the firm has enough cash on hand to meet its payment obligations. If a department suddenly goes over budget, or if revenues fall short of predicted levels, the finance department needs to make adjustments to the investments to increase the cash holdings.

Financial management also uses forecasting and simulation to evaluate alternatives. When financial planners lay out investments for the future year, they need to forecast the cash flow at various points in time, which entails estimating monthly revenue and expenses. New investments and projects have to be scheduled properly to make sure returns and maturity dates provide adequate cash flow.

Several computerized financial modeling tools are available, such as the Interactive Financial Planning System (IFPS). Similar to spreadsheets but geared toward financial models and scheduling, IFPS enables financial analysts to monitor transactions, evaluate models, and examine the results of various simulations.

It can be difficult to identify problems in financial information systems. One common symptom is when a firm consistently has problems meeting its cash-flow needs. However, this symptom could also be caused by rapid growth of a company or by considerable variation in demand for the company's products. Similarly, inaccurate economic and financial forecasts could be symptoms of problems in the information systems. Or they could be random errors caused by unpredictable events. Likewise, it is unreasonable to blame the information system if it fails to pick winning investments every time, because it is difficult to guarantee success. Nonetheless, if several of these problems show up in a firm, it would be wise to dig deeper to determine whether the financial staff is receiving the information and modeling support they need.

## Example

A common problem in finance is the necessity to derive projected financial statements for future years. In particular, financial analysts are often interested in balance sheet and income statement projections to examine future earnings potential.

| Cash | $33,562 | Accounts Payable | $32,872 |
|------|---------|------------------|---------|
| Receivables | 87,341 | Notes Payable | 54,327 |
| Inventories | 15,983 | Accruals | 11,764 |
| Total Current Assets | 136,886 | Total Current Liabilities | 98,963 |
| | | | |
| | | Bonds | 14,982 |
| | | Common Stock | 57,864 |
| Net Fixed Assets | 45,673 | Retained Earnings | 10,750 |
| Total Assets | $182,559 | Liabilities + Equity | $182,559 |

Consider the simple balance sheet and income statement presented in Figures 9.6 and 9.7. Although real-world statements contain more detail, these examples will illustrate the model.

The balance sheet and the income statement are interrelated. Additions to retained earnings on the income statement will be added to the total retained earnings in the balance sheet. Interest paid on the bonds and accounts payable from the balance sheet will appear on the income statement. Similarly, if the amount of common stock changes, changes in dividends will appear on the income statement. These interrelationships do not matter much for data in the current year, because those numbers are not likely to change. However, they will play a role when we examine the projected statements for 1997.

The first step in creating the projected statements is to forecast some of the underlying numbers, such as sales and operating costs. Various statistical and marketing techniques can be used to derive these figures. They are commonly expressed as percentage changes from the prior year. We also need to forecast the effects of these changes on the balance sheet. The simplest method is to assume that the underlying financial ratios will remain constant. For instance, if sales increase by 10 percent, the basic balance sheet accounts (cash, accounts receivable, etc.) should also increase by 10 percent. The model can be made more realistic by using a more sophisticated method.

With a spreadsheet, it is relatively easy to add these forecasts to the income statement and balance sheet. First make the changes to the sales and costs. By using a

| Sales | $97,655 | Tax Rate 1996 | 40% |
|-------|---------|---------------|-----|
| Operating Costs | 76,530 | Dividends 1996 | 60% |
| Earnings before Interest and Tax | 21,125 | Shares Outstanding 1996 | 9,763 |
| | | | |
| Interest | 4,053 | | |
| Earnings before Tax | 17,072 | | |
| Taxes | 6,829 | | |
| Net Income | 10,243 | | |
| | | | |
| Dividends | 6,146 | | |
| Additions to Retained Earnings | 4,097 | | |
| | | | |
| Earnings per Share | $0.42 | | |

separate cell to hold the percent increase, it will be easier to experiment with different values. The second step is to compute the forecasts on the balance sheet entries for cash, accounts receivable, inventories, accounts payable, and accruals. Now, because increased sales result in more income, you need to increase the balance sheet entry for retained earnings by the amount gained from the income statement. Use a formula to combine the old value with the gain for the next year. Of course, it is not likely that the balance sheet will continue to be balanced. In order for the firm to increase sales, it will have to obtain more capital.

There are several ways to increase capital, such as issuing more stock or selling bonds. In a real-world setting, you would examine both methods to see which provides the greatest contribution to profits. Figure 9.8 illustrates the steps needed for the sales of bonds.

Notice that no matter which method you choose, there is a feedback relationship between the income statement and the balance sheet. If a spreadsheet is used for the computations, it will indicate that there is a **circular reference.** In other words, the amount of bonds needed will depend on the retained earnings, but the retained earnings depend on the interest cost of the bonds. In this situation, the feedback is normal and the circular reference does not mean there is an error. However, it will take the spreadsheet a few tries to come up with the correct answer. You will have to tell the spreadsheet to recalculate several times. The values should eventually **converge** to a final solution. In some cases, if interest rates or dividend rates were greater than 100 percent, the numbers would **diverge** and would never reach a solution. Feedback systems that diverge are **unstable** and will not survive.

**FIGURE 9.8**

Financial projections. For most companies, a spreadsheet can be used to estimate changes to the balance sheet and income statement. First compute the increase in sales and costs. Then estimate the affects on cash, accounts receivable, accounts payable, and accruals. Compute the change in retained earnings and use the balance sheet to estimate the need for additional funds. If funds are raised through bond sales, the interest expense increases, altering the income statement. This circular relationship should converge to a stable solution.

| **Balance Sheet projected 1997** | | | |
|---|---|---|---|
| Cash | $36,918 | Accts Payable | $36,159 |
| Acts Receivable | 96,075 ② | Notes Payable | 54,327 ② |
| Inventories | 17,581 | Accruals | 12,940 |
| Total Cur. Assets | 150,576 | Total Cur. Liabilities | 103,427 |
| | | Bonds | 14,982 |
| Net Fixed Assets | 45,673 | Common Stock | 57,864 ③ |
| | | Ret. Earnings | 14,915 |
| Total Assets | $196,248 | Liabs + Equity | 191,188 |
| | | Add. Funds Need | 5,060 |
| | | Bond int. rate 5% | ④ |
| | | Added Interest | $253 |

| **Income Statement projected 1997** | |
|---|---|
| Sales | $107,421 |
| Operating Costs | 84,183 ① |
| Earn. before int. & tax | 23,238 |
| ⑤ Interest | 4,306 |
| Earn. before tax | 18,931 |
| taxes | 8,519 |
| Net Income | 10,412 |
| Dividends | 6,274 |
| Add. to Ret. Earnings | $4,165 |
| Earnings per share | $0.43 |
| Tax rate 1997 | 45% |
| Dividend rate 1997 | 60% |
| Shares outstanding | 9763 |
| Sales increase | 10% |
| Operations cost increase | 10% |

① Forecast sales and costs.

② Forecast cash, accts receivable, accts payable, accruals.

③ Add gain in retained earnings.

④ Compute funds needed and interest cost.

⑤ Add new interest to income statement.

**MARKETING**  Marketing departments are responsible for market research, sales forecasting, management of the sales staff, advertising, and promotion. In some firms they also process orders and manage the design of new products and features. Processing orders is essentially a transaction-processing task. The others involve tactical or strategic questions that are more complex, so we will focus on those tasks.

## Research and Forecasting

An enormous amount of data is available for market research. Figure 9.9 presents some of the common data available for marketing purposes. Internally, the marketing department maintains records of sales and basic customer attributes. With some firms, there can be a longer distance between the firm and the final customer. For instance, manufacturers typically sell products to wholesalers, who place the products in individual stores, where they reach the final customer. In these cases it is more difficult to identify customer needs and forecast sales. There will be delays in receiving sales data because the retailers and wholesalers typically place bulk orders. Additionally, it is more difficult to identify customer preferences because their purchases are filtered through other companies.

Marketing departments also have access to data that is collected by other firms. In a manufacturing environment marketers might get raw sales data from the wholesalers and retailers. On the retail side, with the pervasiveness of checkout scanners, it is now possible to buy daily and hourly sales records from thousands of stores in various cities. This data contains sales of your products as well as rivals' products.

Several marketing models are used to evaluate consumer preferences, forecast sales, and analyze promotion opportunities. For instance, attribute models enable marketing researchers to analyze the importance of product attributes. Consider an automobile. It has measurable attributes such as gas mileage, color, number of seats or doors, price, and cargo space. It also has subjective attributes encompassing style, performance, handling, and ride. Which of these attributes are most important to consumers? What trade-offs are customers willing to make? For example, how much gas mileage are they willing to give up for better performance?

There are also models designed to help marketers choose among the various promotion alternatives. A key concept in marketing today is the use of *target marketing,* in which the goal is to find the consumers who are specifically interested in your products. Advertising and promotions should highlight the relevant features for the people who will see them. To perform target marketing, you need to know which product features appeal to each group. You also need audience characteristics for

**FIGURE 9.9**
COMMON MARKETING
DATA SOURCES
There are three primary
sources of marketing
data: internal
collections, specialty
research companies,
and government
agencies. Detailed data
is available on the
industry, customers,
regions, and
competitors.

| INTERNAL | PURCHASE | GOVERNMENT |
|---|---|---|
| Sales | Scanner data | Census |
| Warranty cards | Competitive market analysis | Income |
| Customer service lines | Mailing & phone lists | Demographics |
| Coupons | Subscriber lists | Regional data |
| Surveys | Rating services (e.g., Arbitron) | Legal registration |
| Focus groups | Shipping, especially foreign | Drivers license |
| | | Marriage |
| | | Housing/construction |

**Reality Bytes**     **9–3**  DELIVERY IN THE EUROPEAN MARKET

The European Union (EU) expanded in 1992. Federal Express realized that if it was going to address the phenomenal growth opportunities that this presented, it would have to be positioned to provide overnight delivery services the day that the EU opened. As a result, it developed a predictive model to assist it in forecasting the location and size of the greatest needs. In addition, Federal Express had to select hardware that would be flexible and powerful enough to keep up with the rapidly changing marketplace.

John Kalmbach, an analyst with the stock brokerage firm of Merrill, Lynch, and Company, summed up the growing international market: In his opinion there is a revolution in the worldwide distribution of goods. Manufacturers in Europe and Japan emphasize low inventories and fast delivery. The one who can offer the fastest service at the best price wins in the marketplace.

Federal Express's projection of the growing importance of the European market led the service to install minicomputers to maintain the large amount of customer-targeted data that is necessary to move with each package. An intricate electronic data interchange (EDI) network was also installed to provide the immediate flow of information among locations.

Thomas Murphy, Federal Express's managing director of international systems development in Memphis, Tennessee, justified the cost of the minicomputer installation because of the additional record-keeping that Federal Express required for its European customers. The record for each airbill is about 2,000 bytes. Personal computers can serve as front ends. The fault tolerance and high-volume processing required by Federal Express necessitates AS/400s to record and keep track of all of the information to require delivery within the European Union.

The European Union poses challenges to U.S. delivery companies. In the early 1990s, Federal Express decreased its commitment to Europe. It still delivers packages between the United States and Europe, but has limited deliveries between European nations.

United Parcel Service (UPS) has also experienced problems, both managerial and from culture clashes. In the early 1990s, UPS lost more than $1 billion. Spanish drivers staged a one-month strike over working conditions. In France, top executives abandoned a local shipping company after it was acquired by UPS. Spanish and German workers also complained about the UPS ban on employees having beards.

each advertising method. For instance, who reads newspapers regularly, and how do they differ from people who watch television sitcoms?

Along with data collection, MIS can help evaluate the models. Computers are used to identify categories and to perform statistical analyses. Marketing survey data is combined with statistics about advertising media. Data from warranty registration cards, discount coupons, and checkout scanners is analyzed to spot changes in preferences, evaluate the effectiveness of promotional campaigns, and provide leads for future promotions. Additionally, in some businesses such as Paramount (Reality Bytes 9–4) which is in the entertainment industry, information systems can be used to track thousands of products and their current status in each market.

Errors or failures in marketing information systems can have serious consequences. Errors in processing orders will result in products not delivered correctly and will create irate ex-customers. Errors in models such as incorrect forecasts or erroneous target information will result in a decline in sales. However, because there are many possible causes of declining sales, more detailed questions are needed to spot the cause. It is difficult to spot errors in the marketing models or in the data being used. It is important that these components be thoroughly tested.

**Reality Bytes** 9–4 PARAMOUNT PICTURES CORPORATION: SALES MANAGEMENT SYSTEM

Paramount Pictures installed a personal computer-based sales management information system to enable salespeople to immediately check the availability of a television series or film for a specific market. The system is connected via modem to Paramount's mainframe system in New York. The system replaced the manual system of consulting a book for availability, and the book had to be constantly updated by hand.

The new system presented the world as a giant grid with each product and its availability presented by market. The product, such as "MacGyver" or "Happy Days," is shown on one axis with the availability in a particular market on the other. A blank space at a row and column intersection indicated that a particular product had not been sold in that market. In this way, the system attempted to pin-

point a niche so salespeople could concentrate on it. This also enabled the salesperson to immediately confirm availability and whether that program has been licensed in that market. Providing customers with this information while they were on the telephone greatly increased the likelihood that the sale would be completed at the time of the original telephone call.

Paramount based its decision to develop the system on the decline in ticket sales and the increased number of employee retirements that reduced the knowledge base on which the sales force could rely. Forecasting growth in the number of worldwide customers, Paramount decided to invest in the sales management system so it could improve the delivery of information to those offices.

## Customer Service

A major focus of marketing is to improve service to the customer. Information systems and decision support systems are useful for identifying consumer demands and keeping track of customer attributes. Walgreens (Reality Bytes 9–5) shows that customer databases can provide better service.

Marketing decisions often entail determining customer preferences. Interviews and data collection are an important first step. Analyzing conflicting data is a challenge that often requires sophisticated decision support tools.

**Reality Bytes**      **9–5**  **WALGREENS DRUG STORES**

Prescription drugs are a multimillion dollar business. Strict licensing and drug control laws prevent individual doctors from stocking and dispensing prescription drugs. As a result, pharmacies have developed into a major component of the health delivery system.

During the 1950s and 1960s people chose a pharmacist based on a personal relationship, not unlike the one that existed between a doctor and patient. Norman Rockwell-like paintings portrayed the pharmacist as the local health practitioner who personally formulated drugs and could take the time to explain the purposes of the drugs that the physician prescribed. For many, it was the personal relationship with the privately owned pharmacy that determined a customer's choice and allegiance to a pharmacist.

The 1980s brought changes to the retail pharmaceutical market. Pharmacists no longer wanted to be available 12 hours per day, 9:00 A.M. to 9:00 P.M. Pharmaceutical research became extremely sophisticated, requiring that drugs be purchased and dispensed rather than formulated on site. Demographics also changed. People were no longer living in small towns or clustered neighborhoods. The residential population had shifted to major suburban centers.

Walgreens recognized that it could not provide up to 24-hour-per-day pharmacy service and still maintain a one-to-one relationship between the pharmacist and the client. If the population was to successfully shift from an independently owned to a chain pharmacy for prescriptions, another marketing factor would have to be found.

In 1985 Walgreens began the Internet Pharmacy Project. As the marketing program states, this computerized database enables any pharmacist at any location in the Walgreens chain to find and fill any prescription in the system. Walgreens built a pharmacy information system on the belief that this factor could become the single most important reason to choose a pharmacist. This system is particularly useful to customers on vacation or for customers who travel longer distances to their jobs.

## Example

Consider the fictional company Ikimasu, which sells customized watches. Ikimasu buys watch components from a group of suppliers. The watch faces and bands are customized for specific companies. For example, companies buy watches with their logos to give as sales incentives and rewards. Tourist locations buy watches to sell as souvenirs. Sporting teams and special-events organizers also buy them for the same reasons.

The marketing department initially determines that monthly sales reports do a good job tracking company sales, but they need more marketing information. In particular, marketing needs a way to measure the effectiveness of marketing promotions. They decide to create a marketing information system to track Ikimasu's sales, sales by competitors, and the results of a weekly customer survey. The survey is from the final customers who buy the watches. The survey teams ask customers about quality, style, and value. The results are summarized as a number between 1 and 100, where 100 is the best score. All three promotions will be tested. First marketers will run with no promotions for six weeks, then each promotion will be tested separately for six weeks each.

After the six-month experiment is completed, the new system has collected enough data to begin modeling how product promotions affect sales at Ikimasu. The results of the survey are displayed in Figure 9.10. Based on this data, a marketing research consultant estimated the effects of the three types of promotions. These four equations represent a model of how sales respond to the different promotions. The estimated equations are shown in Figure 9.11.

**FIGURE 9.10**

Analysis of marketing promotions. Three different promotions were tested and we examined the affect on sales, competitor sales, and customer satisfaction. Even with this limited data set, it is difficult to determine the effect of each promotion from the raw data.

| | **Week** | **Our sales ($)** | **Competition sales ($)** | **Customer survey rating** |
|---|---|---|---|---|
| no promo | 1 | 36725 | 86524 | 45 |
| | 2 | 37564 | 87349 | 46 |
| | 3 | 35835 | 86783 | 42 |
| | 4 | 38256 | 88653 | 48 |
| | 5 | 38698 | 89875 | 47 |
| | 6 | 37865 | 85762 | 43 |
| promo 1 | 1 | 38854 | 87654 | 47 |
| | 2 | 38933 | 88534 | 47 |
| | 3 | 39452 | 92576 | 46 |
| | 4 | 38762 | 93765 | 46 |
| | 5 | 38896 | 91543 | 47 |
| | 6 | 37602 | 89243 | 46 |
| promo 2 | 1 | 38210 | 89456 | 48 |
| | 2 | 39786 | 90765 | 52 |
| | 3 | 42986 | 88976 | 54 |
| | 4 | 43140 | 89653 | 55 |
| | 5 | 43976 | 89763 | 56 |
| | 6 | 43786 | 89076 | 54 |
| promo 3 | 1 | 47532 | 88753 | 42 |
| | 2 | 43876 | 90753 | 41 |
| | 3 | 42087 | 92764 | 38 |
| | 4 | 40123 | 93765 | 36 |
| | 5 | 38742 | 94109 | 37 |
| | 6 | 35673 | 93875 | 36 |

**FIGURE 9.11**

PROMOTION RESULTS Marketing analysis. Regression analysis of the data in Figure 9.10 provides an indication of the differences between the promotions. In particular, the negative signs on coefficients for promotions 1 and 3 could indicate problems.

With no promotions:
$$sales = 20{,}865 + 342 * consumer + 339 * week$$
*consumer survey average = 45*

Promotion 1:
$$sales = 42{,}370 - 62 * consumer - 211 * week$$
*consumer survey average = 47*

Promotion 2:
$$sales = 13{,}448 + 501 * consumer + 545 * week$$
*consumer survey average = 53*

Promotion 3:
$$sales = 44{,}808 + 98 * consumer - 2067 * week$$
*consumer survey average = 38*

**Reality Bytes** ◣ **9–6** NEWMONT MINING CORPORATION

Newmont Mining Corp., headquartered in Denver, was having problems with its personnel records in the latter 1980s. Its gold mining sites in Nevada were having trouble keeping up with the hundreds of personnel records. With a booming business, managers could not even keep up with daily employee recordkeeping, much less with the hundreds of reports required by governmental agencies.

The human resource management (HRM) personnel were falling behind on daily records because they were spending too much time completing reports on absenteeism, training, payroll, and equipment used in each job. Each of the reports stored data in different formats and required manual procedures with considerable rekeying of data and frequent errors. HRM employees wasted a lot time searching for paper documents. The volume of data was huge and growing daily as the company expanded. HRM staff realized that personnel records, payroll, and benefits applications all required the same base data. The key was to integrate the three applications. The goal was to build a centralized database for the main HRM applications.

Central data is now stored in the corporate Unisys A17 machine in Denver. Processing for the Newmont Gold Mining division's payroll, personnel tracking, and benefits is performed on a Unisys A12 at the mine site in Carlin, Nevada. HRM applications for other divisions are processed in Denver. HRM employees use personal computers at various sites to update the main database. Various security levels are assigned to each clerk to provide for security and integrity of the data.

The primary advantages of the system are the increase in productivity for the HRM department. Although it has not resulted in a decrease in the number of HRM employees, staff are now able to concentrate on more complicated tasks.

Now, Newmont faces a new challenge: The corporation is phasing out its Unisys mainframes in favor of a collection of Unisys minicomputers running the Unix operating system. The information system is being converted to a client-server approach. The existing HRM system will have to be converted. In the process, the HRM department would like to add new data to the system, such as hazardous materials experience, training levels, transfers, and salary and performance review data. The eventual goal is to maintain all of the records online.

---

the employee an equivalent job on return to the company. With thousands of employees, a computerized listing of jobs and skills will help HRM staff find employees to take over the job vacated by the employee on leave. It can also be used to search for equivalent new positions when the employee returns.

## Performance Evaluations

A substantial change in the past few years has been the shift from fixed pay rates and standardized raises to a merit pay system that rewards workers based on their performance. This method uses regular performance appraisals to evaluate each employee. These appraisals can be computerized. When each department is given a budget for raises, the manager evaluates each person on the basis of performance, position within the salary range, years of service, and other factors. Computer software can help the manager evaluate various raises. It enables the manager to try out various possibilities, check for consistency, and stay within budget. The software also can automatically monitor compliance with nondiscrimination laws.

## Example

An important HRM task in any organization is the need to allocate raises. Using a merit pay system, each employee is evaluated on the basis of factors related to his

Several software packages assist decision makers in human resource management. For example, the Info:PE package tracks and evaluates data from applicants through employees. It also tracks and analyzes job positions and creates analysis and reports required by government agencies.

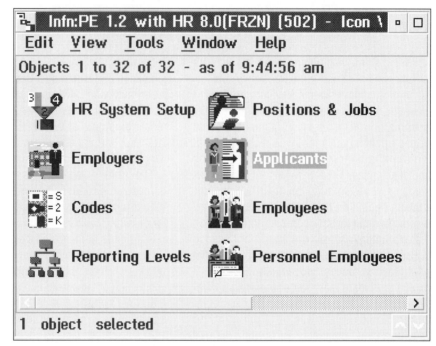

or her job. Typically, each manager is given a fixed amount of money to allocate among the employees. The goal is to distribute the money relative to the performance appraisals, provide sufficient incentives to retain employees, and meet equal employment opportunity guidelines. Many of these goals are conflicting, especially with a finite amount of money available. To set the actual raises, managers need to examine the raw data. On the other hand, a graph makes it easier to compare the various goals.

A few specialized software packages can help you determine merit raises. However, as shown in Figure 9.13, it is possible to create a small system using a spreadsheet. A spreadsheet that can display a graph alongside the data tables is particularly useful. Assume that the company wishes to give a certain portion of the raise based on the average performance ratings. The amount of money per point (currently $100) can be changed. Each person can be given an additional market adjustment raise. The total departmental raises cannot exceed the allocated total ($10,000).

The goal is to fill in the market adjustment column so that the raises match the performance appraisals. As illustrated by the graph in Figure 9.14, the manager can evaluate both absolute dollar raise or the percent increase. The total departmental raises should be equal to $10,000. By displaying the graph next to the last columns in the spreadsheet, it is possible to watch the changes as you enter the data. This immediate feedback makes it easier to set the raises you prefer.

## PRODUCTION AND DESIGN

Although the major world economies are dominated by service industries, manufacturing is still an important component of many firms. Because of the economic issues, manufacturers in industrialized nations have increased their reliance on machines and robots. Advanced computer capabilities have enabled robots to perform more complex tasks. There are several other uses of computers in manufacturing, including

| | | | | MERIT PAY | | | | RAISE POOL | | $10000 | | |
|---|---|---|---|---|---|---|---|---|---|---|---|---|
| | PERFORMANCE | | | PCT | SALARY RANGE ($000) | | | CURRENT | MERIT | MARKET | TOTAL | |
| NAME | R1 | R2 | R3 | PERF. | HIGH | LOW | AVG. | SALARY | $100 | ADJUST. | RAISE | RAISE % |
| Caulkins | 9 | 7 | 6 | 73% | 37.5 | 28.4 | 36.4 | 35.8 | 733 | | 733 | 2.0% |
| Jihong | 3 | 6 | 7 | 53% | 18.9 | 15.4 | 16.3 | 17.9 | 533 | | 533 | 3.0% |
| Louganis | 8 | 7 | 7 | 73% | 30.2 | 26.7 | 28.9 | 29.5 | 733 | | 733 | 2.5% |
| Naber | 9 | 8 | 8 | 83% | 23.2 | 19.5 | 21.4 | 19.8 | 833 | | 833 | 4.2% |
| Spitz | 3 | 4 | 3 | 33% | 22.4 | 17.3 | 18.4 | 17.5 | 333 | | 333 | 1.9% |
| Weissmuller | 5 | 4 | 6 | 50% | 60.4 | 32.5 | 45.2 | 53.2 | 500 | | 500 | 0.9% |
| Department | 6 | 6 | 6 | | 32.1 | 22.2 | 21.9 | 21.7 | 3665 | | 3665 | 2.4% |
| Corporate | 5 | 6 | 5 | | | 124 | 9.2 | 18.9 | 18.9 | | | |

**FIGURE 9.13**

Merit pay analysis. With a merit system, salary increases should be related to performance evaluations (denoted r1, r2, r3). Managers are typically given a fixed pool of money to distribute among the employees. Employee raises should be based on merit evaluations, current salary, and the salary range for the job. Market adjustments are often paid to attract workers in high-demand fields. A spreadsheet can be used to model the effects of various policies. In this example, the manager has allocated $100 for each merit percentage point. The rest of the money will be given as market adjustments. The effects of the adjustments can be seen in the graph displayed in Figure 9.14.

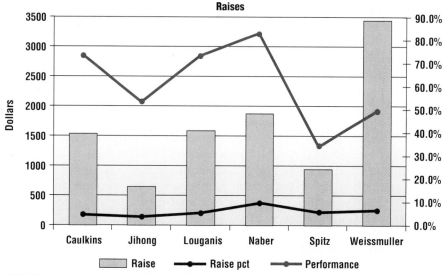

**FIGURE 9.14**

Performance evaluation. Using a separate y-axis for the two types of data and overlaying line plots on the bar chart makes this graph easier to read. If this graph is dynamically linked to the salary table, the manager can make salary changes and instantly compare the raises to the performance ratings.

Reality Bytes ▲ 9-7 DEL MONTE FOODS

In 1991, Del Monte Foods was purchased by 50 employee investors through a leveraged buyout. More recently, Del Monte has teamed with EDS Corporation to revamp its manufacturing systems nationwide. It has focused on this aspect of its company with the intent of improving the efficiency of the plant floor operations.

The two-year, multimillion dollar effort is built on 24 IBM AS/400 minicomputers, packaged application software, and a large Systems Network Architecture-based computer network. It will be run from Del Monte's corporate data center in San Francisco. The new system promises an integrated corporate manufacturing database. The 24 IBM minicomputers match the 24 canning plants and distribution centers that will operate in a hub and spoke format. Six AS/400s will serve as hubs and 18 smaller models will operate as communication processors and print spooling machines.

process control, inventory management, and product design. Sometimes, as with Del Monte (Reality Bytes 9-7), operations can be improved simply by integrating data from all of the plants.

## Process Control

**Process control** is the use of computers to monitor and control the production machines and robots. Production lines generally use many different machines, each requiring several adjustments or settings. If each machine has to be set up separately, it can take days or weeks to change a production line. Similarly, it can be difficult to spot problems when you have to monitor hundreds of settings. If the machines support standard interfaces, they can be connected to a central computer control facility. The computer can monitor all of the measurements generated by the machines, and some adjustments can be made automatically by the computer. Similarly, engineers can change the entire production line by indicating changes on a computer screen. The computer sends the appropriate commands to set up each machine. These systems are also used to monitor quality control measures.

As illustrated by Logan Aluminum (Reality Bytes 9-8), one important benefit of integrated process control systems is improved quality. Identifying problems requires continuous monitoring of the process. In fact process monitoring is a key component of the ISO 9000 quality standards. The ISO 9000 standards are used to verify a firm's commitment to quality design and production.

The distribution of products is often included as a problem in production. Routing salespeople and delivery vehicles is a complex problem in computer science and production management. The goal of finding the shortest route is a classic problem that is difficult to solve for a large number of stops. Grocery stores, like Associated Grocers (Reality Bytes 9-9), have found substantial benefits from computers in improving their distribution systems.

## Inventories, MRP, CIM and JIT

Manufacturing requires raw materials. It also requires products to be tracked through the entire production process to shipment. There are many ways to organize and monitor a production line. Hence, there are many ways to build information systems that support production. One of the oldest production management methods focuses on inventory management. The objective was to maintain sufficient raw materials to keep the line running yet hold costs down by keeping inventories as small as possible.

## Reality Bytes    9–8  LOGAN ALUMINUM AND QUALITY CONTROL

Logan Aluminum operates one of the most modern aluminum rolling mills in the world. It is located near Russellville, Kentucky. The firm uses highly automated equipment to produce aluminum sheets used in the production of beverage cans. In a highly competitive market, the managers have identified quality as being critical to their success.

Logan Aluminum built an enterprise information system called TAS (Technical Application System), that tracks the production and quality data. TAS produces reports and graphs on various functions such as scrap analysis and enables users to ask ad hoc queries. It is also used to maintain quality.

With many complex, interrelated machines, it can be difficult to identify cause-and-effect relationships. As Chris Mohr (process development team leader) notes, "We may change a parameter on one machine, for example, that produces an effect several steps down the line. With the data access that TAS provides, we are better able to separate the 'noise' from true cause-and-effects. This means we can make decisions that are more objective and scientific."

Many manufacturing companies base their information systems on the manufacturing line. A popular system was based on the operations management concepts of **material requirements planning (MRP).** In most MRP systems, the production line drives the information system. At each stage in production, the MRP system evaluates the usage rates of raw materials and determines the necessary inventory levels. If managers or designers alter the production lines, they can use existing data and simulations to determine approximate inventory levels for the new production. Production management has traditionally relied on mathematical models from queuing theory, economic inventory theory, and simulation to determine the best flow of production and the required supplies of materials and labor. Simonds Cutting Tools (Reality Bytes 9-10) shows that modern MRP systems also enable managers to track individual parts back to the original suppliers—an important step in improving quality.

## Reality Bytes    9–9  ASSOCIATED GROCERS

Computers have greatly assisted transportation and distribution systems because of their ability to track and direct truck and other vehicle routings. They are able to optimize the best routes and provide much better guidelines about how to combine multiple deliveries and pickups than could be developed by hand.

Recently written software programs have enabled personal computers to be used for this task because graphics software enables the routes to be graphically represented. Lower costs and increased power have also contributed to the increased use of personal computers in this function. Migration to the personal computer for these functions has also enabled smaller firms that could not afford the greater investment of large systems to take advantage of the cost savings from these distribution programs. Today, these programs handle everything from equipment maintenance to packaging for efficient distribution.

Associated Grocers is one company that has implemented computerized route systems into its distribution network. Associated is a loose association of small, independent grocery stores that was formed to try to remain competitive with the large chains. Because their deliveries are smaller and less frequent, computerization enables these grocers to combine routes, further reducing transportation costs.

Since computerizing, Associated Grocers has improved its on-time delivery from 85 to 99 percent and has reduced the miles driven by 21 percent. On-board computers have even improved gas mileage by 2.8 miles per gallon by monitoring the driver's shifting patterns.

## Reality Bytes    9–10  SIMONDS CUTTING TOOLS

Simonds Cutting Tools based in Fitchburg, Massachusetts, manufactures industrial machines that cut metal, wood, or paper. Simonds has 850 employees working in nine manufacturing and distribution facilities in the United States as well as England, Germany, and Canada. With a mature product line, managers were looking to expand sales in the international markets. However, Ross George, the president, notes that "Our manufacturing systems simply could not guarantee the quality needed to penetrate many foreign markets."

Although Simonds had a satisfactory order entry and MRP system, managers were unable to obtain the information they needed to design new products. The company invested in a new **computer integrated manufacturing (CIM)** system known as MAPICS/DB to run on the company's IBM AS/400 and IBM 4361 computers. The system enables managers to track and identify every aspect of production. For instance, managers can identify all of the vendors who supplied parts for a finished product and which production machines were involved because the production information is linked to the order-entry system. With the system, they have decreased overtime and smoothed the work flow.

The system has also enabled Simonds to dramatically improve the quality of its products. With the information provided by the new system, the company has applied for the ISO 9000 quality standard rating that qualifies them to ship products to European nations. The International Organization of Standards (ISO) 9000 statement requires manufactures to provide detailed production information on each item. Without the new CIM software, Simonds was unable to document the materials and production involved with individual units.

**Manufacturing Resource Planning (MRP II)** represents an integrated approach to production. It combines materials planning with scheduling and process control. The objective is to build a "demand-pull" system that is based on projected sales. In a demand-pull production line, the sales department provides detailed estimates of production needs for a certain time period. The system then computes the labor and raw materials needed to manufacture the products. It searches for an optimal production schedule and creates inventory orders needed to meet the schedule.

A key feature of most production lines is that they rarely behave exactly as they were predicted. There are thousands of things that can change, from marketing departments rearranging schedules to meet rush orders, to broken equipment, to labor shortages or engineering design changes. Any change in one part of the process will affect the others. Production management systems such as MRP II are designed to enable managers to evaluate alternative schedules and choose the most cost effective solutions.

Led by Toyota of Japan, a popular manufacturing technique is to rely on **just-in-time (JIT)** production, where the raw materials arrive at the manufacturing line just as they are needed, so the manufacturer saves money by holding less inventory. However, JIT requires that the suppliers know exactly how much to deliver. If you change production schedules, the suppliers have to be notified. Likewise, if a supplier cannot make a shipment on time, you need to find an alternative supplier. Hence, JIT requires more communication between suppliers and manufacturers. Computer communications, such as EDI, can be used to transfer the orders quickly with less chance for mistakes.

Increased flexibility is another major consideration facing producers today. Yet each change in schedule or product feature requires realigning suppliers and optimizing the production line. To support the new manufacturing systems, many producers have invested heavily in sophisticated information systems. The computer-integrated manufacturing (CIM) technique was introduced in the mid-1980s. In a

Computers are used to track inventory levels, receipts, and shipments. Sophisticated warehouse information systems automatically route boxes to storage and switch conveyor systems to send packages to trucks waiting at the loading docks.

truly integrated environment, every element of the production would be monitored and controlled through the computer system. Figure 9.15 illustrates the basic concepts of a computer-integrated, demand-pull manufacturing system. The sales department estimates sales of each product. The information system uses past manufacturing data to create a production schedule that produces the desired products for the least cost and best quality. The computer then generates just-in-time orders for the suppliers. If there is a change in demand or problems in the production line, changes

**FIGURE 9.15**

Production models. Production requires careful control over purchasing, inventories, scheduling, ordering, and shipping. Optimization models and forecasts play an important role in reducing costs. Integrated manufacturing systems enable companies to produce products on a demand-pull basis. Based on customer orders or forecasts, optimal production schedules are computed and raw materials are automatically ordered through EDI systems.

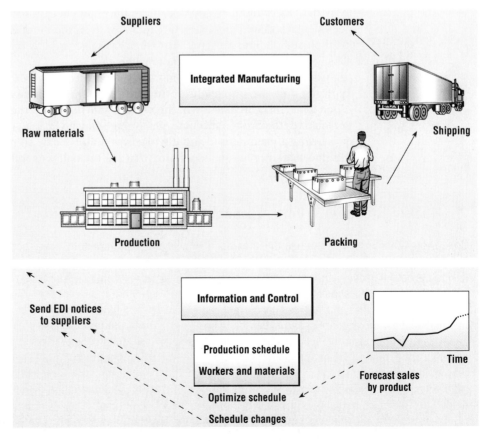

are made in the information system. The computer then reschedules the jobs and issues new orders to the suppliers. As supplies are delivered, they are recorded and the computer directs them to the appropriate production area. There have been many claims made for the potential capabilities of CIM, but to date, few companies have managed to create a truly integrated environment.

## Product Design

As discussed in Chapter 8, computers are heavily used in the design process. **Computer-aided design (CAD)** programs are used to create engineering drawings. CAD programs make it easy to modify drawings. They also make it easier to keep track of material specifications. They can perform spatial and engineering estimates on the designs, such as surface or volume calculations. Individual pieces can be tested on the screen to be sure they fit together correctly. The diagrams can be used by modeling software to examine structural features or perform initial wind-tunnel tests. There are even machines available that will take the diagrams directly from the computer and produce prototypes of the parts. For instance, an engineer could create a replacement gear. The prototype is too soft to be used for real work, but it can be tested to be sure the design is correct. The amazing aspect of these tools is that the prototypes often can be produced in less than an hour. Lockheed Martin (Reality Bytes 9–11) uses computer systems to link various stages of the design process and reduce the cost and time of developing new products.

## Example

Queuing theory is a tool that is often used in production management. It can be used to model problems such as service lines for retail checkouts, the number of medical personnel needed in an emergency room, or even the number of bathrooms needed in an office building. A useful example in manufacturing is the number of repair persons needed to maintain a group of machines.

Consider a company that has 10 machines that produce the same product. Typically they use only eight of the machines; the other two are kept as backups. When a machine breaks down, the work is transferred to the backups, and a repair person fixes the broken machine. On average, any given machine will function for 15 days before a malfunction, and it typically requires 2 days to make the repairs. Using this information, plus an assumption that the breakdowns follow an exponential dis-

---

 **Reality Bytes**     **9–11** LOCKHEED MARTIN AERO AND NAVAL SYSTEMS DIVISION

Concurrent engineering integrates the design and manufacturing functions. It boosts competitiveness by linking the design, manufacturing, marketing, purchasing, and financial applications of the company.

Lockheed Martin has implemented concurrent engineering. All new projects are spearheaded by teams. Each team is composed of individuals from design, manufacturing, product support, procurement, fabrication, quality management, and information systems. After a contract is signed, the team's first task is to work with information systems to develop the right

combination of software and hardware to execute the contract. Concurrent technology has enabled Lockheed Martin to realize substantial benefits in two key areas:

- Bids have been able to be reduced by 20 to 30 percent because less time and material are wasted in manufacturing.
- The Control Components Division plans to reduce its new-product development cycle 40 to 50 percent through the computer-assisted integration of major departments.

tribution, the queuing theory model generates the probability that any number of machines will be broken on a given day. These probabilities also depend on the number of repair workers available. For example, if two machines fail at the same time, one worker could be assigned to each machine.

There are six input parameters to this model: number of backup machines, number of repair workers, mean time to failure, mean repair time, cost of the workers, and cost of lost production. The primary output of the model is the sum of the costs from lost production and the cost of the repair workers. The objective is to hire the number of workers that leads to the lowest cost. With the base data in this example, the least cost point is to hire two repair technicians. The model enables the manager to examine the input data more closely. For example, it is easy to see what happens if the average failure time is closer to 25 days instead of 15, or if it takes 3 days to repair average breakdowns.

There are several specialized programs that make it easier to evaluate more complex queuing theory models. However, it is possible to evaluate this small model in a spreadsheet, as indicated in Figure 9.16. The only hard part is deriving the probability

| PRODUCTION QUEUING MODEL | | | | | | | | |
|---|---|---|---|---|---|---|---|---|
| NUMBER OF REPAIR PERSONS | | | | | | | | |
| Backups | 2 | Mean time to failure | | 15 | days | | | |
| Loss per | $ per day | Mean repair time | | 2 | days | | | |
| Machine | 500 | Avg daily repairer cost | | 150 | | | | |
| | | | | | | | | |
| | | # REPAIRERS | 1 | # REPAIRERS | 2 | # REPAIRERS | 3 | |
| MACHINES WAITING TO BE FIXED | COST OF LOST PRODUCTION | PROBABILITY # MACHINES WAIT TO FIX | EXPECTED $ LOSS | PROBABILITY # MACHINES WAIT TO FIX | EXPECTED $ LOSS | PROBABILITY # MACHINES WAIT TO FIX | EXPECTED $ LOSS | |
| 0 | 0 | 0.1324 | 0 | 0.3162 | 0 | 0.3422 | 0 | |
| 1 | 0 | 0.1413 | 0 | 0.3373 | 0 | 0.3650 | 0 | |
| 2 | 0 | 0.1507 | 0 | 0.1799 | 0 | 0.1947 | 0 | |
| 3 | 500 | 0.1607 | 80 | 0.0959 | 48 | 0.0692 | 35 | |
| 4 | 1000 | 0.1500 | 150 | 0.0448 | 45 | 0.0215 | 22 | |
| 5 | 1500 | 0.1200 | 180 | 0.0179 | 27 | 0.0057 | 9 | |
| 6 | 2000 | 0.0800 | 160 | 0.0060 | 12 | 0.0013 | 3 | |
| 7 | 2500 | 0.0427 | 107 | 0.0016 | 4 | 0.0002 | 1 | |
| 8 | 3000 | 0.0171 | 51 | 0.0003 | 1 | 0.0000 | 0 | |
| 9 | 3500 | 0.0046 | 16 | 0.0000 | 0 | 0.0000 | 0 | |
| 10 | 4000 | 0.0006 | 2 | 0.0000 | 0 | 0.0000 | 0 | |
| | | | 747 | | 137 | | 68 | |
| | | worker cost | 150 | worker cost | 300 | worker cost | 450 | |
| | | total | 897 | total | 437 | total | 518 | |

**FIGURE 9.16**

Production model to determine optimal number of repair persons. The goal is to minimize total costs. Parameters include number of repair workers, number of backup machines, mean time to failure, mean repair time, the cost of additional workers and the cost of lost production. For one to three repairers, the spreadsheet uses probabilities to estimate the number of machines waiting to be fixed to get the expected loss. Varying the parameters leads to different outcomes.

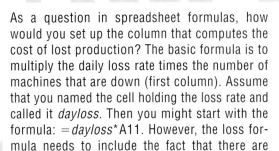

**SPREADSHEET FORMULA**

As a question in spreadsheet formulas, how would you set up the column that computes the cost of lost production? The basic formula is to multiply the daily loss rate times the number of machines that are down (first column). Assume that you named the cell holding the loss rate and called it *dayloss*. Then you might start with the formula: $=dayloss*$A11. However, the loss formula needs to include the fact that there are backup machines available, so you might try something like: $=dayloss*$(A11 − *backups*). Except, what happens when A11 = 1 and *backups* = 2? The loss is negative? Assume that we can-

not sell any production beyond that produced by the original eight (nonbackup) machines. Then, the *negative loss* should really be zero, since the extra production is not worth anything. In other words, if A11 − *backups* is negative, the value in the cell should be zero. There are two basic ways to indicate this condition in a spreadsheet. One method is to use the =IF statement: =IF (A11 − *backups* > 0, +*dayloss*(A11 − *backups*), 0). A slightly faster method is to use the =MAX statement: =MAX(*dayloss*(A11 − *backups*), 0). Notice that with the =MAX approach, the A11 − *backups* term is only entered once.

estimates. The derivation for this example occurs in a separate section of the spreadsheet and is not shown in the example. Although the equations are not overly complicated, they require specialized knowledge. A business manager would rely on an operations research expert to set them up. The box discusses some of the problems you might face in setting up this problem with a spreadsheet.

This example also illustrates the concept of choosing a goal as described in Chapter 3. The discussions of the example to this point have assumed that the number of backup machines (two) is fixed, and that our goal is to determine the number of repair workers to employ. However, it might be cheaper to buy more backup machines instead of hiring more workers. The same model can be used to answer this new question. You first need to know how much it costs to acquire more machines. If these machines are large, you might have to build additional space to store them. Then you need to examine the total costs (lost production, workers, machines) for a combination of different numbers of backup machines and repair workers.

**GEOGRAPHIC INFORMATION SYSTEMS**

Many aspects of business can benefit by modeling problems as geographical relationships. For instance, to choose the site of retail outlets, you need to know the location and travel patterns of your potential customers. Manufacturing can be made more efficient if you know the locations of raw materials, suppliers, and workers. Similarly, locations of distribution warehouses need to be chosen based on retail outlets, manufacturing facilities, and transportation routes. There are thousands of other geographical considerations in business, such as, monitoring pollution discharges, routing and tracking delivery vehicles, classifying areas for risk of crimes and fire, following weather patterns, or tracing migration paths of fish for commercial fishing. **Geographic information systems (GIS)** have been designed to identify and display relationships between business data and locations. Arc Info and MapInfo are two of many commercial GIS packages available.

A GIS begins with the capability of drawing a map of the area you are interested in. It might be a world or national map that displays political boundaries. It might be a regional map that emphasizes the various transportation routes or utility lines. It might be a local map that displays roads or even buildings. An oil exploration company might use a map that displays three-dimensional features of a small area. A shipping company could use ocean maps that display three-dimensional images of the ocean passageways. The level of detail depends on the problem you wish to solve.

### Maps and Location Data

There are two basic ways to create and store the underlying maps: as pictures or as digitized map data. Digital map data provides the most flexibility. Besides being easier to change, digital maps enable you to zoom in and see more detail. Each item is stored by its location as measured by latitude and longitude and sometimes its elevation. Most U.S. digital maps are based on data that the Bureau of the Census created for the 1990 national census, known as TIGER. The Bureau of the Census has every road and house number entered into a giant database. Because of privacy reasons, they will not sell house locations, but you can get the range of street numbers for each city block. The U.S. Department of Defense has digital data available for many areas, including international locations and often includes elevation data. However, keep in mind that the systems being mapped are constantly changing, so even digital maps often contain missing, incomplete, or inaccurate data.

Once you have the base maps, the objective is to overlay additional data on the maps. For example, you can obtain census data that displays average consumer characteristics such as income, house price, and number of autos within each geographic area. The GIS could be used to plot different colors for each income level. Next you can overlay the locations of your retail stores. If you are selling a high-price item like Cadillac (Reality Bytes 9–12), you want to locate the stores in areas of higher income.

Although you can buy base geographical data, how do you know the location of your retail stores? Or, how do you plot the locations of delivery vehicles, or police cars, or trains? The easiest answer today is to use the **Global Positioning System (GPS),** which is a set of satellites maintained by the U.S. government. A portable receiver tuned to the satellites will identify your location in latitude, longitude, and elevation (if it can reach four satellites) within 50 feet. Several hand-held units are

### Reality Bytes          9–12   CADILLAC AND GIS

Even before Elvis, the Cadillac name represented quality cars. From the image alone, the cars carried a premium price. Dealerships were typically located in higher-income neighborhoods or near prosperous business districts.

As migration from the cities increased, and suburbs grew, the demographics of the neighborhoods changed between the 1960s and the 1990s. General Motors used a GIS to mark the locations of existing dealers. Census and marketing data was used to highlight the incomes of various neighborhoods. As a result, GM realized that many dealerships were no longer close enough to high income areas. Several hundred dealerships were relocated.

available for a few hundred dollars. If you work for the department of defense, you can get receivers that will identify your location within a few millimeters, but you need appropriate security clearances to obtain these receivers. In 1996, the U.S. government announced that it would enable consumer use of full-resolution measurements in "five to ten years."

As a model, the GIS makes it easier to spot relationships among items. Revere National (Reality Bytes 9-13) uses this approach to target billboards to specific companies. Visual presentations are generally easy to understand and are persuasive. A GIS can be an effective means to convince management that neighborhoods have changed and that you need to move your retail outlets. A GIS can also be used for simulations to examine alternatives. For example, a GIS oriented to roadmaps can compute the time it would take to travel by different routes, helping you establish a distribution pattern for delivery trucks.

## Example

Consider the problem faced by a manager in a small retail chain that has stores located in 10 Florida cities. They sell a combination of hard goods (such as cleaning supplies, snack items, and drapery rods), and soft goods (mostly clothing). For the most part, profit margins on soft goods are higher than for hard goods. However, total sales of hard goods seems to be better than those of soft goods—except in certain stores. The manager has been unable to find a reason for the difference, but a friend who has lived in Florida longer suggested that there might be some geographical relationship. The basic numbers are presented in Figure 9.17.

Because there are only 10 cities, it might be possible to identify patterns in the data without using a GIS. However, an actual firm might have several hundred or a few thousand stores to evaluate. In this case, it is much more difficult to identify relationships by examining the raw data. It is better to use a GIS to plot the data.

| City | 1980 Pop | 1990 Pop | 1980 PER-CAPITA INCOME | 1990 PER-CAPITA INCOME | 1980 HARD-GOOD SALES (000) | 1980 SOFT-GOOD SALES (000) | 1990 HARD-GOOD SALES (000) | 1990 SOFT-GOOD SALES (000) |
|---|---|---|---|---|---|---|---|---|
| Tampa | 271,523 | 280,015 | 6441 | 15,081 | 767.4 | 851.0 | 953.4 | 1009.1 |
| Tallahassee | 81,548 | 124,773 | 6310 | 14,578 | 595.4 | 489.7 | 843.8 | 611.7 |
| Perry | 8,254 | 7,151 | 5727 | 11,055 | 300.1 | 267.2 | 452.9 | 291.0 |
| Orlando | 128,291 | 164,693 | 6735 | 16,958 | 425.7 | 509.2 | 691.5 | 803.5 |
| Ocala | 37,170 | 42,045 | 6175 | 12,027 | 359.0 | 321.7 | 486.2 | 407.3 |
| Miami | 346,865 | 258,548 | 6084 | 16,874 | 721.7 | 833.4 | 967.1 | 1280.6 |
| Jacksonville | 540,920 | 635,230 | 6767 | 15,316 | 990.2 | 849.1 | 1321.7 | 1109.3 |
| Gainesville | 81,371 | 84,770 | 6150 | 13,672 | 365.2 | 281.7 | 550.5 | 459.4 |
| Fort Myers | 36,638 | 45,206 | 6483 | 16,890 | 535.2 | 652.9 | 928.2 | 1010.3 |
| Clewiston | 5,219 | 6,085 | 7645 | 13,598 | 452.0 | 562.5 | 367.6 | 525.4 |

**FIGURE 9.17**

Geographic sales data. We suspect that sales of hard and soft goods are related to populaton and income. We also want to know whether there are regional patterns to the sales.

Different colors can be used to highlight large increases in sales. By overlaying this data with the population and income data, it is easier to spot patterns. In Figure 9.18 notice that there is a correlation between population and total sales. Also, notice that sales in the northern cities are concentrated more in hard goods than in the southern cities.

## Reality Bytes ▶ 9–13 REVERE NATIONAL CORP.

Today, when most companies think about advertising, the managers tend to focus on television, radio, magazines, and newspapers. The almost-forgotten billboard (or outdoor advertising) industry garners only 2 percent of the corporate advertising dollars. Outdoor advertising faces several drawbacks, such as restrictions on creating new signs and a decline in the tobacco industry (which cannot advertise on television).

Competition from the four other advertising media also place pressures on outdoor advertising. These industries have sophisticated data-gathering techniques that identify the consumers being reached. Advertisers use this data to target their ads to a specific audience and type of consumer. Until now, the billboard industry lacked detailed data on who saw the signs. Although the advertisers know that thousands of people drive by specific billboards every day, they had no way to identify the characteristics of the viewers.

Revere National specializes in outdoor advertising and is acutely aware of the problems facing the industry. Although headquartered in Baltimore, the firm has a large number of billboards in Philadelphia, San Antonio and some smaller cities. They decided that improved information could help them convince advertisers to spend more money on outdoor advertising.

Revere National chose three software packages to create an integrated mapping and demographics geographic information system. The three components are Prime from the New York consumer polling company: Scarborough Research Corp, MapInfo from MapInfo Corp, and software by Marketing Information Services of America (MISA), which collects data about people driving by billboards.

The three systems work together to provide a complete picture of the billboard audience. Scarborough collects personal data from consumers such as what movies they have seen, where they go on vacation, and what beer they drink. The software enables Revere to examine facts and patterns between various products with target groups. MapInfo enables researchers to display the demographic data based on zip codes. The system color-codes each region based on sales of certain products. By highlighting the location of each billboard, advertisers are given a first look at who sees the boards. However, the third component is also required. Revere's research on its 2,000 Philadelphia-area boards indicates that 90 percent of the people who see a billboard are just driving past and do not live in the area—hence the need for the traffic analysis by MISA. MISA researchers sit by each board and collect license plate numbers of passing cars. Using the state's motor vehicle records, they identify the home zip code of each driver.

Adding this information to the MapInfo maps provides an accurate picture of who sees each board. Maps are drawn showing the demographic characteristics of viewers. It makes it easy for advertisers to select a board that reaches it target audience.

Todd Schwartzrock, director of marketing, notes that Revere is spending a "lot of money" on the project. Most of the money is going to buy the demographic data. For example, demographic data from Scarborough costs approximately $20,000 per region. Despite the expense, Schwartzrock believes the system will pay for itself, noting "I can see it increasing our sales by up to 50 percent." Revere's Philadelphia sales manager, Dave Hammes, also notes that "We've achieved something that will totally change the way this industry is looked at." The Outdoor Advertising Association of America, led by Gordon Hughes, also recognizes the strategic aspect of the project, noting that "Revere is on the leading edge of what our industry as a whole needs to be doing with computers."

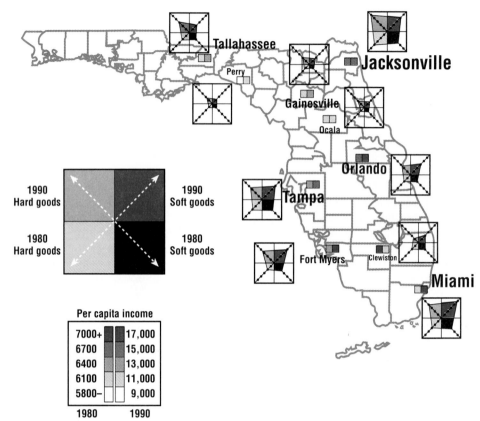

Geographic-based data. It is difficult to display this much data without overwhelming managers. Notice that the sales (radar) graphs use size and shape to highlight total sales, and the changing sales mix. Income is color-coded in a smaller graph. Notice in the sales graphs that the northern counties experienced a greater increase in sales in hard goods compared to the southern counties.

## SUMMARY

Managers use many different models to solve problems. Each discipline might have hundreds of different models. You will use many different models in your career. Keep in mind that there are similarities among many of the business models, and distinct patterns in how MIS provides support for those models. Foremost in MIS support is the ability to retrieve the data needed to evaluate the models. The graphics capabilities of personal computers contributes enormously to the ability of managers to evaluate choices, interpret the results, and make decisions.

Every day, new software packages are created to help managers design and evaluate business models. Some of these tools are designed to solve specific tasks, such as a marketing management package to evaluate customer surveys, or a financial investment system to monitor and identify trends in the prices of financial instruments. Other generic

### A MANAGER'S VIEW

Middle-level managers continuously face tactical-level decisions: How can operations be reorganized to improve the business? Each discipline has its own set of problems and creates its own models. Information systems help managers make tactical decisions by providing data, evaluating models, and presenting output in a variety of formats. As you study models in your chosen discipline, remember the tools that MIS provides. Learn to use them. They will help you make better decisions, and they will help you understand the models. Many times, building a simple spreadsheet and experimenting with changes in the data will help you understand a model and how it is used to solve business problems.

tools, such as spreadsheets, can be used to build whatever model you create.

## KEY WORDS

activity-based costing (ABC), 410
circular reference, 416
computer-aided design (CAD), 430
computer-integrated
　manufacturing (CIM), 428
converge, 416
diverge, 416

geographic information system
　(GIS), 432
Global Positioning System
　(GPS), 433
just-in-time (JIT) inventory, 428
manufacturing resource planning
　(MRP II), 428

material requirements planning
　(MRP), 437
process control, 426
unstable feedback, 416

## REVIEW QUESTIONS

1. Describe the use of models in the disciplines of: accounting, finance, marketing, human resource management, and production.
2. What similarities exist between sample models presented for the various departments?
3. What is a circular reference in a spreadsheet? Does it always mean there is an error in the spreadsheet?
4. What does it mean to say that a feedback loop *diverges?*
5. How are computers used to help manufacturing firms design products and control the manufacturing process?
6. Describe three decisions in finance that could benefit from the use of a DSS.
7. How can a DSS help the HRM department support laws that affect employees?
8. How is a geographic information system different from a package that just draws maps?
9. Describe four examples of businesses that would benefit from the use of a GIS.

## EXERCISES

1. Use the accounting example of activity-based costing. Build a spreadsheet that computes the ABC schedule in the text. Now, create a second version of the table to use for next year's forecast. Salaries are projected to increase by 5 percent in every area, except in *process sales orders,* where they will increase by 6 percent. New fringe benefits will add another 1 percent to everyone's benefits. Supplies are expected to change as follows: process sales orders, source parts, and schedule parts: +5 percent. Reissue purchase orders, expedite customer orders, resolve supplier quality, expedite supplier orders: +7 percent. The others will decrease by 4 percent. Fixed costs will be the same in all areas, except request engineering change and resolve problems which will decrease by 20 percent. Given these changes, compute the new totals. Create a set of graphs that will show how these changes will affect the company.

2. Build the balance sheets and income statements shown in the finance example. Convert the example so that the increase in capital is financed through the sale of stock (assume the price stays the same). In this example, is it better to issue stocks or to sell bonds?

3. From the marketing example, compute a new set of numbers and draw a similar graph given the costs of the promotions: Promo 1: $1,000 up front, Promo 2: $300 per week, Promo 3: $1,000 up front. (Advanced option: Use statistics to estimate the equations in the text.) Trivia Question: What does *ikimasu* mean?

4. Use a spreadsheet to create the example from the HRM section. Fill in the market adjustment column so that raises match the performance appraisals. Remember, total raises cannot exceed $10,000.

5. From the production example, assuming that we currently have one repair worker and two backup machines. The total cost of a machine is $112,500, but it has a useful production life of six years (1,500 days). Assuming we use eight machines for production, how many backup machines and how many repair workers should we employ?

6. For one discipline (accounting, finance, marketing, human resources, economics, production management), find three models. List the assumptions, input and output variables, and the model or equations. Describe a business example where each model would be used.

7. For each of the models in the previous exercise, build a spreadsheet that evaluates the model and presents the output in a manner that makes it easier to make the decision. For most models, you should be able to draw a graph.

8. Interview a local manager to find a specific problem that can benefit from use of a model. Obtain sample data (from the manager, or industry averages, or make it up if it's proprietary). Create a DSS to evaluate the data. How does the decision compare to the manager's (or your) initial guess?

9. Find four sources of data that you might use in a DSS for financial investments. Is the data available in computer form? Is it up-to-date? Optional: How much does it cost?

10. Create an example of a spreadsheet that contains a circular reference. Show two examples, one that converges to a stable solution, and one that diverges.

11. Describe three examples of how a geographic information system can be used to improve decisions. No more than one of them should be in a government agency.

12. Using the sample GIS data and the picture, can you identify any other potential relationships? What other information would you like to see? Can you measure how the different factors affect sales? (Hint: Use statistical techniques.)

| DEPARTMENT | CUSTOMERS/MONTH |
| --- | --- |
| Clothing—Children | 180 |
| Clothing—Men | 150 |
| Clothing—Women | 180 |
| Electronics | 200 |
| Furniture | 150 |
| Household | 250 |
| Linen | 300 |
| Shoes | 300 |
| Sports | 400 |
| Tools | 340 |

 **DeptStor Database**

You are a midlevel manager for a small department store. You have collected a large amount of data on sales for 1995. Your transaction system kept track of every sale (order) by customer. Most customers paid by credit card or check, so you have complete customer data. Walk-in customers who paid cash are given a separate customer number, so you still have the sales data.

You are trying to determine staffing levels for each department. You know that the store becomes much busier during the end-of-the-year holiday season. For summer months, you have thought about combining staff from the departments. From conversations with experienced workers, you have determined that there is a maximum number of customers that can be handled by one person in a department. These numbers are expressed as monthly averages in the table.

You are thinking about combining workers from some of the departments to save on staffing—especially over the spring and summer months. However, working multiple departments makes the sales staff less efficient. There are two considerations in combining staff members. First, if any of the departments are reduced to a staff of zero, sales in that department will drop by 10 percent for that month. Second, total staffing should be kept at the level defined by the monthly averages. If average staffing (total across all departments) falls below the total suggested, then sales in all departments will fall by 2 percent for each tenth of a percentage point below the suggested average.

13. Using the database and a spreadsheet, determine how many workers we need in each department for each month. Present a plan for combining departments if it can save the company money. Assume that sales members cost an average of $1,000 a month. Two queries have already been created by the MIS department and are stored in the database. They are SalesbyMonth and SalesCountByMonth. The first totals the dollar value; the second counts the number of transactions.

14. Write a report to upper management designating the appropriate sales staff levels for each department by month. Include data and graphs to support your position. Hint: Use a spreadsheet that lets you enter various staffing levels in each department in each month, then calculate any sales declines.

15. Obtain the data on the latest advertising campaign from the Web site (or direct from the HTML file if a Web site is not set up for you). For each product category, compute net profits: Net = (Revenue − Costs) − Advertising expenses − Employee cost (Assume employees are hired at the suggested average level.)

**Rolling Thunder Database**

1. **Production model.** Evaluate the daily production levels and capacities. Identify any bottlenecks in production. Is there excess capacity in any of the steps?

2. **Production model.** Evaluate our inventory strategy. Determine whether it is feasible to operate with a just-in-time inventory for some of the components or tubing. (Hint: How often do we use each part. How large are part orders/deliveries? How much do we spend on each order? How much money do we tie up in holding inventory? Do we ever run out of parts?)

3. **Production model.** Management wishes to cut costs. Based on 1994 orders, evaluate the effect on production of altering the number of assembly stations. Consider values of 3, 4, 5, and 6. Perform a similar analysis for paint stations. We particularly want to examine how these changes would affect the average number of days to build a bicycle.

4. **Marketing model.** Managers are thinking about expanding production facilities and would like to know the value of such an expansion. If we increase the capacity of assembly, painting, and shipping, we will probably need more order takers. How busy are the current order lines, and how many new order-entry clerks should we hire if we want to expand production by 10 percent (also consider 20 percent and 40 percent increases). (Hint: Estimate how long each order call will last by the length of time it takes to fill out the order form. Also consider the number of calls that arrive at the same time—busy periods. Consider looking at other firms/industries.)

5. **Marketing model.** Evaluate existing sales by location. Try to obtain external data on demographic characteristics for our customers. Present a marketing plan describing our customers and the type of bicycles they purchase. Provide suggestions on how we might expand our sales by locating similar customers.

6. **Forecast model.** Management wants to know how many bicycles can be sold in the next year. Using internal data, economic data, and industry trends, provide a forecast for the number of bicy-

cles that could be sold (with no production constraints). If possible, provide a breakdown by type of model or frame material.

7. **Finance model.** Extract the appropriate financial data and build a spreadsheet to compute the standard financial ratios. Compare the ratios to other medium-size manufacturers. Based on this analysis what changes should be made to improve the financial performance of the firm?

8. **Finance model.** The firm wants to expand production next year and wants to create another assembly station. The initial cost of the equipment is $50,000. The purchase will entail additional repair and maintenance costs of $100 per month for the next five years (the estimated life of the equipment). Should we buy it?

9. **HRM model.** Build a spreadsheet to compare the production/output of each employee. Compare the production to the salary. Could we reduce the size of the workforce?

10. **HRM model.** Assume that management allocates a 5 percent increase in salaries across the company (excluding managers and the CEO, whose raises are determined by the board). Create a merit evaluation for each of the employees (make up the data if it does not exist). Then determine the new salaries for each worker, based on his or her merit evaluations, level of experience and current salaries. You cannot exceed the overall 5 percent increase for the company. Use any necessary graphs and analysis to explain your choices.

11. **Accounting model.** Build a report that creates the standard income and balance sheets. Create/assume data as necessary, such as outstanding stock.

12. **Accounting model.** Analyze the cash flow. Determine whether there are problems with the existing procedures.

13. **Accounting/Finance model.** Forecast cash flow needs for the next year. Suggest investments and schedule maturities, receipts, and payments to minimize costs for the coming year.

14. **Accounting/Finance model.** Create an application to track financial investments and cash flow needs.

15. **Teamwork.** Most of these models/questions can be combined and solved as an integrated model by a team.

## ADDITIONAL READING

Anthes, Gary H. "Phoenix Maps Out Plan," *Computerworld*, June 14, 1993, p. 81. [City of Phoenix]

Aragon, Lawrence. "Change Agents; Pay Is Rising for IT Executives Who Can Shake It Up," *PC Week*, March 27, 1995, p. E1. [UPS]

Bucken, Michael. "UPS Repaves Gateway to IS: Realigns Help Desks to Speed Aid to Users, Customers," *Software Magazine*, May 1995, p. 52. [UPS]

Davis, Leila. "On the Fast Track to HR Integration," *Datamation*, September 15, 1991, pp. 61-65. [Newmont Mining]

Fitzgerald, Michael. "UPS Delivers New Bar-Code System to Public Domain," *Computerworld*, November 29, 1993, p. 38. [UPS]

Francett, Barbara. "Shining Spots on the Retail Horizon," *Computerworld*, May 13, 1991, p. 97. [Walgreen]

"Frontiers of Finance," *The Economist*, October 9, 1993, (Survey pp. 1-22). [A survey of financial techniques, models, and some existing applications]

Hamilton, Rosemary. "Lotus Ships CD-Networker," *Computerworld*, October 12, 1992, p. 59. [One Source and Europe]

Hoffman, Thomas. "Brokerages Seeing IS Dividends," *Computerworld*, November 29, 1993, p. 1. [Brokerage firm technology]

————. "Phoenix Police Use CASE, Other Tools to Speed Work," *Computerworld*, August 16, 1993, p. 81. [City of Phoenix]

Hogan, Mike and Leslie Crawford. "Our 15 Favorite Products for Life on the Road," *PC World*, November 1995, pp. 281-283. [Mapping and GIS tools]

Jones, Dennis. "John Kadar Interview," *Enterprise Systems Journal*, May 1995, pp. 10-12. [Federal Express]

King, Julia. "Invasion of the Body Patchers," *Computerworld*, September 27, 1993, p. 113. [Paramount Pictures]

Korzeniowski, Paul. "Manufacturers Debate Platform Futures," *Software Magazine*, August 1995, pp. 71-75. [Del Monte]

Leinfuss, Emily. "Synchronizing Remote Data with Home Databases," *Data Based Advisor*, October 1995, pp. 93-96. [Federal Express]

Levine, Ron. "Managing the Move; During Its Client-Server Migration, an IS Shop Discovers DCE," *Internetwork*, April 1995, pp. 1-2. [Associated Grocers]

"Lockheed Martin Setting $1.7B Consolidation," *Electronic News*, July 3, 1995, pp. 12-13. [Lockheed Martin]

Margolis, Nell. "High Tech Gets It There on Time," *Computerworld*, July 2, 1990, p. 77. [Federal Express]

Mason, David and Mary Johnston Turner. "A Time for Change," *Communications Week*, November 6, 1995, p. 31. [Federal Express]

Merrill, Kevin. "Technology Service: New Markets Call," *Computer Reseller News*, October 30, 1995, p. 65. [Federal Express]

Nash, Kim S. "Signing On-Line Yields Productivity Benefits," *Computerworld*, November 18, 1991, p. 29. [UPS]

Pare, Terence. "A New Tool for Managing Costs," *Fortune*, June 14, 1993, pp. 124-129. [A discussion of Activity Based Accounting]

Pastore, Richard. "Prescribing Real-Time Remedies," *Computerworld*, July 24, 1989, p. 41. [Walgreen]

Radosevich, Lynda. "Users See Notes Net Potential," *Computerworld*, February 21, 1994, p. 1. [Associated Grocers]

Ricciuti, Mike. "Here Come the HR Client/Server Systems!", *Datamation*, July 1, 1992, pp. 37-39. [Brief descriptions of new HRM offerings with a focus on integration]

Stahl, Stephanie. "Technology Hits the Road," *Information Week*, September 18, 1995, pp. 188-190. [Federal Express]

Steinberg, Don. "Billboard Ad Company Uses Demographic Software," *InfoWorld*, March 7, 1994, p. 62. [Revere National]

Thyfault, Mary E. "Global Communications Get Real," *Information Week*, November 13, 1995, pp. 34-38. [One Source and Europe]

"UPS Offers Parcel Tracking Online," *Newsbytes*, June 26, 1995, p. NEW2824721. [UPS]

Vacca, John R. "Providing the Tools to Penetrate," *Midrange Systems*, May 12, 1992, pp. 47-48. [Simonds Cutting Tools]

Vitiello, Jill. "Logan Says 'I Can' to Paperless Automation," *Computerworld*, October 28, 1991, p. 77. [Logan Aluminum]

Wagner, Mitch. "Lockheed Martin Outpaces IS Cuts," *Computerworld*, November 13, 1995, p. 24. [Lockheed Martin]

"Wall Street: Refugees from Physics Find Joy as 'Derivatives Geeks'," *Scientific American*, April 1994, pp. 126,128. [Physicists on Wall Street]

Wexler, Joanie M. "Cosmos2: Fedex's Next Generation," *Computerworld*, February 11, 1991, p. 29. [Federal Express]

Wilder, Clinton. "Corporate Culture Key to IS Success," *Computerworld*, May 22, 1989, p. 61 [Federal Express]

# CASES *Delivery Companies*

Statistics indicate that transportation workers use computers slightly less often than the general population. In particular, they spend less time with word processors and spreadsheets than most workers using computers.

SOURCE: Computer Use in the United States, U.S. Bureau of the Census.

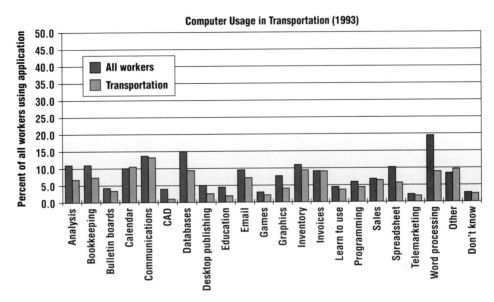

**Computer Usage in Transportation (1993)**

For many years, there was basically one company that delivered packages: the postal service (USPS). Gradually, local delivery companies arose in large cities. Some cartage firms specialized in large items. Others, like the bike messengers, promised immediate delivery of small items. United Parcel Service (UPS) emphasized delivery of larger packages between businesses. They gradually expanded to delivering products directly to customers. Federal Express (FedEx) was founded by Fred Smith, with the goal of delivering small packages overnight to anyplace in the United States.

The USPS is essentially a private organization, but they are subject to control by Congress. Several laws directly affect their operations and the actions of the other companies. In particular, no one but the USPS may deliver mail (or anything else) to individual household mailboxes. At the same time, Congress requires the USPS to provide equal service to *every* mailbox in the nation for the same price. So, a letter sent across the street costs the same as a letter sent to a remote location in Alaska. The USPS is also required to provide free mailing for members of Congress and reduced prices for not-for-profit organizations. At one point, they were reimbursed for this service, but in recent years, Congress has not provided complete funding. The USPS also faces civil service laws that influence their hiring and firing of employees. Other delivery companies are not subject to these constraints. As a result, they are free to charge higher prices based on delivery distance.

Package delivery companies face several problems. Perhaps the most important is the routing of packages and scheduling of flights and crews. Based on historical data, the companies know approximately how many packages will need to be delivered to any city. They still need to be wary of extreme situations, where an extra flight might be needed to handle the shipments to particular destinations. Each day, some flights and their crews will have to be routed at the last minute to handle extra loads on certain routes.

On the surface, it would seem that there is little difference among package delivery companies. Except for price (and convenience), why would it matter which company carries your packages? Federal Express challenged this thinking by introducing package tracking. Any time after Federal Express picks up your package, you can call and determine its location. From the standpoint of a customer, the system provides peace-of-mind, enabling you to verify that the package will arrive on time. Equally importantly, tracking individual packages reduces the chance of a package getting lost. Providing this service required a considerable investment in information technology. But it provided Federal Express with an advantage over the competitors, who were then forced to create their own tracking systems.

## CASE *Federal Express*

In an effort to continue to add value for the customer, Federal Express has launched Cosmos2, a 3½ year project that represents a 100 person effort to build a new infrastructure for the current system. According to Ron Ponder, Federal Express's chief information officer, this new project will enable the delivery company to substantially improve in four areas:

- Totally relational databases.
- Distributed computing.
- The automation of the routing and sorting process.
- A substantial increase in processing speed.

The relational database will enable users to construct their own views of relationships among data rather than following predetermined definitions. This means that the users can search on their own criteria rather than choose from a format provided by others.

The dispatch stations will serve as a distributed, peer-to-peer computing environment. The aim is to offload some transaction processing from the mainframe and place more information closer to the station personnel. This is accomplished by pushing out to each dispatch station the data it needs to manage. This enables the stations to access only the data they need.

The routing and sorting process was further automated during the summer of 1991 when Courier printers were installed in every Federal Express van. The printers print a smart label for each package. The label will not only be recognizable by the human eye; it will also be able to be scanned. When Cosmos2 is fully implemented, software will reside in the Supertracker to route and sort packages. In fact, the Supertracker will beep if a package is placed in the wrong container. The system has grown to the point where there are 46,000 Supertrackers, 1,400 quad racks, 2,400 station bases, and 26,000 mobile radio units.

Continued improvements in the price-performance ratio for the personal computer will enable Federal Express to perform more functions on a distributed basis. This will provide remote users with the ability to serve their own information needs while insuring a smooth flow of information. An important facet of this program is the installation of personal computers at 8,000 of its leading customers. Using EDI, the computers will be able to streamline order-processing services for the customer by calculating sizes, weights, and delivery schedules at the customer's office.

Long-term information systems and telecommunications planning is crucial to Federal Express's intent to expand its delivery services around the world. To accomplish this goal, Ponder has developed a five-year plan that is updated every six months. The plan focuses on applications in financial and corporate systems, air and ground transportation operations, and customer service. It details the rollout of hardware, software, and communications. In Ponder's opinion, the standardization of the communication network is more important to Federal Express than specific technologies. Currently, each of the offices in the 119 countries that Federal Express serves has its own computer system. The goal is to develop core applications that can be transferred to different locations and customized around the edges. Currently, specific applications are integrated across different systems and countries. However, there is no universal program that will enable employees to walk into any office and immediately query and generate reports from the computer system. Such a program would greatly increase the productivity that results from technological transfer.

### Digital Assistant Dispatch System

The Digital Assistant Dispatch System (DADS) notifies couriers when customers on their routes request pickups or have questions about deliveries. DADS enables drivers to be more efficient; there is less doubling back to pick up or deliver to route customers. Before DADS, drivers used a more traditional radio dispatch system.

DADS enables managers to track courier movements. Drivers reacted negatively to this use of technology to track their behavior so closely. Some couriers even went so far as to turn DADS off and go back to the old way of operation.

Resistance subsided when couriers realized that their jobs could be easier if they used the tool. Instead of trying to call dispatchers on the phone to check on a pickup or delivery and risking getting a busy signal, couriers checked their computer screen. Because the computer tracked everything, it was easier to look it up rather than remember to write everything down.

According to Dennis Jones, Federal Express CIO, laboratory tests are not enough for a successful implementation. A lot is learned by putting the system into the hands of the people who will actually use it.

### QUESTIONS

1. What role does technology play in the strategic direction of Federal Express?
2. How does Cosmos2 support the strategic mission of Federal Express?
3. How will Cosmos2 improve Federal Express's competitive position?

4. How will Cosmos2 prevent the entry of other competitors into the overnight delivery business?

5. How does the installation of 8,000 personal computers at Federal Express's leading customers affect the bargaining power of the buyers of overnight delivery service? How will it affect the bargaining power of the other suppliers of the service?

6. In what ways will Cosmos2 and the Supertracker alter the industry structure as it currently exists?

7. On the price versus quality matrix, where does Federal Express place its product? How does this placement prevent its competitors from undercutting it in either price or quality?

8. How does Cosmos2 change the decision-making process for both the Federal Express carrier and the late night sorter in the Atlanta hub?

9. How will other new technologies, facsimile transmission and electronic communication—affect the future strategic direction of Federal Express?

10. What problems are addressed by the DADS routing system?

11. Why did employees resist the use of DADS? What could Federal Express have done to decrease this resistance?

## CASE  *United Parcel Service*

United Parcel Service (UPS) is the largest package distribution company in the world. In 1990 it delivered nearly 2.9 billion packages in more than 180 countries and territories through 254 local outlets. That same year, its revenue totaled $13.6 billion.

Recognizing that technology will play an increasingly critical role in its expansion strategy, UPS is planning an $80 million data-processing and telecommunications center. This center will become the information hub for a global network of more than 1,750 facilities. The expenditure for the center will be in addition to the $1.4 billion communications plan that was implemented in 1986.

The proposed hub will house IBM and Tandem mainframes, DEC and Data General midrange computers, and IBM and compatible personal computers. Its focus will be on distributed processing that will integrate networks, goals, employees, and customers.

One of the problems that UPS faces is the fluctuation in the demand for its shipping services. Because each package is individually recorded and traced, the entry of data about each package is a major bottleneck in the system, especially during the Christmas season. To address this bottleneck, UPS developed a new in-

house imaging system. Named the Advanced Label Imaging System (ALIS), it reads air-freight documents at 35 sites nationwide. Third-shift workers now use ALIS to scan 650,000 to 750,000 labels a night. Technically, the data is fed into microcomputers on Novell Token-Ring LANs. The data is then uploaded to a mainframe in Paramus, New Jersey.

On the data-access side, representatives at 61 sites can retrieve images on microcomputers in response to customer inquiries. One scan of the shipping label can retrieve the recipient's signature, the package's weight, the time of delivery, and remarks from the shipping labels. Microcomputers on Novell Token-Ring LANs run the system at most scanning sites.

UPS has also made a substantial investment in LAN technology. Since 1990, it has installed 254 local area networks. UPS justified this installation because it permits the design of in-house developed systems to take advantage of the networked environment. Because all of the systems must operate on a worldwide basis, it was not efficient for people in the district offices to write their own software. As a result, programming was concentrated with corporate support staffers.

The LANs have increased productivity and justified their own costs. Marc Dodge, manager of LAN services at UPS, summarized the rationale for the decision to convert to LANs: "Our biggest single concern (before LANs were installed) was productivity. Our people were playing musical terminals and they spent a lot of time waiting for file conversion and vacant terminals."

One year after the LANs were installed, Dodge was able to document substantial cost savings. Prior to their installation, not enough terminals could be attached to the minicomputers. With the LANs, the cost of clerical labor has been reduced from $1.57 to $1.47 per one hundred keystrokes (1987 to 1988 figures). Spread across 500 million keystrokes per week, the cost advantage was substantial.

The LANs also enable UPS to keep an extra 5 percent of the equipment and supplies in reserve to enable a 24-hour turnaround on repairs for most equipment failures. The location of the LAN support group in the Louisville hub has made it possible to "piggyback" on the overnight parcel distribution to become an overnight network support system. Repair parts and support materials can be shipped easily throughout the system for arrival the next day. This "piggyback" system provides quick turnaround, substantial backup support, and cost-justification. The LANs have also enabled the technical support to be decentralized. Local sites now handle 90 percent of the technical support questions.

UPS is also employing hand-held computer technology to improve its delivery record accuracy and recordkeeping. By mid-1992, at a cost of $350 million, they plan to implement the microprocessor-based Delivery Information Acquisition Device (DIAD). This laptop model will capture customer signatures electronically. The 11-by-14 inch units contain a keypad, infrared bar code scanner, an LCD screen, and an electronic signature pad. The device will help drivers eliminate paper forms for pickup, tracking, and delivery of packages. The electronic capture of the signature and the scanning and direct key entry of the data will reduce paperwork and the possibility of human error for the drivers.

At the start of each day, each driver will pick up his or her DIAD. It will have been preprogrammed with the day's route. To access this route information, the driver will be prompted to key-enter certain codes. When each package is delivered, the customer will sign the DIAD signature pad with a stylus, and the signature will appear on the DIAD screen. The driver then accesses the location of the next stop. At the end of the day, the DIAD will be placed back in the cradle to enable the data to be transferred to the central computer while the unit is being recharged. By storing the information in the central UPS computer, the customer can receive immediate information regarding the package sent that day. An automated information retrieval system searches the database for the requested shipment. A signature verification or other proof of delivery can then be printed out for the customer.

The DIAD system was initially tested in Mississippi in late 1990. In December 1991, the test was spread to more than 2,000 drivers in 80 centers around the country. Plans were to implement use of the device fully to the 65,000 U.S. drivers at a total cost of more than $350 million. Five thousand units will be retained in stock as spares.

According to Nick Snider, DIAD project manager, "It's important to let our customers know that we are serious about advancing in the field of technology to provide better service. This new system will significantly reduce the time it will take to respond to a customer inquiry."

Parallel to the DIAD system, UPS is developing an online information retrieval system. Named the Delivery Information Automated Lookup System (Dials), the system will eliminate paper entirely from the delivery process. The Dials system is based on an OS/2 graphical user interface rather than traditional DOS commands.

In its efforts to address the European market, UPS will use microcomputer-based Novell local area networks. UPS managers feel that the networks will provide them with more assistance behind the scenes. In Europe, UPS will focus on freight handling at overseas transfer points. Using these hubs, UPS is working on a strategic system that will speed across-the-border package processing.

UPS's system must also deal with customs issues. This is particularly the case because tariff regulations require United Parcel Service to retain information on deliveries for up to 18 months. To comply with these requirements, UPS must send the bill of lading to the receiving country before the package is shipped. Customs officials inspect the bills and pick certain packages for instant delivery, making it possible for a package to be shipped from customs the day it arrives. The new system increases the efficiency of this system and reduces the cost of maintaining these records.

### QUESTIONS

1. How can United Parcel Service use information from the DIAD and Dials systems to develop predictive models of their service needs?
2. The United Parcel Service System primarily collects and reports information regarding packages and customers. What enhancements would you recommend to the system to convert this information to an abstract computer model?
3. All of the information gathered from the DIADs is stored in a database in Louisville. How can this database assist United Parcel Service to market toward the following groups?
   a. The top 100 senders of parcels.
   b. The top 100 receivers of parcels.
4. The DIAD system can be considered to be a dynamic model. How does the information that it collects change over time?
5. Computerized statistical packages assist in the evaluation of customer data. How can factor and regression analysis be applied to the information gathered by the DIAD system?
6. What decision variables can be controlled by management and thus have an influence over the output variables?
7. When the DIAD and DIAL systems were being considered for development there was a great deal of discussion regarding whether they would be an optimum or satisficing solution. If you were making this decision, what factors would you have considered in your efforts to decide whether to pursue the optimum or the satisficing solution?
8. How will information regarding who are the heaviest and lightest users of UPS assist the company to market and price its services?

### CASE *UPS Revisited*

As competition increases in the delivery industry, UPS is finding it necessary to change its policies and procedures. Unfortunately, not all of the changes are well-received. In 1994, the workers' union imposed the first-ever U.S. strike against UPS. Although it was quickly settled, some issues remain unresolved. UPS's position as the largest delivery company in America remains unchallenged. The 1993 annual revenue of $17.8 billion (profits were $809 million) was twice that of Federal Express. With 128,000 trucks and 458 aircraft, UPS controls three-fourths of the ground-parcel market. UPS is committed to maintaining this lead.

UPS has traditionally achieved its high service records through strict policies and controls over the drivers. The UPS methodology spells out everything from how fast drivers should walk (three feet per second), to how many packages to pick up and deliver (an average of 400 a day), to how to hold their keys (teeth up, third finger). UPS has a corps of more than 3,000 industrial engineers to study every process, make improvements, and create new policies for the drivers. Computer routing software is used to establish fixed routes for the drivers. Slower drivers are monitored by managers with stopwatches. Drivers are willing to accept these strict controls in exchange for $40,000 and up salaries, along with good potential for promotion to management.

To increase productivity and satisfy customers, UPS management implemented several changes in 1994, including computerized tracking of all packages, bulk discounts on large shipments, higher limits on package weights (increased from 70 to 140 pounds), and earlier guaranteed delivery times. Although customers like the changes, they all make more work for the drivers. Kent Nelson, the CEO, acknowledges that the changes place more demands on the workers. However, it is less an increase in physical labor and more an issue that "What is getting more difficult is the variety of services and things they have to remember."

The increased emphasis on speed has caused some problems, such as the situation experienced by driver Robert Duncan in Midway, Georgia. He was delivering a hobby kit to an elderly man who had to fetch the COD payment. Because of the approaching air deadline, Mr. Duncan could not wait and had to take the package back: "He started screaming and calling me all kinds of names. I felt bad, but I didn't want a supervisor chewing me out for missing the air deadline."

To compete with Federal Express and Roadway Package System (RPS), UPS found it necessary to implement product tracking and spent $2 billion on the bar code and database technology. The system has cut down on paperwork for the drivers, but many fear that UPS is using the data to more closely monitor their activities. Drivers are also expected to explain all of the 20 new services (such as customs clearing) to

customers. As a result of these increased expectations, UPS is finding it necessary to hire more highly educated drivers. But there is some fear that the more educated workforce will be more independent and less likely to accept the strict rules. Rigid adherence to the rules has caused a few additional problems. For instance, in Seattle, a judge ordered UPS to pay $12 million to 2,000 drivers because UPS was forcing them to work through lunch.

SOURCE: Robert Frank, "As UPS Tries to Deliver More to Its Customers, Labor Problems Grow," *The Wall Street Journal*, May 23, 1994, pp. A1, A5. Reprinted by permission of *The Wall Street Journal*, © 1994 Dow Jones & Company, Inc. All rights reserved.

### QUESTIONS

1. How has the product-tracking system benefited management and customers at UPS? What are the benefits to drivers? What are the costs?
2. What problems are being experienced by the drivers? What is the cause of the problems?
3. Can technology help minimize the problems UPS is experiencing?
4. What decisions are made by drivers? Why does UPS have so many rules?
5. Could technology help the drivers make better decisions? Would such a system increase or decrease driver flexibility?

### CASE  *City of Phoenix GIS*

The City of Phoenix is busy building several geographic information systems. An application for the police department is tied to a new PACE (Police Automated Computer Entry) system. The PACE system is largely based on a Field Interrogation (FI) database. The database stores reports from patrol officers. One thing that all police officers hate is paperwork. It typically takes officers 45 minutes to complete basic reports about each incident. Yet, paperwork is crucial for communication and legal aspects of the job. With the new PACE system, officers telephone their reports to a data-entry clerk, who immediately types it into the system. The PACE system also prompts for additional information if appropriate.

Once the reports are entered in the FI database, they are immediately available to all officers via a CAD/MDT (computer-aided dispatch/mobile data terminal) in each patrol car. They are also sent to the appropriate department (e.g., homicide or burglary) for review and additional information.

The system has already proven useful at tracking down criminals. The "Yogurt Bandit" was linked to robberies of 15 yogurt shops, stores, and banks in 1990. Using the FI database, a detective matched the description of the bandit with a person seen in the area. After they obtained a partial license plate number, police searched parking lots in the area and identified the suspect's car. They staked out the car and waited for the suspect to appear.

With additional changes, the PACE system will carry additional information about crime locations, including floor plans and descriptions. Designers are adding a geographic information system (GIS) component. With this system, officers will be able to get up-to-date maps and information about various areas and buildings throughout the city. For example, police and fire personnel will get immediate information on environmental and chemical hazards at emergency sites. The GIS can also track individual patrol cars and help dispatchers route the nearest officer to an emergency. The GIS can also be tied to the emergency 911 system. When an emergency call is received at the station, the ISDN phone system automatically identifies the phone and plots the location on a map. The GIS can instantly locate the nearest available patrol and emergency vehicles. On confirmation from the dispatcher, the system sends the call details, a map, and other relevant data to the patrol's CAD/MDT system.

The City of Phoenix is building a complete GIS to map its water, sewer, and transportation systems. The project consists of a 5 gigabyte database that displays and identifies every store, street, zone-boundary, land parcel, and water and sewer line in the 400-square-mile city. The city has allocated $7.6 million over five years to build the system.

The system can provide data to city planners and to specialists in various departments. It can locate water lines, track zoning requests, and produce maps showing crime trends, high-growth areas, and environmental hazard sites.

In one application, the system can automatically process requests for liquor licenses, by evaluating various rules regarding distance from churches and schools. Another application handles 22,000 requests

a year to search property records for questions of ownership, environmental and maintenance issues.

Designers also plan to use the system to optimize routes for city garbage collection, compensating for one-way streets and almost daily changes. The system will eventually be able to notify neighbors when someone applies for a zoning change. It will keep records on street maintenance. It can monitor building permits and inspections. The water department will be able to examine potential changes in flows and pressure as the city expands.

## QUESTIONS

1. What costs are involved in building the GIS? What are the potential benefits?
2. What additional GIS applications might exist for the City of Phoenix? Designers have mentioned that they already have more than 50 applications planned.
3. As the city puts increasing amounts of data and personal records on the computer, what privacy and security issues will city leaders face? Contrast their system with the situation in England, where homeowners complained when London officials suggested that they wanted to start keeping (paper-based) records on prices from property sales. What threats should Phoenix guard against?
4. Identify the major objects in the new system (either the police system or the GIS). Specify the major attributes and functions for each object class.
5. Draw a data flow diagram for the new police system.
6. Major cities can afford the expenses of a huge GIS. Can smaller cities create a similar system, or would it be too expensive? That is, can the system be scaled down far enough to make it affordable? Find the components that could be used to create a GIS for a city of around 10,000 people in 25 square miles.

## DISCUSSION ISSUE

### *Simulation*

Geordi is head of marketing for a new product introduction code named *red-clay*. Tasha is the head of finance and accounting. Deanna is the person who developed the red-clay product and is responsible for the overall project. They are in the middle of a small argument over whether they should begin production of the product.

Geordi:    According to the computer simulations, by running these ads at the target 18–24 year old group, we can expect an initial response rate of 19.2 percent. But we're also interested in repeat purchases. By extrapolating the statistics from our experiences with the big-sky product, we anticipate repeat buying of two items a month by 5 percent of the target group. If the product gains momentum, long-run market share should stabilize around 35 percent. At this point, there is insufficient data to determine whether the product will be fully accepted.

Tasha: In other words, we're supposed to risk the entire project based on these numbers generated from the computer. I don't like it.

Deanna: Actually, we believe the values are low. In my discussions with the participants after the study, I sensed that they were much more enthusiastic than the numbers indicate.

Geordi: In fact, Tasha, we deliberately chose conservative values to use in the simulations. If Deanna is right, this product could be hot. We might even show a major profit in the first six months.

Tasha: But, that's all speculation. This model has no relationship to reality. I could just as easily find 10 people who hate the product. I was talking to my niece the other day, and she says it's revolting.

Deanna: Now Tasha, you know we can't make decisions based on the responses of one person. We scientifically selected the participants . . .

Tasha: That was just an example. I'm much more concerned about these computer projections. I don't understand how the computer produced these results. Instead of wasting time with simulations, I think we should talk to real people.

Geordi: If you want, I can print out the computer model equations for you. But they're from state-of-the-art market research, and they might be hard to follow. Plus, last time I checked, there were 50 pages of equations.

Tasha: Are you saying that consumers have to compute 50 pages worth of equations to decide whether they want to buy this product!?

Geordi: No, no. The equations are just used by the computer to describe how customers behave.

Tasha: But how do we know the equations are right? Are you saying the computer can tell you whether I will buy the product?

Deanna: No, of course not. But we don't need to predict responses of individuals. We focus on how the entire target group will respond.

Tasha: We don't seem to be getting anywhere. I still don't see how we know whether the computer is right. If it's wrong, we lose a lot of money. I don't see how the computer can analyze every possibility. For instance, what happens if the product appeals to the 15–18 year old group? Won't that create a negative status effect on our target group?

Geordi: We talked about that possibility early on, but we don't think it's important enough to include in the model. There are hundreds of minor possibilities, but we don't have time to include all of them.

Tasha: In other words, your model only includes things *you* thought were important. That's even worse. Why didn't you just make up the sales projections, instead of hiding them behind some phony model?

Deanna: I sense that we have reached an impasse. Perhaps we should take a break and come back later. Geordi, perhaps you could prepare a small demonstration of the model. And Tasha, remember that we still have to make a decision. We can't always predict the exact future; sometimes even a little information is better than none.

## QUESTIONS

1. Is Tasha right—are simulations just a way for Geordi to invent whatever numbers he wants?
2. How accurate can we make the results from models and simulations? How easy would it be to force a model to produce the results we want?
3. What would you gain by manipulating simulations and models to produce the results you want? What are the costs (short run and long run)?
4. Is it possible to verify the accuracy of simulations and models? Are some models easier to evaluate than others?
5. What knowledge or background do you need to evaluate models? Do you think managers can accurately evaluate models from other disciplines (such as accountants evaluating marketing models)?
6. Should we distrust all models and simulations? What uses do they have?

# *Financial Definitions*

Several standardized methods have been created to analyze business financial data. These numbers are easily computed from the standard reported accounting data. The various financial ratios are particularly useful to highlight potential problems. The ratios can be compared against industry averages that are published by various companies.

The basic definitions are presented here with brief comments on their usage. You can find more detailed analysis and interpretation in any introductory finance textbook.

## BASIC ACCOUNTING REPORTS

The balance sheet summarizes the firm's assets, liabilities, and owner's equity (net worth) at a particular point in time. The income statement details the receipts and profits during a specified time period. The statement of owner's equity or retained earnings statement covers the same time period as the income statement and displays the changes in ownership data.

BALANCE SHEET

| ASSETS | | CLAIMS | |
|--------|--|--------|--|
| Cash | | Accounts Payable | |
| Securities | | Notes Payable | |
| Receivables | | Accruals | |
| Inventories | | Bonds Payable | |
| *(total)* | Current Assets | Provisions for Taxes | |
| | | *(total)* | Total Liabilities |
| Gross Plant & Equip. | | | |
| *less* Depreciation | | Common Stocks | |
| | Net Plant & Equip. | Retained Earnings | |
| | | *(total)* | Total Net Worth |
| *(add)* | Total Assets | *(add)* | Total Claims |

INCOME STATEMENT

| | |
|---|---|
| Net Sales | *(gross sales − returns and discounts)* |
| *less* Cost of goods sold | *(inventory, purchases, transportation, etc.)* |
| | Gross Profit |
| Selling costs | |
| General & administrative | |
| Building leases | |
| *(total)* | Operating expenses |
| *(subtract to get)* | Gross operating income |
| *(less)* | Depreciation |
| *(equals)* | Net operating income |
| *(add)* | Other income   *(royalties, etc.)* |
| *(equals)* | Gross income |
| Interest on notes payable | |
| Interest on mortgage | |
| Interest on bonds | |
| *(total)* | Other expenses |
| *(subtract to get)* | Net income before taxes |
| *(subtract)* | Federal income taxes |
| | Net income |

STATEMENT OF
RETAINED EARNINGS

| | |
|---|---|
| *(Starting)* | Retained earnings |
| *(add)* | Net income |
| *(equals)* | Total |
| *(subtract)* | Dividends |
| *(equals)* | Ending retained earnings |

FINANCIAL RATIO
CALCULATIONS

| PROFITABILITY |
|---|

$$\text{Profit margin} = \frac{\text{Net income before taxes}}{\text{Net sales}}$$

$$\text{Earnings per share (EPS)} = \frac{\text{Net income after taxes} + \text{dividends}}{\text{Number of shares outstanding}}$$

$$\text{Return on equity (ROE)} = \frac{\text{Net income after taxes}}{\text{Equity (book value)}}$$

$$\text{Price earnings ratio (P/E)} = \frac{\text{Average market price per share}}{\text{EPS}}$$

| LIQUIDITY |
|---|

$$\text{Current ratio} = \frac{\text{Current assets}}{\text{Current liabilities}}$$

$$\text{Quick (or Acid) test} = \frac{\text{Current assets} - \text{Inventories}}{\text{Current liabilities}}$$

| ACTIVITY RATIOS |
|---|

$$\text{Asset turnover} = \frac{\text{Net sales}}{\text{Total assets}}$$

$$\text{Inventory turnover} = \frac{\text{Cost of goods sold}}{\text{Inventory}}$$

$$\text{Average collection period} = \frac{\text{Accounts receivable}}{\text{Sales per day}}$$

| LEVERAGE RATIOS |
|---|

$$\text{Debt ratio} = \frac{\text{Total debt}}{\text{Total assets}}$$

$$\text{Times interest earned} = \frac{\text{Income before taxes} + \text{Interest charges}}{\text{Interest charges}}$$

# Interpretation

## Profitability Ratios

There are many ways to evaluate profitability in a firm. Some people look at gross profit (income); others rely on net income. Profit margin is a common measure, but it varies considerably by industry. Return on assets and return on equity more closely reflect the earnings received by investors. The DuPont method shows these two values are closely related. The DuPont method also highlights a key feature of ROA. Firms can increase ROA by increasing their profit margin (possibly selling products at a higher price) or by increasing their turnover (dropping the price and selling more items at lower profit). A quick examination of these two values will tell you a key strategy of the firm.

## Liquidity Ratios

Liquidity ratios evaluate whether a firm can meet its short-term obligations. Higher values mean it is easier to cover current expenses, but values that are too high imply too much money is sitting idle. The quick ratio is the most conservative, where values greater than 1.0 imply a firm can pay off current debts almost immediately.

## Activity Ratios

The activity ratios indicate how well the firm is handling day-to-day operations. In particular, a low *asset turnover* would imply the firm has excess capacity. A low *inventory turnover* implies they are not handling inventory very well or that sales are dropping. A low *average collection period* indicates that the firm is slow to collect from its customers. As usual, *high* and *low* are relative terms and must be compared to industry averages.

## Debt Ratios

The basic *debt ratio* indicates the share of financing that came from borrowing instead of equity (stocks). This value is highly variable. Some managers prefer to borrow heavily; others rely on equity. Relatively high values imply that it will be difficult for the firm to borrow additional money—an important piece of data if you are looking to invest heavily in new technology. The *times interest earned ratio* measures the firm's ability to pay interest costs from operating income. If the ratio is low, the firm is struggling to cover its debt payments.

DUPONT ANALYSIS

$$\text{Profit margin} \times \text{Total asset turnover}$$

$$ROA = \frac{\text{Net income}}{\text{Sales}} \times \frac{\text{Sales}}{\text{Total assets}}$$

$$ROA \times \text{Leverage}$$

$$ROE = \frac{\text{Net income}}{\text{Total assets}} \times \frac{\text{Total assets}}{\text{Common equity}}$$

# CHAPTER 10

# Complex Decisions and Artificial Intelligence

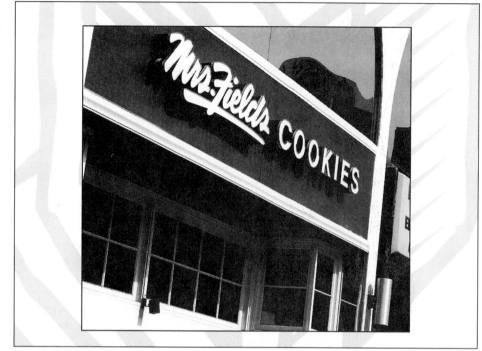

## MRS. FIELDS, INC.

In 1977, Debbie Fields opened a small cookie store in Palo Alto, California, defying conventional wisdom that "No one will pay 75 cents for a cookie." The store specialized in chocolate chip cookies made from a recipe generous in chocolate chips. It became an overnight success. Mrs. Fields cookies struck a responsive chord in the taste buds of the Palo Alto residents. Today, these cookies are available nationwide at more than 635 licensed franchises.

Randy Fields, the "mister" in Mrs. Fields cookies, was a Stanford graduate with a great deal of programming experience. From the beginning, he insisted on the implementation of computers throughout the stores. Even so, problems began to develop in his efforts to keep track of the rapidly expanding chain of stores.

As the company continued to grow, more than 20 people were serving on the headquarters staff. The sales-tracking system required managers to key in sales information on Touch-tone telephones. It worked fine with 25 locations. However, by 1985 it was falling apart under the burden of 136 stores. In addition, Mrs. Fields cookies had just bought a 70-store chain in the east that would have to be immediately integrated into the reporting system. Thus, Randy Fields made the timely decision to hire Paul Quinn, an expert in systems development, to head the MIS area.

The vision for Mrs. Fields cookies was to grow so quickly that no one would be able to catch up. With such an aggressive mission, the owners needed more than just an information management system to stay on top. Quinn had an idea. Because Mrs. Fields had started from an idea that defied conventional wisdom, why not remain innovative in the design of the new computer system? To answer this question, Randy Fields and Paul Quinn embarked on a program to develop an integrated store system that would use expert systems technology.

**OVERVIEW**    What functions do computers perform best? The short answer is: basic computations and processing large sets of data. Modern computer systems are also good at creating graphs and reports. All of these traits are useful for building transaction-processing and decision support systems. But in these situations, the computer is relatively passive. Designers and managers perform all of the analysis and "thinking." The computer provides data, performs calculations, and produces output at the direction of the managers. Can computers do more?

Most people do not have perfect recall and cannot perform billions of mathematical calculations per second. However, people can solve problems and make decisions, and they can deal with symbolic and subjective data. To make decisions in an uncertain world, we make judgments and guesses.

There are certain tasks that people do very easily: recognize a family member across a street, know the difference between a tree and a flower, communicate in a spoken (natural) language, learn new tasks. So far, it has been difficult to create computer systems that can perform these types of tasks.

Most experts believe we are a long ways away from creating machines that can *think*. However, computers can help with certain complex problems. In particular, diagnostic problems are common in business. A machine might need repairs and you have to find the cause, or sales are slipping in one region and you want to find the best method to increase them. You could turn to a consultant or expert to help solve diagnostic problems.

Consider a related question: What functions do machines perform better than humans? To use machines wisely, we must analyze their capabilities and compare them to the relative advantages of humans. Of course, scientific progress continually improves technology and expands the capabilities of machines. Several techniques, like the neural network illustrated in Figure 10.1, have arisen from research into artificial intelligence. Each new technique raises similar questions. How can the technology be used to solve problems and make better decisions? Is the technology cost effective? Sometimes new technology is exciting and it is easy to forget that it must be carefully analyzed to determine its true value.

**FIGURE 10.1**

Computer analysis of data and models. Research into "intelligence" has led to some decisions that can be analyzed and "solved" by computers. Expert systems and neural networks are two tools that are being used to help make decisions. These tools are used to make faster, more consistent decisions.

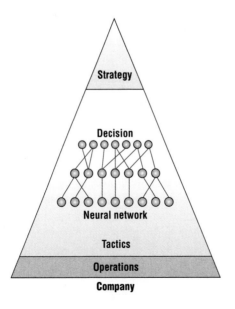

**INTRODUCTION**   Few business problems are straightforward. In these cases, we simply create a set of rules or procedures to follow. A computer can often be programmed to follow these basic procedures. As long as the business behaves in a predictable manner, the rules apply and the computer can handle the details. However, many business problems are less structured and cannot be solved so easily. Additionally, problems often involve data that is not well defined. For example, it is straightforward to create a computer system to handle inventory because the computer can easily keep track of item numbers and quantity sold. Consider the more difficult problem faced by a manager who has to decide where to locate a new plant. Some attributes are measurable, such as distance from suppliers, cost of land, and taxes. Other features are difficult to quantify: quality of the labor force, attitudes of government officials, and long-run political stability of the area.

Many problems involve nonnumeric data and complex interrelationships among the various factors. Without computers, businesses often call in experts or hire consultants to help solve these problems. Special software programs called **expert systems (ES)** provide many of these features. As indicated by their use at The Broadway department stores (Reality Bytes 10–1), expert systems can be used to identify problems and to suggest answers.

From the beginning, researchers and computer designers have known that humans perform some tasks much better than computers can. These differences led researchers to investigate how people solve problems and investigate how humans think. The research into techniques that might make computers "think" more like humans is

---

### ◥ Reality Bytes ◣   10–1   THE BROADWAY, DIVISION OF CARTER HAWLEY HALE STORES, INC.

The Broadway is a Los Angeles-based chain of 43 department stores that performs 57 million customer transactions per year. The retail chain has fully automated its management functions with a variety of components. These include interactive gift registries, credit processing, and sales transactions.

The management knowledge base was named the Area Sales Manager Expert System Consultant (ASMESC). The system includes six modules of sales techniques, staffing, product knowledge, product procurement, floor layout, and motivation. It was built by enlisting eight of the top-producing sales managers to provide the rules for the system. These individuals committed substantial time to interviews to set the ground rules for the system. Ongoing interviews were then conducted to continue to gather information and update the knowledge base.

At The Broadway, area sales managers are assigned to handle the everyday management of the store. The responsibilities of this position include the supervision of the store salespeople and the analysis of sales reports and interactions with customers. Six-month retail sales strategies are projected based on market trends, fashions, and fads. ASMESC uses specific data from each of the stores such as sales per hour and current inventory compared to previous year's sales. Based on this input, the ASMESC can pinpoint areas of concern as well as strong management strategies and characteristics.

The ASMESC was beta tested in two Southern California locations during the Spring of 1988. When sales figures in these two stores showed a marked improvement, the system was deployed to the rest of the locations. Currently the system runs on the company's IBM mainframes. Discussion is continuing about spreading the influence of the system in two directions. First, the system is projected to be delivered on personal computers to every one of Carter Hawley Hale's 114 stores. Second, work is being completed on a Staple Stock Advisor. This component of the system will focus on the ordering and inventory processes of the 1.5 million different stock items that each store carries.

known as **artificial intelligence (AI).** There is some question as to whether it will ever be possible to build machines that can think the same way humans do. Nonetheless, the research has led to some useful tools that perform more complex analysis and can solve difficult problems. These tools attempt to mimic the processes used by humans in a simpler form that can be processed by a computer system.

 **TRENDS**

As businesses began to use computers, the easy problems were solved first, such as the highly structured transaction processing systems discussed in Chapter 4. But from the earliest days of computers, people have dreamed of machines that could solve more complex problems. One recurring question is whether or not machines can ever solve problems the same way as humans. Some of the earliest professional comments on artificial intelligence (AI) came from discussions by British mathematician Alan Turing and his co-workers in the 1940s. Books by Hubert Dreyfus provide a quick, critical review of the history of AI research.

At first (1957–1962), researchers tried to define intelligence and attempted to write programs that could solve general problems. In particular, a great deal of effort and money was expended on software that would automatically translate documents—especially from Russian to English. However, after spending about $20 million, the researchers gave up in 1966. Two additional groups of AI researchers were busy: Newell, Shaw, and Simon at Carnegie and Papert and Minsky at MIT. Newell, Shaw, and Simon created a "General Problem Solver" that could prove some basic theorems in mathematics, when it was given the basic assumptions and prior theorems.

When it became impossible to extend the early research into more general problems, AI research changed directions. From 1962 to 1967, research focused on "Semantic Information Processing" (which was the title of a book by Marvin Minsky). Researchers also began to suggest that to create intelligent machines, they first needed to understand how the human brain worked. So they began to build models of human thought. An interesting program called STUDENT was written by Brobow, a graduate student working under Minsky. STUDENT could solve basic algebra "story problems"

by examining key words (*is* for *equals, into* for *divide,* etc.).

Research again changed from 1967–1972 as workers focused on narrower subjects. Another MIT researcher (Weinograd) created a program called SHRDLU. SHRDLU displayed a set of geometric figures (boxes, pyramids, circles) and would answer questions or manipulate them in response to written commands. Within its limited area, it could understand fairly complex written statements.

From 1972 to 1977, research again narrowed its scope and focused on specific problems or "knowledge domains." The foundations of expert systems came from this early work. Feigenbaum at Stanford created Dendral, a system that contained rules and complex knowledge of chemical reactions. Shortliffe built a classic expert system called MYCIN, which assisted physicians in identifying meningitis and other blood infections.

The years from 1977 to 1997 have seen an expansion of research in AI, including robotics, pattern matching, language comprehension, and voice recognition. We have also seen the commercialization of many of the AI innovations, especially expert systems.

In the early years, researchers were optimistic about the possibilities presented by "thinking machines." In 1953, Turing suggested that by the end of the century, we would have "intelligent" machines. As technical advisor for the 1967 film *2001,* Marvin Minsky assured Kubrik that Turing was pessimistic, and we would see "intelligent" machines well before the end of the century. In 1957, Herbert Simon also suggested that his General Problem Solver would eventually show signs of intelligence. Although these predictions were overly optimistic, the ideas and results of this research have led to computer systems capable of solving more complex problems.

For example, humans are very good at recognizing patterns, so techniques have been created to help machines identify patterns. Engineers are continuing to work on robots that can see, pick up diverse objects, and walk. Research continues into speech recognition and machine vision. In addition to application in manufacturing, these capabilities would make it easier for humans to communicate with machines.

**SPECIALIZED PROBLEMS: COMPLEX, REPETITIVE DECISIONS**

Imagine your life as a top-notch manager. Co-workers perceive you as an expert and value your advice and problem-solving skills. You are constantly answering questions and there are always more problems than you can handle. You are using decision support systems and integrated information technology to perform your job better and more efficiently, but it is not enough. Can technology help you with more complex decisions and problem solving?

From another perspective, when you encounter new problems with different, complex models, it would be helpful to have an expert assist you with applying and understanding the models. Yet experts or consultants are expensive and not always available. Can we somehow capture the knowledge and methods of experts and use technology to make this knowledge available to workers throughout the company?

Expert systems have proven useful for many problems. The goal of an expert system is to enable novices to achieve results similar to those of an expert. The users need to understand the basic problem, learn the terminology, and be able to answer questions. For example, a typical patient would not be able to use a medical expert system, because the questions and terms would not make any sense.

Think of an expert system as a consultant in a box. The consultant can only solve certain specific problems. For example, perhaps a retail store manager needs to estimate buying patterns for the next few months. The manager might call a marketing consultant to survey buyers and statistically search for patterns. The consultant will ask questions to determine the basic objectives and identify

---

 **BUSINESS TRENDS**

Several events are driving the trend toward using temporary workers in business. First, smaller firms find it difficult to hire specialists on a permanent basis. Second, the Family Leave Act requires most firms to allow workers extended leaves for family health reasons. In many cases, firms will elect to hire temporary workers to fill these absences.

Information technology has value for the company in both of these situations. First, instead of hiring consultants, it is increasingly possible to purchase expert systems that incorporate the knowledge of specialist consultants. For instance, software can help general managers solve marketing problems, such as creating and evaluating consumer surveys. These expert systems can provide a

manager with in-depth support for specialized problems at reasonable prices and complete flexibility.

In the case of the Family Leave Act, it is easy to envisage a business that rotates workers every three to six months as some go on leave, others return, and new temporary workers are hired. Each time workers change jobs, they need to be retrained. Although change can be beneficial (insights and skills from one area might lead to new solutions in other departments), it can also be disruptive. Expert systems can be used to train workers and ensure consistency of decisions and customer support.

problems. Similarly, a production manager might be having problems with a certain machine. The manager might call a support line or a repair technician. The advice in this situation will be quite different from the marketing example because the topics (or domains) of the two problems are different. It would be difficult to create one computer program that could help you with both types of problems. On the other hand, there are similarities in the approach to the two problems. Computerized expert systems are designed to solve narrow, specialized problems. Each problem can be relatively complex, but it must be reasonably well defined. Many business problems fall into this category, and expert systems can be built for each problem.

 **EXPERT SYSTEMS APPLICATIONS**

### DIAGNOSTIC PROBLEMS

Many situations present a set of symptoms. Experts analyze these symptoms and search for a common cause. Interpretations are sometimes vague, use incomplete data, and can be hard to express in "rational" terms.

### SPEED

Some decisions are only moderately complex but are made hundreds or thousands of times. The ability to make these decisions rapidly (and correctly) improves customer satisfaction and can lead to an advantage over the competition.

### CONSISTENCY

From operational to legal consequence there are many advantages to making decisions consistently. Presented with the same basic inputs, the firm needs to reach the same conclusion, regardless of irrelevant factors.

### TRAINING

Automated support for repetitive decisions can be useful for training new employees. As the workers use the system, they will learn the business rules that make up their job.

## Diagnostic Problems

Several problems in the world can be classified as diagnostic situations. These problems arise when the decision maker is presented with a set of symptoms and is asked to find the cause of the problem, as well as solutions. Consider a firm that uses a complex machine. If the machine breaks down, production stops until it is fixed. Additionally, maintenance tasks have to be performed every day to keep the machine running. The company hires an engineer to perform these tasks. The engineer also knows which adjustments to make if various symptoms appear. This system has been working well, and the company wishes to expand to other locations with a franchise system. The problem is that there is only one engineer, and it would be too expensive to have a highly trained engineer at each location.

One possible solution would be to set up a phone link between the franchises and the engineer. One person at each franchise would be trained in the basics of the machine. If problems arise, the person could call the engineer. The engineer would ask specific questions, such as "What do the gauges show?" The answers will lead the engineer to ask other questions. Eventually, the engineer makes recommendations based on the answers.

Of course, if there are many franchises, the engineer will be too busy to solve all of the problems. Also, if the businesses are located in different countries, the time dif-

Exsys is one of the leading suppliers of expert system development tools. One of their latest releases builds expert systems that run as a Web site on the Internet. Companies could use this system to provide advanced advice to customers 24 hours a day.

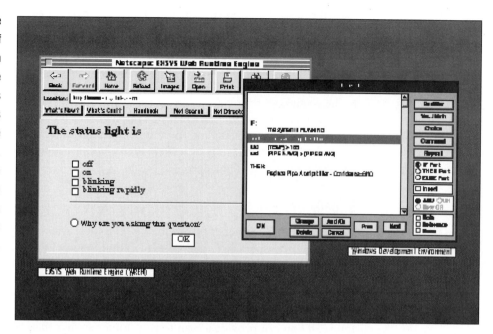

ferences may not allow everyone enough access to the engineer. A better solution is to create a computerized expert system. All of the expert's questions, recommendations, and rules can be entered into a computer system that is distributed to each franchise. If there is a problem, the on-site person turns to the expert system. The system asks the same questions that the engineer would and arrives at the same recommendations. The example of Ford's warranty validation system (Reality Bytes 10–2) shows that expert system can also be used to make sure that franchisees follow complicated sets of rules.

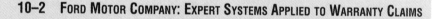

### ◤ Reality Bytes ◣  10–2  FORD MOTOR COMPANY: EXPERT SYSTEMS APPLIED TO WARRANTY CLAIMS

An important part of each new car sale is the warranty repair after the sale. To link repair to the dealer and ultimately new car sales, Ford Motor Company administers its warranty program through local dealerships. After mechanics complete a warranty repair, they submit a claim to headquarters and request a reimbursement from Ford to cover the cost of the parts and labor. Each claim is verified and paid within a 24-hour period.

Because the validation program checks for a number of variables, a complicated system named Automated Claims Entry System is required to verify each claim. Invalidated claims are returned to the claims review department with an appropriate error message explaining why the reimbursement was denied. The ESCAPE expert system was written to expedite the review process and speed payment to each dealership. The expert system was written to replace the COBOL code because the new sales plans and warranty programs had become much more complex. The large volume of changes made the COBOL program too difficult to recode to reflect these changes. An average of 1,000 daily claims are processed through the ESCAPE program each evening.

ESCAPE represents the situation where a set of well-defined rules and principles can be more effectively represented using expert system techniques. Expert systems provide savings by reducing the maintenance and development effort needed for complicated rule-driven processes. Secondly, it allows for quicker and more reliable changes to the base expert system program.

Expert systems also have the ability to explain their recommendations. While running the ES, the user can ask it to explain why it asked a particular question or why it arrived at some conclusion. The ES traces through the answers it was given and explains its reasoning. This ability helps the user gain confidence in the decisions, allows mistakes to be corrected, and helps the users remember the answer for future reference.

The business world offers many examples of diagnostic situations, such as identifying causes of defects, finding the source of delays, and keeping complex equipment running. The common characteristic is that you are faced with a set of symptoms, and you need to find the cause.

## Speedy Decisions

Other situations can benefit from the use of expert systems. Even if a problem is not exceedingly complex, we could use an expert system to provide faster responses or to provide more consistent recommendations. There are many advantages to be gained if you can make a decision faster than your competitors do. If you can identify a trend in stock prices before anyone else, you can make a higher profit. If you can answer customer questions faster, they will be more likely to shop with you in the future. If you can provide a loan to a customer sooner than anyone else, you will do more business. In extreme cases, earlier decisions can save lives, as indicated by Children's Hospital of Boston (Reality Bytes 10–3), which developed a system to monitor and evaluate patient lab results.

---

### ◤ Reality Bytes ◢    10–3   CHILDREN'S HOSPITAL OF BOSTON

Children's Hospital of Boston is developing an artificial intelligence-based just-in-time intervention system. It is unique because it fits into and is built on the overall hospital information systems infrastructure. In doing so, the expert intervention system draws upon the hospital's primary information system to analyze combinations of information for immediate action.

An example of the use of the expert system is the system's ability to collect the results of a patient's lab test, recognize a change that presents potential problems with the medication previously prescribed, and then issue an immediate alert regarding the health of the patient.

The artificial intelligence component represents the final stage in a four-year, $25-million systems infrastructure project. The project was built in three stages. These included basic systems connectivity, applications communications, and full integration.

---

Transaction-processing systems keep much of the basic data that we need to make decisions. Decision support systems help us analyze that raw data. Both of these tools enable us to make decisions faster than trying to make the decision without any computers. However, it still takes time for a human to analyze all of the information.

Consider the case of a bank loan. In order to get a loan, you go to the bank and fill out a loan application form. You tell the loan officer why you want the loan and provide basic data on income and expenses. Depending on the amount of money involved, the banker will probably check your credit history, get appraisals on any collateral, and might need to get approval by a review officer or loan committee. All of these actions take time.

Now, consider the steps involved with a computerized process. First, you need to tell the bank that you want a loan. Instead of driving to the bank, you could use the telephone. With a pushbutton phone, you enter information directly into the bank's computer. The computer would give you a choice of loan types (car, boat, personal, etc.) and you push a button to select one. You enter the amount of money you want to borrow. The next step is to check your credit history. Your income, expenses, and credit record are available to the bank from national credit reporting agencies. The bank might also have its own database. The bank's computer could be connected to credit agency computers to collect additional data on your credit history.

To make the final decision, the bank needs a set of rules. These rules take into account the size of the loan, the value of the collateral, as well as your income, expenses, credit history, and existing loans. When the bank has determined the proper rules, the computer performs the analyses. If the bankers trust the rules, the computer could make the final decision. For example, there would be no need for a loan officer to be involved in simple decisions, such as making small car loans to customers with large savings accounts. With an expert system, a bank can cut the loan-approval period down to a few minutes on the phone.

Many other decisions need to be made rapidly. The first step in all of these cases is to make sure that the transaction-processing system provides the necessary raw data. The second step is to create a set of rules for making the decision. The difficulty lies in finding these rules. For some problems, there are well-defined rules that can be trusted. For other problems, the rules may not exist. In this case, the company will probably still need a human to make the final decision.

## Consistency

The example of the bank loan demonstrates another advantage of expert systems. Business decisions are subject to a wide variety of nondiscrimination laws. An expert system can be used to provide consistent decisions. The rules followed by the ES can be set up to avoid illegal discrimination. Businesses also have credit ratings, which are often determined by Credit Clearing House (CCH) (Reality Bytes 10-4). CCH uses an expert system to make the "easy" decisions, which speeds up the process by allowing humans to focus on the more complicated cases. It also leads to consistent application of the rules.

Consider the loan example. If each loan officer makes individual decisions, it is hard to determine whether they are consistent with corporate policy. Each individual decision would have to be checked to make sure it was nondiscriminatory. On the other hand, a committee could spend several weeks creating a set of lending rules that can be verified to be sure they are legal and ethical. As long as the bank employees follow the recommendations of the ES, the outcome should not be discriminatory. Because there should be few cases where the loan officer overrules the ES, managers will have more time to examine each of these circumstances.

Many business decisions need to be performed consistently to avoid bias and to treat people equally. Loans, pricing, raises, and promotions are some examples. However, there can be problems with using a computer system to enforce standards. The main difficulty lies in creating a set of rules that accurately describe the decisions and standards. For example, it might be useful to have a set of rules regarding raises and promotions, but think about what happens if an employee's job does not fit the basic rules. Organizations continually change, which means the rules have to be

## Reality Bytes  10-4 CREDIT CLEARING HOUSE

Good credit is a prerequisite for business transactions. For clothing or other products to be shipped to a retailer, the manufacturer must be assured that credit can be extended and the bills will subsequently be paid. A division of Dun and Bradstreet, the Credit Clearing House (CCH) provides risk-management assessments for apparel industry manufacturers, wholesalers, jobbers, and marketers. It assigns credit ratings and dollar-specific credit recommendations to each of the retail customers.

The preparation of CCH credit recommendations requires careful review by a staff of trained analysts who examine data from a number of business information reports and maintain a database of credit ratings on 200,000 businesses. Although necessary, this process involves accessing and checking a series of data reports. Because the analysis is quantitative and repetitive, it provides an excellent opportunity for the application of an expert system. Many of the components of the process are generic and can be reused in other searches. The up-front investment in the expert system would greatly reduce the amount of time each search and report would subsequently take.

Three results can follow from a CCH application:

- A decision is made to offer a recommendation to extend credit and a dollar guideline.

- A "no-guideline" decision means that credit should not be extended or the credit limits have already been exceeded.
- A "knockout" is a case for which the system is not able to make a recommendation or to give a dollar guideline. It is subsequently referred directly to analysts for review.

The goal is to reduce the number of "knockout decisions" while maintaining the accuracy of the decision. As subsequent knockouts are evaluated, their results can be codified and integrated into the expert system, further reducing the number of knockouts. Currently the decisions made by the system result in a 98.5 percent agreement with those that were developed by hand.

Another advantage of using an expert system is a great reduction in turnaround time. Credit decisions that used to take up to three days to make can now be completed in three to five seconds. Increased accuracy with speed enables the apparel manufacturer to serve the retailer better and with more accuracy. Equally important, marketing and other sales efforts can be focused on those companies that have the best credit rating.

monitored and changed regularly. The Ontario Department of Corrections (Reality Bytes 10-5) illustrates how expert systems can help enforce standards in the presence of changing rules.

## Training

Training employees is closely associated with problems of consistency. All organizations must train employees. If the tasks are complex and the decisions highly

## Reality Bytes  10-5 ONTARIO DEPARTMENT OF CORRECTIONS

The Ontario Department of Corrections uses a knowledge-based system to develop prison sentences. The system lists and relates several factors that are used to make decisions regarding how long a prisoner will be incarcerated. These include escape attempts, consecutive and concurrent sentences, parole violations, offender's age, and credit for good behavior. Because rules and regulations frequently change based on legislative and regulatory requirements, the system helps the department keep current at all its locations.

unstructured, it can take years for employees to learn the rules and gain the experience needed to deal with problems. Two features of expert systems help employees learn. First, employees learn what questions need to be asked. In particular, after using the system for a while, certain groups of questions will occur together. Second, most expert systems have provisions for explaining their answers (and the motivation for each question). At any point, an employee can ask the expert system why it asked a certain question or why it reached a conclusion. Using an expert system to tutor new employees, Bank of America (Reality Bytes 10–6) cut training time in half.

---

### ◥ Reality Bytes ◢   10–6  BANK OF AMERICA'S CREDIT CARD DIVISION NEW EMPLOYEE TUTOR

Each year the credit card division of the Bank of America receives, and by law must respond to, 240,000 letters from customers who may express dissatisfaction with a particular product or service. Training individuals to respond in a uniform manner is a formidable task.

To address this training need, Bank of America developed the Automated Customer Service Expert System (ACE). The expert system reduces the average training time for a new employee from six to two or three months. The "case" management aspect helps to track the status of all pending cases. It also enables the customer service representatives to prioritize work-in-process.

The major challenge to the development of the expert system was not the acquisition of knowledge from the experts. Rather, it was the difficulty of applying federal banking regulations to programming logic. The regulations require a complex procedure of interpreting each case. Rapidly changing laws also made it difficult to keep current.

The bank approached this problem by using a spreadsheet tool to build a separate condition-action matrix. The condition, the customer's particular dispute, is listed on the vertical axis. Each cell has a value that the customer representative responds to. Smalltalk, an object-oriented programming language from ParcPlace Systems, navigates a series of these matrices to link the sum of the conditions together.

ACE prompts the customer service representative to answer questions to resolve the customer disputes about the transaction. It is the expert system, however, that generates the diagnosis to ultimately provide an appropriate solution.

The second phase of ACE will incorporate a mainframe interface that will enable transaction data to be downloaded to the expert system. In the third phase, the expert system will be integrated into a local area network environment. The complete program will enable all the cases to be stored on a file server. This will make it possible for the customer service manager to review all of the data at a single location.

---

**DECISION SUPPORT SYSTEMS AND EXPERT SYSTEMS**

Consider a small example. You wish to fly from Miami to Phoenix for Thanksgiving. You go to a travel agent who uses a computer reservation system to display the basic flight information. If there are seats available on the flights that you prefer, the computer records your name and prints a ticket. But, what happens if there are no open seats on the flights that you prefer? The computer system simply displays a message. You and the travel agent then have to find alternatives. The computer system is passive. It only provides basic information about schedules, availability, and prices.

Perhaps the computer designers have built a more sophisticated system that has decision support features. Now, when you have trouble finding a flight, the travel agent asks the computer to display a list of all open seats, sorted by price. It shows a graph of available seats arranged by price and departure times. A well-organized presentation of the data can make it easier for you to choose a flight.

**FIGURE 10.2**

Expert systems are designed to help novices achieve the same results as experts. An expert uses symbolic and numeric knowledge along with rules to analyze a situation and make a decision. Knowledge engineers create a computerized knowledge base that is used to assist novices.

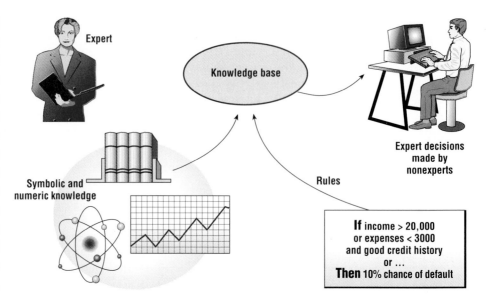

Can the computer do even more? Look at the problem from another perspective. Why do we have travel agents? In the early days of flight reservation systems, the travel agent was necessary because passengers did not have access to computer terminals. Also, the agents needed special training to use the software. Today, it is easy to use a personal computer to make your own reservations. Does that mean we do not need travel agents anymore? That's a question many people are asking. However, consider what happens when the computer reveals that no direct flights are available. For about the same price, you are offered a choice of three other flights with stops in Atlanta, Dallas, or St. Louis. Initially, you might not care which route you take. Now, suppose your travel agent says that the Atlanta airport is renovating the terminals so you would have to spend four hours sitting in a dusty, noisy room with no food service. Or perhaps the agent will tell you that the Dallas airport is 20 miles from the city, so you'll have to spend five hours sitting at the airport instead of sightseeing. This expert advice, based on additional data and rules, will affect your decision.

Figure 10.2 indicates how the additional knowledge of the travel agent can make a difference in your decision. If this knowledge were incorporated into the computer system, it would become an expert system. Such a system would enable a novice traveler to make decisions as well as the experienced travel agent.

In practice, there is no solid line between decision support and expert systems, but Figure 10.3 highlights the primary differences. One of the most important differences is that the expert system evaluates rules and suggests a result or action. Sometimes, as in the case of A.C. Nielson and Frito-Lay (Reality Bytes 10–7), decision support systems collect data that can then be analyzed by expert systems. In the case

**FIGURE 10.3**

DSS versus ES. An expert system has a different goal and a different approach than a decision support system. A DSS is used by a trained decision maker to collect data, analyze models and produce output. An ES is built to provide advice to nonexperts and guide them to make a better decision.

|  | **DSS** | **ES** |
| --- | --- | --- |
| Goal | Help user make decision | Provide expert advice |
| Method | Data–model–presentation | Asks questions, applies rules, explains |
| Type of problems | General, limited by user models | Narrow domain |

## Reality Bytes     10–7   A. C. NIELSON

Supermarket scanned data has been available for the past decade. However, only recently have programs been powerful enough to evaluate this data and make recommendations for marketing changes. To manage the exponentially growing volume of this data, A. C. Nielson, Information Resources, and Metaphor Computer Systems have developed "quasi-expert systems." These systems automatically break down brand performance within regions, detail how competitive products are doing, which promotions work, and which store displays are attracting the most customers.

Frito-Lay receives daily sales information from hand-held terminals operated by 10,000 Frito-Lay salespeople. Information about 100 product lines in 400,000 stores is translated to company computer screens in easy-to-read charts. Red indicates a sales drop, yellow a slowdown, and green an upsurge. Current projections are that the new system eliminates a day of paperwork from each salesperson's weekly

schedule. This time savings enables salespeople to spend more time servicing accounts in the stores.

The decision support systems are seen as crucial in the expensive and highly competitive refrigerated and frozen food shelves. Armed with this information, salespeople from the food companies can demonstrate improved sales and margins immediately to the major food chains. Smaller, local companies are finding it even more difficult to compete because of the high barriers to entry that such a system presents.

Some analysts argue, however, that responding so quickly to sales information could focus on short-term gains at the expense of long-term brand loyalty. Quick reorientations in product promotions do not provide enough time for the consumers to realize the full benefit of the marketing plan. Equally important, it is essential to remember that no matter how recent the data is, it is still historical data. The best marketing decisions are those that most accurately take into account future variables.

of expert systems, users must always be careful to understand how the expert system is evaluating the choices. If the system is using short-term rules, but the users prefer to focus on the long term, use of the expert system can lead to problems.

**BUILDING EXPERT SYSTEMS**

At first glance, you would suspect that expert systems are hard to create. However, except for one step, which is hard, tools exist to make the job easier. Expert system shells help nonprogrammers create a complete expert system. The area that causes the most problems when you are creating expert systems is finding a cooperative expert who fully understands and can explain the problem. Some problems are so complex that it is difficult to explain the reasoning process. Sometimes the expert may rely on vague descriptions and minor nuances that cannot be written down. Even though expert systems can deal with these types of problems, it might take too long to determine the entire process. Also, if you transfer the expert's knowledge to a computer, the expert might worry about losing his or her job.

The system developed by Nynex (Reality Bytes 10–8) to handle problems with telephone switches is a good example of steps needed to create an expert system. On the other hand, it can be time consuming to determine all of the rules needed for an expert system. Techniques such as KADS (Reality Bytes 10–9) have been developed to create a library of rules that can be used by many people throughout the company.

Most expert systems are built as a knowledge base that is processed or analyzed by an inference engine. A **knowledge base** consists of basic data and a set of rules. In most situations, an *inference engine* applies new observations to the knowledge base and analyzes the rules to reach a conclusion.

## Reality Bytes    10–8  NYNEX CORPORATION: MAX

Nynex Corporation has developed MAX, an artificial intelligence-based system, to automate its telephone trouble-screening process. Ed Power is a former tester who was familiar with telephone company computerized switching systems. He set the stage for the system by proposing a four-phased development process:

1. *Preliminary Proof-of-Concept Studies.* At this stage, the MAX team presented Power with problems. He then explained how he would solve them and why. The team turned Power's responses into rules for an expert systems-based prototype.

2. *Expansion of the Prototype.* At this stage the team sought to expand the prototype into a fully functional system with a broadened knowledge base. One mistake the team made at this stage was to "hardwire" too much. In doing so, team members sought to develop a one-to-one relationship between problems and potential solutions.

3. *Arbitration Level.* The arbitration phase saw the development of system rules to use in selecting among equally valid alternatives.

4. *Modification.* This phase involved the modification of the database to address the particulars of the local service center. Using local experts, the team would alter the database dependent on the particular type of equipment in use. This enabled the knowledge base to be tuned for each service center.

The basic steps to create an expert system are: (1) analyze the situation and identify needed data and possible outcomes; (2) determine relationships between data and rules that are followed in making the decision; (3) enter the data and rules into an expert system shell; and (4) design questions and responses. A *knowledge engineer* is often hired to organize the data, help devise the rules, and enter the criteria into the expert system shell, or supervise programmers as they create an expert system.

## Reality Bytes    10–9  KADS (KNOWLEDGE ACQUISITION, AND DOCUMENT STRUCTURING)

In Europe, KADS technology provides models to address generic medical, industrial, and business problems. Procedurally, these include diagnosis, configuration, modeling, and control.

KADS saves time in the problem development cycle. It eliminates the necessity of asking the expert each time to verbalize the decision-making sequence of a problem. Instead, a knowledge engineer can go to a library of design models and readily observe the types of knowledge that must be acquired before interviewing the expert. This greatly improves the efficiency of the process by focusing the time spent with the expert. In addition, solutions learned in one model can be applied to the next.

Source: "KADS Tool: Too Cool!" *AI Expert*, October 1993, p. 44.

## Knowledge Base

A knowledge base is more than a simple database. It consists of data but also contains rules, logic, and links among data elements. In most cases, it contains less structured and more descriptive data. For example, an ES for medicine might have a list of symptoms that contains items like "high temperature," and "intense muscle pain." This

**Reality Bytes**     **10–10**    SCHLUMBERGER'S LOG QUALITY MONITORING SYSTEM

Schlumberger has developed an oil field services and utility measurement system to assist its oil field engineers. The system's primary task is to enhance the performance of well-trained field engineers in oil field exploration. It does this by applying oil well geology data to the information services division.

Rather than using the programming talents of a knowledge engineer to build the expert system, Schlumberger asked the oil engineers or domain experts to build their own system using an expert system shell. This caused the engineers to be more directly involved, ultimately leading to a more successful system.

Another unique feature was the use of an integrated knowledge-based edit tracking system to provide reassurance to computer-naive experts. This safety net enabled users to test the procedures the computer developed against those that they knew worked from their experience. Doing so enabled the program to capture even more expert knowledge. As the experts' confidence in the program grew, so did their reliance in the program. This resulted in an substantial increase in productivity. An additional benefit is the high-performance graphics front-end that enables the field engineer to quickly pinpoint and respond to problems with a faster rate of response.

knowledge base is the reason why the problem must be narrow in scope. Even narrow, well-defined problems can require large amounts of information and thousands of rules or relationships. The real challenge in building expert systems is to devise the knowledge base with its associated rules. Schlumberger (Reality Bytes 10–10) chose to have the users design their expert system, figuring the users knew the rules better than anyone else.

There are three types of expert systems in use today. They are defined by how the knowledge base is organized: by rules, frames, or cases.

### Rules

The heart of a rule-based ES is a set of logical rules. These **rules** are often complicated. Consider some of the rules that might be needed for an ES to evaluate bank loans, as shown in Figure 10.4. This example has been simplified to keep it short. There will usually be hundreds of rules or conditions to cover a wide variety of

**FIGURE 10.4**
**SAMPLE RULES FOR BANK LOAN**

First, compute the monthly income before taxes.

Next, compute the monthly payment of the loan.

If the payment is greater than 5% of income:

    Compute total of other loans payments.

    Compute payments as percent of monthly income.

    If this percent is less than 25%:

        If the new loan is less than 10%, make loan.

    Else:

        If total monthly expenses are less than 40% of income, make the loan.

    Else:

        If less than 50% and has been a customer for more than 5 years or if less than 60% and has been a customer for 10 years and has lived at the same address for 5 years, make the loan.

**FIGURE 10.5**

Decision tree for sample bank loan expert system. Parts of a knowledge base are often expressed as a decision tree. Each answer to a question leads to additional questions and eventually to a decision. Notice that questions sometimes require numeric answers but can also rely on subjective comments.

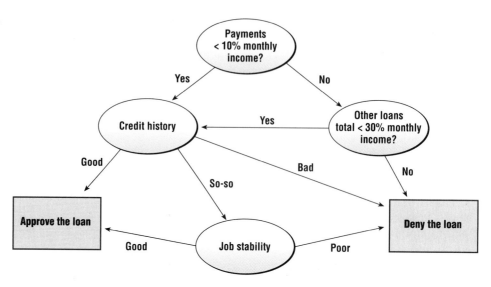

situations. Rules are often presented as If . . . Then . . . Else . . . statements. They can include Boolean conjunctions such as and, or, not. Figure 10.5 presents a portion of a *decision tree* that visually displays the rules.

The difficulty with any ES lies in determining these rules. Some of them will be easy. Others will be complex. Most of them will come from the expert. Unfortunately, most people do not usually express their thoughts in the form of these rules. Although we might follow rules of this sort, they can be difficult to express. It is even more difficult to remember all of the rules at one time. For instance, say you have lived in the same place for five years. A new person moves into the neighborhood. She asks you to describe the best ways to get to school, the mall, and the grocery store. Then she asks you for the best shortcuts if one of the roads is closed. This problem is relatively simple, but can you sit down right now and provide a complete list of all the rules?

### Frame- and Case-Based Reasoning

Another type of expert system uses a more complex type of information known as a frame. A rule-based expert system connects relatively small chunks of data based on numbers and key words. A frame-based system deals with entire frames or (screens) of data at one time. Marvin Minsky, one of the pioneers in AI research, emphasized the importance of frames. A *frame* consists of a related set of information that humans group together. Sometimes groupings can be arbitrary. In the lending example, one frame might consist of all of the basic customer data (loan amount, purpose, credit history, monthly payment, etc.). It could also include a picture of the item to be purchased.

Frames can be linked through hypertext, where selecting a key word on one frame leads to a related frame. In the loan example displayed in Figure 10.6, a loan officer might select the keyword *boat* to bring up a frame listing additional conditions to be examined for boat loans. Frames can also be linked through logic rules. After the loan officer enters the base data on the initial loan screen, the inference engine evaluates the data and displays new screens to collect additional data or to make a recommendation. In this situation, a frame-based system operates much like a rule-based system, but with larger chunks of data. Frames are objects that can contain

**FIGURE 10.6**

Frame-based ES for bank loan example. Instead of asking hundreds of detailed questions, some decisions are better suited to the use of frames. Each frame contains a group of related items. On analyzing the data, the ES uses internal rules to present the next frame.

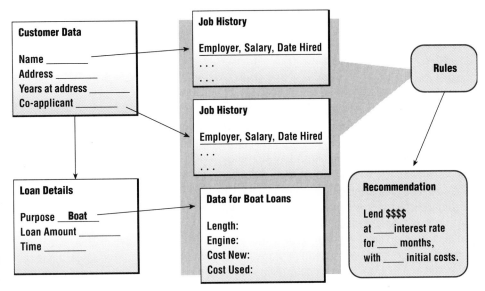

attributes and other objects. Frames can be defined that perform specific functions or operations.

**Case-based reasoning** is similar to frames, because it deals with larger pieces of data. The difference lies in the type of data contained in each frame: Entire cases (or situations) are described in one frame. As workers encounter problems and develop solutions, they write a short description of the situation. These cases are then available to solve future problems. When a manager encounters a problem, he or she asks the expert system to search the cases for similar situations. If the system finds a related case, the manager can retrieve the solution that was used. Many times, the initial workers will also leave notes and descriptions of related problems. Rather than match by words, the system attempts to match by occurrences of a certain activity. General Dynamics (Reality Bytes 10–11) used this approach to keep track of lost and damaged parts.

Case-based reasoning is particularly applicable to the higher-level components of business. For many years, strategic planners have tried to capture and record specific instances of an activity. If different problems in business could be identified, codified, and searched, it would be easier to train new managers to participate in strategic solutions for the business. The difficulty, of course, is categorizing the variables. Previously, someone had to categorize all of the individual cases by using a keyword system. The user would then search for a case by using the predefined set of keywords.

In case-based reasoning, the case approach is conceptual rather than based on individual words. As a result, the traditional Boolean rules do not work well. Through categorization, case-based reasoning connects frames and allows searching to be accomplished on larger components by searching for concepts and ideas instead of keywords.

## Knowledge Engineers

With the importance of descriptive data and complex rules, it can be difficult to determine how an expert system should function. In many cases, it is difficult for

## Reality Bytes    10–11   GENERAL DYNAMICS ELECTRIC BOAT DIVISION

The Electric Boat Division of General Dynamics has used Case-based reasoning to keep track of and repair lost, defective, or damaged parts. This area included any situation that did not conform to a standard requirement.

The programming team developed a case-based reasoning system that would interactively ask users for information about nonconformance. The system then searched its documentation knowledge base to find cases that represent the best potential resolutions.

Stuart Brown, project engineer, originally wanted to take a database approach. This would enable each project group to come up with its own solution every time. Although the database let him store and access information about various nonconforming solutions, it did not work; because it did not provide a way to evaluate the results.

Next Brown looked at expert rule-based systems. The system was too brittle, however, to be rule-directed. According to Brown, "If one rule was changed, the group had to start all over again."

The two most traditional searching mechanisms were discounted in the effort to develop the parts system. Databases search on a specific item of data. This technique can be expanded to include connectors such as *if, then, and,* and *or.* If, however, a "higher-level" search is needed, the system often cannot match accordingly. Expert systems search based upon a rule designation. A series of events is entered into the system. Rules then drive the system as it compares each event to determine whether it matches the defined rule. If a match is found, the system proceeds to the next level of comparison.

Case-based reasoning became the technology of choice because it changed the paradigm for the searching process. Engineers approached the nonconforming part problem from a case rather than a part basis. This meant that the engineers indexed and searched for a solution based on the instances or examples of what was wrong. They did not do so based on defective parts. As a result, case-based reasoning became the methodology of choice because it enabled searching to be accomplished by case occurrence rather than defective part.

human experts to express how they make decisions. Once these obstacles are overcome, the data and rules need to be described in a form that the computer can understand and evaluate.

With the increasing use of expert systems, ES specialists have evolved during the last few years. Knowledge engineers are trained to deal with experts to derive the rules needed to create an expert system. The engineers also convert the data and rules into the format needed by the expert system. The format varies depending on the type of expert system being created. Some systems require a series of if-then rules; others operate from decision trees or tables, and some require the engineer to build and link frames.

When there are several experts involved in a problem or when it will take considerable time to develop the system, it will be better to hire a knowledge engineer to design and build the expert system. When workers thoroughly understand the issues, with some additional training they can be the knowledge engineers and build their own system.

### Creating an ES

There are two basic ways to create an expert system: (1) hiring a programmer to write custom software or (2) using commercial ES shell software to evaluate rules. For some problems, you can also buy a prepackaged solution, but the system was originally created by one of the two basic methods.

Older expert systems were typically written using a special language like LISP or Prolog. These languages work well with text data but require specially trained programmers, making it very expensive to create an ES this way. These two languages are still in use today, but programmers are also using object-oriented languages like C++ to build expert systems.

More commonly today, an ES is built from an **expert system shell.** This program provides a way to collect data, enter rules, talk to users, present results, and evaluate the rules. To create an ES, you just need to know what data you need and all of the rules. Once you express this knowledge base in the format used by the shell's inference engine, the shell takes care of the other problems. There are many ES shells available on a wide variety of computers.

To understand how to create an ES, consider the bank loan example. A typical dialogue with the user (the loan clerk) appears in Figure 10.7. Notice that the ES begins by asking some basic information-gathering questions. The responses of the user are underlined. Once the basic data is collected, the ES performs some computations and follows the built in rules. Notice that the ES follows the rule that asks for the other loan payments. However, the loan clerk does not know about this rule, so he or she asks for clarification. This ability to ask questions is a powerful feature of expert systems.

Once you have collected all of the rules involved in the problem, you enter them into the ES shell. The shell lets you type in the questions you want to ask the user. You define the calculations and tell the shell how to look up any other information you need (e.g., the interest rates for auto loans). You then enter the conditions that tell the shell what questions to ask next. If there are many rules with complex interactions, it is more difficult to enter the rules into the shell. However, as illustrated in Figure 10.8, it is generally easier to use a shell than to have programmers create the system from scratch in LISP or Prolog.

One advantage of ES shells is that you generally have to enter only the basic rules and data. As the user enters the data, the shell performs the calculations and follows

**FIGURE 10.7**

Bank loan sample screen. An expert system carries on a dialog with the user. The ES asks questions and uses the answers to ask additional questions. The user can ask the ES to explain a decision or a question. Hence the ES can be used for training purposes.

```
              Welcome to the Loan Evaluation System.
What is the purpose of the loan? car
How much money will be loaned? 10,000
For how many years? 5

The current interest rate is 10%.
The payment will be $212.47 per month.

What is the annual income? 24,000

What is the total monthly payments of other loans?
Why?

Because the payment is more than 10% of the monthly income.
What is the total monthly payments of other loans? 50.00

The loan should be approved, because there is only a 2% chance
of default.
```

FIGURE 10.8

Expert system development. Once the knowledge is provided by an expert, there are two basic methods used to build an ES. One method is with an expert system shell, or software that already knows how to store and evaluate rules and handle the user interface. The other approach is to hire programmers and write the entire ES from scratch. Special-purpose languages like LISP and Prolog make the job a little easier, but custom programming is still expensive and time-consuming.

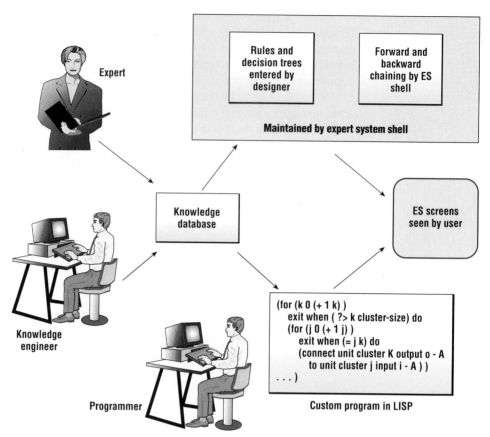

the rules. The shell also automatically answers the user questions. You do not have to be a computer programmer to create an ES with a shell. With training, many users can create their own expert systems using a shell. However, there are many dangers inherent in ES development, so it helps to have someone evaluate and test the resulting system.

## Reasoning

Expert systems usually perform two types of reasoning: forward chaining and backward chaining. **Forward chaining** is where the shell traces your rules from the data entry to a recommendation. In the bank example, forward chaining is used to display the questions and perform the calculations. For example, when the ES realizes that the payment amount is greater than 10 percent of the customer's monthly income, the corresponding rule is utilized. The ES works down the list of rules and evaluates each condition. If the condition is true, the ES does whatever the rule says, and we say that the rule has been fired or **triggered.** Eventually, if all the rules have been entered correctly, the system follows the rules and reaches a conclusion. Generally, the system will present some information indicating how sure it is of the decision. In the example, it uses historical data to indicate only a 2 percent chance of default on the loan.

With **backward chaining,** the user enters a "conclusion" and asks the expert system to see whether the rules support that conclusion. Consider the lending example using the decision tree displayed in Figure 10.5. The bank is investigating the possibility of discrimination and has pulled representative applications from several categories of borrowers. For each of the applicants, the manager wants to determine whether that person should have been granted a loan. A backward chaining expert system begins with the hypothesized conclusion (e.g., that the applicant should have been granted the loan). It examines rules by looking at the conclusion and decides whether the premise supports the conclusion. For example, it might note that there is a poor credit history, hence the loan could not have been granted on the strength of past credit. So the ES next evaluates job stability. If job stability was "good," it traces back and re-examines the credit history. If it finds that credit history was "bad," it concludes that the applicant should not receive the loan. The backward chaining continues until the conclusion is found to be supported or rejected, or there is insufficient data to make a decision.

As you attempt to create an expert system, you should take a broad look at the rules before you begin. Some tasks and decisions simply cannot be described in enough detail to justify the use of an expert system. For example, Manufacturer's Hanover Trust Bank (Reality Bytes 10–12) attempted to model the decisions of their financial traders. However, in many cases, there were no clear-cut rules. It will be difficult to get projects of this sort to work.

---

### ◢ Reality Bytes ◢ 10–12 MANUFACTURER'S HANOVER TRUST BANK: INVESTMENT BANKING SECTOR

At Manufacturer's Hanover Trust Bank of New York a knowledge-based expert system assists securities traders in the buy-and-sell process. The Technical Analysis and Reasoning Assistant, a securities and foreign exchange trading application, is built on the Knowledge Engineering Environment of Intellicorp.

The most difficult part of creating the ES was obtaining expert knowledge from the bank's "experts." Trading provides no clear-cut answers. According to Bruce Conner, vice-president of the investment banking sector, "A good trader may be right only 65 percent of the time. This leaves a wide margin for error. Since each trader has a different philosophy or approach to trading, the system had to be able to be tailored to each trader."

This project was extended in 1989 with the development of the Inspector. This auditing tool for off-market trading was developed using Neuron Data's Nexpert Object Tool. The goal of this system was to ensure trades were made for reasonable rates at reasonable times while maintaining large transaction volumes.

SOURCE: Mitch Betts, "Expert System Joins Fraud Squad," *Computerworld*, May 7, 1990, p. 111.

Sabina Skulsky, "Success Often Elusive for Advanced Tech Group," *Computerworld*, July 9, 1990, p. 88. Copyright 1990 by Computerworld, Inc., Framingham, MA 01701—Reprinted from *Computerworld*.

---

## Limitations of Expert Systems

Expert systems are useful tools that can be applied to several specialized problems. However, there are several important drawbacks to their design and use. First, they can only be created for specific, narrowly defined problems. Some complex problems contain too many rules with too many interactions. It quickly becomes impossible to express all of the interrelationships. For example, it is currently impossible to create a medical diagnostic system that covers all possible diseases. However, Mycin, an early ES, was created to assist doctors in diagnosing infectious blood disorders, which is a much narrower field.

Another problem that users and designers have encountered is that it can be difficult to modify the knowledge base in an expert system. As the environment or problem changes, we need to update the expert system. The changes are

**COMMON LIMITATIONS OF EXPERT SYSTEMS**

- *Fragile Systems:* If the underlying process changes or the environment generates changes, the rules need to be revised. Changes in one rule might force us to rebuild the entire system.
- *Mistakes:* Who is responsible when an expert system makes a mistake? The expert? Several experts? The novice operating the ES? The company that uses it? The company who created it? The knowledge engineers who built it?

- *Vague Rules:* Many times the domain expert cannot completely describe the rules.
- *Conflicting Experts:* If there are conflicting experts or rules, who will decide? Which one is right?
- *Unforeseen Events:* What happens if the ES faces an unexpected problem or a new event? Experts solve these problems through creativity and learning. Expert systems cannot.

relatively easy to make if they affect only a few rules. However, many expert systems use hundreds of interrelated rules. It is not always clear which rules need to be altered, and changes to one rule can affect many of the others. In essence, as the situation changes, the company is forced to completely redesign the expert system. In fast-changing industries, it would cost too much to continually redesign an expert system. In the lending example, a policy change based on monthly income would be relatively easy to implement. On the other hand, some changes in policy would force us to completely redesign the expert system. For instance, we might decide to grant loans to almost everyone but charge riskier people higher interest rates.

Probably the greatest difficulty in creating an expert system is determining the logic rules or frames that will lead to the proper conclusions. It requires finding an expert who understands the process and can express the rules in a form that can be used by the expert system.

## Management Issues of Expert Systems

Creating and building an expert system involves many of the same issues encountered in building any other information system. For instance, the problem must be well-defined, the designers must communicate with the users, and management and financial controls must be in place to evaluate and control the project.

However, expert systems raise additional management issues. Two issues are particularly important: (1) If we transfer the knowledge from an expert to an expert system, is there still a need for the expert, and (2) what happens when the expert system encounters an exception that it was not designed to solve?

The answer to the first question depends on the individual situation. In cases where the problem is relatively stable over time, it is possible to transfer expert knowledge to software—enabling the firm to reduce the number of experts needed. If this action results in layoffs, the experts will need additional incentives to cooperate with the development of the system. In other cases, the firm will continue to need the services of the experts to make changes to the ES and to solve new problems. Before starting an ES project, managers need to determine which situation applies and negotiate appropriately with the experts.

The second problem can be more difficult to identify. Consider what happens when the workers rely on an expert system to make decisions and management cuts costs by hiring less-skilled workers. The workers no longer understand the system or the procedures—they simply follow decisions made by the rules in the ES. If an exception arises, the ES may not know how to respond or it may respond inappropriately. A customer would be left to deal with an underskilled, unmotivated worker who does not understand the process and cannot resolve the problem.

**ADDITIONAL SPECIALIZED PROBLEMS**

Further research in artificial intelligence examined how humans are different from computers. This research led to tools that can be used for certain types of problems. Some of the ideas come from the early days of computers, but it has taken until now for machines to be developed that are fast enough to handle the sophisticated tasks. Ideas in AI have come from many disciplines, from biology to psychology to computer science and engineering.

There are six broad areas where humans are noticeably better than computers: pattern recognition, performing multiple tasks at one time, movement, speech recognition, vision, and language comprehension. Some of these concepts are related, but they all represent features that would make machines much more useful. Even with current technological improvements, most observers agree that it will be several years before these features are available.

---

## ▼ BUSINESS USES OF RESEARCH IN ARTIFICIAL INTELLIGENCE ▲

*Expert Systems:* Building systems that help novices achieve the results of experts.

*Pattern Recognition:* Identifying patterns in sound, vision, and data. Driven by neural network research.

*Voice and Speech Recognition:* Recognizing users by voice, and converting spoken words into written text.

*Language Comprehension:* Understanding the meaning in written (or spoken) text.

*Massively Parallel Computers:* Performing thousands of tasks simultaneously to solve complex problems.

*Robotics and Motion:* Building machines that have a high range of movement, physical sensitivity, and the ability to navigate.

*Statistics, Uncertainty, and Fuzzy Logic:* Finding ways to solve statistical problems easier. Dealing with associations and comparative data.

---

### Pattern Recognition and Neural Networks

One of the early issues in AI research was the question of how human brains worked. Some people suggested that to make intelligent computers, the computers would have to work the same way as the human brain does. An important conclusion from this research is that humans are good at pattern recognition.

Humans use pattern recognition thousands of times a day. It enables us to recognize our co-workers, to spot trends in data, to relate today's problems to last year's changes. There are many problems in business that could benefit from machines that could reliably recognize patterns. What characteristics do "good" borrowers have in common? How will changes in the economy affect next year's sales? How are sales affected by management styles of the sales managers?

Pattern recognition is used by people to solve problems. It is one of the reasons we use cases to teach you to solve business problems. If you notice that a problem is similar to a case you have seen before, you can use your prior knowledge to solve the problem. Imagine how useful it would be if an expert system could recognize patterns automatically. For example, Mellon Bank uses a neural network to spot credit card fraud. In some cases, it identified fraudulent patterns before the human investigators spotted them. It is faster and more accurate than an earlier expert system. The original expert system looked at a limited number of variables and indicated 1,000 suspects a day—far more than actually existed, and too many for the investigators to keep up with. The new neural network system examines more variables, lists fewer false suspects, and adjusts its methods on its own.

A finance manager might use a form of pattern recognition to search for patterns in the financial markets to forecast future movements. Of course, with thousands of other people searching for patterns, the patterns would not last very long. Similarly, a banker might use pattern recognition to classify loan prospects.

One current technique that is used to spot patterns is neural networks. Initial study indicated that the brain is a collection of cells called *neurons* that have many connections to each other. Each of these cells is relatively simple, but there are approximately 100 million of them. In some respects, a neuron resembles a simple computer. It can be at rest (off), or it can fire a message (on). A neuron responds to other cells (input) to send messages to other neurons (output). A collection of these cells is called a **neural network.** Human neural cells are actually more complicated, but researchers have focused on this simplified form.

Computer researchers have been able to build similar networks using computer software. There are also computer chips available today that function as neural networks. Most of the existing examples are small. There are two ways to measure these networks: (1) the number of neurons and (2) the number of interconnections between the individual cells. It is fairly easy to increase the number of cells, but the number of possible interconnections increases very rapidly. For instance, if there are four cells, there are six possible connections. With 10 cells, there are 45 connections. With 1,000 cells, there are half a million connections. In general if there are $N$ cells, there are $N(N-1)/2$ possible connections. For many purposes, we will not need every possible connection, but you can see that if there are millions of cells, we would still want to incorporate a large number of connections. Most existing networks use only a few thousand cells.

Figure 10.9 presents a version of how a neural network converts an array of input sensors into a hidden layer and then stores patterns on output layer. One useful feature of the neural network approach is that it is fairly good at identifying patterns even if some of the inputs are missing.

What can a neural network do that cannot be done with traditional computers? The basic answer is "nothing." However, they provide a new way of thinking about problems. More importantly, with hardware specifically designed to process neural networks, some difficult problems can be solved faster than with traditional computers. The primary objective of neural networks is the ability to store and recognize patterns. A well-designed network is capable of identifying patterns (such as faces or sounds) even if some of the data is missing or altered. The army has designed a neural network system to process visual data that can drive a vehicle at speeds up to 55 miles per hour.

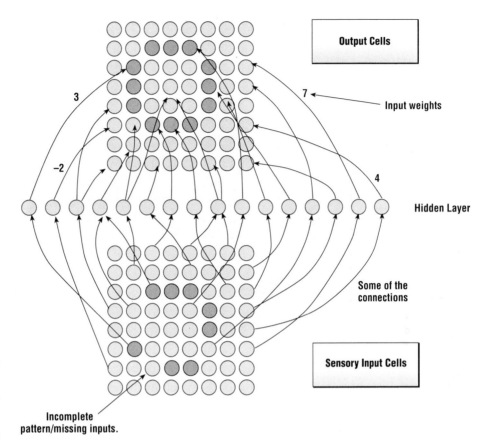

**FIGURE 10.9**
Neural net for pattern matching. Input cells convert data to binary form. The required hidden layer recodes the inputs into a new internal representation. The connections represent outputs from the lower layers. When total input levels exceed some value, the receiving cell fires. Any cell can be connected to many other cells. Input weights are determined by training. The output cells are triggered when total input levels from the connections exceed some threshold. Note that a pattern can be recognized even if some input cells are wrong.

Another advantage that researchers hope to achieve with neural networks is the ability to simplify training of the computer. In the discussion of expert systems, we noted that changes in the business often mean that knowledge engineers have to redesign the entire expert system. A neural network has a limited ability to "learn" by examining past data. Feeding it proper examples establishes the interconnection weights that enable the network to identify patterns. In theory, neural networks have the ability to learn on their own. In practice, the learning stage is the most difficult component of building a neural network. Most times the designer has to understand the problem and provide hints to the network, along with good sample data. In many ways, training a neural network uses basic properties of statistics related to data sampling and regression.

## Machine Vision

There are many uses for machine vision in manufacturing environments. Machines are used in optical character recognition, welding and assembly, and quality control. Mechanical sensors have several advantages over humans. They do not suffer from fatigue, they can examine a broader spectrum of light (including ultraviolet and infrared), and they can quickly focus at many different levels (including microscopic).

On the other hand, traditional computer systems are literal in their vision. It is hard for computers to compare objects of different sizes or to match mirror images. It is hard for machines to determine whether differences between objects are minor and should be ignored or if they are major distinguishing features.

The Department of Defense has funded Carnegie Mellon University to develop software that is used to automatically drive vehicles. One system (Ranger) is used in an army ambulance that can drive itself over rough terrain for up to 16 km. ALVINN is a separate road-following system that has driven vehicles at speeds over 110 kph for as far as 140 km.

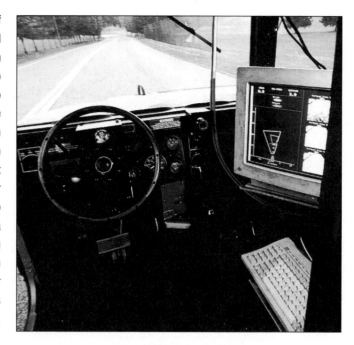

Say you are shown a picture of your instructor, and someone adds or subtracts features to it, such as bigger eyebrows, longer hair, or glasses. In most cases, you would still recognize the face. Computers would have a great deal of difficulty with that problem because they see pictures as a collection of dots (or lines). How does the computer know which changes are important and which are minor?

If computers were better at pattern recognition, there would be thousands of uses for vision recognition systems in manufacturing and business. Neural networks have shown some success in these solving these problems, but they are still somewhat slow and inaccurate. Again, problems that have a narrower scope are easier to solve. For example, the U.S. Post Office uses optical scanners to recognize handwritten zip codes on mail. Yet they rely on humans to read (and key in) addresses and cities.

## Voice and Speech Recognition

We hardly need to discuss the benefits of having a machine that can understand human speech. Most people can speak faster than they can type, so voice input to create and edit documents would save a considerable amount of time and money. Voice input is useful for hands-free operations. A quality control worker might need both hands to inspect a product. Speech recognition enables the worker to take notes that can be edited and printed later. Surgeons gain the same advantages. Additionally, voice input would eliminate the need for a keyboard, and possibly a monitor, making computers much more portable. Dreams of advanced speech recognition have been around for at least 40 years, but we still do not have a system that can recognize continuous speech as effectively as humans.

There are two main types of speech recognition systems available today. Both types are available on personal computers. The first type, such as the system by DragonDictate (Reality Bytes 10–13), must be trained before it can be used. The user speaks a list of words and the computer stores the base patterns. Once the system has been trained, the computer tries to match each word. The words must be spoken clearly and separately. A more advanced form of speech recognition does not require

## Reality Bytes ◢ 10-13 DragonDictate from Dragon Systems, Inc.

DragonDictate is the first commercial, general purpose, voice-driven word processor. It enables personal computer users to use word processors, spreadsheets, and databases to draft memos, reports, or papers completely by speaking rather than typing. Applications include use by the disabled, people in "hands-busy/eyes-busy" environments (such as radiologists who must read x-rays and dictate diagnoses in the dark) and business people who want to exploit the advantages of computer technology but do not know how to type.

Based on a vocabulary of 30,000 words, DragonDictate can recognize discrete words that are separated by a pause of about one quarter of a second. As long as words are consistently pronounced, the program can "learn" the individual's accent and manner of speaking. The more the individual uses it and as time progresses, the program adapts more closely to the individual speaking style of the user. If a word sounds the same but has more than one spelling, DragonDictate displays a list of like-sounding words so that the user can select an alternative with a single keystroke or voice command.

The recognition software uses acoustic word models to identify the sound of a word and statistical language models to establish the likelihood of the word in a given context. Each time the user dictates a word, the system updates the models with information about the user's speech pattern. DragonDictate is currently being extended to German, Spanish, French, Italian, and Dutch.

training. Some manufacturers (such as IBM) offer systems that can understand a dictionary of up to 2,000 words spoken by any native (North American) English speaker. On fast computer systems, the computer can even recognize continuous speech (no pauses).

Nonetheless, speech recognition is still in its infancy. Some difficulties include the fact that most speakers pronounce words differently because all languages have various dialects. Even people who speak the same language sometimes have difficulty understanding various accents. A second problem is homonyms. Words like *to, too,* and *two* cannot be distinguished based on sound. We determine the difference based on how they are used. Third, it is difficult to determine punctuation based on sound. Many English sentences can completely change meaning if the punctuation is changed. Finally, in order to correctly understand someone, it is necessary to understand the context of the statement. For example, slang can be particularly hard to understand. The phrase "It's bad" can have many meanings. Finally, the interpretation of language changes over time. Hence, a computer that wishes to understand human speech will have to be capable of learning new phrases and new interpretations. Consider the two interpretations presented by Figure 10.10, which could be commands spoken to the computer.

**FIGURE 10.10**
VOICE RECOGNITION AND PUNCTUATION

There are inherent problems with voice recognition. Punctuation and implicit meaning are two difficult areas. Even communication between people has frequent misinterpretations.

See what happens when you give a computer the first set of instructions, but it does not hear the commas correctly and thinks you said the second line:

```
(1)  Copy the red, file the blue, delete the yellow mark.
(2)  Copy the red file, the blue delete, the yellow mark.
```

Consider the following sentence, which can be interpreted by humans but would not make much sense to a computer that tries to interpret it literally.

```
I saw the Grand Canyon flying to New York.
```

Despite all of these difficulties, work has been progressing steadily on voice input devices. It is possible that within the next few years there will be voice input systems available for many more tasks. These systems will not be *perfect,* but they will be *acceptable.* The point is that communication between humans is not perfect, so we cannot expect communication between machines and humans to be perfect either.

## Language Comprehension

Related to voice recognition is the issue of language comprehension, or the ability of the computer to actually understand what we are saying. Technically the two topics are separate, since it might be possible to have a machine understand what we type onto a keyboard. Language comprehension exists when the machine actually understands what we mean. One test of comprehension would be the ability of the computer to carry on a conversation. In fact, Alan Turing, a British pioneer in the computer field suggested the **Turing test** for computer intelligence. In this test, a human judge communicates with a machine and another person in a separate room. If the judge cannot determine which user is the machine and which is a person, the machine should be considered to be intelligent. Some people have tested this concept (using specific topics). Other people have noted that perhaps you do not have to be intelligent to carry on a conversation.

Language comprehension would be useful because it would make it easier for humans to use computers. Instead of needing to learn a language such as SQL to access data, imagine being able to get answers to questions asked in English (or some other **natural language**). Of course, any natural language has its limitations. The greatest danger with language comprehension is that the machine will interpret your question incorrectly, and give you the "right" answer to the "wrong" question.

 **LANGUAGE TRANSLATION**

One useful application of language comprehension is the ability to translate human speech from one language to another. Early translators in the 1960s and 1970s were crude, relying on straight substitutions of dictionary words. More recent translator programs can handle conjugation, idioms, and some evaluation of context. The most remarkable device to date is a tabletop machine invented by Sony that can translate spoken Japanese into English with a delay of only a few seconds.

## Speed and Massively Parallel Computers

For many years, one advantage that humans had over machines was that people are capable of performing several tasks at the same time. Related to this capability is the concept that the human brain is organized as a collection of billions of relatively simple cells. Researchers quickly realized that although the computer industry continually produces faster processors, there are limits to how quickly they can be improved. Consequently, designers have been investigating computers that use hundreds or thousands of relatively inexpensive processors. This parallel, distributed-processing model enables the computer to work on many tasks at the same time. In some situations, such a machine could solve problems thousands of times faster than a traditional design. Some companies are experimenting with massively parallel machines that have 30 to 60 *thousand* processors.

Parallel processors enable the machine to work faster because each processor can work on one part of the job. The machine can literally do many operations at the same time. The catch is that to be useful, you need tasks that can be split into thousands of smaller pieces. What types of jobs are specially suited for these processors? Many mathematical computations can be split into pieces. These problems typically use computations on sets of numbers called *matrices.* Many scientific, engineering and statistical problems can be expressed in terms of matrices. Graphics is another area that can be enhanced with parallel processing. Images on a screen can be expressed as collections of thousands of dots or as vectors (matrices). The spectacular graphics you see in science fiction movies were probably generated on a parallel-processing supercomputer. Parallel processors are also used to search huge databases, by assigning each processor to one section of the database. Figure 10.11 shows how it is straightforward to use massively parallel systems for matrix computations, because each processor can be assigned to an independent calculation.

Neural networks are another example of problems that can benefit from using massively parallel machines. Computations for sections of the network, or each input cell, can be assigned to one processor. A common difficulty with these systems is the need to share data and organize the problem so each processor can function independently.

## Robotics and Motion

Modern manufacturing relies heavily on robots, and the capabilities of robots continually increase. Most existing robots are specialized machines that perform a limited number of tasks, such as welding or painting. In many firms, there is little need for a general-purpose robot that can "do everything." However, one area that remains troublesome is the ability of machines to move. Making a machine that can navigate through an unknown or crowded area is especially difficult. Some work is being done

**FIGURE 10.11**

Massively parallel processing. One way to deal with some complex problems is to split them into thousands (or millions) of smaller tasks. With a massively parallel-processing machine, there are thousands of small (inexpensive) processors. Each processor is assigned a portion of the job. They are particularly useful for tasks involving large matrices.

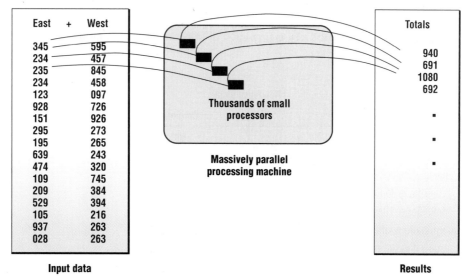

| East | + | West |
|------|---|------|
| 345 | | 595 |
| 234 | | 457 |
| 235 | | 845 |
| 234 | | 458 |
| 123 | | 097 |
| 928 | | 726 |
| 151 | | 926 |
| 295 | | 273 |
| 195 | | 265 |
| 639 | | 243 |
| 474 | | 320 |
| 109 | | 745 |
| 209 | | 384 |
| 529 | | 394 |
| 105 | | 216 |
| 937 | | 263 |
| 028 | | 263 |

**Thousands of small processors**

**Massively parallel processing machine**

| Totals |
|--------|
| 940 |
| 691 |
| 1080 |
| 692 |
| . |
| . |
| . |

**Input data**                    **Results**

in this area. In 1992, a group of researchers created a machine that could navigate through a room at the rate of about a foot per hour.

Although science fiction writers have already devised thousands of uses for "intelligent" robots, there is still a long ways to go. Part of the problem is that the concept of robots is closely tied to the issues of vision, pattern recognition, and intelligence. In order to navigate a crowded room, a robot needs to be able to see objects. It must also recognize each object and have a basic understanding of its characteristics. For instance, a robot needs to recognize and know the difference between a table and a wall to understand that it can go around a table but not a wall.

## Statistics, Uncertainty, and Fuzzy Logic

Many situations can benefit from the use of applied statistics. Statistics enable us to examine large sets of data and spot patterns and relationships. It also enables us to define the concept of uncertainty. In life, we can rarely predict any outcome with complete certainty. There is always a chance that some random event will arise, affecting our system and producing a different outcome. By assigning probabilities to various events, we can evaluate the effect of these random events.

The catch is that statistics is a relatively complex field, and it is often hard to apply in practice. Evaluating millions of data points, determining interactions, and estimating probabilities is not an easy task, even with top-of-the-line computer tools. These tasks often require the services of an expert in statistical analysis. Yet, people face uncertainty every day and manage to make decisions. Sometimes we might not make the "best" decision, but we have found ways to cope with the main issues. One common method of coping is our ability to use subjective and incomplete descriptions. When a person declares that "it is cold outside," listeners in the same area understand the statement. Yet, "cold" is a subjective term. Forty degrees can be cold to a resident of Phoenix, but it would be considered "pleasant" to a resident of Wisconsin in mid-January.

It is possible to model these concepts with statistical definitions that involve means and standard deviations. However, it can be difficult to derive the underlying statistical functions and implement them for each situation. To overcome these limitations, Lofti Zadeh created a system that attempts to mimic the way humans perceive uncertainty. His definition of fuzzy sets and fuzzy logic use definitions of subjective terms like *cold, hot, sometimes, fast,* and *slow.* The logic system defines a way to combine these terms to reach descriptive "conclusions." Figure 10.12 illustrates that the key is that each definition refers to a range.

**FIGURE 10.12**

Subjective definitions. Many human tasks are characterized by subjectivity. When we say that the weather is "cold" we rarely specify an exact temperature. Instead, we are making a comparison to a reference point. Distances farther from the reference point provide a stronger impression of the change. Machine systems can be based on these principles using statistics or "fuzzy-logic" definitions. These interpretations often make it easier for people to deal with machines.

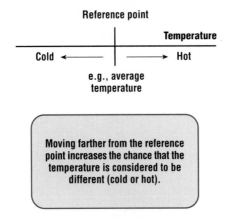

In 1994, Charles Elkan showed that fuzzy logic is conceptually similar to more traditional methodologies. However, manufacturers (especially Japanese companies) have found it easier to design products using fuzzy logic. The fuzzy definitions also correspond with the way humans perceive the machine. Fuzzy logic is used in washing machine settings, elevator controls, and bullet train controllers (where operators can set controls like *hotter* or *faster*).

**DSS, ES, AND AI**

The differences among decision support systems, expert systems, and artificial intelligence can be confusing at first. Take a simple problem and see how a computer system based on each method might operate. A common problem for many businesses is determining how much inventory they should hold. Figure 10.13 discusses the differences among a DSS, ES, and AI approach to the inventory problem.

In the simplest transaction-processing system, the manager would enter a reorder point into the database for each inventory item. The computer would monitor the daily sales, and whenever the reorder point was reached, it would place a new order or perhaps print a daily listing of all products that needed to be ordered.

One problem with the simple method is trying to decide what number to use for the reorder point, and how many items should be ordered each time. There is a management model that can be used to determine the *economic order quantity* (EOQ). Under certain assumptions, the model tells you when and how much to reorder if you know specific values such as the cost of reordering, the holding cost of the inventory, and how fast items are being removed (sold). There are more complex versions of the model. A decision support system could provide the basic data values, and it could evaluate the various models. It might graph the sales and inventory trends to help you make your decision. It could even perform some simulations to show you what might happen under different sales assumptions.

**FIGURE 10.13**

Comparison of techniques. A DSS could collect sales and cost data. It would then automatically monitor sales and send messages to suppliers at appropriate reorder points. An ES could help managers decide if they should use economic order quantity or just-in-time inventory. An AI would examine past sales and inventory data and make recommendations on which inventory method should be used.

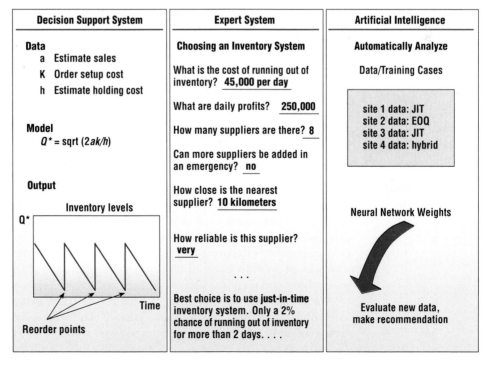

| Decision Support System | Expert System | Artificial Intelligence |
|---|---|---|
| **Data**<br>  a   Estimate sales<br>  K   Order setup cost<br>  h   Estimate holding cost<br><br>**Model**<br>  $Q^* = \text{sqrt}\,(2ak/h)$<br><br>**Output**<br> Inventory levels graph with $Q^*$, Time, Reorder points | **Choosing an Inventory System**<br><br>What is the cost of running out of inventory?  **45,000 per day**<br><br>What are daily profits?  **250,000**<br><br>How many suppliers are there?  **8**<br><br>Can more suppliers be added in an emergency?  **no**<br><br>How close is the nearest supplier?  **10 kilometers**<br><br>How reliable is this supplier?  **very**<br><br>. . .<br><br>Best choice is to use **just-in-time** inventory system. Only a 2% chance of running out of inventory for more than 2 days. . . . | **Automatically Analyze**<br><br>Data/Training Cases<br><br>site 1 data: JIT<br>site 2 data: EOQ<br>site 3 data: JIT<br>site 4 data: hybrid<br><br>Neural Network Weights<br><br>Evaluate new data, make recommendation |

During the last few years, many companies have moved away from the EOQ approach to inventory. Instead, they use a just-in-time (JIT) system. In order for JIT to work, it requires close cooperation with the suppliers. In many cases, it requires your firm's computer to send and receive messages from the suppliers' computers. The big question faced by companies is which inventory method they should use. The choice depends on factors such as the costs of running out, cooperation of suppliers, and distance from suppliers. If you had to answer this question for many different products or stores, it might be helpful to create an expert system. An expert could create the rules. Individual managers would then use the system to evaluate each product or store.

What if we had a computer system that could automatically determine the rules for the expert system? An artificially intelligent machine could look at the underlying data (sales, costs, suppliers, etc.) and derive the rules that indicate when you should use EOQ models and when you should use JIT inventory systems. It might even come up with a completely different system.

## MACHINE INTELLIGENCE

What would it take to convince you that a machine is intelligent? The Turing test has been proposed as one method. Many other tests have been proposed in the past. At one time, people suggested that a machine that could win at chess would be intelligent. Today's chess playing computers have beaten all but the top human players. Another test proposed was the ability to solve mathematical problems—in particular, the ability to solve mathematical proofs. An early AI program created in the 1950s could do that. Today, for a few hundred dollars, you can buy programs that manipulate mathematical symbols to solve equations.

Some people have suggested that intelligence involves creativity. Creativity is probably as hard to measure as intelligence. Even so, there are examples of computer creativity. A few years ago, a programmer developed a system that created music. The interesting feature of the program was that it allowed people to call on the phone and vote on the music. The computer used this feedback to change its next composition. Not only was the computer creative, it was learning and adapting, albeit in a limited context.

Although there are limited business applications to much of this current research, there are two main reasons for staying abreast of the capabilities. First, anything that makes the computer easier to use will make it more useful and these techniques continue to improve. Second, you need to understand the current limitations to avoid costly mistakes.

## OBJECT ORIENTATION

A recent application of AI techniques has arisen in the context of networks and object orientation. A key problem with networks is searching for information across thousands of machines, each of which might use different definitions and protocols. Although networks dramatically improve communication, there are problems with maintaining the "interpretation" of the information from various systems. At heart, networks are built to transmit raw bits of data. Network managers commonly focus on hardware connections, access controls, and transmission of simple data formats.

We increasingly need to think of networks as transmitting entire objects—composed of data, pictures, spreadsheets, sounds, and video. From a pure transmission standpoint, any object can be decomposed into raw data bits and sent between computers. Where we run into problems is transferring objects between different software and different computers. For example, we could create a report object on one computer. We could then send it across a network to a colleague using different software on a different computer. The problem is that our coworker probably will not be able to use or modify the object. To transmit objects across a network, the hardware and software on each end must know how to use the object. It would be similar to sending a videotape to a friend in a different country. Although the tape can be sent across the "network," unless your friend has a machine that is compatible with yours, the tape is useless.

Having a global network that enables users to connect to hundreds of different computers poses additional problems. Each machine might require different commands to perform basic tasks. At this point in time, users need to know the commands and idiosyncrasies of each computer they wish to use. Throw in the fact that the hardware and software are constantly changing, and it becomes difficult to integrate data across these diverse operating environments.

One solution to this problem is to create software agents (Reality Bytes 10–14). *Agents* are object-oriented programs designed for networks that are written to perform specific tasks in response to user requests. The concept of object-orientation is important, because it means that agents know how to exchange object attributes and they have the ability to activate object functions in other agents. The tasks could be simple, such as finding all files on a network that refer to a specific topic. One key feature of agents is that they are designed to communicate with each other. As long as your agent knows the abilities or functions of another agent, they can exchange messages and commands. General Magic is a pioneering company that created a standard programming language for agents. With this language, agents can transfer themselves and run on other computers. Agents also have a degree of "intelligence." They can be given relatively general commands, which the agents reinterpret and apply to each situation they encounter.

## Reality Bytes ▸ 10–14 Sample Agents

Maxims is an agent that runs on a Macintosh computer to help users handle e-mail. It prioritizes, sorts, and deletes mail messages based on user preferences. It learns these preferences by observing the user read mail. For example, Maxim could quickly learn that you always delete messages broadcast to multiple users. Over time, it adds rules and gets better at predicting which messages you want to read. The same system that drives Maxim was used to create a scheduling agent. It helps users schedule meetings with groups of people. It remembers preferences, such as which people prefer morning meetings, and learns to assign priorities to various meetings.

NewT is a learning agent that filters news items for users. It monitors the huge stream of data produced by the Internet Usenet (Netnews). The user enters basic search criteria and NewT waits for matching articles. Items that match are presented to the user. As the user accepts or rejects them, NewT learns the user preferences and updates its internal rules. Users can share their preferences with colleagues by giving *trained* agents to other users.

A slightly different approach is used by Ringo, which is an agent that searches for and recommends music to users. With this system, Ringo agents talk to each other. As users listen to new music, they tell their Ringo agent if they liked it. As the agents talk with each other, they search for users with similar preferences. When they find them, they report the new music ratings back to their primary user.

**FIGURE 10.14**

Software agents. A personal software agent might be used to book a vacation. It would take your initial preferences and communicate with other agents to find sites that matched your preferences. It might also be able to negotiate prices with competing resorts.

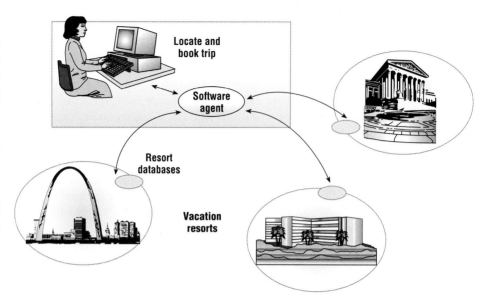

Consider an example illustrated by Figure 10.14. You have been working hard and decide to take a vacation. You want to go to a beach but do not have much money to spend. You are looking for a place where you can swim, scuba dive, and meet people at night. But you also want the place to have some secluded beaches where you can get away from the crowds and relax. You could call a travel agent and buy a package deal, but every agent you called just laughs and says that next time you should call three months ahead of time instead of only three days. You suspect that a beach resort probably has last-minute cancellations and you could get in, but how do you find out? There are thousands of possibilities. If all of the resort computers had automatic reservation agents, the task would be fairly easy. You would start an agent on your computer and tell it the features you want. Your agent sends messages to all of the automated resort agents looking for open spots at places that matched your features. When your agent finds something close, it brings back details and pictures to display on your screen. When you decide on a resort, the agent automatically makes the reservations.

Notice three important features of software agents. First, the agents need to know how to communicate. It is not as simple as transmitting raw data. They must understand the data and respond to questions. Second, imagine the amount of network traffic involved. In the vacation search example, your agent might have to contact thousands of other computers. Now picture what happens when a thousand other people do the same thing! Third, all of the agents are independent. You, and other computer owners, are free to create or modify your own agent. As long as there are standard methods for agents to exchange attributes and activate functions, they can be modified and improved. For instance, you might program your agent to weight the vacation spots according to some system, or you might teach it to begin its search in specific locations.

Programmers have begun to incorporate expert system and other AI capabilities into these agents. By adding a set of rules, the agent becomes more than just a simple search mechanism. The more complex the rules, the more "intelligent" it becomes, which means you have to do less work. In fact, software agents have the potential to dramatically increase the research in AI. Currently, because of limited standards and the difficulty of creating them, there are few examples of useful agents. As increasing numbers of people use agents and begin demanding more intelligence, it will become profitable for researchers to work harder at building reliable, intelligent software.

## SUMMARY

Complex decisions, such as diagnostic problems, require more sophisticated computer tools. Expert systems can be used to solve complex problems if the problem can be narrowed down to a specific problem. Expert systems ask questions of the users and trace through rules to make recommendations. The systems can also trace backward through the rules to explain how they arrived at various questions or conclusions. Expert systems can be built using shells that contain the logic needed to process the rules.

Research into making machines more intelligent has led to several techniques and tools that can be useful in solving some problems. Pattern recognition is being studied with neural networks. Pattern recognition problems are involved in handwriting and voice recognition, vision systems, and in statistical applications. Researchers are also working on robotics and motion—especially combined with vision systems that will enable robots to navigate their way through new areas. Massively parallel computers are being created to speed up computations of problems that can be examined in thousands of separate pieces.

These techniques are still young and have many limitations. One of their most important uses will

be the ability to improve the interaction between computers and humans. The better that computers can be adapted to humans, the easier it will be to use them. Voice recognition and language comprehension systems are important steps in that direction. Although current technology is still somewhat limited, considerable progress has been made over the last few years.

### A MANAGER'S VIEW

Research in artificial intelligence has led to tools that are useful to managers. In particular, expert systems are used to make repetitive decisions rapidly and more consistently using novice employees. Although they are powerful, expert systems can only be used to solve problems in a narrow domain. Even then, they can be hard to modify as the business changes. Neural networks represent a new approach to using computers. They are much better than most other systems at recognizing patterns and have been applied in scanners, handwriting recognition, vision systems, and speech recognition. Advances in robotics, motion, massively parallel computation, and vision systems offer additional capabilities for specific problems.

## KEY WORDS

| | | |
|---|---|---|
| artificial intelligence (AI), 456 | expert system shell, 471 | neural network, 476 |
| backward chaining, 472 | forward chaining, 472 | rules, 467 |
| case-based reasoning, 469 | knowledge base, 465 | triggered, 472 |
| expert system, 455 | natural language, 480 | Turing test, 480 |

## REVIEW QUESTIONS

1. What types of problems are particularly well-suited to expert systems?
2. What are the major differences between a decision support system and an expert system?
3. Do you think consumers would be happier if major decisions in banks were made by expert systems? Or would customers prefer to use a bank that advertised all decisions were made by humans?
4. What steps are involved in creating an expert system?
5. What research is being done in artificial intelligence?
6. Describe three situations that could benefit from the use of pattern recognition.
7. What types of problems are suited for massively parallel computer systems?
8. What tasks can benefit from existing voice recognition technology?
9. What are the three basic types of expert systems?
10. How is backward chaining used in expert systems?
11. How is case-based reasoning different from rule-based expert systems?
12. What is the Turing test? Do you think it is a reasonable test?
13. Why is it so hard to create a machine that can understand natural language?

## EXERCISES

1. Interview local managers or search the recent literature to find three diagnostic problems that could benefit from the use of expert systems. Where would you find an expert to assist with each of the situations?

2. What would it take to convince you that a computer system was intelligent? How close are existing computer systems to this standard? Do you think we might see intelligent machines within the next 5 or 10 years? Within your lifetime?

3. Interview an expert in some area and create an initial set of rules that you could use for an expert system. If you cannot find a cooperative expert, try researching one of the following topics in your library: fruit tree propagation and pruning (what trees are needed for cross-pollination, what varieties grow best in each region, what fertilizers are needed, when they should be pruned), requirements or qualifications for public assistance or some other governmental program (check government documents), legal requirements to determine whether a contract is in effect (check books on business law).

4. Search the computer literature to find the current state-of-the-art in voice and speech recognition. How many words can the best system recognize? What about continuous speech? Does it require training?

5. For the following problems identify those that would be best suited for an expert system and those that would use a decision support system. Explain why.

   • Investing in the stock market.
   • Annual evaluation of suppliers and negotiation support.
   • Choosing a marketing campaign.
   • Customer telephone support lines for questions and problems (not orders).

   • Monitoring and Identifying causes of inventory shrinkage.

6. Describe how artificial intelligence techniques could be used to enhance software agents. What additional capabilities could they be given? Give an example of the application of a "more intelligent" agent.

7. Assume that you have a software agent to handle your personal mail and other tasks on the Internet. Write a set of rules for your agent to follow.

8. Describe a situation, other than the vacation search example, where you would want to use software agents to perform some task. Describe the features of all agents, including attributes and functions that they can perform.

9. Who will pay for the creation of software agents? What about the use of the agents? Should (or could) users be charged every time their agent calls another one? What about network usage? What would happen if your agent used your telephone to connect to thousands of other agents?

 **Rolling Thunder Database**

1. Identify an area in which an expert system could help. Be specific and explain the advantages of using an ES for that area. Where would you find an expert to assist with creating the knowledge domain?

2. Describe how new technologies might be used to improve decisions at the Rolling Thunder Bicycle company. What experimental and future technologies should we watch closely? If you could create an "intelligent" computer system for the company, what would it do and how would it be used to increase profits?

## ADDITIONAL READING

Anthes, Gary. "AI Makes Mark in Corporate World," *Computerworld*, May 18, 1992, p. 87. [Whirlpool help line; A. C. Nielson and supermarkets]

"Bank of America on America Online," *Newsbytes*, August 18, 1995, p. NEW08180006. [Bank of America]

Betts, Mitch. "Romancing the Segment of One," *Computerworld*, March 5, 1990, p. 63. [Bank of America]

Booker, Ellis. "IS Puts New Spin on Service," *Computerworld*, October 28, 1991, p. 14. [Whirlpool help line]

Braly, Daman. "National Jewish Center Launching Disease-Management Message," *Health Management Technology*, September 1995, pp. 20–22. [Hospitals]

———. "Shaking Up the Foundation," *Health Management Technology*, August 1995, pp. 16–19. [Hospitals]

Bylinsky, Gene. "Computers That Learn by Doing," *Fortune*, September 6, 1993, pp. 96-102. [Examples of AI in business]

Campbell, Jeremy. *The Improbable Machine*. New York: Simon and Schuster, 1989. [Comments and history of AI research]

Cortese, Amy. "D&B Installs Instant-Analysis Service," *Computerworld*, May 14, 1990, p. 30. [Credit Clearing House]

"Creating a Corporate Strategy for Imaging and Document Management," *Datamation*, October 15, 1995, pp. 54-66. [Hospitals]

"Customer Unit Reorg Foreshadows Enterprise, Solution Provider Revamps," *Windows Watcher*, May 1995. [A.C. Nielson and supermarkets]

Daly, Ellis Booker. "Cellular Carriers Gain New Fraud-Detection Weapon," *Computerworld*, November 1, 1993, p. 71. [Using pattern recognition to spot theft of cellular phones]

Doyle, T.C. "The Empire Strikes Back," *VARbusiness*, September 1, 1995, pp. 58-64. [A.C. Nielson and supermarkets]

Dreyfus, Hubert L. *What Computers Still Can't Do*. Cambridge: MIT Press, 1992. [Update of the 1972 and 1979 books on the difficulties of AI and the current limits of technology, including critical review of history of AI research]

Dyzel, Bill. "Talking to Windows with DragonDictate," *Windows Sources*, December 1995, p. 60. [Speech recognition]

"E-Banking: FSTC Unveils Electronic Check Technology—Secure, Versatile Instrument for Electronic Commerce," *EDGE, On & About AT&T*, September 25, 1995, p. 41. [Bank of America]

Edmonds, Ernest L., Candy R. Jones, and B. Soufi. "Support for Collaborative Design: Agents and Emergence," *Communications of the ACM*, July 1994, pp. 41-47. [Software agents]

Fitzgerald, Michael. "Cooking with Expert Systems," *Computerworld*, October 15, 1990, p. 45. [Mrs. Fields]

———. "AI (Quietly) Goes Mainstream," *Computerworld*, July 29, 1991, p. 59. [Ontario Department of Corrections]

Francett, Barbara. "Parallel Technology Finds Home in Data Warehouse," *Software Magazine*, May 1995, pp. 63-66. [The Broadway/Carter Hawley Hale]

Genesereth, Michael and S. Ketchpel. "Software Agents," *Communications of the ACM*, July 1994, pp. 48-53. [Software agents]

Grace, Tim. "Solomon Beefs Up Service to VARs," *Computer Reseller News*, September 4, 1995, p. 22. [A.C. Nielson and supermarkets]

Hill, Christian. "Electronic 'Agents' Bring Virtual Shopping a Bit Closer to Reality," *The Wall Street Journal*, September 27, 1994, pp. A1, A6. [AT&T adopts General Magic technology to build software agent system. Attempting to set up national network for retailing]

Hogan, Mike. "Quicken Taps into Online Banking," *PC/Computing*, November 1995, p 84. [Bank of America]

Johnson, Bob. "An Enterprise Toolkit at Your Service," *Software Magazine*, October 15, 1995, pp. 33-40. [Schlumberger]

Knowlee, Anne. "Bank Services; Many Offer Rudimentary Options, But More Are Coming," *PC Week*, October 30, 1995, p. 104. [Bank of America]

———. "Electronic Commerce; Securing Transactions Over the Net," *PC Week*, October 30, 1995, pp. 102-103. [Bank of America]

Koegler, Scott. "Speech Recognition Solutions: Speaking Your Mind," *Infoworld*, November 27, 1995, pp. 92-99. [Speech recognition]

Maes, Pattie. "Agents That Reduce Work and Information Overload," *Communications of the ACM*, July 1994, pp. 31-40. [Software agents]

Medina, Diane. "Awash in Technology: Whirlpool Spins Out New Network to Improve Customer Service," *Information Week*, November 4, 1991, p. 46. [Whirlpool help line]

Moran, Robert. "IBM Stirs Expert Systems into SAA Development," *Computerworld*, January 8, 1990, p. 8. [Mrs. Fields]

Mulqueen, John T. "Spending Spree Hits a Bump; Network Budgets Continue to Grow, But Managers See a Slowdown in Increases in the Year Ahead," *Communications Week*, July 17, 1995, pp. 58-59. [Hospitals]

Newquist, H.P. "Competition from the Unlikeliest of Places," *AI Expert*, May 1995, pp. 46-47. [expert systems at Ford]

Norman, Donald. "How Might People Interact with Agents," *Communications of the ACM*, July 1994, pp. 68-71. [Software agents]

Radding, Alan. "AI in Action," *Computerworld*, July 29, 1991, p. 61. [Nynex and MAX; General Dynamics, Electric Boat]

Riecken, Doug. "A Conversation with Marvin Minsky about Agents," *Communications of the ACM*, July 1994, pp. 23-29. [Software agents]

———. "Intelligent Agents," *Communications of the ACM*, July 1994, pp. 18-21. [Software agents]

Rifkin, Glenn. "CYC-ED Up," *Computerworld*, May 10, 1993, p. 104. [Doug Lenat's effort to program 10 million "common-sense" rules into a computer]

Roberts, Erica. "Virtual-LAN Standard Push," *Communications Week*, June 12, 1995, p. 5. [Hospitals]

Slater, Derek. "IS at Your Service," *Computerworld*, January 20, 1992, p. 71. [Whirlpool help line]

"Solution Providers Must Now Earn 'Partner' Status," *Windows Watcher*, August 1995. [A.C. Nielson and supermarkets]

"Specialized Financial Applications," *Wall Street & Technology*, December 15, 1994, p. 95. [The Broadway/Carter Hawley Hale]

"Speech Recognition System Passes the Test," *Computing Canada*, December 7, 1994. [Speech recognition]

"Speech Recognition: Still Not There Yet," *Computing Canada*, August 2, 1995. [Speech recognition]

Sterling, Bruce. "The Status Symbol of the '90s," *Computerworld*, October 31, 1992, p. 4. [Science fiction writer's perspective on technology, including predictions on the use of agents]

Stevens, Larry. "There's No Magic Genie in a New System," *Computerworld*, November 11, 1990, p. 101. [Schlumberger]

Tanaka, David. "St. Paul's Hospital Tests Virtual Medicine with ATM Link," *Computing Canada*, May 10, 1995, p. 40. [Hospitals]

Vizard, Michael. "Secret Agents of Software," *Computerworld*, August 9, 1993, p. 31. [Agents that learn by watching the users]

Wexler, Joanie M. "IBM Ships Decision Tool," *Computerworld*, October 2, 1989, p. 23. [The Broadway/Carter Hawley Hale]

Zadeh, Lotfi. "The Calculus of Fuzzy If/Then Rules," *AI Expert*, 1992.

# CASES *Customer Service*

Workers in business services rely on computers. In particular, they use them for word processing, communication, graphics and email.

Source: Computer Use in the United States, U.S. Bureau of the Census.

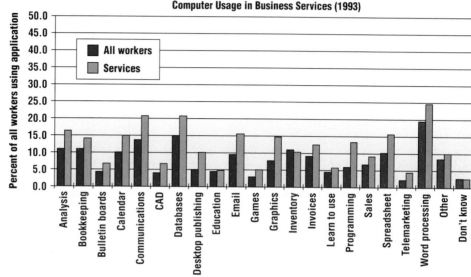

Computer Usage in Business Services (1993)

Managers of many organizations talk about providing customer service and improving consumer satisfaction. Few are able to carry through with this promise. Technology can help. It can also increase isolation and cause more problems.

Many of the business trends of the past few years have made it difficult to improve customer service. Cutting the workforce makes it harder to maintain contact with customers. Installing automated sales systems often persuades managers to focus on statistics instead of the human aspects of transactions. Increased internationalization means customers and companies can be separated geographically and culturally. Management by methodology and franchises can help by moving decision making and responsibility closer to the customer. However, without support and information, pushing decisions to lower-level employees can also lead to chaos.

Customer service can mean many things. For companies like Mrs. Fields, it means providing exactly what customers want, when they want it. A related concept is the issue of *mass customization,* the ability to provide customized products to anyone, at mass-production prices. These techniques require in-depth knowledge of the customer base, and the ability to instantly change production lines.

Customer service includes the necessity of keeping a customer happy after the sale. Some retail stores go so far as saying that any product can be returned at any time. However, firms selling large appliances can-

not rely on such a blanket promise. Companies like General Electric and Westinghouse need a way to resolve problems and answer questions over the phone to avoid returns and complaints.

## CASE *Mrs. Fields Retail Operations Intelligence System Modules*

Mrs. Fields cookies has built its retail system on a series of integrated software modules. All of the components run on a personal computer linked to an IBM AS/400 or System 38 minicomputer installed at the Utah headquarters. The goal of the integrated software is to provide an accurate analysis of the business conditions and personnel situations. The primary benefit of this arrangement is that the information that the managers provide keeps coming back to them in a reorganized fashion that will make it useful for decision making.

The Daily Sales Capture collects all of the sales information by product each day. It graphically breaks down the sales and compares the total sales to the hours worked by the employees.

The Sales Reporting and Analysis Module compares each day's sales to levels of the previous week, month, and year. This includes information by day as well as an average from the previous time period. This enables the manager to quickly grasp the success of each day's effort. An added advantage is the amount of information that the system provides in regard to actual versus projected sales.

The Employee Time Collection Module enables each employee to punch in and out on the store's personal computer. Each night the data is uploaded to the corporate computers. The efficiencies that the system provides reduces to 5 the number of employees on the corporate staff necessary to cut the checks for 7,000 employees.

The Intracomputer Communications and Form Mail Module uses electronic mail to link all the stores to the home office and regional and district managers. Debbie Fields uses Phone Mail to talk to her managers and to share the positive and negative reinforcements of the business. This enables her to put her voice in every store. In her opinion, it also eliminates much of the error and delay normally associated with paper memos. In addition to Phone Mail, Debbie uses Form Mail to respond to standard messages from the field. This enables her to scan her computer messages to discriminate between those messages that are important and those that can be referred to a staff member to handle.

The Repair and Maintenance Module assists the manager to pinpoint mechanical and electrical problems. Through a series of prompts, it walks the manager through a simple schematic of what steps to take to isolate what is wrong and repair it. If this doesn't work, the repair request is logged and a work order is immediately submitted to the store. When the repair is completed, the store uses the computer to indicate that work was done and the vendor's bill gets paid.

The Skill Testing Module maintains the staffing/skills standards on a companywide basis. This ensures that proper training occurs, minimizes test supervision, and reduces cheating through a variable set of questions.

The Inventory Control Module provides weekly inventory alerts to the headquarters that specific supplies for specific stores must be ordered.

The Tax and License Module tracks tax and licensing requirements at the various locations. It accomplishes this by maintaining a database of the laws and regulations in the locations where Mrs. Fields maintains stores.

The Lease Management Module keeps an up-to-date record of the lease requirements and the schedule of when the payments have been made.

The Labor Scheduler schedules employees based on knowledge of labor and workforce conditions. This includes the labor laws of a particular state, employee work preferences, and store characteristics. Cleaning and inventory tasks, skills, and staffing needs during important days are also taken into account. Once the employee data is entered, the scheduler draws up a work schedule, including breaks, that will optimize the hourly employees' time. A Gantt chart identifies bottleneck tasks. This enables the store manager to minimize overtime while providing a schedule that is more responsive to the individual workers' needs.

The Interviewing Module is designed to provide standardization in the way store managers assess the potential of prospective store personnel. Applicants begin by filling out a standard questionnaire on the personal computer. The possibility of consistency is increased by ensuring that each employee answers the same set of interactive interview questions. This ensures that all new employees are asked the same questions corporatewide. Based on the applicant's responses to the basic questions, the system can generate probe questions and identify major concerns or areas that need additional information.

The Personnel Administrator system generates a personnel folder and a payroll entry for a new applicant in Park City, Utah, and comes back to remind the local manager when it is time to submit the performance evaluation. It administers the written skills test and updates the records with the results. Eventually, the entire personnel manual will be on the computer so that it can be searched easily and updated from the central office.

The Daily Production Planner is an expert system that serves as an interactive appointment book, diary, and to-do list. Thirty minutes before the stores open, all store managers log into the system and enter specific information about the day. For example, cookies sell differently dependent upon whether the day is a holiday, weekend, or workday. The enthusiasm and milling crowds of a parade day may greatly increase the demand for cookies. Weather conditions can also be entered into the equation.

After the information is entered, the Planner projects a full day of the amount of cookies that should be baked each hour. As the day progresses, sales figures are automatically fed from the cash registers into the computer. The directions are then updated dependent on the actual store traffic and number of cookies sold. This enables the product mix of the baking to be adjusted to reflect the actual traffic of that day. The system charts hourly progress versus projection and makes recommendations on how to keep the cookies selling. For example, if the customer count is appropriate for the day but the average check is down crew members are encouraged to do more suggestive selling. On the other hand, if the customer count is down, then the computer recommends that the manager provide more sampling in front of the store.

At the end of the day, the Daily Production Planner compares performance to projections and stores this data for use in weekly, monthly, and yearly averages.

## QUESTIONS

1. Classify each of the modules to indicate the primary function: transaction-processing, decision support, or expert system.
2. Identify the type of problem being addressed by each system (e.g., diagnostic, speed).

## CASE *Mrs. Fields Cookies*

| SAMPLE DAILY PRODUCTION SCHEDULE | |
|---|---|
| 6:30 A.M. | Bake 87 oatmeal muffins |
| | Bake 23 fruit muffins |
| 7:30 A.M. | Bake 45 cookies, semisweet, with nuts |

Every night the managers at over 635 Mrs. Fields Cookie stores, 120 La Petite Boulangerie bakery-cafes, and 15 combination shops strike a few keys on their computers to automatically dial the corporate office's 800 number. The store's computer then uploads data that includes inventory reports, new employee forms, labor schedules, and time cards. The system also provides the day's hour-by-hour sales reports along with a record of bank deposits. The menu-driven program can even help a manager diagnose a broken mixer.

The next morning a manager or store controller calls up the overnight figures from the 50–75 stores he or she monitors through an account on an IBM System/38. The report makes it easy to pinpoint actual versus expected production, sales, and labor figures. The manager can focus on those areas and stores that appear to be presenting the most difficulty.

Mrs. Fields' information system was designed to support the front-line fast-food manager and provide central management with a bird's-eye view of the operations. It also enables the store manager to focus on their skills as salespeople rather than financial skills.

This system saves Mrs. Fields cookies more than $700,000 a year in paper-processing expenses by having all of the forms online. Two rules have governed Mrs. Fields' endeavors in expert systems:

- If a machine can do it, a machine should do it. People should do only what only people can do.
- The company will only maintain one database. Everything, including cookie sales, payroll records, suppliers' invoices, inventory reports, and utility charges will go into the same database. A single database means that no one has to waste time completing separate forms and answering the same question twice. It also means that the system can do most of the rote

work while freeing people to interact with other people, both employees and customers.

Despite its size, Mrs. Fields cookies has not franchised. Franchising enables the corporate headquarters to extend responsibility and accountability down to the store level. This is not without cost, however. Franchising reduces the control that the headquarters can exercise over the individual installation. It also means that revenues and profits must be shared with the local franchisee. Fields asserts that no other food retailer has been able to open so many outlets while still retaining the direct, day-to-day control over the individual stores that Mrs. Fields does.

### Employee Hiring and Tracking

Corporatewide, Mrs. Fields hires 50 new employees each day. Most of them receive minimum wage. They begin by filling out their job application on the personal computer. To assist the manager when the application process moves to the interview stage, the PC simultaneously develops questions specific to the applicant. Some employees turn out to be better workers than others. The computerized applications enable Mrs. Fields to compare the applications of the top-notch employees with those who quit or who are fired. This enables questions to be identified that are good predictors of an employee's future.

What distinguishes this system from a normal MIS application is expert systems. Mrs. Fields wanted to keep the executive staff to a minimum while not sacrificing proper management. As with any retail store, financial and scheduling problems can be quite complex. Expert systems provide the company with a way to transfer proper management knowledge to the stores. This was accomplished by bringing the data to the experts (store controllers), so that the experts could redistribute their analysis of that data and suggestions back to the store locations.

Paul Quinn, vice-president of MIS, stated,

> With today's technology, it's much more efficient and effective to bring the data to the decision makers. Then, a handful of people can look at what decisions need to be made, find out what's in common or repetitive about the decision, incorporate that knowledge into an expert system, and then redistribute the expert system. This way, it is like having hundreds of experts at each store location.

Store expertise was not limited to financial and scheduling issues. Even less-structured tasks like hiring new employees and preventing internal theft were pursued. The system was able to generate suggested questions that a manager should ask prospective employees in a face-to-face interview based upon answers to his or her online application. Further, the system was able to reduce internal theft from 8 percent to 1 percent by identifying possible areas of theft and the most likely solutions to identified problems.

Yet everything is not all growth at Mrs. Fields cookies. In 1988, Mrs. Fields reported a loss of $10 million as compared to a net profit of $17.6 million in 1987. On London's Over-the-Counter Market, the price of shares fell from a high of $4.83 in 1987 to a low of $0.44 in 1988. In early February 1988, a joint venture with the Paris-based Midial S.A. to distribute cookies in the 12-nation European community was withdrawn. Several reasons have been listed for this turn in events:

- *Limited Number of Top-Flight Locations.* Mrs. Fields works best in cities and shopping malls where there is enough foot traffic to support a fundamentally single-product shop. The company has most of the limited number of these top-flight store locations covered. To experience further growth, the company cannot rely solely on the U.S. cookie market.

- *Difficulty in Expanding Internationally.* Local customs and regulations make it difficult to expand internationally, even with local partners.

- *Diversification into Multiproduct Cafes and Stores.* La Petite Boulangerie is the first effort of Mrs. Fields to expand their product line. Expansions into these areas often present increased overhead and cost-control issues.

- *Cookie Craze May Be Leveling Off.* With an increased emphasis on health and cholesterol control, the cookie craze may have peaked.

Mrs. Fields was successful in developing a unique system that provides excellent management of an unstructured and complex environment. The system was so successful that the company has developed a spinoff company that only sells the computer software used in Mrs. Fields' system. Named the Retail Operations Intelligence System, the package is adapted to running any franchise-based operation.

SOURCE: Sara Hedberg, "Where's AI Hiding," *AI Expert,* April 1995, p. 17.

## QUESTIONS

1. What items are included in the knowledge base for Mrs. Fields' expert system?
2. Does the expert system in Mrs. Fields' knowledge base use forward or backward chaining?
3. What impact does the fact that Mrs. Fields primarily hires 18–25 year olds have on the type of expert system that the company uses?
4. How can the expert system reduce the amount of time that the manager spends with paperwork and increase the amount of time that the manager spends "managing" employees?
5. How does Mrs. Fields' expert system provide a strategic advantage for the company compared to the cookie sales of David's Cookies and other local brands?
6. What advantages does Mrs. Fields' expert system provide to the accountants in corporate headquarters? What impact do the expert systems have on the size of middle management in the company?
7. How does the fact that cookie production can be adjusted by the hour affect the efficiency of Mrs. Fields' stores?
8. How can Mrs. Fields' corporate headquarters use the expert system to improve the effectiveness of the advertising program?
9. How can Mrs. Fields' corporate headquarters use the expert system to gather and project data on new cookies that are being tested?

## CASE  *General Electric: Customer Help Line*

Since 1982, General Electric has provided an Answer Center with a toll-free phone number for buyers of GE products. GE prides itself on having answers ready for almost all of the calls that come to the line. The Louisville, Kentucky, customer service center is part of the $6 billion appliance division.

When a call is received, the representative brings up a computerized list of symptoms and possible causes. Working through the checklist, the representative can often help the customer fix the problem on the spot. If the problem requires a technician, the caller is switched to the GE Service Center to schedule an appointment or get phone numbers of local service representatives.

The system consists of a huge text database containing problems and responses to more than 1 million problems. The computerized version can retrieve answers in less than two seconds, and is considerably easier to use than the old repair manuals of the "old days." As products are introduced or changed, the data is continually updated by four full-time programmers. An index allows representatives to search the database with a few key words.

The center employed 225 people and handled 3.5 million service calls in 1991. Each representative handled more than 100 calls a day. Twelve product specialists are on call for problems not recorded in the database. They also provide more detailed information for people who choose to fix more complicated problems themselves.

By asking customers to call the helpline when they encounter a problem, GE gains immediate feedback on problems. The system keeps customers happy by providing answers to many common questions. The service representatives also provide advice on how to best use the products and on how to care for them.

An additional feature of the immediate feedback is that GE can spot potential problems. If GE suddenly sees a new problem encountered by many people, the service representatives are instructed to ask more detailed questions. It is much easier for engineers to spot problems and correlations with direct comments from the users.

GE also uses the system to help convince customers to buy new appliances. The system provides repair costs and pricing and feature data for new appliances. The system also recommends callers to dealers who are participating in special promotional deals.

After careful consideration, GE does not collect customer data. They learned that customer prefer to remain anonymous. GE's manager of consumer communications and telemarketing, William Waers, notes that "We don't take the caller's name unless we have their permission, and we don't use any automatic [phone] number identification."

Although this information would undoubtedly be useful to the marketing department, GE determined that customers are more willing to use the system and ask "embarrassing" questions if they do not have to give their name.

GE is contemplating changes to the system, such as graphics and a graphical user interface. However, they are cautious about making changes, because they need to support 3.5 million calls a year. Annette Mattingly, information technology team leader, notes that although technology is important, the system is successful because of the employees. For service representatives, GE employs college-educated workers, provides good training for them and gets a low turnover rate.

SOURCE: Alan Radding, "GE Answers Call to Evolve 10-year-old Help Line," *Computerworld*, January 20, 1992, p. 72. Copyright 1992 by Computerworld, Inc., Framingham, MA 01701—Reprinted from *Computerworld*.

## CASE *Whirlpool: Customer Service*

In 1967, Whirlpool was one of the first companies in the United States to create a toll-free customer support line: the "Cool Line." Gary Lockwood, the director of consumer assistance at Whirlpool's North American Appliance Group, notes that "we're constantly looking for technologies that improve service." In 1992, the Whirlpool support line handled 1.6 million calls from customers. The calls were handled by 100 customer representatives located in Knoxville, Tennessee. By 1995, they anticipated handling 9 million calls a year.

To improve customer support, in 1988 Whirlpool surveyed customers to determine how they could provide "excellence in service." From the problems identified in that survey, in 1991, Whirlpool built a new customer support system. The system incorporated state-of-the-art imaging technology and expert systems. It uses ISDN links between the Knoxville offices and the headquarters in Benton Harbor, Michigan.

When a customer calls the toll-free number, an AT&T ISDN PBX receives the call, complete with the calling party's area code and phone number. The phone number is routed to a special processor from Aristacom International. The processor scans a DB2 database on one of Whirlpool's IBM computers. If the number is found in the files, the associated customer information is retrieved and is routed with the call to a customer service representative. The system can automatically route the call to the service agent who last spoke with the customer.

The networked personal computers on the agents' desks are connected to 10 CD-ROM drives containing more than 150,000 pages of images from 20 years' of service and product manuals. Agents can call up text and detailed schematics in less than two seconds.

When service agents receive a call, they can use an expert system from Aion Corp. to help diagnose the problem. The stored images of the products and their schematics enable the service agents to communicate with the consumer. By looking at the same images (one real, one in the computer), the agent can more easily identify problems and explain the problems.

In 1992, Whirlpool Corp. won an award from the American Association for Artificial Intelligence for its AI system that helps customer service representatives troubleshoot problems. In addition to improved customer service and satisfaction, Whirlpool estimates that the system saves $4 to $6 million annually.

### QUESTIONS

1. What types of problems and questions are the service agents likely to encounter?
2. What types of data are involved in these two systems? What transactions level problems make this situation difficult to solve?
3. What are the similarities and differences between the GE and Whirlpool approaches? How might they differ in costs?
4. As a consumer, which of the two systems would you prefer to deal with?

5. What advantages are provided by expert system technology in this problem?
6. As a consumer with a problem, would you notice the difference if the service agent uses a graphics-based system?
7. Which of the two systems would require more training for the service agents?
8. How can these systems be used to increase sales?

## CASE  *Channel 4: Commercial Breaks*

If Americans ever think about British television, the images from the BBC being rebroadcast on American PBS come to mind. Yet, the UK also has a commercial television network known as Channel 4. Channel 4 broadcasts its programs nationwide, with four-minute breaks for commercials. The advertisements are typically different for each geographic region, but companies can purchase "supermacros" or combinations of regions. These supermacro commercials are scheduled to run at the same time in each market. Six supermacro regions are available to the advertisers.

There are two primary aspects to operating the commercial channel: (1) Marketing representatives have to sell all of the available ad slots, and (2) someone has to schedule the ads to run at the proper time in each market. Unfortunately, these two steps are not always independent. Some advertisers want their commercials to run first (or last). It can be difficult to combine these constraints across various advertisements, especially when factoring in the requirement that supermacro commercials must run at the same time in each market. There can be as many as 50 advertisements in different sequences within every four-minute break.

Channel 4 began with a staff of four scheduling experts. Each day, they got a list of ads that were sold from the central Bull 9000 database. They would manually generate the schedule and put the sequenced list back on the computer for distribution to the transmitters. Sometimes unresolvable conflicts would arise. Other times, the experts would make errors, requiring compensation to the customers (typically in the form of free ads). In some cases, a schedule might leave unsold time slots. If the sales representatives could be notified early enough, then they could offer discounts to fill those slots.

Stephen Ottner, the manager of information systems, sums up the conflict: "It's a very critical end of the business. On the sales side, they're trying to make it later and later before they close the books and put everything down to air, and on the transmission side, they're trying to get things earlier and earlier."

Channel 4 managers knew they needed a better way to schedule the commercial breaks. They considered several automated systems, hoping to decrease the time and effort involved. They contemplated building an expert system, incorporating the knowledge of the existing schedulers. However, Merlin Inkley, the airtime manager, noted that the job is "not impossible to do manually, but it's very difficult."

Eventually, Channel 4 found XpertRule, from Attar Software in Lancashire, England. Akeel Attar, the managing director at Attar Software, comments on the difficulties faced with automating the scheduling system: "The problem is that while the constraints are known, there are no known [solution] strategies. Decision making is an area of expertise that can be captured, but with optimization of schedules, experts intuitively work by trial and error."

As a result, XpertRule is not a traditional expert system. Instead, it uses a genetic algorithm that follows a "survival of the fittest" method. It first generates random solutions to the problem. Then it tests the solutions against the constraints and rates them. Taking the best solutions, it combines them randomly ("mating"). These new "child" solutions are tested and scored. The process repeats for a fixed number of generations, and the computer identifies the best acceptable solution. The departmental staff members then check the results to fine-tune the schedule.

The new system is used iteratively by the staff members, because it can find solutions (on a personal computer) in a few seconds. The fine-tuning can be performed by almost anyone with a background in the area. It no longer requires the use of four experts working full time. It has also cut down on the number of errors.

SOURCE: Elisabeth Heichler, "Expert System Keeps UK TV Ads in Line," *Computerworld*, December 20, 1993, p. 30. Copyright 1993 by Computerworld, Inc., Framingham, MA 01701—Reprinted from *Computerworld*.

### QUESTIONS

1. Why is it so difficult to schedule the commercials on Channel 4?
2. How is the Channel 4 scheduling process different from that faced by networks in the United States?
3. Why did Channel 4 choose to avoid traditional expert systems?
4. What problems might be encountered with the genetic algorithm technique?
5. How does the new system help Channel 4 provide better customer service?

## DISCUSSION ISSUE

### *Who Owns Knowledge?*

There is an important ethical question involving expert systems. Remember that developing an ES requires the assistance of a cooperative expert. Why should an expert cooperate? Listen as Alvy (the CEO) tries to get Annie (the expert) to participate in a new ES project.

Alvy: Hi, Annie. We've got a new project I think you're really going to like. You get to show off a little. We're going to build an expert system to handle quality control. I asked my VPs, and they all said you're the best. Whenever they have a question, they come to you. Your knowledge is going to be the foundation for the new expert system.

Annie: Well, it's nice to know that everyone likes my work. But, I'm a little worried. I heard about the new project, and I've done some reading on expert systems. It seems to me that when you've built your new system, you won't need me around anymore. Are you saying I need to look for a new job?

Alvy: No, no. We really love your work. That's why you've been chosen for this project. It's really quite an honor. We'll take you off your normal duties for a while so you can devote time to the developers, but we want you here.

Annie: But what will I be doing when the system is complete? It took me 15 years of hard work to learn everything. I still have 10 years to retirement. I'm not sure it's possible, but if your fancy new machine takes everything I know, then what's left for me? What are you planning? Drain all my knowledge and throw me away like an empty beer can?

Alvy: Whoa, slow down. I don't really know how this stuff works, but the programmers are just going to ask you a bunch of questions. We're planning on taking at least six months. After that, it'll be another year before the system is completely tested and ready to go. We've got plenty of time to worry about what happens after that.

Annie: That's not good enough. I've invested a lot of time and energy. I've always worked hard for this company. If I'm going to lose my job in a year, I want to know now. I'd be better off if I start looking now.

Alvy: You're blowing this situation out of proportion. I never said anything about you losing your job. When the project's over, it may change a little. We'll have to see how everything works out. When we get out of this recession and get that new plant built, I'll be looking for a manager. It's long term, but if you keep up the good work, you'll be on the short list for that job.

Annie: Hey, I don't need your empty promises. You've been talking about that plant for 10 years. The way I see it, you need me for this expert system. If I walk out of here today, you don't get your system, and I get a new job somewhere else doing what I love.

Alvy: Come on, you've been a loyal employee for years. You've struggled with us through the hard times. It won't be much longer, and I'll be able to reward you the way I always intended. Besides, we trained you. You got all that knowledge from our company. We paid you through all those years. Now we want to use that information. You never complain when the VPs ask you questions.

Annie: Well . . . I don't know . . .

Alvy: Look, I didn't realize it would bother you so much. We don't need to nail this down today. Why not take the afternoon off and think about it. Call Susie in MIS if you want more information on what the programmers need. Let's get together again next week. In the meantime, I'll talk to the VPs and the directors and see whether we can scrape together a raise or a bonus or something.

### QUESTIONS

1. Do you think Annie should go along? Will she be able to keep her job? Will the job be the same?
2. Do you think the company should be able to force Annie to participate? How can they make her participate?
3. Do you think this situation is realistic? Do you think you might some day be in Annie's shoes? What can you do to avoid that situation?

# CHAPTER 11

# Strategic Analysis

**WHAT YOU WILL LEARN IN THIS CHAPTER**

How does a company interact with the business environment through external agents? What are the basic methods of obtaining a competitive advantage? How can information technology be used to gain a competitive advantage? How is technology used to search for an advantage over rivals? What are the costs and potential dangers of being on the leading edge of technology?

American Airlines uses its Sabre Web page (http://www.sabre.com) to provide information about the company and to list flight schedules and make flight and hotel reservations for customers on the Web.

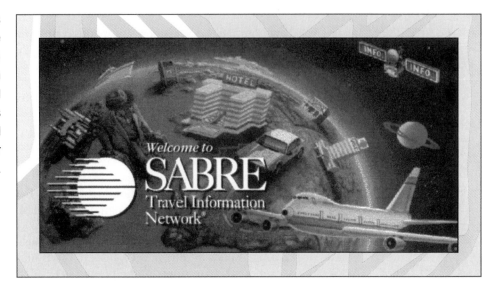

## AMERICAN AIRLINES SABRE

In their efforts to be competitive for the business and pleasure traveler, airlines have placed increasing demands on their reservation systems. The requirement for instantaneous response is a given. However, travelers are intensifying their demand for preassignment to their seats, preissued boarding passes, and more varieties of in-flight menus and movies.

Today travelers even want "one-stop" reservations for all their needs. Hotels and rental car agencies have linked themselves to the reservation systems to enable travelers to complete all of their travel arrangements at one location and through one computer system. Frequent-flyer and hotel programs are similarly linked together. Joint arrangements encourage travelers to stay at participating hotels after flying on a particular airline. When they do so, bonus points are given in award programs that involve linked fly/stay weekends.

To meet these increasingly sophisticated reservation demands, American Airlines developed the Sabre system. This strategic business tool is an advanced database system that provides instantaneous reservation service to travel agents across the country. Specific pricing categories can be introduced, complicated connections planned, and seats reserved all in one action. By enlisting a large number of travel and ticket agencies, American Airlines can use its information system to insure that its seats and flights are filled first.

Ticket agents are more likely to book flights that are listed first. At one time, Sabre always listed American's flights first, increasing the likelihood that the reservations would be made on American instead of competing airlines.

The strength of the Sabre system is its ability to instantaneously link a number of smaller databases. Currently, American is involved in an extensive development program that will further improve this ability. American is experimenting with image processing, expert systems, cooperative processing, local area networks, and a corporatewide office automation network. These new techniques will further improve Sabre's ability to book the entire itinerary for a trip through one reservation system.

**OVERVIEW**  As the world economy has become more competitive, firms have become more ambitious in seeking a means to gain a strategic advantage. As illustrated in Figure 11.1,
they are searching for methods that make them unique. Finding these opportunities
can be difficult. Information technology is a tool that has proved useful at providing a
competitive edge through innovative products, better service, lower costs, and
improved quality.

Setting strategic directions is often performed at the top management levels of
the firm. Because only a few students will become corporate leaders, it might seem
that this chapter is not as important to you. Besides the fact that you might be one of
the few who run a major firm someday, there are two basic reasons why you need to
understand the strategic uses of information technology. First, strategy requires creativity. Having more people in a firm searching for competitive advantages means
more ideas. Even if it is not part of your job description, good ideas are likely to be
rewarded. Second, recall that many jobs are in small businesses. In a small business,
you do not have the luxury of hiring specialists to focus on strategic questions. All
managers are expected to contribute to the growth of the firm.

**INTRODUCTION**  In some ways, information systems designed for competitive advantage are not much
different than transaction processing and decision support systems. In many cases,
advantages over your rivals can result from changes in the basic transaction process-

**FIGURE 11.1**
Strategies. Managers
are increasingly being
asked to find ways to
give their firm an
advantage over the
competition.
Information systems
can help identify areas
that can provide a
competitive edge.
Information systems
can also directly
provide services and
advantages that are not
offered by your rivals.

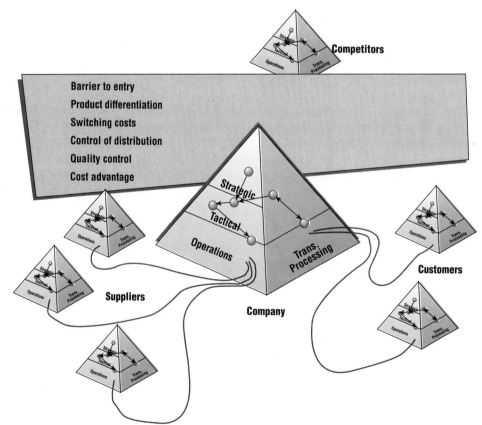

ing systems and business methods. The real difference with strategy lies in its goal: to change the way the business operates and gain an advantage over the other firms in the industry.

Creating strategic systems requires that you understand the entire firm and its relationship with external agents in the environment, such as suppliers, consumers, workers, and rivals. Many systems have been devised to help you analyze and create

---

### ▼ TRENDS ◣

Ideas and concepts for managing businesses are constantly changing. Many current practices are often traced to Alfred Sloan, who drove the consolidation and expansion of General Motors from 1920 to 1956. Management techniques evolve over time and ideas come from many sources. Through the 1950s, many companies focused on making production more efficient. In the 1950s and 1960s, U.S. firms expanded into wider markets, both nationally and internationally. In the 1970s, managers were preoccupied with the economic changes brought on by oil price rises and consequent shocks of high inflation and high interest rates. The 1970s and 1980s also saw the emergence of increased international competition—for example, between 1960 and 1985, U.S. imports as a percent of GNP increased from 5.6 percent to 11.5 percent.

Despite these general trends, most companies find it difficult to change. As a result, as the business environment changes, a company might lose its focus, or new competitors may appear. Periodically, executives need to examine the overall position of the firm to see whether there might be a better strategy or a new way to gain an advantage over rival firms. Michael Porter, in his book *Competitive Strategy: Techniques for Analyzing Industries and Competitors,* took the lead in showing executives how to re-examine their business and search for competitive advantages.

Through the 1960s and 1970s, the use of MIS was largely governed by its capabilities and the immediate needs of the organizations. The most common MIS objective was to save money and time by automating transaction-processing tasks. The projects were evaluated on the basis of how much money they could save. Eventually, managers came to realize that computer systems have other advantages. A new technology might enable the firm to provide better service to customers. The company that is the first implementer of a technology might find it easier to attract customers, giving it a competitive advantage over the other firms. For example, the first banks that installed ATMs to provide 24-hour access gained an advantage over their competitors. Warren McFarlan was one of the first writers to analyze how information technology could be used to gain a competitive advantage.

Several classic cases are commonly used as examples to illustrate the strategic uses of information systems. The earliest examples come from the airline industry. In the 1960s and 1970s, United Airlines and American Airlines spent millions of dollars to develop online reservation systems Apollo (1971) and Sabre. The Apollo system was spun off in 1987 and renamed Covia. In 1988, Covia, British Airways, SwissAir, and KLM formed Galileo. These systems did more than simply sell tickets—they kept track of customers and flights. When the airline industry was deregulated new competitors appeared (such as People's Express). Despite having higher operating costs, the larger airlines were able to survive many of these challenges by using their information systems. With their reservation systems, they were able to charge different prices for different passengers (business and tourist class). Another competitive feature of their systems was that they listed their own flights first. Congress eventually decided this practice was unethical because they were charging other airlines to list flights on the system. The reservation systems are also used to track frequent flyers, which encourages customers to use one airline.

**FIGURE 11.2**
Harvard strategy analysis. Strategy determines the identity of a firm. Formulating strategies is only the first step. As an effective manager, you must also be able to implement strategies.

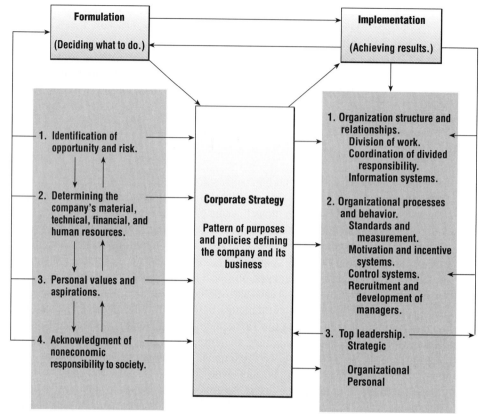

corporate strategies. Figure 11.2 outlines the basic process. A common thread in gaining competitive advantage is to improve the ties and communication with suppliers and consumers. Electronic communication can provide automatic data collection, minimize errors, and create faster responses.

Information systems can provide a competitive advantage through increasing the barriers to entry and controlling distribution channels. Services from information systems can be used to differentiate your product from the others in the market or even to create entirely new products. Computer systems might give you an edge by being the lowest cost producer, or through improved quality management.

 **BUSINESS TRENDS**

Business statistics indicate a clear trend toward the increased importance of service-oriented firms. Service firms are well suited to certain strategic uses of information systems. In particular, product differentiation, product quality, and new products are typically useful strategies. In many service industries, information is the primary product, so technology is especially valuable.

The financial industry provides several strategic examples, such as the Merrill Lynch Cash Management Account, ATMs, or new financial instruments created by brokers. Similarly, Federal Express uses tracking information to differentiate its service from its rivals' offerings. Likewise, the airlines used their reservation systems to give them a competitive advantage in transportation services.

Designing strategic systems can be a dangerous task. There are many opportunities to fail. One complication is that development costs are high. Some strategic systems use new technology, which carries higher costs and a greater risk of incompatibilities and other problems. It is also important to remember that attempts to monopolize a market are illegal, and strategic systems can sometimes come close to breaking the antitrust laws.

The most difficult aspect of strategic systems is coming up with ideas that might give you an advantage. One way to get ideas is to see what firms in other industries have done. You never know when some of the techniques and tricks used by other companies might be useful to you.

## THE COMPETITIVE ENVIRONMENT

One of the important trends facing most businesses today is the increased level of competition. Improved telecommunications and faster delivery services mean that local firms face competition from regional and national firms. Local firms have to compete against national mail-order companies, which offer wide selections, next-day delivery, and low prices. Computer databases, home shopping channels, and toll-free phone numbers make it easier for consumers to compare prices, putting pressure on all firms.

Large national retailers and franchises put pressure on local stores. They also compete against themselves for market territories. Their size gives them leverage in dealing with manufacturers. By purchasing in large quantities, they can negotiate lower prices. Their high volume also makes it easier for them to buy from foreign producers.

Several international trends are creating increased competition. The international search for lower manufacturing costs puts pressure on firms to cut their costs. For instance, the Japanese have moved production to other Asian nations to build television sets. Decreasing trade barriers throughout the world also creates larger markets.

Competition is increasing in many industries, but it is particularly intense in the restaurant and fast food industry. Competition encourages firms to hold down costs, provide more variety, and provide new and better service to customers.

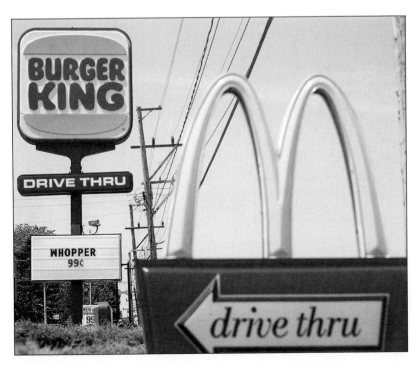

As Eastern European economies rebuild, as the European Union takes shape, and as Mexican incomes increase, consumers will be able to buy more products. Although the prospect of these increased sales is enticing to U.S. manufacturers, there are some complications. If a competitor gets established first, it will be stronger and harder to compete with in the United States. New firms will arise or expand in these international markets, giving them a stronger base to increase sales in the United States, providing for increased competition.

**EXTERNAL AGENTS**     Competitive advantage can be gained by establishing or changing relationships between the firm and its **external agents.** External agents consist of suppliers, customers, rivals, potential new entrants, substitute products, and sometimes the government. Figure 11.3 portrays these relationships in Porter's **five forces model.** From a systems perspective, each of these entities is outside the control of the firm. Yet, they strongly affect the company. Through improved ties to these agents, they become part of your system, which can be used to improve the competitive position of the firm. Figure 11.4 illustrates the various relationships that exist with modern companies.

## Customers

To a retail outlet, customers are likely to be individual people. A large manufacturer may have several levels of customers, ranging from wholesale firms that buy in bulk, then sell to distributors, which deliver products to retailers, where the final customer purchases the product. Having more intermediate levels between the manufacturer and the customer can make it much harder to manage the firm.

An important goal in any company is to satisfy the customers. If there are many layers of buyers between the company and the ultimate consumer, it can be difficult to determine what the customer wants. Similarly, the layers create delays that make it

**FIGURE 11.3**

Porter's five forces model. Strategies often involve external agents: customers, suppliers, competitors, the threat of new entrants, and substitute products.

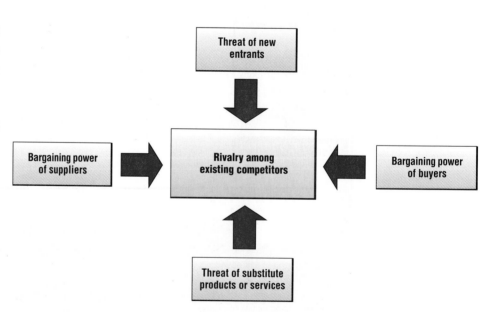

**FIGURE 11.4**
Production chain.
Modern companies
have ties to hundreds
or thousands of
entities. Sometimes a
company will own
several pieces of the
production chain
(vertical integration).
Sometimes the
company might expand
horizontally by building
related businesses.
Each linkage requires
communication and
offers the possibility
for strategic gain.

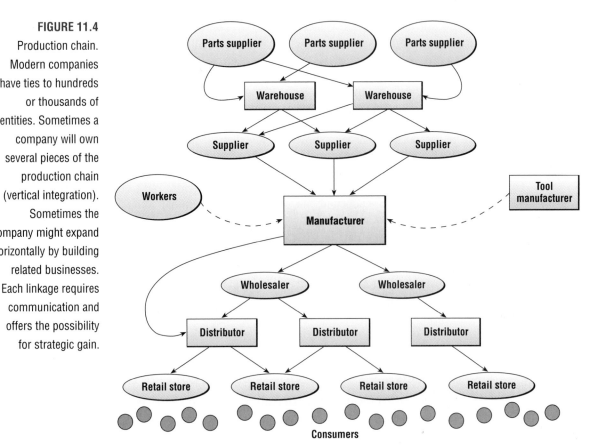

difficult for the retailer to order and obtain the products. For example, with older, slower manufacturing processes, merchants have to place most orders for the Christmas season around July—five or six months before the sales would occur. What happens if the economy changes or some event causes people to suddenly demand a different product? The retailer, manufacturer, and customers all suffer as a result of these long lead times.

The intermediate layers also cause confusion about what the customers want, because it is hard to identify the customer. To the manufacturer, is the customer the wholesale firm that buys the products, the retailer, or the final consumer? It is often wise to focus on the final consumer, but the manufacturer has to consider the needs of the retailer as well. For example, in the bicycle industry, one company found a new way to package its bicycles so that they could be assembled (by the retailer) in half the normal time. This particular situation helped both the retailer and the final consumer, but imagine what happens when the manufacturer receives conflicting demands from the various "customers."

As illustrated by Florida Power and Light (Reality Bytes 11–1), a common strategic goal is to "get closer to the customers." Information systems can be used to strengthen the ties among the customers, manufacturers, and various intermediaries. For example, you could build electronic ordering systems, with terminals in the retail stores to capture current sales levels. The systems could also be used to send new product information to the customers, or collect feedback on various attributes, or to provide immediate answers to question from retailers and customers.

**Reality Bytes** ◣ 11–1 Florida Power and Light

Florida Power and Light is a $5 billion utility that supplies power to the Miami, Florida, area. In the supply of power it was a monopoly. Its customers had little individual bargaining power. Yet FP&L believed it needed to improve its perception among its customers because collectively they could demand that another power company serve the area.

FP&L began by asking its customers to define what quality meant to them. FP&L then tabulated the responses and identified those areas where its customers said it needed the most improvement. The customers identified blackouts as their primary complaint with FP&L.

To respond, FP&L developed a computer model to track information about blackouts and record the exact component that failed and why it failed. Based on this information, the utility was able to better equip its crews to repair elements that were most likely to fail. This enabled it to dispatch a crew with the right equipment to the site of the failure, reducing blackouts by more than 20 percent.

The new program also reduced the time it takes to repair the failure and end the blackout. This was particularly important for FP&L's computer customers. The survey indicated that computer users could sustain their operations for an hour. A longer blackout affected their ability to do their jobs. The computer model was again called on to analyze those outages that exceeded one hour in length. Particular efforts were directed to develop the knowledge and the parts inventory to greatly reduce the number of these blackouts.

## Suppliers

Suppliers can provide individual parts, entire products, or even services (such as a bank that lends money). Three major issues involving suppliers are: price, quality, and delivery schedules. Just as with customers, problems can arise when there are many layers of suppliers. For instance, increased layers can result in longer delays between ordering and delivery, because the supplier has to contact its supplier, who contacts its supplier.

Quality management is also more difficult when there are several layers of suppliers. A fundamental element of **total quality management (TQM)** states that quality must be built into every process and item. Picture the problems that arise if we measure quality only in terms of the output at the manufacturer. When a defective product is found, we have no information about the cause. How can the problem be corrected? We need to know where each component came from and evaluate the quality as soon as possible. For instance, if there is a defective product, we could check each component to determine its original manufacturer. The manufacturer could be notified of problems, and we could search other items for similar defects. The manufacturer could use this data to identify problems with individual production lines.

Information systems can be used to build electronic ties to suppliers. Common uses of these systems include placing orders, tracking shipments, monitoring quality control, notifying partners of changes in plans, and making payments. Electronic links provide faster responses, better recordkeeping, and fewer errors. They also offer the potential strategic benefits described in the next section.

## Rivals, New Entrants, and Substitutes

The goal of a strategic approach is to derive a competitive advantage over the **rivals,** or other firms in the industry. There could be many competitors or just a few larger rivals. The competition could take place in a small town, across a nation, or world-

**Reality Bytes**    **11–2**  AIRLINE RESERVATION SYSTEMS

| | |
|---|---|
| Sabre | American Airlines |
| Galileo | United Airlines |
| Pars | Northwest and TransWorld Airlines |
| DatasII | Delta Airlines |
| System One | Eastern/Continental Airlines |
| Sahara | Various U.S./International Airlines |

The advantages that an airline reservation system provides have caused many of the leading airlines to develop their own database systems. These systems promise the increased benefit of one-stop reservations for all of a traveler's needs.

The systems are extremely costly to develop, however. First, the database of routes and seats must be maintained on an instantaneous basis. Second, the customer/traveler list must also be updated instantaneously. Third, the magnitude of the database in terms of information and time requires that sophisticated programs be written to access the data quickly and efficiently. The increasing demands in terms of access, size, and time require that these programs constantly be fine-tuned and updated.

wide. One of the first steps in any strategic analysis is to identify the primary competitors and to assess their strengths and weaknesses.

One issue to remember about competition is that it never stops. Coming up with one strategic idea is not good enough. For example, American Airlines and United Airlines spent millions of dollars to build reservation systems as strategic systems. Today, all major airlines have access to these systems (Reality Bytes 11–2), and each airline must continually work to improve its system to provide new enticements to customers. Similarly, automobile companies designed computerized diagnostic systems to improve services offered by repair shops (Reality Bytes 11–3).

**Reality Bytes**    **11–3**  AUTOMOBILE REPAIR DIAGNOSTICS

Automobile dealerships have long faced the difficulties of automobile repair. Stocking and maintaining parts for a constantly changing and aging sales base presents major inventory and carrying charges. Finding and training skilled mechanics is complicated by the increasing complexity of computerized engines and power drives. The precision of the engines has made their diagnosis and fine-tuning difficult to analyze and accomplish.

To address these needs and use service as a competitive advantage, the major automobile companies have invested heavily in computerized engine diagnostic systems. They are offered to dealers not only with promises of improved service but also as productivity boosters for the mechanics in the garage. If the computerized systems can accurately diagnose the difficul-

ties, the mechanics can go to work to correct them much more quickly.

Ford Motor Company is offering its dealers the Service Bay Diagnostic System ($35,000). General Motors has named its system Techline T-100 ($18,000–$20,000). Chrysler has called its program the Mopar Diagnostic System (leased at $295–$595 per month). All of the systems work the same way and look like a large tool box with a television screen on top. The technician plugs the machine into the car. The machine runs a series of more than two dozen tests that give the technician a good picture of what is and is not working in the engine. This assists the technician to isolate his or her investigation to the area most likely to be the cause of the problem.

Today, all of the manufacturers have essentially the same systems. In some cases, they might offer improvements over your ideas, which will put the originator at a disadvantage. However, the firm that first implements a new strategy can gain recognition and market share. It is important to remember that companies must continually improve and seek new opportunities.

A related issue is the concept of potential competitors or entrants in the business. In some cases, you might identify the major rivals, implement a strategy, and then immediately lose everything as new firms enter your business. Entrants might build their firms from scratch, like the way Burger King built new stores in the same areas as McDonald's restaurants. Alternatively, other firms may increase the sales of products that are similar to your products. Substitute products are related economically by the degree to which consumers are willing to use one product instead of the other. A classic example comes from the late 1970s, when the U.S. economy faced high inflation rates and banks were subject to limits on the interest rates they could pay on deposits. Merrill Lynch, the stock brokerage firm, introduced a service enabling customers to store their money in a wide variety of financial instruments that paid significantly higher interest rates than did checking accounts, and still write checks on the account. Many larger customers took their money away from banks and put it in these asset accounts. These new accounts were perceived as close substitutes for traditional bank services, and people transferred huge sums of money out of the banking system.

The key point is that you need to take a broad look at your firm and the industry. Know who your competitors are and how they operate. Are there other products or services offered by other industries that might attract your customers? If you make a change in the way you do business, find out how it will affect your rivals. Determine how changes will alter the industry. Will they provide an opening for firms in other industries?

## Government Regulations

In any economy, government intervention has a strong influence on the firm. There are myriad government agencies, regulations, taxes, and reports. The situation multiplies for multinational firms that are subject to the regulations of many nations. These agencies and regulations can have strong effects on the profitability of a firm. Generally, an individual firm has no control over government regulations, but sometimes suggestions can lead to modifications. For instance, it is now possible to submit some documents to government agencies in computer form. In fact, some reports (such as 10K or 10Q financial reports) are *required* to be filed electronically. Electronic forms can decrease your storage costs and make it easier to find documents that have been stored for long periods of time.

## IS TECHNIQUES TO GAIN COMPETITIVE ADVANTAGE

Competitive advantage may be achieved with many techniques in business. Information technology is one area that may provide several opportunities. In general, there is no reason to believe that MIS techniques are better than other methods. However, some firms have experienced considerable success from using these techniques, so they are well worth considering. Additionally, the rapid changes in technology often lead to competitive advantages if your firm is the first to find a creative use for the new technology. The other side of the coin is that untested new technologies may not work as planned. Hence, the pioneer is taking a risk—if the project fails, the development costs may put the firm at a competitive disadvantage.

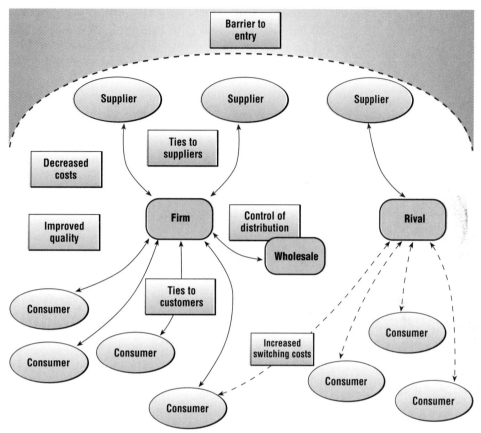

The fundamental mechanisms for gaining competitive advantage are barriers to entry, switching costs, lower production costs, product differentiation, control over distribution channels, innovation, and quality control. These techniques are illustrated in Figure 11.5. The question we wish to examine is how information systems can take advantage of these techniques.

## Barriers to Entry

A fundamental concept of economics is that in order to make extra profits, you need some mechanism to prevent other firms from entering the industry. Otherwise, as soon as your firm develops a strategy that pays higher returns, other firms will flock to the industry and drive the prices and profits down. Figure 11.6 summarizes the

- Economies of scale (size).
- Economies of scope (breadth).
- Product differentiation.
- Capital requirements.
- Cost disadvantages (independent of size).
- Distribution channel access.
- Government policy.

common **barriers to entry.** One common way that information systems create barriers to entry is from their cost. Consider what happens when you create a new information system that provides additional services, like banks did with ATMs. Customers soon expect all firms to offer those services. If a new company wishes to enter the industry, it will have to spend additional money to buy the computers and create the systems to offer those services. The information system raises the cost of entering the industry. A classic example of this situation was the introduction of People's Express Airlines (Reality Bytes 11–4) in 1981. The CEO of People's Express stated that he knew the airline needed a reservation system to compete effectively with other airlines, but after raising $100 million to start the airline, the top man-

### ▼ Reality Bytes ▲ 11–4 PEOPLE'S EXPRESS AIRLINE (CLASSIC CASE)

In 1981, Donald Burr's People's Express Airlines was the darling of the airline industry and American management. In four years the fledgling airline grew to a $2 billion company. People's Express was cited in *In Search of Excellence* as an ideal American business because of its flat organizational structure and compensation plan that based reward on stock growth. All employees, whether "customer representatives" or pilots, were viewed as equally valuable to the company. Growth seemed to be unlimited and the airline could not process applications or reservations fast enough. Yet, on January 18, 1985, People's Express Airlines declared bankruptcy. Soon thereafter, the parts of the empire that Burr constructed were auctioned off and the routes redistributed.

The basic philosophy driving People's Express was to make air travel available to everyone. At its peak, People's low fares brought thousands of students, the elderly, and the middle class through Newark, New Jersey. The waits were horrendous and the service was chaotic. Yet the $29 fare made the hassle worth it, particularly when the other airlines were charging five times as much. People's fares allowed the carrier to book and fly full planes.

As long as the flights were full, the profits were easy to calculate: Determine the price of the fuel and the equipment and employee cost per flight of the plane; determine a per flight fare that would provide a profit when the expenses were subtracted; and repeat this formula across the flight pattern. Keep the fares so low that the flight would always be booked. By developing the demand in this new market segment, Burr felt that he had found a formula for success that could not be broken.

This approach looked promising until American Airlines used its Sabre reservation system to implement "yield pricing." Through advance ticketing and other restrictions, American was able to discount seats that would otherwise have gone unsold because of People's low fares. The flying public now had a choice. They could continue to fly on People's Express Airlines and deal with the chaos and the crowds, or they could make reservations and fly on American Airlines with comfort. Besides, they could fly directly and not go through Newark. The snack and soft drink were free. The remainder of the seats were sold at full price to business people who could not plan far enough ahead to make advance reservations.

People's vision was a good one. It centered on cost-cutting and motivating the workforce. Certainly over-expansion and the lack of a marketing focus contributed to the failure of People's Express. However, a third major factor was the failure to integrate technology into solving its business problems. Before its first plane left the ground, People's decided not to duplicate American and United Airline's sophisticated reservation systems. Instead, the carrier opted for "a big, dumb computer" that stored passengers' names but could not do sophisticated pricing.

Another reason People's shied away from technological development was that the airline lacked the internal expertise to build or even buy a reservation system. In 1983, the carrier contracted with NCR Corporation to build a system to handle yield management. After 18 months, the project failed. According to Burr, the failure was due to poor communication on both sides and a lack of management attention.

agement found it impossible to raise the additional $100 million needed to create the reservation system.

Computer systems might also be used to create more direct barriers to entry. For instance, as a manufacturer you could build a computer system that is tied to retail stores. The stores would use the system to place orders, and to inquire about products, warranties, and delivery schedules. You might be able to forbid the stores from using the system to connect to any other manufacturers. If the stores gain advantages from the new system, they will end up placing more orders from you, and you will keep out potential competitors. However, you will have to be careful not to violate antitrust regulations.

## Distribution Channels

Controlling **distribution channels** is a method of gaining competitive advantage that is similar to creating barriers to entry. The Japanese economy has long been a classic example of controlling distribution channels, although the role of information systems is minimal. In Japan, sales relationships are developed over long periods of time, and companies have many interrelationships and ties. In particular, distribution of products from manufacturers to retailers is controlled by a few large companies that are loosely organized into support groups. If you want to sell products in Japan, you must build a relationship with one of these companies. American executives have often complained about the problems they experience in dealing with these distributors, which creates a barrier to selling U.S. products in Japan. Although there is disagreement on the cause of the problems, the ability to control distribution channels can be an effective strategy to maintain market share and deter rivals. The distributors gain power through their close personal ties to the customers. For example, in Japan, most new automobiles are sold by salespeople who call on customers at their homes.

Information systems can be used to control distribution channels. As a manufacturer, you could build a computer link to the retail stores. In addition to providing faster ordering and more information, you encourage the store to order directly from your company and avoid competitors. For example, Levi Strauss, the jeans manufacturer, has installed such a system in some retail chains. Assume that you work for a competitor and you call on the retail store to convince the buyers to carry your products. Probably the first question you will be asked is whether the store can order your jeans through the Levi Strauss computer link. If the answer is "no," the store manager is going to be less willing to buy your products.

Now, imagine the confusion that can result for the poor retail manager who wishes to sell similar products from three companies. What happens if each company has its own private computer link? Does the manager need to have three different computer terminals and to learn three different systems?

Partly because of the loss of access to distribution channels and partly because of the confusion resulting from having multiple systems, attempts are being made to standardize some electronic relationships. An important component of electronic data interchange (EDI) is to define standards so that managers only have to work with one system and everyone has reasonable access to that system. If EDI does become standardized, there will be fewer opportunities to control distribution channels with information systems. However, businesses might still be able to gain a competitive edge by providing better, more sophisticated electronic services through the links. For example, expert systems might be used to provide faster responses to retailer and consumer questions.

## Switching Costs

An interesting strategic capability of information systems is their ability to create **switching costs** for your consumers. Consider the case of a brokerage firm that creates a system that enables you to manage your accounts with your personal computer. You buy and sell financial instruments and write checks against your account. The computer automatically tracks your portfolio, notifies you of major changes, and automatically sweeps uninvested cash into interest bearing assets. At the end of the year, it prints a complete summary of your transactions for tax purposes.

Now, what happens if another broker offers you the same capabilities? Will you switch to a new firm? You might, but it depends on what other incentives the company offers. If everything else is the same, most people would be reluctant to change since they incur costs to switch. For example, you would have to learn how to use the new system. Additionally, you would have to reenter your investment data and program new reports and graphs. If you are one of the first firms to create a new system, switching costs can be powerful tools to maintain your market share. As examined in Chapter 1, Baxter Healthcare is a classic case (Figure 11.7) of creating switching costs with an information system.

## Lower Production Costs

In some cases, an effective strategy is to become the lowest-cost producer. If you can consistently sell your product for lower prices than your competitors do, you will

**FIGURE 11.7**
**GAINING A COMPETITIVE ADVANTAGE**
Several classic cases illustrate some important methods of acquiring a competitive advantage. Understanding these cases will help you identify potential strategies in other situations. They will also help you communicate with IS professionals.

---

*Barriers to Entry*

The additional costs of creating a sophisticated information system make it harder for firms to enter the industry. Classic case: People's Express.

*Distribution Channels*

Control over distribution prevents others from entering the industry. Case: Movie distribution to theater chains.

*Switching Costs*

Consumers are reluctant to switch to a competitor if they have to learn a new system or transfer data. Classic Case: Baxter Healthcare.

*Lower Production Costs*

Using technology to become the least-cost producer gives an advantage over the competition. Classic case: Wal-Mart.

*Product Differentiation*

Technology can add new features to a product or create entirely new products that entice consumers. Classic cases: Federal Express and Merrill Lynch.

*Quality Management*

Monitoring production lines and analyzing data are important aspects of quality control. Improving quality leads to more repeat sales. Classic case: Digital Equipment Corp.

*The Value Chain*

Evaluating the entire production process identifies how value is added at each step. Combining steps or acquiring additional stages of the value chain can lead to greater profits. Case: Boeing Information Systems.

have an important advantage. However, consumers need to believe that your products are as good as the competition's.

Computer systems have long been used to decrease costs. Transaction-processing and accounting systems decrease administrative costs. Robots and process control systems can be used to control manufacturing costs. Inventory systems are used to track parts and reduce inventory ordering and holding costs. Marketing systems might be used to create better target marketing, with advantages of improved response and lower marketing costs. Financial systems that control investments and cash flow also can result in decreased costs.

## Product Differentiation and New Products

Another strategic use of information systems is the ability to create new or different products. If you can add features to your product so that consumers believe it is different from the competition, you will be able to make more money.

A classic case of using technology to create a new product is portrayed by Merrill Lynch (Reality Bytes 11-5).

A classic case of using information systems to modify a product for competitive advantage came from Federal Express—an overnight package delivery company. Federal Express was the first major delivery company to track individual packages. The service places bar codes on every package and scans them every time the package is moved. By storing this data in a central database, Federal Express employees can tell customers exactly where any package is located. Besides decreasing the number of lost packages, this system provides a new service for customers. Nervous customers can use the information to determine when a package will be delivered. The information system tracks the current location of each package. When the system

---

### ▼ Reality Bytes ▶  11-5  MERRILL LYNCH CASH MANAGEMENT ACCOUNT (CLASSIC CASE)

Until the 1970s, banks and other financial institutions were treated differently by the government than stock brokers such as Merrill Lynch. Financial institutions could not sell stocks, and there were limits on interest rates that could be paid to depositors. Brokerage companies focused on investments in stocks. In this environment, Merrill Lynch created its Cash Management Account (CMA). For a minimum sum of $25,000, investors could open a new account with Merrill Lynch. The account was similar to a bank account. The money could be placed in risk-free government bonds or it could be used to purchase stocks and bonds. The money could be obtained with minimal problems, including writing checks against the account. In short, the CMA became a bank account for medium and large investors. The primary advantage to the CMA over traditional bank accounts was that there were no government restrictions on the interest rates. As commercial interest rates rose in the late 1970s and early 1980s,

huge sums of money left the banking industry and were deposited in the CMA.

Merrill Lynch used its information system to offer additional features, such as automatic transfers between accounts, overnight repurchases and sales of government bonds, and automatic investments and sales of stocks. All the investment options were controlled by individual investors. Banks could not offer these services because of governmental restrictions, and other brokerage firms did not have the information systems. This use of information technology gave an advantage to Merrill Lynch.

While Merrill Lynch was not known for other innovations, it is one of the largest financial institutions in the United States, with a balance sheet comparable to Citicorp's. In 1995, the brokerage firm had 44,000 employees and operated in 31 countries. The 1994 profit amounted to 18.6 percent return on equity.

was created it provided a unique service to customers. To consumers, Federal Express is offering not just package delivery but also information on the location of the package. This **product differentiation** will help attract customers and might allow the company to charge higher prices.

In some cases, information systems can be used to create entirely new products or services. For example, many banks offer "sweep accounts" to customers who place large sums of money in their bank accounts. There are variations, but the purpose of a sweep account is to automatically place money into higher-interest-bearing assets. For instance, you might need cash available during the day to cover any withdrawals. But if you do not make major withdrawals at night, the bank could lend your money to some-one for overnight use. The bank needs a sophisticated information system to keep track of which customers are participating, monitor what limits they have imposed, and auto-matically transfer the money to the borrower's accounts. (As a side note, you might wonder who wants to borrow money for just one night. There are many possibilities, but two major players are governments and large banks. Some interesting international possibilities also arise by lending across time zones.) Customers receive more interest. Borrowers have access to more funds, and banks make money on the transaction fees and interest differentials. These accounts can only be provided by investing in new information systems. The check-analysis services provided by SunTrust Bank (Reality Bytes 11-6) illustrate another innovative banking feature.

## Quality Management

Firms can gain a competitive advantage by offering higher-quality products. Through the 1980s, surveys indicated that owners reported fewer problems with automobiles manufactured by Japanese firms compared to those produced by U.S. manufacturers.

---

 **Reality Bytes**    **11-6**   SunTrust Bank

Commercial banking consists of providing services to other businesses. Some typical services are credit lines, letters of credit, check processing, and invest-ments. There is tremendous competition to provide services to large customers. To gain a competitive advantage, banks are providing new services, as well as competing on the basis of price.

Traditionally, banks simply process all checks that are presented to them. With the huge volume of checks and federal requirements to process checks in a short period of time, banks do not have time to examine the signature on a check. Improved photo-copiers and low-cost laser printers have made it easy for forgers to create false checks. Several companies have lost millions of dollars.

SunTrust Bank offers a new service for checking accounts of commercial customers. Each day, the commercial firm sends a computer file that lists all of the legitimate checks that were written by the com-pany. When the bank receives the checks for payment, its computers examine the company file. If the check is in the list, it is paid. A list of the checks that do not appear in the main list is sent to the client's accounting department. The accounting department examines the list of unexpected checks. If the check is legitimate, the accountants notify the bank to pay it. Otherwise, the bank refuses to honor the check.

Notice that in addition to providing a new service, this system also strengthens ties to the bank's com-mercial customers. More contact with good service makes it more likely that the company will purchase additional services. The system also increases switch-ing costs. A company would be reluctant to switch banks because the staff would have to create new communication links, store data in a different format, and process different reports.

This difference in quality gave the Japanese firms a competitive advantage. Similarly, Motorola is one of the leading proponents of total quality management. The company is constantly encouraging its suppliers to work at improving quality through the entire manufacturing process.

Information systems have a role in improving quality management. For starters, they can be used to collect data about quality measures. If quality measures come directly from production machines, there can be an overwhelming amount of data. In other cases, quality measures might be collected electronically from your suppliers. Collecting data seems like an obvious idea, but the huge amount of data complicates the process. In many cases, manufacturers have trouble identifying the original source when a component fails. Often, just knowing which suppliers cause the most problems is a useful step in quality management. This data can also help the supplier. Failure data can be used by the supplier to pinpoint the source of problems. Since 1992, nations in the European Union (EU) have been requiring firms to improve quality by complying with the statements in the ISO 9000 (International Organization of Standards) directive. ISO 9000 requires companies to measure quality at all stages of production. Any firm that wishes to sell products or parts to firms in the EU must build an information system to monitor quality and provide information to customers.

No machine is perfect. There is always an element of error in the output. The difficult part is to determine which errors imply that the machine needs to be readjusted. Decision support systems can be used to improve quality. **Statistical quality control (SQC)** is an important tool. Several statistical calculations and graphs are used to determine whether fluctuations are purely random or represent major changes that need to be corrected.

Expert systems can also be employed to control errors and locate the source of the problems. Consider a production line that has 50 major machines. Additionally, several hundred parts are purchased from external suppliers. The final product has thousands of parts and hundreds of assembly operations. Total quality management requires that quality be monitored at each step of the process. A typical problem facing a machine operator is that a machine might be straying off the baseline and needs to be corrected. The operator can face several questions, such as: Which adjustment should be made? Should we overcorrect to compensate for the prior errors? Was the problem caused by this machine, or did earlier operations contribute? If corrections are made now, how will they affect other machines down the line? An experienced operator might be able to answer some of these questions. On the other hand, an expert system might be helpful at solving the more complex problems. Digital (Reality Bytes 11–7) used expert systems to improve quality and cut the cost of installing minicomputers. Digital's weak performance in the 1990s also illustrates the difficulty in maintaining a competitive advantage as the market changes.

## The Value Chain

One method of searching for areas that might provide you with strategic benefits is to examine the entire **value chain** of the industry. As shown in Figure 11.8, the key feature of a value chain is to examine each step of production and determine how value is added at each step. If some steps show larger increases in value than others, they will be key points to target for strategic action. The second objective of value chain analysis is to encourage decision makers to examine

**Reality Bytes     11-7   Digital's Use of Expert Systems (Classic Case)**

In the 1970s, Digital Equipment Corporation was experiencing problems with installation of its computers. Many times, various components were purchased and delivered that would not work together. Similarly, installers found that the delivered equipment was often missing necessary cables. The basic problem was that Digital offered many computers, each with different options. Additionally, new versions of hardware typically required different cables and were often incompatible with earlier models. As the number of combinations multiplied, it became impossible for salespeople to keep track of which components worked together and which options were needed for each package. Although the installers and customer service representatives would eventually solve the problems encountered by each customer, the time,

money, and negative images were detrimental to Digital.

To combat these problems, Digital created an expert system called Xcon, that evaluates every order. As new models and peripherals are created, the engineers add the requirements to the expert system. The expert systems works as an engineer to evaluate each sale and make sure the necessary components are included. Use of this system improved the quality of the final product along with reducing costs, giving Digital an advantage over its rivals. The system has an average success rate of 90 percent, versus about 70 percent for human operators. Because of this success, Digital continues to expand its use of expert systems throughout the company, with hundreds of expert systems in use today.

**FIGURE 11.8**

Value chain. The value chain illustrates the essential operations in a business. Every firm has operations for purchasing, production, shipping, marketing, and customer service. These processes are supported by the organization of the firm, human resources management, technology development, and procurement services. Providing services desired by customers contributes to the profit margin of the firm.

the bigger picture in the industry. In many cases, a firm can benefit by expanding its operations beyond its traditional activities. For instance, an automobile manufacturer (Ford) might buy a car rental agency (Hertz). Now the manufacturer can control a large consumer of its products and control the sale of the used vehicles. The Boeing company (Reality Bytes 11–8) similarly broadened its market by spinning off its computer services division, enabling it to offer services to consumers such as NASA.

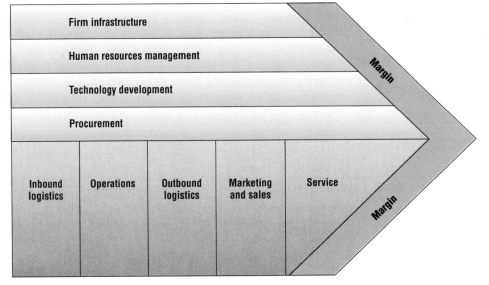

**Reality Bytes** ◣ **11–8** BOEING COMPUTER SERVICES: THE VALUE CHAIN

In 1989, Boeing Computer Services sold $1.5 billion in systems integration work. Eighty-five percent was attributable to federal jobs; 15 percent to commercial ones. According to Mike Little, vice-president of information services,

> We expect the commercial percentage to go up a bit. Our focus, however, will continue to be primarily the U.S. government. A significant element of our strategy is to take advantage of our presence, expertise, and experience in telecommunications and network integration on the federal side and to leverage that to grow our commercial sales.

Boeing Computer Services fits nicely into the value chain of its parent, the Boeing Company. The largest percentage, 76 percent, of Boeing Computer Services' income comes from work it does for the Boeing Company. The next largest income generator is the

National Aeronautics and Space Administration. BCS's primary work is in telecommunications and networking. Other commercial target areas include document-management systems involving image-processing and electronic data interchange.

BCS is most famous for its 1984 10-year contract to design, install, and operate an integrated digital network for NASA's business and engineering needs. Known as the NASA Program Support Communications Network, its hub is at the Marshall Space Flight Center. The network links 17 NASA centers and 100,000 users nationwide. At each center, the network manages an average of 13,000 telecommunications devices. In building the network, BCS was responsible for coordinating over 800 suppliers, subcontractors, and vendors. By 1992, BCS dropped all outside contracts to concentrate on supporting the all-digital design of the new 777 aircraft.

**THE SEARCH FOR INNOVATION**

Industry and academic leaders are constantly searching for ways to improve organizations and gain a competitive advantage. Illustrated by Figure 11.9, one method to organize the search is to examine the primary processes of the firm: research, engineering and design, manufacturing, logistics and supply, marketing, sales and order management, service, and general management. Each of these processes has its own

**FIGURE 11.9**

Process innovation. Production consists of the processes of supply logistics, manufacturing, and sales management. These processes are directly supported by design, engineering, and marketing. Research and customer service support all of the processes; top management organizes and controls the firm. Technology can provide innovations in all of these processes.

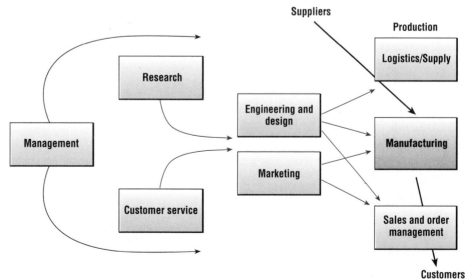

inputs, outputs, and objectives. Analyzing them in detail enables managers to spot problems and to search for innovative opportunities.

The following sections present general ideas for each of these processes that have generated interest and some success. Most of them use technology to improve the process or to help the processes work together better. Keep in mind that in any firm, there can be many ways of improving processes. Relying on information technology is not always the best answer.

Just coming up with a new corporate strategy is difficult, but it is not enough. As indicated by Figure 11.10, an effective strategic plan must also describe the changes in the process, identify the new data needs, and describe how the information system will be changed to support the new strategy. Figure 11.11 summarizes the capabilities of IT to support innovation.

## Research

Research in firms varies enormously depending on the industry and the overall corporate strategy. At a minimum, most firms at least have a product development team that is constantly searching for new products or improvements in existing products. Some companies, like 3M, DuPont, AT&T, or Intel, spend considerable sums of money on basic research to create entirely new products. To these firms, strategic advantage comes from being the leader in the industry with a constant cycle of new products.

IT support for research takes the form of computer analysis and modeling, statistical analysis of data, project management and budgeting, and workgroup technologies that make it easy for researchers to collaborate and share information with each other and with managers throughout the company.

## Engineering and Design

Engineering and design processes are responsible for converting theoretical research into new products. Engineers establish manufacturing procedures, design new equipment, and coordinate suppliers with production. In particular, the design process must optimize the production line to minimize costs and retain high quality.

**FIGURE 11.10**
Developing strategies. Market measures and firm performance measures are used to highlight problems and opportunities. Corporate strategies are developed from process improvements and innovations. Potential strategies are evaluated and prioritized. Processes are re-engineered and new systems are designed and implemented.

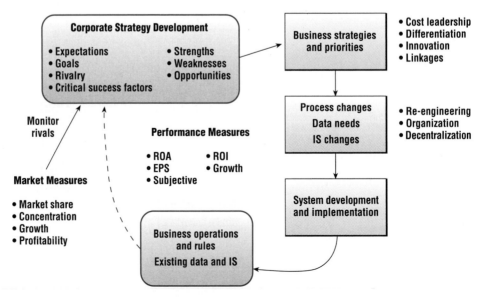

**FIGURE 11.11**
THE SEARCH FOR
INNOVATION
Information technology
provides many
opportunities for
improving the
fundamental business
processes. IT is used
to improve
communication,
decrease costs, reduce
design times, monitor
customers and rivals,
and improve
customer service.

| AREA | INFORMATION TECHNOLOGY SUPPORT |
|---|---|
| Research | Analysis and modeling, project management, workgroup support, databases, decision support. |
| Engineering and Design | CAD/CAM, testing, networks, workgroup support. |
| Manufacturing | Mass customization, links from customers and suppliers, robotics, quality monitoring, expert systems for maintenance, production databases, business integration tools. |
| Logistics and Supply | Just-in-time linkages, forecasts, models, links for design, transaction processing. |
| Marketing | Frequent buyer databases, target market and media analysis, survey design and analysis, multimedia promotion design, links between customers and design teams. |
| Sales and Orders | Portable computers for salesperson contact, expert systems for order customization and configuration, workgroup tools for customer support. |
| Service | Phone support systems, location monitoring and scheduling of service people, expert system diagnostics, databases. |
| Management | Enterprise information systems, links to service providers (accountants, consultants, etc.), e-mail, bulletin boards, decision support systems, personal productivity tools, workgroup support. |

Support for engineering and design takes the form of CAD/CAM systems that make it easy to create, modify, store, and share new designs. If these systems are coupled to integrated design databases, engineers can more easily reuse prior results. Tying into production databases enables the engineers to model and test various aspects of their designs. Engineers can also be supported with expert systems that help them analyze production aspects of their designs. As General Motors engineers design new cars, software helps them improve the layout to simplify production and to use existing components. Engineers are also being supported by workgroup technologies that make it easy to share designs and receive input from teams of workers throughout the company.

## Manufacturing

There are four key features to production: costs, speed or timing, quality, and flexibility. Competing through lower costs and higher quality are time-honored means of gaining a competitive advantage. They might not be sufficient today. Increasingly, firms are turning to **mass customization** in an attempt to gain market share. Twenty or 30 years ago, the large firms in an industry were content to build huge plants, gain economies of scale, and aim at the mass market. This approach tended to leave niches open for competing firms. The problem with this strategy is that it allows rival firms to gain a toehold, which they might use to build market share and eventually compete directly against your primary market. Today's firms are trying to shift production fast enough so that they can cover virtually all of the niche markets.

Mass customization requires an IT system that links the sales system directly to the production line and through to supply. It also involves heavy use of robotics that are configurable directly from one computer. Other uses of IT include expert systems for maintenance and diagnostics. Japanese firms have long been proponents of preventive maintenance. If you wait until a machine breaks, it is too late. Expert systems can be used to schedule routine maintenance and spot problems before they cause problems. IT systems are also heavily used to monitor quality and suggest improvements.

## Logistics and Supply

The implementation of just-in-time (JIT) inventory systems is largely credited to Japanese manufacturers. Today they are used by manufacturers worldwide. Manufacturers attempt to cut costs by holding minimal inventories. Instead, inventories are maintained by the suppliers, who deliver the products to the assembly line just as they are needed. The system can only work if the suppliers and factories are linked electronically—often there is only a one- or two-hour delay between ordering and delivery.

Suppliers are often involved in the design phase. Their knowledge is useful in identifying supply availability, costs, and substitutability of components. Sometimes, it is difficult to locate suppliers for equipment. Computer networks like IndustryNet help firms connect with potential suppliers, identifying equipment, parts, and prices.

## Marketing

A well-known application of IT to improve marketing is the use of frequent-buyer databases that identify major customers. More traditional point-of-sale transaction systems can be leveraged by identifying preferences and rapidly spotting patterns or trends. At the tactical level, expert systems are used to help analyze data and perform statistical trend analysis. Geographic information systems are being used by leading firms to identify patterns and possibilities for new sales. Information systems can also be used to link firms more closely to external marketing firms for research data, communication, and development of promotional materials.

Multimedia tools are being used by leading firms to develop initial ideas for advertising and promotional campaigns. Companies like General Motors are also using video tools and computer dissemination of video to link customers and marketing closer to the design team.

## Sales and Order Management

Sales and order management are often handled simply as an operations or transaction-processing area. However, in the last 10 years, several firms have used technology to gain a competitive advantage by improving the way they handle sales and orders. Frito-Lay's use of hand-held computers is a classic example. The systems enabled managers to more closely track their own sales, sales of competitors, and other external factors. For certain industries, the concept can be extended further to installing workstations at the customer sites that tap into your central databases. Federal Express and Baxter Healthcare both used this technology to gain a leadership position.

Leading firms are also using expert system to assist customers in choosing the products and options that best match their needs. These systems assist order-takers and improve sales by matching customer needs. Expert systems are similarly used to improve configuration and shipping.

Workgroup technologies, e-mail, and expert systems all combine to give more power to the front-line workers dealing directly with customers. Resolving problems and meeting customer needs faster can improve customer satisfaction and cut costs.

## Service

Service industries and service-based processes (like accounting, MIS, and law) have their own problems and opportunities. Technology is used to support services with on-site, portable computers. These systems enable workers to have complete access to information almost anywhere in the world. Leading companies are building specialized databases to support their service workers, such as the "answer line" databases that support General Electric and Whirlpool customer service representatives.

Systems are built that monitor locations of service personnel, enabling firms to identify the closest workers to problems and to fine-tune schedules throughout the day. Complex products are increasingly being sold with internal diagnostic systems that automatically notify service departments. Similarly, companies are cutting costs and reducing repair time by building expert systems to diagnose problems.

## Management

One of the more dramatic IT support mechanisms for management is an enterprise information system. By giving top managers better access to data, it allows them to identify and correct problems faster. More sophisticated models can be built to examine alternatives—especially to analyze the potential reactions of rivals in a competitive situation.

Larger firms are building electronic links to their strategic partners, for instance, by providing electronic access to corporate data to accounting and legal firms. These links enable the external partners to keep a closer eye on the firm, speeding the identification of problems and assisting them in spotting broad patterns and opportunities.

Executives are also increasingly turning to electronic conferencing tools and workgroup software, even e-mail. With these systems, executives can cover more areas and deal with more people than through the phone or through face-to-face contact. Some studies have shown that in traditional conversations managers spend as much as 50 percent of the time on personal "chit-chat." Electronic systems (although they might be less personal) tend to be more efficient. On the other hand, some companies have been restricting employee access to electronic networks (especially the Internet) because they waste too much time on personal communications.

Another approach taken by management is the move toward standardization: the effort to make all jobs similar, routine, and interchangeable. By reducing jobs to their most basic level, they become easier to control and easier to support or replace with information technology. Franchises make good use of this concept. At the same time, management jobs in some companies are being reformulated as teams of knowledge-workers. In the past, managers worked on fixed tasks within the corporate hierarchy. Today, you are more likely to be hired for your specific skills and knowledge. As the needs of the company change, you will work with different teams at solving problems and creating new products and services. Personal computers and client-server technologies are often used to support these management teams. Instead of relying on one central computing facility, each team has its own set of resources that is shared over networks throughout the company.

**COSTS AND DANGERS OF STRATEGIES**

Strategic uses of information systems can be seductive. There are many interesting cases in which companies have created innovative information systems. Inventing strategic alternatives requires a considerable amount of creativity. It is easy to get caught up in the excitement of designing new approaches and to forget about the risks. Evaluation of any project requires weighing the risks against the potential gains.

| STRATEGY | SKILLS AND RESOURCES REQUIRED | ORGANIZATIONAL REQUIREMENTS | RISKS |
|---|---|---|---|
| Differentiation | • Strong marketing.<br>• Product engineering.<br>• Basic research skills.<br>• Distribution channel acceptance and cooperation. | • Internal coordination, R&D, production, and marketing.<br>• Incentives for innovation.<br>• Resources to attract creative and skilled labor. | • Competitors imitate.<br>• Customers do not accept differences.<br>• Cost is too high. |
| Cost Leadership | • Continued capital investment.<br>• Process engineering.<br>• Continuous quality improvement.<br>• Tight supervision of labor and costs.<br>• Products designed for low-cost production.<br>• Low-cost distribution. | • Tight cost control.<br>• Frequent, detailed control reports.<br>• Highly structured organization.<br>• Incentives based on quantitative measures. | • Competitors imitate.<br>• Technology changes.<br>• Lose production or distribution advantage. |
| Customer-Supplier Links | • Influence with partners.<br>• Communication channels.<br>• Standards or agreements. | • Flexibility to respond to customers.<br>• Service-culture.<br>• Ability to adapt to emergencies. | • Security threats.<br>• Changing standards.<br>• Competitors copy with more links. |

**FIGURE 11.12**

Implementing strategy can be difficult, costly, and time consuming. Firms generally choose one primary strategy and then build the resources and shape the organization to best support that strategy.

Although it is often difficult to measure the potential gains and risks, it is important to consider all consequences. By their nature, strategic changes can alter the entire course of the firm. Figure 11.12 summarizes the skills, organizational effects, and risks involved with several strategies.

Robert Morison and Kirtland Mead ("A Hard Look at Strategic Systems") pointed out that it is easy to misinterpret the various classic cases regarding strategic use of technology. For example, in many cases, the true strategy does not lie in the computer system; instead, the gains came from changing the way the business operates. For instance, the gains experienced by American Hospital Supply (Baxter Healthcare Reality Bytes 11–11) came about because they improved the way their customers (hospitals) handled supplies and inventory. The computer system facilitated this change but was not necessarily responsible for it. In other words, rather than search for a *killer* strategic computer system, it is wiser to identify ways to improve the overall business.

## High Capital Costs

One of the important considerations in strategic analysis is the cost. Strategic changes often involve implementing new technology before any of your competitors. Yet new

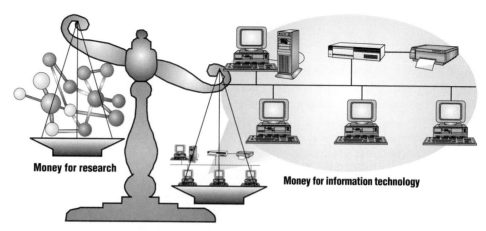

**FIGURE 11.13**
Dangers of strategy. When developing and choosing strategies, you must always remember that innovations can be risky and often carry high capital costs. Although it may be exciting to spend millions of dollars on technology, it can destroy the firm if you do not have enough resources to support research and operations.

**Money for research**

**Money for information technology**

technology tends to carry high costs. Manufacturers of technology may not have reached economies of scale, and they might have monopoly power over prices through patent rights. Additionally, the IS teams will have less experience with the technology, so it will take longer to implement and may result in missteps and require additional testing. For instance, Morison and Mead report that "It took six years and $350 million before American Airlines' Sabre travel agency reservation system started paying off." As Figure 11.13 notes, these costs might take away money from other projects.

It can be difficult to estimate the cost of major projects—especially when they involve new technologies. There are many examples of MIS projects going over budget and beyond deadlines. Additionally, strategic projects often require major capital outlays up front, but increased revenues do not appear until much later.

A big question with new technology is trying to decide when it should be implemented. There is an inherent conflict. If you offer an innovative service from the technology before your competitors, you can gain a competitive advantage. However, if you wait, the costs will be lower. In making this decision, you will also have to guess what action your competitors will take.

## When the Competition Follows

Another difficulty with strategic systems is that much of the advantage comes from creating a service that is not offered by your rivals. Once you introduce the service, your rivals will watch the customer response closely. If the customers begin to switch to your firm, your rivals will undoubtedly create a system to offer the same services. At that point, you lose most of the competitive advantage. Even worse, you might end up with an escalating "war" of technology, as depicted in Figure 11.14. Although the competition is good for the customer, the increased expenditures can cause problems for the company if the ideas do not work as well as you expected. Kash n' Karry (Reality Bytes 11-9) experienced problems when its attempt to gain a strategic advantage did not pay off. On the other hand, Federal Express (Reality Bytes 11-10) uses the same technology (object orientation) to create a competitive advantage. There are differences between industries, and you must carefully evaluate the costs and potential profits.

The gains to technology occur from when you first implement the strategy to the point that your rivals follow. For example, almost all of the major overnight delivery services now provide the ability to track shipments. If the system is easy to create,

**Reality Bytes**    **11–9**    KASH N' KARRY

Kash n' Karry is a Tampa-based chain of 132 retail grocery stores with about $1 billion in annual sales. In 1993, management was concerned about increased competition. Managers decided to build a strategic information system. Win Burke, vice-president of a software company that worked closely with Kash n' Karry, observes that "They felt a very flexible, very reactive information system would allow them to be quicker and more nimble in making pricing and inventory changes and decisions."

Over a two-year time period, the company built an object-oriented warehousing application and a promotional pricing system. The warehouse system tracks and catalogs damaged and returned items from stores. The pricing system is part of an executive information system that enables senior managers to monitor store sales. The two projects are estimated to have cost about $1.5 million to create.

In early 1995, Kash n' Karry pulled the plug on its development team. The chain faced too much debt and filed for bankruptcy protection. As part of the reorganization, the company outsourced the entire MIS department to GSI, a French outsourcing company. Development of additional systems was canceled. Denise Matthys, the MIS employee in charge of coordinating the outsourcing project, summarizes the issues: "I think we probably were a little too far out on the leading edge, and we learned a lot from it. But we have to remember that we're in retail and we sell groceries."

SOURCE: Julia King, "Back to Basics: Supermarket Chain Shelves Object Plans, Outsources IS," *Computerworld,* March 20, 1995, pp. 1, 117. Copyright 1995 by Computerworld, Inc., Framingham, MA 01701. Reprinted from *Computerworld.*

**FIGURE 11.14**

Strategy dangers: Competition follows. One complication with strategies is that your competitors will implement a similar system. Over time, you will be forced to expand your system and provide additional features. In a healthy industry, this competition can generate new services, new customers, and greater profits. It is important to evaluate the long-run effects on the industry while analyzing strategic options.

you may not gain much. However, it is likely that customers who switched to your firm will stay, so you can gain a larger share of the market.

On the other hand, if your strategic ideas do not pay off, your rivals will gain, because you will likely lose most of the money invested in the project. Some firms use this tactic to great advantage. They allow smaller firms to take the risk and experiment with new technologies. If the project succeeds, the large firm steps in with

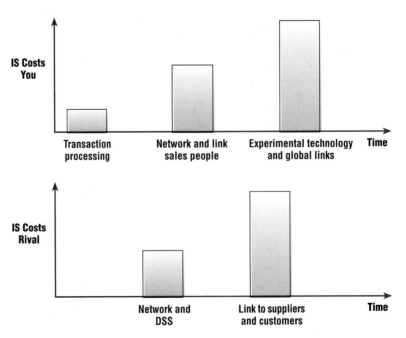

**Reality Bytes**    **11–10   FEDERAL EXPRESS AND OBJECT ORIENTATION**

Federal Express has long relied on technology to build a competitive advantage. The courier took the lead in the delivery industry with its package tracking system, tracing the flow of more than 2 million packages a night. In the early 1990s, Federal Express introduced desktop software for customers, enabling them to track packages from their own desks. It also keeps track of shipping charges and usage. In the mid-1990s, Federal Express is turning its focus to object-oriented design. In particular, the courier is attempting to improve IT quality and reduce maintenance costs by defining a set of basic objects. These object definitions can be reused throughout all of the projects.

Daniel Sweeney, architectural planning manager, notes that

- Information technology should map to business.
- Object technology maps well to Federal Express.
- The key to objects is process management.

- The key to process is configuration management.

Objects at Federal Express are derived from the essential process: delivering packages. Basic objects consist of items like packages, shipping orders, customers, vehicles, planes, and employees. Consistency and quality are enhanced by building a single definition of each of these objects and sharing it across all applications. With reusable objects, Sweeney believes that it will be easier and faster to alter the information systems. For instance, changes in the application often can be made by altering a few properties or functions within one or two objects. With an object design, these changes are made in one location, and the rest of the application is unaffected, reducing the probability of errors.

SOURCE: Daniel Sweeney, architectural planning manager at Federal Express, satellite broadcast.

more money and more clout and creates its own improved version. About the only risk they take is that the smaller firm might become successful enough to grab a serious share of the market.

## Changing Industry

An intriguing problem that can arise is that even if your strategic project succeeds, the company might lose because your project has changed the industry. Consider an insurance company that sells software to companies to allow them to track insurance deductions and payments to workers. The insurance company decides that it can add a program to also compute payroll, so the companies could drop their existing payroll software. These features appear to give the company an edge over its rivals in the insurance industry. The problem is that there are many more companies that create payroll software. It is very simple for these companies to add insurance capabilities to their existing software. The actions of the insurance company encourage the payroll software firms to move into the insurance market. Illustrated in Figure 11.15, the insurance company suddenly has hundreds of new competitors and could lose customers.

## Sharing Data

One common technique in strategic systems is to share your data with customers and suppliers. Two questions arise from this situation. First, do you really want suppliers and customers to have access to the data? Second, can you control their access to protect other data? Security and control issues are examined in detail in Chapter 14. The main point to think about here is what might happen as your customers gain access to your data. Consider the situation of a supplier to General Motors. To save

**FIGURE 11.15**
Changing industry and government intervention. A complication with strategy is it might alter the industry. A firm in Industry 1 might use IT to attract customers from a different industry. Because of this expansion, the firm gains new competitors (from Industry 2). While competition is often beneficial, you must thoroughly analyze the effect of the new competition before embarking on changing the industry. In a related manner, sometimes changes in government regulations alter relationships between industries, as in the telephone and cable-TV markets with passage by Congress of the 1996 Telecommunications bill.

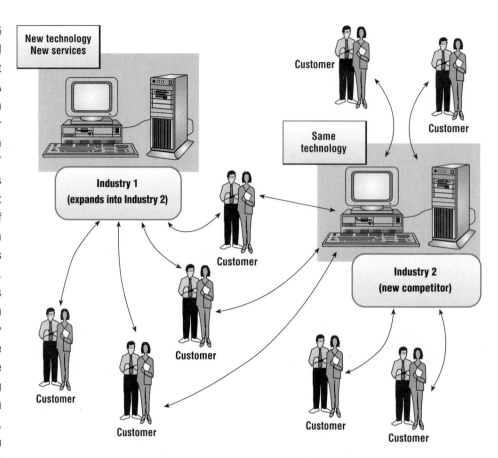

costs and improve communications, GM wants you to connect your computer to the GM factory computers. GM intends to use the links to place orders, monitor quality data, and track shipments. Are you willing to give GM access to your computer? Can you control the information that the large corporation is allowed to see? Maybe to check on orders GM will also be able to determine how much you are producing for other companies. Or maybe GM will gain access to your supplier lists and raw material prices. Even if the GM managers are ethical and do not reveal this data to anyone else, you still might worry. What happens when you have to negotiate prices with GM the next time? If the corporation has access to your data, you might be concerned that it could influence the negotiations. Figure 11.16 illustrates the need for security systems that will enable you to control the access to your data.

## Government Intervention

You have to be careful when considering strategic maneuvers. Many potential strategies violate **antitrust laws.** For example, many barriers to entry are illegal, as is price discrimination. In fact, attempts to monopolize a market are forbidden by the Sherman Antitrust Act. Price fixing and other forms of collusion are also outlawed. Information system agreements between competitors could be scrutinized by the Justice Department or the Federal Trade Commission.

If government agents choose strict interpretations of the laws, it could complicate many information system issues. For instance, firms might be discouraged from

**Reality Bytes** ▲ **11–11** Bᴀxᴛᴇʀ Hᴇᴀʟᴛʜᴄᴀʀᴇ (Cʟᴀssɪᴄ Cᴀsᴇ)

American Hospital Supply gained a competitive advantage by using technology to show hospitals how to reduce their inventories. Although this technique was successful, it also demonstrated to Baxter Healthcare that the technique was successful. Baxter is a large manufacturer of hospital supplies that bought out AHS in 1985.

This purchase enables Baxter to reduce the total inventory in the system. The company can use the AHS warehouses in each city to hold its inventory and does not need to keep inventory at Baxter's plants. Managers also get instant data on demand for products and make more money by eliminating the firm in the middle.

Presumably Baxter paid market price when it bought AHS, so the investments by AHS were not wasted. However, the strategic investment changed the industry so that AHS no longer exists.

After the purchase, Baxter did not stand still. Michael Heschel, Baxter's corporate vice-president of information resources, discusses three IT goals Baxter is pursuing:

- Make as much data as possible available throughout the $6.8 billion corporation.
- Implement leading-edge manufacturing technology.
- Push the computing function out into the business units and down to the most feasible functional level.

One of the primary goals is to push information and decision making down to the customer level, both to reduce costs and to satisfy customers.

One problem Baxter encountered was that for five years after the purchase of AHS, the company still operated two completely different order-processing and distribution systems: one for AHS, and one for Baxter.

Baxter executives decided that to maintain its lead, the company needed to continually adapt and improve the ASAP order system. In 1990, Baxter began upgrading the 7,000 terminals installed at customer sites. Five hundred of them were replaced with personal computers. The PCs provide the hospital managers with direct access to their purchasing and product-use patterns. Another of Baxter's long-run plans is to expand its networks in overseas markets.

In 1994, Baxter International along with three other hospital suppliers began cooperating to produce a standardized electronic ordering system. With existing proprietary systems, hospitals often need multiple computer systems with different terminals to place orders with multiple suppliers.

The new system is designed to link the major suppliers and reduce paperwork. Organizers hope to add electronic catalogs, payments, and database searches to the system.

forming consortiums that define standards. Agreements to share disaster backup facilities might be outlawed. Computer links to customers might be seen as limiting competition. So far, the U.S. agencies have allowed all of these activities to proceed without interference. However, there is always the chance that other nations or different political administrations will view the issues differently.

In the 1980s, the government was relatively lenient about antitrust issues, including those regarding information systems. However, one interesting case arose with the airline reservation systems. For many years, American Airlines and United Airlines had the leading reservation systems. Other airlines could list flights on the systems, but they had to pay money for each ticket sold through the system. A conflict eventually arose, because the airlines that created the system programmed it to list their flights first. Flights from other airlines were often listed on separate screens, so travel agents and customers were encouraged to choose flights from the airline that built the system. Although this mechanism did not directly violate antitrust laws, Congress decided to pass a new law, making the practice illegal. Lawmakers decided that as long as the other airlines had to pay for

**FIGURE 11.16**

Security complications. Improving communication and sharing data are common themes in using technology for competitive advantage. This need to share data with "outsiders" makes it more difficult to protect your internal data. Security systems can provide some protections, but the more outsiders who are involved, the more difficult it is to provide adequate security.

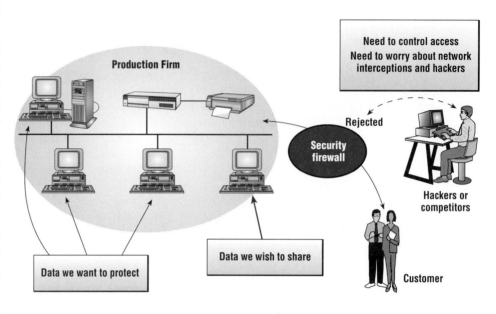

access to the system, everyone should have an equal chance at being listed first. The point is that even though the initial action was not illegal, Congress has the ability to pass new laws and remove the advantages, so you cannot assume that the benefits will last.

## OPERATIONS, TACTICS, STRATEGY

Strategic plans involving information technology are not created from thin air. The systems are based on improved or expanded use of operations- and tactical-level systems.

Consider the airline reservations systems, which began life as transaction-processing systems, reducing costs and making it easier for people to get the flights they want. Similarly, banking systems like ATMs and debit cards were targeted at improving transactions. Yet, these systems all had a strategic component: Being the first organization to implement these systems led to better customer service and increased market share.

Tactical-level systems can also provide strategic advantages. Making better decisions faster creates improved products, more loyal customers, and lower costs. Building decision support systems, enterprise information systems, expert systems, and AI techniques helps to reduce the bureaucracy of middle management. Two important strategic consequences arise: (1) more control and authority are pushed down to customer service agents, enabling them to solve problems faster and meet the needs of the customer; and (2) top executives gain more information and control over the business—making it easier to identify problems, enact new strategies, and respond faster to changes in the business environment.

Overall, there are two important lessons to be learned regarding strategic uses of technology: (1) computer systems can provide value beyond simple cost cutting; and (2) strategic gains are often fleeting, requiring continual upgrades and investment in new technology. Because new technology is expensive, and innovations do not always succeed, it can be risky being on the leading edge. Each firm needs to decide *when* it should adopt new technology. Being first carries not only high costs and more risk but the opportunity for greater rewards, as well as a certain image. Being a technology follower has the advantage of reducing costs. Each industry contains both types of firms.

## SUMMARY

Information systems can provide benefits beyond traditional cost saving. Competitive advantages can be gained by creating barriers to entry and gaining control over distribution channels. Using information systems to build ties to suppliers and customers can provide lower costs and better quality products. Computer systems also provide incentives for customers to remain with your company if they incur costs of learning new systems and transferring data when switching to a competitor. Information systems can also be used to differentiate your products from the others in the marketplace. Similarly, innovative services offered with the help of technology can entice customers and expand your market.

You can search for competitive advantages by examining Porter's external forces of rivals, customers, suppliers, substitute products, and new entrants. You can also search for strategies in research, engineering, and design. In manufacturing, you can look for ways to decrease costs and improve logistics. In marketing, potential gains can be found in better understanding of customer wants, as well as sales and order management. Services can be supported through better information flows and workgroup products. Management can be helped with better data and better decision tools.

### A MANAGER'S VIEW

With increased competition, every manager is being asked to identify ways to improve the company and find an advantage over the rivals. Gaining a competitive edge is not easy. Examining the entire value chain is a useful place to start. Information systems can provide data and evaluate models to help you identify strategic applications. Information systems can also provide direct advantages by creating a barrier to entry, gaining control over distribution, cutting costs, improving quality, and improving ties between suppliers and customers.

There are many risks to strategic systems. They tend to be expensive and difficult to create. Any gains created may disappear when competitors pick up the technology and imitate your offerings. Additionally, making strategic changes to your firm might alter the industry, which might adversely affect your firm. And if these problems are not enough to discourage you, remember that attempts to monopolize a market are illegal, so you have to make sure that your plans do not violate governmental regulations.

## KEY WORDS

antitrust laws, 526
barriers to entry, 510
distribution channels, 511
external agents, 504
five forces model, 504

mass customization, 519
product differentiation, 514
rivals, 506
statistical quality control (SQC), 515

switching costs, 512
total quality management (TQM), 506
value chain, 515

## REVIEW QUESTIONS

1. Briefly describe four techniques that can be used to gain competitive advantage.
2. How is strategic analysis related to the environment aspect of the systems approach?
3. What are external agents?
4. What are the costs and dangers of strategic implementations?
5. For a large manufacturing firm, who are the customers? How many different types of customers can there be?
6. Why are barriers to entry important to gain a competitive advantage?
7. How does control over distribution channels give a firm a competitive advantage?

8. How can information systems be used to gain control over distribution channels?
9. How might EDI limit firms from gaining control over the distribution channels?
10. What are switching costs, and how can they give a company a competitive advantage?
11. How can information systems be used to enhance product differentiation and create new products?
12. What role is played by information systems in improving quality management?
13. What is the value chain and how is it used to search for competitive advantage?

## EXERCISES

1. Consider a small service firm such as a physician, dentist, accountant, or law office. Is it possible for such an office to use computers to gain a competitive advantage? To start, identify the customers, suppliers, and rivals. Do you think the "natural" switching costs are high or low—that is, how often do customers switch to competitors? Which of the major techniques do you think would be the most successful (barriers to entry, switching costs, quality control, lower prices, ties to customers or suppliers, etc.)?

2. How long can firms maintain an advantage using an information system? Research one of the classic cases and find out how long it took for the competitors to implement a similar information system (for example, Merrill Lynch and its Cash Management Account, American Airlines and the Sabre System, Levi-Strauss and its Levi-Link ordering system, or Federal Express and its tracking system). Find out when the system was implemented, identify the competitors, and find out when they implemented similar systems. Did the original company continue to update its strategy? Collect data on sales and profits for the firms to see whether there were major changes.

3. Choose a country other than the United States, Canada, Japan, or a Western European nation. (In particular, select a developing nation perhaps in South America, Africa, Eastern Europe, or Southeast Asia.) Research the communication and information system facilities available to firms in that country. Do you think firms in the United States have a competitive advantage over those firms? If so, what could the firms (or nations) do to overcome that advantage? How will the countries compare five years from now?

4. Read through the industry cases for each chapter in the book. Identify the firms that have chosen to be technology leaders and those that are followers. What other differences can you find between the firms (profits, sales, employees)?

5. Pick an industry. Find two firms in the industry— one a technology leader, the other a follower. Get the financial information on those firms for the last five years. Find analyst summaries of their operations. Compare the two firms. Are there differences in finances, operating methods, or customers?

 **Rolling Thunder Database**

1. Identify the competition in the industry. Who are existing rivals? Who are potential rivals? Be sure to carefully define the industry. Consider using SIC codes.

2. Perform a value chain analysis of the company. Could they improve profits by expanding vertically or horizontally? Are there additional products that we should consider offering?

3. What data do we collect? Can it be used to achieve greater value? Would other firms be interested in our data? Are there possibilities for alliances with other companies?

4. We have the opportunity to purchase a chain of retail bicycle stores. Evaluate the strategic aspects of this proposed acquisition. What will be the effect on the information systems? Can the existing information system be used to improve the operations of the retail stores? What additions and improvements would be needed?

## ADDITIONAL READING

"A Question of Support," *Computerworld*, November 5, 1990, p. 124. [Boeing computer services]

Adhikar, Richard. "Support Shops Call on Automated Tools," *Software Magazine*, May 1995, pp. 48-54. [Digital's use of expert systems]

"Airline to Give Its Agents Wireless Access to Databases," *PC Week*, January 23, 1995. [Airlines]

"American Airlines Signs Long-Term CDPD Contract," *Communications Week*, January 16, 1995. [Airlines]

Andrews, K.R. *The Concept of Corporate Strategy. 3rd ed.* Burr Ridge: Richard D. Irwin, 1987. [Basic text on designing corporate strategy]

Barney, Lee. "Data Warehousing Tames a Cyclone of Information," *Wall Street & Technology*, June 1995, pp. 68-71. [Merrill Lynch and brokerage trading systems]

"Best Practices: Creating Shared Knowledge Bases Gives IT an Edge in C/S Development," *PC Week*, February 6, 1995. [Airlines]

Bicknel, David. "The Politics of Failure," *Computer Weekly*, July 6, 1995, pp. 28-29. [Department of Defense]

Brewin, Bob. "Hidden Funding Would Double Pentagon's IT Spending," *Federal Computer Week*, July 10, 1995, pp. 38-39. [Department of Defense]

Carley, William M. "Did Northwest Steal American's Systems?" *The Wall Street Journal*, July 7, 1994, pp. A1, A8. [Airlines]

Constance, Paul. "Ivory I-CASE Tower Crumbles," *Government Computer News*, March 4, 1996, pp. 46-47. [Department of Defense]

Constance, Paul. "Don't Slip Softly into the Swamp; Navy and Air Force Guides Help Software Managers Avoid Common Traps," *Government Computer News*, October 30, 1995, pp. 39-40. [Department of Defense]

"Creating a Corporate Strategy for Imaging and Document Management," *Datamation*, October 15, 1995, pp. S4-S16. [Department of Defense]

"Defense Department Plots Private ATM Strategy," *Network World*, February 6, 1995. [Department of Defense]

Dellecove, Jr., Tam. "Wireless Off the Ground: American Airlines Counts on Cellular Technology to Shorten Delays in Airports," *Information Week*, May 29, 1995, pp. 33-34. [Airlines]

"DOD Frets Over Proposed Cuts in ARPA's TRP," *Electronic News*, March 13, 1995. [Department of Defense]

"DOD Spells Out How It Will Shift Its Traffic to FTS 2000," *Government Computer News*, 2/6/95. [Department of Defense]

Endoso, Joyce. "Hilmes Will Tighten the Belt on Army ADP," *Government Computer News*, January 20, 1992, p. 52. [Department of Defense]

Evers, Andy. "Review of New Developments in Text Retrieval Systems," *Journal of Information Science*, 1994, pp. 438-443. [Florida Power and Light]

Foley, John. "Infoglut; New Tools Can Help Tame an Ocean of Data," *Information Week*, October 30, 1995, pp. 30-34. [Merrill Lynch]

Francett, Barbara. "Relational DBs Rev Up for High-End TP," *Software Magazine*, October 1995, pp. 87-91. [Hyatt reservations]

Hoffman, Thomas and Mitch Betts. "Scheduling Software Ignites Airline Battle," *Computerworld*, August 28, 1995, p. 16. [Airlines]

"IT Flight Plan," *PC Week*, May 8, 1995, pp. E1-E3. [Airlines]

Kay, Emily. "The Incredible Shrinking Client," *Information Week*, November 13, 1995, pp. 50-55. [Hyatt reservations]

Labich, Kenneth. "Is Herb Kelleher America's Best CEO?" *Fortune*, May 2, 1994, pp. 44-53. [Airlines]

Leonard-Baston, Dorothy. "The Case for Integrative Innovation: An Expert System at Digital," *Sloan Management Review*, Fall 1987, pp. 7-19. [Digital's use of expert systems]

Lovejoy, Paula. "Investors Bank on OS/2 for Reliability and Low Costs," *PC Week*, April 16, 1990, pp. 69-70. [Merrill Lynch, Canada]

"Magnificent Merrill," *The Economist*, April 15, 1995, Survey 15. [Survey section on Wall Street, firms, challenges, finance]

Manning, Ric. "Kelleher Calls Workers and Innovation Keys to Southwest's Success," *Louisville Courier-Journal*, January 26, 1994, p. B12. [Airlines]

McFarlan, F. Warren. "Information Technology Changes the Way You Compete," *Harvard Business Review*, March 1984, pp. 98-103. [Classic discussion of using IT for competitive advantage]

Messmer, Ellen. "DOD Goes on the SONET Offensive," *Network World*, October 23, 1995, p. 8. [Department of Defense]

Moad, Jeff. "Virtual Expert," *PC Week*, August 7, 1995, pp. E1-E2. [Department of Defense]

Moore, John. "Outsourcing," *Federal Computer Week*, July 17, 1995, pp. 1-2. [Department of Defense]

Morison, Robert F. and Kirtland C. Mead. "A Hard Look at Strategic Systems," *Indications*, January 1989. [Myths and issues in strategic systems]

Newquist, Harvey. "The Magic Kingdom of AAAI," *AI Expert*, October 1991, pp. 59-61. [American Airlines AI]

"No-Frills Flights and Cheaper Networking, Too," *LAN Times*, January 23, 1995. [Airlines]

O'Brian, Bridget. "Ticketless Plane Trips, New Technology Force Travel Agencies to Change Course," *The Wall Street Journal*, August 13, 1994, pp. B1, B9. [Airlines]

"Pardon Me, Is This Seat Taken?" *PC Week*, April 3, 1995. [Airlines]

Pastore, Richard. "Coffee, Tea and a Sales Pitch," *Computerworld*, July 3, 1989, p. 1. [Airlines and People's Express]

Pearl, Daniel. "Airlines Squawk Over Screen-Hogging," *The Wall Street Journal*, August 13, 1994, p. B1. [Airlines]

Porter, Michael. *Competitive Advantage: Creating and Sustaining Superior Performance*. New York: Free Press, 1985. [Updated discussion of strategy and competitive advantage]

Porter, Michael. *Competitive Strategy: Techniques for Analyzing Industries and Competitors*. New York: Free Press. [An early book on competitive advantage]

"Portfolio Accounting/Management Systems," *Wall Street & Technology*, December 15, 1994. [Merrill Lynch and brokerage trading systems]

Rapoza, Jim. "Project KickStart Does Just What Its Name Says," *PC Week*, October 30, 1995, p. 90. [Merrill Lynch]

Rogers, Amy. "Apollo Launches Software-Development Subsidiary," *Communications Week*, October 16, 1995, pp. 24–15. [Airlines]

Safer, Andrew. "Electronic Commerce Takes Atlantic Canada by Storm," *Computing Canada*, June 7, 1995, p. 54. [Independent Grocers (IGA)]

Smith, Laura. "Boeing to Shave IT." *PC Week*, June 12, 1995, p. E3. [Boeing computer services]

"Southwest Soars with Ticketless Travel," *LAN Times*, April 24, 1995. [Airlines]

"Technology Changes; So Should Executives," *Computing Canada*, December 7, 1994. [Airlines]

Terdoslavich, William. "Improving the Inns and Outs: Hyatt Hotels Is Using ATM-Like Kiosks to Speed Up Customer Reservations," *Computer Reseller News*, July 31, 1995, pp. 511–512. [Hyatt reservations]

"Textbook Solutions: Text Retrieval Products Let You Find Your Information Needle in the Data Haystack," *HP Professional*, April 1995. [Florida Power and Light]

"The House That Data Built: Data Warehousing Gives Corporations a Competitive Advantage with Better Data Analysis," *HP Professional*, December 1994. [Florida Power and Light]

"The Net Is Nice to Visit, But I Never Wanted to Work There—Until Now," *Windows Magazine*, April 1995. [Hyatt reservations]

"Ticketless Plane Reservations Fly on Client/Server System," *PC Week*, January 30, 1995. [Airlines]

"Trading Department Support Systems," *Wall Street & Technology*, December 15, 1994. [Merrill Lynch and brokerage trading systems]

"Using EDI Effectively—Reports Available from NTIS," *The OSINetter Newsletter*, July 1995. [Department of Defense]

Vitale, Michael. "The Growing Risks of Information Systems Success," *MIS Quarterly*, December 1984, pp. 327–334. [Potential problems with information system strategies]

Wade, Betsy. "Who Gets the Good Seats? Only Airlines Know for Sure," *New York Times News Service*, reprinted in *The Tennessean*, October 24, 1993, p. 6J. [Airlines]

Wagner, Mitch. "Merrill Lynch Embraces NT for Branch Office Automation Project; Company Joins Financial Shops Jumping on NT Bandwagon," *Computerworld*, October 16, 1995, p. 47. [Merrill Lynch]

"Where's AI Hiding?" *AI Expert*, April 1995. [Digital's use of expert systems]

Wilder, Clinton. "Don't Save a Seat: Baxter Healthcare Doesn't Settle for the Leading Edge," *Computerworld Premier 100*, September 11, 1989, pp. 48–51. [Baxter Healthcare]

Wilder, Clinton. "Prize-Winning Utility's IS Tripped Up by Big Chill," *Computerworld*, January 8, 1990, p. 116. [Florida Power and Light]

Wilder, Clinton. "Don't Blame the System," *Computerworld*, July 3, 1989, p. 42. [Airlines and People's Express]

Wilhelm, Steve. "Boeing's Massive Computer Unit Focuses on Sole Client," *Puget Sound Business Journal*, December 18, 1992, pp. 8–9. [Boeing computer services]

Winslow, Ron. "Four Hospital Suppliers Will Launch Common Electronic Ordering System," *The Wall Street Journal*, April 12, 1994, p. B8. [Baxter Healthcare]

"World Wide Web Servers," *Open Information Systems*, September 1995. [Department of Defense]

# CASES *Airlines*

Consider the use of computers by executives. Executives use computers far more than the average worker. In particular, note the heavy emphasis on computers for word processing, communication, databases, analysis, and spreadsheets.

SOURCE: Computer Use in the United States, U.S. Bureau of the Census.

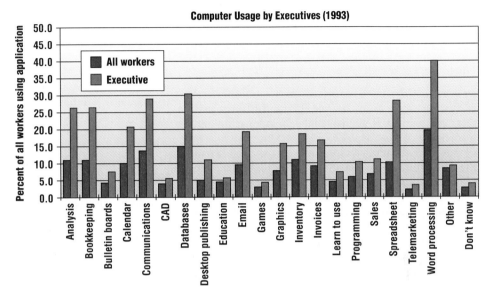

**Computer Usage by Executives (1993)**

Before 1978, running a U.S. airline was relatively straightforward. Almost all of the operations were controlled by the Federal Aviation Administration (FAA) or the Civil Aeronautics Board (CAB). Access to airports was limited and prices were subject to approval by the CAB. Competition was "friendly" and consisted largely of nonprice items like food service. Initially, when the U.S. government decided to deregulate the industry, little changed. The large airlines (United, Eastern, TWA, American Airlines, Pan Am, and a few others) were reluctant to change their operations. They had a system (methodology) that worked relatively well, and it consistently generated profits.

Management life changed dramatically when a few small airlines began offering an innovative approach to airline management. The changes began with a few small airlines in California (like Air West), even before national deregulation. The national market was attacked by People's Express. People's Express offered radically cheaper air fares—sometimes less than $50 a flight. The larger airlines scrambled to compete. With a higher cost structure, the large airlines were at a disadvantage. Then they learned how to use their reservation systems to charge different prices for each person who buys a ticket. Direct competition on pricing and better service (more flights, direct flights, food service, etc.), coupled with some management problems by People's Express eventually spelled the end of People's Express. However, once the door was opened, competition continued. Today, the large air-

lines are suffering again, and the smaller, low-cost airlines are succeeding—notably Southwest Airlines.

Running a modern airline is a complex task. Thousands of decisions need to be made every day. Considering reservations, maintenance, crew scheduling, gate assignments, and investments, airline managers face difficult problems. Faced with stiff competition and low profit margins, the airline that makes the best decisions will be the one that survives. Management information systems can play a key role in determining which firms will succeed. Computerized reservations systems are a key component of the airline decision-making processes. In fact, they have become so important that in the 1980s, the airlines spun off the reservations systems into separate companies. These companies now compete against each other for access to travel agents' desks and for business from nonairline industries, like hotels and car rentals.

The use of information technology has gone through many stages in the airline industry. Initially, the reservation systems were designed just to handle the transaction data for reservations. Yet, the designers made a key decision to save all of the transaction data instead of discarding it when a flight ended. When the airlines faced competition from discounters in the 1980s, they used this data to institute a differential pricing scheme that collected more money from business travelers. By the late 1980s, the airlines further improved the systems to identify and track frequent flyers. The systems were also modified to list their own flights first, encouraging agents to book flights on one airline. Airlines have also implemented technology to make other decisions, such as scheduling. These cases demonstrate the importance of continual improvements and change—to get and hold a competitive advantage.

## CASE *American Airlines*

American Airlines began work on a computerized reservation system in the late 1950s. Up until that time, reservations were maintained on index cards and blackboards.

The Sabre system was introduced in 1963. It began as a nonglamorous plan to computerize flight schedule planning. Previous to this, these schedules were also maintained by hand. The tediousness of this process and the restrictions of airline regulation meant that schedules could not be changed very often. However, as the number of flights increased and cities opened larger airports, the complexity of scheduling became even more intense.

In 1963, when Sabre was introduced, it processed 85,000 telephone calls, 40,000 confirmed reservations, and 20,000 ticket sales. The first Sabre terminal was installed in a travel agency in 1976. Max Hopper, who conceptualized Sabre at American Airlines, saw his task as greater than just computerizing flight schedules. He believed that technology could drive the airline industry and provide a strategic advantage to any airline that would make a sufficient investment to capitalize on it.

American Airlines has realized the important role that the Sabre system continues to play in maximizing utilization. The airline's continued commitment to the system provides many strategic advantages in terms of revenue generation and the maximization of flight patterns.

Hopper sees the era of the "massive, centralized, proprietary computer system" as coming to a close. In his opinion, the marketplace advantages of collecting and manipulating more data than anyone else are diminishing in importance. Today, Hopper sees information technology today as being more pervasive and less potent. He feels that this means the focus should shift from being the first to build proprietary electronic tools to being the best at using and improving technology to make an organization the best in its business.

What does this mean for the Sabre system? The Sabre system was built upon well-developed expertise in hardware evaluation, project management for software development, and systems integration. A great deal of custom-written software was created during 20 years to accomplish these rather lofty goals. Today, the database contains 45 million fares with up to 40

million changes per month. At its peak periods, Sabre handles 2,000 messages per second and initiates more than 500,000 passenger name records every day. Sabre now operates in more than 14,500 subscriber locations in 45 countries. As a result of this proliferation, travel agents account for more than 80 percent of all passenger tickets issued as compared to 40 percent in 1976.

The next phase, InterAAct, is much different in its approach. It is built on hardware and software provided by third-party vendors. These include workstations from AT&T, IBM, and Tandy, and minicomputers from Hewlett-Packard. Microsoft Windows and Hewlett-Packard's NewWave Presentation Software provide the operating system base. The local area network technology comes from Novell. "Dumb terminals" in travel agent and airline reservation offices are being replaced by workstations that are capable of intensive local processing.

Strategically, InterAAct presents itself as an electronic travel supermarket, a computerized middleman for all the suppliers of travel and related services. In addition to air and auto reservations, these include Broadway shows, packaged tours, and currency rates. InterAAct was conceptualized in 1987, with rollout beginning in June 1988. Four principles guided the rollout:

- *Access.* The platform had to give each employee access to the entire system. To accomplish this, developers focused on a single workstation that was easy to use and operated with a standard user interface throughout the company.
- *Comprehensive.* The platform had to be comprehensive. It had to have the capability to connect all managerial levels and computing centers within a company. It had to connect to other companies' platforms.
- *Cost Savings.* The project had to generate substantial savings through productivity gains that had to be quantified in advance. The product had to be rolled out in stages to ensure that these savings were evident.
- *Organizational Implications.* The project had to be managed as much as an organizational issue as a technological one. Time had to be spent to realign how work was performed and decisions were made.

To accomplish these objectives, American listed several alternatives.

- Break up the mainframe base to take advantage of information sharing through more powerful personal workstations (hardware alternatives).

- Move more of the computing power to the end users so that they can have a greater influence in the alternatives that they can select to plan travel arrangements (hardware and software alternatives).
- Introduce menu-driven, easier-to-understand accesses to the system. Provide the opportunity to download particular databases to reduce connect time (software alternatives).
- Use the collective information gained from the Sabre system to project future route distributions and marketing promotions (data alternatives).
- Market the Sabre database. Names, addresses, and demographics from airline passengers provide an attractive resource of successful potential customers for most companies (data alternatives).

More specifically, InterAAct is focused on reducing several areas of frustration and delay not addressed by the Sabre system. An in-depth analysis was conducted of how 300 American employees in different parts of the company spent their time. The results of this analysis indicated that additional automation would only produce enough savings to result in a 10 percent return on American's investment. Nonetheless, American made the financial commitment to the project because managers felt that the soft benefits from the project would boost the returns on InterAAct above the hurdle rate. These would be in the areas of better decisions, faster procedures, and more effective customer service.

The market also changed on the travel agency side. To provide better service to their customers, travel agents prefer a system that provides the most comprehensive and unbiased method to choose the best fare for the passenger. Today, American receives little reservation advantage from the system. Schedules and fares are not treated differently from the other 650 airlines that use the system. American pays the same booking fees as other airlines. The ticket-writing and boarding-pass capacity works similarly for American as it does for other airlines.

American is looking further than the airline industry. A joint venture with Marriott, Hilton, and Budget Rent-a-Car named AMRIS has been formed to focus on a computerized-reservation and yield-management system for the hotel and rental car agencies. The reservation system has been named Confirm and promises to provide yield-management software to any hotel or rental car agency that wants to become involved in the system.

## QUESTIONS

1. What are the business implications for each of the alternatives listed for the InterAAct project?

2. What are some of the cross-referencing data items that American would want to include in a relational data base for InterAAct?

3. Why did American decide to continue with the InterAAct database even when it could not be cost-justified?

4. Data Independence, Integrity, Accuracy, and Redundancy are essential for any database to function efficiently. How is each of these elements addressed in the InterAAct database system?

5. Given that American Airlines no longer enjoys the strategic lead it once had with the Sabre system, how would you recommend that they roll out the InterAAct system during the implementation stage?

6. What specific criteria would you outline for management to review the success or failure of the InterAAct system during the Implementation and Evaluation Stage?

7. How will InterAAct change the daily work of reservation agents in travel agencies across the country?

8. Why does Max Hopper see the era of the "massive, centralized, proprietary computer system" coming to a close?

## CASE *American Airlines Artificial Intelligence Applications*

American Airlines has written and maintains two knowledge-based internal applications. The Maintenance Operations Controller Advisor (MOCA) and American Assistant Load Planner uses knowledge-based systems to handle more work without expanding staff. It does this by embedding the expertise of the human decision makers and leveraging it across the workgroup. The MOCA is the largest knowledge-based system that has been developed. It is a maintenance and engineering application to route aircraft to the proper location with specified time periods for required checkup and maintenance.

The flying public is probably more familiar with American's round-trip frequent-flyer expert system. In 1990, American Airlines offered its frequent flyers a free round-trip pass in return for flying three round trips anywhere in its entire network. Awarding passes for free trips based on round trips had never been done in the industry before. Prior to this, airlines had based their awards on the number miles flown, the number of segments, segment miles flown, or specific hub activity. The difficulty with awarding flights based on round-trip flights was that there were many variables that had to be considered to determine when a frequent-flyer club member begins and ends a round trip.

The best way to accomplish this task was to employ an expert system that was able to identify round trips so they could be properly credited to club members.

Development of the project on a personal computer and subsequent porting to a mainframe enabled the project to be turned around in 15 weeks instead of the 11 to 12 months a similar project would take if it were done on the mainframe.

The airline hub and spoke system makes defining a round trip particularly difficult. The most complex type of round trip to define is the "broken-jaw" trip. This is where one or more segments in the middle of a trip is missing. In this case, a customer may have switched airlines or completed a part of a trip by driving from one airport to another.

In addition to these logical definition problems, the knowledge base had to be able to rapidly process large amounts of data. Specifically, the records of 1 million frequent-flyer card holders who had flown round trips had to be identified from among the 10 million flight segments in the system. This all had to be done with an error rate of less than 2 percent.

The system was developed on an IBM Personal System/2 Model 80 personal computer and was ported to an IBM 3090 mainframe. The knowledge system was built on Inference Corporation's Automated Reasoning Tool for Information Management.

The issue of cost is an important consideration in any analysis of the system. One measure is the reduction in error rate in the reporting to customers. Dropping the error rate from 2 to 1 percent translates into the number of complaints called to the system dropping from 20,000 to 10,000.

The cost of the system must be evaluated not just in terms of the dollars required to build the system but also with respect to the revenue requirements of the frequent-flyer program. A true evaluation of cost, however, must be explained in terms of the revenue damage that would have occurred if the competitive offering had not been responded to. From this standpoint the system was successful. The number of segments flown during the qualifying period was more than 10 percent greater than had been forecast by the marketing department.

## QUESTIONS

1. What advantages does the American Airlines frequent-flyer expert system provide that give it an edge over the competition?
2. Why is the list of customers collected in the knowledge base of the expert system so important to the airlines?
3. What is the role of mathematical algorithms in the determination of the rules for the expert system?
4. Why is ability to do the early work on the expert system on the personal computer so important to the reduction of programming costs?
5. What aspects of the demographics of the workforce at American Airlines make the Maintenance Operations Controller Advisor (MOCA) and American Assistant Load Planner so crucial to the future success of the airline?
6. What quantitative measures would you use to evaluate the effectiveness of the expert system? What marketing benefits does the system provide?
7. What were the benefits of building these systems by using an expert system shell rather than using COBOL or C code?
8. Given the shrinking number of airlines in this country, what enhancements would you recommend in future upgrades for the system?

## CASE *Computerized Reservation Systems (CRS) 1994*

To keep track of the increasing numbers of airlines reservations worldwide, computerized reservation systems have become some of the largest nonmilitary computer systems in the world. CRSs are organized on a transaction basis to provide access and availability to online services. Their functions are constantly changing because providers of new and diverse forms of travel such as car rentals, hotels, and trains, are interested in adding their schedules to the system. Smaller airlines and travel agencies are also clamoring to be part of the systems.

### Sabre System

The Sabre system, owned by American Airlines, is the largest airline reservation system. Sabre has several features in addition to booking flights.

*Air Travel Manager* is Personal ExpertWare's new front end for Eaasy Sabre, a reservation system accessible online. This Windows- and CompuServe-based package simplifies the process of selecting flights and routings, making reservations, and receiving your tickets. It can handle all types of flights, from simple round trips to multiple-leg, open-ended fares. The interface makes querying Eaasy Sabre easier and faster by letting you see only the information that you need to see, without the airline codes.

*Air Traffic Manager* filters Sabre, picking out the relevant information for you and organizing it more accessibly. Air Travel Manager requires both CompuServe and Eaasy Sabre accounts and lists for $149.

*Confirm.* In 1987, AMR Corporation, the holding company for American Airlines, entered a $125 million deal with Budget Rent-A-Car Corp., Hilton Hotels

Corp., and Marriott Corporation to develop the Confirm car rental and hotel reservation system. Soon thereafter, development fees escalated rapidly. By October 1992, things had gone so awry that AMR sued its partners for changing project requirements. AMR was facing a great deal of financial difficulty because of the airline industry price wars. The three partners countersued AMR, saying the holding company misrepresented its system development expertise and final system costs. In early 1994, AMR settled for an undisclosed amount to dissolve the partnership and the business.

## Galileo International

The first Computer Reservation System was established by United Airlines in 1971. Originally called Apollo, it was eventually renamed Covia and spun off as an independent affiliate in 1987. In 1988, Covia, British Airways, SwissAir, and KLM formed Galileo. Today the system processes more than 2 million bookings for more than 500 airlines each day. Based in Rosemont, Illinois, the company has a 30 percent market share by location. It provides services to more than 30,000 travel agencies in 50 countries. Galileo is owned by airline partners including United, USAir, Aer Lingus, British Airways, Air Canada, Austrian Airlines, SwissAir, and KLM Royal Dutch Airlines.

The actual computers for the Galileo system are in Denver, Colorado. Three hundred employees, 23 mainframe computers, and 13 diesel backup generators maintain the growing number of products and databases.

Galileo feels it is set apart from its competitors by its technology platform. Because the airline industry has a lot of peaks and valleys, the data center is constructed to focus on peaks. To preserve space, the car-reservation and fare functions have been moved to personal computers. In that way, the capacity can be easily supplemented when peak periods occur.

In the United States, the Galileo System is distributed by Apollo Travel Services and is marketed under the name of Apollo. Worldwide, Galileo and Apollo have nearly 100,000 dedicated terminals. One-hundred fifty airlines provide a direct link to the Galileo computers with access to flight schedules, seating availability, and fares.

Galileo has added a number of enhancements to its offerings:

- *Focal Point,* a Windows-based product, enables travel agents to use software such as word processors or databases that are then plugged into Galileo.

- *Global Access Software* bridges the Galileo and Apollo databases to enable travel agents access to global travel information. This eliminates the former necessity to have local travel agents. One agent can now handle changes worldwide.
- *GlobalFares* is a database that enables travel agents to automatically search for the lowest international and domestic fares.
- *PrivateFares* is a customized supplement to GlobalFares that enables travel agents to include specially negotiated fares.
- *CarMaster* and *RoomMaster* streamline car and hotel bookings by allowing travel agents to narrowly define their searches. This enables the system to have access to every major car-rental company worldwide and to 35,000 hotel properties.
- *Apollo Spectrum* uses CD-ROM technology to provide a travel agent with maps and other information about clients' destinations. This program enables travel agents to print out maps of areas and show their clients exactly how to get to their locations.
- *Leisure Shopper* is a specialized travel database focused on tours, cruises, and package vacations.
- *Covia Technologies* automates gate signs, monitors, and baggage-control systems at airports.

According to Greg Conley, president, "Galileo is like a grocery store. We offer an electronic shelf for the airlines to put their services on for the buyer to see."

A scripting language enables the travel agent to work in English rather than the traditional CRS commands. Previously, agents had to know the three-letter codes for airports and two-letter codes for airlines. Scripts enable the agent to enter the English word and have the computer translate it to the CRS code. The cut-and-paste feature enables the user to bring information from the Galileo database into the word processor and then through the fax to the client. Productivity is improved through the elimination of data entry.

CRSs are so large that they can only be owned by a few major airlines. Until recently, smaller airlines were allowed to list their flight rates and schedules on CRSs but not to conduct sales or reservation transactions on them. In May 1994, three of the four largest reservation systems—the Apollo, Worldspan and System One CRSs—stopped displaying information for smaller airlines, saying users would have to pay. Southwest Airlines, the most profitable U.S. carrier, as well as many others, decided not to do so. Southwest has initiated a new strategy by making microcomputers, modems, and ticket printers available to travel agents. The American Society of Travel Agents (ASTA) is critical of both the CRS decision and Southwest's response.

No-frills domestic airlines are making use of information technology through no-frills information systems. Companies such as Southwest Airlines, ValuJet Airlines, Kiwi International Airlines, and Reno Air rely on personal computers and client/server technology, outsourcing, off-the-shelf software, networks, and the elimination of paper forms to reduce costs and service while keeping profits high.

Technology use has enabled low-cost, short-haul carriers to increase their share of domestic passenger miles by a factor of four to 13 percent since the mid-1980s. Most unique has been Southwest which was the only profitable major U.S. airline in 1993. According to Southwest vice-president of Systems Robert W. Rapp, "Much of Southwest's success depends upon channels of ticket distribution. Technology enables airlines to change channel."

PC-based, the Southwest Air Travel reservation system enables agents to dial toll-free directly into the system to book flights and issue tickets. Other airlines operate ticketless. This keep-it-simple approach reduces the requirements to simply making the reservation rather than issuing a ticket.

### Canada

Advantis is a new business unit formed in March through a joint venture between IBM and Air Canada of Montreal. The network will be part of the IBM Global Network and be based in Winnipeg. Advantis Canada includes the computer and network services operations of Air Canada and the Gemini Group.

In another new joint venture named Newnetco, IBM Canada is making a cash payment of $50 million to Air Canada for the Gemini network. The new company will assume the information-processing operations of the airline. The outsourcing deal between Newnetco and Air Canada is expected to be worth about $800 million from 1994 to 2000.

Newnetco will act as the network host for the internal reservation systems of Air Canada, other smaller airlines, VIA Rail, and the Department of National Defense. Because it is being combined with the IBM Network Services Company, the new company will also serve clients as diverse as Sears, which uses it to connect its operations across the country, and the National Hockey League, which sends information and statistics over the network after every game.

The Gemini network, which Newnetco is taking over, runs on a fiber optic T-1 backbone from Vancouver to Quebec City. It connects to about 38,000 terminals worldwide. Ninety percent of them are in Canada. That network is linked to another 100,000 terminals worldwide. IBM's Network Services Company was formed in 1993 to provide network operations and outsourcing activities. It uses the IBM Information Network (IIN), which has existed in Canada since 1988. The Canadian version connects to IIN services in the United States and around the world to provide System Network Architecture (SNA) connectivity for inter- and intraorganizational connections. Newnetco's services will include custom network solutions for individual outsourcing requirements, connectivity services, international network services, networking software that will create terminal emulation solutions for hardware systems, and messaging services such as electronic mail. Although Newnetco will take over Gemini's physical network, Galileo Canada will assume control of the computerized reservation system side of the Gemini operation. Galileo Canada will supply Canadian travel agents with automated travel information and booking capabilities. It will use Gemini's Apollo software and Newnetco's computer and telecommunications network.

In the past, Gemini has estimated that the travel agency side of the computer reservation system market in Canada is worth about $120 million a year. Galileo Canada now holds about 50 percent of that market.

Galileo Canada will assume control of the computer reservation system of the Gemini Group and in turn will become a major outsourcing customer of Newnetco. Also providing support to Newnetco will be IBM's outsourcing operation, ISM Information System Management Corp. Estimates place the current value of the Canadian reservation system market at $120 million per year.

Before the merger, Gemini was an airline reservations system joint venture between Air Canada and Canadian Airlines International Ltd. of Calgary. The two national airlines dissolved the partnership after Canadian entered into an alliance with American Airlines, which runs its own reservation system.

IBM and Air Canada also formed another new company, Galileo Canada Inc. Based in Toronto and wholly owned by Air Canada, Galileo has taken over the marketing of Gemini's reservation system software. All Canadian data on the Gemini reservation system was transferred to American Airlines' Sabre system on November 5, 1994.

### European Reservation System

In Europe, the main battle between reservation systems involves the following reservation systems:

Amadeus, owned by Lufthansa and Air France

Sabre, owned by American Airlines

The European Commission has ruled that Sabre must separate its booking data from that of American Airlines. Manual systems are now completely incapable of supporting the huge volume of passengers traveling at the same time. Because any downtime could result in the loss of millions of dollars, these systems must be completely reliable. As an example of the magnitude of the transactions, Sabre uses 12 mainframes to process as many as 3,596 messages per second.

## Games with Technology

Almost since the day reservation systems were installed, the airlines began using them to gain advantages over their rivals. For a long time, the airlines who owned the reservation system would place their own flights at the top of the list. Because each screen could hold only five or six listings, rival flights were often placed several pages down on the list. The U.S. Congress eventually decided that because all firms were charged a fee to list their flights, they should have an equal (random) shot at appearing at the top of the list. In 1994, travel agents (and American Airlines) began accusing others—notably United Airlines—of a new game. They alleged that UA was deliberately listing flights two or three times, thus filling up the screen with their own flights and hiding others. An example provided was a flight from Chicago to Dusseldorf. The listing showed one American flight, a United flight through Frankfort, a Lufthansa flight, and a United flight transferring in Frankfort to Lufthansa. The last three flights were all the same, because United was "code sharing" with Lufthansa but actually flying only one plane. United claims that the listing represented "three different products in the market."

Another interesting capability of the airlines lies in seat assignments. Anyone who flies regularly knows that some seats on a specific plane are better than others. For example, seats directly over the wing tend to have emergency exit doors. Federal regulations require a minimum space for these doors—which means these seats have substantially more leg room than other seats in coach class. Also, many flyers prefer seats near the front of the plane, because those seats enable them to get off the plane sooner (and easier). In September 1992, Delta Airlines began saving these "preferred" seats for late-booking, full-fare business customers and for frequent flyers. Northwest Airlines instituted a similar policy in May 1993. American, TWA, United, and Continental Airlines have

similar systems in place. Essentially, the computer system flags certain seats on each flight that are only available to frequent flyers (with high mileage records) or full-fare customers.

## Northwest Airlines

A more serious complaint beginning in 1991 was still being examined in 1994. According to the *The Wall Street Journal* (July 7, 1994), the basic allegations are as follows. In the late 1980s, Northwest Airlines wanted to build a "yield-management" system that would enable it to set the thousands of fares to maximize its revenue. The basic problem of a modern reservation system is to determine how many customers will book the flight later and be willing to pay a higher price. The remaining seats can be offered early at a discount. The challenge lies in choosing the correct number of seats to sell early. However, Northwest managers were not certain that they could build the system. They were leery of investing $30 million when they could not be sure of its success. On the other hand, they knew that they needed a new system. A 1991 Northwest study notes that "We do not accurately know the revenue impact of planned price decisions . . . Existing decision support tools are ancient . . . We are forgoing revenue streams estimated to be at least $150 million per year."

In 1990, Northwest attempted to purchase the basic fare-setting system from American Airlines. Northwest also tried to purchase a mathematical "spill table" that was used to predict how often a plane would be filled and passengers would be "spilled" or delayed to another flight. American's president, Robert Crandall, replied that the systems were "too strategic—and thus too valuable—to sell for money." However, he did offer to trade it for rights to a Chicago–Tokyo route worth $300 to $400 million. Northwest declined the opportunity. Instead, the airline hired John Garel away from American's yield-management department. They proceeded to hire several other managers from American.

American Airlines was upset with the loss of its managers and began a lawsuit, claiming that Northwest was attempting to steal its trade secrets. In the process, American determined that a PC disk of the spill tables was somehow transferred to Northwest. Other internal American documents are also alleged to have been taken. Northwest representatives claimed that the spill tables and information from American were never used when they upgraded their AIMS fare-setting system. They also argued that the basic techniques used by American were public knowledge available freely to anyone.

## CASE *Southwest Airlines and Other Discount Airlines*

One of the fiercest battles in the airline industry is being pressed by the discount airlines. Inspired by Southwest Airlines, which began flying in Texas in 1971, companies like Valujet Airlines are springing up across the nation. The discounters concentrate on holding costs down, flying popular routes, and offering several flights a day.

For several years, Southwest Airlines was the most profitable airline in the United States. By charging very low fares, the carrier rapidly attracted passengers in each new market. When Southwest moved into Louisville, Kentucky, within seven months the carrier captured 15 percent of the total passenger traffic and 21 percent of the traffic in a typical month. In 1993, the U.S. Department of Transportation noted that it was the "principal driving force for changes occurring in the airline industry."

Southwest's flamboyant leader, Herb Kelleher, claimed not to rely on strategic planning, which he called "regurgitating the same mistakes you made before." Instead, he credited his employees and the company's willingness to try innovative ideas. He illustrated his point with a story from the early days, when a competitor tried to put Southwest out of business by cutting fares in half on a profitable route: "We said, okay, you can fly them for less money, or you can fly with us and we'll give you a free bottle of whiskey. We became the largest liquor distributor in that part of Texas."

Another story revolves around its ticketing system. Southwest sells more tickets from instant ticket machines than any other airline. However, customers often complained that their tickets were lost or damaged. Mr. Kelleher notes that "People said they don't look like a ticket. We had a proposal from our systems guys to spend $4 million to print a ticket that looked more like a ticket."

Kelleher received another suggestion from an employee he refers to as the "smartest guy in the company": "He almost finished high school. In Oklahoma.

He said 'Herb, why don't we print on it: This Is A Ticket?'"

Southwest Airlines cuts costs in several ways. The line flies only one type of aircraft (Boeing 737) to simplify maintenance and training and to minimize spare parts inventory. The attendants don't serve meals, and the planes have had coat closets removed to enable passengers to disembark faster, enabling the airline to turn around a plane and put it back in the air in about 15 minutes—far faster than the hour or more that it takes other airlines. Faster turnaround means that an average Southwest plane makes 10 flights a day—twice as many as competing airlines—making more efficient use of the airline's capital.

Labor costs in the airline industry make up 30 percent of the operating costs. With 80 percent of its employees members of unions, Southwest pays salaries and benefits similar to those at other airlines. In 1992, average wages at Southwest were $44,035 versus $45,801 at American and $54,380 at United Airlines. However, as shown in the table, Southwest employees are far more productive than those at other airlines.

Analysts attribute a large portion of the success of Southwest to its leader, Herb Kelleher. He has created a culture of personal service and enjoyment among employees that is unmatched by any other airline (and probably unique among major corporations). In terms of hiring, Kelleher has noted that "What we are looking for first and foremost is a sense of humor." For instance, during delays at the gate, ticket attendants have awarded prizes to the passenger with the largest hole in his or her socks.

Southwest concentrates on short-haul flights and avoids the hub system. Its average flight is 375 miles long, with an average fare of $58. In advertising, Southwest emphasizes that it is a substitute for driving. Before Southwest entered the Louisville-to-Chicago route, about 8,000 people flew to Chicago each week. Shortly after the airline began flying the route in 1993, 26,000 people a week made the trip by air.

Despite the no-frills approach, Southwest has repeatedly won the Department of Transportation's

|  | AMR | DELTA | NORTHWEST | SOUTHWEST | UAL | USAIR |
|---|---|---|---|---|---|---|
| Cost per available seat mile | 8.9 cents | 9.4 cents | 9.1 cents | 7.0 cents | 9.6 cents | 10.8 cents |
| Passengers per employee | 840 | 1114 | 919 | 2,443 | 795 | 1118 |
| Employees per aircraft | 152 | 134 | 127 | 81 | 157 | 111 |

"Triple Crown"—most on-time flights, best baggage handling, and highest customer satisfaction.

Another method of holding costs down is to avoid paying travel agent commissions. By booking its own reservations (often on personal computer-based systems), and not issuing tickets, Southwest avoids overhead costs and keeps the full fare. Almost 50 percent of all ticket sales are made directly to customers, with an estimated annual savings of $30 million.

For several years, Southwest Airlines was able to get its flights listed on the major reservation systems—for free. Traditionally, airlines paid for the listings by paying a commission for every flight booked through the reservation system. Southwest listed its flights, but had travel agents call a toll-free number to actually book the tickets. In 1994, the reservation systems cracked down and began charging just for listing flights. Southwest refused to pay the fees and was dropped from three of the four major systems. Despite the change, Southwest continues to show 15 percent year-to-year increases in traffic. To further decrease ticketing costs, Southwest provides flight information on the Internet. The company has also moved away from tickets. To reserve a flight, customers give operators a credit card number, then simply show a driver's license at the boarding gate.

Increasingly, travelers are bypassing the traditional travel agent reservation systems. Frequent flyers who stick with one airline simply call the airline's toll-free numbers. Computer-literate travelers have access to Easy Sabre and PARS, the American Airline and Northwest Airline reservation systems available through online services. More than a million customers book their own flights through these systems. Large businesses are developing internal travel staffs and making arrangements directly with airlines to cut their costs.

## QUESTIONS

1. Identify the operations, tactical, and strategic capabilities of airline reservation systems.
2. What do you think the airline reservation system will look like in 10 years? Will it operate similarly to the way it does now? Will we still have travel agents?
3. How did the use of reservation systems change over time?
4. What is the value of the data collected by the reservation systems (after the flight is completed)? What other uses might there be for this data? Could the airlines sell it to other companies?
5. As a consumer, what objections might you have if the airlines chose to sell their data to other companies? Would you have any choice or recourse if a reservation system sold data about you?
6. What is next in this industry? Can airlines find another use for technology to give them a competitive advantage?
7. What problems do airlines have in protecting their technology? Do you think models and techniques should be in the "public domain" available to anyone?
8. Given the uses and advantages of the big reservation systems, how can airlines like Southwest Airlines survive? (Hint: Use additional research.)
9. How does Southwest's strategy differ from those of the other airlines? How does its corporate strategy affect its IT choices?
10. What portion of an airline's success comes from its information systems? How has Southwest been successful where People's Express failed?
11. As a traveler, which reservation methodology do you prefer: the traditional travel agent reservation, booking your own through a computer system, or calling an airline directly? Is there a market segmentation effect in which certain types of travelers prefer each method?
12. How do the European and Canadian airline reservation systems differ from those in the United States? Are the differences attributed to strategy, culture, market, or governments?

## CASE  *Ethics: Using the Computer to Exchange Price Information*

Steven B. Elkins, senior director of marketing systems development at Northwest Airlines, has given an inside account of how airlines send messages to each other to fight fare cuts in their most important markets. According to Elkins, Northwest viewed fare wars as an "atomic bomb" and followed a "golden rule" to ward them off.

Elkins asserted that airlines use signaling over the computerized reservation system to convey their intent to rival airlines. Signals are included in the thousands of fare changes that are submitted to the computer pricing network in Washington. Another component of the signal is the fare expiration date. One competitor might set a fare to run through December. A matching fare might be set to expire in October. Fares that a carrier does not want to offer always have an expiration date in the hope that the competition will match it.

Elkins' testimony came during a suit by International Travel Arrangers, a wholesale tour firm, against Northwest Airlines. The suit alleges that Northwest conspired to restrain trade and monopolize the Minneapolis-St. Paul airport.

Elkins gave the example of Northwest Airlines lowering fares on night flights that were flying with empty seats in a number of routes from Minneapolis to West Coast cities. Continental Airlines swiftly responded by cutting prices to match Northwest's fares. The Continental fares were set to expire one or two days after they were introduced. According to Elkins, Northwest felt that Continental was using this price change to send a message that the airlines did not want Northwest to set reduced night-coach fares in those markets.

Northwest disagreed with this message. It filed new cheap fares from Houston to the West Coast with short expiration dates with the Airline Tariff Publishing network. This was important because Houston is an important base for Continental. Elkins said Northwest lowered these fares "so that Continental would stop trying to undermine our attempt to compete by offering lower fares on specific flights."

Some economists and antitrust attorneys view such back-and-forth pricing activity as normal competitive activity. Consumers often temporarily benefit from this practice. Others believe the practice results in higher prices for consumers and stifles competition. They believe that slashing fares to "discipline" other airlines is particularly against competitive pricing because it often results in larger airlines trying to control smaller ones.

According to Elkins, Northwest priced according to the Golden Rule. He did not allow his pricing analyst to initiate actions in another carrier's market for fear of what the other carrier would do to retaliate. Elkins felt this was a method to avoid the fare wars that hurt industry profits in the past.

In Elkins' view, the most frequent cause for price wars was one carrier using competitive pricing to invade the hub of another airline. Because the carrier is not able to offer as much direct service, the invading carrier competes by offering discount prices on connecting flights through its own hub. Elkins advised his policy analysts not to "initiate such 'beggar thy neighbor' pricing in other carriers' nonstop markets without provocation. Such pricing initiatives are the number one cause of 'fare wars' and I am determined that Northwest will not be blamed for them this winter."

Based on Elkins' testimony, the Justice Department is examining these techniques. Investigators have requested information regarding how Airline Tariff Publishing can be used to influence rivals' fare changes. Industry experts state that every airline signals others electronically. According to Elkins, "These are 'universal truths' that are equally applicable to Northwest, Republic, Western, Continental, TWA, or any other domestic airline."

## QUESTIONS

1. Do you think the "signaling" described by Elkins is ethical?
2. Would these price signaling methods be possible without the technology used by airlines?
3. How does information technology raise new ethical issues?
4. As a middle-level manager working for an airline, if you believed these techniques were unethical, what would you do?

## CASE  *Custom Courses Help Airlines Train*

Airlines are investing in Macintosh-based technology for reservation-service marketing, training of ground crews and flight attendants, and devising flight plans and tracking flights.

Northwest Airlines built a Systems Operation Control (SOC) center (1990), which makes decisions about planning, maintenance and flight dispatch, The Mac system was chosen over solutions from DEC because of its low cost and because it offered connectivity with the airline's Unisys mainframe. SOC organizes those data sources into a centralized or distributed environment. So much time had been spent training people on all the different systems. The SOC provided one platform to communicate with all of Northwests' systems. The SOC has 300 Mac IICI systems that can each communicate with the Unisys and IBM mainframes and Unix workstations.

Several specific Mac applications were designed by Bryan Bourn and his group of operations analysts with St. Paul, Minnesota-based Northwest.

Aircraft Situation Display (ASD) takes positioning information on all active flights off the mainframes and overlays the plane's position on maps showing the location of airports and geographical boundaries. Dispatchers also have at their disposal a variety of tools to measure distances between the flight and any relevant points on the map.

"[ADS is] a real-time tracking mechanism," said Doug Zifler, director of operations automation. "At any time, you can click on a flight number and see where the plane is en route."

The Mac is also used to display the weather graphics that are fed continuously into the network 24 hours a day by a service provider. The 8-bit gray-scale and color satellite images and charts are received by a Macintosh in a proprietary format but are converted to PICT format for display on the Mac using a HyperCard external command (XCMD) written by Northwest.

In the old days, the dispatcher had a dumb terminal that would talk to the mainframe. If the dispatcher wanted a map, he would have to pick up a phone, dial up by modem, and then make the connections. He would then wait for the image to be painted on screen one line at a time. To get another image he would have to dial up again. Nowadays, you can open up as many windows on your screen as RAM allows.

Flight information display systems provide dispatchers and planners with a list of arriving and departing flights, updated in real time. Northwest created "rainbow charts," which are laminated charts that use colors to indicate the airline fleet assignment for a day. This system replaced the manual process where someone actually sits down to color in which planes will be taking which routes and where the layovers will be.

The company also has a Mac application that will run "what-if" scenarios on the rainbow charts for its dispatchers and planners. This system enables the immediate indication of the cancellation of one flight and the replacement by another. It is an intelligent scheduling application used by the people doing aircraft routing.

American Airlines has applied Macromedia's Authorware Professional Macintosh courseware to its AMR Training and Consulting Group. Computer-based courses have been developed for topics ranging from how to use AA's computer reservation system to how to package hazardous materials for air shipping. Testing functions are built into the courseware. Using Authorware, AMR developed more than 200 hours of computer-based training material, including videos (starring American Airlines employees), lessons, quizzes, and tests. The development of these programs was expedited by setting up Authorware "templates" that served as models for the rest of the programs. The courseware describes everything from how to use the computer reservation system to one on "dangerous goods" that describes how to package hazardous materials for shipment on airplanes.

The program is ideally focused on training new employees, who spend five to seven weeks going through the lessons and being tested on the material they learn. Testing is an automatic feature built into the Authorware courseware. A test template presents students with up to 50 questions. They can browse the questions, skip questions, return to them, and bookmark questions that they've answered but want to recheck. Once they are satisfied, students can request that the test be scored. The program grades the test and tells them which questions are right and wrong. It then enables them to go back and review their answers.

The templates, developed for both the Mac and Windows, have been so successful that the company has sold them to other firms, including Delta Air Lines, Sprint Communications Co., and the Federal Aviation Administration. Once a template has been developed for a test or a lesson, it is just a matter of entering the relevant content. A complex model can be developed without being a programmer.

Air France has equipped its U.S.-passenger sales force with PowerBook 170s. Instead of brochures and slide shows, sales representatives take the laptops on sales calls. With the click of a mouse, the company's more than 70 U.S. sales reps can access statistical profiles of travel agencies, commercial accounts, or individual passengers. Graphs and charts showing aircraft seating charts can also be displayed from the PowerBook. The company, which services Paris and the rest of Europe from nine U.S. locations, has also developed custom software through which users can access Air France's reservations computer.

### QUESTIONS

1. What training programs are the airlines putting onto computers? What additional training could be added?
2. What advantages are provided by computerized training as opposed to traditional teaching methods? What are the drawbacks?
3. Do the training systems provide any strategic advantages?

### CASE *A New Reservation System for Hyatt Hotels*

Hyatt Hotels originally operated its reservations system on two central IBM 4381 mainframes. The reservation system was written in assembly language and ran on a host-based operating system called a Transaction Processing Facility (TPF). It was developed to support the high transaction volumes required in airline reservation systems. The combination of assembler and TPF made the reservation system prohibitively complex and costly to modify and upgrade.

Hyatt's other applications, including Hymark and a reporting application, were developed using primitive second-generation languages or outdated third-generation language tools.

In planning to rewrite its system, Hyatt decided to reduce risk by downsizing its applications one by one, starting with the simplest and saving the most complex for last. Following the strategy of only writing software related to its core competencies, Hyatt decided to outsource applications that did not support critical business operations. As a result, Hyatt outsourced its nationwide payroll, covering 50,000 employees, to Automatic Data Processing (ADP) and its accounting applications to a local service provider.

Hyatt chose to rewrite Spirit, Hymark, and the reporting application first. Each rewrite took less than a year. Hyatt was able to expedite the rewrite by matching the functionality of existing host-based applications instead of adding new functions and features.

In 1987, Hyatt installed AT&T 3B2 Unix processors in a majority of its hotels to run hotel operations such as finance, reservations, and sales. In 1988, it began the process of transferring this program to a series of Unix multiprocessors. In so doing, Hyatt replaced its mainframes with five high-end Pyramid Technology ES Series Unix multiprocessing machines and implemented a relational database management system from Informix Software. Host applications were rewritten using Informix's fourth-generation language (4GL) software development tools. Hyatt also replaced its IBM System Network Architecture (SNA) network with a TCP/IP backbone and international packet-switching network to connect the company's 165 hotels around the world to its central data center in Oak Brook, Illinois.

By embarking on the project, Hyatt accepted a great deal of risk. The hotel chain invested $15 million in new hardware, software, and network equipment as well as programming and maintenance services. At the time, no company had deployed Pyramid processors or Informix's DBMS and tools on the scale Hyatt planned. Many industry observers believed that the combination of Unix processors and 4GL-based applications would not support the level of performance required for a mission-critical applications such as Hyatt's reservation system. Further, at that time few companies ran mission-critical applications across a nationwide TCP/IP network.

Based on this concern for risk, Hyatt adopted a number of practices to reduce the risk that it might incur:

- *Rewriting vs. re-engineering.* Hyatt was concerned that, if it tried to re-engineer applications as well as rewrite them, it would prolong the downsizing process indefinitely. A one-to-one rewrite of host application functionality enabled the company to gain the cost-savings of unplugging the mainframe earlier. Once Hyatt completed the migration, it revisited each application and added functionality that users had been urging for years.

- *Strong partnership with core vendors.* To further reduce the risk of implementing untested programs, Hyatt established a strong partnership with its core vendors, Informix and AT&T. Six Informix employees trained Hyatt programmers to code in Informix 4GL. Programmers experienced with 4GLs supplemented the internal staff. Ten AT&T employees worked full time to help employees configure and test the Pyramid boxes to ensure they provided the performance Hyatt required.

Both Informix and AT&T viewed the Hyatt project as a high-visibility account. Their willingness to partner with Hyatt was a major reason they won the contract. This level of partnership made it easier for Hyatt to troubleshoot problems and overcome rough spots in the migration.

- *Small teams.* Hyatt kept its development teams small and gave them complete independence to avoid making the project larger or more complex than it already was. Between Hyatt and Informix, only 15 programmers were assigned to rewrite the three core applications. Young programmers, most of whom were under 30 years old, were chosen for the team. Hyatt found these individuals more open to new ways of developing code and not bound by traditional development methodologies.

- *Frequent evaluations.* Hyatt divided the project into manageable pieces that were designed to yield deliverables every four to six months. This enabled the progress to be carefully monitored and success determined early on.

- *Regular risk assessments.* Prior to each phase of the project, a risk assessment was conducted to described all the things that could go wrong and what would be done to fix them. Identifying potential risks up front enabled the team to take precautions to address the pitfalls ahead.

- *Careful benchmarking.* Risks were also reduced by performing exhaustive benchmarks prior to cutting over each application. The reservation system was moved into testing six months prior to the final cut-over. An automatic transaction-generation utility was used to simulate typical transaction loads. This benchmarking trial enabled evaluation of the performance of the Informix 4GL code and the Informix database. Response times could be enhanced, performance fine-tuned, and bugs worked out prior to full deployment.

Hyatt finished the project in 1990, when it moved the hotel's mission-critical global reservation system to the open systems platform. An important consideration of the project was the migration to the new system without disrupting service. Because of the ongoing needs of the reservation system, Hyatt considered two basic alternatives for the implementation.

- *Gradual rollout.* This method would gradually bring one hotel after another onto the new system while supporting the remaining hotels on the old system. This would mean that hotels would be working with different sets of data, making it difficult to keep everything in sync.

- *Cut-over.* Hyatt could cut over all the hotels at once but run the system only to book reservations after a specified date in the future. This would mean that agents would have to use two terminals to book reservations.

Hyatt decided that the simplest, quickest, and most cost-effective way to implement the new reservation system was to cut over all the hotels at once. It did so on a Friday night, when reservation volumes are at their lowest. Two months prior to the cut-over, Hyatt began uploading all reservations made during the day to the new Informix database. Thus, on the night of the cut-over, the new and existing reservations were essentially in sync; Hyatt had to worry only about uploading that day's reservations into the Informix database. To ensure that the conversion went smoothly, Hyatt instituted a number of test and backup procedures that it performed during the weekend to avert any loss of data and to guarantee adequate performance. A plan was also in place to back out of the new system at any time during the weekend if there were significant problems. The cut-over went smoothly, and Hyatt was able to unplug its mainframes shortly thereafter.

Hyatt's global reservation system enables in-house service representatives as well as independent travel agents to check the availability and pricing of rooms in each of Hyatt's 165 hotels and resorts and book reservations. The system runs 24 hours a day, seven days a week, and is critical to Hyatt's revenues and cash flow.

Important advantages of the new system include the following:

- *A call-in center.* Hyatt maintains a nationwide reservation center in Omaha, Nebraska, where 400 customer service representatives take customer calls and book hotel rooms. The representatives are connected online to the reservation system located in Hyatt's data center in Oak Brook, Illinois. A T1 line links the Omaha and Oak Brook sites.
- *Local reservations.* The system also allows individual hotels to book their own reservations. Each hotel runs a reservation application on at AT&T 3B2 or Hewlett-Packard Unix 800 Series midrange processor. These processors also run a variety of other hotel-specific applications, such as operations and finance. Reservations are made in conjunction with the central reservation system that automatically notifies the local reservation system every time a Hyatt agent in Omaha or an independent travel agent books a hotel room. In turn, each hotel sends a status message back to the central reservation system every half hour stating how many rooms are still available. Because the reservation updates are not completed in real time and agents work from different inventories, this distributed approach sometimes results in inconsistent data. To ensure that each hotel will be working from the most up-to-date data, the local reservation system will be phased out and all hotels migrated to the central reservation system in Oak Brook.
- *Travel agents.* More than 150,000 independent travel agents have a direct link to the reservation system through an industry-sponsored service (Spirit) that connects hotel and airline reservation systems. Established by the major hotel companies to ease the requirements of interfacing their systems with multiple airline computer reservation systems, the service gives travel agents up-to-the-minute room availability and the ability to book rooms directly through Hyatt's central reservation system. About 40 percent of all reservations made through Spirit are now booked by independent travel agents.

Hyatt continues to enhance the applications by adding new functionality and interconnecting the program with new and existing hotel systems. The database in Spirit has been enhanced through the replacement of generic descriptions of room types with detailed inventories of room types and characteristics for each hotel. Spirit can now show the availability of a room in a Hawaiian Hyatt hotel with a king-size bed and an ocean view. Previously, Spirit would show only the availability of a room with a king-size bed but no other features. These additions were made possible by the inclusion of tables within Informix that contain each hotel's room types.

The new system has enabled Hyatt to cut its annual information systems operating costs by 30 percent, including maintenance, software licensing, hardware upgrades, training, and labor. More importantly, Hyatt now has a flexible system that it is able to modify and scale to meet new business opportunities and market demands.

To keep the system competitive, upgrades are constantly being developed using Rapid Application Development. Eight, compared to two, new releases of the core applications are released each year. The ability to rapidly enhance applications has enabled Hyatt to provide superior customer service and maintain a competitive advantage in its fast-paced industry.

In addition, Hyatt has been able to maintain one-second or better response times for all mission-critical applications with both Hymark, its centralized sales and marketing application, and Spirit, the global reservation system. Hyatt books more than $750 million a year through these systems.

In addition to enhancements to its current systems, Hyatt has developed several new client-server application that it has integrated with existing systems. Hyatt has deployed a function room and catering application in all its hotels. The client-server application, developed using Powersoft's PowerBuilder, enables individual hotels to keep track of events booked at the hotel and the availability of meeting rooms and catering services. This information is stored on a Gupta SQLbase database on a local server. Each night, the information is uploaded into Hyatt's Hymark sales and marketing application. This enables a salesperson in Dallas to log into Hymark and check the availability of meeting rooms and catering services in all Hyatt hotels. The salespeople can then use Hymark to book the function rooms and services.

- *Integrated systems.* In addition, Hyatt has integrated the Hymark and Spirit reservation system so that bookings made in one automatically appear in the other. The synchronization is achieved through nightly batch updates.

Hyatt has been able to significantly improve the quality of its customer service by interconnecting its core applications and providing up-to-date information to its sales and marketing force. The new systems have also enabled Hyatt to deploy a national sales force that can book rooms and functions in any Hyatt hotel, no matter where it is located. This combination has enabled the company to boost sales significantly.

To gain real benefits from downsizing, Hyatt was willing to assume high levels of risk. In doing so, it aggressively moved all applications off the mainframe in a four-year period, including a mission-critical application that drives the company's multimillion-dollar daily operations. Hyatt was willing to work with young companies with relatively unproven technology. It also mixed and matched technologies from different vendors, all while trying to keep its computing environment as homogeneous as possible. Hyatt did not waste time and resources playing systems integrator to a multitude of incompatible technologies. Finally, Hyatt followed an aggressive implementation schedule designed to minimize the duration of the conversion and maximize the long-term cost-savings. Since unplugging the mainframe, Hyatt has been able to go back and enhance its core applications, substantially improving efficiency and customer service.

Hyatt did take significant precautions to minimize risk. It outsourced noncritical applications to reliable third parties with strong track records. It partnered with its core vendors and made them accountable for the project's ultimate success or failure. It minimized risks through careful benchmarking and regular risk assessments.

## QUESTIONS

1. What advantages did Hyatt gain by installing its new system? What risks did the hotel chain face?
2. How did the steps taken by Hyatt help protect the data and ensure a smooth implementation?
3. Why did Hyatt choose *not* to re-engineer the reservation systems at the time the company upgraded? What were the potential drawbacks? What other advantages might the hotel chain have gained?
4. What strategic advantages are provided by the new system compared with the old reservation system? As a customer, what features would you see?
5. Of all the methods to gain competitive advantage, which are the strategic focus of the Hyatt reservation system?
6. What similarities does the Hyatt reservation system have with the airline reservation systems?
7. Could the Hyatt reservations have been incorporated into one of the airline systems? What would be the advantages and disadvantages to Hyatt in making such a move?
8. As a competitor to Hyatt, how would you respond? Would creating a similar system be sufficient? What improvements might you add?
9. As a traveler, how would you like to see reservations handled?
10. What do you think the hotel reservation process will be like in 10 years?

## CASE *Merrill Lynch Canada*

The trading floor for Merrill Lynch Canada handles institutional trades of money-market instruments such as municipal bonds and Treasury bills. Its clients include large insurance companies and banks around the world. Transactions are large. Multimillion-dollar offerings are common. The time frame is short. An entire municipal bond issue can be sold off in a matter of hours.

Transaction recording is mission-critical for Merrill Lynch. Every transaction counts. System errors, lost data, or downtime can mean the loss of thousands of dollars in the volatile securities market. Because the company cannot afford to have the system fail, trading has always been done on a mainframe platform. It is nonstop and large enough to keep track all of the transactions that occur during the day.

The difficulty with mainframe-based systems, however, has been the length of time it takes for the information to be collected and entered. According to Bob Jull, president of the software house that built the system for Merrill Lynch, "Trading has always been done on the back of an envelope. Traders yell their trades and keep a blotter on their desk of the ones that were successful. At the close of the day they write them on a big board so they can be consolidated. This enables the inventory to be brought up-to-date."

Technology has enabled the trading strategies to become more sophisticated and immediate. Individual traders must make better informed decisions more quickly. They can no longer base their decisions on the results from the previous day's trades. They must respond based on the current inventory position of the company.

Technology has also enabled auditors to keep better track of the trades that are made during the day. The more quickly these trades are recorded, the sooner errors can be caught and corrected. The computer can construct a list of all of the trades that have been completed. This list becomes an audit trail that can later be traced to find discrepancies. A balance can occur between the total number of trades for the day and the number of trades by each trader, stock, commodity, seller, or purchaser.

To expedite the flow of data, the new system at Merrill Lynch is built on the OS/2 Presentation Manager graphical user interface. This application allows real-time updates on inventory. This includes those instruments that have been sold and those that remain to be sold.

Procedurally, the project involves two phases. The first uses two network servers to maintain the base inventory of trades at the close of each day. Clerks collect the information from the traders and enter the data into a batch-processing system. Consolidated profit-and-loss statements are then produced overnight.

The second phase uses the Presentation Manager on the client side to implement real-time inventory updates. Using a mouse or the keyboard, a trader can pick an item from the inventory summary screen. If the other fields, such as asking or selling price, have not changed, the trader only needs to enter the quantity bought or sold. The inventory is then immediately updated in real time and sent through the network to the other traders.

This system brings a number of advantages to the trading floor. Traders want to concentrate their attention on the trade. They have little time or patience to learn how to use the computer. As a result, the computer interface must be easy-to-use with a quick response time. According to Anna Ewing, assistant vice-president of information systems, "The trader's response has been very positive and intuitive. They've learned the system without a user's guide."

The second advantage is the ability to interact with a number of inputs at the same time. A trader may be talking to a customer on the telephone, shouting to another trader on the floor, and watching a Reuters and Dow Jones screen as well as his or her personal bond portfolio. The windowing nature of the OS/2 operating system enables the trader to keep track of all of these events simultaneously on the same screen. Through the system's minimize feature the trader can focus on one screen while leaving the others running for immediate availability.

The third advantage is strategic. Technology has improved the ability of the trader to capture and use information. This has enabled trades to occur more quickly and with much smaller margins. As a result, traders must be able to respond with increased speed and precision to market openings. According to Jull, "The application is so critical that it has justified the expense."

Fourth, the system presents a number of economic savings for Merrill Lynch. Jull estimates that the personal computer-based local area network cost about half as much as the comparable mainframe or mini version. Anna Ewing set a payback period of two years: "In spite of the overruns associated with the risks and delays in product availability, we were able to achieve the requirements on a very cost-effective platform that encourages end-user computing."

Finally, the new application provides reliability. SQL Server on the OS/2 provides a high-performance database management system not previously available in a PC LAN environment. It allows data to be mirrored by being written and maintained on two distinct servers. Thus, if one server goes down, the other is available as a backup. The crucial nature of the application makes this immediate switching capability essential for its success.

Overall, Ewing has been pleased with the implementation. In her opinion, the only downside was the difficulty of working with a developing operating system. However, the ability to view and interact with a number of screens at the same time has made the program a perfect match for the traders at Merrill Lynch.

In the United States, Merrill Lynch resolved a similar issue by installing 25,000 workstations running Windows-NT. The newer multitasking operating system is connected to Windows-NT servers running the Sybase DBMS. Brokers use the system to access client information, news, investment information, and stock market data.

## QUESTIONS

1. What steps did Merrill Lynch implement to reduce resistance to its new trading program?
2. How is the new system changing the type and location of the job structure at Merrill Lynch?
3. What incentives were implemented to encourage the employees to cooperate with and even embrace the change?
4. How will the new system affect the strategic direction of Merrill Lynch's business?
5. Which of the five forces in Michael Porter's model will this system most help Merrill Lynch protect against?
6. Which generic strategy is Merrill Lynch using to implement a sustainable competitive advantage?
7. Where does Merrill Lynch's new system fit into the value chain?
8. How will the new system improve the reliability and maintainability of Merrill Lynch's trades?
9. How will the new system improve Merrill Lynch's ability to find errors throughout the day and balance the books at the end of the day?
10. What is the value of an audit trail for those who must ensure that the trades are reported accurately?

## CASE    *IGA to Implement Network Links to Challenge Big Chains*

Large national grocery and department chains are rapidly cutting into the profit base for the local grocery stores. These small independent supermarkets have found it increasingly difficult to compete with the lower margins, higher volume, and ultimately lower prices of the large chains.

By affiliating with the Independent Grocer's Alliance, or IGA, small grocery stores are finding a way to remain competitive. An affiliation of 3,600 autonomous supermarkets, IGA is installing client-server systems to manage membership and accounting services.

IGA is owned by 21 national wholesalers that sell to member stores. As such, it provides everything from name brands through IGA private-label goods through its wholesaling network. In addition to manufacturing and distribution, it coordinates joint marketing programs with national brands, coordinates national advertising, manages the labeling and packaging of IGA brand products, and obtains bulk rates on supermarket equipment.

As director of information systems, Jim Anderson's goal is to increase economies of scale by making 3,600 individual stores act as one. To accomplish this, he is building a technology infrastructure that will help retailers trim costs and match competitors' margins. Client-server technology will enable the stores to develop the same power as large chains to gather data and present a common view of the world.

IGA's old system was supported by software running on an IBM/36 minicomputer. Since that system was 10 years old, the information it provided was insufficient for today's sophisticated and complex marketplace. To accomplish the task of re-engineering this system, Anderson looked for software that would address the two primary business processes of managing its member database and running its financial systems. To accomplish this, he looked for a relational database management system, hardware independence, and reliable network connections.

The new system is built on Enterprise by FourGen Software and the Association Management System by Smith, Abbott, and Company. Enterprise provides the billing and financial systems. AMS manages the membership database and processes information on owner-wholesalers and national brand vendors. By linking the member and financial systems, IGA will be able to bill members directly for equipment, packaging, and other supplies simultaneous with the payment of these bills for its members. IGA used CASE tools to write this link and handle updating between the systems.

To round out the first phase of the new system, IGA standardized its office automation software on Microsoft Office, Lotus cc:Mail, and Quark desktop publishing.

The second phase of the program is to link the 3,600 independent retailers into a single network to gather and share sales and marketing information. This will greatly improve IGA's ability to negotiate with vendors. To accomplish this objective, all the stores will be brought to a minimum level of technology. Although some small chains have their own LANs, other stores are still paper-based.

Several prerequisites must be met before this goal can be accomplished. The first is to make sure that the member stores understand the cost savings and marketing advantages that can be realized through this integrated technology. The second is the construction of an inventory of available computer equipment. Once these steps are completed and committed to, IGA can specify the hardware, software, and communications platforms for this new system.

## QUESTIONS

1. Which aspects of Porter's model are being used by IGA to stay competitive?
2. In integrating the stores, what problems are faced by IGA that are different from those of national chains?

3. As technology improves, becomes smaller, and is cheaper, will it be beneficial to IGA? How would these changes affect the difference between IGA and traditional chains like Kroger?

## CASE *The Department of Defense Adopts a "Lag Technology" Strategy*

Beginning in 1980, the U.S. Department of Defense adopted a cutting-edge technological strategy. Their objective was to invest heavily in technology to purchase the leading hardware and software. This was in keeping with the administration's strategy to use technology to accelerate the military's abilities in these areas. Major investments were made in research, equipment, and software to enhance both weapons and administration.

In 1990, the Defense Management Review recommended a policy of "waiting a couple of years" before investing in new technology. The strategy was articulated by Lieutenant General Jerome Hilmes, director of army information systems for command, control, communications, and information: "By waiting a couple of years, especially when it comes to electronic communications, we can get something adequate. However, for mission-critical systems and the high-tech battlefield, the latest technology will still be employed."

Mission-critical systems are those that are essential for the safety and security of the military forces. They include research and development in high technology warfare. Nonmission-critical areas include the accounting, purchasing, and payroll functions of the military. Adopting a "lag technology" perspective in relation to ordinary ADP programs and administrative processing enables more resources to be focused in those areas that are essential for military success. This is particularly the case when the government is cutting back in overall spending, including in the military area. A lag technology strategy will also enable the government to take advantage of a falling price curve in these noncritical areas.

Upfront costs are not the only reasons for not buying the latest technologies. Parts, maintenance, and support can also be more expensive when related to the latest products. Because fewer people have worked with the equipment, there are fewer individuals to call for assistance. This makes the information that is obtained more difficult to identify and more expensive to access. Risk is also increased with the newest equipment. Even though careful analysis may be completed, the market may move in a direction different from the one most logical when the purchase decision was made.

The writing and implementation of standards are another way to contain computer costs. Standards ensure the exchangeability and thus portability of equipment. One method of accomplishing standardization is to develop a standard data dictionary to define database items across departments. For example, in the Army alone there are 47 ways to describe social security numbers. A standard data dictionary would consolidate these numerous descriptions and streamline the communications process among computer systems.

### QUESTIONS

1. Why did Lieutenant General Hilmes make such an explicit distinction between mission-critical and nonmission-critical elements in his description of the new Department of Defense strategy?
2. What would be some other examples of mission-critical and nonmission-critical military applications?
3. The case listed a number of advantages to waiting before making investments in noncritical areas. What are some reasons for moving forward immediately in these purchase areas?
4. How does standardization enable computer equipment to be easily moved between locations?
5. How does standardization help to control costs?
6. What rule could you write to assist a new recruit to distinguish between mission-critical and non-mission-critical areas?
7. Which of the generic strategies is Lieutenant General Hilmes following when he advocates that the Department of Defense adopt a "lag technology"?
8. Where do the mission critical and nonmission-critical technologies fit on the value chain?

## DISCUSSION ISSUE

### *Strategy or Power*

In looking at the various cases involving the use of the information systems to gain a competitive advantage, one pattern often emerges. Many of the examples (such as American Airlines and Baxter Healthcare) consist of suppliers using information systems to change the relationship with their customers. Although this change in the relationship can benefit both parties, the possibility always exists that one of the groups may eventually choose to abuse the power created by the change. In the following example, Oliver, Avery and

Lamar work for an accounting firm. One of their clients is a small business run by Mitch and Abby.

Oliver: Look, we're starting to feel pressure in this business. We're having a lot of trouble keeping our smaller clients. Lately, even some of our larger clients have been complaining about the cost of our services. We need to find some way to expand our services and keep our current clients.

Avery: Well, Oliver, we've been looking at this problem for quite some time. There seem to be only a few options. Obviously we don't want to cut our fees. We've cut our internal costs as far as we can. Based on economic projections, the number of accounting firms is increasing faster than the client base, so we can't expect things to get any better. But, Lamar here has an idea that has some merit . . .

Lamar: Thanks, Avery. I've been talking to our junior staff members and a couple of clients. It seems that a large portion of our time is spent just collecting data from some of our clients. Although most of the larger clients have computerized accounting systems, we still do taxes and audits from the printouts. For the smaller clients, we spend a lot of time just organizing their data. Sure, we charge them for our time, but as soon as a hungry competitor offers to do the paperwork for a lower price, the clients jump ship.

Oliver: Sure, that makes sense; because of our higher overhead, we can't price our services as low as some of these small firms. So what's the answer?

Lamar: Well, the main idea is to handle everything on the computer. Let's take our main computers and connect them to all of our clients. For the larger clients, we'll concentrate on getting direct access to their databases. Whenever we need data, we'll just pull it directly from the client computer, feed it into one of our auditing or tax packages, do some quick analyses, and create the final reports. It'll really speed up the process and cut down on errors. Plus, we'll be able to concentrate more on the analytical services, such as looking for better tax strategies.

Avery: That seems to fit with our goals of cutting costs and offering more services, but what about the small clients that don't use much in the way of computers?

Lamar: With the smaller clients, we'll offer a complete accounting system that runs from our computers. Basically, we'll provide their complete information system. With current telecommunications technology, it's easy to set up. It doesn't really matter where the computers are located. And we've already got most of the software we need.

Oliver: Okay, so we can run with lower costs. I still don't want to cut prices. How does this system help keep clients?

Lamar: Once the clients are on the system, they won't want to switch. Even if a competitor comes up with a similar idea, it would cost the clients too much time and effort to change to another system. Once we get them hooked, they're locked in.

Avery: Yes, that's the best part. Here's how I see the plan. We go to our customers and offer them a short-term discount to switch to the system. Tell them we want to use them as demo sites . . .

Oliver: I get it; we make the same offer to everyone, just to get them on the system.

Avery: That's right, plus we train their staff members. Get them used to the system. After a year or so, we start to raise our rates. In the meantime, we write a couple of reports showing how much the system is saving them. Collect a couple numbers that show how much we spent on training their people and setting up the system for them. Then, if they complain about their bills and start talking about switching to another firm, we give them a report showing how much it'll cost them to switch.

Lamar: Plus, we can tell them the costs are because of their increased business—part of which they earned because of getting better reports from us.

Oliver: And because we have all of their data, it should be easy to make these reports say anything we want. I like it . . .

*(Later, at one of the clients.)*

Mitch: Hi, Abby. Lamar from the accounting firm just made us an interesting offer. He said his firm is offering a new service. It will handle all of our accounting for a fixed fee. And they're offering a special deal if we agree to let them use us as a demo site . . .

Abby: I don't know, Mitch. Maybe they found out we've been talking to other firms, and they're just trying to keep us interested.

Mitch: Nah, I don't think that has anything to do with it. They've got a whole new system. Lamar was really excited. They're going to computerize everything.

Abby: But we can't afford a big computer system. We've talked about it before . . .

Mitch: That's the best part. We don't have to buy the computer. All of the records are kept on their computer. We just use a couple of smart cash registers that transfer the data over the phone lines.

Abby: But what if we ever want to switch companies? How do we get our data?

Mitch: Relax, I asked Lamar about that. He said it's like medical records. The accountants will give us whatever reports we want. If we ever switch companies, they'll give all of the data to the new firm.

Abby: Well, maybe . . . And you said they're giving us a break on the prices? What do we have to do to get that? How can they afford it?

Mitch: Lamar said that officially, we might have to let some potential customer wander through the store to check out the system. They won't see any of the data; they'll just make sure the system works. But don't worry, he hinted that it was just a formality. He's really looking out for us on this one—said he

pulled a few strings to get us the offer. He hinted that they're making money because the new computer system is so efficient.

Abby: Hey, I've got an idea. It sounds like they really want us to use this system. Maybe we can use that to negotiate with them a little . . .

Mitch: Sure. Let's call Lamar and tell him it's still too expensive. We'll drop a hint that someone else made us a better offer for a similar service. Quick, what was the name of that company we talked to last week?

## QUESTIONS

1. Do you think the accounting firm's decision to use the information system to build stronger ties with clients is a good idea?

2. Do you agree with the accounting firm's approach to implementing the system and the plan to increase prices?

3. As a partner in the accounting firm, if you choose to go this route, how would you present and sell it to the clients?

4. Do you think Mitch and Abby examined all of the issues before making their decision? What else should they consider?

5. Do you think Mitch and Abby are taking the right approach in negotiating with Lamar? Is it ethical?

6. As a client, would you accept this offer even if you know what the accounting firm is planning? What could you do to protect your interests?

# Designing and Managing Information Systems

**How do managers organize and control information systems?** Because of their importance in a modern firm, information systems must be carefully planned, designed, and maintained. Business managers are increasingly involved in designing and organizing MIS resources. Managers need to understand the difficulties faced in systems development to understand the rules and processes. As technology changes, the organization of business operations and the MIS resources is changing. By identifying these changes, business managers can improve their operations and make better use of new information technologies.

Changes in technology and business cause fundamental changes in society. These changes affect everything from education to government to our daily lives as employees and citizens. Changing technology brings new responsibilities and problems. As managers and citizens we will face many new decisions. We must always remember our ethical responsibilities to other members of society.

# *Systems Development*

Air traffic control is a difficult job requiring intense concentration. Aging computer systems make the job more difficult, but the FAA has found it even more difficult to design and build a new air traffic control system.

## FEDERAL AVIATION ADMINISTRATION
Governmental control over aviation began in 1911, when Connecticut passed regulations governing the flights of planes. Although the federal government played an early role through the department of defense, control over civilian flights was not formalized until the creation of the Civil Aeronautics Board (CAB) in 1944 as a division of the Commerce Department. The Federal Aviation Administration (FAA) was created in 1958 and the CAB was merged into the new agency. In 1966, the FAA (and CAB) was made part of the Department of Transportation (DOT). The Airline Deregulation Act of 1978 effectively dismantled most functions of the CAB.

The FAA is charged with controlling civilian and military uses of U.S. airspace. The FAA is also responsible for modernizing the airways, installing radar, and training air traffic controllers. Probably their best-known function is control over commercial flights and routes to maintain safety and efficiency. With 50,000 flights a day among 300 major airports, the FAA has a huge task.

Despite the complications of size, weather, and delays, the airline industry has suffered relatively few disasters. The current accident rate is about 1 passenger fatality per 100 million passenger miles—far less than the accident rate caused by automobile traffic. Of the accidents that do arise, about half are typically attributed to human error, with one-third of those being caused by pilot error.

There are several other governmental agencies involved in aviation. The National Weather Service produces up-to-the-minute weather forecasts. The Federal Communication Commission allocates radio frequencies and rules. The National Ocean Survey creates the maps and charts used for navigation. The National Aeronautics and Space Administration supports aviation research. International flights are governed by the UN-sponsored International Civil Aviation Organization (ICAO) formed in 1944 and moved under the aegis of the United Nations in 1947.

The FAA has a computer system to help it control the thousands of daily flights. However, the system was created in the early 1960s. It has been patched and upgraded, but most of the hardware and software are based on decades-old technology. On several occasions, the FAA attempted to upgrade the facilities, but complications have forced the agency back to the old technology.

**OVERVIEW**

By now you should have some ideas on how MIS can help you in your job. Working as a manager, you will develop many ideas involving technology that you want to try. So how do you turn your ideas into an actual system? For complex systems, you will undoubtedly turn to experts for help: computer programmers and systems analysts. In order to communicate effectively with these people, you need to understand a little bit about how they do their jobs and the techniques that are available. Part of that understanding involves learning a little about the problems that are likely to arise when you develop computer systems. As illustrated in Figure 12.1, there are several different ways to create computer systems. Non-MIS managers are often involved in deciding which method to use, so you need to know the benefits, costs, and limitations of each method.

As a manager, you need to understand the problems and limitations facing MIS departments. You need to know why it can take MIS so long to create even small systems. Additionally, more and more often, managers and workers are expected to develop their own small systems (known as **end-user development**). The lessons learned from large MIS projects can help you create your own small system—particularly with implementation problems and solutions.

**INTRODUCTION**

There is a fundamental dilemma faced by anyone developing a computer application. Most problems are so large they have to be split into smaller pieces. The difficulty lies in combining the pieces back into a complete solution. Often each piece is assigned to a different team, and sometimes it takes months to complete each section. Without a solid plan and control, the entire system might collapse. Thousands of system development projects have failed or been canceled because of these complications.

Partly because of the problems that have been encountered in the past, and partially because of technological improvements, there are several techniques avail-

**FIGURE 12.1**

It is not easy to create information systems to support business needs (strategy, tactics, and operations). Three basic techniques are systems development life cycle, prototyping, and end-user development. As a manager, you will participate in each of these methods. You will sometimes have to choose which method to use.

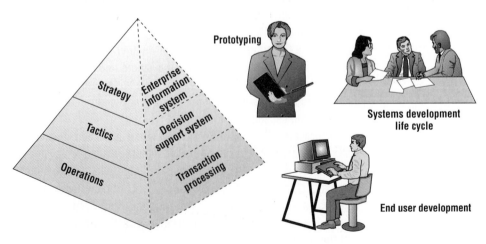

## TRENDS

In the earliest days, computers were used for simple mathematical computations. Most of the time, an individual recognized a problem to be solved, programmed the computer, and used the output. With only one or two people involved in the process, it was much easier to develop computer software. Everyone understood the problems and goals, so there were minimal communication problems. Because everyone knew how to program the computer, there was little reason to worry about creating an interface that was easy to use.

As computer use expanded to transaction processing, the situation changed, but only a little. Managers asked programmers to build systems that generated reports identical to the manually created reports already in use. Programmers concentrated on making efficient use of the computer. Data-entry clerks typed the data onto cards in a specific format. Final reports were sent to managers. The managers never actually used the computers. In fact, knowledge of computers was considered to be a menial, technical problem and something that good managers should avoid. In any case, there were few problems with communication because formulas, report layout, and data types could be copied from the existing manual system. Because managers only cared about the final reports, changes were written on the existing reports and programmers made the

modifications. Since only a few trained people actually used the computer and because computer time was expensive, the user interface consisted of a few simple commands punched onto cards. The programs were short and simple, and programmers designed the systems in their heads or on a few scraps of paper.

Later, as computer use spread and computers were shared by large numbers of people, the separate professions of programmer and systems analyst evolved. Users would request help from the MIS department to solve a particular problem, and a team of analysts and programmers would be assigned. The analysts would interview the users at the start of the project and create system specifications for the programmers. A few days (or weeks or months) later, the MIS team would present what it believed was the completed project. Often users would express some disappointment in the results and adjustments would be made. Sometimes the system never did do exactly what the users wanted. As time elapsed, the business and the needs of the users would change. To control these changes, MIS departments began asking users to "sign off" on the project at various steps, agreeing not to change the specifications. This approach attempted to freeze the system while the analysts modeled it. Unfortunately, the actual business rarely stayed frozen.

able to develop computer systems. The most formal approach is known as the **systems development life cycle (SDLC).** As indicated in Figure 12.2, large organizations that develop several systems use this method to coordinate the teams, evaluate progress, and ensure quality development. Most organizations have created their own versions of SDLC. Any major company that uses SDLC also has a manual that is several inches thick (or comparable online documentation) that lays out the rules that MIS designers have to follow. Although these details vary from firm to firm, all of the methods have a common foundation. The goal is to build a system by analyzing the business processes and breaking the problem into smaller, more manageable pieces.

Improvements in technology improve the development process. The powerful features of commercial software make it easier to build new applications. Programmers and designers can work with larger, more powerful objects. For example, instead of programming each line in COBOL, a report can be created in a few minutes using a database management system or a spreadsheet. **Prototyping** is a design

**FIGURE 12.2**
EXAMPLES OF
SYSTEM
DEVELOPMENT
METHODOLOGIES
Several companies
specialize in developing
systems, and they have
built their own
methodologies to
coordinate teams,
evaluate progress, and
identify problems. All
of these approaches
are similar.

*Andersen Consulting,* a division of Arthur Andersen & Co., is the largest worldwide consulting firm in management information systems. It conducts major installations using a proprietary methodology called Method/1. Method/1 uses four phases in the development process: plan, design, implement, and maintain.

*McKinsey and Co.,* a strategic consulting firm, examines organizations with a copyrighted "Seven S" model. The seven S's are structure, systems, style, staff, skills, strategy, and shared values.

*Ed Yourdon,* a computer programmer credited with standardizing programming in replaceable components, applies a self-developed method of tools and techniques. His method uses graphical diagrams to model the hardware and software on which the system is based.

*Information Engineering Workbench (IEW),* a structured systems-development methodology, uses planning, analysis, design, and construction to increase the productivity of systems analysts. Developed by Knowledgeware, IEW uses object-oriented modeling concepts to involve the users in systems planning, analysis, and design. To increase the speed of the data-processing environment, the data-processing expenditure must be justified by its link to top management's directions and goals. By identifying how technology can best aid the strategic goals of the business, development is focused on systems that provide the most benefit for the company.

technique that takes advantage of these new tools. The main objective of prototyping is to create a working version of the system as quickly as possible—even if some components are not included in the early versions. The third method of creating systems, *end-user development,* relies on users to create their own systems. This method typically uses advanced software (such as spreadsheets and database management systems) and requires users who have some computer skills.

It is important to be careful when you implement any new system. Case studies show that major problems have arisen during implementation of systems. In fact, some organizations have experienced so many problems that they will deliberately stick with older, less useful systems just to avoid the problems that occur during implementation. Although changes can cause problems, there are ways to deal with them during implementation.

There have been some spectacular failures in the development of computer systems. Projects always seem to be over budget and late. Worse, systems are sometimes developed and never used because they did not solve the right problems or they are impossible to use. Several design methods have been created to help prevent these problems. Each method has advantages and drawbacks. As a result, they tend to be suitable for different types of problems.

### Individual Programming

**EARLY METHODS**    At heart, development of information systems comes down to the work of individuals. Despite advances in technology, the emphasis on teamwork, and the use of methodologies, development of systems remains a craft. To understand the implications, consider that there can be a 10-fold (or greater) difference in capability and productivity between programmers. Despite our best efforts, projects still fail (Reality Bytes 12–1). The success of any project depends on the skills and capabilities of the individual programmers and system analysts. Hiring, training, and keeping talented workers are crucial components in developing systems.

---

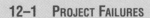

**Reality Bytes    12–1  PROJECT FAILURES**

MIS is littered with systems development projects that have failed—some of the projects cost millions of dollars. A few examples were outlined in 1993 by Peter Neumann.

A relatively recent case comes from Bank of America. In the mid-1980s, the bank spent $23 million on a five-year project to develop a new computerized accounting system for the trust department called MasterNet. After the entire organization converted to the new system and dropped the old version, the staff found that the new system did not work properly. They spent another $60 million trying to make the new system work—and failed. The entire project was scrapped, but the errors caused customers to switch banks and withdraw billions of dollars from their accounts.

In 1983, Blue Cross and Blue Shield of Wisconsin hired EDS to build a $200 million computer system. Although it was delivered on time, it did not work correctly. It issued $60 million in duplicate checks and overpayments. It took almost three years to fix the system.

There are many examples of development problems with Department of Defense contracts. For instance, the GAO reports that the C-17 cargo plane built by Douglas Aircraft had a $500 million overrun because of problems developing the avionics software. Similarly, an extra $1 billion was spent to improve the air-defense software of the B-1 bomber, and experts believe the software never did operate properly.

---

A few techniques were developed to assist individual programmers and analysts. For a short time, programmers were encouraged to visualize programs with *flow charts*. Although a few programmers still use flow charts, others first outline their plans using pseudocode. *Pseudocode* is used to describe the logic of a program or outline a system. It uses basic programming techniques but ignores issues of syntax.

These techniques are also used to communicate with users. Consider a system that requires complex logic or involved computations. Most programmers will not be experts in the interpretation of the equations, so they will rely on the users to verify the accuracy of the final system. As part of that process, the programmer or analyst will describe the program using pseudocode. The analyst will use the pseudocode to illustrate how the system will fit with the underlying business process. As a manager, there are situations in which you will want to check the pseudocode to verify that the program performs computations correctly. Figure 12.3 provides an example of pseudocode for developing a financial system that evaluates projects based on present-value costs. As an accountant or financial analyst involved with this project, you would be responsible for reading the pseudocode segments to make sure the logic and computations are correct.

*Project Evaluation (given a discount factor)*

Get list of cost items from the user
   (Description, value, time-incurred, probability-factor,
   category . . .)

Examine each item in the list:
Compute the present value of the cost:
   $PV = Cost / ( (1 + rate) \wedge time)$

Multiply by the probability factor:
   $EV = probability * PV$

If item is in a special category,
   Then add or subtract correction:
   category = Land          Add 10%
   category = Overhead      Subtract 5%
   category = Labor         Add 15%
End If

Accumulate the total value

End of list

Return the Total value

## Top-Down and Bottom-Up Design

In the 1970s, there was considerable discussion of whether systems (and programs) should be designed following a top-down or a bottom-up approach. With a **top-down design,** the analyst begins by modeling the "big-picture" situation. Early methods called for analyzing the entire corporation. To save time, top-down analysis generally begins with the highest business level that will be affected by the system. As shown in Figure 12.4, the goal is to start at the top and list all of the business functions (marketing, accounting, etc.). All of these functions are broken into processes, each of which is supported by business activities. Eventually, a complete picture of the firm (or subsystem) is created that contains any desired level of detail.

The main purpose of a top-down approach is to examine problems in the context of the entire system. It is particularly useful at comparing problems from different areas of the company. For instance, perhaps problems are found in marketing, accounting, and inventory management. Which problem should be solved first? Are the problems related? If we work on one problem, can we use some of the same techniques to solve the others? Because a top-down approach examines the entire system, it can answer these questions. The biggest drawback to the top-down approach is that it can take forever—literally. Because of the complexity and the continuous changes in most organizations, it is impossible to build a complete systems model of the organization.

A **bottom-up design** is somewhat like the advertisement: *Just do it.* Whenever a problem arises, the first objective is to solve it. If marketing, accounting, and inventory all need new systems, independent teams are assigned to develop them. The teams work closely with the individual departments but might not interact with each

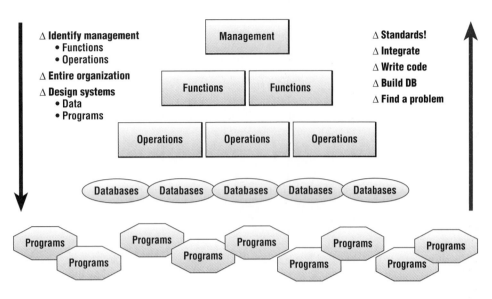

**FIGURE 12.4**

Top-down and bottom-up design. The top-down approach begins by examining the entire organization and seeks to improve the overall operations by making changes to the most critical areas. Bottom-up design identifies problems and solves them. By following standards and sharing data through a DBMS, the individual pieces should eventually fit together. Most organizations use a combination of the two methods: top-down to set long-term goals and maintain internal consistency and bottom-up to solve day-to-day problems and to get systems built on time.

other. The advantage is that each problem gets solved relatively quickly and the users have control over how the system works. The drawback is that the company ends up with different systems that will probably not work together. For example, it will be difficult for the accountants to retrieve data from the marketing department.

Today, most people recognize that systems analysis and development requires a combination of features from both bottom-up and top-down designs. One common approach is to orient systems development to database management systems. The database administrator defines standards. The standards are designed from a top-down perspective to meet the needs of the entire organization. Teams of developers then solve the bottom-up problems of the individual departments. As long as they follow the database standards, the resulting systems should fit together.

Compare these problems to the **data flow diagram (DFD)** techniques introduced in Chapter 3. A DFD has only five elements (and two of those are arrows). It displays an overall view in the first two or three levels, and detailed descriptions are presented with additional levels. It can be built from the top down by starting at the context diagram and filling in each level for the entire company. It can also be built from the bottom up by working on detail views first and combining them into the final set of diagrams. Again, corporate standards are used to ensure that all designers use similar terms and that the pieces fit together.

## The Need for Control

**SYSTEMS DEVELOPMENT LIFE CYCLE**

The systems development life cycle (SDLC) was designed to overcome the problems that arose with large projects that involve many users and require thousands of hours of development by multiple analysts and programmers. Difficulties with runaway projects are shown in Figure 12.5. Some causes of problems are highlighted in Figure 12.6.

Before the use of the SDLC method, several related problems were common. It was hard to coordinate and control the various programmers and analysts, so there were duplicated efforts. Individual programmers created portions of a system that

**FIGURE 12.5**
Runaway projects. Managers fear runaway projects, but they still occur. Some projects end up two to five times over budget and behind schedule. Some projects are canceled because they never meet their objectives. Some fail because of design problems and conflicts among users, management, and developers. An important step in managing projects is to identify when the project becomes a runaway project.

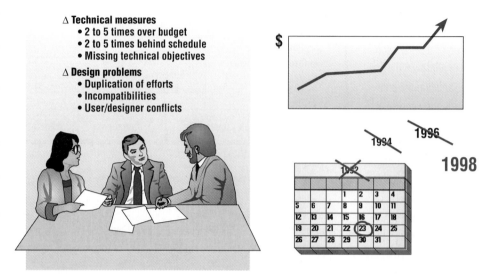

△ **Technical measures**
  • **2 to 5 times over budget**
  • **2 to 5 times behind schedule**
  • **Missing technical objectives**
△ **Design problems**
  • **Duplication of efforts**
  • **Incompatibilities**
  • **User/designer conflicts**

would not work together. Users did not always have much input into the process. When they did have input, there were conflicts between users, and analysts did not know which approach to use. With long-term projects, programmers were promoted to other areas or left for different companies. New employees had to learn the system and determine what others had done before they could proceed. Similarly, new users would appear (through promotions and transfers), and existing users would change the specifications of the system. These problems often lead to runaway projects—projects that are significantly late and over budget. Even today, there are many instances of runaway projects. In fact, as illustrated by the examples, there are enough problems to support a separate division of the accounting firm, KPMG Peat Marwick (Reality Bytes 12–2).

These problems are related through the issue of control. It is impossible to prevent users from changing the specifications and to prevent employees from taking

---

▼ **BUSINESS TRENDS: TEMPORARY WORKERS** ▶

One pattern that caused problems for MIS in the past was the high turnover in the MIS staff. Many times, projects were finished by completely different groups of MIS employees than the ones who began the project. This turnover created a strong need for control on projects to make sure the newcomers could understand the project, and to provide increased communication between the MIS department and the users.

As companies begin to rely on more temporary workers, the same problems arise. If MIS workers take family leaves, they are likely to be assigned a different job on return. Similarly, businesses are using more consultants to create the initial projects. Support and revisions are often performed by other employees. Although the outside contracts simplify the management involvement during the creation of the project, managers need to ensure that certain design standards are followed, and documentation is provided to allow the system to be modified later.

| Top 5 Reasons for Success | Top 5 Reasons for Failure |
|---|---|
| User involvement | Lack of user input |
| Executive management support | Incomplete requirements |
| Clear requirements | Changing requirements and specifications |
| Proper planning | Lack of executive support |
| Realistic expectations | Lack of technical skills |

SOURCE: Adapted from Rosemary Cafasso, "Few IS Projects Come in on Time, on Budget," *Computerworld*, December 12, 1994, p. 20. Copyright 1994 by Computerworld, Inc., Framingham, MA 01701. Reprinted from *Computerworld*.

other jobs. Likewise, large projects involving many analysts and programmers will always have problems with coordination and compatibility (Business Trends). The goal of SDLC was to design a system that can handle all of these problems.

## Introduction to SDLC

An important feature of the SDLC approach is that it is a comprehensive method. Some organizations (such as EDS) that specialize in systems development have hundreds of pages in manuals to detail all the steps and rules for using SDLC. Fortunately, it is possible to understand SDLC by looking at a smaller number of steps. As illustrated in Figure 12.7, there are five basic phases to the SDLC approach: (1) feasibility and planning, (2) systems analysis, (3) systems design, (4) implementation, and (5) maintenance and review.

Actually, just about any systems development methodology uses these five steps. They differ largely in how much time is spent in each section, who does the work,

 Reality Bytes  12–2 KPMG Runaway Systems Management Practice

KPMG Peat Marwick has developed a unique section in its Information Technology Practice to address the threat of substitute products or services. It has established the Runaway Systems Management Practice to repair messes left by other systems integrators. Jules Ghedina, partner in charge of Peat Marwick's Technology Resource Center, estimates that at least one-third of all systems integration projects now underway fit into the runaway category. In Ghedina's opinion, these projects are two to five times over budget, two to five times behind schedule, and are missing their technical objectives.

One of the causes of a runaway information systems project is the lack of a rigorous work plan. Instead, management is conducted by the "seat-of-the-pants." Consequently, there is no clear standard against which to compare performance. Nor is there a clear work plan against which to measure performance.

The first step to regain control is to impose strict project standards, plans, and practices on the entire project team. The second step is to make certain that the people who are going to use the system have input into what the system will look like.

### RUNAWAY PROJECT EXAMPLES

*Allstate Insurance.* The Allstate project was originally slated to be an $8 million project that was to be completed and running by 1987. Five years later, costs were projected to be $100 million and the project was still at least a year away from completion.

*UK Department of Social Security.* The Department of Social Security's "Operational Strategy" was originally to have cost £713 million. By 1991, that figure had grown to £2000 million with completion scheduled for April 1992.

**FIGURE 12.7**

Systems development life cycle. Sometimes SDLC is known as the waterfall methodology because each step produces outputs that are used in the next step. The existing system is studied for problems and improvements. A new design is analyzed for feasibility. In-depth analysis generates the business requirements. Systems design turns them into a technical design that is implemented, creating a new system. This new system is analyzed and the process continues.

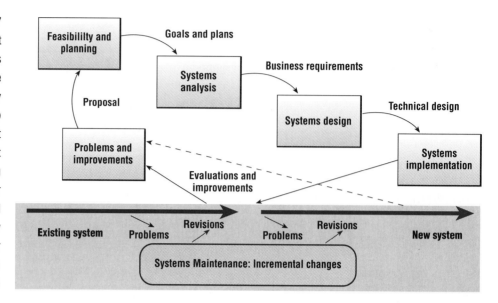

and in the degree of formality involved. The SDLC is by far the most formal method, so it offers a good starting point in describing the various methodologies.

## Feasibility and Planning

The basic premise of **systems analysis** was presented in Chapter 3. The primary goal of the systems analysis stage is to identify problems and determine how they can be solved with a computer system. In formal SDLC methodologies, the first step in systems analysis is a **feasibility study.** A feasibility study is a quick examination of the problems, goals, and expected costs of the system. The objective is to determine whether the problem can reasonably be solved with a computer system. In some cases, maybe there is a better (or cheaper) alternative, or perhaps the problem is simply a short-term annoyance and will gradually disappear. In other cases, the problem may turn out to be more complex than was thought and involve users across the company. Also, some problems may not be solvable with today's technology. It might be better to wait for improved technology or lower prices. In any case, you need to determine the scope of the project to gain a better idea of the costs, benefits, and objectives.

The feasibility study is typically written so that it can be easily understood by non-programmers. It is used to "sell" the project to upper management and as a starting point for the next step. Additionally, it is used as a reference to keep the project on track, and to evaluate the progress of the MIS team. Projects are typically evaluated in three areas of feasibility: economics, operations, and technical. Is the project cost-effective or is there a cheaper solution? Will the proposed system improve the operations of the firm, or will complicating factors prevent it from achieving its goals? Does the technology exist and does the firm have the staff to make the technology work?

When the proposal is determined to be feasible, the MIS team leaders are appointed and a plan and schedule are created. The schedule contains a detailed listing of what parts of the project will be completed at each time. Of course, it is extremely difficult to estimate the true costs and completion dates. Nonetheless, the schedule is an important tool to evaluate the status of the project and the progress of the MIS teams. Figure 12.8 summarizes the role of planning and scheduling in providing control for projects.

**FIGURE 12.8**

Development controls. A complex system requires careful management. Without planning and control, any project will become a runaway. Control begins with a detailed plan and performance targets that enable managers to evaluate progress and identify problems. System control is provided by standardized practices and procedures to ensure that teams are producing compatible output. User input and control ensure that the final project will actually be useful.

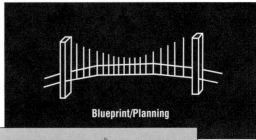

- **Detailed work plan**
- **Performance targets**
- **Practices and procedures**
- **User input and control**

**Blueprint/Planning**

## Systems Analysis

Once a project has been shown to be feasible and it is approved, work can begin on a full-fledged analysis. The first step is to determine how the existing system works and where the problems are located. The technique is to break the system into pieces. Smaller pieces are easier to understand and to explain to others. Also, each piece can be assigned to a different MIS team. As long as they work from the same initial description and follow all of the standards, the resulting pieces should fit back together.

Diagrams are often created to illustrate the system. The diagrams are used to communicate among analysts and users, other analysts, and eventually the programmers. Data flow diagrams are a common method to display the relationships that were determined during systems analysis. The diagrams represent a way to divide the system into smaller pieces. As illustrated by AT&T (Reality Bytes 12–3), these pieces can then be distributed to smaller design teams.

 **Reality Bytes** 12–3 **AT&T**

In 1989, the U.S. District Court ruled that AT&T could no longer rely on regional Bell operating companies to provide billing services for its credit card. AT&T found itself with the huge task of replacing its entire calling card system by January 1, 1992.

In response, AT&T introduced an information system using 42 mainframes to meet its international marketing needs to more than 40 million subscribers. Using COBOL code, the effort would require 350 million person-years to complete. However, Index Technology's PC Prism has helped the calling card

development team deal with AT&T's complicated organizational structure. PC Prism was used to identify AT&T's internal and external goals and appropriate customer services and needs. Information and models are translated by design and analysis systems into detailed business-process flow diagrams. This technique has enabled system development to be broken down so that it can be completed on micro-and mini-computers. This method has resulted in the project running ahead of schedule.

**FIGURE 12.9**
Visual tables of contents. Programs are usually split into smaller modules. The user interface is typically divided into screens. A VTOC displays how the screens (and modules) are related to each other. Managers should carefully check the VTOC to be certain that it performs all of the necessary operations.

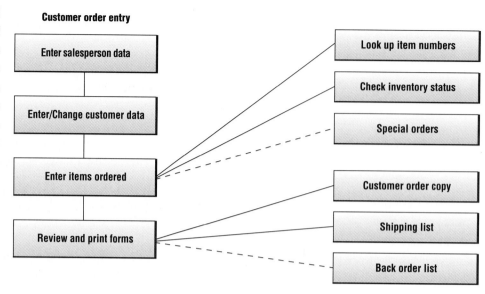

**FIGURE 12.9**
Visual tables of contents. Programs are usually split into smaller modules. The user interface is typically divided into screens. A VTOC displays how the screens (and modules) are related to each other. Managers should carefully check the VTOC to be certain that it performs all of the necessary operations.

A **visual table of contents (VTOC)** is sometimes used to show how modules of a system are related. Versions of the technique are also used to display *menu trees*. Analysts will lay out the user interface before any programming takes place. By reading through the VTOC, you can get a feel for how the system will work. It is easy for the analyst to make changes or additions at this point. Figure 12.9 presents a simple example of a VTOC. In some cases, the analyst will build the menu system so that users and managers can work through the choices to see how the system might operate. At this stage, users should verify that the system contains all of the desired functions, that the system is easy to understand, and that common tasks do not require an excessive number of keystrokes.

Graphics tools provide a useful way to communicate with the user and to document the user requirements. Figure 12.10 discusses the major differences. However, they do not speed up the development process. Producing, changing, and storing documentation can be a significant problem. Yet these tools are necessary because they make it easier for the user to control the final result. One increasingly common

**FIGURE 12.10**
Comparison of diagramming tools. Systems designers use many graphical tools. Each tool has a specific purpose and is suitable for certain tasks. For example, the *data flow diagram* is good for illustrating processes and activities. An *entity relationship diagram* is designed to show how data and objects relate to each other. A *structure chart* is used to highlight how a program will be used.

|  | DATA FLOW DIAGRAM | ENTITY RELATIONSHIP DIAGRAM | STRUCTURE CHART OR VTOC |
|---|---|---|---|
| Purpose | Show processes and flow of data | Describe entities and how they are related | Show modules and usage flow |
| Classification | Process | Data structure | Module structure |
| Object orientation | No | Yes | No |
| Decomposition | Increasingly detailed levels of process | By entities or object inheritance | By program structure or usage steps |

solution is to keep all of the documentation on the computer. This method reduces the costs, makes it easier for everyone to share the documentation, and ensures that all users have up-to-date information for the system.

At the end of the analysis phase, the MIS team will have a complete description of the business requirements. The problems and needs are documented with text, data flow diagrams, and other figures depending on the methodology followed.

## Systems Design

The third major step of the SDLC is to design the new system. During this step, the new system is typically designed on paper. The objective of **systems design** is to describe the new system as a collection of modules or subsystems. By subdividing the total project, each portion can be given to a single programmer to develop. As the pieces are completed, the overall design ensures that they will work together. Typically, the diagrams created during the analysis phase can be modified to indicate how the new system will work. The design will list all of the details, including data inputs, system outputs, processing steps, database designs, manual procedures, and feedback and control mechanisms. Backup and recovery plans along with security controls will be spelled out to ensure that the database is protected.

In traditional SDLC methods, managers and users will be shown various components of the system as they are completed. The managers will have to *sign off* on these sections to indicate that they meet the user needs. This signature is designed to ensure that users provide input to the system. If there are many diverse users, there can be major disagreements about how the system should function. Sign offs require users to negotiate and formally agree to the design. It is relatively easy to make design changes at this stage. If everyone attempts to make changes at later stages, the cost increases dramatically.

In terms of physical design, some of the hardware and software will be purchased. Programmers will write and test the program code. As indicated in Figure 12.11, in most large projects, the actual coding takes only 15 to 30 percent of the total development time. Initial data will be collected or transferred from existing systems. Manuals and procedures will be written to instruct users and system operators on how to use the system.

Once the designer has created base modules and sample inputs and outputs, the users are invited to a structured walkthrough. A **structured walkthrough** is a review process where the objective is to reveal problems, inaccuracies, ambiguities,

**FIGURE 12.11**

Systems design effort. G. Davis and M. Olson observed that only a portion of total development effort is used in programming. The analysis and design stages require the bulk of the development time. With today's use of code generators and overseas programmers, the actual programming component can be reduced even further.

| STAGE | PROCEDURE | APPROXIMATE % OF EFFORT |
|---|---|---|
| Analysis | Feasibility | 5 |
| | Requirements | 15 |
| | Conceptual design | 5 |
| Design | Physical design | 20 |
| | Programming | 25 |
| | Procedure development | 10 |
| Implementation | Conversion | 15 |
| Maintenance and review | Review | 5 |
| | Maintenance | Not included |

**VIRTUS WALKTHROUGH**

An application of structured walkthrough occurs in the design/build environment. To work effectively, designers must be able to visualize space in three dimensions, engineers need calculations to size structural elements, and builders must be able to track time and estimate costs. Virtus WalkThrough is a spatial-design visualization product that enhances this process by producing three-dimensional models. This product enables users to make 3-D models, such as buildings, and "walk" through them in real time. It does this by displaying plane, perspective, front, and side views of a design environment in adjacent windows. The environment can be manipulated on-screen in the planar view, with revisions instantly appearing in all four windows. The user can place a window on the wall and WalkThrough will show the view in full color. When rooms are joined with the Connection tool, adjacent objects share features. This enables users to "walk" through doors and "see" through windows. The package includes a library of 3-D clip art that can be added to the rooms.

The structured walkthrough is an extremely successful development technique. This formal methodology enables colleagues to inspect and comment on system deliverables. In doing so, they provide feedback on correcting faults and looking at the root cause of errors.

and omissions in the systems design before the program code is finalized. The users are presented with a prototype or mockup of the proposed system. It is easier to spot problems and make suggestions by observing how the actual system might appear. A similar process has long been used in architecture, where the architect first builds a cardboard model of the project. Virtus WalkThrough has gone a step farther and created a computerized system that enables customers to view buildings on the computer screen. Similar tools exist in MIS with which a designer can quickly piece together displays that illustrate how each screen might look and how the user will see the system. The number of walkthroughs used depends on the amount of time users and programmers can spend on reviewing the designs. The walkthroughs also provide management with feedback regarding the time schedule and anticipated costs of the project, because they are often scheduled in the original feasibility study.

The output of the design stage consists of a complete technical specification of the new system. It includes as many details as possible—sometimes leading to thousands of pages (or computer files) of description.

One of the difficulties in the design stage is sometimes called "creeping elegance." As the system is being built analysts, programmers, and users all want to include additional features. Although many of the features are good ideas, the continual evolution of the system causes additional delays. It also complicates testing, because changes in one section can affect the rest of the system. Go Corporation (Reality Bytes 12–4) experienced these problems when designing its first hand-held personal computer.

### Systems Implementation

Systems implementation involves installation and changeover from the previous system to the new one, including training users and making adjustments to the system. The major issues are summarized in Figure 12.12. Many nasty problems can arise at this stage. You have to be extremely careful in implementing new systems. First, users are probably nervous about the change already. If something goes

## Reality Bytes ► 12–4 GO CORPORATION

Go Corporation was created in 1987 to create a hand-held personal computer that recognized handwriting instead of relying on typing. Jerry Kaplan, the CEO, discusses the problems and adventures in his book (*Startup: A Silicon Valley Story*). The primary focus was on the development of the operating system, Penpoint, which would perform the necessary hand-writing recognition and handle basic filing tasks. The hardware was being developed by other companies.

The operating system presented a completely new user interface, where pen strokes were interpreted as commands. For example, slash meant delete and tapping the pen on the screen was used to select an item. Designing the system presented many problems because every issue was new. As the deadlines slipped and costs mounted, Jerry Kaplan noted some common problems:

> Most of the engineers were occupied with simpli-fying portions of the program to reduce its size. But in the course of rewriting, everyone was proposing improvements that would tend to increase its size. Penpoint was succumbing to a

disease known as feature creep—the irresistible temptation for engineers to load a product down with their favorite special features. Before unnec-essary additions hardened around their feet like concrete, the senior technical managers staged meetings called Feature Court, with "Judge Wapner" presiding. Each side would argue its case, and a binding decision was made on the spot. Despite these efforts, the system seemed to grow like a cancer. No sooner were we able to save some space than a new, indispensable requirement would emerge.

At the same time, Go Corporation was pressured by a competitive product from Microsoft that was based on the Windows operating system. Go Corporation was eventually absorbed by AT&T, which had financed much of the operations. The Penpoint operating sys-tem finally made it to market in 1995.

SOURCE: Jerry Kaplan, *Startup: A Silicon Valley Adventure Story,* Houghton Mifflin Co., 1994. (Excerts in "The Startup, *Fortune,* May 29, 1995, pp. 110–120.)

---

**FIGURE 12.12**

Systems implementation. When changing operations with a new system, you must be careful to encourage users to change. An important step in making a smooth transition is to involve the users at every step of the design, and make the system flexible enough to adapt to different users. Education and training, sufficient testing, and formal plans all make for easier implementations.

wrong, they may never trust the new system. Second, if major errors occur, you could lose important business data.

A crucial stage in implementation is final testing. Testing and quality control must be performed at every stage of development, but a final systems test is needed before

- Final testing
- Involve users
- Education and training
- Flexibility
- Recognize how the system will affect the business
- Encourage users to change
- Implementation plans

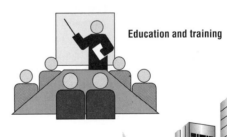
Education and training

Changing business operations

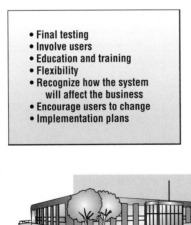

staff entrust the company's data to the new system. Occasionally, small problems will be noted, but their resolution will be left for later. In any large system, there are bound to be errors and changes. The key is to identify them and determine which ones must be fixed immediately. Smaller problems are often left to the software maintenance staff.

Change is an important part of MIS. Designing and implementing new systems often causes changes in the business operations. Yet, many people do not like changes. Changes require learning new methods, forging new relationships with people and managers, or perhaps even loss of jobs. Changes exist on many levels: in society, in business, and in information systems. Changes can occur because of shifts in the environment, or they can be introduced by internal **change agents.** Left to themselves, most organizations will resist even small changes. Change agents are objects or people who cause or facilitate changes. Sometimes it might be a new employee who brings fresh ideas; other times changes can be mandated by top-level management. Sometimes an outside event such as arrival of a new competitor or a natural disaster forces an organization to change. Whatever the cause, people tend to resist change. However, if organizations do not change, they cannot survive. The goal is to implement systems in a manner that recognizes resistance to change but encourages people to accept the new system. Effective implementation involves finding ways to reduce this resistance. Sometimes, implementation involves the cooperation of outsiders such as suppliers. Dillard's Department Stores (Reality Bytes 12–5) was having trouble convincing suppliers to cooperate, so the managers used brute force. However, these methods can often fail or cause repercussions.

## Reality Bytes ▲     12–5   EDI at Dillard's

A major implementer of electronic data interchange is Dillard's Department Stores. Like many retailers, Dillard's began its direction toward EDI by requesting rather than requiring it. Ray Heflin, chief of EDI, described the approach that influenced 70 percent of its suppliers to move to EDI: "I went one-on-one with sales representatives and presidents. Then we had three seminars—full-day presentations of what we wanted to do with EDI and the schedules we recommend."

Yet, to be successful, Dillard's needed 100 percent of the suppliers to supply its products this way. As a result, Heflin provided pressure on the rest to get their attention. When suppliers missed their first EDI implementation deadline, Dillard's charged them $25 per subsequent paper transaction. When they missed the final deadline at the end of 1991, Dillard's discontinued doing business with them. In Heflin's view, that was the only way to accomplish the goal. In his opinion, "People don't get educated unless they've got to get educated."

### Involve Users

An important process in reducing resistance to change is to involve the users in the design of the new system. There are three main advantages of user contributions. First, the users will get the system they need. Second, the users will understand the project better and it will be easier to use. Third, user contributions provide a sense of ownership, minimizing **user resistance** and promoting use of the final system.

At a minimum, user participation can begin by allowing users to design the reports and customize the input screens. Even moderately trained users can create report layouts and sample input screens using spreadsheets, word processors, or database management systems. Early involvement by users helps ensure that the users get worthwhile systems that are easier to use. Additionally, it gives them more time to adapt to the concept of change and see how it might benefit them.

Keep in mind that many computer systems are designed to improve the business operations and reduce costs. Often, these improvements arise by eliminating jobs. In these cases, it is hard to expect users to be enthusiastic about the new system. They are not likely to be cooperative if they are asked to help design the system that takes away their jobs. Even if employees are promised jobs in other areas, they are likely to be apprehensive about the changes. When jobs do need to be cut, experience from layoff specialists shows that it is best to determine job cuts up front and establish a clear policy before you begin implementing the new system.

### Education and Training

Anyone except aggressive risk takers will be nervous about a new system if they know nothing about it. A key component of any implementation strategy is user education and training. Even generic education courses that explain how computers work and how they can help are useful. Specific training classes on the actual system are even more useful. Many companies pay for training when it directly affects an employee's job. Companies also encourage workers to continue their general education by covering at least some of the costs.

Training classes give managers the chance to answer questions from the users and minimize the amount of misinformation floating through the grapevine. Additionally, the MIS development team gets feedback on the system and can make last-minute changes or record suggestions for future enhancements.

In some cases, a variety of training methods should be scheduled. Some experienced users may prefer a simple handout explaining the goals and the primary commands available. Some users will need extensive, personal support and encouragement. Some companies are experimenting with video and multimedia training tools. For example, a personal computer tutoring system could be used to simulate the operation of the new system. Users can work at their own pace and are quizzed periodically to see whether they understand the basic operations. In addition to being accessible 24 hours a day, some people might feel more comfortable with computer training, especially if they can study at home or in their office. No one needs to know if they make mistakes, and they can ask "silly" questions without being embarrassed.

### Flexibility

It is important that systems be flexible so they can be adjusted by the users. Simple things like being able to set screen colors, mouse sensitivity, and keyboard speed can be critical to keeping users happy. They are also useful for users with physical challenges. Some people have difficulty seeing certain colors and they are much more productive if they can choose their own colors.

The items that can be controlled by users will be different for each system. For instance, sometimes users may be allowed to change report titles or even calculations. In other cases, these variables may be governed by legal or security constraints. The key is to give the users as much control as possible while maintaining the integrity of the data. An added benefit from this flexibility is that if users are able to make their own changes, there will be less need for system changes later.

### Recognize How the System Will Affect the Business

Computer systems often change the way the business operates. These changes are not always anticipated. For example, when ATMs were installed in banks, the goal was to give customers easier access to their money. A second objective was to decrease the bank's operational costs by decreasing the workload on the human tellers. Early bank studies indicated that each ATM transaction cost the bank $0.50, whereas a human teller cost the bank $1 per transaction. Initially consumers were reluctant to change, but they eventually shifted transactions to the ATMs—primarily simple deposits and withdrawals. However, human tellers are now dealing with more complicated transactions, making their jobs more difficult. As a bank manager, if you simply looked at the number of transactions processed by tellers before ATMs and after ATMs, you might conclude that the tellers were less productive. By failing to notice the change in complexity, you would make bad decisions.

In general, technology has traditionally created more jobs for society. However, they are almost always different jobs, usually in different industries. Hence, some workers can lose their jobs. Additionally, the newly created jobs may require more education, or might be in a different state, or even another country. Some workers will not want to change jobs. Others will have difficulty moving to new areas—especially in dual-income families.

These changes have to be communicated to the users as soon as possible. The more opportunity employees have to adjust to the changes, the easier it will be for them. Several firms exist with the sole purpose of providing support for displaced workers. They help with searching for new jobs and finding educational or retraining opportunities.

### Encourage Users to Change

A common management technique is to make sure that the payment system incentives match the goals of the organization. Consider the situation of a bank teller. Perhaps a portion of the teller's pay is based on the number of transactions processed in a day. When ATMs are installed, if a manager concludes that teller productivity has declined, the tellers might be denied raises or promotions. A teller who foresees this problem would definitely resist the change to ATMs. One solution is to change the payment structure so the tellers are not penalized for the changing nature of their jobs.

Even if the business operations are not substantially altered, implementing a new system can cause reduced productivity while employees learn to operate the new system. Employees whose pay is based on performance will resist changes, because even a temporary decline in productivity will result in less money. A common solution is to provide additional training to help the users learn the system faster. During the training period, it might be appropriate to base employee pay on original productivity levels.

### Implementation Plans

Because implementation is so important, several techniques have been developed to help implement new systems. Direct cutover is an obvious technique, where the old system is simply dropped and the new one started. If at all possible, it is best to avoid this technique because it is the most dangerous to data. If anything goes wrong with the new system, you run the risk of losing valuable information because the old system is not available. The various methods are displayed in Figure 12.13.

In many ways, the safest choice is to use parallel implementation. In this case, the new system is introduced alongside the old one. Both systems are operated at the same time, until you determine that the new system is acceptable. The main draw-

**FIGURE 12.13**

Conversion options. When you implement a new system, there are several possible conversion methods. In most cases, direct cutover should be avoided because of the disruptions and potential for lost data. Parallel conversion entails running both systems simultaneously, which is safe but can become expensive and time consuming. With multiple stores or business units, pilot introductions of phased implementations are common. For pilot testing, designers can bring extra workers, managers, and systems designers to one location and work out the problems with the system. Once the system is running well, it can be implemented at other locations. With a phased implementation, a system can be introduced slowly throughout the company (e.g., by department). Projects can also be phased in by modules.

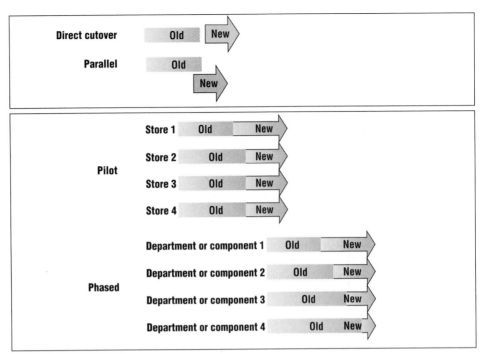

back to this method is that it can be expensive because data has to be entered twice. Additionally, if users are nervous about the new system, they might avoid the change and stick with the old method. In this case, the new system may never get a fair trial.

There are several intermediate possibilities, called *phased implementation.* For example, if you design a system for a chain of retail stores, you could pilot test the first implementation in one store. By working with one store at a time, there are likely to be fewer problems. If problems do arise, you will have more staff members around to overcome the obstacles. When the system is working well in one store, you can move to the next location. Similarly, even if there is only one store, you might be able to split the implementation into sections based on the area of business. You might install a set of computer cash registers first. When they work correctly, you can connect them to a central computer and produce daily reports. Next you can move on to annual summaries and payroll. Eventually the entire system will be installed.

## Maintenance

Once the system is installed, the MIS job has just begun. Computer systems are constantly changing. Hardware upgrades occur continuously, and commercial software tools may change every year. Users change jobs. Errors may exist in the system. The business changes, and management and users demand new information and expansions. All of these actions mean the system needs to be modified. The job of overseeing and making these modifications is called **software maintenance.**

The pressures for change are so great that in most organizations today as much as 80 percent of the MIS staff is devoted to modifying existing programs. These changes can be time consuming and difficult. Most major systems were created by teams of programmers and analysts over a long period. In order to make a change to a program, the programmer has to understand how the current program works. Because the program was written by many different people with varying styles, it can be hard

Reality Bytes     12–6   DuPont: RDB Expert Maximizes Database Efficiency

At DuPont a department of engineers is charged with analyzing the quality control of its database applications. Engineers regularly test and evaluate the database retrieval system to make certain that the information that it provides is accurate. Unfortunately, this system had become bogged down with many iterations of changes and adjustments. As a result, a team of database experts was investing one to two weeks per examination to manually examine the data. RDB Expert reduced this time frame by running through the tedium of massive data collection in less than two hours.

Developed by the *Digital Equipment Corporation,* RDB Expert tunes and optimizes database performance by analyzing its logical design, transaction workload, data volume, and system environment. Following this analysis, it generates executable code to develop a new design or restructure an old one.

Using RDB Expert in a field test, Greg Ballance has been able to improve performance by 20 percent. The large, complex applications that the tool developed eliminate much of the groundwork necessary to complete the database evaluation. It has done so by providing a snapshot of the databases under different load conditions. It then identifies which queries are important and then examines only those identified to be such. As a result, quality control specialists can examine the databases more often and with greater precision.

to understand. Finally, when a programmer makes a minor change in one location it can affect another area of the program, which can cause additional errors or necessitate more changes.

Digital Equipment Corporation has created an expert system that helps users such as DuPont (Reality Bytes 12–6) fine-tune their databases. By speeding up the process, maintenance costs are reduced, data integrity is improved, and users gain faster access to the data.

One difficulty with software maintenance is that every time part of an application is modified, there is a risk of adding defects (bugs). Also, over time the application becomes less structured and more complex, making it harder to understand. At some point, a company may decide to replace or improve the heavily modified system. There are several techniques for improving an existing system, ranging from rewriting individual sections to restructuring the entire application. The difference lies in scope—how much of the application needs to be modified. Older applications that were subject to modifications over several years tend to contain code that is no longer used, poorly documented changes, and inconsistent naming conventions. These applications are prime candidates for restructuring, during which the entire code is analyzed and reorganized to make it more efficient. More importantly, the code is organized, standardized, and documented to make it easier to make changes in the future.

## Evaluation

An important phase in any project is evaluating the resulting system. As part of this evaluation, it is also important to assess the effectiveness of the particular development process. There are several questions to ask. Were the initial cost estimates accurate? Was the project completed on time? Did users have sufficient input? Are maintenance costs higher than expected? The assessment items are summarized in Figure 12.14.

Evaluation is a difficult issue. How can you as a manager tell the difference between a good system and a poor one? In some way, the system should decrease

**FIGURE 12.14**

Evaluation of completed projects. When projects are completed, the design team should evaluate the project and assess the development procedures. Cost and time estimates can be used to improve estimates for future projects. System performance issues can be addressed with future upgrades. It is important that the system achieve project goals and provide users with necessary tools and support.

| Feasibility Comparison | |
|---|---|
| Cost and Budget | Compare actual costs to budget estimates. |
| Time Estimates | Was project completed on time? |
| Revenue Effects | Does system produce additional revenue? |
| Maintenance Costs | How much money and time are spent on changes? |
| Project Goals | Does system meet the initial goals of the project? |
| User Satisfaction | How do users (and management) evaluate the system? |
| System Performance | |
| System Reliability | Are the results accurate and on time? |
| System Availability | Is the system available on a continuous availability? |
| System Security | Does the system provide access to authorized users? |

costs, increase revenue, or provide a competitive advantage. Although these effects are important, they are often subtle and difficult to measure. The system should also be easy to use and flexible enough to adapt to changes in the business. If employees or customers continue to complain about a system, it should be re-examined.

A system also needs to be *reliable*. It should be available when needed, and should produce accurate output. Error detection can be provided in the system to recognize and avoid common problems. Similarly, some systems can be built to tolerate errors, so that when errors arise, the system recognizes the problem and works around it. For example, some computers exist today that automatically switch to backup components when one section fails, thereby exhibiting **fault tolerance.**

An important concept for managers to remember when dealing with new systems is that the evaluation mechanism should be determined at the start of the project. Far too often, the question of evaluation is ignored until someone questions the value of the finished product. It is a good design practice to ask "What would make this system a good system when it is finished?" or "How can we tell a good system from a bad one in this application?" Even though these questions may be difficult to answer, they need to be asked. The answers, however incomplete, will provide valuable guidance during the design stage.

Recall that every system needs a goal, a way of measuring progress toward that goal, and a feedback mechanism. Traditionally, control of systems has been the task of the computer programming staff. Their primary goal was to create error-free code, and they used various testing techniques to find and correct errors in the code. Today, creating error-free code is not a sufficient goal.

We have all heard the phrase, "The customer is always right." The meaning behind this phrase is that sometimes people have different opinions on whether a system is behaving correctly. When there is a conflict, the opinion that is most important is that of the customer. In the final analysis, customers are in control because they can always take their business elsewhere. With information systems, the users are the customers and the users should be the ones in control. Users determine whether a system is good. If the users are not convinced that the system performs useful tasks, it is not a good system.

## Strengths and Weaknesses of SDLC

The primary purpose of the SDLC method of designing systems is to provide guidance and control over the development process. As summarized in Figure 12.15, there are strengths and weaknesses to this methodolgy. SDLC management control is vital for large projects to ensure that the individual teams work together. There are also financial controls to keep track of the project expenses. The SDLC steps are often spelled out in great detail. The formality makes it easier to train employees, and to evaluate the progress of the development. It also ensures that steps are not skipped—such as user approval, documentation, and testing. For large, complex projects, this degree of control is necessary to ensure the project can be completed. Another advantage of SDLC is that by adhering to standards while building the system, programmers will find the system easier to modify and maintain later. The internal consistency and documentation make it easier to modify. With 80 percent of MIS resources spent on maintenance, this advantage can be critical.

In some cases the formality of SDLC causes problems. Most importantly, it increases the cost of development and lengthens the development time. Remember that often less than 25 percent of the time is spent on actually writing programs. A great deal of the rest of the time is spent filling out forms and drawing diagrams.

The formality of the SDLC also causes problems with projects that are hard to define. SDLC works best if the entire system can be accurately specified in the beginning. That is, users and managers need to know *exactly* what the system should do long before the system is created. That is not a serious problem with transaction-processing systems. However, consider the development of a complex decision support system. Initially, the users may not know how the system can help. Only through working with the system on actual problems will they spot errors and identify enhancements.

Although some large projects could never have been completed without SDLC, its rigidity tends to make it difficult to develop many modern applications. Additionally, experience has shown that it has not really solved the problems of projects being over budget and late. As a result of this criticism, many people are searching for alternatives. One possibility is to keep the basic SDLC in place and use technology to make it more efficient. Other suggestions have been to replace the entire process with a more efficient development process, such as prototyping. Consider the assistance of technology first.

**FIGURE 12.15**

Strengths and weaknesses of SDLC. The SDLC methodologies were created to control large, complex development projects. They work fairly well for those types of processes. SDLC does not work as well for small projects that require rapid development or heavy user involvement with many changes.

| STRENGTHS | WEAKNESSES |
|---|---|
| Control. | Increased development time. |
| Monitor large projects. | Increased development costs. |
| Detailed steps. | Systems must be defined up front. |
| Evaluate costs and completion targets. | Rigidity. |
| Documentation. | Hard to estimate costs, project overruns. |
| Well-defined user input. | User input is sometimes limited. |
| Ease of maintenance. | |
| Development and design standards. | |
| Tolerates changes in MIS staffing. | |

**CASE TOOLS: CAN TECHNOLOGY HELP MIS?** Software development with SDLC can be time consuming and expensive. In the past few years, several new software tools have been developed to help MIS in these tasks. They fall under the heading of **computer aided software engineering (CASE).** There are two main categories of CASE tools: one for software development and another for maintaining existing systems. Similar to Kaiser Permanente, many companies have a substantial backlog of MIS projects that could take years to complete. They are searching for ways to help them design and build systems faster. Johnson & Johnson (Reality Bytes 12–7) used a CASE tool that wrote the actual program code to design a new system in a fraction of the time it would have taken using traditional methods.

Sophisticated CASE tools (like IEF) combine both categories of features. For system development, CASE tools help analysts draw and maintain several types of diagrams, including data flow diagrams. Screen editors are used to design reports and data-entry screens. The software automatically creates a data dictionary that can be used to enforce design standards and share information among team members. CASE

---

**◤ Reality Bytes ◤ 12–7 JOHNSON & JOHNSON GREAT BRITAIN**

Johnson & Johnson is the world's largest producer of health care products for the consumer, pharmaceutical, and professional markets. The patient care division is part of the professional group that produces health care products for use in hospitals and the community. The company's leadership in the health care industries requires that orders be filled and delivered in an expeditious manner.

In 1989, J&J used the same distribution system for both the consumer and professional divisions of the company. Neither were adequately served, because six days often passed between orders and deliveries. The collection of the orders to run them as a batch process often added three days to the delivery schedule just for computer processing.

In an effort to expedite this system, J&J decided to develop a new delivery system. The goal was to collate 600 orders each day from a product range of more than 3,000. These orders would be distributed to more than 2,500 delivery points throughout Great Britain with 99 percent of the deliveries to be made within three days. The medical nature of the business demanded that development and conversion to the new program be completed in only six months.

This short time frame necessitated that a CASE tool be chosen for development. Although J&J's staff had a good working knowledge of the distribution system, they had only a limited understanding of the company's current software. The uniform code and menu-driven generation that CASE technology provides enabled the developers to quickly adapt to the new environment. As a result, they were able to complete the delivery system project far faster than they would have been able to if they had coded everything under the traditional method.

Short time frames and CASE tools place a greater emphasis on the individuals involved in the computer decision-making process. At J&J, the business managers defined the distribution mechanism and set pricing policies that would combine orders into a cost-justifiable package. Distribution engineers charted the system and documented the flow from the time the order reached the plant to when the product left the warehouse. Computer analysts took these specifications and developed a CASE procedure that would carry them out into the distribution environment. Operations personnel ensured that the sufficient computers were available to run the system.

Once the system was in place, immediate users could sit at the computer and enter orders directly from the telephone or from computer-coded order-entry cards. Pickers then retrieved the orders from the bins in the warehouses and prepared the shipping parcels using the preprinted orders and shipping labels. The improved processing ability of the new CASE system enabled the goal of three-day order-to-delivery goal to be met.

## KAISER PERMANENTE HMO

Kaiser Permanente, the largest health maintenance organization (HMO) in the United States, is using computer-aided software engineering (CASE) technology to improve efficiency and cut administrative and health care costs. The systems development area views this as a better way to improve the quality of the systems in a shorter time frame than traditional programming.

Before the CASE program began at Kaiser, the programming backlog was more than 100 work-years. As a result, the company implemented Texas Instruments' Information Engineering Facility (IEF) as its integrated CASE product. The changeover to CASE paralleled the purchase of intelligent workstations to replace terminals. Kaiser sees the CASE implementation as an essential component of its strategic plan to remain viable in the competitive health care market. CASE tools will enable Kaiser to respond more quickly to the demands of an increasingly demanding health care environment.

tools today can use all of this information to create the final source code. The computer does the actual programming based on the design specifications. Besides saving time, it eliminates one source of errors.

In terms of maintenance, there are some exciting software tools available. The basic technique is called **reverse engineering.** In reverse engineering, the goal is to take older software (sometimes known as **legacy systems**) and rewrite it to modernize it and make it easier to modify and enhance. Reverse engineering tools consist of software that reads the program code from the original software. For example, if a programmer is asked to modify the payroll program, she could first use the CASE tool to examine the payroll software. This tool will put the payroll package into modern structured code, drop unused code, highlight the sections that are heavily used, and standardize all of the variable names. Some software can even create the underlying diagrams, input screens, and reports. Then the programmer can make changes to these design documents and rebuild the program automatically.

One other tool that is available to the MIS department is a database management system (DBMS), usually coupled with a fourth-generation language. Using this tool instead of an older language such as COBOL can be as much as 10 times faster. It is easier to create sophisticated programs with fewer errors. The database systems also allow some portability so that if the company buys a new computer, the old data and software can be transferred to it with only minor changes. Finally, both end users and MIS workers can use the DBMS to answer many questions without needing to write a computer program.

One drawback to CASE tools is that they are relatively expensive, both for the software and the training for the MIS department. CASE tools increase MIS productivity, but only if the workers are fully trained in the development methodology.

**PROTOTYPING AND RAPID APPLICATION DEVELOPMENT (RAD)**

Prototyping has been proposed as a method to use for systems that are not overly complex and do not involve too many users or analysts. Just as automobile engineers design prototypes before attempting to build the final car, MIS programmers can build early versions of systems. These systems are then continually modified until the user is satisfied.

The first step in designing a system via prototyping is to talk with the user. The analyst then uses a fourth-generation language and a DBMS to create approximately

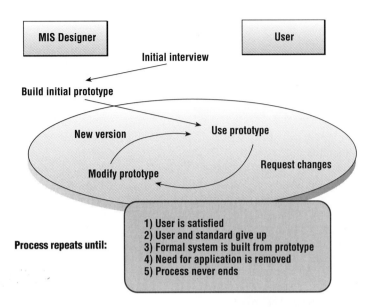

what the user wants. This first step generally requires only a couple of weeks. The business user then works with the prototype and suggests changes. The analyst makes the changes and this cycle repeats until the user is satisfied or decides that the system is not worth pursuing. The emphasis is on getting a working version of the system to the user as fast as possible, even if it does not have all the details. Figure 12.16 illustrates the cycle involved in prototyping.

The major advantage of prototyping is that users receive a working system much sooner than they would with the SDLC method. Additionally, the users have more input so they are more likely to get what they wanted. Finally, remember that a large portion of MIS time is spent making changes. A system designed with the prototyping method is much easier to change because it was designed to be modified from the start.

In the early stages of design, a prototype is analogous to the scale models that automobile and aircraft designers use for wind-tunnel tests or to the cardboard scale models that architects use to show potential buyers what the finished building will look like. The initial mockup may not actually have any computer code. It might be a collection of input screens and reports that look like they were produced by the computer system. The primary value of these simulated results is to enable the user to actually see the planned results. Users often have difficulty telling designers what they want beforehand. They can react to sample output by saying what they like or dislike, or what needs to be added to the output to make it more useful to the end user.

With today's latest development tools, however, the prototype may be more than a mockup. It may be used to create a substantial portion of the final code. Using CASE tools and database management systems, error-free code can be generated almost instantly from the prototype descriptions. These tools also build documentation automatically, making it easier for the designer, and the maintenance programmer.

Tools available for prototyping include presentation tools such as Hollywood, Toolbook, or Dan Bricklin's Demo, which can show a series of computer screens and demonstrate the look and feel of the finished product. More powerful fourth-generation languages and database management systems can generate actual applications including input files, interactive screens, reports, and executable code without

Developing systems is generally a team effort among MIS developers and business users. Groupware, CASE, and development tools are often used to facilitate communication and coordination.

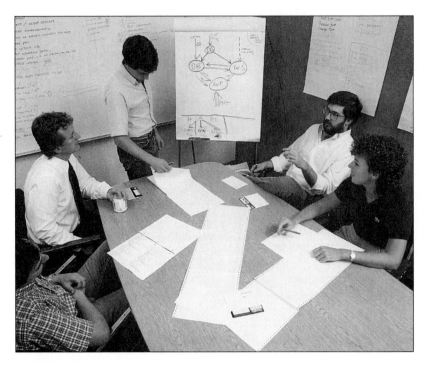

requiring programming. Other specialized tools such as expert system shells enable the designer to work with complex logical rules to create a finished product for certain types of applications.

The process of building a preliminary prototype, trying it out, refining it, and trying again is referred to as the *iterative process* of systems development. In the traditional SDLC approach, there was some iteration, but it is limited to a defined stage. The formal sign-off procedure was instituted specifically to restrict changes beyond some point in the development cycle. With the prototyping approach, iteration is planned and modern prototyping tools make it easy to modify the application. Further, because the prototyping tools allow a preliminary model to be created much faster, the user gets a working model much earlier in the design process. Therefore, the repeated changes are less likely to delay the completion.

Prototyping is especially helpful in situations where there will be heavy user interaction with the system, where the needed output is uncertain, and in some decision support applications where the logic is hard to determine in advance. Prototyping fosters a spirit of experimentation. It does not matter if there is some uncertainty regarding the path to the desired results or even uncertainty about the desired results. Prototyping enables you to try out a possible solution to see how it flies and to keep repeating this process until users are satisfied.

There are some drawbacks or complications to the use of prototyping. First, problems arise if several users are involved. Imagine what happens if each user wants different changes and they cannot agree on how the system should behave. One of the reasons for user sign-offs in SDLC is to force users to agree before you create the system. For large projects, several different prototypes of reports and input screens could be used to help users evaluate the various choices.

There are some more subtle drawbacks to prototyping. Picture yourself as an MIS manager where the analysts all use prototyping exclusively. Most of the time the analysts are talking with the users and making simple changes. How do you know when the project is finished? How do you know whether the analyst is a hard worker or just making endless minor changes? How do you tell a user to stop making trivial changes? Under the SDLC method, you have predefined targets (milestones) and you know exactly what each person is supposed to accomplish. As a manager responsible for completing projects and allocating raises, which method would you prefer?

*Rapid application development (RAD)* bears some similarities to prototyping. Notably, the goal is to build a system much faster than with traditional SDLC methods. Using many of the same tools (database management system, high-level languages, graphical toolkits, and objects), highly trained programmers can build systems in a matter of weeks or months. Using workgroups, communication networks, and CASE tools, small teams can speed up the development and design steps.

## DEVELOPING SYSTEMS REQUIRES TEAMWORK

Designing and developing systems is much easier if the entire system can be built by one person. In fact, that is one of the strengths of recent tools—they enable a single person to build more complex systems. However, many information systems—especially those that affect the entire organization—require teams of IS workers. As soon as multiple designers, analysts, and programmers are involved, we encounter management and communication problems. MIS researchers have measured the effects of these problems. One study by DeMarco and Lister showed that on large projects, 70 percent of developer's time is spent working with others. Jones noted that team activities accounted for 85 percent of the development costs. There seem to be substantial areas for improvement in systems development by focusing on teamwork. Two promising techniques are joint application development and collaborative support systems.

## Joint Application Development (JAD)

One of the most difficult steps in creating any new system is determining the user requirements. What does the system need to do and how will it work? This step is crucial. If the designers make a mistake here, the system will either be useless or will need expensive modifications later. Prototyping and SDLC take different approaches to this problem. With SDLC, analysts talk with users and write reports that describe how the system will operate. Users examine the reports and make changes. This approach is time-consuming and difficult for users because they only see paper notes of the proposed system. Prototyping overcomes some of the problems by letting users work with actual screens and reports. But use of prototyping is hard to expand beyond one or two users.

Some companies overcome the problems of SDLC by prototyping each input screen and report with one or two primary users. Once the main concepts have been designed, the analysts formalize the system and get approval from other users. The designs are then given to programmers to create with the traditional SDLC development methods.

Recall that an important reason for using SDLC is to obtain the views and agreement of many users. Using traditional interview methods and paper documentation, this process often takes several months. Each change has to be re-examined by other users, and disagreements have to be resolved.

A technique known as *joint application development (JAD)* was created to speed up the design stage. With JAD the main system is designed in an intense three-to five-day workshop. Users, managers, and systems analysts participate in a series of intense meetings to design the inputs (data and screens), and outputs (reports) needed by the new system.

By putting all of the decision makers in one room at the same time, conflicts are identified and resolved faster. Users and managers gain a better understanding of the problems and limitations of technology. The resulting system has greater value for users and managers because it more closely matches their needs. There is less need for changes later, when they become more expensive, so the system is cheaper to create.

The biggest drawback to JAD is that it requires getting everyone together at the same time for an extended period of time. Even for moderately complex systems, the meetings can run eight hours a day for three to five days. Most managers (and users) find it difficult to be away from their jobs for that length of time. Higher-level managers are also needed at these meetings ensure that the system provides the appropriate reports and information. Finally, the meetings can only succeed if they are led by a trained facilitator. The facilitator keeps the discussions moving in the right direction, minimizes conflicts, and encourages everyone to participate. At the end of the sessions, the systems development team should have a complete description of the proposed system. CASE tools are often useful in taking notes, building sample screens, and creating report layouts.

## Collaborative Development Technologies

Vessey and Sravanapudi suggest there are three levels of tasks in developing systems. Level 1 consists of tasks that cannot be shared. Level 2 represents sharing of work products. For example, a systems analyst creates design specifications that are used by programmers to create the system. Level 3 represents typical group sharing that is not dependent on particular products. It consists of general communication, scheduling, and keeping track of people and progress. Any collaborative system designed to support systems development must provide support for Levels 2 and 3.

In designing systems, Level 2 (teamwork) tasks can be supported in three basic areas: control, information sharing, and change monitoring. Figure 12.17 illustrates

**FIGURE 12.17**

Teamwork support for systems development. Development projects rely heavily on teamwork, which requires three levels of coordination: control, information sharing, and change monitoring [Vessey and Sravanapudi]. Control entails setting access controls so that only authorized people can read and alter specific information. Information sharing entails providing networks and communication, keeping all data consistent, and avoiding problems with concurrency. Change monitoring entails keeping track of which developers made changes to the project and when they were made.

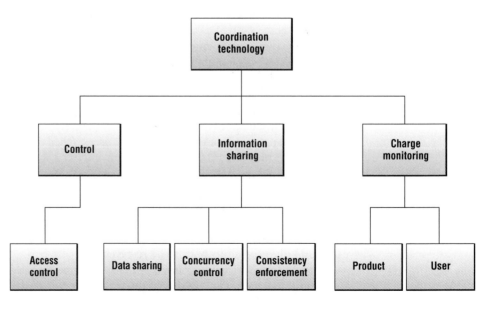

these components of coordination technology. Control is primarily a security problem, in which each person needs to limit the access to his or her work but still support sharing with the team members who need access. Information sharing consists of basic data sharing so that team members are dealing with the same basic set of data. Any time we share data, we need to be concerned about concurrency. The collaborative system must make sure that two people do not attempt to change the same item at the same time. Additionally, if conflicts do arise among files used by workers, the system should spot the problem and notify the team. Consistency and enforcement of standards are crucial aspects of building systems. Each team member must follow precise standards so that the subsystems work together.

Change monitoring is crucial in a large system. Team leaders need to know what changes have been made and who made them. Change lists help minimize duplication of effort and enable team managers to monitor progress and develop schedules. It is also important to monitor maintenance changes once the system is installed. If anything goes wrong, MIS can quickly find the likely cause. It is also important to monitor usage by analysts and programmers. Both from a security standpoint and to assist in solving problems, it helps to know which people made each change.

MIS development teams can benefit from the same types of support systems that are available for general management. In particular, the integration and groupware tools discussed in Chapter 7 are useful. Communication systems, setting appointments, sharing documents, and joint development of reports are all useful tools.

Vessey and Sravanapudi evaluated four CASE tools to determine how well they implemented the features needed to support teamwork. In general, the tools implemented only 39 percent of 35 basic features they identified. Most of the strength was in information sharing (54 percent), followed by control (29 percent) and monitoring (25 percent). Groupware support was minimal, so CASE tools would need to be supplemented with other groupware products.

## OBJECT-ORIENTED AND EVENT-DRIVEN DEVELOPMENT

The concept of **object-oriented development** has received considerable attention during the past few years. In some ways, the base design techniques are not much different from traditional SDLC techniques. In other ways, object orientation requires a completely new way of thinking about systems development. The ultimate goal of the object-oriented approach is to build a set of *reusable* objects and procedures. The idea is that eventually, it should be possible to create new systems or modify old ones simply by plugging in a new module or modifying an existing object.

An *object* can be anything from an icon on a computer screen to an accounting statement. Objects have a set of characteristics or attributes, and methods or operations that can be performed on objects. Figure 12.18 shows sample attributes and methods for a set of related bank account objects. Notice that properties and methods are *inherited.* New objects based on other objects acquire the same properties and methods. Designers need only define the additional properties and functions that make the new objects different. Once the base *classes* (collections of objects) are defined, new objects can be created with minimal effort.

One key difference between object orientation and other development methods is the way processes or functions are handled. With objects, all functions are *embedded* in the definition of the object—the object comes first. The object approach reverses the treatment of processes and data. With SDLC, illustrated by a data flow diagram, the emphasis is on processes, and data (attributes) is passed between processes.

**FIGURE 12.18**

Object orientation is a relatively new approach. Objects represent entities in the real world. Each object has a name, properties (attributes or data), and methods (functions) that it can perform. Objects can be defined from other objects as in this object hierarchy. The lower levels inherit the properties and methods of the prior definitions. Hence, new objects can be created (in both the real world and in the computer system) with minimal effort.

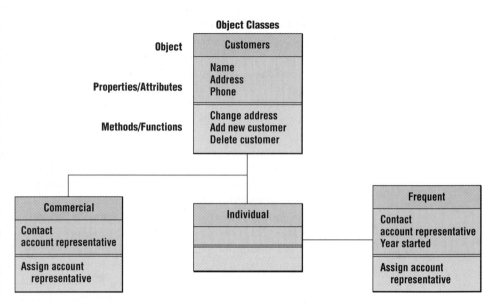

One goal of an object-oriented approach is to create a set of information system building blocks. These objects and procedures could be purchased from commercial software companies (such as a spreadsheets from Microsoft or a database system from Oracle). MIS programmers or consultants can create additional objects tailored for your specific company or department. Once the basic blocks are in place, end users or MIS analysts can select the individual pieces to create a complete system. Hence, as Figure 12.19 indicates, less time is needed for implementation, as long as the analysis and design are performed carefully. On the other hand, the up-front costs of designing and building these objects can be quite high. Additionally, the tools and techniques tend to require substantial retraining of the existing MIS staff. Both of these types of costs have caused some companies to avoid object-oriented methods.

Although object-oriented techniques are still being developed, many companies are already headed in this direction. One effect of this type of development is that much of the traditional programming is moved to commercial companies that specialize in creating software components. Other companies hire analysts who focus on the business needs and put together the appropriate modules. These analysts need to

**FIGURE 12.19**

SDLC versus object-oriented. Initial design of an object-oriented approach takes more effort than with SDLC. However, once the objects are properly defined, it is much easier to create and implement a new system.

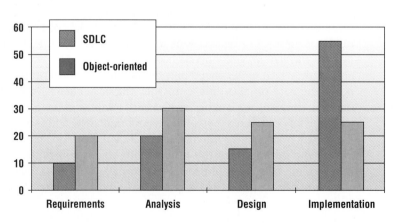

understand business, be able to identify problems, and know how information systems can be used to solve them.

Another new feature of modern programming is the emergence of **event-driven systems.** In older programs, the programmer was responsible for building a complete, sequential program that defined and controlled every step taken by the user. Modern, window-based software does not follow a sequential process. Instead, actions by users generate events. The programs respond to these events and alter data or offer additional choices. Typical events include mouse clicks pointing to items on the screen, keystrokes, changes to values, or transmissions from other systems.

As a user, you will be asked to help identify important objects along with their attributes and functions. You will also want to determine specific events and rules. In any business application, the underlying business rules define interrelationships between the objects. As certain events occur, data elements will be changed or added. For example, as shown in Figure 12.20, when an item is sold, several actions take place: recording the sale, updating inventory levels, and perhaps notifying customer service. You cannot assume that the analyst or programmer automatically knows all of these rules. To get a system that works well, managers and users must communicate these relationships and events to the system designer.

## END-USER DEVELOPMENT

The term *end-user development* simply means that users do all of the development work themselves. In many ways, it resembles prototyping, except that users (instead of analysts from the MIS department) create and modify the prototypes. Clearly the main advantage is that users get what they want without waiting for an MIS team to finish its other work and without the difficulty of trying to describe the business problems to someone else.

There are two basic reasons why end-user development is increasingly popular. First, most MIS organizations are facing a two- or three-year backlog of projects. That means that if you bring a new project to MIS, the designers will not even start on it for at least two years (unless you give up some other project). The second reason is that software tools are getting more powerful and easier to use at the same time.

**FIGURE 12.20**
Objects and events. Most modern systems are event-driven in the sense that the programs are written as small modules that are triggered when some event happens. Instead of writing some monolithic code that controls every user action, developers create objects whose functions are executed in response to a change in the business environment or at the direction of the user.

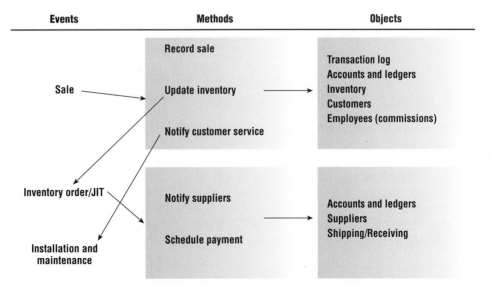

Today it is possible for users to create systems with a spreadsheet in a few hours that 10 years ago would have taken MIS programmers a month to build with third-generation languages. As tools become more powerful and more integrated, it becomes possible to create even more complex systems. Reread the discussion of software integration in Chapter 7 and picture the reports you can create using off-the-shelf software. Five years ago, most users would not dream of being able to create these reports. Today, with windowing software you can build systems that share data with many users across the corporate networks—simply by pointing to items with a mouse. The advantages of end-user development are similar to those in prototyping. In particular, users get what they want, and they get working systems sooner.

The potential problems of end-user development are not always easy to see. Most of them arise from the fact that users generally lack the training and experience of MIS analysts and programmers. For instance, systems produced by end users tend to be written for only one person to use. They are oriented to working on stand-alone personal computers. The systems are often customized to fit the needs of the original users. Additionally, most users do not write documentation, so others will have difficulty using the products. Because of lack of training, users rarely perform as much testing as they should. The systems lack security controls and are hard to modify. Think about the problems you encounter when you are given a spreadsheet that was created by the person who held the job before you.

Other problems stem from the bottom-up approach inherent in end-user development. People in different areas of the company will wind up working on the same problem, when it could have been solved once by MIS. Data tends to be scattered throughout the company, making it hard to share and wasting space. Not following standards generates incompatibilities among systems, making it difficult to combine systems created by different departments or even by people within the same department.

End users are limited by the capabilities of commercial software. The initial systems may work fine, but as the company grows and changes, the commercial software might be unable to support the necessary changes. As a result, some users have created systems that produce incorrect answers, take too long to run, or lose data.

The last, and possibly most important, complication is that end-user development takes time away from the user's job. Some users spend months creating and modifying systems that might have been created by MIS programmers in a fraction of the time. One of the reasons for creating an MIS department is to gain efficiency from

## BUSINESS TRENDS: DOWNSIZING

As businesses become smaller and shift increased responsibility down to lower levels of managers, these managers will become more responsible for determining their own information needs and for creating portions of information systems. As a manager, to get the information system that you need, it becomes increasingly important that you understand the process, advantages, and disadvantages of the systems development methods: SDLC, prototyping, and end-user development. At a minimum, you will be involved in the selection of the method, initial design, and implementation. As development tools grow more powerful, an increasing number of systems and modifications will be created by managers and other users.

using specialists. If users are spending too much time creating and revising their own applications, the company needs to consider hiring more MIS personnel.

**WHEN TO CALL FOR HELP**

The bottom line is that managers often have to decide which method is most suitable for developing a particular system. If the project is large and expensive, and affects important assets of the company, the choice of SDLC is fairly clear-cut. If a user simply needs computations for a one-time decision, it is faster and cheaper to have the user create the model using a spreadsheet. However, in many cases, there is not an obvious answer. A project might start out small, then suddenly grow. Similarly, a spreadsheet that was created by a user for one purpose might be passed around the company and used by others to make crucial decisions.

There is not much difference between projects created by end users and those that use prototyping. In a sense, virtually any project could be started by end users. As shown in Figure 12.21, the trick is to learn when to call for help by understanding the limitations of the methods. If the project is used by many people, affects critical portions of the business, or grows beyond the capabilities of prepackaged software, then MIS programmers can be called in to expand it, test it, create documentation, make it more flexible, or create an entirely new system.

Modern MIS departments have devised many ways to help users develop new systems other than the traditional analysts and programmers working on SDLC projects. Two methods that are discussed in more detail in Chapter 13 are moving MIS employees out to the departments and the creation of an information center. In both cases, the goal is to have MIS employees responsible for assisting users. This assistance can be offered in many forms, such as helping decide which hardware and software to purchase, answering questions about software, offering classes in using software and creating systems, testing user-developed systems for errors and incompatibilities, and building prototypes.

**FIGURE 12.21**
WHEN TO CALL MIS FOR HELP
As companies struggle to cut costs, end-user managers are increasingly responsible for developing their own computer applications. As software tools improve, managers can develop complex systems. Yet, there are times when it is best to get help and approval from an MIS team— especially when the application involves critical operations.

Many people will use the system:
- PC versus central computer.
- Need documentation.
- Individual user differences.
- Need to train users.

Commercial software limitations.

User time is expensive.

Mission-critical application:
- Additional testing.
- Many modifications.
- Need security and control.

Need to integrate:
- Use corporate data.
- Tie to existing software.
- Connect to network.

Database integrity:
- Avoid duplicate data.
- Verify changes to corporate data.

**COMBINING METHODOLOGIES**

In actual practice, most companies use a combination of the various methods to create systems. Figure 12.22 summarizes the features of the primary methods used to design and build information systems. Note that the methods are roughly listed in declining order of control and formality. Keep in mind that these techniques can be combined so that projects gain the benefits of each method. For example, large projects that require control and oversight benefit from using SDLC and other MIS-controlled methods. Even in these projects, prototyping and JAD are often used for reports and input screens. An MIS analyst will meet with users and quickly build sample screens and reports using CASE tools and personal computer-based software. Users alter the designs and they are adjusted until the users are satisfied. Then the prototype designs are turned over to the SDLC team to be programmed into the main system.

Some projects might begin as end-user systems to solve problems within one department As the application expands and more users become involved, a RAD or SDLC team might be called in to standardize processes, convert the data, and build a shared application for the entire company.

Similarly, a company might use SDLC techniques (especially standards and testing) to create an initial set of objects. Once these objects are created, a team can use prototyping and RAD techniques to build new systems. Likewise, companies will purchase prewritten components as much as possible. It is almost always cheaper to buy components that already exist. These components can range from application software like database management systems to object libraries that can be customized for each company.

Any modern company with a large enough MIS staff is continuously experimenting with all of these design methods. Creating software is an expensive, time-consuming process. Firms are constantly searching for techniques and methodologies that will improve the process and lead to better systems.

| | SDLC | RAD | OBJECTS | JAD | PROTOTYPING | END USER |
|---|---|---|---|---|---|---|
| Control | formal | MIS | standards | joint | user | user |
| Time frame | long | short | any | medium | short | short |
| Users | many | few | varies | few | one or two | one |
| MIS staff | many | few | split | few | one or two | none |
| Transaction or DSS | trans. | trans. or DSS | trans. or DSS | DSS | DSS | DSS |
| Interface | minimal | minimal | Windows | crucial | crucial | crucial |
| Documentation and training | vital | limited | in objects | limited | weak | none |
| Integrity and security | vital | vital | in objects | limited | weak | weak |
| Reusability | limited | some | vital | limited | weak | none |

**FIGURE 12.22**

Choosing design methodologies. With a wide variety of potential applications, we need several design methodologies. Each methodology has advantages and disadvantages and is suited for different applications. When choosing a methodology, you should also consider the training and background of the users and development team. The chart shows how each method supports several basic functions in the development of systems. The appropriate software tool can be found by matching the project characteristics to the strengths of each methodology.

**PURCHASING COMMERCIAL SOFTWARE**

One important trend in the last few years is the growing importance of commercially available software. Hardware has been continually improving in performance. Many platforms are becoming standardized, like Microsoft Windows on personal computers and Unix on mid-range workstations. These two trends encourage the development and acceptance of commercial software packages. For example, no company would try to write its own word-processing software because several low cost packages are readily available commercially. Increasingly, commercial packages handle many common tasks—especially transaction processing and financial reporting and accounting tasks.

In the past, the trade-off between buying versus creating your own software was a shortage of acceptable alternatives and performance problems with "generic" applications. Both of these problems are minimized with faster machines and the widespread adoption of a few basic platforms. Today, several commercial applications exist to handle all of the basic tasks of managing a company. The software vendor is responsible for basic operations and for improving its product. By selling to many companies, the development costs are spread out and the software can be purchased for substantially less than it would cost for one company to produce the application. Individual companies modify the application to provide additional features that support their own business processes. As illustrated by Sun Hydraulics (Reality Bytes 12–8), the individual application components can be combined to create customized applications.

One important concept to remember is that even if you choose to purchase commercial software, you must still perform many of the basic feasibility and analysis steps—especially for complex, expensive software. Comparing and evaluating software can be just as time consuming as the traditional analysis stage in the SDLC methodology.

◥ **Reality Bytes** ◣ **12–8** APPLYING VISUAL BASIC PROGRAMMING AT SUN HYDRAULICS

Sun Hydraulics Corporation is a Sarasota, Florida-based maker of hydraulic cartridge valves, such as those used in fork lifts. Sun Hydraulics began custom development with a database access application named CatNav. Sales support users navigate through the company's product catalog with it. Sales individuals can use this Windows application to type in a selection and find a product. The program did not take off, however, because most people used a word processor and were not interested in using other programs.

To address this need, Windows programmer Chris Barlow applied a component model to his company's custom-computing needs, orchestrating the components with Visual Basic. Having used Visual Basic for two and a half years, Chris's team turned CatNav into a Dynamic Data Exchange (DDE) program. The team then added a CatNav icon to Microsoft Word for Windows' toolbar, using its WordBasic resident language (which is compatible with VB). Users can now type a product code in Word, click the CatNav icon, and see the information they need in the Word docu-

ment. The programming team linked Visual Basic to Word to launch CatNav, feed it the code, and then paste CatNav's answer into Word.

Visual Basic has enabled Sun to improve its code maintenance. The format of the database, the databases themselves, or word processors can be changed independently of one other. Performance issues are addressed with Dynamic Link Libraries.

Barlow uses Visual Basic to integrate third-party code into his applications. This code includes

- Spreadsheet custom controls from FarPoint Technologies Inc., of Richmond, Virginia.
- Advanced-debugging tool called Spyworks from Desaware of San Jose, California.
- Data Widgets from Sheridan Software Systems Inc. of Melville, New York, for enhanced database access.
- Internal programs such as a custom control convert local times to Greenwich Mean Time. This puts transactions from around the world in the same timeframe.

## SUMMARY

Systems development can be a difficult task. Many projects have failed because they cost much more than anticipated or they did not produce useful systems. Large projects are especially difficult to control because there can be conflicting goals, it is hard to ensure that subsystems work together, business needs change during the development process, and there is turnover among the MIS employees. The systems development life cycle evolved as a means to deal with the complexity of large systems and provide the necessary controls to keep projects on track.

Systems analysis techniques are used to break projects into manageable pieces. Various graphing tools, such as data flow diagrams, are used to display the relationships between the components. Systems design techniques use the results of the analysis to create the new system. The new system consists of interconnected modules. Each module has inputs, outputs, processing steps, database requirements, manual procedures, and controls. At various stages in the design process, managers and users are asked to sign off on the proposed system, indicating that they will accept it with no further changes.

In contrast to the rigid control embodied in the SDLC method, the prototyping approach is iterative and creates an early working model of the system. Users and managers can see the proposed input screens and reports and make changes to them. As the project develops, the prototype goes from a simple mockup to a working system. Prototyping is sometimes used in conjunction with SDLC during the design phase to lay out input screens and reports.

A third way to build systems is for end users to develop their own projects using fourth-generation tools such as database management systems, spread-

> ### A MANAGER'S VIEW
> As a manager in a large company, you will work closely with the MIS department to modify and build systems that support your operations. You need to be aware of the problems facing MIS staff to understand the reasons for their rules and methods. Managers are increasingly being asked to develop their own systems and to participate more heavily in the design of new reports and forms. The details of analysis, design, testing, and implementation will be useful regardless of the method used. As a manager, you also need to know the advantages and drawbacks of various development methods; you will often have to choose the method that is best suited to solving your problems.

sheets, and other commercial software. As the capabilities of commercial software tools increase, users can develop more complex systems. The backlog facing MIS also encourages users to develop their own systems. The potential dangers of user development, such as lack of testing, incompatibilities, and unnecessary duplication, can be controlled by having MIS teams available to assist end users.

All three methods of developing systems involve five basic steps: feasibility and planning, systems analysis, design, implementation, and maintenance. Prototyping and end-user development typically focus on the design stage. However, managers need to remember that implementation problems can arise with any new system, regardless of how it was created. Similarly, there will always be a need to maintain and modify existing applications. It is easy to forget these steps when users develop their own software.

## KEY WORDS

## REVIEW QUESTIONS

1. What is pseudocode, and why would a manager need to be able to read it?
2. What are the differences between top-down and bottom-up design? How do current methods use both techniques?
3. Why was the systems development life cycle method created and used?
4. What are three common methods to develop systems?
5. What are the major phases in the SDLC method?
6. Which stage of the SDLC method uses the most MIS resources today?
7. Why do legacy systems cause problems for MIS? How might reverse engineering help?
8. What activities are involved in systems analysis?
9. What activities are involved in the systems design stage?
10. What activities are involved in systems implementation?
11. How can resistance to change be managed?
12. Describe the major implementation techniques.
13. What are the drawbacks to the SDLC method?
14. How can CASE tools help the MIS department?
15. What types of projects are best suited to prototyping?
16. What are the advantages of prototyping over SDLC?
17. What projects are best suited to end-user development?
18. What is the purpose of the object-oriented approach to development?
19. Why is end-user development becoming more common?

## EXERCISES

1. If you have access to a CASE tool, use it to create the data flow diagrams illustrated in Chapter 3. Add another level of detail to the diagrams. Be sure to create the data dictionary. This assignment is best accomplished with teams. Assign one section of the diagrams to each team member.
2. Interview a local manager to determine the requirements for a new system. Explain which method would be the best approach to develop the system. Estimate how long it would take to complete the project and how much it would cost. Advanced option: Illustrate the new system with a data flow diagram. More advanced: Create the system.
3. Consider an information system for a firm that manufactures furniture. Every day, production managers get shipping invoices that detail the supplies that were delivered that day. Production orders come in from the marketing department, listing each product and the options that need to be included. Once a week, the production team gets a quality report from sales outlets listing problems they have encountered with the products. Manufacturing is split into several component groups that are further split into teams. For instance, one component group makes sofas and recliners, another makes tables and chairs. Teams include frame groups, upholstery, woodworking, and finishing. Once a week, each team creates a report that lists the products that were completed, the materials used in each product, statistical quality measures on each component, and the amount of time spent on each step. Using an object-oriented approach and based on what you know (or can find out) about furniture, create a list of objects that might be used in building an information system for this company. Show the relationships among the objects. Hint: One important object is *forms*.
4. Interview computer users to determine how they feel about their current system. Do they like it? What are the major advantages and drawbacks? How long have they used it? When was it changed last? Are there changes users want to see? Are they willing to accept changes? How are relations with the MIS workers? Who initiates changes, users or MIS? If users proposed a new project, how long would it take for MIS to get to it (how long is the backlog)? Team approach: Have each team member interview a different person (some users, some in MIS). Combine your results to get a picture of the entire company. Do users agree with each other? Does the MIS department agree with the users? Do they see the same problems? Hint: If you do not have access to another company, you can always find computer users in the university.

## ADDITIONAL READING

"All 208 Million Tax Returns Get Electronic Scrutiny on Arrival," *Government Computer News*, March 6, 1995. [IRS]

Asbrand, Deborah. "Client/Server: The Bedrock of New Business," *InfoWorld*, September 18, 1995, pp. 53–61. [IRS]

"ATC Upgrades: User Fees or Trust Fund," *Federal Computer Week*, October 9, 1995. [FAA]

Barker, Paul. "KPMG to Delve into Issue of Fraud and IT," *Computing Canada*, August 2, 1995, p. 12. [System development examples]

Bass, Brad. "GSA Official Blasts FAA Attempts to Blame Woes on Buying Process," *Federal Computer Week*, September 4, 1995, pp. 3–4. [FAA]

"Big Brother's Watching, But This Time It Could Be You," *Government Computer News*, December 12, 1994. [IRS]

"Bringing Harmony to Business Systems; Why Interoperability Is Critical to Businesses and Their Strategic Computer Systems," *Information Week*, October 2, 1995. [Bechtel]

Cafasso, Rosemary. "Few IS Projects Come In On Time, On Budget, *Computerworld*, December 12, 1994, p. 20. [Statistics on development problems, based on survey by The Standish Group: The High Cost of Chaos]

Carney, Dan. "FAA Confirms Wilcox as $475M WAAS Winner," *Federal Computer Week*, August 7, 1995, p. 3. [FAA]

"Clinton's '96 Budget: More IT, Same Money," *Government Computer News*, February 20, 1995. [FAA]

Constance, Paul, James M. Smith, and Florence Olsen, "IRS RC Buy Is on Hold Yet Again," *Government Computer News*, July 3, 1995, p. 3. [IRS]

DeMarco, T. and T. Lister. *Peopleware*. New York: Dorset House, 1987. [Hints and problems developing useful systems]

Dorobek, Christopher. "Congress Weighs FAA Reform Options," *Government Computer News*, October 16, 1995, p. 63. [FAA]

Doyle, T.C. "The Empire Strikes Back," *VARbusiness*, September 1, 1995, pp. 58–64. [Johnson & Johnson Great Britain]

"FAA's $500 Million Navigation Contract Takes Flight," *Federal Computer Week*, April 10, 1995. [FAA]

Gill, Phillip J. "Bechtel Consolidates Its Global Reach With Satellite," *Computerworld*, January 30, 1989, p. 32. [Bechtel]

"Government Must Join the Throngs Tooling Along the Internet," *Government Computer News*, March 6, 1995. [IRS]

Grimm, Vanecca Jo. "FAA to Spend $65M on Stopgap Replacements for Old Computers," *Government Computer News*, August 7, 1995, p. 3. [FAA]

Haight, Timothy. "All You Need to Know About the Future of Business," *Network Computing*, October 1, 1995, pp. 58–59. [DuPont and Digital expert systems]

Hanna, Mary. "Net Growth Outpaces Expertise," *Software Magazine*, July 1995, pp. 41–46. [Johnson & Johnson Great Britain]

"IRS Beefs Up Its Phone Filing System," *Government Computer News*, July 17, 1995, p. 8. [IRS]

"IRS Puts the 500 Most Popular Tax Forms on the Internet," *Government Computer News*, February 6, 1995. [IRS]

"IRS Rolls Out RFP for Treasury Department Acquisition 2," *Federal Computer Week*, January 23, 1995. [IRS]

"IT Projects Still Fail to Deliver, Says Research," *Computer Weekly*, March 2, 1995. [System development examples]

Jackson, William. "FAA and GSA Renew Their Dogfight Over Air Traffic Control Modernization," *Government Computer News*, September 18, 1995, p. 73. [FAA]

Jackson, William. "FAA Sticks With Loral On Air Traffic System Contract," *Government Computer News*, May 15, 1995, p. 8. [FAA]

Jackson, William. "FAA System Will Improve Flow of Air Traffic Over Oceans," *Government Computer News*, October 2, 1995, p. 70. [FAA]

Jackson, William. "No Voice Traffic Jams for FAA System," *Government Computer News*, June 19, 1995, p. 14. [FAA]

Jackson, William. "Unions Balk at Privatizing FAA Systems Modernization," *Government Computer News*, June 19, 1995, p. 87. [FAA]

Johnson, Maryfran. "DuPont Employs Expert to Increase Database Benefit," *Computerworld*, 2/18/91, p. 30. [DuPont and Digital expert systems]

Jones, T.C. *Programming Productivity*, New York: McGraw Hill, 1986. [Evaluating and measuring productivity, costs of teamwork]

Juneau, Lucie. "Luring Consumers with Conspicuous Efficiency," *Computerworld*, September 14, 1992, p. 37. [Dillard's]

Kaplan, Jerry. *Startup: A Silicon Valley Adventure Story*. Houghton Mifflin Co, 1994. (Excerts in: "The Start Up," *Fortune*, May 29, 1995, pp. 110–120.) [Go Corporation]

Konsynski, Benn. "Advances in Information System Design," *Journal of Management Information Systems*, Fall, 1984, pp. 5–32. [Summary of software development methods]

"Make Your Own Reality with WalkThrough Pro," *Computer Shopper*, July 1995. [Virtus WalkThrough]

"Mandate Is to Ensure Software Will Fly," *Government Computer News*, March 20, 1995. [FAA]

Masnat, Sam. "A New Voice for Air Traffic: VSCS Is Fault-Tolerant," *Government Computer News*, July 31, 1995, pp. 55–56. [FAA]

Masud, Sam. "New Bells Are Ringing at IRS," *Government Computer News*, October 16, 1995, pp. 44–45. [IRS]

Monroe, John Stein. "FAA Taps Loral to Fly Program Upgrade," *Federal Computer Week*, May 8, 1995, pp. 20–21. [FAA]

Monroe, John Stein. "TRW Nabs $231M Support Pact," *Federal Computer Week*, June 19, 1995, p. 1. [FAA]

Nash, Jim. "EDI Sprinters Find Partners on Slow Track," *Computerworld*, March 5, 1990, p. 1. [Dillard's]

Nash, Jim. "When Push Comes to Shove," *Computerworld*, March 5, 1990, p. 12. [Dillard's]

Naumann, Justus and Milton Jenkins. "Prototyping: The New Paradigm for Systems Development," *MIS Quarterly*, Spring 1982. [Description, uses and advantages of prototyping]

Neumann, Peter. "System Development Woes," *Communications of the ACM*, October 1993, p. 146. [System development problem examples]

"On a Wing and a LAN," *LAN Magazine*, December 1994. [FAA]

Power, Kevin. "Given Outsourcing, Privatizing Trend, OMB Plans to Overhaul Circular A-76," *Government Computer News*, July 17, 1995, p. 90. [FAA]

Rifkin, Glenn. "CEOs, PCs Don't Mix Well," *Computerworld*, April 17, 1989, p. 82. [Tootsie Roll]

Rothfeder, Jeffrey. "Invasion of Privacy," *PC World*, November 1995, pp. 152–161. [IRS]

"Routing Software Uses Compression to Speed Traffic," *Government Computer News*, March 20, 1995. [FAA]

Ryan, Stephan M. "FAA's Bailout Betrays Citizens, Benefits Lawyers," *Government Computer News*, September 18, 1995, p. 29. [FAA]

Smith, James M. "IRS Spends $1B for Next Five Years of Systems Support," *Government Computer News*, July 17, 1995, p. 82. [IRS]

Smith, James M. "Treasury's $109M PC Award Opposed; Sysorex Exec Claims Concept Automation Failed to Meet Requirements," *Government Computer News*, July 17, 1995, p. 6. [IRS]

Stedman, Craig. "Kaiser Prescribes On-Line Patient Care; Middleware to Link Systems, Medical Facilities," *Computerworld*, May 22, 1995, p. 63. [Kaiser Permanente]

Taft, Darryl K. "Data Protection: Feds Go Under Deep Cover: Resellers Support New Encryption System," *Computer Reseller News*, September 2, 1995, pp. 117–118. [IRS]

"Technology Pioneers," *PC Week*, October 30, 1995, p. E3. [Kaiser Permanente]

"The Taxman Cometh, Toting a ThinkPad," *PC Week*, March 20, 1995. [IRS]

Vessey, Iris and Ajay Sravanapudi. "Case Tools as Collaborative Support Technologies," *Communications of the ACM*, January 1995, pp. 83–95. [Description of collaborative support goals and evaluation of some CASE tools]

"Virtus Browser, Tools Go 3-D," *PC Week*, September 25, 1996. [Virtus WalkThrough]

"Virtus to Send 3-D to the Web," *MacWEEK*, July 17, 1995. [Virtus WalkThrough]

Walker, Charles. "Are Aircraft Software Tests Up to Scratch?" *Computer Weekly*, June 22, 1995, p. 16. [FAA]

"Where's AI Hiding?" *AI Expert*, April 1995. [IRS]

Willmott, Dan. "Startup. (Read Only)," *PC Magazine*, June 27, 1995, p. 69. [Go Corporation]

# CASES *Government Agencies*

Government employees make heavy use of computers for word processing, communication (including email), and databases. Many public administration jobs entail the collection, analysis, and dissemination of data.

Source: Computer Use in the United States, U.S. Bureau of the Census.

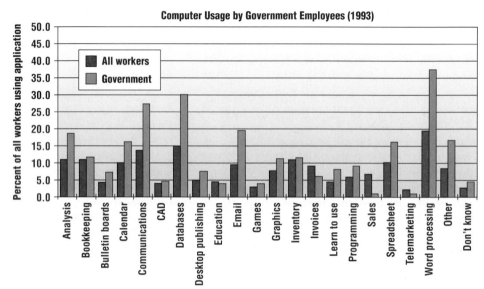

**Computer Usage by Government Employees (1993)**

Governmental agencies have several unique problems. The most important one is that funding is subject to changes in the political climate. With each election, an agency runs the risk of having to change direction, cancel projects, or provide support for new tasks.

On the other hand, from an economic perspective, most government agencies are not subject to economic pressures. Consequently, they may not have the same incentives to economize and minimize costs that are faced by businesses.

The third critical feature of most government agencies is that they tend to serve large numbers of people—especially at the federal level. These large organizations collect huge amounts of data. Even today, much of governmental data is stored on paper.

Most governmental agencies have dealt with the size issue by maintaining large staffs, and combining of decentralized management with centralized controls. Traditionally, government organizations have paid lower salaries than commercial businesses. Although the salaries are supplemented with benefits and job security, governmental agencies often face high turnover rates and changes in personnel. To compensate for these problems, the agencies rely heavily on procedures. There are rules for every conceivable circumstance. As new situations and decisions arise, new rules are created. Given these challenges, there is no surprise that most people perceive government agencies as large bureaucracies, filled with endless forms and strange rules.

There are many obvious uses for computers in government agencies. During a few minutes of observation, anyone can generate ideas that could improve agency performance, making life easier for the workers and citizens. However, the real challenges have always arisen in creating and implementing these ideas.

Although there are many success stories regarding computer implementation within government agencies, there are also some costly failures. The Federal Aviation Administration and the Internal Revenue Service cases present some of the difficulties that have arisen.

Be careful when you read these cases. Do not simply blame the problems on "typical government mismanagement." Many of these problems also exist within businesses. Always remember that we are searching for answers and methods that will overcome the obstacles and complications.

## CASE *Federal Aviation Administration (FAA)*

The FAA is charged with overseeing all public (nonmilitary) flight operations in the United States related to safety and access to the air. They establish safety criteria, issue licenses for pilots, and create air worthiness certificates for planes. They also operate the air traffic control system throughout the United States. Funding for the agency is generated through user fees and taxes on aircraft fuel, tires, and airline tickets. By 1990, the Aviation Trust Fund held $41 billion, built up during the prior 20 years. The FAA is an executive agency and theoretically operates under the direct control of the U.S. president. However, tax rates and expenditures are established by Congress.

Air traffic control in the United States is an exceedingly complex problem. In 1994, the 300 major airports generated 50,000 flights a day. Air traffic control is responsible for scheduling the takeoffs, landings, and flight paths of all these flights. By 1990, 455 million passengers a year were flying on U.S. airlines.

Traffic control is organized into three levels: nationwide U.S. airspace, 20 regional air traffic centers, and individual airports. Air traffic control operators at each airport have immediate control over takeoffs and landings. Regional operators watch traffic within their defined airspace. Systemwide control is provided by the Central Flow facilities located in Washington, D.C. The Central Flow managers examine traffic across the entire United States and resolve conflicts and problems that arise among regions. The 40 traffic management specialists plan each day in advance, creating alternative routings for aircraft because of problems arising from snowstorms, accidents, and closed runways.

### Early Systems

The early traffic control system was built with hardware and software from Sperry-Rand/Univac, a computer company that was purchased in the mid-1980s by Burroughs. The combined company is now called Unisys. The airport-based traffic control computers were based on 256K bytes of main memory and performed 500,000 instructions per second. The original systems were installed in the early 1960s. The 20 regional centers had their own computers—IBM 9020 machines that were custom made for the FAA in the 1960s.

### Improvements

In 1981, the FAA was given approval for a comprehensive new system to upgrade the computer system. New airports, such as Dallas-Fort Worth, coupled with deregulation of the airline industry in 1978 led to huge increases in air traffic. The $12 billion plan called for replacement of 12 major systems over the course of 12 years. An additional 80 smaller projects were included in the plan.

By 1990, only 1 of the 12 systems had been replaced and the project was $15 billion over the original budget, and an average of four years late. The one project that was completed was known as Host, because it called for replacement of the mainframe computers at the 20 regional control centers. IBM installed its 3083 mainframes on schedule, but was $16 million over budget. Even then, the 3083s were technologically obsolete at the time they were installed because the newer IBM 3090-class machines had been available for a year.

The FAA has been criticized several times for a lack of oversight and control in developing new systems. In 1980, the Senate Appropriations committee noted that "The FAA has no ongoing, well-defined, and systematic management approach to evaluating software and operational cost, capacity, and performance of the current system to meet projected short-range workloads."

The General Accounting Office (GAO), the watchdog of Congress, echoed that sentiment several times later.

### Advanced Automation System

One of the more visible components of the plan is the Advanced Automation System (AAS), which is designed to provide updated tracking displays to the controllers. It was supposed to be completed by 1990, but at that time was delayed until 1993. The system is designed to use IBM RS-6000 computers to display flight information, schedules, and current location along with weather fronts. The color systems will have higher resolution, be easier to read, and carry more information.

In 1994, an internal study of the AAS showed that the project was still two years behind schedule and probably would fall back another two years before completion. The project to that time has cost $2.3 billion and is estimated to eventually cost about $7 billion. David Hinson, FAA administrator, announced that he was replacing top managers on the project, dropping portions of uncompleted work, and demanding performance guarantees from the contractors. One system being canceled is the Area Control Computer Complex, which was designed to interconnect the host computers at the airport and regional levels.

### Problems

Air traffic controllers have been reporting problems with existing systems for years:

- In 1992, West Coast air traffic was delayed for several hours. An IBM 3083 at the regional station crashed. In the process, it removed the identification labels from the radar screens of controllers from Oregon to Los Angeles. The controllers switched to an older backup system but had to increase plane separation from the typical 3 miles up to 20 miles. Pilots and controllers used radio communication and manually filed flight plans to compensate. Ron Wilson, a spokesman for the San Francisco airport, notes that although there are frequent disruptions, "The FAA computer failures generally don't last long, just long enough to screw things up."

At Oakland, California, an average of three times a month the controllers' screens fail and controllers have a few seconds to memorize the position, speed, course, altitude and destination of the 12 planes they are typically guiding. Then their screens go blank for at least 10 seconds. Sometimes when the screens come back online, they are missing critical data.

- Joel Willemssen, assistant director of the U.S. GAO's Information Management and Technology Division, reported that 70 percent of the 63 largest airports in the United States have experienced problems with blank or flickering computer screens. John Mazor, a spokesman for the Airline Pilots Association, notes the problems cause "delays, diversions, and—in the worst possible cases—accidents. It's not as dangerous as you might think, but it's not something you want to have happen to you."
- The Los Angeles basin region consists of 21 airports handling 6.5 million flights a year. The GAO notes that the FAA computers in the region have repeatedly suffered from the loss of critical data and slow responses because of the overload.

### Alternatives

The FAA and its constituents are aware of these problems and several solutions have been proposed. Evaluating the proposals is complicated by the fact that each organization has different objectives.

- Private pilots have objected to the FAA plans, led by the Aircraft Owners and Pilots Association (AOPA) of 300,000 noncommercial owners. The AOPA has proposed a satellite-based system that the assocation estimates would save $6 billion over the current AAS proposal. The FAA response is that "satellites aren't a replacement for the current [system]." The commercial airlines are also resisting the proposal, and suggesting that it should be delayed until 2010.
- In the meantime, because the new AAS is not available, the FAA is trying to make do with the existing Univac terminals. For starters, they are increasing the internal memory systems with modern technology. The FAA also awarded a $150 million contract to Unisys to either refurbish older machines or open up an old production line to produce more of the 15- to 20-year-old terminals. Much of the equipment, the 30-bit Univac terminals, radar-gathering, and data-filtering units, are still based on vacuum tubes.
- IBM is continuing work on the contract. Observing that it is the largest contract they ever received, the workers note that they underestimated the complexity of the problem. They also experienced problems with the Ada compilers and limited support environment. The project was estimated to require 2 million lines of new code. There is some belief by the GAO that even if the project is completed, it will be obsolete.
- The GAO and FAA have considered additional options, such as entirely new systems from IBM or from BDM Corp. However, the alternatives have been rejected because they are too risky or would take too long to implement.
- Airlines and governments in other nations are also upset at FAA plans to implement a satellite-based locating and instrument landing system (ILS). International airlines prefer to have a worldwide standard system, but they are concerned about using a satellite system that is controlled by the U.S. Department of Defense.

### QUESTIONS

1. What systems development problems are being experienced by the FAA?
2. Is the AAS a "runaway system?" What characteristics does it exhibit?
3. What alternatives are available to resolve the problems experienced by the FAA?
4. Are the problems encountered by the FAA due to the problem complexity, systems methodology, lack of control and oversight, economics, or some other source?
5. What mistakes were made by the FAA in developing the new system?
6. What complications in this case make the FAA system difficult to create?
7. What tools and techniques exist to help resolve the problems?
8. Why was it possible for one programmer to build the expert system in two months? How does the answer to this question provide help for the rest of the FAA?
9. How can you solve the problems at the FAA? Write a detailed plan.
10. What problems do you expect to encounter in solving the FAA problem? What political and organizational do you expect to encounter?

# CASE *The Internal Revenue Service (IRS)*

Between personal and business returns, the IRS processes more than 200 million tax returns a year. Some of the returns are simple one-page forms; others run to thousands of pages of supporting documents. Overall, the service handles more than 1 billion information documents a year. The IRS brings in more than $1 trillion in tax revenue a year. The IRS has 10 regional service centers that are responsible for processing and storing individual forms. In 1989, it cost the IRS $34 million just to store the paper documents.

Until 1990, all documents at the IRS were stored as paper records in a central warehouse. Documents were organized according to the year of filing. As a result, if a taxpayer had a problem or question that covered multiple years, the citizen had to schedule multiple meetings with IRS officials to correct problems for each of the years. In some cases, it could take weeks or months just to get the files. Occasionally, the IRS found it was faster to ask the taxpayer for a copy of the return. By the early 1990s, this problem was resolved by having each of the 10 service centers store digital images of the tax returns, making them available to agents on their terminals. Even so, the IRS knows that it needs more automation, especially the ability to scan the returns directly into a computerized information system.

Of course, automation sometimes creates additional problems, such as the situation faced by Dickie Ann Conn. The IRS determined that she owed $67,714 in back taxes. As a result, she was sent a bill for more than $1 billion in interest and penalties. On challenge, the IRS admitted that there was an error in the interest computation.

## IRS History of Automation Problems

The IRS seems like a logical candidate for improved automation. The benefits of faster processing, fewer mistakes, and easier access to data ought to save a considerable amount of money. The computer's ability to search the data, automatically match transactions, and analyze each return presents several additional opportunities that can either cut costs or raise additional revenue. Managers at the IRS are fully aware of the potential, and they have proposed several systems over the years. The problem has been in implementation and in getting Congress to support the plans.

In the late 1960s, the IRS knew that it needed to redesign its basic systems, and began planning for a system to be installed in the 1970s. Congress eventually killed the plan for two main reasons: it was too expensive, and Congress was concerned about security and taxpayer privacy. The IRS then focused on keeping its existing computers running.

In 1982, the existing system was nearing capacity and the IRS established the Tax System Redesign program. It was a major redesign and consisted of three major components. According to the GAO, changes in management resulted in the system never getting past the design stage. A new assistant commissioner in 1982 embarked on design of a new system that would carry the IRS through the 1990s. Initial costs were estimated at $3 to $5 billion over the entire project. The primary objective was to replace the old central tape-based system with an online database. Eventually optical technology would be used to scan the original documents and store the data in the database. A new communication system would carry the data to any agent's workstation. By 1989, initial planning had already cost the IRS more than $70 million, with no concrete proposal or results.

The main computer systems were replaced at the IRS service centers in 1985. The change in the systems was almost disastrous for the IRS. The change delayed returns processing, leading to delays in refunds that cost the IRS millions of dollars in interest payments. IRS employees worked overtime but still could not keep up. Rumors were flying that some employees were dumping returns to cut down their backlog. Because of the delays and backlogs, the IRS managed to audit only about half the usual number of returns.

In 1986, the IRS initiated a plan to provide 18,000 laptop computers to make its field auditors more productive with its Automated Examination System (AES). Unfortunately, the service bought the Zenith laptops a full year before the software was ready. The system was written in Pascal and was delivered to agents in July 1986. The system was designed to help examine Form 1040 returns. Its biggest drawback was that it used 18 different diskettes, requiring agents to continually swap disks. From privatization efforts by the Reagan administration, the system was subcontracted to outside developers. As IRS funding was cut, programmers with experience in Pascal were cut. The system had to be rewritten in C.

A survey in 1988 revealed that 77 percent of the agents were dissatisfied with the software and it was used by only one-third of them. By 1989, the IRS revised the software and managed to reduce it to eight disks. Overall, by 1989, the AES project was more than six years behind schedule, and the GAO observed that it would be $800 million over the original budget. The IRS originally anticipated that the AES would produce $16.2 billion in additional revenue over nine years by making agents more productive. The GAO disputed those numbers, noting that "the IRS has been unable to verify that the use of laptops has actually resulted in the examination of additional returns or increased tax revenues."

In 1990, the White House cut funding for the program from $110 million down to $20 million.

### Tax System Modernization

By 1989, the IRS knew that it desperately needed to redesign its entire system for collecting taxes and processing information. In hearings before Congress, Senator David Pryor (D-Ark.) noted that the 1960s-era IRS computers were headed for a "train wreck" in the mid-1990s. The GAO estimated the original project would cost between $3 and $4 billion. The projected date for implementation slipped from 1995 to 1998.

The overall Tax System Modernization (TSM) design calls for a centralized online database, smaller departmental systems containing local information that are tied together with a nationwide network. Tax return data would be entered with a combination of electronic filing and optical scanners.

By 1991, the estimated cost of the plan had expanded to $8 billion. Although it was anticipated that the system would cut $6 billion in costs, the TSM plan was rapidly attacked by members of Congress. Three studies of the TSM plan by the GAO were released in early 1991:

- The GAO was concerned that optical technology was not sufficiently advanced to perform the tasks demanded by the IRS. The GAO urged greater emphasis on electronic filing.
- The GAO was concerned about management issues such as transition planning, progress measurement and accountability.
- The GAO and Sen. John Glenn (D-Ohio) voiced concerns about security.

GAO official Howard Rhile notes that "This is a serious omission in view of the fact that the IRS intends to allow public access . . . to some of its systems and because concerns over the security of taxpayer information helped doom the first [IRS] modernization effort in the late 1970s."

Despite these misgivings, the IRS was committed to the TSM plan. Fred Goldberg, IRS commissioner, agreed with the GAO findings but observed that

> We have been running our business essentially the same way, using essentially the same computer and telecommunications systems design for 25 years. [Existing systems] will perform well and achieve incremental improvements for the next few years . . . Our best judgment is that [OCR] technology will be there when we need it, by the end of the decade.

By 1992, the situation was worse. Shirley Peterson, the new commissioner of internal revenue, stated at a Congressional hearing that "Our systems are so antiquated that we cannot adequately serve the public. The potential for breakdown during the filing season greatly exceeds acceptable business risk . . . Some components of these computers are so old and brittle that they literally crumble when removed for maintenance."

In December 1991, the IRS awarded a 12-year, $300-million contract to TRW to help manage the process and provide planning and system integration services.

The new system is ambitious, calling for 60 major projects, two dozen major purchases, 20 million lines of new software, and 308 people just to manage the purchasing. Despite their efforts, elements of the IRS modernization plan were stalled because of purchasing difficulties. In July 1991, the IRS awarded a billion-dollar Treasury Multiuser Acquisition Contract (TMAC) to AT&T. The goal was to standardize purchasing for the IRS and the Treasury Department by routing all purchases through one vendor. The contract was challenged by other vendors and overturned. The contract was re-bid and AT&T won a second time. IBM (one of the original protesters) again objected to the process, noting that the IBM bid of $708 million was less than the $1.4 billion bid by AT&T.

In 1993, the IRS acknowledged that the TSM Design Master Plan needed to be rewritten. In particular, it had to focus on business aspects instead of technology. To better coordinate technical planning with IRS needs, the agency established a research and development center funded by $78.5 million of federal money but run by the private sector. The center is responsible for providing technical assistance and strategic planning for the TSM. The IRS also established a high-level "architect office" to evaluate technologies and their likely uses.

Through 1992, the IRS had spent $800 million on TSM. In 1993, new IRS estimates indicate that TSM will cost $7.8 billion above the $15.5 billion needed to keep existing systems running. The new system is expected to generate $12.6 billion in total benefits by 2008 through reduced costs, increased collections, and interest savings. Additionally, the improved processes should save taxpayers $5.4 billion and cut 1 billion hours from their time spent with the IRS.

The IRS asked Congress for a 1996 allocation of $1.03 billion, a substantial increase from the $622 million it spent on automation in 1995. However, Hazel Edwards from the General Accounting Office noted that "After eight years and an investment of almost $2 billion, IRS's progress toward its vision has been minimal."

IRS Commissioner Margaret Milner Richardson denies the GAO claims, noting "I think we have made significant progress, not minimal progress . . . but we do know we can and must do more."

The IRS situation represents a typical dilemma for Congress. The IRS claims that by spending more money, it will be possible to create a system that finally works. The GAO believes it is impossible to complete the entire project envisioned by the IRS. The GAO believes the IRS should focus on smaller projects that can be completed in one to two years.

## Electronic Filing

The IRS introduced electronic filing in 1986, when 25,000 forms were filed electronically. By 1990, 4.2 million people filed for tax refunds electronically. In 1992, the number increased to 10 million filers.

The primary target of electronic filing is the millions of individual taxpayers who will receive refunds. To control the process and ensure that documents are properly filed, electronic filing is only available through authorized tax preparers. The IRS is deliberately avoiding providing access to individual taxpayers. As a result, taxpayers who use the system pay an additional charge to the preparer. However, the electronic system provides for refunds within a couple of weeks.

Electronically filed returns cost the IRS one-tenth the processing cost of paper forms. They also eliminate the cost of paper storage. The IRS notes that it is able to store 800,000 returns on one side of a 12-inch optical disk.

For taxpayers with easy returns, the IRS is simplifying the process even further—providing for filing over the telephone. In a 1992 pilot, 117,000 Ohio taxpayers filed for refunds using TouchTone phone calls. The system was expanded nationwide in 1994. It can only be used by taxpayers who qualify to use the 1040EZ form. A replacement form (1040-TEL) must still be signed and filed with the IRS, along with the W-2 (withholding) statements.

## Automated Under-Reporter (AUR)

The Automated Under-Reporter (AUR) is another component of the TMS. The AUR is a system designed to monitor returns and identify people who are most likely to underpay their taxes. The system was first installed in 1992 at the Ogden, Utah, regional center. The system pulls data from the service center's Unisys 1180 mainframe. It is downloaded across a local area network to a Sequent Computer System S-81 minicomputer, and from there it is sent to one of 240 networked Unix workstations on the employees' desks.

The system automatically matches distribution documents (such as 1099s and W-2s) with the filings of individual taxpayers. Mark Cox, assistant IRS commissioner for information systems development, notes that in trials with the AUR "We've been able to cut down the rework of cases from 25 percent to less than 5 percent. We see this type of work enabling us to share in more of a connectivity mode."

The system uses an Oracle Corp database running SQL to match data from various sources. It also performs basic tax computation and helps agents send notices to taxpayers. Managers note that although the new system has not improved the speed of the agents, it has cut down the error rates. As agents become familiar with the system, they expect productivity to improve.

In 1991, the Ogden center processed 26 million tax returns, collecting $100 billion in tax payments. It processed $9 billion in refunds. In 1992, it won the Presidential Award for Quality for improved tax processing by saving the government $11 million over five years.

## Currency and Banking Retrieval System

In 1988, Congress passed a new law in an attempt to cut down on crime (notably drug dealing) and to provide leads to people who significantly underreport their income. Every cash transaction over $10,000 is required by federal law to be reported to the IRS on a Form 8300. The IRS created the Currency and Banking Retrieval System to match these forms against the filer's tax return. The system automatically identifies people who had large cash purchases but claimed little income. However, because of a programming error, the system missed forms covering $15 million in cash transactions between 1989 and 1990.

The problem stemmed from the fact that the IRS used the same code number on the 8300 forms that it had been using on other cash transaction forms. The IRS later assigned separate codes for each form. But when programmers created the new matching programs, they did not know that there were now two codes for each transaction.

The system was corrected in 1991 and by 1992 was used to process more than 1 million queries a year.

Jennie Stathis of the GAO notes that there are additional problems with the Form 8300. In particular, the filings are often incomplete or contain incorrect taxpayer identification numbers. The IRS is developing software that will allow businesses to automatically verify the taxpayer ID numbers before the customer completes the purchase.

## Document Processing System and Service Center Recognition/Image Processing System (SCRIPS)

In 1994, the IRS awarded a $1.3 billion contract to the IBM Federal Systems Co. to design a document processing system that by the late 1990s will convert virtually every tax return to digital form. A day after the contract was awarded, IBM sold the Federal Systems Co. to Loral Corp for $1.52 billion.

The 15-year systems integration contract calls for having the system online in 1996. The plan calls for scanning incoming tax forms. Special software will digitally remove the form layout and instructions, leaving just the taxpayer data. OCR software will then convert the characters (including handwritten numbers) into computer data.

The system was scheduled for initial installation at the Austin, Texas, regional center in August 1995. Plans call for installing it at Ogden, Utah, Cincinnati, Ohio, Memphis, Tennessee, and Kansas City, Missouri, by 1998.

Despite the popularity of electronic filing, the IRS still sees a need for the OCR system. The IRS anticipates receiving 252 million paper filings in the year 2001.

SCRIPS is a less ambitious project ($88 million) that was awarded in 1993 to Grumman Corp.'s Data Systems unit. SCRIPS was designed to capture data from four simple IRS forms that are single-sided. SCRIPS was supposed to be an interim solution that would support the IRS until DPS could be fully deployed. However, delays have pushed back the delivery of the SCRIPS project.

Interestingly, Grumman Data Systems was the loser in the contest for the DPS contract. The IRS noted that Grumman failed a key technical test.

### Security Breaches

In 1993, Sen. John Glenn (D-Ohio) released an IRS report indicating that 386 employees took advantage of "ineffective security controls" and looked through tax records of friends, neighbors, relatives, and celebrities at the Atlanta regional IRS office. Additionally, five employees used the system to create fraudulent returns, triggering more than 200 false tax refunds. Additional investigations turned up more than 100 other IRS employees nationwide with unauthorized access to records. Glenn observed that the IRS investigation examined only one region and looked at only one of 56 methods that could be use to compromise security. He noted that "I'm concerned this is just the tip of a very large iceberg."

The IRS itself noted that the TSM program "greatly increases the risk of employee browsing, disclosure, and fraud," because of the online access to the centralized databases.

Margaret Richardson, commissioner of internal revenue, noted that the system used by the perpetrators was 20 years old and was used by 56,000 employees. It met all federal security standards, using passwords and limiting access based on job descriptions. The IRS found the problems in Atlanta by examining records of database access from 1990 to 1993. Because the system generated 100 million transactions a month, the data is stored on magnetic tape, making it difficult to search.

In 1989, the IRS arrested Alan N. Scott, of West Roxbury, Massachusetts, for allegedly submitting 45 fraudulent returns via the new electronic filing system. The IRS claims the man received more than $325,000 in refunds.

The IRS requires tax return preparers to fill out an application before it issues an access code. Mr. Scott apparently used a fake taxpayer ID number and lied on the application form to gain the access number. The IRS claims he then submitted false returns using bogus names and taxpayer ID numbers to get refund checks ranging from $3,000 to $23,000.

IRS officials note that the electronic filings actually made it easier to identify the problem, because the computer could scan the data earlier than if it had been submitted by hand. Once the situation was identified, the IRS was able to immediately lock out further transactions from Mr. Scott's access number.

### IRS Budget

Like any Congressional agency, the IRS budget is set by Congress and approved by the president. In 1995, the Clinton administration asked Congress to increase the IRS budget by 10 percent—allocating the money to improving the information systems and procedures at the IRS to make them more effective. Congress responded by cutting the IRS budget by 2 percent. The Clinton budget called for $8.23 billion, the Congressional numbers cut the budget from $7.48 billion in 1995 to $7.35 billion in 1996. Congress did grant a slight increase in the budget for tax system modernization. Rep. Jim Lightfoot (R-Iowa) observed that "without modernization, I think you're throwing good money after bad. The IRS is still working out of cardboard boxes. It's basically that bad."

### QUESTIONS

1. What problems have been experienced by the IRS in developing its information systems?
2. How are these problems related to the service's systems development methodologies?
3. What other factors are involved in causing the IRS difficulties?

4. Is the IRS pushing technology too hard? For example, are the OCR systems technically reasonable?

5. The GAO thinks the IRS should place more emphasis on electronic filing. Is the GAO correct, or is the IRS approach better? Write a proposal supporting one of the two sides, emphasizing costs, benefits, risks, and opportunities.

6. Why was the State of Virginia able to build an integrated system by 1991 when the IRS still does not have the same capabilities?

7. Are there any ways to speed up the development of systems for the IRS? What would be the costs and risks?

8. Are the IRS problems the result of technology or management difficulties?

9. What would be the advantages and drawbacks to outsourcing the IRS information systems, similar to the UK approach? How does that approach differ from the methods used by the IRS?

10. Write a 5-year and 10-year management plan for the development and adoption of technology at the IRS. Be sure to include transition and implementation details.

11. Why did the IRS choose private banks to develop the Electronic Payments System? Could this technique be used for other systems?

12. Why would NationsBank choose to focus on object-oriented technology instead of a traditional database system to build the Electronic Federal Tax Payments System?

13. What are the differences between the IRS proposals and the GAO suggestions? What are the advantages of each approach?

## CASE  *The Bechtel Group: Linking the Company's Technology into a Cohesive System*

The Bechtel Group is a $5 billion construction company that develops, engineers, builds, and operates major construction sites around the world. Its projects have included the Hoover Dam, the San Francisco-Oakland Bay Bridge, the James Bay hydroelectric plant in northeastern Quebec, and the Metro subway system in Washington, DC.

The Bechtel Group's relationship to technology has been early and long. It was an early investor in technology to plot and control its construction projects. However, the diversity of its projects and their geographic dispersion led to a proliferation of computers, protocols, and programs. To meet information needs that develop with each new project, each unit developed its own way of managing information. Although the technology worked well at the unit and project levels, there was no way to gain synergy among projects. In the opinion of many, this lack of coordination led to a considerable reinventing of wheels.

Management decided that considerable value would result if all the technology in the company could be linked. Engineers in diverse corners of the world could learn from each other if they could communicate easily by computer and compare notes regarding the same software/engineering programs.

To meet the challenge of integration, Bechtel formed an interdisciplinary task force composed of individuals from information services, technical services, engineering, construction, procurement, and cost scheduling project management. George Conniff, manager of the Industrial Business Line and former manger of information services, set the charter for the Automation Integration Methods group (AIM): "Develop policies and strategies to focus technology and automation on developing a competitive advantage."

Like most business groups, the task force began by placing a moratorium on the runaway development of software. This gave the team time to establish standards for the programs that would be developed. At the time the task force also placed a tight control on the purchase of hardware. Standards needed to be established in this area as well to prevent the proliferation of an incompatible infrastructure.

AIM focused on a strategy that would provide an infrastructure that enables Bechtel to distribute work; share data; and communicate quickly, efficiently, and with a great deal of user-friendliness. The team pursued and obtained a strong commitment from senior management to support them with overall strategy and funding. AIM chose to standardize on the DECNet OSI network, IBM, and Compaq as the standard personal computers, the Oracle database platform, Lotus 1-2-3 as the standard spreadsheet, and WordPerfect as the word processor. The group personally catalogued and examined more than 2,000 software applications in the company and chose 110 standard applications. They then delegated the implementation of these standards to information services.

Once a program was established to standardize equipment, systems, and software, the next step became one of linking the pieces all together. This project, called Distributed Project Execution (DSE), was put in place to enable any Bechtel employee to share information among clients, suppliers, permanent offices, project sites, and offshore technical centers through a sophisticated, networked, telecommunications system.

DSE added a bold new dimension to the Bechtel's communication system. Previously people had to be moved to the work. Advances in voice, graphics, and data technology enabled the work to be moved to the people. With AIM and DSE, a small, focused project team on location can tap into the expertise of any of Bechtel's engineering or research staff without bearing the expense and the inconvenience of having them travel to the specific location. An example of this new technique involves a time-critical refinery project in the United Kingdom. The computer network enabled the design work to be distributed to offices in London, Houston, and Gaithersburg, Maryland. This enabled the design to be completed concurrently in these three locations without the time and expense of moving the team to London for the project.

The ultimate goal of DSE is a seamless network. This would allow easy access to information from all over the company and the outside world by those who need it. Even though individual projects differ, Bill Howard, vice-president of information technology—futures group, believes 80 percent of the systems to manage them are the same across organizational lines. Howard feels that the ultimate success of DSE will depend on the ability of the information technology group to train people at all levels of the company to use the systems. This will not only make everyone more computer-conversant, it will also develop a team mentality among the users.

Howard believes the work at Bechtel has only begun. To meet the ever-expanding challenges, he has divided his Information Technology Futures Group into three areas:

- Research and development examines new technologies that Bechtel might use to develop the next generation of technology.
- Group marketing and strategy looks beyond Bechtel's present business strategies toward the next planning horizon.
- Information technology seeks to position Bechtel to provide new information-technology-based services and products to Bechtel clients.

Ultimately, Howard believes that his area can open a totally new area of technology services for Bechtel's clients. In his opinion, information services are a natural extension of the engineering services that Bechtel already provides. He believes the same abilities are necessary in both fields. These include project management, procurement, and financial skills.

Fine-tuning these skills will enable Bechtel to take the next step and become a true systems integrator. The next step in this process will be for Bechtel to begin bidding on projects in which the information system is the whole project, not just a component of the engineering or construction job. Toward this end, Bechtel has selected its six in-house programs with the strongest commercial value and packaged them for sale. One system involves a program that enables engineers to develop designs in three dimensions, "walk through" the projects, and visualize the completed computerized designs. Another presents project management in a way that it can be applied to specialized engineering design analysis, such as charting the piping or the electrical circuits for a building.

In keeping with its goal to sell stand-alone information services, Bechtel has acquired Technological Applications, Inc. (TAI), of Jacksonville, Florida. This acquisition includes a wide range of expert information systems for the monitoring, manufacturing, and analysis of engineering projects. One example of an expert system application is a nuclear power plant system to monitor the control of room temperatures and vibrations. The expert system identifies where a problem is and suggests steps to fix it. Another example is the use of artificial intelligence to manage the codes and materials involved in pipe welding. A third type would be to provide information about chemical spills.

Howard analyzes Bechtel's new directions in this way:

> The pace of change is accelerating. It's a whole new era. The nature of work and organization for a company like ours is being redefined. We have the tools to do things better, faster, and more accurately than ever. Our job now is to bring the abilities of the users up to the level of the technology that's at our disposal.

## QUESTIONS

1. Using the systems development life-cycle approach, break the Bechtel Automation Integration Methods developments into the steps of the systems life-cycle.
2. Parallel the Bechtel technology case to the systems analysis, design, implementation, and maintenance four-step process.
3. How will Bechtel's approach change the traditional roles of computer programmer and systems analyst in the company?
4. Using data flow diagrams, represent the time-critical refinery project in the United Kingdom.
5. A data store is a place in which data is stored for some time period while it is waiting to be processed or used by some other part of the system. What items would a construction/engineering company like Bechtel keep in a data store?
6. How would the module concept of programming assist the Automation Integration Methods group to categorize and integrate all of the programs that Bechtel had developed on an ad hoc basis?

7. What specific steps would you recommend to Bill Howard to prevent his new initiatives from becoming as unfocused as Bechtel's previous programs?

## CASE *Tootsie Roll Industries: Online Processing for Effective Sales Management*

Based in Chicago, Tootsie Roll Industries is a $180-million corporation that manufactures a line of confectionery products, the most famous of which is Tootsie Roll candy.

To track its orders and manufacturing processes, Tootsie Roll contracted with Sequent Computer Systems to install its online transaction-processing system (OLTP). The primary concept of OLTP is that many users can update a common database simultaneously. It is based on the principle that each transaction contains a finite set of entries. Each user as well has a fixed set of options when working with each transaction. For example, a sales order has a fixed form. Users are only allowed to enter, modify, or delete information in certain fields on the form. Because these information updates are predictable, the entry process can be systematized for maximum performance.

Using this principle, OLTP can be used to expedite sales order entry, general ledger posting, inventory updating, and personnel-records management. Rather than collecting sales orders or inventory records on paper forms and routing them to data-entry operators, OLTP allows information to be entered immediately into the system. Thus, reports produced from the database will always contain the latest information.

In 1989, Tootsie Roll replaced the company's aging mainframe-based system with a Sequent OLTP system. According to Ellen Gordon, president,

> Tootsie Roll can now look at the previous day's orders and see which region was ahead of its sales projection or which plant needs more work. We can play "what if," looking at information any way we want it, whenever we want it.
>
> Having access to such up-to-date information makes a tremendous difference. We don't have to call up our technology department and ask them to run a report, and have them tell us they can't run it exactly the way we need it, or that it'll take some extra programming to do that particular report.

At Tootsie Roll, the OLTP system significantly improved the company's information flow. Under the old centralized paper-based system, two or three data-entry operators processed orders. Managers had to wait up to a month for data about sales, production, and inventory. The new Sequent system gathers data from dozens of workstations scattered throughout the warehouses and plants. This enables managers to analyze data that is current through the previous day through predefined reports as well as custom queries.

Up-to-date access provides important information for marketing and sales managers as well. The query system is particularly important for them because they can examine the data by customer, market, region, product, or any of the 25,000 Tootsie Roll accounts. Hence, managers can spot trends more quickly and manage potential problems before they occur.

The ability to develop customized statistical reports in real time has enhanced the effectiveness managing the marketing regions. Instant online reports focusing on the statistically significant areas and data enable managers to concentrate on accounts that show the most growth potential. They can also experiment with new sales plans much more easily and make judgments much sooner about the effectiveness of these programs.

SOURCE: Glenn Rifkin, "CEOs, PCs Don't Mix Well," *Computerworld*, April 17, 1989, p. 82. Copyright 1989 by Computerworld, Inc., Framingham, MA 01701—Reprinted from *Computerworld*.

### QUESTIONS

1. What goals did Tootsie Roll want to achieve through its online processing system?
2. At Tootsie Roll, the time required for production feedback decreased from two months to one day. How would this fact assist the managers and supervisors in charge of the production process to be more efficient and cost effective?
3. Before the OLTP system was installed, sales and marketing managers were always complaining that they did not have good enough data to make strategic marketing decisions. What did they mean by this statement? How were these concerns addressed by the new system?
4. If you were consulting with the sales staff at Tootsie Roll, what steps would you add to their sales analysis that would enable them to better evaluate and control their efforts?
5. How is online transaction processing different from more traditional computer programs?

## DISCUSSION ISSUE

*Users versus Developers*

One of the most difficult aspects of creating software is enhancing the communication between users and designers. Let's listen in on a typical discussion between an analyst (Khalil) and a manager (Charlie).

Charlie:   But you said the entire project would be finished three months ago. Now you're telling me it will take another six months?

Khalil:   Look, we were on schedule until a couple of my people quit. The real problem is that your staff kept changing their minds. When we started the marketing research system, you said we did not have to worry about tracking customer coupons. After everyone signed off on the requirements step, you suddenly decide to add these features. We had to go back and start over. That's why we're behind the original schedule.

Charlie:   Wait a minute. We didn't care about the coupons until our competitor suddenly decided to expand operations in the Western region. I can't control what our rivals do. I don't remember "signing off" on anything. All I know is that once a month, you sent me a whole stack of papers to read that had nothing to do with my job. And after that first week of meetings, I never saw you for six months. If you had stopped in sooner, I could have told you about the coupons.

Khalil:   This is a big project, and we have been busy. If you want the coupon tracking, we'll do it, but it's going to take another six months. You're lucky we can even squeeze it in. We've got other problems. Your employees can't agree on the form and content of some of these reports. We need you to pick one type. Also, to save time, we're going to skip this first report and just give you the combined data on this second report. We don't see any reason to duplicate the data. Last, we need to know the formula you use to make this calculation.

Charlie:   No. We need all of the reports exactly the same as we use now. Don't change anything. I don't know the exact formula. I think Michel has it. Ask her. Uh oh, I have another meeting in two minutes. Don't change the reports, just add the coupon tracking. Oh, and we have a new employee (Jack) and he has some great new ideas. Be sure you talk to him.

*Six months later . . .*

Khalil:   Hi, I'm Khalil. What happened to Charlie?

Michel:   He was promoted to marketing VP. When are we going to get the marketing research system?

Khalil:   It's in alpha test now, but we're going to wait on the new 9350 series before implementing. We're having some I/O channel problems, plus I think the 9350 will support Token Ring directly.

Michel:   Huh? I don't know what you're doing, but we needed this system a year ago. We're desperate. Jack created this great spreadsheet program. It gives us some of the reports we want now, but your staff won't give us access to the data we need.

Khalil:   I can write a COBOL program to pull out some data for you, but we can't let your spreadsheets change any of the information. We can't trust the PCs, and there's no way to set up the security and integrity tests we need. You'd be better off waiting until we get the whole system running.

Michel:   Well, we can't trust you either. We're just going to keep working on the PCs. At least we have something. Anyway, I've got bigger problems right now. I just heard that we're expanding into New England by buying out another company. I have to fly out there and check out their marketing plans and hire a couple more staff members.

Khalil:   What? No one told me. We'll need a bigger computer, and we have to change . . . Wait. Do you know what computer that company is using?

## QUESTIONS

1.   Whose fault is it that the marketing project is six months behind schedule?
2.   Do you think the project will ever be finished?
3.   Should the marketing department be given access to the corporate data? Should the staff be allowed to change the data?
4.   Is there a solution to these problems—Perhaps a different development method or different tools?
5.   What can be done to improve the communication between the users and MIS department?

# CHAPTER 13

# Organizing Information System Resources

BankAmerica uses its Web site (http://www.bankamerica.com) to provide basic information about the company and its services. By 1995, some other banks began offering rudimentary banking services over the Internet.

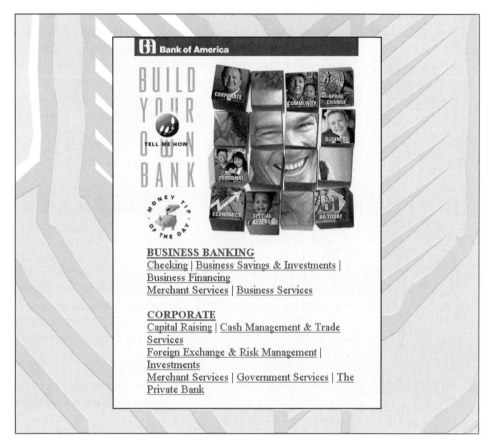

## CONTINENTAL BANK

Few industries have faced the level of strategic upheaval that has revolutionized the banking industry. For generations, banking was an institution. Its buildings were symbolized by tall, white columns and stability. When a person joined a bank, he or she remained "a banker" until retirement. The regulation of interest rates kept competition to a minimum. When someone needed to borrow money, be it for a home or a car, they always went to a bank.

Today the bank's image and operations are much different. Car companies, department stores, and credit unions are only a few of those who are in the financial services industry. Deregulation during the early 1980s removed many of the restrictions that protected banks from competition. As a result, banks have had to change from "banker's hours" to their customers' hours. In doing so, they have had to redefine their market segment and who their customers really are.

One of the banks hardest hit by change was the Continental Bank of Chicago. In May 1984, Reuters reported rumors that the bank's loans to Latin American countries and oil-gas drillers were in jeopardy. Within days, Japanese money managers refused to redeposit several billion dollars in overnight accounts. Internal improprieties also contributed to the growing lack of trust in the bank.

By July 1984, Continental declared bankruptcy. Because it was the seventh largest bank in the United States, the Federal Deposit Insurance Corporation felt that closing its doors would result in a major financial crisis. In order to keep the bank solvent, the FDIC took more than an 80 percent interest in what was once the seventh largest bank in the United States.

**OVERVIEW**

The role of the MIS department is to help you achieve business goals. But before you start to think of them as your personal genie, keep in mind that the MIS staff works for the entire company. As illustrated by Figure 13.1, the challenge is to organize the MIS resources to support everyone with a minimum of conflicts.

In addition to systems development, many tasks need to be done to ensure that companies make efficient use of their MIS resources. But why should business managers care about how the MIS resources are organized? In smaller businesses, the answer is simple: There is no strong MIS department, so you have to do the job yourself. The answer is more complex in larger businesses that have well-established MIS departments. A basic answer lies in the fact that MIS departments face many challenges that impose constraints on their choices. Managers and users need to understand these constraints to learn why MIS departments cannot always fulfill their requests. Managers also need to determine the best method for building systems they need.

One of the key constraints facing MIS is that information within an organization needs to be accessible to everyone. There is a long history in U.S. companies of independent pockets of information being created that cannot be shared. In fact, there is a long-running conflict in many companies between individual demands and the corporate need to share data. The competing demands between this centralization and decentralization influence almost every aspect of how companies create and use information. Managers and users can play a key role in resolving the underlying conflicts.

**INTRODUCTION**

The capabilities of application software are impressive. Because of these tools, business people using personal computers are solving problems in a few hours that never would have been attempted five years ago. With these powerful tools available to the average business person, it is easy to wonder why a company needs an MIS department. That's a good question, and the answers keep changing through the years.

MIS departments provide many important services. For example, think about what happens when a new version of your word processor is released. Someone has to install the software, distribute the manuals, convert old document files to the new

**FIGURE 13.1**

Organizing information system resources. Making effective use of information systems requires organizing the MIS resources: Hardware, software, data, and personnel. A key decision involves positioning the resources in the organization which revolves around decentralization versus centralization. The goal is to balance the need for central control and the value of decentralized decisions.

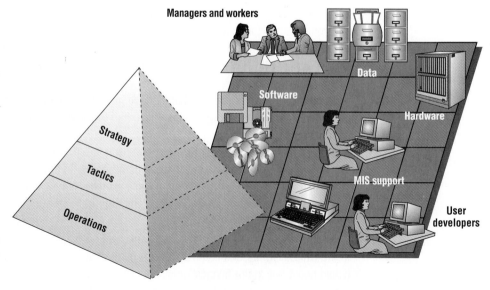

---

## TRENDS

There were few management issues with the earliest computers. They were big, required specially designed rooms, and highly trained programmers and operators. These computers were used for basic computations. As a result, the computers were placed in a central location. All data and software were stored with the computer. Because the early machines had limited communication capabilities, the MIS personnel were also located with the machines.

As the price of computers dropped and capabilities increased, they were used for more tasks. The machines, data, and software continued to be stored in central locations. Many companies put them in large rooms surrounded by glass, so managers could show visitors that the company was pursuing "modern" solutions. Eventually, companies realized that these "glass-houses" were a security risk. Most companies now hide their main computers behind locked doors and security guards.

In the 1970s, many companies purchased midrange computers. These computers were easier to operate and individual departments could afford to buy one for their own use. It represented the beginning of hardware **decentralization.** Many companies now had computers scattered throughout the firm. Software, data, and some MIS personnel followed the machines to the departments. In many cases, the hardware, software, and data were incompatible with the central computers. As long as the machines and data were used only by a single department, the problems were minimal. However, many MIS departments spent a good portion of the 1970s trying to get these machines and user departments to share data.

In the 1980s, the move toward decentralization accelerated with the introduction of personal computers. The competition in microcomputer technology has created hardware that is as powerful as most large central computers at a fraction of the price. Most companies today have an average of slightly less than one computer per employee. The key concern is that as hardware becomes distributed throughout the organization, software, data and the need for support will follow. If computers and data are completely decentralized, it is difficult to share data among workers.

The local area networks of the late 1980s were a response to the need to share data and hardware. However, even with a LAN, there are many ways to organize the various information resources.

In the 1990s, as personal computers become increasingly powerful, it becomes more tempting to shift data to these machines. This increased control by individuals can alter the structure of the company, as the conflict between centralization and decentralization intensifies.

---

format, and show people how to use the new features. Now imagine the problems involved when there are 5,000 workers using this software.

According to statistics collected by *Computerworld,* large companies spend about 5 percent of their sales revenue on the MIS area. For a company with a billion dollars in sales, that amounts to $50 million a year spent on MIS. This money pays for personal computers, central computers, communications, software, and MIS personnel to manage it all. The primary tasks undertaken by the MIS department are software development, setting corporate computing standards, hardware administration, database administration, advocacy and planning, and end-user support.

Small businesses usually do not have a separate MIS department. That does not mean these duties are ignored. Even in small businesses, someone has to be responsible for these MIS functions. However, small businesses generally do not attempt to develop their own software. Even relying on commercial software requires that time be spent on determining data needs and evaluating software packages.

## THE CHANGING ROLE OF MIS

The role of the MIS department has changed over time. In many respects, it is in the middle of a fundamental change. In the past, MIS departments focused on creating information systems and controlling data—particularly transaction data. Today, as explained by the Gartner Group (an IS consulting firm), the objectives of MIS are:

• Provide transparent access to corporate data.

• Optimize access to data stored on multiple platforms for many groups of users.
• Maximize the end-user's ability to be self-sufficient in meeting individual information needs.

These changes represent a shift in attitude. It moves toward the goal of increasing support for workers, not their replacement, so employees can do their jobs better on their own.

Probably the most important MIS decision facing business today is the issue of centralization. Because personal computers have a huge price/performance advantage over larger computers, there is a major incentive to decentralize the hardware. Yet, there are some serious complications with complete decentralization. There are many strategies for organizing information resources to gain the advantages of both centralization and decentralization. The management goal is to find the combination that works best for each situation. Before examining the alternatives, you need to understand the basic MIS roles.

**MANAGING THE INFORMATION SYSTEMS FUNCTION**

Many times in your career you will find yourself heavily involved with members of the MIS department. In the case of a small business, you might be in charge of the one or two MIS personnel. At some time, you might be the company liaison to an outsourcing vendor, MIS contractor, or consultant. In all of these situations, you will be responsible for planning, monitoring, and evaluating the MIS organization. You will have to make decisions and answer questions like: Is the MIS department doing a good job? Should the company be spending more money on MIS? Is it getting a good value for its current spending? Are there other methods that would be more efficient or save money?

As many companies have found, it is difficult to evaluate the MIS function. There are few objective measures. Changes in technology make the process more difficult. Innovations in hardware and software often make it easier to build and maintain information systems. However, there is a cost to buying new equipment. There is also a cost to continually retraining workers and modifying databases and reports. The goal of management is to find the appropriate balance between the need to update and the costs.

Management of information systems begins by understanding the roles of MIS. The MIS function is responsible for hardware and software acquisition and support. MIS staff provide access to corporate data and build applications. They support end-user development with training and help desks. MIS workers set corporate data standards and maintain the integrity of the company databases. All of these functions have to be organized, performed, and evaluated on a regular basis.

The issue of new technology points out the importance of planning. The only way to control costs and evaluate MIS benefits is to establish a plan. Plans need to be detailed so actual results can be compared to the plan. Yet plans need to be flexible enough to adapt to unexpected events and new technology. You also need to formulate contingency plans for events that might occur.

One key issue in managing information technology is organizing the MIS function so that it matches the structure of the firm. Centralization versus decentralization has been a key issue in the organization of MIS resources. Networks and powerful personal computers have led to more options supporting decentralization of information. The increased options are useful, but they create more issues managers must examine. To understand the advantages and drawbacks of MIS options, we must first examine the roles of MIS.

## MIS ROLES

Good information systems do not simply materialize from thin air. Providing timely, accurate, and relevant information requires careful planning and support. Creating effective information involves maintaining hardware, providing software training and support, supporting end-user development, defining and controlling access to databases, establishing corporate standards, and researching the competitive advantages of new technologies. The basic roles of MIS are outlined in Figure 13.2.

### Hardware Administration

Managers should not have to be computer experts to use their computers. Consider the work involved in buying a new computer. The computer industry has been changing rapidly—both with personal computers and with larger computers. Major changes occur in computer hardware continuously. For example, Intel (the designer of processors for most IBM-compatible personal computers) produced five major versions (plus additional variations) of microprocessors between 1982 and 1993. Each processor was more than twice as fast as the prior version and provided new features. Similar changes are constantly being made to the video capabilities, printers, networks, and storage devices.

**FIGURE 13.2**
MIS roles. The MIS department is responsible for hardware administration, software development, and training and support. MIS staff establish corporate computing standards, provide access to corporate data, and support end-user development. The MIS department also plays an advocacy role, presenting the IS benefits and strategies to the executive officers.

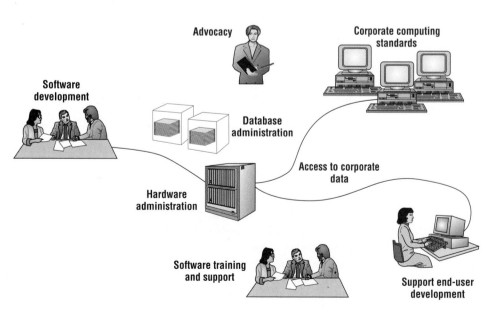

While computer reliability has increased considerably in the last ten years, installing, repairing, and modifying hardware is still an important job. Many companies rely on the original vendor or outside service firms to provide a rapid response to problems.

Every time the hardware changes, there are new uses for computers. As computers gain speed and capabilities, they can be used to solve more difficult problems. As the price declines, computers can be used for even more tasks. An enormous amount of time is required for MIS watchers just to keep track of the changes in the industry. Someone has to keep abreast of these changes. It does not make sense for every manager to be an expert on the current state of computer hardware. Instead of duplicating this effort, it is best to make the MIS department responsible for maintaining current computer information.

When users want to purchase new computers, they can go to the MIS department for information and advice. Some businesses provide a company computer store to allow users to test new computers. The MIS department can then deliver and set up the computers with the appropriate software already installed. This specialization means that users do not have to spend large amounts of time keeping up with changes in the computer industry. It also allows companies to buy hardware and software in large quantities to get better discounts. By working with standard hardware and software, MIS staff can make sure that all the pieces will work together. The MIS department also takes care of repairing the existing computers. If a computer breaks down, someone has to identify the problem and install replacement parts or notify the vendor.

Hardware devices also need routine maintenance. Printers have to be cleaned and toner cartridges replaced. Disk drives need to be reorganized, reformatted, or realigned. Networks sometimes need to be reorganized because accounts are added or deleted almost daily. These small tasks can quickly multiply if there are thousands of users.

## Software Support

Software generally requires more support than hardware does. MIS staff can help users decide which software to purchase and can install it. Users need to be trained to use various software features. Whenever workers change jobs or a company hires new workers, they need to be trained. Similarly, commercial software versions change almost every year, implying more training for users. Additionally, someone has to install the new copies on the machines, manuals have to be distributed, and data files sometimes have to be converted.

Just as in other areas of business, MIS jobs have become highly specialized. For instance, many advertisements for MIS jobs look like someone spilled a bowl of alphabet soup on the page. Companies often search for technical skills involving specific hardware and software.

Unfortunately, this approach to jobs causes problems for MIS personnel. In order to find other jobs or to advance in their current position, they have to acquire increasingly detailed knowledge of specific hardware and software packages. Yet, with

rapid changes in the industry, this knowledge can become obsolete in a year or two. These changes mean employees have to continually expand their knowledge and identify software and hardware approaches that are likely to succeed.

On the other hand, businesses need to keep their current applications running. With thousands of hours invested in current systems, companies cannot afford to discard their current practices and adopt every new hardware and software system that shows some promise.

When users have difficulty getting the computer to do what they want, it is time saving to have someone to call for help. Most commercial software companies provide telephone support for their products. However, many of them charge extra for this support. In many cases, it is better for MIS to support users directly. Besides the possibility of lower costs, the MIS department has a better understanding of the business problems. Also, many users are now combining information from several packages. For example, you might put a spreadsheet and a graph into a word-processed document. If different companies created the three programs and you have trouble, which one of the three software companies do you call? Your own MIS department will have experience with all three packages, and should be able to identify the cause of the problems.

## Access to Corporate Data

In many organizations, massive data is stored on centralized computers. This basic data is often maintained by the MIS department. Users need this data for various reports. The marketing department may need the last 18 months of sales data in order to forecast the next 6 months. One important role of the MIS department is to help users access this information. Two basic items are needed to provide access to the data: hardware connections and software.

In terms of hardware, the MIS department is responsible for providing the physical connections between the machines. Besides the initial installation, considerable effort can be required to maintain these networks. Modern local area networks have many components scattered throughout the firm's buildings. Maintenance personnel need substantial expertise and patience to identify and correct problems that arise. Similarly, when someone wants to rearrange a large office, it might be necessary to change the network wiring. When computers are changed or someone wants access to other computers, the MIS personnel are responsible for changing the network.

In terms of software, the MIS department has to make sure that the information is provided in a format that can be used by the personal computers. MIS personnel have to be certain the users are authorized to access the data. The software has to maintain all necessary security provisions to make sure the data remain accurate. The personal computers also may need additional software to access the corporate network.

Network specialists can be involved in every aspect of the network, from installing and analyzing cables to configuring accounts and monitoring security over company networks. While communication between two computers is relatively straightforward, larger networks are much more difficult to install and maintain. Just tracking connection problems and identifying cables can be a full-time job.

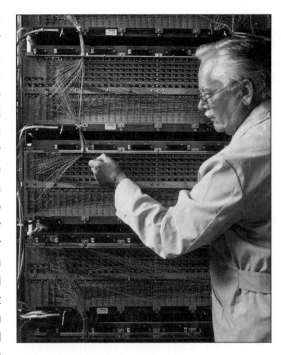

## Software Development

Chapter 12 explains the three common approaches to developing software: systems development life cycle, prototyping, and end-user development. Regardless of the method used, someone has to be in charge of each project. Also, because several projects are likely to be proposed at the same time, someone has to evaluate the feasibility of the projects and decide which ones should be undertaken first. Similarly, someone has to monitor the progress of all projects to keep them on track and avoid budget overruns.

The additional tasks of analysis and software design in the SDLC and prototyping methods have already been explained. The role of MIS personnel with end-user development is not as clear. Consider an extreme situation. If a company relies on prepackaged software and applications created by end users, would the company need an MIS staff? The basic answer is that someone still has to perform some of the MIS tasks, but he or she is likely to be an employee of an individual business unit instead of an MIS department.

## Support for End-User Development

Many application packages include programming capabilities. For example, a manager may create a spreadsheet to calculate sales commissions. Each week, new sales data is entered and the spreadsheet automatically produces summary reports. It would be better to have a clerk enter this new data instead of a manager. To make the clerk's job easier, the manager uses the macro capabilities in the spreadsheet to create a set of menus and help messages. Similarly, using a word processor's macro facilities, a legal department can create standard paragraphs for various contracts. With them, a secretary can type one word to display a prewritten warranty paragraph. In theory, even complex applications traditionally provided by the MIS

Training and education are increasingly important functions of the MIS department. With hardware and software changing on a daily basis, employees must constantly learn new tools and techniques.

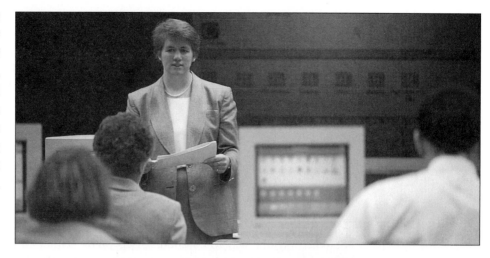

department, such as accounting systems, could be programmed by end users with prepackaged software.

Several problems can arise from end-user programming. Techniques that are acceptable for small projects may lead to errors and delays with large systems. Programming major applications requires obtaining information from users and managers. Applications designed for corporate use require extensive checking of data and security provisions to ensure accuracy. The software often needs to run on different operating systems and local networks.

The MIS department can provide assistance to minimize these problems. MIS personnel can assist end users in collecting ideas from other users. They can help in testing the applications to verify the accuracy and make sure the software works with other applications. MIS can provide tools and help end users in documenting their applications and moving them to new operating systems or new hardware. Programmers can write special routines to overcome limitations of commercial software that might arise. MIS staffs also maintain help desks or information centers to answer user questions and help users debug applications.

## Corporate Computing Standards

Over time, MIS has learned that the firm gets into trouble if all of the people work independently. In the 1960s, applications such as payroll, accounting, and customer order processing were developed independently. During the 1970s companies had to spend large amounts of money getting all of the pieces to work together. In the 1980s, personal computers arrived and the problems got worse.

Reacting to the problems created by these incompatibilities, MIS professionals at different companies developed **standards.** If all vendors used standard formats for files, hardware connections, and commands, products from different vendors could be used together. Today, there are standards for everything: data, hardware, software, report layouts, and coffee pots.

It is unlikely that the computing world will ever see complete cooperation among vendors. There are three factors that prevent products from working together. First, standards are often ambiguous or incomplete. Human languages always have some ambiguity, and there is no way to determine whether the description actually covers every possible situation. A second problem is that standards

**Reality Bytes  13–1  GILLETTE**

Patrick Zilvitis is directing Gillette in re-engineering its IS structure. He is emphasizing international standards, which is particularly important because two-thirds of Gillette's business is done outside the United States. Every employee of the division is held accountable for making IS strategy a top priority.

incorporate what is known about a topic at the time the standard is developed. Computing technologies change rapidly. Often, vendors can produce better products by not following the standards. Then new standards have to be developed. A third problem occurs because vendors want to distinguish their products from the offerings of competitors. If there were standards that perfectly described a product, there would be only one way to compete: price. Many vendors find that it is more profitable to offer features beyond what is specified in the standards, enabling the developers to charge a higher price.

Even though it is not possible to create perfect industry standards, there are advantages to creating companywide standards. They enable firms to buy products at lower prices. Most large businesses have special purchase agreements with hardware and software vendors. Buying in bulk allows them to get better prices. Similarly, it is easier to fix hardware if all the machines are the same. Likewise, it is much more convenient to upgrade just one word-processing package for 200 computers, instead of 20 different brands. Similarly, training is less expensive and time consuming if everyone uses the same software and hardware. Finally, standards make it easier for employees to share information across the company. Standards are especially important in a company like Gillette (Reality Bytes 13–1) which has offices around the world.

Some organizations forget that standards cannot be permanent. Hardware and software change almost continuously; new products arrive that are substantially better than existing standard items. Similarly, as the business changes, the standards often have to be revised. Also, there are exceptions to just about any policy. If one department cannot do their job with the standard equipment, MIS must make an exception and then figure out how to support this new equipment and software. American College Testing (Reality Bytes 13–2) illustrates the importance of maintaining flexibility and adaptability of IT support.

**Reality Bytes  13–2  AMERICAN COLLEGE TESTING SERVICE**

The American College Testing Service (ACT) is a $60 million nonprofit service company based in Iowa City. Its primary mission is to develop and administer educational assessment and placement instruments. It is most familiar to high school students who take its tests as a method of evaluation for admission to college.

The information services division maintains in-house administrative and program support and major research efforts. Other programs, including all finan-cial and accounting transactions, are outsourced. According to David Siebert, ACT's chief information officer, the company has made a strategic decision not to make major investments in technology to be able to stay on the edge with reduced risk.

Because particular examinations can grow by orders of magnitude overnight, the computer area must be flexible. As a result, systems must be flexible enough to grow easily or be able to be moved from one platform to another.

## Data and Database Administration

Databases are crucial to the operation of any company. Keeping the databases up-to-date and accurate does not happen by chance. Larger organizations employ a **database administrator (DBA)** to be responsible for maintaining the corporate database. The DBA is responsible for maintaining the databases, monitoring performance of the database management system, and solving day-to-day problems that arise with the databases.

Companies also need someone to coordinate the definition of the data. Large organizations might hire a separate **data administrator (DA),** smaller companies will pass this role to the DBA. The DA is responsible for defining the structure of the databases. The DA has to make certain the data is stored in a form that can be used by all the applications and users. He or she is responsible for avoiding duplicate terms (e.g., customer instead of client). Additionally, the DA provides for **data integrity,** which means that the data must contain as few errors as possible.

The DA is also required to maintain security controls on the database. The DA has to determine who has access to each part of the data, and specify what changes users are allowed to make. Along the same lines, companies and employees are required by law to meet certain privacy requirements. For instance, banks are not allowed to release data about customers except in certain cases. In Europe, there are much stricter privacy rules. If a firm operates a computer facility in many European countries, the company must carefully control access to all customer data. Some nations prohibit the transfer of customer data out of the country. The DA is responsible for understanding these laws and making sure the company complies with them.

Finally, because today's databases are so crucial to the company, the business needs a carefully defined disaster and recovery policy. Typically that means the databases have to be backed up every day. Sometimes, a company might keep continuous backup copies of critical data on separate disk drives at all times. MIS has to plan for things that might go wrong (fires, viruses, floods, hackers, etc.). If something does affect the data or the computer system, MIS is responsible for restoring operations. For instance, an alternate computing site might be needed while the original facilities are being repaired. All of this planning requires considerable time.

## Advocacy Role

The MIS department is headed by a single manager. That person often is called the *chief information officer (CIO).* The CIO position might be a vice-president or one level below that. A major portion of this job involves searching for ways in which the information system can help the company. In particular, the CIO searches for and advocates strategic uses of MIS. The goal is to use the computer in some way that attracts customers to provide an advantage over the competitors. As illustrated by Du Pont (Reality Bytes 13–3), the CIO is also responsible for organizing the MIS department to fit the needs of the company.

---

▼ Reality Bytes ▲    13–3  DuPont and Company

Cinda Hallman, vice-president of information systems at DuPont, played a key role in cutting the annual budget by $1 billion. Working with a leadership team of 15 of DuPont's IS managers, she mapped out a three-year plan to consolidate data centers, leverage procurement with buyers, and reduce the use of outside contractors. This strategy resulted in a $400 million reduction in costs.

Whenever a new technology is introduced, someone has to be responsible for deciding whether it will be worth the expense to make a change. If there is no one in this **advocacy role** who evaluates the existing systems and comparing them to new products, an organization is probably not often going to get new equipment. Even when many users are dissatisfied with an existing system, they will have a better chance of acquiring new technology if they can voice their complaints through one highly placed person. Along these lines, the CIO is responsible for long-run planning in terms of information technology.

**MIS JOBS**    A wide variety of jobs are available in MIS. Some of the jobs require a technical education such as that for programmers. Specialized positions are available in data communications and database management. On the other hand, **systems analysts** require an extensive knowledge of business problems and solutions. Some entry-level operator jobs require only minimal training. On the other end of the scale, analysts may eventually become team leaders or managers. The entire MIS function is coordinated by chief information officers.

As you might expect, salaries depend on experience, individual qualifications, industry, location, and current economic conditions. Shown in Figure 13.3, there are essentially four job tracks in MIS departments: operations, end-user support, networks, and systems development. Computer operators are hired for tasks like loading paper, loading tapes and canceling jobs that fail. Many of these tasks are being automated. Entry-level operator jobs do not require a college degree, but there is little room for advancement. End-user support consists of training users, answering questions, and installing software. Network management involves installing network hardware and software, diagnosing problems, and designing new

**FIGURE 13.3**

IS salaries. As in any field, salaries depend on experience. However, in IS, they also depend heavily on technical skills. Programmer/analysts with current skills and experience in new technologies find it easier to get jobs and obtain higher salaries. Note that there is a wide variety of jobs in IS, each requiring different types of skills.

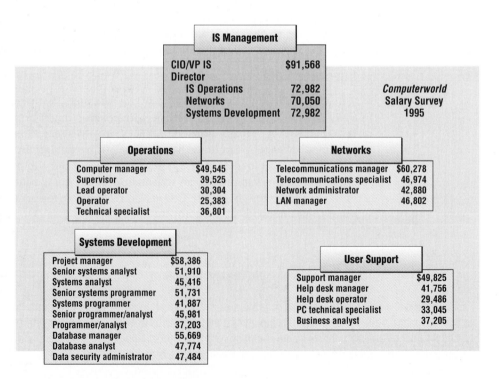

| | SYSTEMS ANALYST | | COMPUTER PROGRAMMER | | TEXTILE WORKER | |
|---|---|---|---|---|---|---|
| | SALARY | BENEFITS | SALARY | BENEFITS | PER HOUR | BENEFITS |
| United States | 46,757 | 14,443 | 36,022 | 10,578 | 8.74 | 2.87 |
| Japan | 51,938 | 12,581 | 42,316 | 9,415 | 14.12 | 9.53 |
| Germany | 49,286 | 15,821 | 40,124 | 13,951 | 13.12 | 7.38 |
| France | 44,050 | 27,113 | 26,311 | 19,210 | 9.73 | 6.76 |
| Britain | 41,808 | 9,680 | 25,529 | 5,718 | 8.23 | 2.04 |
| India | 2,248 | 3,196 | 1,769 | 2,206 | 0.41 | 0.15 |
| Mexico | 20,794 | 15,057 | 14,917 | 11,161 | 1.68 | 1.25 |
| Hong Kong | 51,277 | 12,185 | 28,211 | 6,404 | 3.33 | 0.52 |

Data in U.S. dollars. Sources: Towers Perrin, Werner International, American Textile Manufacturers' Institute. Printed in *The Economist,* July 30, 1994. Differences can be affected by other factors, such as cost of living, productivity, access to equipment, and transportation and communication costs.

networks. Systems development includes programming, systems analysis, and database administration.

Every year, *Computerworld* surveys workers in the industry and publishes average salaries. Job placement firms like Robert Half also collect data on salaries. This data can be useful to you if you are searching for a job or thinking about a career in MIS. As a business manager, the numbers will give you an indication of the costs entailed in building and maintaining information systems. Basic averages are listed in Figure 13.3 As indicated by Figure 13.4, costs vary enormously by nation, which is leading some U.S. companies to use programmers from India, Scotland, and Russia.

One way to see the changes occurring in MIS is to look at the types of skills that businesses are looking for in MIS applicants. Arnett and Litecky (*Journal of Systems Management*) analyzed MIS job ads for 10 U.S. cities. Figure 13.5 shows that of all the job ads, 40 percent were related to personal computers or local area networks. By comparison, jobs for traditional COBOL programming constituted only 19 percent of the total. Part of the difference might arise because personal computer skills are newer or it is easier to find COBOL programmers and firms might not need to resort to newspaper advertisements. Nevertheless, the increased emphasis on distributed computing is an indication of its growing importance.

| SKILL | PERCENTAGE OF ALL POSITION ADS* |
|---|---|
| PC/LAN | 40.2% |
| Relational DBMS | 28.1% |
| Unix | 22.0% |
| C | 19.6% |
| COBOL | 19.4% |

*Total is greater than 100 percent because ads can request more than one skill (Arnett and Litecky, 1994).

**CENTRALIZATION
AND
DECENTRALIZATION**

One of the most pressing questions facing businesses today is the issue of **centralization.** Interestingly, many of the discussions apply to the entire firm, not just to the information systems. Large companies that grew up as monolithic centralized corporations are considering breaking into smaller units with more decentralized control. Smaller firms, such as Directel (Reality Bytes 13–4), are also experimenting with decentralization. Even within the same industry, firms can try different approaches, as shown by three insurance companies (Reality Bytes 13–5).

Almost none of the issues of centralization and decentralization are new—politicians, economists, and organizational theorists have debated them for hundreds of years. The basic argument for centralization revolves around the need to coordinate activities and efficiencies that can be gained from large-scale operations. Proponents of decentralization argue that moving control to smaller units produces a more flexible system that can respond faster to market changes, encourage individual differences, and innovate.

As with many arguments, there are different answers for different circumstances, and it is rare that the extreme choices are best. Wise managers will attempt to gain the advantages of both approaches. With information systems, there are four basic areas that are subject to centralization or decentralization: hardware, software, data,

---

 **Reality Bytes**     **13–4**    DIRECTEL

Directel, a small catalog company in Columbus, Ohio, has moved the management information systems group from the finance and operations department, where it was originally located, to a separate division within the company. This enables the company to support its present capabilities while preparing for future changes. Liaisons have been established between the MIS department and personnel from the office, warehouse, and administrative staffs.

---

 **Reality Bytes**     **13–5**    INSURANCE COMPANY CENTRALIZATION

The organization of the information system in insurance companies can follow one of three models: centralized, decentralized, or hybrid.

- *Highly centralized.* Massachusetts Mutual has a highly centralized IS department. Measures of success are based on overall statistics for the entire organization.
- *Highly decentralized.* Unum is a highly decentralized IS department. The responsibility for the cost of managing its $80 million IS program is distributed to individual business units. Because the company has a niche-oriented business strategy, this makes the IS department more responsive to Unum's unique product lines. John

Alexander, director of IS, recognizes that there are cost savings that could be realized by performing functions across product lines. However, he feels that so much time would have to be spent gaining concurrence from the business units that ultimately it is cheaper to implement the programs in the individual departments.

- *Hybrid.* The Hartford takes a hybrid approach. IS authority is centralized with the division of IS resources across functional business units. IS spending is based on the business units' assessment of their IS needs.

## THE COST OF COMPUTERS

The cost of a computer consists of much more than hardware. The costs include even more than the software and data. In 1995, Forrester Research, Inc., estimated that large companies spend $3,830 annually to maintain each personal computer. Improved technology and standards are expected to cause costs to drop by 50 percent. The largest expense is providing one support person for every 50 personal computer users, which amounts to $1,420 per user. Breakdowns amount to about six days of lost time a year, adding up to $1,350 per personal computer.

and staffing. Determining the best way to organize information resources requires that managers understand the advantages and disadvantages for each of these areas.

## Hardware

Hardware resources are often a strong cause of changes in MIS. In particular, today's move toward decentralization is being driven by one important factor: the cost of hardware. Typical estimates of the cost of large central computers indicate that they cost around $50,000 per MIPS (million instructions per second). The cost of personal computers is somewhere around $50 per MIPS. Although it is difficult to compare the features between the two types of machines, it is hard to ignore a computer that costs a thousand times less. Virtually all of the new computing power installed in companies in the last few years has been in the form of personal computers.

### Centralization

The biggest advantage of centralized IS hardware is that it is easier to share hardware, software, and data with multiple users. Complete centralization is shown in Figure 13.6. Consider a simple example. If a company installs an expensive printer in one user's office, it will be difficult for other users to get access to the printer. On the other hand, with only one central computer, all of the hardware, software, and data will be located in one place. All users can be given equal access to these

**FIGURE 13.6**

Complete centralization. For many years, computers were expensive and there were few communication networks. Consequently, hardware, data, software, and MIS personnel were centrally located. Data was sent to the computer for processing and printed reports were distributed throughout the company. Users only dealt indirectly with MIS.

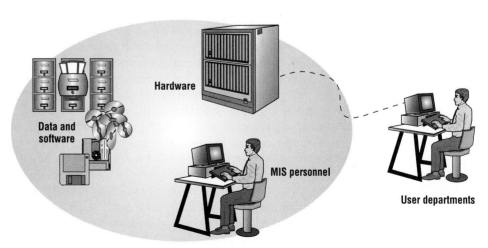

Data and software

Hardware

MIS personnel

User departments

**Reality Bytes     13–6   United States Steel: Consolidation of Computing Centers**

The United States Steel Division of USX Corporation is based in Pittsburgh, Pennsylvania. In 1990, it consolidated its two data centers into one supercenter. This combination saved $5 million and reduced its workforce by 25 percent.

facilities. By keeping all hardware, software, and personnel in one location, it is easier to avoid duplication and keep costs down, as illustrated by United States Steel (Reality Bytes 13–6).

Along the same lines, centralized hardware also makes it easier to control user access to the information system. By storing all data on one machine, it is easy to monitor all usage of the data. In a sense, all user access to data must first be approved by the MIS department. Any data alteration or transfer is much easier to control if it takes place on one machine.

There are also some cost advantages to maintaining centralized hardware. First, there is less duplication and more efficient use of the hardware. How often is a personal computer used? When a user is working on some other task, the machine usually sits idle on the desk. On the other hand, if one user stops processing jobs on a central computer, the additional resources (memory, disk space, processing time) are automatically allocated to other jobs.

Centralized purchasing can also be used to save money. It is easier to standardize equipment if it is not spread throughout the company. It is generally possible to obtain discounts from vendors by buying larger quantities. Centralized purchases also make it easier to keep track of the amount of money spent on information technology. When user departments are responsible for all IT purchases, the lack of centralized control can lead to duplication of hardware.

### Decentralization

Decentralization of hardware carries its own advantages. First, there is less chance of a total breakdown. If your computer breaks, everyone else can continue working. You might even be able to borrow someone else's machine.

With decentralization, users can obtain personalized equipment. Perhaps a financial analyst needs an extremely fast machine to process complex equations. Or maybe a marketing representative needs a portable computer to collect data from clients. An advertising specialist could use special high-resolution graphics to help design promotions. In each case, the company saves money by buying each user exactly what he or she needs, and not forcing everyone to use one standardized product.

Currently, the third advantage is the most important: price. Any slight cost advantage from using centralized computers is destroyed by the enormous price advantage of personal computers. Of course, some of today's high-performance personal computers can be used as a central computer. Even so, users need some device to access that computer, and it does not cost much to give the devices the additional capabilities of separate personal computers. As observed by the Gartner Group, notice the trend in worldwide sales of computer systems displayed in Figure 13.7. The percentage of value spent on micros (defined as machines with a cost less than $25,000) has been steadily increasing since 1980. This trend is likely to continue or accelerate.

**FIGURE 13.7**
While sales of all computers have increased, there is no question that microcomputer sales have increased faster than any other computer. Sources: Gartner Group and Dataquest.

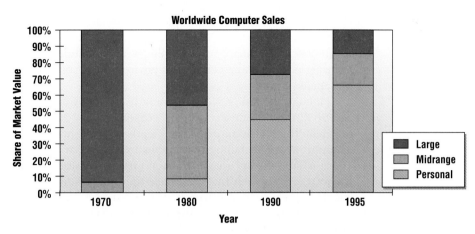

Worldwide Computer Sales

## Software and Data

Wherever there is hardware, it is also necessary to provide software. Nonetheless, it is possible to centralize some aspects of software, even though there are decentralized computers. The goal is to capture the advantages of both methods at the same time. Data files are similar to software files, but there are some additional features to consider when choosing where to store the data.

### Software Centralization

If software is standardized and purchased centrally, it is possible to negotiate lower prices from software vendors. In many cases, it is not necessary to purchase a separate copy of software for each user. Instead, a license is purchased that allows a specific number of people to use the software at one time. Because it is unlikely that every user will need the same software at the same time, this method can save a considerable amount of money. Additionally, if everyone uses the same basic software, there are fewer compatibility problems and it is easy for users to exchange data with coworkers. Similarly, upgrades, training, and assistance are much simpler if there are a limited number of packages to support. Imagine the time and effort involved if the company needs to upgrade a spreadsheet on 5,000 separate machines. Some companies have reported that by the time they managed to upgrade the entire company, an even newer version was released.

One difficulty with centralized software is that loading and running software across a network can be slower than if it is installed on each machine. Even with high-speed networks and fast file servers, users will notice that the applications load and run slower across the network. The problem is exacerbated when several users request the same application at the same time.

### Software Decentralization

Forcing users to choose identical packages can lead to major arguments between users and the MIS department. Many times users have different requirements or perhaps they simply have different preferences. If one group of users prefers the software that is different from the corporate standard, why should everyone in the company be forced to use the same tools? Cost becomes less of an issue as software prices drop. Support might be a problem, but major software packages today are similar. Data incompatibilities often can be resolved with conversion software.

To some extent, users should have the ability to customize their software to match their preferences. Today, most software packages enable users to choose colors, mouse or keyboard responsiveness, and locations to store personal files. If this software is moved to a centralized environment, you have to be careful to preserve this ability.

One complication with enabling users to choose different software is that it can be difficult to determine the configurations of each machine. If a user has a problem, the MIS support person needs to know what software is installed on the machine. When installing new hardware and software, the support team needs to know what software exists on each target machine. Managers also need to track software usage when they purchase upgrades and to verify compliance with software licenses. Several software tools exist to help the MIS department track software usage and report on the configuration of each computer. A small file is installed on each computer that reports on the software, hardware, and configuration of each machine.

### Data Centralization

The most important feature of centralized data is the ability to share it with other users. Large central computers and minicomputers were designed from the ground up to share data. They were designed to solve the problems of allowing concurrent access and to protect the integrity of the data. Similarly, they have security facilities that enable owners of the data to specify which users can and cannot have access to the data. Centralized systems also monitor access and usage of the data to prevent problems.

Another important feature of centralized data is the ease of making backups. When all databases are stored on one machine, a single operator can be hired to maintain daily backups. If data files are lost, it is easy to restore them from the backups. With the data on one machine, it is easy to ensure that all files are regularly backed up. Contrast this situation with distributed personal computers, where users are generally responsible for making their own backup copies. How often do you personally make backups? Every night?

### Data Decentralization

The strongest advantage to decentralizing data is that it gives users better access to the data. Storing data where it is used provides faster access because it minimizes transmission time. Similarly, many people find it easier to access data when it is stored on their own personal computers—they know how the files are organized. Users also have complete control of the data and can prevent anyone else from even knowing that it exists. For data that does not need to be shared, this control presents no problems. However, scattered control of data can interfere with other users when many people need access to the data. An example of complete decentralization—including data, hardware, and personnel—is displayed in Figure 13.8.

Data replication is sometimes used to provide the advantages of decentralized data—and still provide companywide access. With replication, the database is copied to multiple servers throughout the company. Users work on their local copies, which provide fast access to the data. The changes are copied to the other servers at regular intervals, so everyone has access to the latest data. This technique is often used with groupware products to distribute spreadsheets and word-processed documents.

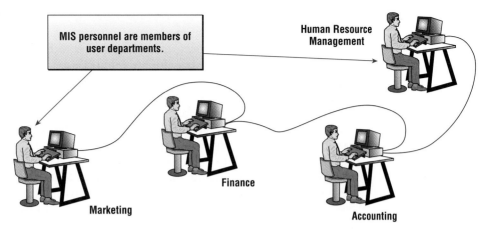

**FIGURE 13.8**
Complete decentralization. Each department maintains its own hardware, software, and data. Corporate standards and a network enable workers to utilize data across the company. MIS personnel are members of the user departments and support tasks within that department.

## Personnel

When most users think about decentralization, they often forget about the information systems personnel. Traditionally, the MIS roles have been performed by centralized MIS staffs. However, as hardware becomes more decentralized there are increasing pressures to decentralize the personnel by having them report directly to user departments. Mutual Benefit Life Insurance (Reality Bytes 13–7) used automation and decentralization to cut costs. However, many MIS personnel resist these changes.

### Centralization

Most of the advantages of a centralized MIS staff accrue to the MIS workers. For example, MIS workers often feel more comfortable with other MIS specialists. Centralization creates a group of homogeneous workers who share the same education and experiences. Moving MIS workers to user departments places them in a minority position.

One implication of this situation is seen by looking at the career path of an MIS worker. In a centralized environment, workers are typically hired as programmers. They eventually become systems analysts. Some move on to become team or project leaders, and a few can look forward to becoming managers of IS departments and perhaps a CIO someday. If programmers are moved to user departments (say human resources), what career path do they have? Maybe they could become team leader or manager of the HRM department, but they would be competing with HRM specialists for those positions.

  **Reality Bytes** **13–7  MUTUAL BENEFIT LIFE INSURANCE COMPANY**

Mutual Benefit Life Insurance Company is automating operations and reducing staff in an effort to cut costs and improve service to its customers. When the company changed the focus of its computer jobs to use microcomputers, Charles McCaig, the director of information systems, was also given responsibility to control human resources. Job realignments were made with emphasis on the best uses of people by exploiting technology.

Centralization also makes it easier for the company to provide additional training to MIS staffers. Because hardware and software changes occur constantly, MIS employees need to continually learn new tools and techniques. If they are all located in a central facility, it is easy to set up training classes and informal meetings to discuss new technologies.

Centralization also gives the firm the ability to hire MIS specialists. If there are 50 positions available, two or three can be set aside for workers specializing in areas such as database administration or local area networks. If all workers are distributed to user areas, the individual departments will be less willing to pay for specialists.

Lastly, when the entire MIS staff is centralized, it is easier to see how much MIS is costing the firm. If the MIS functions are dispersed to user departments, they may be performed on a part-time basis by various employees. It is difficult to control the costs and evaluate alternatives when you don't know how much is being spent.

### Decentralization

The primary advantage to decentralized MIS staffing is that the support is closer to the users. As a result, they receive faster responses to questions and problems. More importantly, as the MIS staffers spend more time with the users, they gain a better understanding of the problems facing the users' department. Communication improves and problems are easier to identify and correct. These are powerful advantages to the individual departments and have the potential to create much better development and use of information systems.

### The Help Desk

One issue with decentralized MIS support is that it can be expensive to place MIS personnel in each department. Many companies compromise by creating a help desk that is staffed by MIS employees who specialize in helping business managers. When business managers have questions, workers at the help desk provide answers. Typical problems involve personal computers, networks, and access to corporate databases. One advantage for business managers is that they do not have to search for answers—they simply call one number. This system can also cut costs and ensure consistent support. The knowledge of the support workers is easily shared throughout the company. It is also easier to train and evaluate the workers.

To provide more decentralized support, some companies are using their networks to provide more detailed help to business departments. They set up a special program in the background on each personal computer. When someone calls for help, the microcomputer specialist can see the user's screen and take control of the user's machine. This method simplifies communication between the user and the specialist, making it easier to solve problems and make changes immediately. Of course, it also raises several security issues, because the help desk personnel could monitor any machine at any time.

**CLIENT-SERVER SOLUTIONS**

Centralization and decentralization are also strongly affected by the cost of telecommunications. With high transmission costs and slow speeds, companies formerly had few choices in determining the layout or architecture of the information technology. Most companies relied on clusters of separate data centers. Owing to recent changes in telecommunications (declining costs, increased bandwidth, and increased reliability), firms have moved to more flexible arrangements that use technology distributed throughout the company.

**FIGURE 13.9**

Summary of benefits of centralization and decentralization. There are advantages to both centralization and decentralization of the MIS resources. The ultimate objective is to design an MIS organization to benefit from as many of the advantages as possible by combining both centralization and decentralization.

| | CENTRALIZATION | DECENTRALIZATION |
|---|---|---|
| Hardware | Share data. <br> Share expensive hardware. <br> Control purchases. <br> Control usage. <br> Less duplication. <br> Efficient use of resources. | Less chance of breakdown. <br> Users get personalized machines. <br> Microcomputers are cheaper. |
| Software | Compatibility. <br> Bulk buying discounts. <br> Easier training. <br> Ease of maintenance. | Different user preferences. <br> Easier access. <br> Customization. |
| Data | Easy backup. <br> Easier to share. <br> Less duplication. <br> Security control & monitoring. | Not all data needs to be shared. <br> Easier and faster access. <br> Control and politics. |
| Personnel | Similar worker backgrounds. <br> Easier training. <br> Straightforward career path. <br> Specialized staff. <br> Easier to see and control costs. | Faster response to users. <br> More time with users. <br> Better understanding and communication. <br> Different career path. |

Figure 13.9 summarizes the benefits of centralization and decentralization. However, in practice, no company is completely centralized or completely decentralized. Each firm must find a point that balances the benefits and costs of the each method. In order to investigate this process, it helps to look at the extreme situations first. Figure 13.6 illustrates how many MIS were organized in the days of central computers. The hardware, software, data and personnel were all situated in one location. Data was typically collected manually from the business, reports were printed at the computer, and copies were distributed to the users. Data sharing existed, but only among applications on the central computer.

## ▼ BUSINESS TRENDS: DECENTRALIZATION ◣

One of the key trends in business in the 1990s has been the move toward decentralized management. The objective is to empower the managers who are close to the customers, enabling them to provide better service. However, if the overall management becomes more decentralized, features of the information system must also be decentralized. Serious problems arise when the information system does not match the organizational structure.

In MIS, the move toward decentralization is complicated by the fact that the information system must also support centralized goals. For instance, consolidated reports are produced for accounting, employee records, and environmental summaries. As a result, managers have to search for creative solutions that provide decentralized control yet produce the needed centralized information.

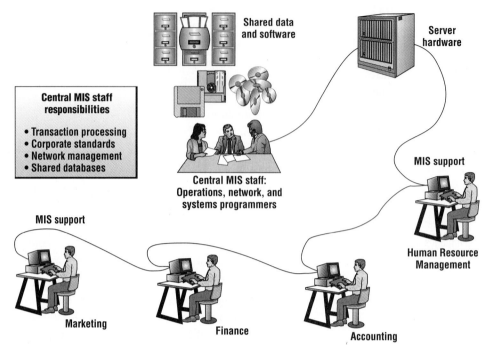

Many small businesses began with a different MIS organization. They were unable to afford large central computers, so they relied on personal computers. Although they rarely have the money to pay for MIS workers, the MIS functions still have to be performed. The roles are typically filled on a part-time basis by other employees. Today, many of these businesses have installed LANs that provide some capabilities to share data. However, data and software are often stored on many different computers. Figure 13.8 illustrates the situation of a highly decentralized information system.

Although these two extremes have their uses, an intermediate position can do a better job of providing advantages offered by both methods. There are many possibilities: Consider the various arrangements of hardware, software, data, and personnel. There are also many ways to decentralize or centralize each component. One common intermediate method is known as the client-server approach.

The **client-server model** separates all of the components into two categories: servers or clients. The functions associated with the server tend to be centralized, whereas the client components and tasks are dispersed among the users. The terms client and server deliberately imply a relationship between the two types of machines. Servers tend to be larger, faster computers with operating systems designed for multiuser access and control. Clients are typically microcomputers that are set up for use by one person at a time. Figure 13.10 shows a version of a client-server approach. To see the usefulness of this approach, examine the four components: hardware, software, data, and personnel.

## Hardware

The arrangement of the hardware is the most distinctive feature of the client-server model. It consists of one or more computers designated as servers. Managers and workers use client microcomputers that are attached to the servers through a local

**Reality Bytes**    **13-8**    **BLACK AND DECKER INFORMATION FLOW**

In the early 1980s Black and Decker faced increased pressure from Japanese, Korean, and Chinese competitors in the production of small electric tools and appliances. Although their reputation in North America for quality and durability was strong, the company was facing increased price competition from abroad. Because the tools and appliances were priced in the $15–$30 range, consumers increasingly viewed them as expendable commodities rather than products that would be retained for a long period of time.

Reduced sales caused Black and Decker to realize that the company needed to change the output of its production efforts. This change in focus was made clear when Nolan Archibald became chairman and announced his "cut-and-build" turnaround program. Black and Decker began to work with suppliers to develop a seamless flow of information from the plant floor to the store shelf.

Archibald has been successful in increasing sales and earnings; yet he feels more must be done in the information services area to improve the ability to report the strides being made in other parts of the company. According to Archibald, "We couldn't get information into the hands of managers to run things as well as we'd have liked."

Based on Archibald's directive, Sid Diamond, the new vice-president of information services, introduced three new information services approaches at Black and Decker. One of his initiatives has been the introduction of the "push-and-pull" philosophy. Development resources and computing power are pushed as close to the output, or end user, as possible by consolidating computer hardware resources. In doing so, Diamond has reduced information systems costs from 2.5 percent to 2 percent of sales.

The second approach Black and Decker has taken toward improving information services has been to purchase PRC Inc., a computer services firm. Diamond wants to team with PRC to initiate projects that interface imaging with e-mail. The goal is to enable the engineering and other groups to more quickly distribute their output throughout the company.

Third, Black and Decker is trying to offload as much processing as possible from the mainframes to personal computers. The goal is to have 800 million instructions per second (MIPS) reside on mainframe and midrange computers and 3,000 MIPS distributed on personal computers and workstations throughout the enterprise. To further assist with the transfer of computing to the end users, systems development staff have been moved to the business units.

---

area network. The servers are typically centrally located. They might be high-end microcomputers, midrange computers, or mainframes. These servers and the network are selected and maintained by the MIS staff. They provide all of the necessary concurrency and security controls to grant multiple users access to data at the same time. Black and Decker (Reality Bytes 13–8) argues that one of the purposes of the client-server approach is to push the information systems down to the users as much as possible.

The client computers are generally personal computers designed for the use of a single person. They can be purchased by the individual users or departments (decentralized), or the company might set up a bulk purchase agreement with vendors. Oftentimes companies set up help desks or information centers that help users select standard hardware, configure it and install it, and handle repairs. Users gain the advantage of decentralized choice, and the company gains the advantages of having standardized machines.

Printers and other peripherals can be located with the servers, at individual client computers, or in departmental offices. Departmental printers are relatively popular because they can be monitored by a few key employees yet still provide

| IMMEDIATE 1 TO 2 YEARS USERS | NEAR-TERM 3 TO 5 YEARS SYSTEM INTEGRATION | LONG-TERM 6 TO 10 YEARS IT EFFICIENCY |
|---|---|---|
| Better access to data | Tighter integration across the company | Resource utilization |
| Increased participation | Faster IT responses | New technology |
| Improved productivity | Business process re-engineering | Adaptive systems |

convenient access by most employees. Through the network, print jobs can be sent to any of the available printers. If one printer breaks down, the job can be routed to another printer.

## Software and Data

One of the primary goals of a client-server system is to provide the advantages of centralized control of software and data. Commercial software that is used by several users is stored on the servers. Only one copy of the software is needed, reducing the amount of storage space needed and making it easier to provide updates. The server keeps track of the number of people currently using the software to make sure it stays below the number authorized by the purchase license. The basic advantages of the client-server approach are summarized in Figure 13.11.

Data that will be shared with colleagues is also stored on the server—typically with a database management system. Transaction-processing systems can collect data and produce the traditional reports. These reports and the underlying data are stored on the server and can be accessed from the client computers.

Mail messages, data, and reports can be sent to other users. They are first stored on the server and forwarded to the users. In the case of multiple servers, the network operating system keeps track of the users and routes the messages to the appropriate servers, and then on to the user's client machine.

The network can also be used to provide data backup for each personal computer. With the appropriate software installed on each machine, data is automatically forwarded to the server for backup. As long as the personal computer is not turned off, the process is automatic and invisible to the user, making it easy to provide daily (even hourly) backup of all the data in the company.

## Personnel

The issue of centralized MIS personnel is perhaps the most complicated. With a local area network, it is easy to move hardware, software, and data around the company. It is not as easy to move people (Reality Bytes 13–9). However, the network can be used by MIS personnel to provide assistance to users. For example, say you are using a spreadsheet to build a marketing decision support model, and you encounter a problem trying to create a graph. If your system was set up for network support, you simply call the MIS help desk. An MIS applications programmer can access your computer across the network, correct the problems, and set up your graph, all without leaving the office.

The MIS department maintains responsibility for the company's transaction-processing systems, which provide the bulk of the shared data in the firm. They also set up the servers and maintain the network. In order to ensure that everyone has access, the MIS department defines the databases and sets standards for hardware and software.

Some MIS personnel can be moved to user departments. In addition to helping with day-to-day problems, they can work on prototyping more complex applications.

Reality Bytes  13–9 CLIENT-SERVER CAVEATS

As summarized by the Gartner Group, an information systems consulting firm, some early results on the client-server approach indicate some problems:

- Because support for central large computers typically continues, hardware costs rise (because personal computers cost more than simple terminals).

- System management problems of client-server networks are enormous. The management tools that exist for large centralized computers do not yet exist for PC-based distributed networks.
- The change to a client-server approach requires new staff skills, and the approach is likely to be resisted.

With their knowledge of the user requirements, they can serve as liaisons to the SDLC development team when major projects are designed.

## Peer-to-Peer Systems

Client-server systems are not the only way to achieve a balance between centralization and decentralization. In fact, in many ways, they represent an intermediate step toward a more distributed system. Remember that firms still need to support the legacy systems that were created through the 1970s and 1980s. These centralized systems were designed to capture and process the transaction data of the companies. It is not easy to throw them away, especially since it takes time to build replacement systems. As a result, it is easiest to leave the central data on these machines and make them servers. The clients are typically personal computers that are connected to the servers over a local area network. Because most personal computers were designed for single users, they tend to work best when dealing with one user at a time. They are acceptable as clients, but early personal computers were limited in their ability to deal with many users simultaneously. As personal computer hardware, operating systems, and software improve, it becomes easier to connect personal computers directly to each other instead of relying on centralized servers. In a peer-to-peer system, any computer can be a server, a client, or both. This type of system allows greater flexibility in terms of storing and accessing data. However, many problems need to be resolved, such as security controls. Additionally, by scattering data across hundreds or thousands of computers, it becomes difficult for users to find the data they need. The basic issues in decentralizing control and distributing information system resources are summarized in Figure 13.12.

**OBJECT ORIENTATION**

The use of decentralized or distributed computing has two conflicting effects on the use of objects. First, it increases the need for an object-oriented approach. However, it is much harder to manage objects in a distributed environment.

Almost all of the object-oriented development has occurred in the workstation worlds of Unix and personal computers. To date, little object development takes place in centralized transaction processing. There are two reasons for the use of objects on workstations. First, the development of graphical user interfaces is greatly simplified by using an object approach. Second, it is easier for users to find and manipulate data scattered throughout a distributed system if the data is stored as objects. If objects are defined consistently across the organization, once managers learn the properties and uses of an object (e.g., customer data), they will be able to access that object anywhere it is used in the company.

**FIGURE 13.12**
Decentralization summary. Some organizations are moving toward a completely distributed environment, where each subunit becomes independent but connected. Each division is responsible for its own profits and costs. Information systems are the responsibility of each department. Communication systems are used to share data with other units and to improve transaction processing.

| DECENTRALIZATION ISSUES | | |
| --- | --- | --- |
| **ORGANIZATIONAL IMPACT** | **STRENGTHS** | **WEAKNESSES** |
| Are operations interdependent? | End users gain control. | Possible short-term bias in decision making. |
| • Planning<br>• Development | Supports workgroups. | Might not be optimal use of resources for corporation. |
| • Physical resources<br>• Operations | Enables new organizational structures. | Corporatewide interests can be lost. |
| Can subunits relate solely through information and messages? | Increased organizational flexibility. | IS staff might lose cohesiveness and support. |
| Does corporate culture support decentralization? | | |

The problem with objects in a distributed environment is easily spotted by the "If" statement in the last paragraph. With one or two centralized computers, it is relatively easy to ensure that all object definitions are the same and that everyone can get access to them. As hardware, data and software get distributed throughout the company, it becomes increasingly difficult to maintain standards.

Consider a situation that will become increasingly common. A manager in one department creates a report using object tools and linking data from a variety of sources. The report works well—as long as it remains on the machine that created it. Problems arise when the report is passed electronically to managers using other machines in different locations. The objects in the report might not be accessible to the other managers, or they might be reached through different access paths. Similarly, managers in other locations probably use different software and hardware, and they might not be compatible with the objects on the report.

The industry is beginning to work on this problem, but it could be several years before the details are ironed out. One project is known as the **Common Object Request Broker Architecture (CORBA).** This model was largely developed in the Unix community to enable objects to communicate with each other across networks. In 1994, Microsoft announced that its own *Object Linking and Embedding (OLE)* protocol would eventually incorporate the CORBA standards. Eventually products based on these systems will be able to locate and share objects across networks. In the meantime, control of objects is a management issue that will require company standards, careful supervision, and considerable training and support.

## CHANGE AND OUTSOURCING

In theory, the client-server approach offers many advantages, and many organizations have adopted or are considering variations of it. The only problem is that it can be difficult to change a company from its existing organization to a client-server approach. Existing systems that keep the company running were built and modified throughout decades. Most of the hardware and software were designed to be stand-alone systems; they were not intended to function as servers that exchange data with client computers. Firms have millions of dollars and millions of lines of code tied up in these systems. They cannot simply be discarded.

Second, even if a company decides to go with a client-server approach, there are still hundreds of alternatives. Some of these decisions are risky, because some hardware and software choices will not survive the vagaries of the marketplace. The transition from existing systems to a new approach is complicated by the need to maintain the current system while exploring risky alternatives. Consider the problem from the standpoint of a firm in 1995. The existing mainframe systems are getting older, and the company needs to consider transferring to a client-server approach. The catch is that it is too hard to choose the appropriate technology. The best guess is that within a couple of years, the technology will stabilize, but what should the company do in the meantime? Purchasing new mainframes is an expensive proposition—especially if they will be discarded when the company switches to a client-server system. Yet, the firm is unwilling to risk a transfer to immature technology.

Partly because of changes, partly because of the distributed nature of the client-server approach, many firms have seen an increase in support costs when they convert to a client-server approach. In some cases, the support costs exceed the cost savings from using lower-cost machines. On the other hand, the increased costs often arise because of increased computer usage by managers.

One approach to this dilemma that some companies have taken is known as **outsourcing.** With outsourcing, the company sells its central computers and transfers portions of the MIS staff to a service company such as Electronic Data Systems (EDS) or ISSC, the IBM subsidiary. The company signs an agreement to use the services of the outsourcing firm for a fixed number of years. Depending on the agreement, the outsourcing firm can be responsible for anything from machine operation and maintenance, to development of new systems, to telecommunication services. The leading outsourcing companies are listed in Figure 13.13.

Electronic Data Systems (EDS) is a large outsourcing firm. They provide a wide variety of MIA services to clients in many industries. Their Web site (http://www.eds.com) provides an overview of their services and operations as well as information on career opportunities.

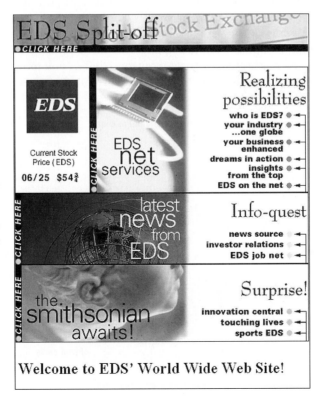

| COMPANY | ESTIMATED 1991 ANNUAL OUTSOURCING REVENUE (MILLIONS) | COMPANY | ESTIMATED 1995 ANNUAL OUTSOURCING REVENUE (MILLIONS) |
|---|---|---|---|
| EDS | $1,200 | EDS | $10,050* |
| Computer Sciences | 400 | IBM | 3,900 |
| IBM | 350 | Computer Sciences | 3,370* |
| Fiserv | 225 | Andersen Consulting | 3,450* |
| Systematics | 225 | Perot Systems | 500 |
| Perot Systems | 160 | Affiliated Computer | 425 |
| Affiliated Computer Systems | 155 | Fiserv | 375 |
| Shared Medical Systems | 140 | Systematics | 350 |
| First Financial Management | 80 | | |
| Others | 600 | Others | 1,600 |
| Total | $5,526 | Total | $21,320 |

Nell Margolis, "Outsourcing Boom Over? You Ain't Seen Nothin'," *Computerworld,* January 13, 1992. Data from Merrill Lynch & Co. Estimated outsourcing revenue.

*Actual 1994 sales, from Kevin Helliker and Louise Lee, "EDS Now Has to Prove the Value of Independence," *The Wall Street Journal,* August 8, 1995.

Outsourcing has primarily been used to decrease operating costs or to get the initial money from the sale of the machines. In particular, the company gains an infusion of cash through the sale of the machines. Some firms have stated that they chose outsourcing because it enables them to focus on their core business and not worry about maintaining computers and designing systems. Figure 13.14 illustrates conditions under which it is useful to consider outsourcing. As you move away from the center of the diagram, outsourcing becomes less useful. The most common uses of out-

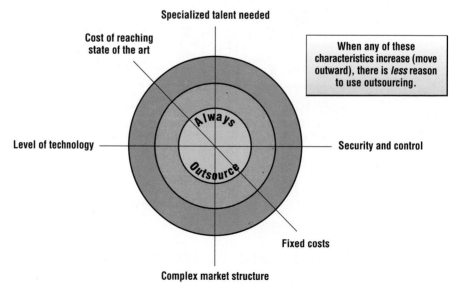

sourcing are for straightforward applications of technology, including personal computer installation and servicing, maintenance of legacy systems, and routine application development.

On the other hand, situations that are unique or require advanced uses of information technology are best handled internally. For example, complex markets that benefit from strategic applications require the knowledge and experience of employees who work for the company. Likewise, situations that require tight security are easier to control if they remain in-house. Another reason to avoid outsourcing is when the outsourcing firm will have to pay the same costs that you face—because they will charge for an additional profit margin, the final cost can be higher. Examples include applications with high fixed costs or that require high-levels of expensive state-of-the-art equipment or specialized MIS talent.

Competitive pressures are also leading many managers to consider outsourcing their information systems. As technology continues to change, it becomes increasingly difficult for general business managers to keep up with the technology. Each change brings requests for new hardware and software, and the need to reevaluate the use of technology within the firm. Changing technology also requires continual retraining of the information systems staff. At the same time, middle-level management positions are being cut, and managers are asked to take on more tasks. In these circumstances, Figure 13.15 shows that it is easy to see why companies decide to transfer IS management to an expert through outsourcing.

There are drawbacks to outsourcing. First, there might be a slight increase in security risk because the MIS employees have weaker ties to the original company. On the other hand, outsourcing providers are likely to have stricter security provisions than an average firm does. A bigger question is the issue of who is responsible for identifying solutions and new uses of technology for the firm. If MIS workers are employed by an external firm, will it be their job to search for new applications? If not, who will?

**FIGURE 13.15**

Outsourcing forces. Firms are being pushed to cut margins. Many are focusing on their core competencies, leaving little time for wrestling with technology. At the same time, as the large outsourcing firms gain customers, their efficiency improves and they can offer more services and more specialists at better rates.

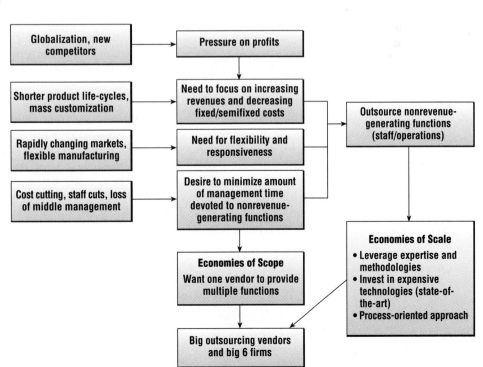

## SUMMARY

One of the more difficult problems facing MIS departments and company executives is the conflict between centralization and decentralization. These issues were involved in many decisions during the last 5 to 10 years, from politics to corporate organizations, to the way in which MIS fits into the organization. Although there is no single answer that applies to all situations, there has been a distinct trend during the last few years toward decentralization. In larger organizations, this propensity has been hampered by the highly centralized organizations and computer systems that have been in place for the last 30 years.

Decentralization of MIS can occur in any of four areas: hardware, software, data, and MIS personnel. Economics is driving the decentralization of hardware because of tremendous price performance values in personal computers. The challenge is to accommodate this decentralization without losing the benefits of centralization. One option would be a completely decentralized information system, where each user and department is responsible for its own information. A more flexible option being pursued by many companies is an intermediate strategy involving the client-server approach. The goal of this approach is to capture the benefits of both decentralization and centralization.

Benefits to centralized hardware include economies of scale, easier maintenance, and better prices through negotiation strength. The primary benefit of decentralized hardware is the ability of users to acquire and control exactly the components they need. There are also substantial price advantages to personal computers at this point in time.

Benefits of centralized software management include easier upgrades and control over purchases and access, along with compatibility across the organization. The primary benefit to decentralization is increased flexibility and control gained by users. Similarly, the main benefit to centralized data is increased control over access, providing sched-

uled backups, and making it easier to share data. On the other hand, decentralization gives users a stronger ownership role, easier access (to their own data), and personal control.

Benefits to centralized MIS personnel accrue mainly to the MIS staff: It is easier to support training, MIS workers offer support to each other, and it is easier to hire specialists. The primary advantage of decentralization is better communication with users and faster response to user problems.

Some companies find it profitable to sell portions of their computer facilities to outside organizations such as IBM and EDS, in a transaction known as outsourcing. Outsourcing provides a short-term increase in cash for the company, access to computer specialists, and the ability to concentrate on the company's primary business. However, firms requiring specialized talent, high security and control, high levels of recent technology, new state-of-the-art information technology, or complex market structures should avoid outsourcing and retain in-house management of the information function.

> **A MANAGER'S VIEW**
>
> Identifying problems, making decisions, and building systems are not enough to keep a company running. Most organizations have an MIS department to build, maintain and evaluate information technology. As a general business manager, you need to be aware of the various ways of organizing MIS resources: hardware, software, data, and personnel. The MIS resources must support the needs and organization of the business. When the MIS organization differs from the business system, there will be conflicts. You need to watch for these problems and adjust the organization or MIS as needed. The client-server approach is often used to attain the benefits of centralization and decentralization at the same time.

## KEY WORDS

advocacy role, 618
centralization, 620
client-server model, 628
Common Object Request Broker
   Architecture (CORBA), 632

data integrity, 617
data administrator (DA), 617
database administrator (DBA), 617
decentralization, 609

outsourcing, 633
standards, 615
systems analyst, 618

## REVIEW QUESTIONS

1. What are the basic roles of the MIS department?
2. What types of MIS jobs are available?
3. What are the advantages of centralizing computer hardware? What are the advantages of decentralization?
4. What are the advantages of centralizing computer software? What are the advantages of decentralization?
5. What are the advantages of centralizing computer data? What are the advantages of decentralization?
6. What are the advantages of centralizing computer personnel? What are the advantages of decentralization?
7. How does the client server approach combine benefits of centralization and decentralization in terms of hardware, software, and personnel?
8. What are the potential advantages of outsourcing computer facilities? What are the drawbacks?

## EXERCISES

1. Interview computer users and managers in a local firm (or your university) and determine the degree of decentralization in their information system organization. Talk to several users and see whether their perceptions agree. Are they receiving all of the advantages of centralization and decentralization? If not, how could the system be modified to gain these benefits without significantly increasing the drawbacks? Be sure to analyze hardware, software, data, and personnel.
2. Interview some computer science majors to determine what types of jobs they are looking for. Also, interview some business-oriented MIS majors and compare the responses. Ask the subjects whether they would prefer working for a centralized IS department or within a decentralized department. What reasons do they give? Do they have a minor in a business discipline? (Team approach: Each team member should interview a different person, then combine the results and look for similarities and differences.)
3. Using salary surveys and local advertisements, find typical salaries for various MIS jobs in your area.
4. Make a list of symptoms you would expect to see in a company that has centralized databases and MIS personnel; but has decentralized its departments, and users have just bought hundreds of new personal computers in the last three years.

5. Make a list of symptoms you expect to see in a company that is "too decentralized." That is, company users are free to choose any hardware and software, and databases are maintained by each department. Data is shared through reports that are printed in each department and forwarded to other departments on paper. There is no central MIS staff and no CIO. Treat it as a company that started small using personal computers and grew but did not come up with a centralized information system approach.

 **Rolling Thunder Database**

1. Describe the organization of the existing information system. What changes would enable the system to run better? If the company doubles in size in three years, what organizational changes do you recommend for the information system?
2. How should the company handle typical information system tasks like data backup, creating employee accounts, maintaining hardware, selecting new hardware and software, and so on?
3. Would you recommend a centralized or decentralized approach to information systems at the Rolling Thunder Bicycle company? Who is currently in charge of the major components? What problems can we anticipate if we continue with the existing structure?

## ADDITIONAL READING

"12 Years Of High-Tech History on CD-ROM," *Newsbytes*, August 18, 1995.[Visa]

Ambrosio, Johanna. "Global Softwhere?" *Computerworld*, August 2, 1993, p. 74. [Black and Decker]

Arnett, Kirk P. and C.R. Litecky. "Career Path Development for the Most Wanted Skills in the MIS Job Market," *Journal of Systems Management*, February 1994, pp. 6–10.

"Banking on the Net," *Communications Week*, August 14, 1995. [Visa]

Betts, Mitch. "Banc One Writes Down Mainframe Role," *Computerworld*, April 16, 1990, p. 10. [Banc One]

Betts, Mitch. "FILES with Faces," *Computerworld*, December 14, 1992, p. 93. [Banc One]

Betts, Mitch. "Shadow Spending Haunts IS," *Computerworld*, July 26, 1993, p. 1. [Gillette]

Booker, Ellis. "Data Dowsed in Midwest Floods," *Computerworld*, July 19, 1993, p. 6. [Meredith]

"Client/Server Finds Homes for Organs in a Heartbeat," *InfoWorld*, August 28, 1995. [American Management Systems]

"Consulting Firm Sees Flexibility as Good Business," *Telecommuting Review: the Gordon Report*, March 1995. [American Management Systems]

"Contracts Prepare DOD for Life After CHCS Deployment," *Government Computer News*, April 17, 1995. [American Management Systems]

Doyle, T.C. "It's No Longer Too Early to Get In," *VARbusiness*, May 1, 1995, pp. 54–60.

Feuche, Michael. "Data Center Automation," *Computerworld*, August 27, 1990, p. 59. [US Steel]

Fitzgerald, Michael. "Clear VISTAs for Continental Bank," *Computerworld*, August 13, 1990, p. 51. [Continental Bank]

Fitzgerald, Michael. "The Challenge of Change," *Computerworld*, August 13, 1990, p. 57. [Continental Bank]

Halper, Mark. "EDS Losing Out on Client/Server," *Computerworld*, February 28, 1994. p. 30. [Meredith]

Halper, Mark. "Outsourcers: Saviors or Charlatans?" *Computerworld*, August 2, 1993, p. 63. [US Steel]

Helliker, Kevin and Louise Lee. "EDS Now Has to Prove the Value of Independence," *The Wall Street Journal*, August 8, 1995, pp. B1, B4. [EDS and outsourcing]

Hoffman, Thomas. "No More Middleman," *Computerworld*, July 17, 1995, p. 55.

"How Much Is That Ant in the Window?" *The Economist*, July 30, 1994, p. 63. [Labor costs for programmers and analysts in various nations]

"Instant Credit," *PC Week*, July 3, 1995, p. E3.

"Internet Security Advances, But Skepticism Remains: Money Transactions Increasing as Communication Grows More Secure," *Computer Shopper*, December 1995. [Visa]

"Internet Security: Open Market Offers Software That Makes the Internet Safer for Business; Protection Measures Free to Both Web Businesses & Users," *EDGE: Work-Group Computing Report*, October 16, 1995, p. 17. [Banc One]

King, Julia. "Banking: A Few Glimmers Amid the Gloom," *Computerworld*, November 4, 1991, p. 105. [Continental Bank]

LaPlante, Alice. "Growth Is Relative," *Computerworld*, September 14, 1992, p. 18. [Massachusetts Mutual, Unum and The Hartford]

"Managing Unruly Desktop Computers Costs Businesses Dearly," *The Wall Street Journal*, February 16, 1995, p. A1. [Maintenance costs of personal computers]

"Marketing on the 'Net: You Can Gain an Edge with an Internet Home Page," *VARbusiness*, July 1995. [American Management Systems]

"More on Visa/MasterCard Internet Security Deal," *Newsbytes*, July 26, 1995. [Visa]

"'Net Security Agreement Disintegrates," *Communications Week*, October 2, 1995. [Visa]

"Pursuing Web Security, MasterCard, Visa Team; VeriSign Intros Digital ID," *Electronic Marketplace Report*, July 4, 1995. [Visa]

Redditt, Kay Lewis and Thomas M. Lodahl. "Leaving the IS Mothership," *CIO Magazine*, October 1988. [Decentralization advantages and disadvantages, emphasizing MIS staffing]

Rifkin, Glenn. "A Bank that Systems Helped Build," *Computerworld*, February 20, 1989, p. 70. [Banc One]

"SAP Boosts Customer Support; Expands Service, Products to Capitalize On Its Popularity, *InfoWorld*, October 2, 1995. [Black and Decker]

Stern, Gabriella and Clare Ansberry. "Its Acquisition Binge Has Loaded Banc One with Maze of Branches," *The Wall Street Journal*, April 11, 1994, pp. A1, A6. [Banc One]

Sullivan-Trainor, Michael. "The Push for Proof of Information Systems Payoff, *Computerworld*, April 3, 1989, p. 55. [Mutual Benefit Life Insurance]

"Visa & Worlds Inc. to Offer 3-D Internet Banking," *Newsbytes*, August 10, 1995. [Visa]

"Visa, MasterCard Plan Internet Venture," *Los Angeles Times*, June 23, 1995. [Visa]

"Visa, MasterCard Spar Over 'Net Payment," *Communications Week*, October 9, 1995. [Visa]

"Warehouse Wake-Up Call," *InfoWorld*, November 20, 1995. [American Management Systems]

Wells, Rob. "Journey of a Credit Card Purchase in Digital Age," *The Tennessean*, December 19, 1993, p. 4E. [Visa]

"Where's AI Hiding?" *AI Expert*, April 1995. [Black and Decker]

"Who Wins Home Banking?" *Forbes*, August 14, 1995. [Visa]

Wilder, Clinton. "Be All You Can Be: Maslow as IS Guidepost," *Computerworld*, February 19, 1990, p. 63. [Mutual Benefit Life Insurance]

Wingfield, Nick. "Digital IDs to Help Secure Internet: Certifying Authorities to Promote Electronic Commerce," *InfoWorld*, October 23, 1995, p. 12. [Banc One]

## CASES  *Financial Institutions*

Banking and finance firms have long been leaders in the use of information technology. Workers rely on them for word processing, communication and e-mail. IT usage for transaction processing is indicated in the bookkeeping and database categories. Decision support usage shows up in analysis and spreadsheets.

SOURCE: Computer Use in the United States, U.S. Bureau of the Census.

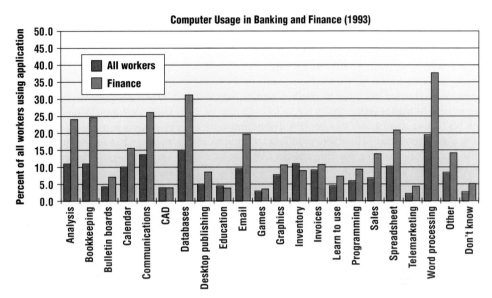

**Computer Usage in Banking and Finance (1993)**

Percent of all workers using application

Legend: ■ All workers  ■ Finance

Categories: Analysis, Bookkeeping, Bulletin boards, Calendar, Communications, CAD, Databases, Desktop publishing, Education, Email, Games, Graphics, Inventory, Invoices, Learn to use, Programming, Sales, Spreadsheet, Telemarketing, Word processing, Other, Don't know

Major changes have taken place in financial institutions in the last ten years. The next ten promise to be just as exciting. The banking environment in the United States is unique among major countries—in the early 1990s, there were about 14,000 financial institutions in the United States. Most countries have 1 or 2 (almost always less than 20) national banks.

From the 1930s to the 1970s, banking in the United States was a relatively staid industry. Virtually all aspects of banking were controlled by the government, including pricing (interest rates), markets, and advertising. Federal and state laws combined to categorize most banks into narrow markets. The huge inflation rates of the early 1970s were a major shock to the banking system. Savings and loans that relied on fixed-rate housing loans were severely pressed; most did not survive. Banks were pressured by the flow of money out of the banking system into government bonds and stocks—assisted by the innovative accounts created by Merrill Lynch & Co. As a result of these pressures, Congress changed the banking laws—removing restrictions and encouraging financial institutions to compete. As savings and loans failed in one region, bank examiners began to encourage out-of-state banks to buy up the remaining assets.

Recognizing the changes occurring in the industry, and the ever-expanding boundaries of cities, state governments began to tolerate banks that operated across multiple states. In 1994, the federal government repealed the laws that prevented banks from fully competing across the nation. As the final barriers are removed, the "consolidation" of the banking industry will accelerate.

Along with regulatory changes, technology is providing even more impetus for change. Today, almost all banks support ATMs and electronic payments through the *Automated Clearing House (ACH)*. There are various levels of telephone service, ranging from account summaries to transfers between accounts to automatic loan approvals. More aggressive banks are expanding the use of debit cards with local merchants. On the commercial side, bankers are increasingly asking for access to borrower's computer records, to monitor sales and cash flow on a continuous basis.

As the business world changes, banks will have to change and adapt. Although most payments are still made by paper (checks), there is increasing demand for automated payments (EDI) and electronic access to accounts. As commercial use of the Internet expands, banks need to devise an electronic payment system that is relatively secure.

Remember that "money" today is largely an abstract concept. For the most part, funds are merely an accounting entry at your bank. Money exists only as an entry on the bank's computer. The primary purpose of a bank is to provide services to its customers. Technology and attention to accuracy and needs of the customer will continue to drive the industry.

# CASE *Continental Bank*

Three years after the bankruptcy, when Thomas Theobald was appointed as the chief executive officer of Continental Bank in 1987, he needed to move quickly to redefine its direction. He did so by announcing a bold new strategy to concentrate in the investment banking business. This led to the sale of the company's consumer business as well as some marginal commercial businesses.

To be successful, any change this drastic requires a comprehensive plan. Theobald identified technology as the vehicle to accomplish this change. An extremely sophisticated technology would be necessary to identify a select group of customers and provide a superior level of service to them. To accomplish his goals, Theobald hired John Gigerich. Gigerich went immediately to work to introduce the Vision for Information Systems Technology Architecture or Vista. Extensive interviews were conducted and systems development set in place. Based upon this information, a methodology was established to use a systems life-cycle process to redirect Continental to more focused customer strategy.

## Continental Bank's Information Technology Methodology

The goal of Continental Bank's methodology was to shift the image of the bank from one that competes for both retail and commercial customers to one that concentrates solely on corporations, institutional investors, and high-income individuals. To accomplish this goal, the information system was shifted from a mainframe-based, transaction-processing organization to one in which information would primarily be maintained through workstations. *Relationship banking* would link customer companies to individual bankers who would be responsible for keeping the customer satisfied with Continental's service. By knowing each customer, the relationship banker could identify and sell added services. Operated correctly, this would identify new products for each client, thereby thwarting the competition.

## Continental Bank's Vista Program

In 1989 Continental Bank launched an ambitious information system to parallel its redirected business strategy. After declaring bankruptcy in 1987 and being placed under the protection of the Federal Deposit Insurance Corporation, the bank refocused its energies on a new group of customers: the middle-sized corporation located in the Midwest. Because of its previous difficulties, the bank knew that it had to be better than its competition in its chosen market segment.

To accomplish its goals, Continental launched a major initiative to restructure its information system.

John Gigerich, chief information officer, chose the IBM OS/2 workstation platform and the AS/400 because of its multitasking capabilities. Through the use of processes running in simultaneous windows, the corporate banker could now access all of a client's accounts at once and even move funds between accounts as changes occur in his or her portfolio or the market.

Vista is built on the database concept. Every bank must maintain databases of the various account types that are available to its customers. Continental is the first bank to access these databases not just to respond to customer's questions but actually to redirect the funds in the most profitable way.

Gigerich views manager and user input as crucial to the success of the Vista project. Continental constructed a methodology and questionnaires to ensure that the business units would have sufficient input into programming the system. Only after all of the managers had the opportunity to describe their work flow processes were the program specifications allowed to be developed.

Begun in the spring of 1989, Continental Bank's Vista program provides a good example of the systems life-cycle process. Vista was much more than a piecemeal update of the bank's systems and technology. It was an effort to totally re-evaluate the ways in which information is being obtained, distributed, and used at the bank.

Vista's goals were to identify the bank's strategic information requirements, provide an overall statement of the bank's technology directions for planning and budgeting, and develop a stronger appreciation among business units of how automation can open competitive opportunities. Vista called for a great deal of time to be spent analyzing the current operations of the bank, charting the problems and opportunities, and making specific recommendations regarding future directions.

## From Transaction Processing to Decision Making

The computer is no longer a tool that just speeds up clerical and other transactions. It is now a valuable decision-making device that organizes information to better present business decisions, make options clearer, and improve the management process. As a result of this power, increased security must be put in place to protect the bank's information and assets.

At Continental, computers have established themselves as essential in the transaction-processing area. They have long been used to process checks and balance loan and other service agreements. Today, however, computers are assisting bank employees to make decisions as well as balance accounts.

Undoubtedly, you are most familiar with the bank's use of transaction processing. As a manager, you may be involved with the daily updating of customer accounts with new information that includes deposits, loans, and cleared checks. Or you may be responsible for monitoring a customer's line of credit or account balance. The interactive nature of transaction processing enables you to enter data directly into the database. This makes sure that the customer's records are maintained on an accurate and up-to-date basis. As the bank changes to provide even more services to its customers, you will be able to do more than just rapidly enter data. Eventually, you will be called on to assist customers by recommending the best investment combination based upon each customer's unique personality and return objectives.

Moving from transaction processing to management information systems presents important opportunities—and challenges. Rather than being constrained to simply inputting data, users can now query the system to pinpoint important variables. For example, it is now possible for you to list all of a customer's checks above a certain amount or written after a given date. A sudden jump in the number of withdrawals by an older customer can raise a red flag that an appointed individual from the bank should examine the account and contact the individual.

The introduction of the OS/2 operating system on the PS/2 enabled MIS to take an important step forward. Multitasking, its most important new function, enables a number of functions and databases to be run at the same time on the same computer. Previously, a customer's accounts had to be individually accessed and manually compared. Now, with multitasking, all of a customer's accounts can be examined and compared at the same time. At one time, information in the loan department was kept separate from that in business development. This meant that a customer's current loan information could not easily be compared to his or her available credit or savings account. Equally important, the customer had to deal with a lending officer who was different from the individual on the savings side of the bank. For the customer this meant more telephone calls to individuals who were only tangentially familiar with his or her account.

With the advent of management information systems and multitasking capability on the PS/2, a customer's loan, line of credit, and savings accounts can now be examined by the same bank officer using OS/2 on the same computer. This innovation enabled that officer to focus his or her expertise on understanding the specific business needs of a customer rather than becoming immersed in the specific nuances of the loan program.

Consolidating the breadth of a customer's accounts at the Bank resulted in a number of advantages. It also presented important challenges to the information access area. Improved customer orientation means that an officer who was previously limited to a single data set must now become proficient in accessing a broader range of data. Equally important, he or she is required to have access to all of the information for a particular customer in a number of different databases.

Two major factors contribute to the success of a customer-focused, multiaccount system. First is the amount of information that is accessed. The more information that can be used to make a decision, the better that decision will be. The second is the ability of the system to organize and present data in a succinct and understandable manner. The clearer the summary information is and the more it matches the needs of the decision maker, the better and more accurate will be the ultimate decision.

### Security and Risks

Ironically, the two greatest strengths of a multiaccount system can also be its greatest weaknesses. Consolidating large amounts of information from diverse sections of the corporation leads to the increased risk of unauthorized access or the loss of integrity due to improper maintenance. Bringing information together from many different segments of the organization and from many different computer systems presents a number of access problems. Levels of protection are required as the user accesses and retrieves information from multiple local area networks and mainframes. Integrity must be maintained as data is transferred across systems and combined.

The ITS Technology Risk Management Planning Group is addressing the information access issues of management information systems. Defining technology needs, layering passwords, establishing policies and procedures, and developing training programs all contribute to a risk-managed information environment. Business resumption plans will ensure that these directions will continue, even after an emergency.

### Outsourcing

By 1990, Continental Bank decided to outsource its MIS department. The bank contracted with IBM to handle all of its data processing needs. Several factors were considered in the decision:

- Once the decision is made, it is difficult to reverse.
- The information systems operation should be examined to determine whether the consolidation of data centers, standardization of equipment, centralization of the purchase of supplies,

ancellation of the maintenance agreements, nd the elimination of unused support will fect significant cost savings.

osts will not be absorbed from outsourcing. An ternal group must be established to manage he vendor and interfaces between internal and outsourced operations.

Tangible and intangible benefits and hidden costs must be analyzed. Outsourcing makes it possible for an institution to remove certain assets from its balance sheet. This enables closer compliance with the Financial Institutions Reform, Recovery, and Enforcement Act.

• Determination must be made whether the sharing of resources with other users can effect economies of scale.

The negatives of outsourcing consisted of:

• Outsourcing can reflect a loss of confidence by senior management in the information systems function. Assurances must be given to control costs and the ability to satisfy user departments.

• Business knowledge must be integrated into the decision to ensure that concentration will not focus more on technology than on the solutions.

• Efforts must be extended to demonstrate the availability of open and honest communications between the users and senior management to prevent a deterioration of trust.

• Outsourcing can lead to an overemphasis on technology to the extent that time and attention are diverted from the development of business solutions for the company involved.

• An application-development methodology and operational standards need to be put in place to ensure that the implementation of the outsourcing agreement occurs in a manner that can be audited.

• Compensation and benefit packages must be examined to ensure that the best technicians in the information systems group will be maintained.

Companies likely to benefit from outsourcing were:

• Financially stressed companies seeking outsourcing help.
• Companies with the need for the assumption of financial responsibility for all equipment and vendor agreements.
• Companies unable to cover long-term debt.
• Companies that are willing to trade off long-term strategic advantage for short-term cost savings.

### Sellout

By 1993, Continental Bank was purchased by BankAmerica of San Francisco. The IS development project was canceled and all accounts were shifted to the BankAmerica system. Most of the employees and operations were transferred to BankAmerica, and the main offices continued to be staffed under the new management. The outsourcing contract was dissolved and operations were transferred to BankAmerica staff.

### QUESTIONS

1. What problems did Continental Bank face?
2. What strategic decisions did Continental managers make to solve their problems?
3. What role was played by the information system?
4. Were the plan and implementation scheme reasonable?
5. Why did Continental Bank outsource the IS department? What did the bank gain or lose?
6. What went wrong? Why did Continental sell out to BankAmerica? Did the outsourcing decision play a role?
7. Write an alternative plan that might have saved Continental Bank.

### CASE *Banc One*

In 1960, Banc One was the eight hundreth largest bank in the United States. In 1990, it was the eighth largest. The Columbus, Ohio, institution consists of 81 separate banks, encompassing 1,333 branches. The majority of growth has occurred in the last 10 years, when Banc One purchased 112 banks, quintupling its employment in the process. Overall, the process has been profitable for Banc One, showing a net income of $1.14 billion in 1993 ($2.98 a share). The bank has established a 25-year string of profits as of 1994. However, 1994 profits were negatively affected by a $36 billion contract in interest-rate derivatives, when Banc One got caught (along with several other large firms) betting that interest rates would continue to fall.

### Local Control

The primary focus of Banc One is retail banking, emphasizing consumer deposits and loans, with some loans to small businesses. The bankers have attempted to keep their status as a "folksy" community bank, spreading their name through word-of-mouth and support for local, rural communities.

Over the years, Banc One maintained its profitability through keeping costs down. However, controlling 81 banks, each with its own board of directors and chief executive officer, has tended to raise costs lately. The Texas branches alone have 24 separate presidents with their own boards and administrative staffs.

Instead of consolidating management on purchasing new "partners," Banc One has kept the local managements and encouraged them to cut their own costs. The local managers are free to set salaries, hire employees, and market their banking services. This approach is helpful in encouraging other banks to sell to Banc One.

Overall, the system of localized control has worked well, although the purchase of MCorp in Texas in 1990 required some additional persuasion. The new bank was encouraged to drop its two chefs (the French chef earned $80,000, the Tex-Mex chef $65,000). Still, expanding operations in Texas has led to increased costs.

One consequence of the localized management approach is that most of the banks still have separate data processing facilities and run different software. However, in 1993, Banc One did consolidate 13 credit card centers down to four.

For more recent acquisitions, Banc One created a SWAT team of 150 experts. The acquired banks can "purchase" IS services from Banc One Services Corp. at 90 percent of the market price. The division consists of 1,650 employees, with an annual budget of $293 million. Federal regulations give an acquiring bank a weekend to convert a new bank onto the acquirer's systems. The SWAT team works straight through to install hardware, load software, and convert data to the new system.

### Changing Customer Needs

While operating costs are important to Banc One, a larger problem is looming in the area of customer service. Industrywide, total household assets held by banks peaked in 1980. Since then, consumers have spread assets into stocks and bonds—largely through mutual fund investments. This change in the industry makes it difficult to grow using the traditional retail banking philosophies. Other banks have countered by forming alliances with brokerage firms. In 1993, Mellon Bank Corp. of Pittsburgh purchased Boston Co. and Dreyfus Corp. NationsBank allied with Dean Witter, Discover & Co., to provide more investment services to its customers. Banc One CEO John McCoy admits that the bank needs to change: "We really want to be a one-stop shopping center. We need to change how we take care of the retail customer."

In the early 1990s, the bank began installing small investment counseling centers in its banks. Instead of associating with established brokerage houses, the bank prefers to train its own employees. John Fisher, a retired senior vice-president, notes that "Banc One's feeling is customer satisfaction will be greater if we learn to do this ourselves."

### Technology

For the past decade or more, Banc One has had a firm grasp of the strategic uses of technology. It was through a partnership with Banc One that Merrill Lynch & Co. was able to create its innovative Cash Management Account. The bank was also a pioneer in the implementation of ATMs, credit card processing, and electronic funds transfers among brokerage houses. Commenting on the bank's successes with strategic planning and information technology, John McCoy notes that "We think of ourselves as being in three businesses: (1) running banks, (2) buying and improving banks, and (3) taking advantage of technology in running our banks."

Rather than focus on a single solution or technology, McCoy observes that the bank has always been open to trying new ideas:

> We've always tried to be doers. We are willing to allow people to try a lot of things. If there are 100 possibilities of things to do and you do three of them, you're probably not going to be very successful. But if there are 100 ideas and you do 80 of them, you're likely to have a pretty high success rate. There may be only 20 that are successful, but you'll hit 18 of them.

As part of this strategy, McCoy is careful to keep an eye on each attempt, cutting off the ones that do not look promising: "All we ask is that whatever is tried be measured, so that if something isn't working out the way it's supposed to, we can cut it out. We've had more than our share of disasters or dumb things we've tried. But you have to have those to have successful ones."

### Downsizing

In 1990, Banc One began a five-year plan to move to personal computers. Terry Lowder, vice-president of the IS unit, commented that "For a given application [now on the mainframe], we expect to offload 50 percent to 90 percent of the processing cycles to another platform."

The decision was largely driven by the increased demand for applications by the managers. The mainframes were not keeping up with the demands. The long-run plan is to use the central mainframes as database servers, handling high-volume transaction processing. The big systems will continue to be used for batch routines such as sending bills and printing statements.

The personal computers will eventually be connected via local area networks, probably through intermediate midsize computers. The workstations will collect data from the appropriate mainframe databases and deliver it to the workstation applications. Lowder expects to see productivity benefits from improved response times and declining costs as the workstations pick up the processing demand.

### Re-engineering a New Approach

In 1992, Banc One was awarded the first *Computerworld* "excellence in re-engineering" award. With the help of EDS, Banc One built a new bank management system that consolidates all account information by customer. Although the concept of providing complete information seems logical to anyone who has studied banks or MIS, it is a recent innovation in the banking industry. In 1992 (see table), Banc One was also ranked number one among MIS peers and consultants in a *Computerworld Premier 100* survey.

In the early days of banks, most customers rarely had more than one or two types of accounts: a checking account and a savings or loan account. With paper-based systems, transactions were posted on the individual accounts—by account number. In modern banking relationships, customers can easily have dozens of separate accounts, including checking, money market, certificates of deposit (each handled separately), house loans, auto loans, second mortgages, and investments. Traditional bank systems treat each account separately and store data by the accounts. For a manager to get complete information on one customer, data has to be retrieved from each separate account.

In 1986, Banc One began development of the Strategic Banking System, which uses central mainframes to store all transaction data for customers. The system, with 10 million lines of code, cost more than $100 million to build. It was initially installed for use at 23 branches and will be extended to the others. Although the primary customer data is stored on central mainframes, managers at the individual branches rely on networks of personal computers to examine

and analyze the data. They can use the system to retrieve a complete customer profile. It can also generate data for all customers in a given household, or of all customers who work for a certain employer. The system is designed to hold 12,000 pieces of data about each customer.

Benefits of the new system include improved accuracy, because the database has integrity rules that automatically check the data. Equally importantly, the new system provides data to managers to improve cross-selling products, which have increased by 15 percent to 20 percent. Donald McWhorter, president of Banc One, emphasizes the strategic importance of the system when he notes that "We want a system that gives us everything there is to know about that customer and incidentally does handle the transaction . . . We decided we're in the information business, not the transaction business."

The system enables bank representatives to spend more time analyzing patterns and helping customers, instead of entering data and tracking down information. Mitchell Zoellner, director of implementation and support, comments that "The more you know about the customers, the more you can target them for a specific type of product pertinent to their financial picture or lifestyle."

EDS assigned 200 employees to the project and interviewed 300 Banc One employees to determine the design parameters needed for the new system. Approximately 80 percent of the development costs were borne by EDS—in exchange for the right to resell the application to other banks. As a result of cross-agreements, the first release was installed by Norwest Corp. in Minneapolis in 1989. The system faced typical development problems and ran about two years behind schedule. Although this arrangement seems to negate the strategic advantages of the system, Linda Antrim, a Banc One marketing manager, claims that "No bank will ever know the software as well as we do. More importantly, the real competitive advantage is not the software but the way that bankers exploit that tool."

| SELECTED IT STATISTICS FOR BANC ONE | 1993 | 1992 | 1991 | 1990 | 1989 | 1988 |
|---|---|---|---|---|---|---|
| IT Rank | 1 | 11 | 40 | 9 | 5 | 24 |
| IS Budget $ | 387 M | 293 M | 258 M | 235 M | 170 M | 150 M |
| IS Budget % | 6.5 | 7.15 | 7.36 | 7.00 | 6.22 | 8.00 |
| Processor value $ | 93 M | 79 M | 52 M | 40 M | 60 M | 50 M |
| Processor value % | 1.5 | 1.93 | 1.48 | 1.00 | 2.19 | 3.00 |
| PCs per employee | 1 | 1 | 1.04 | 0.58 | 0.58 | 0.2 |
| %IS Budget—training | 4 | 4.0 | 4.7 | 5.0 | 5.0 | 5.0 |
| %IS Budget—staff | 27.9 | 30.7 | 31.0 | 30.0 | 36.0 | 30.0 |

SOURCE: *Computerworld Premier 100*

## QUESTIONS

1. What management problems are created when organizations use acquisitions to grow as rapidly as Banc One? In the case of banks, how does MIS complicate acquisitions?
2. When a team moves in to convert a bank to the Banc One system, what problems are the members likely to encounter? What MIS tools and systems will they need? Devise an initial plan that the team can follow when converting a new bank. Be sure to include contingency plans.
3. What aspects of the Banc One MIS are centralized? Which ones are decentralized? How has the MIS department changed over time?
4. What are the benefits and drawbacks to Banc One's overall management scheme of local management?
5. As interstate banking increases, what features will consumers want? How will MIS be involved in providing these features? How should the bank and MIS be organized to best deliver these features?
6. What benefits are provided by the new integrated customer information system at Banc One? Why did banks wait until 1990 to begin implementing this type of system?
7. What are the advantages and drawbacks of Banc One's decision to have EDS build the new integrated system? Will Banc One be able to gain competitive advantages with this plan?
8. How is Banc One different from Continental Bank? How do these differences affect the style and design of the information system?

## CASE  *Visa International*

Statistics in 1994 indicate that Visa International is the leading credit card agency, holding approximately 50 percent of the market. MasterCard holds 27 percent, and American Express, 20 percent. Almost 300 million Visa credit cards have been issued.

As an organization, Visa is owned by its member banks. It exists solely to promote and process the credit cards issued by those banks. Processing the cards entails making electronic connections worldwide among 20,000 financial institutions and 10 million merchants in 247 countries.

VisaNet is the network that links the various computers. The system uses 9 million miles of fiber optic cable. Worldwide, in 1993 the network handled 11,000 transactions per minute. By 1998, the annual volume on the network should reach $1 trillion. The network has been growing at a rate of about 14 percent a year. There is plenty of opportunity for growth. Charles Russell, Visa International president in 1993, noted that in 1992, only 15 percent of all retail sales were made by credit card.

Despite the large volume, Visa tries to process each transaction within 20 seconds. If the process takes any longer, the customer and merchant get upset. Consider the steps involved in processing a single transaction:

1. Your credit card is swiped through a terminal that reads the card number and expiration date from the magnetic stripe on the back.
2. The terminal calls one of the 1,400 small Visa computers that are connected to the primary network.
3. The Visa computer contacts your bank's computer and requests authorization. The computer checks several conditions:
   *a.* It checks a central file to see whether your card was reported stolen.
   *b.* It verifies that your purchase would not put you over your credit limit.
   *c.* It examines your buying pattern to see whether the purchase is unusual—which might represent a stolen card.
4. If all conditions are met, the computer sends a notice back through the system to the original merchant.
5. If your bank's computer is not available or is too busy, the Visa computer will automatically authorize the sale, as long as it falls below a certain level.
6. During the next couple of days, your bank's computer will forward payment to the merchant's bank. Although the payment could be made immediately, banks typically negotiate a delay of 3½ days, which used to be half the average float time for payments made by check.

## QUESTIONS

1. What aspects of the Visa processing are centralized? Which ones are decentralized?
2. What operational problems are encountered by Visa? How does the IS design help minimize these problems?
3. As more transactions, including ATMs and debit cards, are routed on the network, what threats and vulnerabilities exist?

## CASE *American Management Systems*

Founded in 1970, American Management Systems is a $225 million, 2,800-employee computer consulting company. It has completed more than 500 integration projects for 40 of the 50 largest U.S. banks, 5 of the 10 largest insurance companies, more than 90 federal agencies, and more than 50 of the Fortune 100 companies.

AMS focuses its efforts on its traditional vertical and horizontal customers. This is primarily for projects in the $1- to 10-million range for the world's largest companies. Its vertical niche is the sale of computer integration services to the financial community, state, local, and federal government, and higher education. About 75 to 80 percent of its computer integration revenues come from commercial contracts.

AMS also stresses horizontal areas of expertise. These include its own CASE tool, a life-cycle productivity system, document imaging, expert systems, cooperative processing, and integration involving IBM's System Application Architecture. AMS sees its role in these areas as both education and integration. It feels that it often must educate its customers regarding the possibilities before it can sell them on the advantages that the new technology provides.

AMS is focused on a customer base that reinforces its vertical and horizontal expertise. It is also trying to develop new business in specifically targeted areas, specifically the telecommunications consulting market. To gain credibility in this market, AMS has developed a TieLine family of billing, administrative, and client-interface software for telecommunications companies. After a company buys this standardized platform, the TieLine system can be customized to address the individual needs of each customer.

AMS has used the TieLine system to win a spot as subcontractor to IBM for a contract with Centel Corporation to install its new automated billing system. AMS has also formed a joint venture with Bell Atlantic Corporation to make Bell Atlantic Systems Integration Corporation. BASIC applies technology to improving telephone company billing systems. Based on these linkages, AMS is trying to win other telecommunications projects with other companies around the world.

### QUESTIONS

1. What advantages does AMS receive from focusing its energies on its traditional vertical and horizontal customer base?
2. Why is AMS extending beyond its traditional technology consulting markets?
3. From your reading of the case, what percentage of AMS's efforts is placed in the new venture? Why does AMS concentrate so much of its resources in its traditional markets?
4. How will the new system improve the reliability and maintainability of AMS's business?
5. What arguments would you use to convince your boss to choose AMS to develop a new system you need?

## CASE *Meredith Corporation*

Meredith Corporation in Des Moines, Iowa, publishes magazines such as the *Ladies Home Journal* and *Better Homes and Gardens*. In spite of the fact that it employed 221 information systems workers, its fulfillment center—the area that updates subscriptions—was falling further and further behind in technology. Most of the systems were homegrown PL/1 applications that were 15 to 20 years old. Almost all of the resources were committed to maintenance. When subscribers called to update their subscriptions, the telephone operators had to switch to separate computer systems for each publication.

Terry Marksberry, vice-president of the fulfillment division, was hired to radically update the technology skills of the information services area. To expedite the process, he outsourced all of the operations to EDS. EDS agreed to hire all 221 workers and move their skills from mainframe to become client-server-based.

EDS promised to rebuild the skill base of the staff as well as manage the day-to-day operations. Only a small corporate staff was left to plan the future. Marksberry concentrated on planning for the future. He developed a client-server architecture based on Sun/Unix servers networked to Windows-based personal computers running Informix and Sybase relational database software.

According to Marksberry, the most difficult part has been the transition for the former information systems staff: "It's just as hard for EDS to do this retraining as it would have been for us. IS has traditionally been a focal point of change within the corporation. Lately, it's ridiculous. People have to throw away almost everything they know about technology and start over. That's extraordinarily difficult."

### QUESTIONS

1. Why did Meredith choose to outsource its computer operations? What did the corporation gain? What are the potential costs?
2. In five years, if Meredith chooses to drop the outsourcing contract, what problems might the corporation encounter?
3. If you were CEO of Meredith Corporation, what could you have done to avoid (or minimize) the problems encountered by the fulfillment division?

## DISCUSSION ISSUE

### *Outsourcing*

*Outsourcing* is a new term for an old concept in MIS. Rather than own the computers and hire a large MIS staff, a company may choose to let a specialized firm run the entire computer operations. Two of the largest firms specializing in running computer operations for other companies are EDS and IBM. For a fee, these companies will provide the main computers, communication links, software, and even software development and maintenance. The current debate over outsourcing began when Kodak decided to let IBM run its main computer operations. Most likely part of the decision was caused by the expenses incurred by Kodak when they lost a patent infringement suit to Polaroid, but there are many other issues involved and several other large firms have chosen not to run their own computer operations. Listen to Paul (VP of finance) and Corie (VP of MIS) of the fictional MegaPark Corporation, as they try to decide whether their firm should switch to outsourcing:

**Paul:** Look at the charts. If we sell off our old computers and transfer the MIS staff to EDS, we can save $5 million a year.

**Corie:** But what about the employees? Some of them have been with us for 15 years. What if they don't want to move? What if they don't like EDS management? What about their seniority and pensions and . . .

**Paul:** Who cares? We need to cut costs. At least they'll have jobs.

**Corie:** Well, let's look at those costs. What happens when the outside firm raises its prices? We're at their mercy.

**Paul:** Wait a minute. Now you're worried about increasing costs? You've been in here every year begging for more money! At least with outsourcing we get a set price schedule. You always overspend your budget. In the last five years, your budget has increased three times as fast as the rest of the company, and you still want more.

**Corie:** Ouch. Well, what about service and responsibility to the users? As long as MIS is located here, I can deal with user problems immediately. We get together with them for lunch and play softball with the users. Because we see them all the time, we know what they want.

**Paul:** EDS didn't say anything about a softball team, but your people spend most of the time on the phone anyway. With all of the communication networks they have, what difference does it make where the MIS team is located? Besides, EDS said they have more than 200 people with experience working in our industry, plus immediate access to thousands of others. And they are hiring most of our people as well.

**Corie:** But can EDS be as responsive as we can? We've worked hard to reduce our MIS decision-making process and to involve users in all decisions. If a user department needs something, we can decide in a couple of weeks whether to commit resources to it. EDS personnel would take months to go through their decision-making process. We know the industry, and we know the people who work here.

**Paul:** One of our competitors, Grand Consolidated, Limited, has used outsourcing for three years. The company increased its market share by 11 percent, mostly at our expense. Maybe the outsourcing didn't help, but it surely didn't hurt!

**Corie:** All right. What about security? I'll bet you forgot that one. When all of our customer data is stored on our machines in our building, I know how to protect it. Now you're going to put all of this important information in someone else's computer. Even worse, EDS already handles one of our competitors. How do we know Grand Consolidated won't get access to our information?

**Paul:** Get real, Corie. We sell pet rocks. We don't have any secret data.

**Corie:** Of course we do. What about our employee evaluations? What about our plans for future products? What about our sales data concerning which products do well with which types of customers? What about our evaluations of our competitors? Of course, there's also our evaluations of environmental pollution legislation and which legislators might be sympathetic to our positions. Then, there's . . .

**Paul:** All right, all right. I get the idea. We'll have to get EDS to establish some encryption system or something to protect our data. EDS must be doing something like that for the other companies it supports. I'm sure there're ways to protect our data.

**Corie:** What about our new ad campaign? That is all computer generated. Same thing with the designs for next year's models. Which reminds me—we had to get some special equipment for those projects. How will we do that in the future?

Paul: EDS says it can get us any equipment we need. And the managers there said with their company's size they can get it at better prices. Plus, we don't have to buy the hardware, so we don't get stuck with expensive, obsolete equipment. EDS always has the newest hardware.

Corie: How about strategic uses of MIS? I've been thinking about some ways we can tie in to our suppliers' computers and improve our quality control. And I've been talking with some of our distributors so that we can get access to their computers and get better information on sales. Who is going to think up these ideas? Who will nail down the details? Who . . .

Paul: You will, Corie. You're not going anywhere. Besides, since you no longer have to worry about the day-to-day details, you'll have more time to work on these big projects. You've raised some good points, and I really want to ask EDS about its security provisions and get

our lawyers to look things over, but I've made up my mind.

Corie: I'm not happy about it, but it might work out. Those computers were getting old. I wanted to replace them but I figured that within five years we'd switch to PC networks, so it would be a waste of money to buy new central computers today. Maybe the outsourcing will work until we're ready to switch to PC networks. If we outsource, will we ever be able to move MIS back in house?

## QUESTIONS

1. What are the reasons a company might wish to outsource its information management?
2. What are the possible dangers in outsourcing?
3. How should a company evaluate the success or failure of its move to outsourcing?
4. If a company chooses to outsource its information management, how much of the MIS functions should the company keep in-house?
5. If you were an employee of an MIS department and your company decided to outsource, what would be your considerations in deciding whether to take a job with the company hired to do the information management?

# CHAPTER 14

# Information Management and Society

Harvard Pilgrim Health Care. As one of the largest HMOs in the U.S., HPHC understands the necessity of computerizing medical and billing records. Yet, the issue of huge databases of individual medical records raises several concerns about privacy.

## HARVARD PILGRIM HEALTH CARE

Harvard Pilgrim Health Care (HPHC), located in Burlington, Massachusetts, was founded in 1969 by the dean of the Harvard Medical School. With 520,000 members in 1992, it controls about 25 percent of the market share in New England and is the nation's sixth largest health maintenance organization (HMO). From the start, the managers knew they wanted to automate many of the traditional patient records. Their early efforts led to a hierarchical database that was essentially used in a batch mode. Physicians had to ask assistants to go to the front offices and look up basic patient information. Although many medical providers have highly automated systems to track patient billing data, HPHC was one of the first to integrate basic patient charting data. The goal was to provide better information for physicians, nurses, and assistants to make better decisions. The initial automated system held 1.5 million patient records.

Like many other medical providers, HPHC noted that paper-based records caused problems. For example, the cost of the staff for transcribing physician notes, filing, and organizing patient records was costing HPHC up to $5 per patient visit. Beyond the economic issues, important data (such as test results) was occasionally lost—resulting in retesting or re-examining patients.

In 1991, the Institute of Medicine (IOM) noted that medical information systems were "remarkably similar to the patient record of 50 years ago." IOM studies also noted that 79 percent of the time, lab results were missing from patient charts; 30 percent of the time, entire charts were unavailable during a patient visit; and 11 percent of the patient cases studied had no charts at all. Even when patient charts did exist, they tended to be overwhelming—the average size could be measured in pounds: 1.5 pounds, in fact. Yet, in 1992, of 600 HMOs surveyed, only HPHC had any form of automated patient medical record system.

**OVERVIEW**     The other chapters show how to use information systems to help perform business jobs, from personal tasks to helping the company gain a competitive edge. They also show that information technology is altering jobs and companies. As illustrated by Figure 14.1, companies do not exist in a vacuum, so technology is also affecting the "environment," or society.

How would you work if you suddenly lost all of your data or if your computers could not run? How long could a modern company survive without technology? There are a variety of threats to information and technology. Managers need to evaluate those possibilities and make contingency plans. Although technology may increase our vulnerability, it also provides tools to protect data. You need to understand how basic security systems work and how they are used to protect information.

**INTRODUCTION**     If nothing else, history has shown that technological change is inevitable. Competitive economics virtually guarantees that the search for new products, new manufacturing techniques, and other ways to gain competitive advantage will continue.

Changes in technology often affect society. It can change individuals, jobs, education, governments, and social interactions. As components of society, each group has rights and responsibilities to others, such as a "right" to **privacy** and obligations regarding ethics. As Figure 14.2 indicates, companies and governments collect data about many aspects of our lives.

Effects on individuals can be beneficial or detrimental. Often, a change in technology can help one set of individuals and harm another group. Typical problems include loss of privacy, depersonalization, and changing incentives or motivations. Advantages include lower prices, and better products and service.

The effects on jobs is hard to predict, but most observers conclude that workers will require more education and training. In the past, most authorities feel that increases in technology generally led to an increase in the number of jobs. However, many of the new jobs require higher levels of education, and the workers displaced by the technology rarely have the qualifications needed for the new jobs. Technology also has an effect on crime. As illustrated by Security Pacific (Reality Bytes 14–1), computers can be used to steal millions of dollars.

**FIGURE 14.1**
Information management and society. Every organization and individual exists in a social environment. Changes in the firm and changes in technology affect the environment. Changes in the environment can affect the firm. An understanding of these interactions will make you a better manager.

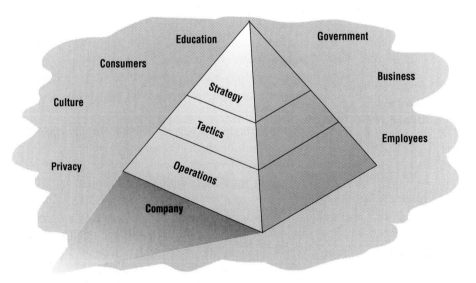

**FIGURE 14.2**
Privacy? There are many different records that are kept on our lives. Some are maintained by governmental organizations, some by private companies. Some records are protected by privacy regulations; most are not.

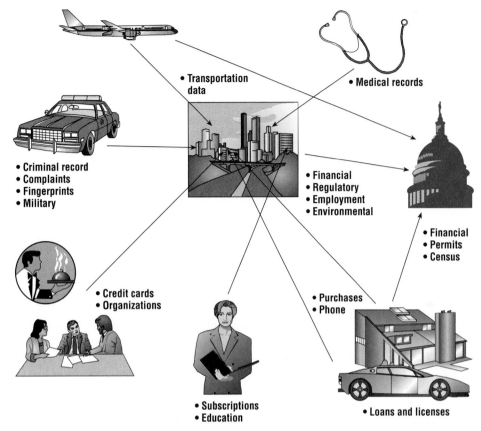

- Transportation data
- Medical records
- Criminal record
- Complaints
- Fingerprints
- Military
- Financial
- Regulatory
- Employment
- Environmental
- Financial
- Permits
- Census
- Credit cards
- Organizations
- Purchases
- Phone
- Subscriptions
- Education
- Loans and licenses

In addition to the increased demand, technology has provided new teaching methods. Although there is considerable debate over the costs and benefits of technology in education, there is usually a place for technology—even if only as a specialized technique. However, most educators remember the early claims of how

  **Reality Bytes**    **14–1  COMPUTER CRIME**

In October 1978, Security Pacific National Bank in California was robbed of more than $10 million. Bank officials were not even aware of the loss until the FBI notified them several days later. The money was stolen electronically by Stanley Mark Rifkin, who had worked as a consultant for the bank.

The electronic funds department of the bank routinely transferred between $2 billion and $4 billion dollars a day. Employees used a secret code to authorize the transfer of the money. The code was changed daily.

On October 25, 1978, Rifkin went to the wire room of the bank. He stated that he was working on an efficiency study, and the employees let him in. He found the secret code posted on a wall and wrote down the numbers. He went to a pay phone called the wire room and said he was an employee of the international department. Using the code numbers, he asked them to transfer $10.2 million to an account in New York. He later transferred the money to Switzerland. He used the money to buy diamonds from the Soviet government.

Then he brought the diamonds back to the United States and proceeded to tell several people how he had robbed the bank. One of them, his attorney, called the FBI. He was arrested in San Diego with the diamonds on November 5.

The industrial revolution in the late 18th century caused many changes to society. Before the revolution, workers were predominantly employed as craftsmen, farmers, or lesser-skilled laborers. Mechanization brought standardization and assembly lines, for which jobs were reduced to simple, repetitive tasks.

As transportation improved, people moved from farms to cities, and cities spread to suburbs. Communication systems improved and linked the populations back together. Better product distribution mechanisms changed the way products are sold. Companies (such as Sears, through its cata- logues) began to distribute products nationally instead of relying on small local stores. National and international markets developed with every change in the communication and transportation systems.

These changes were so strong that philosophers and writers began to take note of how technological changes can affect society. From the bleak pictures painted by Dickens, Marx, and Orwell, to the fantastic voyages of Verne, Heinlein, and Asimov, we can read thousands of opinions and predictions about how technology might affect the political, economic, and social environments.

television was going to revolutionize education. Fifty years later, television is beginning to play a role in education, but it is still hampered by the limited availability of two-way links.

Governments attempt to control these impacts of technology by creating laws, but laws often bring their own problems. Also, in times of rapid change, laws rarely keep up to the changes in technology. Governments are also directly affected by improved communication facilities. For example, technology makes it possible for governments to better understand the needs of the citizens and provide more avenues for communication.

Technology can alter any number of social interactions. Social groups can gain or lose power, and types or methods of criminals are altered. Additionally, society can become dependent on technology, which is not necessarily bad, but it causes problems if the technology is removed or substantially altered.

**INDIVIDUALS**    Information technology plays an important role in the lives of most individuals. Many jobs are directly involved in the collection, processing, and evaluation of data. Performance of many workers is continually monitored by computers. As consumers, virtually our entire lives are recorded and analyzed. Governments maintain massive files on all public aspects of our lives.

Although data has been collected on citizens for many years, recent improvements in technology raise greater concerns about privacy. As computer capabilities increase, it becomes possible to collect, integrate, and analyze the huge volume of data. Using publicly available data, it is possible to collect an amazing amount of data on any person.

## Privacy

Recall the use of technology to improve marketing discussed in Chapter 9. Marketing and sales can be improved by maintaining databases of consumer information and tracking sales and preferences at the customer level. Combining government statistics

**Reality Bytes** 14–2 **TRW**

TRW runs a large consumer credit agency. They maintain financial data on about 90 million people in the United States. Whenever you apply for a loan, the lending institution often purchases a credit report from TRW. The report contains records of your payments on loans, bills, and credit cards. These reports are used by almost every financial institution today. The next time you apply for credit (or look at any credit card application), check the fine print for the section that indicates you grant the company permission to examine your credit files. If you have too many late payments, credit agencies will refuse to lend you money.

Federal consumer laws give you the right to examine your files—for a fee. You also have the right to include a letter and comments in your credit file. These comments are automatically provided to anyone who retrieves your credit history. For example, if you are late in paying a bill, you can attach a short explanation. Most companies forward these explanations to TRW for inclusion in your file.

Picture the size of this database. It keeps track of monthly payments by millions of consumers. It not only records problems, it keeps track of when you pay every major loan. Credit agencies receive a listing of the average number of days late (or early) that you pay your bills. With millions of consumers, myriad transactions are posted to this database every day.

With all of these transactions, imagine how difficult it is to keep the data accurate. In 1991, TRW acciden-

tally recorded every Norwich, Vermont, homeowner as delinquent in paying property tax. The population of Norwich consists largely of doctors, lawyers, professors, and other professionals, who were understandably upset about the mistake. As a result, TRW now allows consumers to examine their credit files once a year without paying a fee. Federal law also grants consumers the right to a free copy of the report if they are denied credit based on the report.

Consumers Union (which publishes *Consumer Reports*) noted from an informal survey of their employees, that 48 percent of their credit reports had errors and 19 percent had major errors that would be sufficient to deny them credit. However, the Associated Credit Bureau (consisting of the major credit agencies) claims that less than 1 percent of the records are in error.

There are two important lessons to learn from this example. First, as a consumer, you have to be careful today concerning your credit history. All of your financial transactions are available across the nation. Second, as managers, we need to be careful to maintain the accuracy of customer data. One method is to provide customers access to their files so they can verify the accuracy and make changes or comments. All three of the major credit agencies have toll-free phone numbers: TRW, 800–232–2879; Trans Union, 800–848–4046, Equifax, 800–441–9025.

and data from market research firms with geographical data can provide a precise picture of consumer demands. As demonstrated by TRW (Reality Bytes 14–2), Ritz Carlton, and American Express (Reality Bytes 14–3), it also might represent an invasion of privacy for individuals. With databases available even to small companies, it is easy to acquire basic data on any individual. For instance, phone numbers and addresses for approximately 80 million U.S. households can be obtained for around $150 on CD-ROMs. Voter registration, motor vehicle, and property records are routinely sold by state and local governments. However, the omnibus crime bill of 1994 placed restrictions on the sales of some governmental data—especially to individuals.

It is easy to obtain lists from universities, clubs and social organizations, magazine subscriptions, and mail-order firms. Statistical data can be purchased from the U.S. government. Although most U.S. agencies are forbidden from releasing specific individual observations until 50 years after the collection date, statistical averages can be highly accurate. By combining the statistical averages with your address, your

Reality Bytes     14–3    RITZ-CARLTON

Ten years ago, it was common for guests at the Ritz-Carlton hotels to have to wait in line to check out. These delays frustrate customers and encourage them to stay at other hotels.

Now, Ritz-Carlton uses a reservation system from Covia that keeps track of expected departure times for its guests. This additional information enables the hotels to schedule more workers at key times and minimize the lines.

Candace Zimmerman, director of reservations, notes that the system is also used to maintain a list customer preferences. For example, desk clerks, waiters, and other staff members "write things down they overhear in elevators or comments dropped at check-out time." This data is available to employees at all Ritz-Carlton hotels to anticipate the needs of the guests, such as room preferences and wine choices.

Do you think hotels should collect this type of data? How can they control the accuracy?

Do you think employees might reveal this information to other people?

### AMERICAN EXPRESS

In early 1994, ABC reported on the "Day One" show that tobacco companies increased the nicotine content of cigarettes to encourage people to smoke more. ABC claims that a confidential tobacco indus-

try insider, "Deep Cough," provided the information. The largest tobacco company, Philip Morris, sued ABC for $10 billion, claiming libel. Philip Morris then attempted to find the informant. With no success on its own, Morris subpoenaed 13 companies for travel records of the two ABC producers of the show. In particular, the company wanted travel and charge records on the ABC corporate credit card for producer Walt Bogdanich and his assistant producer, Keith Summa.

Despite arguments that this search would violate "freedom of the press," a Richmond, Virginia, judge ruled against ABC. Although ABC quickly filed an appeal and gained an injunction, Philip Morris's lawyers worked faster. They immediately requested the information from American Express. American Express immediately provided the data, and then some. Philip Morris asked for data from a one-month period when they believed the informant met with the producers. American Express provided receipts for seven years of data. The company also included corporate credit card receipts for at least six other journalists who were never involved in the dispute.

American Express spokespeople says they "deeply regret these errors" but apparently violated no laws. Credit card companies are not subject to the same regulations as commercial banks and credit reporting agencies like TRW.

actual income might be estimated to within a few thousand dollars. Also, there have been problems in the past with law enforcement and government employees selling personal data to private investigators. In 1981, 18 people were accused of selling social security information, including six government employees (*Government Computer News,* January 6, 1992, p. 58).

In the United States, there are few laws or regulations regarding data held by private organizations. However, several federal laws control the use of data collected by government agencies. For example, federal agencies are restricted from sharing databases except in specific situations. In most cases the FBI cannot access the IRS data without special permits. In terms of collection and use of data by private companies, there are few restrictions. Contrary to popular belief, there is no "right to privacy" specified in federal law. However, an element of privacy is contained in a few scattered federal laws and some state laws. For example, one federal law prohibits movie rental stores (and libraries) from disclosing lists of items rented by individuals.

Because most people prefer to maintain their privacy, companies have an ethical (and sometimes legal) obligation to respect their wishes. Individuals can always ask

## INTERNATIONALIZATION: PRIVACY

Different countries have different laws regarding protection of consumer data. In particular, some European nations have stricter controls than does the United States. There has been some discussion among these nations (notably France), that firms should be forced to keep consumer data within the originating country; that way it is still subject to the local laws. If a U.S. firm transmits its local French database back to the United States, the data can no longer be controlled by French law. Although such restrictions would be difficult to enforce, companies have an ethical obligation to support the laws of the nation in which they operate.

The United Kingdom has a requirement that all databases involving personal data must be registered with the data protection agency.

The European Union in general has a restriction on trading data that states that personal data can only be transferred to another country if the nation supports "adequate" protection of personal data. According to *Network World,* the EU is considering a requirement that all businesses register databases containing personal data. Additionally, businesses would be required to obtain individuals' permission to collect or process the data. They would also have to notify the individual each time the data is reused or sold.

companies not to distribute personal data. Companies should give consumers the option of protecting personal data by building it into their databases and informing consumers whenever companies collect data.

### Employee Privacy

Computers have created other problems with respect to individual privacy. They are sometimes used to monitor employees. Computers can automatically track all of the work done by each person. Some employers post this data on public bulletin boards to encourage employees to work harder (Reality Bytes 14-4). There is software

## Reality Bytes          14–4   MONITORING WORKERS

As more and more data is stored on the computer, it becomes easier to use the computer to monitor employees. "Twenty-six million employees nationwide already have their work tracked electronically. Ten million have their work evaluated and their pay based on computer-generated statistics." Some organizations even post these statistics on bulletin boards—which is humiliating to the slower workers. For instance, data-entry clerks may have their keystroke speeds and error rates displayed. The problem is that it is easy for computers to monitor some activities. Some organizations even monitor the amount of time that employees spend in the washroom. Unfortunately, it is not as easy to know how to use the resulting statistics. The 9to5 organization recommends that any organization planning to use computer monitoring should follow certain rules:

- Notify workers of all surveillance and how it is used, and allow workers complete access to their personnel files.
- Establish grievance procedures to appeal unfairly or incorrectly collected data.
- Establish meaningful standards by collecting work statistics by workgroup rather than by individual, by barring the use of monitoring results to discipline workers, and by sampling performance periodically, rather than continuously.
- Use employees' input in establishing standards.

available for local area networks that enables managers to see exactly what every employee is doing—without the employee knowing they are being watched. Some employers read their employees' electronic mail messages. Currently, all of these activities are legal in the United States. However, they can be intimidating to employees and seem to have little managerial value.

### Protecting Your Privacy

Despite the shortage of laws, there are several actions you can take to protect your privacy and restrict access to personal data. First, it is your responsibility to notify employers and companies you deal with to not distribute your personal data. You can also ask them why they need personal data and whether it is optional or required. In particular, all federal agencies are required to explain why they need data from you and the purposes for which it will be used. You can also write to direct marketing associations and file a request that your name not be included in general mailings or unsolicited phone calls. By using variations of your name or address, such as changing your middle initial, you can keep track of which organizations are selling personal data. In some cases, you can refuse to give out personal data (such as a social security or taxpayer identification number). If a private company insists, simply stop doing business with it. In a world where firms increasingly rely on a single number for identification, it is important that you protect that number (Reality Bytes 14–5).

With most government agencies and with banks, creditors, and credit-reporting agencies, you have the ability to check any data that refers to you. You have the right to disagree with any inaccurate data and request that it be changed. You can also file letters of explanation that are reported with the original data. In 1994, Congress updated the Fair Credit Reporting Act of 1970. The new version requires credit bureaus to verify disputed information within 30 days or delete it. Businesses that provide data to the credit agencies would also be required to investigate claims of incorrect information. The bill also limits who can have access to the data stored by the credit agencies and controls how it can be used in direct marketing campaigns. In 1994, according to the Associated Press, the bureaus processed 450 million files, selling 1.5 million records a day and handling almost 2 billion pieces of data every month.

 **Reality Bytes**    14–5  SOCIAL SECURITY NUMBERS

Sometime in 1989, Jeffrey McFadden of Anderson, Indiana, obtained the social security number and birth date of William Kalin from military records. McFadden used them to get a photo ID card from the Kentucky Bureau of Motor Vehicles that contained his own photo and a false address. Using the false ID, McFadden opened a checking account and wrote more than $6,000 in bad checks.

On May 8, 1989, Indiana State Police arrested Kalin for forgery. Even though he had no prior record of

criminal activity, Kalin spent two days in jail before posting bail. Police eventually tracked down a photograph taken by a business that cashed one of the bad checks. The charges against Kalin were dropped when the photo did not match.

Kalin sued McFadden for loss of wages, legal expenses, inconvenience, humiliation, and mental anguish. In 1994 he was awarded $10,000.

**Reality Bytes**     14–6   PROBLEMS WITH SOCIAL SECURITY NUMBERS

Computer systems have the potential to cause serious problems for people. Most governmental computer systems use numbers to identify people. For instance, the federal government issues social security numbers (SSN), and states issue license numbers for drivers. The problem is that people tend to believe that these numbers are always correct—especially if they are stored in a computer. Peter Neumann provides these examples:

- After Terry Dean Rogan lost his wallet with driver's license and credit cards, someone impersonating Rogan committed two murders and two robberies, which resulted in a warrant being placed in the National Crime Information Center (NCIC) database. Rogan was arrested five times in 14 months, despite trying to get the NCIC records corrected on discovering the problem after his first arrest. (He eventually sued and won $55,000 from the Los Angeles police.)
- Martin Lee Dement spent two years in Los Angeles County jail because of botched use of

the then-new California Automated Latent Print System; a manual check of another suspect's fingerprints finally cleared him.
- A masquerader parlayed a bogus '"duplicate" driver's license for Teresa Stover into $30,000 in credit card charges. The same department of motor vehicles branch in Bailey's Crossroads, Virginia, issued thousands of bogus licenses, allegedly for only a nominal bribe.
- A front-page article by Yasmin Anwar in the *San Francisco Chronicle* (August 30, 1991) noted that felonies for stealing, selling, or otherwise misusing SSNs are on the rise in the United States. For example, someone discovered 12 people were fraudulently using her SSN; another person found that someone using her SSN had obtained 16 credit cards in her name and charged $10,000; and a third discovered that her unemployment benefits had already been collected by five other people!

## Dehumanization

Companies should also be aware that many people find technology to be dehumanizing. Several years ago Citicorp, a large bank based in New York, exhibited this **dehumanization** when it attempted to force people with small accounts to use automated teller machines instead of human tellers. The attempt lasted about a week and irritated many customers, because they preferred to deal with humans. Similarly, many people feel they should be recognized by their name, and not have to rely on a number for identification. Companies can often minimize problems by using numbers only for internal identification and rely on a combination of name and address or phone number when they deal with customers.

## Loss of Jobs

JOBS     There is no question that technology causes some workers to lose their jobs. In the 19th century, Luddites reacted to textile automation by destroying machines. Information technology is no exception. Norbert Weiner, a computer pioneer in the 1940s, predicted a major depression would result from computers replacing workers. Despite these predictions, during the last 100 years technology has increased the number of jobs and raised the standard of living of most workers. Since the introduction of computers in the 1950s, the world's economies have grown and incomes have increased. However, individual workers can lose jobs in the short run. Even in the long run, lower-skilled workers experience greater difficulty in finding new jobs.

**FIGURE 14.3**

SOURCE: U.S. Bureau of Labor Statistics (*The Economist,* February 11, 1995, p. 22). Today there is no guarantee that your job will continue to exist. Demand for specialists changes constantly. Jobs that are well-defined and require little innovation or thought can usually be performed easily by computers.

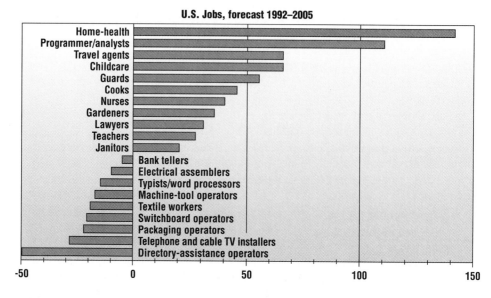

Figure 14.3 shows the changes in jobs for the next few years that are anticipated by the Bureau of Labor Statistics.

Most experts believe that technology increases the total number of jobs. New technology creates demand for designers, manufacturing firms to produce it, and people to maintain and repair it. Computer hardware also creates demands for software programmers. Additionally, technology can cause the economy to grow, creating more jobs in all sectors. There are indications that the new jobs created by technology tend to be higher paying, physically safer, and less repetitive than those replaced by technology. Information technology can also reduce product prices, raising the standard of living by enabling people to buy more goods.

On the other hand, technology typically causes some workers to lose their jobs. Unfortunately, many of these displaced workers cannot be retrained for the new jobs created by the technology. Similarly, the new jobs might not pay as much money, have lower status, or might be less desirable work environments.

Governments have created several programs to provide benefits of money, retraining, and relocation to workers who lose their jobs. As managers, we need to understand the effects on employees when we introduce new technology. Many corporations provide ongoing educational payments and training classes to help workers improve their skills. Others provide out-placement services to help unemployed workers in their job search.

As individuals, we need to remember that changing technology can eliminate virtually any job. One of the best plans is to continue your education and learn new skills. Remember that technology continually changes. Some of the skills you learn today will be obsolete in a couple of years. We must all continually learn new skills and adapt to changes. Applying these skills in your current job adds experience that will help you find a new job. It also benefits your current employer and might help you keep your job or stay with the company if new technology makes your current job obsolete.

The concept of continually acquiring new skills sounds straightforward. However, many times you will have to choose among multiple technologies. Guessing wrong can lead you to invest time and money in a technology or skill that fades away. As you become more involved with technology, you will increasingly find it necessary to "predict" the future. Identifying trends and deciphering fact from rumor are important skills to learn.

## Physical Disabilities

Technology offers many possibilities to provide jobs for workers with physical disabilities. In fact, in 1992, the U.S. Congress passed the Americans with Disabilities Act, stating that companies are not allowed to discriminate against disabled employees. Common uses of technology include the use of scanners and speech synthesizers for visually impaired workers; voice input devices and graphics displays for workers who cannot use keyboards; and telecommuting for those who work from home.

## Telecommuting

The fact that about 70 percent of U.S. jobs are service-based jobs raises interesting possibilities for workers. Many services like accounting, legal advice, education, insurance, investments, data analysis, computer programming, and consulting are not tied to a physical location. As a service provider, you could be located anywhere and still perform your job—as long as you have the appropriate telecommunications system. As communication improves to include video links and faster document transfer, even more jobs can be performed from remote locations.

Some companies are experimenting with home-based workers, especially in cities like Los Angeles and New York with long commute times. Some workers like the concept; others try it for a few months and return to a traditional workplace job. There are several advantages and complications from the perspective of the worker, the firm, and society.

If a substantial number of workers choose to work from home, the firm gains two main advantages: (1) decreased costs through smaller offices, and (2) flexibility in hiring additional workers on a contract basis. Some people have predicted that companies might also gain from increased use of part-time workers, thus avoiding the cost of insurance and other benefits. The greatest complication to the firm is evaluating and managing employees. Without daily personal contact, including conversations, it is harder to spot problems and make informal suggestions as corrections.

Telecommuting sounds appealing to those who spend hours in traffic commuting to work. Most knowledge workers can easily purchase the computer equipment needed to work at home. It is more difficult to provide the self-motivation and organization to be an effective worker. On the other hand, there are fewer interruptions from coworkers.

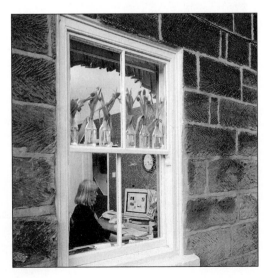

To the worker, the most obvious benefit lies in reducing the time and expense of commuting to work. The biggest drawback lies in the loss of personal contact and daily ritual of a typical work schedule. Depending on your home environment, there can be substantially more interruptions and distractions at home. It is also more difficult to "get away" from your job. Working from home on a flexible schedule requires strong motivation and organization. Before you choose to work at home, talk to someone with experience.

A few firms have experimented with intermediate telecommuting options. As indicated in Figure 14.4, the firm leases smaller offices in city suburbs and workers operate from these satellite offices instead of one central location. The offices are linked by high-capacity telecommunication lines. Workers keep a traditional office environment but cut their commuting costs. Businesses maintain traditional management control but do not save as much money.

A few people have speculated about the effects on society if there is a large shift to telecommuting. At this point, there is not much evidence to support any of the hypotheses, but many of them focus on negative aspects. People could become isolated. Jobs could become highly competitive and short-term. Firms could list projects on the network and workers would compete for every job. Workers would essentially become independent contractors and bear the responsibilities and costs of insurance, retirement, and other benefits, with little or no job security. They would also have no loyalty to any particular firm. Firms could become loose coalitions of workers and teams that are constantly changing, with little control over future directions. It is hard to predict what will really happen, but by understanding the negative effects, they become easier to avoid.

**FIGURE 14.4**
Telecommuting. In the simplest form of telecommuting, individual workers connect to office computers from their homes. An intermediate method has been used to avoid the problems of distractions and the cost of creating a home office. Workers report to satellite centers in their suburban neighborhood. Workers retain a structured environment but reduce their travel time.

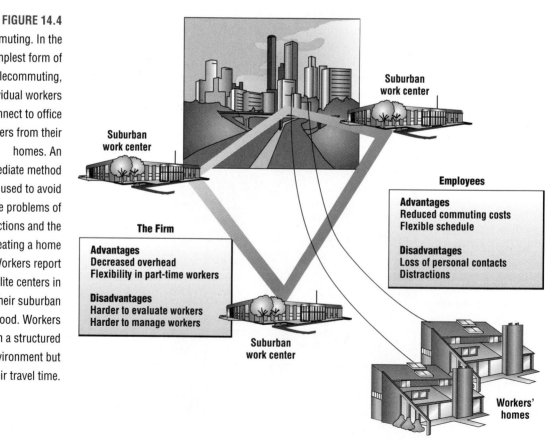

Suburban work center

Suburban work center

Suburban work center

**Employees**
**Advantages**
Reduced commuting costs
Flexible schedule

**Disadvantages**
Loss of personal contacts
Distractions

**The Firm**
**Advantages**
Decreased overhead
Flexibility in part-time workers

**Disadvantages**
Harder to evaluate workers
Harder to manage workers

Workers' homes

**EDUCATION AND TRAINING**  For hundreds of years, the principles and techniques of education have changed only slightly. As new technologies are introduced, people have often declared that the world of education would change markedly. Yet, few technologies have had a lasting impact on education. Television is a classic example. Although movies and news reports are sometimes used for teaching purposes, the role of television in formal education is minimal. However, it is used for informal education and for training—especially with the availability of videotapes for teaching specific tasks.

One of the drawbacks to video education is the lack of interaction and feedback. Multimedia tools that combine video, sound, and computer interaction represent one attempt to surmount this limitation. However, there are three basic problems with applying technology to education. First, technology is often expensive—especially compared to traditional methods. Second, it is time consuming to create lessons, and generally they are difficult to change. Third, there is little conclusive evidence that the techniques are equal to or superior to existing techniques. Especially in light of the first two problems, it is difficult to test the new technologies. In many cases, by the time prices have fallen and lessons are created, an even newer technology emerges.

Despite these obstacles, technological innovations are often used for specialized teaching purposes. For instance, interactive and multimedia computer tools can be used to provide more in-depth study for advanced students or to handle repetitive drills for those students needing extra work. Increasingly available two-way video links are used to connect teachers and students in remote locations.

New technologies are also used in business settings for retraining classes, partly to reduce the cost of hiring instructors and partly because the lessons are available to workers at any time, and can be studied at whatever speed the student desires.

**GOVERNMENT**  Governments can be slow to adopt new technologies. Typically, government agencies have limited budgets, long procurement cycles, and requirements for special allocations to acquire new technology. They tend to have smaller IS staffs, who also receive less pay than their counterparts in private business. Additionally, government projects tend to be large and involve thousands of people, which makes them expensive, harder to create, and more difficult to implement.

Nonetheless, governments are definitely affected by changes in technology. For example, many people believe that the fall of the centralized Eastern European governments was hastened by the improved communication facilities provided by computer networks and facsimile machines.

In the United States, the federal government has begun to provide information and responses to questions via bulletin board systems. It is even possible to send electronic mail to the president. Almost all federal data is available in computer form. There are computerized indexes to help you locate data produced by the government. Even municipal governments are beginning to post notices and data on computer-based bulletin boards.

Technology is also used by politicians campaigning for office. For many years government officials have used databases to track letters and comments, to solicit contributions, and to tailor speeches to specific audiences. More direct use of technology occurred during the 1992 presidential campaign, during which some of the candidates used technology to create what they called "electronic town meetings," where citizens could call in questions and watch the candidate respond over television.

Several people have mentioned the possibility of creating electronic voting systems to provide faster tallies of votes. Potential problems exist in identifying the voters and preventing them from voting more than once. However, in 1994, several states implemented limited technology-based voting systems. Using these systems, voters can now vote any time within a two-week period—instead of standing in line on one particular day.

**SOCIAL INTERACTIONS**

As any good science fiction book illustrates, advances in technology can alter society in many different ways. Sometimes the responses are hard to predict, and they often occur gradually, so it can be difficult to spot patterns. At the moment, there appear to be three patterns that are important: crime, social group power, and equal access to technology. The issue of crime is more complicated, so it is covered in its own section.

## Social Group Legitimacy

One interesting feature of technology is that it has substantially lowered communication costs, including the costs of producing and distributing information to large public groups. For example, desktop publishing systems enable groups to create professional-quality documents at low cost. Additionally, video production facilities are easily affordable by any group, and access to mass markets is provided free through *public-access channels* on cable television. Computer bulletin board systems are accessible to anyone with a computer and a modem for a small monthly fee. These technologies enable small groups to reach a wider audience for minimal cost.

There is nothing wrong with the concept of **social group legitimacy**—in fact it is loosely protected by the "freedom of speech" provisions in the U.S. Constitution. Just remember that even "free" speech has many restrictions—including those related to defamation (Reality Bytes 14–7). The only catch is that with growing professionalism of small-group productions it becomes harder to distinguish fact from fiction, and it is harder for the public to tell the difference between mainstream, professional commentary and radical extremists. For example, do you believe stories that are printed in *The New York Times?* What about stories printed in supermarket tabloids that sport titles like: "Space Alien Eats Movie Star?" What if a radical group printed its own daily newspaper with slightly less radical stories? How would you know whether articles were true?

The same issues can be applied to television broadcasts. With his "War of the Worlds" broadcast, Orson Welles shocked many listeners because they had come to accept radio broadcasts as fact. With existing technology, it is possible to create realistic-looking fictional broadcasts. It is not even necessary to resort to tricks such as hidden explosive charges. It is possible to create computer-generated images that exceed the quality of broadcast signals, so they appear to be realistic. Advertisers have made heavy use of these techniques. Every time you watch a commercial, you should remind yourself that a portion of what you are seeing is probably a computer-generated image. Now, imagine what would happen if an extremist organization used this same technology to create newscasts with altered pictures.

## Access to Technology

Picture a world in which financial instruments are traded electronically, goods are purchased through computer-television systems, libraries are converted to electronic media, and businesses require suppliers to exchange data over computer links. Large portions of the United States and Europe are getting closer to this scenario every day. Now, what happens to the individuals in poorer nations who can barely afford to eat,

**Reality Bytes** ◣ **14–7** ᴇʟᴇᴄᴛʀᴏɴɪᴄ Sᴛᴏᴄᴋ Mᴀɴɪᴘᴜʟᴀᴛɪᴏɴ

The issue of deciphering fact from fiction can be especially difficult when you rely on purely electronic communications like the Internet. In any society, there are people who rely on guile, subterfuge, and greed to take money from other citizens. Most people learn to recognize techniques and signs, especially nonverbal communication cues, when they are approached by strangers asking for money. In the new world of international electronic communications, these cues are missing, and it can be hard to identify good advice from bad. Electronic communications provide hustlers with the ability to reach millions of people with a single message and to circumvent the personal safeguards built up in most people.

The big three commercial networks (CompuServe, Prodigy, and America Online Inc), observe that there are almost 2.5 million investors using their services. Investor bulletin boards, on which users post tips and discuss ideas, are one of the most popular services.

Some people have tried to take advantage of this huge population. A common technique is to buy shares in a penny stock, then invent a claim about some hot new product, breakthrough, or invention and post a message on the bulletin boards. If even a few people respond to the claim, the security's price skyrockets, the swindler sells out fast, and the new investors lose. A case in point is Wye Resources, Inc., a penny stock company from Thunder Bay, Ontario. In January 1994, based on glowing claims described on the Prodigy service, its stock price jumped from $0.30 to $1.85 a share. The Ontario Securities Commission closed down trading for alleged violations of security regulations.

Another interesting case arose in August 1993. Epitope, Inc, a Beaverton, Oregon, company filed a federal suit against Karl Kipke, a Kansas City broker. Kipke allegedly sent out damaging messages about Epitope on the Prodigy bulletin board. He was sued for defamation that drove the stock price down. Mr. Kipke denied knowing that the information was incorrect. He eventually settled out of court.

much less invest in personal and national information systems? If the means of production are based on technology and certain groups do not have access, the gap between the **haves and have-nots** will widen. In addition to the suffering caused by this inequity, social theory indicates that large diversity can lead to unstable societies and violence.

Some companies have worked to give others access to technology. For example, WordPerfect encourages businesses to donate old copies of the word-processing software to high schools when they upgrade to a newer version. On the international front, businesses can donate older personal computers to organizations for shipment to other countries. After 3 to 5 years, the technology is often out of date for the United States, but even old technology is better than nothing in some countries. For many years (during the *cold war*), the United States strictly controlled the export of technology. In 1995, the United States finally relaxed most of the restrictions but retained limitations on the export of some software and **encryption** products. It is wise to check with a lawyer or customs agents before attempting to export current technology.

## E-mail Freedom

Some organizations have observed an interesting feature when they first replace paper mail with electronic mail systems. The first people to use the technology are generally younger, more likely to take risks, and bolder than the typical employee. If the top management levels accept and respond to electronic messages, they are likely to get a different perspective on the organization, its problems and potential solutions. E-mail systems provide a means for employees (and sometimes customers) at the lower levels to bypass the hierarchy of middle management. A few directed comments and words of encouragement can enhance this effect, which is useful if managers are searching for new approaches to solving problems.

## Liability and Control of Data

Virtually all of our legal structures and interpretations were created before the advent of a computerized society. Although federal and state governments have passed a few laws specifically to address problems with computer interaction, most legal systems still rely on laws and definitions created for a paper-based world. Sometimes these concepts do not fit well in a computerized environment. For example, how would you classify the operator of a bulletin board system? Is that person a publisher of information, like a newspaper? Or is the sys op a vendor offering disk space to anonymous writers? In particular, are the owners of bulletin board systems responsible for the content of messages posted on their systems? To date, the court systems have tended to make the decision based on whether the owners exercise "editorial control." In 1995, the New York supreme court ruled that Prodigy can be sued for libel. An anonymous writer posted a message that was highly critical of the financial status of a certain firm. The firm claimed that the comments were false and sued Prodigy for publishing false information. Since its inception, Prodigy has maintained a policy of forbidding people to post "profane" messages. The Prodigy staff use software to scan messages. The court noted that these actions constitute editorial control, so Prodigy can be treated as any other publisher of information (like a newspaper).

## Transactions and Money

In an electronic world where there is no physical exchange of items, how can people make payments? It is possible to purchase software, data, pictures, music, and other data over electronic networks. There are complications making payments over open networks. The seller needs to verify the authenticity of the payment, and the buyer needs to be certain that only the authorized cost will be charged. One method is to use traditional credit card numbers, but the buyer has little control over the card number once it is given to a vendor. Someone might intercept the card number and use it to make additional purchases. Although encryption could minimize these problems, problems remain with unscrupulous vendors. A vendor could take card numbers for legitimate sales, then use the card to make additional purchases. It would be difficult to prevent wide-scale fraud, especially on an international network. A third problem is that buyers might wish to remain anonymous. Perhaps they do not want their every purchase recorded.

Several companies have proposed methods to deal with these problems. As illustrated in Figure 14.5, most involve the use of a trusted third party (like a bank). *Digital cash* is an example, where buyers can make anonymous purchases on a network, and sellers are assured of receiving payment. Consumers transfer "real money" to the third party and receive one-time-use digital cash numbers. These numbers can be given to a vendor, who returns them to the third party for an account credit. Other methods, like the NetBill system, use the third party to verify authenticity of the buyer and seller. The third party completes the transaction by transferring the money between accounts and forwarding a decryption key to the buyer.

**THREATS TO INFORMATION**

There are many potential threats to information systems and the data they hold. The complicated aspect is that the biggest **information threat** is from legitimate users and developers. Purely by accident, a user might enter incorrect data or delete important information. A designer might misunderstand an important function and the system will produce erroneous results. An innocent programming mistake could result in incorrect or destroyed data. Minor changes to a frail system could result in a cascading failure of the entire system.

We can detect and prevent some of these problems through careful design, testing, training, and backup provisions. However, modern information systems are extremely complex. We cannot guarantee they will work "correctly" all of the time. Plus, the world poses physical threats that cannot be avoided: hurricanes, earthquakes, floods, and so on. Often, the best we can do is build contingency plans that enable the company to recover as fast as possible. The most important aspect of any disaster plan is to maintain adequate backup copies. With careful planning, organization, and enough money, firms are able to provide virtually continuous information system support.

A second set of problems arises from the fact that as technology changes, so do criminals. Today, only a desperate person would rob a bank with a gun. The probability of being caught is high and the amount of money stolen is low. Not that we wish to encourage anyone to become a thief, but the computer offers much easier ways to steal larger amounts of money. Consider the example of some thieves in West Hartford, Connecticut. In 1993, they stole an ATM from a warehouse and installed it at a shopping mall. They put a small amount of money in the machine and disabled the existing machine to encourage people to use theirs. When customers entered their personal identification numbers (PINs) to withdraw money, the ATM recorded the numbers. The thieves used the numbers to create their own ATM cards, which they used to withdraw thousands of dollars from ATMs along the East Coast.

**FIGURE 14.5**

Electronic transactions. One difficulty with electronic transactions is the need for electronic payments. Large payments or monthly payments can be made through most banks in the form of "real" money in checking accounts. These methods can be cumbersome and expensive for small transactions. Several companies have proposed standards for the creation of "digital cash." The goal is to create an electronic form of money that can be verified, is inexpensive to use, can support anonymity, and cannot be easily counterfeited.

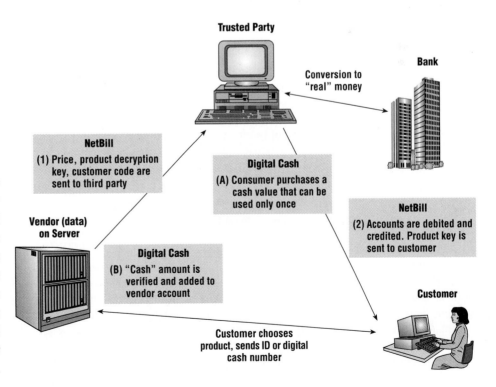

**Trusted Party**

**Bank**

Conversion to "real" money

**NetBill**
(1) Price, product decryption key, customer code are sent to third party

**Digital Cash**
(A) Consumer purchases a cash value that can be used only once

**NetBill**
(2) Accounts are debited and credited. Product key is sent to customer

**Vendor (data) on Server**

**Digital Cash**
(B) "Cash" amount is verified and added to vendor account

**Customer**

Customer chooses product, sends ID or digital cash number

## FIGURE 14.6

Threats to information. By far, the most serious threats are from "insiders": employees, mistakes, consultants and partnerships. Businesses have to trust insiders to stay in operation, but we need to put limits on the access to data. It is possible for outsiders to break into most computer systems, but it is fairly difficult and often relies on the support of a person inside the company. Viruses can be a serious problem in terms of the time required to clean them out. You must constantly back up your work to keep it safe.

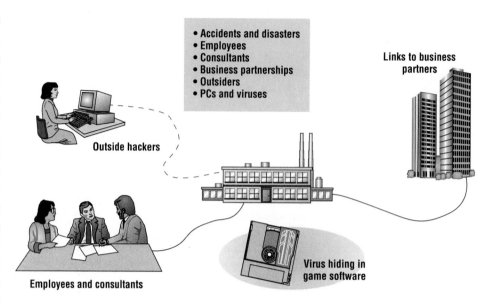

- Accidents and disasters
- Employees
- Consultants
- Business partnerships
- Outsiders
- PCs and viruses

Links to business partners

Outside hackers

Employees and consultants

Virus hiding in game software

It is important to determine the potential threats to computer security described by Figure 14.6. For example, there were several well-publicized cases in the 1980s involving computer security. Most of these problems arose from **hackers** who used modems and personal computers to break into company computers. Similar publicity arose in the mid-1990s with respect to Internet hackers. Because these cases received so much attention, many people thought that their biggest problem was wild teenagers with cheap personal computers. If you were to spend most of your computer security budget to combat this threat, it would be a waste of money. In practice, most computer crimes are committed by people inside the company.

## Employees

Employees are the heart of any company. Companies function and succeed by trusting their employees. Although almost all employees are honest and diligent, there is always the chance that one employee will use the company's knowledge, experience, and trust to misappropriate resources.

It can be difficult to identify people who might cause damage to the firm. Many companies today use psychological tests, background checks, and random drug tests to indicate potential problems. Most companies are wary of employees whose

### BUSINESS TRENDS: TEMPORARY WORKERS

As businesses increasingly rely on temporary workers and consultants, the security risks increase. In general, permanent workers have a greater incentive to keep the company healthy. Additionally, it is more difficult to assess the character of temporary workers. Also, with higher turnover rates, it is more diffi-cult to identify problems and to prove responsibility. On the other hand, any schemes or thefts would have to be short-term oriented. For instance, a thief would avoid long-term schemes that steal small amounts over long periods of time.

**Reality Bytes** ◥  **14–8   ICI DATA TAPES**

ICI is a giant European company that originally spe-cialized in the production of chemicals. In 1977, Rodney Cox was 25 years old and was employed as a computer programmer at a data-processing center in The Netherlands. He was upset that his boss, Geoffrey Cowlin, would not promote him. After Cox's repeated grumbling, Cowlin fired him.

During the next weekend, Cox drove to the data center, and with the help of security staff, loaded more than 1,000 computer data tapes into his station wagon. The tapes contained detailed financial records and plans for the entire European operations of ICI. Cox then drove to the company headquarters in

Rotterdam. Again, with the help of the security offi-cers, he collected all of the backup tapes and drove away. He now had the only copies of the financial data of the company. They would be worth a fortune to ICI's competitors. It would also cost ICI millions of dollars to recreate the lost data.

The next day, Cox phoned Cowlin and demanded $400,000 in exchange for the tapes. Cowlin immedi-ately called the Dutch police, who brought in Scotland Yard and Interpol. They eventually agreed to meet Cox in London and pay the ransom for the tapes. When Cox and his brother-in-law arrived to collect the ransom, they were arrested, and the tapes were recovered.

employment has been terminated. Businesses follow specific steps when employees leave, being particularly careful to remove the employees' access to company com-puters. The ICI situation (Reality Bytes 14–8) presents one example of problems.

A more complicated problem arises with MIS employees. Programmers and ana-lysts have to be trusted. Without them, there would be no software. However, it is generally best if the programmers are not the users of the program. Companies enforce a separation of duties among staff programmers and users. Think about what might happen if a bank teller was also responsible for writing the computer program used by tellers. It would be easy to use the software to steal money from different accounts. Auditing transaction-processing systems is an important task for auditors.

Unscrupulous programmers have also been known to include "time bombs" in their software. Whenever the software runs, it checks a hidden file for a secret word. If the programmer leaves the company, the secret word does not get changed. When the program does not find the correct word, it starts deleting files (Reality Bytes 14–9). On large projects, these bombs can be impossible to spot (until they go off). The damage can usually be minimized by keeping good backups. Another danger area is that programmers might include a trap door or secret password that allows them to gain access to the software even if they leave the company. Sometimes these trap doors are installed innocently—to enable programmers to make corrections

 **Reality Bytes** ◥  **14–9   TIME BOMBS**

In the mid-1980s, a programmer at an insurance com-pany in Texas lost his job. Not an unusual occurrence, but he had created a "time bomb" in the applications that he wrote for the company. Every day when he went to work, he entered a password in the computer. When he was fired, he could not log on to the com-

puter. When the programs that he had written did not get the new password, they began deleting information on the computer. Hundreds of paychecks were delayed because of this destruction. The programmer was arrested and convicted of malicious destruction of cor-porate information.

faster. The important point is to make sure they are removed when the system is permanently installed.

An interesting class of threats to securing your data arises from negligence instead of deliberate actions by the users. For instance, employees might accidentally delete data. Or, carrying disks, tapes or even laptop computers past magnetic fields can sometimes damage the files. In these cases, the best bet is to have backups readily available. More complicated problems arise when laptop computers are lost or even stolen. In addition to the data stored on the machines, the files often hold passwords for corporate computers. Many laptops provide passwords and encrypt the data to minimize these problems. One other problem that falls into this category is a warning to be careful about how you dispose of old tapes, disks, and computer equipment. In 1990, the U.S. Department of Justice sold some out-of-date equipment and tapes to a broker in Kentucky for $45. Unfortunately, the DOJ did not erase all of the data from the tapes. It turned out to be a serious problem, because the tapes contained names and addresses of people in the Justice Department's witness protection program. Businesses run similar risks when they send computer equipment out for repairs.

In general, the best way to minimize problems from employees stems from typical management techniques. Hire workers carefully, treat employees fairly, have separation of jobs, use teamwork, and maintain constant checks on their work.

## Consultants

Consultants present the same potential problems as employees. However, consultants tend to be hired for a short time, so the firm knows even less about them than about regular employees. Consultants are generally used for specialized jobs, so there may not be any internal employees who can adequately monitor their work.

## Business Partnerships

As computers spread throughout every aspect of business, many companies are sharing their data. For example, General Motors asks its suppliers to provide all information electronically. This electronic data interchange (EDI) means that business information is processed faster and with fewer errors. The problem is that in many cases, it means GM gives other companies considerable access to GM's computer, and vice versa. For instance, if GM is thinking about increasing production, the managers might want to check supplier production schedules to make sure the suppliers can provide enough parts. To do it electronically, GM needs access to the suppliers' computers.

## Outsiders

There is some threat from outsiders who might dial up your computer and guess a password. Most of these threats can be minimized by using some common sense. For example, in the 1980s, some groups gained access to computers because the operators never changed the default password that was shipped with the computer! In most cases, these threats can be controlled through the use of dial-back modems; however, as noted in the Department of Defense case, networks can cause additional problems.

## Personal Computers and Viruses

Personal computers represent a major point of vulnerability to companies today. Most microcomputer operating systems have limited security capabilities. Most do not

### HACKERS

The U.S. General Accounting Office reported that Dutch computer hackers electronically broke into 34 U.S. Department of Defense computers. The hackers managed to copy and even change information related to military operations in the Persian Gulf war. Although the information was sensitive, it was nonclassified. Most of the data involved personnel records. The thieves used the Internet computer network to access the government computers by using "widely known loopholes such as default passwords and flaws in computer operating systems." The lapse in security was actually caused by poor computer management. "The GAO reported in May 1990 that none of the agencies had fully implemented planned security controls, and only 38 percent of the 145 security plans had been put into place." In a separate incident, Israeli officials reported in September that "an 18-year-old hacker had penetrated computers at the Pentagon and retrieved classified information related to the Patriot missile." Also, an Australian hacker is accused of causing a NASA computer to shut down for 24 hours.

have passwords, they cannot prevent files from being changed, and they do not keep track of usage and changes. Because many of them are connected to networks and to larger computers, they can be dangerous to computer security. If someone gets access to a microcomputer, he or she generally can gain access to the other computer systems in the company.

One particularly dangerous threat to personal computers comes in the form of a software program called a **virus.** As illustrated in Figure 14.7, a computer virus is a small program that hides inside another program. Someone might write a game and give it to you to play. If you like the game, you will pass it around to friends. Hiding inside the game is a small piece of code. Every time you run the game, this piece of code copies itself to other files on your computer. Even if you stop playing the game, the virus will still be on your computer, hiding in the other software. A virus can

**FIGURE 14.7**
Virus activity. Once a virus is loaded on your computer, you will need an antivirus software package to remove the virus. Several versions are available at low cost. A virus can come from any software that supports executable code. Because most packages use macro programming languages, even documents can contain viruses.

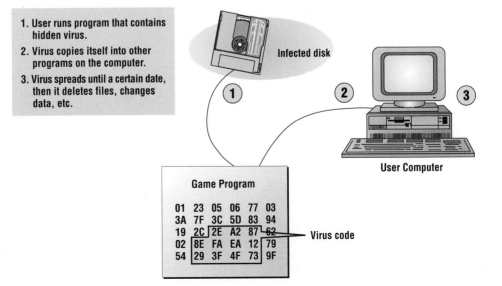

**Reality Bytes**  **14–10** VIRUS ATTACKS

Novell, Inc., which produces local area network software, was forced to notify 3,800 customers that a December 1991 release of some software was infected by the Stoned III virus. Other vendors have experienced similar virus attacks. To minimize these problems, most companies screen their software with antivirus software before shipping the disks. However, some new viruses are able to avoid detection from the antivirus software. Although it is possible for computers to be infected with software purchased from commercial firms, companies are more likely to have problems with software carried by employees. A study of 600 firms by the National Computer Security Association found that "43 percent of virus infections occurred after employees brought an infected disk to work." Only 9 percent were caused by commercial software and demonstration disks.

**FIGURE 14.8**

VIRUS DAMAGE

Computer viruses can be expensive. It takes time to clean up all infected computers. Over one-third of the firms reported that it cost them more than $2000 per incident to recover from a virus attack. While antivirus software helps, many people do not use it. Also, new viruses can sneak in before antivirus software is modified to spot them. Hence, in early 1996, 49 percent of the reported virus problems stemmed from the introduction of the Word.concept macro virus.

quickly infect every computer in a company. Finally, at some point in time (perhaps a Friday the 13th or Michelangelo's birthday), the virus becomes active. It might display a harmless message or it might destroy all the files on your computer. A trickier virus might search for computer passwords stored on your personal computer and send them to a competitor.

A virus can be picked up from many sources. There have even been cases where a virus has been hidden on disks that were sent directly from commercial software vendors (Reality Bytes 14–10). Antivirus software will search your computer for known viruses; commonly available packages are listed in Figure 14.8. Until microcomputers gain additional levels of security, viruses will remain a problem. Again, the first rule of safety is to *always* have backups of your data and software. Even the backups might become infected, but if a virus destroys the files on your computer, at least you can recover the data. Because of the expanding capabilities of software, it is now possible to pick up a virus just by "reading" a document or spreadsheet file. Current software contains an internal programming language that can be used to carry and spread a virus. So far, these viruses are relatively easy to identify and to eliminate. Most software packages have a technique to disable programs (macros) when you open the document, for example, hold down the SHIFT key when you open the document.

| DAMAGE | PERCENT OF FIRMS REPORTING PROBLEM IN 1991 | PERCENT OF FIRMS REPORTING PROBLEM IN 1996 |
|---|---|---|
| Loss of productivity | 62 | 81 |
| Message and lockup | 41 | 62 |
| Corrupted files | 38 | 59 |
| Lost data | 30 | 39 |
| Unreliable applications | 24 | 35 |
| System crash | 23 | 30 |

SOURCES: Michael Alexander, "Infection risk not spurring use of antivirus software," *Computerworld*, December 16, 1991, p. 49 and by Computerworld, Inc., Framingham, MA 01701—Reprinted from *Computerworld*.

Gary H. Anthes, "Old, new viruses swarm PC users," *Computerworld*, May 6, 1996, p. 55.

**COMPUTER SECURITY**

Transaction and accounting data is clearly valuable to a company and needs to be protected. There are three major security issues: (1) unauthorized disclosure of information, (2) unauthorized modification and (3) unauthorized withholding of information. As an example of the first problem, you would not want your competitor to get access to your new marketing plans. An example of the second problem would be if employees could modify their payroll records to change their pay rates. The third problem is less obvious, but just as important. Imagine what would happen if you needed to look at the latest inventory to decide how much to reorder, but the computer refused to give you access.

## Manual and Electronic Information

Protection of information is a topic that has existed forever. Not surprisingly, the strongest developments in security have come from the military. The armed services lead the way both in manual and electronic security. Military funding has paid for much of the development of computer security. Because manual security precautions existed long before computers, the initial work in computer security focused on applying these older techniques. Nevertheless, there are some major differences that arise from storing information electronically. To see the complications added by electronic storage of information, consider a hypothetical case of two spies looking for a letter. Juan has gained access to a personal computer, but Mike is in a musty basement library full of paper files.

Mike is not even sure he is in the right place. There are thousands of documents in the basement, and the letter might even be stored in some other building. The computer that Juan is searching is large enough to hold all of the company's information, so he only has to look in one place. For his search, Juan just uses the computer database. In seconds, he finds what he wants. He copies the letter to a disk, turns off the machine and walks out the door. Mike is still walking up and down aisles in the basement trying to read file tags with his flashlight. When he finally finds the letter, he uses his trusty spy camera to take pictures of the letter, hoping they will be legible. Now he has to put the letter back exactly as he found it so no one can tell he copied it.

Obviously it is much easier to locate and copy data stored on computers. Even more importantly, it is easier to change the data. In many cases, data on computers can be changed without anyone knowing that the file was altered. It is even theoretically possible for a person to break into a computer by using the phone system or a computer network. The intruder does not have to physically enter the building.

## Backup Protection

One of the most important steps in protecting the information assets of the company is the use of backups. Data needs to be backed up on a regular basis. For some firms, that means making backup copies every night. In other cases, it means that sensitive data sets have to be duplicated as soon as they are created. With centralized computers, it is relatively easy to have the machines automatically make copies of data that was changed during the day. In a completely decentralized environment, it is more difficult to make the copies. In many cases, users have to be responsible for making their own backups. Unfortunately, most users are reluctant to take the time to make daily backups of their work. That is where local area networks come in handy. Properly designed networks allow the MIS staff to connect to individual user machines and make the backups automatically. Of course, backup tapes have to be stored in a safe location. Also, you must be careful when you discard old data tapes to make sure they have been erased.

SunGard is a premier provider of computer backup facilities and disaster planning services. Its fleet of Mobile Data Centers can be outfitted with a variety of distributed systems hardware and delivered to a disaster site within 48 hours.

Along with the data, it is useful to make arrangements for backing up the computer hardware. What happens to a company if a disaster—such as a flood, fire, or hurricane—strikes the computer center? How long can a company survive without the management information system? Today, there are many ways to plan for and recover from potential disasters. Some companies make arrangements with similar firms in other locations. If one company experiences problems, it would move the processing to the data center of the other company. Of course, each company needs to have sufficient computer capabilities to support both operations.

A more common approach today is to contract with a disaster recovery services provider, such as SunGard Services, Inc. (Reality Bytes 14-11). Service providers like

**Reality Bytes**     **14–11**  SUNGARD RECOVERY SERVICES

SunGard Recovery Services Inc. has been a leading provider of total business recovery solutions since 1978. The company founded the industry and offers recovery services throughout North America. In addition to providing backup facilities, the company provides business continuity planning software and consulting services through its subsidiary, SunGard Planning Solutions Inc.

SunGard's Comprehensive Business Recovery[SM] services include: computer hot-sites and cold-sites, electronic vaulting for data backup, network recovery, remote testing and recovery, and work group recovery services for voice, data, and LAN systems.

Services are delivered through SunGard's network of MegaCenters®, and MetroCenters® as well as its fleet of Mobile Data Centers stationed at strategic points nationwide.

SunGard's Mobile Data Centers (shown in picture), are custom-designed units that can be outfitted with a variety of distributed systems hardware configured to replace any designated system when disaster strikes. Mobile Data Centers can arrive at the site of a disaster within 48 hours of notification. On making the appropriate network connections, the Mobile Data Center enables a company to quickly and easily restore operations from any parking lot near the original data facility.

SunGard provide access to their commercial recovery facilities and provide several levels of support for various fees. One common level of support, called a **hot site,** consists of a fully configured computer center. Specific computer equipment is already installed and ready for immediate use. When the MIS staff declares a disaster, they install the backup tapes on the hot-site computers, and use telecommunication lines to run the day-to-day operations. Another alternative is to contact for a **cold site,** which provides fully functional computer room space, without the computer equipment. If a disaster occurs, either the company or the disaster recovery services provider can arrange for the necessary equipment to be shipped to the cold-site. There can be a delay of several days before the new data center will be operational.

For computer operations that absolutely must never be interrupted, some firms utilize a backup computer that is continuously running to maintain a complete copy of the daily operations. All data is maintained simultaneously at both locations. If problems arise with one machine, the second one takes over automatically.

Although there are several options available for central computers, there are fewer disaster plan alternatives for personal computers. Of course, the first step is to provide regular backups of the data and software. But, if a disaster wipes out the company's personal computer, what options are available? If you need only 20 or 30 machines, you might be able to buy them from a local vendor, but they often maintain small inventories to keep their costs down. Even large manufacturers like IBM and Compaq experience backlogs and might not be able to meet your needs. One useful alternative is to encourage your employees to buy computers for their use at home. If a disaster strikes, they can use modems and work out of their homes until you have time to set up new facilities and new hardware. Many companies provide generous computer purchase plans for their employees to encourage them to buy their own computers.

## User Identification

One difficulty with providing computer security lies in identifying the user. In a manual security system, a guard can be used to physically identify each person by asking to see identification. There are few vision systems available for computers and they are expensive. The most common method of identifying users to computers is with a password.

### Passwords

Each user is given an account name and a password that are known only to the computer and the user. If someone correctly enters both the name and the password, the computer assumes it must be the user. This method is cheap, fast, and does not require too much effort by the user. However, there are problems. The biggest difficulty is that users are afraid of forgetting their password, so they choose words that are easy to remember. Unfortunately, passwords that are easy to remember tend to be obvious to other people. For instance, *never* use the words *password* or *secret* as a password. Similarly, do not use the names of relatives, pets, or celebrities. Most of these can be obtained by looking in a phonebook or asking someone you know. In fact, you should not use any actual words. Most people use only a couple thousand words in typical conversation. The goal is to make it hard for someone to guess the password. You need to choose passwords from the largest possible set of characters and numbers. There are two other rules about passwords: Change them often and never write them down. If you forget a password, the system administrator will let you create a new one. For additional security, many computer systems require users to change their passwords on a regular basis, such as every 30 or 60 days.

One drawback to passwords is that we need too many of them. Everything from ATM cards to phone calls to computer accounts uses passwords or *personal identification numbers (PINs)*. It is difficult to remember several different passwords, especially if you choose random letters and numbers and change them often. With so many passwords, it is tempting to write them down, which defeats their purpose. Some computer network security systems use a security server. Users log in once and the security server gives them access to all of the authorized servers. The system is most useful on large networks.

Passwords are not a perfect solution to identifying users. No matter how well they are chosen or how often they are changed, there is always a chance that someone could guess the password. They are so risky that U.S. government top-secret information is stored on computers that cannot be connected to phone lines. By physically preventing outsiders from using the computers, there is a smaller chance that the information could be compromised.

### Biometrics

**Biometrics** is a field of study that is trying to determine how to identify people based on biological characteristics. The most promising devices are fingerprint and handprint readers. As shown in Figure 14.9, there is even a device that "reads" a thermal pattern of the user's face. Most of these devices can be connected to terminals or personal computers, or used as door locks to identify and verify authorized users. Their biggest drawbacks are that they are not 100 percent accurate and they are more expensive than using passwords. There has also been some work done on retina scanners that read the blood-vessel pattern at the back of the eye. Some people have tried to use voice recognition systems, but their accuracy is too low. Think about what happens if you have a cold. You would not be allowed to use your computer.

There are some potential advantages to biometric security devices. The user does not have to remember anything or carry keys around. They are reasonably accurate. The most common mistake is to prevent legitimate users from gaining access. Biometric scanners are difficult to fool by an unauthorized person. However, remember that no computer security system is perfect. Pretend you are writing a spy novel. How would a cold-blooded spy get around a fingerprint reader?

**FIGURE 14.9**

Biometric devices. Several methods exist to identify a person based on biological characteristics. Common techniques include fingerprint, handprint readers, and retinal scanners. More exotic devices include body shape sensors and this thermal facial reader from Technology Recognition Systems which uses infrared imaging to identify the user.

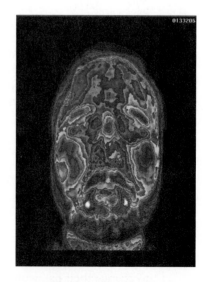

## Access Control

As long as the computer can identify each user, it can control access to any piece of data. As manager of the marketing department, you could allow other managers to read the sales data but not change it. Similarly, the accounting department could allow managers to see the accounts payable data, but only the accounting department would be able to modify the data and write new checks. With a good security system, it is possible for the human resources manager to allow employees to look up work phone numbers in the corporate database but not to see salaries or other confidential information.

The common access controls available are: read, write, execute, and delete. With these security features, the owner of the information can give other users exactly the type of access they need.

## Alternative Security Measures

### Audits

Accountants have long known that in order to maintain security over data, it is necessary to perform audits. There are too many ways for unscrupulous people to make changes to stored information. Audits are used to locate mistakes and to prevent fraud. Existing criminology practice states that in many cases, the threat of getting caught (by an audit) will convince most people to be more careful and to avoid fraudulent behavior. The same principles extend to security audits. By monitoring computer activity, auditing financial records, and periodically checking to see whether everyone is obeying security regulations, users are encouraged to follow the security guidelines of the company.

Of course, audits cost money and they interfere with the daily operations of the firm. As a result, it is important to schedule audits carefully, and to keep an eye on the costs as well as the potential benefits. There are several professional organizations (such as the EDP Auditors Association (Reality Bytes 14-12) designed to help security employees learn more about the latest technologies and to teach them what to look for in audits. The American Institute of Certified Public Accountants (AICPA) also provides standards and audit guidelines that are useful at combatting fraud.

### Physical Access

Because it is so difficult to provide logical security to a computer, other mechanisms have been developed. Many of them rely on controlling physical access to the computer.

 Reality Bytes     14–12  EDP Auditors

Founded in 1970, the Electronic Data Processing Auditors Association sponsors seminars and conferences to assist its member auditors to analyze the accuracy and security of the organizations in which its members are employed. The association offers courses that provide continuing education credits. These courses bring its members up to date on the latest technologies and what to look for in terms of audit and security violations. With the proliferation of computer hardware and software systems, these meetings provide essential training and evaluation tools to the auditors in their efforts to evaluate and secure their companies' computer systems.

**FIGURE 14.10**

Dial-back modem. (1) User calls computer. (2) Modem answers. (3) User enters name and password. (4) Modem hangs up. (5) Modem dials phone number in database. (6) User machine answers. (7) User gets access. If a hacker tries to call (with a stolen name and password), the company modem will call back to the employee's phone and get no verification. Dial-back modems do present a problem for employees who travel frequently.

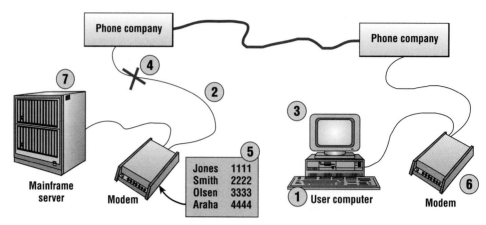

For instance, computers and terminals should be kept in controlled areas. They must certainly be kept away from visitors and delivery people. Many types of locks and keys can be used to protect terminals and personal computers. Similarly, all documents should be controlled. Paper copies of important reports should be shredded.

It is relatively easy to prevent outsiders from calling a computer. There are modems that have a dial-back feature. As shown in Figure 14.10, when an employee calls the computer from home, the modem answers and asks for a name and password. If the name and password are entered correctly, the modem hangs up the phone. Next, it looks up the name in a table and dials the corresponding phone number. Even if someone steals your password, it will not do any good unless he or she calls from your home phone.

### Monitoring

Another effective security provision is to monitor access to all of the data. Most large computers can keep track of every change to every file. They can keep a log of who accesses each file. They keep track of every time someone incorrectly enters a password. An audit trail of every file change can be provided to management. That means it is possible to find out who changed the salary data, what time it was changed, and from which terminal. All financial data is routinely audited by both internal and external auditors. Sometimes hidden control data is used to make sure procedures are followed.

### Hiring and Employee Evaluation

Because many problems are caused by "insiders," it makes sense to be careful when you hire employees. Employers should always check candidates' references. In more extreme situations, employers can check employee backgrounds for criminal records. There are several instances of disgruntled employees causing security problems. In many cases, the best security solution is to establish close relationships with your employees and encourage teamwork. Employees who work closely together can defuse potential problems and informally monitor the work of other employees.

## Encryption

Remember that personal computers were originally designed for only one user at a time, so most of them have minimal security provisions. But what if you have a spreadsheet file that you need to protect so that others cannot read it? Or what if your corporate strategy files are stored on your laptop, and the laptop is stolen? Similarly, what if you need to send a disk to a subsidiary in another country? How can you protect the data from being read in these cases?

Encryption is a method of modifying the original information according to some code, so that it can only be read if the user knows the decryption key. Encryption can be used to transmit information from one computer to another. Information stored on a computer also can be encrypted. Even if someone guesses a password and gains access to the computer, the files will be gibberish without the encryption key—just like a scrambled cable TV signal.

There are two basic types of encryption. Most methods use a single key to both encrypt and decrypt a message. For example, the **Data Encryption Standard (DES)** method uses a single key. Although DES is a U.S. standard, versions of it are available throughout the world. A second method uses both a **private key** and a **public key.** Whichever key is used to encrypt the message, the other key must be used to decrypt it. The **Rivest-Shamir-Adelman (RSA) algorithm** is an example of a method that uses two keys. RSA protection is available on a wide variety of computers.

Methods that use two keys have some interesting uses. The trick is that everyone knows your public key, but only you know the private key. Consider the example shown in Figure 14.11, in which Makiko and Takao want to send messages to each other using electronic mail. Makiko first types a letter. Then she encrypts the message with Takao's public key. This message can only be decrypted and read when Takao uses his private key. No one else can decrypt the message to read or change it. However, someone might be able to destroy the message before Takao gets it.

There is a second use of dual key systems called **authentication.** Let's say that Takao wants to send a message to Makiko. To make sure that only she can read it, he encrypts it with her public key. However, he is worried that someone has been sending false messages to Makiko using his name. Takao wants to make sure that Makiko knows the message came from him. If Takao also encrypts the message with his private key, it can only be decrypted with Takao's public key. When Makiko receives the message, she applies her private key and Takao's public key. If the message is readable, then it must have been sent by Takao. This situation is displayed in Figure 14.12.

Encryption should be seriously considered for any communications that are sent between computers. Without encryption, it is relatively easy for unauthorized

**FIGURE 14.11**
Dual-key encryption. Makiko sends a message that only Takao can read. With a dual-key system, one key encrypts the message, the other decrypts it. Once Takao's public key is applied to the message, only Takao's private key will retrieve the message. Keys are usually very large prime numbers.

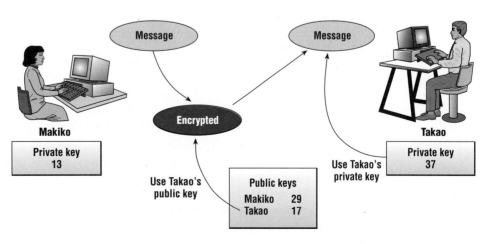

Message

Message

**Encrypted**

**Makiko**

Private key
13

Use Takao's
public key

Public keys

Makiko    29
Takao     17

Use Takao's
private key

**Takao**

Private key
37

**FIGURE 14.12**
Dual-key encryption for message authentication. Takao sends a message to Makiko. Using his private key ensures that the message must have come from him. Using Makiko's public key prevents anyone else from reading the message. Dual-key systems require that a trusted machine be available to hold the public keys.

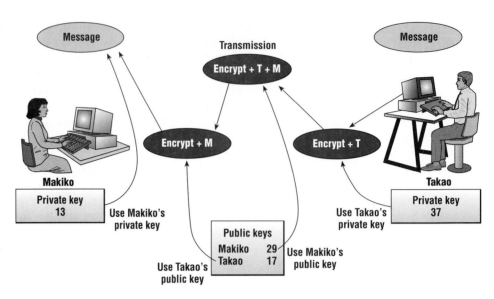

people to deliberately or accidentally read the messages. Encryption is available with many personal computer software packages. Almost all spreadsheets and word processors permit you to encrypt your file when you save it. To read it back, you have to enter the correct password. You also can buy utility packages that will encrypt your entire disk drive, which can be useful for users who travel with their laptop computers. To retrieve any data on the disk drive, you have to enter the correct key value.

## Encryption, Privacy, and Public Needs

It is easy to find situations for which firms and consumers need encryption to protect transactions and verify the identity of the participants. The demand increases as more transactions are moved online with little or no physical documentation. When phone conversations move to radio networks (cellular phones), we need to worry more about industrial espionage. Even simple messages deserve protection from a nosy co-worker. With faster hardware and improved software, it is easy to encrypt virtually any transaction, message or phone call.

However, it is just as easy for drug dealers to encrypt their messages and lock their spreadsheets. Unethical government officials and lobbyists can just as easily prevent anyone else from reading their communications. Criminals of all types can use public networks for their own communications, knowing that no one can decipher their messages. Likewise, foreign governments could use technology to hide their actions from public scrutiny.

Various law enforcement agencies and departments in the U.S. government believe that the widespread use of encryption will hinder their ability to identify and prosecute criminals. They are also concerned about making this technology available worldwide. In response to these problems, the U.S. government has taken three basic actions: (1) export of strong encryption is denied—products using strong encryption are currently classified as "munitions" and prohibited from export. However, a lawsuit was filed in 1995 challenging this treatment of encryption. (2) Various branches of the government, notably the top-secret National Security Agency (NSA) are rumored to have several supercomputers for code-

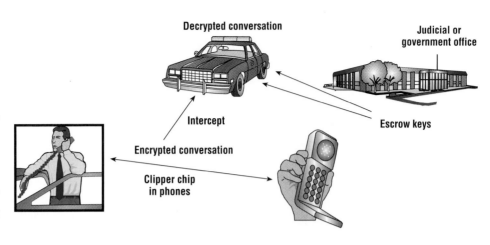

**FIGURE 14.13**
The Clipper chip. The U.S. government is concerned that citizens and foreigners will use encryption for "undesirable" purposes, such as spying and committing crimes. The National Security Agency created a secret method of encrypting messages, including digital phone transmissions. Every encryption device can be broken with two special keys (numbers) that are held in escrow by judicial or governmental agencies. On receiving court permission, police would be able to decrypt any message or conversation.

breaking. (3) The U.S. government has created a secret encryption method that is being sold as the **Clipper chip.** It is primarily designed for use in oral communications (on phones), but can be used in any digital transmission. As Figure 14.13 illustrates, the Clipper chip has a unique feature: it uses two special **escrow keys.** Every chip has a unique number and two special key numbers. The plan is that these escrow keys will be filed with two governmental agencies. If the government suspects criminal activity, an official will obtain a judicial warrant to retrieve the keys. With these keys, the official can instantly decrypt any message using that specific chip. Following complaints by people concerned about privacy, the government chose to make use of the Clipper chip optional. However, it is required for use by (nonmilitary) governmental agencies. The government is hoping that official demand for products using the Clipper chip will drive prices down far enough to encourage use by private companies.

## Users

**RESPONSIBILITY AND ETHICS**

Computer users have certain responsibilities in terms of computer security and privacy. First, they have an obligation to obey the laws that pertain to computers. The U.S. government and some states, along with other nations, have laws against computer crimes. Other laws regarding stealing have also been applied to computer crimes. One law that has received much attention is the copyright law. European and U.S. copyright laws prohibit the copying of software except for necessary backup. It is the responsibility of users to keep up with the changes in the laws and to abide by them. In the last few years, software publishers have increased their efforts to stop illegal copying of software, called **software piracy** (Reality Bytes 14–13).

Although it might seem to be trivial, making illegal copies of software (or videotapes, or other copyrighted works) can cause several problems. First, it takes money away from the legal owners of the software, which reduces their incentive to create new products. Second, you run the risk of hurting your employer. If employees illegally copy company-purchased software, the owners of the copyright can sue the employer. Third, copying software provides an illegal advantage over your competitors. A small design firm might decide to copy a $20,000 CAD design system instead of buying it. Consequently, honest firms are hurt because the original firm will be able to make lower bids on jobs because their costs are lower. Fourth, as an individual, you

**Reality Bytes**     **14–13  DAVY JONES LOCKER: PIRACY**

Until 1992, 43-year-old Richard Kenadek ran an international user bulletin board system (BBS) from his home in Millbury, Massachusetts. The system had dozens of modems, allowing users to exchange messages and download software. In June 1992, Kenadek was one of the first people charged with criminal violation of U.S. copyright laws. The Software Publishers Association (a trade group) is also suing Kenadek for civil damages. A new law passed after Kenadek was raided would provide even harsher penalties (up to five years in prison and $250,000 in fines).

The U.S. Attorney, Donald Stern, charged Mr. Kenadek with knowingly allowing people to transfer copyrighted software from his bulletin board. Allegedly, subscribers who paid $99 a year were given access to a special account containing commercial software. Stern observed that "The pirating of commercial software through the operation of clandestine computer bulletin boards seriously jeopardizes the investment of money and personnel

which software companies put into the development of new programs."

In his defense, Kenadek's lawyer, James Reardon, claims that he acted to prevent people from copying software off the bulletin board. He posted a warning message stating:

> From now on there will be NO MORE uploading of Copywrited [sic] Software!!! . . . I will NOT TOLERATE the uploading of any more Copywrited Files.

Stern countered by noting that Kenadek could have used software to scan for illegal copies of software and delete them. He also claimed that Kenadek kept software online that was designed to be downloaded "for evaluation only."

SOURCE: Junda Woo, "Copyright Laws Enter the Fight against Electronic Bulletin Board," *The Wall Street Journal*, September 27, 1994, p. B14. Reprinted by permission of *The Wall Street Journal*, © 1994 Dow Jones & Company, Inc. all rightrs reserved.

have a reputation to defend. If your friends, colleagues, or employers learn that you are willing to break the law by copying software; they can easily believe that you are willing to break other laws.

Users of computer systems also have an obligation as part of **computer ethics** to customers and clients (Reality Bytes 14–14) Most information in computer databases is confidential information. It should not be revealed to anyone except authorized employees. Some nations have laws to protect this privacy. If you find a company violating these laws, it is your responsibility to question the practice.

Users have an obligation to use the information provided by computer applications appropriately. When a user sets up calculations in a spreadsheet, the user must realize that those calculations might be wrong. The calculations must be tested and the information produced should always be checked for reasonableness. You should not believe information solely because it comes from a computer. All data should be verified.

## Programmers and Developers

Programmers would never get jobs if they could not be trusted. This trust is one of the most crucial requirements to being a programmer. As a programmer or developer, not only do you have to be honest, you must also avoid any appearance of dishonesty. For example, practical jokes involving security violations can be dangerous to your career.

Programmers have more responsibilities than many other employees. Software is used in many critical areas. If a programmer attempts a job that is beyond his or her capabilities, crucial errors may be introduced. For example, consider what might happen if an underqualified person took a job programming medical life support systems.

**Reality Bytes** ◢ 14-14 Selling Your Life

A company called *Nationwide Electronic Tracking (NET)* advertised that it had

"instant access" to a wide range of "confidential" computer data. For fees ranging from $5 to $175, NET promised, it could provide customers with data on virtually anyone in the country—private credit reports, business histories, driver's license records, even personal social security records and criminal history backgrounds.

This type of information could be valuable to a business person. For example, you could check out employees, customers, or even competitors. The catch is that most of this information is confidential.

Last week, NET was identified by the FBI as one player in a nationwide network of brokers and private investigators who allegedly were pilfering confidential personal data from U.S. government computers and then selling them for a fee to lawyers, insurance companies, private employers, and other customers.

Police officers in various cities have been charged with selling information obtained from computer searches of local and federal databases. Besides the invasion of privacy issue, there is another serious problem with these databases:

The security of the FBI's database has long been a concern to civil libertarians, because roughly half of its arrest records are incomplete, failing to record whether charges were dropped or even whether a suspect was ultimately acquitted.

SOURCE: Michael Isikoff, "Illegal Selling of Stolen Computer Files Threatens Privacy," *The Washington Post*, printed in *The Atlanta Journal/The Atlanta Constitution*, December 28, 1991, p. C8.

If he or she made a mistake, a person might die. Although mistakes can be made by anyone, they are more likely to arise when a programmer attempts too difficult of a job.

Along the same lines, programmers have an obligation to test everything they do. It also means that companies have the responsibility to provide adequate time for programmers to perform the tests. The important step is to identify components that are critical and to build in safeguards.

There have been enormous increases in the demand for software in the last decade. At the same time, new tools allow programmers to create much more complex applications. But our ability to create this new software has far outstripped our ability to ensure that it is error free. Even commercial programs, such as word processors and spreadsheets, still have errors that can cause problems. In spite of the best efforts of conscientious, talented people, software used appropriately can produce erroneous information.

Liability for erroneous information produced by software has not been fully established yet. Laws and court decisions during the 1990s should settle many aspects of who is responsible when software makes mistakes or fails. A related issue is the extent to which the user is responsible for correctly entering information needed by the program and for using the information produced by the program appropriately.

## Companies

Every company has obligations to society, customers, employees, and business partners. In terms of society, a firm must obey all relevant laws. For customers, firms must ensure privacy of data. That means companies will collect only the data that they truly need. The data must be safeguarded so that only those who need it for their job have access. If customer information is sold or distributed for other purposes, customers should be notified. Consumers must be allowed to remove their names from any distribution lists.

For employees, a company must provide training and monitoring (compliance programs) to ensure they understand the laws and are following them. Firms must provide sufficient funds to allow the employees to meet their individual responsibilities. Companies must provide enough time and money to adequately test software. Firms have an obligation to allow their employees a certain amount of privacy. For instance, companies have no reason to routinely monitor and read employees' electronic mail messages.

Companies are required to abide by all partnership agreements. In terms of computers, they must safeguard all data acquired from partners. They must not use the data in a manner that would injure the firms involved.

## Governments

Federal, state, and local governments have obligations to establish laws that provide a means for those unfairly injured to allow them to gain compensation from those who did the damage. Until the 1980s, there were relatively few laws at any level specifically directed at computer usage. Instead, laws intended for other purposes were stretched to cover computer crimes. Frequently, citing mail fraud laws was the only recourse. Some criminals were not convicted because the crime was considered "victimless" by the jury or the injured corporation declined to prosecute.

Starting in the mid-1980s, the federal government and nearly every state passed new laws concerning computer crime. The 1984 Computer Fraud and Abuse Act outlawed unauthorized access to data stored in federal government computers. In 1986, the Computer Fraud and Abuse Act and the Electronic Communications Privacy Act were enacted. The Computer Fraud and Abuse Act makes it a federal crime to alter, copy, view or damage data stored in computers subject to federal law. The law provides fines of up to $100,000 and up to 20 years in prison. The Computer Abuse Amendments Act of 1994 expanded the original definitions to include transmission of harmful code such as viruses. It also distinguishes between actions taken "with reckless disregard" for potential damages (misdemeanor) and intentionally harmful acts (felony). It also modified the language so that crimes causing damages of more than $1,000 or involving medical records are within federal jurisdiction. Additionally, it placed controls on states in terms of selling drivers' license records.

Most states have enacted similar laws for the few computers that might not be subject to federal law. European countries have been ahead of the United States in developing legislation to deal with computer crime.

Legislation, enforcement, and judicial interpretation have not kept up with changes in technology. A major question that is unresolved is the extent to which copyright law applies to the "look and feel" of software. For example, Lotus corporation sued Borland because Borland's Quattro Pro spreadsheet used menu titles similar to those used by the Lotus 123 spreadsheet. Some people are calling for legislation making it illegal to write a computer virus program, although there is some question that such a law might be an unnecessary restriction on freedom of speech or freedom of the press. In fact, there is considerable discussion over whether electronic mail and bulletin board operators should be treated as members of the press and receive first amendment protections.

In terms of enforcement, most federal, state, and local agencies have few, if any, officers devoted to solving computer crimes. In fact, many software piracy cases have been pursued by U.S. Secret Service agents. One complication is that most law enforcement agencies lack proper training in computer usage and investigation of computer crimes.

## SUMMARY

Technological change and increasingly aggressive use of information systems by businesses have several consequences. Technology affects individuals, their jobs, educational systems, governments, and society as a whole. Businesses have to be careful to protect the privacy of consumers and workers. Security provisions, disclosure policies, and audits are used to ensure that data is only used for authorized purposes. To ensure accuracy, it is crucial to allow customers (and workers) to examine relevant data and make changes.

Technology is generally believed to increase the total number of jobs available. However, the workers displaced by the introduction of technology are rarely qualified for the new jobs. Businesses and governments need to provide retraining and relocation to help those workers who lose their jobs. Sometimes technology allows physically disabled people to work in jobs they might not otherwise be able to perform.

Improved communication networks, huge databases, and multimedia tools provide possibilities for education and training in the public and business sectors. However, because of high development costs, technology tends to be used for specialized training.

Governments have long been involved in data collection, and technology enables them to work more efficiently. Of course, many political observers would argue that perhaps governments should not be *too* efficient. For example, it would be difficult for businesses to operate in an environment where the laws were changed every day. Technology also has the potential to improve communication between citizens and their representatives.

There are other interactions between technology and society. One feature is that lower prices, improved capabilities, and ease-of-use have made improved communication available to virtually any size group—providing a wider audience for small extremist groups. The new technologies also offer the ability to alter pictures, sound, and video, making it difficult to determine the difference between fact and fiction. Another important social issue is providing access to technology for everyone. It would be easy to create a world or nation consisting of *haves* and *have-nots* in terms of access to

> ### A MANAGER'S VIEW
> As a manager, you need to understand how businesses, technology, and society interact. Dealing with changes in privacy and security threats will become increasingly important to managing a company. Evaluating changes in society will also give you an advantage in the marketplace; it is important to know your customers. As a citizen, you need to be aware of the negative and positive effects of technology. In particular, changes in technology often lead to changes in political power and control. As a manager and a citizen, you are obligated to make ethical decisions and to understand the consequences of your actions.

information. Those with information would be able to grow and earn more money, while those lacking the data would continually lose ground.

Increasing dependence on technology brings with it new threats to the security of the firm. Managers need to recognize and evaluate these threats and understand some of the techniques used to minimize them. The most common threats come from inside the company, in terms of workers, consultants, and business partnerships. These threats are difficult to control, because firms have to trust these individuals to do their jobs. Training, oversight, audits, and separation of duties are common means to minimize the threats. Depending on the communication systems used, there are threats from outsiders and viruses that can access computers with modems, over networks, or by intercepting communications. Dial-back modems, access controls, encryption, and antivirus software are common techniques to combat these threats.

Working in today's business environment means more than just doing your job. Each individual and firm has ethical obligations to consumers, workers, other companies, and society. In addition to obeying the laws, it is important for workers and companies to remember that the data in information systems refers to real people. The lives of people can be adversely affected by inaccurate data, poorly designed information systems, or abuse of the information.

## KEY WORDS

authentication, 679

biometrics, 676

Clipper chip, 681

cold site, 675

computer ethics, 682

Data Encryption Standard (DES), 679

dehumanization, 659

encryption, 665

escrow key, 681

hackers, 668

haves and have-nots, 665

hot site, 675

information threat, 667

privacy, 652

private key, 679

public key, 679

Rivest-Shamir-Adelman (RSA) algorithm, 679

social group legitimacy, 664

software piracy, 681

virus, 671

## REVIEW QUESTIONS

1. What privacy problems are individuals likely to experience as the use of computers and availability of data increase?
2. Do employees need to worry about the data collected by their employers?
3. Do you think increasing use of computers causes a loss of jobs? What about in the past or in the future?
4. How are computers helping disabled people to perform jobs?
5. How can computers be used in education and training?
6. Do you think state, local, and federal governments are making efficient use of computers? What privacy controls exist? Should there be additional controls?
7. In what ways have computers affected society and organizations? Will these patterns continue? Are there other important patterns that might arise?
8. What are the basic threats to information systems?
9. Why is computer security different from security for paper information?
10. How do computers recognize individual users?
11. What types of access control are typically available to restrict access to your data?
12. What alternative security measures can be used to minimize security risks?
13. How can data encryption be used to verify the author of a document or order?
14. What are the ethical responsibilities of users in terms of information systems?

## EXERCISES

1. If you have access to a local area network or a multiuser system that allows sharing of data, create a word-processed document and assign the proper security rights so that someone else in your class (or your instructor) can read the file but cannot alter it. As a team project, grant access only to your team members.
2. Team project: All team members should create a short spreadsheet. Protect each one with a password. Now, swap files and see whether team members can guess your password. You must be able to restore your file without writing down your password. As an experiment, one team member should choose a password that is easy to guess.
3. Team project: Split into two groups. Individuals in each group will type a page of text into a word processor (pick any full page from the textbook). To start, everyone will work on the project independently, but there is a deadline of no more than two days. Second, team members will pair up and type the document a second time. This

time, while one person types the document, the other one will time his or her performance and count mistakes at the end. The goal is to find the team member who is fastest and makes the fewest mistakes. The trick is that each person's work will be monitored at all times. Now, when all members of the team have completed their tasks, get the team back together and answer the following questions. Was there more pressure while you were being watched? Were you nervous? More attentive? Were you faster the second time? Did you make more mistakes? Would you object to working under these conditions on a daily basis?

4. Obtain a copy of antivirus software (most universities have a site license for one) and check all of your disks for viruses. Did the program find any? How long did it take check all of your disks? Do you often use disks on different computer systems? Do you know whether these systems are tested on a regular basis?

5. As a manager, you have an opening for a new employee. While checking the background of one applicant, you learn that two years ago he (or she) was fired from a job for deliberately accessing computer files of other employees and destroying data. One of your colleagues suggested that the incident means the person must know a lot about computers, which would be useful in your department. Are you willing to hire this person? Why or why not? If you are somewhat willing to hire the applicant, what questions would you ask in an interview, or what additional information would you want to see?

6. Imagine that a company develops a device that can drive a car, unassisted, on any major road. After the system is in use for two years, someone is killed in a car accident where one of the vehicles uses this new system. Should the injured people be allowed to sue the company that sells the system? What about the programmers who created it? What if the company knows that there is a 1 percent chance that an accident will occur while the system is being used? However, without the system, there is a 10 percent chance that you will be involved in an accident. Do these statistics change your answer? Do you think a system of this type should be required to have a 0 percent chance of error? Is such a level possible? Would you buy and use a system if these probabilities were true?

7. Do you think governmental agencies should share data about citizens? For example, should

the FBI be able to access IRS records to locate suspected criminals? Should the FBI be allowed to access files from state and local governments? For instance, should all arrest records be automatically relayed to a central database? Should medical records be accessible to law enforcement agencies? Say that it is technically possible for the FBI to build a national database that contains DNA records for all citizens. If all medical records (from accidents, blood tests, and medical treatment) were computerized and automatically forwarded to the FBI, the agents could easily locate virtually any criminal.

 **Rolling Thunder Database**

1. What privacy problems might exist at Rolling Thunder? What rules or procedures should we enact to avoid problems?

2. What data access controls should we implement? Examine each data table and the input forms. Determine who should have "ownership" rights and decide which groups should have read or modify privileges.

3. What threats (physical and logical) exist to our information system? What steps should we take to minimize these threats and minimize problems?

4. What employee procedures and background checks should we perform to protect our information systems?

## ADDITIONAL READING

"$10,000 Awarded to Man Whose Identity Was Stolen," Associated Press, *Louisville Courier-Journal*, February 4, 1994, p. B6. [Impersonation using an SSN]

Alexander, Michael. "Infection Risk Not Spurring Use of Anti-Virus Software," *Computerworld*, December 16, 1991, p. 49. [Viruses]

Alexander, Michael. "Shrink-Wrapped Viruses on Rise," *Computerworld*, January 6, 1992, p. 8. [Viruses]

Anthes, Gary H. "Old, New Viruses Swarm PC Users," *Computerworld*, May 6, 1996, p. 55. [Viruses]

Bequai, August. *Technocrimes*. Lexington, MA: Lexington Books, 1989. [Security Pacific and other cases]

Betts, Mitch. "Health Fraud: Computers at War," *Computerworld*, September 13, 1993, pp. 1, 14. [Health insurance billing]

Bozman, Jean S. "Fault-y Tales: Mainframes Rock 'n Roll," *Computerworld*, October 30, 1989, p. 6. [Disaster recovery services]

Cohen, Laurie P. and Alix M. Freedman. "American Express Sends a Statement That's Quite Wrong," *The Wall Street Journal*, February 24, 1995, pp. A1, A6. [American Express releases data]

Emshwiller, John R. "How Low-Key Style Let a Con Man Steal Millions from Bosses," *The Wall Street Journal*, December 4, 1995, pp. A1, A7. [Donald Peterson]

Emshwiller, John R. "Looking for a New Bookkeeper? Beware of this One," *The Wall Street Journal*, December 19, 1994, pp. B1, B2. [Donald Peterson]

Gottschalk, Jr., Earl C. "Stock Hustlers Exploit On-Line Services," *The Wall Street Journal*, June 21, 1994, pp. C1, C13. [Electronic stock manipulation]

Hoffman, Thomas. "Imaging Cures Hospital's Paper Woes: Memorial Sloan-Kettering Saving More Than $140K/Year with a Healthy Dose of Document Imaging," *Computerworld*, June 29, 1992, p. 74, [Hospitals]

"Invasion of Privacy," *PC World*, November 1995. [TRW records]

"Is Nothing Private?" *Business Week*, September 4, 1989. [TRW records]

Joyce, Edward. "Time Bomb: Inside the Texas Virus Trial," *Computer Decisions*, December 1988. [Programmer misdeeds]

Kay, Emily. "Strong Medicine," *Corporate Computing*, August 1992, pp. 153–157. [Hospitals]

Kennedy, Michael. "The Role of Networking in the Health Care Environment," *Telecommunications*, September 1995, p. 55. [Hospitals]

Livingston, Dennis. "Network Heals a Medical Center," *Systems Integration*, September 1991, pp. 48–51. [Hospitals]

Malnig, Anita. "Multimedia Moves into Medical Training," *MacWeek*, June 22, 1992, pp. 36–37, [Hospitals]

Miller, Michael W. "Data Tap: Patient's Records Are Treasure Trove for Budding Industry: Doctors' and Pharmacies' Files Are Gathered and Mined for Use by Drug Makers; Firms Say Names Are Deleted," *The Wall Street Journal*, February 27, 1992, p. A1. [Hospitals]

Nash, Jim. "Imaging Heals Hospital's Sick File System," *Computerworld*, March 2, 1992, pp. 43–44. [Hospitals]

*Network World*, January 27, 1992, p. 27. [Some international privacy restrictions]

Neumann, Peter G. "Inside Risks," *Communications of the ACM*, January 1992, p. 186. [Dangers of social security numbers]

"No Place Like Home?" *The Wall Street Journal*, October 14, 1994, pp. R1–R28. [Special section on home offices, with discussion of benefits and pitfalls. Includes stories by several entrepreneurs]

Nussbaum, Gerald. "Charting Vital Signs: Computers Boost Patient Care," *Corporate Computing*, August 1992, pp. 203–204. [Hospitals]

Nussbaum, Karen. "Workers Under Surveillance," *Computerworld*, January 6, 1992, p. 21. [Monitoring of workers]

Parker, Donn B. *Crime by Computer*. New York: Scribner, 1976. [Early cases of computer fraud and abuse]

Radosevich, Marcia. *Computerworld*, September 3, 1993, p. 14. [Health insurance billing]

"Ritz-Carlton," *Computerworld*, July 19, 1993, p. 91. [Ritz-Carlton data collection]

Roberts, Ralph and Pamela Kane. *Compute!'s Computer Security*. Greensboro, NC: Compute! Books, 1989 [Basic elements of computer security]

Samuelson, Pamela. "Legally Speaking: Can Hackers Be Sued for Damages Caused by Computer Viruses?" *Communications of the ACM*, June 1989. [Legal analysis of computer viruses]

Saul, Stephanie. "What Inmate Workers Know About Outsiders Causes Worry," *Louisville Courier Journal*, November 28, 1994, p. C8. [Data privacy]

Simpson, Charlie. "Imagine That Xpoint and ImagePlus Help Hospital Systems Operate Efficiently," *Midrange Systems*, April 7, 1992, p. 36. [Hospitals]

Smith, James M. "VA Finishes Hardware Upgrade at 67 Medical Centers," *Government Computer News*, August 3, 1992, p. 12. [Hospitals]

Stoll, Clifford. *The Cuckoo's Egg: Tracking a Spy Through a Maze of Computer Espionage*. New York: Doubleday, 1989. [Fascinating story of a spy searching US networks]

"Technology and Unemployment: A World Without Jobs?" *The Economist*, February 11, 1995, pp. 21–23. [Excellent analysis of the effects of technology on jobs, including references to studies]

Whiteside, Thomas. *Computer Capers: Tales of Electronic Thievery, Embezzlement and Fraud*. New York: Crowell, 1978. [Early cases of computer fraud and abuse]

Young, Joy. "Quality Patient Care Boosted by MUMPS," *Computers in Healthcare*, June 15, 1992, pp. 14–15. [Hospitals]

# CASES  *Health Care*

The healthcare industry is beginning to expand its use of IT. Common uses include communication, word processing, and databases. Of course, within this service industry, some healthcare employees use computers more than others.

SOURCE: Computer Use in the United States, U.S. Bureau of the Census.

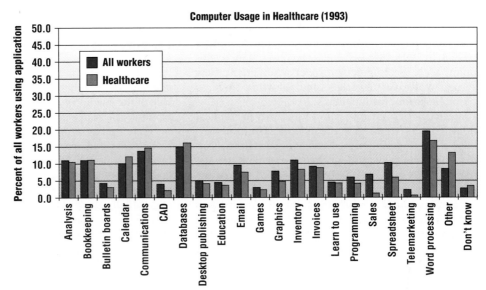

**Computer Usage in Healthcare (1993)**

As the average age of the U.S. population continues to rise, the demand for health care increases. For most people, health care is a sensitive topic. Since Hippocrates, ethical analyses and laws have been created to ensure competency and quality in health care. Some strict regulations apply to medical records and medical communications. Physicians, patients, and health care employees all have strong reasons for the maintenance of accurate records.

In the "old days," most health care records were maintained on paper by personal physicians and a local hospital. With today's world of specialists, HMOs, and managed health care, patients records are passed from physician to physician and to insurance agencies. Government agencies are increasingly involved in health care decisions as well. To function with minimal errors and high quality control, everyone in the system needs access to medical records. Yet, the existing paper-based system means that only one person can see the records at a time. It also increases the likelihood that files will be lost or misplaced in transit.

Several proposals have been made for computerizing medical records. Individual hospitals and physicians have experimented with computerization. There are still many unresolved issues regarding accessibility, standardization, and liability. Some U.S. government proposals have called for national health care cards that will hold personal medical data. Others have called for national medical databases. There are problems that need to be resolved with all of the proposed solutions.

## CASE  *Different Approaches to Medical Records*

### HARVARD PILGRIM HEALTH CARE

Medical decisions made by physicians are obviously important, because they directly affect the lives of patients. Keeping accurate records is a major factor in diagnoses, treatment, and preventing future problems. As the cost of medical care increases, health care providers have become more "business oriented" and now focus on controlling costs as well as providing quality care. For several years, medical providers have used information systems to track financial aspects of the business, such as billing and accounts receivable.

Throughout the medical community, there has been a reluctance to computerize patient records. Some state and federal regulations apply to medical records. For instance, in some cases physical signatures are required to be on file to authorize treatments and some drug prescriptions. Although many states allow electronic authorization for treatment, confusion about the laws is often cited as a reason for maintaining a paper-based system. Health care professionals have also been reluctant to use computerized systems. For example, Ginger Dankese, a senior medical assistant at Harvard Pilgrim Health Care (HPHC), notes that medical care is "a lot more personal with a paper chart. You have to get used to looking at a patient and the computer at the same time. If someone's sick, you don't want him talking to the back of your head."

Physicians have also worried that computerized systems will force them to spend more time on clerical matters. For instance, in re-engineering the tasks at HPHC, Thomas Pyle, the CEO, attempted to push more jobs over to the physicians, including forcing them to enter their own data into the new computer system. In 1991, Pyle was encouraged to resign. At this point, there is disagreement over whether the new system will save physician time, allowing them to spend more time with patients.

Resistance to change is not unknown in medical information systems. A Veterans Administration (VA) hospital in Tuscaloosa, Alabama, converted its information system from an older Digital minicomputer system to a LAN consisting of Intel 486-based microcomputers. The system performed standard business and accounting functions. However, one pharmacist was upset with the new system. With the old system, he would start a print request on Friday afternoon and leave for the day because it took so long to print. With the new system, he was forced to work Friday afternoons because the printouts were created almost immediately.

HPHC has high hopes for the system. The goal is to create integrated, easy-to-use systems for each functional area, including administration (e.g., scheduling appointments, membership enrollment, and billing), pharmacy (e.g., prescriptions, checking for drug interactions, and monitoring excessive prescriptions and use of addictive drugs), lab work (e.g., scheduling and reporting of results), and clinical (e.g., diagnoses, exam results, and physician notes).

The system is eventually designed to be integrated among applications and across all of the health centers managed by HPHC. It will enable physicians, clerks, nurses, emergency personnel, and even patients access to the same base information—subject to access rights to protect privacy and prevent unauthorized changes. For example, patients can use the system to get basic medical advice from their homes. The overall goal is to provide physicians with a better way to examine the huge amounts of sometimes conflicting data.

The system is based on Apple Macintosh computers on physician and clerical desktops. These microcomputers and some terminals are connected via an Ethernet network to a Digital VAX 6500, which functions as a large database server. As other health centers are added to the system, they will be networked over T1 data links from the phone companies.

HPHC initially tried to develop the system with in-house staffing but decided the facility needed additional technical assistance. In late 1988, HPHC created a new firm in conjunction with EDS (known as InterPractice Systems or IPS), headed by Dr. Al Martin, who was a medical director at HPHC. In January 1991,

HPHC opened a clinic in Burlington, Massachusetts, to test the system. Almost 100 doctors, clinicians, and designers were involved in the initial design of the system. By 1992, development costs were around $8.5 million. However, HPHC believes they can save around $4 per member for each month, amounting to at least $21.6 million a year.

HPHC and IPS have made the system easy for physicians to use by relying heavily on the graphical interface of the Macintosh. For example, if a doctor receives a phone call from a patient, he or she clicks on an icon to open the basic file. Icons are displayed to indicate prior visits and information about the patient. For instance, a pencil indicates administrative data and a face represents a personal visit. By pointing to a problem list, the doctor gets a list of problems reported by the patient, along with details recorded about each visit. With the system, the doctor can make immediate recommendations over the phone without having to search through paper records and call back later.

IPS and HPHC are experimenting with more sophisticated features, such as direct access by customers from their homes. By using the system to diagnose minor ailments and suggest over-the-counter remedies, HPHC was hoping it would reduce the 35 percent of office visits that are medically unnecessary. So far, this portion of the system has not been heavily used. Another useful feature of this part of the system is that it contains rules to automatically notify HPHC personnel in emergency situations. For instance, if a patient requests advice about poisoning and selects specific options on a menu, the system notifies medical personnel to call the patient and provide emergency care if necessary. However, there is reason to believe that most patients will be uncomfortable with using the computer system.

## LUTHERAN HOSPITAL IN LA CROSSE, WISCONSIN

A key component of intensive care units (ICU) is monitoring patient vital signs and maintaining records of physician orders, as well as treatments such as administration of drugs. For several years, Hewlett-Packard has sold automatic monitoring devices such as the CareVue 9000. However, hospitals have been reluctant to use the new technology. In a 1992 survey, only 17 percent of responding hospital IS executives noted that they had implemented bedside systems. Another 32 percent said they were considering implementation of bedside-monitoring systems.

In many ways, the bedside-monitoring systems are analogous to the point-of-sale or barcode systems used by retail merchants. The goal is to automatically collect data as close to the source as possible. The systems capture and store data from heart-rate and blood-pressure devices. They have graphics-based screens to allow nurses and doctors to enter additional information. In the future, they could even be tied to the hospital's base information system, for example, to store historical patient records or notify billing.

As the system collects basic patient data, it enables nurses to record additional observations. It reduces measurement and computational errors. By generating standard reports, the system frees nurses to spend more time providing patient care. The system tracks progress over time and draw graphs that allow physicians to spot trends.

Lutheran Hospital measured nursing activity before and after implementing the CareVue system. With the system in place, nurses spent 22 percent less time making charts, which effectively doubled the amount of time they could spent with patients. By eliminating overtime charting, Lutheran save the equivalent of a full-time employee.

## INDIAN RIVER MEMORIAL HOSPITAL

Indian River Memorial Hospital in Vero Beach, Florida, chose a different approach to the problem of managing patient records. The hospital's new system still uses paper-based forms, but in a different manner. First, hospital and insurance forms are stored electronically and are printed at nursing stations or in emergency rooms as they are needed. The computer adds bar codes to record basic patient identifiers. After the forms have been filled in, they are eventually scanned back into the computer system as images and filed by their bar code identifiers. The forms are indexed and stored on an IBM AS/400. They can be viewed by physicians, nurses and administrative personnel through terminals.

## SAN JOSE MEDICAL CENTER

The San Jose Medical Center trauma facility has implemented a similar medical imaging system, but it relies on IBM microcomputers and Wang workstations. The center switched to the computer-based filing system because the director of records estimated the cost of retrieving a single paper file could run as high as $13. Currently only 40 percent of each patient's file is handled by the computer, but the staff hopes to improve to 95 percent.

## COLUMBIA-PRESBYTERIAN MEDICAL CENTER OF NEW YORK

Columbia-Presbyterian (CPMC) is a large teaching medical center in New York, associated with Columbia University and scattered across 13 buildings at the main site. With 1,512 beds and 5,000 physicians,

nurses, and researchers, CPMC has a mission not only to provide quality care but to train medical students and to pursue medical research.

Funded by Columbia University and the National Institute of Health, the CPMC is building a new hospital and research information system. The system will eventually integrate data from five components:

- The Clinical Information System provides electronic access to patient data. Because a patient may see many different medical personnel in different locations, paper-based reports are hard to use. This subsystem maintains data about lab results such as blood tests, reports from treatment centers such as endoscopy and obstetrics, surgical reports, as well as admission and discharge information.

- The Administrative Information System provides standard accounting data to the local offices. It includes an integrated word processor so secretaries and researchers can create and share documents. It also contains a centralized phone directory.

- The Clinical Research Support System assists authorized researchers in finding and downloading patient data. For example, CPMC is adding the capability of scanning for certain patient conditions and automatically notifying interested researchers when particular diseases or conditions appear.

- Basic Science Research Support is designed to give researchers access to computer databases across the country. Researchers also have their own databases on their lab computers such as DNA sequences and research in molecular biology.

- The Scholarly Information System provides physicians with electronic access to research journals and the MEDLINE biomedical index. When a physician finds a relevant article he or she can use the system to request that the article be faxed to the office.

A major task of the CPMC IS staff is to provide network access to all of the equipment and people at the medical center. Along with providing access, they are concerned about providing appropriate security facilities to protect patient privacy.

## DEPARTMENT OF DEFENSE COMPOSITE HEALTH CARE SYSTEM

The U.S. Department of Defense operates 200 medical facilities throughout the United States. With the help of Science Applications International Corp., the DOD is building a $2-billion information system designed for the Digital VMS environment. The four-plus year development project, begun in 1988, experienced typical delays and cost overruns. It was criticized by many people—some of whom had a financial interest in encouraging the DOD to consider alternative systems. The Government Accounting Office (GAO) has also been critical of the system, noting that it lacks a critical archiving facility to hold historical patient data. In early stages, the GAO also suggested that the system had the unfortunate ability to store a patient's data in many separate locations—potentially causing problems if a medical provider accidentally saw only part of the patient's data. The system has been designed in pieces, and the full system was not designed to be operational until 1994. The GAO warned the DOD that use of parts of the system could lead to problems. The GAO was particularly concerned about the lack of an inpatient order entry (IPOE) module. Doctors at various hospitals, including the Walter Reed Medical Center, were critical of the system. In particular, they noted that the system is cumbersome, slow, and contains data errors, such as not recording the proper physician's name with patient orders.

Developers of the system agreed that the user interface needed to be improved, noting that the system works, but they had difficulty getting physicians to use it. The inpatient order entry system (IPOE), with which physicians record treatment orders, was particularly troublesome. Despite the objections, the DOD continues to press on with development and deployment of the system. Officials cite the potential savings of $4 to $5 billion over three years. They also note that any system is preferable to antiquated paper-based processes.

## QUESTIONS

1. Identify the decision support components involved in each of medical center cases. Does one factor have a higher priority than others?
2. What basic problems are the information systems designed to overcome? What are the potential benefits?
3. What similarities exist among the cases at the different medical centers?
4. What problems are being faced by the Department of Defense? What features or ideas would you want the DOD to "borrow" from the other examples?
5. As a patient, what reactions would you have to a medical center in which the physicians and nurses heavily used computers? What problems would you expect to encounter? What are the potential benefits to you?
6. What are the advantages and disadvantages of a computerized patient system to the caregivers (e.g., nurses and physicians)? Do they have to worry about loss of jobs?
7. In comparing each of the systems, what potential problems exist in the longer run? Consider the cases of a patient or a physician who moves from one area of the country to another. How could these issues be resolved? What factors will hinder the potential solutions?
8. Why do you think it has taken so long for hospitals and medical centers to begin implementing patient-care decision support systems?
9. What types of access should be allowed to patient medical information? Can individuals limit the use of their medical data? Should they be allowed to?

## CASE  *Health Insurance and Billing*

Health care and payment of it is a major topic for employees, businesses, governments, and insurance companies. As the U.S. population ages, increasing amounts of money are being spent on health care. By some reports (*Corporate Computing,* 1992), American corporations spent 45 percent of their after-tax profits on health insurance in 1990. Medical care is the fastest growing segment of federal government expenditures and has led to calls for renovations in health care financing across America.

Several years ago, to simplify recordkeeping, issuance of bills, and payments, the health insurance industry created a standardized set of codes collectively known as ICD-9 as identifiers for all medical procedures. They are five-digit codes grouped into DRGs (diagnosis-related group). When physicians and other health care providers record patient diagnoses and treatments, they add the appropriate ICD-9 code numbers. These codes are submitted to patient's insurance company for reimbursement. Insurance companies have predefined "usual and customary" charges that apply for each code, which represent the amount of money insurers will pay for the itemized procedures.

From the provider's standpoint, one difficulty with the codes is that there are thousands of them. Also, for most major procedures, there will be several different ICD-9 codes that might apply to the particular treatment. As a result, the provider has to choose which codes best represent the treatment that was provided. They also have to be careful to include all of the appropriate codes, because many treatments require a combination of related codes.

To assist the providers, several companies have created software that enables the physician to search for the proper codes based on the treatment that was performed. Some expert systems exist that will search for alternative combinations and display related choices. The physician then chooses among the groups for the set of codes that most closely matches the treatment that was performed.

Most of these software packages are integrated with patient billing and record systems. Once the physician (or an assistant) enters the appropriate codes, the data is stored with the patient records and a bill is printed for the patient and for the insurance company. Some packages automatically call the appropriate insurance companies (or government agency for Medicaid and Medicare) and transfer the statements electronically.

Because of the difficulty of choosing the proper code, there is the potential for abuse. According to Marcia Radosevich (*Computerworld,* September 13, 1993, p. 14), president of Health Payment Review, most insurance billing fraud involves billing for work that was never done. Also, even though the vast majority of medical providers are conscientious and honest, estimates are that dishonesty and mistakes in coding result in overpayments of 1 percent of health care spending, or almost $8 billion in 1992.

Many of the billing packages sold to medical providers specifically advertise that they will increase the amount of payments received from insurance companies. Although such claims may be legitimate, there are some reports of abuses. One common trick is to break a treatment into smaller parts and bill for each of the parts. For example, Health Payment Review illustrates how a physician might submit a bill with four codes totaling $7,082 for arthroscopic knee surgery, which should be billed only as code 29881 for a total payment of $2,670.

| CODE | ITEM | PAYMENT |
| --- | --- | --- |
| 27570 | Manipulation of the knee | $   473 |
| 29870 | Diagnostic arthroscopy | 1,371 |
| 29875 | Limited synovectomy | 2,568 |
| 29881 | Knee arthroscopy/meniscectomy | 2,670 |
| Total | | $7,082 |

Many situations involve careful judgments. For instance, many of the software systems designed for providers automatically list any related diagnoses. The provider is supposed to choose the set of codes that represents the most accurate diagnosis. However, it would be tempting to automatically choose the option that generates the highest fees.

More blatant forms of billing fraud exist. For one example, a physician billed 10 different insurance companies for performing 48 surgical procedures in a single day, which was physically impossible. Currently, almost all insurance companies (and government programs) review major claims. With training and experience, they can spot the unbundling shown in the arthroscopic knee example. However, a single insurer cannot easily spot fraud that is routed through several insurance companies.

The Clinton administration proposed major revisions to health care and payments in the United States. One of the provisions called for more use of electronic data interchange (EDI). In most cases, the amount of paperwork, time, and cost of handling claims could be decreased by submitting claims electronically and making payments automatically. Some insurers worried that it would become more difficult to detect fraud and abuse of the coding system.

To decrease costs and improve the processing speed, some insurance companies are turning to expert systems created specifically to help detect "unusual" billing patterns. Companies such as Health Payment Review, GMIS, and Medicode have created software that analyzes statements to detect the unbundling problems and other potential fraud situations.

## QUESTIONS

1. How do computerized insurance filing systems help medical care providers?
2. What are the basic decisions involved?
3. Identify the components of a decision support system that are used by hospitals.
4. In a health insurance company, how can information systems be used to cut costs and detect fraud?
5. Assume you have the authority to revise the entire information system of recording and billing medical care from patient records to treatment to billing to payment. Devise a better system. What problems or hindrances do you expect to encounter?
6. Is it socially responsible for medical care providers to use billing systems that might increase their revenue?
7. Is it acceptable for companies to create billing systems that tell providers that they can increase revenue by "unbundling" ICD-9 codes and other questionable practices? If you were working as a manager (or programmer) at a software company and found out the company specialized in "creative" billing software, what would you do?

## CASE  *Post Office Release of Address Lists*

The United States Postal Service is working on the first computerized list of American addresses. This list would provide a regularly cleaned and updated list to direct mail advertisers. The post office plans to license the electronic list to private database companies that sell personal information to mailers, investigators, and debt collectors. The plan is to restrict the use of the list and not attach names to the addresses.

Before this project, the postal service never had a single list of the nation's 100 million addresses, even for internal purposes. The post office is legally forbidden from making available to the public for any purpose, any list of names and addresses. The postal service says this directory will not be a violation of this law because the service will carefully monitor the database companies that use the list. The focus on the sales will be to correct current mailing lists rather than to make new ones.

According to Ed Burnett, an Englewood, New Jersey, direct mail consultant, "This is the best thing since sliced bread to correct the mail that isn't delivered."

Privacy experts are equally concerned by the proposal. The top database companies can already construct lists for 80 percent of the American households by cross-referencing telephone books, driver's-license files, and hundreds of other sources. Looking for new sources of revenue, the companies have begun to sell data to private detectives, credit collectors, and government agencies.

Janlori Goldman, director of the American Civil Liberties Union's Project on Privacy and Technology, states that "The Post Office is providing this information for commercial profit. It seems like a first step in the wrong direction."

The post office already collects change-of-address forms into one computer file and sells it to 20 companies. The companies charge $2 to check a thousand names. Post office officials justify this sale because "They pick only the most reliable concerns for the change-of-address program and regulate them intensely."

Another initiative is a program in Akron, Ohio, to help customers keep records of their Christmas card mailing lists. Customers give the post office their mailing lists and receive free bar-coded mailing labels. The post office proposed to keep the lists on disk so they could be updated each year.

A second proposal is to add two more numbers to the nine-digit postal code so that the zip code would correspond directly with each unique address. Once implemented, bulk mailers would receive an additional discount for using all 11 digits. Tests of the new system have been successful and the post office is accelerating the project.

Robert Ellis Smith, publisher of the "Privacy Journal" newsletter, is concerned about a government agency assigning a special number to each household: "One of the values of American life is that it allows enough flexibility for people not to be enumerated and accountable at every point of their lives."

SOURCE: Colleen O'Hara, "USPS Turns to Electronic Forms." *Federal Computer Week,* August 28, 1995. pp. 20–21. Reprinted with permission of *Federal Computer Week.* Copyright 1996, FCW Government Technology Group. All rights reserved.

### QUESTIONS

1. As a marketer, how would you use a guaranteed mailing list that contains every address in the United States? What other data would you use to target your customers?
2. As a consumer, do you object to receiving unsolicited mail? Would you prefer to receive no mail from advertisers? Do you read unsolicited mail? Make purchases using it?
3. How could con artists or other criminals use this information to perpetrate scams?
4. Are there some people who would experience problems if their home addresses were publicly available to everyone?

## CASE  *Donald Peterson: Bookkeeper*

Nathan J. International Inc. is a small clothing manufacturer in Huntington Beach, California, with three retail stores. In 1993, Celia Imperiale, the owner, advertised for a bookkeeper. A man calling himself Michael Hammond answered the ad. From his resume, he seemed ideal. He had worked as a bookkeeper for more than 20 years in stable jobs with only two firms. Imperiale called the phone number given for his previous employer and was given a glowing recommendation. She was unable to reach the earliest employer, but that was in a different city and the job was almost 12 years before. Hammond seemed knowledgeable about accounting and computers. He also mentioned that he was covered by his wife's health insurance and so would not need coverage. Ms. Imperiale hired Hammond, noting that "he seemed the perfect employee."

Imperiale notes that although he operated "very slowly, almost at a snail's pace," Hammond performed his job reliably until one Friday in December—the day that the outside auditor was scheduled to perform the quarterly check of the books. Hammond disappeared completely. He took his personnel file, along with a private file Imperiale kept in her office. He also took several credit card applications that had been sent to Imperiale.

The auditor quickly noticed that there was $44,000 missing from the business accounts. Apparently, Hammond would pick up the cash receipts from each of the retail stores. He would make up a deposit slip and show everything to Imperiale. But on the way to the bank, he wrote a new deposit slip for about 10 percent of the value, pocketing the other 90 percent. He covered the difference by changing account values in the computer and by not paying federal and state taxes. After leaving Nathan J., he ran up $2,000 of bills using the credit card applications he acquired from Imperiale's office.

Jeff Nelson, a detective with the Huntington Beach police department, notes that the man claiming to be Hammond more often used the name David Shelton. However, Nelson has traced him through 15 different aliases. He appears to have performed similar scams with several other companies in California. Elaine Hutchison, owner of Paragon Equities Inc., a property-management company in Long Beach, claims that "Michael Gordon" stole $72,000 from her business. In addition to pocketing cash, he would create fake suppliers on the computer and then send checks to accounts that he controlled. Authorities believe he is responsible for embezzling at least $600,000 from more than seven small businesses.

Police credit Shelton with being cautious and inventive. He drove nondescript cars and parked them away from work so people would not spot them. He typically stayed in flop-houses, with minimal records kept and at low cost. He often used accomplices at the flop-houses to answer the phone and give job recommendations. He did not socialize with colleagues and avoided having his photograph taken. In the only photograph detectives could obtain, Shelton had his back to the camera. Bank records show that Shelton used his cash to buy gold bullion, which they have been unable to trace.

Postscript: This story ran in *The Wall Street Journal* in April 1994. Two days later, the *Journal* reported that another small California business owner identified Donald Peterson (his real name) from the police sketch that appeared with the article. He was arrested and charged.

Although Peterson is spending time in jail, most of the money remains missing, and he feels no remorse for his crimes. He goes on to note that his actions were "a good learning experience" for the victims and would encourage them to become better business people. He says that when he gets out of prison this time (he was previously incarcerated in the 1970s), he hopes to present seminars on avoiding fraud or possibly to get a job "perhaps in accounting."

## QUESTIONS

1. What can small businesses do to protect itself from people like Peterson?
2. What computer controls could be established to minimize these types of problems?
3. How will these controls (manual and computer) affect the operation of the business, employee attitude, and costs?
4. Why did Peterson target small businesses? What differences exist between small and large businesses that might make it easier for criminals?
5. Is there any way police might have caught up with Peterson sooner? For example, could the employers have collected additional information? What consequences would these actions have in terms of employee and personal privacy?

## CASE *Protecting Information in Directories and Electronic Databases*

CD-ROM and online technology make it possible for data to be read directly onto a person's hard disk drive. Printed directories can be easily scanned into a standard word-processing platform. All of these technologies make it difficult to maintain the competitive advantage of databases.

In *Feist Publications Inc.* v. *Rural Telephone Services Company,* decided in April 1990, the U.S. Supreme Court ruled that a competitor could copy a telephone white pages directory serving 7,700 people in rural Kansas. In a unanimous decision, the court ruled that "sweat of the brow" in compiling banks of data does not qualify a directory for copyright protection. The court went on to hold that compilations of publicly available data must be arranged or selected in some original or creative way to warrant copyright protection. The court left to future decisions the question of how much "original and creative" work was necessary to protect data entered into the computer.

A federal judge in Atlanta has ruled that the Yellow Pages, not the White Pages, is subject to copyright because of the unique way in which it is arranged. The Federal Appeals Court in New York ruled that a directory of businesses in Chinatown could copy information from a competitor.

The *Feist* case opens new doors to those companies who use data collected by other entities. Ultimately, this may create more competition and lower prices for directories. Several additional cases have been brought since the *Feist* case:

- *Trade-mark Search.* A trademark search firm appeared before a federal judge asking him to declare public a database of state-registered trademarks owned by its chief competitor.

- *PhoneDisc USA Company.* PhoneDisc markets computerized telephone directories. It has been electronically scanning all 3,500 White Pages telephone directories published in the United States. PhoneDisc also uses overseas labor to enter many of the names. The company currently markets names, addresses, and phone numbers of 80 million U.S. consumers and 11 million businesses.

- *Marquis Who's Who.* The publishers of *Marquis Who's Who* are writing the preface of the next edition to stress the creative process necessary to assemble the names and biographies of significant individuals. The new preface will specifically spell out the special characteristics of the book, including its secret and "unique standards" of selection.

- *Standard & Poors.* Standard & Poors has added a clear plastic wrap with rules for the use of the data that is being sent. By opening the wrap, the user agrees to the terms of the agreement. These include an agreement not to use the "Register in any manner which competes with or substitutes for Standard & Poors." Based on similar issues in "shrink-wrapped" software, this technique might not be effective if the purchaser has no ability to influence the terms of the "agreement."

- *Southwestern Bell.* Southwestern Bell is putting its trademark on each of the white pages in its directories. This would make it illegal for competitors to photocopy its pages.

- *American Business Information Systems.* This marketer of electronic directories of every business in the United States puts a software device on its CD-ROMs that make them unusable after a year. Of course, the data is out of date by that time, because approximately 20 percent of phone directory listings change in a year.

Companies that enter, market, and maintain databases are working to make their work "original and creative." Those that will be most successful at building this barrier are companies that have developed a sophisticated directory established in a niche market. By definition, electronic databases may be the most difficult to protect. The effectiveness of a database is that it is comprehensive; making a database comprehensive removes one of the attributes of creativity that will protect it from being copied.

## QUESTIONS

1. What are the benefits of a copyright system? Why would the courts consider some data to be uncopyrightable?
2. What are the benefits and costs of the phone companies creating their own electronic directories?
3. As more information is moved to online directories, how will companies protect their copyrights? Even if they can protect the data, how will they charge users to recoup their costs?
4. Assume you can rewrite copyright and patent laws from scratch. Outline a new policy that can be applied to data created and transmitted with modern technology. (Hint: This is a hard question. Do some research to see what other people propose.)

## CASE  *Giving Employees Access to Data*

An important privacy and security consideration is to hire employees whom you can trust. Although most companies are careful, they can sometimes make mistakes.

One day, Beverly Dennis, a grandmother in Ohio, was upset when she received a 12-page sexually graphic letter. The letter was sent by an inmate in a Texas prison who is serving a 6½ year sentence for breaking into a house and raping a woman. Dennis is obviously concerned, but what does this case have to do with information systems?

It all began with a Nebraska company called Metromail Corp., which sent surveys to thousands of people promising free products and coupons in exchange for filling out the survey. The completed surveys were processed by a New York company, Computerized Image, which hired Texas prisoners to type the data into computers. The goal of the program was to teach the prisoners useful skills, but it gave them access to personal data.

Many other states have implemented similar job-training programs. Companies gain cheap labor, and inmates learn useful skills and have a chance to earn a job when they leave. TWA uses youthful offenders in California to work as overflow reservationists. During peak times, calls are automatically routed to special phones at the Ventura County prison. In one incident, a former inmate participant was charged with using a caller's credit card number to charge thousands of dollars of merchandise.

Several states use prisoners to enter public data from lawsuits and wills into computers. Although this information is in the public record, the process often gives prisoners access to names, addresses, and social security numbers.

## QUESTIONS

1. What are the advantages to society from these prisoner work programs? What are the drawbacks?
2. Is there some way to gain the advantages of these programs and avoid or minimize the drawbacks demonstrated in these cases?
3. Even if we pass laws prohibiting this practice, could similar problems arise? Should companies avoid hiring any ex-convict?
4. As consumers, what safeguards can we take to prevent similar problems? If a similar situation arises, what protections do we have?

## CASE  *HMM: Protecting Information*

Michael has been working as a department manager for Heavy Metal Manufacturing (not a real company) for the last five years. The company produces custom parts ands tools for use in large construction equipment. Last year, HMM made a profit of $5.8 million dollars on sales of $95.7 million. There are 250 full-time employees. When large contracts are due, the company typically hires an additional 200 part-time employees and consultants. Most of the employees work in the manufacturing department. About 75 of them are in management or clerical positions.

The company has several long-term contracts with customers such as John Deere, Case, and Caterpillar. Smaller firms and local repair shops also buy parts and tools directly from HMM's factory. The marketing and sales department is headed by Mary Johns. There are 10 full-time salespeople who spend most of their time traveling to the larger clients. They all have laptop computers that they use to place orders, check production status, and forward customer complaints and requests to Mary. About 25 percent of their communication traffic consists of customer requests to change specifications, shipment dates, or delivery locations.

As head of purchasing, David Honin is in charge of finding supplies and materials and getting them to the factory in time for processing. His department also handles payments to the vendors. Every week, he produces a list of supplies that are scheduled to be delivered the following week. Once a month, the department sends checks to the suppliers and provides a report on the orders and payments to the accounting department. Lately, the production managers have been complaining about supplies not showing up as scheduled.

Last year, HMM installed a new database management system to keep track of the various orders, customers, and supplies. The database system was created by a group of outside consultants and has been working well. It enables salespeople to keep up with customer requests and to check on suppliers and schedules to estimate how long it will take to produce special orders. Most of the employees have been pleased with the new system. However, the accountants have been complaining about the inability to transfer data from the DBMS directly into their accounting system.

Cindy Werner, the CEO, has just called Michael to a meeting. They have known each other since college, and she trusts him completely. An external accounting firm has just notified her that they believe a large sum of money is missing. At this point, she trusts only Michael and the accounting firm, and she needs to find out what happened to the money.

At first, Michael believes this will be an easy job: The accountants will check the books for discrepancies, he will provide information about various employees, and the guilty people will be identified. After talking with the external accountants, the problem does not sound easy any more. The basic accounting records seem to be in order. All of the accounts match, and there is no indication of missing money, materials, or products. If someone is stealing from the firm, he or she is also changing the computer records to cover the trail.

However, the accounting team noticed a problem when they tried to find a special tool. The manufacturing department produced a batch of tools on July 22. A week later, they noticed a minor defect in one unit and they decided to fix the others. They tracked down all but one tool. When the auditors found out three weeks later, they became curious and wanted to know whether the tool ever got fixed. John in manufacturing told them he asked the sales reps to bring it back for inspection, but it never showed up. The accounting team contacted the marketing people, who said they never got the request from John. The accountants decided to call the firm that purchased the tool. When they were unable to contact anyone at the firm, they became suspicious and contacted Cindy.

The customer files reveal that the firm in question was a good local customer that buys several products every week. However, on closer examination, there is a problem. The section of the city where the firm is located is zoned for commercial/retail use only. There should not be a production company located in that area, yet the marketing records show that it is supposed to be a custom manufacturer.

Michael immediately suspects two salespeople: Mark and Susan, who both joined the company about a year ago. He notices that Mark is in charge of this particular account. He remembers meeting the two at a company picnic, where they stayed together and seemed to avoid the other employees. It seemed strange at the time and looks suspicious now. After talking with the accountants, they decide the best approach is to set a trap.

With the help of Cindy, Michael sets up a new production run of a special tool. This tool is expensive but is used by many different manufacturers and can be easily sold—just the sort of item someone would be inclined to steal. Cindy and Michael make plans to secretly number each tool so it can be identified later. In the meantime, Sam, one of the junior partners in the accounting firm, approaches the suspicious "manufacturing" customer. After a week, he finds the owners and convinces them that he needs one of the special tools. He convinces them that he needs it immediately and offers them a price slightly above the current market value.

The other members of the accounting team begin contacting other customers, banks, and suppliers. After a couple weeks, they have enough data to make some initial estimates. By comparing these records to the data stored in the company accounting system, they estimate that HMM is missing between $1.5 and $2.5 million. When Cindy hears these numbers, she agrees to let Michael and the team go ahead with their plan.

After a week, Mark records a sale of the tool to the suspicious company. The accountants can find no record of a payment from the firm. When Sam buys the tool from the company and finds the hidden identification number, the police are notified. They arrest Mark, Susan, and the owners of the company. However, when the district attorney hears about the case, she refuses to prosecute, stating that there is not sufficient evidence and the defendants would have a strong case of entrapment.

### QUESTIONS

1.  What did Michael do wrong in his investigation? If you had Michael's job, what would you have done to investigate the case?
2.  At this point, it is probably too late to catch the people who have been stealing because they have undoubtedly heard about Mark and Susan. In any case, you would like to know who is guilty and find out how they did it so you can avoid future problems. What steps would you take at this point? What additional information do you need, and how can you get it?
3.  What rules and procedures should have been in place at HMM to prevent this type of crime? Would these rules interfere with the operations of the company? What would it cost to enforce them (e.g., more staff, more computers, or something else)?

4.  When should the police be called in to investigate crimes of this sort? Do police departments have the resources and training to investigate these problems? If the police are unable to help, who would you call?

### CASE  *MRH: Metro Receiving Hospital*

Metro Receiving Hospital (not a real facility) has a problem. Its insurance company is canceling its coverage. The hospital just lost its sixth lawsuit involving qualifications of physicians and nurses.

MRH is an older facility with 825 beds and is located in the center of a city. It used to handle a wide variety of cases. Today, it specializes in trauma cases and short-term intensive care. Almost none of the patients stays more than one week. The Midwestern metropolitan area has a population of around 1 million people—mostly poor.

The hospital has trouble hiring physicians. The salaries are low, it's in a bad part of the city, and working conditions are hectic, with out-of-date equipment. There are almost 500 physicians on staff, along with 1,400 nurses and 50 pharmacists. Roughly 45 percent of the medical staff is young; they graduated within the last five years. Most of the workers in this group will work at the hospital for three years or less. Staffing is also difficult for administrative positions. Pay is low and there is limited support for training. As a result, morale is low and only 15 percent of the administrative workers have stayed at MRH more than three years.

There is an old centralized computer system that was created 15 years ago. It handles payroll and patient billing. One newer feature is its ability to exchange data directly with the insurance companies. As a result, MRH can check eligibility requirements for new patients and submit bills directly to the insurance companies. However, most of their patients don't have jobs, so medical support comes from various government programs.

The hospital recently experienced some problems with a few physicians. An investigative reporter found that three of them had their licenses revoked in other states before they came to MRH. Three others were once found guilty of sexually abusing their patients. Additionally, two pharmacists had felony convictions for illegally distributing drugs. As a result of the stories, the local citizens are complaining and politicians have established commissions to investigate the hospital.

After several meetings, it has been suggested that the hospital begin intensive background checks of the existing staff members and all job applicants. After considerable discussion, the state has agreed to allow MRH to connect two computer terminals to the state and regional police files. Through this system, the hospital can get access to all seven regional criminal record systems in the United States. It also gives investigators access to the FBI and NCIC databases, including the new automated fingerprint identification system. With this system, all employees and job applicants can be screened for arrests and criminal records.

After one year, comments on the new system are mixed. Five job applicants were rejected because the computer files revealed potential problems. However, two of them have sued the hospital claiming that the data was incorrect. Surveys of the medical staff indicate that morale is even lower than it was last year. Rumors have been circulating that one of the administrators routinely uses the police files to check on all employees (and friends, relatives, and neighbors).

Additionally, many people suspect that one of the administrators is using the computer link to operate a separate business. He uses the system to search for missing people, especially spouses who are delinquent in paying alimony and child support. He also searches for missing children (especially those taken by divorced parents).

## QUESTIONS

1.  Why would a hospital install a link to police computers?
2.  What problems might arise from the use of the computer search?
3.  Who is (or should be) responsible for the accuracy of the data (and its effect on hiring)?
4.  Is there any way to prevent abuse of the link to the crime database? Would computer controls be successful?
5.  Should governments and police departments allow other people and businesses access to their databases? If one type of business is given access, should the states be forced to allow other businesses to apply? Will they have a choice?
6.  What limits should be placed on access to government crime databases?

## DISCUSSION ISSUE

### *Security Limits?*

In many ways, it is impossible to provide complete security to any data. The ultimate protection would be to hide or destroy data so that no one could ever see it. Of course, no one could use the data. Problems arise because some people need to use data, but the organization also needs to control who can see and use certain information. One of the most difficult aspects of computer security is controlling access without interfering with the business and employee privacy.

Jenny has been working for a large company for the last three years. Axel was hired two months ago—he is a little more enthusiastic in his use of computers. Axel also has little faith in central administrators and rules.

*(Office, 9:15 A.M.)*

Axel:   Hey Jenny, check out these silly new rules. These guys have gone too far this time. It says here that certain employees can only access these accounts during working hours!

Jenny:  Really? Did you see the new PCs that MIS just delivered? They have warning stickers and special screws. We're not even allowed to open the cases.

Axel:   What are they worried about anyway? There's nothing in there to steal. Besides, it wouldn't take 30 seconds to get that screw out.

Jenny:  I don't know. I guess they're worried about us altering the machines. Or maybe they're afraid we'll do something to the network interface card to break security on the network.

Axel:   Well, too bad. I need to install my CD-ROM, and I'm not going to sit around and wait for tech support to get here. These rules are getting ridiculous.

*(Security center, 7:02 P.M.)*

Billy:    Hey Taggert, check out this report from the computer activity monitor. It says that Jenny down in finance is still logged in.

Taggert:  So, I've seen her work late some nights. She's on the authorized list, isn't she?

Billy:    Yeah, but I swear I passed her in the hall when I got back from dinner. Hang on, let's check the security logs . . . Yeah. There it is. She checked out at 6:32 P.M. Let's see . . . Yeah, the parking garage gate records show she drove out at 6:38 P.M. That doesn't give her time to get home and call in.

Taggert: Okay, then let's see who's logged on . . . The network monitor says the activity is coming from a machine in her office area. Run a quick personnel scan and see who hasn't checked out from that area yet. I'll start the logs so we can record everything.

Billy: The only one left is that new guy: Axel. His security background check came up negative, but there's not a lot of information about him. No suspicious associations, just a typical college graduate . . .

Taggert: Well, do a quick financial scan on him. The computer logs show Jenny's machine going online right about when his machine was switched off. I'm getting some weird feedback from his machine. Remind me to check out the security card in his computer later.

Billy: Well, there's nothing unusual in this credit analysis. Just the usual: He was late with a couple rent payments, some heavy credit card purchases, . . . wait, he did just buy a new car. Think it means anything?

Taggert: Maybe. Hang on, let's bring up the machine he's using . . . There. Now we can see everything he's doing.

Billy: Sure, but it doesn't make much sense to me. Looks like he's running some sort of statistical analysis . . . That's a report writer and a word processor running in the background. How do we know it's Axel? Maybe Jenny forgot and left her machine running?

Taggert: Hang on a second, wait until we get some keyboard activity. OK, there we go. Now, bring up the security camera over here . . . Yeah, there he is . . .

Billy: What's that on the side? Looks like a dismantled PC . . .

Taggert: Yeah, that's probably why I had trouble earlier. Well, I don't know what he's doing, but we've got him on at least two major security violations. The access one is a felony. That's enough for me. Send a termination notice to human resources, and let's go get him out of here. I'm locking up his computer now.

*(Office, 8:18 P.M.)*

Billy: Okay, Axel, hold it right there.

Axel: What the . . .? Who are you guys?

Taggert: Corporate security. Come with us . . .

Axel: What? Look, if it's about the computer, I can explain, mine broke, and . . .

Taggert: We don't want to hear it. You can confess tomorrow. Your boss can decide if we call in the police. Either way, you're out of here. Billy, escort him out. Then follow him home. Make sure he's here by 8:00 tomorrow morning. If he tries to leave, call the police and have him arrested.

## QUESTIONS

1. Do you think Axel is guilty of violating computer security laws? Is there enough evidence to prove it? Even if no laws were broken, should he lose his job for violating company procedures?

2. Assuming Axel really is guilty, what additional evidence might you try to collect? What risks does the company face if it lets him continue while security people look for more evidence?

3. Are these security capabilities available today? As an executive, would you create a security system like this one? Would you tell the employees about its capabilities or keep it a secret?

4. As a worker, how would you feel about working for a company with this type of security system? Would you want the company to tell you about all of its security capabilities?

5. Assume that you are in Axel's position (and that you are innocent). Your boss tells you that you must have a major report finished by 8:00 A.M. tomorrow morning. After she leaves, your computer breaks down. You try to fix it but don't succeed. You remember that your boss' computer has the same capabilities as yours and automatically connects to the network when you turn it on (the password is supplied by her startup program). What would you do? If you know about all of the security features—what would you do?

# Glossary

**10Base-T:** A system of connecting computers on a LAN using twisted-pair cable. The method relies on compression to increase raw transfer rates to 10 megabits per second.

**Access speed:** A measure of disk drive speed. Loosely, the time it takes a disk drive to move to a particular piece of data.

**Accounting journal:** Raw financial transaction data are collected by the accounting department and stored in a journal. Modern accounting requires the use of a double-entry system to ensure accurate data.

**Activity-based costing (ABC):** ABC allocates costs by examining a detailed breakdown of the production activities. The cost of each process is computed for each different product. The detail provides a better picture of the production cost for each item.

**Advocacy role:** Someone in MIS, usually the chief information officer, who bears responsibility for exploring and presenting new applications and uses of MIS within the company.

**Agent:** An object-oriented program designed for networks that is written to perform specific tasks in response to user requests. Agents are designed to automatically communicate with other agents to search for data and make decisions.

**American National Standards Institute (ANSI):** An organization responsible for defining many standards, including several useful information technology standards.

**Antitrust laws:** A variety of laws that make it illegal to use monopoly power. Some basic (economic) actions to achieve a competitive advantage are illegal. Strategic plans must be evaluated carefully to avoid violating these laws.

**Archie:** A database that determines what features are displayed on different gopher menus on the Internet. You can use archie to find specific sources of data. Only the gopher menu items are searched, not the actual data files. Use veronica to search the data files.

**Artificial intelligence (AI):** An attempt to build machines that can think like humans. Techniques evolved from this research help solve more complex problems. Useful techniques include expert systems, neural networks, massively parallel computers, and robotics.

**American Standard Code for Information Interchange (ASCII):** A common method of numbering characters so they can be processed. For instance, the letter $A$ is number 65. It is slowly being replaced by the ANSI character set table and the use of international code pages that can display foreign characters.

**Assumptions:** Models are simplifications of real life, so they require assumptions about various events or conditions.

**Asynchronous Transfer Mode (ATM):** A packet-based network system that uses high-speed transmission lines (150 megabits and over) and routers to maximize network efficiency and throughput.

**Attributes:** Descriptions of an object or entity. For example, a customer object would at least have attributes for name, phone number, and address.

**Audit trail:** The ability to trace any transaction back to its source. In accounting, transaction values are accumulated on the general ledger and used to create reports. An audit trail is a set of marks or records to point back to the original transaction.

**Authentication:** The ability to verify the source of a message. Dual-key systems are a useful technique. The sender uses a private key to encrypt the message. The recipient applies the sender's public key. If the decrypted message is readable, it had to have come from the alleged sender, because the keys always work in pairs.

**Backbone:** A high-speed communication line that links multiple subnetworks. It is usually a fiber optic line.

**Backward chaining:** In an expert system, the user enters a "conclusion" and asks to see whether the rules support that conclusion.

**Barriers to entry:** Anything that makes it more difficult for new firms to enter an industry. Several possibilities would violate antitrust laws. An acceptable barrier is the increased use of information systems, which raises the cost of entering an industry because a rival would have to spend additional money on information technology.

**Beginners All-purpose Symbolic Instruction Code (BASIC):** An early computer programming language designed to be easy to program and to teach. Visual Basic is a current version for Windows programming.

**Benchmark:** A set of routines or actions used to evaluate computer performance. By performing the same basic tasks on several machines, you can compare their relative speeds. Benchmarks are especially useful when the machines use different processors and different input and output devices.

**Binary data:** A collection of ones and zeros called bits. Computer processors operate only on binary data. All data forms are first converted to binary.

**Biometrics:** A field of study that is trying to determine how to identify people based on biological characteristics. The most common devices are fingerprint and handprint readers.

**Bit:** The smallest unit of data in a computer. All data is converted to bits or binary data. Each bit can be in one of two states: on or off. Bits are generally aggregated into collections called a byte.

**Bitmap:** A method of storing images. The picture is converted to individual dots that are stored as bits. Once a picture is stored in bitmap form, it is difficult to resize. However, bitmaps are good for displaying photographic images with subtle color shading.

**Board of directors:** A group of people paid to oversee and evaluate the decisions of the company. Technically the CEO reports to the board of directors, but they are charged more with reviewing the CEO's decisions. Most boards have the authority to remove a CEO, but many board members are selected by the CEO.

**Boolean search:** Searching for data by using the logic operators AND, OR, and NOT conditions in a WHERE statement, for example, find a list of customers where city = "Detroit" and age > 50 and do not own a car.

**Bottom-up development:** An approach to designing and building systems in which workers build system components to solve each problem as it arises. Eventually the pieces are combined to create an integrated system. The method relies on standards and controls to facilitate cooperation and integration. *See also* Top-down development.

**Brainstorming:** A group technique in which each individual is asked to come up with possible suggestions to a problem. Any ideas are useful, regardless of how wild they are. Even fanciful ideas could stimulate someone else to improve it or to explore a related area.

**Broadband communications:** A communications system in which more than one signal travels over the medium at the same time, for instance, using a cable to carry telephone calls, computer data, and video signals at the same time.

**Broadcasts:** A technique of transmitting messages using radio, micro, or infared waves. Broadcast messages are sent to all devices in a certain area. Others in the vicinity can also receive the messages.

**Browser:** A software tool that converts World Wide Web data into a graphical page with hypertext links. Using standard (HTML) commands, companies can offer data and additional links to users. Users simply click on individual words and pictures to retrieve additional data and move to other network sites.

**Bulletin board system (BBS):** Similar to a typical bulletin board, except that people access it from computers. The BBS enables users to store comments, pictures, and files for other people to retrieve. Bulletin boards are usually organized by topics and can be searched for specific phrases or comments. They are a useful way to disseminate information that is of interest to many different people.

**Bus:** Most computers have special slots called a bus to provide high-speed connections to other devices. Various manufacturers make boards that fit into these slots. The processor can exchange data with these other devices, but performance is sometimes constrained by the design of the bus.

**Bus network:** A network organizing scheme in which each computer is attached to a common transmission medium. Protocols are needed to determine when a machine can transmit and to recover from collisions.

**Byte:** A collection of bits. Traditionally, 8 bits make up one byte. From binary arithmetic, an 8-bit byte can hold 2 to the 8th power, or 256, possible numbers. In many systems a byte is used to hold one character.

**C:** A powerful programming language that is flexible and creates efficient code. A language commonly used to build complex applications, and to create commercial software products.

**C++:** An object-oriented extension of the C programming language. It is commonly used to build commercial software. It produces efficient code and supports the development of reusable objects.

**Cache:** A buffer between the processor and a slower device such as a printer, disk drive, or memory chips. The cache generally consists of high-speed memory. Data is transferred in bulk to the cache. It is then pulled out as it is needed, freeing up the processor to work on other jobs instead of waiting for the slower device to finish.

**Carrier-Sense, Multiple-Access/Collision Detection (CSMA/CD):** A communications protocol that determines how computers will behave on a shared-medium network. Ethernet protocols rely on CSMA/CD. Other alternatives are Token Ring and packet switching.

**Case-based reasoning:** An expert system approach that records information in the form of situations and cases. Users search for cases similar to their current problem and adapt the original solution.

**CD-ROM:** Compact disk-read only memory. Data is stored and retrieved with a laser. A special machine is required to create data on a CD-ROM. Used to hold data that does not change very often. Useful for multimedia applications because a disk can hold about 650 megabytes of data. The format used to store music CDs.

**Centralization:** A business scheme for performing most operations and making management decisions from one location in an organization. MIS organization can be examined in four areas: hardware, software, data, and personnel. *See also* Decentralization.

**Change agents:** Objects or people who cause or facilitate changes. Sometimes the change agent might be a new employee who brings fresh ideas, other times change can be mandated by top-level management. Sometimes an outside event such as a competitor or a hurricane forces an organization to change.

**Change drivers:** Concepts or products that have altered the way businesses operate. Classic examples include: bar code scanners in retail stores, hand-held miniterminals or notebooks by delivery firms and salespeople, and reservation systems by travel and entertainment industries.

**Charge-back system:** A scheme for charging other internal departments for services. For example, some firms charge departments a fee based on how often they use the central computer. The goal was to ration a limited resource by avoiding free use.

**Chart of accounts:** A listing of all of the accounts and subaccounts in the general ledger. It must be defined ahead of time for each business.

**Chief executive officer (CEO):** The head of a company. The person ultimately responsible for setting the direction and policies of the firm. Usually the CEO is also the chairperson of the board of directors.

**Chief information officer (CIO):** The person who is in charge of the MIS organization within a firm, charged with overseeing operations, setting MIS priorities, and being a top-level advocate for MIS. Also develops and supports strategy for the firm.

**Circular reference:** In a spreadsheet, a set of cells that eventually refer to each other. In the simplest example, cell A1 would use values stored in cell A2, but cell A2 uses the value stored in A1. This technique is sometimes used to create an iterative solution to a model.

**Classes:** Base descriptions of objects. Technically, classes describe generic attributes and methods. Objects are a specific instance of a class.

**Client-server organization:** A method of organizing the MIS function so that some operations are centralized while others are decentralized. The client-server model separates all of the components into two categories: servers or clients. The functions associated with the server tend to be centralized, whereas the client components and tasks are dispersed among the users.

**Client-server network:** A network configuration in which a few machines are used as file servers and the others (clients) are independent workstations. Shared data is first sent to a file server where it can be examined or transferred by another client.

**Clip art:** Artwork created and sold to be used by nonartists. Hundreds of collections are available of people, places, buildings, and other objects. Clip art images are often used to create presentations and illustrate reports.

**Clipboard:** The method used to transfer data between software packages in windows-oriented operating environments. All objects that are cut or copied are placed onto the clipboard, ready to be pasted to another location or another package. Clipboard viewers exist to show the current contents of the clipboard. Some software systems allow a clipboard to hold several cuttings. Many automatically delete the older cuts—keeping only the most recent.

**Clipper chip:** An encryption method created by the U.S. top-secret National Security Agency (NSA). It uses a secret algorithm to encrypt and decrypt digital messages. It was particularly designed for digital voice communication. Its key feature is the use of two escrow keys assigned to each chip. If the police decide they want to listen to a conversation between two suspects, they can get a court order, collect the escrow keys and instantly decrypt the call.

**Closed loop:** A system or piece of computer code in which every step in a control mechanism is contained inside the system, and does not utilize external input. *See also* Feedback.

**Closed system:** A system that is entirely self-contained and does not respond to changes in the environment. Most closed systems eventually fail due to entropy.

**Coaxial cable:** A cable used to transmit data. Cable television is a widespread application. The inner cable is surrounded by a plastic insulator, which is surrounded by a wire mesh conductor and an outer casing. The wire mesh insulates the internal signal wire from external interference.

**Cold site:** A facility that can be leased from a disaster backup specialist. A cold site contains power and telecommunication lines but no computer. In the event of a disaster, a company calls the computer vendor and begs for the first available machine to be sent to the cold site.

**Collision:** In networks, a collision arises when two computers attempt to broadcast messages at the same time. The network protocols need to identify the situation and determine which machine will go first.

**Column:** A vertical part of a table that holds data for one attribute of an entity in a database or spreadsheet. For example, a table to describe automobiles will have columns for make, model, and color.

**Command-line interface:** A method of controlling the computer by typing commands. The user must generally memorize specific commands. Older machines still use them because GUI systems require too much overhead. Some people prefer command lines, because it is faster to type one or two commands than to manipulate an image on the screen.

**Common Business-Oriented Language (COBOL):** An early programming language designed to handle typical transaction processing tasks. Its death has been predicted for years, but it is hard to throw away billions of lines of code.

**Common Object Request Broker Architecture (CORBA):** A model largely developed in the Unix community that will enable objects to communicate with each other across networks. In particular, it is designed to enable users to combine different data types from various software vendors into a single compound document. The data could reside on any server on the network.

**Competitive advantage:** Something that makes your company better or stronger than your rivals. Examples include lower costs, higher quality, strong ties to loyal customers, and control over distribution channels.

**Compound document:** A document that incorporates different types of data: text, graphics, sound, and video. The different objects might be transmitted across a network to be included in a final document.

**Computer-integrated manufacturing (CIM):** Using a computer to control most of the production equipment in a manufacturing environment. The computer can monitor the production statistics. It is also used to set individual machine controls.

**Computer information system (CIS):** *See* Management information system (MIS).

**Computer ethics:** The concept that all of us have an obligation with respect to data. For example, managers have a responsibility to customers to protect personal data, to collect only data that is truly needed, and to give customers the ability to correct errors in personal data.

**Computer-aided design (CAD):** Programs that are used to create engineering drawings. CAD programs make it easy to modify drawings. They also make it easier to keep track of material specifications. They can perform spatial and engineering estimates on the designs, such as surface or volume calculations.

**Computer-aided software engineering (CASE):** Computer programs that are designed to support the analysis and development of computer systems. They make it easier to create, store, and share diagrams and data definitions. Some versions even generate code. There are two categories of CASE tools: software development and maintenance of existing systems.

**Concatenated key:** In relational databases, a key that consists of more than one column. The columns are combined to yield a unique primary key.

**Concurrency:** A situation that arises when applications attempt to modify the same piece of data at the same time. If two people are allowed to make changes to the same piece of data, the computer system must control the order in which it processes the two requests. Mixing the two tasks will result in the wrong data being stored in the computer.

**Context diagram:** The top level of a data flow diagram that acts as a title page and displays the boundaries of the system and displays the external entities that interact with the system.

**Converge:** The ability of an iterative model to stabilize on a fixed solution. The alternative is that values continually increase and never reach a solution.

**Critical success factors:** A limited number of concrete goals that must be met for the organization to be successful. Identifying these key factors helps determine the strategic directions and highlights the areas that can benefit from improved information systems.

**Cut, copy, paste:** A common mechanism used to transfer and link data between different software packages. The data to be transferred is marked. When it is cut or copied, it is placed on the clipboard. Switching to the second package, the object is pasted into the appropriate location. Dynamic and static links are specified through options in the "paste special" menu. With the cut option, the original object is deleted. With copy, the original is unchanged.

**Data:** Data consists of factual elements (or opinions or comments) that describe some object or event. Data can be thought of as raw numbers.

**Data administrator:** MIS manager who is charged with overseeing all of the data definitions and data standards for the company to ensure that applications can share data throughout the company.

**Data dictionary:** Contains all of the information to explain the terms used to define a system. Often includes report descriptions, business rules, and security considerations.

**Data encryption standard (DES):** An older method of encrypting data that was commonly used by financial institutions. With current computer capabilities that can break a DES-encrypted message, DES is no longer considered a secure encryption system.

**Data flow diagram (DFD):** A diagramming technique used to analyze and design systems. It shows how a system is divided into subsystems and highlights the flow of data between the processes and subsystems. It displays processes, external entities, files, data flows, and control flows.

**Data independence:** Separating programs from their data definition and storage. The main advantage is that it is possible to change the data without having to change the programs.

**Data integrity:** (1) A concept that implies data is as accurate as possible. It means the database contains few errors. (2) Keeping data accurate and correct as it is gathered and stored in the computer system.

**Data store:** A file or place where data is stored. In a realistic setting, a data store could be a computer file, file cabinet, or even a reference book.

**Data types:** To humans, there are four basic types of data: text and numbers, images, sound, and video. Each data type must be converted to binary form for computer processing.

**Data warehouse:** A single consolidation point for enterprise data from diverse production systems. The data is typically stored in one large file server or a central computer. Because legacy systems are difficult to replace, some data is copied into a data warehouse, where it is available for management queries and analysis.

**Database:** A collection of related data that can be retrieved easily and processed by computers. A collection of data tables.

**Database administrator (DBA):** (1) A person appointed to manage the databases for the firm. The DBA needs to know the technical details of the DBMS and the computer system. The DBA also needs to understand the business operations of the firm. (2) A management person in the MIS department charged with defining and maintaining the corporate databases. Maintaining data integrity is a key component of the job.

**Database management system (DBMS):** Software that defines a database, stores the data, supports a query language, produces reports, and creates data-entry screens.

**Decentralization:** Moving the major operations and decisions out to lower levels within the firm. In MIS, decentralization has largely been led by the declining cost and improved capabilities of personal computers. *See also* Centralization.

**Decision biases:** Without models and careful analysis, decisions made by people tend to be biased. There are several biases in each of the four systems categories: data acquisition, processing, output, and feedback.

**Decision support system (DSS):** Systems to use data collected by transaction processing systems to evaluate business models and assist managers to make tactical decisions. They have three major components: data collection, analysis of models, and presentation.

**Decision tree:** A graphical representation of logic rules. Each possible answer to a question or situation leads to a new branch of the tree.

**Default value:** A value that is automatically displayed by the computer. Users can often override the default by deleting the old value and entering a new one. The goal is to choose a value that will almost always be entered, so the user can skip that item.

**Dehumanization:** Some people feel that technology isolates people and decreases our contact with other members of society. Treating people as identification numbers and summary statistics can lead managers to forget the human consequences of their decisions.

**Descriptive model:** A model that is defined in words and perhaps pictures. Relationships between objects and variables tend to be subjective. Useful for an initial understanding of a system but difficult to evaluate by computer.

**Desktop Publishing (DTP):** The art of creating professional documents with personal computers and small laser printers. Beyond basic word processing, DTP software provides controls to standardize pages, improve the page layout, and establish styles.

**Detail section:** The section in a report that is repeated for every row in the associated tables. It is often used for itemized values, whereas group and page footers are used for subtotals.

**Diagnostic situations:** Spotting problems, searching for the cause, and implementing corrections. Examples include responding to exception reports to identify problems and potential solutions, and determining why the latest marketing approach did not perform as well as expected.

**Dial-back modem:** A special modem placed on a central computer. When a user attempts to log in, the dial-back modem breaks the connection and calls back a predefined phone number. Its use minimizes the threat of outsiders gaining access to the central computer.

**Digital cash:** An electronic version of money that is provided and verified by a trusted third party. It consists of an encrypted number for a specified value that can only be used one time. It provides for verifiable and anonymous purchases using networks.

**Distribution channel:** Products are rarely distributed directly from the manufacturer to the final customer. There are layers of distributors in between. If a producer can gain control over this means of getting the product to consumers, the producer can prevent new rivals from entering the industry. Improved communication systems offer the possibility of eroding control over some distribution channels.

**Diverge:** The property of an iterative model where successive computations keep leading to larger values (in magnitude). The model never reaches a stable solution. Generally due to insufficient or incorrect feedback mechanisms.

**Documentation:** Descriptions of a system, its components, the data, and records of changes made to the system.

**Domain server:** A computer on the Internet that converts mnemonic names into numeric Internet addresses. The names are easier for humans to remember, but the computers rely on the numeric addresses.

**Download:** To transfer files from a remote computer to a local computer (usually a personal computer). *See also* Upload.

**Drill down:** To use an information system to get increasingly detailed data about a company. In an enterprise information system, the ability to look at overall company data, then select breakdowns by regions, departments, or smaller levels.

**Dual-key encryption:** A method of encrypting a message that requires two keys: one to encrypt and one to decrypt. One of the keys is a public key that is

available to anyone. The other key is private and must never be revealed to other people. RSA is a popular dual-key encryption system. Dual-key systems can also be used to authenticate the users.

**Dynamic data exchange:** An early method of linking data from multiple sources with the Windows operating system. The software packages literally send messages to other software packages, which enables them to combine and update data. *See also* dynamic integration and Object Linking and Embedding (OLE).

**Dynamic integration:** A means of linking data from multiple documents. One compound document (or container) can hold data objects created by other software. As the original data is changed, it is automatically updated in the container document. *See also* Static integration.

**E-mail:** Electronic mail, or messages that are transmitted from one computer user to another. Networks transfer messages between the computers. Users can send or retrieve messages at any time. The computer holds the message until the recipient checks in.

**Electronic data interchange (EDI):** Exchanging transaction data with entities outside the control of your firm. Private connections can be established directly between two firms. Public networks are also being formed where one provider collects data and routes it to the appropriate client.

**Encryption:** A method of modifying the original information according to some code, so that it can only be read if the user knows the decryption key. It is used to safely transmit data between computers.

**End-user development:** Managers and workers are to develop their own small systems using database management systems, spreadsheets, and other high-level tools.

**Enterprise information system:** A type of decision support system that collects, analyzes, and presents data in a format that is easy to use by top executives. To achieve this objective, the EIS is based on a model of the entire company. In most cases the model is presented graphically and the executives retrieve information by pointing to objects on the screen.

**Enterprise network:** A network that connects multiple subnetworks across an entire firm. Often, the networks use different protocols and different computer types, which complicates transmitting messages.

**Ergonomics:** The study of how machines can be made to fit humans better. One of the main conclusions of this research in the computer area is that individuals need to be able to adjust input (and output) devices to their own preferences.

**Escrow key:** In an encryption system, it is a special key that can be used by government officials to decrypt a secret conversation. The Clipper chip uses escrow keys.

**Ethernet:** A network communications protocol that specifies how machines will exchange data. It uses a broadcast system in which one machine transmits its message on the communication medium. The other machines listen for messages directed to them.

**Event-driven approach:** (1) A user-interface approach where the user controls the sequence or operations and the software responds to these events. Events can range from a simple key-press to a voice command. (2) Modern, window-based software does not follow a sequential process. Instead, actions by users generate events. The programs respond to these events and alter data or offer additional choices. Typical events include mouse clicks pointing to items on the screen, keystrokes, changes to values, or transmissions from other systems.

**Exception report:** Report that is triggered by some event to signify a condition that is unusual and needs to be handled immediately.

**Executive information system (EIS):** *See* Enterprise information system.

**Exhaustive testing:** Testing every possible combination of inputs to search for errors. Generally not a feasible option, so most computer systems will always contain errors.

**Expert system (ES):** The goal of an expert system is to help a novice achieve the same results as an expert. They can handle ill-structured and missing data. Current expert systems can only be applied to narrowly defined problems. Diagnostic problems are common applications for expert systems.

**Expert system shell:** A program that provides a way to collect data, enter rules, talk to users, present results, and evaluate the rules for an expert system.

**Export:** An older method of exchanging data among various software packages. One package exports the data by storing it in a format that can be read by other software. Object Linking and Embedding is a more powerful way to exchange data.

**EBCDIC:** Extended Binary Coded Decimal Interchange Code. A method of numbering characters so they can be processed by machines. Used exclusively by large IBM and compatible computers. *See also* ASCII.

**External agents:** Entities that are outside the direct control of your company. Typical external agents are customers, suppliers, rivals, and governments. Competitive advantages can be found by producing better-quality items or services at a lower cost than your rivals. Also, many firms have strengthened their positions by building closer ties with their suppliers and customers.

**External entity:** Objects outside the boundary of a system that communicate with the system. Common business examples include suppliers, customers, government agencies, and management.

**Facsimile (Fax):** A combination scanner, transmitter, and receiver that digitizes an image, compresses it, and transmits it over phone lines to another facsimile machine.

**Fault-tolerant computer:** A computer or a system that is designed to continue functioning properly even if some of the components fail. Fault-tolerant machines rely on duplication of subsystems with continuous monitoring and automatic maintenance calls.

**Feasibility study:** A quick examination of the problems, goals and expected costs of a proposed system. The objective is to determine whether the problem can reasonably be solved with a computer system.

**Feedback:** Well-designed systems have controls that monitor how well they meeting their goal. The information measuring the goals and providing control to the system is known as feedback.

**Fiber optic cable:** A thin glass or plastic cable that is internally reflective. It carries a light wave for extended distances and around corners.

**File server:** Computer on a network that is used to hold data and program files for users to share. To be effective, it should use a multitasking operating system.

**File Transfer Protocol (FTP):** A standard method of transferring files on the Internet. If you control a computer, you can give other users access to specific files on your computer without having to provide an account and password for every possible user.

**Five forces model:** Michael Porter's model used to search for competitive advantage. The five forces are: rivals, customers, suppliers, potential competitors, and substitute products.

**Flow chart:** An old pictorial method for describing the logic of a computer program. It has largely been replaced by pseudocode.

**Font size:** An important characteristic of text is its size. Size of type is typically measured in points. For reference, a capital letter in a 72-point font will be approximately 1 inch high.

**Forward chaining:** In an expert system, the ES traces your rules from the data entry to a recommendation. Forward chaining is used to display questions, perform calculations, and apply rules.

**Frame:** A related set of information that humans group together. Sometimes groupings can be arbitrary. A concept used in discussing AI applications and human cognition.

**Frame relay:** A network communication system that uses variable-length packets. It is useful for high-speed, large bursts of data. It is being used for long-distance network communications.

**Franchise:** A means of organizing companies. Independent operators pay a franchise fee to use the company name. They receive training and benefit from the name and advertising of the parent company. They purchase supplies from the parent company and follow the franchise rules.

**Front-end processor:** A simple communications device for large central computers that accepted all of the terminal wires and then assigned each user to an open communications port on the computer. This device decreased the number of physical access ports required on the computer.

**Functions:** *See* Methods.

**Fuzzy logic:** A way of presenting and analyzing logic problems that is designed to handle subjective descriptions (e.g., hot and cold).

**General ledger:** A collection of accounts that break financial data into specific categories. Common categories include accounts receivable, accounts payable, inventory, and cash.

**Geographic information system (GIS):** Designed to identify and display relationships among business data and locations. Used to display geographical relationships. Also used to plot delivery routes and create maps.

**Gigabyte:** Approximately 1 billion bytes of data. Technically, 1,024 to the third power (or 2 to the thirtieth), which is 1,073,741,824. The next highest increment is the terabyte.

**Global positioning system (GPS):** A system of 24 satellites created by the U.S. Department of Defense. The civilian receivers will identify a location to within about 50 feet. Used for navigation, tracking vehicles, and plotting delivery routes.

**Gopher:** A set of menus that are used to find information on various machines on the Internet. Although it is loosely organized by category, you generally need to know approximately where to find the data you want.

**Graphical User Interface (GUI):** A GUI system is based on a graphics screen instead of simple text, and users perform tasks by clicking a mouse button on or manipulating objects on the screen. For example,

copies are made by dragging an item from one location on the screen to another. Pronounced as "gooey."

**Group breaks:** Reports are often broken into subsections so that data in each section is grouped together by some common feature. For example, a sales report might group items by department, with subtotals for each department.

**Group decision support system (GDSS):** A type of groupware that is designed to facilitate meetings and help groups reach a decision. Each participant uses a networked computer to enter ideas and comments. Votes can be recorded and analyzed instantly. Comments and discussion are automatically saved for further study.

**Groupware:** Software designed to assist teams of workers. There are four basic types: communication, workflow, meeting, and scheduling. The most common is communication software that supports messages, bulletin boards, and data file transfers and sharing.

**Hacker:** Primarily used to indicate a person who devotes a great deal of time trying to break into computer systems.

**Hardware:** Hardware consists of the physical equipment used in computing.

**Haves and have-nots:** Shorthand description of saying that countries that have more resources can use those resources to develop new technologies and change the marketplace, making it harder for the less fortunate nations to catch up. In terms of information, there is some concern that shifting an economy to computer networks will make it hard for some nations to do business with those who can afford to invest heavily in information technology.

**High-Definition Television (HDTV):** Transmission of television signals in digital form. It provides clearer reception. It also supports encrypted transmissions so broadcasters can control who receives the images. HDTV also supports compression, so more data (better pictures or more channels) can be transmitted in the same frequency space.

**Hot links:** *See* Dynamic integration.

**Hot site:** A facility that can be leased from a disaster backup specialist. A hot site contains all the power, telecommunication facilities, and computers necessary to run a company. In the event of a disaster, a company collects its backup data tapes, notifies workers, and moves operations to the hot site.

**Icon:** A small picture on a computer screen that is used to represent some object or indicate a command. A classic example is the trash can used to delete files on the Apple Macintosh.

**Image:** A graphic representation that can be described by its resolution and the number of colors. They can be stored as bit-mapped or vector images.

**Import:** An older method of exchanging data among various software packages. Most software (e.g., a database management system) can export or store data in a text file format. Another software package (e.g., a spreadsheet) can import or retrieve this data. Object Linking and Embedding is a more powerful way to exchange data.

**Inference engine:** Within an expert system, the inference engine applies new observations to the knowledge base and analyzes the rules to reach a conclusion.

**Information:** Information represents data that has been processed, organized, and integrated to provide insight. The distinction between data and information is that information carries meaning and is used to make decisions.

**Information center:** An MIS group responsible for supporting end users. It typically provides a help desk to answer questions, programmers who provide access to corporate databases, training classes, and network support people to install and maintain networks.

**Information system:** A collection of hardware, software, data, and people designed to collect, process, and distribute data throughout an organization.

**Information threats:** There are two classes of threats to information: (1) physical, in the form of disasters; and (2) logical, which consists of unauthorized disclosure, unauthorized modification, and unauthorized withholding of data. The primary source of danger lies with insiders: employees, ex-employees, partners, or consultants.

**Inheritance:** Classes of objects are created or derived from other object classes. Each derived class inherits the attributes and methods of the prior class. For example, a savings account object can be derived from an account object. The savings account object will automatically have the same attributes and methods. Attributes and methods specific to the savings account can be added.

**Input devices:** People do not deal very well with binary data, so all data forms must be converted into binary form for the computer. Input devices—for example, keyboards, microphones, and bar code readers—make the conversion.

**Input-Process-Output:** A shorthand description of a subsystem. Each subsystem receives inputs and performs some process. The output is passed to another subsystem.

**Integrated data:** The practice of combining data from many sources to make a decision. Data can come from different departments throughout the business, and it can come in many different forms. Networks, groupware, and products that support dynamic linking are all useful tools to integrate data to make better decisions.

**Integrated Services Digital Network (ISDN):** A set of services, and a transmission and control system, offered by telephone companies. It uses complete digital transmission of signals to improve transmission speed and quality.

**Internet:** A collection of computers loosely connected to exchange information worldwide. Owners of the computers make files and information available to other users. Common tools on the Internet include e-mail, ftp, archie, veronica, gopher, telnet, and the World Wide Web.

**Iterative solution:** Building a model and evaluating it until the parameter values converge to a fixed solution. Sometimes an iterative model will diverge and never reach an acceptable solution. *See also* Circular reference.

**Joint application development (JAD):** A method to reduce design time by putting everyone in development sessions until the system is designed. Users, managers, and systems analysts participate in a series of intense meetings to design the inputs (data and screens), and outputs (reports) needed by the new system.

**Just-in-time (JIT) inventory:** A production system that relies on suppliers delivering components just as they are needed in production, instead of relying on inventory stocks. JIT requires close communication between manufacturers and suppliers.

**Kilobyte:** Approximately one thousand bytes of data. Technically it is 2 to the tenth, or 1,024.

**Knowledge:** Knowledge represents a higher level of understanding, including rules, patterns, and decisions. Knowledge-based systems are built to automatically analyze data, identify patterns, and recommend decisions.

**Knowledge base:** Within an expert system, the knowledge base consists of basic data and a set of rules.

**Knowledge engineer:** A person who helps build an expert system by organizing the data, devising the rules, and entering the criteria into the expert system shell. Trained to deal with experts to derive the rules needed to create an expert system. The engineer also converts the data and rules into the format needed by the expert system.

**Legacy systems:** Information systems that were created over several years and are now crucial to operating the company. They probably use older technology, and the software is difficult to modify. However, replacing them is difficult and likely to interfere with day-to-day operations. Any changes or new systems must be able to work with the older components.

**Local area network (LAN):** A collection of personal computers within a small geographical area, connected by a network. All of the components are owned or controlled by one company.

**Lycos:** (Named for the Wolf spider). Software that searches Web sites, catalogs each page it finds and records the links for future searching. Lycos searches for the most popular Web sites to catalog in its database. You can use the database to search for data you need.

**Magnetic hard drives:** Magnetic hard drives (or disk drives) consist of rigid platters that store data with magnetic particles. Data is accessed by spinning the platters and moving a drive head across the platters to access various tracks.

**Magnetic ink character recognition (MICR):** A special typeface printed with ink containing magnetic particles. It can be read rapidly and reliably by computers. Banks are the primary users of MICR. Checks are imprinted with MICR routing numbers. MICR readers are more accurate than straight OCR because they pick up a stronger signal from magnetic particles in the ink.

**Mail filters:** Programs that automatically read e-mail and sort the messages according to whatever criteria the manager prefers. Junk mail can be discarded automatically.

**Management information system (MIS):** An MIS consists of five related components: hardware, software, people, procedures, and databases. The goal of management information systems is to enable managers to make better decisions by providing quality information.

**Manufacturing Resource Planning (MRP II):** An integrated approach to manufacturing. Beginning with the desired production levels, we work backward to determine the processing time, materials, and labor needed at each step. These results generate schedules and inventory needs. Sometimes known as a demand-pull system.

**Mass customization:** The ability to modify the production line often enough to produce more variations of the main product. The goal is to cover virtually all of the niche markets.

**Materials requirements planning (MRP):** An early production system, where at each stage of production, we evaluate the usage of materials to determine the optimal inventory levels.

**Mathematical model:** A model that is defined by mathematical equations. This format is easy to use for forecasts and for simulation analyses on the computer. Be careful not to confuse precision with accuracy. A model might forecast some value with great precision (e.g., 15.9371), but the accuracy could be quite less (e.g., actual values between 12 and 18).

**Media:** For the means of transmissions, connecting computers in a network. Common methods include twisted-pair and coaxial cable; fiber optic lines; and radio, micro, and infrared waves.

**Megabyte:** Loosely, 1 million bytes of data. Technically, it is 1,048,576 bytes of data, which is 2 raised to the 20th power.

**Megaflops:** Millions of floating-point operations per second. A measure of the processor speed, it counts the number of common arithmetical operations that can be performed in one second.

**Megahertz:** One million cycles per second, a measure of the clock chip in a computer, which establishes how fast a processor can operate.

**Menu tree:** A graphical depiction of the menu choices available to users in a system.

**Metadata:** Describes the source data, and the transformation and integration steps, and defines the way the database or data warehouse is organized.

**Methods:** Descriptions of actions that an object can perform. For example, an employee object could be hired, promoted, or released. Each of these functions would necessitate changes in the employee attributes and in other objects. The methods carry out these changes.

**Microsecond:** One-millionth of a second. Few computer components are measured in microseconds, but some electrical devices and controllers operate in that range. One microsecond compared to one second is the same as comparing one second to 11.6 days.

**Million instructions per second (MIPS):** A measure of computer processor speed. Higher numbers represent a faster processor. However, different brands of processors use different instruction sets, so numbers are not always comparable.

**Millisecond:** One-thousandth of a second. Disk drives and some other input and output devices perform operations measured in milliseconds. One millisecond compared to one second is the same as comparing 1 second to 16.7 minutes.

**Model:** A simplified, abstract representation of some real-world system. Some models can be written as mathematical equations or graphs, others are subjective descriptions. Models help managers visualize physical objects and business processes. Information systems help you build models, evaluate them, and organize and display the output.

**Modem:** Modulator-demodulator. A device that converts computer signals into sounds that can be transmitted (and received) across phone lines.

**Morphing:** Digital conversion of one image into another. The term is an abbreviation of *metamorphosis.* True morphing is done with digital video sequences, where the computer modifies each frame until the image converts to a new form.

**Multimedia:** The combination of the four basic data types: text, sound, video, and images (animation). In its broadest definition, multimedia encompasses virtually any combination of data types. Today, it typically refers to the use of sound, text, and video clips in digitized form that are controlled by the computer user.

**Multitasking:** A feature of operating systems that enables you to run more than one task or application at the same time. Technically, they do not run at exactly the same time. The processor divides its time and works on several tasks at once.

**Musical Instrument Data Interchange (MIDI):** A collection of standards that define how musical instruments communicate with each other. Sounds are stored by musical notation and are re-created by synthesizers that play the notes.

**Nanosecond:** One-billionth of a second. Computer processors and memory chips operate at times measured in nanoseconds. One nanosecond compared to 1 second is the same as comparing 1 second to 31.7 years.

**Natural language:** A human language used for communication with other humans, as opposed to a computer programming language or some other artificial language created for limited communication.

**Network interface card (NIC):** The communication card that plugs into a computer and attaches to the network communication medium. It translates computer commands into network messages and server commands.

**Network operating system (NOS):** A special operating system installed on a file server, with portions loaded to the client machines. It enables the machines to communicate and share files.

**Neural network:** A collection of artificial neurons loosely designed to mimic the way the human brain operates. Especially useful for tasks that involve pattern recognition.

**Neuron:** The fundamental cell of human brains and nerves. Each of these cells is relatively simple, but there are approximately 100 million of them.

**News groups:** A set of electronic bulletin boards available on the Internet. Postings are continuously circulated around the network as people add comments.

**Normalization:** A set of rules for creating tables in a relational database. The primary rules are that there can be no repeating elements and every nonkey column must depend on the whole key and nothing but the key. Roughly, it means that each table should refer to only one object or concept.

**Numbers:** One of the basic data types, similar to text on input and output. Attributes include precision and a scaling factor that defines the true size or dimension of the number.

**Object:** A software description of some entity. It consists of attributes that describe the object, and functions (or methods) that describe the actions that can be taken by the object. Objects are generally related to other objects through an object hierarchy.

**Object hierarchy:** Objects are defined from other base objects. The new objects inherit the properties and functions of the prior objects.

**Object Linking and Embedding (OLE):** A standard created by Microsoft for its Windows operating system to create compound documents and dynamically link data objects from multiple software packages. You begin with a compound document or container that holds data from other software packages. These data objects can be edited directly (embedded). Most OLE software also supports dynamic linking.

**Object orientation:** An approach to systems and programming that classifies data as various objects. Objects have attributes or properties that can be set by the programmer or by users. Objects also have methods or functions that define the actions they can take. Objects can be defined from other objects, so most are derived from the four basic data types.

**Object-oriented development:** The ultimate goal of the object-oriented approach is to build a set of reusable objects and procedures. The idea is that eventually, it should be possible to create new systems or modify old ones simply by plugging in a new module or modifying an existing object.

**One-to-many relationship:** Some object or task that can be repeated. For instance, a customer can place many orders. In database normalization, we search for one-to-many relationships and split them into two tables.

**Open operating system:** An operating system that is supposed to be vendor neutral. It should run on hardware from several different vendors. When a buyer upgrades to a new machine, the operating system and software should function the same as before.

**Open system:** An open system learns by altering itself as the environment changes.

**Operating system:** A basic collection of software that handles jobs common to all users and programmers. It is responsible for connecting the hardware devices, such as terminals, disk drives, and printers. It also provides the environment for other software, as well as the user interface that affects how people use the machine.

**Operations level:** Day-to-day operations and decisions. In a manufacturing firm, machine settings, worker schedules, and maintenance requirements would represent management decisions at the operations level. Information systems are used at this level to collect data and perform well-defined computations.

**Optical character recognition (OCR):** The ability to convert images of characters (bitmaps) into computer text that can be stored, searched, and edited. Software examines a picture and looks for text. The software checks each line, deciphers one character at a time, and stores the result as text.

**Optimization:** The use of models to search for the best solutions: minimizing costs, improving efficiency, or increasing profits.

**Output devices:** Data stored in binary form on the computer must be converted to a format people understand. Output devices—for example, display screens, printers, and synthesizers—make the conversion.

**Outsourcing:** The act of transferring ownership or management of MIS resources (hardware, software and personnel) to an outside MIS specialist.

**Packets:** Network messages are split into packets for transmission. Each packet contains a destination and source address as well as a portion of the message.

**Packet switching network:** A communications protocol in which each message is placed into smaller packets. These packets contain a destination and source address. The packets are switched (or routed) to the appropriate computer. With high-speed switches, this protocol offers speeds in excess of 150 megabits per second.

**Page footer:** Data that are placed at the bottom of each page in a report. Common items include page totals and page numbers.

**Page header:** Data that is placed at the top of every page in a report. Common items include the report title, date, and column labels.

**Parallel processing:** Using several processors in the same computer. Each processor can be assigned different tasks, or jobs can be split into separate pieces and given to each processor. There are a few massively parallel machines that utilize several thousand processors.

**Parameter:** Variables in a model that can be controlled or set by managers. They are used to examine different situations or to tailor the model to fit a specific problem.

**Peer-to-peer network:** A network configuration in which each machine is considered to be an equal. Messages and data are shared directly between individual computers. Each machine continuously operates as both a client and a server.

**Photo-CD:** A standardized system created by Kodak to convert photographs to digital (bitmap) form and store them on optical disks.

**Pixel:** Picture element, or a single dot on an image or video screen.

**Point-of-sale (POS) system:** A means of collecting data immediately when items are sold. Cash registers are actually data terminals that look up prices and instantly transmit sales data to a central computer.

**Polymorphism:** In an object design, different objects can have methods that have the same name but operate slightly differently. For example, a checking account object and a savings account object could each have a method called pay interest. The checking account might pay interest monthly, whereas the savings account pays it quarterly.

**Precision (numeric):** In computers, numeric precision represents the number of digits stored to the right of the decimal point. So, 10.1234 is more precise than 10.12, however, it is not necessarily more accurate. The original value might not have been measured beyond two digits.

**Prediction:** Model parameters can be estimated from prior data. Sample data is used to forecast future changes based on the model.

**Primary key:** A column or set of columns that contains data to uniquely identify each row in a relational database table. For example, each customer must have a unique identifier, possibly a phone number or an internally generated customer number.

**Privacy:** (1) The concept that people should be able to go about their lives without constant surveillance, that personal information about people should not be shared without their permission. (2) Collecting personal data only when you have a legitimate use for it, allowing customers to correct and remove personal data. Protecting confidential data so that it is not released to anyone. Giving customers to option so you do not sell or lease their personal data.

**Private key:** In a dual-key encryption system, the key that is protected by the owner and never revealed. It is generally a very large number.

**Problem boundary:** The line that identifies the primary components of the system that are creating a specific problem. Subsystems inside the boundary can be modified to solve the problem or enhance the system. Subsystems outside the boundary cannot be altered at this time.

**Procedures:** Procedures are instructions that help people use the systems. They include items such as user manuals, documentation, and procedures to ensure that backups are made regularly.

**Process:** An activity that is part of a data flow diagram. Systems can be built to process goods or to process data. Most information system work focuses on processes that alter data.

**Process control:** The use of computers to monitor and control the production machines and robots. Production lines generally use many different machines, each requiring several adjustments or settings. Computer control simplifies and speeds the setup.

**Process control system:** A computerized system that monitors and controls a production line. Some systems are completely linked so that a central computer can set up machines on an entire assembly line.

**Process innovation:** Evaluating the entire firm to improve individual processes, and to search for integrated solutions that will reduce costs, improve quality, or boost sales to gain a competitive advantage. *See also* Re-engineering.

**Processor:** The processor is the heart of a computer. It carries out the instructions of the operating system and the application programs.

**Product differentiation:** The ability to make your products appear different from those of your rivals, thus attracting more customers. Information systems have been used to alter products and provide new services.

**Properties:** *See* Attributes.

**Protocols:** A set of definitions and standards that establish the communication links on a network. Networks are often classified by their choice of protocol. Common protocols include Ethernet, Token Ring, and TCP/IP.

**Prototyping:** An iterative system design technique that takes advantage of high-level tools to rapidly cre-

ate working systems. The main objective of prototyping is to create a working version of the system as quickly as possible, even if some components are not included in the early versions.

**Pseudocode:** A loosely structured method to describe the logic of a program or outline a system. It uses basic programming techniques but ignores issues of syntax and relies on verbal descriptions.

**Public key:** In a dual-key encryption system, the key that is given to the public. Each person wishing to use dual-key encryption must have a different public key. The key works only in tandem with the user's private key.

**Query by example (QBE):** A visual method of examining data stored in a relational database. You ask questions and examine the data by pointing to tables on the screen and filling in templates.

**Random access memory (RAM):** High-speed memory chips that hold data for immediate processing. On most computers, data held in RAM is lost when the power is removed, so data must be moved to secondary storage.

**Rapid application development (RAD):** The goal of building a system much faster than with traditional SDLC methods. Using powerful tools (database management system, high-level languages, graphical toolkits, and objects), highly trained programmers can build systems in a matter of weeks or months. Using workgroups, communication networks, and CASE tools, small teams can speed up the development and design steps.

**Read Only Memory (ROM):** A type of memory on which data can be stored only one time. It can be read as often as needed but cannot be changed. ROM keeps its data when power is removed, so it is used to hold certain core programs and system data that is rarely changed.

**Reduced instruction set computer (RISC):** When designing a RISC processor, the manufacturer deliberately limits the number of circuits and instructions on the chip. The goal is to create a processor that performs a few simple tasks very fast. More complex problems are solved in software. Because RISC processors require fewer circuits, they are easier to produce.

**Redundant Array of Inexpensive Disks (RAID):** Instead of containing one large drive, a RAID system consists of several smaller drives. Large files are split into pieces stored on several different physical drives. The data pieces can be duplicated and stored in more than one location for backup. RAID systems also provide faster access to the data, because each of the drives can be searching through their part of the file at the same time.

**Re-engineering:** A complete reorganization of a company. Beginning from scratch, you identify goals along with the most efficient means of attaining those goals, and create new processes that change the company to meet the new goals. The term *re-engineering* and its current usage were made popular in 1990 by management consultants James Champy and Michael Hammer.

**Relational database:** A database in which all data is stored in flat tables that meet the normalization rules. Tables are logically connected by matching columns of data. System data, such as access rights, descriptions, and data definitions are also stored in tables.

**Repetitive stress injury (RSI):** An injury that occurs from repeating a stressful action. For instance, several people have complained that constant typing damages their wrists. Ergonomic design, adjusting your workspace, and taking breaks are common recommendations to avoid repetitive stress.

**Report:** A printed summary or screen display that is produced on a regular basis by a database management system. The main sections of a report are: report header, page header, group/break header, detail, group/break footer, page footer, and report footer.

**Request for proposal (RFP):** A list of specifications and questions sent to vendors asking them to propose (sell) a product that might fill those needs.

**Resolution:** The number of dots or pixels displayed per inch of horizontal or vertical space. Input and output devices, as well as images and video, are measured by their resolution. Higher values of dots-per-inch yield more detailed images.

**Reverse engineering:** The process of taking older software and rewriting it to modernize it and make it easier to modify and enhance. Reverse engineering tools consist of software that reads the program code from the original software and converts it to a form that is easier to modify.

**Rivals:** Any group of firms that are competing for customers and sales. Similar to competitors, but "competition" carries an economic definition involving many firms. Even an industry with two firms can experience rivalry.

**Rivest-Shamir-Adelman (RSA):** Three mathematicians who developed and patented a dual-key encryption system. The term often refers to the encryption technique. It is based on the computational difficulty of factoring very large numbers into their prime components.

**Rocket scientists:** Mathematically trained financial analysts who build complex mathematical models of the stock market and help create and price new securities.

**Router:** A communication device that connects subnetworks together. Local messages remain within each subnetwork. Messages between subnetworks are sent to the proper location through the router.

**Row:** A horizontal element that contains all of the data to describe an entity or object in a relational database or spreadsheet.

**Rules:** A set of conditions that describe a problem or a potential response. Generally expressed as "If . . . Then" conditions. Used by expert systems to analyze new problems and suggest alternatives.

**Sampler:** An input device that reads electrical signals from a microphone and stores the sound as a collection of numbers. It measures the frequency and amplitude of the sound waves thousands of times per second.

**Scalability:** The ability to buy a faster computer as needed and transfer all software and data without modification. True scalability enables users to buy a smaller computer today and upgrade later without incurring huge conversion costs.

**Scrolling region:** On a data entry form, a subform or section that is designed to collect multiple rows of data. Much like a spreadsheet, the user can move back and forth to alter or examine prior entries.

**Secondary storage:** Data storage devices that hold data even if they lose power. Typically cheaper than RAM, but slower. Disk drives are common secondary storage devices.

**Serifs:** The small lines, curlicues, and ornamentation on many typefaces. They generally make it easier for people to read words and sentences on printed output. Sans serif typefaces have more white space between characters and are often used for signs and displays that must be read from a longer distance.

**Sign-off:** In a systems development life-cycle approach, the approval that managers must give to forms, reports, and computations at various stages of the development. This approval is given when they sign the appropriate documents.

**Simulation:** Models are used to examine what might happen if we decide to make changes to the process, to see how the system will react to external events, or to examine relationships in more detail.

**Social legitimacy:** At one time, mainstream organizations were identified by the quality of their presentation and their image. Large firms spend millions of dollars on graphic artists, professional designers, and professional printing. The decreasing cost of computers enables even small organizations to create an image that is hard to distinguish from large organizations.

**Software:** A collection of computer programs that are algorithms or logical statements that control the hardware.

**Software maintenance:** The act of fixing problems, altering reports, or extending an existing system to improve it. It refers to changes in the software, not to hardware tasks such as cleaning printers.

**Software piracy:** The act of copying software without paying the copyright owner. With few exceptions (e.g., backup), copying software is illegal. Companies and individuals who are caught have pay thousands of dollars in penalties and risk going to jail. It is commonly accepted that piracy takes money away from the development of improved software.

**Software suites:** Collections of software packages that are designed to operate together. Theoretically, data from each package can be easily shared with data from the others. So word processors can incorporate graphics, and spreadsheets can retrieve data from the database management system. Suites are often sold at a substantial discount compared to buying each package separately.

**Sound:** One of the basic data types. There are two methods to describe sound: samples or MIDI. Digitized (sampled) sound is based on a specified sampling and playback rate, and fits into frequency and amplitude (volume) ranges.

**Speech Recognition:** The ability of a computer to capture spoken words, convert them into text, and then take some action based on the command.

**SQL:** A structured query language supported by most major database management systems. The most common command is of the form: SELECT *column list* FROM *table list* JOIN *how tables are related* WHERE *condition* ORDER BY *columns*.

**Standard operating procedures:** A set of procedures that define how employees and managers should deal with certain situations.

**Standards:** An agreement that specifies certain technical definitions. Standards can be established by committees or evolve over time through market pressures. As technology changes, new standards are created.

**Static integration:** A means of combining data from two documents. A copy of the original is placed into the new document. Because it is static, changes made to the original document are not automatically updated. *See also* Dynamic integration.

**Statistical quality control (SQC):** The statistical analysis of measurement data to improve quality. Several statistical calculations and graphs are used to determine whether fluctuations are purely random or represent major changes that need to be corrected.

**Strategic decisions:** Strategic decisions involve changing the overall structure of the firm. They are long-term decisions and are unstructured. They represent an attempt to gain a competitive advantage over your rivals. They are usually difficult and risky decisions. MIS support for strategic decisions typically consists of gathering, analyzing, and presenting data on rivals, customers, and suppliers.

**Structured decisions:** Decisions that can be defined by a set of rules or procedures. They can be highly detailed, but they are defined without resorting to vague definitions.

**Structured walkthrough:** A review process in which the objective is to reveal problems, inaccuracies, ambiguities, and omissions in the systems design before the program code is finalized. The users are presented with a prototype or mockup of the proposed system.

**Switching costs:** The costs incurred in creating a similar information system when a customer switches to a rival firm. Information technology creates switching costs because customers would have to convert data, re-create reports, and retrain users.

**Synthesizer:** An electronic device to convert electrical signals into sound. One basic technique is FM synthesis, which generates and combines fixed waves to achieve the desired sound. A newer method combines short digitized samples of various instruments with waveforms to create more realistic sounds.

**Sysop:** System operator. Person in charge of an electronic bulletin board who organizes files and controls access and privileges.

**System:** A collection of interrelated objects that work toward some goal.

**Systems analysis and design:** A refinement of the scientific method that is used to analyze and build information systems.

**Systems analyst:** A common job in MIS. The analyst is responsible for designing new systems. Analysts must understand the business application and be able to communicate with users. Analysts must also understand technical specifications and programming details.

**Systems development life cycle (SDLC):** A formal method of designing and building information systems. There are five basic phases: (1) feasibility and planning, (2) systems analysis, (3) systems design, (4) implementation, and (5) maintenance and review.

**T1, T3:** An older communication link provided by phone companies. Used to carry digitized analog signals, it is being replaced with ISDN links. T1 refers to a group of 24 voice-grade lines and can carry 1.544

megabits per second (Mbps). A T2 trunk line is equivalent to 96 voice circuits providing 6.312 Mbps. T3 provides 44.736 Mbps, and T4 can carry 139,264 Mbps. Services can be leased at any of these levels, where greater bandwidth carries higher costs.

**Table:** A method of storing data in a relational database. Tables contain data for one entity or object. The columns represent attributes, and data for each item is stored in a single row. Each table must have a primary key.

**Tactical decisions:** Tactical decisions typically involve time frames of less than a year. They usually result in making relatively major changes to operations but staying within the existing structure of the organization. MIS support consists of databases, networks, integration, decision support systems, and expert systems.

**Telnet:** A method supported on the Internet that enables users of one computer to log on to a different computer. Once logged on to the new system, the user is treated as any other user on the system.

**Terabyte:** Approximately 1 trillion bytes of data. Technically, it is 2 to the fortieth power.

**Text:** The simplest of the four basic data types, it also includes numbers. In its most basic form, text is made up of individual characters, which are stored in the computer as numbers. More sophisticated text is described by its typeface, font size, color, and orientation (rotation).

**Token Ring:** A communications protocol that describes when each machine can send messages. A machine can only transmit when it receives a special message called a token. When the message is finished or a time limit is reached, the token is passed to the next machine.

**Top-down development:** An approach to designing and building systems that begins with an analysis of the entire company and works down to increasing detail. A complete top-down approach is usually impossible because it takes too long to analyze everything. *See also* Bottom-up development.

**Total quality management (TQM):** A management doctrine that states that quality must be built into every process and item. Every step and each person must be dedicated to producing quality products and services.

**Transaction-processing system:** Transactions are exchanges between two parties. Transaction-processing systems record and collect this data for the organization. This data forms the foundation for all other information system capabilities. MIS support typically consists of databases, communication networks, and security controls.

**Transborder data flow (TBDF):** The transfer of data across national boundaries. Some countries place restrictions on the transfer of data, especially data that relates to citizens (and of course, data related to "national security"). Some people have discussed taxing the flow of data.

**Triggered rule:** In an expert system, if a rule is used in an application, it is said to have been triggered or fired.

**Trojan horse:** A special program that hides inside another program. Eventually, when the main program is run, the Trojan horse program might delete files, display a message, or copy data to an external computer.

**True color:** Humans can distinguish about 16 million colors. Devices that can display that many colors are said to display true color. It requires the device to use 3 bytes (24 bits) for each pixel.

**Turing test:** A test proposed by Alan Turing in which a machine would be judged "intelligent" if the software could use conversation to fool a human into thinking it was talking with a person instead of a machine.

**Twisted-pair cable:** Common dual-line wire. Often packaged as three or four pairs of wires. The cable can be run for only a limited distance, and the signal is subject to interference.

**Typeface:** A defined way to draw a set of text characters. Several thousand typefaces have been created to meet different artistic and communication needs. A common characterization is serif and sans serif typefaces.

**Unix:** A popular operating system created by Bell Labs. It is designed to operate the same on hardware from several different vendors. Unfortunately, there are several varieties of Unix, and software that operates on one version often must be modified to function on other machines.

**Unstable model:** A model that cannot be solved for a single solution. The solution might continually diverge, or it could oscillate between several alternatives. Generally due to insufficient or incorrect feedback mechanisms.

**Upload:** To transfer files from a local computer (usually a personal computer) to a distant computer. *See also* Download.

**Usenet:** *See* News groups.

**User resistance:** People often resist change. Implementation of a new system highlights this resistance. Managers and developers must prepare for this resistance and encourage users to change. Education and training are common techniques.

**Value chain:** A description of the many steps involved in creating a product or service. Each step adds value to the product or service. Managers need to evaluate the chain to find opportunities to expand the firm and gain more sales and profits.

**Vector image:** A stored collection of mathematical equations, representing lines, circles, and points. These equations can be rescaled to fit any output device or to any desired size. Users deal with the base objects, not the mathematical definitions.

**Veronica:** A software tool that searches all of the currently connected gophers. You enter a list of keywords, and veronica tells you which computers might have data about that topic. Be careful when you select keywords, or you might get back a gigantic list that will take forever to transmit.

**Video:** One of the basic data types. Video combines the attributes of images and sound. An important attribute is the frames-per-second definition. U.S. standard video operates at 30 frames-per-second, movie films run at 24 frames-per-second. Digitizing video requires capturing and playing back the frames at the appropriate speed.

**View:** A stored query. If you have a complex query that you have to run every week, you (or a database specialist) could create the query and save it as a view with its own name. It is then treated much like a simple table.

**Virtual reality (VR):** Virtual reality describes computer displays and techniques that are designed to provide a realistic image to user senses, including three-dimensional video, three-dimensional sound, and sensors that detect user movement that is translated to on-screen action.

**Virus:** A malicious program that hides inside another program. As the main program runs, the virus copies itself into other programs. At some point, the virus displays a message, shuts down the machine, or deletes all of the files.

**Visual BASIC:** A modern variation of the BASIC programming language created by Microsoft for application programming in Windows. A variation resides inside many of the Microsoft applications, enabling programmers to manipulate and exchange data among the database, spreadsheet, and word processor.

**Visual table of contents:** A graphical design method that shows how modules of a system are related. Versions of the technique are also used to display menu trees.

**Voice mail:** A messaging system similar to telephone answering machines but with additional features like message store and forward. You can use your computer to send messages to co-workers. There are tools that will read e-mail and fax messages over the phone, so managers can stay in touch while they are away from the computer.

**Voice Recognition:** The ability of a computer to capture spoken words and convert them into text.

**Webmaster:** Specialized IS worker who is responsible for creating, maintaining, and revising a company's World Wide Web site. Webmasters use technical and artistic skills to create sites that attract browsers.

**Wide area network (WAN):** A network that is spread across a larger geographic area. In most cases, parts of the network are outside the control of a single firm. Long-distance connections often use public carriers.

**Window:** A portion of the computer screen. You can move each window or change its size. Windows enable you to display and use several applications on the screen at one time.

**Windows NT:** A relatively new operating system created by Microsoft. Its goal is to function exactly the same on several different types of hardware. Software that runs on one machine can be transferred directly and run on other machines that support this operating system.

**Wisdom:** A level above knowledge. Wisdom represents intelligence, or the ability to analyze, learn, adapt to changing conditions, and create knowledge.

**Workflow software:** A type of groupware that is designed to automate forms handling and the flow of data in a company. Forms and reports are automatically routed to a list of users on the network. When each person adds comments or makes changes, it is routed to the next process.

**Workstations:** Computers attached to a network, designed for individual use. Typically, personal computers.

**World Wide Web (WWW):** A first attempt to set up an international database of information. Web browsers display graphical pages of information, including pictures. Hypertext connections enable you to get related information by clicking highlighted words.

**WORM (Write Once, Read Many) disk:** Similar to a CD-ROM, but it is easier to store data. Once data is written on the disk, it cannot be changed. Early WORM drives were superseded by lower-cost drives that can store data in standard CD-ROM format.

**WYSIWYG:** What you see is what you get. With a true WYSIWYG system, documents will look exactly the same on the screen as they do when printed. In addition to format, it means that the printer must have the same typefaces as the video display. Color printers use a system to match the colors on the monitor.

# Organization Index

# Subject Index

## A

Access rights, 191, 215, 677
Access speed, 70, 213
Accounting
  controls, 408
  decision example, 410
  statements, 407
  strategic support, 409
  transaction processing, 161, 407
Accounting cycle, 162
Accounting journal, 161
Accounting system, 18, 77, 98, 160-164, 316, 407, 513, 559, 615
Activity based costing (ABC), 410
Advocacy role, 617
Agent, 102, 146, 485
ANSI, 155, 272
ANSI-X12, 155, 277
Antitrust laws, 526
Application generator, 191, 211
Application software, 76
  analysis and computations, 77
  calendars, 80
  communication
    graphics and presentation, 78
    voice and mail, 79
    writing, 77
  organizing resources, 80
  research, 76
  schedules, 80
Archie, 280
Artificial intelligence (AI), 456, 483
  creativity, 484
  machine vision, 477
  pattern recognition, 475
  robotics, 481
  speech recognition, 478
ASCII, 48, 333
Assumptions, 10, 115, 238, 255, 326, 379
Asynchronous Transfer Mode (ATM), 275
Attributes, 47, 112, 191, 273, 417, 484, 583
Audit trail, 163, 678
Authentication, 675, 679

## B

Backbone, 267
Backup, 75, 213, 256, 526, 567, 617, 624, 673, 667, 672
Backward chaining, 472
Bandwidth, 57, 266, 271, 626
Barriers to entry, 465, 509
Benchmark, 61
Binary data, 46, 273, 308
Biometrics, 676

Bitmap, 49, 66
Bits, 46, 57, 69, 266, 484
Boolean search, 224
Bottom-up design, 560
Business integration, 316, 323
  communication, 324
  compound documents, 313, 324
  databases, 325
  joint authorship, 326
  teamwork, 326
  workgroups, 327
Business and technology trends
  decentralization, 15
  franchises, 13
  internationalization, 17
  management by methodology, 13
  service-oriented business, 18
  small business, 14
  temporary workers, 16
Brainstorming, 336
Break header, 210
Broadcasts, 52, 264, 413
Browser, 279
Bulletin board system (BBS), 252, 278, 682
Bus network, 305
Business integration, 14, 316, 505
Business models, 372, 406
Business Operations, *See* Operations level, 21, 104, 143, 189, 329, 366, 528, 560,
Business trends, 11
Byte, 46, 48

## C

C, 619
C++, 471, 619
Cable, 262-263
Cache, 59
Calendar, 80, 255
Carrier Sense-Multiple-Access/ Collision Detection (CSMA/CD), 306
Case based reasoning, 468
Centralization, 27, 620-625
Change agent, 570
Chargeback, 142
Chart of accounts, 161, 164
Chief executive officer (CEO), 13, 252, 387
Chief information officer (CIO), 617
Circular reference, 381, 416
Classes, *See* Objects–classes
Clip art, 78
Clipboard, 343
Clipper chip, 680
Closed system, 99

CMYK, 79
Coaxial cable, 263
COBOL, 189, 192, 196, 389, 459, 557, 565
Cold site, 674
Collision, 306
Column, 191, 237, 338, 381
Command line interface, 74
Commercial database, 221-223, 322
Common Object Request Broker Architecture (CORBA), 320, 632
Communication, 9, 11, 12, 77, 101, 151, 248, 259, 324, 430, 479, 503, 520, 559, 565, 572, 618, 626, 661
Compatibility, 75, 271, 332, 561, 615, 623
Competition, 13, 17, 64, 118, 334, 503, 506, 523, 575, 616
Competitive advantage, 26, 123, 146, 327, 508, 575, 611
  costs and dangers, 521
  external agents, 24, 523
  information system uses, 508, *Also see* Strategic information systems
  innovation, 517
Complex decisions, 3, 372, 455
  language comprehension, 480
  machine vision, 477
  parallel operations, 480
  pattern recognition, 475
  reasoning, 472
  robotics and motion, 481
  statistics and uncertainty, 482
  voice and speech recognition, 478
Compound document, 313, 324
Computer
  input, 46, 65
  output, 46, 68
  process, 60
  secondary storage, 70
Computer aided design (CAD), 255, 369, 430, 519, 681
Computer aided software engineering (CASE), 104, 577
Computer based training, 54
Computer ethics, 681–684
Computer gloves, 56
Computer Information System (CIS), 6
Computer integrated manufacturing (CIM), 318, 426
Concatenated key, 192
Concurrency, 157, 330, 583, 624
Consistency, 195, 333, 369, 370, 424, 461, 576
Context diagram, 104, 561
Converge, 416
Cost accounting, 410
Critical success factors, 123
Cultural differences, 286

# Photo Credits